ORCHESTRAL MUSIC IN PRINT

1983 SUPPLEMENT

Edited by

Margaret K. Farish

Music-In-Print Series

MUSICDATA, INC.
Philadelphia, 1983

The Music-In-Print Series to date:

Vol. 1. Choral Music In Print - Sacred Choral Music (1974)
Vol. 2. Choral Music In Print - Secular Choral Music (1974)
Choral Music In Print: 1976 Supplement (Out of print)
Sacred Choral Music In Print: 1981 Supplement
Secular Choral Music In Print: 1982 Supplement
Vol. 3. Organ Music In Print (1975)
Vol. 4. Classical Vocal Music In Print (1976)
Vol. 5. Orchestral Music In Print (1979)
Orchestral Music In Print: 1983 Supplement
Educational Section of Orchestral Music In Print (1978)
Vol. 6. String Music In Print, Second Edition (1973)

Music-In-Print Series: ISSN 0146-7883

Music-In-Print Annual Supplement 1983

Music-In-Print Annual Supplement: ISSN 0192-4729

Printed by Port City Press, Baltimore, Maryland

Musicdata, Inc.
3 Maplewood Mall
Philadelphia, Pennsylvania 19144

Library of Congress Cataloging in Publication Data
Farish, Margaret K.
      Orchestral music in print. 1983 supplement.

      (Music-in-print series, ISSN 0146-7883)
      "Supplement to Orchestral music in print . . . 1979. It
contains listings obtained since that date, including
those which appeared in the Music-in-print annual
supplements of 1980, 1981, and 1982"—P.
      1. Orchestral music—Bibliography. I. Title.
II. Series.
ML128.O5F33 Suppl.   016.785   83-13336
ISBN 0-88478-014-7

Contents

Preface

This volume is a supplement to *Orchestral Music In Print,* published in 1979. It contains listings obtained since that date, including those which appeared in the *Music-In-Print Annual Supplements* of 1980, 1981 and 1982. In addition to recent issues of new works and editions, there are some entries for earlier publications from catalogs not previously available.

The publisher is, of course, the only dependable source of information on music currently in print. The entries in this supplement were compiled from catalogs and lists sent each year by publishers in this country and abroad. As in *Orchestral Music In Print,* all works for eleven or more players are included, with the exception of those scored solely for wind instruments. Music for solo instruments or voices with orchestra is listed in both volumes, but this *Supplement* does not contain information on new publications for chorus and orchestra. These entries will be found in the supplements devoted to *Choral Music In Print.*

In *Orchestral Music In Print* a main entry appears under the name of the composer and includes, whenever possible, the instrumentation and duration. If the work is available from more than one publisher, all editions are listed under one uniform title. This system has been followed in this volume. However, since it is a supplement, instrumentation and duration are not shown for new editions of works listed in the base volume.

Although most publishers send excellent catalogs, some do not provide all of the information needed for a complete entry. Often the missing elements can be added by the editor, if the composer and the title can be identified. Unfortunately, this is not always possible. Without the full name and dates it is difficult to know which member of a musical family is the composer and, even more frequently, which work is offered. For example, if "Concerto in D" by a prolific 18th century composer is listed by half a dozen publishers, it is impossible to tell whether six different concerti or six editions of one concerto are available. In these circumstances, each is listed separately with a Musicdata Identification Number (MIN) for the benefit of the computer which is programmed to treat all works with identical titles as multiple editions. A similar system is used for common titles, such as "Minuet". The repetition of identical titles indicates lack of information. The works may be the same; only an examination of the scores will provide proof.

The works of each composer are listed alphabetically by title. Because the computer-based system does not permit changes in this order, entries for collections will not always precede those for individual works, as they do in most music library files. *Symphonies* will come before *Symphony,* but *Suites* will follow *Suite.* For most titles of this nature, the English form of the plural has been used but there are, inevitably, a few exceptions. The most important of these is *Concerto.* The Italian plural has been adopted in this case to accommodate the unalterable *Concerti Grossi.*

Once again, it is a pleasure to thank Northwestern University and the staff of the Music Library for invaluable assistance, and to acknowledge my debt to all who participated in the preparation of this volume: Walter A. Frankel, Nancy K. Nardone, Thomas R. Nardone, Martha N. Harden, Mark Resnick.

Evanston, Illinois
June, 1983

Margaret K. Farish

Guide to Use

THE MUSIC-IN-PRINT SERIES

The Music-In-Print series is an ongoing effort to identify all music available throughout the world. The intention is to cover all areas of music as rapidly as resources permit, as well as to provide a mechanism for keeping the information up-to-date.

Since 1973, Musicdata, Inc., has solicited catalogs and listings from music publishers throughout the world. Using the information supplied by co-operating publishers, the series lists specific editions in appropriate volumes.

It is often difficult to define the boundaries between the various broad areas of music covered by the volumes in the series. The definition of sacred and secular choral music varies from publisher to publisher; some major choral works are no longer listed in Orchestral Music, reflecting changing editorial practice; some solo vocal music is in Orchestral Music; etc. The user is advised to consult the preface to individual volumes for greater definition of scope. Use of more than one volume may well be necessary to identify an edition of a work.

Editorial policy is to include as much information as the publisher supplies, within the limits of practicality. An attempt is made to bring together different editions of a composition under a single title.

MUSIC-IN-PRINT ANNUAL SUPPLEMENT

The Music-In-Print series is kept up to date by means of the Music-In-Print Annual Supplement. Each year's Supplement contains a separate section updating each volume already published in the Music-In-Print series. The updates are cumulative, so that only the latest Supplement is needed, in addition to the base volumes of the series. As additional volumes are published, corresponding sections are added to the Annual Supplement. When special supplements or revised editions of the base volumes are published, the listings from the Annual Supplement are incorporated in them and dropped from the Supplement, thus starting the cycle over again.

GENERAL ARRANGEMENT

Within each catalog in the Music-In-Print series the user will find a comprehensive listing of the works of music publishers throughout the world. The arrangement of this listing is a single alphabetic interfiling of composers' names, titles of works, and cross references. The title under the composer's name serves as the focus for major information on each composition. In the absence of a composer the title in the main list is the focal point. In order to bring together all different editions of a composition under a uniform and/or structured title, many musical form titles are translated into English (so, Konzert becomes Concerto, Fantaisie becomes Fantasy, etc.).

For each title there are two types of information: a) generic information about the composition and b) specific information pertaining to the editions which are in print. Included in the generic information category are the uniform title of the composition, a structured title for the work (e.g., Concerto No. 2 In D Minor; Cantata No. 140), a thematic catalog number or opus and number designation, the larger source from which the work was taken, and remarks.

Following the generic information about the piece is the information about the individual editions. This information includes the arranger, the published title of the edition if different from the uniform title, the language of the text (for vocal works), instrumentation required for performance, the duration of the work in minutes (') and seconds ("), a difficulty rating assigned to the edition by the publisher or editor, the format of the publication, publisher, publisher's number, and price or rental information concerning the edition.

Following is an example of a typical entry under a composer:

MOZART, WOLFGANG AMADEUS (1756-1791)
Nozze Di Figaro, Le: Overture
[4']
2.2.2.2. 2.2.0.0. timp,strings
sc,parts RICORDI-IT rental (M1)
"Marriage of Figaro, The: Overture"
sc,parts BREITKOPF-W f.s. (M2)

In this entry under the composer, Wolfgang Amadeus Mozart, the title of an excerpt, "Overture", follows the original title of the complete work, "Nozze Di Figaro, Le". It is scored for 2 flutes, 2 oboes, 2 clarinets, 2 bassoons, 2 horns, 2 trumpets, timpani and strings. Duration is approximately 4 minutes. The code RICORDI-IT indicates the publisher of the first listed edition; score and parts are offered by this publisher on rental. The sequence number (M1) marks the end of the information on this edition. The English title "Marriage Of Figaro, The: Overture" is given for the next edition which is published by BREITKOPF-W; score and parts for this edition are for sale.

The full names and addresses of all publishers or U.S. agents are given in the publisher list which follows the list of editions at the end of the book.

Following is an example of an entry with a structured title:

MOZART, WOLFGANG AMADEUS (1756-1791)
   Symphony No. 25, [excerpt]
      (Gordon, Philip) 2.1.2.1.al-
         sax. ten-sax. 2.2.1.1. timp,perc,
         strings [3'] (Menuetto, [arr.])
      PRESSER sets $7.50, and up, sc
      $1.50   (M3)

Here a structured title "Symphony No. 25," requires a different form of listing. The excerpt, "Menuetto", has been arranged by Philip Gordon for 2 flutes, oboe, 2 clarinets, bassoon, alto saxophone, tenor saxophone, 2 horns, 2 trumpets, trombone, tuba, timpani, percussion and strings. Duration is three minutes. The publisher, PRESSER, offers sets of parts priced at $7.50 and up. A separate score is available for $1.50.

INSTRUMENTATION

Instrumentation is given in the customary order. When a work is scored for full orchestra, the number of wind players required is indicated by two groups of numbers—four for woodwinds (flute, oboe, clarinet, bassoon) and four for brass (horn, trumpet, trombone, tuba). Other instruments are listed by name, or abbreviated name. A number placed before a named instrument indicates the number of players. A slash is used for alternate instrumentation.

The common auxiliary wind instruments are not mentioned by most publishers. For example, 2.2.3.3. for woodwinds indicates the work is scored for two flutes, but it *may* include a piccolo part which can be played by one of the flutists. Similarly, it is possible that parts for English horn, bass clarinet and contrabassoon are provided but no additional players will be required. If the publisher does specify the auxiliary instruments required, this information is given either in parentheses (the number of players is not affected) or after a plus sign (an additional player is needed).

Example:

   2(pic).2+opt ob.3(opt bass-clar).2+contrabsn.
   4.2.3.0+opt tuba. timp,2-3perc,harp,cel/pno,
   strings

This example is scored for 2 flutes and piccolo (played by one of the flutists), 2 oboes plus an optional third oboe, 3 clarinets (one may play the optional bass clarinet part), 2 bassoons plus contrabassoon (additional player required), 4 horns, 2 trumpets, 3 trombones, optional tuba, timpani, percussion (2 or 3 players), harp, celeste or piano, and strings.

Choral parts are given as a list of voices (e.g. SATB, TTBB, etc.). Vocal solo parts are given as a list of voices followed by the term "solo" or "soli".

Solo instrumental parts are listed following the complete orchestration of a work.

The term "orch" may be substituted for a detailed listing if the publisher has not provided the instrumentation for orchestral works.

REMARKS

The remarks are a series of codes or abbreviations giving information on the seasonal or other usage of the piece, the type of music, and the national origin and century for folk or anonymous pieces. (These codes also make it possible to retrieve, from the data base developed for the Music-In-Print series, specialized listings of music for particular seasons, types, etc.) Following this Guide to Use will be found a complete List of Abbreviations.

SEQUENCE NUMBERS

An alphanumeric number, appearing on the right margin, has been assigned to each edition represented in this catalog. These are for the purpose of easing identification and location of specific entries.

PRICES

We can give no assurances of the accuracy of stated prices. The prices of editions have been increasing steadily over the last few years, yet we have thought it helpful to give the user a U.S. dollar figure, where available. The publishers should be consulted directly for current prices.

CROSS REFERENCES

In order to provide the user with as many points of access as possible, the Music-In-Print series has been heavily cross-referenced. For example, the first example by Mozart, illustrated above, may be located under either its Italian or English title in the main alphabet, as well as under the composer. Therefore, the following cross references would exist in the main alphabet:

NOZZE DI FIGARO, LE: OVERTURE
   see Mozart, Wolfgang Amadeus

and

    MARRIAGE OF FIGARO, THE: OVERTURE see
        Mozart, Wolfgang Amadeus, Nozze Di
        Figaro, Le: Overture

and in addition, the following cross reference would be found under the composer's name:

    Marriage of Figaro, The: Overture
        *see Nozze Di Figaro, Le: Overture

Cross references are employed also to assist in the search for works frequently identified by popular names or subtitles, such as the "Surprise" Symphony of Haydn and the "Jupiter" Symphony of Mozart.

COLLECTIONS

An attempt has been made to provide the user with access to pieces contained within collections, while still keeping the work within reasonable bounds of time and space. Accordingly, the following practices have been adopted:

If the members of a collection are published separately, they are listed individually, regardless of the number of pieces involved. If the collection is only published as a whole, the members are listed only if they do not exceed six in number. For larger collections, a code is given indicating the number of pieces and whether or not the contents are listed in the publisher's catalog. For example,

    CC18L indicates a collection of 18 pieces which are
        listed in the publisher's catalog
    CC101U indicates a collection of 101 pieces which
        are *unlisted* in the publisher's catalog
    CCU indicates a collection of an unknown number of
        pieces

Whenever the members are listed, they are also cross-referenced to the collection. For example, consider the following entry:

    FIVE VOLUNTARIES, [ARR.]
      (Maxwell Davies) 3.3.2.1, 3.3.0.0.
        timp,perc,strings,cont sc,parts
        SCHOTT 10994 f.s.
        contains: Attaignant, Pierre,
          Magnificat; Clarke, Jeremiah,
          King William's March; Clarke,
          Jeremiah, Serenade; Couperin,
          Louis, Sarabande; Croft, William,
          March Tune   (F1)

Published by Schott, edition number 10994, this collection edited by Maxwell Davies contains five members, which are not published separately. Under each of the members there is a cross reference saying 'see FIVE VOLUNTARIES, [ARR.]'.

If the members were also published separately, the cross references in both directions would say 'see also'. If the members were *only* published separately (i.e., the collection were not published as a whole) then the cross reference under the collection would read 'see' and under the members, 'see from'. Thus, 'see' and 'see also' direct the user to information concerning publication, while 'see from' provides access to the collection of which a given publication is a part.

Another problem is the cataloging of untitled collections. These are collections of several pieces published as a whole, but having no overall title. In this case, the publication information is given under the first piece listed, together with the cross reference 'contains also,' followed by the titles of the other members. Under each of the other members, the cross reference 'see' directs the user to the entry for the first member.

List of Abbreviations

The following is a general list of abbreviations developed for the Music-In-Print series. Therefore, all of the abbreviations do not necessarily occur in the present volume. Also, it should be noted that terms spelled out in full in the catalog, e.g. woodwinds, tuba, Easter, Passover, folk, Swiss, do not appear in this list.

A	alto	camb	cambiata	ea.	each
acap	a cappella	Can	Canadian	ECY	End of Church Year
acord	accordion	cant	cantata	educ	educational material
Adv	Advent	Carib	Caribbean	elec	electric
Afr	African	CC	collection	Ember	Ember Days
Agnus	Agnus Dei	CCU	collection, unlisted	Eng	English
al-clar	alto clarinet	CCUL	collection, partially listed	Epiph	Epiphany
al-fl	alto flute	cel	celesta	eq voices	equal voices
al-sax	alto saxophone	Cen Am	Central American	Eur	European
Allelu	Alleluia	cent	century	evang	evangelistic
Anh.	Anhang (supplement)	Chin	Chinese	Eve	Evening
anti	antiphonal	chord	chord organ		
arr.	arranged	Circum	Circumcision		
Asc	Ascension	clar	clarinet		
ASD	All Saints' Day	cloth	clothbound		
aud	audience	cmplt ed	complete edition	F.	thematic catalog of the instrumental works of Antonio Vivaldi by Antonio Fanna
Austral	Australian	Cnfrm	Confirmation		
		Commun	Communion		
B	bass	cong	congregation	f.s.	for sale
Bald	Baldwin organ	Conn	Conn organ	fac ed	facsimile edition
Bar	baritone	cont	continuo	Fest	festivals
bar horn	baritone horn	contrabs-clar	contrabass clarinet	Finn	Finnish
bar-sax	baritone saxophone	contrabsn	contrabassoon	fl	flute
bass-clar	bass clarinet	cor	chorus	Fr	French
bass-fl	bass flute	cor pts	choral parts		
bass-sax	bass saxophone	cor-resp	choral response		
bass-trom	bass trombone	Corpus	Corpus Christi		
bass-trp	bass trumpet	cradle	cradle song	Gd.Fri.	Good Friday
bds	boards	cym	cymbals	Ge.	thematic catalog of the works of Luigi Boccherini by Yves Gerard
Belg	Belgian				
Benton	thematic catalog of the works of Ignace Pleyel by Rita Benton				
Bibl	Biblical			Gen	general
Boh	Bohemian			Ger	German
boy cor	boys' chorus			Giegling	thematic catalog of the works of Giuseppe Torelli by Franz Giegling
Braz	Brazilian				
Bryan	thematic catalog of the symphonies of Johann Wanhal by Paul Bryan	D.	thematic catalog of the works of Franz Schubert by Otto Erich Deutsch		
				girl cor	girls' chorus
bsn	bassoon	Dan	Danish	glock	glockenspiel
BVM	Blessed Virgin Mary	db	double bass	gr. I-V	grades I-V
BWV	Bach-Werke-Verzeichnis; thematic catalog of the works of J.S. Bach by Wolfgang Schmieder	db-tuba	double-bass tuba	Greg	Gregorian chant
		dbl cor	double chorus	gtr	guitar
		Ded	Dedication	Gulbransen	Gulbransen organ
		degr.	degree		
BuxWV	Buxtehude-Werke-Verzeichnis; thematic catalog of the works of Dietrich Buxtehude by G. Kärstadt (Wiesbaden, 1974)	desc	descant		
		diff	difficult	Hamm	Hammond organ
		Dounias	thematic catalog of the violin concertos of Giuseppe Tartini by Minous Dounias	Harv	Harvest
				Heb	Hebrew
C.Landon	numbering of the keyboard sonatas of Joseph Haydn by Christa Landon			Helm	thematic catalog of the works of C.P.E. Bach by Eugene Helm
		Doxol	Doxology		

Hill	thematic catalog of the works of F.L. Gassmann by George Hill	liturg	liturgical	Perger	thematic catalog of the instrumental works of Michael Haydn by Lothar Perger
Hob.	thematic catalog of the works of Joseph Haydn by Anthony van Hoboken	Longo	thematic catalog of the sonatas of Domenico Scarlatti by Alessandro Longo	pic	piccolo
Holywk	Holy Week	Lowrey	Lowrey organ	pic-trp	piccolo trumpet
horn	French horn			pipe	pipe organ
hpsd	harpsichord			pno	piano
Hung	Hungarian	Magnif	Magnificat	pno-cond sc	piano-conducting score
HWC	Healey Willan Catalogue	mand	mandolin	pno red	piano reduction
		manuscript	manuscript (handwritten)	Pol	Polish
		med	medium	Polynes	Polynesian
		men cor	mens' chorus	pop	popular
Ind	Indian	Mex	Mexican	Port	Portuguese
inst	instruments	Mez	mezzo-soprano	PreClass	Pre-Classical
ipa	instrumental parts available	MIN	Musicdata Identification Number	Proces	processional
ipr	instrumental parts for rent	min sc	miniature score	Psntd	Passiontide
Ir	Irish	mix cor	mixed chorus	pt, pts	part, parts
Isr	Israeli	Morav	Moravian		
It	Italian	Morn	Morning		
		mot	motet	quar	quartet
				quin	quintet
J-C	thematic catalog of the works of G.B. Sammartini by Newell Jenkins and Bathia Churgin	Neth	Netherlands	Quinqua	Quinquagesima
Jap	Japanese	NJ	Name of Jesus		
Jew	Jewish	No.	number		
jr cor	junior chorus	Nor Am	North American	rec	recorder
Jubil	Jubilate Deo	Norw	Norwegian	Reces	recessional
		Nos.	numbers	Refm	Reformation
		Nunc	Nunc Dimittis	rent	for rent
				Req	Requiem
K.	thematic catalog of the works of W.A. Mozart by Ludwig, Ritter von Köchel; thematic catalog of the works of J.J. Fux by the same author			Royal	royal occasion
				Rum	Rumanian
		ob	oboe	Russ	Russian
		oct	octavo	RV	Ryom-Verzeichnis; thematic catalog of the works of Antonio Vivaldi by Peter Ryom
Kaul	thematic catalog of the instrumental works of F.A. Rosetti by Oskar Kaul	offer	offertory		
		Op.	Opus		
		Op. Posth.	Opus Posthumous		
kbd	keyboard	opt	optional, ad lib		
Kirk-patrick	thematic catalog of the sonatas of Domenico Scarlatti by Ralph Kirkpatrick	ora	oratorio		
		orch	orchestra		
		org	organ	S	soprano
		org man	organ, manuals only	s.p.	separately published
Kor	Korean			Sab	Sabbath
Krebs	thematic catalog of the works of Karl Ditters von Dittersdorf by Karl Krebs			sac	sacred
				sax	saxophone
				sc	score
		P., P.S.	thematic catalogs of the orchestral works of Antonio Vivaldi by Marc Pincherle	Scot	Scottish
				sec	secular
				Septua	Septuagesima
		Palm	Palm Sunday	Sexa	Sexagesima
L	listed	pap	paperbound	So Am	South American
Landon	numbering of the keyboard trios of Joseph Haydn by H.C.R. Landon	Paymer	thematic catalog of the works of G.B. Pergolesi by Marvin Paymer	sop-clar	soprano clarinet
				sop-sax	soprano saxophone
		Pent	Pentecost	Span	Spanish
Lat	Latin	perc	percussion	speak cor	speaking chorus
		perf mat	performance material	spir	spiritual
		perf sc	performance score	sr cor	senior chorus
				study sc	study score
				Swed	Swedish

SWV	Schütz-Werke-Verzeichnis; thematic catalog of the works of Heinrich Schütz by W. Bittinger (Kassel, 1960)	U	unlisted	WoO.	work without opus number; used in thematic catalogs of the works of Beethoven by Kinsky and Halm and of the works of J.N. Hummel by Dieter Zimmerscheid
		UL	partially listed		
		unis	unison		
		US	United States		
		vcl	violoncello	Wq.	thematic catalog of the works of C.P.E. Bach by Alfred Wotquenne
T	tenor	vibra	vibraphone		
tamb	tambourine	vla	viola		
temp blks	temple blocks	vln	violin	Wurlitzer	Wurlitzer organ
ten-sax	tenor saxophone	voc pt	vocal part	WV	Wagenseil-Verzeichnis; thematic catalog of the works of G.C. Wagenseil by Helga Scholz-Michelitsch
Thanks	Thanksgiving	voc sc	vocal score		
Thomas	Thomas organ	VOCG	Robert de Visée, Oeuvres Complètes pour Guitare edited by Robert Strizich		
TI	thematic catalog of the works of Francisco Tarrega by Mijndert Jape				
timp	timpani	Whitsun	Whitsuntide	Xmas	Christmas
treb	treble	WO	without opus number; used in thematic catalog of the works of Muzio Clementi by Alan Tyson	xylo	xylophone
Trin	Trinity				
trom	trombone				
trp	trumpet	Wolf	thematic catalog of the symphonies of Johann Stamitz by Eugene Wolf	Z.	thematic catalog of the works of Henry Purcell by Franklin Zimmerman
TWV	Telemann-Werke-Verzeichnis; thematic catalog of the works of G.P. Telemann by Mencke and Ruhncke				
		wom cor	womens' chorus		

ORCHESTRAL MUSIC

A

A.B.C. OR ADVENTURE - BEDTIME STORY - CELEBRATION see Rypdal, Terje

A CAPRICCIO, FOR VIOLIN AND ORCHESTRA see Schonherr, Max

A MO' DI FANTASIA see Bossi, [Marco] Enrico

A MODO DE CONCIERTO see Pablo, Luis de

A.S.C. see Lenot, Jacques

..A-.TA-LON-, FOR SOLO VOICE AND ORCHESTRA see Holt, Simeon ten

A VOUS see Beurden, Bernard van

AALLON KEHTOLAULU, FOR SOLO VOICE AND ORCHESTRA, [ARR.] see Jarnefelt, Armas

AAMUN AUTEREESSA, FOR SOLO VOICE AND ORCHESTRA see Palmgren, Selim

ABACADA see Talarczyk, Jozef

ABACO, EVARISTO FELICE DALL'
  (1675-1742)
  Concerto, Op. 6, No. 6, in F [14']
    string orch,cont
    (Luck, R.) sc BREITKOPF-W PB 5083
    f.s., pts BREITKOPF-W OB 5083
    f.s.   (A1)

  Concerto, Op. 6, No. 7, in A [12']
    string orch,cont
    (Luck, R.) sc,pts GERIG BG 915 f.s.
                                  (A2)

ABBANDONO, L', FOR SOLO VOICE AND ORCHESTRA see Blangini, Giuseppe Marco Maria Felice

ABDUCTION FROM THE SERAGLIO, THE: OVERTURE see Mozart, Wolfgang Amadeus, Entfuhrung Aus Dem Serail, Die: Overture

ABEL ET CAIN, FOR SOLO VOICE AND ORCHESTRA see Frid, Geza

ABEND, DER, FOR SOLO VOICE AND ORCHESTRA see Diepenbrock, Alphons

ABENDLIED, [ARR.] see Schumann, Robert (Alexander)

ABENDMUSIK see Dressel, Erwin

ABENDSTERN see Strauss, Josef

ABIDE WITH ME see Monk

ABONNENTEN WALZER see Strauss, Eduard

ABOUT see Dijk, Jan van

ABSCHIED see Leeuw, Reinbert de

ABSCHIED see Vogel, Wladimir

ABU HASSAN: OVERTURE see Weber, Carl Maria von

ABWANDLUNGEN EINES ALTENGLISCHEN VOLKSLIEDES see Dressel, Erwin

ABYSS AND CARESS, FOR TRUMPET AND ORCHESTRA see Dlugoszewski, Lucia

ACADEMIC FESTIVAL OVERTURE see Brahms, Johannes, Akademische Festouverture

ACCANTO, FOR CLARINET AND ORCHESTRA see Lachenmann, Helmut Friedrich

ACH HERR, LASS DEINE LIEBEN ENGELEIN, FOR SOLO VOICE AND STRING ORCHESTRA see Tunder, Franz

ACHTUNG, LOS! see Diederich, Fritz

ACIS AND GALATEA: AS WHEN THE DOVE, FOR SOLO VOICE AND ORCHESTRA see Handel, George Frideric

ACIS AND GALATEA: LOVE SOUNDS THE ALARM, FOR SOLO VOICE AND ORCHESTRA see Handel, George Frideric

ACIS AND GALATEA: O RUDDIER THAN THE CHERRY, FOR SOLO VOICE AND ORCHESTRA see Handel, George Frideric

ACIS AND GALATEA: WOULD YOU GAIN THE TENDER CREATURE, FOR SOLO VOICE AND ORCHESTRA see Handel, George Frideric

ACKER, DIETER (1940-   )
  Concerto for Violin and Orchestra
    [31']
    3.2+English horn.2+bass clar.2+
      contrabsn. 4.3.3.1. 2perc,harp,
      pno,strings
    BREITKOPF-W perf mat rent   (A3)

  Symphony No. 1 [30']
    3.2+English horn.2+bass clar.2+
      contrabsn.alto sax.tenor
      sax.bass sax. 4.3.3.1. 4perc,
      2harp,pno/cel,strings
    BREITKOPF-W perf mat rent   (A4)

ACQUEFORTI DELLA VECCHIA MILANO see Nascimbene, M.

ACTAEON, FOR HORN AND ORCHESTRA see Bennett, Richard Rodney

ACTIONEN WALZER see Strauss, Josef

AD AQUAM see Dijk, Jan van

AD FESTUM LETITIE see Badings, Henk

AD LIBITUM see Serocki, Kazimierz

AD MARGINEM, FOR FLUTE, VIOLIN, VIOLA, AND ORCHESTRA see Raxach, Enrique

ADAGIO, ALLEGRETTO EN ALLEGRO see Roos, Robert de

ADAGIO E RONDO VARIATO, FOR PIANO AND ORCHESTRA see Renzi, Armando

ADAGIO ET STRETTO see Amy, Gilbert

ADAGIO PER ARCHI [3']
  string orch
  (Cammarota, C.) sc ZANIBON 5343 f.s.,
    pts ZANIBON 5344 f.s.   (A5)

ADAGIO UND FUGE IN C MINOR, K. 546 see Mozart, Wolfgang Amadeus

ADAM, A.
  Bravour-Variationen Uber Ein Thema
    Von Mozart, For Solo Voice, Flute
    And Orchestra [6']
    1.2.2.2. 2.0.0.0. strings,fl
      solo,high solo
    (Schmidt, Gustav) RIES perf mat
      rent   (A6)

ADAM, ADOLPHE-CHARLES (1803-1856)
  Cantique De Noel
    "O Holy Night" LUCKS 02459 set
    $12.00, pts $.75, ea.   (A7)

  Farfadet, Le: Overture [5']
    1+pic.2.2.2. 4.2.3.0. timp,perc,
      strings
    KALMUS 1676 sc $6.00, set $20.00
                                    (A8)

  If I Were King: Overture *see Si
    J'Etais Roi: Overture

  O Holy Night *see Cantique De Noel

  Poupee De Nuremberg, La: Overture
    [5']
    1+pic.2.2.2. 4.2.3.0. timp,perc,
      strings
    KALMUS 1697 sc $6.00, set $30.00
                                    (A9)

  Si J'Etais Roi: Overture
    "If I Were King: Overture" LUCKS
    05003 sc $9.50, set $16.00, pts
    $1.40, ea.   (A10)

ADAMS, BYRON
  Concerto for Trumpet and String
    Orchestra
    string orch,trp solo
    BRASS PRESS min sc $5.00, solo pt
    $2.00, sc,pts rent   (A11)

ADELAIDE, FOR SOLO VOICE AND ORCHESTRA see Beethoven, Ludwig van

ADEPTEN WALZER, DIE see Strauss, Johann, [Jr.]

ADESTE FIDELIS see Wade

ADIEU see Mesritz van Velthuysen, Anny

ADIEU see Ruyneman, Daniel

ADIEU, ROBERT SCHUMANN, FOR SOLO VOICE AND ORCHESTRA see Schafer, R. Murray

ADLER, SAMUEL HANS (1928-   )
  Feast Of Lights, The
    sc TRANSCON. 990175 $10.00   (A12)

ADLGASSER, ANTON CAJETAN (1729-1777)
  Symphonies, Four
    see SALZBURG, PART 2

ADORATION see Bordewijk-Roepman, Johanna

ADORO TE, FOR SOLO VOICE AND ORCHESTRA see Mengelberg, Kurt Rudolf

AEP, DE HOND EN DE VIS, DEN see Stallaert, Alphonse

AESCHBACHER, WALTHER (1901-1969)
  Chaconne, Variationen, Fuga Und Coda
    *Op.30
    AMADEUS BP 2618 f.s.   (A13)

  Symphony, Op. 50
    string orch
    AMADEUS BP 2680 f.s.   (A14)

AESOP FABLER SUITE see Gutche, Gene

AFFICHE POUR LA REOUVERTURE DU MAGASIN see Dijk, Jan van

AFORISMEN see Bon, Willem Frederik

AFRICAINE, L': O PARADIS, FOR SOLO VOICE AND ORCHESTRA see Meyerbeer, Giacomo

AFRICAN SUITE: DANSE NEGRE see Coleridge-Taylor, Samuel

AFRIKANERIN QUADRILLE, DIE see Strauss, Johann, [Jr.]

AFTERNOON OF A FAUN see Debussy, Claude, Prelude A L'Apres-Midi D'Un Faune

AFTERTONES OF INFINITY see Schwantner, Joseph

AGER, KLAUS (1946-   )
  Dolce Raggio Di Sole Perduto, Un
    [15']
    fl,clar,bsn,perc,strings,pno solo
    MODERN 2078 perf mat rent   (A15)

AGGREGATES SONORES see Kayn, Roland

AGITATO see Nelhybel, Vaclav

AGRELL, JOHAN JOACHIM (1701-1765)
  Concerto for Oboe and String
    Orchestra [11'30"]
    string orch,cont,ob solo
    (Eriksson, Bo) sc,pts BUSCH HBM 070
    f.s.   (A16)

AGRIPPINA: OVERTURE see Handel, George Frideric

AH CRUDEL!, FOR SOLO VOICE AND ORCHESTRA see Haydn, [Franz] Joseph

AH! PERFIDO, FOR SOLO VOICE AND ORCHESTRA see Beethoven, Ludwig van

AH, SE EDMONDO ZU "HELENE" VON MEHUL, FOR SOLO VOICE AND ORCHESTRA see Weber, Carl Maria von

AH SE IN CIEL, BENIGNE STELLE, FOR SOLO VOICE AND ORCHESTRA see Mozart, Wolfgang Amadeus

AH, TU NON SENTI, FOR SOLO VOICE AND ORCHESTRA see Haydn, [Franz] Joseph

AHLGRIMM, HANS (1904-1945)
  Concerto for Trumpet and Orchestra in
    F [15']
    0.2.0.2. 2.0.0.0. strings,trp
      solo
    sc,pts LIENAU rent   (A17)

  Concerto for Violin and Orchestra in
    D minor [27']
    2.2.2.2. 2.2.0.0. timp,strings,
      vln solo
    sc,pts LIENAU rent   (A18)

  Komm, Susser Tod. Variationen Uber
    Ein Thema Von J.S. Bach [28']
    2+pic.2.2.2+contrabsn. 4.2.3.0.
      timp,perc,strings
    sc,pts LIENAU rent   (A19)

AHLUND, ULRIK (1951-   )
  Sentens Pro Utopia *Op.12
    2.2.2.2. 3.2.2.1. timp,2perc,
      strings
    sc STIM perf mat rent   (A20)

AIDA: CELESTE AIDA, FOR SOLO VOICE AND ORCHESTRA see Verdi, Giuseppe

AIDA: FINALE, ACT 4, SCENE 2, FOR SOLO VOICES AND ORCHESTRA see Verdi, Giuseppe

AIDA: MARCIA see Verdi, Giuseppe

AIDA: O PATRIA MIA, FOR SOLO VOICE AND ORCHESTRA see Verdi, Giuseppe

AIDA: PRELUDIO, ACT I see Verdi, Giuseppe

AIDA: RITORNA VINCITOR, FOR SOLO VOICE AND ORCHESTRA see Verdi, Giuseppe

AIDA: TRIUMPHAL MARCH AND BALLET see Verdi, Giuseppe, Aida: Marcia

AILBOUT, HANS
Bei Uns Ist Alle Tage Sonntag
RIES f.s. (A21)

Im Rosengarten Von Sanssouci (Niel) RIES f.s. (A22)

Lauschige Nachte
RIES f.s. (A23)

Mit Zopf Und Reifrock
RIES f.s. (A24)

Rhapsodie Catalan
RIES f.s. (A25)

Vor Einer Taverne
RIES f.s. (A26)

AILLEURS see Sato, Kimi

AIMANT LA ROSE, FOR SOLO VOICE AND ORCHESTRA see Rimsky-Korsakov, Nikolai

AIR AND GAVOTTE see Foote, Arthur

AIR ON THE G STRING see Bach, Johann Sebastian, Suite No. 3 in D, BWV 1068, Second Movement

AIR ON THE G STRING see Bach, Johann Sebastian, Suite No. 3 In D, BWV 1068, Second Movement, [arr.]

AIRS DE BALLET: GALOP, [ARR.] see Drigo, Riccardo

AIRS DE BALLET: PIZZICATO, [ARR.] see Drigo, Riccardo

AIRS DE BALLET: ROMANCE, [ARR.] see Drigo, Riccardo

AIRS ET RITOURNELLES see Suter, Robert

AJDIC, ALOJZ (1939-)
Koncertantna Glasba, For Horn And Orchestra [9']
2(pic).2.2(bass clar).2(contrabsn). 4.2.3.0. timp,strings,horn solo
"Musique Concertante, For Horn And Orchestra" DRUSTVO DSS 875 perf mat rent (A27)

Musique Concertante, For Horn And Orchestra *see Koncertantna Glasba, For Horn And Orchestra

AKADEMISCHE FESTOUVERTURE see Brahms, Johannes

AKHENATEN see Gutche, Gene

AKIBA, FOR SOLO VOICE AND ORCHESTRA see Vredenburg, Max

AKOETEST see Masseus, Jan

AKPABOT, SAMUEL
Three Nigerian Dances [9']
string orch,timp
OXFORD 97.714 sc $5.00, pts $.80, ea. (A28)

AKWAN see Wilson, Olly

AL FINE see Winkler, Gerhard

ALASKAN SYMPHONY see Sawyer, Wilson, Symphony No. 1

ALBINONI, TOMASO (1671-1750)
Concerti, Four, For Stringed Instruments
(Shapiro, M.) string orch,cont sc PRESSER $6.00
contains: Concerto, Op. 5, No. 8, in F; Concerto, Op. 5, No. 10, in A; Concerto, Op. 7, No. 7, in A; Concerto, Op. 7, No. 10, in B flat (A29)

Concerto in C, MIN 633
(Upmeyer, W.) KALMUS A3269 sc $3.00, set $7.50, pts $1.50, ea., kbd pt $1.75, solo pt $1.50 (A30)

Concerto in G, MIN 42
string orch,cont,fl solo
(Scheck-Ruf) sc SYMPHON 527 f.s., pts SYMPHON 528 f.s. (A31)

Concerto, Op. 5, No. 1, in B flat
string orch,cont,vln solo
(Kolneder) EULENBURG GM323P f.s.

ALBINONI, TOMASO (cont'd.)

(Piccioli, G.) sc DE SANTIS DS 859 f.s., pts DE SANTIS DS 860A-D f.s. (A33)

Concerto, Op. 5, No. 8, in F
see Concerti, Four, For Stringed Instruments

Concerto, Op. 5, No. 10, in A
see Concerti, Four, For Stringed Instruments

Concerto, Op. 7, No. 3, in B flat
string orch,cont,ob solo
(Kolneder) EULENBURG GM341P f.s. (A34)

Concerto, Op. 7, No. 5, in C
string orch,cont,2ob soli
(Kolneder) EULENBURG GM343P f.s. (A35)

Concerto, Op. 7, No. 7, in A
see Concerti, Four, For Stringed Instruments

Concerto, Op. 7, No. 10, in B flat
see Concerti, Four, For Stringed Instruments

Concerto, Op. 9, No. 2, in D minor
string orch,cont,ob solo INTERNAT. perf mat rent (A36)

Concerto, Op. 9, No. 9, in C, [arr.]
(Lauth, A.) 2trp,hpsd,strings [11'25"] COSTALL C.3645 perf mat rent (A37)

ALBRECHTSBERGER, JOHANN GEORG (1736-1809)
Symphonies, Five
see AUSTRIAN CLOISTER SYMPHONISTS

Symphony in D, MIN 34
(Fodor) (special import only) sc EMB 6196 f.s. (A38)

ALBUM DI DISEGNI see Orthel, Leon

ALCANDRO, LO CONFESSO (I),FOR SOLO VOICE AND ORCHESTRA see Mozart, Wolfgang Amadeus

ALCESTE: DIVINITES DU STYX, FOR SOLO VOICE AND ORCHESTRA see Gluck, Christoph Willibald, Ritter von

ALCESTE: INCIDENTAL PIECES see Handel, George Frideric

ALCESTE: OVERTURE see Gluck, Christoph Willibald, Ritter von

ALCHYMIST, DER: OVERTURE see Spohr, Ludwig (Louis)

ALCINA: OVERTURE AND DANCES see Handel, George Frideric

ALEOST see Lawhead, D.V.

ALESSANDRO, RAFAELE D' (1911-1959)
Concerto for Oboe and String Orchestra, Op. 79
string orch,ob solo
EULENBURG E10065 f.s. (A39)

Tema Variato *Op.78
AMADEUS BP 2661 f.s. (A40)

ALESSANDRO STRADELLA: OVERTURE see Flotow, Friedrich von

ALEXANDER'S FEAST: OVERTURE see Handel, George Frideric

ALEXANDRINE POLKA see Strauss, Johann, [Jr.]

ALFANO, FRANCO (1876-1954)
Tre Liriche, For Solo Voice And Orchestra [8']
1.1.1. 1.1.0.0. perc,cel,harp, pno,strings,solo voice
sc CARISCH 19876 perf mat rent (A41)

ALFVEN, HUGO (1872-1960)
Midsommarvaka - Swedish Rhapsody No. 1 *Op.19
LUCKS 08637 sc $13.00, set $30.00, pts $1.40, ea. (A42)

ALI BABA: ENTR'ACTE AND BALLET MUSIC see Cherubini, Luigi

ALICE SYMPHONY, AN see Del Tredici, David

ALICE SYMPHONY, AN: THE LOBSTER QUADRILLE see Del Tredici, David

ALKEMA, HENK (1944-)
Intrada [8']
2.2.2.2. 2.2.3.1. timp,perc,harp, strings
DONEMUS perf mat rent (A43)

Mandala [4']
string orch
sc DONEMUS f.s., perf mat rent (A44)

ALL' UNGHERESE, FOR VIOLIN AND ORCHESTRA see Wilhelmj, August

ALLA POLACCA, FOR VIOLIN AND ORCHESTRA see Wilhelmj, August

ALLDAHL, PER-GUNNAR (1943-)
Knaverlek, For Two Key Fiddles And String Orchestra
string orch, 2 key fiddles
sc STIM perf mat rent (A45)

ALLEGRA PIAZZETTA, L': SUITE see Mortari, Virgilio

ALLEGRETTO see Delden, Lex van

ALLEGRIA, L', FOR SOLO VOICE AND ORCHESTRA see Kox, Hans

ALLEGRO see Fries, Herbert

ALLEGRO, ADAGIO EN VARIATIES see Ruiter, Wim de

ALLEGRO APPASSIONATO FOR PIANO AND ORCHESTRA see Saint-Saens, Camille

ALLEGRO APPASSIONATO FOR VIOLONCELLO AND ORCHESTRA see Saint-Saens, Camille

ALLEGRO BRILANTE see Korinek, Miloslav

ALLEGRO BRILLANTE, FOR PIANO AND CHAMBER ORCHESTRA see Panni, Marcello

ALLEGRO DA CONCERTO, FOR PIANO AND ORCHESTRA see Pedrollo, Arrigo

ALLEGRO FOR STRINGS see Bois, Rob du

ALLEGRO, IL PENSIEROSO, ED IL MODERATO, L': LET ME WANDER, NOT UNSEEN, FOR SOLO VOICE AND STRING ORCHESTRA see Handel, George Frideric

ALLEGRO, IL PENSIEROSO, ED IL MODERATO, L': SWEET BIRD, FOR SOLO VOICE AND ORCHESTRA see Handel, George Frideric

ALLEGRO MARCIALE, PASTORALE UND FUGE see Scarlatti, Domenico

ALLEGRO, MENUETT UND RONDINO see Mozart, Leopold

ALLELUIA TIMPANIS see Bedford, David

ALLEZ HOP see Berio, Luciano

ALLMACHT, DIE, "GROSS IST JEHOVA", FOR SOLO VOICE AND ORCHESTRA, [ARR.] see Schubert, Franz (Peter)

ALMA GRANDE E NOBIL CORE, FOR SOLO VOICE AND ORCHESTRA see Mozart, Wolfgang Amadeus

ALMACKS QUADRILLE see Strauss, Johann, [Jr.]

ALOIS, JOHANN URBAN
Sinfonia in D, MIN 41
2ob/2fl,strings
(Hoffmann, A.) sc,pts MOSELER 40.133 f.s. (A46)

ALONE see Grieg, Edvard Hagerup, Einsame, Der, For Solo Voice And Orchestra

ALRE LIEFFELICKEN EEN, EEN see Horst, Anton van der

ALSINA, CARLOS ROQUE (1941-)
Decisions [15']
2.1.3.1. 2.2.2.1. 3perc,2vln,vla, 2vcl,db
sc ZERBONI 8410 f.s., pts ZERBONI 8411 rent (A47)

Senales [14']
2.1.3.1. 2.2.2.0. perc,pno,2vln, vla,vcl,db
(score special import only) sc ZERBONI 8374 f.s., perf mat rent (A48)

Stucke [17']
3.3.4.3. 4.3.2.1. timp,perc, strings
(score special import only) sc ZERBONI 8320 f.s., perf mat rent (A49)

ALSO SPRACH ZARATHUSTRA see Strauss, Richard

ALT-NIEDERLAND see Unger, Hermann

ALTDEUTSCHE LIEDER, FOR SOLO VOICE AND ORCHESTRA see Lothar, Mark

ALTEN SEGELSCHIFFE TRAUMEN, DIE, FOR SOLO VOICE AND ORCHESTRA see Ebert, Wolfgang

ALTENBURG, MICHAEL (1584-1640)
Drei Intraden Zu Advent Und Weihnacht (Egidi, A.) "Three Entradas For Advent And Christmas" KALMUS A4567 sc $3.00, set $6.25, pts $1.25, ea. (A50)

Three Entradas For Advent And Christmas *see Drei Intraden Zu Advent Und Weihnacht

ALTER BAUERNTANZ see Urack, Otto

ALTERATION see Zinsstag, Gerard

ALTITUDES see Ratiu, Horia

ALVIMARE, PIERRE D.'
see DALVIMARE, MARTIN-PIERRE

AM, MAGNAR
Concerto for Double Bass and Orchestra [17']
2(pic).2(English horn).2(bass clar).2(contrabsn). 6.2.2.0. timp,perc,harp,strings,db solo NORGE (A51)

Pa Glytt...:(Ajar), For Doublebass And Orchestra *see Concerto for Double Bass and Orchestra

AM ENDE DES REGENBOGES see Raxach, Enrique

AM RHEIN, AM DEUTSCHEN RHEIN, FOR SOLO VOICE AND ORCHESTRA see Ries, Franz

AMARILLI see Caccini, Giulio

AMAZING GRACE
(Mayfield, Larry; Skillings, Otis) SINGSPIR 7704 $19.95 (A52)

AMAZONE, DIE: AUF DEM KOSTUMFEST see Blon, Franz von

AMAZONE, DIE: OVERTURE see Blon, Franz von

AMAZONE, DIE: POTPOURRI see Blon, Franz von

AMAZONE, DIE: QUADRILLE see Blon, Franz von

AMBASCIA see Bossi, [Marco] Enrico

AMBER WAVES see Gould, Morton

AMBIENTE see Braun, Peter Michael

AMBROSIO, ALFREDO D' (1871-1914)
Concerto for Violin and Orchestra, Op. 29, in B minor [25']
2+pic.2.2.2. 4.2.3.0. timp,harp, strings,vln solo KALMUS 2293 sc $30.00, set $40.00 (A53)

AMDAHL, MAGNE
Bagatelle for Alto Flute and String Orchestra
string orch,pno,alto fl solo NORGE (A54)

Concertino for Trumpet and Orchestra 2.2.2.2. 4.2.3.0. perc,strings, trp solo NORGE (A55)

Elegy for Trombone and Orchestra 2(pic).2(English horn).2(bass clar).2(contrabsn). 2.1.1.0. timp,perc,strings,trom solo NORGE (A56)

Elemntum *see Symphony No. 1

Norsk Stemning [4'30"]
2.2(English horn).2(bass clar).2. 2.3.2.0. perc,pno/cel,strings, elec bass NORGE (A57)

Symphony No. 1 [23']
6(3pic).4(English horn).5(bass clar).4(contrabsn). 6.4.3.1. timp,perc,harp,pno/cel,strings NORGE (A58)

AMERICA
(Luck, Arthur) "My Country 'Tis Of Thee" LUCKS HYMNS 11 set $9.00, pts $.65, ea. contains also: Auld Lang Syne (A59)

AMERICA 1776-1876-1976 see Reif, Paul

AMERICA, THE BEAUTIFUL
(Mayfield, Larry; Skillings, Otis) SINGSPIR 7703 $19.95 (A60)

AMERICA THE BEAUTIFUL see Ward

AMERICAN IN TOKYO, AN see Hattori, Ryoichi

AMERS see Boucourechliev, Andre

AMICO FRITZ, L': INTERMEZZO see Mascagni, Pietro

AMICO FRITZ, L': PRELUDIO see Mascagni, Pietro

AMONG THE STARS see Weingartner, (Paul) Felix von, Unter Sternen, For Solo Voice And Orchestra

AMOR EST UN OISEAU REBELLE, L' see Bizet, Georges, Carmen: Habanera, For Solo Voice And Orchestra

AMOR NOW TILTING NIGHT see Dlugoszewski, Lucia

AMOURETTE see Filipucci, Edmond

AMPHITRYON: OVERTURE see Rogers, Bernard

AMRAM, DAVID WERNER (1930-)
En Memoria De Chano Pozo [10']
2.2.2.2. 4.2.3.1. 4perc,strings, fl solo,elec bass solo,pno solo PETERS P66752 perf mat rent (A61)

Ode To Lord Buckley, For Saxophone And Orchestra [18']
2.2.2.2. 2.2.2.1. timp,perc, strings,alto sax solo PETERS 66858 perf mat rent (A62)

Trail Of Beauty, The, For Solo Voice And Orchestra
2.1(English horn).3.3. 4.2.3.1. timp,perc,harp,strings,ob soli, Mez solo PETERS P66704 perf mat rent (A63)

AMSEL, DIE, FOR SOLO VOICE AND ORCHESTRA see Tiessen, Heinz

AMSTERDAM, FOR SOLO VOICE AND ORCHESTRA see Voormolen, Alexander Nicolas

AMY, GILBERT (1936-)
Adagio Et Stretto [19']
3.3.3.3. 4.3.3.1. 4perc,harp,pno& cel,strings sc UNIVER. UE 16755 f.s., perf mat rent (A64)

Echos XIII [14']
fl,pic,clar,bass clar,bsn,vln, vla,vcl,db,horn solo,trom solo, harp solo,pno solo sc UNIVER. UE 16672 $25.00, perf mat rent (A65)

AN DEN KNABEN ELIS see Goosen, Jacques

AN DEN UFERN DER WOLGA see Muhr, Ferry

AN DER MOLDAU POLKA see Strauss, Johann, [Jr.]

AN DER SCHONEN BLAUEN DONAU see Strauss, Johann, [Jr.]

AN DER SCHONEN BLAUEN DONAU, [ARR.] see Strauss, Johann, [Jr.]

AN DER WOLGA POLKA see Strauss, Johann, [Jr.]

AN DIE LIEBE, FOR SOLO VOICE AND ORCHESTRA see Chemin-Petit, Hans

AN DIE MUSIK, FOR SOLO VOICE AND ORCHESTRA, [ARR.] see Schubert, Franz (Peter)

ANACREON: BALLET MUSIC see Cherubini, Luigi

ANACREON: OVERTURE see Cherubini, Luigi

ANAGRAMMA see Sagvik, Stellan

ANAKREONS GRAB, FOR SOLO VOICE AND ORCHESTRA see Wolf, Hugo

ANAKREONTICA, FOR SOLO VOICE AND ORCHESTRA see Davies, Peter Maxwell

ANALGETIKA see Sagvik, Stellan

ANALOGUES see Dorward, David

ANATOLIA-ORCHESTERSUITE see Tuzun, Ferit

ANCIENT GREEK MARCH see Skalkottas, Nikos

AND SO IT GOES see Lindroth, Peter

ANDALUSISCHE STRASSENMUSIK see Pero, Hans

ANDANTE see Ravanello, Oreste

ANDANTE APPASSIONATO see Becce, Giuseppe

ANDANTE CANTABILE, [ARR.] see Tchaikovsky, Piotr Ilyich

ANDANTE FOR FLUTE AND ORCHESTRA IN C see Mozart, Wolfgang Amadeus

ANDANTE FOR STRING ORCHESTRA see Mayer, William Robert

ANDANTE FUNEBRE see Svendsen, Johan (Severin)

ANDANTE UND RONDO UNGARESE, FOR BASSOON AND ORCHESTRA see Weber, Carl Maria von

ANDANTINO GRAZIOSO, [ARR.] see Chopin, Frederic

ANDERSEN, ALFRED (1869-1952)
Aus Norwegens Berg Und Tal [12']
2.2.2.2. 2.2.1.0. timp,perc, strings sc,pts LIENAU rent (A66)

Naiades, Les
2.2.2.2. 2.0.0.0. strings sc,pts LIENAU rent (A67)

ANDERSON, LEROY (1908-1975)
Arietta
3.2.2.2.opt 2alto sax.opt tenor sax. 4.3.3.0.opt tuba. opt perc, strings [2'40"] WOODBURY $14.00 (A68)
string orch [2'40"] WOODBURY $4.50 (A69)

Balladette
string orch [2'40"] WOODBURY $4.50 (A70)
3.2.2.2.opt 2alto sax.opt tenor sax. 4.3.3.0.opt tuba. perc, strings [2'40"] WOODBURY $14.00 (A71)

Birthday Party [2'15"]
3.2.2.2. 4.3.3.1. 3perc,strings WOODBURY rent (A72)

Captains And The Kings, The [2'45"]
3.2.2.2.opt 2alto sax.opt tenor sax. 4.3.3.1. 3perc,strings WOODBURY $16.00 (A73)

Clarinet Candy [2'45"]
3.2.4.2.opt 2alto sax.opt tenor sax. 4.3.3.1. 3perc,strings WOODBURY $18.00 (A74)

Golden Years, The [3'20"]
3.2.2.2.opt 2alto sax.opt tenor sax. 4.3.3.1. perc,strings WOODBURY $14.00 (A75)

Home Stretch [2'30"]
3.2.2.2.opt 2alto sax.opt tenor sax. 4.3.3.1. 3perc,strings WOODBURY $16.00 (A76)

Lullaby Of The Drums [3'15"]
3.2.2.2. 4.3.3.1. 4perc,strings WOODBURY rent (A77)

Waltz Around The Scale [2'40"]
3.2.2.2. 4.3.3.1. 5perc,strings WOODBURY rent (A78)

ANDRASOVAN, TIBOR (1917-)
Concerto for Harpsichord and String Orchestra [18']
string orch,hpsd solo SLOV.HUD.FOND O-460A perf mat rent (A79)

Dukla-Brana Slobody
3.3.3.3. 4.4.3.1. timp,perc,harp, strings "Dukla-The Gate To Freedom" SLOV.HUD.FOND O-445A perf mat rent (A80)

Dukla-The Gate To Freedom *see Dukla-Brana Slobody

ANDREA CHENIER: LA MAMMA MORTA, FOR SOLO VOICE AND ORCHESTRA see Giordano, Umberto

ANDREA CHENIER: UN DI ALL' AZZURRO
SPAZIO, FOR SOLO VOICE AND
ORCHESTRA see Giordano, Umberto

ANDREA O I RICONGIUNTI see Tutino,
Marco

ANDRES, WALTER (1904-   )
Ouverture Zu Einem Heiteren Spiel
*Op.34 [10']
2(pic).1.2.1. 2.2.2.0. timp,cym,
strings
RIES perf mat rent   (A81)

ANDRIESSEN, HENDRIK (1892-1981)
Attente Mystique, L', For Solo Voice
And Orchestra
2.2.2.2. 4.0.0.0. strings,S solo
[20'] sc DONEMUS f.s., perf mat
rent   (A82)

Aube Spirituelle, L', For Solo Voice
And Orchestra [6']
2.2.2.2. 2.0.0.0. strings,Mez
solo
sc DONEMUS f.s., perf mat rent
                         (A83)

Cantique Spirituel, For Solo Voice
And String Orchestra [4']
string orch,S/T solo
sc DONEMUS f.s., perf mat rent
                         (A84)

Canzone [5']
2.2.2.2. 4.3.3.1. timp,perc,harp,
strings
sc DONEMUS f.s., perf mat rent
                         (A85)

Fiat Domine, For Solo Voice And
String Orchestra [3']
string orch,Mez solo
sc DONEMUS f.s., perf mat rent
                         (A86)

Invitation Au Voyage, L', For Solo
Voice And Orchestra [6']
2.2.2.2. 2.0.0.0. strings,Mez
solo
sc DONEMUS f.s., perf mat rent
                         (A87)

Maria Zart, Von Edler Art, For Solo
Voice And String Orchestra [3']
string orch,Mez solo
sc DONEMUS f.s., perf mat rent
                         (A88)

Philomela: Berceuse, For Solo Voice
And Orchestra [3']
3.2.2.2. 4.2.2.0. timp,harp,
strings,S solo
sc DONEMUS f.s., perf mat rent
                         (A89)

Trois Pastorales, For Solo Voice And
Orchestra [6']
2.2.3.2. 2.2.0.0. timp,perc,harp,
cel,strings,Mez solo
(Flothuis, M.) sc DONEMUS f.s.,
perf mat rent   (A90)

ANDRIESSEN, JURRIAAN (1925-   )
Branles Gaulois, Les, For Accordion
And Orchestra [20'30"]
2ob,2horn,hpsd,strings,acord solo
DONEMUS perf mat rent   (A91)

Cave, The, For Violoncello And
Orchestra [15']
3.0.3.0. 0.3.2.1. pno,elec pno,
Hamm, hpsd (ampl.), vcl solo
(ampl.)
sc DONEMUS f.s., perf mat rent
                         (A92)
Celebrazione, La (Sinfonia No. 8)
[17']
2.2.2.2. 2.2.0.0. timp,strings
sc DONEMUS f.s., perf mat rent
                         (A93)

Concerto for Flute and Orchestra
[24']
1.2.2.2. 2.2.0.0. timp,perc,harp,
strings,fl solo
DONEMUS   (A94)

Pavane [5']
3.3.3.3. 4.3.3.1. timp,2perc,
strings
sc MOLENAAR 14.1562.08 f.s.   (A95)

Perpetual Movement [12']
8vln,2vla,2vcl,db,electronic tape
DONEMUS sc f.s., pts rent   (A96)

Rococo-Concerto, For Clarinet And
Orchestra
orch,clar solo MOLENAAR 14.1404.08
f.s.   (A97)

Say Cheese [13']
2.2.2.2. 4.3.3.1. timp,3perc,
strings
DONEMUS perf mat rent   (A98)

Sinfonia No. 8 *see Celebrazione, La

Thy Black Is Fairest, For Solo Voice
And Orchestra [14']
pno,strings,Bar solo
DONEMUS perf mat rent   (A99)

ANDRIESSEN, JURRIAAN (cont'd.)

Vier Revius Liederen, For Solo Voice
And String Orchestra
org/hpsd,strings,Mez solo
sc DONEMUS f.s., perf mat rent
                         (A100)

ANDRIESSEN, LOUIS (1939-   )
Hymn To The Memory Of Darius Milhaud
[4']
2.2.2.2. 4.2.2.1. pno,strings
DONEMUS perf mat rent   (A101)

Mausoleum [30']
0.0.0.0. 8.3.4.0. 2perc,cym,
2harp,2pno,bass gtr,4vla,4vcl,
2Bar
DONEMUS sc f.s., pts rent   (A102)

Nocturnen, For Solo Voice And
Orchestra [9']
2.2.2.2. 2.0.2.0. timp,perc,harp,
pno/cel,strings,S solo
sc DONEMUS f.s., perf mat rent
                         (A103)

Staat, De, For Solo Voices And
Orchestra [40']
0.4.0.0. 4.4.4.0. 2harp,2pno,elec
gtr,elec bass,4vla, 4 female
voices
sc DONEMUS f.s., perf mat rent
                         (A104)

Symfonie Voor Losse Snaren [25']
7vln,3vla,3db
"Symphony For Open Strings" sc
DONEMUS f.s.   (A105)

Symphony For Open Strings *see
Symfonie Voor Losse Snaren

Tijd, De [45']
8.0.4.0. 0.6.0.0. 2pno,2harp,
Hamm,2bass gtr,2vibra,6-8perc,
strings, women's voices, 2crot
"Time" DONEMUS f.s.   (A106)

Time *see Tijd, De

ANDRIESSEN, WILLEM (1887-1964)
Drie Liederen, For Solo Voice And
Orchestra
2.2.2.2. 4.2.0.0. timp,strings,Mez
solo sc DONEMUS f.s., perf mat
rent
contains: Hei Met De Wolken Zoo
Wit; Herinnering; O Man Van
Smarte   (A107)

Hei Met De Wolken Zoo Wit
see Drie Liederen, For Solo Voice
And Orchestra

Herinnering
see Drie Liederen, For Solo Voice
And Orchestra

O Man Van Smarte
see Drie Liederen, For Solo Voice
And Orchestra

ANDRIX, GEORGE (1932-   )
Five Pieces For Orchestra
2.2.2.2. 2.2.2.1. timp,perc,
strings
SEESAW perf mat rent   (A108)

Variations for Orchestra
2.2.3.2. 4.3.3.1. 2perc,timp,
strings
SEESAW perf mat rent   (A109)

ANFANGEN AUFHOREN see Bredemeyer,
Reiner

ANGELIQUE see Loffler, Willy

ANGELS WE HAVE HEARD ON HIGH
(Luck, Arthur) LUCKS HYMNS 2 set
$10.00, pts $.65, ea. contains
also: Handel, George Frideric, Joy
To The World   (A110)

ANGELUS see Bossi, [Marco] Enrico

ANGELUS. PRIERE AUX ANGES GARDIENS see
Liszt, Franz

ANGOT QUADRILLE see Strauss, Eduard

ANICCA see Ung, Chinary

ANIMALEN, FOR SOLO VOICE AND ORCHESTRA
see Werle, Lars-Johan

ANMUT UND WURDE see Juon, Paul, Suite,
Op. 94

ANNA BOLENA: OVERTURE see Donizetti,
Gaetano

ANNA KARENINA: SUITE NO. 1 see
Robbiani, Igino

ANNA KARENINA: SUITE NO. 2 see
Robbiani, Igino

ANNACA, FOR SOLO VOICES AND CHAMBER
ORCHESTRA see Sagvik, Stellan

ANNEAU D'ARGENT, L' see Chaminade,
Cecile

ANNEAU DU TAMARIT, L', FOR VIOLONCELLO
AND ORCHESTRA see Ohana, Maurice

ANNEN-POLKA see Strauss, Johann, [Jr.]

ANNIE LAURIE, FOR SOLO VOICE AND
ORCHESTRA
LUCKS 02165 set $3.75, pts $.75, ea.
                         (A111)

ANNUNCIAZIONE, L' see Lavagnino, Angelo
Francesco

ANROP, FOR SOLO VOICE AND ORCHESTRA see
Lundquist, Torbjorn

ANTHONY OF PADUA'S FISH SERMON see
Mahler, Gustav, Knaben Wunderhorn,
Des: Des Antonius Von Padua
Fischpredigt, For Solo Voice And
Orchestra

ANTICANTI see Morthenson, Jan W.

ANTICHE MUSICHE DI VIRGINALISTI
INGLESI, [ARR.]
(Margola, F.) string orch [14'] sc
ZANIBON 3951 f.s., pts ZANIBON 3952
f.s.   (A112)

ANTICO SOLE, FOR SOLO VOICE AND
ORCHESTRA see Malipiero, Riccardo

ANTIGONE see Hvoslef, Ketil

ANTIQUE see Bordewijk-Roepman, Johanna

ANTONSEN, IVAR
Piece Of Orchestra, A
1.1.2.1. 2.1.1.0. strings
NORGE   (A113)

ANZAGHI, DAVIDE (1936-   )
Ermosonio
4.3.4.3. 4.3.3.1. vibra,harp,pno,
cel,timp,perc,strings
sc ZERBONI 8422 f.s., pts ZERBONI
8423 rent   (A114)

APARTMENT HOUSE 1776 see Cage, John

APERGHIS, GEORGES (1945-   )
Concerto Grosso [50']
0.0.3.2. 0.0.3.1. 4perc,temple
blocks,pno,4vcl,db,electronic
tape,MezBarB soli, actress
AMPHION A 297 perf mat rent   (A115)

APOKALYPTISCHE PHANTASIE see Hauer,
Josef Matthias

APOLLO UND HYACINTHUS: PRELUDE see
Mozart, Wolfgang Amadeus

APPELONA see Voormolen, Alexander
Nicolas

APPLEFONIA see Oosterveld, Ernst

APPRENTI SORCIER, L' see Dukas, Paul

APPUNTI PER UN NOTTURNO see Bettinelli,
Bruno

APRES UN REVE, FOR DOUBLE BASS AND
ORCHESTRA, [ARR.] see Faure,
Gabriel-Urbain

APRES UN REVE, FOR TROMBONE AND
ORCHESTRA, [ARR.] see Faure,
Gabriel-Urbain

APRES UN REVE, FOR VIOLA AND ORCHESTRA,
[ARR.] see Faure, Gabriel-Urbain

APRES UN REVE, FOR VIOLONCELLO AND
ORCHESTRA, [ARR.] see Faure,
Gabriel-Urbain

AQUAMARIN see Wagner, Josef

ARABESCHI, FOR FLUTE, PIANO AND
ORCHESTRA see Castiglioni, Niccolo

ARANJUEZ see Fischer-Larsen, Eric

ARC OF LIFE see Krenek, Ernst

ARCADELT, JACOB (ca. 1505-1568)
Ave Maria
see RICREAZIONI DI ANTICHE MUSICHE
CLASSICHE, SERIE III: MUSICHE
ANTICHE ITALIANE

ARCANA, FOR SOLO VOICE AND CHAMBER
ORCHESTRA see Schafer, R. Murray

ARCO-11 see Malec, Ivo

ARCUS see Holler, York

ARDITI, LUIGI (1822-1903)
    Bacio, Il, For Solo Voice And
        Orchestra
        "Kiss, The" LUCKS 02118 sc $8.00,
        set $10.00, pts $.75, ea.   (A116)

    Kiss, The *see Bacio, Il, For Solo
        Voice And Orchestra

    Parla-Walzer
        RIES f.s.   (A117)

    Parla-Walzer, For Solo Voice And
        Orchestra [6']
        2.2.2.2. 4.2.3.0. timp,perc,harp,
        strings,high solo
        (Gaebel, Kurt) RIES perf mat rent
                                     (A118)

ARE ALL AMERICANS MADE OF PLASTIC? see
    Meijering, Chiel

ARENA see Kormann, H.L.

ARENA-KLANGE see Bortz, Alfred

ARENAS see Kletsch, Ludwig

ARENSKY, ANTON STEPANOVICH (1861-1906)
    Concerto for Piano and Orchestra, Op.
        2, in F
        KALMUS 1296 sc $35.00, set $40.00
                                     (A119)
    Dream On The Volga: Overture
        LUCKS 05008 sc $6.00, set $16.00,
        pts $1.00, ea.   (A120)
    Suite, Op. 7 [20']
        2+pic.2.2.2. 4.2.3.1. timp,perc,
        strings
        KALMUS 2556 sc $35.00, set $65.00
                                     (A121)
    Symphony No. 1, Op. 4, in G minor
        [33']
        2+pic.2.2.2. 4.2.3.1. timp,perc,
        strings
        KALMUS 2382 sc $40.00, set $80.00
                                     (A122)
    Variations On A Theme Of Tchaikovsky
        *Op.35a [15']
        string orch
        BROUDE BR. sc $3.50, set $8.75, pts
        $1.75, ea.   (A123)
        LUCKS 05023 sc $4.00, set $4.75,
        pts $.95, ea.   (A124)

ARGENTO, DOMINICK (1927-   )
    In Praise Of Music: Seven Songs For
        Orchestra [30']
        3(pic,alto fl).3(English
        horn).3(bass
        clar).3(contrabsn). 4.3.3.2.
        timp,perc,pno/cel,harp,strings
        min sc BOOSEY HPS 927 $9.50, perf
        mat rent   (A125)

    Royal Invitation
        sc BOOSEY $8.00   (A126)

    Water Bird Talk, A [45']
        1.1.1.0. 1.0.0.0. harp,pno,cel,
        perc,strings
        BOOSEY perf mat rent   (A127)

ARIA see Bach, Johann Sebastian, Suite
    No. 3 In D, BWV 1068, Second
    Movement, [arr.]

ARIA, FOR TWO VIOLIN AND STRING
    ORCHESTRA see Uccellini, Marco

ARIA DA CHIESA see Chailly, Luciano

ARIA DE LA FOLIA ESPANOLA see Henze,
    Hans Werner

ARIA DEL MOLINO, L', FOR SOLO VOICES
    AND ORCHESTRA see Sinigaglia, Leone

ARIA E BURLESCA see Soresina, Alberto

ARIA E FINALE see Handel, George
    Frideric

ARIA E SCHERZO, FOR CLARINET AND STRING
    ORCHESTRA see Gabucci, A.

ARIA FIAMMINGA
    see Ricreazioni Di Antiche Musiche
    Classiche, Serie I: Musiche Antiche
    Italiane

ARIA IN G, FOR VIOLIN AND ORCHESTRA see
    Mayuzumi, Toshiro

ARIA NO. 1, [ARR.] see Bach, Johann
    Sebastian

ARIA TRISTA E RONDO GIOCOSO see
    Badings, Henk

ARIA VARIATA see Martini, [Padre]
    Giovanni Battista

ARIADNE AUF NAXOS, FOR SOLO VOICE AND
    ORCHESTRA, [ARR.] see Haydn,
    [Franz] Joseph, Arianna A Naxos,
    For Solo Voice And Orchestra,
    [arr.]

ARIANNA A NAXOS, FOR SOLO VOICE AND
    ORCHESTRA see Haydn, [Franz] Joseph

ARIANNA A NAXOS, FOR SOLO VOICE AND
    ORCHESTRA, [ARR.] see Haydn,
    [Franz] Joseph

ARIETTA see Anderson, Leroy

ARIETTA FOR STRINGS see Dello Joio,
    Norman

ARINA'S DROOM see Boer, Ed de

ARIOSO, FOR SOLO VOICE AND STRING
    ORCHESTRA see Sibelius, Jean

ARIOSO, [ARR.] see Bach, Johann
    Sebastian

ARIOSO FOR VIOLA AND STRING ORCHESTRA,
    [ARR.] see Bach, Johann Sebastian

ARKADISCHE SUITE see Kempff, Wilhelm

ARLESIENNE, L': SUITE NO. 1 see Bizet,
    Georges

ARLESIENNE, L': SUITE NO. 1, [ARR.] see
    Bizet, Georges

ARLESIENNE, L': SUITE NO. 2 see Bizet,
    Georges

ARLESIENNE, L': SUITE NO. 2, [ARR.] see
    Bizet, Georges

ARLESIENNE, L': SUITES NOS. 1 AND 2 see
    Bizet, Georges

ARMEN BALL POLKA see Strauss, Johann,
    [Jr.]

ARMENIAN RHAPSODY NO. 3 see Hovhaness,
    Alan

ARMIDA: OVERTURE see Haydn, [Franz]
    Joseph

ARNIC, BLAZ (1901-1970)
    Three Tales For A Young Pianist, For
        Piano And String Orchestra *see
        Tri Pravljice, For Piano And
        String Orchestra

    Tri Pravljice, For Piano And String
        Orchestra [15']
        string orch,pno solo
        "Three Tales For A Young Pianist,
        For Piano And String Orchestra"
        DRUSTVO DSS 831 perf mat rent
                                     (A128)

ARNO HOLZ-LIEDER, FOR SOLO VOICE AND
    ORCHESTRA see Goosen, Jacques

AROLDO: OVERTURE see Verdi, Giuseppe

ARONADA see Mestres-Quadreny, Josep
    Maria

ARPINO-OUVERTURE see Terpstra, Koos

ARRIGO, GIROLAMO (1930-   )
    Dalla Nebbia Verso La Nebbia
        6vcl,6db
        RICORDI-IT 132310 f.s.   (A129)

    Infrarosso [13']
        1.1.2.0. 1.0.1.0. 2perc,harp,pno,
        cel,2vln,vla,vcl,db
        sc BRUZZI S-052 $13.00, perf mat
        rent   (A130)

    Shadows [16']
        4.2.4.2.4sax. 4.4.3.1. 2perc,
        vibra/xylo,timp,2harp,pno,cel,
        vla,vcl,db
        BRUZZI SV-049 perf mat rent (A131)

ARS COMBINATORIA see Babbitt, Milton
    Byron

ART OF THE FUGUE: CONTRAPUNCTUS NO.1,
    [ARR.] see Bach, Johann Sebastian,
    Kunst Der Fuge, Die: Contrapunctus
    No. 1, (arr.)

ARTIST'S LIFE see Strauss, Johann,
    [Jr.], Kunstlerleben Walzer

ARUTUNIAN, ALEXANDER (1920-   )
    Concerto for Trumpet and Orchestra
        INTERNAT. perf mat rent   (A132)

ASCANIO IN ALBA: OVERTURE see Mozart,
    Wolfgang Amadeus

ASCENSIO see Buchtger, Fritz

ASHKENAZY, BENJAMIN (1940-   )
    Caprice 4-1 [14']
        2.2.2.2.alto sax. 4.3.3.0. timp,
        perc,strings
        DONEMUS perf mat rent   (A133)

    Metamorphosis 4-6-2-1 [25']
        2.2.3.2. 4.3.3.0. 2perc,2harp,
        pno,strings
        DONEMUS perf mat rent   (A134)

ASIOLI, BONIFAZIO (1769-1832)
    Sinfonia Azione Teatrale Campestre
        see NORTHERN ITALIAN SYMPHONY,
        1800-1840, THE

ASTERES see Casagrande, Alessandro

ASTRIAB, JAN (1937-   )
    Diphthong 2 [20']
        3.3.3.3. 4.3.4.1. perc,elec pno,
        strings
        fac ed POLSKIE $16.00   (A135)

AT THE CRADLE, FOR SOLO VOICE AND
    ORCHESTRA see Grieg, Edvard Hagerup

AT THE CROSS
    see Songs Of The Cross

ATALANTA: CARE SELVE, FOR SOLO VOICE
    AND STRING ORCHESTRA see Handel,
    George Frideric

ATATURK IN WAR AND PEACE see Firat,
    Ertugrul

ATHALIE: KRIEGSMARSCH DER PRIESTER see
    Mendelssohn-Bartholdy, Felix

ATHALIE: WAR MARCH OF PRIESTS see
    Mendelssohn-Bartholdy, Felix,
    Athalie: Kriegsmarsch Der Priester

ATMOSPHERES, FOR 4 FLUTES AND STRINGS
    see Bozza, Eugene

ATTENTE MYSTIQUE, L', FOR SOLO VOICE
    AND ORCHESTRA see Andriessen,
    Hendrik

ATTILA: OH DOLORE!, FOR SOLO VOICE AND
    ORCHESTRA see Verdi, Giuseppe

AU PAYS OU SE FAIT LA GUERRE, FOR SOLO
    VOICE AND ORCHESTRA see Duparc,
    Henri

AUBADE see Francaix, Jean

AUBADE A NINON see Lacombe, Paul

AUBADE MARINE, FOR VIOLONCELLO AND
    ORCHESTRA see Larsson, S. Roger

AUBE SPIRITUELLE, L', FOR SOLO VOICE
    AND ORCHESTRA see Andriessen,
    Hendrik

AUBER, DANIEL-FRANCOIS-ESPRIT
    (1782-1871)
    Domino Noir, Le: Overture
        KALMUS 1911 sc $15.00, set $30.00
                                     (A136)
    Fra Diavolo: Overture
        LUCKS 05031 sc $6.50, min sc $4.50,
        set $23.00, pts $1.40, ea.   (A137)
    Masaniello: Overture *see Muette De
        Portici, La: Overture
    Muette De Portici, La: Overture
        "Masaniello: Overture" LUCKS 05032
        sc $6.50, min sc $4.50, set
        $23.00, pts $1.40, ea.   (A138)

AUER, GERHARDT (1925-   )
    Concertino for Viola and Orchestra
        2.2.2.2. 2.0.0.0. strings,vla
        solo
        SLOV.HUD.FOND 0-220A perf mat rent
                                     (A139)

AUF DEM CANALE GRANDE, FOR SOLO VOICE
    AND ORCHESTRA see Ebert, Wolfgang

AUF DEN SPUREN EINES REHES see
    Kotscher, Edmund

AUF DER JAGD see Strauss, Johann, [Jr.]

AUF EIN ALTES BILD "IN GRUNER
    LANDSCHAFT", FOR SOLO VOICE AND
    ORCHESTRA see Wolf, Hugo

AUF FERIENREISEN see Strauss, Josef

AUF SONNIGEN STRASSEN see Rust,
    Friedrich Wilhelm

AUF ZUM TANZE see Strauss, Johann,
    [Jr.]

AUFERSTEHUNG see Graner, Georg,
    Symphony No. 1

AUFFORDERUNG ZUM TANZ, [ARR.] see
    Weber, Carl Maria von

AUFKLANGE see Hausegger, Siegmund von

AUFLOSUNG see Verhaar, Ary

AUFTAKTE see Bredemeyer, Reiner

AUGENSPRACHE see Strauss, Eduard

AULA-LIEDER WALZER see Strauss, Eduard

AULD LANG SYNE
    see America

AUMANN, FRANZ JOSEF (1728–1797)
    Symphony
        see AUSTRIAN CLOISTER SYMPHONISTS

AURA see Maderna, Bruno

AURORA see Hamilton, Iain

AURORA E DANZA see Marti, Heinz

AURORAS OF AUTUMN, THE, FOR OBOE AND
    ORCHESTRA see Hekster, Walter

AUS DEM RECHTSLEBEN WALZER see Strauss,
    Eduard

AUS DEM STEGREIF see Geisler, Willy

AUS DEM ZYKLUS "NIETZSCHE LIEDER" OP.
    26, FOR SOLO VOICE AND ORCHESTRA
    see Bleyle, Karl

AUS DEN BERGEN WALZER see Strauss,
    Johann, [Jr.]

AUS DER STUDIENZEIT WALZER see Strauss,
    Eduard

AUS FINNLAND see Palmgren, Selim, From
    Finland

AUS GALANTER ZEIT see Klaas, Julius

AUS ITALIEN see Strauss, Richard

AUS LIEB' ZU IHR POLKA see Strauss,
    Eduard

AUS MEINER HEIMAT see Brase, Fritz

AUS NORWEGENS BERG UND TAL see
    Andersen, Alfred

AUSTRIA MARSCH see Strauss, Johann,
    [Jr.]

AUSTRIAN CLOISTER SYMPHONISTS
    (Freeman, Robert N.; Meckna, Michael)
    sc GARLAND ISBN 0-8240-3814-2
    $90.00 "The Symphony", Vol. B-VI
    contains: Albrechtsberger, Johann
        Georg, Symphonies, Five; Aumann,
        Franz Josef, Symphony;
        Paradeiser, Marian (Carl),
        Symphonies, Three; Schneider,
        Franz, Symphony; Zechner, Johann
        Georg, Symphonies, Two   (A140)

AUTOBUMMEL see Luft, Gerd

AUTOGRAPH WALZER see Strauss, Johann,
    [Jr.]

AUTOMNE, L', FOR SOLO VOICE AND
    ORCHESTRA see Bon, Willem Frederik

AUTUMN 60 see Cardew, Cornelius

AVALANCHE: SUITE see Kraft, William

AVE MARIA see Arcadelt, Jacob

AVE MARIA see Henselt, Adolph von

AVE MARIA, FOR SOLO VOICE AND ORCHESTRA
    see Rieder, Ambrosius

AVE MARIA, FOR SOLO VOICE AND
    ORCHESTRA, [ARR.] see Gounod,
    Charles Francois

AVE MARIA, FOR SOLO VOICE AND
    ORCHESTRA, [ARR.] see Schubert,
    Franz (Peter)

AVE MARIA, FOR SOLO VOICE AND STRING
    ORCHESTRA see Voormolen, Alexander
    Nicolas

AVE MARIA, FOR SOLO VOICE, OBOE AND
    STRING ORCHESTRA see Hofmann,
    Wolfgang

AVE MARIA, [ARR.] see Gounod, Charles
    Francois

AVE MARIA, [ARR.] see Schubert, Franz
    (Peter)

AVIDOM, MENACHEM (1908–   )
    Volkssinfonie
        study sc ISRAELI IMP 539 f.s.
                                        (A141)
AWAY IN A MANGER see Luther, Martin

B

B 9 634 ORADOUR SUR GLANE see Zosi,
    Giuliano

"B" FOR ORCHESTRA see Newman, Theodore
    Simon

BABA YAGA see Liadov, Anatol
    Konstantinovich

BABBITT, MILTON BYRON (1916–   )
    Ars Combinatoria [19']
        2(pic).0.English horn.1(bass
        clar).2(contrabsn). 2.2.1.1.
        3perc,harp,cel,pno,strings
    PETERS 66878 perf mat rent   (B1)

BABER, JOSEPH W. (1937–   )
    Divertimento, Op. 32, No. 4 [9']
        string orch
        sc OXFORD 92.705 $6.00, pts OXFORD
        $1.00, ea.   (B2)

BABES IN TOYLAND: MARCH OF THE TOYS see
    Herbert, Victor

BABES IN TOYLAND: SELECTION see
    Herbert, Victor

BABES IN TOYLAND: SELECTIONS see
    Herbert, Victor

BABY, DAS: OVERTURE see Heuberger,
    Richard

BACCIO DI MANO, UN, FOR SOLO VOICE AND
    ORCHESTRA see Mozart, Wolfgang
    Amadeus

BACH, CARL PHILIPP EMANUEL (1714–1788)
    Concerto for Flute and String
        Orchestra in A [19']
        string orch,fl solo
    INTERNAT. perf mat rent   (B3)

    Concerto for Flute and String
        Orchestra in G
    INTERNAT. perf mat rent   (B4)

    Concerto for Harpsichord and String
        Orchestra in C minor, Wq. 31
        string orch,hpsd/pno solo
        (Balla, Gyorgy) sc,pts NAGELS
        NMA 253 f.s.   (B5)

    Concerto in D, MIN 20, [arr.]
        (Steinberg, M.) LUCKS 07234 sc
        $7.50, set $11.50, pts $1.15, ea.
                                     (B6)
    Concerto in D, MIN 808, [arr.]
        (Steinberg) BROUDE BR. sc $6.00,
        set $12.50, pts $1.25, ea.   (B7)

    Sinfonia, Wq. 183, No. 1, in D
        KALMUS 5555 sc $9.00, set $20.00
                                     (B8)
    Sinfonia, Wq. 183, No. 3, in F
        KALMUS 5554 sc $9.00, set $20.00
                                     (B9)
    Symphonies, Six
        (Gallagher, Charles C.; Helm, E.
        Eugene) sc GARLAND
        ISBN 0-8240-3821-5 $90.00 "The
        Symphony", Vol. C-VIII
        contains: Symphony, Wq. 173, in
        G; Symphony, Wq. 175, in F;
        Symphony, Wq. 176, in D;
        Symphony, Wq. 179, in E flat;
        Symphony, Wq. 180, in G;
        Symphony, Wq. 181, in F   (B10)

    Symphony, Wq. 173, in G
        see Symphonies, Six

    Symphony, Wq. 175, in F
        see Symphonies, Six

    Symphony, Wq. 176, in D
        see Symphonies, Six

    Symphony, Wq. 179, in E flat
        see Symphonies, Six

    Symphony, Wq. 180, in G
        see Symphonies, Six

    Symphony, Wq. 181, in F
        see Symphonies, Six

    Symphony, Wq. 183, No. 1, in D
        LUCKS 07233 sc $10.00, set $14.00,
        pts $1.50, ea.   (B11)

    Symphony, Wq. 183, No. 3, in F
        LUCKS 09130 sc $12.00, set $16.00,
        pts $1.50, ea.   (B12)

BACH, ERIK
Dangerous Dreams
3.3.3.3. 4.3.3.1. timp,perc,harp,
strings
SAMFUNDET perf mat rent   (B13)

BACH, JOHANN BERNHARD (1676-1749)
Overture No. 1 in G minor
string orch,cont,vln solo
(Fareanu) KALMUS 5207 sc $6.00,
perf mat rent, set $9.00, pts
$1.50, ea.   (B14)

BACH, JOHANN CHRISTIAN (1735-1782)
Cease Awhile, For Solo Voice And
Orchestra
KALMUS A4571 sc $3.00, set $5.00,
pts $.60, ea.   (B15)

Concerto for Bassoon and Orchestra in
B flat
sc EMB $10.00   (B16)

Concerto for Bassoon and Orchestra in
E flat
sc EMB $10.00   (B17)

Concerto for Harpsichord and String
Orchestra, Op. 1, No. 4
string orch,hpsd/pno solo
LUCKS 00167 sc $7.00, set $10.00,
pts $1.00, ea.   (B18)

Midst Silent Shades, For Solo Voice
And Orchestra
KALMUS A4569 sc $3.00, perf mat
rent, set $12.00, pts $1.00, ea.
                               (B19)

Overture in B flat, MIN 82
2.2.2.0. 0.1.0.0. perc,strings
without db
sc,pts HARMONIA 2191 f.s.   (B20)

Overtures, Op. 3, Nos. 1-6 *see
Sinfonia, Op. 3, Nos. 1-6

Overtures, Op. 3, Nos. 1-6 *see
Sinfonias, Op. 3, Nos. 1-6

Sinfonia Concertante in A
LUCKS 08902 sc $14.50, set $25.00,
pts $1.75, ea.   (B21)

Sinfonia Concertante in E flat
KALMUS 4477 sc $12.00, set $15.00
                               (B22)

Sinfonia in B flat, [arr.] *see
Zanaida: Overture, [arr.]

Sinfonia, Op. 6, No. 3, in E flat
(Gmur, Hanspeter) sc,pts NAGELS
NMA 239 f.s.   (B23)

Sinfonia, Op. 6, No. 6, in G minor
(Stein) LUCKS 06200 sc $29.50, set
$33.25, kbd pt $19.75, pts $5.50,
ea.   (B24)

Sinfonias, Op. 3, Nos. 1-3
KALMUS 5208 set $12.00, perf mat
rent, pts $1.50, ea.   (B25)

Sinfonias, Op. 3, Nos. 1-6
"Overtures, Op. 3, Nos. 1-6" KALMUS
A4574 pts $3.00, ea., set $24.00,
perf mat rent   (B26)

Sinfonias, Op. 3, Nos. 4-6
KALMUS 5209 set $12.00, perf mat
rent, pts $1.50, ea.   (B27)

Zanaida: Overture, [arr.] (Sinfonia
in B flat, [arr.])
2.2.2.0.opt bsn. 0.2.0.0. timp,
strings sc,pts HARMONIA 3158 f.s.
                               (B28)

BACH, JOHANN CHRISTOPH (1642-1703)
Lamento "Ach, Dass Ich Wassers Gnug
Hatte", For Solo Voice And
Orchestra
org,strings,A solo
(Schneider, M.) sc BREITKOPF-W
PB 4832 f.s., pts BREITKOPF-W
OB 4832 f.s.   (B29)

BACH, JOHANN SEBASTIAN (1685-1750)
Air, [arr.] *see Suite No. 3 In D,
BWV 1068, Second Movement, [arr.]

Air On The G String *see Suite No. 3
in D, BWV 1068, Second Movement

Air On The G String *see Suite No. 3
In D, BWV 1068, Second Movement,
[arr.]

Aria *see Suite No. 3 In D, BWV
1068, Second Movement, [arr.]

Aria No. 1, [arr.] (from Cantata No.
78)
(Lauth, A.) 2trp,hpsd,strings [6']
COSTALL C.3646 perf mat rent
                               (B30)

BACH, JOHANN SEBASTIAN (cont'd.)

Arioso, [arr.]
see Four Bach Gems
(Gui, V.) 2.3.0.2. 2.0.0.0. strings
[6'] min sc CARISCH 18727 f.s.,
perf mat rent   (B31)

Arioso For Viola And String
Orchestra, [arr.] (from Cantata
No. 156: Ich Steh' Mit Einem Fuss
Im Grabe)
string orch,vla solo LUCKS 00751 sc
$2.75, set $3.75, pts $.75, ea.
                               (B32)

Art Of The Fugue: Contrapunctus No.1,
[arr.] *see Kunst Der Fuge, Die:
Contrapunctus No. 1, (arr.)

Bist Du Bei Mir, For Solo Voice And
String Orchestra, [arr.] *BWV
508
(Luck) string orch,solo voice LUCKS
02919 sc $2.50, set $3.00, pts
$.60, ea.   (B33)

Bist Du Bei Mir, [arr.] *BWV 508
(Nelhybel, Vaclav) string orch,opt
ob,opt solo voice sc,pts BARTA
B 124 $7.50, pts BARTA $.60, ea.
                               (B34)

Brandenburg Concerti Nos. 1-3 *BWV
1046-1048, CC3L
min sc LEA 27 $2.40   (B35)

Brandenburg Concerti Nos. 1-6 *BWV
1046-1051
sc DEUTSCHER f.s.   (B36)
min sc RICORDI-IT PR 733 $9.95
                               (B37)
(reprint of Bach Gesellschaft
edition, 1871) study sc DOVER
23376-6 $6.95 contains also:
Suites Nos. 1-4, BWV 1066-1069
                               (B38)
min sc ZEN-ON 890241 f.s.   (B39)

Brandenburg Concerti Nos. 4-6 *BWV
1049-1051, CC3L
min sc LEA 28 $2.40   (B40)

Brandenburg Concerto No.1 In F *BWV
1046
min sc UNIVER. PH93 $2.75   (B41)
BROUDE BR. sc $5.50, set $13.50,
pts $1.00, ea.   (B42)
LUCKS 07148 sc $4.75, set $7.50,
min sc $2.50, pts $.70, ea., kbd
pt $2.00   (B43)

Brandenburg Concerto No.2 In F *BWV
1047
min sc UNIVER. PH 94 $2.75   (B44)
BROUDE BR. sc $5.50, set $11.50,
pts $1.00, ea.   (B45)
LUCKS 08170 sc $4.75, set $5.50,
min sc $2.50, pts $.70, ea., kbd
pt $2.00   (B46)

Brandenburg Concerto No.3 In G *BWV
1048
min sc UNIVER. PH95 $2.75   (B47)
BROUDE BR. sc $5.50, set $12.50,
pts $1.00, ea.   (B48)
LUCKS 08171 sc $4.75, set $7.00,
min sc $2.50, pts $.70, ea., kbd
pt $2.00   (B49)

Brandenburg Concerto No.4 In G *BWV
1049
min sc UNIVER. PH96 $2.75   (B50)
BROUDE BR. sc $5.50, set $12.50,
pts $1.25, ea.   (B51)
LUCKS 08357 sc $5.00, set $6.50,
min sc $2.50, pts $.95, ea., kbd
pt $2.00   (B52)

Brandenburg Concerto No.5 In D *BWV
1050
min sc UNIVER. PH97 $2.75   (B53)
BROUDE BR. sc $5.50, set $12.50,
pts $1.25, ea.   (B54)
LUCKS 08172 sc $5.00, set $4.75,
min sc $2.50, pts $.95, ea., kbd
pt $2.50   (B55)

Brandenburg Concerto No.6 In B Flat
*BWV 1051
min sc UNIVER. PH98 $2.75   (B56)
BROUDE BR. sc $5.50, set $10.00,
pts $1.25, ea.   (B57)
LUCKS 05056 sc $5.00, set $4.75,
min sc $2.50, pts $.95, ea., kbd
pt $2.00   (B58)

Cantata No. 35: Geist Und Seele Wird
Verwirret, For Solo Voice And
Orchestra
KALMUS A4492 sc $14.00, perf mat
rent, set $16.00, pts $2.00, ea.
                               (B59)

Cantata No. 51: Jauchzet Gott In
Allen Landen, For Solo Voice And
Orchestra
LUCKS 08966 sc $4.00, set $9.00,
min sc $2.50, pts $.75, ea., kbd

BACH, JOHANN SEBASTIAN (cont'd.)

pt $2.50   (B60)

Cantata No. 53: Schlage Doch,
Gewunschte Stunde, For Solo Voice
And Orchestra
(attributed to Bach; actually
composed by Georg Melchior
Hoffmann) LUCKS 08967 sc $3.00,
set $3.00, min sc $2.50, pts
$.50, ea.   (B61)

Cantata No. 82: Ich Habe Genug, For
Solo Voice And Orchestra
LUCKS 08987 sc $4.50, set $6.00,
min sc $2.50, pts $1.00, ea., kbd
pt $3.00   (B62)

Cantata No. 170: Vergnugte Ruh',
Beliebte Seelenlust, For Solo
Voice And Orchestra
KALMUS A4526 sc $8.00, set $6.00,
pts $1.00, ea.   (B63)

Cantata No. 202: Weichet Nur,
Betrubte Schatten, For Solo Voice
And Orchestra
LUCKS 03108 sc $5.00, set $7.00,
min sc $2.50, pts $1.00, ea., kbd
pt $3.00   (B64)

Cantata No. 209: Non Sa Che Sia
Dolore, For Solo Voice And
Orchestra
KALMUS A4531 sc $6.00, set $9.00,
pts $1.50, ea.   (B65)

Chaconne, [arr.]
(Casella, A.) 4.3.4.3. 4.3.4.0.
timp,org,strings [18'] manuscript
CARISCH   (B66)
(Nielsen, R.) string orch [18'] sc
CARISCH 18726 f.s., min sc
CARISCH 18726A f.s., pts CARISCH
18752 f.s.   (B67)

Chorale Preludes, Three, [arr.]
2.3.3.3. 4.3.3.1. timp,strings min
sc CARISCH 16838 perf mat rent
contains: Ich Ruf' Zu Dir, Herr
Jesus, [arr.]; In Dulci Jubilo,
[arr.]; Liebster Jesus, Wir
Sind Hier, [arr.]   (B68)

Chorales, Two, [arr.]
(Gui, V.) 2.3.0.2. 4.0.0.0. strings
min sc CARISCH 20324 perf mat
rent
contains: Herzlich Tut Mich
Verlangen, [arr.] [5']; Kommst
Du Nun, Jesus, Von Himmel
Herunter, [arr.] [5']   (B69)

Chorales, Two, [arr.]
(Luck) string orch LUCKS 08467 sc
$1.50, set $3.75, pts $.75, ea.
contains: Ich Will Hier Bei Dir
Stehen, [arr.]; Was Gott Tut,
Das Ist Wohlgetan, [arr.]   (B70)

Come, Sweet Death, [arr.] *see Komm,
Susser Tod, [arr.]

Concerti For Three And Four
Harpsichords
sc DEUTSCHER f.s.
contains: Concerto for 3
Harpsichords and String
Orchestra, No. 1, in D minor,
BWV 1063; Concerto for 3
Harpsichords and String
Orchestra, No. 2, in C, BWV
1064; Concerto for 4
Harpsichords and String
Orchestra in A minor, BWV 1065
                               (B71)

Concerti For Three Claviers, Two
min sc LEA 56 $2.40
contains: Concerto for 3
Harpsichords and String
Orchestra, No. 1, in D minor,
BWV 1063; Concerto for 3
Harpsichords and String
Orchestra, No. 2, in C, BWV
1064   (B72)

Concerti For Two Claviers, Two
min sc LEA 147 $2.40
contains: Concerto for 2
Harpsichords and String
Orchestra, No. 1, in C minor,
BWV 1060; Concerto for 2
Harpsichords and String
Orchestra, No. 2, in C, BWV
1061   (B73)

Concerto for Harpsichord and
Orchestra, No. 6, in F, BWV 1057
[20']
2rec/2fl,strings,hpsd solo
KALMUS 5147 sc $12.00, perf mat
rent, set $16.00, pts $1.50, ea.
                               (B74)

BACH, JOHANN SEBASTIAN (cont'd.)

Concerto for Harpsichord and String
    Orchestra, No. 1, in D minor, BWV
    1052
    min sc LEA 97 $2.40 contains also:
    Concerto for Harpsichord and
    String Orchestra, No. 2, in E,
    BWV 1053   (B75)

Concerto for Harpsichord and String
    Orchestra, No. 2, in E, BWV 1053
    see Bach, Johann Sebastian,
    Concerto for Harpsichord and
    String Orchestra, No. 1, in D
    minor, BWV 1052

Concerto for Harpsichord and String
    Orchestra, No. 3, in D, BWV 1054
    min sc LEA 98 $2.40 contains also:
    Concerto for Harpsichord and
    String Orchestra, No. 4, in A,
    BWV 1055; Concerto for
    Harpsichord and String Orchestra,
    No. 5, in F minor, BWV 1056 (B76)

Concerto for Harpsichord and String
    Orchestra, No. 4, in A, BWV 1055
    see Bach, Johann Sebastian,
    Concerto for Harpsichord and
    String Orchestra, No. 3, in D,
    BWV 1054

Concerto for Harpsichord and String
    Orchestra, No. 5, in F minor, BWV
    1056
    see Bach, Johann Sebastian,
    Concerto for Harpsichord and
    String Orchestra, No. 3, in D,
    BWV 1054
    BROUDE BR. sc $6.00, set $11.00,
    pts $1.25, ea.   (B77)
    min sc INTERNAT. 1037 $3.50 (B78)
    LUCKS 00083 sc $3.75, set $4.75,
    min sc $2.50, pts $.95, ea. (B79)

Concerto for Harpsichord and String
    Orchestra, No. 7, in G minor, BWV
    1058
    LUCKS 00003 sc $5.00, set $5.00,
    min sc $2.50, pts $1.00, ea.
                                  (B80)

Concerto for 2 Harpsichords and
    String Orchestra, No. 1, in C
    minor, BWV 1060
    see Concerti For Two Claviers, Two

Concerto for 2 Harpsichords and
    String Orchestra, No. 2, in C,
    BWV 1061
    see Concerti For Two Claviers, Two
    LUCKS 00005 sc $5.00, set $4.75,
    pts $.95, ea.   (B81)

Concerto for 3 Harpsichords and
    String Orchestra, No. 1, in D
    minor, BWV 1063
    see Concerti For Three Claviers,
    Two
    see Concerti For Three And Four
    Harpsichords

Concerto for 3 Harpsichords and
    String Orchestra, No. 2, in C,
    BWV 1064
    see Concerti For Three Claviers,
    Two
    see Concerti For Three And Four
    Harpsichords
    LUCKS 00008 sc $6.00, set $5.00,
    min sc $2.50, pts $1.00, ea.
                                  (B82)

Concerto for 4 Harpsichords and
    String Orchestra in A minor, BWV
    1065
    see Concerti For Three And Four
    Harpsichords
    LUCKS 00009 sc $6.00, set $4.75,
    min sc $2.00, pts $.95, ea. (B83)

Concerto for Viola and String
    Orchestra in A, BWV 1055, [arr.]
    (Mohr) string orch,cont,vla solo
    [15'] PETERS perf mat rent (B84)

Concerto for Violin and Orchestra in
    D minor, BWV 1059
    *reconstruction
    (Frotscher) LUCKS 01031 sc $13.00,
    set $12.50, pts $1.50, ea. (B85)

Concerto for Violin and String
    Orchestra, No. 1, in A minor, BWV
    1041
    min sc LEA 96 $2.40 contains also:
    Concerto for Violin and String
    Orchestra, No. 2, in E, BWV 1042;
    Concerto Movement For Violin And
    Orchestra In D   (B86)
    min sc BOOSEY 265 $6.00   (B87)
    LUCKS 00547 sc $3.75, set $4.75,
    min sc $2.50, pts $.95, ea. (B88)

Concerto for Violin and String
    Orchestra, No. 2, in E, BWV 1042
    see Bach, Johann Sebastian,

BACH, JOHANN SEBASTIAN (cont'd.)

Concerto for Violin and String
    Orchestra, No. 1, in A minor, BWV
    1041
    LUCKS 00548 sc $3.75, set $4.75,
    min sc $2.50, pts $.95, ea. (B89)

Concerto for 2 Violins and String
    Orchestra in D minor, BWV 1043
    BROUDE BR. set $9.00, pts $1.25,
    ea.   (B90)
    LUCKS 00500 sc $4.00, set $4.75,
    min sc $2.50, pts $.95, ea., kbd
    pt $1.50   (B91)

Concerto Movement For Violin And
    Orchestra In D
    see Bach, Johann Sebastian,
    Concerto for Violin and String
    Orchestra, No. 1, in A minor, BWV
    1041

Four Bach Gems
    (Zinn, William) string orch
    EXCELSIOR cmplt ed $10.00, pts
    $2.50, ea.
    contains: Arioso, [arr.]; Fugue
    in G minor, [arr.]; Prelude in
    E, [arr.] (from Partita, BWV
    1006); Suite No. 3 In D, BWV
    1068, Second Movement, [arr.]
    (Air, [arr.])   (B92)

Fughetta Sopra "Queste Sole Dieci
    Sante Preci"
    see RICREAZIONI DI ANTICHE MUSICHE
    CLASSICHE, SERIE V: MUSICHE
    ANTICHE ITALIANE

Fugue in C
    see RICREAZIONI DI ANTICHE MUSICHE
    CLASSICHE, SERIE III: MUSICHE
    ANTICHE ITALIANE

Fugue in G minor, [arr.]
    see Four Bach Gems

Fugues, Five, [arr.]
    (Mozart, W.A.) string orch (K.405)
    sc,pts MOSELER M 40.136 f.s.
                                  (B93)

Gavottes From French Suites No. 5 And
    6, [arr.]
    string orch LUCKS 01454 sc $3.00,
    set $5.00, pts $1.00, ea.   (B94)

Giant Fugue *see Wir Glauben All' An
    Einem Gott, [arr.]

Herzlich Tut Mich Verlagen, [arr.]
    see Chorales, Two, [arr.]

Ich Ruf' Zu Dir, Herr Jesus, [arr.]
    see Chorale Preludes, Three, [arr.]

Ich Will Hier Bei Dir Stehen, [arr.]
    see Chorales, Two, [arr.]

In Dulci Jubilo, [arr.]
    see Chorale Preludes, Three, [arr.]
    LUCKS 08815 sc $5.00, set $19.00,
    pts $.75, ea.   (B95)
    (Reed, Alfred) 2+pic.2+English
    horn.2+bass clar.2+contrabsn.
    4.3.3.1. timp,perc,strings KALMUS
    A5476 sc $5.00, perf mat rent,
    set $24.00, pts $.75, ea.   (B96)

Jesu Bleibet Meine Freude, [arr.]
    (Luck) "Jesu, Joy Of Man's
    Desiring, [arr.]" LUCKS 02340 sc
    $4.00, set $8.00, pts $.75, ea.
                                  (B97)
    (Reed, Alfred) "Jesu, Joy Of Man's
    Desiring, [arr.]" 3.2+English
    horn.2+bass clar.2+contrabsn.
    4.3.3.1. timp,harp,strings KALMUS
    A5468 sc $6.00, perf mat rent,
    set $30.00, pts $1.00, ea. (B98)

Jesu, Joy Of Man's Desiring, [arr.]
    *see Jesu Bleibet Meine Freude,
    [arr.]

Kanons, Vierzehn, BWV 1087, [arr.]
    (Meylan, Raymond) ob,English horn,
    bsn,trom,strings sc,pts NAGELS
    NMA 242 f.s.   (B99)

Kanons, Vierzehn, BWV 1087, [arr.]
    (Goldmann) 1.2.0.1. 2.1.1.0. hpsd,
    strings DEUTSCHER perf mat rent
                                  (B100)

Komm, Susser Tod, [arr.]
    (Reed, Alfred) "Come, Sweet Death,
    [arr.]" 3.2+English horn.2+bass
    clar.2+contrabsn. 4.3.3.1. timp,
    strings KALMUS A5475 sc $5.00,
    perf mat rent, set $21.00, pts
    $.75, ea.   (B101)
    (Stokowski, Leopold) 3.2+English
    horn.0+bass clar.1+contrabsn.
    4.3.4.1. timp,harp,strings [4']
    KALMUS A5517 sc $4.00, perf mat
    rent, set $14.00, pts $.75, ea.

BACH, JOHANN SEBASTIAN (cont'd.)

                                  (B102)
Kommst Du Nun, Jesus, Von Himmel
    Herunter, [arr.]
    see Chorales, Two, [arr.]

Kunst Der Fuge, Die, [arr.]
    (Klemm; Weymar) string orch sc,pts
    RIES f.s.   (B103)

Kunst Der Fuge, Die: Contrapunctus
    No. 1, (arr.)
    (Nelhybel, Vaclav) "Art Of The
    Fugue: Contrapunctus No.1,
    [arr.]" string orch sc,pts BARTA
    B 106 $6.00, pts BARTA $.60, ea.
                                  (B104)

Liebster Jesus, Wir Sind Hier, [arr.]
    see Chorale Preludes, Three, [arr.]

Mein Jesu, [arr.] (from Schemelli's
    Gesang-Buch)
    (Stokowski, Leopold) string orch
    [6'] KALMUS A5518 sc $2.00, set
    $3.00, pts $.60, ea.   (B105)

Mein Jesu, Was Fur Seelenweh, [arr.]
    (Reed, Alfred) "My Jesus, Oh What
    Anguish, [arr.]" 3.2+English
    horn.2+bass clar.2+contrabsn.
    4.3.3.1. timp,strings KALMUS
    A5479 sc $5.00, perf mat rent,
    set $21.00, pts $.75, ea.   (B106)

Musical Offering: Ricercare, [arr.]
    *see Musikalisches Opfer:
    Ricercare A 6, [arr.]

Musikalisches Opfer: Ricercare A 6,
    [arr.]
    (Lenzewski, G.) "Musical Offering:
    Ricercare, [arr.]" string orch
    [10'] KALMUS A1093 sc $3.50, set
    $4.50, pts $.75, ea.   (B107)
    (Webern, Anton) min sc UNIVER.
    PH465 $8.50   (B108)

My Jesus, Oh What Anguish, [arr.]
    *see Mein Jesu, Was Fur
    Seelenweh, [arr.]

Passepieds, Two
    string orch,cont
    sc,pts PETERS H 73 f.s.   (B109)

Pieces Arranged In The Form Of A
    Suite
    (Schmutzler, L.) string orch KALMUS
    A4559 sc $4.50, set $5.00, pts
    $1.00, ea.   (B110)

Prelude And Fugue In C Minor, [arr.]
    (Wilson) 2.2.2.2. 2.2.0.0. timp,
    perc,harp,cel,strings [5'] SCOTUS
    325-X perf mat rent   (B111)

Prelude and Fugue in G, [arr.]
    (Galliera, A.) 2.2.2.2. 4.2.0.0.
    timp,strings [10'] manuscript
    CARISCH   (B112)

Prelude, Chorale, And Fugue, [arr.]
    (Abert) LUCKS 05062 sc $10.00, set
    $20.00, pts $2.00, ea.   (B113)

Prelude in B minor, [arr.] (from Das
    Wohltemperierte Klavier, Part I,
    No. 24, BWV 869)
    (Stokowski, Leopold) string orch
    [5'] KALMUS A5519 sc $3.00, set
    $3.00, pts $.75, ea.   (B114)

Prelude in E, [arr.] (from Partita,
    BWV 1006)
    see Four Bach Gems

Schafe Konnen Sicher Weiden, [arr.]
    (Reed, Alfred) "Sheep May Safely
    Graze, [arr.]" 3.2+English
    horn.2+bass clar.2. 4.3.3.1.
    timp,strings KALMUS A5478 sc
    $5.00, perf mat rent, set $27.00,
    pts $1.00, ea.   (B115)

Schmucke Dich, O Liebe Seele, For
    Violoncello And String Orchestra,
    [arr.]
    (Vaughan Williams, Ralph) string
    orch,vcl solo [10'] OXFORD perf
    mat rent   (B116)

Sheep May Safely Graze, [arr.] *see
    Schafe Konnen Sicher Weiden,
    [arr.]

Siciliano From Sonata In C Minor, BWV
    1017, [arr.]
    (Stokowski, Leopold) string orch
    [3'30"] KALMUS A5520 sc $2.50,
    set $3.00, pts $.60, ea.   (B117)

Sinfonia No. 9
    see RICREAZIONI DI ANTICHE MUSICHE
    CLASSICHE, SERIE III: MUSICHE
    ANTICHE ITALIANE

BACH, JOHANN SEBASTIAN (cont'd.)

So Gehst Du Nun, Mein Jesu, Hin,
   [arr.]
   (Reed, Alfred) "Thus Do You Fare,
   My Jesus, [arr.]" 3(pic).2+
   English horn.2+bass clar.2+
   contrabsn. 4.3.3.1. timp,perc,
   strings KALMUS A5477 sc $5.00,
   perf mat rent, set $22.00, pts
   $.75, ea.   (B118)

Suite in G minor, BWV 1070
   string orch,kbd
   (David) KALMUS 5418 sc $3.50, set
   $9.00, pts $1.50, ea.   (B119)

Suite, No. 1, in C, BWV 1066
   min sc BOOSEY 261 $3.00   (B120)
   sc RICORDI-IT PR616 f.s.   (B121)
   LUCKS 05064 sc $3.00, set $5.50,
   min sc $2.50, pts $.75, ea., kbd
   pt $2.00   (B122)
   (Gruss, Hans) min sc BAREN. TP 192
   $3.25   (B123)
   (Soldan) BROUDE BR. sc $5.50, set
   $10.75, pts $1.00, ea.   (B124)

Suite No. 2 in B minor, BWV 1067
   sc RICORDI-IT PR617 $2.50   (B125)
   LUCKS 05063 sc $3.00, set $4.75,
   min sc $2.50, pts $.75, ea., kbd
   pt $2.00   (B126)
   (Gruss, Hans) min sc BAREN. TP 193
   $3.25   (B127)
   (Soldan) BROUDE BR. set $9.00, pts
   $1.00, ea., kbd pt $2.75   (B128)

Suite No. 3 in D, BWV 1068
   LUCKS 05065 sc $3.00, set $7.75,
   min sc $2.50, pts $.75, ea., kbd
   pt $2.00   (B129)
   (Gruss, Hans) min sc BAREN. TP 194
   $3.25   (B130)
   (Soldan) BROUDE BR. sc $5.50, set
   $12.00, pts $1.50, ea.   (B131)

Suite No. 3 In D, BWV 1068, Second
   Movement, [arr.]
   see Four Bach Gems
   (Luck) "Air On The G String" string
   orch LUCKS 05052 sc $2.00, set
   $3.75, pts $.75, ea.
   (Stokowski, Leopold) "Aria" string
   orch [5'30"] KALMUS A5516 sc
   $2.50, set $3.75, pts $.75, ea.
                                 (B133)

Suite No. 4 in D, BWV 1069
   min sc BOOSEY 264 $3.00   (B134)
   LUCKS 05066 sc $3.00, set $8.75,
   min sc $2.50, pts $.75, ea., kbd
   pt $3.00   (B135)
   (Gruss, Hans) min sc BAREN. TP 195
   $3.25   (B136)
   (Soldan) BROUDE BR. sc $5.50, set
   $16.00, pts $1.25, ea.   (B137)

Suites Nos. 1-4, BWV 1066-1069
   see Bach, Johann Sebastian,
   Brandenburg Concerti Nos. 1-6
   min sc ZEN-ON 890251 f.s.   (B138)
   min sc LEA 55 $2.40   (B139)
   min sc,cloth PETERS 578 $25.00
                                 (B140)
   "Vier Ouverturen, BWV 1066-1069" sc
   DEUTSCHER f.s.   (B141)

Tempo Di Sonata, [arr.]
   (Sonzogno, C.) 2.2.3.3. 4.3.3.1.
   timp,strings [8'] manuscript
   CARISCH   (B142)

Thus Do You Fare, My Jesus, [arr.]
   *see So Gehst Du Nun, Mein Jesu,
   Hin, [arr.]

Toccata And Fugue In C For Organ:
   Adagio, [arr.]
   (Stokowski, Leopold) 3.2+English
   horn.1+bass clar.2+contrabsn.
   4.4.4.1. glock,timp,bass drum,
   harp,strings [3'30"] KALMUS A5515
   sc $3.00, perf mat rent, set
   $13.00, pts $.75, ea.   (B143)

Toccata And Fugue In C: Largo, [arr.]
   (La Rotella, P.) 1.1.2.2. 2.2.3.0.
   strings [4'] min sc CARISCH 17137
   f.s., perf mat rent   (B144)

Toccata In C: Adagio E Fuga, [arr.]
   (Sonzogno, C.) 2.2.2.2. 4.2.2.1.
   harp,strings [10'] sc CARISCH
   18742 perf mat rent   (B145)

Toccata in F, [arr.]
   (Parelli, A.) 3.3.3.3. 4.3.3.1.
   timp,strings [8'] sc CARISCH
   18904 perf mat rent   (B146)

Trio, BWV 585, in C minor, [arr.]
   (Besley) 1.1.2.2. 2.1.0.0. timp,
   strings,vln solo,ob solo [6']
   KALMUS A4316 sc $6.00, perf mat
   rent, set $15.00, pts $1.00, ea.
                                 (B147)

BACH, JOHANN SEBASTIAN (cont'd.)

Verschollene Solokonzerte In
   Rekonstruktionen *CC8L
   (Fischer) sc DEUTSCHER f.s.
   contains Concerti BWV 1052, BWV
   1055, BWV 1056, BWV 1060, BWV
   1061, BWV 1053, BWV 1059, BWV
   1063   (B148)

Vier Ouverturen, BWV 1066-1069 *see
   Suites Nos. 1-4, BWV 1066-1069

Was Gott Tut, Das Ist Wohlgetan,
   [arr.]
   see Chorales, Two, [arr.]

Wir Glauben All' An Einem Gott,
   [arr.]
   (Stokowski, Leopold) "Giant Fugue"
   3.2+English horn.3+bass clar.2+
   contrabsn. 5.3.3.2. timp,strings
   [4'] KALMUS A5521 sc $5.00, perf
   mat rent, set $12.00, pts $1.00,
   ea.   (B149)

BACH, VINCENT (1890-1976)
   Hungarian Melodies, For Cornet And
   Orchestra [7']
   2.2.2.1. 2.2.2.1. perc,pno,vln,
   vcl,db,cornet solo
   MARGUN BP 1019   (B150)

BACH, WILHELM FRIEDEMANN (1710-1784)
   Sinfonia in D, MIN 108 [18']
   2.2.0.1. 2.0.0.0. cont,strings
   study sc PETERS EP 8456 $17.50,
   perf mat rent   (B151)

Sinfonia in D minor
   2fl,strings
   LUCKS 05069 sc $3.50, set $6.25,
   pts $1.15, ea.   (B152)

Sinfonia in F
   string orch,cont
   LUCKS 01457 sc $4.00, set $4.00,
   pts $.95, ea., kbd pt $2.00
                                 (B153)

BACHIANAS BRASILEIRAS NO. 7 see Villa-
   Lobos, Heitor

BACIO, IL, FOR SOLO VOICE AND ORCHESTRA
   see Arditi, Luigi

BACK, SVEN-ERIK (1919-   )
   Stories
   2.2.2.2. 2.2.2.0. timp,2perc,pno,
   strings,6perc soli,opt
   electronic tape
   STIM   (B154)

BADINGS, HENK (1907-   )
   Ad Festum Letitie
   see Drie Kerstliederen, For Solo
   Voice And Orchestra

Aria Trista E Rondo Giocoso
   1.0.1.0. 0.0.0.0. harp,pno,
   strings
   sc DONEMUS f.s., perf mat rent
                                 (B155)
Bij Een Doode
   see Liederen Van Dood En Leven, For
   Solo Voice And Orchestra

Concerto for Flute, Oboe, Clarinet
   and Orchestra, No. 3 [27']
   0.0.1.3. 4.4.3.1. timp,3perc,
   strings,fl solo,ob solo,clar
   solo
   DONEMUS   (B156)

Coplas, For Solo Voice And Orchestra
   [5']
   2.2.2.2. 2.2.0.0. timp,perc,
   strings,A solo
   sc DONEMUS f.s., perf mat rent
                                 (B157)
Dies Est Letitie
   see Drie Kerstliederen, For Solo
   Voice And Orchestra

Drei Duetten, For Solo Voices And
   String Orchestra
   string orch,SA soli sc DONEMUS
   f.s., perf mat rent
   contains: Ghele Bloemkens; Hoe
   Schone Staet Die Linde; Stil
   Ende Vredsaem   (B158)

Drie Kerstliederen, For Solo Voice
   And Orchestra
   2.2.2.1. 3.2.1.0. timp,perc,harp,
   cel,strings,S solo sc DONEMUS
   f.s., perf mat rent
   contains: Ad Festum Letitie; Dies
   Est Letitie; Puer Nobis
   Nascitur   (B159)

Eindeloos
   see Liederen Van Dood En Leven, For
   Solo Voice And Orchestra

BADINGS, HENK (cont'd.)

Ghele Bloemkens
   see Drei Duetten, For Solo Voices
   And String Orchestra

Hoe Schone Staet Die Linde
   see Drei Duetten, For Solo Voices
   And String Orchestra

Liederen Van Dood En Leven, For Solo
   Voice And Orchestra
   2.2.3.2. 3.2.3.0. timp,2perc,harp,
   cel,strings,T solo sc DONEMUS
   f.s., perf mat rent
   contains: Bij Een Doode;
   Eindeloos; Maanlicht; Morgen
                                 (B160)

Maanlicht
   see Liederen Van Dood En Leven, For
   Solo Voice And Orchestra

Morgen
   see Liederen Van Dood En Leven, For
   Solo Voice And Orchestra

Puer Nobis Nascitur
   see Drie Kerstliederen, For Solo
   Voice And Orchestra

Sinfonietta
   2.0.2.0. 0.2.0.0. perc,strings
   sc,pts HARMONIA 2507 f.s.   (B161)

Stil Ende Vredsaem
   see Drei Duetten, For Solo Voices
   And String Orchestra

Suite Of Dutch Dances No. 2
   2+pic.2.2.1. 2.2.2.0. perc,
   strings
   sc,pts HARMONIA 2792 f.s.   (B162)

Vier Wiegeliedjes, For Solo Voice And
   String Orchestra, [arr.]
   (Nobel, F. de) string orch,A/Mez
   solo sc DONEMUS f.s., perf mat
   rent   (B163)

BAD'NER KURPARK-TRADITION, VERSION 3
   see Grims-land, Ebbe

BAEKERS, STEPHAN (1948-   )
   Concerto for Chamber Orchestra [15']
   1.1.1.1. 2.2.0.0. pno,strings
   without db
   sc DONEMUS f.s., perf mat rent
                                 (B164)
Musique Pour Orchestre De Chambre
   [10']
   0.0.1.1. 1.1.0.0. pno,strings
   DONEMUS sc f.s., pts rent   (B165)

BAFADIS see Delden, Lex van

BAGATELLE see Rixner, Josef

BAGIN, PAVEL (1933-   )
   Three Songs, For Solo Voice And
   Orchestra *see Tri Spevy, For
   Solo Voice And Orchestra

Tri Spevy, For Solo Voice And
   Orchestra [11']
   1.1.2.2. 2.0.0.0. harp,cel,vibra,
   strings,S solo
   "Three Songs, For Solo Voice And
   Orchestra" SLOV.HUD.FOND KH-71
   perf mat rent   (B166)

BAGLEY, E.E.
   National Emblem March
   set LUCKS 08689 $16.00   (B167)

BAGLIORI see Guarino, Carmine

BAGUENA SOLER, JOSE (1908-   )
   Cuatro Lieder, For Solo Voice And
   Orchestra
   sc PILES 2030-V f.s.   (B168)

Microsuite
   sc PILES 2050-P f.s.   (B169)

BAHN FREI POLKA see Strauss, Eduard

BAIRD, TADEUSZ (1928-1981)
   Canzona [16']
   3.3.3.3. 4.3.3.1. timp,perc,
   strings
   study sc PETERS EP 8466 $18.50,
   perf mat rent   (B170)

Concerto Lugubre, For Viola And
   Orchestra
   sc PETERS P8381 $42.50, perf mat
   rent   (B171)

Stimmen Aus Der Ferne, For Solo Voice
   And Orchestra [18']
   4.2.2.2. 4.3.3.0. 2perc,2harp,
   strings,Bar solo
   PETERS perf mat rent   (B172)

BAIRD, TADEUSZ (cont'd.)

Szenen, For Violoncello, Harp And
Orchestra
3.3.3.3. 4.3.3.0. timp,perc,
strings,vcl solo,harp solo
sc LITOLFF,H 8442 $25.00, ipr
(B173)

BAISER DE LA FEE, LE: DIVERTIMENTO see
Stravinsky, Igor

BAKFARK, BALINT (VALENTIN) (1507-1576)
Three Lute Fantasies, [arr.] *CC3U
(Darvas) min sc EMB K91 $3.50
(B174)

BAL, LE see Dusapin, Pascal

BAL CHAMPETRE QUADRILLE see Strauss,
Johann, [Jr.]

BAL LUNAIRE see Stuppner, Hubert

BALADA, LEONARDO (1933-   )
Homage To Casals [9']
2.2.2.2. 3.3.3.1. timp,3perc,
harp,pno,strings
study sc SCHIRM.G $12.00   (B175)

Homage To Sarasate [8']
2.2.2.2. 3.3.3.1. timp,3perc,
harp,pno,strings
study sc SCHIRM.G $18.00   (B176)

BALADE POUR ROBERT D'ESTOUTEVILLE see
Henkemans, Hans

BALADO, JUAN (? -1832)
Sinfonia in D minor
see SYMPHONY IN MADRID, THE

BALAKIREV, MILY ALEXEYEVICH (1837-1910)
Islamey, [arr.]
LUCKS 08998 sc $18.00, set $40.00,
pts $1.50, ea.   (B177)
(Liapunov) 4.2.3.2. 4.4.3.1. timp,
perc,2harp,strings [12'] KALMUS
5325 sc $18.00, perf mat rent,
set $40.00, pts $1.50, ea. (B178)

Overture On The Themes Of Three
Russian Folk Songs [7']
2.2.2.2. 2.2.3.0. timp,strings
KALMUS 5380 sc $12.00, perf mat
rent, set $18.00, pts $1.00, ea.
(B179)

BALES, RICHARD HORNER (1915-   )
Stony Brook
string orch
PEER sc $8.00, set $30.00   (B180)

BALFE, MICHAEL WILLIAM (1808-1870)
Bohemian Girl, The: Then You'll
Remember Me, For Solo Voice And
Orchestra
LUCKS 02263 set $8.50, pts $.75,
ea.   (B181)

BALKAN see Knumann, Jo

BALKOM, SJEF VAN (1922-   )
Engelse Suite, For Flute And
Orchestra
opt clar,opt perc,pno,strings,fl
solo
sc DONEMUS f.s., perf mat rent
(B182)

BALL GESCHICHTEN WALZER see Strauss,
Johann, [Jr.]

BALL PROMESSEN WALZER see Strauss,
Eduard

BALLABILI IN MODO ISTRIANO see Svara,
Danilo

BALLADE see Beekhuis, Hanna

BALLADE, FOR SOLO VOICE AND ORCHESTRA
see Henkemans, Hans

BALLADE DES PENDU, FOR SOLO VOICE AND
ORCHESTRA see Bunge, Sas

BALLADESKER MARSCH see Dressel, Erwin

BALLADETTE see Anderson, Leroy

BALLATA CAVALLERESCA see Castelnuovo-
Tedesco, Mario

BALLATA DELL'ANGOSCIA see Casagrande,
Alessandro

BALLATELLA see Bossi, [Marco] Enrico

BALLCHRONIK WALZER see Strauss, Eduard

BALLET DE COUR: LA CANARIE see Pierne,
Gabriel

BALLET DE COUR: MENUET DU ROY see
Pierne, Gabriel

BALLET DE COUR: PASSA-MEZZO see Pierne,
Gabriel

BALLET DE COUR: PASSEPIED see Pierne,
Gabriel

BALLET DE COUR: PAVANE ET SALTARELLO
see Pierne, Gabriel

BALLET DE COUR: RIGAUDON see Pierne,
Gabriel

BALLET EGYPTIEN see Luigini, Alexandre

BALLET MUSIC see Lully, Jean-Baptiste
(Lulli)

BALLET MUSIC, [ARR.] see Gluck,
Christoph Willibald, Ritter von

BALLET SUITE, [ARR.] see Rameau, Jean-
Philippe

BALLETTO see Dalla Vecchia, Wolfango

BALLETTO see Malipiero, Riccardo

BALLETTO see Schmelzer, Johann Heinrich

BALLETTO, [ARR.] see Marini, Biagio

BALLETTO FOR ORCHESTER see Werdin,
Eberhard

BALLETTPROBE see Paasch, Leopold

BALLO IN MASCHERA, UN: DI TU SE FEDELE,
FOR SOLO VOICE AND ORCHESTRA see
Verdi, Giuseppe

BALLO IN MASCHERA, UN: ERI TU CHE
MACCHIAVI, FOR SOLO VOICE AND
ORCHESTRA see Verdi, Giuseppe

BALLO IN MASCHERA, UN: MA DALL' ARIDO
STELO DIVULSA, FOR SOLO VOICE AND
ORCHESTRA see Verdi, Giuseppe

BALLO IN MASCHERA, UN: MA SE M'E FORZA
PERDERTI, FOR SOLO VOICE AND
ORCHESTRA see Verdi, Giuseppe

BALLO IN MASCHERA, UN: SAPER VORRESTE,
FOR SOLO VOICE AND ORCHESTRA see
Verdi, Giuseppe

BALLSTRAUSSCHEN POLKA see Strauss,
Johann, [Jr.]

BAMBOLINA see Mielenz, H.

BANCQUART, ALAIN (1934-   )
Symphonie Concertante, For Harp And
Instrumental Ensemble [18']
alto fl,ob,English horn,bass
clar,bsn,horn,2trp,trom,2vln,
vla,vcl,db,harp solo
RICORDI-FR R.2301 perf mat rent
(B183)

Symphonie De Chambre [20']
2.2.2.2. 2.2.2.0. fl solo,vcl
solo
RICORDI-FR R.2285 perf mat rent
(B184)

Symphony, MIN 112 [40']
4.4.4.0. 4.4.4.0. 6perc,2elec
gtr,strings
RICORDI-FR R.2283 perf mat rent
(B185)

Symphony No. 2 [16']
2.3.3.3. 4.2.3.0. perc,strings
RICORDI-FR perf mat rent   (B186)

BANDITEN GALOPP POLKA see Strauss,
Johann, [Jr.]

BANDITENSTREICHE: OVERTURE see Suppe,
Franz von

BANGE NACHT see Becce, Giuseppe

BANK, JACQUES (1943-   )
Fan It
3.3.3.3. 3.3.3.1. strings
sc DONEMUS f.s., perf mat rent
(B187)

Pathetique [9']
3.2.2.2. 2.2.2.0. timp,perc,
strings
sc DONEMUS f.s., perf mat rent
(B188)

Recorders, For Recorder And Orchestra
[18']
strings,perc,rec solo
DONEMUS   (B189)

BANTZ, JOHANN ANDREA
(fl. ca. 1680-   )
Suite, MIN 90
string orch,cont sc,pts HUG GH8799
f.s.   (B190)

BARANOVIC, KRESIMIR (1894-1975)
Chinesische Erzahlung [90']
2(pic).2(English horn).2.1.
3.3.0.0. timp,2perc,harp,pno,
cel,strings
BREITKOPF-W perf mat rent   (B191)

BARASOU, FOR SOLO VOICE AND CHAMBER
ORCHESTRA see Sakac, Branimir

BARBARESK see Thommessen, Olav Anton

BARBER OF SEVILLE, THE: OVERTURE see
Rossini, Gioacchino, Barbiere Di
Siviglia, Il: Overture

BARBER OF SEVILLE: OVERTURE see
Paisiello, Giovanni, Barbiere Di
Siviglia, Il: Overture

BARBETTA PADOVANO, JULIO CESARE
(ca. 1540-1603)
Pavana
see RICREAZIONI DI ANTICHE MUSICHE
CLASSICHE, SERIE II: MUSICHE
ANTICHE ITALIANE

BARBIERE DI SIVIGLIA, IL: DUNQUE IO
SON, FOR SOLO VOICES AND ORCHESTRA
see Rossini, Gioacchino

BARBIERE DI SIVIGLIA, IL: ECCO RIDENTE
IN CIELO, FOR SOLO VOICE AND
ORCHESTRA see Rossini, Gioacchino

BARBIERE DI SIVIGLIA, IL: LA CALUNNIA,
FOR SOLO VOICE AND ORCHESTRA see
Rossini, Gioacchino

BARBIERE DI SIVIGLIA, IL: LARGO AL
FACTOTUM, FOR SOLO VOICE AND
ORCHESTRA see Rossini, Gioacchino

BARBIERE DI SIVIGLIA, IL: OVERTURE see
Paisiello, Giovanni

BARBIERE DI SIVIGLIA, IL: OVERTURE see
Rossini, Gioacchino

BARBIERE DI SIVIGLIA, IL: UNA VOCE POCO
FA, FOR SOLO VOICE AND ORCHESTRA
see Rossini, Gioacchino

BARCAROLA see Henze, Hans Werner

BARCAROLE D'AMORE see Fischer-Larsen,
Eric

BARCAROLLE see Pylkkanen, Tauno
Kullervo, Venhelaulu, For Solo
Voice And Orchestra

BARCHEGGIO, IL: SERENATA A TRE, FOR
SOLO VOICES AND ORCHESTRA see
Stradella, Alessandro

BARCHEGGIO, IL: SINFONIA see Stradella,
Alessandro

BARGIELSKI, ZBIGNIEW (1937-   )
Concerto for Violin and Orchestra
[21']
4.4.4.4.alto sax. 4.4.4.1. pno,
elec gtr,3perc,strings,vln solo
sc POLSKIE f.s.   (B192)

BARNBY, [SIR] JOSEPH (1838-1896)
Now The Day Is Over
see Cruger, Johann, Now Thank We
All Our God

BAROLSKY, MICHAEL (1947-   )
Sternengesang [12']
1.2.0.2. 2.0.0.0. 3perc,strings
BREITKOPF-W perf mat rent   (B193)

BARQUE D'OR see Mesritz van Velthuysen,
Anny

BARRAQUE, JEAN (1928-1973)
Concerto for Clarinet, Vibraphone and
Orchestra [40']
2.2.1.3.alto sax.tenor
sax.baritone sax. 1.1.1.0.
harp,hpsd,gtr,vln,vla,vcl,clar
solo,vibra solo
BRUZZI SV-050 perf mat rent (B194)

BARRAUD, HENRY (1900-   )
Offrande A Une Ombre
min sc BOOSEY 1036 $4.00   (B195)

Rapsodie Cartesienne
BOOSEY 741 min sc $7.50, sc rent
(B196)

Rapsodie Dionysienne
min sc BOOSEY 747 $7.50   (B197)

BARSANTI, FRANCESCO (ca. 1690-1772)
Concerti Grossi, Six *CC6U
string orch KALMUS 5423 set $28.00,
perf mat rent, pts $3.50, ea.
(B198)

Overture, Op. 4, No. 2
string orch,cont
sc SCHOTTS 71 U0186 $13.50, pts
SCHOTTS $1.75, ea.   (B199)

BARTA, LUBOR (1928-1972)
Symphony No. 3 [18']
2+pic.2.2+clar in E flat.2.
4.3.3.1. timp,perc,strings
study sc CESKY HUD. AP 1822 f.s.,

BARTA, LUBOR (cont'd.)

    perf mat rent   (B200)

BARTERED BRIDE, THE: OVERTURE see
    Smetana, Bedrich, Prodana Nevesta:
    Overture

BARTOK, BELA (1881-1945)
    Mikrokosmos: Five Pieces, [arr.]
    (Serly, Tibor) string orch min sc
    BOOSEY 27 $4.00   (B201)

BARTOLOZZI, BRUNO (1911-   )
    Immagine, For Solo Voice And Chamber
    Orchestra [12']
      2.0.2.1. 1.1.0.0. timp,perc,xylo,
      vibra,cel,harp,2vln,vla,vcl,db,
      S solo
    sc BRUZZI SV-001 $28.00, perf mat
    rent   (B202)

    Memorie [14']
      4.1.1.1. 0.3.0.0. perc,3gtr,
      strings
    sc ZERBONI 8139 f.s., perf mat rent
                                     (B203)
    Sentimento Del Sogno, For Solo Voice
    And Orchestra [9']
      3.2.3.2. 3.3.2.0. timp,perc,xylo,
      vibra,harp,pno,strings,S solo
    BRUZZI SV-005 perf mat rent (B204)

BARTOS, JAN ZDENEK (1908-   )
    Concerto Da Camera, For Viola And
    String Orchestra [16']
      string orch,vla solo
    SUPRAPHON AP 2710 perf mat rent
                                     (B205)

BARUFFE CHIOZZOTTE, LE: OVERTURE see
    Sinigaglia, Leone

BASCARSIJA BLACKSMITHS, THE see Lavrin,
    Anton, Kovaci Na Bascarsiji

BASILI, FRANCESCO (1767-1850)
    Sinfonia in D minor
    see NORTHERN ITALIAN SYMPHONY,
    1800-1840, THE

BASKISCHER TANZ see Heuser, Ernst

BASSETT, LESLIE (1923-   )
    Concerto for 2 Pianos and Orchestra
      3.2.3.2(contrabsn). 4.2.3.1.
      4perc,strings,2pno soli
    PETERS P66719 perf mat rent (B206)

BASTIEN UND BASTIENNE: OVERTURE see
    Mozart, Wolfgang Amadeus

BASTON, JOHN (ca. 1700-   )
    Concerto for Guitar and String
    Orchestra
      string orch,gtr solo
    sc,pts BOTE GB 51 f.s.   (B207)

BAT, THE: LAUGHING SONG see Strauss,
    Johann, [Jr.], Fledermaus, Die:
    Mein Herr Marquis, For Solo Voice
    And Orchestra

BAT, THE: OVERTURE see Strauss, Johann,
    [Jr.], Fledermaus, Die: Overture

BATTAGLIA DI LEGNANO, LA: OVERTURE see
    Verdi, Giuseppe

BATTALIA see Biber, Heinrich Ignaz
    Franz von

BATTISTA, IL see Caldara, Antonio

BATTLE HYMN OF THE REPUBLIC
    (Mayfield, Larry; Skillings, Otis)
    SINGSPIR 7701 $19.95   (B208)

BATTLE HYMN OF THE REPUBLIC see Steffe,
    William

BAUCHTANZ see Becce, Giuseppe

BAUERN-POLKA see Strauss, Johann, [Jr.]

BAUMANN, MAX (1917-   )
    Suite Moderne
      2.2.0.2. 0.0.0.0. perc,strings
    sc,pts SCHWANN S 2282 f.s.   (B209)

BAUR, JURG (1918-   )
    Carmen-Variationen [15']
      2.2.2.2. 3.2.3.0. timp,2perc,
      harp,strings
    BREITKOPF-W perf mat rent   (B210)

    Concerto for Violin and Orchestra,
    No. 2
      2.2.2.2. 4.2.3.0. timp,perc,harp,
      strings,vln solo
    study sc BREITKOPF-W PB 5060 f.s.,
    perf mat rent   (B211)

    Sentimento Del Tempo, For 3 Woodwinds
    And Orchestra
      0.0.0.0. 2.2.2.0. timp,4perc,
      harp,strings,ob solo,clar solo,

BAUR, JURG (cont'd.)

      bsn solo
    BREITKOPF-W perf mat rent   (B212)

    Sinfonische Metamorphosen Uber
    Gesualdo [20']
      2+pic.2+English horn.2+bass
      clar.2+contrabsn. 4.3.3.1.
      timp,4perc,harp,cel,strings
    BREITKOPF-W perf mat rent   (B213)

BAURISCHE FESTMUSIK see Jentsch, Walter

BAVICCHI, JOHN ALEXANDER (1922-   )
    Mont Blanc Overture
      2(opt pic).0.opt ob.2(opt bass
      clar).1. 2.3.3.0.opt tuba.
      timp,perc,strings
      (string supplement A available for
      $10.00) OXFORD sc $8.00, set
      $23.00   (B214)

BAYRISCHE HOCHZEIT see Rixner, Josef

BAZELON, IRWIN ALLEN (1922-   )
    De-Tonations, For Brass Quintet And
    Orchestra [20']
      study sc NOVELLO 2793-92 $13.75
                                   (B215)
    Short Symphony (Testament To A Big
    City)
      sc BOOSEY $6.50   (B216)

BAZLIK, MIROSLAV (1931-   )
    Five Little Elegies *see Pat' Malych
    Elegii Pre Slaciky

    Pat' Malych Elegii Pre Slaciky [10']
      string orch
      "Five Little Elegies" SLOV.HUD.FOND
      KH-400 perf mat rent   (B217)

BEAR SYMPHONY see Haydn, [Franz]
    Joseph, Symphony No. 82 in C

BEATRICE ET BENEDICT: OVERTURE see
    Berlioz, Hector (Louis)

BEAU MONDE QUADRILLE, LE see Strauss,
    Johann, [Jr.]

BEAUTIFUL DREAMER, FOR SOLO VOICE AND
    STRING ORCHESTRA, [ARR.] see
    Foster, Stephen Collins

BEAUTIFUL HELEN, THE: OVERTURE see
    Offenbach, Jacques, Belle Helene,
    La: Overture

BEAUTIFUL MELUSINE see Mendelssohn-
    Bartholdy, Felix, Marchen Von Der
    Schonen Melusine

BEAUTIFUL SAVIOUR
    see Kocher, For The Beauty Of The
    Earth

BEC-5 see Fox, Frederick Alfred (Fred)

BECCE, GIUSEPPE (1881-1973)
    Andante Appassionato
      LIENAU f.s.   (B218)

    Bange Nacht
      LIENAU f.s.   (B219)

    Bauchtanz
      LIENAU f.s.   (B220)

    Cuore Vibrante *Op.31
      LIENAU f.s.   (B221)

    Feierlicher Aufmarsch
      LIENAU f.s.   (B222)

    Finale-Glucklicher Ausgang
      LIENAU f.s.   (B223)

    Im Zaubergarten
      LIENAU f.s.   (B224)

    Intermezzo Lirico *Op.13
      LIENAU f.s.   (B225)

    Komische Verfolgung Und Flucht
      LIENAU f.s.   (B226)

    Legende D'Amour *Op.11
      LIENAU f.s. contains also: Serenade
      D'Amalfi, Op.14   (B227)

    Ouverture Mignonne
      LIENAU f.s.   (B228)

    Preludio A Un Dramma
      LIENAU f.s.   (B229)

    Scene Passionnee *Op.23
      LIENAU f.s.   (B230)
      LIENAU f.s. contains also: Serenata
      Della Laguna, Op.32   (B231)

    Serenade
      see Becce, Giuseppe, Visione
      Orientale

BECCE, GIUSEPPE (cont'd.)

    Serenade D'Amalfi *Op.14
      see Becce, Giuseppe, Legende
      D'Amour

    Serenata Della Laguna *Op.32
      see Becce, Giuseppe, Scene
      Passionnee

    Serenata Mignonne *Op.34
      LIENAU f.s.   (B232)

    Serenata Napolitana *Op.33
      LIENAU f.s.   (B233)

    Spannender Dialog Mit Pausen
      LIENAU f.s.   (B234)

    Tempelweihe
      LIENAU f.s.   (B235)

    Tragische Intermezzo
      LIENAU f.s.   (B236)

    Visione Orientale
      LIENAU f.s. contains also: Serenade
                                   (B237)

BEDFORD, DAVID (1937-   )
    Alleluia Timpanis [8']
      4.4.4.4. 6.4.2+bass trom.1. timp,
      6perc,opt org,opt rec,strings
    sc UNIVER. UE 16121 $16.50, perf
    mat rent   (B238)

BEDOUIN CARAVAN IN THE DESERT see
    Meijering, Chiel

BEECKE, (FRANZ) IGNAZ VON (1733-1803)
    Symphony in C minor
    see SEVEN SYMPHONIES FROM THE COURT
    OF OETTINGEN-WALLERSTEIN (1773-
    1795)

BEECROFT, NORMA (1934-   )
    Improvvisazioni Concertanti No.3
    [15']
      2.2.2.2. 4.2.2.1. timp,2perc,
      strings,fl solo
    sc UNIVER. UE 16147 f.s., perf mat
    rent   (B239)

BEEKHUIS, HANNA (1889-   )
    Ballade
      see Vier Liederen, Naar Aanleiding
      Van Oud-Hollandsche Melodieen,
      For Solo Voice And Orchestra

    Chi-King, For Solo Voice And
    Orchestra
      2.2.2.2. 4.2.3.1. 3perc,harp,
      strings,Bar/Mez solo sc DONEMUS
      f.s., perf mat rent
      contains: Chinesisches
        Soldatenlied; Klage Der Garde;
        Mude Soldat, Der   (B240)

    Chinesisches Soldatenlied
      see Chi-King, For Solo Voice And
      Orchestra

    D'Une Qui Faisait La Longue
      see Trois Serenades, For Solo Voice
      And Orchestra

    Keizer Van Zweden, De
      see Vier Liederen, Naar Aanleiding
      Van Oud-Hollandsche Melodieen,
      For Solo Voice And Orchestra

    Klage Der Garde
      see Chi-King, For Solo Voice And
      Orchestra

    Kwatrijnen En Nachtstilte, For Solo
    Voice And String Orchestra [5']
      string orch,A solo
      sc DONEMUS f.s., perf mat rent
                                   (B241)
    Lentedans [6']
      1.0.1.0. 0.1.0.0. pno, strings
      without vla, db
      sc DONEMUS f.s., perf mat rent
                                   (B242)
    M'Aymerez-Vous Bien?
      see Trois Serenades, For Solo Voice
      And Orchestra

    Mude Soldat, Der
      see Chi-King, For Solo Voice And
      Orchestra

    Nachtegael Die Sanck Een Liedt, De
      see Vier Liederen, Naar Aanleiding
      Van Oud-Hollandsche Melodieen,
      For Solo Voice And Orchestra

    Trois Serenades, For Solo Voice And
    Orchestra
      2.2.2.2. 2.0.0.0. timp,perc,harp,
      strings,Mez solo sc DONEMUS f.s.,
      perf mat rent
      contains: D'Une Qui Faisait La
        Longue; M'Aymerez-Vous Bien?;
        Voici La Douce Nuit De Mai
                                   (B243)

BEEKHUIS, HANNA (cont'd.)

Vier Liederen, Naar Aanleiding Van
Oud-Hollandsche Melodieen, For
Solo Voice And Orchestra
3.2.2.2. 4.2.3.1. timp,perc,harp,
cel,strings,A solo sc DONEMUS
f.s., perf mat rent
contains: Ballade; Keizer Van
Zweden, De; Nachtegael Die
Sanck Een Liedt, De;
Wachterlied   (B244)

Voici La Douce Nuit De Mai
see Trois Serenades, For Solo Voice
And Orchestra

Wachterlied
see Vier Liederen, Naar Aanleiding
Van Oud-Hollandsche Melodieen,
For Solo Voice And Orchestra

BEERS, JACQUES (1902-1947)
Concerto for Solo Voice, Saxophone,
Piano and Orchestra
1.1.1.1.alto sax. 1.1.1.0. pno,
strings,S solo
sc DONEMUS f.s., perf mat rent
(B245)

Dominus Regit Me (Psalm No. 23)
see Tre Psalmi, For Solo Voice And
Orchestra

Exultare Justi In Domino (Psalm No.
33)
see Tre Psalmi, For Solo Voice And
Orchestra

Manyanas Liebeslieder, For Solo Voice
And Orchestra [17']
3.1.3.2. 3.2.2.0. timp,perc,
vibra,strings,S solo
sc DONEMUS f.s., perf mat rent
(B246)

Psalm No. 5 *see Verba Mea Auribus

Psalm No. 23 *see Dominus Regit Me

Psalm No. 33 *see Exultare Justi In
Domino

Tre Psalmi, For Solo Voice And
Orchestra
3.3.3.3. 2.2.2.0. timp,perc,harp,
strings,A/Bar solo sc DONEMUS
f.s., perf mat rent
contains: Dominus Regit Me (Psalm
No. 23); Exultare Justi In
Domino (Psalm No. 33); Verba
Mea Auribus (Psalm No. 5)
(B247)

Verba Mea Auribus (Psalm No. 5)
see Tre Psalmi, For Solo Voice And
Orchestra

BEETHOVEN, LUDWIG VAN (1770-1827)
Adelaide, For Solo Voice And
Orchestra
LUCKS 02428 sc $5.00, set $6.00,
pts $.75, ea.   (B248)

Ah! Perfido, For Solo Voice And
Orchestra *Op.65
LUCKS 02473 sc $6.50, set $7.50,
min sc $2.50, pts $.75, ea.
(B249)

Christus Am Olberge: I Love The Lord,
For Solo Voice And Orchestra
LUCKS 03342 sc $4.00, set $8.00,
pts $.60, ea.   (B250)

Christus Am Olberge: Oh My Heart Is
Sore, For Solo Voice And
Orchestra
LUCKS 03340 sc $4.00, set $8.00,
pts $.60, ea.   (B251)

Concerti For Piano And Orchestra,
Nos. 1-5
min sc RICORDI-IT PR 1239 $16.95
(B252)

Concerto for Piano and Orchestra, No.
1, Op. 15, in C
min sc BOOSEY 211 $6.00   (B253)
min sc PETERS 602 $7.00   (B254)
min sc ZEN-ON 890541 f.s.   (B255)
LUCKS 00011 sc $11.00, set $16.50,
pts $1.40, ea.   (B256)

Concerto for Piano and Orchestra, No.
2, Op. 19, in B flat
min sc PETERS 603 $7.00   (B257)
min sc ZEN-ON 890542 f.s.   (B258)
LUCKS 00012 sc $11.00, set $14.50,
pts $1.40, ea.   (B259)

Concerto for Piano and Orchestra, No.
3, Op. 37, in C minor
BROUDE BR. set $22.50, pts $1.75,
ea.   (B260)
min sc PETERS 604 $7.50   (B261)
min sc ZEN-ON 890543 f.s.   (B262)
LUCKS 00013 sc $11.00, set $18.00,
pts $1.40, ea.   (B263)

BEETHOVEN, LUDWIG VAN (cont'd.)

Concerto for Piano and Orchestra, No.
4, Op. 58, in G
min sc UNIVER. PH43 $7.00   (B264)
BROUDE BR. set $22.50, pts $1.75,
ea.   (B265)
min sc PETERS 605 $7.50   (B266)
min sc ZEN-ON 890544 f.s.   (B267)
LUCKS 00014 sc $9.50, set $18.00,
pts $1.40, ea.   (B268)

Concerto for Piano and Orchestra, No.
5, Op. 73, in E flat
BROUDE BR. set $27.50, pts $2.00,
ea.   (B269)
min sc PETERS 606 $8.50   (B270)
min sc ZEN-ON 890545 f.s.   (B271)
LUCKS 00015 sc $15.00, set $20.00,
pts $1.65, ea.   (B272)

Concerto For Violin And Orchestra In
C, Fragment *see Konzertsatz For
Violin And Orchestra In C, [arr.]

Concerto for Violin and Orchestra,
Op. 61, in D
min sc UNIVER. PH45 $4.00   (B273)
BROUDE BR. sc $16.50, set $27.50,
pts $1.75, ea.   (B274)
min sc PETERS 601 $6.00   (B275)
min sc ZEN-ON 890546 f.s.   (B276)
LUCKS 00501 sc $10.00, set $16.50,
min sc $3.00, pts $1.40, ea.
(B277)
(Schmidt-Gorg, J.) sc HENLE HN 325
$24.75   (B278)

Consecration Of The House *see Weihe
Des Hauses, Die

Coriolan Overture *Op.62
BROUDE BR. set $20.00, pts $1.25,
ea.   (B279)
LUCKS 05094 sc $8.00, set $15.00,
min sc $2.50, pts $1.15, ea.
(B280)
min sc ZEN-ON 890551 f.s.   (B281)

Creatures Of Prometheus, The:
Overture *see Geschopfe Des
Prometheus, Die: Overture

Deutsche Tanze, Zwolf
LUCKS 09083 sc $4.00, set $13.00,
pts $.95, ea.   (B282)

Deutsche Tanze, Zwolf, WoO. 8
3.2.2.2. 2.3.0.0. timp,perc,
strings
(Kovacs) "German Dances, Twelve,
WoO. 8" sc EULENBURG E10077 f.s.,
perf mat rent   (B283)

Egmont *Op.84
BREITKOPF-W perf mat rent   (B284)

Egmont: Overture
min sc UNIVER. PH44 $3.00   (B285)
BROUDE BR. set $17.75, pts $1.25,
ea.   (B286)
min sc ZEN-ON 890553 f.s.   (B287)
LUCKS 05095 sc $3.75, set $14.00,
min sc $2.00, pts $.95, ea.
(B288)

Emperor Concerto *see Concerto for
Piano and Orchestra, No. 5, Op.
73, in E flat

Eroica Symphony *see Symphony No. 3,
Op. 55, in E flat

Fantasy for Piano, Chorus and
Orchestra, Op. 80
LUCKS 00017 sc $9.00, set $21.00,
min sc $2.50, pts $1.40, ea., cor
pts $.25, voc sc $1.00, kbd pt
$2.00   (B289)

Fidelio: Abscheulicher, Wo Eilst Du
Hin, For Solo Voice And Orchestra
LUCKS 02357 sc $4.00, set $8.00,
pts $.75, ea.   (B290)

Fidelio: Gott, Welch' Dunkel Hier,
For Solo Voice And Orchestra
2.2.2.2. 4.0.0.0. timp,strings,T
solo
BREITKOPF-W perf mat rent   (B291)
LUCKS 02222 sc $4.00, set $8.00,
pts $.75, ea.   (B292)

Fidelio: Hat Man Nicht Auch Gold
Beineben, For Solo Voice And
Orchestra [3']
2.2.2.2. 2.0.0.0. strings,B solo
BREITKOPF-W perf mat rent   (B293)
LUCKS 03159 sc $4.00, set $8.00,
pts $.75, ea.   (B294)

Fidelio: O Namenlose Freude, For Solo
Voices And Orchestra
LUCKS 02046 sc $4.00, set $8.00,
pts $.75, ea.   (B295)

BEETHOVEN, LUDWIG VAN (cont'd.)

Fidelio: O War Ich Schon Mit Dir
Vereint, For Solo Voice And
Orchestra
LUCKS 02955 sc $4.00, set $8.00,
pts $.75, ea.   (B296)

Fidelio: Overture
BROUDE BR. set $20.00, pts $1.00,
ea.   (B297)
LUCKS 05096 sc $6.50, set $16.50,
min sc $2.00, pts $.95, ea.
(B298)
min sc ZEN-ON 890554 f.s.   (B299)

Fur Elise, [arr.]
LUCKS 01694 sc $2.00, set $5.00,
pts $.60, ea.   (B300)

German Dances, Twelve, WoO. 8 *see
Deutsche Tanze, Zwolf, WoO. 8

Geschopfe Des Prometheus, Die:
Overture
"Creatures Of Prometheus, The:
Overture" BROUDE BR. set $17.00,
pts $1.25, ea.   (B301)
"Prometheus: Overture" LUCKS 05106
sc $5.75, set $9.50, min sc
$2.00, pts $.95, ea.   (B302)

Gratulations-Menuett Und Tanze Fur
Orchester *CCU
sc,pap HENLE 4061 $39.00, sc,cloth
HENLE 4062 $46.25 Beethoven Werke
Series II, Volume 3   (B303)

Grosse Fuge, [arr.] *Op.133
(Weingartner) string orch LUCKS
01458 sc $5.00, set $10.00, pts
$2.00, ea.   (B304)

King Stephen: Overture *see Konig
Stephan: Overture

Konig Stephan: Overture
"King Stephen: Overture" LUCKS
08503 sc $10.00, set $20.00, min
sc $2.50, pts $1.15, ea. (B305)

Kontretanze, Zwolf
LUCKS 08625 sc $2.75, set $9.50,
pts $.75, ea.   (B306)

Kontretanze, Zwolf, WoO. 14
1.2.2.2. 2.0.0.0. perc,strings
sc EULENBURG E10038 f.s., perf mat
rent   (B307)

Konzertsatz For Violin And Orchestra
In C, [arr.]
(Hellmesberger) "Concerto For
Violin And Orchestra In C,
Fragment" 1.2.0.2. 2.2.0.0. timp,
strings,vln solo [19'] KALMUS
A1286 sc $25.00, perf mat rent,
set $25.00, pts $2.00, ea., solo
pt $2.00   (B308)

Landlerische Tanze, Sechs, WoO. 15
[10']
string orch without vla
(Biba, O.) sc,pts DOBLINGER DM 697
f.s.   (B309)

Leonore Overture No. 1 *Op.138
LUCKS 05101 sc $10.00, set $20.00,
pts $1.40, ea., min sc $2.50
(B310)

Leonore Overture No.3 *Op.72a
min sc UNIVER. PH18 $3.00   (B311)
BROUDE BR. set $25.00, pts $1.50,
ea.   (B312)
min sc ZEN-ON 890552 f.s.   (B313)
LUCKS 05100 sc $8.00, set $20.00,
min sc $2.50, pts $1.25, ea.
(B314)

Menuette, Zwolf, WoO. 7
3.2.2.2. 2.2.0.0. timp,strings
(Beyer) sc EULENBURG E10014 f.s.,
perf mat rent   (B315)

Musik Zu Einem Ritterballett, [arr.]
2.0.2.0. 2.2.0.0. strings sc,pts
HARMONIA 1536 f.s.   (B316)

Pastorale Symphony *see Symphony No.
6, Op. 68, in F

Prometheus: Overture *see Geschopfe
Des Prometheus, Die: Overture

Quartet, Op. 18, No. 4, in C minor,
[arr.]
(Spengel, H.L. von) 1.2.2.2.
2.2.3.0. timp,strings [18']
ORLANDO rent   (B317)

Romance for Violin and Orchestra, No.
1, Op. 40, in G
min sc PETERS 676 $4.50 contains
also: Romance for Violin and
Orchestra, No. 2, Op. 50, in F
(B318)
LUCKS 00554 sc $2.25, set $8.00,

BEETHOVEN, LUDWIG VAN (cont'd.)

min sc $2.50, pts $.95, ea.
contains also: Romance for Violin
and Orchestra, No. 2, Op. 50, in
F   (B319)

Romance for Violin and Orchestra, No.
2, Op. 50, in F
see Beethoven, Ludwig van, Romance
for Violin and Orchestra, No. 1,
Op. 40, in G
see Beethoven, Ludwig van, Romance
for Violin and Orchestra, No. 1,
Op. 40, in G

Rondo for Piano and Orchestra in B
flat, WoO. 6
LUCKS 00143 sc $3.75, set $10.50,
pts $.95, ea.   (B320)

Ruinen Von Athen, Die: Overture
*Op.113
min sc UNIVER. PH89 $3.00   (B321)
LUCKS 08502 sc $7.00, set $22.00,
min sc $2.00, pts $1.40, ea.
                                     (B322)
"Ruins Of Athens, The: Overture"
min sc PETERS 862 $5.00   (B323)

Ruinen Von Athen, Die: Turkischer
Marsch
LUCKS 05108 sc $2.75, set $9.50,
pts $.75, ea.   (B324)
"Ruins Of Athens, The: Turkish
March" BROUDE BR. set $10.00, pts
$.75, ea.   (B325)

Ruins Of Athens, The: Overture *see
Ruinen Von Athen, Die: Overture

Ruins Of Athens, The: Turkish March
*see Ruinen Von Athen, Die:
Turkischer Marsch

Short Symphony, [arr.] (from Sonata,
Op. 6)
(Keuning) 2.1.2.0. 0.2.0.0. timp,
strings sc,pts HARMONIA 3108 f.s.
                                     (B326)

Symphonies, Nos. 1-5
min sc RICORDI-IT PR 650 $16.95
                                     (B327)

Symphonies, Nos. 6-9
min sc RICORDI-IT PR 651 $16.95
                                     (B328)

Symphony No. 1, Op. 21, in C
min sc UNIVER. PH7 $3.50   (B329)
BROUDE BR. set $27.50, pts $1.75,
ea.   (B330)
study sc DOVER 23377-4 $7.50
contains also: Symphony No. 2,
Op. 36, in D; Symphony No. 3, Op.
55, in E flat   (B331)
min sc ZEN-ON 890501 f.s.   (B332)
LUCKS 05109 sc $8.00, set $17.00,
min sc $3.50, pts $1.40, ea.
                                     (B333)

Symphony No. 2, Op. 36, in D
see Beethoven, Ludwig van, Symphony
No. 1, Op. 21, in C
BROUDE BR. set $32.50, pts $2.00,
ea.   (B334)
min sc ZEN-ON 890502 f.s.   (B335)
min sc UNIVER. PH8 $4.50   (B336)

Symphony No. 3, Op. 55, in E flat
see Beethoven, Ludwig van, Symphony
No. 1, Op. 21, in C
BROUDE BR. set $42.50, pts $2.25,
ea.   (B337)
min sc ZEN-ON 890503 f.s.   (B338)
min sc UNIVER. PH9 $5.00   (B339)

Symphony No. 4, Op. 60, in B flat
min sc UNIVER. PH10 $5.00   (B340)
BROUDE BR. set $30.00, pts $2.25,
ea.   (B341)
study sc DOVER 23378-2 $6.50
contains also: Symphony No. 5,
Op. 67, in C minor   (B342)
min sc ZEN-ON 890504 f.s.   (B343)

Symphony No. 5, Op. 67, in C minor
see Beethoven, Ludwig van, Symphony
No. 4, Op. 60, in B flat
BROUDE BR. set $42.50, pts $2.25,
ea.   (B344)
min sc ZEN-ON 890505 f.s.   (B345)
min sc UNIVER. PH1 $4.50   (B346)

Symphony No. 6, Op. 68, in F
min sc UNIVER. PH3 $5.00   (B347)
BROUDE BR. set $42.50, pts $2.25,
ea.   (B348)
study sc DOVER 23379-0 $7.50
contains also: Symphony No. 7,
Op. 92, in A   (B349)
min sc ZEN-ON 890506 f.s.   (B350)

Symphony No. 7, Op. 92, in A
see Beethoven, Ludwig van, Symphony
No. 6, Op. 68, in F
BROUDE BR. set $40.00, pts $2.25,
ea.   (B351)
min sc ZEN-ON 890507 f.s.   (B352)

BEETHOVEN, LUDWIG VAN (cont'd.)

min sc UNIVER. PH11 $6.50   (B353)

Symphony No. 8, Op. 93, in F
min sc UNIVER. PH4 $6.00   (B354)
BROUDE BR. set $40.00, pts $2.25,
ea.   (B355)
study sc DOVER 23380-4 $7.95
contains also: Symphony No. 9,
Op. 125, in D minor   (B356)
min sc ZEN-ON 890508 f.s.   (B357)

Symphony No. 9, Op. 125, in D minor
see Beethoven, Ludwig van, Symphony
No. 8, Op. 93, in F
BROUDE BR. set $67.50, pts $3.25,
ea.   (B358)
min sc ZEN-ON 890509 f.s.   (B359)
min sc UNIVER. PH30 $7.00   (B360)

Tarpeja: Triumph-Marsch
LUCKS 05119 sc $3.00, set $7.00,
pts $.60, ea.   (B361)

Trauermarsch, [arr.] (from Sonata,
Op.26)
2.2.2.2. 2.2.3.0. timp,strings [5']
LIENAU perf mat rent   (B362)

Weihe Des Hauses, Die *Op.124
"Consecration Of The House" min sc
PETERS 863 $5.50   (B363)
"Consecration Of The House" LUCKS
05120 sc $11.00, set $20.00, min
sc $2.00, pts $1.15, ea.   (B364)

Wiener Tanze, Elf
KALMUS 5556 sc $4.00, set $11.00
                                     (B365)

BEGLI OCCHI VEZZOSI, FOR SOLO VOICE AND
ORCHESTRA see Haydn, [Franz] Joseph

BEGRUNDAN see Blomberg, Erik

BEGRUSSUNG see Klebe, Giselher

BEHEMOTH see Pierce, (Anne) Alexandra

BEHERRSCHER DER GEISTER, DER: OVERTURE
see Weber, Carl Maria von

BEHIND THE VEILS OF WORDS see Leeuw,
Charles van der

BEHLER, ALBERT
Sinfonia No. 2
2ob,2trp,hpsd,strings
sc,pts HARMONIA 2108 f.s.   (B366)

BEHREND, SIEGFRIED (1933-   )
Bon Jour, Ma Belle, For Solo Voice
And Orchestra
LUCKS 02136 set $8.00, pts $.75,
ea.   (B367)

BEI UNS IST ALLE TAGE SONNTAG see
Ailbout, Hans

BEI UNS Z'HAUS see Strauss, Johann,
[Jr.]

BEIDEN GRENADIERE, DIE, FOR SOLO VOICE
AND ORCHESTRA, [ARR.] see Schumann,
Robert (Alexander)

BEKKU, SADAO (1922-   )
Symphony No. 2 [29']
3(pic).2+English horn.2+bass
clar.2+contrabsn. 4.3.3.1.
timp,perc,xylo,vibra,cel/pno,
harp,strings
ONGAKU perf mat rent   (B368)

BEKRANZTER KAHN see Roos, Robert de

BELA KRIZANTEMA, FOR SOLO VOICES AND
ORCHESTRA see Bozic, Darijan

BELIEVE ME IF ALL THOSE ENDEARING YOUNG
CHARMS, FOR SOLO VOICE AND
ORCHESTRA
LUCKS 02933 sc $3.00, set $3.75, pts
$.75, ea.   (B369)

BELLA MIA FIAMMA, FOR SOLO VOICE AND
ORCHESTRA see Mozart, Wolfgang
Amadeus

BELLA ROSITA see Litkiewicz, Alfred

BELLE DU JOUR see Curtis-Smith, Curtis
O.B.

BELLE HELENE, LA: OVERTURE see
Offenbach, Jacques

BELLE MOLINARA, LA: DUETTO, FOR SOLO
VOICES AND ORCHESTRA see Paisiello,
Giovanni

BELLINI, GABRIELE (1936-   )
Concerto for Horn and Orchestra [14']
2.2.2.2. 0.2.1.0. 5perc,strings,
horn solo
sc,pts ZANIBON 4754 rent   (B370)

BELLINI, VINCENZO (1801-1835)
Capuleti E I Montecchi, I: Sinfonia
"Romeo And Juliet: Overture" KALMUS
A4665 sc $15.00, perf mat rent,
set $20.00, pts $1.25, ea.   (B371)

Gratias Agimus, For Solo Voice And
Orchestra [12']
1.0.1.0. 0.2.0.0. strings,S solo
sc BRUZZI S-061 $7.50, perf mat
rent   (B372)

Norma: Casta Diva, For Solo Voice And
Orchestra
LUCKS 02296 sc $6.50, set $10.50,
pts $.75, ea.   (B373)

Norma: Deh! Con Te, Mira O Norma, For
Solo Voices And Orchestra
LUCKS 02347 sc $9.00, set $14.00,
pts $.95, ea.   (B374)

Norma: Sinfonia
LUCKS 05125 sc $8.50, set $14.00,
pts $1.40, ea.   (B375)

Pirata, Il: Sinfonia
KALMUS A4677 sc $15.00, perf mat
rent, set $22.00, pts $1.25, ea.
                                     (B376)

Puritani, I: Qui La Voce; Vien
Diletto, For Solo Voice And
Orchestra
LUCKS 02210 sc $7.00, set $11.50,
pts $.75, ea.   (B377)

Romeo And Juliet: Overture *see
Capuleti E I Montecchi, I:
Sinfonia

Sonnambula, La: Cara Compagne; Come
Per Me Sereno; Sovra Il Sen, For
Solo Voice And Orchestra
LUCKS 02477 sc $10.00, set $19.00,
pts $.95, ea.   (B378)

Tecum Principium, For Solo Voice And
Orchestra
2.2.2.2. 2.0.0.0. strings,S solo
sc CARUS 40.062-01 f.s., voc sc
CARUS 40.062-03 f.s., pts CARUS
f.s.   (B379)

BELLMAN, CARL MIKAEL (1740-1795)
Bellman-Svit, For Solo Voice And
Orchestra, [arr.]
(Bjorlin, Ulf) 2.4.2.2. 4.3.0.0.
timp,strings,solo voice STIM perf
mat rent   (B380)

BELLMAN-SVIT, FOR SOLO VOICE AND
ORCHESTRA, [ARR.] see Bellman, Carl
Mikael

BELSAZER, FOR SOLO VOICE AND ORCHESTRA
see Bosmans, Henriette

BELSHAZZAR'S FEAST: SUITE, [ARR.] see
Sibelius, Jean

BEN-HAIM, PAUL (1897-   )
Symphonic Metamorphosis On A Bach
Chorale
study sc ISRAELI IMP 594 f.s.
                                     (B381)

Symphony No. 2
study sc ISRAELI IMP 537 f.s.   (B382)

BENDA, FRIEDRICH LUDWIG (1752-1792)
Sinfonia, MIN 964
string orch
LUCKS 01763 sc $3.00, set $4.75,
pts $.95, ea.   (B383)

BENDA, GEORG ANTON (JIRI ANTONIN)
(1722-1795)
Sinfonia No. 2 in G, [arr.]
2.2.2.0. 0.2.0.0. strings sc,pts
HARMONIA 2209 f.s.   (B384)

BENEDICT, [SIR] JULIUS (1804-1885)
Capinera, La, For Solo Voice And
Orchestra
"Wren, The" LUCKS 02072 set $8.00,
pts $.75, ea.   (B385)

Wren, The *see Capinera, La, For
Solo Voice And Orchestra

BENEDICTUS see Mackenzie, [Sir]
Alexander Campbell

BENES, JURAJ (1940-   )
Intermezzo No. 2 [21']
12vcl
SLOV.HUD.FOND 0-404 perf mat rent
                                     (B386)

Memoire
alto fl,clar in A,bsn,flugelhorn,
horn,db tuba,harp,9vln,3db
SLOV.HUD.FOND perf mat rent   (B387)

Music for Trumpet, Percussion and
Strings [13']
perc,vibra,marimba,strings,trp
solo

BENES, JURAJ (cont'd.)

    SLOV.HUD.FOND O-243 perf mat rent
                             (B388)

BENGALISCHER LICHTERTANZ see Esslinger,
    Ferdinand Adam

BENNETT, RICHARD RODNEY (1936-   )
    Actaeon, For Horn And Orchestra
        sc NOVELLO 2491 $13.75   (B389)

    Concerto for Double Bass and
        Orchestra
        sc,pts NOVELLO rent   (B390)

    Concerto for Harpsichord and
        Orchestra [22']
        study sc NOVELLO 2789-92 $12.50
                             (B391)

    Concerto for Violin and Orchestra
        2.2.1.2. 4.2.3.1. timp,perc,harp,
          pno,strings,vln solo
        NOVELLO sc $15.10, sc,pts rent
                             (B392)

    Zodiac
        2.3.3.3. 4.3.3.1. timp,perc,pno,
          harp,strings
        NOVELLO sc $12.40, sc,pts rent
                             (B393)

BENNETT, [SIR] WILLIAM STERNDALE
    (1816-1875)
    Symphonies, Three
        (Temperley, Nicholas) sc GARLAND
          ISBN 0-8240-3813-4 $90.00 "The
          Symphony", Vol. E-VII
          contains: Symphony in A; Symphony
          in G minor, MIN 202; Symphony
          in G minor, MIN 203   (B394)

    Symphony in A
        see Symphonies, Three

    Symphony in G minor, MIN 202
        see Symphonies, Three

    Symphony in G minor, MIN 203
        see Symphonies, Three

BENVENUTI, ARRIGO (1925-   )
    Canoni Enigmatici [12']
        2.1.3.0.2sax. 2.1.2.1. timp,
          3perc,xylo,vibra,gtr,carillon,
          glock,harp,cel,pno,org,strings
        BRUZZI S-002 perf mat rent (B395)

    Debris [14']
        1.1.1.1. 2.1.1.0. timp,glock,
          xylo,vibra,gtr,pno,harp,4vln,
          2vla,2vcl,db
        sc BRUZZI S-041 $10.00, perf mat
        rent   (B396)

    Et Inquietam Cor Nostrum [10']
        2.1.1.1. 1.1.0.0. xylo,vibra,
          harp,pno,vln,vla,vcl,db,
          electronic tape,solo voice
        BRUZZI S-054 perf mat rent (B397)

    Pot Pourri [10']
        1.1.2.1. 1.1.1.0. 2perc,harp,pno,
          cel,2vln,vla,vcl,db
         sc BRUZZI S-051 $25.50, perf mat
        rent   (B398)

    Ricomposizione [10']
        2.1.1.1. 1.1.0.0. xylo,vibra,
          harp,pno,2vln,vla,vcl,
          electronic tape
        BRUZZI S-054 perf mat rent (B399)

    Schemi E Cadenze [10']
        string orch,opt fl BRUZZI S-069
        perf mat rent   (B400)

BENVENUTO CELLINI: OVERTURE see
    Berlioz, Hector (Louis)

BERATTELSE see Blomberg, Erik

BERCEUSE see Jarnefelt, Armas

BERCEUSE see Schubert-Weber, S.

BERCEUSE see Trojahn, Manfred

BERCEUSE, LA see Strauss, Johann, [Jr.]

BERCEUSE GASCONNE see Lacombe, Paul

BERG, GUNNAR (1909-   )
    Essai Accoustique
        2.1.2.2. 1.1.1.0. perc,strings
        SAMFUNDET perf mat rent (B401)

    Mutationen
        2.2.2.2. 2.2.0.0. perc,harp,
          strings
        SAMFUNDET perf mat rent (B402)

    Passacaglia
        3.2.4.3.alto sax. 4.4.3.1. 3perc,
          strings
        SAMFUNDET perf mat rent (B403)

BERG, OLAV
    Concertino for Trumpet and Orchestra
        [13']
        2.2.2.2. 4.2.3.1. timp,perc,
          strings,trp solo
        NORGE   (B404)

BERGE, SIGURD (1929-   )
    Music To The Gudbrandsdals Play, The
        3.0.3.0. 0.4.3.2. 3euphonium,
          perc,12vln,lute,gtr
        NORGE   (B405)

BERGEIJK, GILIUS VAN (1946-   )
    Opwaartsche Wegen [30']
        1.2.2.0.alto sax. 4.1.0.0. 2perc,
          2vln,vla
        sc DONEMUS f.s., perf mat rent
                             (B406)

    Orkestspel [20'-25']
        2.2.2.2. 2.0.0.0. 8vln,4vla,2vcl,
          db
        sc DONEMUS f.s., perf mat rent
                             (B407)

BERGEL, BERND (1909-   )
    Two Movements For Strings
        string orch
        study sc ISRAELI IMP 567 f.s. (B408)

BERGER, HANS
    Chez Nous [6']
        3(pic).2(bass clar).2. 4.3.3.1.
          2perc,harp,strings
        RIES perf mat rent   (B409)

BERGER, THEODOR (1905-   )
    Capriccio, Op. 3a [5']
        2(pic).2(English horn).2(bass
          clar).2. 2.2.0.0. perc,strings,
          2vln soli
        RIES perf mat rent   (B410)

    Impressionen *Op.8 [20']
        2.1+English horn.2(bass clar).2.
          4.2.3.0. timp,2perc,harp,
          strings
        RIES perf mat rent   (B411)

BERGHORN, ALFRED (1911-1978)
    Konzertante Sinfonie *Op.34 [32']
        1.1.1.1. 1.1.1.0. timp,strings
        RIES perf mat rent   (B412)

BERGKRISTALL see Bussotti, Sylvano

BERIO, LUCIANO (1925-   )
    Allez Hop [28']
        3.3.4.3+3sax. 4.4.3.1. timp,harp,
          pno,cel,glock,vibra,marimba,
          elec gtr,perc,strings
        ZERBONI perf mat rent   (B413)

    Chemins IV On Sequenza VII, For Oboe
        And Strings [10']
        3vln,3vla,3vcl,db,ob solo
        (in the US available from AMP)
        UNIVER. perf mat rent   (B414)

    Ritorno Degli Snovidenia, Il, For
        Violoncello And Orchestra [19']
        3.2.3.2+alto sax. 2.2.2.1. pno,
          3vln,3vla,3vcl,2db,vcl solo
        (in the US available from AMP) sc
        UNIVER. UE 16649 f.s., perf mat
        rent   (B415)

    Scene [12']
        2+2pic.2+English horn.2+clar in E
          flat+bass clar.2+contrabsn.alto
          sax. 3.3.3.1. timp,2perc,harp,
          cel,pno,strings
        (in the US available from AMP)
        UNIVER. perf mat rent   (B416)

BERIOT, CHARLES-AUGUST DE (1802-1870)
    Concerto for Violin and Orchestra,
        No. 7, Op. 76, in G
        LUCKS 00503 set $14.00, pts $1.15,
          ea.   (B417)

    Concerto for Violin and Orchestra,
        No. 9, Op. 104, in A minor
        LUCKS 00504 set $14.00, pts $1.15,
          ea.   (B418)

    Fantaisie Ballet *see Scene De
        Ballet, For Violin And Orchestra

    Scene De Ballet, For Violin And
        Orchestra *Op.100
        "Fantaisie Ballet" LUCKS 00572 set
        $23.00, pts $1.15, ea.   (B419)

BERKELEY, MICHAEL
    Concerto for Oboe and String
        Orchestra [25']
        string orch,ob solo
        OXFORD perf mat rent   (B420)

    Fantasia Concertante [21']
        1.2.0.2. 2.0.0.0. strings
        OXFORD perf mat rent   (B421)

    Flames [12']
        3.3.3.3. 4.3.3.1. timp,3perc,
          harp,strings

BERKELEY, MICHAEL (cont'd.)

    OXFORD perf mat rent   (B422)

    Meditations [14']
        string orch
        OXFORD perf mat rent   (B423)

    Primavera [6']
        3.3.3.3. 4.3.3.1. timp,2perc,
          harp,strings,opt cor
        OXFORD perf mat rent   (B424)

    Uprising [21']
        2.2.2.2. 2.2.0.0. timp,strings
        OXFORD perf mat rent   (B425)

    Wild Winds, The [12']
        1.1.2.1. 2.1.0.0. perc,pno,
          strings,S solo
        OXFORD perf mat rent   (B426)

BERLIN, JOHAN DANIEL (1714-1787)
    Symphony in D
        see SYMPHONY IN NORWAY, THE

BERLIN, JOHAN HENRICH (1741-1807)
    Symphony in C
        see SYMPHONY IN NORWAY, THE

BERLIOZ, HECTOR (LOUIS) (1803-1869)
    Beatrice Et Benedict: Overture
        LUCKS 05138 sc $9.50, set $23.00,
          min sc $2.50, pts $1.40, ea.
                             (B427)

    Benvenuto Cellini: Overture
        2.2.2.4. 4.4+2cornet.3.1. timp,
          perc,strings
        LUCKS 05139 sc $9.50, set $28.00,
          min sc $2.50, pts $1.40, ea.
                             (B428)
        sc LIENAU f.s.   (B429)

    Carnaval Romain, Le *Op.9 [9']
        2(pic).2(English horn).2.4. 4.2+
          2cornet.3.0. timp,perc,strings
        "Roman Carnival" min sc PETERS 620
        $4.00
        "Roman Carnival" LUCKS 05144 sc
        $8.00, set $23.00, min sc $2.50,
        pts $1.15, ea.   (B431)
        "Romischer Carneval" sc,pts LIENAU
        rent   (B432)

    Corsaire, Le *Op.21 [7']
        2.2.2.4. 4.2+2cornet.3.1. timp,
          strings
        COSTALL perf mat rent   (B433)
        LUCKS 05043 sc $9.50, set $28.00,
        min sc $2.50, pts $1.40, ea.
                             (B434)

    Damnation De Faust, La: Ballet Des
        Sylphes
        "Damnation Of Faust: Dance Of The
        Sylphes" LUCKS 05142 sc $3.75,
        set $9.50, min sc $2.00, pts
        $.75, ea.   (B435)

    Damnation De Faust, La: Chanson De La
        Puce, For Solo Voice And
        Orchestra
        "Damnation Of Faust: Flea Song"
        LUCKS 03360 sc $4.00, set $8.00,
        pts $.60, ea.   (B436)

    Damnation De Faust, La: Marche
        Hongroise
        "Damnation Of Faust: Hungarian
        March" LUCKS 05140 sc $5.00, set
        $13.50, min sc $2.00, pts $.60,
        ea.   (B437)

    Damnation De Faust, La: Marche
        Hongroise, Ballet Des Sylphes,
        Menuet Des Follets
        "Dannazione Di Faust, La: Marcia
        Ungherese, Balletto Dei Silfi,
        Minuetto Dei Folletti" sc
        RICORDI-IT PR913 f.s.   (B438)

    Damnation De Faust, La: Menuet Des
        Follets
        "Damnation Of Faust: Dance Of The
        Sprites" KALMUS A1305 sc $6.00,
        perf mat rent, set $20.00, pts
        $1.00, ea.   (B439)
        "Damnation Of Faust: Dance Of The
        Sprites" LUCKS 05141 sc $3.75,
        set $13.50, min sc $2.00, pts
        $.75, ea.   (B440)

    Damnation De Faust, La: Serenade De
        Mephisto, "Devant La Maison", For
        Solo Voice And Orchestra
        LUCKS 03090 sc $4.00, set $8.00,
        pts $.75, ea.   (B441)

    Damnation De Faust, La: Voici Des
        Roses, For Solo Voice And
        Orchestra
        LUCKS 03356 sc $4.00, set $8.00,
        pts $.75, ea.   (B442)

    Damnation Of Faust: Dance Of The
        Sprites *see Damnation De Faust,
        La: Menuet Des Follets

BERLIOZ, HECTOR (LOUIS) (cont'd.)

Damnation Of Faust: Dance Of The
   Sylphes *see Damnation De Faust,
   La: Ballet Des Sylphes

Damnation Of Faust: Flea Song *see
   Damnation De Faust, La: Chanson
   De La Puce, For Solo Voice And
   Orchestra

Damnation Of Faust: Hungarian March
   *see Damnation De Faust, La:
   Marche Hongroise

Dannazione Di Faust, La: Marcia
   Ungherese, Balletto Dei Silfi,
   Minuetto Dei Folletti *see
   Damnation De Faust, La: Marche
   Hongroise, Ballet Des Sylphes,
   Menuet Des Follets

Death Of Cleopatra, For Solo Voice
   And Orchestra *see Mort De
   Cleopatre, La, For Solo Voice And
   Orchestra

Enfance Du Christ, L': Prelude, Part
   II, "La Fuite En Egypte"
   LUCKS 08994 sc $2.75, set $7.50,
   pts $.95, ea.   (B443)

Fantastic Symphony *see Symphonie
   Fantastique

Francs-Juges, Les: Overture *Op.3
   [13']
   2.2.2.3. 4.3.3.0. timp,perc,
   strings
   COSTALL perf mat rent   (B444)

Hungarian March
   sets NOVELLO 9029-30 $39.00, and
   up, pts NOVELLO 9584 $1.25, ea.,
   sc NOVELLO 9028 $8.75   (B445)

King Lear Overture *Op.4 [14']
   1+pic.2.2.2. 4.2.3.1. timp,
   strings
   "Roi Lear Overture" COSTALL perf
   mat rent   (B446)

Mort De Cleopatra, La, For Solo Voice
   And Orchestra
   2.2.2.2. 4.2.3.0. timp,strings,S
   solo
   BREITKOPF-W perf mat rent (B447)
   LUCKS 03013 sc $11.50, set $23.00,
   min sc $6.00, pts $1.40, ea.
                              (B448)
   "Death Of Cleopatra, For Solo Voice
   And Orchestra" KALMUS A2575 sc
   $12.00, perf mat rent, set
   $27.00, pts $1.50, ea.   (B449)

Nuits D'Ete, Les, For Solo Voice And
   Orchestra *Op.7
   COSTALL perf mat rent   (B450)

Reverie Et Caprice, For Violin And
   Orchestra *Op.8 [10'30"]
   2.2.2.2. 2.0.0.0. strings,vln
   solo
   BREITKOPF-W perf mat rent (B451)
   COSTALL perf mat rent   (B452)

Roi Lear Overture *see King Lear
   Overture

Roman Carnival *see Carnaval Romain,
   Le

Romeo And Juliet: Love Scene *see
   Romeo Et Juliette: Scene D'Amour

Romeo And Juliet: Queen Mab, Scherzo
   *see Romeo Et Juliette: La Reine
   Mab, Scherzo

Romeo And Juliet: Romeo Alone -
   Festivities At Capulet's *see
   Romeo Et Juliette: Grand Fete
   Chez Capulet

Romeo Et Juliette: Grand Fete Chez
   Capulet
   "Romeo And Juliet: Romeo Alone -
   Festivities At Capulet's" LUCKS
   08393 sc $10.00, set $17.00, pts
   $.95, ea.   (B453)

Romeo Et Juliette: La Reine Mab,
   Scherzo
   "Romeo And Juliet: Queen Mab,
   Scherzo" LUCKS 05145 sc $12.00,
   set $25.00, pts $1.40, ea. (B454)

Romeo Et Juliette: Scene D'Amour
   "Romeo And Juliet: Love Scene"
   LUCKS 08513 sc $5.75, set $9.50,
   pts $.95, ea.   (B455)

Romischer Carneval *see Carnaval
   Romain, Le

BERLIOZ, HECTOR (LOUIS) (cont'd.)

Symphonie Fantastique *Op.14
   min sc ZEN-ON 891501 f.s. (B456)
   LUCKS 08514 sc $25.00, set $60.00,
   min sc $5.00, pts $3.00, ea.
                              (B457)
   "Fantastic Symphony" min sc PETERS
   621 $10.00   (B458)

Symphonie Fantastique: March To The
   Scaffold, [arr.]
   (Carter, Anthony) 2.2.3.2. 4.3.3.1.
   timp,perc,pno/org,strings [6'] sc
   OXFORD 77.865 $9.75, set OXFORD
   $27.50, pts OXFORD $1.15, ea.
                              (B459)

Symphonie Funebre Et Triomphale
   *Op.15
   BREITKOPF-W perf mat rent (B460)

Waverley Overture *Op.2b [9']
   2.2.2.4. 4.3.3.1. timp,strings
   COSTALL perf mat rent   (B461)

BERNIER, RENE (1905-   )
   Offrande A Erard, For Harp And
   Orchestra
   LEDUC perf mat rent   (B462)

BERNSTEIN, LEONARD (1918-   )
   Slava! [6']
   2+pic.2+English horn.3+bass
   clar.2+contrabsn.soprano sax.
   4.3.3.1. elec gtr,pno,timp,
   perc,strings
   BOOSEY perf mat rent   (B463)

Songfest, For Solo Voices And
   Orchestra [40']
   3.3.4.3. 4.3.3.1. harp,timp,perc,
   strings,SMezATBarB soli
   BOOSEY perf mat rent   (B464)

BERTONI, FERDINANDO (GIUSEPPE)
   (1725-1813)
   Sinfonia in C, MIN 73 [9']
   2ob,2trp,strings
   (Bonelli, E.) sc ZANIBON 4072 f.s.,
   pts ZANIBON 4073 f.s.   (B465)

BERWALD, FRANZ (1796-1868)
   Concerto for Violin and Orchestra,
   Op. 2, in C sharp minor
   sc BAREN. BA 4904 f.s., perf mat
   rent   (B466)

Estrella De Soria: Overture
   2.2.2.2. 4.2.3.0. timp,strings
   KALMUS 5420 sc $12.00, perf mat
   rent, set $35.00, pts $2.25, ea.
                              (B467)
   (Castegren, Nils) BAREN. BA 6756
   perf mat rent   (B468)

Konzertstuck for Bassoon and
   Orchestra
   KALMUS 5421 sc $9.00, perf mat
   rent, set $30.00, pts $2.00, ea.
                              (B469)

Sinfonie Singuliere (Symphony No. 5
   in C) [30']
   2.2.2.2. 4.2.3.0. timp,strings
   KALMUS 5419 sc $21.00, perf mat
   rent, set $50.00, pts $3.00, ea.
                              (B470)

Symphony No. 5 in C *see Sinfonie
   Singuliere

BESCHWINGTES ZWISCHENSPIEL see Lurmann,
   Ludwig

BESSERE ZEITEN WALZER see Strauss,
   Eduard

BETTINELLI, ANGELO (1878-1913)
   Carovane Notturne [12']
   3.3.2.2. 4.2.3.1. timp,harp,cel,
   perc,strings
   manuscript CARISCH   (B471)

Saraband [10']
   3.2.2.2. 4.2.3.1. timp,perc,harp,
   strings
   manuscript CARISCH   (B472)

BETTINELLI, BRUNO (1913-   )
   Appunti Per Un Notturno [10']
   1.1.1.1. 2.1.0.0. perc,vibra,
   strings
   sc CARISCH 22045 f.s., perf mat
   rent   (B473)

Cinque Liriche Di Montale, For Solo
   Voice And Orchestra [29']
   fl,clar,strings,S solo
   sc CARISCH 21284 f.s., pts CARISCH
   rent   (B474)

Divertimento for Harpsichord and
   Orchestra
   3.2.2.2. 2.1.0.0. timp,perc,
   strings,hpsd solo
   sc CARISCH 22052 f.s., perf mat
   rent   (B475)

BETTINELLI, BRUNO (cont'd.)

Fantasia Concertante, For String
   Quartet And Orchestra [19']
   3.2.2.2. 4.2.2.0. perc,pno,
   strings,string quar soli
   CARISCH 20877 perf mat rent (B476)

Movimento Sinfonico [8']
   3.2.3.2. 4.3.3.1. timp,perc,pno,
   strings
   CARISCH perf mat rent   (B477)

Musica Per 12 [10']
   11strings,hpsd
   perf mat rent sc CARISCH 21920, pts
   CARISCH 21920A   (B478)

Psalm No. 4 for Solo Voice and
   Orchestra [16']
   1.1.1.1. 2.2.0.0. timp,2pno,
   strings,S solo
   sc,pts ZANIBON D236 rent   (B479)

Ricercari [11']
   fl,ob,clar,bsn,2horn,pno,strings
   sc,pts ZANIBON D249 rent   (B480)

Sinfonia No. 2 [33']
   2+pic.2+English horn.2+bass
   clar.2+contrabsn. 4.3.3.1.
   timp,strings
   sc,pts ZANIBON D210 rent   (B481)

Sinfonia No. 3 [20']
   string orch
   sc,pts ZANIBON D220 rent   (B482)

Sinfonia No. 5
   sc RICORDI-IT 132360 f.s. (B483)

Studio
   sc RICORDI-IT 132179 f.s. (B484)

Varianti
   sc RICORDI-IT 131687 f.s. (B485)

BETULIA LIBERATE, LA: SINFONIA see
   Holzbauer, Ignaz

BETWEEN BRIDGES, FOR TRUMPET AND
   CHAMBER ORCHESTRA see Cytron,
   Warren A.

BETWEEN TWO WORLDS, FOR SAXOPHONE AND
   ORCHESTRA see Hekster, Walter

BEURDEN, BERNARD VAN (1933-   )
   A Vous
   5.1.1.0. 0.0.0.0. perc,pno 4-
   hands,strings
   sc DONEMUS f.s., perf mat rent
                              (B486)

Concerto for Accordion and Orchestra
   [12']
   2.2.2.2. 2.2.2.0. timp,perc,
   strings,acord solo
   sc DONEMUS f.s., perf mat rent
                              (B487)

Konsertante Muziek, For Viola And
   Orchestra [15']
   2.2.2.2. 2.2.2.1. perc,vla solo
   sc DONEMUS f.s., perf mat rent
                              (B488)

BEWEGINGEN see Vries, Klaas de

BEWEGTES SPIEL see Ritter, Helmut

BEWEGUNGEN see Friedrichs, Gunter

BEYERMAN-WALRAVEN, JEANNE (1878-1969)
   Zieke Buur, Uit: "Fantomen" Van F.
   Pauwels, De, For Solo Voice And
   Orchestra [15']
   4.3.3.4. 4.3.3.1. timp,perc,
   2harp,cel,strings,A solo
   sc DONEMUS f.s., perf mat rent
                              (B489)

BI-CENTURION see Gutche, Gene

BIALAS, GUNTER (1907-   )
   Gestiefelte Kater, Der: Szenen Und
   Ballettmusik [14']
   2+pic.2.2.2+contrabsn. 4.3.3.1.
   timp,2perc,pno,strings
   BAREN. BA 6776 perf mat rent (B490)

Introitus - Exodus [26']
   2+pic.2.2.2+contrabsn. 4.3.3.1.
   timp,3perc,harp,strings,org
   solo
   BAREN. BA 6716 perf mat rent (B491)

Weg Nach Eisenstadt, Der [16']
   1(pic).2.0.2. 2.0.0.0. timp,
   strings
   study sc BAREN. BA 6774 f.s., perf
   mat rent   (B492)

BIBALO, ANTONIO (1922-   )
   Symphony No. 2 [35']
   2(pic).2(English horn).2(bass
   clar).2(contrabsn). 4.3.3.0.
   timp,2perc,harp,strings
   sc HANSEN-DEN WH 29652 $41.75
                              (B493)

BIBER, CARL (? -ca. 1750)
    Sonata for 2 English Horns
      see Biber, Carl, Sonata for 2 Oboes

    Sonata for 2 Oboes
      2ob/2English horn,bsn,strings
      without vla,cont
      sc UNIVER. UE 25A005 $12.00, set
      UNIVER. UE 25B005 $13.00, pts
      UNIVER. $2.00, ea. contains also:
      Sonata for 2 English Horns (B494)

    Sonata Sancti Ioannis Nepomunceni
      [5']
      2bsn,strings without vla,cont,vln
      solo,vcl solo
      sc UNIVER. UE 25A006 $9.50, set
      UNIVER. UE 25B006 $12.50, pts
      UNIVER. $1.75, ea.   (B495)

    Sonatas For Clarino, Three
      strings without vla,cont, clarino
      solo
      sc UNIVER. UE 25A002 $12.50, set
      UNIVER. UE 25B002 $13.00, pts
      UNIVER. $1.75, ea.   (B496)

    Sonatas For Clarino, Two
      4trp in C,bsn,timp,strings
      without vla,cont,vln solo,
      clarino solo
      sc UNIVER. UE 25A003 $12.00, set
      UNIVER. UE 25B003 $13.00, pts
      UNIVER. $2.00, ea.   (B497)

    Sonatas For Trumpets, Two
      4trom,bsn,timp,strings without
      vla,cont, 4 clarini
      sc UNIVER. UE 25A004 $12.00, set
      UNIVER. UE 25B004 $13.00, pts
      UNIVER. $2.00, ea.   (B498)

BIBER, HEINRICH IGNAZ FRANZ VON
    (1644-1704)
    Battalia
      string orch,cont
      (Blahnik, Joel) KERBY set $20.00,
      sc $6.00   (B499)

BICENTENNIAL FANFARE see Proto, Frank

BIENER, GUSTAV (1926-   )
    Kleine Suite
      string orch
      sc SCHWANN S 2277   (B500)

BIERBAUM-LIEDER, FOR SOLO VOICE AND
    ORCHESTRA see Bordewijk-Roepman,
    Johanna

BIJ EEN DOODE see Badings, Henk

BIJL, THEO VAN DER (1886-1971)
    Convoi d'Une Pauvre Fille, Le, For
      Solo Voice And Orchestra [5']
      2.3.3.2. 0.0.0.0. harp,cel,
      strings,med solo
      sc DONEMUS f.s., perf mat rent
                                   (B501)
    Douleur Chretienne, La, For Solo
      Voice And Orchestra [4']
      2.2.2.2. 4.0.0.0. harp,strings,
      low solo
      sc DONEMUS f.s., perf mat rent
                                   (B502)
    Errants, Les, For Solo Voice And
      Orchestra [4']
      2.2.2.2. 4.0.0.0. harp,cel,
      strings,med solo
      sc DONEMUS f.s., perf mat rent
                                   (B503)
    Zu Wem Spreche Ich Heute?, For Solo
      Voice And Orchestra [5']
      2.2.2.3. 4.0.0.0. harp,org,cel,
      strings,low solo
      sc DONEMUS f.s., perf mat rent
                                   (B504)

BIJOUTERIE QUADRILLE see Strauss,
    Johann, [Jr.]

BIJOUX POLKA see Strauss, Johann, [Jr.]

BIJVANCK, HENK (1909-1969)
    Harpzangen Van Koning David, For Solo
      Voice And Orchestra [20']
      2.2.2.3. 4.3.2.2. timp,perc,
      2harp,strings,A/Mez solo
      sc DONEMUS f.s., perf mat rent
                                   (B505)

BILBAO see Fischer-Larsen, Eric

BILDER EINER AUSSTELLUNG, [ARR.] see
    Mussorgsky, Modest Petrovich,
    Pictures At An Exhibition, [arr.]

BILDER VOM JAHRMARKT, FOR FLUTE AND
    ORCHESTRA see Zieritz, Grete von

BILUCAGLIA, CLAUDIO (1946-   )
    Lied, For Solo Voice And Instrumental
      Ensemble [15']
      1.1.0.0. 0.1.0.0. pno,perc,vibra,
      2vln,vla,vcl,S solo
      sc ZERBONI 8127 f.s., pts ZERBONI
      8128 rent   (B506)

BIN NUR EIN ARMER DICHTER see Geisler,
    Willy

BINKERD, GORDON WARE (1916-   )
    Symphony No. 1
      sc BOOSEY $12.00   (B507)

    Symphony No. 2
      sc BOOSEY $10.00   (B508)

    Symphony No. 3
      sc BOOSEY $10.00   (B509)

BIOGRAMMA see Maderna, Bruno

BIRD, ARTHUR (1856-1923)
    Gavotte And Valse Menuet [6']
      string orch sc MARGUN BP 1042
      $2.50, perf mat rent   (B510)

    Impromptu for Violoncello and Chamber
      Orchestra [6']
      1.1.2.1. 2.0.0.0. strings,vcl
      solo
      MARGUN BP 1044 perf mat rent (B511)

    Melodie, For Violin And Orchestra
      *Op.5,No.1 [4']
      2.2.2.2. 2.0.0.0. timp,strings,
      vln solo
      MARGUN BP 1045 perf mat rent (B512)

    Spanish Dance *Op.9,No.2 [4']
      2.2.2.2. 2.2.0.0. timp,perc,
      strings,vln solo
      MARGUN BP 1046 perf mat rent (B513)

    Two Pieces, For Flute And Orchestra
      *Op.17 [8']
      0.2.2.2. 2.0.0.0. perc,harp,
      strings,fl solo
      MARGUN BP 1043 perf mat rent (B514)

    Two Poems For Orchestra *Op.25 [7']
      2.2.2.2. 2.2.0.0. timp,perc,
      strings
      MARGUN BP 1002 perf mat rent (B515)

BIRTH OF MUSIC, THE see Keuning, Hans
    P.

BIRTHDAY PARTY see Anderson, Leroy

BIRTWISTLE, HARRISON (1934-   )
    Carmen Arcadiae Mechanicae Perpetuum
      [12']
      1(pic).1.1(bass
      clar).1(contrabsn). 1.1.1.0.
      marimba,strings, electric piano
      sc UNIVER. UE 16166 $38.00, perf
      mat rent   (B516)

    Melencolia I, For Clarinet, Harp And
      String Orchestra [20']
      string orch,clar solo,harp solo
      sc UNIVER. UE 16128 $21.00, perf
      mat rent   (B517)

    Silbury Air
      1.1.1.1. 1.1.1.0. perc,harp,pno,
      strings
      sc UNIVER. 50 16141 $62.00   (B518)

    Visions Of Francesco Petrarca, The,
      For Solo Voice, Instrumental
      Ensemble And School Orchestra
      [65']
      1.1.1.0. 1.1.1.0. 2vln,vcl,Bar
      solo, and school orchestra
      sc UNIVER. UE 14176 f.s., perf mat
      rent   (B519)

BIS (EVOCATION), FOR PIANO AND
    ORCHESTRA see Groot, Cor (Cornelius
    Wilhelmus) de

BISATTA see Runnstrom, William

BISCHOF, RAINER (1947-   )
    Deduktionen *Op.7 [13']
      string orch
      sc,pts DOBLINGER rent   (B520)

BISGAARD, LARS
    Passacaglia
      3.2.3.3. 4.2.2.1. timp,5perc,cel,
      harp,strings
      SAMFUNDET perf mat rent   (B521)

BISHOP, [SIR] HENRY (ROWLEY)
    (1786-1855)
    Lo, Here The Gentle Lark, For Solo
      Voice And Orchestra
      LUCKS 02002 sc $3.75, set $6.00,
      pts $.75, ea.   (B522)

BIST DU BEI MIR, FOR SOLO VOICE AND
    STRING ORCHESTRA, [ARR.] see Bach,
    Johann Sebastian

BIST DU BEI MIR, [ARR.] see Bach,
    Johann Sebastian

BITTE SCHON POLKA see Strauss, Johann,
    [Jr.]

BIZET, GEORGES (1838-1875)
    Amor Est Un Oiseau Rebelle, L' *see
      Carmen: Habanera, For Solo Voice
      And Orchestra

    Arlesienne, L': Suite No. 1
      LUCKS 05160 sc $12.00, set $30.00,
      min sc $3.00, pts $1.40, ea.
                                   (B523)
    Arlesienne, L': Suite No. 1, [arr.]
      (Hoffmann) 2.2(English
      horn).2.2.alto sax. 4.4.3.0.
      timp,perc,harp,pno,strings BROUDE
      BR. set $40.00, pts $1.75, ea.
                                   (B524)
    Arlesienne, L': Suite No. 2
      LUCKS 05161 sc $12.00, set $30.00,
      min sc $5.00, pts $1.40, ea.
                                   (B525)
    Arlesienne, L': Suite No. 2, [arr.]
      (Hoffmann) 2.2(English
      horn).2.2.alto sax. 4.4.3.0.
      timp,perc,harp,pno,strings pts
      BROUDE BR. $1.50, ea.   (B526)
    Arlesienne, L': Suites Nos. 1 And 2
      min sc ZEN-ON 890851 f.s.   (B527)

    Carmen: Air De Fleur, For Solo Voice
      And Orchestra
      "Fleur Que Tu M'Avais Jetee, La"
      LUCKS 02060 sc $3.75, set $8.00,
      pts $.75, ea.   (B528)
    Carmen: Chanson Du Toreador, For Solo
      Voice And Orchestra
      "Carmen: Toreador Song" LUCKS 02029
      sc $3.75, set $7.50, pts $.75,
      ea.   (B529)
    Carmen: En Vain Pour Eviter, For Solo
      Voice And Orchestra
      LUCKS 03109 sc $4.00, set $8.00,
      pts $.75, ea.   (B530)
    Carmen: Entr'actes II, III, IV [6']
      2(pic).2(English horn).2.2.
      4.2.3.0. timp,perc,harp,strings
      KALMUS A1320 sc $10.00, perf mat
      rent, set $30.00, pts $1.50, ea.
                                   (B531)
      LUCKS 10279 sc $10.00, set $30.00,
      pts $1.50, ea.   (B532)

    Carmen Fantasy, For Violin And
      Orchestra
      (Sarasate) LUCKS 00505 set $28.00,
      pts $1.60, ea., solo pt $2.00
                                   (B533)
    Carmen: Gypsy Song
      LUCKS 02994 sc $3.75, set $11.50,
      pts $.75, ea.   (B534)
    Carmen: Habanera, For Solo Voice And
      Orchestra
      "Amor Est Un Oiseau Rebelle, L'"
      LUCKS 02021 sc $3.75, set $11.50,
      pts $.75, ea.   (B535)
    Carmen: Je Dis Que Rien Ne
      M'Epouvante, For Solo Voice And
      Orchestra
      LUCKS 02003 sc $3.75, set $7.50,
      pts $.75, ea.   (B536)
    Carmen: Je Suis Escamillo, For Solo
      Voices And Orchestra
      LUCKS 03376 sc $4.00, set $8.00,
      pts $.60, ea.   (B537)
    Carmen: Je Vais Danser En Votre
      Honneur, For Solo Voices And
      Orchestra
      LUCKS 03141 sc $7.00, set $14.00,
      pts $.75, ea.   (B538)
    Carmen: Marche
      (Tobani) LUCKS 05155 set $11.00,
      pts $.95, ea.   (B539)
    Carmen: Parle-Moi De Ma Mere, For
      Solo Voices And Orchestra
      LUCKS 02442 sc $5.00, set $12.00,
      pts $.75, ea.   (B540)
    Carmen: Prelude
      LUCKS 09039 sc $5.50, set $18.00,
      pts $.95, ea.   (B541)
    Carmen: Seguedille, For Solo Voices
      And Orchestra
      LUCKS 02166 sc $3.75, set $7.50,
      pts $.75, ea.   (B542)
    Carmen: Si Tu M'Aimes, For Solo
      Voices And Orchestra
      LUCKS 03378 sc $4.00, set $8.00,
      pts $.60, ea.   (B543)
    Carmen: Suite No. 1
      BROUDE BR. sc $6.00, set $25.00,
      pts $1.50, ea.   (B544)
      LUCKS 05158 sc $8.00, set $20.00,
      min sc $3.00, pts $.95, ea.
                                   (B545)

BIZET, GEORGES (cont'd.)

Carmen: Suite No. 2
    BROUDE BR. set $25.00, pts $1.50,
    ea.   (B546)
    LUCKS 05159 sc $8.00, set $20.00,
    min sc $4.00, pts $.95, ea.
                                           (B547)

Carmen: Toreador Song *see Carmen:
    Chanson Du Toreador, For Solo
    Voice And Orchestra

Fleur Que Tu M'Avais Jetee, La *see
    Carmen: Air De Fleur, For Solo
    Voice And Orchestra

Jeux D'Enfants, [arr.] *Op.22
    LUCKS 05164 sc $15.00, set $24.00,
    min sc $4.00, pts $1.20, ea.
                                           (B548)

Ouvre Ton Coeur, For Solo Voice And
    Orchestra
    LUCKS 02480 sc $4.00, set $8.00,
    pts $.75, ea.   (B549)

Pecheurs De Perles, Les: Au Fond Du
    Temple Saint, For Solo Voices And
    Orchestra
    LUCKS 03334 sc $4.00, set $12.00,
    pts $.75, ea.   (B550)

Pecheurs De Perles, Les: Comme
    Autrefois Dans La Nuit Sombre,
    For Solo Voice And Orchestra
    LUCKS 02479 sc $4.00, set $8.00,
    pts $.75, ea.   (B551)

Pecheurs De Perles, Les: Je Crois
    Entendre Encore, For Solo Voice
    And Orchestra
    LUCKS 02215 sc $4.00, set $12.00,
    pts $.75, ea.   (B552)

Pecheurs De Perles, Les: Prelude
    LUCKS 05130 sc $8.00, set $18.00,
    pts $.95, ea.   (B553)

Symphony No. 1 in C
    sc UNIVER. UE 10687 $57.00, set
    UNIVER. UE 10688 $114.00, pts
    UNIVER. $8.00, ea.   (B554)

Variations Chromatiques, [arr.]
    (Weingartner) 2.2.2.2. 4.2.3.0.
    timp,perc,harp,strings [12']
    KALMUS 5268 sc $15.00, perf mat
    rent, set $32.00, pts $1.50, ea.
                                           (B555)

BJELINSKI, BRUNO (1909-   )
Brasilianische Sinfonietta
    2(pic).1.1.1. 2.2.0.0. timp,
    4perc,pno,strings,opt jr cor/
    wom cor
    BREITKOPF-W perf mat rent   (B556)

Concerto for Clarinet and String
    Orchestra [23']
    string orch,clar solo
    BREITKOPF-W perf mat rent   (B557)

Petit Concert, For Piano And Chamber
    Orchestra [10']
    0.1.2.1. 0.2.0.0. timp,perc,
    strings,pno solo
    BREITKOPF-W perf mat rent   (B558)

BJORKLUND, STAFFAN (1944-   )
Sinfonia Concertante [18']
    2.2.2.2. 4.2.2.0. timp,perc,harp,
    pno,strings
    sc STIM perf mat rent   (B559)

BJORLIN, ULF (1933-   )
Sailor's Life, For Solo Voice And
    Orchestra
    2.2.2.2. 4.2.0.0. timp,perc,
    strings,solo voice
    STIM perf mat rent   (B560)

BLACHER, BORIS (1903-1975)
Blues, Espagnola Und Rumba
    Philharmonica
    12vcl
    study sc BOTE f.s.   (B561)

Dance Scenes [35']
    2+pic.2.2.2. 2.2.0.0. timp,perc,
    strings
    BOOSEY perf mat rent   (B562)

Dance Suite (from Dance Scenes) [18']
    2+pic.2.2.2. 2.2.0.0. timp,perc,
    strings
    (Drew) BOOSEY perf mat rent (B563)

BLACK EYES see Flothuis, Marius

BLACK LION DANCES see Cole, Hugo

BLACKFORD, RICHARD
Sinfonie Poliziane [25']
    2.2.2.2. 4.3.3.1. timp,harp,
    strings
    OXFORD perf mat rent   (B564)

BLAKE, DAVID (1936-   )
Concerto for Violin and Orchestra
    NOVELLO study sc $17.20, sc,pts
    rent   (B565)

BLAKE, (JAMES HUBERT) EUBIE (1883-1983)
Charleston Rag, [arr.]
    (Schuller, Gunther) 0(pic).0.1.0.
    0.1.1.1. perc,pno,2vln,vla,vcl,
    db, trap set [4'] MARGUN MM 3 set
    $15.00, sc $3.00   (B566)

BLANGINI, GIUSEPPE MARCO MARIA FELICE
(1781-1841)
Abbandono. L', For Solo Voice And
    Orchestra [3']
    1.0.1.1. 2.0.0.0. strings,S solo
    manuscript CARISCH   (B567)

BLANQUER, AMANDO
Sinfonietta
    sc PILES 2070-P f.s.   (B568)

BLAUBART QUADRILLE see Strauss, Josef

BLAUE FONTANE, DIE, FOR PIANO, HARP AND
STRING ORCHESTRA see Bortz, Alfred

BLAUWVINGERS see Boer, Ed de, Fantasy,
Op. 8

BLAVET, MICHEL (1700-1768)
Concerto for Flute and String
    Orchestra in A minor [13']
    string orch,fl solo
    INTERNAT. perf mat rent   (B569)

BLENDINGER, HERBERT (1936-   )
Concerto Barocco, For Trumpet And
    Orchestra [18']
    2.2+English horn.2.2. 2.2.0.0.
    timp,strings,trp solo
    ORLANDO rent   (B570)

Concerto for Viola and Orchestra, Op.
    38 [19']
    3.2.2.2+contrabsn. 3.3.3.1. timp,
    perc,harp,strings,vla solo
    ORLANDO rent   (B571)

Sinfonietta [15']
    2.2.2.2. 2.2.3.0. timp,perc,harp,
    strings
    ORLANDO rent   (B572)

BLEYLE, KARL (1880-1969)
Aus Dem Zyklus "Nietzsche Lieder" Op.
    26, For Solo Voice And Orchestra
    [12']
    2.2(English horn).2.2. 3.0.0.0.
    timp,perc,harp,strings,S/A solo
    BREITKOPF-W perf mat rent   (B573)

Legende *Op.28 [10']
    2+pic.2+English horn.2+bass
    clar.2. 4.3.3.1. timp,perc,
    harp,cel,strings
    BREITKOPF-W perf mat rent   (B574)

BLISS, [SIR] ARTHUR (1891-1975)
Conquest Of The Air
    sc BOOSEY $25.00   (B575)

BLITZ see Clementi, Aldo

BLOCH, AUGUSTYN (1929-   )
Layers Of Time *see Warstwy Czasu

Warstwy Czasu [10']
    9vln,3vla,2vcl,db
    "Layers Of Time" sc POLSKIE f.s.
                                 (B576)

BLOCH, ERNEST (1880-1959)
Concerto Symphonique, For Piano And
    Orchestra
    min sc BOOSEY 70 $35.00   (B577)

BLOMBERG, ERIK (1922-   )
Begrundan [6']
    2.2.2.0. 0.2.0.0. timp,strings
    sc STIM perf mat rent   (B578)

Berattelse [8']
    2.2.2.2. 2.2.2.1. strings
    STIM   (B579)

Brev [3']
    2.2.2.1. 1.2.1.0. strings
    sc STIM perf mat rent   (B580)

Festspel [5']
    2.2.2.0. 0.2.0.0. timp,2perc,
    strings
    sc STIM perf mat rent   (B581)

Flykt [7'30"]
    2.2.2.1. 1.2.2.0. timp,strings
    sc STIM perf mat rent   (B582)

Gyckelspel [5']
    2.2.2.2. 2.2.0.0. timp,perc,
    strings,opt db
    sc STIM perf mat rent   (B583)

BLOMBERG, ERIK (cont'd.)

Inspel [4']
    2.2.2.1. 2.0.0.0. timp,strings
    sc STIM perf mat rent   (B584)

Intoning [9']
    2.2.2.2. 2.2.2.1. timp,perc,
    strings
    sc STIM   (B585)

Kvade [5']
    2.2.2.2. 2.2.2.1. timp,strings
    STIM   (B586)

Lyrism [6']
    2.2.2.2. 2.2.2.1. strings
    STIM   (B587)

Obstinato [7']
    2.2.2.2. 2.2.2.0. timp,perc,
    strings
    sc SUECIA ENO 311 perf mat rent
                                 (B588)

Puts [7']
    2.2.2.2. 2.2.2.0. timp,strings
    sc STIM perf mat rent   (B589)

Rop [4']
    2.2.2.1. 1.2.1.0. timp,harp,
    strings
    sc STIM perf mat rent   (B590)

Sentiment [4']
    2.2.2.1. 1.2.1.0. timp,strings
    sc STIM perf mat rent   (B591)

Spelmansstamma [7']
    2.2.2.2. 2.2.2.1. timp,strings
    STIM   (B592)

Svensk Bolero [3'30"]
    2.2.2.2. 2.2.2.0. strings
    sc STIM   (B593)

Svensk Bouree [5']
    2.2.2.2. 2.2.2.1. timp,perc,
    strings
    STIM   (B594)

Utspel [5']
    3.2.2.3. 3.3.3.1. timp,5perc,
    strings
    sc STIM perf mat rent   (B595)

Uttoning [7']
    2.2.2.2. 2.2.2.1. timp,strings
    STIM   (B596)

Vagspel [4']
    2.2.2.0. 0.2.0.0. timp,perc,
    strings
    sc STIM perf mat rent   (B597)

BLOMMANDE RONN, FOR SOLO VOICE AND
ORCHESTRA see Lundkvist, Per

BLON, FRANZ VON (1861-1945)
Amazone, Die: Auf Dem Kostumfest
    1+pic.2.2.2. 4.2.3.0. timp,perc,
    strings
    sc,pts LIENAU rent   (B598)

Amazone, Die: Overture
    2.2.2.2.2alto sax.tenor sax.
    4.2.3.0. harp,timp,perc,strings
    sc,pts LIENAU rent   (B599)

Amazone, Die: Potpourri
    2(pic).2.2.2. 4.2.3.0. harp,timp,
    perc,strings
    sc,pts LIENAU rent   (B600)

Amazone, Die: Quadrille
    2.2.2.2. 4.2.3.0. timp,perc,
    strings
    sc,pts LIENAU rent   (B601)

Erste Preis, Der
    2(pic).2.2.2. 4.2.3.0. timp,perc,
    strings
    sc,pts LIENAU rent   (B602)

Fest-Ouverture [8']
    2.2.2.2. 4.2.3.1. harp,timp,perc,
    strings
    sc,pts LIENAU rent   (B603)

Hoch Lebe Der Wein
    1+pic.2.2.2. 4.2.3.0. timp,perc,
    strings
    sc,pts LIENAU rent   (B604)

Idealen, Dem
    2(pic).2.2.2. 4.2.3.0. timp,perc,
    strings
    sc,pts LIENAU rent   (B605)

Im D-Zug
    LIENAU f.s.   (B606)

Liebestraum
    2.2.2.2. 4.0.0.0. strings
    LIENAU f.s.   (B607)

BLON, FRANZ VON (cont'd.)

    Melitta
        2+opt fl.2.2.2. 4.2.3.0. harp,
        timp,strings
        LIENAU f.s.   (B608)

    Puppen-Menuett
        string orch
        LIENAU f.s.   (B609)

    Sizilietta
        2.2+English horn.2.2.alto
        sax.tenor sax. 2.2.1.0. timp,
        perc,strings
        sc,pts LIENAU f.s.   (B610)

    Wenn Aus 1000 Blutenkelchen
        LIENAU f.s.   (B611)

    Zum Rendez-Vous
        1+pic.2.2.2. 4.2.3.0. timp,perc,
        strings
        LIENAU f.s.   (B612)

BLUE DANUBE WALTZ, [ARR.] see Strauss,
    Johann, [Jr.], An Der Schonen
    Blauen Donau, [arr.]

BLUES, ESPAGNOLA UND RUMBA
    PHILHARMONICA see Blacher, Boris

BLUETTE POLKA see Strauss, Johann,
    [Jr.]

BLUME, KARL (1883-1947)
    Markische Seen
        LIENAU f.s.   (B613)

    Sonne Im Laub
        LIENAU f.s.   (B614)

BLUMEN IM WIND see Busch, Hans

BLUMEN-SERENADE see Mielenz, H.

BLUMEN UND STERNE see Wismar, R.

BLUMER, THEODOR (1881-1964)
    Capriccio [9']
        2(pic).2.2.2. 3.2.1.0. timp,perc,
        harp,strings
        RIES perf mat rent   (B615)

    Immortellen-Walzer [7']
        2.2.2.2. 2.2.1.0. timp,perc,harp,
        strings
        sc RIES f.s., perf mat rent   (B616)

    Lustspiel-Ouverture *Op.75 [10']
        2+pic.2.2.2. 4.3.3.1. timp,perc,
        harp,strings
        sc RIES f.s., perf mat rent   (B617)

BLUTENZAUBER see Kosubek, Herbert

BOCCACCIO: HAB ICH NUR DEINE LIEBE, FOR
    SOLO VOICES AND ORCHESTRA see
    Suppe, Franz von

BOCCACCIO QUADRILLE see Strauss, Eduard

BOCCHERINI, LUIGI (1743-1805)
    Concerto for Violoncello and
        Orchestra in B flat, Ge. 482,
        [arr.]
        (Grutzmacher) 2ob,2horn,strings,vcl
        solo LUCKS 00616 sc $7.50, set
        $11.00, pts $.95, ea.   (B618)

    Easy Dances For Strings
        LUCKS 01460 sc $4.00, set $5.00,
        pts $1.00, ea.   (B619)

    Minuetti, Due, In D And E Flat,
        [arr.]
        (Hellmesberger) LUCKS 09193 sc
        $3.00, set $5.00, pts $1.00, ea.
                                       (B620)
    Minuetto In G
        string orch
        KALMUS A4576 sc $3.00, set $3.75,
        pts $.75, ea.   (B621)

    Minuetto, Op. 11
        string orch LUCKS 05715 sc $2.75,
        set $4.75, pts $.95, ea.   (B622)

    Overture In D, Op. 43 *see Sinfonia,
        Ge. 521, Op. 43, in D

    Siciliana
        string orch
        KALMUS A4560 sc $1.00, set $4.50,
        pts $.75, ea.   (B623)

    Sinfonia, Ge. 470, Op. 38, No. 4, in
        G
        fl/ob,bsn,horn,strings
        sc,pts DOBLINGER DM 624 f.s.   (B624)

    Sinfonia, Ge. 490, in D
        opt 2ob, opt 2horn,strings
        sc ZANIBON 5825 f.s., pts ZANIBON
        5826 f.s.   (B625)

BOCCHERINI, LUIGI (cont'd.)

    Sinfonia, Ge. 491, Op. 7, in C
        2ob,2bsn,strings
        sc,pts DOBLINGER DM 602 f.s. (B626)

    Sinfonia, Ge. 493, Op. 21, No. 1, in
        B flat
        2fl/2ob,2horn,strings
        sc,pts DOBLINGER DM 609 f.s. (B627)

    Sinfonia, Ge. 494, Op. 21, No. 2, in
        E flat
        2fl/2ob,2horn,strings
        sc,pts DOBLINGER DM 610 f.s. (B628)

    Sinfonia, Ge. 495, Op. 21, No. 3, in
        C
        2fl/2ob,2horn,strings
        sc,pts DOBLINGER DM 611 f.s. (B629)

    Sinfonia, Ge. 496, Op. 21, No. 4, in
        D
        2fl/2ob,2horn,strings
        sc,pts DOBLINGER DM 612 f.s. (B630)
        sc,pts DOBLINGER DM 601 f.s. (B631)

    Sinfonia, Ge. 497, Op. 21, No. 5, in
        B flat
        2fl/2ob,2horn,strings
        sc,pts DOBLINGER DM 613 f.s. (B632)

    Sinfonia, Ge. 498, Op. 21, No. 6, in
        A
        2fl/2ob,2horn,strings
        sc,pts DOBLINGER DM 614 f.s. (B633)

    Sinfonia, Ge. 500, in D
        2horn,strings
        sc,pts DOBLINGER DM 631 f.s. (B634)

    Sinfonia, Ge. 503, Op. 12, No. 1, in
        D
        2ob,2horn,strings
        sc,pts DOBLINGER DM 603 f.s. (B635)

    Sinfonia, Ge. 504, Op. 12, No. 2, in
        E flat
        2ob,2horn,strings
        sc,pts DOBLINGER DM 604 f.s. (B636)

    Sinfonia, Ge. 505, Op. 12, No. 3, in
        C
        2fl,2horn,strings
        sc,pts DOBLINGER DM 605 f.s. (B637)

    Sinfonia, Ge. 506, Op. 12, No. 4, in
        D minor
        2ob,2horn,strings
        sc,pts DOBLINGER DM 606 f.s. (B638)

    Sinfonia, Ge. 507, Op. 12, No. 5, in
        B flat
        2fl,2horn,strings
        sc,pts DOBLINGER DM 607 f.s. (B639)

    Sinfonia, Ge. 508, Op. 12, No. 6, in
        A
        2fl,2horn,strings
        sc,pts DOBLINGER DM 608 f.s. (B640)

    Sinfonia, Ge. 509, Op. 35, No. 1, in
        D
        2ob,opt bsn,2horn,strings
        sc,pts DOBLINGER DM 615 f.s. (B641)

    Sinfonia, Ge. 510, Op. 35, No. 2, in
        E flat
        2ob,opt bsn,2horn,strings
        sc,pts DOBLINGER DM 616 f.s. (B642)

    Sinfonia, Ge. 511, Op. 35, No. 3, in
        A
        2ob,opt bsn,2horn,strings
        sc,pts DOBLINGER DM 617 f.s. (B643)

    Sinfonia, Ge. 512, Op. 35, No. 4, in
        F
        2ob,opt bsn,2horn,strings
        sc,pts DOBLINGER DM 618 f.s. (B644)

    Sinfonia, Ge. 513, Op. 35, No. 5, in
        E flat
        2ob,opt bsn,2horn,strings
        sc,pts DOBLINGER DM 619 f.s. (B645)

    Sinfonia, Ge. 514, Op. 35, No. 6, in
        B flat
        2ob,opt bsn,2horn,strings
        sc,pts DOBLINGER DM 620 f.s. (B646)

    Sinfonia, Ge. 515, Op. 37, No. 1, in
        C
        fl,2ob,2bsn,2horn,strings
        sc,pts DOBLINGER DM 621 f.s. (B647)

    Sinfonia, Ge. 517, Op. 37, No. 3, in
        D minor
        fl,2ob,2bsn,2horn,strings
        sc,pts DOBLINGER DM 623 f.s. (B648)
        KALMUS 5206 sc $10.00, perf mat
        rent, set $19.00, pts $1.50, ea.
                                       (B649)
    Sinfonia, Ge. 518, Op. 37, No. 4, in
        A
        fl,2ob,2bsn,2horn,strings

BOCCHERINI, LUIGI (cont'd.)

    sc,pts DOBLINGER DM 625 f.s.   (B650)

    Sinfonia, Ge. 519, Op. 41, in C minor
        2ob,2bsn,2horn,strings
        sc,pts DOBLINGER DM 626 f.s.   (B651)

    Sinfonia, Ge. 520, Op. 42, in D
        2ob,2bsn,2horn,strings
        sc,pts DOBLINGER DM 627 f.s.   (B652)

    Sinfonia, Ge. 521, Op. 43, in D
        2ob,bsn,2horn,strings
        sc,pts DOBLINGER DM 628 f.s.   (B653)
        KALMUS A4570 sc $7.00, perf mat
        rent, set $12.00, pts $1.25, ea.
                                       (B654)
    Sinfonia, Ge. 522, Op. 45, in D minor
        2ob,2bsn,2horn,strings
        sc,pts DOBLINGER DM 629 f.s.   (B655)

    Sinfonia, Ge. 523, Op. 10, No. 4, in
        C
        2ob,bsn,2horn,gtr,strings
        sc,pts DOBLINGER DM 630 f.s.   (B656)

BOCHSA, ROBERT-NICOLAS-CHARLES
    (1789-1856)
    Concerto for Harp and String
        Orchestra, No. 3, Op. 293
        (Robert, F.) string orch,harp solo
        COSTALL C.3648 perf mat rent
                                       (B657)
BODA DE LUIS ALONSO, LA: INTERMEDIO NO.
    4 see Gimenez, Jeronimo

BODE, HERMANN (1859-1934)
    Jugendubermut
        LIENAU f.s.   (B658)

    Nixentanze
        LIENAU f.s.   (B659)

    Pfeil, Der
        LIENAU f.s.   (B660)

    Spruhteufelchen
        LIENAU f.s.   (B661)

BODENSOHN, ERNST FRIEDRICH WILHELM
    Concerto for Flute, Alto Flute,
        Viola, Violoncello and String
        Orchestra [30']
        string orch,fl solo,alto fl/
        English horn solo,vla solo,vcl
        solo
        BODENS EA 52 f.s.   (B662)

    Concerto for Flute and String
        Orchestra, No. 2 [17']
        string orch,fl solo
        BODENS EA 41 f.s.   (B663)

    Concerto for Flute, Clarinet,
        Violoncello and String Orchestra
        [35']
        string orch,fl solo,clar solo,vcl
        solo
        BODENS EA 44 f.s.   (B664)

    Concerto for Flute, Oboe and String
        Orchestra [30']
        string orch without vln,fl solo,
        ob solo
        BODENS EA 42 f.s.   (B665)

    Illumination, For Flute And Orchestra
        [5']
        2.2.2.2. 4.2.3.3. perc,strings,fl
        solo
        BODENS EA 23 f.s.   (B666)

BOEDIJN, GERARD H. (1893-1972)
    In Nachtschaduw, For Solo Voice And
        Orchestra *Op.94
        1.1.1.1. 2.1.0.0. timp,perc,
        strings,Bar solo
        sc DONEMUS f.s., perf mat rent
                                       (B667)
BOEHMER, KONRAD (1941-   )
    Canciones Del Camino [20'30"]
        2.3.5.2. 6.4.4.4. 2timp,2perc,
        2harp,pno,strings
        DONEMUS perf mat rent   (B668)

    Lied Uit De Verte, For Solo Voice And
        Orchestra [20']
        2.4.2.2. 4.2.3.1. timp,2perc,pno,
        vln,vla,vcl,db,S/Mez solo, gtr
        (ampl.)
        sc DONEMUS f.s., perf mat rent
                                       (B669)
BOER, ED DE (1957-   )
    Arina's Droom *Op.6 [12']
        2.2.2.2. 2.1.0.0. 3-4perc,cel,
        strings
        DONEMUS   (B670)

    Blauwvingers *see Fantasy, Op. 8

    Concertino On A Dutch Folksong, For
        Violoncello And Orchestra *Op.7,
        No.2 [13']
        3.2.2.2. 2.0.0.1. 3perc,cel,
        strings,vcl solo

BOER, ED DE (cont'd.)

DONEMUS f.s. (B671)

Damon, Der
see Galgenlieder, For Solo Voice
And Orchestra

Es Pfeift Der Wind
see Galgenlieder, For Solo Voice
And Orchestra

Fantasy, Op. 8 [20']
3.2.2.2. 4.2.3.0. timp,2perc,
strings
DONEMUS (B672)

Feuerprobe
see Galgenlieder, For Solo Voice
And Orchestra

Galgenlieder, For Solo Voice And
Orchestra *Op.5
6.1.5.3. 4.2.2.1. 4perc,harp,pno,
cel,strings,Bar solo DONEMUS sc
f.s., pts rent
contains: Damon, Der; Es Pfeift
Der Wind; Feuerprobe;
Gruselett; Plotzlich;
Wiederhergestellte Ruhe, Die
(B673)

Gruselett
see Galgenlieder, For Solo Voice
And Orchestra

Hommage Aan Dimitri Schostakowitsch
3.2.2.0. 3.3.3.1. 2perc,harp,pno,
strings
DONEMUS sc f.s., pts rent (B674)

Plotzlich
see Galgenlieder, For Solo Voice
And Orchestra

Wiederhergestellte Ruhe, Die
see Galgenlieder, For Solo Voice
And Orchestra

BOER, JAN DEN (1932-   )
Rondeaux Amoureux, For Solo Voice And
Orchestra [6']
2.2.1.2. 2.2.0.0. timp,strings,
low solo
sc DONEMUS f.s., perf mat rent
(B675)

BOESMANS, PHILIPPE (1936-   )
Concerto for Piano and Orchestra
[26']
4.3.3.2. 4.4.3.1. harp,pno,glock,
5perc,strings,pno solo
JOBERT perf mat rent (B676)

BOGUSLAWSKI, EDWARD (1940-   )
Symphony No. 1 [27']
4.4.4.4. 6.4.4.0. 6perc,2pno,
2harp,strings,cor
sc POLSKIE f.s. (B677)

BOHDANOWICZ, BAZYLI (1754-1819)
Symphony in D
see SYMPHONY IN POLAND, THE

BOHEME, LA: ADDIO DI MIMI, FOR SOLO
VOICE AND ORCHESTRA see Puccini,
Giacomo

BOHEME, LA: CHE GELIDA MANINA, FOR SOLO
VOICE AND ORCHESTRA see Puccini,
Giacomo

BOHEME, LA: MIMI TU NON TORNI, FOR SOLO
VOICES AND ORCHESTRA see Puccini,
Giacomo

BOHEME, LA: MUSETTA'S WALTZ see
Puccini, Giacomo, Boheme, La:
Quando Me'n Vo Soletta, For Solo
Voice And Orchestra

BOHEME, LA: O SOAVE FANCIULLA, FOR SOLO
VOICES AND ORCHESTRA see Puccini,
Giacomo

BOHEME, LA: QUANDO ME'N VO SOLETTA, FOR
SOLO VOICE AND ORCHESTRA see
Puccini, Giacomo

BOHEME, LA: SI, MI CHIAMANO MIMI, FOR
SOLO VOICE AND ORCHESTRA see
Puccini, Giacomo

BOHEME, LA: VECCHIA ZIMARRA, FOR SOLO
VOICE AND ORCHESTRA see Puccini,
Giacomo

BOHEMIAN GIRL, THE: THEN YOU'LL
REMEMBER ME, FOR SOLO VOICE AND
ORCHESTRA see Balfe, Michael
William

BOHM, CARL
Mouche, La, [arr.]
(Dressel, Erwin) 2.2.2.2. 2.0.0.0.
timp,triangle,strings [3'] sc
RIES f.s., perf mat rent (B678)

BOHM, KARL (1844-1920)
Calm As The Night *see Still Wie Die
Nacht, For Solo Voice And
Orchestra

Still Wie Die Nacht, For Solo Voice
And Orchestra
"Calm As The Night" LUCKS 02503 set
$7.50, pts $.75, ea. (B679)

BOHMISCHE KIRMES see Mietzner, Heinz

BOIELDIEU, FRANCOIS-ADRIEN (1775-1834)
Calife De Bagdad, Le: Overture
LUCKS 05178 sc $7.00, set $16.00,
min sc $4.50, pts $1.25, ea.
(B680)

Dame Blanche, La: Overture
LUCKS 05180 sc $7.50, set $15.00,
min sc $4.50, pts $1.15, ea.
(B681)

Jean De Paris: Overture
BREITKOPF-W perf mat rent (B682)

BOIS, ROB DU (1934-   )
Allegro For Strings [8']
9vln,3vla,2vcl,db
sc DONEMUS f.s., perf mat rent
(B683)

Concertino [8']
2.1.1.0. 0.1.0.0. 3perc,pno,
strings
sc DONEMUS f.s., perf mat rent
(B684)

Concerto for Violin and Orchestra
4.2.3.2sax. 4.3.2.1. perc,harp,
pno/elec org,2elec gtr,mand,
strings,vln solo
sc DONEMUS f.s., perf mat rent
(B685)

Concerto for 2 Violins and Orchestra
[21']
2.2.2.2. 2.2.2.0. timp,perc,harp,
strings,2vln soli
DONEMUS perf mat rent (B686)

Flower Given To My Daughter, A
2.2.3.3.alto sax(tenor sax).
2.2.2.1. acord,perc,pno,3db
sc DONEMUS f.s., perf mat rent
(B687)

Skarabee [4']
2.2.2.2. 2.2.2.0. timp,2perc,
strings
MOLENAAR 14.1560.08 f.s. (B688)

Tre Pezzi [3']
2.1.1.1. 1.1.0.0. perc,strings
sc DONEMUS f.s., perf mat rent
(B689)

BOISDEFFRE, CHARLES-HENRI-RENE DE
(1838-1906)
Reverie *Op.52 [4']
harp,strings,vla d'amore/vln/vla/
vcl solo
KALMUS 2620 sc $3.00, set $5.00
(B690)

Suite Lorraine *Op.92 [14']
2+pic.2.2.2. 4.2.3.0. timp,harp,
strings
KALMUS 3180 sc $30.00, set $30.00
(B691)

BOISMORTIER, JOSEPH BODIN DE
(1689-1755)
Concerto for Bassoon and String
Orchestra
string orch,hpsd,bsn solo
OISEAU perf mat rent (B692)

Concerto in D, MIN 43
string orch,cont,vcl solo
min sc SYMPHON 581 f.s., pts
SYMPHON 583 f.s. (B693)

BOITO, ARRIGO (1842-1918)
Mefistofele: Ecco Il Mondo, For Solo
Voice And Orchestra
LUCKS 03228 sc $3.75, set $7.50,
pts $.75, ea. (B694)

Mefistofele: L'Altra Notte, For Solo
Voice And Orchestra
LUCKS 02481 sc $3.75, set $7.50,
pts $.75, ea. (B695)

Mefistofele: Son Lo Spirito, For Solo
Voice And Orchestra
"Mefistofele: Song Of The Whistle"
LUCKS 03289 sc $7.50, set $18.00,
pts $.75, ea. (B696)

Mefistofele: Song Of The Whistle
*see Mefistofele: Son Lo Spirito,
For Solo Voice And Orchestra

BOKES, VLADIMIR (1946-   )
Concerto for Piano and Orchestra, Op.
21 [24']
2.2.2.2. 4.2.2.1. xylo,vibra,
strings,pno solo
SLOV.HUD.FOND 0-458 perf mat rent
(B697)

Symphony No. 2 [40']
4.4.5.5. 6.3.2.1. strings
SLOV.HUD.FOND 0-489 perf mat rent
(B698)

BOKES, VLADIMIR (cont'd.)

Three Dances *see Tri Tance

Tri Tance
string orch
"Three Dances" SLOV.HUD.FOND 0-481A
perf mat rent (B699)

BOLCOM, WILLIAM (1938-   )
Concertante For Violin, Flute, Oboe
And Orchestra [18']
1.1.3.2. 2.1.0.0. harp,strings,
vln solo,fl solo,ob solo
MARKS rent (B700)

BOLERO see Longo, Achille

BOLERO SINFONICO see Ingenbrand, Josef

BOLZONI, GIOVANNI (1841-1919)
Gavotta
string orch
LUCKS 08210 sc $2.75, set $4.75,
pts $.95, ea. (B701)

Minuetto
string orch
LUCKS 07287 sc $2.75, set $4.75,
pts $.95, ea. (B702)

Ruscello, Il [4']
string orch
pts CARISCH 18847 perf mat rent
(B703)

BON, ANDRE (1946-   )
Ode [13']
2.2.2.2. 2.0.0.0. timp,strings
AMPHION A 391 perf mat rent (B704)

BON, MAARTEN (1933-   )
Boreal, For Violin And Percussion
[6']
16perc,vln solo
DONEMUS (B705)

Sieben, Jedenfalls Sieben [11']
0.0.1.0.soprano sax. 0.0.0.0.
2pno,2elec org,2cel,2marimba,
2vibra,2xylo,vln
sc DONEMUS f.s., perf mat rent
(B706)

BON, WILLEM FREDERIK (1940-   )
Aforismen [15']
9vln,3vla,2vcl,db
sc DONEMUS f.s., perf mat rent
(B707)

Automne, L', For Solo Voice And
Orchestra [10']
3.3.3.3. 4.4.3.1. 4perc,harp,
strings,Bar solo
DONEMUS perf mat rent (B708)

Concerto for Oboe and Strings [17']
8vln,2vla,2vcl,db,English horn&
ob&ob d'amore&Heckelphone solo
sc DONEMUS f.s., perf mat rent
(B709)

1999 [Dix-Neuf Cent Quatre-Vingt-Dix-
Neuf], 4 Propheties De
Nostradamus, For Solo Voice And
Orchestra [14']
2.2.3.2. 4.3.3.0. timp,3perc,
2harp,pno,strings,S solo
sc DONEMUS f.s., perf mat rent
(B710)

Ete, L', For Solo Voice And Orchestra
[14']
3.3.3.2. 4.4.3.1. timp,perc,harp,
cel,vibra,strings,A solo
sc DONEMUS f.s., perf mat rent
(B711)

Hiver, L', For Solo Voice And
Orchestra [10']
3.3.3.3. 4.2.3.1. 3perc,harp,
strings,T solo
DONEMUS perf mat rent (B712)

Printemps, Le, For Solo Voice And
Orchestra [10']
3.3.3.2. 4.2.3.1. timp,6perc,
harp,strings,S solo
DONEMUS perf mat rent (B713)

BON JOUR, MA BELLE, FOR SOLO VOICE AND
ORCHESTRA see Behrend, Siegfried

BOND, VICTORIA (1945-   )
C-A-G-E-D
string orch
SEESAW perf mat rent (B714)

Equinox: Suite
2.2.2.2. 4.3.3.1. timp,perc,harp,
pno,strings
SEESAW perf mat rent (B715)

BONDON, JACQUES (1927-   )
Concerto D'Octobre, For Clarinet And
String Orchestra
ESCHIG sc,pts rent, min sc f.s.
(B716)

Lumiere Eclatee, La, For Solo Voice
And Orchestra
sc,pts ESCHIG f.s. (B717)

BONDT, CORNELIS DE (1953-   )
  Kompositie [15']
    5.4.6.4. 4.5.4.2. strings
    DONEMUS perf mat rent   (B718)

BONELLI, ETTORE (1900-   )
  Sei Variazioni Su Un Tema Di A.
    Corelli
    ob,strings
    sc ZANIBON 5216 f.s.   (B719)

  Visione Eroica [26']
    2+pic.2+English
      horn.2.0.contrabsn. 4.3.3.1.
      3timp,5perc,cel,harp,strings
    sc ZANIBON 3595 rent, pts ZANIBON
      3596 rent   (B720)

BONHEUR, LE see Mesritz van Velthuysen,
  Anny

BONNEAU, PAUL (1918-   )
  Deux Caprices En Forme De Valse, For
    Flute And String Orchestra
    string orch,opt harp/pno,fl solo
    LEDUC perf mat rent   (B721)

BONONCINI, GIOVANNI (1670-1747)
  Camilla Triofante, La: Wie Du Mir, So
    Ich Dir
    strings,opt winds,cont
    sc HEINRICH. 8847 f.s., pts
      HEINRICH. 8848 f.s.   (B722)

  Sonata, Op. 3, No. 10, in D
    2trp,strings,cont
    sc,pts MUS. RARA 41.657-20 f.s.
                                  (B723)

BONSEL, ADRIAAN (1918-   )
  Proloog [10']
    3.3.3.2. 4.2.3.0. 4perc,strings
    DONEMUS sc f.s., pts rent   (B724)

  Vrede-Oorlag-Vrede?, Moto-Perpetuo?
    [13']
    3.3.3.3.alto sax. 4.3.3.1. perc,
      2harp,strings
    sc DONEMUS f.s., perf mat rent
                                  (B725)

BONTEMPELLI, MASSIMO (1878-1960)
  Partita Alla Popolare [14']
    1.1.1.1. 1.0.0.0. strings
    manuscript CARISCH   (B726)

BOOGAARD, BERNARD VAN DEN (1952-   )
  Concertino for Harp, Guitar and
    Orchestra [10']
    1.1.2.1. 1.1.1.0. perc,pno,
      strings,harp solo,gtr solo
    DONEMUS perf mat rent   (B727)

  Concerto for Piano and Orchestra in D
    [20']
    3.3.4.3. 4.2.1.1. timp,3perc,
      2harp,strings,pno solo
    sc DONEMUS f.s., perf mat rent
                                  (B728)

  Concerto for Piano and Orchestra, No.
    2 [22']
    2.1.3.2. 1.1.2.0. 2perc,strings,
      pno solo
    DONEMUS   (B729)

  Profiel, For Harpsichord And
    Orchestra [20']
    0.2.0.2. 0.0.2.0. 4rec,10vln,
      3vla,2vcl,db,hpsd solo
    sc DONEMUS f.s., perf mat rent
                                  (B730)

BOOGIE AGITATO see Klebe, Giselher

BOONE, CHARLES N. (1939-   )
  San Zeno-Verona
    study sc SALABERT $23.00   (B731)

BOOREN, JO VAN DEN (1935-   )
  Epitaphe Villon, L', For Solo Voice
    And Orchestra
    3.3.3.0. 4.3.3.1. timp,3perc,
      strings,med solo
    sc DONEMUS f.s., perf mat rent
                                  (B732)

  Geographie Interieure [16']
    4.4.4.4. 4.4.3.1. 4perc,harp,pno,
      strings
    DONEMUS   (B733)

  Sinfonia Jubilata, No. 1 [17']
    4.3.4.2. 4.4.3.1. timp,3perc,
      harp,strings
    sc DONEMUS f.s., perf mat rent
                                  (B734)

  Souvenir [7']
    4.4.4.3. 4.3.3.1. timp,2perc,
      harp,cel,strings
    DONEMUS sc f.s., pts rent   (B735)

BORA see Kotonski, Wlodzimierz

BORDEWIJK-ROEPMAN, JOHANNA (1892-1971)
  Adoration
    see Bierbaum-Lieder, For Solo Voice
      And Orchestra

BORDEWIJK-ROEPMAN, JOHANNA (cont'd.)

  Antique
    see Illuminations, Les, For Solo
      Voice And Orchestra

  Bierbaum-Lieder, For Solo Voice And
    Orchestra
    3.2.2.2. 1.1.2.0. cel,harp,strings,
      S solo sc DONEMUS f.s., perf mat
      rent
    contains: Adoration; Gigerlette;
      Schwarze Laute, Die; Sei
      Getrost   (B736)

  Bottom
    see Illuminations, Les, For Solo
      Voice And Orchestra

  Fleurs
    see Illuminations, Les, For Solo
      Voice And Orchestra

  Gigerlette
    see Bierbaum-Lieder, For Solo Voice
      And Orchestra

  Holland, For Solo Voice And Orchestra
    [3']
    2.3.2.2. 4.3.3.0. perc,harp,
      strings,A solo
    sc DONEMUS f.s., perf mat rent
                                  (B737)

  Ik Wensche U, For Solo Voice And
    String Orchestra [2']
    string orch,S solo
    sc DONEMUS f.s., perf mat rent
                                  (B738)

  Illuminations, Les, For Solo Voice
    And Orchestra
    2.3.2.2. 2.2.0.0. timp,perc,harp,
      strings,S solo sc DONEMUS f.s.,
      perf mat rent
    contains: Antique; Bottom; Fleurs
                                  (B739)

  Kroaie Enden Puyt, De, For Solo Voice
    And Orchestra [2']
    3.3.2.3. 2.2.1.0. harp,strings,S
      solo
    sc DONEMUS f.s., perf mat rent
                                  (B740)

  Oranje May-Lied, For Solo Voice And
    Orchestra [3']
    3.3.2.2. 2.3.3.1. timp,perc,
      strings,S solo
    sc DONEMUS f.s., perf mat rent
                                  (B741)

  Schwarze Laute, Die
    see Bierbaum-Lieder, For Solo Voice
      And Orchestra

  Sei Getrost
    see Bierbaum-Lieder, For Solo Voice
      And Orchestra

BOREAL, FOR VIOLIN AND PERCUSSION see
  Bon, Maarten

BOREC - UVERTURA NA PARTIZANSKE TEME
  see Svara, Danilo

BORG, KIM
  Laulelmia Saimaalta, For Solo Voice
    And Orchestra *Op.13
    2.1.2.1. 1.0.0.0. vibra,strings,
      solo voice
    FAZER perf mat rent   (B742)

  Laulua Aleksis Kiven Sanoihin, 7, For
    Solo Voice And Orchestra *Op.27,
    CC7U
    2.2.2.2. 2.2.0.0. timp,2perc,cel/
      pno,strings,solo voice FAZER perf
      mat rent   (B743)

  Suomalaista Kansanlaulua, 20, For
    Solo Voice And Orchestra *CC20U
    1.1.1.1. 1.0.0.0. timp,strings,solo
      voice FAZER perf mat rent   (B744)

BORGHI, LUIGI (ca. 1745-ca. 1806)
  Cadenzas, For Violin, Op. 11
    see Six Violin Concertos And Sixty-
      Four Cadenzas

  Concerti for Violin and Orchestra,
    Op. 2
    see Six Violin Concertos And Sixty-
      Four Cadenzas

  Concerti for Violin and Orchestra,
    Op. 3
    see Six Violin Concertos And Sixty-
      Four Cadenzas

  Six Violin Concertos And Sixty-Four
    Cadenzas
    (Banat, Gabriel) 2ob,2horn,strings,
      vln solo pts JOHNSON $75.00
    "Masters of the Violin", Vol. 1
    contains: Cadenzas, For Violin,
      Op. 11; Concerti for Violin and
      Orchestra, Op. 2; Concerti for
      Violin and Orchestra, Op. 3
                                  (B745)

BORIS GODUNOV: CHANSON DE VARLAAM see
  Mussorgsky, Modest Petrovich

BORIS GODUNOV: HALLUCINATION SCENE.
  SCENE OF THE CLOCK, FOR SOLO VOICE
  AND ORCHESTRA see Mussorgsky,
  Modest Petrovich

BORIS GODUNOV: MONOLOGUE OF BORIS, FOR
  SOLO VOICE AND ORCHESTRA see
  Mussorgsky, Modest Petrovich

BORNENES JUUL, [ARR.] see Gade, Niels
  Wilhelm

BORODIN, ALEXANDER PORFIRIEVICH
  (1833-1887)
  In The Steppes Of Central Asia
    BROUDE BR. set $20.00, pts $1.25,
      ea.   (B746)
    min sc ZEN-ON 892651 f.s.   (B747)
    LUCKS 05186 sc $7.50, set $17.00,
      min sc $2.50, pts $.95, ea.
                                  (B748)

  Nocturne From String Quartet No. 2,
    [arr.]
    (Dolan, James) "Quartet: Slow
      Movement, [arr.]" string orch
      [6'] NEW MUSIC WEST perf mat rent
                                  (B749)

  Nocturne From String Quartet No. 2
    For Violin And Orchestra, [arr.]
    (Rimsky-Korsakov, N.) 2.2.2.2.
      2.2.0.0. timp,strings,vln solo
      [8'] KALMUS A4575 sc $4.00, perf
      mat rent, set $12.00, pts $.75,
      ea.   (B750)

  Quartet: Slow Movement, [arr.] *see
    Nocturne From String Quartet No.
    2, [arr.]

BOROGYIN, A.P.
  see BORODIN, ALEXANDER PORFIREVICH

BORRIS, SIEGFRIED (1906-   )
  Intrada No. 4 *Op.77,No.4
    string orch
    sc HEINRICH. 8849 f.s., pts
      HEINRICH. 8850 f.s.   (B751)

BORSCHEL, ERICH (1907-   )
  Landlermusik
    RIES f.s.   (B752)

BORSTLAP, JOHN (1950-   )
  Invocazione [10']
    2.3.3.2. 3.3.3.2.0. perc,harp,pno,
      cel,strings
    DONEMUS perf mat rent   (B753)

  Variations for Piano and String
    Orchestra [17']
    string orch,pno solo
    DONEMUS   (B754)

BORTZ, ALFRED (1882-   )
  Arena-Klange
    RIES f.s.   (B755)

  Blaue Fontane, Die, For Piano, Harp
    And String Orchestra [6']
    string orch,pno solo,harp solo
    sc RIES f.s., perf mat rent   (B756)

  Capriccio, Op. 72 [5']
    2.2.2.2. 4.2.3.1. timp,2perc,opt
      harp,strings
    sc RIES f.s., perf mat rent   (B757)

  Handwerker-Suite *Op.58 [20']
    2.1.2.2. 2.2.2.0. timp,perc,opt
      harp,strings
    RIES perf mat rent   (B758)

  Humoreske [4']
    2(pic).2.2.2. 4.2.3.0. timp,perc,
      harp,strings
    RIES perf mat rent   (B759)

  Kleine Carmen
    RIES f.s.   (B760)

  Szenen Einer Mondnacht *Op.75 [20']
    string orch
    RIES perf mat rent   (B761)

BORTZ, DANIEL (1943-   )
  October Music [10']
    string orch
    GEHRMANS ENO 6036   (B762)

BORUSSIA MARSCH see Spontini, Gaspare

BOSMANS, HENRIETTE (1895-1952)
  Belsazer, For Solo Voice And
    Orchestra [10']
    3.2.2.2. 4.2.2.0. timp,perc,harp,
      cel,strings,A solo
    sc DONEMUS f.s., perf mat rent
                                  (B763)

  Concert Piece for Flute and Orchestra
    [12']
    1.0.1.1.3sax. 1.1.1.0. perc,pno,
      strings,fl solo
    sc DONEMUS f.s., perf mat rent

BOSMANS, HENRIETTE (cont'd.)

(B764)

BOSSI, [MARCO] ENRICO (1861-1925)
A Mo' Di Fantasia [6']
   2.2.2.2. 2.0.0.0. timp,harp,cel,
   org,pno,strings
   manuscript CARISCH   (B765)

Ambascia
   see Ricreazioni Di Antiche Musiche
   Classiche, Serie VI: Musiche
   Antiche Italiane

Angelus (from Op. 118, No. 4)
   see RICREAZIONI DI ANTICHE MUSICHE
   CLASSICHE, SERIE IV: MUSICHE
   ANTICHE ITALIANE

Ballatella
   see Ricreazioni Di Antiche Musiche
   Classiche, Serie VI: Musiche
   Antiche Italiane

Canzone
   see Ricreazioni Di Antiche Musiche
   Classiche, Serie VI: Musiche
   Antiche Italiane

Canzone Nordica
   see Ricreazioni Di Antiche Musiche
   Classiche, Serie VI: Musiche
   Antiche Italiane

Concert Piece for Organ and
   Orchestra, Op. 130
   0.0.0.0. 2.3.3.1. timp,bells,
   strings,org solo
   manuscript CARISCH   (B766)

Fantasia Sinfonica, For Organ And
   Orchestra *Op.147 [20']
   0.0.0.0. 4.0.0.0. harp,strings,
   org solo
   manuscript CARISCH   (B767)

Fatemi La Grazia
   see RICREAZIONI DI ANTICHE MUSICHE
   CLASSICHE, SERIE IV: MUSICHE
   ANTICHE ITALIANE

Fughetta (from Op. 118, No. 2)
   see RICREAZIONI DI ANTICHE MUSICHE
   CLASSICHE, SERIE IV: MUSICHE
   ANTICHE ITALIANE

Kermesse
   see Ricreazioni Di Antiche Musiche
   Classiche, Serie VI: Musiche
   Antiche Italiane

Marcia Nuziale [6']
   3.2.2.2. 4.3.3.1. timp,perc,harp,
   strings
   manuscript CARISCH   (B768)

Nenia
   see Ricreazioni Di Antiche Musiche
   Classiche, Serie VI: Musiche
   Antiche Italiane

Overture [6']
   2.2.2.2. 4.2.3.1. timp,strings
   manuscript CARISCH   (B769)

Quattro Pezzi [10']
   string orch
   manuscript CARISCH   (B770)

Ricreazioni Di Antiche Musiche
   Classiche, Serie VI: Musiche
   Antiche Italiane
   string orch sc CARISCH 21341 rent,
   pts CARISCH 21342 rent
   contains: Ambascia; Ballatella;
   Canzone; Canzone Nordica;
   Kermesse; Nenia; Ronda Dei
   Lillipuzzi; Tempo Di Scherzo
                                   (B771)

Ronda Dei Lillipuzzi
   see Ricreazioni Di Antiche Musiche
   Classiche, Serie VI: Musiche
   Antiche Italiane

Santa Caterina Da Siena
   1.1.0.0. 4.2.0.0. perc,harp,cel,
   harmonium,string quar,vln solo
   manuscript CARISCH   (B772)

Scherzo in F [6']
   2.2.2.2. 2.2.0.0. timp,cel,
   strings
   manuscript CARISCH   (B773)

Sposalizio, For Violin, Violoncello
   And Orchestra [16']
   harp,org,strings,vln solo,vcl
   solo
   manuscript CARISCH   (B774)

Tempo Di Scherzo
   see Ricreazioni Di Antiche Musiche
   Classiche, Serie VI: Musiche
   Antiche Italiane

BOSSI, [MARCO] ENRICO (cont'd.)

Theme and Variations [20']
   3.3.3.3. 4.3.4.1. timp,perc,harp,
   cel,bells,strings
   manuscript CARISCH   (B775)

Tre Momenti Francescani *Op.140
   [22']
   3.3.2.2. 4.2.3.1. timp,perc,harp,
   cel,bells,strings
   manuscript CARISCH   (B776)

Tre Pezzi Sinfonici [12']
   3.2.3.2. 4.3.3.1. timp,strings
   manuscript CARISCH   (B777)

Ultimo Canto [5']
   0.0.2.2. 4.0.3.1. timp,harp,
   strings
   manuscript CARISCH   (B778)

Viandante, Il [6']
   3.3.3.2. 4.3.3.1. timp,perc,harp,
   strings
   manuscript CARISCH   (B779)

BOSSI, RENZO (1883-1965)
Fantocci Animati [14']
   2.1.1.1. 2.2.0.0. timp,harp,cel,
   pno,strings
   manuscript CARISCH   (B780)

Frammenti Lirici, For Solo Voice And
   String Orchestra [10']
   string orch,solo voice
   sc CARISCH 17259 rent, pts CARISCH
   17259A rent   (B781)

Intermezzo Nostalgico [5']
   1.1.2.2.sax. 2.2.2.1. timp,perc,
   harp,strings
   min sc CARISCH perf mat rent (B782)

Nell'anno 1000: Preludio [6']
   2.2.2.2. 4.2.3.1. timp,org,harp,
   strings
   manuscript CARISCH   (B783)

Sinfonia, Op. 11, in A [25']
   3.3.3.2. 4.2.3.1. timp,perc,harp,
   strings
   manuscript CARISCH   (B784)

Tempo Di Concerto, For Trumpet And
   Orchestra [6']
   timp,strings,trp solo
   manuscript CARISCH   (B785)

Tre Rifrazioni Sonore [25']
   3.2.2.2. 4.3.3.1. timp,perc,cel,
   strings
   manuscript CARISCH   (B786)

Trilogia Cristiana, For Violoncello
   And Orchestra [29']
   perc,pno,strings,vcl/vln solo
   manuscript CARISCH   (B787)

Villotta [15']
   3.2.3.2. 4.3.3.1. timp,perc,harp,
   cel,strings
   sc CARISCH 21334 perf mat rent
                                   (B788)

BOSSLER, KURT (1911-1976)
Metamorphosen, For 2 Trumpets And
   Orchestra
   perc,strings,2trp soli
   [9'] MÜLLER f.s.   (B789)

Triptychon, For Flute And Orchestra
   timp,strings,fl solo
   [9'] MÜLLER f.s.   (B790)

BÖTTCHER, EBERHARD
Fantasia Sinfonica [10']
   2.2.2.2. 2.2.1.0. timp,strings
   NORGE   (B791)

BOTTESINI, GIOVANNI (1821-1889)
Concerto for Double Bass and
   Orchestra, No. 2, in B minor
   [20']
   1.2.0.2. 2.0.0.0. timp,strings,db
   solo
   sc,pts DOBLINGER rent   (B792)

Duo Concertant Sur Les Themes Des
   "Puritains", For Violoncello,
   Doublebass And Orchestra [14']
   2+pic.2.2.2. 4.2.3.1. timp,perc,
   strings,vcl solo,db solo
   (Starr, Mark) sc,pts BILLAUDOT rent
                                   (B793)

Passione Amorosa, For Double Bass And
   Orchestra [12']
   2.2.2.2. 2.2.0.0. timp,strings,db
   solo
   INTERNAT. perf mat rent   (B794)

BOTTOM see Bordewijk-Roepman, Johanna

BOUCOURECHLIEV, ANDRE (1925-   )
Amers
   1(pic,alto fl).2(English
   horn).3(bass clar).1. 1.1.1.0.
   2perc,harp,cel,2vln,vla,vcl,db
   LEDUC sc, pts rent   (B795)

Nom d'Oedipe, Le [115']
   2.0.2.0. 0.0.2.0. 9perc,harp,
   2vcl,2db
   AMPHION perf mat rent   (B796)

BOULEZ, PIERRE (1925-   )
Notations [25']
   3.2.2.2. 3.3.3.1. timp,8perc,
   3harp,cel,strings
   UNIVER. perf mat rent   (B797)

BOULOGNE, JOSEPH (CHEVALIER DE ST.-
   GEORGES)
   see SAINT-GEORGES, JOSEPH BOULOGNE DE

BOUQUET QUADRILLE see Strauss, Johann,
   [Jr.]

BOURGAULT-DUCOUDRAY, LOUIS-ALBERT
   (1840-1910)
   Rapsodie Cambodgienne [12']
   3.2(English horn).2+bass clar.4.
   4.4.3.1. timp,perc,2harp,
   strings
   KALMUS 3259 sc $25.00, set $75.00
                                   (B798)

BOURLAND, ROGER (1952-   )
Rhapsody for Clarinet and Orchestra
   [9']
   2(pic).2.0.2. 2.0.0.0. perc,
   strings,clar solo
   MARGUN BP 1003 perf mat rent (B799)

BOURREE UND GONDOLIERA, FOR VIOLIN AND
   ORCHESTRA, [ARR.] see Ries, Franz

BOUTON DE ROSE, LE: TENEBRE E LUCE see
   Drigo, Riccardo

BOYCE, WILLIAM (1711-1779)
Symphonies Nos.1-8
   (Gobermann, Max) min sc UNIVER.
   PH471 $13.00   (B800)

BOZAY, ATTILA (1939-   )
Pezzo Concertato No. 2, For Citara
   And Orchestra *Op.24
   orch, citara solo
   (special import only) sc EMB 10215
   f.s.   (B801)

Pezzo D'Archi *Op.14
   string orch
   (special import only) sc EMB 10201
   f.s.   (B802)

BOZIC, DARIJAN (1933-   )
Bela Krizantema, For Solo Voices And
   Orchestra [30']
   1(pic).1(English horn).1(bass
   clar).0(contrabsn). 3.2.1.1.
   timp,5perc,pno,elec org,
   strings,SBar&narrator
   "White Chrysanthemum, For Solo
   Voices And Orchestra" DRUSTVO
   DSS 770 perf mat rent   (B803)

White Chrysanthemum, For Solo Voices
   And Orchestra *see Bela
   Krizantema, For Solo Voices And
   Orchestra

BOZZA, EUGENE (1905-   )
Atmospheres, For 4 Flutes And Strings
   [8']
   8vln,3vla,3vcl,2db,4fl soli
   LEDUC perf mat rent   (B804)

Concertino for Tuba and Orchestra
   [17']
   1.1.1.1. 1.1.1.0. timp,perc,
   strings
   LEDUC perf mat rent   (B805)

BRAAL, ANDRIES DE (1909-   )
Concertante Muziek [20']
   1.1.1.1. 1.1.0.0. timp,perc,pno,
   xylo,strings
   sc DONEMUS f.s., perf mat rent
                                   (B806)

Groote Vogel, De, For Solo Voice And
   Orchestra [4']
   1.1.1.0. 2.0.0.0. strings,Bar
   solo
   sc DONEMUS f.s., perf mat rent
                                   (B807)

Koraalfantasie, Over Psalm 91, For
   Trumpet And String Orchestra
   string orch,trp solo
   sc DONEMUS f.s., perf mat rent
                                   (B808)

BRABANT, FOR SOLO VOICE AND ORCHESTRA
   see Leeuw, Ton de

BRABANTSE RAPSODIE see Schoonenbeek,
   Kees

BRAGA, GAETANO (1829-1907)
  Santa Lucia, For Solo Voice And
    Orchestra
    (Luck) LUCKS 02298 set $15.00, pts
    $.75, ea.   (B809)

BRAHMS, JOHANNES (1833-1897)
  Academic Festival Overture *see
    Akademische Festouverture

  Akademische Festouverture *Op.80
    [12']
    3.2.2.3. 4.3.3.1. timp,perc,
    strings
    study sc BREITKOPF-W PB 3693 f.s.
                                     (B810)
    "Academic Festival Overture" BROUDE
    BR. set $35.00, pts $1.75, ea.
                                     (B811)
    "Academic Festival Overture" LUCKS
    05199 sc $7.00, set $30.00, min
    sc $2.50, pts $1.40, ea.   (B812)

  Canzone In B Flat, For Violoncello
    And Orchestra (from Op. 55) [8']
    2.2.2.2. 4.2.0.0. timp,strings,
    vcl solo
    BREITKOPF-W perf mat rent   (B813)

  Chorale Prelude: Es Ist Ein Ros'
    Entsprungen, [arr.]
    (Scott, E.) "Lo, How A Rose E'er
    Blooming" 2.0.1.1. 0.0.0.0.
    strings KALMUS A4622 sc $3.00,
    perf mat rent, set $9.00, pts
    $1.00, ea.   (B814)

  Chorale Preludes, Eleven, [arr.]
    *Op.122, CC11U
    (Thomson, Virgil) sc BOOSEY $15.00
                                     (B815)
  Chorale Preludes, Five, [arr.]
    *Op.122
    (Angerer, Paul) "Funf
    Choralvorspiele, [arr.]" string
    orch [14'] DOBLINGER f.s.   (B816)

  Complete Concerti
    pap DOVER ISBN 0-486-24170-X $10.95
    contains: Concerto for Piano and
    Orchestra, No. 1, Op. 15, in D
    minor; Concerto for Piano and
    Orchestra, No. 2, Op. 83, in B
    flat; Concerto for Violin and
    Orchestra, Op. 77, in D;
    Concerto for Violin,
    Violoncello and Orchestra, Op.
    102, in A minor   (B817)

  Concerto for Piano and Orchestra, No.
    1, Op. 15, in D minor
    see Complete Concerti
    min sc ZEN-ON 891141 f.s.   (B818)

  Concerto for Piano and Orchestra, No.
    2, Op. 83, in B flat
    see Complete Concerti
    min sc ZEN-ON 891142 f.s.   (B819)

  Concerto for Violin and Orchestra,
    Op. 77, in D
    see Complete Concerti
    min sc ZEN-ON 891145 f.s.   (B820)
    LUCKS 00506 sc $12.00, set $28.00,
    min sc $3.50, pts $1.75, ea.
                                     (B821)
  Concerto for Violin, Violoncello and
    Orchestra, Op. 102, in A minor
    see Complete Concerti
    study sc INTERNAT. 747 $6.00 (B822)
    min sc PETERS 526 $8.50   (B823)
    LUCKS 00507 sc $14.00, set $30.00,
    pts $1.75, ea.   (B824)

  Drei Lieder, [arr.]
    2.2.2.2+contrabsn. 4.2.3.0. timp,
    strings KALMUS 2698 sc $4.00, set
    $20.00
    contains: In Summer Fields;
    Lullaby; True Love   (B825)

  Feldeinsamkeit, For Solo Voice And
    Orchestra, [arr.] *Op.86,No.2
    LUCKS 02798 sc $3.00, set $7.50,
    pts $.75, ea.   (B826)

  Funf Choralvorspiele, [arr.] *see
    Chorale Preludes, Five, [arr.]

  Hungarian Dance No. 4 *see
    Ungarischer Tanz No. 4, [arr.]

  Hungarian Dances No. 1, 3, And 10
    *see Ungarische Tanze Nos. 1, 3,
    And 10, [arr.]

  Hungarian Dances No. 5 And 6 *see
    Ungarische Tanze Nos. 5 And 6,
    [arr.]

  Hungarian Dances Nos. 1, 3, And 10
    *see Ungarische Tanze Nos. 1, 3,
    And 10, [arr.]

BRAHMS, JOHANNES (cont'd.)

  In Summer Fields
    see Drei Lieder, [arr.]

  In Waldeseinsamkeit, For Solo Voice
    And Orchestra, [arr.] *Op.85,
    No.6
    LUCKS 02824 set $7.50, pts $.75,
    ea.   (B827)

  Liebesliederwalzer, [arr.] *Op.52
    (Herman) string orch LUCKS 05205 sc
    $3.75, set $7.00, pts $1.40, ea.
                                     (B828)
  Lo, How A Rose E'er Blooming *see
    Chorale Prelude: Es Ist Ein Ros'
    Entsprungen, [arr.]

  Lullaby
    see Drei Lieder, [arr.]

  Meine Liebe Ist Grun, For Solo Voice
    And Orchestra, [arr.] *Op.63,
    No.5
    LUCKS 02379 sc $4.00, set $7.50,
    pts $.75, ea.   (B829)

  Rhapsody for Solo Voice, Chorus and
    Orchestra, Op. 53
    (Alto Rhapsody) LUCKS 02834 sc
    $5.50, set $11.50, pts $.75, ea.
                                     (B830)
  Serenade, Op. 11, in D
    min sc PETERS 559 $7.00   (B831)

  Symphonies, Nos. 1-4
    min sc RICORDI-IT PR 611 $16.95
                                     (B832)
  Symphony No. 1, Op. 68, in C minor
    min sc UNIVER. PH130 $5.00   (B833)
    pts BROUDE BR. $2.00, ea.   (B834)
    min sc ZEN-ON 891101 f.s.   (B835)
    (Gerdes) min sc PETERS 9580A $8.50
                                     (B836)
  Symphony No. 2, Op. 73, in D
    min sc UNIVER. PH131 $5.00   (B837)
    pts BROUDE BR. $3.00, ea.   (B838)
    min sc ZEN-ON 891102 f.s.   (B839)
    (Gerdes) min sc PETERS 9581A $8.50
                                     (B840)
  Symphony No. 3, Op. 90, in F
    min sc UNIVER. PH132 $4.00   (B841)
    pts BROUDE BR. $3.00, ea.   (B842)
    min sc ZEN-ON 891103 f.s.   (B843)
    (Gerdes) min sc PETERS 9582A $8.50
                                     (B844)
  Symphony No. 4, Op. 98, in E minor
    min sc UNIVER. PH133 $3.00   (B845)
    pts BROUDE BR. $2.50, ea.   (B846)
    min sc ZEN-ON 891104 f.s.   (B847)
    (Gerdes) min sc PETERS 9583A $8.50
                                     (B848)
  Tragic Overture *see Tragische
    Ouverture

  Tragische Ouverture *Op.81 [11']
    3.2.2.2. 4.2.3.1. timp,strings
    study sc BREITKOPF-W PB 3694 f.s.
                                     (B849)
    "Tragic Overture" BROUDE BR. set
    $35.00, pts $1.75, ea.   (B850)
    "Tragic Overture" LUCKS 07291 sc
    $7.00, set $30.00, min sc $2.50,
    pts $1.40, ea.   (B851)

  True Love
    see Drei Lieder, [arr.]

  Ungarische Tanze Nos. 1, 3, And 10,
    [arr.]
    "Hungarian Dances No. 1, 3, And 10"
    LUCKS 07666 sc $7.00, set $23.00,
    min sc $2.50, pts $1.40, ea.
                                     (B852)
    "Hungarian Dances Nos. 1, 3, And
    10" 2+pic.2.2.2. 4.2.0.0. timp,
    perc,strings BROUDE BR. sc $5.00,
    set $27.50, pts $1.50, ea.   (B853)

  Ungarische Tanze Nos. 5 And 6, [arr.]
    (Parlow) "Hungarian Dances No. 5
    And 6" LUCKS 05204 sc $7.00, set
    $28.00, pts $1.40, ea.   (B854)

  Ungarischer Tanz No. 4, [arr.]
    (Juon) "Hungarian Dance No. 4"
    LUCKS 05203 sc $5.00, set $15.00,
    pts $.75, ea.   (B855)

  Variationen Uber Ein Thema Von Joseph
    Haydn *Op.56a [17']
    3.2.2.3. 4.2.0.0. timp,triangle,
    strings
    min sc UNIVER. PH134 $3.00   (B856)
    study sc BREITKOPF-W PB 3692 f.s.
                                     (B857)
    "Variations On A Theme By Haydn"
    BROUDE BR. set $22.50, pts $1.75,
    ea.   (B858)
    "Variations On A Theme By Haydn"
    LUCKS 05214 sc $8.50, set $18.00,
    min sc $2.50, pts $1.15, ea.
                                     (B859)

BRAHMS, JOHANNES (cont'd.)

  Variations On A Theme By Haydn *see
    Variationen Uber Ein Thema Von
    Joseph Haydn

  Vier Ernste Gesange, For Solo Voice
    And Orchestra, [arr.] *Op.121
    LUCKS 02889 set $9.00, pts $.60,
    ea.   (B860)

  Wiegenlied, For Solo Voice And
    Orchestra, [arr.] *Op.49,No.4
    LUCKS 02004 set $7.50, pts $.75,
    ea.   (B861)

BRAMBACH, CASPAR JOSEPH (1833-1902)
  Ouverture Zu "Tasso" *Op.30 [9']
    2.2.2.2. 4.2.3.0. timp,strings
    sc,pts LIENAU rent   (B862)

BRANDENBURG CONCERTI NOS. 1-3 see Bach,
  Johann Sebastian

BRANDENBURG CONCERTI, NOS. 1-6 see
  Bach, Johann Sebastian

BRANDENBURG CONCERTI NOS. 4-6 see Bach,
  Johann Sebastian

BRANDENBURG CONCERTO NO. 1 IN F see
  Bach, Johann Sebastian

BRANDENBURG CONCERTO NO.2 IN F see
  Bach, Johann Sebastian

BRANDENBURG CONCERTO NO. 3 IN G see
  Bach, Johann Sebastian

BRANDENBURG CONCERTO NO.4 IN G see
  Bach, Johann Sebastian

BRANDENBURG CONCERTO NO. 5 IN D see
  Bach, Johann Sebastian

BRANDENBURG CONCERTO NO.6 IN B FLAT see
  Bach, Johann Sebastian

BRANDSTROM, CHRISTER (1951-   )
  Sinfonia Ecologica *see Symphony No.
    1, Op. 25

  Symphony No. 1, Op. 25 [32']
    3.3.3.3. 4.3.2.2. timp,2perc,
    harp,cel,strings
    STIM   (B863)

BRANDTS-BUYS, JAN (1868-1933)
  Concerto for Piano and Orchestra, Op.
    15 [25']
    2.2.2.2+contrabsn. 4.2.0.0.
    strings,pno solo
    sc,pts LIENAU rent   (B864)

BRANLES GAULOIS, LES, FOR ACCORDION AND
  ORCHESTRA see Andriessen, Jurriaan

BRASE, FRITZ (1884-1940)
  Aus Meiner Heimat *Op.11 [27']
    2.2.2.2. 4.2.3.0. timp,perc,
    strings
    sc,pts LIENAU f.s.   (B865)

  Donegal
    sc,pts RIES f.s.   (B866)

  Irische Lustspiel-Ouverture
    RIES f.s.   (B867)

BRASILIANISCHE SINFONIETTA see
  Bjelinski, Bruno

BRAUN, PETER MICHAEL (1936-   )
  Ambiente [20']
    2.2.2(bass clar).2.soprano sax.
    2.2+cornet.2.0.baritone horn.
    timp,3perc,harp,strings
    (ob or clar may be substituted for
    sop sax; trp may be substituted
    for cornet; tuba may be
    substituted for baritone horn) sc
    BREITKOPF-W BG 1229 perf mat rent
                                     (B868)
BRAUNFELS, BERTEL
  Neues Federspiel Nach Versen Aus "Des
    Knaben Wunderhorn", For Solo
    Voice And Chamber Orchestra *see
    Braunfels, Walter

BRAUNFELS, WALTER (1882-1954)
  Neues Federspiel Nach Versen Aus "Des
    Knaben Wunderhorn", For Solo
    Voice And Chamber Orchestra
    (composed with Braunfels, Bertel)
    [15']
    1.1.1.1. 1.0.0.0. strings,solo
    voice
    RIES perf mat rent   (B869)

  Serenade, Op. 20 [23']
    3.1+English horn.2.2. 4.2.0.0.
    timp,perc,harp,strings
    RIES perf mat rent   (B870)

BRAUTSHAU POLKA see Strauss, Johann,
    [Jr.]

BRAVNICAR, MATIJA (1897-1977)
    Dance Burlesque *see Plesna Burleska

    Divertimento for Piano and String
        Orchestra [10']
        string orch,pno solo
        DRUSTVO DSS 834 perf mat rent
                                        (B871)

    Metamorphoses De Danse [18']
        2(pic).2.2.2. 4.2.3.1. timp,
        3perc,harp,pno,strings
        DRUSTVO DSS 773 perf mat rent
                                        (B872)

    Plesna Burleska [8']
        2(pic).2(English horn).2.2.
        4.2.3.1. timp,2perc,harp,
        strings
        "Dance Burlesque" DRUSTVO DSS 805
        perf mat rent   (B873)

    Simfonicna Antiteza [15']
        2(pic).2(English horn).2.2.
        4.2.3.1. timp,2perc,harp,
        strings
        "Symphonic Antithesis" DRUSTVO
        DSS 806 perf mat rent   (B874)

    Symphonic Antithesis *see Simfonicna
        Antiteza

BRAVOUR-VARIATIONEN UBER EIN THEMA VON
    MOZART, FOR SOLO VOICE, FLUTE AND
    ORCHESTRA see Adam, A.

BREAKTHROUGH see Suchon, Eugen, Prielom

BREDEMEYER, REINER (1929-   )
    Anfangen Aufhoren [8']
        3.3.3.3. 4.2.3.1. timp,strings
        PETERS   (B875)

    Auftakte [10']
        4.3.4.4. 4.4.3.1. timp,perc,
        strings
        PETERS   (B876)

    Concerto for Oboe and Orchestra [22']
        3.3.0.2. 2.1.1.0. timp,vibra,
        strings,ob solo
        sc PETERS EP 5545 f.s., perf mat
        rent   (B877)

    Spiel Zu 45 [15']
        2.1.1.2. 1.2.1.1. 3perc,strings
        PETERS   (B878)

BREIT, BERT (1927-   )
    Suite Sportive [20'40"]
        1(pic).1.1.0. 1.3.3.0. timp,perc,
        pno/hpsd,strings
        ORLANDO rent   (B879)

BRENNENDE LIEBE see Strauss, Josef

BRERO, CESARE (1908-1973)
    Concerto for String Orchestra [8']
        sc CARISCH 18894 perf mat rent
                                        (B880)

BRESGEN, CESAR (1913-   )
    Concerto for Trombone and Orchestra
        2.2.2.2. 3.2.0.0. timp,perc,harp,
        cel,strings,trom solo
        BREITKOPF-W perf mat rent   (B881)

    Concerto for 2 Violoncelli and
        Orchestra
        2(pic).1.2(bass clar).0. 2.1.1.0.
        timp,perc,strings,2vcl soli
        BREITKOPF-W perf mat rent   (B882)

    Elegy [11']
        12vcl
        BREITKOPF-W perf mat rent   (B883)

    Elegy for Flute and String Orchestra
        [12'30"]
        string orch,fl solo
        sc,pts DOBLINGER rent   (B884)

    Elenka, For Balalaika, Harp And
        Orchestra [25']
        1(pic).1.2.1. 2.1.1.0. timp,perc,
        strings,balalaika solo,harp
        solo
        BREITKOPF-W perf mat rent   (B885)

    Samiotissa [20']
        2(pic).2(English horn).2.2.
        4.2.2.0. timp,perc,harp,strings
        sc,pts DOBLINGER rent   (B886)

BREUKER, W.
    Export Vivaldi
        orch MOLENAAR 14.1567.08 f.s.
                                        (B887)

BREUNICH, JOHANN MICHAEL (1699-1755)
    Concerto in G [17']
        string orch,cont,fl solo
        BODENS EA 54 f.s.   (B888)

BREV see Blomberg, Erik

BREVIK, TOR (1932-   )
    Cattle Call And Summer Night, For
        Solo Voice And Orchestra *see
        Lokketrall Og Somar-Natta, For
        Solo Voice And Orchestra

    Festintrade (composed with
        Storbekken, Egil)
        2.2.2.2. 2.2.2.0. timp,perc,
        strings
        NORGE   (B889)

    Lokketrall Og Somar-Natta, For Solo
        Voice And Orchestra (composed
        with Storbekken, Egil)
        0.1.0.0. 1.0.0.0. strings,solo
        voice
        "Cattle Call And Summer Night, For
        Solo Voice And Orchestra" NORGE
                                        (B890)

    Meeting The Orchestra, For Narrator
        And Orchestra
        2.2.2.2. 2.2.2.0. timp,perc,
        strings,narrator
        NORGE   (B891)

BRIAN, HAVERGAL (1876-1972)
    Symphony No. 8
        study sc MUS.VIVA f.s.   (B892)

    Symphony No. 10
        study sc MUS.VIVA f.s.   (B893)

    Symphony No. 21
        study sc MUS.VIVA f.s.   (B894)

    Symphony No. 22
        study sc MUS.VIVA f.s.   (B895)

BRICKWORK see Eisma, Will, Metselwerk

BRIDE ELECT MARCH, THE see Sousa, John
    Philip

BRIDGE, FRANK (1879-1941)
    Oration
        sc FABER $30.00   (B896)

BRINGS, ALLEN STEPHEN (1934-   )
    Concerto Da Camera No. 3
        string orch,fl solo
        SEESAW perf mat rent   (B897)

    Concerto for Orchestra [16']
        2(pic).2.2.2. 2.2.1.0. timp,perc,
        strings
        sc MIRA $28.00, perf mat rent
                                        (B898)

    Cradle Song, A
        2.2.2.2. 2.2.2.0. harp,strings,
        solo voice
        MIRA perf mat rent see from Three
        Songs Of Blake And Donne, For
        Solo Voice And Orchestra   (B899)

    Never Seek To Tell Thy Love
        2.2.2.2. 2.2.2.0. harp,2timp,
        perc,strings,solo voice
        MIRA perf mat rent see from Three
        Songs Of Blake And Donne, For
        Solo Voice And Orchestra   (B900)

    Song
        2.2.2.2. 2.2.2.0. harp,strings,
        solo voice
        MIRA perf mat rent see from Three
        Songs Of Blake And Donne, For
        Solo Voice And Orchestra   (B901)

    Three Songs Of Blake And Donne, For
        Solo Voice And Orchestra *see
        Cradle Song, A; Never Seek To
        Tell Thy Love; Song   (B902)

    Two Pieces For Orchestra
        3.3.3.3. 4.3.3.1. timp,3perc,
        harp,strings
        SEESAW perf mat rent   (B903)

BRITAIN, RADIE (1908-   )
    Pygmalion Overture
        3.3.3.3. 4.3.3.1. timp,perc,harp,
        strings
        SEESAW perf mat rent   (B904)

BRITTEN, [SIR] BENJAMIN (1913-1976)
    Canadian Carnival *Op.19
        sc BOOSEY $9.00   (B905)

    Lachrymae, For Viola And String
        Orchestra *Op.48a
        min sc BOOSEY 904 $3.50   (B906)

    Phaedra, For Solo Voice And Orchestra
        *Op.93
        sc FABER $24.00   (B907)

    Prince Of The Pagodas: Prelude And
        Dances
        3.3.3.3.alto sax. 4.3.3.1. timp,
        perc,harp,pno,strings
        min sc BOOSEY HPS 919 $39.00 (B908)

    Suite On English Folk Tunes "A Time
        There Was..." *Op.90 [14']
        2(pic).2(English horn).2.2.

BRITTEN, [SIR] BENJAMIN (cont'd.)
        2.2.0.0. timp,2perc,harp,
        strings
        sc FABER FM 199 f.s., perf mat rent
                                        (B909)

BROCKWAY, HOWARD A. (1870-1951)
    Cavatina, For Violin And Orchestra
        [5']
        0.0.1.0. 2.0.0.0. strings,vln
        solo
        MARGUN sc $5.00, pts $10.00 (B910)

BROEKMAN, DAVID (1899-1958)
    Concerto for Piano, Percussion and
        Orchestra [35']
        3.2.3(clar in E flat,bass
        clar).2. 4.4.3.1. timp,harp,
        cel,strings,4perc,strings,pno solo
        MARGUN BP 1004 perf mat rent (B911)

    Concerto for Violin and Orchestra
        [38']
        2.2(English horn).2(bass clar).2.
        4.3.3.1. timp,perc,harp,
        strings,vln solo
        MARGUN BP 1005 perf mat rent (B912)

    Symphony No. 2 [30']
        3.3.3(clar in E flat).3. 4.4.3.1.
        timp,perc,harp,strings
        MARGUN BP 1007 perf mat rent (B913)

    Variations On A Theme By Valerius
        [9']
        string orch
        MARGUN BP 1036 perf mat rent (B914)

BROGGI, A.M. (1918-   )
    Tre Movimenti [15'30"]
        3.2.1.2. 2.1.1.0. vibra,timp,
        perc,strings
        sc CARISCH 21689 rent, pts CARISCH
        21690 rent   (B915)

BROKIGA BLAD see Sorenson, Torsten

BROMAN, STEN
    Overture
        3.2.2.2. 4.4.3.1. timp,perc,cel,
        strings
        sc,pts STIM rent   (B916)

BRONS see Schat, Peter

BRONS, CAREL (1931-   )
    They Are Telling Us [14']
        2.2.2.2. 2.2.0.0. perc,strings,
        2harp soli
        DONEMUS perf mat rent   (B917)

BROWN, CHRISTOPHER (1943-   )
    Sonata, Op. 42
        string orch
        CHESTER JWC 55140 min sc $33.75,
        pts rent   (B918)

    Sun Rising, The *Op.45
        2.2.2.2. 4.3.3.1. timp,perc,
        strings
        min sc CHESTER $27.75   (B919)

BROZAK, DANIEL (1947-   )
    Genitum [15']
        2.2.2.2. 2.2.2.1. 4perc,strings
        DONEMUS perf mat rent   (B920)

    Slunovrat [30']
        3.3.3.3. 4.3.3.1. timp,6perc,
        strings
        "Solstice, The" DONEMUS perf mat
        rent   (B921)

    Solstice, The *see Slunovrat

    Voiles, Les *see Zavoje

    Zavoje [11']
        fl,tuba,strings
        "Voiles, Les" DONEMUS perf mat rent
                                        (B922)

BRUCE
    Memories Of You (composed with
        Duckworth)
        4-20strings
        SEESAW perf mat rent   (B923)

BRUCH, MAX (1838-1920)
    Concerto for Violin and Orchestra,
        No. 1, Op. 26, in G minor
        BROUDE BR. set $27.50, pts $1.50,
        ea.   (B924)
        LUCKS 00508 sc $17.00, set $23.00,
        min sc $3.00, pts $1.40, ea.
                                        (B925)

    Hebrew Songs
        LUCKS 00602 sc $8.00, set $25.00,
        pts $1.40, ea.   (B926)

    Kol Nidrei, For Double Bass And
        Orchestra, [arr.] *Op.47
        2.2.2.2. 4.3.3.1. timp,harp,
        strings,db solo [6'] INTERNAT.
        perf mat rent   (B927)

BRUCH, MAX (cont'd.)

Kol Nidrei, For Trombone And
Orchestra, [arr.] *Op.47
(Voisin, Roger) 2.2.2.2. 4.2.3.0.
timp,harp,strings,trom solo [6']
INTERNAT. perf mat rent   (B928)

Kol Nidrei, For Viola And Orchestra,
[arr.] *Op.47
2.2.2.2. 4.2.3.0. timp,harp,
strings,vla solo [6'] INTERNAT.
perf mat rent   (B929)

Kol Nidrei, For Violin And Orchestra,
[arr.] *Op.47
2.2.2.2. 4.2.3.0. timp,harp,
strings,vln solo [6'] INTERNAT.
perf mat rent   (B930)

Kol Nidrei, For Violoncello And
Orchestra *Op.47 [6']
2.2.2.2. 4.2.3.0. timp,harp,
strings,vcl solo
BROUDE BR. set $20.00, pts $1.00,
ea.   (B931)
INTERNAT. perf mat rent   (B932)
LUCKS 00601 sc $6.50, set $16.00,
pts $.95, ea.   (B933)

Romance for Viola and Orchestra, Op.
85 [9']
1.1.2.2. 3.2.0.0. timp,strings,
vla solo
KALMUS 5422 sc $7.00, perf mat
rent, set $17.00, pts $1.00, ea.
                              (B934)

Schottische Fantasie, For Violin And
Orchestra *Op.46
"Scotch Fantasy" LUCKS 00414 sc
$17.00, set $33.00, pts $1.65,
ea.   (B935)

Scotch Fantasy *see Schottische
Fantasie, For Violin And
Orchestra

BRUCHMANN, KLAUS PETER (1932-   )
Concertino for Violoncello and
Orchestra [7']
2.2.2.2. 4.3.3.1. timp,perc,db,
vcl solo
ORLANDO rent   (B936)

Kriminallegro [6']
string orch
ORLANDO rent   (B937)

Rhythmische Ouverture [5']
2.2.2.2. 4.3.3.0. timp,perc,
strings
ORLANDO rent   (B938)

BRUCKNER, ANTON (1824-1896)
Erinnerung, [arr.]
(Andriessen, Hendrik) 2.2.2.0.
0.0.0.0. harp,strings DONEMUS
perf mat rent   (B939)

Overture in G minor
2.2.2.2. 2.2.3.0. timp,strings
sc UNIVER. 51 06570 $24.00   (B940)

Symphony in F minor
(Nowak) 2.2.2.2. 4.2.3.1. timp,
strings [47'] (1863 version) sc
MUSIKWISS. BR55 $16.00, perf mat
rent   (B941)

Symphony No. 1 in C minor [50']
3.2.2.2. 4.2.3.0. timp,strings
(second version, 1890-91)
MUSIKWISS. study sc f.s., pts
rent   (B942)
(Haas) (Linz Version; each movement
available separately) KALMUS 5496
sc $35.00, perf mat rent, set
$75.00, pts $4.00, ea.   (B943)

Symphony No. 2 in C minor
(Haas) (each movement available
separately) KALMUS A5497 sc
$40.00, perf mat rent, set
$75.00, pts $4.00, ea.   (B944)

Symphony No. 3 in D minor
2.2.2.2. 4.3.3.0. timp,strings
sc,pts LIENAU rent   (B945)
[65'] (first version, 1873)
MUSIKWISS. study sc f.s., pts
rent   (B946)

Symphony No. 3 in D minor, Second
Movement [18'30"]
2.2.2.2. 4.3.3.0. timp,strings
(Adagio No. 2, 1876) study sc
MUSIKWISS. f.s.   (B947)

Symphony No. 4 in E flat [60']
2.2.2.2. 4.3.3.0. timp,strings
(first version, 1874) MUSIKWISS.
study sc f.s., pts rent   (B948)

Symphony No. 4 in E flat, Finale
2.2.2.2. 4.3.3.1. timp,strings
[18'] study sc MUSIKWISS. f.s.

BRUCKNER, ANTON (cont'd.)
                              (B949)
Symphony No. 5 in B flat
(Haas) (each movement available
separately) KALMUS A 5498 sc
$50.00, perf mat rent, set
$80.00, pts $4.50, ea.   (B950)

Symphony No. 8 in C minor [52']
3.3.3.3. 8.3.3.1. timp,perc,harp,
strings
sc,pts LIENAU rent   (B951)

BRUCKNER DIALOGUE see Einem, Gottfried
von

BRUDER STUDIO POLKA see Strauss, Eduard

BRUHNS, NICHOLAUS (1665-1697)
Jauchzet Dem Herrn Alle Welt, For
Solo Voice And String Orchestra
(Psalm No. 100) [12']
string orch,hpsd,opt trp,S solo
(Walter, G.A.) BREITKOPF-W perf mat
rent   (B952)

Psalm No. 100 *see Jauchzet Dem
Herrn Alle Welt, For Solo Voice
And String Orchestra

BRUN, HERBERT (1918-   )
Gestures
1.1.1.1. 1.1.1.0. perc,vln,vla,db
SMITH PUB sc $16.50, pts $18.50
                              (B953)

BRUNELLI, LOUIS JEAN (1925-   )
Essay For Cyrano [21']
3.3.3.3. 4.3.3.1. timp,perc,harp,
strings
BOOSEY perf mat rent   (B954)

BRUNETTI, GAETANO (1744-1798)
Symphonies, Nine *CC9U
(Jenkins, Newell) sc GARLAND
ISBN 0-8240-3801-0 $90.00 "The
Symphony", Vol. A-V   (B955)

BRUNI-TEDESCHI, ALBERTO (1915-   )
Diario Marino [45']
3.3.3.sax. 4.3.3.1. 4timp,harp,
pno,cel,vibra,xylo,glock,gtr,
2perc,strings,speaking voice
sc ZERBONI 8339 f.s., pts ZERBONI
8340 rent   (B956)

Fantasia-Recitativo Quasi Una Danza,
For Piano And Orchestra
ZERBONI 8883-4   (B957)

BRUNNENNYMPHE, FOR VIOLIN AND ORCHESTRA
see Kugerl, H.

BRUNS, VICTOR (1904-   )
Concerto for Trumpet and Orchestra,
Op. 50
1.1.1.1. 3.0.1.0. timp,perc,
strings,trp solo
BREITKOPF-L perf mat rent   (B958)

BRUSCHETTINI, M. (1896-   )
Giugno, For Solo Voice And Orchestra
[3']
1.1.1.1. 1.0.0.0. timp,pno,
strings,S solo
manuscript CARISCH   (B959)

BRUST, HERBERT (1900-1968)
Drei Masurentanze *Op.41 [8']
1.1.1.0. 0.1.1.0. timp,perc,pno,
strings
RIES perf mat rent   (B960)

BRUTET ACKORD see Lindgren, Par

BRUYNEL, TON (1943-   )
Translucent II [10']
string orch,electronic tape
DONEMUS   (B961)

BRUYNS, HENK
Schlittenpferde, Die
RIES f.s.   (B962)

BUCCHI, VALENTINO (1916-1976)
Concerto Di Concerti
string orch,vln solo,vla solo,vcl
solo,db solo
sc CARISCH CM 21950 f.s., perf mat
rent   (B963)

Concerto for Piccolo and String
Orchestra [10']
string orch,pic/fl solo
sc CARISCH 21943 f.s., pts CARISCH
21943A rent   (B964)

Concerto In Rondo, For Piano And
Orchestra
FORLIVESI perf mat rent   (B965)

Concerto Lirico, For Violin And
String Orchestra [12']
string orch,vln solo
sc CARISCH 21935 f.s., pts CARISCH
21396 f.s.   (B966)

BUCCHI, VALENTINO (cont'd.)

Fantasy for String Orchestra [12']
string orch
f.s. sc CARISCH 21648, pts CARISCH
21649   (B967)

Incipit Per Archi, Un [10']
string orch
f.s. sc CARISCH 21933, pts CARISCH
21933A   (B968)

Pianto Delle Creature, For Solo Voice
And Orchestra [13']
2.2.2.2. 4.2.2.0. timp,perc,pno,
strings,solo voice
sc CARISCH 20751 f.s., pts CARISCH
rent   (B969)

BUCHT, GUNNAR (1927-   )
Clairobscur, En [12']
2.2.2.2. 2.2.0.0. perc,harp,7vln,
2vla,2vcl,db
STIM   (B970)

Concerto for Violin and Orchestra
[23']
2.2.2.2. 4.2.3.1. timp,4perc,
harp,cel,strings,vln solo
BUSCH HBM 069 perf mat rent   (B971)

Georgica [20'30"]
4.4.4.3. 4.4.4.2. 2timp,4perc,
2harp,cel,strings
sc STIM   (B972)

Sinfonia Concertante for Flute,
Viola, Harp and Orchestra [22']
2.2.2.2. 4.2.3.1. timp,perc,
strings,fl solo,vla solo,harp
solo
STIM   (B973)

Symphony No. 7
study sc SUECIA ENO 295 f.s. (B974)

BUCHTGER, FRITZ (1903-1978)
Ascensio [12']
2.1.2.1. 2.1.1.1. strings
ORLANDO rent   (B975)

Concertino for Oboe, Violin,
Violoncello and String Orchestra
[15']
string orch,ob solo,vln solo,vcl
solo
ORLANDO rent   (B976)

Hepzibah [15']
1.2.2.2. 0.1.0.0. strings
ORLANDO rent   (B977)

Kaiserliche Botschaft, Eine, For Solo
Voice And Orchestra [7'35"]
2.2.2.2. 2.3.2.0. timp,perc,
strings,Bar solo
ORLANDO rent   (B978)

Schichten-Bogen [20']
2.2.2.2. 2.2.2.0. perc,strings
ORLANDO rent   (B979)

Vor Der Tur, For Solo Voice And
Orchestra [50']
2.1.2.2. 0.0.0.0. perc,strings,
solo voice
ORLANDO rent   (B980)

BUDAPEST see Lamparter, Omar

BUDDE, KURT
Dramatische Ouverture *Op.28 [15']
3(pic).2(English horn).2.2.
4.3.3.1. 3timp,2perc,harp,
strings
RIES perf mat rent   (B981)

BUDER, ERNST ERICH (1896-1962)
Festival Ouverture [6']
2.2.2.2. 3.2.3.0. timp,perc,harp,
strings
sc RIES f.s., perf mat rent   (B982)

Kavalkade
RIES f.s.   (B983)

Komplimente
RIES f.s.   (B984)

Landliche Suite
RIES f.s.   (B985)

BUFFONESCA PICCOLA see Kowalski, Julius

BULL, JOHN (ca. 1562-1628)
Due Composizioni
(Guerrini, G.) string orch sc
ZANIBON 4503 f.s., pts ZANIBON
4504 f.s.
contains: Duke Of Brunswick's
Alman, The; King's Hunt, The
                              (B986)

Duke Of Brunswick's Alman, The
see Due Composizioni

BULL, JOHN (cont'd.)

King's Hunt, The
see Due Composizioni

BULL, OLE BORNEMANN (1810-1880)
Quartetto Per Un Violino Solo, [arr.]
(Ronnes, Robert)
2.2.2.3(contrabsn). 4.4.3.1.
perc,strings,vln solo NORGE
(B987)

BULLERIAN, HANS (1885-   )
Mazurka
sc,pts RIES f.s.   (B988)

BUND, HANS
Charmeur, Der
RIES f.s.   (B989)

Erinnerung An Ein Ballerlebnis
RIES f.s.   (B990)

In Spanischen Garten [4']
2.2.2.2. 4.2.3.0. 2perc,pno,
strings
RIES perf mat rent   (B991)
RIES f.s.   (B992)

Kleine Suite
RIES f.s.   (B993)

Rue De Plaisir
RIES f.s.   (B994)

Spanischer Tanz
RIES f.s.   (B995)

BUNGE, SAS (1924-1980)
Ballade Des Pendu, For Solo Voice And
Orchestra [11']
2.2.2.2. 2.0.0.0. timp,perc,harp,
strings,A/B solo
sc DONEMUS f.s., perf mat rent
(B996)

BUNTE BALLE see Ritter, Helmut

BUNTE LICHTER see Kleine, Werner

BUREN, JOHN VAN (1952-   )
Romance for Orchestra [7']
MODERN 2114 rent   (B997)

BURGERSINN WALZER see Strauss, Johann,
[Jr.]

BURKHARD, WILLY (1900-1955)
Kleine Konzertante Suite *Op.79
[16']
1(pic).2.2.2. 2.2.1.0. timp,perc,
harp,strings
study sc BAREN. BA 6767 f.s., perf
mat rent   (B998)

BURLAS, LADISLAV (1927-   )
Music for Violin and Orchestra [20']
3.2.3.2. 4.3.3.1. timp,perc,xylo,
bells,pno,strings,vln solo
SLOV.HUD.FOND 0-452A perf mat rent
(B999)

BURLESCA see Rapalo, Ugo

BURLESCA see Urack, Otto

BURLESCA, FOR HORN AND ORCHESTRA see
Laburda, Jiri

BURLESCA, FOR PIANO AND ORCHESTRA see
Piccioli, Giuseppe

BURLESKE see Moser, Rudolf

BURLESKE see Riege, Ernst

BURLESKE, FOR PIANO AND ORCHESTRA see
Strauss, Richard

BURLETTA see Juon, Paul, Konzertstuck
for Violin and Orchestra, Op. 97

BURRATTINI see Guarino, Carmine

BURSCHENWANDERUNG POLKA see Strauss,
Johann, [Jr.]

BURTON, S.
Dithyramb
study sc SALABERT $23.00   (B1000)

BUSCH, CARL (1862-1943)
Elegy, Op. 30, in D minor
string orch
KALMUS A4573 sc $3.00, set $3.75,
pts $.75, ea.   (B1001)

BUSCH, HANS
Blumen Im Wind
RIES f.s.   (B1002)

BUSH, GEOFFREY (1920-   )
Noctambule
sc NOVELLO 9031 $8.75, set NOVELLO
9032 $34.75, pts NOVELLO 9585   (B1003)

BUSONI, FERRUCCIO BENVENUTO (1866-1924)
Concerto for Violin and Orchestra,
Op. 35a, in D [20']
3.2.2.2. 4.2.3.1. timp,perc,
strings,vln solo
KALMUS 5211 sc $20.00, perf mat
rent, set $40.00, pts $1.50, ea.
(B1004)

Fantasia Contrappuntistica, [arr.]
(Beaumont, A.) harp,cel,pno,strings
[35'] BREITKOPF-W perf mat rent
(B1005)

BUSSOTTI, SYLVANO (1931-   )
Bergkristall
sc RICORDI-IT 132081 $30.00 (B1006)

Nottetempo: Danza Di Bufera
sc RICORDI-IT 132728   (B1007)

Semi Di Gramsci, I
orch,string quar soli
sc RICORDI-IT 131874 f.s.   (B1008)

BUTTERWORTH, ARTHUR (1923-   )
Green Wind [5'30"]
2.2.2.2. 2.0.0.0. timp,perc,harp,
strings
sc,pts HINRICHSEN rent   (B1009)

BUXTEHUDE, DIETRICH (ca. 1637-1707)
Chaconne In E Minor, [arr.]
(Chavez, Carlos) 2+2pic.2+English
horn.3+bass clar.2+contrabsn.
4.3.3.1. timp,strings [7'] sc
KALMUS A7008 $7.00   (B1010)

Fughetta
see RICREAZIONI DI ANTICHE MUSICHE
CLASSICHE, SERIE III: MUSICHE
ANTICHE ITALIANE

C

C-A-G-E-D see Bond, Victoria

CAAMANO, ROBERTO (1923-   )
Suite, Op. 9
string orch
min sc BARRY-ARG 1045 $3.50   (C1)

CABALLERO, M.F. (1835-1906)
Gigantes Y Cabezudos
string orch
KALMUS 5425 pno-cond sc $6.00, perf
mat rent, set $10.00, pts $2.00,
ea.   (C2)

CABO RASO-GUT SO see Rhinow, H.J.

CACAVAS, JOHN (1930-   )
Day The Orchestra Played, The, For
Narrator And Orchestra
sc BOOSEY $5.00   (C3)

CACCIA see Holten

CACCIA, FOR HORN AND ORCHESTRA see
Montico, Mario

CACCINI, GIULIO (1546-1618)
Amarilli
see RICREAZIONI DI ANTICHE MUSICHE
CLASSICHE, SERIE V: MUSICHE
ANTICHE ITALIANE

CACHEMIRIENNE, LA see Drigo, Riccardo

CADENZAS, FOR VIOLIN, OP. 11 see
Borghi, Luigi

CAGE, JOHN (1912-   )
Apartment House 1776
PETERS   (C4)

Quartets I-VIII, Version For 24
Players [40']
1.2.1.2. 2.0.0.0. strings
sc,pts PETERS P66686 rent   (C5)

Quartets I-VIII, Version For 41
Players [40']
2.2.2.2. 2.2.0.0. strings
sc,pts PETERS P66687 rent   (C6)

Quartets I-VIII, Version For 93
Players [40']
3.4(English horn).4(clar in E
flat,bass clar).3. 6.4.3.1.
strings
sc,pts PETERS P66688 rent   (C7)

Renga [30'-40']
78 parts for instruments and-or
voices
sc,pts PETERS P6818 rent   (C8)

Score And 23 Parts
23 instruments and-or voices and
tape
sc,pts PETERS P6815 rent   (C9)

Thirty Pieces For Five Orchestras
[30']
3(pic,alto fl).3(English
horn).3(bass
clar).3(contrabsn). 5.5.6.0.
timp,2perc,pno,strings
PETERS 66879 perf mat rent   (C10)

CAGLIOSTRO IN WIEN: OVERTURE see
Strauss, Johann, [Jr.]

CAGLIOSTRO QUADRILLE see Strauss,
Johann, [Jr.]

CAID, LE: LE TAMBOUR-MAJOR, FOR SOLO
VOICE AND ORCHESTRA see Thomas,
Ambroise

CAIN BALLET see Newman, Theodore Simon

CAIO MARIO: OVERTURE see Cimarosa,
Domenico

CAJKOVSKIJ, PETR ILJIC
see TCHAIKOVSKY, PIOTR ILYICH

CAKEWALK: SUITE see Kay, Hershy

CALDARA, ANTONIO (1670-1736)
Battista, Il (Sinfonia No. 2 in C)
string orch,cont
(Nowak, L.) sc,pts DOBLINGER DM 769
f.s.   (C11)

Gerusalemme Convertita (Sinfonia, No.
7, in D)
string orch,cont
(Nowak, L.) sc,pts DOBLINGER DM 774
f.s.   (C12)

CALDARA, ANTONIO (cont'd.)

Gesu Presentato Nel Tempio (Sinfonia,
No. 9, in B flat)
string orch,cont
(Nowak, L.) sc,pts DOBLINGER DM 776
f.s.   (C13)

Gioseffo Che Interpreta I Sogni
(Sinfonia, No. 10, in E minor)
string orch,cont
(Nowak, L.) sc,pts DOBLINGER DM 777
f.s.   (C14)

Martirio Del S. Terenzio, Il
(Sinfonia No. 1 in F)
string orch,cont
(Nowak, L.) sc,pts DOBLINGER DM 768
f.s.   (C15)

Morte d'Abel, La (Sinfonia, No. 3, in
F minor)
string orch,cont
(Nowak, L.) sc,pts DOBLINGER DM 770
f.s.   (C16)

Morte E Sepultura Di Christo
(Sinfonia, No. 4, in B minor)
string orch,cont
(Nowak, L.) sc,pts DOBLINGER DM 771
f.s.   (C17)

Naboth (Sinfonia, No. 11, in D minor)
string orch,cont
(Nowak, L.) sc,pts DOBLINGER DM 778
f.s.   (C18)

Passione Di Gesu Signor Nostro, La
(Sinfonia, No. 12, in A minor)
string orch,cont
(Nowak, L.) sc,pts DOBLINGER DM 779
f.s.   (C19)

S. Elena Al Calvario (Sinfonia, No.
6, in G minor)
string orch,cont
(Nowak, L.) sc,pts DOBLINGER DM 773
f.s.   (C20)

S. Pietro In Cesarea (Sinfonia, No.
5, in B flat)
string orch,cont
(Nowak, L.) sc,pts DOBLINGER DM 772
f.s.   (C21)

Sedecia (Sinfonia, No. 8, in B flat)
string orch,cont
(Nowak, L.) sc,pts DOBLINGER DM 775
f.s.   (C22)

Sinfonia No. 1 in F *see Martirio
Del S. Terenzio, Il

Sinfonia No. 2 in C *see Battista,
Il

Sinfonia, No. 3, in F minor *see
Morte d'Abel, La

Sinfonia, No. 4, in B minor *see
Morte E Sepultura Di Christo

Sinfonia, No. 5, in B flat *see S.
Pietro In Cesarea

Sinfonia, No. 6, in G minor *see S.
Elena Al Calvario

Sinfonia, No. 7, in D *see
Gerusalemme Convertita

Sinfonia, No. 8, in B flat *see
Sedecia

Sinfonia, No. 9, in B flat *see Gesu
Presentato Nel Tempio

Sinfonia, No. 10, in E minor *see
Gioseffo Che Interpreta I Sogni

Sinfonia, No. 11, in D minor *see
Naboth

Sinfonia, No. 12, in A minor *see
Passione Di Gesu Signor Nostro,
La

CALGACUS see McGuire, Edward

CALIBAN UPON SETEBOS see Rosenboom,
David

CALIFE DE BAGDAD, LE: OVERTURE see
Boieldieu, Francois-Adrien

CALM AS THE NIGHT see Bohm, Karl, Still
Wie Die Nacht, For Solo Voice And
Orchestra

CALM SEA AND PROSPEROUS VOYAGE see
Mendelssohn-Bartholdy, Felix,
Meeresstille Und Gluckliche Fahrt

CALTABIANO, SEBASTIANO (1899-   )
Due Preludi [17']
3.3.3.3. 4.3.3.1. timp,perc,
2harp,cel,bells,strings
min sc CARISCH 16132 perf mat rent
                                  (C23)

Overture in F [8']
2.2.2.2. 4.2.1.0. timp,strings
sc CARISCH 17113 perf mat rent
                                  (C24)

Prometeo [16']
3.3.3.3. 4.3.3.1. timp,perc,
2harp,strings
sc CARISCH 16840 perf mat rent
                                  (C25)

Visione Di S. Martino [16']
3.3.3.3. 4.3.3.1. timp,perc,1-
2harp,cel,bells,strings
min sc CARISCH 15776 perf mat rent
                                  (C26)

CAMBIALE DI MATRIMONIO, LA: OVERTURE
see Rossini, Gioacchino

CAMELIEN POLKA see Strauss, Johann,
[Jr.]

CAMILLA TRIOFANTE, LA: WIE DU MIR, SO
ICH DIR see Bononcini, Giovanni

CAMILLERI, CHARLES (1931-   )
Concerto for Piano and Orchestra, No.
1
ROBERTON perf mat rent   (C27)

Concerto for Piano and Orchestra, No.
2
ROBERTON perf mat rent   (C28)

Cosmic Visions
string orch
ROBERTON perf mat rent   (C29)

CAMILLUCCI, GUIDO (1912-   )
Due Danze [9']
1.1.1.0. 1.0.0.0. pno,strings
sc CARISCH 19458 f.s., perf mat
rent   (C30)

CAMINITI, G. (1895-1971)
Concerto for Violoncello and
Orchestra in A [25']
3.3.2.2. 4.2.3.1. perc,harp,pno,
strings,vcl solo
manuscript CARISCH   (C31)

CAMMAROTA, CARLO (1905-   )
Concerto for Piano and Orchestra
[27']
2.2.2.2. 4.2.3.1. timp,strings,
pno solo
sc ZANIBON 4329 rent, pts ZANIBON
4333 rent, solo pt ZANIBON 4297
                              (C32)

Divergenze [20']
2.2.2.2. 4.3.3.1. timp,cym,
strings
sc ZANIBON 5167 rent, pts ZANIBON
5168 rent   (C33)

CAMPIELLO, IL: INTERMEZZO, ACT II;
RITORNELLO, ACT III see Wolf-
Ferrari, Ermanno

CAMUSSI, EZIO (1877-1956)
Piccola Suite [6']
3.2.2.2. 2.2.3.1. timp,perc,cel,
harp,bells,xylo,strings
manuscript CARISCH   (C34)

CANADIAN CARNIVAL see Britten, [Sir]
Benjamin

CANCIONES DEL CAMINO see Boehmer,
Konrad

CANNABICH, CHRISTIAN (1731-1798)
Concerto Alla Pastorale In C [8']
1.1.0.1. 1.0.0.0. strings
(Bodart, Eugen) MANNHEIM E 28-56
f.s.   (C35)

Pastorale, No. 1, in D [14']
2.2.0.2. 2.0.0.0. strings
(Bodart, Eugen) MANNHEIM E 26-56
f.s.   (C36)

Pastorale, No. 2, in D [6']
2.2.0.2. 2.0.0.0. strings,org
(Bodart, Eugen) MANNHEIM E 10-57
f.s.   (C37)

Sinfonia Pastorale In F [7']
2.2.0.2. 2.0.0.0. strings,org
(Bodart, Eugen) MANNHEIM E 2-57
f.s.   (C38)

CANONE I see Schumann, Robert
(Alexander)

CANONE II see Schumann, Robert
(Alexander)

CANONI ENIGMATICI see Benvenuti, Arrigo

CANTA IN PRATO, FOR SOLO VOICE AND
STRING ORCHESTRA see Vivaldi,
Antonio

CANTA IN PRATO, FOR SOLO VOICE AND
STRING ORCHESTRA, RV 636 see
Vivaldi, Antonio

CANTATA NO. 35: GEIST UND SEELE WIRD
VERWIRRET, FOR SOLO VOICE AND
ORCHESTRA see Bach, Johann
Sebastian

CANTATA NO. 51: JAUCHZET GOTT IN ALLEN
LANDEN, FOR SOLO VOICE AND
ORCHESTRA see Bach, Johann
Sebastian

CANTATA NO. 53: SCHLAGE DOCH,
GEWUNSCHTE STUNDE, FOR SOLO VOICE
AND ORCHESTRA see Bach, Johann
Sebastian

CANTATA NO. 82: ICH HABE GENUG, FOR
SOLO VOICE AND ORCHESTRA see Bach,
Johann Sebastian

CANTATA NO. 170: VERGNUGTE RUH',
BELIEBTE SEELENLUST, FOR SOLO VOICE
AND ORCHESTRA see Bach, Johann
Sebastian

CANTATA NO. 202: WEICHET NUR, BETRUBTE
SCHATTEN, FOR SOLO VOICE AND
ORCHESTRA see Bach, Johann
Sebastian

CANTATA NO. 209: NON SA CHE SIA DOLORE,
FOR SOLO VOICE AND ORCHESTRA see
Bach, Johann Sebastian

CANTATORIUM CARNEVALE, FOR SOLO VOICES
AND ORCHESTRA see Toebosch, Louis

CANTERBURY CONCERTO, FOR PIANO AND
ORCHESTRA see Straesser, Joep

CANTI see Castiglioni, Niccolo

CANTI DELL'ESILIO, I, FOR SOLO VOICE
AND ORCHESTRA see Porrino, Ennio

CANTI DI STAGIONE, FOR SOLO VOICE AND
ORCHESTRA see Porrino, Ennio

CANTI PER SANT'ALESSANDRO: INTERLUDIO,
FOR SOLO VOICE AND ORCHESTRA see
Gavazzeni, Gianandrea

CANTI SERENI, I, FOR SOLO VOICE AND
ORCHESTRA see Pizzini, Carlo
Alberto

CANTI V, FOR HARPSICHORD AND CHAMBER
ORCHESTRA see Jorns, Helge

CANTICLE OF THE EVENING BELLS, FOR
FLUTE AND ORCHESTRA see Schwantner,
Joseph

CANTICO DI VITTORIA, FOR SOLO VOICE AND
ORCHESTRA see Guerrini, Guido

CANTICUM see Olsen, Sparre

CANTICUM ZACHARIAE, FOR SOLO VOICE AND
ORCHESTRA see Salva, Tadeas

CANTIQUE DE NOEL see Adam, Adolphe-
Charles

CANTIQUE SPIRITUEL, FOR SOLO VOICE AND
STRING ORCHESTRA see Andriessen,
Hendrik

CANTO DE LI AUGEI, IL, FOR SOLO VOICE
AND ORCHESTRA see Kopelent, Marek

CANTO DE LOS MARRANOS, FOR SOLO VOICE
AND ORCHESTRA see Levy, Marvin
David

CANTO DELL'OSPITE, FOR SOLO VOICE AND
ORCHESTRA see Sinigaglia, Leone

CANTO DI TERRA D'ORO, IL see Martino,
Aladino di

CANTO INFERNALE, FOR SOPRANO AND
ORCHESTRA see Laman, Wim

CANTO MISTICO see Ravanello, Oreste

CANTO POR VICTOR JARA, FOR VIOLONCELLO
AND ORCHESTRA see Jahn, Thomas

CANTO VARIATO, FOR VIOLONCELLO AND
ORCHESTRA see Dressel, Erwin

CANTU, MARIO (1903-1961)
Andante [3']
1.1.1.1. 1.0.0.0. strings
manuscript CARISCH   (C39)

CANTU, MARIO (cont'd.)

Impressioni Dolomitiche [16']
3.3.3.2. 4.3.3.1. timp,perc,
2harp,pno,cel,strings
sc CARISCH 17120 perf mat rent
(C40)

Poema Ligure [15']
3.3.3.2. 4.3.3.1. timp,perc,cel,
2harp,pno,bells,strings
sc CARISCH 17101 perf mat rent
(C41)

CANTUS AMORIS see Flothuis, Marius

CANTUS I (VERANDERUNGEN EINES CHORALES
VON J.S. BACH, BWV 60) see
Dittrich, Paul-Heinz

CANTUS II - UNUM NECESSARIUM, FOR SOLO
VOICE AND ORCHESTRA see Dittrich,
Paul-Heinz

CANZON A 3, MIN 19 see Cavalli,
(Pietro) Francesco

CANZON A 4, MIN 20 see Cavalli,
(Pietro) Francesco

CANZON A 6, MIN 21 see Cavalli,
(Pietro) Francesco

CANZON A 8, MIN 22 see Cavalli,
(Pietro) Francesco

CANZON A 10, MIN 23 see Cavalli,
(Pietro) Francesco

CANZON A 12, MIN 24 see Cavalli,
(Pietro) Francesco

CANZONA see Baird, Tadeusz

CANZONA see Frescobaldi, Girolamo

CANZONE see Andriessen, Hendrik

CANZONE see Bossi, [Marco] Enrico

CANZONE see Lombardi, Luca

CANZONE see Marschera, F.

CANZONE see Nordio, Cesare

CANZONE, FOR VIOLIN AND ORCHESTRA see
Wahlberg, Rune

CANZONE DEGLI UCCELLI, LA see Francesco
da Milano

CANZONE D'ESTATE, FOR VIOLIN AND
ORCHESTRA see Ricci Signorini,
Antonio

CANZONE IN B FLAT, FOR VIOLONCELLO AND
ORCHESTRA see Brahms, Johannes

CANZONE NORDICA see Bossi, [Marco]
Enrico

CANZONETTA see Mendelssohn-Bartholdy,
Felix

CANZONETTA, FOR CLARINET AND ORCHESTRA
see Pierne, Gabriel

CANZONI AMOROSE DEL DUECENTO, FOR SOLO
VOICES AND ORCHESTRA see Henkemans,
Hans

CAPDENAT, PHILIPPE (1934-   )
Cassation [26']
2.2.2.2. 2.0.0.0. strings
AMPHION A 382 perf mat rent   (C42)

Stimuli Pour Sources Sonores
Aleatoires Et Instruments
AMPHION A 270 perf mat rent   (C43)

CAPINERA, LA, FOR SOLO VOICE AND
ORCHESTRA see Benedict, [Sir]
Julius

CAPITAN FRACASSA, FOR VIOLIN AND
ORCHESTRA see Castelnuovo-Tedesco,
Mario

CAPITAN MARCH, EL see Sousa, John
Philip

CAPITAN SPECTACULAR, EL, [ARR.] see
Sousa, John Philip

CAPRICCIO BRILLANTE, FOR PIANO AND
ORCHESTRA see Mendelssohn-
Bartholdy, Felix

CAPRICCIO BRILLANTE ON "JOTA ARAGONESE"
see Glinka, Mikhail Ivanovich

CAPRICCIO ESPAGNOL see Rimsky-Korsakov,
Nikolai

CAPRICCIO FUGATO see Scarlatti,
Domenico

CAPRICCIO ITALIEN see Tchaikovsky,
Piotr Ilyich

CAPRICCIO OKINAWA see Kanai, Kikuko

CAPRICCIO PIAN' E FORTE see Ruders,
Poul

CAPRICCIO RITMICO see Dressel, Erwin

CAPRICCIO SCIVOLANDO see Kess, Ludwig

CAPRICCIOSA, LA, FOR VIOLIN AND
ORCHESTRA see Ries, Franz

CAPRICE 4-1 see Ashkenazy, Benjamin

CAPRICE EN FORME DE VALSE, [ARR.] see
Saint-Saens, Camille

CAPRICE FANTASTIQUE see Dressel, Erwin

CAPRICE FOR ORCHESTRA see Fountain,
Primous

CAPRICE VIENNOIS, [ARR.] see Kreisler,
Fritz

CAPRIOL SUITE, VERSION FOR STRING
ORCHESTRA see Heseltine, Philip
("Peter Warlock")

CAPRIOLEN see Rixner, Josef

CAPTAINS AND THE KINGS, THE see
Anderson, Leroy

CAPULETI E I MONTECCHI, I: SINFONIA see
Bellini, Vincenzo

CAPUZZI, ANTONIO (1753-1818)
Concerto for Double Bass and
Orchestra in D, MIN 4 [20']
0.2.0.0. 2.0.0.0. strings,db solo
(Malaric, R.) sc,pts DOBLINGER rent
(C44)

CARACOL see Englert, Giuseppe Giorgio

CARDELLINO, IL see Vivaldi, Antonio,
Concerto, RV 428, Op. 10, No. 3, in
D, P. 155, F.VI no. 14

CARDELLO, ROLF
Pausenlos Im Ring
RIES f.s.   (C45)

CARDEW, CORNELIUS (1936-   )
Autumn 60 [10']
sc UNIVER. UE 15444 $8.00, perf mat
rent   (C46)

CARL, GENE (1953-   )
Presentiment °see Voorgevoel

Voorgevoel [16']
3.3.3.3. 4.4.3.1. timp,3perc,
harp,strings
"Presentiment" DONEMUS   (C47)

CARLEVARO, A. (1914-   )
Concerto Del Plata, For Guitar And
Orchestra
sc BARRY-ARG $25.00   (C48)

CARLSTEDT, JAN (1926-   )
Trittico Galante, For Oboe And String
Orchestra
string orch,ob solo
sc,pts,solo pt STIM perf mat rent
(C49)

CARMEN: AIR DE FLEUR, FOR SOLO VOICE
AND ORCHESTRA see Bizet, Georges

CARMEN ARCADIAE MECHANICAE PERPETUUM
see Birtwistle, Harrison

CARMEN: CHANSON DU TOREADOR, FOR SOLO
VOICE AND ORCHESTRA see Bizet,
Georges

CARMEN: EN VAIN POUR EVITER, FOR SOLO
VOICE AND ORCHESTRA see Bizet,
Georges

CARMEN: ENTR'ACTES II, III, IV see
Bizet, Georges

CARMEN FANTASIE, FOR VIOLIN AND
ORCHESTRA see Waxman, Franz

CARMEN FANTASY, FOR VIOLIN AND
ORCHESTRA see Bizet, Georges

CARMEN: GYPSY SONG see Bizet, Georges

CARMEN: HABANERA, FOR SOLO VOICE AND
ORCHESTRA see Bizet, Georges

CARMEN: JE DIS QUE RIEN NE M'EPOUVANTE,
FOR SOLO VOICE AND ORCHESTRA see
Bizet, Georges

CARMEN: JE SUIS ESCAMILLO, FOR SOLO
VOICES AND ORCHESTRA see Bizet,
Georges

CARMEN: JE VAIS DANSER EN VOTRE
HONNEUR, FOR SOLO VOICES AND
ORCHESTRA see Bizet, Georges

CARMEN: MARCHE see Bizet, Georges

CARMEN: PARLE-MOI DE MA MERE, FOR SOLO
VOICES AND ORCHESTRA see Bizet,
Georges

CARMEN: PRELUDE see Bizet, Georges

CARMEN: SEGUEDILLE, FOR SOLO VOICES AND
ORCHESTRA see Bizet, Georges

CARMEN: SI TU M'AIMES, FOR SOLO VOICES
AND ORCHESTRA see Bizet, Georges

CARMEN: SUITE NO. 1 see Bizet, Georges

CARMEN: SUITE NO. 2 see Bizet, Georges

CARMEN: TOREADOR SONG see Bizet,
Georges, Carmen: Chanson Du
Toreador, For Solo Voice And
Orchestra

CARMEN-VARIATIONEN see Baur, Jurg

CARNAVAL DES ANIMAUX, LE see Saint-
Saens, Camille

CARNAVAL ROMAIN, LE see Berlioz, Hector
(Louis)

CARNIVAL IN PARIS see Svendsen, Johan
(Severin)

CARNIVAL OF THE ANIMALS see Saint-
Saens, Camille, Carnaval Des
Animaux, Le

CARNIVALSBILDER see Strauss, Johann,
[Jr.]

CARO MIO BEN, FOR SOLO VOICE AND STRING
ORCHESTRA, [ARR.] see Giordani,
Giuseppe

CAROL OF THE BELLS see Leontovich, M.

CAROVANE NOTTURNE see Bettinelli,
Angelo

CARPENTER, GARY (1951-   )
Concerto for Orchestra [20']
3.3.3.3. 4.3.3.1. timp,3perc,
harp,pno,strings
DONEMUS perf mat rent   (C50)

Eight Drops In The Ocean
MODERN 2061 perf mat rent   (C51)

Three Dance Sequences 'The Continuing
Story' [16']
3.2.3.2. 4.2.2.1. 4perc,harp,
strings
DONEMUS perf mat rent   (C52)

CARPI, FIORENZO (1918-   )
Concerto for Flute and Chamber
Orchestra [12'30']
2clar,2bsn,pno,perc,strings,fl
solo
sc,pts ZANIBON D242 rent   (C53)

Gregorians Sketches [15']
2.2.3.1.sax. 1.1.0.0. 2perc,harp,
cel,xylo,gtr,strings
manuscript CARISCH   (C54)

Sonata Notturna, For Flute, Violin
And Strings [11']
4vln,3vla,2vcl,db,fl solo,vln
solo
sc,pts ZANIBON D251 rent   (C55)

Varianti [13']
0.2.0.2. 0.2.2.0. drums,strings
sc,pts ZANIBON D269 rent   (C56)

CARRIBEAN ISLANDS see Miller, Charles

CARROUSEL, FOR SOLO VOICES AND
INSTRUMENTAL ENSEMBLE see Globokar,
Vinko

CARTER, ELLIOTT COOK, JR. (1908-   )
Symphony Of Three Orchestras, A
sc AMP $42.50   (C57)

CARULLI, FERDINANDO (1770-1841)
Concerto for Flute, Guitar and
Orchestra in G, MIN 46 [15']
2ob,2horn,strings,fl solo,gtr
solo
(Chiesa, R.) sc ZERBONI 8135 f.s.,
pts ZERBONI 8136 rent   (C58)

CASAGRANDE, ALESSANDRO (1922-1964)
Asteres [23']
2.2.2.2. 4.3.3.1. timp,perc,
vibra,harp,bells,strings
sc CARISCH 21773 rent, pts CARISCH
21774 rent   (C59)

CASAGRANDE, ALESSANDRO (cont'd.)

Ballata dell'Angoscia [22']
2.2.2.2. 4.3.3.1. perc,timp,harp,
strings
manuscript CARISCH   (C60)

Tempo Sinfonico, For Piano And
Orchestra [12']
1.1.1.1.sax. 4.4.0.0. perc,timp,
bongos,strings,pno solo
manuscript CARISCH   (C61)

Tre Divertimenti [18']
1.1.1.1. 2.0.0.0. timp,harp,
strings
manuscript CARISCH   (C62)

CASAGRANDE, E. (1926-   )
Prismes, For Solo Voice And String
Orchestra [5']
string orch,solo voice
sc ZANIBON 5643 f.s.   (C63)

CASELLATI, GINO (1890-   )
Elegy [6']
string orch
sc,pts ZANIBON 5257 rent   (C64)

CASSOLI, M. (1930-   )
Concertino "Al Modo Antico" In E
Flat, For Violoncello And String
Orchestra [12']
string orch,vcl solo
sc ZANIBON 5878 f.s., pts ZANIBON
5879 f.s.   (C65)

CASTALDO, JOSEPH F. (1927-   )
Lacrimosa [23']
string orch
sc PEER $7.00   (C66)

CASTELLANA see Chagrin, Francis

CASTELLI DI GIULIETTA E ROMEO, I, FOR
PIANO AND ORCHESTRA see Pedrollo,
Arrigo

CASTELNUOVO-TEDESCO, MARIO (1895-1968)
Ballata Cavalleresca
FORLIVESI perf mat rent   (C67)

Capitan Fracassa, For Violin And
Orchestra
FORLIVESI perf mat rent   (C68)

Cipressi
FORLIVESI perf mat rent   (C69)

Sirenetta E Il Pesce Turchino
FORLIVESI perf mat rent   (C70)

CASTIGLIONI, NICCOLO (1932-   )
Arabeschi, For Flute, Piano And
Orchestra
orch,fl solo,pno solo
sc RICORDI-IT 132020 f.s.   (C71)

Canti [8']
2.2.2.2. 2.2.1.0. timp,perc,harp,
pno,vibra,strings
ZERBONI perf mat rent   (C72)

Concertino Per La Notte Di Natale
sc RICORDI-IT 132924   (C73)

Inverno In-Ver
sc RICORDI-IT 132107 f.s.   (C74)

CATTINI, UMBERTO (1922-   )
Cinque Carmi Di Catullo, For Solo
Voice And Orchestra [11']
2.2.2.2. 2.2.0.0. timp,harp,
strings,solo voice
manuscript CARISCH   (C75)

Divertimento [10']
string orch
manuscript CARISCH   (C76)

Musica Per Antichi Poeti Italiani,
For Solo Voice And Orchestra [6']
fl,clar,strings,S solo
sc,pts ZANIBON D246 rent   (C77)

Partita [12']
pno,strings
manuscript CARISCH   (C78)

Tre Poesie Di Salvatore Quasimodo,
For Solo Voice And Orchestra [5']
1.1.0.1. 1.1.0.0. pno,strings,S
solo
sc,pts ZANIBON D252 rent   (C79)

CATTLE CALL AND SUMMER NIGHT, FOR SOLO
VOICE AND ORCHESTRA see Brevik,
Tor, Lokketrall Og Somar-Natta, For
Solo Voice And Orchestra

CAUCASIAN SKETCHES see Ippolitov-
Ivanov, Mikhail Mikhailovich

CAVALIERE ROMANTICO, IL see Toni, Alceo

CAVALLERIA RUSTICANA: ADDIO ALLA MADRE,
FOR SOLO VOICE AND ORCHESTRA see
Mascagni, Pietro

CAVALLERIA RUSTICANA: BADA SANTUZZA,
FOR SOLO VOICES AND ORCHESTRA see
Mascagni, Pietro

CAVALLERIA RUSTICANA: BRINDISI, "VIVA
IL VINO SPUMEGGIANTE", FOR SOLO
VOICE AND ORCHESTRA see Mascagni,
Pietro

CAVALLERIA RUSTICANA: IL CAVALLO
SCALPITA, FOR SOLO VOICE AND
ORCHESTRA see Mascagni, Pietro

CAVALLERIA RUSTICANA: INTERMEZZO see
Mascagni, Pietro

CAVALLERIA RUSTICANA: NO, NO TURIDDU,
RIMANI, FOR SOLO VOICES AND
ORCHESTRA see Mascagni, Pietro

CAVALLERIA RUSTICANA: PRELUDIO E
SICILIANA see Mascagni, Pietro

CAVALLERIA RUSTICANA: TURIDDU MI TOLSE
L'ONORE, FOR SOLO VOICES AND
ORCHESTRA see Mascagni, Pietro

CAVALLERIA RUSTICANA: VOI LO SAPETE,
FOR SOLO VOICE AND ORCHESTRA see
Mascagni, Pietro

CAVALLI, (PIETRO) FRANCESCO (1602-1676)
Canzon A 3, MIN 19
strings,org
sc,pts EULENBURG GM734 f.s.   (C80)

Canzon A 4, MIN 20
strings,org
sc,pts EULENBURG GM733P f.s.   (C81)

Canzon A 6, MIN 21
0.0.0.0. 0.0.2.0. strings,org
sc,pts EULENBURG GM732P f.s.   (C82)

Canzon A 8, MIN 22
0.0.0.0. 0.0.4.0. strings,org,
hpsd
sc,pts EULENBURG GM731P f.s.   (C83)

Canzon A 10, MIN 23
0.0.0.0. 0.0.5.0. strings,org,
hpsd
sc,pts EULENBURG GM730P f.s.   (C84)

Canzon A 12, MIN 24
0.0.0.0. 0.2.4.0. strings,org,
hpsd
sc,pts EULENBURG GM735P f.s.   (C85)

CAVALLI, EUGENIO
Divertimento for Viola and String
Orchestra [8']
string orch,vla solo
sc,pts RARITIES $12.00   (C86)

CAVATINA, FOR VIOLIN AND ORCHESTRA see
Brockway, Howard A.

CAVE, THE, FOR VIOLONCELLO AND
ORCHESTRA see Andriessen, Jurriaan

CEASE AWHILE, FOR SOLO VOICE AND
ORCHESTRA see Bach, Johann
Christian

CECILIA, FOR SOLO VOICE AND ORCHESTRA
see Sinigaglia, Leone

CEDAR AND THE PALM, THE see Kalinnikov,
Vassili Sergeievich

CELEBRATION see McLennan, John Stewart

CELEBRATION PRELUDE see Dorward, David

CELEBRATIONS see Douw, Andre

CELEBRAZIONE, LA see Andriessen,
Jurriaan

CELLA AZZURRA, LA see Rocca, Lodovico

CELTIC DANCES see Mathias, William

CENDRILLON SUITE NO. 1: LE SOMMEIL DE
CENDRILLON see Massenet, Jules

CENDRILLON SUITE NO. 2: LES FILLES DE
NOBLESSE see Massenet, Jules

CENDRILLON SUITE NO. 3: MENUET see
Massenet, Jules

CENDRILLON SUITE NO.4: LES TENDRES
FIANCES see Massenet, Jules

CENDRILLON SUITE NO. 5: LES MANDORES
see Massenet, Jules

CENDRILLON SUITE NO. 6: LA FLORENTINE
see Massenet, Jules

CENDRILLON SUITE NO. 7: MARCHE DES
PRINCESSES see Massenet, Jules

CENERENTOLA, LA: NACQUI ALL'AFFANNO -
NON PIU MESTA, FOR SOLO VOICE AND
ORCHESTRA see Rossini, Gioacchino

CENERENTOLA, LA: OVERTURE see Rossini,
Gioacchino

CENTENNIAL WALTZ see Strauss, Johann,
[Jr.]

CENTRI-FUGA see Holt, Simeon ten

CEPHALE ET PROCRIS: BALLET SUITE,
[ARR.] see Gretry, Andre Ernest
Modeste

CEREMUGA, JOSEF (1930-   )
Concerto Da Camera, For Wind Quintet
And String Orchestra
string orch,wind quin soli sc
PANTON 1784 f.s.   (C87)

CERVETTI, SERGIO (1940-   )
Six Sequences For Dance
fl,horn,5perc,cel,pno,elec gtr,
vcl
MOECK 5033 sc $31.00, pts rent
(C88)

CESKOSLOVENSKA PREDOHRA see Ocenas,
Andrej

CESSATE OMAI CESSATE, FOR SOLO VOICE
AND STRING ORCHESTRA see Vivaldi,
Antonio

CESTI, MARC' ANTONIO (1623-1669)
Tu Mancavi A Tormentarmi Crudelissima
Speranza, [arr.]
(Stokowski, Leopold) harp,strings
[6'] KALMUS A5522 sc $4.00, set
$4.50, pts $.75, ea.   (C89)

CHABRIER, [ALEXIS-] EMMANUEL
(1841-1894)
Joyeuse Marche
LUCKS 07310 sc $9.50, set $32.00,
pts $1.40, ea.   (C90)

Roi Malgre Lui, Le: Fete Polonaise
LUCKS 08976 sc $18.00, set $30.00,
pts $1.60, ea.   (C91)

CHACONNE see David, Johann Nepomuk

CHACONNE, [ARR.] see Bach, Johann
Sebastian

CHACONNE IN E MINOR, [ARR.] see
Buxtehude, Dietrich

CHACONNE, VARIATIONEN, FUGA UND CODA
see Aeschbacher, Walther

CHADWICK, GEORGE WHITEFIELD (1854-1931)
Symphonic Sketches
KALMUS 3448 sc $40.00, set $90.00
(C92)

Symphonic Sketches: A Vagrom Ballad
2(pic).1+English horn.2+bass
clar.2. 4.2.3.0. timp,perc,
harp,strings
KALMUS 3451 sc $12.00, set $30.00
(C93)

Symphonic Sketches: Hobgoblin
2+pic.2.2+bass clar.2. 4.2.0.0.
timp,perc,harp,strings
KALMUS 3450 sc $15.00, set $38.00
(C94)

Symphonic Sketches: Jubilee And Noel
3.3.3.2. 4.2.3.0. timp,perc,harp,
strings
KALMUS 3449 sc $15.00, set $38.00
(C95)

CHAGRIN, FRANCIS (1905-1972)
Castellana
sets NOVELLO 9034-35 $31.75, and
up, sc NOVELLO 9033 $7.75, pts
NOVELLO 9586 $1.25, ea.   (C96)

CHAIKOVSKII, PETR IL'ICH
see TCHAIKOVSKY, PIOTR ILYICH

CHAILLEY, JACQUES (1910-   )
Solmisation
6vln,2vla,2vcl,db
sc,pts LEDUC f.s.   (C97)

CHAILLY, LUCIANO (1920-   )
Aria Da Chiesa [4']
string orch
sc,pts ZANIBON D240 rent   (C98)

Contrappunti A Quattro Dimensioni
sc RICORDI-IT 132207 f.s.   (C99)

Due Pezzi, For Violin And Orchestra
[8']
1.1.1.1. 1.1.1.0. cym,strings,vln
solo
sc,pts ZANIBON D250 rent   (C100)

CHAILLY, LUCIANO (cont'd.)

Hochetus Et Rondellus [6']
pno,timp,strings
sc,pts ZANIBON D222 rent   (C101)

Piccole Serenate [12']
string orch
sc,min sc ZANIBON 4887 f.s., pts
ZANIBON 4888 f.s.   (C102)

Ricercare [8']
string orch
sc ZANIBON 4761 f.s., pts ZANIBON
4762 f.s.   (C103)

Sonata Tritematica No. 7 [20']
string orch
sc CARISCH 21326 rent, pts CARISCH
20327 rent   (C104)

Suite for String Orchestra [12']
string orch
sc,pts ZANIBON D293 rent   (C105)

Toccata [8']
string orch
sc ZANIBON 4763 f.s., pts ZANIBON
4764 f.s.   (C106)

Tre Episodi Per Fanfara E Orchestra
FORLIVESI perf mat rent   (C107)

Triplum No. 1 For Violin, Harpsichord
And String Orchestra [12']
string orch,vln solo,hpsd solo
sc ZANIBON 5498 rent, pts ZANIBON
5499 rent   (C108)

Triplum No. 2 For Violin, Piano And
Orchestra [14']
2.2.2.2. 2.2.2.0. timp,4perc,
strings,vln solo,pno solo
sc ZANIBON 5508 rent, pts ZANIBON
5509 rent   (C109)

CHAMBER CONCERTO see Nasveld, Robert

CHAMBER CONCERTO, FOR VIOLA AND STRING
ORCHESTRA see Genzmer, Harald

CHAMBER SYMPHONY NO.2 see Schoenberg,
Arnold

CHAMINADE, CECILE (1857-1944)
Anneau d'Argent, L'
"Silver Ring, The" see Selection Of
Songs, [arr.]

Chanson Espagnole
see Selection Of Songs, [arr.]

Concertino for Flute and Orchestra,
Op. 107, in D
LUCKS 00796 sc $10.00, set $20.00,
pts $1.40, ea.   (C110)

Fiances, Les
see Selection Of Songs, [arr.]

Madrigal
see Selection Of Songs, [arr.]

Ritournelle
see Selection Of Songs, [arr.]

Roundel
see Selection Of Songs, [arr.]

Selection Of Songs, [arr.]
(Geehl) 1(pic).1(English
horn).2.1.2soprano sax. 2.2.1.0.
perc,harp,strings KALMUS A5501 sc
$5.00, perf mat rent, set $18.00,
pts $1.50, ea.
contains: Anneau d'Argent, L',
"Silver Ring, The"; Chanson
Espagnole; Fiances, Les;
Madrigal; Ritournelle; Roundel
(C111)

Silver Ring, The *see Anneau
d'Argent, L'

CHAMPAGNER-POLKA see Strauss, Johann,
[Jr.]

CHANDOSCHKIN, IWAN
see KHANDOSHKIN, IVAN

CHANSON DU DESESPOIR, FOR VIOLONCELLO
AND ORCHESTRA see Schuback, Peter

CHANSON ESPAGNOLE see Chaminade, Cecile

CHANSON GEORGIENNE, FOR SOLO VOICE AND
ORCHESTRA, [ARR.] see Rachmaninoff,
Sergey Vassilievich

CHANSON SANS PAROLES see Stuhec, Igor

CHANSON TRISTE, [ARR.] see Kalinnikov,
Vassili Sergeievich

CHANT, LE, FOR SOLO VOICE AND ORCHESTRA
see Knapik, Eugeniusz

CHANT DE ROSSIGNOL, LE see Stravinsky,
Igor

CHANT DU MENESTREL, FOR VIOLONCELLO AND
ORCHESTRA see Glazunov, Alexander
Konstantinovich

CHANT SUR LA MORT D'HAYDN, FOR SOLO
VOICE AND ORCHESTRA see Cherubini,
Luigi

CHAPULTEPEC see Chavez, Carlos

CHARIVARI QUADRILLE see Strauss,
Johann, [Jr.]

CHARLATAN MARCH, THE see Sousa, John
Philip

CHARLESTON RAG, [ARR.] see Blake,
(James Hubert) Eubie

CHARMEUR, DER see Bund, Hans

CHARPENTIER, GUSTAVE (1860-1956)
Louise: Depuis Le Jour, For Solo
Voice And Orchestra
LUCKS 02232 sc $4.75, set $9.50,
pts $.75, ea.   (C112)

CHARPENTIER, JACQUES (1933-   )
Concerto No. 6 for Oboe and String
Orchestra
string orch,ob solo
sc LEDUC f.s.   (C113)

Concerto No. 8 for Horn and String
Orchestra
string orch,horn solo
LEDUC sc, pts rent   (C114)

Concerto No. 9 for Violoncello and
String Orchestra
string orch,vcl solo
LEDUC sc, pts rent   (C115)

Et L'Imaginaire Se Mit A Danser
(Symphony No. 5)
3.2.2.2. 4.3.3.1. strings
LEDUC study sc f.s., pts rent
(C116)

Symphony No. 4 [20']
2.2.2.2. 4.3.3.1. timp,3perc,
strings
LEDUC perf mat rent   (C117)

Symphony No. 5 *see Et L'Imaginaire
Se Mit A Danser

Symphony No. 6
study sc LEDUC f.s., perf mat rent
(C118)

Vitraux Pour Notre Dame, For Solo
Voice And String Orchestra [20']
string orch,high solo
sc LEDUC f.s.   (C119)

CHARPENTIER, MARC-ANTOINE
(ca. 1636-1704)
Marche De Triomphe
2.2+English horn.0.2. 0.2.1.1.
timp,cont,strings
(Lambert, G.) COSTALL perf mat rent
(C120)

Noels Pour Les Instruments [18']
2.0.0.0. 0.0.0.0. org/hpsd,
strings
sc UNIVER. UE 25A022 $17.50, set
UNIVER. UE 25B022 $33.00, pts
UNIVER. $3.50, ea.   (C121)

(Lambert, G.) COSTALL perf mat rent
(C122)

Offerte Pour Les Instruments
2fl,2ob,2bsn,tuba,org,strings
(Lambert, G.) COSTALL perf mat rent
(C123)

CHARSIGAUD see Smit, Sytze

CHASSE, LA see Haydn, [Franz] Joseph,
Symphony No. 73 in D

CHASSE, LA see Hoffmeister, A.,
Symphony in D

CHATONS DE PARIS, LES, FOR ACCORDION
AND STRING ORCHESTRA see Groot, Cor
(Cornelius Wilhelmus) de

CHATS, LES, FOR SOLO VOICE AND
ORCHESTRA see Diepenbrock, Alphons

CHATSCHATURJAN, ARAM
see KHACHATURIAN, ARAM

CHAUN, FRANTISEK (1921-   )
Five Pictures
sc PANTON 1590 f.s.   (C124)

CHAUSSON, ERNEST (1855-1899)
Poeme, For Violin And Orchestra
*Op.25
LUCKS 00550 sc $12.00, set $21.00,
pts $1.25, ea.   (C125)

CHAUSSON, ERNEST (cont'd.)

Symphony, Op. 20, in B flat
study sc INTERNAT. 876 $8.75 (C126)

Tempete, La *Op.18
2.2.2.2. 2.2.3.0. timp,perc,harp,
strings
KALMUS 5322 sc $9.00, perf mat
rent, set $20.00, pts $1.00, ea.
(C127)

Viviane *Op.5
3(pic).2.2.3. 4.3.3.1. timp,
strings
KALMUS 5324 sc $12.00, perf mat
rent, set $22.00, pts $1.25, ea.
(C128)

CHAVEZ, CARLOS (1899-1978)
Chapultepec
sc KALMUS A7011 $16.00   (C129)

Concerto for 4 Horns and Orchestra
sc KALMUS A7013 $16.00   (C130)

Concerto for Violin and Orchestra
sc KALMUS A7000 $23.00   (C131)

Symphony No. 3
BOOSEY 829 min sc $9.00, sc $12.00
(C132)

Symphony No. 6
sc KALMUS A7012 $30.00   (C133)

CHAYNES, CHARLES (1925-   )
Concerto for Clarinet and Orchestra
LEDUC perf mat rent   (C134)

Onze Visages Ou L'Antifugue
6vln,2vla,2vcl,db
sc,pts LEDUC   (C135)

Pour Un Monde Noir, For Solo Voice
And Orchestra [32']
2(pic).3.2(bass clar).3. 4.3.3.1.
timp,perc,pno,harp,strings,S
solo
RICORDI-FR R.2279 perf mat rent
(C136)

CHEMIN-PETIT, HANS (1902-1981)
An Die Liebe, For Solo Voice And
Orchestra [16']
0.2.0.1. 0.0.0.0. harp,strings,S
solo
sc LIENAU f.s.   (C137)

Concerto for Orchestra in D [26']
2.2.2.2. 4.2.3.1. timp,strings
sc,pts LIENAU rent   (C138)

Concerto for Recorder, Harpsichord
and Orchestra [14']
perc,strings,rec solo,hpsd solo
sc,pts LIENAU rent   (C139)

Festliche Musik [13']
2+pic.2+English horn.2+bass
clar.2+contrabsn. 4.3.3.1.
2harp,timp,perc,strings
sc,pts LIENAU rent   (C140)

Orchesterprolog [17']
2.2.2.2. 4.3+opt 3trp.3.1. timp,
perc,strings
sc,pts,min sc LIENAU rent   (C141)

Symphony No. 1 in A minor [32']
2.2.2+bass clar.2+contrabsn.
4.2.3.0. org,timp,perc,strings
sc,pts LIENAU rent   (C142)

Von Der Eitelkeit Der Welt, For Solo
Voice And Orchestra [15']
0.2.0.1. 0.0.0.0. strings,Bar
solo
sc LIENAU f.s.   (C143)

CHEMINEMENTS see Lefebvre, Claude

CHEMINS IV ON SEQUENZA VII, FOR OBOE
AND STRINGS see Berio, Luciano

CHERUBINI, LUIGI (1760-1842)
Ali Baba: Entr'acte And Ballet Music
[9']
(Reinecke) KALMUS A4563 sc $10.00,
perf mat rent, set $19.00, pts
$1.00, ea.   (C144)

Anacreon: Ballet Music [6'30"]
2.2.2.2. 4.0.3.0. timp,strings
KALMUS 5311 sc $12.00, perf mat
rent, set $15.00, pts $.75, ea.
(C145)

LUCKS 10559 sc $12.00, set $15.00,
pts $.75, ea.   (C146)

Anacreon: Overture
min sc PETERS 692 $4.50   (C147)

Chant Sur La Mort d'Haydn, For Solo
Voice And Orchestra
(Spada, Pietro) sc BSE $15.75, perf
mat rent   (C148)

CHERUBINI, LUIGI (cont'd.)

Deux Journees, Les: Overture
"Water Carrier, The: Overture" min
sc PETERS 828 $4.00   (C149)

Eliza: Overture [8']
2.2.2.2. 4.0.0.0. timp,strings
KALMUS 5309 sc $15.00, perf mat
rent, set $20.00, pts $1.25, ea.
(C150)

Faniska: Overture [8']
2.2.2.2. 2.2.1.0. timp,strings
KALMUS 5310 sc $18.00, perf mat
rent, set $20.00, pts $1.25, ea.
(C151)

Lodoiska: Overture [11']
2.2.2.2. 2.2.1.0. timp,strings
KALMUS 5308 sc $15.00, perf mat
rent, set $20.00, pts $1.25, ea.
(C152)

Overture, MIN 93 [12']
1.2.2.2. 4.2.3.0. timp,strings
(Gruetzmacher) KALMUS A4562 sc
$12.00, perf mat rent, set
$32.00, pts $1.50, ea.   (C153)

Water Carrier, The: Overture *see
Deux Journees, Les: Overture

CHEVALIER DE SAINT-GEORGES
see SAINT-GEORGES, JOSEPH BOULOGNE DE

CHEZ NOUS see Berger, Hans

CHI-KING, FOR SOLO VOICE AND ORCHESTRA
see Beekhuis, Hanna

CHI SA, CHI SA, QUAL SIA, FOR SOLO
VOICE AND ORCHESTRA see Mozart,
Wolfgang Amadeus

CHI VIVE AMANTE, FOR SOLO VOICE AND
ORCHESTRA see Haydn, [Franz] Joseph

CHIAROSCURO see Druckman, Jacob Raphael

CHIAROSCURO see Kelterborn, Rudolf

CHIHARA, PAUL SEIKO (1938-   )
Concerto for Saxophone and Orchestra
[18']
2.2.2.2. 4.3.3.1. timp,2perc,
harp,strings,sax solo
PETERS perf mat rent   (C154)

Mistletoe Bride [31']
2(pic).2.2.2. 4.2.3.1. timp,
2perc,harp,pno/cel,strings,
electronic tape
sc,pts PETERS P66801 perf mat rent
(C155)

CHILDREN'S SONGS, [ARR.]
(Kirkland, Camp) CRESPUB CP-IN 7+9
$15.00 see also Seven+
Orchestration Series, Group 2
(C156)

CHINESE NIGHTINGALE, THE see Deursen,
Anton van

CHINESISCHE ERZAHLUNG see Baranovic,
Kresimir

CHINESISCHES SOLDATENLIED see Beekhuis,
Hanna

CHINI, ANDRE (1945-   )
Norrsken, For Organ, Electronic
Equipment And String Orchestra
[12']
string orch,electronic equipment,
org solo
pts,solo pt STIM perf mat rent
(C157)

CH'IO MI SCORDI DI TE, FOR SOLO VOICE
AND ORCHESTRA see Mozart, Wolfgang
Amadeus

CHOPIN, FREDERIC (1810-1849)
Andantino Grazioso, [arr.]
(Becce, Guiseppe) LIENAU f.s.
(C158)
Concerto for Piano and Orchestra, No.
1, Op. 11, in E minor
BROUDE BR. study sc $9.00, set
$35.00, pts $2.25, ea.   (C159)
LUCKS 00022 sc $13.00, set $28.00,
min sc $6.00, pts $1.75, ea.
(C160)
Grande Polonaise Brillante, For Piano
And Orchestra *Op.22
LUCKS 00116 sc $9.50, set $13.00,
min sc $3.00, pts $1.15, ea.
(C161)
Largo Doloroso, [arr.]
(Becce, Guiseppe) LIENAU f.s.
(C162)
Largo Tragico, [arr.]
(Becce, Guiseppe) LIENAU f.s.
(C163)
Polonaise, Op. 40, No.1, [arr.]
(Glazunow) LUCKS 05282 sc $5.50,
set $14.00, pts $1.15, ea. (C164)

CHOPIN, FREDERIC (cont'd.)

Sylphides, Les, [arr.]
(Glazunov, Alexander K.) 2.2.2.2.
4.2.0.0. timp,perc,harp,strings
[26'] (each movement available
separately) KALMUS A1383 sc
$8.00, perf mat rent, set $90.00,
pts $4.00, ea.   (C165)

Variations On "La Ci Darem La Mano",
For Piano And Orchestra *Op.2
2.2.2.2. 2.0.0.0. timp,strings,
pno solo
sc,pts LIENAU rent   (C166)
LUCKS 00104 sc $7.00, set $14.00,
min sc $2.50, pts $1.60, ea.
(C167)

CHOPINIANA see Glazunov, Alexander
Konstantinovich

CHORAI REVISITED see Straesser, Joep

CHORALE AND TOCCATA see Ramovs, Primoz,
Koral In Tokata

CHORALE PRELUDE: ES IST EIN ROS'
ENTSPRUNGEN, [ARR.] see Brahms,
Johannes

CHORALE PRELUDES, ELEVEN, [ARR.] see
Brahms, Johannes

CHORALE PRELUDES, FIVE, [ARR.] see
Brahms, Johannes

CHORALE PRELUDES, THREE, [ARR.] see
Bach, Johann Sebastian

CHORALES, TWO, [ARR.] see Bach, Johann
Sebastian

CHORALES, TWO, [ARR.] see Bach, Johann
Sebastian

CHORALFANTASIE IN A MINOR see Wocke,
Erich

CHRIST AROSE, [ARR.]
(Kirkland, Camp) CRESPUB CP-IN 7+8
$15.00 see also Seven+
Orchestration Series, Group 2
(C168)
CHRIST LAG IN TODESBANDEN, MEDITATION
ON see Cortes, Ramiro

CHRIST THE LORD IS RISEN TODAY
(Mayfield, Larry; Skillings, Otis)
SINGSPIR 7706 $19.95   (C169)

CHRISTENSEN, BERNHARD
Rondo Finale (from The Eternal Trio)
3.3.3.3. 4.3.3.1. timp,pno,
strings, 4 tambours
SAMFUNDET perf mat rent   (C170)

CHRISTIANSEN, HENNING (1932-   )
Forsvundne, Den [19']
3.2.4.3. 4.3.2.1. strings
sc SAMFUNDET 264 perf mat rent
(C171)

CHRISTMAS CONCERTO see Corelli,
Arcangelo, Concerto Grosso, Op. 6,
No. 8, in G minor

CHRISTMAS EVE: POLONAISE see Rimsky-
Korsakov, Nikolai

CHRISTMAS EVE: SUITE see Rimsky-
Korsakov, Nikolai

CHRISTMAS EVE SUITE, [ARR.] see Gade,
Niels Wilhelm, Bornenes Juul,
[arr.]

CHRISTMAS SYMPHONY see Haydn, [Franz]
Joseph, Symphony No. 26 in D minor

CHRISTMAS SYMPHONY see Schiassi,
Gaetano Maria, Sinfonia Pastorale

CHRISTOPH COLUMBUS see Wagner, Richard

CHRISTOU, JANI (1926-1970)
Sinfonia No. 1 for Solo Voice and
Orchestra
sc DE SANTIS DS 887 f.s.   (C172)

CHRISTUS AM OLBERGE: I LOVE THE LORD,
FOR SOLO VOICE AND ORCHESTRA see
Beethoven, Ludwig van

CHRISTUS AM OLBERGE: OH MY HEART IS
SORE, FOR SOLO VOICE AND ORCHESTRA
see Beethoven, Ludwig van

CHRISTUS: HIRTENGESANG see Liszt, Franz

CHROMA see Holler, York

CHROMATIC SQUARE see Tautenhahn,
Gunther

CHRONIQUE ILLUSTREE: GRANDE CHRONIQUE
ILLUSTREE, FOR SOLO VOICE AND
ORCHESTRA see Pousseur, Henri

CHRONIQUE ILLUSTREE: PETITE CHRONIQUE
ILLUSTREE see Pousseur, Henri

CIAIKOVSKI, PIETRO
see TCHAIKOVSKY, PIOTR ILYICH

CICALECCIO DEL MERCATO see Mussorgsky,
Modest Petrovich

CID, DER: OVERTURE see Cornelius, Peter

CID, LE: BALLET SUITE see Massenet,
Jules

CID, LE: PLEUREZ, PLEUREZ MES YEUX, FOR
SOLO VOICE AND ORCHESTRA see
Massenet, Jules

CIELITO LINDO, FOR SOLO VOICE AND
ORCHESTRA see Padilla

CIGALETTES, LES see Filipucci, Edmond

CIGANSKE PIESNE, FOR SOLO VOICE AND
ORCHESTRA see Mikula, Zdenko

CIKKER, JAN (1911-   )
Co Mi Deti Rozpravali [16']
3.3.3.2. 4.3.3.1. timp,perc,
bells,xylo,cel,harp,strings
"What The Children Told Me"
SLOV.HUD.FOND O-443A perf mat
rent   (C173)

Divertimento, Op. 16
string orch
SLOV.HUD.FOND KH-190 perf mat rent
(C174)

Dupak [7']
3.1.2.1. 2.2.1.0. timp,perc,
cimbalom,strings
SLOV.HUD.FOND P-19 perf mat rent
(C175)
East Slovakian Recruiting Song *see
Vychodoslovensky Verbunk

Hviezdnata Noc
3.1.2.1. 2.2.1.0. timp,perc,
cimbalom,strings
"Starry Night" SLOV.HUD.FOND P-18
perf mat rent   (C176)

Midsummer Day *see Na Jana

Na Jana
3.2.2.1. 2.2.1.0. timp,perc,
2cimbalom,strings
"Midsummer Day" SLOV.HUD.FOND P-16
perf mat rent   (C177)

Starry Night *see Hviezdnata Noc

Vychodoslovensky Verbunk [6']
2.1.2.1. 2.2.2.0. perc,cimbalom,
strings
"East Slovakian Recruiting Song"
SLOV.HUD.FOND P-17 perf mat rent
(C178)
What The Children Told Me *see Co Mi
Deti Rozpravali

CILENSEK, JOHANN (1913-   )
Konzertstuck for Flute and Orchestra
sc,quarto PETERS 9687 $35.00, perf
mat rent   (C179)

Konzertstuck for Viola and Orchestra
sc,quarto PETERS 9688 $35.00, perf
mat rent   (C180)

CIMAROSA, DOMENICO (1749-1801)
Caio Mario: Overture [10']
0.2.0.0. 2.0.0.0. strings
(Acciai, G.) sc ZERBONI 8310 f.s.,
pts ZERBONI 8311 rent   (C181)

Concerto for 2 Flutes and Orchestra
in G, MIN 58 [15']
2ob,bsn,strings,2fl soli
INTERNAT. perf mat rent   (C182)

Due Supposti Conti, I (Or) Lo Sposo
Senza Moglie: Overture [10']
0.2.0.0. 2.0.0.0. strings
(Acciai, G.) sc ZERBONI 8308 f.s.,
pts ZERBONI 8309 rent   (C183)

Giannina E Bernardone: Overture
KALMUS 5212 sc $12.00, perf mat
rent, set $22.00, pts $1.50, ea.
(C184)

Italiana In Londra: Overture [10']
0.2.0.0. 2.0.0.0. strings
(Spada, P.) sc ZERBONI 8002 f.s.,
pts ZERBONI 8003 rent   (C185)

Sinfonia in B, MIN 106 [12']
0.2.0.0. 2.0.0.0. strings
sc BREITKOPF-W PB 5068 f.s., pts
BREITKOPF-W OB 5068 f.s.   (C186)

CIMENTO DELL'ARMONIA E DELL'INVENZIONE,
IL, VOL. 1 see Vivaldi, Antonio

CIMENTO DELL'ARMONIA E DELL'INVENZIONE, IL, VOL. 2 see Vivaldi, Antonio

CIMITERO DI GUERRA see Lattuada, Felice

CINCO INVOCACIONES AL CRUCIFICADO, FOR SOLO VOICE AND ORCHESTRA see Montsalvatge, Xavier

CINQ ETUDES see Vliet, Henk van der

CINQ MARS: OVERTURE see Gounod, Charles Francois

CINQUE CARMI DI CATULLO, FOR SOLO VOICE AND ORCHESTRA see Cattini, Umberto

CINQUE DANZE MODERNE see Cumar, R.

CINQUE LIRICHE DI MONTALE, FOR SOLO VOICE AND ORCHESTRA see Bettinelli, Bruno

CINQUE PEZZI PER ARCHI see Grossi, Pietro

CIPRESSI see Castelnuovo-Tedesco, Mario

CIRCULUS VIRTUOSUS, FOR FLUTE, OBOE, CLARINET, BASSOON AND ORCHESTRA see Wahren, Karl Heinz

CIRIBIRIBIN, FOR SOLO VOICE AND ORCHESTRA see Pestalozzi, Heinrich

CLAASSEN, ARTHUR
　　Sans Souci Menuet *Op.1
　　　string orch
　　　LUCKS 08448 sc $1.75, set $4.75,
　　　　pts $.95, ea.　　　　　(C187)

CLAFLIN, [ALAN] AVERY (1898-1979)
　　Symphony No. 2
　　　sc BOOSEY $25.00　　　　(C188)

CLAIR DE LUNE, FOR PIANO AND ORCHESTRA see Sciarrino, Salvatore

CLAIR DE LUNE, FOR SOLO VOICE AND ORCHESTRA see Diepenbrock, Alphons

CLAIR DE LUNE, [ARR.] see Debussy, Claude

CLAIROBSCUR, EN see Bucht, Gunnar

CLARINET CANDY see Anderson, Leroy

CLASSICAL SYMPHONY see Prokofiev, Serge

CLASSICAL SYMPHONY IN A see Skalkottas, Nikos

CLAUDINE VON VILLA BELLA: OVERTURE see Schubert, Franz (Peter)

CLEEVE, STEWART MONTAGU
　　Whitgift Suite
　　　sets NOVELLO 9043-44 $27.75, and
　　　　up, sc NOVELLO 9042 $4.25, pts
　　　　NOVELLO 9589 $1.00, ea.　(C189)

CLEMENTI, ALDO (1925-　　)
　　Blitz [18']
　　　2.1.3.1. 1.2.1.1. cel,pno,harp,
　　　　vibra,2vln,vla,vcl,db
　　　ZERBONI perf mat rent　　(C190)

　　Clessidra [9']
　　　1.1.1.1. 2.0.0.0. 2pno,2vln,vla
　　　sc ZERBONI 8232 f.s., perf mat rent
　　　　　　　　　　　　　　　(C191)

　　Collage [24']
　　　2.2.3.1+2sax. 2.2.1.0. vibra,
　　　　xylo,pno,perc,strings, recorded
　　　　voice
　　　ZERBONI perf mat rent　　(C192)

　　Concerto for Double Bass and
　　　Orchestra
　　　2.2.2.0. 2.2.2.0. cel,glock,
　　　　carillon,6vln,3vla,3vcl,db solo
　　　sc ZERBONI 8240 f.s., perf mat rent
　　　　　　　　　　　　　　　(C193)
　　Concerto for Piano and Orchestra
　　　2.2.0.2. 2.2.2.0. 4vln,4vla,4vcl,
　　　　pno solo
　　　sc ZERBONI 8165 f.s., perf mat rent
　　　　　　　　　　　　　　　(C194)
　　Concerto for Violin and Orchestra
　　　[12']
　　　3.3.0.3. 3.0.0.0. carillon,14vln,
　　　　7vla,7vcl,vln solo
　　　sc ZERBONI 8368 f.s., perf mat rent
　　　　　　　　　　　　　　　(C195)

CLEMENTI, MUZIO (1752-1832)
　　Concerto for Piano and Orchestra in
　　　C, MIN 47 [25']
　　　0.2.0.2. 2.2.0.0. timp,strings,
　　　　pno solo
　　　(Spada, P.) sc ZERBONI 8206 f.s.,
　　　　pts ZERBONI 8207 rent　　(C196)

　　Symphony, Op. 18, No. 1, in B flat
　　　[20']
　　　2.2.0.2. 2.0.0.0. strings

CLEMENTI, MUZIO (cont'd.)

　　　(Spada, P.) sc ZERBONI 8204 f.s.,
　　　　pts ZERBONI 8205 rent　　(C197)

　　Symphony, Op. 18, No. 2, in D [20']
　　　2.2.0.2. 2.0.0.0. strings
　　　(Spada, P.) sc ZERBONI 8228 f.s.,
　　　　pts ZERBONI 8229 rent　　(C198)

CLEMENZA DI TITO, LA: ECCO IL PUNTO - NON PIU DI FIORI, FOR SOLO VOICE AND ORCHESTRA see Mozart, Wolfgang Amadeus

CLEMENZA DI TITO, LA: OVERTURE see Mozart, Wolfgang Amadeus

CLEMENZA DI TITO, LA: PARTO, MA TU BEN MIO, FOR SOLO VOICE AND ORCHESTRA see Mozart, Wolfgang Amadeus

CLEOPATRE I see Mulder, Ernest W.

CLEPATRE II see Mulder, Ernest W.

CLESSIDRA see Clementi, Aldo

CLOCK SYMPHONY see Haydn, [Franz] Joseph, Symphony No. 101 in D

CLOWN see Ketting, Piet

CO MI DETI ROZPRAVALI see Cikker, Jan

COAKLEY, DONALD
　　Once A Canadian Lad [4']
　　　string orch
　　　KERBY 19335 sc,pts $18.00, sc $6.00
　　　　　　　　　　　　　　　(C199)
COALOTTINO II, FOR BASS CLARINET AND STRING ORCHESTRA see Maros, Miklos

COCKSHOTT, GERALD WILFRED (1915-　　)
　　Maddermarket Suite
　　　sets NOVELLO 9046-47 $30.75, and
　　　　up, sc NOVELLO 9045 $5.50, pts
　　　　NOVELLO 9590 $1.25, ea.　(C200)

COHN, JAMES MYRON (1928-　　)
　　Little Circus, The
　　　sc BOOSEY $9.00　　　　　(C201)

COLAS BREUGNON: OVERTURE see Kabalevsky, Dmitri Borisovich

COLDING-JORGENSEN, HENRIK
　　Ballade for Tuba and Chamber
　　　Orchestra [15']
　　　2.1.2.1.alto sax. 1.0.0.0. 2perc,
　　　　4vln,vla,vcl,db,db tuba solo
　　　SAMFUNDET perf mat rent　(C202)

　　Pa Din Taerskel, For Solo Voice And
　　　Orchestra
　　　sc,pts SAMFUNDET 233 perf mat rent
　　　　　　　　　　　　　　　(C203)
COLE, BRUCE (1947-　　)
　　Foundry Of Minstrels [19']
　　　2(pic).2(English horn).2(bass
　　　　clar).2. 4.2.2.1. timp,perc,
　　　　harp,strings
　　　BOOSEY perf mat rent　　　(C204)

COLE, HUGO (1917-　　)
　　Black Lion Dances
　　　sets NOVELLO 9049-50 $64.00, and
　　　　up, sc NOVELLO 9048 $12.50, pts
　　　　NOVELLO 9591 $1.75, ea.　(C205)

COLERIDGE-TAYLOR, SAMUEL (1875-1912)
　　African Suite: Danse Negre *Op.35,
　　　No.4
　　　KALMUS 5424 pno-cond sc $3.00, perf
　　　　mat rent, set $15.00, pts $1.00,
　　　　ea.　　　　　　　　　　(C206)
　　　LUCKS 05302 sc $8.00, set $20.00,
　　　　pts $1.25, ea.　　　　　(C207)

　　Four Characteristic Waltzes *Op.22
　　　KALMUS 5328 sc $15.00, perf mat
　　　　rent, set $30.00, pts $2.00, ea.
　　　　　　　　　　　　　　　(C208)
COLGRASS, MICHAEL (CHARLES) (1932-　　)
　　Deja Vu, For Percussion Quartet And
　　　Orchestra [18']
　　　3(pic,alto fl).0.3(clar in E
　　　　flat,bass clar).3(contrabsn).
　　　　4.3.3.1. 2harp,pno&cel,strings,
　　　　4perc soli
　　　sc FISCHER,C $20.00　　　(C209)

COLLAGE see Clementi, Aldo

COLLAGE see Markovic, Adalbert

COLLECTED POEMS, FOR SOLO VOICES AND ORCHESTRA see Thomson, Virgil Garnett

COLLOQUY FOR STRINGS see La Montaine, John

COLMAL OVERTURE see Winter, Peter von

COLOMBINE POLKA see Strauss, Eduard

COLONIAL VARIANTS see Dello Joio, Norman

COLONNEN WALZER see Strauss, Johann, [Jr.]

COLORS OF YOUTH, THE see Rogers, Bernard

COMBATTIMENTO DI TANCREDI E CLORINDA, IL, FOR SOLO VOICES AND STRING ORCHESTRA, [ARR.] see Monteverdi, Claudio

COMBRAY see Mieg, Peter

COME BACK TO SORRENTO, FOR SOLO VOICE AND ORCHESTRA see Curtis, Ernesto de

COME, SWEET DEATH, [ARR.] see Bach, Johann Sebastian, Komm, Susser Tod, [arr.]

COMEDIANS, THE see Kabalevsky, Dmitri Borisovich

COMEDIANS, THE: GALOP see Kabalevsky, Dmitri Borisovich

COMEDY OVERTURE see Patejdl, Vaclav, Veseloherna Predohra

COMIN' THROUGH THE RYE, FOR SOLO VOICE AND STRING ORCHESTRA
　　string orch,solo voice
　　LUCKS 02182 set $4.50, pts $.75, ea.
　　　　　　　　　　　　　　　(C210)
COMMUNICATION see Kvam, Oddvar S., Symphony No. 2

COMO UNA OLA DE FUERZA Y LUZ, FOR SOLO VOICE, PIANO AND ORCHESTRA see Nono, Luigi

COMPLETE CONCERTI see Brahms, Johannes

COMPLIMENTO see Felderhof, Jan

COMPOSITION see Ogura, Roh

COMPOSIZIONE 5, "NO HAN MUERTO" see Macchi, Egisto

COMPOSIZIONE NO. 3 see Macchi, Egisto

COMPOSIZIONE NO. 4 see Grossi, Pietro

CONCENTUS BIJUGIS, FOR PIANO 4-HANDS AND STRING ORCHESTRA see Novak, Jan

CONCERT AVEC PLUSIEURS INSTRUMENTS NO. 2, FOR VIOLA, VIOLONCELLO AND ORCHESTRA see Dittrich, Paul-Heinz

CONCERT AVEC PLUSIEURS INSTRUMENTS NO. 3, FOR FLUTE, OBOE AND ORCHESTRA see Dittrich, Paul-Heinz

CONCERT ETUDE, FOR TRUMPET AND ORCHESTRA see Goedicke, Alexander

CONCERT FOR ORGAN AND ORCHESTRA, MIN104 see Monnikendam, Marius

CONCERT MUSIC see Maw, Nicholas

CONCERT MUSIC, FOR CLARINET AND ORCHESTRA see Tandler, Juraj, Koncertna Hudba, For Clarinet And Orchestra

CONCERT MUSIC V see Karlins, M. William

CONCERT SUITE, FOR VIOLIN AND ORCHESTRA see Elwell, Herbert

CONCERTANTE, FOR SAXOPHONE AND ORCHESTRA see Constant, Marius

CONCERTANTE DU BALLET DE MIRZA, FOR 2 HARPS AND ORCHESTRA see Gossec, Francois Joseph

CONCERTANTE FOR VIOLIN, FLUTE, OBOE AND ORCHESTRA see Bolcom, William

CONCERTANTE MUSIC III see Riley, Dennis

CONCERTANTE MUZIEK see Braal, Andries de

CONCERTANTE SUITE, FOR VIOLIN AND CHAMBER ORCHESTRA see Schubert, Heinz

CONCERTATO, FOR PIANO AND ORCHESTRA see Svara, Danilo

CONCERTI, FOR TRUMPET AND STRING ORCHESTRA, THREE see Hertel, Johann Wilhelm

CONCERTI, FOR VIOLONCELLO AND STRING ORCHESTRA, THREE see Leo, Leonardo (Oronzo Salvatore de)

CONCERTI, FOUR, FOR STRINGED INSTRUMENTS see Albinoni, Tomaso

CONCERTI FOR OBOE AND ORCHESTRA, FOUR see Handel, George Frideric

CONCERTI FOR ORGAN AND ORCHESTRA NOS. 1-8: OP. 4, NOS. 1-6; OP. 7, NOS. 1-2 see Handel, George Frideric

CONCERTI FOR ORGAN AND ORCHESTRA NOS. 9-16: OP. 7, NOS. 3-6, NOS. 13-16 see Handel, George Frideric

CONCERTI FOR PIANO AND ORCHESTRA, K. 175, 382, 238, 242 see Mozart, Wolfgang Amadeus

CONCERTI FOR PIANO AND ORCHESTRA, K. 246, 271, 365 see Mozart, Wolfgang Amadeus

CONCERTI FOR PIANO AND ORCHESTRA, K. 414, 413, 415 see Mozart, Wolfgang Amadeus

CONCERTI FOR PIANO AND ORCHESTRA, K. 449-451 see Mozart, Wolfgang Amadeus

CONCERTI FOR PIANO AND ORCHESTRA, K. 453, 456, 459 see Mozart, Wolfgang Amadeus

CONCERTI FOR PIANO AND ORCHESTRA, K. 466, 467, 482 see Mozart, Wolfgang Amadeus

CONCERTI FOR PIANO AND ORCHESTRA, K. 488, 491, 503 see Mozart, Wolfgang Amadeus

CONCERTI FOR PIANO AND ORCHESTRA, K. 537, 595, 386, ANH. 64 see Mozart, Wolfgang Amadeus

CONCERTI FOR PIANO AND ORCHESTRA, NOS. 1-5 see Beethoven, Ludwig van

CONCERTI FOR PIANO AND ORCHESTRA NOS. 17-22 see Mozart, Wolfgang Amadeus

CONCERTI FOR PIANO AND ORCHESTRA NOS. 23-27 see Mozart, Wolfgang Amadeus

CONCERTI FOR THREE AND FOUR HARPSICHORDS see Bach, Johann Sebastian

CONCERTI FOR THREE CLAVIERS, TWO see Bach, Johann Sebastian

CONCERTI FOR TWO CLAVIERS, TWO see Bach, Johann Sebastian

CONCERTI FOR VIOLONCELLO AND ORCHESTRA see Haydn, [Franz] Joseph

CONCERTI GROSSI, ELEVEN see Handel, George Frideric

CONCERTI GROSSI, NINETEEN see Handel, George Frideric

CONCERTI GROSSI, SIX see Barsanti, Francesco

CONCERTI MIT ORGELLEIERN see Haydn, [Franz] Joseph

CONCERTI, THREE see Handel, George Frideric

CONCERTINA ALLA BURLA, FOR PIANO AND ORCHESTRA see Orthel, Leon

CONCERTINO "AL MODO ANTICO" IN E FLAT, FOR VIOLONCELLO AND STRING ORCHESTRA see Cassoli, M.

CONCERTINO ALL'ITALIANA see Dalla Vecchia, Wolfango

CONCERTINO CHITARRISTICO see Kox, Hans

CONCERTINO DA CAMERA, FOR FLUTE AND STRING ORCHESTRA IN G, MIN30 see Salieri, Antonio

CONCERTINO DA CAMERA, FOR VIOLONCELLO AND ORCHESTRA see Nelhybel, Vaclav

CONCERTINO DA CHIESA, FOR VIOLIN AND INSTRUMENTAL ENSEMBLE see Hallnas, Eyvind

CONCERTINO DA PRIMAVERA, FOR PIANO AND ORCHESTRA see Visser, Peter

CONCERTINO DE MOTU IMPARI, FOR CLARINET AND ORCHESTRA see Kubizek, Augustin

CONCERTINO DRAMMATICO, FOR VIOLIN, VIOLA AND STRING ORCHESTRA see Koetsier, Jan

CONCERTINO 'IN EXILE', FOR PIANO AND ORCHESTRA see Marez Oyens, Tera de

CONCERTINO MEDITERRANEO, FOR FLUTE AND ORCHESTRA see Stark, Wilhelm

CONCERTINO ON A DUTCH FOLKSONG, FOR VIOLONCELLO AND ORCHESTRA see Boer, Ed de

CONCERTINO PASTORALE see Ireland, John

CONCERTINO PER LA NOTTE DI NATALE see Castiglioni, Niccolo

CONCERTO A DUE CORI, NO. 1 see Handel, George Frideric, Concerto Grosso, No. 27, in B flat

CONCERTO A DUE CORI, NO. 2 see Handel, George Frideric, Concerto Grosso, No. 28, in F

CONCERTO A DUE CORI, NO. 3 see Handel, George Frideric, Concerto Grosso, No. 29, in F

CONCERTO A SOL see Zelenka, Jan Dismas

CONCERTO ABBREVIATO see Radica, Ruben

CONCERTO ALLA PASTORALE IN C see Cannabich, Christian

CONCERTO ALLA RUSTICA see Vivaldi, Antonio

CONCERTO BAROCCO, FOR TRUMPET AND ORCHESTRA see Blendinger, Herbert

CONCERTO BERGAMASCO see Mayr, Johann Simon

CONCERTO BREVE see Graap, Lothar

CONCERTO BREVE, FOR BALLERINA AND ORCHESTRA see Malipiero, Riccardo

CONCERTO BURLESCO, FOR ALTO SAXOPHONE, JAZZ GROUP AND ORCHESTRA see Riedel, Georg

CONCERTO CAPRICCIOSO, FOR PIANO AND ORCHESTRA see Koetsier, Jan

CONCERTO DA CAMERA, FOR VIOLA AND STRING ORCHESTRA see Bartos, Jan Zdenek

CONCERTO DA CAMERA, FOR WIND QUINTET AND STRING ORCHESTRA see Ceremuga, Josef

CONCERTO DA CAMERA NO. 3 see Brings, Allen Stephen

CONCERTO DA CAMERA NO. 3 see Dodgson, Stephen

CONCERTO DA CAMERA NO. 4 see Dodgson, Stephen

CONCERTO DA CAMERA NO. 5 see Dodgson, Stephen

CONCERTO DANS LE GOUT ITALIEN, FOR VIOLIN, VIOLA, VIOLONCELLO AND STRING ORCHESTRA see Mieg, Peter

CONCERTO DEL PLATA, FOR GUITAR AND ORCHESTRA see Carlevaro, A.

CONCERTO DI CONCERTI see Bucchi, Valentino

CONCERTO DILETTO I see Diethelm, Caspar

CONCERTO DILETTO II see Diethelm, Caspar

CONCERTO D'INFANZIA, FOR VOICE AND ORCHESTRA see Prosperi, Carlo

CONCERTO D'OCTOBRE, FOR CLARINET AND STRING ORCHESTRA see Bondon, Jacques

CONCERTO ELEGANTE see Hallberg, Bengt

CONCERTO ENTUSIASTICO see Wittinger, Robert

CONCERTO EROICO, FOR HORN AND ORCHESTRA see Pospisil, Juraj

CONCERTO FOR 6 PERCUSSIONISTS AND ORCHESTRA see Parchman, Gen Louis

CONCERTO FOR HARP AND ORCHESTRA see Handel, George Frideric, Concerto for Organ and Orchestra, No. 6, Op. 4, No. 6, in B flat

CONCERTO FOR PIANO AND ORCHESTRA, 1964 see Marttinen, Tauno

CONCERTO FOR PIANO AND ORCHESTRA NO. 7 see Mozart, Wolfgang Amadeus, Concerto for 3 Pianos and Orchestra, No. 7, in F, K. 242

CONCERTO FOR PIANO AND ORCHESTRA NO. 10 see Mozart, Wolfgang Amadeus, Concerto for 2 Pianos and Orchestra, No. 10, in E flat, K. 365

CONCERTO FOR PIANO AND ORCHESTRA NO. 28 see Mozart, Wolfgang Amadeus, Rondo for Piano and Orchestra in D, K. 382

CONCERTO FOR PIANOLA AND ORCHESTRA see Dijk, Jan van

CONCERTO FOR ROCK GROUP AND ORCHESTRA see Selig, Robert

CONCERTO FOR SHAKUHACHI AND ORCHESTRA see Hirose, Ryohei

CONCERTO FOR TRAUTONIUM AND ORCHESTRA see Genzmer, Harald

CONCERTO FOR VIOLIN AND ORCHESTRA IN C, FRAGMENT see Beethoven, Ludwig van, Konzertsatz For Violin And Orchestra In C, [arr.]

CONCERTO GROSSO A QUATTRO CORI see Stolzel, Gottfried Heinrich

CONCERTO GROSSO IN C (ALEXANDER'S FEAST) see Handel, George Frideric

CONCERTO IN RONDO, FOR PIANO AND ORCHESTRA see Bucchi, Valentino

CONCERTO LIRICO see Wittinger, Robert

CONCERTO LIRICO, FOR VIOLIN AND STRING ORCHESTRA see Bucchi, Valentino

CONCERTO LUGUBRE, FOR FLUTE AND ORCHESTRA see Giannella, Louis

CONCERTO LUGUBRE, FOR VIOLA AND ORCHESTRA see Baird, Tadeusz

CONCERTO MOVEMENT FOR VIOLIN AND ORCHESTRA IN D see Bach, Johann Sebastian

CONCERTO PER ARCHI see Haubenstock-Ramati, Roman

CONCERTO PER EURIDICE, FOR GUITAR AND STRING ORCHESTRA see Novak, Jan

CONCERTO PER LA CANDIDA PACE see Margola, Franco

CONCERTO PER ORCHESTRA DA CAMERA see Pernes, Thomas

CONCERTO: PERCUSSION see Conyngham, Barry

CONCERTO ROMANTICO NO. 2, FOR VIOLONCELLO AND ORCHESTRA see Forino, L.

CONCERTO SEMPLICE, FOR VIOLIN AND ORCHESTRA see Sarkozy, Istvan

CONCERTO SERIOSO, FOR VIOLIN AND ORCHESTRA see Segerstam, Leif

CONCERTO SYMPHONIQUE, FOR PIANO AND ORCHESTRA see Bloch, Ernest

CONCERTONE 1980, FOR VIOLA AND ORCHESTRA see Ketting, Piet

CONCERTONE FOR TWO VIOLINS AND ORCHESTRA IN C, K. 190 see Mozart, Wolfgang Amadeus

CONCERTONE, SINFONIA CONCERTANTE, K. 190, 364 see Mozart, Wolfgang Amadeus

CONCERTSTUK see Wijdeveld, Wolfgang

CONCERVATI FEDELE, FOR SOLO VOICE AND STRING ORCHESTRA see Mozart, Wolfgang Amadeus

CONCIERTO DE TENERIFE, FOR PIANO AND ORCHESTRA see Kuhn, Max

CONCIERTO PARA TRES HERMANAS, FOR GUITAR AND ORCHESTRA see Pizzini, Carlo Alberto

CONCURRENZEN WALZER see Strauss, Johann, [Jr.]

CONFLUENCE see Wordsworth, William

CONFRONTATIONS AND INDOCTRINATIONS, FOR JAZZ QUINTET, BIG BAND AND 19 INSTRUMENTS see Porcelijn, David

CONJUNTOS see Delas, Jose Luis de

CONQUEST OF THE AIR see Bliss, [Sir] Arthur

CONSECRATION OF THE HOUSE see Beethoven, Ludwig van, Weihe Des Hauses, Die

CONSEQUENZEN WALZER see Strauss, Eduard

CONSOLI, MARC-ANTONIO (1941-   )
Odefonia [24']
2(pic).2(English horn).2(bass clar).2. 2.2.1.0. 3perc,4vcl, 2db
MARGUN BP 1008 perf mat rent (C211)

CONSORT MUSIC 1 see Rechberger, Hermann

CONSORT MUSIC 2 see Rechberger, Hermann

CONSORTIEN WALZER see Strauss, Josef

CONSORTS see Rowland, David

CONSTANT, MARIUS (1925-   )
Concertante, For Saxophone And Orchestra [17']
2.2.1.0. 2.2.1.0. perc,harp, strings,alto sax solo
RICORDI-FR R.2249 perf mat rent (C212)

Elementi, Gli, For Trombone And Chamber Orchestra [17']
2horn,strings,trom solo
RICORDI-FR R.2239 perf mat rent (C213)

Harpalyce, For Harp And String Orchestra [10']
string orch,harp solo
RICORDI-FR R.2281-82 perf mat rent (C214)

Nana-Symphonie [35']
3.3.4.3. 4.3.3.1. timp,4perc,pno, cel,harp,org,strings
RICORDI-FR R.2230 perf mat rent (C215)

Ponant 19, For Piano And Instrumental Ensemble [18']
2clar,2sax,4trp,4trom,2perc,2vln, vla,vcl,db,pno solo
AMPHION A 182 perf mat rent (C216)

CONSTANTINIDES, DINOS DEMETRIOS (1929-   )
Concerto for Violin, Violoncello, Piano and Orchestra
2.3.3.2. 4.3.3.1. timp,2perc, strings,vln solo,vcl solo,pno solo
SEESAW perf mat rent (C217)

Dedications For Orchestra
3.2.3.2. 4.3.3.1. timp,2perc, harp,strings
SEESAW perf mat rent (C218)

Designs
string orch
SEESAW perf mat rent (C219)

Symphony No. 1
3.3.3.3. 4.3.3.1. 3perc,strings
SEESAW perf mat rent (C220)

CONTE FEERIQUE see Rimsky-Korsakov, Nikolai

CONTES D'HOFFMANN, LES: BARCAROLLE, "O BELLE NUIT, O NUIT D'AMOUR", FOR SOLO VOICE AND ORCHESTRA see Offenbach, Jacques

CONTES D'HOFFMANN, LES: IL ETAIT UNE FOIS, FOR SOLO VOICE AND ORCHESTRA see Offenbach, Jacques

CONTES D'HOFFMANN, LES: INTERMEDE ET BARCAROLLE see Offenbach, Jacques

CONTES D'HOFFMANN, LES: LES OISEAUX DANS LA CHARMILLE, FOR SOLO VOICE AND ORCHESTRA see Offenbach, Jacques

CONTILLI, GINO (1907-1978)
Variazioni E Notturni, For Solo Voice And Orchestra [20']
3.3.2.2. 4.3.3.1. cel,xylo,vibra, harp,timp,2perc,strings,S solo
sc ZERBONI 8434 f.s., pts ZERBONI 8435 rent (C221)

CONTRAPPUNTI A QUATTRO DIMENSIONI see Chailly, Luciano

CONTRASTS see Rapf, Kurt

CONTRASUBJEKTE. PASSACAGLIA UBER BACH see Stranz, Ulrich

CONTRAVOLUTION see Laman, Wim

CONTRETANZE, FUNF, K. 609 see Mozart, Wolfgang Amadeus

CONTRETANZE, VIER, K. 267 see Mozart, Wolfgang Amadeus

CONTRETANZE, K. 123 see Mozart, Wolfgang Amadeus

CONVERSE, FREDERICK SHEPHERD (1871-1940)
Valzer Poetici, Op. 5, [arr.] (Schuller, Gunther) 3.3.3.2. 4.2.3.1. perc,harp,strings [11']
MARGUN BP 1009 perf mat rent (C222)

CONVOI D'UNE PAUVRE FILLE, LE, FOR SOLO VOICE AND ORCHESTRA see Bijl, Theo van der

CONYNGHAM, BARRY (1944-   )
Concerto: Percussion [20']
2.2.3.2. 4.3.3.1. harp,strings
UNIVER. perf mat rent (C223)

Sky [12']
8vln,2vla,2vcl,db
sc UNIVER. UE 29121 f.s., perf mat rent (C224)

COOPER OF FIFE, THE see Dorward, David

COORNHERT-VARIATIES see Dijk, Jan van

COPE, DAVID
Music For Brass, Strings And Percussion
0.0.0.0. 4.2.2.2. harp,timp, 2perc,strings
SEESAW perf mat rent (C225)

Variations for Piano and Orchestra
3.3.3.3. 4.2.3.1. 3perc,db,pno solo
SEESAW perf mat rent (C226)

COPLAND, AARON (1900-   )
Preamble For A Solemn Occasion
sc BOOSEY $5.00 (C227)

Symphony for Organ and Orchestra
BOOSEY 745 min sc $9.50, sc $25.00 (C228)

Two Pieces
string orch
sc BOOSEY $7.50 (C229)

COPLAS, FOR SOLO VOICE AND ORCHESTRA see Badings, Henk

COPPELIA: VALSE DE LA POUPEE ET CZARDAS see Delibes, Leo

COQ D'OR, LE: INTRODUCTION AND BRIDAL PROCESSION see Rimsky-Korsakov, Nikolai

COQ D'OR, LE: INTRODUCTION AND CORTEGE see Rimsky-Korsakov, Nikolai, Coq D'Or, Le: Introduction And Bridal Procession

COQ D'OR, LE: SUITE see Rimsky-Korsakov, Nikolai

CORAL ISLAND, FOR SOLO VOICE AND ORCHESTRA see Takemitsu, Toru

CORALE SINFONICO, FOR ORGAN AND ORCHESTRA see Gubitosi, Emilia

CORDERO, ROQUE (1917-   )
Elegy for String Orchestra
string orch
PEER sc $8.00, pts rent (C230)

Paz-Paiz-Peace
fl,English horn,bass clar,clar, alto fl,bsn,strings,harp
PEER perf mat rent (C231)

CORELLI, ARCANGELO (1653-1713)
Christmas Concerto *see Concerto Grosso, Op. 6, No. 8, in G minor

Concerti Grossi, Op. 5
(see Geminiani, Francesco) KALMUS (C232)

Concerti Grossi, Op. 6, Nos. 1-6
min sc LEA 145 $2.40 (C233)

Concerti Grossi, Op. 6, Nos. 7-12
min sc LEA 146 $2.40 (C234)

Concerto Grosso, Op. 6, No. 1, in D
string orch,cont,2vln soli,vcl solo
LUCKS 07245 sc $3.75, set $7.75, min sc $2.50, pts $1.15, ea. (C235)

(Woehl) BROUDE BR. sc $4.50, set

CORELLI, ARCANGELO (cont'd.)

$8.00, pts $1.50, ea. (C236)

Concerto Grosso, Op. 6, No. 2, in F
string orch,cont,2vln soli,vcl solo
LUCKS 07241 sc $3.75, set $7.75, min sc $2.50, pts $1.15, ea. (C237)

(Woehl) BROUDE BR. sc $4.50, set $8.00, pts $1.50, ea. (C238)

Concerto Grosso, Op. 6, No. 3, in C minor
string orch,cont,2vln soli,vcl solo
LUCKS 08321 sc $3.75, set $7.75, min sc $2.50, pts $1.15, ea. (C239)

(Woehl) BROUDE BR. sc $4.50, set $8.00, pts $1.50, ea. (C240)

Concerto Grosso, Op. 6, No. 4, in D
string orch,cont,2vln soli,vcl solo
LUCKS 07222 sc $3.75, set $7.75, min sc $2.50, pts $1.15, ea. (C241)

(Woehl) BROUDE BR. sc $4.50, set $8.00, pts $1.50, ea. (C242)

Concerto Grosso, Op. 6, No. 5, in B flat
string orch,cont,2vln soli,vcl solo
LUCKS 07226 sc $3.75, set $7.75, min sc $2.50, pts $1.15, ea. (C243)

(Woehl) BROUDE BR. sc $4.50, set $8.00, pts $1.50, ea. (C244)

Concerto Grosso, Op. 6, No. 6, in F
string orch,cont,2vln soli,vcl solo
LUCKS 07258 sc $3.75, set $7.75, min sc $2.50, pts $1.15, ea. (C245)

(Woehl) BROUDE BR. sc $4.50, set $8.00, pts $1.50, ea. (C246)

Concerto Grosso, Op. 6, No. 7, in D
string orch,cont,2vln soli,vcl solo
LUCKS 07267 sc $3.75, set $7.75, min sc $2.50, pts $1.15, ea. (C247)

(Woehl) BROUDE BR. sc $4.50, set $8.00, pts $1.50, ea. (C248)

Concerto Grosso, Op. 6, No. 8, in G minor
string orch,cont,2vln soli,vcl solo
LUCKS 05312 sc $3.75, set $7.75, min sc $2.50, pts $1.15, ea. (C249)

(Woehl) BROUDE BR. sc $6.00, set $8.00, pts $1.50, ea. (C250)

Concerto Grosso, Op. 6, No. 9, in F
string orch,cont,2vln soli,vcl solo
LUCKS 07282 sc $3.75, set $7.75, min sc $2.50, pts $1.15, ea. (C251)

(Woehl) BROUDE BR. sc $4.50, set $8.00, pts $1.50, ea. (C252)

Concerto Grosso, Op. 6, No. 10, in C
string orch,cont,2vln soli,vcl solo
LUCKS 07283 sc $3.75, set $7.75, min sc $2.50, pts $1.15, ea. (C253)

(Woehl) BROUDE BR. sc $4.50, set $8.00, pts $1.50, ea. (C254)

Concerto Grosso, Op. 6, No. 11, in B flat
string orch,cont,2vln soli,vcl solo
LUCKS 07285 sc $3.75, set $7.75, min sc $2.50, pts $1.15, ea. (C255)

(Woehl) BROUDE BR. sc $4.50, set $8.00, pts $1.50, ea. (C256)

Concerto Grosso, Op. 6, No. 12, in F
string orch,cont,2vln soli,vcl solo
LUCKS 07667 sc $3.75, set $7.75, min sc $2.50, pts $1.15, ea. (C257)

(Woehl) BROUDE BR. sc $4.50, set $8.00, pts $1.50, ea. (C258)

Sarabanda, Giga E Badinerie
BROUDE BR. sc $2.50, set $3.75, pts $.75, ea. (C259)

Suite, MIN 83, [arr.]
1.1.2.0. 0.1.0.0. perc,strings without vla sc,pts HARMONIA 2214 f.s. (C260)

CORELLI, ARCANGELO (cont'd.)

Suite, MIN 764
string orch LUCKS 07780 sc $1.75,
set $3.00, pts $.70, ea.   (C261)

CORIGLIANO, JOHN (1938-   )
Voyage
string orch
SCHIRM.G sc,pts $15.00, sc $3.00,
pts $1.00, ea.   (C262)

CORIOLAN OVERTURE see Beethoven, Ludwig
van

CORNELIUS, PETER (1824-1874)
Cid, Der: Overture
INTERNAT. perf mat rent   (C263)

CORNUCOPIA, FOR TUBA AND ORCHESTRA see
Kraft, William

CORONATION MARCH see Meyerbeer,
Giacomo, Kronungsmarsch

CORPS CELESTE see Norby, Erik

CORREGGIA, ENRICO
Ephemeral 2
gtr,fl,pno,perc,strings
TONOS 7224   (C264)

Murmeln
11strings, flexaton or solo voice
TONOS 7415   (C265)

CORRENTE E GAGLIARDA see Pesenti,
Martino

CORRETTE, MICHEL (1709-1795)
Concerto for Harpsichord and
Orchestra, No. 4, in C
string orch,hpsd/org solo
(Abbott, Alain) sc,pts BILLAUDOT
$25.50   (C266)

CORS ET CORDES, FOR BASSETHORN AND
ORCHESTRA see Keulen, Geert van

CORSAIRE, LE see Berlioz, Hector
(Louis)

CORSARESCA see La Rotella, Pasquale

CORTEGE see Schafer, R. Murray

CORTEGE IN A MINOR see Moszkowski,
Moritz

CORTEGE SOLENNEL, OP. 50 see Glazunov,
Alexander Konstantinovich

CORTEGES see Foccroulle, Bernard

CORTES, RAMIRO (1933-   )
Christ Lag In Todesbanden, Meditation
On [6'19"]
string orch
WIMBLEDN W1200 sc $9.50, pts $1.00,
ea.   (C267)

CORTESE, LUIGI (1899-1976)
Prelude and Fugue [9']
2.2.1.2. 2.2.1.0. harp,strings
sc CARISCH 20327 perf mat rent
(C268)

Serenade [19']
3.2.2.2. 2.2.1.0. pno,strings
sc CARISCH 18358 perf mat rent
(C269)

Tre Salmi, For Solo Voice And
Orchestra [22']
3.3.3.4. 4.4.3.1. timp,cel,harp,
strings,S solo
sc ZERBONI 8193 f.s., pts ZERBONI
8194 rent   (C270)

COSCIA, SILVIO (1899-1977)
Exorcism, The (Faust In The Forest)
[12']
2.2.2.2. 4.3.3.1. timp,perc,harp,
strings
MARGUN BP 1010 perf mat rent (C271)

COSI DUNQUE TRADISCI, FOR SOLO VOICE
AND ORCHESTRA see Mozart, Wolfgang
Amadeus

COSI FAN TUTTE: AH SCOTATI - SMANIE
IMPLACABILE, FOR SOLO VOICE AND
ORCHESTRA see Mozart, Wolfgang
Amadeus

COSI FAN TUTTE: COME SCOGLIO IMMOTO,
FOR SOLO VOICE AND ORCHESTRA see
Mozart, Wolfgang Amadeus

COSI FAN TUTTE: DONNE MIE, LA FATE A
TANTI, FOR SOLO VOICE AND ORCHESTRA
see Mozart, Wolfgang Amadeus

COSI FAN TUTTE: IN UOMINI, IN SOLDATI,
FOR SOLO VOICE AND ORCHESTRA see
Mozart, Wolfgang Amadeus

COSI FAN TUTTE: OVERTURE see Mozart,
Wolfgang Amadeus

COSI FAN TUTTE: PER PIETA, BEN MIO, FOR
SOLO VOICE AND ORCHESTRA see
Mozart, Wolfgang Amadeus

COSI FAN TUTTE: PRENDERO QUEL
BRUNETTINO, FOR SOLO VOICES AND
ORCHESTRA see Mozart, Wolfgang
Amadeus

COSI FAN TUTTE: RIVOLGETE A LUI LO
SGUARDO, FOR SOLO VOICE AND
ORCHESTRA see Mozart, Wolfgang
Amadeus

COSI FAN TUTTE: UN' AURA AMOROSA, FOR
SOLO VOICE AND ORCHESTRA see
Mozart, Wolfgang Amadeus

COSMIC VISIONS see Camilleri, Charles

COSMOGONIE POUR UNE ROSE see Tabachnik,
Michel

COSSETTO, EMIL (1918-   )
Suite Concertante No. 1
pno,strings,fl solo
DRUS.HRVAT.SKLAD. f.s.   (C272)

Suite Concertante No. 2
pno,strings,ob solo
DRUS.HRVAT.SKLAD. f.s.   (C273)

Suite Concertante No. 3
pno,strings,clar solo
DRUS.HRVAT.SKLAD. f.s.   (C274)

Suite Concertante No. 4
pno,strings,bsn solo
DRUS.HRVAT.SKLAD. f.s.   (C275)

Suite Concertante No. 5
pno,strings,horn solo
DRUS.HRVAT.SKLAD. f.s.   (C276)

COSTRETTA A PIANGERE, FOR SOLO VOICE
AND ORCHESTRA see Haydn, [Franz]
Joseph

COTE D'AZUR--NICE see Escher, Rudolf
George

COUNTERBASS, FOR DOUBLE BASS AND STRING
ORCHESTRA see Sermila, Jarmo

COUNTRY SONG see Holst, Gustav

COUPERIN, FRANCOIS (LE GRAND)
(1668-1733)
Parnasse Ou L'Apotheose De Corelli,
Le, [arr.]
(Paillard, J.F.) string orch,cont
sc,pts COSTALL f.s.   (C277)

Soeur Monique Rondo
see RICREAZIONI DI ANTICHE MUSICHE
CLASSICHE, SERIE III: MUSICHE
ANTICHE ITALIANE

COURANTS, FOR TROMBONE AND INSTRUMENTAL
ENSEMBLE see Mestral, Patrice

COURSE DE PRINTEMPS, LA see Koechlin,
Charles

COWEN, [SIR] FREDERIC HYMEN (1852-1935)
In Fairyland: Moonbeam Fairies
[4'30"]
2+pic.2.2.2. 4.2.3.1. timp,perc,
harp,strings
KALMUS A5481 sc $4.00, set $10.00,
pts $1.00, ea.   (C278)

CRADLE SONG, A see Brings, Allen
Stephen

CRADLE SONG FOR A DEAD HORSEMAN see
Sallinen, Aulis, Kehtolaulu
Kuolleelle Ratsumiehelle

CRAMER, JOHANN BAPTIST (1771-1858)
Concerto for Piano and Orchestra, No.
5, Op. 48, in C minor [26']
1.2.0.2. 2.0.0.0. timp,strings,
pno solo
sc,pts LIENAU rent   (C279)

CREATION, THE: IN NATIVE WORTH see
Haydn, [Franz] Joseph, Schopfung,
Die: Mit Wurd' Und Hoheit Angetan,
For Solo Voice And Orchestra

CREATION, THE: WITH VERDURE CLAD see
Haydn, [Franz] Joseph, Schopfung,
Die: Nun Beut Die Flur, For Solo
Voice And Orchestra

CREATION OF THE FEMALE MONSTER, THE:
SUITE see Waxman, Franz

CREATURES OF PROMETHEUS, THE: OVERTURE
see Beethoven, Ludwig van,
Geschope Des Prometheus, Die:
Overture

CRESSWELL, LYELL
Concerto for Violin and Orchestra
[12']
3.3.3.3. 4.3.3.1. timp,5perc,
strings,vln solo
SCOTUS 243-1 f.s.   (C280)

Salm [20']
3.3.3.3. 4.3.3.1. timp,3perc,
harp,strings
SCOTUS 238-5 f.s.   (C281)

CRESTON, PAUL (1906-   )
Fugue (from String Quartet, Op.8)
string orch
SHAWNEE J 73 $10.00   (C282)

CRISANTEMI see Puccini, Giacomo

CRISPINO QUADRILLE see Strauss, Josef

CROFT, WILLIAM (1678-1727)
Oh God, Our Help In Ages Past
see Haydn, [Johann] Michael, O
Worship The King

Overture: Laurus Cruentas [4']
string orch,cont
(Bevan, Maurice) sc OXFORD 27.962
$7.00, perf mat rent   (C283)

CRONICA DE UM DIA DE VERAO, FOR
CLARINET AND STRING ORCHESTRA see
Prado, Jose-Antonio (Almeida)

CROSS SONGS, [ARR.]
(Kirkland, Camp) CRESPUB CP-IN 7+7
$15.00 see also Seven+
Orchestration Series, Group 2
(C284)

CROSSE, GORDON (1937-   )
Concerto for Violin and Orchestra,
No. 2, Op. 26 [35']
4(pic,alto fl).3(English
horn).3(bass clar).3. 4.3.3.1.
timp,3perc,harp,pno,cel,
strings,vln solo
study sc OXFORD 23.128 $30.00, sc,
pts OXFORD rent   (C285)

Concerto for Violoncello and
Orchestra [24']
2.2.2.2. 1.2.2.0. timp,3perc,cel,
pno,strings,vcl solo
OXFORD perf mat rent   (C286)

Dreamsongs *Op.43 [14']
1(pic).1.1+bass clar.1. 2.1.1.0.
perc,harp,cimbalom,strings
OXFORD perf mat rent   (C287)

Play Ground [30']
3.3.3.3. 4.3.3.1. timp,5perc,
harp,cel,pno,strings
OXFORD perf mat rent   (C288)

Suite No. 1 (from Story Of Vasco,
The)
3(2pic).3(English horn).2+bass
clar.3. 4.3.3.1. timp,3perc,opt
cimbalom,pno&cel,harp,strings
OXFORD perf mat rent   (C289)

Symphony No. 1 [20']
2(pic,alto fl).2(English
horn).2(bass clar).2. 2.0.0.0.
timp,perc,harp,strings
study sc OXFORD 77.814 $6.20, perf
mat rent   (C290)

CRUCIUS, HEINZ
Elegie
RIES f.s. contains also: Ries,
Franz, Gondoliera   (C291)

Leben Lang, Ein
see Crucius, Heinz, Sommer In
Amalfi

Saragossa
RIES f.s. contains also: Winkler,
Gerhard, Tarentina, La   (C292)

Sommer In Amalfi
RIES f.s. contains also: Leben
Lang, Ein   (C293)

Ungarische Vision
RIES f.s.   (C294)

CRUEGER, JOHANN
see CRUGER, JOHANN

CRUGER, JOHANN (1598-1662)
Now Thank We All Our God
(Luck, Arthur) LUCKS HYMNS 9 set
$10.00, pts $.65, ea. contains
also: Barnby, [Sir] Joseph, Now
The Day Is Over   (C295)

CRUMB, GEORGE (1929-   )
Echoes Of Time And The River
sc KALMUS A7004 $12.00   (C296)

CRUSELL, BERNHARD HENRIK (1775-1838)
Concerto for Clarinet and Orchestra,
Op. 5, in F minor [25']
1.2.0.2. 2.2.0.0. timp,strings,
clar solo
KALMUS 5181 sc $15.00, perf mat
rent, set $24.00, pts $1.50, ea.
(C297)

CRYPTOGAMEN, FOR SOLO VOICE AND
ORCHESTRA see Schat, Peter

CSARDAS, FOR VIOLIN AND ORCHESTRA see
Monti, Vittorio

CUATRO CANCIONES DE CUNA, FOR SOLO
VOICE AND ORCHESTRA see Letelier
Llona, Alfonso

CUATRO COPLAS, FOR SOLO VOICE AND
ORCHESTRA see Mul, Jan

CUATRO LIEDER, FOR SOLO VOICE AND
ORCHESTRA see Baguena Soler, Jose

CUCKOO AND THE NIGHTINGALE, THE see
Handel, George Frideric, Concerto
for Organ and Orchestra, No. 13, in
F

CUMAR, R. (1906-)
Cinque Danze Moderne [11']
0.0.3.0.2sax. 0.2.1.0. pno,1-
2perc,strings
sc CARISCH 17131 perf mat rent
(C298)

CUNNINGHAM, MICHAEL GERALD (1937-)
Concerto for Trumpet and Orchestra
2.3.3.3. 4.1.3.1. perc,strings,
trp solo
SEESAW perf mat rent (C299)

Irish Symphony
string orch
SEESAW perf mat rent (C300)

Serenade
string orch
SEESAW perf mat rent (C301)

CUORE VIBRANTE see Becce, Giuseppe

CURTIS, ERNESTO DE
Come Back To Sorrento, For Solo Voice
And Orchestra
LUCKS 02521 sc $4.00, set $9.50,
pts $.75, ea. (C302)

CURTIS-SMITH, CURTIS O.B. (1941-)
Belle Du Jour
study sc SALABERT $17.25 (C303)

CUTS AND DISSOLVES see Rihm, Wolfgang

CYBERNETISCH OBJEKT see Porcelijn,
David

CYCLE OF SONGS, FOR SOLO VOICE AND
ORCHESTRA see Fladmoe, Arvid

CYCLOIDEN WALZER see Strauss, Johann,
[Jr.]

CYCLOPHONY VIII see Kox, Hans

CYPRESSES, THE, [ARR.] see Dvorak,
Antonin

CYTHEREN QUADRILLE see Strauss, Johann,
[Jr.]

CYTRON, WARREN A. (1944-)
Between Bridges, For Trumpet And
Chamber Orchestra [14']
MCGIN-MARX perf mat rent (C304)

Windstring Soliloquies, For Speaker
And Chamber Orchestra [11']
MCGIN-MARX perf mat rent (C305)

CZAR AND CARPENTER: OVERTURE see
Lortzing, (Gustav) Albert, Zar Und
Zimmermann: Overture

CZARDAS NO. 3 see Scheibe, W.

CZECHOSLOVAK OVERTURE see Ocenas,
Andrej, Ceskoslovenska Predohra

CZERNIK, W.
Jeu D'Amour
WOITSCHACH f.s. (C306)

CZERNIK, WILLY (1904-)
Rubezahl [26']
3(pic).2(English horn).2+bass
clar.2+contrabsn. 4.3.3.1.
timp,3perc,harp,cel,strings
RIES perf mat rent (C307)

CZINKA PANNA NOTAJA, FOR VIOLIN AND
ORCHESTRA see Hubay, Jeno

CZTERY POLONEZY WERSALSKIE see
Sikorski, Kazimierz

D

DA CHE PENSA A MARITARMI, FOR SOLO
VOICE AND ORCHESTRA see Haydn,
[Franz] Joseph

DAETWYLER, JEAN
Concertino for Guitar and String
Orchestra
string orch,gtr solo
sc,pts PAN 1 f.s. (D1)

Pan Und Die Nymphen, For Flute, Harp
And String Orchestra
string orch,fl solo,harp solo
PAN 2 (D2)

DAG AAN DAG KOMT HIJ EN GAAT see
Mengelberg, Karel

DAGDRIVAREN see Rosenberg, Hilding

D'ALESSANDRO, RAFAELE
see ALESSANDRO, RAFAELE D'

DALLA NEBBIA VERSO LA NEBBIA see
Arrigo, Girolamo

DALLA VECCHIA, WOLFANGO (1923-)
Balletto (Suite No. 2) [35']
2(pic).2.2.2+contrabsn. 0.2.3.0.
2perc,2pno,strings
sc ZANIBON 4534 rent, pts ZANIBON
4535 rent (D3)

Concertino All'Italiana [12']
string orch
sc ZANIBON 4438 f.s., pts ZANIBON
4439 f.s. (D4)

Quattro Momenti Musicali, For Flute
And String Orchestra [18']
string orch,fl solo
sc ZANIBON 4589 f.s., pts ZANIBON
4590 f.s. (D5)

Suite Accademica (Suite No. 1) [35']
2+pic.2+English horn.2+bass
clar.2+contrabsn. 3.3.3.0.
timp,2perc,harp,2pno,strings
sc ZANIBON 4624 rent, pts ZANIBON
4625 rent (D6)

Suite No. 1 *see Suite Accademica

Suite No. 2 *see Balletto

Variati Amorosi Momenti
string orch
sc ZANIBON 5770 f.s., pts ZANIBON
5771 f.s. (D7)

Victoris Laus [20']
string orch,vla solo
sc ZANIBON 5527 rent, pts ZANIBON
5528 rent (D8)

DALL'ABACO, EVARISTO FELICE
see ABACO, EVARISTO FELICE DALL'

DALLAPICCOLA, LUIGI (1904-1975)
Parole Di San Paolo, For Solo Voice
And Orchestra [8']
fl,alto fl,2clar,bass clar,cel,
pno,vibra,xylorimba,harp,Mez/
boy. solo, strings without
violin and double bass
min sc BOOSEY $8.50, perf mat rent
(D9)

Three Questions With Two Answers
[16']
2.3.4.3+sax. 4.2.3.1. harp,cel,
xylo,marimba,vibra,perc,strings
sc ZERBONI 8155 f.s., perf mat rent
(D10)

DALLINGER, FRIDOLIN (1933-)
Panta Rhei [9'30"]
2+pic.2+English horn.2+bass
clar.2+contrabsn. 4.3.3.1.
timp,perc,harp,xylo,vibra,
strings
sc,pts DOBLINGER rent (D11)

DALVIMARE, MARTIN-PIERRE (1772-1839)
Concerto for Harp and Orchestra, No.
2
2.0.2.2. 2.0.0.0. timp,strings,
harp solo
COSTALL perf mat rent (D12)

D'AMBROSIO, ALFREDO
see AMBROSIO, ALFREDO D'

DAME BLANCHE, LA: OVERTURE see
Boieldieu, Francois-Adrien

DAMEN SOUVENIR POLKA see Strauss,
Johann, [Jr.]

DAMENSPENDE see Strauss, Johann, [Jr.]

DAMNATION DE FAUST, LA: BALLET DES
SYLPHES see Berlioz, Hector (Louis)

DAMNATION DE FAUST, LA: CHANSON DE LA
PUCE, FOR SOLO VOICE AND ORCHESTRA
see Berlioz, Hector (Louis)

DAMNATION DE FAUST, LA: MARCHE
HONGROISE see Berlioz, Hector
(Louis)

DAMNATION DE FAUST, LA: MARCHE
HONGROISE, BALLET DES SYLPHES,
MENUET DES FOLLETS see Berlioz,
Hector (Louis)

DAMNATION DE FAUST, LA: MENUET DES
FOLLETS see Berlioz, Hector (Louis)

DAMNATION DE FAUST, LA: SERENADE DE
MEPHISTO, "DEVANT LA MAISON", FOR
SOLO VOICE AND ORCHESTRA see
Berlioz, Hector (Louis)

DAMNATION DE FAUST, LA: VOICI DES
ROSES, FOR SOLO VOICE AND ORCHESTRA
see Berlioz, Hector (Louis)

DAMNATION OF FAUST: DANCE OF THE
SPRITES see Berlioz, Hector
(Louis), Damnation De Faust, La:
Menuet Des Follets

DAMNATION OF FAUST: DANCE OF THE
SYLPHES see Berlioz, Hector
(Louis), Damnation De Faust, La:
Ballet Des Sylphes

DAMNATION OF FAUST: FLEA SONG see
Berlioz, Hector (Louis), Damnation
De Faust, La: Chanson De La Puce,
For Solo Voice And Orchestra

DAMNATION OF FAUST: HUNGARIAN MARCH see
Berlioz, Hector (Louis), Damnation
De Faust, La: Marche Hongroise

DAMON, DER see Boer, Ed de

DAMONE, IL: SINFONIA see Stradella,
Alessandro

DANCE BURLESQUE see Bravnicar, Matija,
Plesna Burleska

DANCE DIVERSIONS see Hurd, Michael

DANCE OF THE ENRAPTURED see Stein, Leon

DANCE OF THE EXULTANT see Stein, Leon

DANCE OF THE JOYOUS see Stein, Leon

DANCE SCENES see Blacher, Boris

DANCE SUITE see Blacher, Boris

DANCE SUITE see Gervaise, Claude

DANCE SUITE see Skalkottas, Nikos

DANCE THROUGH THE LAND OF SHADOWS, THE
see Germeten, Gunnar, Dansen
Gjennom Skuggeheimen

DANCE VARIATIONS see Mathias, William

DANCE VARIATIONS, FOR TWO PIANOS AND
ORCHESTRA see Gould, Morton

DANCES see Osterc, Slavko

DANCING
(George, Thom Ritter) (based on music
of Bizet; Borodin; Corelli;
Offenbach; Paderwski; Strauss,
Josef and Strauss, Johann) sc,pts
ACCURA 044 $75.00 (D13)

DANCING STICKS see Faust, Willi

DANGEROUS DREAMS see Bach, Erik

DANIEL-LESUR
see LESUR, DANIEL

DANNAZIONE DI FAUST, LA: MARCIA
UNGHERESE, BALLETTO DEI SILFI,
MINUETTO DEI FOLLETTI see Berlioz,
Hector (Louis), Damnation De Faust,
La: Marche Hongroise, Ballet Des
Sylphes, Menuet Des Follets

DANNAZIONE E PREGHIERA, FOR SOLO VOICE
AND STRING ORCHESTRA see
Procaccini, Teresa

DANS DER GODEN, DE see Pluister, Simon

DANSE DE FETE see Steffaro, Julius

DANSE ESPAGNOLE, FOR VIOLIN AND
ORCHESTRA see Sarasate, Pablo de

DANSE MACABRE see Saint-Saens, Camille

DANSE NAPOLITAINE see Desormes, I.C.

DANSE ROUMAINE see Gounod, Charles
Francois

DANSE SACREE ET DANSE PROFANE, FOR HARP
AND STRING ORCHESTRA see Debussy,
Claude

DANSEN GJENNOM SKUGGEHEIMEN see
Germeten, Gunnar

DANSES FRANCAISES DU DIX-SEPTIEME
SIECLE
string orch,cont
(Paillard, J.F.) sc,pts COSTALL f.s.
(D14)

DANZA, LA, FOR SOLO VOICE AND ORCHESTRA
see Rossini, Gioacchino

DANZA JERATICA see Gentili, Alberto

DANZA RUSTICA see Farina, Guido

DANZE PER I CINQUE CERCHI see Medin, N.

DANZI, FRANZ (1763-1826)
Concerto for Flute and Orchestra, No.
2, Op. 31, in D minor
0.2.0.2. 2.2.0.0. timp,strings,fl
solo
(Foerster) sc EULENBURG E10079
f.s., perf mat rent   (D15)

Concerto for Flute and Orchestra, No.
4, Op. 43, in D
0.2.0.2. 2.2.0.0. timp,strings,fl
solo
(Foerster) sc EULENBURG E10069
f.s., perf mat rent   (D16)

DARINKA see Koester, Willy

DASCHA see Mielenz, Hans

DAVICO, VINCENZO (1889-1969)
O Luna Che Fai Lume, For Solo Voice
And Orchestra [3']
harp,cel,strings,S solo
manuscript CARISCH   (D17)

DAVID, ADOLPHE ISAAC (1842-1897)
Pluie, La
string orch
"Rain, The" LUCKS 07231 sc $1.75,
set $3.50, pts $.70, ea. (D18)

Rain, The *see Pluie, La

DAVID, FELICIEN-CESAR (1810-1876)
Perle Du Bresil, La: Charmant Oiseau,
For Solo Voice And Orchestra
LUCKS 02073 set $7.50, pts $.75,
ea.   (D19)

DAVID, GYULA (1913-   )
Concerto for Horn and Orchestra
orch,horn solo
(special import only) sc EMB 10163
f.s.   (D20)

DAVID, JOHANN NEPOMUK (1895-1977)
Chaconne *Op.71 [13']
2.2.2.2. 4.2.3.0. timp,perc,
strings
study sc BREITKOPF-W PB 4897 f.s.
(D21)

Concerto for Organ and Orchestra, Op.
61 [20']
2fl,3trom,timp,perc,harp,strings,
org solo
study sc BREITKOPF-W PB 5070 f.s.
(D22)

Concerto for String Orchestra, No. 3,
Op. 74
string orch
study sc BREITKOPF-W PB 5072 f.s.,
perf mat rent   (D23)

Concerto for Violin and Orchestra,
No. 3, Op. 56 [20']
1+pic.1.1+bass clar.1. 2.1.1.0.
timp,perc,strings,vln solo
sc,pts BREITKOPF-W rent   (D24)

Concerto for Violin, Violoncello and
Orchestra, Op. 68
orch,vln solo,vcl solo
study sc BREITKOPF-W PB 4831 f.s.,
perf mat rent   (D25)

DAVID, THOMAS CHRISTIAN (1925-   )
Concerto for Organ and Orchestra
[15']
2+pic.2.2.2+contrabsn. 4.3.3.1.
timp,strings,org solo
solo pt DOBLINGER 02 313 f.s., sc,
pts DOBLINGER rent   (D26)

Concerto for 2 Violins and String
Orchestra [16']
string orch,2vln soli
sc,pts DOBLINGER rent   (D27)

DAVID, THOMAS CHRISTIAN (cont'd.)

Concerto Grosso [18']
string orch
sc,pts DOBLINGER rent   (D28)

DAVIES, PETER MAXWELL (1934-   )
Anakreontica, For Solo Voice And
Orchestra
orch,Mez solo
sc CHESTER f.s.   (D29)

Mirror Of Whitening Light, A [22']
1.1.1.1. 1.1.1.0. perc,cel,vln,
vla,vcl,db
min sc BOOSEY $14.00, perf mat rent
(D30)

Points And Dances From Taverner [18']
alto fl,clar,contrabsn,trp,timp,
hpsd,org,vla,vcl,gtr, alto trom
min sc BOOSEY $3.00, perf mat rent
(D31)

Revelation And Fall, For Solo Voice
And Orchestra
sc BOOSEY $40.00   (D32)

Shakespeare Music
1.1.2.1. 1.0.1.0. perc,gtr,vla,db
BOOSEY 862 min sc $6.25, sc $18.00,
pts rent   (D33)

Symphony [58']
2(pic,alto fl).2(English
horn).2(bass
clar).2(contrabsn). 4.3.3.0.
timp,perc,harp,cel,strings
min sc BOOSEY $23.00, perf mat rent
(D34)

DAVIS, ALLAN GERALD (1922-   )
Divertimento [25']
1.1.1.1. 2.2.0.0. strings
sc OXFORD 97.717 $20.00, perf mat
rent   (D35)

DAY THE ORCHESTRA PLAYED, THE, FOR
NARRATOR AND ORCHESTRA see Cacavas,
John

DE BELLIS, ENZO (1907-   )
Sonata for Violoncello, Piano and
Orchestra [20']
2.2.2.2. 2.2.0.0. timp,perc,
bells,strings,vcl solo,pno solo
sc ZANIBON 4749 rent, pts ZANIBON
4750 rent   (D36)

DE BERIOT, CHARLES-AUGUSTE
see BERIOT, CHARLES-AUGUSTE DE

DE CURTIS, ERNESTO
see CURTIS, ERNESTO DE

DE GRANDIS, RENATO (1927-   )
Melek Nato, Dal Cuore Luminoso
fl,11strings
TONOS 7224   (D37)

Signore Dal Volto Luminoso Alla
Terra, Il [9']
3.3.3.3. 3.4.3.1. harp,cel,hpsd&
pno,3perc,strings
sc ZERBONI 8252 f.s., pts ZERBONI
8253 rent   (D38)

DE KOVEN, (HENRY LOUIS) REGINALD
(1859-1920)
Robin Hood: Armorer's Song, For Solo
Voice And Orchestra
(Luck) LUCKS 02061 sc $5.00, set
$15.00, pts $.75, ea.   (D39)

Robin Hood: O Promise Me, For Solo
Voice And Orchestra
LUCKS 02238 pno-cond sc $1.00, set
$5.00, pts $.50, ea.   (D40)

DE MAYO, FELIPE
see MAYO, FELIPE DE

DE PABLO, LUIS
see PABLO, LUIS DE

DE PAR LES RUES, LA MEMOIRE, FOR FLUTE,
PIANO AND STRING ORCHESTRA see
Lenot, Jacques

DE PROFUNDIS see Pfundt, Reinhard

DE-TONATIONS, FOR BRASS QUINTET AND
ORCHESTRA see Bazelon, Irwin Allen

DE ZUCCOLI, G. (1887-1959)
Elevazione [6']
string orch,opt org
pts ZANIBON 2326 f.s.   (D41)

Notte Di Getsemani, La [14']
3.3.3.3. 4.3.2.1. timp,perc,cel,
harp,strings
sc CARISCH 19871 perf mat rent
(D42)

DEAREST BELIEVE see Giordani, Giuseppe,
Caro Mio Ben, For Solo Voice And
String Orchestra, [arr.]

DEATH AND TRANSFIGURATION see Strauss,
Richard, Tod Und Verklarung

DEATH OF CLEOPATRA, FOR SOLO VOICE AND
ORCHESTRA see Berlioz, Hector
(Louis), Mort De Cleopatre, La, For
Solo Voice And Orchestra

DEBARADEURS QUADRILLE see Strauss,
Josef

DEBAT DU CUER ET DU CORPS DE VILLON, LE
see Henkemans, Hans

DEBRIS see Benvenuti, Arrigo

DEBUSSY, CLAUDE (1862-1918)
Afternoon Of A Faun *see Prelude A
L'Apres-Midi D'Un Faune

Clair De Lune, [arr.]
(Luck) LUCKS 05334 sc $6.00, set
$10.00, pts $.75, ea.   (D43)
(Reed, Alfred) 1.1.2.1.2soprano
sax. 1.2.1.0. perc,harp,pno,
strings KALMUS A5480 sc $7.00,
perf mat rent, set $13.00, pts
$.75, ea.   (D44)

Danse Sacree Et Danse Profane, For
Harp And String Orchestra
string orch,harp solo
BROUDE BR. set $12.50, pts $1.75,
ea.   (D45)
LUCKS 00754 sc $6.75, set $9.50,
pts $.95, ea.   (D46)

Enfant Prodigue, L': Air De Lia, For
Solo Voice And Orchestra
LUCKS 02144 sc $4.00, set $13.50,
pts $.75, ea.   (D47)

Enfant Prodigue, L': Cortege Et Air
De Danse
KALMUS 3453 sc $8.00, set $23.00
(D48)

Jet D'Eau, Le, For Solo Voice And
Orchestra, [arr.]
3.2.2.2. 4.2.0.0. 2harp,cel,
strings,S solo [5'] KALMUS 3452
sc $7.00, set $22.00   (D49)

Mer, La
study sc INTERNAT. 2126 $10.50
(D50)
sc,quarto PETERS 9153 $90.00 (D51)
min sc ZEN-ON 892053 f.s. (D52)
LUCKS 05340 sc $30.00, set $70.00,
min sc $7.50, pts $3.25, ea.
(D53)
(Pommer) min sc PETERS 9153A $19.50
(D54)

Nocturnes
study sc INTERNAT. 1055 $9.50 (D55)
sc,quarto PETERS 9156 $60.00 (D56)
(Pommer) min sc PETERS 9156A $12.00
(D57)

Petite Suite, [arr.]
(Busser) 2.2.2.2. 2.2.0.0. timp,
perc,strings [13'] KALMUS 3454 sc
$25.00, set $35.00   (D58)

Prelude A l'Apres-Midi d'Un Faune
sc,quarto PETERS 9151 $60.00 (D59)
min sc ZEN-ON 892054 f.s. (D60)
"Afternoon Of A Faun" study sc
INTERNAT. 1090 $4.25   (D61)
"Prelude To The Afternoon Of A
Faun" 3.2+English horn.2.2.
4.0.0.0. 2harp,strings, antique
cymbal BROUDE BR. set $25.00, pts
$1.50, ea.   (D62)
(Pommer) min sc PETERS 9151A $14.50
(D63)

Prelude To The Afternoon Of A Faun
*see Prelude A L'Apres-Midi D'Un
Faune

Six Epigraphes Antiques, [arr.] [14']
(Escher, Rudolf) 4.2.2.1. 0.0.0.0.
perc,cel,2harp,strings DONEMUS
perf mat rent   (D64)

DECISIONS see Alsina, Carlos Roque

DECK THE HALLS
(Luck, Arthur) LUCKS HYMNS 1 set
$7.00, pts $.65, ea. contains also:
We Wish You A Merry Christmas (D65)

DECORATIONS ET DECOMPOSITION see Dijk,
Jan van

DECOUST, MICHEL (1936-   )
T.H.T. [12']
2.2.2.2. 2.2.1.1. perc,harp,
strings
SALABERT perf mat rent   (D66)

DEDALO see Turchi, Guido

DEDE, EDMUND (1829-1903)
Mephisto Masque, [arr.]
(Schuller, Gunther) 2.2.2.2.
2.2.2.0. timp,perc,strings,
euphonium/ophicleide solo [5']

DEDE, EDMUND (cont'd.)

MARGUN BP 2019 sc $4.50, pts
$10.00   (D67)

DEDICATION see Schumann, Robert
(Alexander), Widmung, For Solo
Voice And Orchestra, [arr.]

DEDICATIONS FOR ORCHESTRA see
Constantinides, Dinos Demetrios

DEDLER, ROCHUS (1779-1822)
Sinfonia in D [18']
2.0.0.0. 2.2.0.0. timp,strings
(Munster, Robert) ORLANDO rent
(D68)

DEDUKTIONEN see Bischof, Rainer

DEEP RIVER, [ARR.] see Luck, Andrew H.

DEFESCH, WILLIAM
see FESCH, WILLEM DE

DEGEN, JOHANNES (1910-   )
Impressiones Lapponicae *Op.24
2clar,2horn,perc,pno,2vln,2vcl,db
sc STIM perf mat rent   (D69)

Norbotten-Symphonie II [33'30"]
2.2.2.2. 3.3.3.1. timp,2perc,
strings
STIM   (D70)

Vier Temperamente, Die [17']
string orch
STIM   (D71)

DEH, TORNA, MIO BENE!, FOR SOLO VOICE
AND ORCHESTRA see Proch, Heinrich

DEIN BIN ICH see Mozart, Wolfgang
Amadeus, Re Pastore, Il: L'Amero
Saro Costante, For Solo Voice And
Orchestra

DEIN RATH IST WOHL GUT see Grieg,
Edvard Hagerup, Your Advice Is
Good, For Solo Voice And Orchestra,
[arr.]

DEJA VU, FOR PERCUSSION QUARTET AND
ORCHESTRA see Colgrass, Michael
(Charles)

DEKOVEN, REGINALD
see DE KOVEN, (HENRY LOUIS) REGINALD

DEL DIARIO DE UN PAPAGAYO see Smart,
Gary

DEL MORAL, PABLO
see MORAL, PABLO DEL

DEL TREDICI, DAVID (1937-   )
Alice Symphony, An [41']
2(2pic).2.2(clar in E
flat).2(contrabsn). 4.2.2.1.
timp,perc,strings,S solo, folk
group: 2sax, mand, banjo, acord
min sc BOOSEY f.s., perf mat rent
(D72)

Alice Symphony, An: The Lobster
Quadrille [13']
2(2pic).2.2(clar in E
flat).1(contrabsn). 4.2.2.1.
perc,strings,opt S solo, folk
group: 2sax, mand, banjo, acord
BOOSEY perf mat rent   (D73)

Syzygy [26']
0.2pic(fl,alto fl).2(2English
horn).2(bass
clar).2(contrabsn). 1.2.0.0.
tubular bells,strings,S solo
min sc BOOSEY $19.00, perf mat rent
(D74)

Vintage Alice, For Solo Voice And
Orchestra
1(pic).1.1(clar in E
flat).1.2sax. 2.1.1.0. timp,
perc,mand,banjo,acord,strings,S
solo
min sc BOOSEY 818 $28.00   (D75)

DELACOSTE, F.X.
Capriccio [10']
2.2.2.2. 2.0.0.0. timp,3perc,
strings
AMPHION perf mat rent   (D76)

DELALANDE, MICHEL-RICHARD (1657-1726)
Symphonies Pour Les Soupers Du Roi:
Deuxieme Caprice Ou Caprice Que
Le Roy Demandoit Souvent, [arr.]
(Paillard, J.F.) 2ob,bsn,hpsd,
strings sc,pts COSTALL f.s. (D77)

Symphonies Pour Les Soupers Du Roi:
Premier Caprice Ou Caprice De
Villers-Cotterets, [arr.]
(Paillard, J.F.) 2ob,bsn,3trp,timp,
hpsd,strings sc,pts COSTALL f.s.
(D78)

DELALANDE, MICHEL-RICHARD (cont'd.)

Symphonies Pour Les Soupers Du Roi:
Troisieme Caprice, [arr.]
(Paillard, J.F.) 2fl,2ob,2bsn,hpsd,
strings sc,pts COSTALL f.s. (D79)

Symphony No. 1 (from Symphonies De
Noel)
2ob,opt bsn,strings without vla,
kbd
KALMUS 5431 kbd pt $3.00, sc $3.00,
perf mat rent, set $10.00, pts
$1.00, ea.   (D80)

Symphony No. 2 (from Symphonies De
Noel)
2ob,opt bsn,strings without vla,
kbd
KALMUS 5432 kbd pt $5.00, sc $5.00,
perf mat rent, set $15.00, pts
$1.50, ea.   (D81)

Symphony No. 3 (from Symphonies De
Noel)
2ob,opt bsn,strings without vla,
kbd
KALMUS 5433 kbd pt $3.00, sc $3.00,
perf mat rent, set $10.00, pts
$1.00, ea.   (D82)

Symphony No. 4 (from Symphonies De
Noel)
2ob,opt bsn,strings without vla,
kbd
KALMUS 5434 kbd pt $5.00, sc $5.00,
perf mat rent, set $15.00, pts
$1.50, ea.   (D83)

DELAS, JOSE LUIS DE (1928-   )
Conjuntos [22']
fl,alto fl,ob,clar,horn,1perc,
harp,pno,vln,vla,vcl,db,
electronic tape
BREITKOPF-W perf mat rent   (D84)

Imago [14']
fl,alto fl,clar,bass clar,harp,
cel,pno,2perc,vln,vla,vcl
BREITKOPF-W perf mat rent   (D85)

DELDEN, LEX VAN (1919-   )
Allegretto [4']
2.0.0.0. 0.0.0.0. perc, strings
without vla, db
sc DONEMUS f.s., perf mat rent
(D86)

Bafadis *Op.103
3.3.3.3. 4.3.3.1. timp,perc,harp,
strings
MOLENAAR 14.1561.08 f.s.   (D87)

Concerto for 2 Saxophones and
Orchestra, Op. 91 [18']
2.0.2.2. 2.2.0.0. timp,strings,
2soprano sax soli
sc DONEMUS f.s., perf mat rent
(D88)

Concerto for Violin and Instrumental
Ensemble, Op. 104 [17']
2.3.3.3. 4.0.0.0. perc,vln solo
DONEMUS perf mat rent   (D89)

Musica Di Catasto *Op.108 [13']
string orch
DONEMUS   (D90)

Scherzo for Piano and Strings [3']
strings without vla, db, and pno
solo
sc DONEMUS f.s., perf mat rent
(D91)

Tij En Ontij *Op.52 [20']
2.2.2.2. 2.2.0.0. timp,perc,
strings
sc DONEMUS f.s., perf mat rent
(D92)

Trittico *Op.105 [15']
0.2.0.0. 2.0.0.0. strings
DONEMUS perf mat rent   (D93)

DELERUE, GEORGES (1925-   )
Concerto for Horn and String
Orchestra
string orch,horn solo
sc BILLAUDOT $39.00, perf mat rent
(D94)

DELFT, MARC VAN (1958-   )
Symphony No. 1, Op. 1 [37']
3.2.2.3. 4.3.3.1. 6perc,cel,
2harp,strings
DONEMUS f.s.   (D95)

DELIBES, LEO (1836-1891)
Coppelia: Valse De La Poupee Et
Czardas
LUCKS 07327 sc $6.50, set $18.00,
pts $.95, ea.   (D96)

Filles De Cadix, Les, For Solo Voice
And Orchestra
LUCKS 02006 sc $3.75, set $8.50,
pts $.75, ea.   (D97)

DELIBES, LEO (cont'd.)

Lakme: Ah! Viens Dans La Foret, For
Solo Voice And Orchestra
LUCKS 03421 set $12.00, pts $1.00,
ea.   (D98)

Lakme: Air Des Clochettes, For Solo
Voice And Orchestra
"Lakme: Bell Song" LUCKS 02005 sc
$4.75, set $9.50, pts $.75, ea.
(D99)

Lakme: Ballet Music
LUCKS 05171 sc $13.00, set $28.00,
pts $1.50, ea.   (D100)

Lakme: Bell Song *see Lakme: Air Des
Clochettes, For Solo Voice And
Orchestra

Lakme: Fantaisie Aux Divins
Mensonges, For Solo Voice And
Orchestra
LUCKS 02202 set $12.00, pts $1.00,
ea.   (D101)

Lakme: Pourquoi Dans Les Grands Bois,
For Solo Voice And Orchestra
LUCKS 02693 set $12.00, pts $1.00,
ea.   (D102)

Prelude And Mazurka
sets NOVELLO 9052-53 $37.25, and
up, sc NOVELLO 9051 $8.75, pts
NOVELLO 9592 $1.25, ea.   (D103)

Roi S'Amuse, Le
2.2.2.0. 0.2.0.0. perc,strings
sc,pts HARMONIA 2372 f.s.   (D104)

DELIUS, FREDERICK (1862-1934)
Concerto for Violoncello and
Orchestra
min sc BOOSEY 910 $7.50   (D105)

Four Songs For Voice And Orchestra
2.2.2.2. 4.2.0.0. timp,harp,
strings,solo voice
OXFORD perf mat rent   (D106)

Hassan: Intermezzo
see Three Orchestral Pieces

Hassan: Serenade
see Three Orchestral Pieces

Prelude And Idyll, For Solo Voices
And Orchestra
orch,SBar soli
min sc BOOSEY 901 $15.00   (D107)

Three Orchestral Pieces
min sc BOOSEY 23 $7.00
contains: Hassan: Intermezzo;
Hassan: Serenade; Village Romeo
And Juliet, A: The Walk To
Paradise Garden   (D108)

Village Romeo And Juliet, A: The Walk
To Paradise Garden
see Three Orchestral Pieces

DELLO JOIO, NORMAN (1913-   )
Arietta For Strings
string orch
MARKS sc $3.00, set $12.00, pts
$.75, ea.   (D109)

Colonial Variants
sc AMP $35.75   (D110)

DELUGE, LE: PRELUDE see Saint-Saens,
Camille

DEMI FORTUNE POLKA see Strauss, Johann,
[Jr.]

DEMOLIRER POLKA see Strauss, Johann,
[Jr.]

DENCKER, HELMUT (1944-   )
Musik Fur Orchester [10']
3.3+English horn.3+bass clar.2.
4.4.3.1. strings
MODERN 1915 rent   (D111)

DENHOFF, MICHAEL (1955-   )
Sinfonia [17']
3(pic).2+English horn.2.2.
3.3.3.1. 3perc,harp,pno,strings
BREITKOPF-W perf mat rent   (D112)

Tempus Impletum [16']
3.2+English horn.2+bass clar.3.
4.3.3.1. 2perc,pno,strings
BREITKOPF-W perf mat rent   (D113)

Umbrae In Memoriam B.A. Zimmermann,
For Violin, Violoncello And
Orchestra [17']
3(pic).2+English horn.2.2.
4.3.3.0. timp,2perc,pno,
strings,vln solo,vcl solo
BREITKOPF-W perf mat rent   (D114)

DENK ES, O SEELE, FOR SOLO VOICE AND
ORCHESTRA see Wolf, Hugo

DENNEN-SYMFONIE see Meulemans, Arthur,
Symphony No. 3

DENNISON, SAM (1926-   )
Lyric Piece And Rondo, For Tuba And
String Orchestra [8']
string orch,tuba solo
KALMUS 5557 sc $12.00, set $15.00
(D115)

DENZA, LUIGI (1846-1922)
Funiculi-Funicula, [arr.]
LUCKS 09163 set $13.00, pts $.75,
ea.   (D116)

DER DU VON DEM HIMMEL BIST, FOR SOLO
VOICE AND STRINGS see Hofmann,
Wolfgang

DERKSEN, BERNARD (1896-1965)
Liebeswerben
RIES f.s.   (D117)

DES TEUFELS LUSTSCHLOSS: OVERTURE see
Schubert, Franz (Peter)

DESAFIO II, FOR VIOLONCELLO AND STRING
ORCHESTRA see Nobre, Marlos

DESAFIO III, FOR VIOLIN AND STRING
ORCHESTRA see Nobre, Marlos

DESAFIO IV, FOR DOUBLE BASS AND STRING
ORCHESTRA see Nobre, Marlos

DESAFIO VII, FOR PIANO AND STRING
ORCHESTRA see Nobre, Marlos

DESERT POINT see Eliasson, Anders

DESHAYES, PROSPER-DIDIER
(ca. 1745-ca. 1815)
Symphony in D
(Metz, John R.) ("The Symphony",
Vol. D-X) sc GARLAND
ISBN 0-8240-3815-0 $90.00
contains also: Ozi, Etienne,
Symphonies Concertantes In B Flat
And In F (Griswold, Harold E.);
Devienne, Francois, Symphonies
Concertantes In F And B Flat (La
France, Albert; Read, Jesse;
Lott, R. Allen); Viotti, Giovanni
Battista, Symphonie Concertante
in B flat (White, Chappell)
(D118)

DESIGN see Rorem, Ned

DESIGNS see Constantinides, Dinos
Demetrios

DESORMES, I.C. (1841-1898)
Danse Napolitaine
1+pic.2.2.2. 2.2.3.0. perc,strings
KALMUS 5426 pno-cond sc $3.00,
perf mat rent, set $17.00, pts
$1.00, ea.   (D119)

Divertissement Espagnol [10']
2.1.2.1. 3.0.3.1. timp,perc,
strings
KALMUS A5323 sc $5.00, perf mat
rent, set $20.00, pts $1.50, ea.
(D120)

Marche De l'Armee Francaise Au Tonkin
1+pic.2.2.2. 2.2.3.0. perc,
strings
KALMUS A5500 sc $3.00, perf mat
rent, set $12.00, pts $.75, ea.
(D121)

Serenade De Mandolines
string orch
KALMUS 5427 pno-cond sc $3.00, set
$5.00, pts $1.00, ea.   (D122)

DESSAU, PAUL (1894-   )
Drei Intermezzi: Guernica [12']
ob d'amore,English horn,trom,
perc,pno,strings
(Schenker, Friedrich) DEUTSCHER
perf mat rent   (D123)

Music For String Instruments
15strings
sc BOTE f.s.   (D124)

DESTOUCHES, ANDRE-CARDINAL (1672-1749)
Isse: Suite
2.2.0.1. 0.1.0.0. cont,strings
OISEAU perf mat rent   (D125)

DETONI, DUBRAVKO (1937-   )
Vierundfunfzig Endungen [10'-12']
3orch
MODERN 2044   (D126)

DEURSEN, ANTON VAN (1922-   )
Chinese Nightingale, The
2.2.2.2. 2.2.0.0. timp,perc,pno,
strings
sc DONEMUS f.s., perf mat rent
(D127)

DEURSEN, ANTON VAN (cont'd.)

Music For A Non-Existing Musical
2.2.2.2. 2.2.0.0. timp,strings
sc DONEMUS f.s., perf mat rent
(D128)
Variations For 2 Instrumental Choirs
2.2.2.2. 2.1.0.0. timp,S rec,A
rec,T rec,B rec,strings
sc DONEMUS f.s., perf mat rent
(D129)
Variations For 4 Instrumental Choirs
2.2.2.2. 2.2.0.0. perc,4acord,S
rec,A rec,T rec,B rec,strings
sc DONEMUS f.s., perf mat rent
(D130)

DEUTSCHE HERZEN WALZER see Strauss,
Eduard

DEUTSCHE MARCHEN-SUITE see Dressel,
Erwin

DEUTSCHE REIGEN see Lohse, Fred

DEUTSCHE TANZE, DREI, K. 605 see
Mozart, Wolfgang Amadeus

DEUTSCHE TANZE, FUNF, MIT CODA UND
SIEBEN TRIOS see Schubert, Franz
(Peter)

DEUTSCHE TANZE, SECHS, K. 571 see
Mozart, Wolfgang Amadeus

DEUTSCHE TANZE, SECHS, MIN 36 see
Haydn, [Franz] Joseph

DEUTSCHE TANZE, ZWOLF see Beethoven,
Ludwig van

DEUTSCHE TANZE, ZWOLF, WOO. 8 see
Beethoven, Ludwig van

DEUTSCHER CHORAL see Maasz, Gerhard

DEUTSCHER MIT ZWEI TRIOS, [ARR.] see
Schubert, Franz (Peter)

DEUTSCHES BAROCK see Pachernegg, Alois

DEUTSCHLAND UBER ALLES see Haydn,
[Franz] Joseph

DEUTSCHMANN, GERHARD (1933-   )
Kleine Tanze Grosser Meister
string orch
sc HEINRICH. 8853 f.s., pts
HEINRICH. 8854 f.s.   (D131)

DEUX CAPRICES EN FORME DE VALSE, FOR
FLUTE AND STRING ORCHESTRA see
Bonneau, Paul

DEUX JOURNEES, LES: OVERTURE see
Cherubini, Luigi

DEUX MELODIES, FOR SOLO VOICE AND
ORCHESTRA see Diepenbrock, Alphons

DEUX NOCTURNES, FOR SOLO VOICE AND
ORCHESTRA see Hermans, Nico

DEVCIC, NATKO (1914-   )
Concerto for Solo Voice and
Instrumental Ensemble
Ondes Martenot,marimba,vibra,
4vln,4vla,T solo
sc GERIG BG 815 f.s.   (D132)

Istrian Suite
3.3.3.3. 4.2.3.1. timp,perc,
strings
DRUS.HRVAT.SKLAD. f.s.   (D133)

Non Nova
3.3.3.2. 4.3.3.0. timp,perc,
strings
DRUS.HRVAT.SKLAD. f.s.   (D134)

DEVIENNE, FRANCOIS (1759-1803)
Concerto for Clarinet and Orchestra,
Op. 25
0.2.0.0. 2.0.0.0. strings,clar
solo
(Balassa) sc,pts EULENBURG E10145
f.s.   (D135)
Concerto for Flute and Orchestra in
D, MIN 80 [25']
2ob,opt 2horn,strings,fl solo
(Bodensohn, E.) BODENS EA 51 f.s.
(D136)
Concerto for Flute and Orchestra, No.
2, in D [8']
2ob,2horn,strings,fl solo
INTERNAT. perf mat rent   (D137)
Concerto for Flute and Orchestra, No.
5, in G [20']
2ob,2horn,strings,fl solo
(Bodensohn, E.) BODENS EA 53 f.s.
(D138)
Concerto for Flute and Orchestra, No.
7, in E minor [17']
2ob,2horn,strings,fl solo
INTERNAT. perf mat rent   (D139)

DEVIENNE, FRANCOIS (cont'd.)

Symphonies Concertantes In F And B
Flat
see Deshayes, Prosper-Didier,
Symphony in D

DI CAPUA, EDUARDO (1864-1917)
O Sole Mio, For Solo Voice And
Orchestra, [arr.]
LUCKS 03139 set $7.50, pts $.75,
ea.   (D140)

DI MARTINO, ALADINO
see MARTINO, ALADINO DI

DIABOLIN POLKA see Strauss, Johann,
[Jr.]

DIAGONAALMUZIEK see Holt, Simeon ten

DIALOG, FOR TRUMPET AND STRING
ORCHESTRA see Metzler, Friedrich

DIAMOND, DAVID (1915-   )
Concerto for Violin and Orchestra,
No. 3 [16'30"]
4.3.4.3. 4.3.3.1. timp,perc,pno,
harp,strings,vln solo
PEER perf mat rent   (D141)

Romeo And Juliet
min sc BOOSEY HPS 680 $7.50   (D142)

DIARIO MARINO see Bruni-Tedeschi,
Alberto

DIBAK, IGOR (1947-   )
Divertimento, Op. 16 [14']
string orch
SLOV.HUD.FOND perf mat rent   (D143)

Fantasy for Viola and Orchestra [15']
2.2.2.2. 4.0.0.0. timp,4perc,
strings,vla solo
SLOV.HUD.FOND 0-345 perf mat rent
(D144)

DICE BENISSIMO, FOR SOLO VOICE AND
ORCHESTRA see Haydn, [Franz] Joseph

DICHTER UND BAUER: OVERTURE see Suppe,
Franz von

DIDO AND AENEAS: FAREWELL OF DIDO,
[ARR.] see Purcell, Henry

DIDO AND AENEAS: OVERTURE, [ARR.] see
Purcell, Henry

DIDO AND AENEAS: WHEN I AM LAID IN
EARTH, FOR SOLO VOICE AND STRING
ORCHESTRA see Purcell, Henry

...DIE STIMME, DIE ALTE, SCHWACHER
WERDENDE STIMME..., FOR SOLO VOICE,
VIOLONCELLO AND ORCHESTRA see
Wildberger, Jacques

DIEBISCHE ELSTER, DIE: OVERTURE see
Rossini, Gioacchino, Gazza Ladra,
La: Overture

DIEDERICH, FRITZ
Achtung, Los!
RIES f.s.   (D145)

DIEMENTE, EDWARD PHILIP (1923-   )
Dimensions II
strings,electronic tape
SEESAW perf mat rent   (D146)

DIEMER, EMMA LOU (1927-   )
Concert Piece for Organ and Orchestra
2.2.2.2. 4.3.3.1. timp,3perc,
strings,org solo
SEESAW perf mat rent   (D147)

Fairfax Festival Overture
3.2.2.2. 4.3.3.1. timp,perc,pno,
strings
SEESAW perf mat rent   (D148)

DIEPENBROCK, ALPHONS (1862-1921)
Abend, Der, For Solo Voice And
Orchestra [5']
2.3.3.2. 4.0.0.0. strings,S solo
see Drei Lieder, For Solo Voice And
Orchestra
sc DONEMUS f.s., perf mat rent
(D149)
Chats, Les, For Solo Voice And
Orchestra [5']
2.2.3.1. 4.0.0.0. strings,A solo
see Trois Melodies, For Solo Voice
And Orchestra
sc DONEMUS f.s., perf mat rent
(D150)
Clair De Lune, For Solo Voice And
Orchestra [5']
3.3.3.2. 2.0.0.0. strings without
db,S solo
see Deux Melodies, For Solo Voice
And Orchestra
sc DONEMUS f.s., perf mat rent
(D151)

DIEPENBROCK, ALPHONS (cont'd.)

Deux Melodies, For Solo Voice And
    Orchestra
    3.3.3.2. 2.0.0.0. strings without
    db,S solo sc DONEMUS f.s., perf
    mat rent
    contains: Clair De Lune, For Solo
        Voice And Orchestra; Écoutez La
        Chanson Bien Douce, For Solo
        Voice And Orchestra   (D152)

Drei Lieder, For Solo Voice And
    Orchestra
    2.3.3.2. 4.0.0.0. timp,harp,
    strings,S solo sc DONEMUS f.s.,
    perf mat rent
    contains: Abend, Der, For Solo
        Voice And Orchestra; Hinuber
        Wall'ich, For Solo Voice And
        Orchestra; Lied Der Spinnerin,
        For Solo Voice And Orchestra (D153)

Ecoutez La Chanson Bien Douce, For
    Solo Voice And Orchestra
    see Deux Melodies, For Solo Voice
        And Orchestra

En Sourdine, For Solo Voice And
    Orchestra, [arr.]
    (Andriessen, H.) 1.0.0.0. 1.0.0.0.
    12vln,4vla,4vcl,db,low solo sc
    DONEMUS f.s., perf mat rent
                                    (D154)

Es War Ein Alter Konig, For Solo
    Voice And Orchestra, [arr.]
    (Andriessen, H.) 2.1.0.0. 1.0.0.0.
    12vln,4vla,4vcl,2db,A/Bar solo
    [3'] sc DONEMUS f.s., perf mat
    rent   (D155)

Hinuber Wall'ich, For Solo Voice And
    Orchestra [5']
    2.2.3.2. 4.0.0.0. timp,harp,
    strings without db,S/T solo
    see Drei Lieder, For Solo Voice And
        Orchestra
    sc DONEMUS f.s., perf mat rent
                                    (D156)

Hymne An Die Nacht: Gehoben Ist Der
    Stern, For Solo Voice And
    Orchestra [16']
    2.2.3.2. 4.3.3.1. timp,perc,harp,
    strings,S solo
    sc DONEMUS f.s., perf mat rent
                                    (D157)

Hymne An Die Nacht: Muss Immer Der
    Morgen Wiederkommen, For Solo
    Voice And Orchestra [15']
    3.3.3.3. 4.2.3.1. timp,perc,
    2harp,strings,A solo
    sc DONEMUS f.s., perf mat rent
                                    (D158)

Hymne "Wenige Wissen Das Geheimniss
    Der Liebe, For Solo Voice And
    Orchestra
    2.3.3.2. 4.2.3.0. timp,strings,S/
    T solo
    sc DONEMUS f.s., perf mat rent
                                    (D159)

Ik Ben In Eenzaamheid Niet Meer
    Alleen *see Liederen Voor
    Sopraan En Orkest No. 2

Im Grossen Schweigen, For Solo Voice
    And Orchestra [20']
    3.3.4.2. 4.4.3.1. timp,perc,
    2harp,strings,Bar solo
    sc DONEMUS f.s., perf mat rent
                                    (D160)

Kann Ich Im Busen Heisse Wunsche
    Tragen?, For Solo Voice And
    Orchestra [5']
    2.1.2.2. 2.0.0.0. strings,A/Mez
    solo
    sc DONEMUS f.s., perf mat rent
                                    (D161)

Konig In Thule, Der, For Solo Voice
    And Orchestra [5']
    0.2.2.2. 4.1.3.0. timp,perc,
    strings,A solo
    see Twee Balladen, For Solo Voice
        And Orchestra
    sc DONEMUS f.s., perf mat rent
                                    (D162)

Lied Der Spinnerin, For Solo Voice
    And Orchestra
    see Drei Lieder, For Solo Voice And
        Orchestra

Lied Der Spinnerin, For Solo Voice
    And Strings [3']
    horn,S solo, strings without vcl,
    db
    sc DONEMUS f.s., perf mat rent
                                    (D163)

Liederen Voor Sopraan En Orkest No. 2
    [4']
    3.2.3.2. 4.0.0.1. timp,strings,S
    solo
    "Ik Ben In Eenzaamheid Niet Meer
        Alleen" sc DONEMUS f.s., perf mat
    rent   (D164)

DIEPENBROCK, ALPHONS (cont'd.)

Lydische Nacht, For Solo Voice And
    Orchestra [18']
    2.3.3.2. 4.3.3.0. timp,perc,harp,
    strings,Bar solo
    sc DONEMUS f.s., perf mat rent
                                    (D165)

Mignon, For Solo Voice And Orchestra
    [4']
    0.2.3.2. 4.0.0.0. strings without
    db,A solo
    see Twee Balladen, For Solo Voice
        And Orchestra
    sc DONEMUS f.s., perf mat rent
                                    (D166)

Nacht, Die, For Solo Voice And
    Orchestra [16']
    2.2.2.2. 4.1.3.1. timp,perc,harp,
    mand,strings,A/Mez solo
    sc DONEMUS f.s., perf mat rent
                                    (D167)

Puisque l'Aure Grandit, For Solo
    Voice And Orchestra
    see Trois Melodies, For Solo Voice
        And Orchestra

Recueillement, For Solo Voice And
    Orchestra
    see Trois Melodies, For Solo Voice
        And Orchestra

Trois Melodies, For Solo Voice And
    Orchestra
    2.2.3.1. 4.0.0.0. harp,strings,AMez
    soli sc DONEMUS f.s., perf mat
    rent
    contains: Chats, Les, For Solo
        Voice And Orchestra; Puisque
        l'Aure Grandit, For Solo Voice
        And Orchestra; Recueillement,
        For Solo Voice And Orchestra (D168)

Twee Balladen, For Solo Voice And
    Orchestra
    0.2.3.2. 4.1.3.0. timp,perc,
    strings,A solo sc DONEMUS f.s.,
    perf mat rent
    contains: Konig In Thule, Der,
        For Solo Voice And Orchestra;
        Mignon, For Solo Voice And
        Orchestra   (D169)

Vogels, De: Lied Van Den Hop, For
    Solo Voice And Orchestra
    3.3.3.2. 3.3.0.0. timp,perc,harp,
    strings,T solo
    sc DONEMUS f.s., perf mat rent
                                    (D170)

Vondel's Vaart Naar Agrippine, For
    Solo Voice And Orchestra [15']
    2.3.3.2. 4.3.3.1. timp,perc,harp,
    strings,Bar solo
    sc DONEMUS f.s., perf mat rent
                                    (D171)

Wenn Ich Ihn Nur Habe, For Solo Voice
    And Orchestra
    2.2.3.2. 4.0.0.0. timp,strings,S
    solo
    sc DONEMUS f.s., perf mat rent
                                    (D172)

Zij Sluimert, For Solo Voice And
    Orchestra
    0.1.3.1. 4.0.3.0. strings without
    vln,T solo
    sc DONEMUS f.s., perf mat rent
                                    (D173)

DIES EST LETITIE see Badings, Henk

DIETHELM, CASPAR (1926-   )
    Concerto Diletto I *Op.141a
        string orch
        sc,pts AMADEUS GM 634 f.s.   (D174)

    Concerto Diletto II *Op.141b
        string orch
        sc,pts AMADEUS GM 635 f.s.   (D175)

    Concerto for Clarinet and String
        Orchestra
        string orch,clar solo
        sc,pts AMADEUS BP 2451 f.s. (D176)

    Concerto for Recorder and String
        Orchestra
        string orch,A rec solo
        sc,pts AMADEUS BP 2654 f.s. (D177)

    Tripartita *Op.120
        string orch
        AMADEUS GM 550 sc f.s., pts rent
                                    (D178)

DIJK, JAN VAN (1918-   )
    About
        3.2.3.3. 4.3.3.1. timp,6perc,
        harp,strings
        sc DONEMUS f.s., perf mat rent
                                    (D179)

    Ad Aquam
        2.0.0.0. 0.1.0.0. pno,strings,vln
        solo,vcl solo
        sc DONEMUS f.s., perf mat rent
                                    (D180)

    Affiche Pour La Reouverture Du
        Magasin
        3.3.3.3. 4.3.3.1. timp,perc,harp,

DIJK, JAN VAN (cont'd.)

    strings
    sc DONEMUS f.s., perf mat rent
                                    (D181)

    Concertino for Piano and Orchestra,
        No. 3 [6']
        1.0.1.0.alto sax. 1.1.1.0.
        strings without vla, db, and
        pno solo
        sc DONEMUS f.s., perf mat rent
                                    (D182)

    Concertino for Piano and Orchestra,
        No. 4 [8'30"]
        2.0.0.1.sax. 1.1.0.0. strings,pno
        solo
        DONEMUS perf mat rent   (D183)

    Concerto for Organ and Orchestra
        *see Musica Per Organo
        Trentunisono I No. 4

    Concerto for Piano 4-Hands and
        Orchestra [17']
        2S rec,2A rec,perc,pno 4-hands
        soli, strings without vla, db
        sc DONEMUS f.s., perf mat rent
                                    (D184)

    Concerto For Pianola And Orchestra
        [13']
        3.2.2.2. 4.3.3.1. timp,2perc,
        strings, pianola solo
        DONEMUS perf mat rent   (D185)

    Coornhert-Variaties
        clar,strings
        sc DONEMUS f.s., perf mat rent
                                    (D186)

    Decorations Et Decomposition
        5-2.4-2.5-2.5-2. 8-4.4.4.1.
        8perc, pno 4-hands, org, cel,
        strings
        sc DONEMUS f.s., perf mat rent
                                    (D187)

    Duetto Accompagnato, For Saxophone,
        Trombone, And String Orchestra
        string orch,alto sax solo,trom
        solo
        sc DONEMUS f.s., perf mat rent
                                    (D188)

    Gebedt
        see Vijf Liederen, For Solo Voice
            And Orchestra

    Gebenedijd
        see Vijf Liederen, For Solo Voice
            And Orchestra

    Ik Die Bij De Sterren Sliep, For Solo
        Voice And Orchestra [4']
        2.2.3.3. 4.2.3.1. timp,harp,
        strings,Bar solo
        sc DONEMUS f.s., perf mat rent
                                    (D189)

    Interlude, For Violin And Orchestra
        [5']
        2.2.0.0. 0.1.0.0. strings without
        db,vln solo
        sc DONEMUS f.s., perf mat rent
                                    (D190)

    Jesu, Wijs En Wondermachtig
        see Vijf Liederen, For Solo Voice
            And Orchestra

    Kerstliedje
        see Vijf Liederen, For Solo Voice
            And Orchestra

    Kikvorst, De [20']
        3.2.2.2. 2.2.1.0. timp,3perc,opt
        pno,strings
        DONEMUS perf mat rent   (D191)

    Musica Per Organo Trentunisono I No.
        4 (Concerto for Organ and
        Orchestra) [7']
        orch,org solo
        sc DONEMUS f.s., perf mat rent
                                    (D192)

    Nachtstilte
        see Vijf Liederen, For Solo Voice
            And Orchestra

    Pastorale No. 2 [10']
        1.0.1.0. 0.1.1.0. pno,strings
        DONEMUS perf mat rent   (D193)

    Serenade
        1.0.0.0. 0.0.0.0. pno, strings
        without vla, db
        sc DONEMUS f.s., perf mat rent
                                    (D194)

    Sonatina
        2.0.0.0. 0.0.0.0. pno, strings
        without vla, db
        sc DONEMUS f.s., perf mat rent
                                    (D195)

    Theme and Variations, Op. 666 [4']
        3.3.2.3. 2.2.3.1. timp,2perc,
        harp,strings
        DONEMUS   (D196)

    Touch After Finish [10']
        0.0.0.0. 0.1.0.0. pno,org,strings
        sc DONEMUS f.s., perf mat rent
                                    (D197)

DIJK, JAN VAN (cont'd.)

Vijf Liederen, For Solo Voice And
  Orchestra
  1.0.0.0. 0.0.0.0. strings,Bar solo
  sc DONEMUS f.s., perf mat rent
  contains: Gebedt; Gebenedijd;
  Jesu, Wijs En Wondermachtig;
  Kerstliedje; Nachtstilte (D198)

Wat Ben Ik, Dan Een Vogel In De
  Schemering?, For Solo Voice And
  Orchestra [3']
  1.0.3.2. 4.0.0.0. strings,Bar
  solo
  sc DONEMUS f.s., perf mat rent
                                        (D199)

Wijding Aan Mijn Vader, For Solo
  Voice And Orchestra [5']
  3.2.3.3. 3.0.0.0. harp,strings,
  Bar solo
  sc DONEMUS f.s., perf mat rent
                                        (D200)

DIMENSIONS II see Diemente, Edward
  Philip

DINARA GIRL see Gotovac, Jakov

D'INDY, VINCENT
  see INDY, VINCENT D'

DINORAH QUADRILLE see Strauss, Johann,
  [Jr.]

DINORAH: SHADOW SONG see Meyerbeer,
  Giacomo, Pardon De Ploermel, Le:
  Ombre Legere, For Solo Voice And
  Orchestra

DIONISI, RENATO (1910-   )
  Concerto for 2 Pianos and String
    Orchestra [13'35"]
    string orch,2pno soli
    sc ZANIBON 5011 f.s(, pts ZANIBON
    5012 f.s.   (D201)

  Invenzione, For Flute And String
    Orchestra [8']
    string orch,fl solo
    sc,pts ZANIBON D321 rent   (D202)

  Luctus In Ludis, For Solo Voice And
    Orchestra [17']
    2.2.2.2. 2.2.0.0. timp,perc,pno,
    harp,strings,solo voice
    sc ZANIBON 5153 f.s., pts ZANIBON
    5154 f.s.   (D203)

  Piccolo Concerto, For Oboe And String
    Orchestra [14']
    string orch,ob solo
    sc,pts ZANIBON D258 rent   (D204)

  Preludio Sarabanda E Finale [7']
    string orch
    sc,pts ZANIBON D238 rent   (D205)

DIPHTHONG 2 see Astriab, Jan

DIPLOMAT MARCH, THE see Sousa, John
  Philip

DIRECTORATE MARCH, THE see Sousa, John
  Philip

DIRRIWACHTER, WIM (1937-   )
  Promvariaties, Variations On "The
    British Grenadiers" [18']
    2.2.2.2.2sax. 2.2.2.1. timp,
    2perc,strings
    DONEMUS perf mat rent   (D206)

DISCOURSE see Newman, Theodore Simon

DISGRESSIONS see Fontyn, Jacqueline

DISPA, ROBERT (1929-   )
  Concerto for Violin and String
    Orchestra
    string orch,vln solo
    sc DONEMUS f.s., perf mat rent
                                        (D207)

  Concerto for Violoncello and
    Orchestra [21']
    3.2.2.2. 4.3.0.0. timp,3perc,
    acord,2harp,strings,vcl solo
    DONEMUS   (D208)

  Poeme Pour Un Homme Bien-Aime [13']
    3.3.3.3. 4.3.3.1. timp,3perc,pno,
    2harp,strings
    DONEMUS   (D209)

DISPLAY, THE: DANCE SYMPHONY see
  Williamson, Malcolm

DISPUTATIONEN WALZER see Strauss, Josef

DISTRATTO, IL see Haydn, [Franz]
  Joseph, Symphony No. 60 in C

DITHYRAMB see Burton, S.

DITHYRAMBE see Strauss, Josef

DITTERSDORF, KARL DITTERS VON
  (1739-1799)
  Concerto for Harpsichord and
    Orchestra in B flat, MIN 78
    LUCKS 05174 sc $6.00, set $13.00,
    pts $1.50, ea.   (D210)

  Concerto for Piano and String
    Orchestra in A, MIN 84
    string orch,pno solo
    sc,pts HARMONIA 2035 f.s.   (D211)

  Concerto for Violin and Orchestra in
    D, MIN 1
    min sc EMB K214 $6.50   (D212)

  Periodical Overture
    2fl,2ob,strings
    KALMUS 5314 set $9.00, pts $1.00,
    ea., cmplt ed rent   (D213)

  Polonaise In D Major, [arr.]
    (Liebeskind, J.) KALMUS 5307 sc
    $2.50, perf mat rent, set $9.00,
    pts $.50, ea.   (D214)

  Rettung Der Andromeda Durch Perseus,
    Die *see Sinfonia in F, Krebs 76

  Rote Kappchen, Das: Overture [6']
    2.2.2.0.opt bsn. 2.0.0.0. strings
    (Munster, Robert) ORLANDO rent
                                        (D215)

  Sinfonia in A, Krebs 78
    2fl,2bsn,2horn,strings
    KALMUS 5219 sc $9.00, perf mat
    rent, set $16.00, pts $1.50, ea.
                                        (D216)

  Sinfonia in B flat, Krebs 74
    1.2.0.2. 2.2.0.0. timp,strings
    KALMUS 5216 sc $10.00, perf mat
    rent, set $21.00, pts $1.50, ea.
                                        (D217)

  Sinfonia in C, Krebs 93, [arr.]
    (Kretzschmar) 0.2.0.2. 2.0.0.0.
    strings KALMUS 5313 sc $12.00,
    perf mat rent, set $22.00, set
    $1.50, ea.   (D218)

  Sinfonia in C, MIN 85
    2.2.2.0. 0.2.0.0. perc,strings
    sc,pts HARMONIA 2080 f.s.   (D219)

  Sinfonia in D, Krebs 77
    1.2.0.2. 2.2.0.0. timp,strings
    KALMUS 5218 sc $12.00, perf mat
    rent, set $20.00, pts $1.50, ea.
                                        (D220)

  Sinfonia in E flat, Krebs 24, [arr.]
    (Liebeskind, J.) 2ob,2horn,strings
    KALMUS 5220 sc $7.00, perf mat
    rent, set $9.00, pts $1.00, ea.   (D221)

  Sinfonia in F, Krebs 70, [arr.]
    (Liebeskind, J.) 2ob,2horn,strings
    KALMUS 5221 sc $6.00, perf mat
    rent, set $9.00, pts $1.00, ea.   (D222)

  Sinfonia in F, Krebs 76
    2ob,2horn,strings
    KALMUS 5217 sc $10.00, perf mat
    rent, set $13.50, pts $1.50, ea.
                                        (D223)

  Sturz Phaetons, Der *see Sinfonia in
    B flat, Krebs 74

  Versteinerung Der Phineus, Die *see
    Sinfonia in D, Krebs 77

  Verwandlung Der Lycischen Bauern
    *see Sinfonia in A, Krebs 78

DITTRICH, PAUL-HEINZ (1930-   )
  Cantus I (Veranderungen Eines
    Chorales Von J.S. Bach, BWV 60)
    [22']
    2+alto fl.2+English horn.2+bass
    clar.2+contrabsn. 4.3.4.0.
    timp,2perc,pno,strings
    BREITKOPF-W perf mat rent   (D224)

  Cantus II - Unum Necessarium, For
    Solo Voice And Orchestra [20']
    3.3.3.3. 4.3.3.0.0. timp,2perc,
    electronic equipment,electronic
    tape,pno,strings without vln,
    vcl solo,S solo
    sc UNIVER. UE 16749 f.s., perf mat
    rent   (D225)

  Concert Avec Plusieurs Instruments
    No. 2, For Viola, Violoncello And
    Orchestra [20']
    3(pic,alto fl).0.3(bass clar).0.
    0.3.3.0. timp,2perc,perc,
    strings,vla solo,vcl solo
    BREITKOPF-W perf mat rent   (D226)

  Concert Avec Plusieurs Instruments
    No. 3, For Flute, Oboe And
    Orchestra [25']
    3.3.3.2. 4.3.3.0. timp,perc,pno,
    cel,harp,synthesizer,strings
    sc PETERS EP 5544 f.s., pts PETERS
    rent   (D227)

DITTRICH, PAUL-HEINZ (cont'd.)

  Engfuhrung [30']
    2.2.2.2. 2.2.2.0. timp,perc,elec
    org,strings,S solo, solo voices
    PETERS   (D228)

  Illuminations [22']
    3(pic).3(English horn).3(bass
    clar).3(contrabsn). 4.4.4.1.
    timp,3perc,cel&pno,strings
    sc UNIVER. UE 16636 f.s., perf mat
    rent   (D229)

DIVERGENZE see Cammarota, Carlo

DIVERSE DANCES see Gauldin, Robert

DIVERTEREND see Kockelmans, Gerard

DIVERTIMENTI, SEVENTEEN see Mozart,
  Wolfgang Amadeus

DIVERTIMENTO FUR DEN FASCHING-DIENSTAG
  see Eybler, Joseph

DIVERTIMENTO IN G, HOB. II:G1 see
  Haydn, [Franz] Joseph, Cassation in
  G

DIVERTIMENTO ZA SLAVKA OSTERCA see
  Petric, Ivo

DIVERTISSEMENT ESPAGNOL see Desormes,
  I.C.

DIVINA FORESTA, LA see Scalero, Rosario

1999 [DIX-NEUF CENT QUATRE-VINGT-DIX-
  NEUF], 4 PROPHETIES DE NOSTRADAMUS,
  FOR SOLO VOICE AND ORCHESTRA see
  Bon, Willem Frederik

DIXIE JOE
  Schwedische Hochzeitsreise [3']
    2.1.2.1. 2.3.2+bass trom.0. harp,
    gtr,timp,perc,strings
    ORLANDO rent   (D230)

  Sombrero [2']
    2alto sax,elec gtr,gtr,marimba/
    glock,perc,strings
    ORLANDO rent   (D231)

  Tripp-Trapp, Galopp [2']
    2.1.2.1. 2.3.2+opt bass trom.0.
    strings
    ORLANDO rent   (D232)

DLUGOSZEWSKI, LUCIA (1925-   )
  Abyss And Caress, For Trumpet And
    Orchestra [35']
    2.2.1.0. 1.0.2.0. 4vln,3vcl,trp
    solo, timbre pno
    MARGUN BP 2024 perf mat rent (D233)

  Amor Now Tilting Night [25']
    2.1.1.1. 1.2.1.0. 2perc,2vln,vla,
    vcl,db, timbre pno
    MARGUN BP 2025 perf mat rent (D234)

  Strange Tenderness Of Naked Leaping
    [25']
    2.0.0.0. 0.2.0.0. strings
    MARGUN BP 2001 perf mat rent (D235)

DOBRZYNSKI, IGNACY FELIKS (1807-1867)
  Symphony, Op. 15, in C minor
    see SYMPHONY IN POLAND, THE

DR. JEKYLL AND MR. HYDE: SUITE see
  Waxman, Franz

DOCTRINEN WALZER see Strauss, Eduard

DODGSON
  Russian Pieces
    sets NOVELLO 9055-56 $29.75, and
    up, sc NOVELLO 9054 $5.50, pts
    NOVELLO 9593 $1.50, ea.   (D236)

DODGSON, STEPHEN (1924-   )
  Concerto Da Camera No. 3 [15']
    2fl,strings,vln solo
    sc SCOTUS 253-9 f.s.   (D237)

  Concerto Da Camera No. 4 [22']
    strings,pno
    sc SCOTUS 258-X f.s.   (D238)

  Concerto Da Camera No. 5 [19']
    2ob,2bsn,strings
    sc SCOTUS 263-6 f.s.   (D239)

  Concerto for Bassoon and Orchestra
    [19']
    2ob,2horn,strings,bsn solo
    sc,pts SCOTUS 091-9 f.s.   (D240)

  Concerto for Guitar and Orchestra,
    No. 1 [19']
    1.0.3.1. 2.0.0.0. strings,gtr
    solo
    sc,pts SCOTUS 200-8 f.s.   (D241)

DODGSON, STEPHEN (cont'd.)

Concerto for Guitar and Orchestra,
No. 2 [22']
fl,2ob,ob d'amore,2clar,bsn,
3trom,perc,harp,strings,gtr
solo
sc,pts SCOTUS 205-9 f.s.   (D242)

Concerto for Viola da Gamba and
Orchestra [21']
fl,2ob,clar,bsn,2horn,strings,vla
da gamba solo
sc,pts SCOTUS 111-7 f.s.   (D243)

DOHL, FRIEDHELM (1936-   )
Ikaros [12']
2(pic).2(English
horn).2(contrabsn). 2.2.2.0.
3perc,strings
study sc BREITKOPF-W BG 1393 f.s.,
perf mat rent   (D244)

Symphony for Violoncello and
Orchestra
2.2.2.2. 2.2.2.1. 3perc,harp,
strings,vcl solo
[34'30"] sc MOECK 5241   (D245)

DOHNANYI, ERNST VON (1877-1960)
Konzertstuck for Violoncello and
Orchestra, Op. 12, in D
INTERNAT. perf mat rent   (D246)

DOKTOR FAUST: OVERTURE see Smetana,
Bedrich

DOLATSHAHI, DARIUSH
Mirage [15']
2.2.2.2. 4.4.4.1. timp,2perc,
electronic tape,strings
(score and tape available for
$50.00; parts and tape also for
rent) BOELKE-BOM   (D247)

DOLCE NELLA MEMORIA see Grasbeck,
Gottfrid

DOLCE RAGGIO DI SOLE PERDUTO, UN see
Ager, Klaus

DOMHARDT, GERD (1945-   )
Concerto for 2 Violins and Orchestra
3.2.2.2. 4.3.3.1. perc,cel,pno,
strings,2vln soli
sc DEUTSCHER 1439A f.s., pts
DEUTSCHER 1439B f.s.   (D248)

Kammersinfonie No. 2
12strings,perc
sc DEUTSCHER 1704 f.s., perf mat
rent   (D249)

Symphony No. 1
3.3.3.3. 4.3.3.1. timp,perc,pno,
strings
DEUTSCHER perf mat rent   (D250)

DOMINATION OF BLACK see Holloway, Robin

DOMINE MEUS SALUTIS MEAE, FOR SOLO
VOICE AND ORCHESTRA see Rieder,
Ambrosius

DOMINO NOIR, LE: OVERTURE see Auber,
Daniel-Francois-Esprit

DOMINUS REGIT ME see Beers, Jacques

DON ALONZO see Kletsch, Ludwig

DON CARLOS: ELLA GIAMMAI M'AMO, FOR
SOLO VOICE AND ORCHESTRA see Verdi,
Giuseppe

DON CARLOS: O DON FATALE, FOR SOLO
VOICE AND ORCHESTRA see Verdi,
Giuseppe

DON CARLOS: PER ME GIUNTO, O CARLO,
ASCOLTA, FOR SOLO VOICE AND
ORCHESTRA see Verdi, Giuseppe

DON GIOVANNI: BATTI, BATTI, O BEL
MASETTO, FOR SOLO VOICE AND
ORCHESTRA see Mozart, Wolfgang
Amadeus

DON GIOVANNI: DALLA SUA PACE, FOR SOLO
VOICE AND ORCHESTRA see Mozart,
Wolfgang Amadeus

DON GIOVANNI: DEH VIENI ALLA FINESTRA.
SERENADE, FOR SOLO VOICE AND
ORCHESTRA see Mozart, Wolfgang
Amadeus

DON GIOVANNI: FINCH' HAN DAL VINO, FOR
SOLO VOICE AND ORCHESTRA see
Mozart, Wolfgang Amadeus

DON GIOVANNI: FUGGI CRUDELE, FOR SOLO
VOICE AND ORCHESTRA see Mozart,
Wolfgang Amadeus

DON GIOVANNI: IL MIO TESORO, FOR SOLO
VOICE AND ORCHESTRA see Mozart,
Wolfgang Amadeus

DON GIOVANNI: LA CI DAREM LA MANO, FOR
SOLO VOICES AND ORCHESTRA see
Mozart, Wolfgang Amadeus

DON GIOVANNI: MADAMINA! IL CATALOGO,
FOR SOLO VOICE AND ORCHESTRA see
Mozart, Wolfgang Amadeus

DON GIOVANNI: MI TRADI QUELL'ALMA
INGRATA, FOR SOLO VOICE AND
ORCHESTRA see Mozart, Wolfgang
Amadeus

DON GIOVANNI: NON MI DIR BELL'IDOL MIO,
FOR SOLO VOICE AND ORCHESTRA see
Mozart, Wolfgang Amadeus

DON GIOVANNI: NOTTE E GIORNO, FOR SOLO
VOICE AND ORCHESTRA see Mozart,
Wolfgang Amadeus

DON GIOVANNI: OR SAI CHI L'ONORE, FOR
SOLO VOICE AND ORCHESTRA see
Mozart, Wolfgang Amadeus

DON GIOVANNI: OVERTURE see Mozart,
Wolfgang Amadeus

DON GIOVANNI: VEDRAI CARINO, FOR SOLO
VOICE AND ORCHESTRA see Mozart,
Wolfgang Amadeus

DON JUAN see Strauss, Richard

DON JUAN: OVERTURE see Mozart, Wolfgang
Amadeus, Don Giovanni: Overture

DON PASQUALE: BELLA SICCOME UN'ANGELO,
FOR SOLO VOICE AND ORCHESTRA see
Donizetti, Gaetano

DON PASQUALE: IN DER FREMDE WILL ICH
WEILEN, FOR SOLO VOICE AND
ORCHESTRA see Donizetti, Gaetano

DON PASQUALE: O DIESE GLUT IN BLICKEN,
FOR SOLO VOICE AND ORCHESTRA see
Donizetti, Gaetano

DON PASQUALE: OVERTURE see Donizetti,
Gaetano

DON PASQUALE: QUEL GUARDO IL CAVALIERE,
FOR SOLO VOICE AND ORCHESTRA see
Donizetti, Gaetano

DON PASQUALE: SCHON WIE EIN HOLDER
ENGEL see Donizetti, Gaetano, Don
Pasquale: Bella Siccome Un'Angelo,
For Solo Voice And Orchestra

DON PASQUALE: TORNAMI A DIR CHE M'AMI,
FOR SOLO VOICES AND ORCHESTRA see
Donizetti, Gaetano

DON QUICHOTTE: INTERLUDE NO. 1,
"SERENADE" see Massenet, Jules

DON QUICHOTTE: INTERLUDE NO. 2, "LA
TRISTESSE DE DULCINEE" see
Massenet, Jules

DON QUICHOTTE: SUITE see Nabokov,
Nicolas

DON QUICHOTTE SUITE see Telemann, Georg
Philipp

DON QUIXOTE see Strauss, Richard

DON QUIXOTE SUITE see Telemann, Georg
Philipp, Don Quichotte Suite

DONATI, PINO (1907-1975)
Notte, Divina Notte, For Solo Voice
And Orchestra [3']
1.1.1.1. 1.1.1.0. harp,strings,
solo voice
sc CARISCH 21781 perf mat rent
(D251)

Pastorale [8']
1.1.2.1. 2.1.0.1. harp,strings,
solo voice
manuscript CARISCH   (D252)

Pastorale for Solo Voice and
Orchestra [11']
1.1.2.1. 2.1.0.1. strings,A solo
manuscript CARISCH   (D253)

DONATONI, FRANCO (1927-   )
Concerto for Bassoon and String
Orchestra [16']
string orch,bsn solo
sc,pts ZANIBON D328 rent   (D254)

Overture [15'30"]
2+pic.2.2.2. 3.2.1.0. timp,drums,
strings
sc,pts ZANIBON D277 rent   (D255)

DONATONI, FRANCO (cont'd.)

Portrait, For Harpsichord And
Orchestra [18']
3.3.3.3. 3.3.3.1. marimba,vibra,
cel,pno,2harp,timp,perc,
strings,hpsd solo
sc ZERBONI 8337 f.s., perf mat rent
(D256)

DONAU-BLUMEN QUADRILLE see Lumbye, Hans
Christian

DONAUSTRAND, DU WALZERLAND see Kaiser-
Eric, W.

DONAUWEIBCHEN WALTZER see Strauss,
Johann, [Jr.]

DONEGAL see Brase, Fritz

DONIZETTI, GAETANO (1797-1848)
Anna Bolena: Overture
KALMUS A4784 sc $15.00, perf mat
rent, set $30.00, pts $1.50, ea.
(D257)

Concertino for Violin, Viola and
Orchestra in D minor
2fl,2horn,strings,vln solo,vla
solo
RARITIES perf mat rent   (D258)

Don Pasquale: Bella Siccome
Un'Angelo, For Solo Voice And
Orchestra [3']
2.2.0.2. 4.2.3.0. timp,strings,
Bar solo
LUCKS 03423 sc $5.00, set $12.00,
pts $1.00, ea.   (D259)
"Don Pasquale: Schon Wie Ein Holder
Engel" sc,pts LIENAU rent   (D260)

Don Pasquale: In Der Fremde Will Ich
Weilen, For Solo Voice And
Orchestra [7']
2.2.2.2. 2.2.1.0. timp,strings,T
solo
sc,pts LIENAU rent   (D261)

Don Pasquale: O Diese Glut In
Blicken, For Solo Voice And
Orchestra [6']
2.2.2.2. 4.2.3.0. timp,strings,S
solo
sc LIENAU f.s., rent   (D262)

Don Pasquale: Overture
LUCKS 08630 sc $7.50, set $22.00,
pts $1.40, ea.   (D263)

Don Pasquale: Quel Guardo Il
Cavaliere, For Solo Voice And
Orchestra
LUCKS 02451 sc $4.75, set $7.50,
pts $.75, ea.   (D264)

Don Pasquale: Schon Wie Ein Holder
Engel *see Don Pasquale: Bella
Siccome Un'Angelo, For Solo Voice
And Orchestra

Don Pasquale: Tornami A Dir Che
M'Ami, For Solo Voices And
Orchestra
LUCKS 03431 sc $3.75, set $7.50,
pts $.75, ea.   (D265)

Elisir d'Amore, L': Una Furtiva
Lagrima, For Solo Voice And
Orchestra
LUCKS 02101 sc $3.75, set $7.50,
pts $.75, ea.   (D266)

Favorita, La: O Mio Fernando, For
Solo Voice And Orchestra
LUCKS 02148 sc $5.75, set $11.50,
pts $.75, ea.   (D267)

Favorita, La: Overture
KALMUS A4801 sc $12.00, perf mat
rent, set $30.00, pts $1.50, ea.
(D268)

Favorita, La: Spirito Gentil, For
Solo Voice And Orchestra
LUCKS 02055 sc $3.75, set $7.50,
pts $.75, ea.   (D269)

Fille Du Regiment, La: Il Faut
Partir, For Solo Voice And
Orchestra
LUCKS 02302 sc $3.75, set $7.50,
pts $.75, ea.   (D270)

Linda Di Chamounix: O Luce Di Quest'
Anima, For Solo Voice And
Orchestra
LUCKS 02530 sc $9.50, set $11.50,
pts $.75, ea.   (D271)

Linda Di Chamounix: Overture
KALMUS A4828 sc $20.00, perf mat
rent, set $26.00, pts $1.50, ea.
(D272)

Lucia Di Lammermoor: Mad Scene *see
Lucia Di Lammermoor: Scena Della
Pazzia, For Solo Voice And
Orchestra

DONIZETTI, GAETANO (cont'd.)

Lucia Di Lammermoor: Regnava Nel
　Silenzio, For Solo Voice And
　Orchestra
　LUCKS 02384 sc $9.50, set $14.50,
　　pts $.95, ea.　　　　　　(D273)

Lucia Di Lammermoor: Scena Della
　Pazzia, For Solo Voice And
　Orchestra
　"Lucia Di Lammermoor: Mad Scene"
　LUCKS 02049 sc $8.75, set $11.50,
　　pts $.75, ea.　　　　　　(D274)

DONNA BIANCA, FOR SOLO VOICE AND
　ORCHESTRA see Sinigaglia, Leone

DONNA DIANA: OVERTURE see Reznicek,
　Emil Nikolaus von

DONNE CURIOSE, LE: OVERTURE see Wolf-
　Ferrari, Ermanno

DOPPELGESANG, FOR SOLO VOICES AND
　STRING ORCHESTRA see Goosen,
　Jacques

DORATI, ANTAL (1906-　　)
Concerto for Piano and Orchestra
　3.3.3.3. 4.3.3.1. timp,3perc,
　strings,pno solo
　sc ZERBONI 8178 f.s., pts ZERBONI
　8106 rent　　　　　　　　(D275)

Night Music, For Flute And Orchestra
　orch,fl solo
　min sc CHESTER $25.50　　　(D276)

DORFMUSIK see Paulsen, Helmut

DORFSCHWALBEN AUS OSTERREICH see
　Strauss, Josef

DORFSCHWALBEN AUS OSTERREICH, FOR SOLO
　VOICE AND ORCHESTRA see Strauss,
　Josef

DORIAN GRAY SUITE see Kox, Hans

DORILLA: BALLETTI see Vivaldi, Antonio

DORMEUR DU VAL, LE see Escher, Rudolf
　George

DORWARD, DAVID
Analogues [13']
　11strings soli
　SCOTUS 341-1 f.s.　　　　(D277)

Celebration Prelude [4']
　1.2.1.1. 2.2.0.0. timp,perc,
　strings
　sc SCOTUS 218-0 f.s.　　(D278)

Concerto for Piano and Orchestra
　[36']
　3.3.3.3. 4.3.3.1. 2timp,2perc,
　2harp,2db,pno solo
　SCOTUS 298-9 perf mat rent　(D279)

Concerto for Viola and Orchestra
　[16']
　2.2.2.2. 4.3.3.1. timp,perc,harp,
　strings,vla solo
　sc SCOTUS 233-4 f.s.　　(D280)

Concerto for Violin and String
　Orchestra [22']
　string orch,vln solo
　sc SCOTUS 268-7 f.s.　　(D281)

Concerto for Violoncello and String
　Orchestra [30']
　string orch,vcl solo
　sc SCOTUS 228-8 f.s.　　(D282)

Cooper Of Fife, The [8']
　2+pic.2.2.2+contrabsn. 4.3.3.1.
　timp,perc,strings
　sc SCOTUS 223-7 f.s.　　(D283)

Fanfare: The Declaration Of Arbroath:
　Freedom Is A Noble Thing, For
　Solo Voices And Orchestra [7']
　2+pic.2.2.2. 4.3.3.1. timp,perc,
　harp,strings,narrator&Bar solo
　sc SCOTUS 283-0 f.s.　　(D284)

Festivities [14']
　2+pic.2.2.2. 4.3.3.1. timp,3perc,
　harp,pno,strings
　sc SCOTUS 278-4 f.s.　　(D285)

Legend Of The Megaliths [14']
　2+pic.2.2.2. 4.3.3.1. timp,3perc,
　harp,pno,opt gtr,strings
　sc SCOTUS 288-1 f.s.　　(D286)

Ode [19']
　2.0.2.2. 2.0.0.0. timp,strings
　sc SCOTUS 293-8 f.s.　　(D287)

Picayune Suite [14']
　2.2.0.2. 2.0.0.0. strings
　sc SCOTUS 204-0 f.s.　　(D288)

DORWARD, DAVID (cont'd.)

Scottish Waltz [4']
　string orch
　sc SCOTUS 356-X f.s.　　(D289)

Sinfonietta [14']
　string orch
　sc SCOTUS 361-6 f.s.　　(D290)

Sonata Concertante [17']
　string orch
　sc SCOTUS 366-7 f.s.　　(D291)

Summer Interludes [12']
　2.2.2.2. 4.2.3.0. timp,2perc,
　harp,strings
　sc SCOTUS 214-8 f.s.　　(D292)

Symphony No. 1 [28']
　2.2.2.2. 4.3.3.1. timp,perc,harp,
　pno,strings
　sc SCOTUS 209-1 f.s.　　(D293)

Variations On An Old Scots Air
　perc,strings
　sc SCOTUS 371-3 f.s.　　(D294)

Violins Of Autumn, The [13']
　hpsd,strings,vln solo
　sc SCOTUS 219-9 f.s.　　(D295)

DOUBLE HELIX, FOR CLARINET, PIANO AND
　SYMPHONY ORCHESTRA see Manassen,
　Alex

DOUBLE PIECE see Newman, Theodore Simon

DOULEUR CHRETIENNE, LA, FOR SOLO VOICE
　AND ORCHESTRA see Bijl, Theo van
　der

DOUW, ANDRE (1951-　　)
Celebrations [8']
　2.2.2.2. 4.4.3.1. 2-3perc,strings
　DONEMUS f.s.　　　　　　(D296)

Styx [12']
　0.2.0.0. 2.0.0.0. strings
　DONEMUS sc f.s., pts rent　(D297)

Styx, For Violin And String Orchestra
　[17']
　string orch,vln solo
　DONEMUS　　　　　　　　　(D298)

Trois Chants Du Crepuscule, For Solo
　Voices And String Orchestra
　string orch,SS soli
　DONEMUS perf mat rent　　(D299)

DOWLAND, JOHN (1562-1626)
Five Pieces
　string orch
　LUCKS 01471 sc $3.00, set $4.00,
　　pts $.75, ea.　　　　　　(D300)

DR. BIRCHER UND ROSSI see Tischhauser,
　Franz

DRAGONS DE VILLARS, LES: OVERTURE see
　Maillart, Louis Aime

DRAMATIC STUDY see Podprocky, Jozef,
　Dramaticka Studia

DRAMATICKA STUDIA see Podprocky, Jozef

DRAMATISCHE OUVERTURE see Budde, Kurt

DREAM CHILDREN see Elgar, [Sir] Edward
　(William)

DREAM ON THE VOLGA: OVERTURE see
　Arensky, Anton Stepanovich

DREAM TUNNEL, FOR NARRATOR AND
　ORCHESTRA see Kraft, William

DREAMLAND see Mulder, Herman,
　Droomland, For Solo Voice And
　Orchestra

DREAMSONGS see Crosse, Gordon

DREAMSTREAMS, FOR FLUTE AND STRING
　ORCHESTRA see McCulloh, Byron B.

DREI ALTOSTERREICHER-MARSCHE see Kont,
　Paul

DREI DEUTSCHE TANZE see Schumann, Georg

DREI DIALOGE, FOR HORN AND STRINGS see
　Wolschina, Reinhard

DREI DUETTEN, FOR SOLO VOICES AND
　STRING ORCHESTRA see Badings, Henk

DREI GEISHA LIEDER, FOR SOLO VOICE AND
　ORCHESTRA see Verhaar, Ary

DREI GESANGE, FOR SOLO VOICE AND
　ORCHESTRA see Gilse, Jan van

DREI GESANGE, FOR SOLO VOICE AND
　STRINGS see Hofmann, Wolfgang

DREI GESANGE AUS R. TAGORE'S "DER
　GARTNER", FOR SOLO VOICE AND
　ORCHESTRA see Gilse, Jan van

DREI GESANGE AUS R. TAGORE'S
　"GITANJALI" see Gilse, Jan van

DREI INTERMEZZI: GUERNICA see Dessau,
　Paul

DREI INTRADEN ZU ADVENT UND WEIHNACHT
　see Altenburg, Michael

DREI LIEDER, FOR SOLO VOICE AND
　ORCHESTRA see Ellinger, Albert

DREI LIEDER, FOR SOLO VOICE AND
　ORCHESTRA see Diepenbrock, Alphons

DREI LIEDER, FOR SOLO VOICE AND STRINGS
　see Giltay, Berend

DREI LIEDER, [ARR.] see Brahms,
　Johannes

DREI MASURENTANZE see Brust, Herbert

DREI ROMANTISCHE LIEDER, FOR SOLO VOICE
　AND ORCHESTRA see Roos, Robert de

DREI SCHWEDISCHE VOLKSWEISEN see
　Kallstenius, Edvin

DREI STUCKE see Uhl, Alfred

DREI STUCKE, FOR VIOLONCELLO AND
　ORCHESTRA, [ARR.] see Offenbach,
　Jacques

DREI STUCKE: ANDANTE, LARGO, LARGHETTO,
　[ARR.] see Handel, George Frideric

DREI TANZE AUS DEM 14. JAHRHUNDERT see
　Niehaus, Manfred

DREI TEMPI see Kotscher, Edmund

DRESDEN, SEM (1881-1957)
Kerstlied, For Solo Voice And
　Orchestra
　3trom,perc,strings,med solo
　sc DONEMUS f.s., perf mat rent
　　　　　　　　　　　　　　(D301)

Rembrandt's "Saul En David", For Solo
　Voice And Orchestra [16']
　3.3.2.3. 4.3.3.0. timp, 2-3perc,
　harp,cel,strings,S solo
　sc DONEMUS f.s., perf mat rent
　　　　　　　　　　　　　　(D302)

DRESSEL, ERWIN (1909-　　)
Abendmusik *Op.33 [18']
　2.2.2.2. 2.2.0.0. timp,perc,
　strings
　RIES perf mat rent　　　(D303)

Abwandlungen Eines Altenglischen
　Volksliedes *Op.41 [15']
　3(pic).2+English horn.2+bass
　clar.2+contrabsn. 2.2.3.0.
　timp,2perc,harp,strings
　sc RIES f.s., perf mat rent　(D304)

Balladesker Marsch [4']
　2.2.2.2. 4.2.3.0. timp,perc,opt
　harp,strings
　sc RIES f.s., perf mat rent　(D305)

Canto Variato, For Violoncello And
　Orchestra [7']
　2.2.2.2. 2.2.1.0. timp,perc,harp,
　strings,vcl solo
　RIES perf mat rent　　　(D306)

Capriccio Ritmico [5']
　2.2.2.2. 4.2.3.0. timp,perc,harp,
　strings
　sc RIES f.s., perf mat rent　(D307)

Caprice Fantastique [11']
　3(pic).1+English horn.2.2.
　4.2.3.0. timp,perc,harp,strings
　sc RIES f.s., perf mat rent　(D308)

Cassation [16']
　2(pic).2.2.2. 2.2.1.0. timp,perc,
　strings
　sc RIES f.s., perf mat rent　(D309)

Concerto for Oboe, Clarinet, Bassoon
　and Orchestra [20']
　2(pic).1.1.1. 2.2.2.0. timp,
　2perc,harp,strings,ob solo,clar
　solo,bsn solo
　RIES perf mat rent　　　(D310)

Deutsche Marchen-Suite *Op.36 [13']
　2.2.2.2. 2.1.1.0. timp,perc,
　strings
　RIES perf mat rent　　　(D311)

Franzosische Ouverture [7']
　2(pic).2.2.2. 4.2.2.0. timp,perc,
　harp,strings

DRESSEL, ERWIN (cont'd.)

    sc RIES f.s., perf mat rent (D312)

    Freudiger Aufklang [5']
      2(pic).2.2.2. 4.2.3.0. timp,perc,
      harp,strings
      sc RIES f.s., perf mat rent (D313)

    Gardenia [5']
      2.2.2.2. 2.2.2.0. timp,perc,harp,
      strings
      sc RIES f.s., perf mat rent (D314)

    Harlekins Ouverture [5']
      2(pic).2.2.2. 4.2.3.0. timp,perc,
      strings
      sc RIES f.s., perf mat rent (D315)

    Heitere Begegnungen
      sc RIES f.s. (D316)

    Idyllische Suite [15']
      2(pic).1+English horn.2.2.
      2.2.3.0. timp,perc,harp,strings
      sc RIES f.s., perf mat rent (D317)

    Kapriolen Ouverture [7']
      2.2.2.2. 2.2.1.0. timp,perc,harp,
      strings
      RIES perf mat rent (D318)
      RIES f.s. (D319)

    Kleine Komodie *Op.63 [16']
      2(pic).2.2.2. 2.2.2.0. timp,perc,
      harp,strings
      RIES perf mat rent (D320)

    Kunterbunt *Op.40 [18']
      2(pic).2.2.2. 2.2.2.1. timp,perc,
      strings
      RIES perf mat rent (D321)

    Lyrische Tanze *Op.65 [27']
      string orch
      RIES perf mat rent (D322)

    Ouverture Zu Einem Marchenspiel
      *Op.47 [9']
      2.2.2.2. 2.2.1.0. timp,perc,harp,
      strings
      sc RIES f.s., perf mat rent (D323)

    Romanzetta [4']
      2.2.2.2. 2.2.1.0. perc,harp,
      strings
      RIES perf mat rent (D324)
      RIES f.s. (D325)

    Rondoburleske [7']
      2(pic).2.2.2. 2.2.1.0. timp,perc,
      strings
      sc RIES f.s., perf mat rent (D326)

    Schwarzwalder Uhren [8']
      2(pic).2(English horn).2.2.
      4.2.3.0. timp,2perc,harp,
      strings
      sc RIES f.s., perf mat rent (D327)

    Serenade No. 2 in E flat [14']
      string orch
      sc RIES f.s., perf mat rent (D328)

    Serenade, Op. 62 [25']
      string orch
      RIES perf mat rent (D329)

    Sinfonietta Serena [30']
      string orch
      RIES perf mat rent (D330)

    Suite Der Masken *Op.57 [16']
      2(pic).2.2.2. 2.2.1.0. timp,perc,
      harp,cel,strings
      RIES perf mat rent (D331)

    Tanzminiaturen [10']
      2.2.2.2. 2.2.1.0. perc,strings
      RIES perf mat rent (D332)
      RIES f.s. (D333)

    Variationen-Serenade, For Piano And
      Orchestra [11']
      2(pic).2.2.2. 2.2.2.0. timp,perc,
      strings,pno solo
      sc RIES f.s., perf mat rent (D334)

    Walzerreigen [5']
      2.2.2.2. 4.3.3.0. timp,perc,harp,
      strings
      RIES perf mat rent (D335)
      RIES f.s. (D336)

DREYFUS, GEORGE (1928-)
    Lawson's Mates
      sc ALLANS $5.00, perf mat rent
      (D337)

    Symphonie Concertante
      study sc ALLANS $6.25, perf mat
      rent (D338)

    Symphony No. 2
      study sc ALLANS $6.25, perf mat
      rent (D339)

DREYFUS, GEORGE (cont'd.)

    We Belong
      sc ALLANS $10.00, perf mat rent
      (D340)

DRIE CHINEESCHE LIEDEREN, FOR SOLO
VOICE AND ORCHESTRA see Pluister,
Simon

DRIE GEDICHTEN, FOR SOLO VOICE AND
ORCHESTRA see Voormolen, Alexander
Nicolas

DRIE KERSTLIEDEREN, FOR SOLO VOICE AND
ORCHESTRA see Badings, Henk

DRIE LATIJNSE MINNELIEDEREN, FOR SOLO
VOICE AND ORCHESTRA see Mul, Jan

DRIE LIEDEREN, FOR SOLO VOICE AND
ORCHESTRA see Andriessen, Willem

DRIE OUD-NEDERLANDSE LIEDEREN, FOR SOLO
VOICE AND ORCHESTRA see Horst,
Anton van der

DRIGO, RICCARDO (1846-1930)
    Airs De Ballet: Galop, [arr.]
      (Hoffmann) 2+pic.2.2.2. 4.2.3.1.
      timp,harp,strings KALMUS 5213
      pno-cond sc $1.00, set $20.00,
      pts $1.00, ea., cmplt ed rent
      (D341)

    Airs De Ballet: Pizzicato, [arr.]
      (Hoffmann) 2+pic.2.2.2. 4.2.3.1.
      timp,harp,strings KALMUS 5215
      pno-cond sc $1.00, set $11.00,
      pts $.60, ea., cmplt ed rent
      (D342)

    Airs De Ballet: Romance, [arr.]
      (Hoffmann) 2+pic.2.2.2. 4.2.3.1.
      timp,harp,strings KALMUS 5214
      pno-cond sc $2.00, set $15.00,
      pts $.60, ea., cmplt ed rent
      (D343)

    Bouton De Rose, Le: Tenebre E Luce
      [8']
      1+pic.2.2.2. 4.3.3.1. timp,perc,
      harp,strings
      pts ZANIBON 2214 rent (D344)

    Cachemirienne, La [7'30"]
      1+pic.1.2.2. 4.0.3.1. 2timp,bass
      drum,2perc,strings
      sc ZANIBON 4250 f.s., pts ZANIBON
      4251 f.s. (D345)

    Millions d'Arlequin, Les: Valse Des
      Alouettes
      LUCKS 10652 set $10.00, pts $.60,
      ea. (D346)

    Millions D'Arlequin, Les: Valse Des
      Alouettes, [arr.]
      (Hoffmann) 2+pic.2.2.2. 4.2.3.0.
      perc,strings KALMUS 5306 sc
      $9.00, perf mat rent, set $10.00,
      pts $.60, ea. (D347)

DRITTES SEEBILD "GEGEN NORDEN", FOR
SOLO VOICE AND ORCHESTRA see
Trojahn, Manfred

DROBNA GLASBA see Stuhec, Igor

DROOMLAND, FOR SOLO VOICE AND ORCHESTRA
see Mulder, Herman

DROSTE LIEDER, FOR SOLO VOICE AND
STRINGS see Hofmann, Wolfgang

DROTTNINGHOLMS-MUSIQUE see Roman, Johan
Helmich

DRUCKMAN, JACOB RAPHAEL (1928-)
    Chiaroscuro [16']
      3.3.3.2. 4.3.3.1. harp,pno,elec
      org,timp,strings, electric
      piano
      BOOSEY perf mat rent (D348)

    Concerto for Viola and Orchestra
      [18']
      2(pic).alto fl.2(English
      horn).3.2. 4.3.3.1. timp,perc,
      harp,pno,strings,vla solo
      BOOSEY perf mat rent (D349)

    Lamia, For Solo Voice And Orchestra
      [24']
      3.2.4.2. 4.3.2.1. timp,2perc,
      harp,org,strings,solo voice
      min sc BOOSEY HPS 933 $32.00 (D350)

DRUM ROLL SYMPHONY see Haydn, [Franz]
Joseph, Symphony No. 103 in E flat

DRUSCHETZKY, GEORG (1745-1819)
    Concerto for Oboe and Orchestra in B
      flat
      0.0.0.0. 2.0.0.0. strings,ob solo
      (Weinmann) sc,pts EULENBURG E10125
      f.s. (D351)

DU BIST see Verhaar, Ary

DU BIST DIE RUH, FOR SOLO VOICE AND
ORCHESTRA, [ARR.] see Schubert,
Franz (Peter)

DU BOIS, ROB
see BOIS, ROB DU

DU HAST IM BLICK see Funk, Franz

DUBINUSHKA see Rimsky-Korsakov, Nikolai

DUBOIS, PIERRE-MAX (1930-)
    Sonatina for Saxophone and Orchestra
      [8']
      1.0.1.1. 1.0.0.0. timp,perc,
      strings,alto sax solo
      LEDUC perf mat rent (D352)

DUBOIS, THEODORE (1837-1924)
    Suite Miniature
      2.2.2.2. 2.0.0.0. strings
      (in this edition timp and perc
      parts) KALMUS A3338 sc $8.00,
      perf mat rent, set $16.00, pts
      $1.75, ea. (D353)

DUCKWORTH
    Memories Of You *see Bruce

DUE CANTI see Wagner, Richard

DUE CANTI, FOR VIOLIN AND ORCHESTRA see
Ricci Signorini, Antonio

DUE COMPOSIZIONI see Bull, John

DUE DANZE see Camillucci, Guido

DUE FOSCARI, I: CABALETTA DI JACOPO,
FOR SOLO VOICE AND ORCHESTRA see
Verdi, Giuseppe

DUE IMPRESSIONI see Ricci Signorini,
Antonio

DUE INTERMEZZI see Spagnoli, G.

DUE INVENZIONI, FOR PIANO AND ORCHESTRA
see Gorini, Gino

DUE LAUDE, FOR SOLO VOICE AND ORCHESTRA
see Mortari, Virgilio

DUE LIRICHE, FOR SOLO VOICE AND
ORCHESTRA see Torri, M.

DUE LIRICHE TEDESCHE E UN CONGEDO DI
GIOSUE CARDUCCI, FOR SOLO VOICE AND
ORCHESTRA see Mannino, Franco

DUE MOMENTI INTIMI, FOR VIOLONCELLO AND
ORCHESTRA see Ricci Signorini,
Antonio

DUE NOTTURNI see Soresina, Alberto

DUE PAGINE D'ALBUM, FOR SOLO VOICE AND
STRING ORCHESTRA see Porrino, Ennio

DUE PEZZI see Ravanello, Oreste

DUE PEZZI, FOR VIOLIN AND ORCHESTRA see
Chailly, Luciano

DUE PEZZI: HUMORESKE, FOR HORN AND
ORCHESTRA see Sinigaglia, Leone

DUE PEZZI: LIED, FOR HORN AND ORCHESTRA
see Sinigaglia, Leone

DUE PEZZI SACRI see Malipiero, Riccardo

DUE PRELUDI see Caltabiano, Sebastiano

DUE SUPPOSTI CONTI, I (OR) LO SPOSO
SENZA MOGLIE: OVERTURE see
Cimarosa, Domenico

DUE TEMPI see Maegaard, Jan

DUETTO ACCOMPAGNATO, FOR SAXOPHONE,
TROMBONE, AND STRING ORCHESTRA see
Dijk, Jan van

DUISTERNIS see Mulder, Herman

DUKAS, PAUL (1865-1935)
    Apprenti Sorcier, L'
      "Sorcerer's Apprentice, The" study
      sc INTERNAT. 1089 $6.00 (D354)
      "Sorcerer's Apprentice, The" LUCKS
      05419 sc $15.00, set $45.00, min
      sc $5.00, pts $2.00, ea. (D355)

    Sorcerer's Apprentice, The *see
      Apprenti Sorcier, L'

    Symphony in C [38']
      3.3.2.2. 4.3.3.1. timp,strings
      KALMUS 5294 sc $60.00, perf mat
      rent, set $100.00, pts $4.00, ea.
      (D356)

DUKE OF BRUNSWICK'S ALMAN, THE see
Bull, John

DUKLA-BRANA SLOBODY see Andrasovan,
Tibor

DUKLA-THE GATE TO FREEDOM see
Andrasovan, Tibor, Dukla-Brana
Slobody

D'UNA SPOSA MESCHINELLA, FOR SOLO VOICE
AND ORCHESTRA see Haydn, [Franz]
Joseph

D'UNE QUI FAISAIT LA LONGUE see
Beekhuis, Hanna

DUO CONCERTANT SUR LES THEMES DES
"PURITAINS", FOR VIOLONCELLO,
DOUBLEBASS AND ORCHESTRA see
Bottesini, Giovanni

DUODECIMET, [ARR.] see Schnabel, Artur

DUODECIMET NO. 1 see Mertens, Hardy

DUPAK see Cikker, Jan

DUPARC, HENRI (1848-1933)
Au Pays Ou Se Fait La Guerre, For
Solo Voice And Orchestra
LUCKS 03059 sc $8.00, set $15.00,
pts $1.25, ea.　　　　　(D357)

Extase, For Solo Voice And Orchestra
LUCKS 02679 sc $5.00, set $13.00,
pts $1.00, ea.　　　　　(D358)

Invitation Au Voyage, L', For Solo
Voice And Orchestra
LUCKS 02678 sc $8.00, set $17.00,
pts $1.00, ea.　　　　　(D359)

Manoir De Rosemonde, Le, For Solo
Voice And Orchestra
LUCKS 03102 sc $3.75, set $9.50,
pts $.75, ea.　　　　　(D360)

Phidyle, For Solo Voice And Orchestra
LUCKS 02157 sc $4.00, set $12.00,
pts $.75, ea.　　　　　(D361)

Testament, For Solo Voice And
Orchestra
LUCKS 03061 sc $10.00, set $18.00,
pts $1.25, ea.　　　　　(D362)

Vague Et La Cloche, La, For Solo
Voice And Orchestra
LUCKS 03060 sc $15.00, set $22.00,
pts $1.25, ea.　　　　　(D363)

Vie Anterieure, La, For Solo Voice
And Orchestra
LUCKS 03058 sc $4.00, set $9.00,
pts $.75, ea.　　　　　(D364)

DURKO, ZSOLT (1934-　　)
Turner Illustrations, For Violin And
Instrumental Ensemble
14inst,vln solo
(special import only) sc EMB 10208
f.s.　　　　　(D365)

DUSAPIN, PASCAL (1955-　　)
Bal, Le [10']
1.2.2.1.soprano sax. 1.1.1.1.
3vcl,db
JOBERT perf mat rent　　　(D366)

Souvenir Du Silence [9']
7vln,3vla,2vcl,2db
MODERN 2030 rent　　　　(D367)

Timee
JOBERT perf mat rent　　　(D368)

DUSTERE ANMUT see Komorous, Rudolf

DUTILLEUX, HENRI (1916-　　)
Timbres, Espace, Mouvement
4.4.4.4. 4.3.3.1. timp,perc,cel,
harp,strings without vln,vla
HEUGEL study sc $47.50, pts rent
　　　　　(D369)

DUTTON, BRENTON PRICE (1950-　　)
Symphony No. 2
2.2.3.2. 4.3.3.1. perc,strings
SEESAW perf mat rent　　　(D370)

DUVERNOY, CHARLES (1766-1845)
Concerto for Clarinet and Orchestra,
No. 3, in B flat
0.2.0.0. 2.0.0.0. strings,clar
solo
(Fodor) sc,pts EULENBURG E10131
f.s.　　　　　(D371)

DUVOSEL, LIEVEN (1877-1956)
Morgen, Der [8']
2+pic.2+English horn.2+bass
clar.2. 4.3.3.1. timp,3perc,
harp,strings
BREITKOPF-W perf mat rent　(D372)

DVE VDOVY: SAMOSTATNE VLADNU JA VSEMI,
FOR SOLO VOICE AND ORCHESTRA see
Smetana, Bedrich

DVORAK, ANTONIN (1841-1904)
Concerto for Violin and Orchestra,
Op. 53, in A minor
LUCKS 00401 sc $22.00, set $40.00,
min sc $4.00, pts $2.25, ea.
　　　　　(D373)

Concerto for Violoncello and
Orchestra, Op. 104, in B minor
min sc ZEN-ON 891441 f.s.　(D374)
LUCKS 00630 sc $15.00, set $23.00,
min sc $5.00, pts $1.40, ea.
　　　　　(D375)

Cypresses, The, [arr.]
(Suk) string orch KALMUS 5337 sc
$9.00, perf mat rent, set $10.00,
pts $2.00, ea.　　　　　(D376)

Festival March *Op.54a
KALMUS A 4577 sc $7.00, perf mat
rent, set $15.00, pts $.75, ea.
　　　　　(D377)

From The Bohemian Forest: Silent
Woods, For Violoncello And
Orchestra, [arr.] *Op.68,No.5
"Waldesruhe" 1.0.2.2. 1.0.0.0.
strings,vcl solo [6'] INTERNAT.
perf mat rent　　　　　(D378)
"Waldesruhe" LUCKS 00634 sc $4.00,
set $11.50, pts $.95, ea.　(D379)

From The New World　*see Symphony,
Op. 95, in E minor

Gipsy Songs: Songs My Mother Taught
Me, For Solo Voice And Orchestra,
[arr.]
LUCKS 02361 set $7.50, pts $.75,
ea.　　　　　(D380)

Golden Spinning Wheel, The　*Op.109
[20']
2.3.2.3. 4.2.3.1. timp,perc,harp,
strings
KALMUS 5200 sc $20.00, perf mat
rent, set $40.00, pts $1.50, ea.
　　　　　(D381)

Hero's Song　*Op.111 [25']
2.2.2.2. 4.2.3.1. timp,perc,
strings
KALMUS 5199 sc $20.00, perf mat
rent, set $35.00, pts $1.50, ea.
　　　　　(D382)

Humoresque, Op. 101, No. 7, [arr.]
[5']
2.2.2.2. 2.2.1.0. timp,harp,
strings
(Schmid) KALMUS A1434 sc $3.00,
perf mat rent, set $12.00, pts
$.60, ea.　　　　　(D383)

Husitska Overture　*Op.67
LUCKS 05424 sc $12.00, set $18.00,
pts $1.40, ea.　　　　　(D384)

Midday Witch　*Op.108 [15']
3.2.3.2. 4.2.3.1. timp,perc,
strings
KALMUS 5358 sc $12.00, perf mat
rent, set $22.00, pts $1.00, ea.
　　　　　(D385)

Notturno, Op. 40, in B
string orch
LUCKS 01472 sc $3.00, set $5.75,
pts $1.15, ea.　　　　　(D386)

Othello Overture　*Op.93 [13']
2.3.3.2. 4.2.3.1. timp,perc,harp,
strings
KALMUS 5295 sc $20.00, perf mat
rent, set $25.00, pts $1.00, ea.
　　　　　(D387)

Romance for Violin and Orchestra, Op.
11
LUCKS 05193 sc $12.00, set $15.00,
pts $1.00, ea.　　　　　(D388)

Rusalka: Song To The Moon, For Solo
Voice And Orchestra
LUCKS 02359 sc $6.00, set $7.50,
pts $.75, ea.　　　　　(D389)

Serenade, Op. 22, in E
LUCKS 05195 sc $6.00, set $8.75,
pts $1.75, ea.　　　　　(D390)

Serenade, Op. 44, in D minor
pts INTERNAT. 1397 $17.75, min sc
INTERNAT. 1399 $6.00　　(D391)
LUCKS 10669 set $15.00, min sc
$3.50　　　　　(D392)

Slavonic Dance, Op. 72, No. 2, [arr.]
(Richter, Lynne H.) string orch
[4'30"] KENSING. sc $4.50, pts
$1.50, ea.　　　　　(D393)

Slavonic Dances, Nos. 4 And 6
sets NOVELLO 9058-59 $41.75, and
up, sc NOVELLO 9057 $12.50, pts
NOVELLO 9594 $1.00, ea.　(D394)

DVORAK, ANTONIN (cont'd.)

Slavonic Dances, Op. 46
min sc ZEN-ON 891451 f.s.　(D395)

Suite, Op. 39 [25']
2.2+English horn.2.2. 2.2.0.0.
timp,strings
sc,pts LIENAU f.s.　　　　(D396)

Symphony, Op. 70, in D minor
min sc ZEN-ON 891407 f.s.　(D397)

Symphony, Op. 88, in G
min sc ZEN-ON 891408 f.s.　(D398)
LUCKS 08664 sc $25.00, set $47.00,
min sc $6.00, pts $2.75, ea.
　　　　　(D399)

Symphony, Op. 95, in E minor
pts BROUDE BR. $2.75　　　(D400)
min sc ZEN-ON 891409 f.s.　(D401)

Two Waltzes, [arr.] (from Op. 54,
Nos. 1 And 4)
string orch sc,pts AMADEUS GM 651
f.s.　　　　　(D402)

Vanda　*Op.25 [10']
2.2.2.2. 4.2.3.0. timp,strings
KALMUS 5296 sc $12.00, perf mat
rent, set $19.00, pts $1.00, ea.
　　　　　(D403)

Waldesruhe　*see From The Bohemian
Forest: Silent Woods, For
Violoncello And Orchestra, [arr.]

Wild Dove, The　*see Wood Dove

Wood Dove　*Op.110 [18']
3.3.3.2. 4.2.3.1. timp,perc,harp,
strings
"Wild Dove, The" KALMUS 5357 sc
$18.00, perf mat rent, set
$27.00, pts $1.00, ea.　　(D404)

DYKES
Eternal Father Strong To Save
(Luck, Arthur) LUCKS HYMNS 6 set
$9.50, pts $.65, ea. contains
also: Hemy, Faith Of Our Fathers
　　　　　(D405)

Holy, Holy, Holy
see Warren, George William, God Of
Our Fathers

E

E-A-D-G - BLUES see Hudec, Jiri

E-A-D-G - BOOGIE see Hudec, Jiri

EAGLES see Rorem, Ned

EARLY AMERICAN SAMPLER, AN see La
    Montaine, John

EARLY ONE MORNING, FOR PIANO AND
    ORCHESTRA see Scott, Cyril Meir

EARTH COLORS see Selig, Robert,
    Symphony No. 2

EAST SLOVAKIAN RECRUITING SONG see
    Cikker, Jan, Vychodoslovensky
    Verbunk

EASTER STANZAS, FOR SOLO VOICE AND
    ORCHESTRA see Rowland, David

EASY DANCES FOR STRINGS see Boccherini,
    Luigi

EBBE SKAMMELSSON-VARIATIONER see
    Lundin, Dag

EBEL, ARNOLD (1883-1963)
    Sinfonietta Giocosa *Op.39 [35']
        3(pic).2+English horn.2+bass
        clar.2+contrabsn. 4.3.3.1.
        timp,2perc,strings
        RIES perf mat rent   (E1)

EBENHOH, HORST (1930-   )
    Concerto for Percussion and
        Orchestra, Op. 39 [19']
        2+pic.2.2.2+contrabsn. 3.3.3.0.
        timp,strings,2perc soli
        sc,pts DOBLINGER rent   (E2)

    Divertimento, Op. 41 [11']
        string orch
        sc,pts DOBLINGER rent   (E3)

    Kleine Festmusik *Op.45,No.1 [5']
        1.1.3.0. 1.2.0.0. timp,perc,harp,
        strings
        sc,pts DOBLINGER rent   (E4)

EBERHARD, DENNIS (1943-   )
    Ephrata, For Four Percussion Soli And
        Orchestra
        MARGUN   (E5)

    Marginals [15']
        4trom,strings
        MARGUN BP 2002 perf mat rent (E6)

EBERLE, FREDERICK (1853-1930)
    Paraphrase On "A Bird Sang In The
        Linden Tree", Op. 48, [arr.]
        *see Paraphrase On "Ein Voglein
        Sang Im Lindenbaum", Op. 48,
        [arr.]

    Paraphrase On "Ein Voglein Sang Im
        Lindenbaum", Op. 48, [arr.]
        2(pic).2.2.2. 4.2.3.0. timp,perc,
        strings KALMUS A5510 sc $2.00,
        perf mat rent, set $11.00, pts
        $.50, ea.   (E7)
        (Eberle) "Paraphrase On "A Bird
        Sang In The Linden Tree", Op. 48,
        [arr.]" 2+pic.2.2.2. 4.2.3.0.
        timp,perc,strings KALMUS A4580 sc
        $3.00, set $10.00, pts $.50, ea.
                                    (E8)

EBERLIN, JOHANN ERNST (1702-1762)
    Symphonies, Three
        see SALZBURG, PART 2

EBERT, WOLFGANG (1920-   )
    Alten Segelschiffe Traumen, Die, For
        Solo Voice And Orchestra [4']
        2.2.2.2. 4.2.3.0. timp,perc,harp,
        strings,Bar solo
        ORLANDO rent   (E9)

    Auf Dem Canale Grande, For Solo Voice
        And Orchestra [3']
        2.2.2.2. 2.2.1.0. perc,harp,
        strings,S solo
        ORLANDO rent   (E10)

    Lied Vom Fischer Fidolin, Das, For
        Solo Voice And Orchestra [3']
        2.2.2.2. 4.2.3.0. timp,perc,harp,
        strings,Mez solo
        ORLANDO rent   (E11)

ECCLESIASTICAL SYMPHONIES see Wuorinen,
    Charles

ECCO SETTEMBRE, FOR SOLO VOICE AND
    ORCHESTRA see Pick-Mangiagalli,
    Riccardo

ECHOES OF TIME AND THE RIVER see Crumb,
    George

ECHOKONZERT, FOR VIOLONCELLO AND
    ORCHESTRA see Motte, Diether de la

ECHOS XIII see Amy, Gilbert

ECKLEBE, ALEXANDER (1904-   )
    Erinnerung An Mayrhofen [7']
        2.2.2.2. 4.2.3.0. timp,perc,harp,
        strings
        RIES perf mat rent   (E12)
        RIES f.s.   (E13)

    Grusse Aus Holstein [6']
        2.2.2.2. 4.2.3.0. timp,perc,harp,
        strings
        sc RIES f.s., perf mat rent (E14)

ECLIPSE, FOR 2 PIANOS AND INSTRUMENTAL
    ENSEMBLE see Gaussin, Allain

ECLIPSES see Miroglio, Francis

ECOPHONY see Russell, Armand King

ECOUTEZ LA CHANSON BIEN DOUCE, FOR SOLO
    VOICE AND ORCHESTRA see
    Diepenbrock, Alphons

EDER, HELMUT (1916-   )
    Concerto for Violoncello, Double Bass
        and Orchestra, Op. 70
        2(pic).2.2+bass clar.2. 3.2.2.0.
        perc,harp,vibra,cel,strings,vcl
        solo,db solo
        sc,pts DOBLINGER rent   (E15)

    Jubilatio *Op.68 [12']
        1.1.1.1. 1.0.0.0. perc,cel,xylo,
        vibra,strings
        study sc DOBLINGER STP. 417 f.s.,
        sc,pts DOBLINGER rent   (E16)

    Melodia-Ritmica, Op. 59, No. 2
        12vcl f.s. sc DOBLINGER 06 262, pts
        DOBLINGER 06 263, study sc
        DOBLINGER STP 377   (E17)

    Serenade, Op. 69 [20']
        6horn,46strings
        study sc DOBLINGER STP. 416 f.s.,
        sc,pts DOBLINGER rent   (E18)

    Wo Die Trompete Das Thema Beginnt',
        For Violoncello And Orchestra
        *Op.74 [25']
        3(pic).2(English horn).3(bass
        clar).2(contrabsn). 3.2.2.0.
        perc,cel,harp,strings,vcl solo
        DOBLINGER perf mat rent   (E19)

EDUARDO E CRISTINA: OVERTURE see
    Rossini, Gioacchino

EFFIE SUITE see Wilder, Alec, Suite for
    Tuba and Orchestra, No. 1

EGK, WERNER (1901-   )
    Spiegelzeit
        sc SCHOTTS ED 6919 $35.00   (E20)

EGLOGA, FOR FLUTE AND ORCHESTRA see
    Guerrini, Guido

EGMONT see Beethoven, Ludwig van

EGMONT: OVERTURE see Beethoven, Ludwig
    van

EGMONT: OVERTURE see Meulemans, Arthur

EGYPTIAN MARCH see Strauss, Johann,
    [Jr.], Egyptischer Marsch

EGYPTISCHER MARSCH see Strauss, Johann,
    [Jr.]

EHRENBERG, CARL EMIL THEODOR
    (1878-1962)
    Sinfonische Suite *Op.22 [40']
        3(pic).2+English horn.2.2.
        4.2.3.1. 3timp,2perc,harp,cel,
        strings
        RIES perf mat rent   (E21)

EHRET DIE FRAUEN WALZER see Strauss,
    Eduard

EI MIKAAN VIRTA see Sallinen, Aulis

EICHENDORFF-SUITE see Lothar, Mark

EICHINGER, HANS
    Intermezzo Virtuoso, For Piano And
        Orchestra [3']
        2(pic).2.2.2. 3.2.1.0. timp,perc,
        harp,cel,strings,pno solo
        RIES perf mat rent   (E22)

    Zwei Griechische Tanze [7']
        2.2.2.2. 4.2.3.0. timp,perc,harp,
        cel,opt gtr,strings
        RIES perf mat rent   (E23)

EIGHT DROPS IN THE OCEAN see Carpenter,
    Gary

EIGHT RUSSIAN FOLKSONGS see Liadov,
    Anatol Konstantinovich

EIGHT THREE-PART INVENTIONS see
    Koblitz, David

EILPOST see Kletsch, Ludwig

EIN HERZ EIN SINN see Strauss, Johann,
    [Jr.]

EINDELOOS see Badings, Henk

EINEM, GOTTFRIED VON (1918-   )
    Bruckner Dialogue [14']
        2.2.2.2. 4.3.3.1. timp,strings
        BOOSEY perf mat rent   (E24)

    Hunyady Laszlo *Op.59 [18']
        2.2.2.2. 2.2.2.0. timp,perc,
        strings
        study sc PETERS EP 8470 f.s., perf
        mat rent   (E25)

    Ludi Leopoldini *Op.55 [19']
        1.1.1.1. 1.1.1.0. timp,strings
        study sc PETERS EP 8452 f.s., perf
        mat rent   (E26)

EINIGE SCHWIERIGKEITEN BEI DER
    UBERWINDUNG DER ANGST see Gielen,
    Michael Andreas

EINSAME, DER, FOR SOLO VOICE AND
    ORCHESTRA see Grieg, Edvard Hagerup

EINZELSTUCKE, K. 409, 477, 527, 546 see
    Mozart, Wolfgang Amadeus

EINZUGSMARSCH DER BOJAREN see
    Halvorsen, Johan, Entry Of The
    Boyards

EISBRENNER, WERNER (1908-   )
    Spaziergang
        RIES f.s.   (E27)

    Vorspiel Zu Einer Komodie [5']
        2.2.2.2. 3.3.3.1. perc,harp,
        strings
        sc RIES f.s., perf mat rent (E28)

    Zwei Stucke: Allegro Und Adagio [13']
        string orch
        sc RIES f.s., perf mat rent (E29)

EISLER, HANNS (1898-1962)
    Suites Nos. 5, Op. 34 And No. 6, Op.
        40
        sc DEUTSCHER f.s.   (E30)

EISMA, WILL (1929-   )
    Brickwork *see Metselwerk

    Indian Summer, For English Horn And
        Orchestra [8'30"]
        6vln,2vla,2vcl,db,English horn
        solo
        DONEMUS   (E31)

    Little Lane, For Oboe And Orchestra
        [13']
        1.1.2.1. 2.1.1.0. 2perc,pno,6vln,
        3vla,3vcl,2db,ob solo
        sc DONEMUS f.s., perf mat rent
                                    (E32)

    Metselwerk [9']
        2.2.2.2. 2.2.1.0. harp,strings,
        perc solo
        "Brickwork" DONEMUS sc f.s., solo
        pt f.s., pts rent   (E33)

EKLUND, HANS (1927-   )
    Concerto for Horn and Orchestra
        timp,strings,horn solo
        sc GEHRMANS ENO 6060   (E34)

EL-DABH, HALIM (1921-   )
    Lucifer [30']
        1(pic).1(English horn).1.1.
        1.1.1.1. timp,perc,harp,pno,
        strings
        PETERS P66738 perf mat rent (E35)

    Unity At The Crossroad [8']
        3(pic).2.2.2. 2.2.2.0. timp,
        3perc,strings
        PETERS 6385 perf mat rent   (E36)

ELEGIA E CAPRICCIO, FOR VIOLIN,
    DOUBLEBASS AND STRING ORCHESTRA see
    Mortari, Virgilio

ELEGIA ROMANTICA, FOR SOLO VOICE AND
    ORCHESTRA see Nordio, Cesare

ELEGIAC MELODIES see Grieg, Edvard
    Hagerup

ELEGIAC WALTZ see Ridout, Alan

ELEGIE see Crucius, Heinz

ELEGY see Washburn, Robert Brooks

ELEGY FOR THE WHALE see Wilder, Alec

ELEKTROPHOR-POLKA see Strauss, Johann,
[Jr.]

ELEMENTI, GLI, FOR TROMBONE AND CHAMBER
ORCHESTRA see Constant, Marius

ELEMNTUM see Amdahl, Magne, Symphony
No. 1

ELENKA, FOR BALALAIKA, HARP AND
ORCHESTRA see Bresgen, Cesar

ELEVAZIONE see De Zuccoli, G.

ELEVAZIONE see Palafuti

ELEVAZIONE see Zipoli, Domenico

ELEVEN STUDIES FOR ELEVEN PLAYERS see
Rorem, Ned

ELFEN POLKA see Strauss, Johann, [Jr.]

ELFENLIED, FOR SOLO VOICE AND ORCHESTRA
see Wolf, Hugo

ELFERS, KONRAD
Goldrausch (composed with Reichel,
Gerd)
1.1.2.1. 3.3.3.0. timp,perc,harp,
pno,banjo,strings
ORLANDO rent   (E37)

ELGAR, [SIR] EDWARD (WILLIAM)
(1857-1934)
Dream Children *Op.43 [7']
2.2.2.2. 4.0.0.0. timp,harp,
strings
KALMUS 5164 sc $9.00, perf mat
rent, set $19.00, pts $1.00, ea.
(E38)
Elegy, Op. 58
string orch
LUCKS 01473 sc $3.00, set $4.75,
pts $.95, ea.   (E39)
Imperial March *Op.32 [8']
2.2.2.3. 4.3.3.1. timp,perc,
strings
KALMUS 5341 sc $6.00, perf mat
rent, set $18.00, pts $.75, ea.
(E40)
Introduction And Allegro, For String
Quartet And String Orchestra
*Op.47
string orch,string quar soli
LUCKS 08539 sc $8.00, set $12.00,
min sc $3.50, pts $1.50, ea.
(E41)
Light Of Life, The: Meditation [6']
2.2.2.3. 4.2.3.1. timp,perc,harp,
org,strings
KALMUS 5223 sc $5.00, perf mat
rent, set $18.00, pts $.75, ea.
(E42)
Pomp And Circumstance March No. 1 In
D
LUCKS 05460 sc $7.00, set $22.00,
pts $.95, ea.   (E43)
Pomp And Circumstance Marches Nos. 1-
5
min sc BOOSEY 905 $25.00   (E44)
Salut D'Amour *Op.12
LUCKS 05420 sc $4.00, set $10.00,
pts $.75, ea.   (E45)
Sea Pictures, For Solo Voice And
Orchestra
LUCKS 02532 sc $20.00, set $30.00,
pts $1.25, ea.   (E46)
Serenade, Op. 20, in E minor
string orch
BROUDE BR. set $10.00, pts $2.00,
ea.   (E47)
LUCKS 07671 sc $5.00, set $7.00,
pts $1.40, ea.   (E48)
Sospiri *Op.70
BREITKOPF-W perf mat rent   (E49)

ELIAS: DANN WERDEN DIE GERECHTEN
LEUCHTEN, FOR SOLO VOICE AND
ORCHESTRA see Mendelssohn-
Bartholdy, Felix

ELIAS: ES IST GENUG, FOR SOLO VOICE AND
ORCHESTRA see Mendelssohn-
Bartholdy, Felix

ELIAS: HERR GOTT ABRAHAMS, ISAAKS, UND
ISRAELS, FOR SOLO VOICE AND
ORCHESTRA see Mendelssohn-
Bartholdy, Felix

ELIAS: HORE, ISRAEL, FOR SOLO VOICE AND
ORCHESTRA see Mendelssohn-
Bartholdy, Felix

ELIAS: IST NICHT DES HERREN WORT WIE
EIN FEUER?, FOR SOLO VOICE AND
ORCHESTRA see Mendelssohn-
Bartholdy, Felix

ELIAS: JA, ES SOLLEN WOHL BERGE
WEICHEN, FOR SOLO VOICE AND
ORCHESTRA see Mendelssohn-
Bartholdy, Felix

ELIAS: SEI STILLE DEM HERRN UND WARTE
AUF IHN, FOR SOLO VOICE AND
ORCHESTRA see Mendelssohn-
Bartholdy, Felix

ELIAS: SO IHR MICH VON GANZEM HERZEN
SUCHET, FOR SOLO VOICE AND
ORCHESTRA see Mendelssohn-
Bartholdy, Felix

ELIASSON, ANDERS (1947-   )
Concerto for Bassoon and Orchestra
sc REIMERS f.s., perf mat rent
(E50)
Desert Point [13']
string orch
STIM   (E51)
Impronta [11']
2.2.2.2. 4.2.2.0. harp,strings
sc STIM perf mat rent   (E52)

ELIJAH: FOR THE MOUNTAINS SHALL DEPART
see Mendelssohn-Bartholdy, Felix,
Elias: Ja, Es Sollen Wohl Berge
Weichen, For Solo Voice And
Orchestra

ELIJAH: HEAR YE, ISRAEL see
Mendelssohn-Bartholdy, Felix,
Elias: Hore, Israel, For Solo Voice
And Orchestra

ELIJAH: IF WITH ALL YOUR HEARTS see
Mendelssohn-Bartholdy, Felix,
Elias: So Ihr Mich Von Ganzem
Herzen Suchet, For Solo Voice And
Orchestra

ELIJAH: IS NOT HIS WORD LIKE A FIRE?
see Mendelssohn-Bartholdy, Felix,
Elias: Ist Nicht Des Herren Wort
Wie Ein Feuer?, For Solo Voice And
Orchestra

ELIJAH: IT IS ENOUGH see Mendelssohn-
Bartholdy, Felix, Elias: Es Ist
Genug, For Solo Voice And Orchestra

ELIJAH: LORD GOD OF ABRAHAM see
Mendelssohn-Bartholdy, Felix,
Elias: Herr Gott Abrahams, Isaaks,
Und Israels, For Solo Voice And
Orchestra

ELIJAH: O REST IN THE LORD see
Mendelssohn-Bartholdy, Felix,
Elias: Sei Stille Dem Herrn Und
Warte Auf Ihn, For Solo Voice And
Orchestra

ELIJAH: THEN SHALL THE RIGHTEOUS SHINE
see Mendelssohn-Bartholdy, Felix,
Elias: Dann Werden Die Gerechten
Leuchten, For Solo Voice And
Orchestra

ELIS I see Goosen, Jacques

ELISEN POLKA see Strauss, Johann, [Jr.]

ELISIR D'AMORE, L': UNA FURTIVA
LAGRIMA, FOR SOLO VOICE AND
ORCHESTRA see Donizetti, Gaetano

ELIZA: OVERTURE see Cherubini, Luigi

ELJEN A MAGYAR POLKA see Strauss,
Johann, [Jr.]

ELLINGER, ALBERT (1910-1966)
Drei Lieder, For Solo Voice And
Orchestra [14']
2.2.2.2. 4.1.3.0. timp,harp,
strings,A solo
MANNHEIM E 13-60 f.s.   (E53)

ELLINGTON, EDWARD KENNEDY (DUKE)
(1899-1974)
Solitude, [arr.]
string orch
(Gould, Morton) BELWIN rent   (E54)

ELVERHOJ: AGNETES DROM see Kuhlau,
Friedrich

ELVERHOJ: OVERTURE see Kuhlau,
Friedrich

ELWELL, HERBERT (1898-1974)
Concert Suite, For Violin And
Orchestra
orch,vln solo
ACCURA perf mat rent   (E55)

EMMER, HUIB (1951-   )
Montage, For Piano And Instrumental
Ensemble [15']
0.2.3.0.2sax. 2.1.2.0. Hamm,
marimba,bass gtr,vln,2vla,vcl,
2db,pno solo
DONEMUS perf mat rent   (E56)
Rebelle, Le, For Solo Voice And
Orchestra [15']
0.2.2.0.tenor sax. 2.0.1.0.
4perc,pno,2vln,vla,2vcl,2db,S
solo
sc DONEMUS f.s., perf mat rent
(E57)

EMPEROR CONCERTO see Beethoven, Ludwig
van, Concerto for Piano and
Orchestra, No. 5, Op. 73, in E flat

EMPEROR WALTZ see Strauss, Johann,
[Jr.], Kaiser-Walzer

EMPEROR WALTZ, THE, [ARR.] see Strauss,
Johann, [Jr.], Kaiser-Walzer,
[arr.]

EMPFINDSAME MUSIK see Katzer, Georg

EN MEMORIA DE CHANO POZO see Amram,
David Werner

EN MINIATUR POLKA see Strauss, Eduard

EN PASSANT see Manneke, Daan

EN SOURDINE, FOR SOLO VOICE AND
ORCHESTRA, [ARR.] see Diepenbrock,
Alphons

ENCHANTED LAKE see Liadov, Anatol
Konstantinovich

END OF A SPECIMEN, THE see Meijering,
Chiel

ENDSPURT see Geisler, Willy

ENFANCE DU CHRIST, L': PRELUDE, PART
II, "LA FUITE EN EGYPTE" see
Berlioz, Hector (Louis)

ENFANT PRODIGUE, L': AIR DE LIA, FOR
SOLO VOICE AND ORCHESTRA see
Debussy, Claude

ENFANT PRODIGUE, L': CORTEGE ET AIR DE
DANSE see Debussy, Claude

ENGEL, DER, FOR SOLO VOICE AND
ORCHESTRA, [ARR.] see Wagner,
Richard

ENGELSE SUITE, FOR FLUTE AND ORCHESTRA
see Balkom, Sjef van

ENGFUHRUNG see Dittrich, Paul-Heinz

ENGLERT, GIUSEPPE GIORGIO (1925-   )
Caracol [8']
1.1.1.1. 1.0.1.0. strings
HINRICHSEN perf mat rent   (E58)

ENTERTAINMENT NO. 2 see Wilder, Alec

ENTERTAINMENT NO. 4 FOR HORN AND
CHAMBER ORCHESTRA see Wilder, Alec

ENTERTAINMENT NO. 6 see Wilder, Alec

ENTFUHRUNG AUS DEM SERAIL, DIE: ACH ICH
LIEBTE, FOR SOLO VOICE AND
ORCHESTRA see Mozart, Wolfgang
Amadeus

ENTFUHRUNG AUS DEM SERAIL, DIE: DURCH
ZARTLICHKEIT, FOR SOLO VOICE AND
ORCHESTRA see Mozart, Wolfgang
Amadeus

ENTFUHRUNG AUS DEM SERAIL, DIE: FRISCH
ZUM KAMPFE, FOR SOLO VOICE AND
ORCHESTRA see Mozart, Wolfgang
Amadeus

ENTFUHRUNG AUS DEM SERAIL, DIE: HA! WIE
WILL ICH TRIUMPHIEREN, FOR SOLO
VOICE AND ORCHESTRA see Mozart,
Wolfgang Amadeus

ENTFUHRUNG AUS DEM SERAIL, DIE: HIER
SOLL ICH DICH DENN SEHEN, FOR SOLO
VOICE AND ORCHESTRA see Mozart,
Wolfgang Amadeus

ENTFUHRUNG AUS DEM SERAIL, DIE: ICH
BAUE GANZ AUF DEINE STARKE, FOR
SOLO VOICE AND ORCHESTRA see
Mozart, Wolfgang Amadeus

ENTFUHRUNG AUS DEM SERAIL, DIE: MARTERN
ALLER ARTEN, FOR SOLO VOICE AND
ORCHESTRA see Mozart, Wolfgang
Amadeus

ESTHER: NOW PERSECUTION — TUNE YOUR HARPS, FOR SOLO VOICE AND ORCHESTRA see Handel, George Frideric

ESTRELLA DE SORIA: OVERTURE see Berwald, Franz

ESTRO ARMONICO, L', VOL. 1 see Vivaldi, Antonio

ESTRO ARMONICO, L', VOL. 2 see Vivaldi, Antonio

ESTUDIANTINA WALTZ see Waldteufel, Emil

ET INQUIETAM COR NOSTRUM see Benvenuti, Arrigo

ET L'IMAGINAIRE SE MIT A DANSER see Charpentier, Jacques

ETE, L', FOR SOLO VOICE AND ORCHESTRA see Bon, Willem Frederik

ETERNAL FATHER STRONG TO SAVE see Dykes

"ETOILE A PLEURE ROSE...,L'" see Escher, Rudolf George

ETOILE DU NORD, L': OVERTURE see Meyerbeer, Giacomo

ETT NARKES BONDBROLLOP see Ohlsson, Richard

ETTI, KARL (1912-   )
    Fantastische Ouverture [12']
        3.3.3.3. 4.3.3.1. timp,perc,
        strings
        sc,pts DOBLINGER rent   (E78)

    Introduktion Und Rondo Uber Ein
        Franzosisches Kinderlied [7']
        string orch
        DOBLINGER perf mat rent   (E79)

ETTORRE, IGINO (1928-   )
    Tema Con Variazioni [11']
        1+pic.1.1+bass clar.1. 1.1.0.0.
        timp,strings
        sc ZANIBON 5617 f.s., pts ZANIBON
        5618 f.s.   (E80)

EUCALYPTS, FOR FLUTE, HARP, OBOE AND ORCHESTRA see Takemitsu, Toru

EUGENE ONEGIN: ARIA OF LENSKI, FOR SOLO VOICE AND ORCHESTRA see Tchaikovsky, Piotr Ilyich

EUGENE ONEGIN: LETTER SCENE, FOR SOLO VOICE AND ORCHESTRA see Tchaikovsky, Piotr Ilyich

EUGENE ONEGIN: POLONAISE see Tchaikovsky, Piotr Ilyich

EUGENE ONEGIN: WALTZ see Tchaikovsky, Piotr Ilyich

EUGENE ONEGIN: WOHIN, WOHIN SEID IHR ENTSCHWUNDEN see Tchaikovsky, Piotr Ilyich, Eugene Onegin: Aria Of Lenski, For Solo Voice And Orchestra

EUGENE OVERTURE see Svoboda, Tomas

EURYANTHE: OVERTURE see Weber, Carl Maria von

EVANGELISTI, FRANCO (1926-   )
    Random Or Not Random
        2.0.2.2. 2.2.2.0. timp,perc,pno,
        cel,strings
        HINRICHSEN perf mat rent   (E81)

EVASIES see Meulemans, Arthur

EVENING IN THE MOUNTAINS, FOR SOLO VOICE AND ORCHESTRA see Grieg, Edvard Hagerup

EVENING SONG see Schumann, Robert (Alexander), Abendlied, [arr.]

EVENING WITH ANGELS see Holloway, Robin

EVE'S MEDITATION ON LOVE, FOR SOLO VOICE, TUBA AND STRING ORCHESTRA see Tischhauser, Franz

EVOCATION see Jordahl, Robert A.

EVOCAZIONE see Orthel, Leon

EVOCAZIONI see Schubert, Manfred

EVOLUTIO QUAESTIONIS, FOR SOLO VOICE AND CHAMBER ORCHESTRA see Fountain, Primous

EXALTATION, DITHYRAMB AND CAPRICE see Peterson, Wayne Turner

EXCERPT, FOR PIANO AND CHAMBER ORCHESTRA see Shackelford, Randolph Owens

EXCHANGES see Oosterveld, Ernst

EXEMPLUM see Yun, Isang

EXILED see Fountain, Primous

EXORCISM, THE (FAUST IN THE FOREST) see Coscia, Silvio

EXPLORATIONS AND METAMORPHOSES see Williams, Adrian

EXPLOSIONEN UND CANTUS see Kratzschmar, Wilfried, Symphony No. 2

EXPORT VIVALDI see Breuker, W.

EXPRESS POLKA see Strauss, Johann, [Jr.]

EXTASE, FOR SOLO VOICE AND ORCHESTRA see Duparc, Henri

EXTRAVAGANTEN WALZER, DIE see Strauss, Johann, [Jr.]

EXULTARE JUSTI IN DOMINO see Beers, Jacques

EXULTATE see Nystedt, Knut

EXULTET ORBIS GAUDIIS see Vogler, [Abbe] Georg Joseph

EXZENTRISCHER MARSCH see Schilling, Hans Ludwig

EYBLER, JOSEPH (1765-1846)
    Concerto for Clarinet and Orchestra
        in B flat
        2.0.2.2. 2.0.0.0. timp,strings,
        clar solo
        (Weinmann) (original and simplified
        versions by the composer
        included) sc,pts EULENBURG E10132
        f.s.   (E82)

    Divertimento Fur Den Fasching-
        Dienstag [11']
        2(2pic).2.0.2. 2.2.0.0. timp,
        perc,strings without vln
        (Biba, O.) sc,pts DOBLINGER rent
                                        (E83)

EYSER, EBERHARD (1932-   )
    Hjarter Kung: Gagliarda Di Gustav
        Vasa [8']
        1-3.1-3.1-3.1-3.1-3.1-3.0-3.0-1.
        1-4perc, str
        sc STIM   (E84)

    Madrigalillos, For Solo Voice And
        Chamber Orchestra [18']
        fl,ob,clar,alto sax,bsn,vln,vla,
        vcl,db,harp,S solo
        sc STIM perf mat rent   (E85)

    Mordet Pa Gustav III Eller
        Maskeradbalen I Fickformat, For
        Voice And String Orchestra
        [4'30"]
        string orch,opt 1-2clar,bsn,solo
        voice
        sc,pts STIM   (E86)

    Rid I Natt [22'30"]
        3.3.3.3. 4.3.3.1. timp,perc,
        strings
        STIM   (E87)

    Sinfonietta No. 2 [12']
        1.1.1.1. 1.0.0.0. strings
        sc,pts STIM rent   (E88)

    Tonadas [9']
        horn/Wagner tuba,perc,strings
        sc STIM perf mat rent   (E89)

    Tragen Vinner
        study sc SUECIA f.s.   (E90)

F

FACETTES see Lechner, Konrad

FAGELSANG, FOR FLUTE AND ORCHESTRA see Lundkvist, Per

FAHRT NACH TRENTO see Stanke, Willy

FAINT DAWN see Ishii, Maki, Sho-Ko

FAIRFAX FESTIVAL OVERTURE see Diemer, Emma Lou

FAIRY QUEEN, THE: TWO SUITES see Purcell, Henry

FAIRY-TALE SUITE see Suk, Josef, Pohadka Suite

FAIRY TALES see Rimsky-Korsakov, Nikolai, Conte Feerique

FAITH OF OUR FATHERS see Hemy

FALBE, HANS HAGERUP (1772-1830)
    Symphony in D
    see SYMPHONY IN NORWAY, THE

FALCIATORI, I, FOR SOLO VOICE AND ORCHESTRA see Sinigaglia, Leone

FALEGNAME DI LIVONIA, IL: SINFONIA see Pacini, Giovanni

FALLA, MANUEL DE (1876-1946)
    Siete Canciones Populares Espanolas,
        For Solo Voice And Orchestra,
        [arr.] *CC7U
        (Berio, Luciano) 2.1+English
        horn.3.2. 2.2.2.0.db tuba. timp,
        perc,strings,Mez solo UNIVER.
        perf mat rent   (F1)

FALLING ASLEEP IN AN ORCHARD see Flothuis, Marius

FALSO PELLEGRINO, IL, FOR SOLO VOICE AND ORCHESTRA see Sabino, A.

FALSTAFF: E SOGNO? O REALTA?, FOR SOLO VOICE AND ORCHESTRA see Verdi, Giuseppe

FAN IT see Bank, Jacques

FANCHETTI, G.
    Pizzicati-Arabesken *Op.6
        string orch
        LIENAU f.s.   (F2)

FANCY FOR "HARDANGER FIDDLE" AND STRING ORCHESTRA see Madsen, Trygve

FANDANGO see Napravnik, Eduard

FANFARE AND DANCE see Proto, Frank

FANFARE AND MEMORIAL see Yun, Isang

FANFARE: THE DECLARATION OF ARBROATH: FREEDOM IS A NOBLE THING, FOR SOLO VOICES AND ORCHESTRA see Dorward, David

FANISKA: OVERTURE see Cherubini, Luigi

FANTAISIE BALLET see Beriot, Charles-August de, Scene De Ballet, For Violin And Orchestra

FANTAISIE CONCERTANTE see Feld, Jindrich

FANTAISIE CONCERTANTE, FOR HARP AND ORCHESTRA see Jadin, Louis Emanuel

FANTASIA CONCERTANTE see Berkeley, Michael

FANTASIA CONCERTANTE, FOR STRING QUARTET AND ORCHESTRA see Bettinelli, Bruno

FANTASIA CONTRAPPUNTISTICA, [ARR.] see Busoni, Ferruccio Benvenuto

FANTASIA DOPPIA, FOR VIOLIN, VIOLONCELLO AND ORCHESTRA see Svara, Danilo

FANTASIA FOR PIANO AND ORCHESTRA IN C, "DER WANDERER", [ARR.] see Schubert, Franz (Peter)

FANTASIA I see Harper, Edward

FANTASIA II see Harper, Edward

FANTASIA NO. 1 see Thorpe Davie, Cedric

FANTASIA NO. 2 see Thorpe Davie, Cedric

FANTASIA NOTTURNA see Nordio, Cesare

FANTASIA ON A THEME BY TALLIS see
Vaughan Williams, Ralph

FANTASIA ON ONE NOTE see Purcell, Henry

FANTASIA ON THEME OF COUPERIN see
Horovitz, Joseph

FANTASIA-RECITATIVO QUASI UNA DANZA,
FOR PIANO AND ORCHESTRA see Bruni-
Tedeschi, Alberto

FANTASIA SINFONICA see Bottcher,
Eberhard

FANTASIA SINFONICA, FOR ORGAN AND
ORCHESTRA see Bossi, [Marco] Enrico

FANTASIA SOPRA 12 NOTE DEL "DON
GIOVANNI", FOR PIANO AND ORCHESTRA
see Rota, Nino

FANTASIE UBER EIN THEMA VON MOZART see
Ludewig, Wolfgang

FANTASTIC SYMPHONY see Berlioz, Hector
(Louis), Symphonie Fantastique

FANTASTISCHE OUVERTURE see Etti, Karl

FANTOCCI ANIMATI see Bossi, Renzo

FANTOCCI RIBELLI, I see Toni, Alceo

FARANDOLE, [ARR.] see Pierne, Gabriel

FARBERMAN, HAROLD (1929-   )
Concerto for Violin and Orchestra
3.3.3.3. 4.3.3.1. timp,perc,
glock,xylo,vibra,harp,pno,gtr,
strings,vln solo
BELWIN rent   (F3)

Reflected Realities
2.2.3.3. 4.2.3.1. alto sax,timp,
perc,chimes,glock,xylo,vibra,
harp,pno,elec bass,strings,vln
solo
BELWIN rent   (F4)

FAREWELL SYMPHONY see Haydn, [Franz]
Joseph, Symphony No. 45 in F sharp
minor

FARFADET, LE: OVERTURE see Adam,
Adolphe-Charles

FARINA, EDOARDO (1939-   )
Sonata Al Divino Claudio
string orch,trom solo
rent sc CARISCH 21840, pts CARISCH
21841   (F5)

FARINA, GUIDO (1903-   )
Chorale [6']
3.3.3.3. 4.3.3.1. timp,perc,pno,
harp,strings
manuscript CARISCH   (F6)

Danza Rustica [4']
pno,strings
manuscript CARISCH   (F7)

Finta Ammalata, La: Introduzione
3.2.2.2. 4.3.3.1. timp,perc,cel,
harp,strings
manuscript CARISCH   (F8)

Lauda [4']
pno,strings
manuscript CARISCH   (F9)

Pavia [31']
3.3.3.3. 4.5.5.1. timp,perc,pno,
2harp,org/cel,bells,strings
manuscript CARISCH   (F10)

Sinfonia dell'Autunno Pavese [12']
pno,strings
manuscript CARISCH   (F11)

Tempo Di Carnevale: Overture [5']
1.1.2.1. 2.1.1.0. timp,perc,harp,
pno,strings
sc CARISCH 20955 perf mat rent
                              (F12)

Tre Liriche, For Solo Voice And
String Orchestra
string orch,solo voice
manuscript CARISCH   (F13)

FARKAS, FERENC (1905-   )
Jelky Andras Suite
string orch
(special import only) sc EMB 7757
f.s.   (F14)

FARSO, IL see Henkemans, Hans

FASCH, CARL FRIEDRICH CHRISTIAN
Concerto in E, MIN 7
string orch,trp solo,ob d'amore
solo,vln solo
(Hofmann, K.) sc CARUS 40.503-01
f.s., pts CARUS f.s.   (F15)

FAST TRACK POLKA see Strauss, Eduard,
Bahn Frei Polka

FATA MORGANA see Strauss, Johann, [Jr.]

FATEMI LA GRAZIA see Bossi, [Marco]
Enrico

FATINITZA: OVERTURE see Suppe, Franz
von

FATINITZA QUADRILLE see Strauss, Eduard

FAUNE ET LA BERGERE, LE, FOR SOLO VOICE
AND ORCHESTRA see Stravinsky, Igor

FAURE, GABRIEL-URBAIN (1845-1924)
Apres Un Reve, For Double Bass And
Orchestra, [arr.]
1.1.1. 1.0.0.0. strings,db solo
[3'] INTERNAT. perf mat rent
                              (F16)

Apres Un Reve, For Trombone And
Orchestra, [arr.]
(Voisin, Roger) 1.1.1.1. 1.0.0.0.
strings,trom solo [3'] INTERNAT.
perf mat rent   (F17)

Apres Un Reve, For Viola And
Orchestra, [arr.]
1.1.1.1. 1.0.0.0. strings,vla solo
[3'] INTERNAT. perf mat rent
                              (F18)

Apres Un Reve, For Violoncello And
Orchestra, [arr.]
2.2.2.2. 2.0.0.0. strings,vcl solo
[3'] INTERNAT. perf mat rent
                              (F19)

Ballade for Piano and Orchestra, Op.
19
min sc INTERNAT. 1334 $5.25, perf
mat rent   (F20)

Elegy for Violoncello and Orchestra,
Op. 24
2.2.2.2. 4.0.0.0. strings,vcl
solo
sc,pts HAMELLE f.s.   (F21)
LUCKS 00644 sc $4.75, set $11.50,
pts $.95, ea.   (F22)

Nocturne
string orch
LUCKS 05480 sc $3.75, set $4.75,
pts $.95, ea.   (F23)

Pelleas Et Melisande: Sicilienne
LUCKS 08633 sc $3.75, set $9.50,
pts $.95, ea.   (F24)

Pelleas Et Melisande: Suite
BROUDE BR. set $35.00, pts $1.75,
ea.   (F25)
LUCKS 05495 sc $16.00, set $22.00,
pts $1.60, ea.   (F26)

Shylock Suite: Nocturne
BROUDE BR. sc $4.50, set $6.25, pts
$1.25, ea.   (F27)

FAUST, WILLI
Dancing Sticks [3']
2.2.2.1. 2.0.0.0. perc,harp,gtr,
strings
ORLANDO rent   (F28)

Happy End [3']
1.1.2.1. 2.0.0.0. perc,harp,gtr,
strings
ORLANDO rent   (F29)

Holiday For Bows [3']
gtr,perc,strings
ORLANDO rent   (F30)

March Of The Jolly Marksmen [2'45"]
3.0.2.1. 2.2.2.0. perc,harp,gtr,
strings
ORLANDO rent   (F31)

Music-Box-Gavotte [3'55"]
hpsd,gtr,perc,strings
ORLANDO rent   (F32)

FAUST: AIR DES BIJOUX; BALLADE, "IL
ETAIT UN ROI DE THULE", FOR SOLO
VOICE AND ORCHESTRA see Gounod,
Charles Francois

FAUST: AVANT DE QUITTER CES LIEUX, FOR
SOLO VOICE AND ORCHESTRA see
Gounod, Charles Francois

FAUST: FAITES-LUI MES AVEUX, FOR SOLO
VOICE AND ORCHESTRA see Gounod,
Charles Francois

FAUST: JEWEL SONG AND KING OF THULE see
Gounod, Charles Francois, Faust:
Air Des Bijoux; Ballade, "Il Etait
Un Roi De Thule", For Solo Voice
And Orchestra

FAUST: LE VEAU D'OR, FOR SOLO VOICE AND
ORCHESTRA see Gounod, Charles
Francois

FAUST: MON COEUR EST PENETRE, FOR SOLO
VOICES AND ORCHESTRA see Gounod,
Charles Francois

FAUST: OVERTURE see Spohr, Ludwig
(Louis)

FAUST: SALUT, DEMEURE CHASTE ET PURE,
FOR SOLO VOICE AND ORCHESTRA see
Gounod, Charles Francois

FAUST: SERENADE DE MEPHISTO, FOR SOLO
VOICE AND ORCHESTRA see Gounod,
Charles Francois

FAVOLE, FOR SOLO VOICES AND ORCHESTRA
see Soresina, Alberto

FAVORITA, LA: O MIO FERNANDO, FOR SOLO
VOICE AND ORCHESTRA see Donizetti,
Gaetano

FAVORITA, LA: OVERTURE see Donizetti,
Gaetano

FAVORITA, LA: SPIRITO GENTIL, FOR SOLO
VOICE AND ORCHESTRA see Donizetti,
Gaetano

FEAST OF LIGHTS, THE see Adler, Samuel
Hans

FEENMARCHEN WALZER see Strauss, Johann,
[Jr.]

FEIERLICHER AUFMARSCH see Becce,
Giuseppe

FEIERLICHER EINZUG see Strauss, Richard

FEIERLICHES ADAGIO see Seidl, Kurt

FEIERMUSIK see Paulsen, Helmut

FEILER, DROR (1951-   )
Maavak
2pic,2ob,2alto clar in E flat,
2trp,6perc,4db
sc STIM perf mat rent   (F33)

FELD, JINDRICH (1925-   )
Fantaisie Concertante
fl,perc,strings
sc LEDUC f.s., perf mat rent (F34)

FELDEINSAMKEIT, FOR SOLO VOICE AND
ORCHESTRA, [ARR.] see Brahms,
Johannes

FELDERHOF, JAN (1907-   )
Complimento
string orch
sc DONEMUS f.s., perf mat rent
                              (F35)

Gavotte En Rumba [5']
2.0.0.0. 0.0.0.0. perc,pno 4-
hands, strings without vla,
db
sc DONEMUS f.s., perf mat rent
                              (F36)

Introductie En Rondo [11']
2.2.2.2. 2.2.0.0. timp,strings,
opt bells
DONEMUS f.s.   (F37)

FELDMAN, MORTON (1926-   )
Flute And Orchestra [20']
3.3+English horn.3+bass clar.3+
contrabsn. 3.3.4.1. 6perc,harp,
pno,cel,strings,fl solo
sc UNIVER. UE 16529 f.s., perf mat
rent   (F38)

Oboe And Orchestra [18']
4.4.4.4. 3.3.3.1. 3perc,harp,cel&
pno,strings,ob solo
study sc UNIVER. UE16508 f.s., perf
mat rent   (F39)

Orchestra [18']
4.4.4.4. 2.3.3.1. 4perc,harp,
2pno&cel,strings
sc UNIVER. UE 16511 f.s., perf mat
rent   (F40)

FELDMAYER, JOHANN GEORG (1756-1822)
Concerto for 2 Horns and Orchestra in
F [15']
0.2.0.0. 2.0.0.0. strings,2horn
soli
PETERS perf mat rent   (F41)

FELLEGARA, VITTORIO (1927-   )
Studi In Forma Di Variazioni [12']
2.2.2.2. 2.2.0.0. timp,strings
sc ZERBONI 8428 f.s., pts ZERBONI
8429 rent   (F42)

FELSENMUHLE, DIE: OVERTURE see
    Reissiger, Karl Gottlieb

FEM DAGAR I PARIS see Hudecek, Radovan

FENNELLEY, BRIAN (1937-   )
    Quintuplo For Brass Quintet And
        Orchestra [13']
        2(pic).3.3.2. 4.2.3.1. 3perc,
        strings,2trp soli,horn solo,
        trom solo,tuba solo
    MARGUN BP 2049 perf mat rent   (F43)

FERDINAND QUADRILLE see Strauss,
    Johann, [Jr.]

FERENCZY, OTO (1921-   )
    Concerto for Piano and Orchestra
        [26']
        2.3.3.2. 4.2.3.0. timp,4perc,
        strings,pno solo
    SLOV.HUD.FOND 0-485 perf mat rent
                                    (F44)
    Overture [7']
        3.2.2.2. 4.2.3.1. timp,perc,harp,
        strings
    SLOV.HUD.FOND 0-444A perf mat rent
                                    (F45)

FERGUSON, HOWARD (1908-   )
    Partita
    min sc BOOSEY 14 $5.00   (F46)

FERHUDA: 2 INTERMEZZI see Santoliquido,
    Francesco

FERN HILL see Harper, Edward

FERNEYHOUGH, BRIAN (1943-   )
    Terre Est Un Homme, La
        4.4.4.3. 4.4.3.2. timp,4perc,
        2harp,pno,hpsd,cel,cimbalom,
        strings,gtr
    HINRICHSEN perf mat rent   (F47)

    Transit, For Solo Voices And Chamber
        Orchestra [40']
        1.1.1.0. 3.3.3.2. timp,3perc,
        2harp,cel,hpsd,pno,cimbalom,
        gtr,strings,electronic
        equipment,SMezATBarB soli
    sc PETERS EP 7219   (F48)

FERRARI, GIORGIO (1925-   )
    Recital [10']
        1.1.1.1. 2.0.0.0. hpsd,strings
    manuscript CARISCH   (F49)

    Suoni Per Archi [11']
        string orch
    sc ZANIBON 5531 f.s., pts ZANIBON
        5532 f.s.   (F50)

FERRERO
    Siglied
    sc RICORDI-IT 132458 f.s.   (F51)

FERRYMAN'S BRIDE, THE, FOR SOLO VOICE
    AND ORCHESTRA see Sibelius, Jean,
    Koskenlaskian Morsiamet, For Solo
    Voice And Orchestra

FESCH, WILLEM DE (1687-1761)
    Concerto, Op. 3, No. 2, in B flat
        2ob/2fl,strings without vla,cont
        (Ruf) sc SYMPHON 584 f.s.   (F52)

FESCHE GEISTER see Strauss, Eduard

FEST-OUVERTURE see Blon, Franz von

FEST QUADRILLE see Strauss, Johann,
    [Jr.]

FESTA IONTANA see Nordio, Cesare

FESTA SERIA see Schuyt, Nico

FESTINTRADE see Brevik, Tor

FESTIVAL MARCH see Dvorak, Antonin

FESTIVAL MUSIC see Handel, George
    Frideric, Alcina: Overture And
    Dances

FESTIVAL OUVERTURE see Buder, Ernst
    Erich

FESTIVAL OVERTURE see Freso, Tibor,
    Festivalova Predohra

FESTIVAL OVERTURE see Hermans, Nico

FESTIVAL OVERTURE see Hirose, Ryohei

FESTIVAL POLONAISE see Svendsen, Johan
    (Severin)

FESTIVAL PRELUDE see Liszt, Franz

FESTIVALOVA PREDOHRA see Freso, Tibor

FESTIVE OVERTURE see Shostakovich,
    Dmitri

FESTIVITIES see Dorward, David

FESTKLANGE see Liszt, Franz

FESTLICHE MUSIK see Chemin-Petit, Hans

FESTLICHE SONATE see Lang, Walter

FESTLICHER AUFKLANG see Lurmann, Ludwig

FESTLICHER AUFRUF see Sommerlatte,
    Ulrich

FESTLICHER HYMNUS see Schoeck, Othmar

FESTMARSCH IN E FLAT see Strauss,
    Richard

FESTMARSCH ZU SCHILLERS 100JAHRIGER
    GEBURTSTAGSFEIER see Meyerbeer,
    Giacomo

FESTPOLONAISE see Robrecht, Carl

FESTSPEL see Blomberg, Erik

FETIS, FRANCOIS-JOSEPH (1784-1871)
    Concerto for Flute and Orchestra in B
        minor
        2.2.2.0. 2.2.0.0. timp,strings,fl
        solo
    sc EULENBURG GM860 f.s., perf mat
        rent   (F53)

FEUERFEST see Strauss, Josef

FEUERPROBE see Boer, Ed de

FIALA, JOSEPH (1748-1816)
    Concerto for 2 Horns and Orchestra in
        E flat [17']
        2.0.0.0. 2.0.0.0. strings,2horn
        soli
    PETERS perf mat rent   (F54)

    Symphony in C
    see SEVEN SYMPHONIES FROM THE COURT
        OF OETTINGEN-WALLERSTEIN (1773-
        1795)

FIANCES, LES see Chaminade, Cecile

FIAT DOMINE, FOR SOLO VOICE AND STRING
    ORCHESTRA see Andriessen, Hendrik

FIBY, H. (1834-1917)
    Wiegenlied, Op. 32, No. 1
        string orch
    KALMUS A 3278 sc $1.25, set $3.00,
        pts $.50, ea.   (F55)

FIDDLER see Ukmar, Vilko, Godec

FIDELE BURSCHE WALZER see Strauss,
    Eduard

FIDELIO: ABSCHEULICHER, WO EILST DU
    HIN, FOR SOLO VOICE AND ORCHESTRA
    see Beethoven, Ludwig van

FIDELIO: GOTT, WELCH' DUNKEL HIER, FOR
    SOLO VOICE AND ORCHESTRA see
    Beethoven, Ludwig van

FIDELIO: HAT MAN NICHT AUCH GOLD
    BEINEBEN, FOR SOLO VOICE AND
    ORCHESTRA see Beethoven, Ludwig van

FIDELIO: O NAMENLOSE FREUDE, FOR SOLO
    VOICES AND ORCHESTRA see Beethoven,
    Ludwig van

FIDELIO: O WAR ICH SCHON MIT DIR
    VEREINT, FOR SOLO VOICE AND
    ORCHESTRA see Beethoven, Ludwig van

FIDELIO: OVERTURE see Beethoven, Ludwig
    van

FIEDLER, MAX (1859-1939)
    Lustspiel-Ouverture *Op.11 [10']
        2.2.2.2. 4.2.3.0. timp,glock,
        harp,strings
    RIES perf mat rent   (F56)

    Serenade, Op. 15 [25']
        2.2.2.2. 2.2.0.0. timp,perc,
        strings
    RIES perf mat rent   (F57)

FIELD, THE, FOR FLUTE AND ORCHESTRA see
    Ichiyanagi, Toshi

FIERY WIND see Reynolds, Roger

FIGHTER - OVERTURE ON PARTIZAN THEMES
    see Svara, Danilo, Borec - Uvertura
    Na Partizanske Teme

FIGLIO DEL RE, IL, FOR SOLO VOICE AND
    ORCHESTRA see Sinigaglia, Leone

FIGURA ESPOSTA see Hoch, Francesco

FIGUREN IN EINER LANDSCHAFT see Raxach,
    Enrique

FILIPUCCI, AGOSTINO
    Serenade Lointaine
        string orch
    LUCKS 05217 sc $3.75, set $5.75,
        pts $1.15, ea.   (F58)

FILIPUCCI, EDMOND
    Amourette
        2.2.2.2. 2.0.0.0. timp,strings
    KALMUS A4566 sc $2.00, perf mat
        rent, set $15.00, pts $1.50, ea.
                                    (F59)

    Cigalettes, Les
        2.2.2.2. 2.0.0.0. timp,strings
    KALMUS A4547 sc $2.00, perf mat
        rent, set $15.00, pts $1.50, ea.
                                    (F60)

    Marionettes, Les
        2.2.2.2. 2.0.0.0. timp,strings
    KALMUS A4564 sc $2.00, perf mat
        rent, set $15.00, pts $1.50, ea.
                                    (F61)

    Phrynette
        2.2.2.2. 2.0.0.0. timp,strings
    KALMUS A4546 sc $2.00, perf mat
        rent, set $15.00, pts $1.50, ea.
                                    (F62)

FILLE DU REGIMENT, LA: IL FAUT PARTIR,
    FOR SOLO VOICE AND ORCHESTRA see
    Donizetti, Gaetano

FILLES DE CADIX, LES, FOR SOLO VOICE
    AND ORCHESTRA see Delibes, Leo

FILOSOFO DI CAMPAGNA, IL: ARIA DI LENA,
    FOR SOLO VOICE AND STRING ORCHESTRA
    see Galuppi, Baldassare

FILS, [JOHANN] ANTON (1733-1760)
    Sinfonia Periodique No. 2
    BREITKOPF-W perf mat rent   (F63)

FILTZ, ANTON (ANTONIN)
    see FILS, [JOHANN] ANTON

FINALE FARSESCO see Ricci Signorini,
    Antonio

FINALE-GLUCKLICHER AUSGANG see Becce,
    Giuseppe

FINE, IRVING (1914-1962)
    Notturno
        harp,strings
    sc BOOSEY rent   (F64)

FINE, VIVIAN (1913-   )
    Romantic Ode [13']
        string orch,vln solo,vla solo,vcl
        solo
    MARGUN BP 2050 perf mat rent   (F65)

FINGAL'S CAVE OVERTURE see Mendelssohn-
    Bartholdy, Felix, Hebriden, Die

FINK
    While Shepherds Watched Their Flocks
        By Night
    see Jolly Old Saint Nicholas

FINLANDIA see Sibelius, Jean

FINNEY, ROSS LEE (1906-   )
    Concerto for Percussion and Orchestra
        [15']
        3.3.3.3. 4.3.3.1. harp,pno,cel,
        strings,4perc soli
    sc PETERS P66097 $21.50, perf mat
        rent   (F66)

    Concerto for Strings [17'30"]
        string orch
    PETERS P66718 perf mat rent   (F67)

    Narrative, For Violoncello And
        Chamber Orchestra [14']
        1(pic).1.3.0. 2.2.1.0. 2vln,vla,
        db,vcl solo
    PETERS P66691 perf mat rent   (F68)

    Slow Piece, For String Orchestra
        string orch
    NEW VALLEY 146 sc,pts $7.50, pts
        $.75, ea.   (F69)

FINNISSY, MICHAEL (1946-   )
    Long Distance, For Piano And
        Instrumental Ensemble [25']
        fl,3trp,3trom,2vln,2vla,2vcl,db,
        pno solo
    UNIVER. perf mat rent   (F70)

FINTA AMMALATA, LA: INTRODUZIONE see
    Farina, Guido

FINTO STANISLAO, IL: OVERTURE see
    Verdi, Giuseppe

FINZI, GERALD (1901-1956)
    Nocturne- New Year Music
    sc BOOSEY $9.00   (F71)

FIORE DI PIETRA, IL: SUITE NUZIALE see Prokofiev, Serge, Tale Of The Stone Flower: Wedding Suite

FIORILE, FOR SOLO VOICE AND ORCHESTRA see Pick-Mangiagalli, Riccardo

FIORILLO, FEDERIGO (1755-1823)
Sinfonia Concertante in F [16']
0.2.2.0. 2.0.0.0. strings,2ob/ob& clar/2clar soli
(Steinbeck) sc,pts EULENBURG E10124 f.s. (F72)

FIRAT, ERTUGRUL
Ataturk In War And Peace
2.2.2.2. 2.2.1.0. 5perc,pno,cel, harp,strings
SEESAW perf mat rent (F73)

Upheaval
4.3.4.2. 1.3.3.1. 5perc,2pno, strings,pno solo
SEESAW perf mat rent (F74)

FIRE SYMPHONY see Haydn, [Franz] Joseph, Symphony No. 59 in A

FIREBIRD: SUITE, 1919 VERSION see Stravinsky, Igor

FIREWORKS see Stravinsky, Igor

FIRST NOEL, THE see Sandys

FISCHER, JOHANN AUGSBURGIENSIS (1646-1716)
Tafelmusik
string orch,cont
(Engel) KALMUS A1100 sc $3.00, set $4.00, pts $1.00, ea. (F75)

FISCHER, JOHANN CASPAR FERDINAND (ca. 1665-1746)
Praeludium, Fuge Und Gigue
strings,pno
(Schneider) sc,pts HEINRICH. 222 f.s. (F76)

FISCHER-LARSEN, ERIC
Aranjuez
RIES f.s. (F77)

Barcarole D'amore
RIES f.s. (F78)

Bilbao
RIES f.s. (F79)

Toledanische Nacht
RIES f.s. (F80)

FISCHERTANZ see Kletsch, Ludwig

FIVE GERMAN DANCES, CODA AND TRIO see Schubert, Franz (Peter), Deutsche Tanze, Funf, Mit Coda Und Sieben Trios

FIVE GERMAN DANCES WITH CODA AND SEVEN TRIOS see Schubert, Franz (Peter), Deutsche Tanze, Funf, Mit Coda Und Sieben Trios

FIVE LITTLE ELEGIES see Bazlik, Miroslav, Pat' Malych Elegii Pre Slaciky

FIVE MINUETS AND SIX TRIOS see Schubert, Franz (Peter), Menuette, Funf, Und Sechs Trios

FIVE PICTURES see Chaun, Frantisek

FIVE PIECES see Dowland, John

FIVE PIECES see Morthenson, Jan W.

FIVE PIECES, [ARR.] see Purcell, Henry

FIVE PIECES FOR ORCHESTRA see Andrix, George

FIVE SKETCHES see Pfister, Hugo

FLADMOE, ARVID
Cycle Of Songs, For Solo Voice And Orchestra
2.2.0.2. 2.3.0.0. timp,strings, Bar solo
NORGE (F81)

FLAMES see Berkeley, Michael

FLEDERMAUS, DIE: CZARDAS, FOR SOLO VOICE AND ORCHESTRA see Strauss, Johann, [Jr.]

FLEDERMAUS, DIE: DU UND DU see Strauss, Johann, [Jr.]

FLEDERMAUS, DIE: ICH LADE GERN MIR GASTE EIN, FOR SOLO VOICE AND ORCHESTRA see Strauss, Johann, [Jr.]

FLEDERMAUS, DIE: MEIN HERR MARQUIS, FOR SOLO VOICE AND ORCHESTRA see Strauss, Johann, [Jr.]

FLEDERMAUS, DIE: OVERTURE see Strauss, Johann, [Jr.]

FLEDERMAUS, DIE: POLKA FRANCAISE see Strauss, Johann, [Jr.]

FLEDERMAUS, DIE: SELECTION see Strauss, Johann, [Jr.]

FLEDERMAUS, DIE: TICK-TACK POLKA see Strauss, Johann, [Jr.], Tik-Tak Polka

FLEDERMAUS, DIE: WATCH DUET, ACT 2, FOR SOLO VOICES AND ORCHESTRA see Strauss, Johann, [Jr.]

FLEISCHER, WILLY
Suite [14']
string orch
RIES perf mat rent (F82)

FLEUR QUE TU M'AVAIS JETEE, LA see Bizet, Georges, Carmen: Air De Fleur, For Solo Voice And Orchestra

FLEURS see Bordewijk-Roepman, Johanna

FLEURS DU MAL, FOR SOLO VOICE AND ORCHESTRA see Laman, Wim

FLEXIO see Loevendie, Theo

FLIEGE, HERMANN
Gavotte Circus Renz *Op.105 [4']
2(pic).2.2.2. 4.2.3.1. timp,perc, strings
(Dressel, Erwin) sc RIES f.s., perf mat rent (F83)

FLIEGENDE HOLLANDER, DER: DIE FRIST IST UM; WIE OFT IN MEERES TIEFEN SCHLUND, FOR SOLO VOICE AND ORCHESTRA see Wagner, Richard

FLIEGENDE HOLLANDER, DER: OVERTURE see Wagner, Richard

FLIRT see Kochmann, Spero

FLOOD, THE: PRELUDE see Saint-Saens, Camille, Deluge, Le: Prelude

FLORET SILVA see Mul, Jan

FLORIDORO, IL: PER PIETA, FOR SOLO VOICE AND ORCHESTRA see Stradella, Alessandro

FLOSMAN, OLDRICH (1925-)
Partita No. 2
sc PANTON 1753 f.s. (F84)

Village, The *see Partita No. 2

FLOTHUIS, MARIUS (1914-)
Black Eyes *Op.33,No.3
see Four Trifles, For Solo Voice And Orchestra

Cantus Amoris *Op.78
string orch
DONEMUS sc f.s., pts rent (F85)

Es Ist Nacht *Op.3,No.2
see Vier Liederen, For Solo Voice And Orchestra

Falling Asleep In An Orchard *Op.33, No.1
see Four Trifles, For Solo Voice And Orchestra

Four Trifles, For Solo Voice And Orchestra
1.1.2.1.alto sax. 1.1.0.0. timp, perc,harp,cel,vibra,strings,high solo sc DONEMUS f.s., perf mat rent
contains: Black Eyes, Op.33,No.3; Falling Asleep In An Orchard, Op.33,No.1; Look, The, Op.33, No.2; Seal Woman, The, Op.33, No.4 (F86)

Hymnus, For Solo Voice And Orchestra *Op.67 [9']
3.3.3.2. 4.3.3.2. timp,perc,harp, vibra,strings,S solo
sc DONEMUS f.s., perf mat rent (F87)

Kleine Ouverture, For Solo Voice And Orchestra *Op.14 [7']
2.2.3.3. 3.3.3.1. timp,perc,harp, cel,vibra,strings,S solo
sc DONEMUS f.s., perf mat rent (F88)

Look, The *Op.33,No.2
see Four Trifles, For Solo Voice And Orchestra

FLOTHUIS, MARIUS (cont'd.)

Morgen War Von Dir Erfullt, Der *Op.3,No.1
see Vier Liederen, For Solo Voice And Orchestra

Nocturne, Op. 77 [3']
2.2.2.2. 4.2.3.0. timp,perc,harp, strings
DONEMUS perf mat rent (F89)
orch MOLENAAR 14.1558.08 f.s. (F90)

O Nacht *Op.3,No.3
see Vier Liederen, For Solo Voice And Orchestra

Per Sonare Ed Ascoltare, For Flute And Orchestra [20']
4.2.2.2. 4.3.3.1. timp,6perc, 2harp,strings,fl solo
sc DONEMUS f.s., perf mat rent (F91)

Seal Woman, The *Op.33,No.4
see Four Trifles, For Solo Voice And Orchestra

To An Old Love, For Solo Voice And Orchestra *Op.32 [7']
1.0.3.2.alto sax. 2.3.2.0. timp, harp,strings,Mez solo
sc DONEMUS f.s., perf mat rent (F92)

Vier Liederen, For Solo Voice And Orchestra
2.1.2.1. 2.2.0.0. perc,harp,cel, vibra,strings,S solo sc DONEMUS f.s., perf mat rent
contains: Es Ist Nacht, Op.3, No.2; Morgen War Von Dir Erfullt, Der, Op.3,No.1; O Nacht, Op.3,No.3; Wasserfall Bei Nacht, Op.3,No.4 (F93)

Wasserfall Bei Nacht *Op.3,No.4
see Vier Liederen, For Solo Voice And Orchestra

FLOTOW, FRIEDRICH VON (1812-1883)
Alessandro Stradella: Overture [7']
2+pic.2.2.2. 4.2.3.0. timp,perc, strings
min sc UNIVER. PH42 $2.00 (F94)
KALMUS A5505 sc $8.00, perf mat rent, set $20.00, pts $1.00, ea. (F95)

Martha: Ach So Fromm, For Solo Voice And Orchestra
"Martha: M'Appari Tutt' Amor" LUCKS 02180 sc $3.75, set $7.50, pts $.75, ea. (F96)

Martha: Die Letzte Rose, For Solo Voice And Orchestra
"Martha: Tis The Last Rose Of Summer" LUCKS 02079 sc $3.75, set $7.50, pts $.75, ea. (F97)

Martha: Lasst Mich Euch Fragen, For Solo Voice And Orchestra
"Martha: Porter Song" LUCKS 02033 sc $4.00, set $8.00, pts $.60, ea. (F98)

Martha: M'Appari Tutt' Amor *see Martha: Ach So Fromm, For Solo Voice And Orchestra

Martha: Overture
LUCKS 05511 sc $4.00, set $18.00, min sc $4.50, pts $.95, ea. (F99)

Martha: Porter Song *see Martha: Lasst Mich Euch Fragen, For Solo Voice And Orchestra

Martha: Tis The Last Rose Of Summer *see Martha: Die Letzte Rose, For Solo Voice And Orchestra

FLOTTAISON BLEME, FOR PIANO AND ORCHESTRA see Gorli, Sandro

FLOTTES LEBEN POLKA see Strauss, Eduard

FLOWER GIVEN TO MY DAUGHTER, A see Bois, Rob du

FLUGSCHRIFTEN WALZER see Strauss, Johann, [Jr.]

FLUTE AND ORCHESTRA see Feldman, Morton

FLUTE DE JADE, LA, FOR SOLO VOICE AND ORCHESTRA see Knapik, Eugeniusz

FLYING DUTCHMAN, THE: OVERTURE see Wagner, Richard, Fliegende Hollander, Der: Overture

FLYKT see Blomberg, Erik

FOCALES, FOR DOUBLE BASS AND INSTRUMENTAL ENSEMBLE see Mestral, Patrice

FOCCROULLE, BERNARD (1953-   )
  Corteges [14']
    12strings
    MODERN 1955 rent   (F100)

FOLII III see Pusztai, Tibor

FOLK TUNE AND INTERMEZZO, FOR VIOLIN
  AND ORCHESTRA see Jez, Jakob,
  Narodna In Intermezzo, For Violin
  And Orchestra

FOLKSONG see Foss, Lukas

FONGAARD, BJORN
  Three Pieces *Op.10
    string orch
    NORGE   (F101)

FONTYN, JACQUELINE (1930-   )
  Disgressions
    2.1.2.1. 2.1.1.0. timp,2perc,cel,
      harp,strings
    SEESAW perf mat rent   (F102)

  Mouvements Concertantes, For Two
    Pianos And String Orchestra
    string orch,2pno soli
    SEESAW perf mat rent   (F103)

FOOTE, ARTHUR (1853-1937)
  Air And Gavotte
    string orch
    LUCKS 08469 sc $3.75, set $5.75,
      pts $1.15, ea.   (F104)

  Irish Folk Song
    string orch
    LUCKS 08470 sc $3.00, set $5.00,
      pts $1.00, ea.   (F105)

FOR AN UNKNOWN SOLDIER, FOR FLUTE AND
  STRING ORCHESTRA see Johnson,
  Hunter

FOR MOONLIGHT NIGHTS, FOR FLUTE AND
  ORCHESTRA see Ketting, Otto

FOR MOTHER see Ukmar, Vilko, Materi

FOR THE BEAUTY OF THE EARTH see Kocher

FOR THE LAST TIME...! I REPEAT..., FOR
  FLUTE AND ORCHESTRA see Porcelijn,
  David

FOREST, THE see Glazunov, Alexander
  Konstantinovich

FORET, LA see Glazunov, Alexander
  Konstantinovich, Forest, The

FORINO, L. (1868-1936)
  Concerto Romantico No. 2, For
    Violoncello And Orchestra [14']
    2.2.2.2. 4.2.3.1. timp,perc,harp,
      strings,vcl solo
    manuscript CARISCH   (F106)

FORSPILL, FOR VIOLIN AND ORCHESTRA see
  Janson, Alfred, Concerto for Violin
  and Orchestra

FORSTER, CHRISTOPH (1693-1745)
  Symphony in E flat, MIN 216
    2horn,strings,cont
    KALMUS 5428 sc $3.00, set $3.75,
      pts $.75, ea.   (F107)

FORSTER, K.
  Sonata a 7
    2cornetto,bsn,strings,cont
    MUS. RARA 1949B f.s.   (F108)

FORSVUNDNE, DEN see Christiansen,
  Henning

FORTNER, WOLFGANG (1907-   )
  Triptychon
    3.3.3.3. 6.3.3.2. strings
    sc SCHOTTS 71 A6826 $42.00   (F109)

  Variations for Chamber Group [21']
    gtr,harp,hpsd,marimba,pno,strings
    sc SCHOTTS ED 6949 $35.00   (F110)

FORTUNE TELLER, THE: GYPSY LOVE SONG,
  FOR SOLO VOICE AND ORCHESTRA see
  Herbert, Victor

FORTUNE TELLER, THE: ROMANY LIFE, FOR
  SOLO VOICE AND ORCHESTRA see
  Herbert, Victor

FORTUNE TELLER, THE: SELECTION see
  Herbert, Victor

FORZA DEL DESTINO, LA: O TU CHE IN SENO
  AGLI ANGELI, FOR SOLO VOICE AND
  ORCHESTRA see Verdi, Giuseppe

FORZA DEL DESTINO, LA: OVERTURE see
  Verdi, Giuseppe

FORZA DEL DESTINO, LA: PACE, PACE, MIO
  DIO, FOR SOLO VOICE AND ORCHESTRA
  see Verdi, Giuseppe

FORZA DEL DESTINO, LA: SOLENNE IN
  QUEST'ORA, FOR SOLO VOICES AND
  ORCHESTRA see Verdi, Giuseppe

FOSS, LUKAS (1922-   )
  Concerto for Percussion and Orchestra
    study sc SALABERT $22.00   (F111)

  Concerto for Violoncello and
    Orchestra [20']
    2horn,trp,2trom,perc,vibra,harp,
      pno,org,strings,vcl solo
    study sc FISCHER,C $7.50   (F112)

  Folksong
    study sc SALABERT $14.50   (F113)

  Orpheus
    study sc SALABERT $15.50   (F114)

  Quintets For Orchestra [15']
    2.2+English horn.2+bass clar.2.
      3.3.3.1. timp,chimes,elec org,
      strings
    PEMBROKE study sc $15.00, sc,pts
      rent   (F115)

  Salomon Rossi Suite
    study sc SALABERT $11.75   (F116)

FOSSILIEN see Sari, Jozsef

FOSTER, STEPHEN COLLINS (1826-1864)
  Beautiful Dreamer, For Solo Voice And
    String Orchestra, [arr.]
    string orch,harp,solo voice LUCKS
    03140 sc $2.00, set $4.50, pts
    $.75, ea.   (F117)

  Gems Of Stephen Foster, [arr.]
    (Tobani) LUCKS 05524 set $21.00,
    pts $1.25, ea.   (F118)

  Jeannie With The Light Brown Hair,
    For Solo Voice And String
    Orchestra, [arr.]
    string orch,solo voice LUCKS 02541
    sc $2.50, set $3.75, pts $.75,
    ea.   (F119)

  Old Folks At Home, [arr.]
    (Busch) string orch LUCKS 02332 sc
    $2.00, set $3.75, pts $.75, ea.
                                       (F120)

  Twelve Best Loved Songs, [arr.]
    (Zinn, William) string orch
    EXCELSIOR $18.00   (F121)

FOUNDRY OF MINSTRELS see Cole, Bruce

FOUNTAIN, PRIMOUS (1949-   )
  Caprice For Orchestra [6']
    1(alto fl).2.3.2. 4.3.3.0. timp,
      perc,pno,strings
    sc MARGUN BP 2004 $7.50, perf mat
      rent   (F122)

  Concerto for Harp and Chamber
    Orchestra [9']
    1.0.1.0. 0.1.0.0. 3perc,pno,
      strings,harp solo
    sc MARGUN BP 2006 $7.50, perf mat
      rent   (F123)

  Concerto for Violoncello and
    Orchestra [21']
    3(alto fl).3.3.3. 4.3.3.0. timp,
      perc,pno,strings,vcl solo
    MARGUN BP 2005 perf mat rent (F124)

  Evolutio Quaestionis, For Solo Voice
    And Chamber Orchestra [3']
    1.1.1.1. 1.1.1.0. harp,pno,timp,
      3perc,2vln,vla,vcl,db,S solo
    sc MARGUN BP 2007 $4.50, perf mat
      rent   (F125)

  Exiled [13']
    4(alto fl).3.3.2. 4.3.3.1. timp,
      harp,pno,strings
    MARGUN BP 2008 perf mat rent (F126)

  Movement For Orchestra [2']
    2.2.1.0. 2.3.4.1. timp,2perc,pno,
      strings
    MARGUN BP 2010 perf mat rent (F127)

  Osiris [9']
    3.3.3.3. 4.3.3.0. timp,2perc,pno,
      strings
    MARGUN BP 2009 perf mat rent (F128)

FOUR BACH GEMS see Bach, Johann
  Sebastian

FOUR BAGATELLES see Lang, Ivana

FOUR CHARACTERISTIC WALTZES see
  Coleridge-Taylor, Samuel

FOUR CRADLE SONGS, FOR SOLO VOICE AND
  ORCHESTRA see Letelier Llona,
  Alfonso, Cuatro Canciones De Cuna,
  For Solo Voice And Orchestra

FOUR ETUDES see Stravinsky, Igor

FOUR LAST SONGS, FOR SOLO VOICE AND
  ORCHESTRA see Strauss, Richard,
  Vier Letzte Lieder, For Solo Voice
  And Orchestra

FOUR ORCHESTRAL COMPOSITIONS see Sixta,
  Jozef

FOUR PIECES see Osterc, Slavko, Stiri
  Skladbe

FOUR PIECES see Korn, Peter Jona

FOUR POLONAISES OF VERSAILLES see
  Sikorski, Kazimierz, Cztery
  Polonezy Wersalskie

FOUR SEASONS, THE see Proto, Frank

FOUR SEASONS, THE see Vivaldi, Antonio,
  Concerti, RV 269, RV 315, RV 293,
  RV 297

FOUR SENTIMENTS see Wilder, Alec

FOUR SONGS FOR VOICE AND ORCHESTRA see
  Delius, Frederick

FOUR TEXTS IN MUSIC, FOR SOLO VOICE AND
  ORCHESTRA see Gabold, Ingolf

FOUR TRIFLES, FOR SOLO VOICE AND
  ORCHESTRA see Flothuis, Marius

FOX, FREDERICK ALFRED (FRED)
    (1931-   )
  BEC-5
    12strings
    SEESAW perf mat rent   (F129)

FRA DE UNGES VERDEN see Kvam, Oddvar S.

FRA DIAVOLO: OVERTURE see Auber,
  Daniel-Francois-Esprit

FRAGE NICHT see Lersen, Fred

FRAGMENT see Ligeti, Gyorgy

FRAGMENTOS see Ramirez, Luis Antonio

FRAGMENTS FROM THE SONG OF SONGS, FOR
  SOLO VOICE AND ORCHESTRA see La
  Montaine, John

FRAMMENTI LIRICI, FOR SOLO VOICE AND
  STRING ORCHESTRA see Bossi, Renzo

FRAN SALLY, FOR SOLO VOICE AND CHAMBER
  ORCHESTRA see Osterling, Ulf

FRANCAIX, JEAN (1912-   )
  Aubade
    12vcl
    sc SCHOTTS ED 6710 $38.00, pts
    SCHOTTS ED 6794 $62.00   (F130)

  Concerto for Bassoon and Strings
    [18']
    6vln,2vla,2vcl,db,bsn solo
    SCHOTTS FAG 18 $15.50   (F131)

  Concerto for Violin and Instrumental
    Ensemble, No. 2
    2.2.2.2. 2.0.0.0. 6vln,2vla,2vcl,
      db,vln solo
    SCHOTTS ED 6871 $21.00   (F132)

  Divertissement for Bassoon and String
    Orchestra
    string orch,bsn solo
    sc SCHOTTS 71 U00185 $13.50, pts
    SCHOTTS $2.50, ea.   (F133)

  Ouverture Anacreontique
    study sc SCHOTTS ED 6846 $13.50
                                       (F134)

FRANCESCA DA RIMINI. FANTASY see
  Tchaikovsky, Piotr Ilyich

FRANCESCO DA MILANO
    (ca. 1497?-ca. 1573?)
  Canzone Degli Uccelli, La
    see RICREAZIONI DI ANTICHE MUSICHE
    CLASSICHE, SERIE I: MUSICHE
    ANTICHE ITALIANE

FRANCK, CESAR (1822-1890)
  O Lord Most Holy *see Panis
    Angelicus, For Solo Voice And
    Orchestra

  Panis Angelicus, For Solo Voice And
    Orchestra
    "O Lord Most Holy" LUCKS 02324 sc
    $3.75, set $7.50, pts $.75, ea.
                                       (F135)

FRANCK, CESAR (cont'd.)

Prelude. Choral And Fugue, [arr.]
(Pierne) 3(pic).2+English horn.3+
bass clar.4.sarrusophone.
4.3.3.1. timp,perc,2harp,strings
[17'] KALMUS A4545 sc $18.00,
perf mat rent, set $40.00, pts
$1.50, ea.   (F136)

Psyche: 3. Les Jardins D'Eros
LUCKS 05228 sc $5.75, set $20.00,
pts $.95, ea.   (F137)

Psyche: 4. Psyche Et Eros
LUCKS 05229 sc $5.75, set $20.00,
pts $.95, ea.   (F138)

Redemption: Morceau Symphonique No. 5
[14']
2.2.2.2. 4.2.3.1. timp,strings
KALMUS A2602 sc $18.00, perf mat
rent, set $43.00, pts $2.50, ea.
                                  (F139)

Symphony in D minor
pts BROUDE BR. $3.50, ea.   (F140)
min sc PETERS 629 $8.50   (F141)
min sc ZEN-ON 891201 f.s.   (F142)

FRANCKENSTEIN, CLEMENS VON (1875-1942)
Vier Tanze *Op.52
sc,pts RIES f.s.   (F143)

FRANCO, CESARE
see FRANCK, CESAR

FRANCS-JUGES, LES: OVERTURE see
Berlioz, Hector (Louis)

FRANK, ANDREW (1946-   )
Season Of Darkness
2.2.2.1. 2.2.1.0. perc,strings,
contrabsn solo
SEESAW perf mat rent   (F144)

FRANKE-BLOM, LARS-AKE (1941-   )
Concerto for Double Bass and
Orchestra [20']
1.1.1.0. 0.0.0.0. timp,2perc,
harp,strings,db solo
STIM   (F145)

Concerto for Viola and Orchestra
[16']
1.1.1.1. 2.0.0.0. timp,harp,
strings,vla solo
sc STIM perf mat rent   (F146)

FRANKEN, WIM (1922-   )
Concerto in G for Piano and Orchestra
[23']
3.3.3.3. 2.2.1.0. 2perc,strings,
pno solo
sc DONEMUS f.s., perf mat rent
                                  (F147)

FRANKENSTEIN!!, FOR SOLO VOICE AND
ORCHESTRA see Gruber, Heinz Karl

FRANKO, MLADEN (1937-   )
Puppenspiele, For Piano And Orchestra
[6']
2.2.2.0. 2.2.2.0. drums,perc,elec
bass,strings,pno solo
ORLANDO rent   (F148)

Slawia [7'30"]
2.2.2.2. 2.3.2.0. timp,perc,harp,
xylo,strings
ORLANDO rent   (F149)

FRANZL, IGNAZ (1736-1811)
Symphonies In C, In F And In C
(Wurtz, Roland) ("The Symphony",
Vol. C-XI) sc GARLAND
ISBN 0-8240-3816-9 $90.00
contains also: Winter, Peter von,
Symphonie Concertante, Op. 20
(Henderson, Donald); Winter,
Peter von, Colmal Overture
(McCorkle, Donald); Winter, Peter
von, Schlacht-Sinfonie (Johnson,
Thor)   (F150)

FRANZOSISCHE OUVERTURE see Dressel,
Erwin

FRANZOSISCHE OUVERTURE, IN A MINOR see
Telemann, Georg Philipp

FRANZOSISCHE SUITE see Niklas, Ferry

FRATE 'NNAMORATO, LO: CHI DISSE CHE LA
FEMMENA, FOR SOLO VOICE AND STRING
ORCHESTRA see Pergolesi, Giovanni
Battista

FRATE 'NNAMORATO, LO: GNORA CREDITEMI,
FOR SOLO VOICE AND STRING ORCHESTRA
see Pergolesi, Giovanni Battista

FRATE 'NNAMORATO, LO: OGNI PENA CCHIU
SPIETATA, FOR SOLO VOICE AND STRING
ORCHESTRA see Pergolesi, Giovanni
Battista

FRAUEN KAFERIN see Strauss, Johann,
[Jr.]

FRAUENHERZ see Strauss, Josef

FRAUENWURDE WALZER see Strauss, Josef

FRAULEIN TEUFEL: SATANELLA WALZER see
Schwartz, Otto

FREDERICH, OTTO
Nachtlied, For Solo Voice And
Orchestra *Op.10 [10']
2.2+English horn.2+bass clar.2.
2.2.3.0. timp,harp,strings,low
solo
RIES perf mat rent   (F151)

FREDERIKA POLKA see Strauss, Johann,
[Jr.]

FREDRIKSSON, LENNART (1952-   )
Kontemplativa Variationer
3.2.2.2. 4.2.3.1. timp,3perc,
strings
pts STIM perf mat rent   (F152)

Romans, For Violin And String
Orchestra
string orch,vln solo
sc,pts,solo pt STIM perf mat rent
                                  (F153)

FREE LANCE MARCH see Sousa, John Philip

FREE VARIATIONS see Peterson, Wayne
Turner

FREIKUGELN POLKA see Strauss, Johann,
[Jr.]

FREISCHUTZ, DER: DURCH DIE WALDER,
DURCH DIE AUEN, FOR SOLO VOICE AND
ORCHESTRA see Weber, Carl Maria von

FREISCHUTZ, DER: OVERTURE see Weber,
Carl Maria von

FREISCHUTZ, DER: SCHWEIG', SCHWEIG'
DAMIT, FOR SOLO VOICE AND ORCHESTRA
see Weber, Carl Maria von

FREISCHUTZ, DER: UND OB DIE WOLKE SIE
VERHULLE, FOR SOLO VOICE AND
ORCHESTRA see Weber, Carl Maria von

FREISCHUTZ, DER: WIE NAHTE MIR DER
SCHLUMMER, FOR SOLO VOICE AND
ORCHESTRA see Weber, Carl Maria von

FREIWILLIGE VOR! MARSCH see Strauss,
Johann, [Jr.]

FRENCH SUITE see Hoddinott, Alun

FRESCOBALDA, LA, [ARR.]. ARIA CON
VARIAZIONI see Frescobaldi,
Girolamo

FRESCOBALDI, GIROLAMO (1583-1643)
Canzona
see RICREAZIONI DI ANTICHE MUSICHE
CLASSICHE, SERIE V: MUSICHE
ANTICHE ITALIANE

Frescobalda, La, [arr.]. Aria Con
Variazioni
(Caggiano, R.) string orch [8'] sc
ZANIBON 4376 f.s., pts ZANIBON
4377 f.s.   (F154)

Fugue
see RICREAZIONI DI ANTICHE MUSICHE
CLASSICHE, SERIE V: MUSICHE
ANTICHE ITALIANE

Toccata Per La Elevazione
see RICREAZIONI DI ANTICHE MUSICHE
CLASSICHE, SERIE II: MUSICHE
ANTICHE ITALIANE

FRESCOBALDIANA see Giannini, Vittorio

FRESO, TIBOR (1918-   )
Festival Overture *see Festivalova
Predohra

Festivalova Predohra *Op.30
2.2.1.1. 4.4.3.1. perc,harp,
strings
"Festival Overture" SLOV.HUD.FOND
0-59 perf mat rent   (F155)

Sketch, For Solo Voice, Violin And
Orchestra *see Skica, For Solo
Voice, Violin And Orchestra

Skica, For Solo Voice, Violin And
Orchestra [13']
3.2.2.2. 4.2.2.1. timp,perc,harp,
strings,vln solo,S solo
"Sketch, For Solo Voice, Violin And
Orchestra" SLOV.HUD.FOND 0-446A
perf mat rent   (F156)

FRESO, TIBOR (cont'd.)

Suite, Op. 27
hpsd,strings
SLOV.HUD.FOND 0-28A, 0-82A perf mat
rent   (F157)

FRESQUE see Tabachnik, Michel

FREUDENTHAL, OTTO (1934-   )
Concert Piece
trom,timp,perc,strings
pts STIM perf mat rent   (F158)

In Highgate Cemetary
string orch
pts STIM   (F159)

FREUDIGER AUFKLANG see Dressel, Erwin

FREUET EUCH DES LEBENS WALZER see
Strauss, Johann, [Jr.]

FRID, GEZA (1904-   )
Abel Et Cain, For Solo Voice And
Orchestra *Op.15 [13']
3.2.3.3. 4.3.3.1. timp,perc,
2harp,strings,B/A solo
sc DONEMUS f.s., perf mat rent
                                  (F160)

Concertino for Orchestra
orch MOLENAAR 14.1564.08 f.s.   (F161)

Concertino for 2 Trumpets and
Orchestra, Op. 93 [5'30"]
3.2.2.2. 3.0.0.0. timp,2perc,
strings,2trp soli
DONEMUS perf mat rent   (F162)

Concerto for Clarinet and String
Orchestra, Op. 82 [15']
string orch,clar solo
sc DONEMUS f.s., perf mat rent
                                  (F163)

Kinderliedjes II, For Solo Voice And
Orchestra *Op.56a [7']
harp,perc,strings,Mez solo
DONEMUS perf mat rent   (F164)

Music For Violins And Violas *Op.92
[14']
DONEMUS perf mat rent   (F165)

Olifant-Variaties, Op Een Thema Van
Saint-Saens, For Doublebass And
Orchestra *Op.91
string orch,db solo
sc DONEMUS f.s., perf mat rent
                                  (F166)

Podium Suite, For Violin And
Orchestra *Op.3 [12']
2.2.2.2. 1.1.0.0. timp,perc,
strings,vln solo
sc DONEMUS f.s., perf mat rent
                                  (F167)

Schopenhauer-Cantate, For Solo Voice
And Orchestra *Op.22 [15']
2.2.2.2. 1.1.0.0. timp,perc,
strings,Mez solo
sc DONEMUS f.s., perf mat rent
                                  (F168)

FRIDL, HANS
Mein Schones Ungarland
RIES f.s.   (F169)

Rote Tulpen
RIES f.s.   (F170)

So Wie Mein Wien
RIES f.s.   (F171)

FRIEDEMANN, CARL (1862-1952)
Lola *Op.128
2.2.2.2. 4.2.3.0. perc,strings
sc,pts LIENAU rent   (F172)

Slavische Rhapsodie No. 1 *Op.114
[8']
2(pic).2.2.2. 4.2.3.1. timp,perc,
strings
LIENAU f.s.   (F173)

Slavische Rhapsodie No. 3 *Op.297
[11']
2(pic).2.2.2. 4.2.3.1. harp,timp,
perc,strings
sc,pts LIENAU rent   (F174)

Victor-Von-Scheffel-Marsch *Op.134
1.2.2.2. 4.2.3.0. perc,strings
sc,pts LIENAU rent   (F175)

FRIEDEN see Gilse, Jan van

FRIEDENSPALMEN WALZER see Strauss,
Josef

FRIEDRICHS, GUNTER (1935-   )
Bewegungen [15']
1.1.1.1. 1.1.1.0. timp,perc,org,
vcl,strings,pno solo
PEER perf mat rent   (F176)

FRIES, HERBERT
Allegro [8']
    string orch
    ASSMANN   (F177)

Concerto for Clarinet and String
    Orchestra [15']
    string orch,clar solo
    ASSMANN   (F178)

Concerto for Violin and Orchestra
    [31']
    3(2pic).2+English horn.2+bass
    clar.2+contrabsn. 4.3.3.0.
    timp,perc,harp,pno,cel,strings,
    vln solo
    ASSMANN   (F179)

Concerto for Violoncello and
    Orchestra [18']
    3.3.3.3. 4.3.3.0. timp,perc,harp,
    pno,cel,strings,vcl solo
    ASSMANN   (F180)

Symphony [18']
    3.2+English horn.2+bass clar.2+
    contrabsn. 4.3.3.1. timp,2perc,
    harp,strings
    ASSMANN   (F181)

Variations [28']
    3.2.3.3. 4.3.3.0. timp,perc,harp,
    pno,cel,strings
    ASSMANN   (F182)

FRIESLAND see Schouwman, Hans

FRIESLAND, FOR SOLO VOICE AND ORCHESTRA
    see Schouwman, Hans

FRIGOLI-FRIGOLA see Mestres-Quadreny,
    Josep Maria

FRIIS, BORGE
Lenzwind
    RIES f.s.   (F183)

FRISCH, FRECH, FEDERLEICHT see
    Kotscher, Edmund

FRISCH HERAN POLKA see Strauss, Johann,
    [Jr.]

FRISCHER WIND see Stolzenwald, Otto

FRITCHIE, WAYNE
Impressions
    string orch
    SEESAW perf mat rent   (F184)

Music For Orchestra No. 2
    SEESAW perf mat rent   (F185)

FROHER START see Gutzeit, Erich

FROHES LEBEN WALZER see Strauss, Josef

FROHLICHE GEIGEN see Stolzenwald, Otto

FROHLICHES SPIEL see Kletsch, Ludwig

FROM BOHEMIA'S MEADOWS AND FORESTS see
    Smetana, Bedrich, Ma Vlast: Z
    Ceskych Luhu A Haju

FROM BYRON'S DON JUAN: SHIPWRECK AND
    LOVE SCENE, FOR SOLO VOICE AND
    ORCHESTRA see Thomson, Virgil
    Garnett

FROM FINLAND see Palmgren, Selim

FROM THE BOHEMIAN FOREST: SILENT WOODS,
    FOR VIOLONCELLO AND ORCHESTRA,
    [ARR.] see Dvorak, Antonin

FROM THE FOUNTAIN OF YOUTH, FOR GUITAR
    AND ORCHESTRA see Selby, Philip

FROM THE NEW WORLD see Dvorak, Antonin,
    Symphony, Op. 95, in E minor

FROM: THE RECOLLECTION, FOR SOLO VOICE
    AND STRING ORCHESTRA see Voormolen,
    Alexander Nicolas

FROM WOOD AND METAL see Melcher, John

FROMM, FOR SOLO VOICE AND ORCHESTRA see
    Linnala, Eino

FROMM-MICHAELS, ILSE (1888-   )
Passacaglia, Op. 16 [15']
    3(pic).2.2.2. 2.2.2.1. timp,
    strings
    RIES perf mat rent   (F186)

FROMMEL, GERHARD (1906-   )
Concerto in B minor for Piano,
    Clarinet and String Orchestra
    [25']
    string orch,pno solo,clar solo
    RIES perf mat rent   (F187)

FROMMEL, GERHARD (cont'd.)
Neun Gedichte Aus "Sange Eines
    Fahrenden Spielmanns" Von Stefan
    George, For Solo Voice And
    Chamber Orchestra [25']
    1.0.1.1. 1.0.0.0. strings,solo
    voice
    RIES perf mat rent   (F188)

Variationen Uber Ein Eigenes Thema
    [16']
    2(pic).2.2.2. 4.2.3.0. timp,cym,
    harp,strings
    RIES perf mat rent   (F189)

FRUHLING AM LAGO MAGGIORE see Pero,
    Hans

FRUHLINGSLIED see Sibelius, Jean,
    Spring Song

FRUHLINGSSTIMMEN WALZER see Strauss,
    Johann, [Jr.]

FRUMERIE, (PER) GUNNAR (FREDRIK) DE
    (1908-   )
Jungfru Maria, For Solo Voice And
    Orchestra *Op.12,No.1 [6']
    1.1.2.2. 2.2.0.0. timp,perc,harp,
    cel,strings,solo voice
    sc STIM perf mat rent   (F190)

FUCHS, CARL EMIL
Improvisationen [13']
    2fl,3clar,bass clar,harp,strings
    sc RIES f.s., perf mat rent   (F191)

Ungarische Serenade [14']
    2.1.2.1. 2.2.1.0. timp,perc,harp,
    strings
    RIES perf mat rent   (F192)

FUCIK, JULIUS (1872-1916)
Entrance Of The Gladiators [3'30"]
    1(pic).2.2.2. 4.2.3.0. timp,perc,
    strings
    KALMUS A1458 sc $2.00, perf mat
    rent, set $12.00, pts $1.00, ea.
                                   (F193)
    LUCKS 05563 sc $2.00, set $11.50,
    pts $.95, ea.   (F194)

FUGA DEL GATTO see Scarlatti, Domenico

FUGGER-ZEITBILDER see Kaiser-Eric, W.

FUGHETTA see Bossi, [Marco] Enrico

FUGHETTA see Buxtehude, Dietrich

FUGHETTA see Pollarolo, Carlo Francesco

FUGHETTA SOPRA "QUESTE SOLE DIECI SANTE
    PRECI" see Bach, Johann Sebastian

FUGUES, FIVE, [ARR.] see Bach, Johann
    Sebastian

FULEIHAN, ANIS (1900-1970)
Symphony No. 2
    sc BOOSEY $17.50   (F195)

FUNERAL MARCH OF A MARIONETTE see
    Gounod, Charles Francois, Marche
    Funebre D'Une Marionette

FUNERAL MUSIC, FOR SOLO VOICE AND
    ORCHESTRA see Lhotka-Kalinski, Ivo

FUNF BAGATELLEN see Stam, Henk

FUNF CHORALVORSPIELE, [ARR.] see
    Brahms, Johannes, Chorale Preludes,
    Five, [arr.]

FUNF KLEINE STUCKE see Juon, Paul

FUNF LIEDER, FOR SOLO VOICE AND
    ORCHESTRA see Schwickert, Gustav

FUNF ORCHESTERLIEDER, FOR SOLO VOICE
    AND ORCHESTRA see Goosen, Jacques

FUNICULI-FUNICULA, [ARR.] see Denza,
    Luigi

FUNK, FRANZ
Du Hast Im Blick
    RIES f.s.   (F196)

FUR ELISE, [ARR.] see Beethoven, Ludwig
    van

FUR LUSTIGE LEUT' see Strauss, Eduard

FUR P.D. see Goldmann, Friedrich

FURIADE see Stanke, Willy

FURIOSO POLKA see Strauss, Johann,
    [Jr.]

FURLOTTI, ARNALDO (1880-1958)
Samaritana, La: Preludio [4']
    3.3.2.2. 4.3.3.1. timp,strings
    manuscript CARISCH   (F197)

FURST, PAUL WALTER (1926-   )
Rannoch-Concerto, For Horn And
    Orchestra *Op.59 [15']
    2(2pic).2+English horn.2+bass'
    clar.2. 4.3.3.1. timp,perc,
    strings,horn solo
    sc,pts DOBLINGER rent   (F198)

FURST BARIATINSKY MARSCH see Strauss,
    Johann, [Jr.]

FURSTIN NINETTA; NEUE PIZZICATO POLKA
    see Strauss, Johann, [Jr.]

FUSIONEN WALZER see Strauss, Eduard

FUSIONS-DIFFUSIONS see Mestral, Patrice

FUSZWASCHUNG, DIE, FOR SOLO VOICE AND
    ORCHESTRA see Zagwijn, Henri

G

GAATHAUG, MORTEN
  Landscape *Op.14 [12']
    2(pic).2(English horn).2(bass
    clar).2(contrabsn). 4.2.3.1.
    timp,perc,harp,strings
    NORGE   (G1)

GABLENZ MARSCH see Strauss, Josef

GABOLD, INGOLF (1942-   )
  Four Texts In Music, For Solo Voice
    And Orchestra
    sc HANSEN-DEN WH 29543 $31.00   (G2)

GABRIELI, DOMENICO (ca. 1650-1690)
  Sonata in D, MIN 98
    trp,strings,cont
    (XI 4) MUS. RARA 1933B f.s.   (G3)

  Sonata in D, MIN 99
    trp,strings,cont
    (XI 7) MUS. RARA 1954B f.s.   (G4)

  Sonata in D, MIN 100
    trp,strings,cont
    (XI 8) MUS. RARA 1943B f.s.   (G5)

  Sonata No. 2
    trp,strings,hpsd
    (Voisin, Roger) INTERNAT. perf mat
    rent   (G6)

  Sonata No. 3
    trp,strings,org
    (Voisin, Roger) INTERNAT. perf mat
    rent   (G7)

  Sonata No. 4
    trp,strings,org
    (Voisin, Roger) INTERNAT. perf mat
    rent   (G8)

GABRIELIANA see Malipiero, Gian
  Francesco

GABUCCI, A. (1896-1976)
  Aria E Scherzo, For Clarinet And
    String Orchestra [8']
    string orch,clar solo
    sc CARISCH 21786 f.s., pts CARISCH
    21787 f.s.   (G9)

GADE, NIELS WILHELM (1817-1890)
  Bornenes Juul, [arr.] *Op.36
    (Hoffman) "Christmas Eve Suite,
    [arr.]" string orch [8'30"]
    KALMUS 3456 sc $5.00, set $5.00
                                    (G10)

  Christmas Eve Suite, [arr.] *see
    Bornenes Juul, [arr.]

  Concerto for Violin and Orchestra,
    Op. 56, in D minor
    BREITKOPF-W perf mat rent   (G11)

GAEBEL, KURT
  Ouverture Zur Operette "Fatinitza"
    [7']
    2.2.2.2. 4.2.3.0. timp,perc,harp,
    strings
    RIES perf mat rent   (G12)

GAGIC, BOGDAN (1931-   )
  Symphony
    2.3.3.3. 4.3.3.1. 2harp,strings
    DRUS.HRVAT.SKLAD. f.s.   (G13)

GAHER, JOZEF (1934-   )
  Concerto Grosso No. 3
    1.2.2.2. 2.2.0.0. timp,perc,
    strings,fl solo,vln solo,pno
    solo
    SLOV.HUD.FOND 0-484 perf mat rent
                                    (G14)

GALANT KWARTET, FOR SOLO VOICE AND
  ORCHESTRA see Mul, Jan

GALGARIEN see Holm, Mogens Winkel

GALGENLIEDER, FOR SOLO VOICE AND
  ORCHESTRA see Boer, Ed de

GALIMATHIAS MUSICUM, K. 32 see Mozart,
  Wolfgang Amadeus

GALLIERA, ALCEO (1910-   )
  Idillio [8']
    2.2.2.2. 0.0.0.0. timp,bells,
    strings
    manuscript CARISCH   (G15)

GALLIERA, ARNALDO (1871-1934)
  Chorale (from Suite Dionisiaca) [4']
    3.3.3.3. 4.2.3.1. timp,perc,
    2harp,strings
    manuscript CARISCH   (G16)

GALOPPING STRINGS see Steffaro, Julius

GALUPPI, BALDASSARE (1706-1785)
  Filosofo Di Campagna, Il: Aria Di
    Lena, For Solo Voice And String
    Orchestra [3']
    string orch,S solo
    manuscript CARISCH   (G17)

GAMES see Tandler, Juraj, Hry

GAMMALMODIG SVIT see Linde, Bo

GANDINO (1878-1940)
  Novelletta [5']
    2.2.2.2. 2.2.1.0. timp,perc,harp,
    strings
    sc CARISCH 16495 f.s., perf mat
    rent   (G18)

GARCIA MORILLO, ROBERTO
  see MORILLO, ROBERTO GARCIA

GARDENIA see Dressel, Erwin

GARDNER, JOHN LINTON (1917-   )
  Overture Half Holiday
    sets NOVELLO 9066-67 $47.50, and
    up, sc NOVELLO 9065 $8.75, pts
    NOVELLO 9597 $1.50, ea.   (G19)

GARTENFEST, EIN see Schlensog, Martin

GASSMANN, FLORIAN LEOPOLD (1729-1774)
  Symphonies, Seven
    (Hill, George R.) ("The Symphony",
    Vol. B-X) sc GARLAND
    ISBN 0-8240-3807-X $90.00
    contains also: Wanhal, Johann
    Baptist (Jan Krtitel),
    Symphonies, Five (Bryan, Paul)
                                    (G20)

GAULDIN, ROBERT (1931-   )
  Diverse Dances
    sc,pts ACCURA 040 rent   (G21)

GAUSSIN, ALLAIN (1943-   )
  Eclipse, For 2 Pianos And
    Instrumental Ensemble [20']
    1.1.2.1. 1.1.1.1. 4perc,harp,vln,
    vla,vcl,db,2pno soli
    RICORDI-FR R.2262 perf mat rent
                                    (G22)

  Ogive, For Harpsichord And Strings
    [22'-23']
    12strings,hpsd solo
    RICORDI-FR R.2276 perf mat rent
                                    (G23)

GAVAZZENI, GIANANDREA (1909-   )
  Canti Per Sant'Alessandro:
    Interludio, For Solo Voice And
    Orchestra [6']
    3.3.2.3. 4.3.3.1. timp,perc,harp,
    pno,strings,female solo
    manuscript CARISCH   (G24)

  Concerto for Violin and Orchestra
    [25']
    2.2.2.2. 2.2.0.0. timp,perc,pno,
    strings,vln solo
    manuscript CARISCH   (G25)

GAVOTTA see Bolzoni, Giovanni

GAVOTTA see Martucci, Giuseppe

GAVOTTE see Lully, Jean-Baptiste
  (Lulli)

GAVOTTE A LA HENRY see Luck, Arthur

GAVOTTE AND VALSE MENUET see Bird,
  Arthur

GAVOTTE, [ARR.] see Martini, [Padre]
  Giovanni Battista

GAVOTTE CIRCUS RENZ see Fliege, Hermann

GAVOTTE EN RUMBA see Felderhof, Jan

GAVOTTE NO. 2 see Luck, Arthur

GAVOTTE, [ARR.] see Gossec, Francois
  Joseph

GAVOTTES FROM FRENCH SUITES NO. 5 AND
  6, [ARR.] see Bach, Johann
  Sebastian

GAYANE: SABRE DANCE see Khachaturian,
  Aram Ilyich

GAYANE: THREE DANCES see Khachaturian,
  Aram Ilyich

GAYANEH: LA DANZA DELLE SCIABOLE see
  Khachaturian, Aram Ilyich, Gayane:
  Sabre Dance

GAZELLE, DIE see Strauss, Josef

GAZZA LADRA, LA: OVERTURE see Rossini,
  Gioacchino

GEBEDT see Dijk, Jan van

GEBENEDIJD see Dijk, Jan van

GEBET, FOR SOLO VOICE AND ORCHESTRA see
  Wolf, Hugo

GEBHARD, MARTIN ANTON (1776-1836)
  Salve Regina for Solo Voice and
    Orchestra
    fl,org/pno,strings,T/S solo
    [Lat] EULENBURG GM254 set $12.00,
    pts $1.75, ea.   (G26)

GEBURTSTAGSMARSCH see Kuhne, Ferdinand

GEDACHTNISLIEDER, FOR SOLO VOICE AND
  ORCHESTRA see Kox, Hans

GEDENKBLATTER WALZER see Strauss, Josef

GEFESSELTE ORPHEUS, DER see Kohler,
  Siegfried

GEFORS, HANS (1952-   )
  Slits [17']
    2.2.2.2. 4.2.3.0. timp,strings
    STIM   (G27)

GEIGE WEINT, DIE see Wismar, R.

GEISLER, WILLY
  Aus Dem Stegreif
    RIES f.s.   (G28)

  Bin Nur Ein Armer Dichter
    RIES f.s.   (G29)

  Endspurt
    RIES f.s.   (G30)

  Liebeslieder Ohne Worte
    RIES f.s.   (G31)

  Mein Lieblingslied
    RIES f.s.   (G32)

  Melodia
    RIES f.s.   (G33)

  Melodie Und Rhythmus
    RIES f.s.   (G34)

  Musikanten-Suite
    RIES f.s.   (G35)

  Uber Lander Und Meere
    RIES f.s.   (G36)

  Vom Menuett Zum Walzer
    RIES f.s.   (G37)

  Zahide
    RIES f.s.   (G38)

GEISSLER, FRITZ (1921-   )
  Konzertante Fantasie
    1.2.0.0. 2.0.0.0. strings
    DEUTSCHER perf mat rent   (G39)

  Symphony No. 9
    3.3.3.3. 4.3.3.1. timp,perc,
    strings
    sc DEUTSCHER 1711 f.s., perf mat
    rent   (G40)

  Symphony No. 10
    2.2.2.2. 4.3.3.1. harp,timp,perc,
    strings
    sc DEUTSCHER 1716 f.s., perf mat
    rent   (G41)

GEIST, JOHN
  Lake: To ......, The [7']
    BELLA   (G42)

GEIST DES WOIWODEN, DER: CSARDAS see
  Grossmann, Louis

GEISTLICHES KONZERT, FOR SOLO VOICE AND
  ORCHESTRA see Metzler, Friedrich

GELBE NARZISSEN see Ritter, Helmut

GEMINIANI, FRANCESCO (1687-1762)
  Concerti Grossi, Nos. 1-3 (from
    Sonatas, Op. 5, By Corelli)
    string orch,cont,2vln soli,vcl
    solo
    KALMUS A 4578 set $10.50, pts
    $1.50, ea.   (G43)

  Concerti Grossi, Nos. 4-6 (from
    Sonatas, Op. 5, By Corelli)
    string orch,cont,2vln soli,vcl
    solo
    KALMUS A4579 set $10.50, pts $1.50,
    ea.   (G44)

  Concerto Grosso, Op. 3, No. 1, in D
    LUCKS 05241 sc $4.00, set $8.75,
    min sc $3.50, pts $1.15, ea.   (G45)

GEMS OF STEPHEN FOSTER, [ARR.] see
  Foster, Stephen Collins

GENESIS see Rice, Thomas

GENITUM see Brozak, Daniel

GENTILI, ALBERTO (1873-1954)
Danza Jeratica [9']
3.3.3.2. 4.3.3.1. perc,cel,harp,
strings
perf mat rent sc CARISCH 18730, pts
CARISCH   (G46)

Prelude
2.2.2.2. 2.1.0.0. harp,cel,
strings
sc CARISCH 20753 perf mat rent
         (G47)

GENZMER, HARALD (1909-)
Cantata for Solo Voice, Trumpet and
String Orchestra [21']
string orch,trp solo,S/T solo
PETERS perf mat rent   (G48)

Chamber Concerto, For Viola And
String Orchestra
string orch,vla solo
PETERS 8134 sc $20.00, set $22.50,
pts $25.00, $3.75   (G49)

Concertino for Piano and String
Orchestra, No. 2
string orch,pno solo
PETERS 5973 study sc $15.50, sc
$27.50, set $35.00, pts $3.25,
ea., solo pt $15.50   (G50)

Concerto for Organ and String
Orchestra, No. 2 [15']
string orch,org solo
PETERS perf mat rent   (G51)

Concerto for Percussion and Orchestra
[21']
3.2.2.2. 2.2.1.0. strings,perc
solo
PETERS perf mat rent   (G52)

Concerto for Piano and Orchestra, MIN
44 [20']
2(pic).2.2.2. 3.2.0.0. timp,
strings,pno solo
RIES perf mat rent   (G53)

Concerto For Trautonium And Orchestra
[20']
2.2.2.2. 2.2.2.1. strings,
trautonium solo
RIES perf mat rent   (G54)

Music for Orchestra [31']
2.2.2.2. 4.2.1.0. timp,2perc,
harp,strings
PETERS perf mat rent   (G55)

Mystic Trumpeter, The *see Cantata
for Solo Voice, Trumpet and
String Orchestra

Notturno for Horn and String
Orchestra
string orch,horn/vla solo
sc PETERS 8106 $14.00, pts PETERS
$2.25, ea., set PETERS $15.00
         (G56)

Sonatina for String Orchestra
string orch
sc PETERS 8050 $16.00, pts PETERS
$2.75, ea., set PETERS $13.75
         (G57)

Sonatina for String Orchestra, No. 2
string orch
sc PETERS 8156 $18.00, pts PETERS
$3.00, ea., set PETERS $15.00
         (G58)

GEOGRAPHIE INTERIEURE see Booren, Jo
van den

GEORG-TRAKL-LIEDER, FOR SOLO VOICE AND
ORCHESTRA see Goosen, Jacques

GEORGE, EARL ROBERT (1924-)
Thanksgiving Overture, A
sc BOOSEY $9.00   (G59)

GEORGICA see Bucht, Gunnar

GERELLI, ENNIO (1907-1970)
Concerto for Strings and Piano [12']
string orch,pno
sc,pts ZANIBON D231 rent   (G60)

GERMAN, [SIR] EDWARD (EDWARD GERMAN
JONES) (1862-1936)
Gipsy Suite [15']
2.2.2.2. 4.2.3.0. timp,perc,harp,
strings
KALMUS 5348 sc $24.00, perf mat
rent, set $50.00, pts $2.00, ea.
         (G61)

Henry VIII: Three Dances
LUCKS 05587 sc $12.00, set $20.00,
pts $1.40, ea.   (G62)

Nell Gwyn: Three Dances
LUCKS 05586 sc $15.00, set $19.00,
pts $1.40, ea.   (G63)

GERMAN DANCES, SIX, K. 571 see Mozart,
Wolfgang Amadeus, Deutsche Tanze,
Sechs, K. 571

GERMAN DANCES, THREE, K. 605 see
Mozart, Wolfgang Amadeus, Deutsche
Tanze, Drei, K. 605

GERMAN DANCES, TWELVE, WOO. 8 see
Beethoven, Ludwig van, Deutsche
Tanze, Zwolf, WoO. 8

GERMETEN, GUNNAR
Dance Through The Land Of Shadows,
The *see Dansen Gjennom
Skuggeheimen

Dansen Gjennom Skuggeheimen [13'30"]
string orch
"Dance Through The Land Of Shadows,
The" NORGE   (G64)

GERUSALEMME CONVERTITA see Caldara,
Antonio

GERVAISE, CLAUDE (fl. ca. 1550)
Dance Suite
sets NOVELLO 9069-70 $22.50, and
up, sc NOVELLO 9068 $19.25, pts
NOVELLO 9598 $1.00, ea.   (G65)

GERVASIO, RAFFAELE (1910-)
Preludio E Allegro Concertante
perc,pno,strings
sc CARISCH 21867 rent, pts CARISCH
21868 rent   (G66)

GESANG WEYLAS "DU BIST ORPLID, MEIN
LAND", FOR SOLO VOICE AND ORCHESTRA
see Wolf, Hugo

GESANG ZUR NACHT, FOR SOLO VOICE AND
ORCHESTRA see Stuppner, Hubert

GESCHICHTEN AUS DEM WIENERWALD WALZER
see Strauss, Johann, [Jr.]

GESCHICHTEN AUS DEM WIENERWALD WALZER,
FOR SOLO VOICE AND ORCHESTRA see
Strauss, Johann, [Jr.]

GESCHOPFE DES PROMETHEUS, DIE: OVERTURE
see Beethoven, Ludwig van

GESPENSTER see Huber, Nicolaus A.

GESTA see Renosto, Paolo

GESTALT see Hamel, Peter Michael

GESTIEFELTE KATER, DER: SZENEN UND
BALLETTMUSIK see Bialas, Gunter

GESTURES see Brun, Herbert

GESU PRESENTATO NEL TEMPIO see Caldara,
Antonio

GEVECHT, HET, FOR SOLO VOICE AND
ORCHESTRA see Laman, Wim

GEWICKSMANN, VITALI
Symphony No. 3
min sc PETERS 5794 $14.50, perf mat
rent   (G67)

GHELE BLOEMKENS see Badings, Henk

GIANFERRARI, VINCENZO (1859-1939)
Tre Preludi [9']
3.3.3.2. 4.3.3.1. timp,perc,cel,
harp,strings
sc CARISCH 16488 perf mat rent
         (G68)

GIANNELLA, LOUIS (ca. 1778-1817)
Concerto Lugubre, For Flute And
Orchestra [14']
0.2.0.1. 2.2.0.0. timp,strings,fl
solo
(Scimone, C.) sc ZANIBON 5457 f.s.,
pts ZANIBON 5458 f.s.   (G69)

GIANNINA E BERNARDONE: OVERTURE see
Cimarosa, Domenico

GIANNINI, VITTORIO (1903-1966)
Frescobaldiana
sc KALMUS A7015 $20.00   (G70)

Symphony No. 1
sc KALMUS A7014 $50.00   (G71)

GIANT FUGUE see Bach, Johann Sebastian,
Wir Glauben All' An Einem Gott,
[arr.]

GIARDINO MAGICO, IL see Nielsen, Tage

GIARDINO RELIGIOSO see Maderna, Bruno

GIEFER, WILLY (1930-)
Relief [15']
3.3(English horn).3.3(contrabsn).
4.3.3.1. timp,2perc,strings
BREITKOPF-W perf mat rent   (G72)

GIELEN, MICHAEL ANDREAS (1927-)
Einige Schwierigkeiten Bei Der
Uberwindung Der Angst [30'-60']
4.4.4.0. 4.4.4.2. timp,perc,2pno,
2org,30vln
BREITKOPF-W perf mat rent   (G73)

GIETER see Janssen, Guus

GIGANTES Y CABEZUDOS see Caballero,
M.F.

GIGERLETTE see Bordewijk-Roepman,
Johanna

GILSE, JAN VAN (1881-1944)
Drei Gesange, For Solo Voice And
Orchestra
2.2.2.2. 4.3.3.1. timp,harp,
strings,med solo sc DONEMUS f.s.,
perf mat rent
contains: Frieden; Herbststurm;
Konigslied, Das   (G74)

Drei Gesange Aus R. Tagore's "Der
Gartner", For Solo Voice And
Orchestra
3.3.2.2. 4.3.3.0. timp,2harp,cel,
strings,S solo
sc DONEMUS f.s., perf mat rent
         (G75)

Drei Gesange Aus R. Tagore's
"Gitanjali" [14']
2.3.2.2. 4.3.3.0. timp,perc,harp,
cel,strings,S solo
sc DONEMUS f.s., perf mat rent
         (G76)

Erhebung, For Solo Voice And
Orchestra (Symphony No. 3) [55']
3.3.4.3. 6.4.3.1. timp,perc,harp,
strings,S solo
sc DONEMUS f.s., perf mat rent
         (G77)

Frieden
see Drei Gesange, For Solo Voice
And Orchestra

Herbststurm
see Drei Gesange, For Solo Voice
And Orchestra

Konigslied, Das
see Drei Gesange, For Solo Voice
And Orchestra

Symphony No. 3 *see Erhebung, For
Solo Voice And Orchestra

GILTAY, BEREND (1910-1975)
Drei Lieder, For Solo Voice And
Strings [10']
strings without db,A solo
sc DONEMUS f.s., perf mat rent
         (G78)

Gosauer Symphonie [44']
3.2.2.2. 4.3.3.0. timp,perc,
strings
sc DONEMUS f.s., perf mat rent
         (G79)

Kosmochromie I [21']
3.3.3.3. 4.3.3.0. timp,perc,
marimba,vibra,strings,
4loudspeakers
sc DONEMUS f.s., perf mat rent
         (G80)

Kosmochromie II, For String Quartet
And Chamber Orchestra [12']
0.2.0.0. 2.0.0.0. 12vln,3vla,
3vcl,2db,opt electronic tape,
string quar soli
sc DONEMUS f.s., perf mat rent
         (G81)

Sinfonia Piccola [14']
2.2.2.2. 2.0.0.0. timp,perc,
strings
sc DONEMUS f.s., perf mat rent
         (G82)

Symphony No. 2 [26']
2.2.2.2. 3.2.0.0. timp,perc,
strings
sc DONEMUS f.s., perf mat rent
         (G83)

Variazioni Sinfoniche [22']
2.2.2.1. 3.2.0.0. timp,perc,pno
4-hands,strings
sc DONEMUS f.s., perf mat rent
         (G84)

GIMENEZ, JERONIMO (1854-1923)
Boda De Luis Alonso, La: Intermedio
No. 4
LUCKS 06078 sc $35.00, set $50.00,
pts $2.50, ea.   (G85)

GINASTERA, ALBERTO (1916-)
Glosses Sobre Temes De Pau Casals
*Op.48 [18']
3(pic).3(English horn).3(clar in
E flat,bass clar).3(contrabsn).
4.3(piccolo trp).3.1. timp,
perc,harp,pno,cel,harmonium,
strings
BOOSEY perf mat rent   (G86)

GIOCONDA, LA: CIELO E MAR, FOR SOLO
VOICE AND ORCHESTRA see Ponchielli,
Amilcare

GIOCONDA, LA: OMBRE DI MIA PROSAPIA,
FOR SOLO VOICE AND ORCHESTRA see
Ponchielli, Amilcare

GIOCONDA, LA: SELECTION see Ponchielli,
Amilcare

GIOCONDA, LA: SUICIDIO - IN QUESTI
FIERI MOMENTI, FOR SOLO VOICE AND
ORCHESTRA see Ponchielli, Amilcare

GIOCONDA, LA: VOCE DI DONNA, FOR SOLO
VOICE AND ORCHESTRA see Ponchielli,
Amilcare

GIOIELLI DELLA MADONNA, I: INTERMEZZO E
SERENATA see Wolf-Ferrari, Ermanno

GIORDANI, GIUSEPPE (ca. 1753-1798)
Caro Mio Ben, For Solo Voice And
String Orchestra, [arr.]
"Dearest Believe" string orch,solo
voice LUCKS 02058 set $3.00, pts
$.75, ea. (G87)

Dearest Believe *see Caro Mio Ben,
For Solo Voice And String
Orchestra, [arr.]

GIORDANI, TOMMASO (1730-1806)
Sinfonia in E flat, MIN 86
2ob/2fl,2trp,perc,strings
sc,pts HARMONIA 2047 f.s. (G88)

GIORDANO, UMBERTO (1867-1948)
Andrea Chenier: La Mamma Morta, For
Solo Voice And Orchestra
LUCKS 02305 sc $5.00, set $10.00,
pts $.75, ea. (G89)

Andrea Chenier: Un Di All' Azzurro
Spazio, For Solo Voice And
Orchestra
LUCKS 02225 sc $4.00, set $8.00,
pts $.75, ea. (G90)

GIORNI DELUSI, I see Mariatti, Franco

GIORNO DELLA VITA, UN see Ullman, Bo

GIORNO IN CONSERVATORIO, UN see
Viezzer, M.

GIOSEFFO CHE INTERPRETA I SOGNI see
Caldara, Antonio

GIOVANNA D'ARCO: OVERTURE see Verdi,
Giuseppe

GIPSY SONGS: SONGS MY MOTHER TAUGHT ME,
FOR SOLO VOICE AND ORCHESTRA,
[ARR.] see Dvorak, Antonin

GIPSY SUITE see German, [Sir] Edward
(Edward German Jones)

GIUFFRE, GAETANO (1918-   )
Invenzione, For Flute And String
Orchestra
string orch,fl solo
SEESAW perf mat rent (G91)

New York Concerto
2.2.2.2. 4.3.3.0. timp,perc,harp,
strings,pno solo
SEESAW perf mat rent (G92)

GIUFFRE, JAMES PETER (JIMMY)
(1921-   )
Mirrors For Jazz Trio And Orchestra
[16']
0.0.0.0. 2.2.2.0. strings,clar&
fl&soprano sax&bass fl&tenor
sax solo,drums solo,db solo
MARGUN BP 3001 perf mat rent (G93)

Symphonic Movement [5']
3.3.3.3. 4.3.3.1. 3perc,harp,cel,
strings
MARGUN BP 3027 perf mat rent (G94)

GIUGNO, FOR SOLO VOICE AND ORCHESTRA
see Bruschettini, M.

GIULIANI, MAURO (1781-1829)
Concerto for Guitar and String
Orchestra, Op. 36, in A
(Henze) KALMUS A1185 sc $15.00,
perf mat rent, set $25.00, pts
$3.50, ea. (G95)

GIULIO CESARE: PIANGERO, PIANGERO, FOR
SOLO VOICE AND ORCHESTRA see
Handel, George Frideric

GIULIO CESARE: V'ADORO PUPILLE, FOR
SOLO VOICE AND ORCHESTRA see
Handel, George Frideric

GIUSTINO, IL: SINFONIA see Vivaldi,
Antonio

GLADIATOR MARCH, THE see Sousa, John
Philip

GLASER, JAN PIETER
Sinfonia 1-6
2ob,2trp,strings
sc,pts HARMONIA 1855 f.s. (G96)

GLASER, WERNER WOLF (1910-   )
Concerto for Saxophone and String
Orchestra [17']
string orch,soprano sax solo
sc STIM perf mat rent (G97)
STIM (G98)

Divertimento No. 2 [18'30"]
string orch,wind quin
sc STIM perf mat rent (G99)

Martinson-Kantat, For Solo Voices And
Chamber Orchestra
1.1.1.1. 1.1.0.0. strings,AMez
soli
STIM (G100)

Old English Love Songs, For Solo
Voice And Orchestra [23'30"]
2.2.2.2. 2.2.0.0. timp,strings,S/
T solo
pts,solo pt STIM perf mat rent (G101)

Symphony No. 10 [42']
3.3.3.2. 4.2.3.1. timp,4perc,
strings
sc STIM perf mat rent (G102)

Triologia 2 [40']
3.3.3.2. 4.2.3.1. timp,5perc,
harp,strings
sc STIM (G103)

GLAZUNOV, ALEXANDER KONSTANTINOVICH
(1865-1936)
Chant Du Menestrel, For Violoncello
And Orchestra *Op.71
LUCKS 01809 sc $3.00, set $8.00,
pts $.75, ea. (G104)

Chopiniana *Op.46
min sc BELAIEFF BEL 460 $30.00, ipr
(G105)

Concerto for Saxophone and String
Orchestra in E flat [15']
string orch,alto sax solo
KALMUS 5405 solo pt $3.00, sc
$8.00, perf mat rent, set $15.00,
pts $3.00, ea. (G106)

Concerto for Violin and Orchestra,
Op. 82, in A minor
LUCKS 00510 sc $15.50, set $32.00,
min sc $4.00, pts $1.75, ea. (G107)

Cortege Solennel, Op. 50
KALMUS A4645 sc $7.00, perf mat
rent, set $30.00, pts $1.00, ea. (G108)

Forest, The *Op.19 [18']
3.2.2.2. 4.2.3.1. timp,perc,harp,
strings
"Foret, La" KALMUS 5229 sc $25.00,
perf mat rent, set $40.00, pts
$1.50, ea. (G109)

Foret, La *see Forest, The

Intermezzo Romantico *Op.69 [5']
3.2.2.2. 4.2.3.1. timp,strings
KALMUS 5228 sc $8.00, perf mat
rent, set $25.00, pts $1.00, ea. (G110)

Jour De Fete (composed with Liadov,
Anatol Konstantinovich; Rimsky-
Korsakov, Nikolai) [12']
string orch
BELAIEFF BEL416 sc $22.50, pts rent
(G111)

Mazurka *Op.18 [8']
3.2.2.2. 4.2.3.0. timp,perc,
strings
KALMUS 5226 sc $12.00, perf mat
rent, set $35.00, pts $1.50, ea. (G112)

Melodie Et Serenade Espagnole, For
Violoncello And Orchestra *Op.20
"Two Pieces For Cello And
Orchestra" KALMUS A1120 sc
$12.00, perf mat rent, set
$15.00, pts $1.00, ea. (G113)

Mer, La *see Sea, The

Overture On Greek Themes, No. 1, Op.
3
KALMUS A1480 sc $25.00, perf mat
rent, set $40.00, pts $2.00, ea. (G114)

Poeme Lyrique, Op. 12
KALMUS A4354 sc $8.00, perf mat
rent, set $15.00, pts $.75, ea. (G115)

Primavera D'Or, La, For Solo Voice
And Orchestra
LUCKS 02853 set $7.50, pts $.75,
ea. (G116)

Ruses d'Amour: Grand Pas Des Fiances
2+pic.2.2.2. 4.2.3.1. timp,perc,
harp,strings,vln solo,vcl solo

GLAZUNOV, ALEXANDER KONSTANTINOVICH
(cont'd.)

KALMUS A3192 sc $5.00, perf mat
rent, set $15.00, pts $2.00, ea.
(G117)

Sea, The *Op.28 [22']
3.3.3.3. 6.4.3.1. timp,perc,1-
2harp,strings
"Mer, La" KALMUS 5349 sc $27.00,
perf mat rent, set $66.00, pts
$2.00, ea. (G118)

Seasons, The, Op. 67: Spring
3.2.2.2. 4.2.3.1. timp,perc,harp,
cel,strings
KALMUS 5179 sc $7.00, perf mat
rent, set $22.00, pts $1.00, ea. (G119)

Seasons, The, Op. 67: Summer
3.2.2.2. 4.2.3.1. timp,perc,harp,
cel,strings
KALMUS 5178 sc $20.00, perf mat
rent, set $40.00, pts $1.50, ea. (G120)

Triumphal March *Op.40
KALMUS A4646 sc $10.00, perf mat
rent, set $32.00, pts $1.00, ea. (G121)

Two Pieces For Cello And Orchestra
*see Melodie Et Serenade
Espagnole, For Violoncello And
Orchestra

Vendredis Polka, Les (composed with
Liadov, Anatol Konstantinovich;
Sokolov, Nikolai Alexandrovich)
string orch
KALMUS 5429 sc $5.00, set $6.25,
pts $1.25, ea. (G122)

GLIERE, REINHOLD MORITZOVICH
(1875-1956)
Red Poppy, The: Russian Sailors'
Dance
LUCKS 05606 sc $10.50, set $32.00,
pts $1.75, ea. (G123)

Red Poppy, The: Suite
KALMUS A1482 sc $30.00, perf mat
rent, set $80.00, pts $3.50, ea. (G124)

Sirens, The *Op.33 [15']
4.4.4.3. 6.3.3.1. timp,perc,cel,
strings
KALMUS 5297 sc $25.00, perf mat
rent, set $90.00, pts $3.50, ea. (G125)

GLIMPSE INTO THE UNKNOWN, FOR SOLO
VOICE AND ORCHESTRA see Suchon,
Eugen, Pohl'ad Do Neznama, For Solo
Voice And Orchestra

GLINKA, MIKHAIL IVANOVICH (1804-1857)
Capriccio Brillante On "Jota
Aragonese"
LUCKS 07130 sc $14.00, set $25.00,
pts $1.50, ea. (G126)

Life For The Tsar, A: Mazurka
BROUDE BR. sc $5.00, set $15.00,
pts $1.00, ea. (G127)

Life For The Tsar, A: Overture
min sc PETERS 705 $5.00 (G128)

Prince Kholmsky: Overture And
Interlude
2.1.2.2. 2.2.1.0. timp,strings
(Glazunov; Rimsky-Korsakov) min sc
BELAIEFF BEL470 $24.50, ipr
(G129)

Russlan And Ludmilla: Overture
BROUDE BR. set $25.00, pts $1.75,
ea. (G130)
2.2.2.2. 4.3.2.0. timp,strings [4']
INTERNAT. perf mat rent (G131)
LUCKS 05609 sc $5.00, set $18.00,
min sc $3.50, pts $.95, ea. (G132)

Valse-Fantaisie
LUCKS 05272 sc $10.00, set $18.00,
pts $1.50, ea. (G133)

GLOBOKAR, VINKO (1934-   )
Carrousel, For Solo Voices And
Instrumental Ensemble [40']
1.0.2.1.sax. 1.0.0.1. harp,gtr,
acord,elec org,vln,vla,vcl,db,4
solo voices
PETERS perf mat rent (G134)

Kafig, Der
PETERS perf mat rent (G135)

GLOSELUND, FOR SOLO VOICE AND ORCHESTRA
see Kvam, Oddvar S.

GLOSSES SOBRE TEMES DE PAU CASALS see
Ginastera, Alberto

GLUCK, CHRISTOPH WILLIBALD, RITTER VON
(1714-1787)
Alceste: Divinites Du Styx, For Solo
Voice And Orchestra
LUCKS 02007 sc $4.00, set $7.50,

GLUCK, CHRISTOPH WILLIBALD, RITTER VON
  (cont'd.)

    pts $.75, ea.   (G136)

  Alceste: Overture
    2.2.2.3. 2.0.3.0. strings
    sc LIENAU f.s.   (G137)
    (Weingartner) LUCKS 05611 sc $6.75,
    set $11.50, min sc $2.00, pts
    $.95, ea.   (G138)

  Ballet Music, [arr.]
    (Doppler) LUCKS 05612 sc $6.50, set
    $16.00, pts $.75, ea.   (G139)

  Concerto for Flute and Orchestra in
    G, MIN 49
    2horn,strings,fl solo
    (de Reede) sc AMADEUS BP 2051 f.s.,
    pts AMADEUS f.s.   (G140)

  Concerto for Flute and Orchestra in
    G, MIN 381
    LUCKS 01108 sc $3.00, set $9.00,
    pts $1.00, ea.   (G141)

  Iphigenie En Aulide: Overture
    (this edition scored for 2.2.2.2.
    2.2.3.0. timp, str with ending by
    W.A. Mozart) sc,pts LIENAU rent
                                     (G142)
    (Wagner) LUCKS 05615 sc $6.50, set
    $22.00, min sc $2.50, pts $1.40,
    ea.   (G143)

  Orfeo Ed Euridice: Air De Furies
    "Orpheus: Dance Of The Furies"
    LUCKS 08961 sc $1.75, set $8.50,
    pts $.75, ea.   (G144)

  Orfeo Ed Euridice: Ballet Des Ombres
    Heureuses, [arr.]
    (Mottl) "Orpheus: Dance Of The
    Blessed Spirits" LUCKS 08688 sc
    $2.75, set $6.75, pts $.75, ea. (G145)

  Orfeo Ed Euridice: Che Faro Senza
    Euridice, For Solo Voice And
    Orchestra
    LUCKS 02266 sc $2.00, set $3.00,
    pts $.75, ea.   (G146)

  Orfeo Ed Euridice: Overture
    0.2.0.2. 2.2.0.0. timp,strings
    sc LIENAU f.s.   (G147)
    LUCKS 05311 sc $3.75, set $11.50,
    pts $.95, ea.   (G148)

  Orfeo Ed Euridice: So Klag Ich Ihren
    Tod, For Solo Voice And Orchestra
    LUCKS 02940 sc $4.00, set $8.00,
    pts $.60, ea.   (G149)

  Orpheus: Dance Of The Blessed Spirits
    *see Orfeo Ed Euridice: Ballet
    Des Ombres Heureuses, [arr.]

  Orpheus: Dance Of The Furies *see
    Orfeo Ed Euridice: Air De Furies

  Overture in D
    string orch
    LUCKS 05288 sc $5.00, set $8.75,
    pts $1.75, ea.   (G150)

  Symphony in F, MIN 557
    2horn,strings
    LUCKS 01557 sc $6.25, set $8.00,
    pts $1.15, ea.   (G151)

  Symphony in G, MIN 289
    string orch
    LUCKS 05289 sc $6.50, set $7.50,
    pts $1.50, ea.   (G152)

GLUCK, DAS: OVERTURE see Prochazka,
  Rudolf

GLUCKLICH IST, WER VERGISST see
  Strauss, Johann, [Jr.]

GNECCO, FRANCESCO (1769-1810)
  Sinfonia all'Italiana [7']
    1.1.1.1. 2.1.0.0. timp,strings
    sc CARISCH 19467 f.s., pts CARISCH
    20008 f.s.   (G153)

GNOSSIENNES, TROIS, [ARR.] see Satie,
  Erik

GOD OF OUR FATHERS see Warren, George
  William

GOD REST YE, MERRY GENTLEMEN
  (Luck, Arthur) LUCKS HYMNS 23 set
  $15.00, pts $.65, ea. contains
  also: Up On The Housetop   (G154)

GODARD, BENJAMIN LOUIS PAUL (1849-1895)
  Jocelyn: Berceuse, For Solo Voice And
    Orchestra
    (Luck) LUCKS 02456 set $12.00, pts
    $.75, ea.   (G155)

GODARD, BENJAMIN LOUIS PAUL (cont'd.)

  Jocelyn: Suite No. 1
    2+pic.2(English horn).2.2.
    4.4.3.1. timp,perc,harp,strings
    KALMUS 5352 sc $12.00, perf mat
    rent, set $30.00, pts $1.00, ea.
                                     (G156)

  Jocelyn: Suite No. 2
    2+pic.2(English horn).2.2.
    4.2.3.1. timp,perc,harp,strings
    KALMUS 5353 sc $12.00, perf mat
    rent, set $30.00, pts $1.00, ea.
                                     (G157)

GODEC see Ukmar, Vilko

GODRON, HUGO (1900-1971)
  Hommage A Bizet [28']
    1.1.1.1. 0.1.0.0. pno,4vln,2vla,
    2vcl,db
    sc DONEMUS f.s., perf mat rent
                                     (G158)
  Promenades: Fanfare
    3.2.2.2. 2.2.0.0. timp,perc,
    strings
    sc DONEMUS f.s., perf mat rent
                                     (G159)

GOEDICKE, ALEXANDER (1877-1957)
  Concert Etude, For Trumpet And
    Orchestra *Op.49
    set BRASS PRESS $21.00   (G160)

GOEHR, ALEXANDER (1932-   )
  Metamorphosis - Dance
    3.3.3.3. 4.3.3.1. 3perc,harp,
    strings
    study sc SCHOTTS 75 A11300 $8.00
                                     (G161)

GOLABEK, JAKUB (ca. 1739-1789)
  Symphony in D
    see SYMPHONY IN POLAND, THE

GOLD AND SILVER WALTZ see Lehar, Franz,
  Gold Und Silber Walzer

GOLD UND SILBER WALZER see Lehar, Franz

GOLDE, ADOLF
  Wirbelwind [5']
    2(pic).2.2.2. 4.2.3.1. timp,perc,
    harp,strings
    (Dressel, Erwin) RIES perf mat rent
                                     (G162)

GOLDEN AGE, THE: POLKA see
  Shostakovich, Dmitri

GOLDEN AGE DANCES see Keuning, Hans P.

GOLDEN SPINNING WHEEL, THE see Dvorak,
  Antonin

GOLDEN YEARS, THE see Anderson, Leroy

GOLDFISCHLEIN POLKA see Strauss, Eduard

GOLDMANN, FRIEDRICH (1941-   )
  Concerto for Oboe and Orchestra [35']
    3.3.3.3. 4.3.3.0. 5perc,strings,
    ob solo
    sc PETERS EP 5538 f.s., perf mat
    rent   (G163)

  Concerto for Piano and Orchestra
    [28']
    3.3.2.3. 4.3.3.1. timp,perc,
    strings,pno solo
    sc PETERS EP 9590 f.s., perf mat
    rent   (G164)

  Concerto for Violin and Orchestra
    [35']
    3.3.3.3. 4.3.3.0. 5perc,strings,
    vln solo
    sc PETERS EP 5538 f.s., perf mat
    rent   (G165)

  Fur P.D. [5']
    15strings
    PETERS perf mat rent   (G166)

  Inclinatio Temporum [18']
    4.3.3.3. 4.3.3.1. perc,strings
    PETERS   (G167)

  Symphony No. 2 [28']
    4.2.3.2. 4.3.3.0. perc,strings
    PETERS perf mat rent   (G168)

GOLDMARK, KARL (1830-1915)
  Concerto for Violin and Orchestra,
    Op. 28, in A minor
    ERES 1899 rent   (G169)
    LUCKS 00511 sc $20.00, set $32.00,
    pts $1.75, ea.   (G170)

  Konigin Von Saba, Die: Ballet Music
    "Queen Of Sheba, The: Ballet Music"
    KALMUS 5224 sc $10.00, perf mat
    rent, set $35.00, pts $1.50, ea.
                                     (G171)
  Queen Of Sheba, The: Ballet Music
    *see Konigin Von Saba, Die:
    Ballet Music

GOLDMARK, KARL (cont'd.)

  Scherzo, Op. 19, in E minor [5']
    2.2.2.2. 2.2.0.0. timp,strings
    sc,pts DOBLINGER rent   (G172)

GOLDNER BECHER see Rixner, Josef

GOLDRAUSCH see Elfers, Konrad

GOLDSUCHER, DER see Kleine, Werner

GOLOB, JANI (1948-   )
  Nocturne [12']
    string orch
    (outside Yugoslavia this
    publication can be obtained from
    Gerig) sc DRUSTVO   (G173)

GONDOLIERA see Ries, Franz

GOOD KING WENCESLAS
  see Sandys, First Noel, The

GOOSEN, JACQUES (1952-   )
  An Den Knaben Elis
    see Georg-Trakl-Lieder, For Solo
    Voice And Orchestra

  Arno Holz-Lieder, For Solo Voice And
    Orchestra
    2.2.2.1.soprano sax.alto sax.
    1.2.1.0. timp,perc,harp,hpsd,
    harmonium,cel,gtr,vibra,8vln,
    4vla,4vcl,A solo sc DONEMUS f.s.,
    perf mat rent
    contains: In Himmelblauer Ferne;
      In Welken Kronen   (G174)

  Doppelgesang, For Solo Voices And
    String Orchestra
    string orch,TBar soli
    DONEMUS perf mat rent   (G175)

  Elis I
    see Georg-Trakl-Lieder, For Solo
    Voice And Orchestra

  Funf Orchesterlieder, For Solo Voice
    And Orchestra [6']
    4.4.0.0. 4.0.0.0. tam-tam,harp,
    cel,vibra,strings,S solo,
    cowbells
    sc DONEMUS f.s., perf mat rent
                                     (G176)
  Georg-Trakl-Lieder, For Solo Voice
    And Orchestra
    perc,2vibra,harp,7vln,4vla,2vcl,db,
    countertenor DONEMUS sc f.s., pts
    rent
    contains: An Den Knaben Elis;
      Elis I   (G177)

  In Himmelblauer Ferne
    see Arno Holz-Lieder, For Solo
    Voice And Orchestra

  In Welken Kronen
    see Arno Holz-Lieder, For Solo
    Voice And Orchestra

  Orchesterstuck
    4.4.4.4. 6.4.4.0. timp,6perc,
    2harp,strings
    sc DONEMUS f.s., perf mat rent
                                     (G178)
  Symphony No. 1 [15']
    string orch
    DONEMUS   (G179)

GORINI, GINO (1914-   )
  Due Invenzioni, For Piano And
    Orchestra [14']
    1.1.1.1. 1.1.0.0. timp,harp,
    strings,pno solo
    sc CARISCH 18905 perf mat rent
                                     (G180)

GORLI, SANDRO (1948-   )
  Flottaison Bleme, For Piano And
    Orchestra [15']
    4.4.5.4. 6.4.4.0. pno,2harp,
    8perc,strings,pno solo
    sc ZERBONI 8405 f.s., pts ZERBONI
    8406 rent   (G181)

GOSAUER SYMPHONIE see Giltay, Berend

GOSSAMER NOONS, FOR SOLO VOICE AND
  ORCHESTRA see Helps, Robert

GOSSEC, FRANCOIS JOSEPH (1734-1829)
  Concertante Du Ballet De Mirza, For 2
    Harps And Orchestra
    2horn,strings,2harp soli
    (Robert, F.) COSTALL perf mat rent
                                     (G182)
  Gavotte, [arr.]
    string orch KALMUS A1039 sc $4.00,
    set $14.00, pts $1.75, ea.   (G183)

  Symphony in D, MIN 87
    2fl,opt ob,2clar,2trp,strings
    sc,pts HARMONIA 1576 f.s.   (G184)

GOSSEC, FRANCOIS JOSEPH (cont'd.)

Symphony, Op. 12, No. 2, in G
LUCKS 01560 sc $5.00, set $12.00,
pts $1.50, ea. (G185)

GOTHIC CONCERTO, A, FOR HARP AND
ORCHESTRA see Kox, Hans

GOTOVAC, JAKOV (1895-   )
Dinara Girl
3.2.2.2. 4.2.3.1. timp,perc,
strings
DRUS.HRVAT.SKLAD. f.s. (G186)

GOTTERDAMMERUNG: BRUNNHILDA'S SELF-
IMMOLATION see Wagner, Richard,
Gotterdammerung: Brunnhilde
Schlussgesang, For Solo Voice And
Orchestra

GOTTERDAMMERUNG: BRUNNHILDE
SCHLUSSGESANG, FOR SOLO VOICE AND
ORCHESTRA see Wagner, Richard

GOTTERDAMMERUNG: SIEGFRIEDS RHEINFAHRT
see Wagner, Richard

GOTTERDAMMERUNG: SIEGFRIED'S RHINE
JOURNEY see Wagner, Richard,
Gotterdammerung: Siegfrieds
Rheinfahrt

GOTTERDAMMERUNG: TRAUERMUSIK BEIM TODE
SIEGFRIEDS see Wagner, Richard

GOTTERDAMMERUNG: WALTRAUTE'S SCENE see
Wagner, Richard

GOTTSCHALK, LOUIS MOREAU (1829-1869)
Grand Tarantelle, For Piano And
Orchestra, [arr.]
(Kay, Hershy) sc BOOSEY $6.00 (G187)

Night In The Tropics, A, [arr.]
(Hatton, Gaylen) sc BOOSEY $7.00 (G188)

GOULD, MORTON (1913-   )
Amber Waves
sc SCHIRM.G $7.50 (G189)

Dance Variations, For Two Pianos And
Orchestra
sc SCHIRM.G $5.00 (G190)

Elegy
string orch
sc SCHIRM.G $10.00 (G191)

Hymnal
sc SCHIRM.G $8.50 (G192)

Jubilo
sc SCHIRM.G $8.50 (G193)

Memorials
sc SCHIRM.G $7.50 (G194)

Philharmonic Waltzes
sc SCHIRM.G $5.00 (G195)

Saratoga Quickstep
sc SCHIRM.G $10.00 (G196)

Serenade Of Carols
study sc SCHIRM.G $2.00 (G197)

Spirituals
sc KALMUS A7003 $16.00 (G198)

Star-Spangled Overture
sc SCHIRM.G $10.00 (G199)

Symphony Of Spirituals
sc SCHIRM.G $25.00 (G200)

GOUNOD, CHARLES FRANCOIS (1818-1893)
Ave Maria, For Solo Voice And
Orchestra, [arr.]
LUCKS 02082 set $12.00, pts $.75,
ea. (G201)

Ave Maria, [arr.]
(Luck) "Meditation" LUCKS 05054 sc
$3.00, set $8.00, pts $.75, ea. (G202)

Cinq Mars: Overture [6']
2.2.2.2. 4.2.3.0. timp,perc,
strings
KALMUS 5338 sc $5.00, perf mat
rent, set $12.00, pts $.60, ea. (G203)

Danse Roumaine
2+pic.2.2.2. 4.2.3.0. timp,perc,
strings
KALMUS 5333 sc $9.00, perf mat
rent, set $12.00, pts $.60, ea. (G204)

Faust: Air Des Bijoux; Ballade, "Il
Etait Un Roi De Thule", For Solo
Voice And Orchestra
"Faust: Jewel Song And King Of
Thule" LUCKS 02392 sc $4.00, set
$9.00, pts $.75, ea. (G205)

GOUNOD, CHARLES FRANCOIS (cont'd.)

Faust: Avant De Quitter Ces Lieux,
For Solo Voice And Orchestra
LUCKS 02030 sc $3.75, set $7.50,
pts $.75, ea. (G206)

Faust: Faites-Lui Mes Aveux, For Solo
Voice And Orchestra
LUCKS 02008 sc $3.75, set $7.50,
pts $.75, ea. (G207)

Faust: Jewel Song And King Of Thule
*see Faust: Air Des Bijoux;
Ballade, "Il Etait Un Roi De
Thule", For Solo Voice And
Orchestra

Faust: Le Veau D'Or, For Solo Voice
And Orchestra
LUCKS 02242 sc $3.75, set $7.50,
pts $.75, ea. (G208)

Faust: Mon Coeur Est Penetre, For
Solo Voices And Orchestra
LUCKS 02142 sc $7.50, set $14.50,
pts $.75, ea. (G209)

Faust: Salut, Demeure Chaste Et Pure,
For Solo Voice And Orchestra
LUCKS 02267 sc $3.75, set $7.50,
pts $.75, ea. (G210)

Faust: Serenade De Mephisto, For Solo
Voice And Orchestra
"Vous Qui Faites L'Enormie" LUCKS
02306 sc $3.75, set $7.50, pts
$.75, ea. (G211)

Funeral March Of A Marionette *see
Marche Funebre D'Une Marionette

Jeanne D'Arc: Suite No. 1, Vision Et
Dieu Le Veut [7']
2(pic).2.2.2. 4.2.3.1. timp,perc,
harp,strings
KALMUS 5329 sc $12.00, perf mat
rent, set $15.00, pts $.75, ea. (G212)

Jeanne D'Arc: Suite No. 2, Priere De
Jeanne D'Arc [4'30"]
2(pic).2.2.2. 4.2.3.1. timp,perc,
harp,strings
KALMUS 5330 sc $6.00, perf mat
rent, set $10.00, pts $.50, ea. (G213)

Jeanne D'Arc: Suite No. 3, Marche Du
Sacre [3']
2(pic).2.2.2. 4.2.3.1. timp,perc,
harp,strings
KALMUS 5331 sc $8.00, perf mat
rent, set $12.00, pts $.50, ea. (G214)

Marche Funebre D'Une Marionette
"Funeral March Of A Marionette"
BROUDE BR. set $25.00, pts $1.25,
ea. (G215)
"Funeral March Of A Marionette"
LUCKS 05651 sc $8.50, set $16.00,
pts $1.15, ea. (G216)

Marche Nuptiale
2+pic.2.2.2. 4.2+2cornet.3.1.
timp,perc,harp,strings,pno solo
KALMUS A3392 sc $2.50, perf mat
rent, set $20.00, pts $1.00, ea. (G217)

Meditation *see Ave Maria, [arr.]

Mireille: Overture [6']
2.2.2.2. 4.2.3.0. timp,perc,
strings
KALMUS 5332 sc $6.00, perf mat
rent, set $24.00, pts $1.25, ea. (G218)

Romeo And Juliet: Waltz Song *see
Romeo Et Juliette: Valse, "Je
Veux Vivre Dans Ce Reve", For
Solo Voice And Orchestra

Romeo Et Juliette: Ballet Music [15']
2+pic.2.2.2. 4.4.3.1. timp,perc,
harp,strings
KALMUS 3455 sc $20.00, set $60.00 (G219)

Romeo Et Juliette: Nuit D'Hymenee,
For Solo Voices And Orchestra
LUCKS 02561 sc $6.00, set $15.00,
pts $1.00, ea. (G220)

Romeo Et Juliette: Valse, "Je Veux
Vivre Dans Ce Reve", For Solo
Voice And Orchestra
"Romeo And Juliet: Waltz Song"
LUCKS 02134 sc $3.75, set $7.50,
pts $.75, ea. (G221)

Vous Qui Faites L'Enormie *see
Faust: Serenade De Mephisto, For
Solo Voice And Orchestra

GOYANA: FOUR SKETCHES, FOR PIANO AND
STRING ORCHESTRA see Waxman, Franz

GRAAF, CHRISTIAAN E.
Sinfonia No. 4
2fl,2trp,strings
sc,pts HARMONIA 1828 f.s. (G222)

GRAAP, LOTHAR (1933-   )
Concerto Breve
2.1.0.1. 0.1.0.0. timp,strings
sc,pts BREITKOPF-W PB-OB 4056 f.s. (G223)

GRAHN, ULF (1942-   )
Concertino for Piano and String
Orchestra [12'-15']
string orch,pno solo
sc STIM perf mat rent (G224)

Homage A Charles Ives
string orch
SEESAW perf mat rent (G225)

GRANADOS, ENRIQUE (1867-1916)
Tres Danzas Espanolas, [arr.] [13']
(Lamote De Grignon) 2+pic.2(English
horn).2+bass clar.2. 4.2.3.1.
timp,perc,harp,strings KALMUS
A1581 sc $14.00, perf mat rent,
set $30.00, pts $1.50, ea. (G226)

GRAND MARCH FUNEBRE NO. 2 see Luck,
Andrew H.

GRAND TARANTELLE, FOR PIANO AND
ORCHESTRA, [ARR.] see Gottschalk,
Louis Moreau

GRANDE FANFARE see Rossini, Gioacchino

GRANDE POLONAISE BRILLANTE, FOR PIANO
AND ORCHESTRA see Chopin, Frederic

GRANDIS, RENATO DE
see DE GRANDIS, RENATO

GRANER, GEORG (1876-1945)
Auferstehung *see Symphony No. 1

Sinfonia Patetica *see Symphony No.
2

Symphony No. 1 [17']
4(pic).3(English horn).3+bass
clar.3+contrabsn. 6.3.3.1.
harp,cel,timp,perc,strings
sc,pts LIENAU rent (G227)

Symphony No. 2 [18']
3(pic).2(English horn).3(bass
clar).3(contrabsn). 6.3.3.1.
harp,cel,timp,perc,strings
sc,pts LIENAU rent (G228)

GRAPPELLI, STEPHANE (1908-   )
Souvenir De Villingen, [arr.]
(Schuller, Gunther) 2.2.3.2.
4.3.3.1. timp,cel,harp,strings,
vln solo [4'] sc MARGUN BP 3002
$8.00, perf mat rent (G229)

GRASBECK, GOTTFRID (1927-   )
Dolce Nella Memoria
2.2.2.1. 2.0.0.0. timp,strings
AKADEM f.s. (G230)

GRATIAS AGIMUS, FOR SOLO VOICE AND
ORCHESTRA see Bellini, Vincenzo

GRATULATIONS-MENUETT UND TANZE FUR
ORCHESTER see Beethoven, Ludwig van

GRAUN, JOHANN GOTTLIEB (1703-1771)
Concerto Grosso in G
string orch,cont,fl solo,vln
solo,vla solo,vcl solo
sc MULLER 2135 f.s. (G231)

GRAUPNER, CHRISTOPH (1683-1760)
Concerto in G minor, MIN 40
string orch,cont,vla solo
sc,pts MOSELER 40.134 f.s. (G232)

GRAWERT, THEODOR (1858-1927)
Schwedischer Reitersignal-Marsch
2(pic).2.2.2. 4.2.3.0. timp,perc,
strings
sc,pts LIENAU rent (G233)

GREEN, GEORGE C. (1930-   )
Prologue And Fugue
2.2.2.2. 4.2.3.1. timp,perc,pno,
harp,strings
SEESAW perf mat rent (G234)

GREEN, JOHN (1908-   )
Mine Eyes Have Seen [30']
3(pic,alto fl).3(English
horn).2.3(contrabsn).
4.3(flugelhorn).3.1. timp,perc,
2harp,pno/cel,org,synthesizer,
strings,solo voice, jazz group:
tenor sax, trp-flugelhorn, elec
gtr, drum set
BOOSEY perf mat rent (G235)

GREEN WIND see Butterworth, Arthur

GREENSLEEVES, [ARR.]
(Reed, Alfred) KALMUS 5370 sc $10.00,
perf mat rent, set $26.00, pts
$1.00, ea.   (G236)

GREENSLEEVES-PHANTASY see Maessen,
Antoon

GREETING see Holst, Gustav

GREETING PRELUDE see Stravinsky, Igor

GREETINGS FROM HOLLAND see Schuyt, Nico

GREGOR, CESTMIR (1926-   )
Sinfonietta
sc PANTON 1786 f.s.   (G237)

GREGORIANS SKETCHES see Carpi, Fiorenzo

GRESAK, JOZEF (1907-   )
Symphony for Organ and Orchestra
[24']
0.0.0.0. 4.3.3.1. timp,perc,xylo,
bells,strings,org solo
SLOV.HUD.FOND 0-474A perf mat rent
(G238)

GRESS, RICHARD
Variationen Uber Ein Thema Von Mozart
*Op.40 [15']
string orch
RIES perf mat rent   (G239)

GRETCHEN AM SPINNRADE, [ARR.] see
Schubert, Franz (Peter)

GRETRY, ANDRE ERNEST MODESTE
(1741-1813)
Cephale Et Procris: Ballet Suite,
[arr.]
(Mottl) 2.2.2.2. 2.2.0.0. timp,
perc,strings BROUDE BR. sc $6.00,
set $22.50, pts $1.50, ea.   (G240)

Epreuve Villageoise, L': Overture
KALMUS 5551 sc $5.00, set $15.00
(G241)

Kleine Ballett-Musik, [arr.]
(Franko, Sam) 1(pic).2.2.2.
2.2.0.0. timp,perc,strings [7']
RIES perf mat rent   (G242)

Rosiere Republicaine, La: Ballet
Music
2.2.2.2. 2.0.0.0. timp,strings
(Kehr, Gunter) SCHOTTS CON 65 sc
$10.50, set $27.00, pts $2.50,
ea.   (G243)

GRIEG, EDVARD HAGERUP (1843-1907)
Alone *see Einsame, Der, For Solo
Voice And Orchestra

At The Cradle, For Solo Voice And
Orchestra *Op.68,No.5
see Grieg, Edvard Hagerup, Evening
In The Mountains, For Solo Voice
And Orchestra

Concerto for Piano and Orchestra, Op.
16, in A minor
BROUDE BR. study sc $7.50, set
$30.00, pts $1.75, ea.   (G244)
min sc ZEN-ON 891041 f.s.   (G245)
LUCKS 00028 sc $14.00, set $23.00,
min sc $3.50, pts $1.40, ea.
(G246)

Dein Rath Ist Wohl Gut *see Your
Advice Is Good, For Solo Voice
And Orchestra, [arr.]

Einsame, Der, For Solo Voice And
Orchestra *Op.32
"Alone" LUCKS 02389 sc $3.75, set
$7.50, pts $.75, ea.   (G247)

Elegiac Melodies *Op.34
string orch
BROUDE BR. sc $2.50, set $5.00, pts
$1.00, ea.   (G248)
"Heart Wounds; Last Spring" LUCKS
05689 sc $1.75, set $3.75, pts
$.75, ea.   (G249)

Erotik, [arr.] *Op.43,No.5
(Spicker, Max) harp,strings LUCKS
08225 sc $2.00, set $5.00, pts
$1.00, ea.   (G250)

Evening In The Mountains, For Solo
Voice And Orchestra *Op.68,No.4
LUCKS 05697 sc $3.75, set $6.50,
pts $.60, ea. contains also: At
The Cradle, For Solo Voice And
Orchestra, Op.68,No.5   (G251)

Heart Wounds; Last Spring *see
Elegiac Melodies

Holberg Suite *Op.40
string orch
BROUDE BR. set $6.50, pts $1.50,
ea.   (G252)
LUCKS 05679 sc $4.00, set $7.00,
min sc $2.50, pts $1.40, ea.
(G253)

GRIEG, EDVARD HAGERUP (cont'd.)

Huldigungsmarsch *see Sigurd
Jorsalfar: Triumphal March

I Love You, For Solo Voice And
Orchestra, [arr.]
LUCKS 02184 sc $3.00, set $8.00,
pts $.75, ea.   (G254)

Last Spring *see Letzter Fruhling,
For Solo Voice And String
Orchestra

Letzter Fruhling, For Solo Voice And
String Orchestra
string orch,solo voice
"Last Spring" LUCKS 02351 sc $2.50,
set $3.75, pts $.75, ea. (G255)

Lyric Pieces, Two, From Op. 68 [5']
0.1.0.0. 1.0.0.0. strings
KALMUS A1529 sc $4.00, set $4.00,
pts $1.50, ea.   (G256)

Norgwegian Folk Tunes, 19, [arr.]
*Op.66, CC19U
(Olsen, C.G. Sparre) sc NORSK
NMO 9344A f.s., pts NORSK f.s.
(G257)
Norwegian Bridal Procession, [arr.]
*Op.19,No.2
(Halvorsen) LUCKS 05695 sc $9.50,
set $24.00, pts $1.60, ea. (G258)

Peer Gynt: Overture [10']
2+pic.2.2.2. 4.2.3.0. timp,harp,
strings
KALMUS 5166 sc $8.00, perf mat
rent, set $25.00, pts $1.00, ea.
(G259)
Peer Gynt: Suite No. 1 *Op.46
BROUDE BR. set $37.50, pts $2.00,
ea.   (G260)

Peer Gynt: Suite No. 2 *Op.55
LUCKS 05683 sc $13.50, set $33.00,
min sc $5.50, pts $1.75, ea.
(G261)
Schwan, Ein *see Swan, A, For Solo
Voice And Orchestra, [arr.]

Sigurd Jorsalfar: Triumphal March
*Op.56,No.3
"Huldigungsmarsch" LUCKS 05688 sc
$6.00, set $15.00, pts $1.25, ea.
(G262)
Solvejg's Song, For Solo Voice And
Orchestra
LUCKS 02390 sc $3.75, set $4.75,
pts $.75, ea.   (G263)

Suite, No. 1, Op. 38, [arr.] (from
Slatter, Op. 72)
2(pic).2.2.2. 4.3.3.1. timp,perc,
harp,strings
(Sommerfeldt, Oistein) [9'] sc
NORSK NMO 9207 $21.00, perf mat
rent   (G264)

Swan, A, For Solo Voice And
Orchestra, [arr.]
"Schwan, Ein" LUCKS 02288 sc $3.75,
set $4.75, pts $.75, ea. (G265)

Symphonic Dances On Norwegian Themes
*Op.64
LUCKS 08648 sc $18.00, set $40.00,
min sc $5.00, pts $2.25, ea.
(G266)
Three Norwegian Pieces
sets NOVELLO 9072-73 $16.25, and
up, sc NOVELLO 9071 $4.25, pts
NOVELLO 9599 $.75, ea.   (G267)

Three Pieces
sets NOVELLO 9075-76 $29.00, and
up, sc NOVELLO 9074 $4.50, pts
NOVELLO 9600 $1.00, ea.   (G268)

Traum, Ein, For Solo Voice And
Orchestra, [arr.] *Op.48,No.6
LUCKS 02364 set $7.50, pts $.75,
ea.   (G269)

Two Melodies *Op.53
string orch
LUCKS 05741 sc $5.75, set $5.75,
pts $1.15, ea.   (G270)

Two Nordic Melodies *Op.63
string orch
"Two Norwegian Airs" LUCKS 01480 sc
$5.75, set $5.75, pts $1.15, ea.
(G271)
Two Norwegian Airs *see Two Nordic
Melodies

Wedding Day At Troldhaugen, [arr.]
*Op.65,No.6
(Huppertz) 1.1.2.1. 3.2.1.0. perc,
strings [6'] KALMUS A4565 sc
$2.00, perf mat rent, set $15.00,
pts $1.00, ea.   (G272)

GRIEG, EDVARD HAGERUP (cont'd.)

Your Advice Is Good, For Solo Voice
And Orchestra, [arr.]
"Dein Rath Ist Wohl Gut" LUCKS
02365 set $7.50, pts $.75, ea.
(G273)
GRIEND, KOOS VAN DE (1905-1950)
Suite [15']
1.0.0.0. 0.1.0.0. 2pno, strings
without vla, db
sc DONEMUS f.s., perf mat rent
(G274)
GRILLO, GIOVANNI BATTISTA
(? -ca. 1620)
Preludio Sinfonico
3.3.3.3. 4.3.3.1. timp,perc,
2harp,cel,xylo,strings
manuscript CARISCH   (G275)

GRILLO E LA FORMICA, IL, FOR SOLO VOICE
AND ORCHESTRA see Sinigaglia, Leone

GRIMM, FRIEDRICH KARL (1902-   )
Lucrezia Borgia [20']
3(pic).2.2+bass clar.2. 4.2.3.1.
timp,perc,harp,strings
RIES perf mat rent   (G276)

Notturno
sc,pts RIES f.s.   (G277)

GRIMM, HANS HEINZ
Marguerite Und Der Bar, Die [10']
2.2.2.2. 4.3.3.0. timp,perc,harp,
strings
RIES perf mat rent   (G278)

GRIMS-LAND, EBBE (1915-   )
Bad'ner Kurpark-Tradition, Version 3
1.1.2.1. 2.2.1.0. perc,strings
sc STIM perf mat rent   (G279)

GRIS-GRIS see Koblitz, David

GRISEY, GERARD (1946-   )
Jour Contre Jour [21']
2.0.2.0. 1.1.0.0. perc,elec org,
string quin,electronic tape
RICORDI-FR R.2260 perf mat rent
(G280)
Modulations [21']
2.2.2(bass clar).2(contrabsn).
2.2.2.1. 3perc,harp,pno,elec
org,cel,5vln,3vla,2vcl,2db
RICORDI-FR R.2246 perf mat rent
(G281)
Sortie Vers La Lumiere Du Jour [25']
2.0.2.0. 1.1.1.0. 3perc,elec org,
string quin
RICORDI-FR R.2256 perf mat rent
(G282)

Transitoires [20']
4.4.5.2.2sax. 4.4.3.1. 4perc,
harp,bass gtr,org,acord,strings
RICORDI-FR perf mat rent   (G283)

GROET DER MARTELAREN, FOR SOLO VOICE
AND ORCHESTRA see Landre, Guillaume

GROOT, COR (CORNELIUS WILHELMUS) DE
(1914-   )
Bis (Evocation), For Piano And
Orchestra [2']
1.1.2.1. 2.2.1.1. strings,pno
solo
sc DONEMUS f.s., perf mat rent
(G284)
Chatons De Paris, Les, For Accordion
And String Orchestra [17']
string orch,acord solo
DONEMUS perf mat rent   (G285)

GROOT, HUGO DE (1914-   )
Ouverture Romantique
2.0.opt ob.2.0.opt bsn. 2.2.0.0.
strings
sc,pts HARMONIA 2738 f.s.   (G286)

GROOTE VOGEL, DE, FOR SOLO VOICE AND
ORCHESTRA see Braal, Andries de

GROSS WIEN WALZER see Strauss, Johann,
[Jr.]

GROSSE FUGE, [ARR.] see Beethoven,
Ludwig van

GROSSER FESTMARSCH see Wagner, Richard

GROSSI, PIETRO (1917-   )
Cinque Pezzi Per Archi [9']
20vln,10vla,10vcl,8db
BRUZZI S-004 perf mat rent   (G287)

Composizione No. 4 [10']
1.2.2.1. 1.2.1.0. 2vln,vla,vcl,
2db
sc BRUZZI C-010 $20.00, perf mat
rent   (G288)

GROSSMANN, LOUIS
Geist Des Woiwoden, Der: Csardas
RIES f.s.   (G289)

GROTESKNY POCHOD see Kardos, Dezider

GROTESQUE MARCH see Kardos, Dezider, Groteskny Pochod

GROUND, FOR FLUTE AND ORCHESTRA see Werner, Sven Erik

GROV, MAGNE
Concerto for Piano and Orchestra [26']
2.2.2.2. 2.2.1.0. timp,strings, pno solo
NORGE (G290)

GRUBER, FRANZ XAVER (1787-1863)
Silent Night
(Luck, Arthur) LUCKS HYMNS 4 set $7.50, pts $.65, ea. contains also: Redner, Lewis [Henry], O Little Town Of Bethlehem (G291)

GRUBER, HEINZ KARL (1943-   )
Frankenstein!!, For Solo Voice And Orchestra [20']
1(pic).1.1.1. 3.1.1.1. timp,perc, harp,cel,strings,Bar solo
BOOSEY perf mat rent (G292)

GRUSELETT see Boer, Ed de

GRUSSE AUS HOLSTEIN see Ecklebe, Alexander

GUARINO, CARMINE (1893-1965)
Bagliori [14']
2.3.3.3. 4.3.4.0. timp,perc,cel, harp
sc CARISCH 18747 f.s., perf mat rent (G293)

Burrattini [3']
2.3.3.3. 4.3.3.0. timp,perc,xylo, harp,strings
sc CARISCH 18875 f.s., perf mat rent (G294)

Concerto for Piano and Orchestra [24']
2.3.3.2. 2.2.2.0. timp,perc,harp, strings,pno solo
sc CARISCH 21422 rent, pts CARISCH 21423 rent (G295)

Marcia Funebre Per Un Pulcino [3']
3.3.3.3. 4.3.3.1. perc,cel,harp, strings
sc CARISCH 18874 perf mat rent (G296)

GUARINO, MARIO (1900-1971)
Concerto for Violin and Orchestra [30']
3.3.3.3. 4.3.3.1. timp,perc,harp, strings,vln solo
sc CARISCH 21838 perf mat rent (G297)

GUBITOSI, EMILIA (1887-1972)
Concerto for Piano and Orchestra [25']
3.3.2.2. 4.2.4.0. timp,perc, carillon,harp,strings,pno solo
sc CARISCH 19892 perf mat rent (G298)

Corale Sinfonico, For Organ And Orchestra [12']
1.1.0.0. 0.1.2.0. bells,pno,org, strings,org solo
sc CARISCH 19466 perf mat rent (G299)

Sonata In Bianco Minore, For Solo Voices And Orchestra [12']
2.1.1.1. 1.0.0.0. cel,harp,pno, strings, solo voices
manuscript CARISCH (G300)

GUDMUNDSEN-HOLMGREEN, PELLE (1932-   )
Mirror II [31']
3.3.3.3.2sax. 4.3.3.1. pno, strings
sc SAMFUNDET 255 perf mat rent (G301)

GUERRINI, GUIDO (1890-1965)
Cantico Di Vittoria, For Solo Voice And Orchestra [8']
2.2.2.2. 2.0.0.0. pno,strings,B solo
manuscript CARISCH (G302)

Egloga, For Flute And Orchestra [5']
0.1.1.1. 1.0.0.0. perc,harp,pno, strings,fl solo
manuscript CARISCH (G303)

Sette Variazioni Su Un'allemanda Di John Bull [19']
3.2.4.3. 4.3.4.0. timp,perc,cel, 2harp,pno,org,xylo,strings
sc CARISCH 21660 f.s., pts CARISCH 21661 rent (G304)

GUGLIELMI, PIETRO ALESSANDRO (1728-1804)
Virtuosa In Mergellina, La: Terzetto, For Solo Voices And Orchestra [6']
0.2.0.0. 0.0.0.0. strings, solo

GUGLIELMI, PIETRO ALESSANDRO (cont'd.)
voices
manuscript CARISCH (G305)

GUGLIELMO RATCLIFF: INTERMEZZO (PRELUDE, ACT IV) see Mascagni, Pietro

GUGLIELMO RATCLIFF: INTRODUCTION see Mascagni, Pietro

GUGLIELMO RATCLIFF: SOGNO, ACT III see Mascagni, Pietro

GUIDO DEL POPOLO: FRAMMENTI SINFONICI see Robbiani, Igino

GUILLAUME TELL: BALLET, PAS DE SIX see Rossini, Gioacchino

GUILLAUME TELL: OVERTURE see Rossini, Gioacchino

GUILLOU, JEAN (1930-   )
Concerto for Piano and Orchestra [37']
2(2pic).2(English horn).2(bass clar).2(contrabsn). 4.2.2.1. timp,perc,harp,strings,pno solo
LEDUC perf mat rent (G306)

GUIRLANDE, LA see Rameau, Jean-Philippe

GULLBERG, OLOF (1931-   )
Concertino for Chamber Orchestra [8']
1.1.1.1. 1.1.0.0. pno,strings
sc,pts STIM perf mat rent (G307)

Romantiska Miniatyrer [8'30"]
string orch
sc STIM perf mat rent (G308)

Variationer, For Piano And Instrumental Ensemble [7']
fl,clar,bsn,2horn,3vln,2vla,vcl, pno solo
sc STIM perf mat rent (G309)

GUNGL, JOSEPH (1810-1889)
Souvenir De Philadelphia *Op.87
LUCKS 07847 set $11.50, pts $.75, ea. (G310)

GURSCHING, ALBRECHT (1934-   )
Sinfonia Concertante for Harp, Violoncello and Orchestra [19']
2.2.2.2. 3.2.3.1. timp,strings, harp solo,vcl solo
PEER perf mat rent (G311)

GUTCHE, GENE (1907-   )
Aesop Fabler Suite *Op.43
sc HIGHGATE 7.0250.6 $18.00 (G312)

Akhenaten *Op.51 [26']
3.3.3.3. 4.4.3.1. timp,6perc, strings
REGUS $50.00 (G313)

Bi-Centurion *Op.49 [18'7"]
3.3.3.3. 4.4.3.1. timp,4perc, strings
REGUS $25.00 (G314)

Helios Kinetic *Op.52 [18']
3.3.3.3. 4.4.3.1. timp,4perc, strings
REGUS $50.00 (G315)

Icarus *Op.48 [24'53"]
3.3.3.3. 4.4.3.1. timp,6perc, strings
REGUS $35.00 (G316)

Perseus And Andromeda XX *Op.50 [22']
3.3.3.3. 4.4.3.1. timp,4perc, strings
REGUS $40.00 (G317)

GUTZEIT, ERICH
Froher Start
RIES f.s. (G318)

Landlicher Tanz
RIES f.s. (G319)

Offene Fenster, Das [10']
2.2.2.2. 4.3.3.0. timp,perc, strings
RIES perf mat rent (G320)

GYCKELSPEL see Blomberg, Erik

GYMNOPEDIES NOS. 1 AND 3, [ARR.] see Satie, Erik

"GYP THE BLOOD" OR HEARST!? WHICH IS WORST?! see Ives, Charles

GYPSY AIRS see Sarasate, Pablo de, Zigeunerweisen, For Violin And Orchestra

GYPSY BARON, THE: OVERTURE see Strauss, Johann, [Jr.], Zigeunerbaron, Der: Overture

GYPSY BARON, THE: SELECTION see Strauss, Johann, [Jr.], Zigeunerbaron, Der: Selection

GYPSY BARON, THE: TREASURE WALTZ see Strauss, Johann, [Jr.], Zigeunerbaron, Der: Schatz Walzer

GYPSY SONGS, FOR SOLO VOICE AND ORCHESTRA see Mikula, Zdenko, Ciganske Piesne, For Solo Voice And Orchestra

GYROWETZ, ADALBERT (JIROVEC) (1763-1850)
Concerto for Piano and Orchestra, No. 2, Op. 94, in B flat [22']
1.2.2.2. 2.2.0.0. timp,strings, pno solo
(Kiesewetter, Peter) ORLANDO rent (G321)

H

H.M.S. PINAFORE: I'M CALLED LITTLE
BUTTERCUP, FOR SOLO VOICE AND
ORCHESTRA see Sullivan, [Sir]
Arthur Seymour

H.M.S. PINAFORE: REFRAIN, AUDACIOUS
TAR, FOR SOLO VOICE AND ORCHESTRA
see Sullivan, [Sir] Arthur Seymour

H.M.S. PINAFORE: WHEN I WAS A LAD, FOR
SOLO VOICE AND ORCHESTRA see
Sullivan, [Sir] Arthur Seymour

HAB ICH LIEB, FOR SOLO VOICE, VIOLIN
AND STRING ORCHESTRA see Kubizek,
Augustin

HAB ICH LIEB, SO HAB ICH NOT see
Kubizek, Augustin

HABBESTAD, KJELL
Lament, For Solo Voice And Orchestra
[13']
3(pic).3(English horn).3(bass
clar).3(contrabsn). 4.3.3.1.
timp,perc,cel,harp,pno,strings,
S solo
NORGE   (H1)

HACHIMURA, YOSHIO (1938-   )
Logic Of Distraction, The, For Piano
And Orchestra
orch,pno solo
ZEN-ON 999170   (H2)

HAFFNER SYMPHONY see Mozart, Wolfgang
Amadeus, Symphony No. 35 in D, K.
385

HAGELBAUER, C.A.
Heinzelmannchens Brautfahrt
string orch
LIENAU f.s.   (H3)

HAIKU II, FOR SOLO VOICE AND ORCHESTRA
see Leeuw, Ton de

HAIL TO THE SPIRIT OF LIBERTY MARCH see
Sousa, John Philip

HAIMANSKINDER QUADRILLE see Strauss,
Johann, [Jr.]

HAINES, EDMUND (1914-1974)
Pastorale for Flute and String
Orchestra [3']
string orch,fl solo
MARGUN BP 3019 perf mat rent   (H4)

Poem for Viola and Chamber Orchestra
[6']
2.2(English horn).0.1. 1.0.0.0.
harp,strings,vla solo
MARGUN BP 3020 perf mat rent   (H5)

Symphony No. 1 [25']
2.2(English horn).2.2. 4.2.3.0.
timp,perc,strings
MARGUN BP 3021 perf mat rent   (H6)

HALEINES ASTRALES see Matsushita, Shin-
Ichi

HALEVY, JACQUES (1799-1862)
Juive, La: Si La Rigeur Et Vengeance,
For Solo Voice And Orchestra
LUCKS 02034 set $8.00, pts $.60,
ea.   (H7)

HALFFTER, CRISTOBAL (1930-   )
Mizar [20']
2fl,3vln,3vla,2vcl,db,3perc
sc UNIVER. UE 16661 f.s., perf mat
rent   (H8)

Variaciones Sobre La Resonancia De Un
Grito [26']
3clar,3trom,3vcl,pno,hpsd,
electronic tape,electronic
equipment
sc UNIVER. UE 16663 f.s., perf mat
rent   (H9)

HALLBERG, BENGT (1932-   )
Concerto Elegante
string orch, jazz group
pts STIM   (H10)

Quintessence, For Wind Quintet And
String Orchestra
string orch,wind quin soli
pts STIM perf mat rent   (H11)

HALLNAS, EYVIND (1937-   )
Concertino Da Chiesa, For Violin And
Instrumental Ensemble [2']
5krummhorn,5rec,perc,vln solo
sc STIM   (H12)

HALLNAS, EYVIND (cont'd.)
Concerto for Piano and Orchestra [5']
1.2.2.2. 2.2.0.0. timp,strings,
pno solo
sc STIM perf mat rent   (H13)

Lyro-Svit [4'30"]
string orch
sc STIM perf mat rent   (H14)

Preludium Och Intermezzo, For Trumpet
And String Orchestra [6']
string orch,trp solo
sc STIM   (H15)

Sinfonietta [10']
2.2.2.2. 2.2.2.0. timp,perc,
strings
sc STIM perf mat rent   (H16)

HALLNAS, HILDING (1903-   )
Karlekens Ringdans
2.2.2.2. 2.2.0.0. timp,perc,harp,
cel,strings
pts STIM   (H17)

HALVORSEN, JOHAN (1864-1935)
Einzugsmarsch Der Bojaren *see Entry
Of The Boyards

Entry Of The Boyards
"Einzugsmarsch Der Bojaren" LUCKS
05716 sc $8.00, set $20.00, pts
$1.25, ea.   (H18)

HAMANN, BERNHARD
Concerto for Violoncello and
Orchestra, Op. 5 [40']
2(pic).2.2.2+contrabsn. 4.3.2.1.
timp,perc,strings,vcl solo
RIES perf mat rent   (H19)

Rondo Capriccioso, For Violin And
Orchestra *Op.2 [10']
1.2.2.2. 3.0.0.0. strings,vln
solo
RIES perf mat rent   (H20)

Symphonische Impression *Op.6 [13']
3(pic).2+English horn.2(bass
clar).2(contrabsn). 4.3.3.1.
timp,perc,harp,strings
RIES perf mat rent   (H21)

Zwei Stucke, For Violin And Orchestra
[5']
2.2+English horn.0.2. 1.0.0.0.
harp,strings,vln solo
RIES perf mat rent   (H22)

HAMBRAEUS, BENGT (1928-   )
Parade
study sc SUECIA f.s.   (H23)

HAMBURG, JEFF (1956-   )
Symphony in E flat [15']
2.2.2.2. 2.1.1.0. timp,cel,
strings
DONEMUS   (H24)

HAMBURGISCHE TAFELMUSIK see Maasz,
Gerhard

HAMEL, PETER MICHAEL (1947-   )
Gestalt [20']
3(pic,alto fl).2+English horn.2+
bass clar.2+contrabsn. 4.2.3.1.
timp,3perc,pno,strings
study sc BAREN. BA 6782 f.s., perf
mat rent   (H25)

Integrale Musik [22']
inst,electronic tape, solo voices
ORLANDO rent   (H26)

Klangfarben [40']
string orch, opt 2 tanpuras
ORLANDO rent   (H27)

HAMERIK, ASGER (1834-1923)
Symphonie Spirituelle No. 6 *Op.38
string orch
LUCKS 08636 sc $7.50, set $10.50,
pts $1.75, ea.   (H28)

HAMILTON, IAIN (1922-   )
Aurora [12']
3.3.3.3. 4.3.3.1. timp,perc,harp,
strings
study sc PRESSER 416-41102 $15.00
(H29)

HAMLET see Liszt, Franz

HAMLET, [ARR.] see Tchaikovsky, Piotr
Ilyich

HAMLET: CHANSON BACHIQUE, FOR SOLO
VOICE AND ORCHESTRA see Thomas,
Ambroise

HAMLET: INCIDENTAL MUSIC see
Shostakovich, Dmitri

HAMMARSKJOLD PORTRAIT, FOR SOLO VOICE
AND STRING ORCHESTRA see
Williamson, Malcolm

HANDEL, GEORGE FRIDERIC (1685-1759)
Acis And Galatea: As When The Dove,
For Solo Voice And Orchestra
LUCKS 03151 sc $3.75, set $7.50,
pts $.75, ea.   (H30)

Acis And Galatea: Love Sounds The
Alarm, For Solo Voice And
Orchestra
LUCKS 02565 sc $3.75, set $7.50,
pts $.75, ea.   (H31)

Acis And Galatea: O Ruddier Than The
Cherry, For Solo Voice And
Orchestra
LUCKS 02564 sc $3.75, set $7.50,
pts $.75, ea.   (H32)

Acis And Galatea: Would You Gain The
Tender Creature, For Solo Voice
And Orchestra
LUCKS 03189 sc $4.00, set $8.00,
pts $.75, ea.   (H33)

Agrippina: Overture
ob,strings,cont
LUCKS 08538 sc $2.75, set $5.75,
pts $.95, ea.   (H34)

Alceste: Incidental Pieces
0.2.0.2. 0.1.0.0. strings
(David, Hans) KALMUS A1637 sc
$5.00, perf mat rent $12.00,
pts $1.50, ea.   (H35)

Alcina: Overture And Dances
string orch
"Festival Music" LUCKS 01481 sc
$3.00, set $3.75, pts $.75, ea. (H36)

Alexander's Feast: Overture
LUCKS 05303 sc $7.00, set $10.50
(H37)

Allegro, Il Pensieroso, Ed Il
Moderato, L': Let Me Wander, Not
Unseen, For Solo Voice And String
Orchestra
LUCKS 03073 sc $4.00, set $8.00,
pts $.60, ea.   (H38)

Allegro, Il Pensieroso, Ed Il
Moderato, L': Sweet Bird, For
Solo Voice And Orchestra
LUCKS 02901 sc $4.00, set $8.00,
pts $.75, ea.   (H39)

Aria E Finale
see RICREAZIONI DI ANTICHE MUSICHE
CLASSICHE, SERIE III: MUSICHE
ANTICHE ITALIANE

Atalanta: Care Selve, For Solo Voice
And String Orchestra
LUCKS 02694 sc $3.75, set $5.75,
pts $.75, ea.   (H40)

Bourree, MIN 109, [arr.]
(Simpson) pno,string orch [3'] sc
PETERS H 74 f.s., perf mat rent
(H41)

Concerti For Oboe And Orchestra, Four
see Concerti Grossi, Eleven

Concerti For Organ And Orchestra Nos.
1-8: Op. 4, Nos. 1-6; Op. 7, Nos.
1-2 *CC8L
min sc LEA 125 $2.40   (H42)

Concerti For Organ And Orchestra Nos.
9-16: Op. 7, Nos. 3-6, Nos. 13-16
*CC16L
min sc LEA 126 $2.40   (H43)

Concerti Grossi, Eleven
min sc LEA 54 $2.40
contains: Concerti For Oboe And
Orchestra, Four; Concerti
Grossi, Op. 3, Nos. 1-6;
Concerto Grosso In C
(Alexander's Feast)   (H44)

Concerti Grossi, Nineteen *CCU
pap DOVER ISBN 0-486-24187-4 $8.95
(H45)

Concerti Grossi, Nos. 27-29
(Hudson) sc DEUTSCHER 4037 f.s. (H46)

Concerti Grossi, Op. 3, Nos. 1-6
see Concerti Grossi, Eleven
(Hudson) sc DEUTSCHER 4017 f.s.
(H47)

Concerti Grossi, Op. 6, Nos. 1-6
min sc LEA 71 $2.40   (H48)

Concerti Grossi, Op. 6, Nos. 1-12
(Hoffmann; Redlich) sc DEUTSCHER
4016 f.s.   (H49)

Concerti Grossi, Op. 6, Nos. 7-12
min sc LEA 72 $2.40   (H50)

HANDEL, GEORGE FRIDERIC (cont'd.)

Concerti, Three
see Handel, George Frideric, Royal Fireworks Music

Concerto A Due Cori, No. 1 *see Concerto Grosso, No. 27, in B flat

Concerto A Due Cori, No. 2 *see Concerto Grosso, No. 28, in F

Concerto A Due Cori, No. 3 *see Concerto Grosso, No. 29, in F

Concerto for Flute and String Orchestra in D, MIN 79 [20'-22'] string orch,cont,fl/ob solo (Bodensohn, E.) BODENS EA 34 f.s. (H51)

Concerto for Harp And Orchestra *see Concerto for Organ and Orchestra, No. 6, Op. 4, No. 6, in B flat

Concerto for Oboe and String Orchestra in B flat string orch,cont,ob solo MUS. RARA f.s. (H52)

Concerto for Oboe and String Orchestra in G minor string orch,cont,ob solo MUS. RARA f.s. (H53)

Concerto for Oboe and String Orchestra, No. 2, in B flat (Seiffert, M.) KALMUS A3326 sc $5.00, set $8.00, pts $1.50, ea. (H54)

Concerto for Oboe and String Orchestra, No. 3, in G minor string orch,cont,ob solo LUCKS 00797 sc $4.75, set $4.75, pts $.95, ea. (H55)

Concerto for Organ and Orchestra, No. 3, Op. 4, No. 3, in G minor [12'] 2ob,bsn,strings,cont,org solo KALMUS 5351 kbd pt $6.00, sc $6.00, set $6.00, pts $.75, ea. (H56)

Concerto for Organ and Orchestra, No. 4, Op. 4, No. 4, in F LUCKS 00830 sc $5.75, set $11.00, pts $1.15, ea. (H57)

Concerto for Organ and Orchestra, No. 5, Op. 4, No. 5, in F LUCKS 00756 sc $5.75, set $11.50, pts $1.40, ea. (H58)

Concerto for Organ and Orchestra, No. 6, Op. 4, No. 6, in B flat string orch,cont,harp solo sc,pts DOBLINGER DM 839 f.s. (H59) LUCKS 00115 sc $2.50, set $9.50, pts $1.40, ea. (H60)

Concerto for Organ and Orchestra, No. 10, Op. 7, No. 4, in D minor [16'] 2ob,bsn,strings,cont,org solo KALMUS 5350 kbd pt $5.00, sc $8.00, perf mat rent, set $8.00, pts $1.00, ea. (H61)

Concerto for Organ and Orchestra, No. 11, Op. 7, No. 5, in G minor [14'] 2ob,bsn,strings,cont,org solo KALMUS 5326 kbd pt $4.00, sc $6.00, perf mat rent, set $8.00, pts $1.00, ea. (H62)

Concerto for Organ and Orchestra, No. 13, in F [16'] 2ob,bsn,strings,cont,org solo KALMUS 5327 kbd pt $4.00, sc $5.00, perf mat rent, set $8.00, pts $1.00, ea. (H63)

Concerto for Organ and Orchestra, No. 17, in D minor 2ob,bsn,strings,cont,org solo DEUTSCHER perf mat rent (H64)

Concerto Grosso In C (Alexander's Feast) see Concerti Grossi, Eleven

Concerto Grosso, No. 24, in F KALMUS A5473 sc $5.00, set $10.00, pts $1.00, ea. (H65)

Concerto Grosso No. 25 *see Water Music

Concerto Grosso No. 26 *see Royal Fireworks Music

Concerto Grosso No. 27 in B flat DEUTSCHER (H66) KALMUS A2386 sc $10.00, perf mat rent, set $20.00, pts $2.25, ea. (H67)

HANDEL, GEORGE FRIDERIC (cont'd.)

Concerto Grosso No. 28 in F DEUTSCHER (H68) KALMUS A2387 sc $10.00, perf mat rent, set $20.00, pts $2.25, ea. (H69)

Concerto Grosso No. 29 in F DEUTSCHER (H70) KALMUS A2388 sc $10.00, perf mat rent, set $20.00, pts $2.25, ea. (H71)

Concerto Grosso, Op. 3, No. 1, in B flat LUCKS 05305 sc $4.00, set $9.00, min sc $3.25, pts $1.00, ea. (H72)

Concerto Grosso, Op. 3, No. 2, in B flat LUCKS 05306 sc $4.00, set $8.00, min sc $3.25, pts $.95, ea. (H73)

Concerto Grosso, Op. 3, No. 5, in D minor LUCKS 05309 sc $4.00, set $7.75, min sc $3.25, pts $.95, ea. (H74)

Concerto Grosso, Op. 6, No. 1, in G (Weismann) BROUDE BR. set $8.00, pts $1.00, ea. (H75)

Concerto Grosso, Op. 6, No. 2, in F (Weismann) BROUDE BR. sc $5.00, set $8.00, pts $1.00, ea. (H76)

Concerto Grosso, Op. 6, No. 3, in E minor string orch,cont,2vln soli,vcl solo LUCKS 05727 sc $4.00, set $6.75, min sc $2.50, pts $.95, ea. (H77) (Weismann) BROUDE BR. sc $5.00, set $8.00, pts $1.00, ea. (H78)

Concerto Grosso, Op. 6, No. 4, in A minor string orch,cont,2vln soli,vcl solo LUCKS 05728 sc $4.00, set $6.75, min sc $2.50, pts $.95, ea. (H79) (Weismann) BROUDE BR. sc $5.00, set $8.00, pts $1.00, ea. (H80)

Concerto Grosso, Op. 6, No. 5, in D string orch,cont,2vln soli,vcl solo min sc BOOSEY 226 $2.50 (H81) LUCKS 05732 sc $4.00, set $6.75, min sc $2.50, pts $.95, ea. (H82) (Weismann) BROUDE BR. set $8.00, pts $1.00, ea. (H83)

Concerto Grosso, Op. 6, No. 6, in G minor min sc UNIVER. PH129 $4.25 (H84) (Weismann) BROUDE BR. set $8.00, pts $1.00, ea. (H85)

Concerto Grosso, Op. 6, No. 7, in B flat string orch,cont,2vln soli,vcl solo study sc DEUTSCHER 4016B f.s. contains also: Concerto Grosso, Op. 6, No. 8, in C minor; Concerto Grosso, Op. 6, No. 9, in F; Concerto Grosso, Op. 6, No. 10, in D minor; Concerto Grosso, Op. 6, No. 11, in A; Concerto Grosso, Op. 6, No. 12, in B minor (H86) (Weismann) BROUDE BR. sc $5.00, set $8.00, pts $1.00, ea. (H87)

Concerto Grosso, Op. 6, No. 8, in C minor string orch,cont,2vln soli,vcl solo see Handel, George Frideric, Concerto Grosso, Op. 6, No. 7, in B flat min sc BOOSEY 229 $2.50 (H88) LUCKS 05729 sc $4.00, set $6.75, min sc $2.50, pts $.95, ea. (H89) (Weismann) BROUDE BR. sc $5.00, set $8.00, pts $1.00, ea. (H90)

Concerto Grosso, Op. 6, No. 9, in F string orch,cont,2vln soli,vcl solo see Handel, George Frideric, Concerto Grosso, Op. 6, No. 7, in B flat LUCKS 08652 sc $4.00, set $6.75, min sc $2.50, pts $.95, ea. (H91) (Weismann) BROUDE BR. sc $5.00, set $8.00, pts $1.00, ea. (H92)

Concerto Grosso, Op. 6, No. 10, in D minor see Handel, George Frideric, Concerto Grosso, Op. 6, No. 7, in B flat (Weismann) BROUDE BR. set $8.00, pts $1.00, ea. (H93)

HANDEL, GEORGE FRIDERIC (cont'd.)

Concerto Grosso, Op. 6, No. 11, in A string orch,cont,2vln soli,vcl solo see Handel, George Frideric, Concerto Grosso, Op. 6, No. 7, in B flat LUCKS 08654 sc $4.00, set $6.75, min sc $2.50, pts $.95, ea. (H94) (Weismann) BROUDE BR. sc $5.00, set $8.00, pts $1.00, ea. (H95)

Concerto Grosso, Op. 6, No. 12, in B minor see Handel, George Frideric, Concerto Grosso, Op. 6, No. 7, in B flat (Weismann) BROUDE BR. set $8.00, pts $1.00, ea. (H96)

Cuckoo And The Nightingale, The *see Concerto for Organ and Orchestra, No. 13, in F

Drei Stucke: Andante, Largo, Larghetto, [arr.] (Schmitt, Alois) org,strings [11'] RIES perf mat rent (H97)

Esther: Now Persecution - Tune Your Harps, For Solo Voice And Orchestra LUCKS 02863 set $8.00, pts $.75, ea. (H98)

Festival Music *see Alcina: Overture And Dances

Giulio Cesare: Piangero, Piangero, For Solo Voice And Orchestra LUCKS 02839 sc $2.00, set $4.50, pts $.75, ea. (H99)

Giulio Cesare: V'Adoro Pupille, For Solo Voice And Orchestra LUCKS 03034 sc $3.75, set $7.50, pts $.75, ea. (H100)

Hercules: My Father, For Solo Voice And String Orchestra LUCKS 03135 sc $3.75, set $3.50, pts $.75, ea. (H101)

Joshua: O Had I Jubal's Lyre, For Solo Voice And Orchestra LUCKS 02568 sc $2.00, set $3.75, pts $.75, ea. (H102)

Joy To The World see Angels We Have Heard On High

Judas Maccabaeus: Arm, Arm Ye Brave, For Solo Voice And Orchestra LUCKS 02953 sc $2.75, set $7.50, pts $.75, ea. (H103)

Judas Maccabaeus: Overture LUCKS 05169 sc $7.00, set $10.50, pts $.95, ea. (H104)

Judas Maccabaeus: Sound An Alarm, For Solo Voice And Orchestra LUCKS 02201 sc $3.75, set $8.50, pts $.75, ea. (H105)

Larghetto, [arr.] (Muller-Berghaus, C.) 2.2.2.2. 2.2.3.0. timp,harp,opt org, strings [4'] RIES perf mat rent (H106)

Largo, [arr.] *see Serse: Ombra Mai Fu, [arr.]

Messiah: But Who May Abide The Day Of His Coming, For Solo Voice And Orchestra LUCKS 03510 sc $3.75, set $7.50, pts $.75, ea. (H107)

Messiah: Comfort Ye - Every Valley Shall Be Exalted, For Solo Voice And Orchestra LUCKS 02458 sc $3.75, set $3.75, pts $.75, ea. (H108)

Messiah: He Shall Feed His Flock, For Solo Voice And Orchestra LUCKS 02431 sc $3.75, set $7.50, pts $.75, ea. (H109)

Messiah: He Was Despised, For Solo Voice And Orchestra LUCKS 03511 sc $3.75, set $7.50, pts $.75, ea. (H110)

Messiah: How Beautiful Are The Feet, For Solo Voice And Orchestra LUCKS 03119 sc $3.75, set $7.50, pts $.75, ea. (H111)

Messiah: I Know That My Redeemer Liveth, For Solo Voice And Orchestra LUCKS 02432 sc $3.75, set $7.50, pts $.75, ea. (H112)

HANDEL, GEORGE FRIDERIC (cont'd.)

Messiah: Overture, [arr.]
(Prout) LUCKS 05192 sc $7.50, set
$6.00, pts $.75, ea.   (H113)

Messiah: Pastoral Symphony
LUCKS 05735 sc $1.00, set $5.00,
pts $.75, ea.   (H114)

Messiah: Rejoice Greatly, For Solo
Voice And Orchestra
LUCKS 02569 sc $3.75, set $7.50,
pts $.75, ea.   (H115)

Messiah: The People That Walked In
Darkness, For Solo Voice And
Orchestra
LUCKS 03296 sc $3.75, set $7.50,
pts $.75, ea.   (H116)

Messiah: The Trumpet Shall Sound, For
Solo Voice And Orchestra
LUCKS 02570 sc $3.75, set $7.50,
pts $.75, ea.   (H117)

Messiah: Thou Shalt Break Them, For
Solo Voice And Orchestra
LUCKS 03327 sc $3.75, set $7.50,
pts $.75, ea.   (H118)

Messiah: Thus Saith The Lord, For
Solo Voice And Orchestra
LUCKS 02856 sc $1.50, set $3.75,
pts $.75, ea.   (H119)

Messiah: Why Do The Nations, For Solo
Voice And Orchestra
LUCKS 03298 sc $3.75, set $7.50,
pts $.75, ea.   (H120)

Minuetto, Musetta E Gavotta, [arr.]
(Martucci, G.) string orch [9'] sc
CARISCH 11193 rent, pts CARISCH
11194 rent   (H121)

Nun Schweiget, Winde, For Solo Voice
And Orchestra *see Silete Venti,
For Solo Voice And Orchestra

Radamisto: Aria Di Polissena, For
Solo Voice And Orchestra
LUCKS 02425 sc $3.75, set $7.50,
pts $.75, ea.   (H122)

Rinaldo: Lascia Ch'Io Pianga, For
Solo Voice And Orchestra
LUCKS 02342 sc $3.75, set $7.50,
pts $.75, ea.   (H123)

Rinaldo: Lass Mich Mit Tranen Mein
Los Beklagen, For Solo Voice And
Orchestra, [arr.]
(Meyerbeer, Giacomo) [Ger/It]
2.2.2.2. 2.0.0.0. strings,S solo
[5'] sc,pts LIENAU rent   (H124)

Royal Fireworks Music (Concerto
Grosso No. 26)
see Wassermusik - Feuerwerksmusik
min sc LEA 139 $2.40 contains also:
Water Music; Concerti, Three
(H125)
sets NOVELLO 9090-91 $34.50, and
up, sc NOVELLO 9089 $9.75, pts
NOVELLO 9505 $1.00, ea.   (H126)
(Tanabe, Roy) NEW MUSIC WEST perf
mat rent   (H127)

Samson: Honour And Arms, For Solo
Voice And Orchestra
LUCKS 02574 sc $3.75, set $5.75,
pts $.75, ea.   (H128)

Samson: How Willing My Paternal Love,
For Solo Voice And Orchestra
LUCKS 03518 sc $4.00, set $6.00,
pts $.60, ea.   (H129)

Samson: Let The Bright Seraphim, For
Solo Voice And Orchestra
LUCKS 02573 sc $3.75, set $7.50,
pts $.75, ea.   (H130)

Samson: Thy Glorious Deeds Inspir'd
My Tongue, For Solo Voice And
Orchestra
LUCKS 03148 sc $3.75, set $7.50,
pts $.75, ea.   (H131)

Samson: Total Eclipse, For Solo Voice
And Orchestra
LUCKS 03149 sc $3.00, set $7.50,
pts $.75, ea.   (H132)

Samson: Why Does The God Of Israel
Sleep, For Solo Voice And
Orchestra
LUCKS 03150 set $8.00, pts $.75,
ea.   (H133)

Samson: With Plaintive Notes, For
Solo Voice And Orchestra
LUCKS 03224 set $8.00, pts $.75,
ea.   (H134)

HANDEL, GEORGE FRIDERIC (cont'd.)

Scipione: Hear Me! Ye Winds And
Waves!, For Solo Voice And
Orchestra
(Luck) LUCKS 02576 set $17.00, pts
$.75, ea.   (H135)

Semele: 0 Sleep Why Dost Thou Leave
Me?, For Solo Voice And Orchestra
(Luck) LUCKS 02578 sc $2.50, set
$3.75, pts $.75, ea.   (H136)

Semele: Where'er You Walk, For Solo
Voice And Orchestra
LUCKS 02244 sc $3.75, set $7.50,
pts $.75, ea.   (H137)

Serse: Ombra Mai Fu, For Solo Voice
And Orchestra
LUCKS 02307 sc $3.75, set $7.50,
pts $.75, ea.   (H138)

Serse: Ombra Mai Fu, [arr.]
(Luck) "Xerxes: Largo" LUCKS 05733
sc $3.00, set $8.00 pts $.75,
ea.   (H139)
(Molinari) "Largo, [arr.]" sc
RICORDI-IT PR548 f.s.   (H140)

Serse: Overture And Sinfonia
(Kneusslin) LUCKS 10156 sc $9.00,
set $10.50, pts $1.75, ea.   (H141)

Silete Venti, For Solo Voice And
Orchestra
0.1.0.1. 0.0.0.0. strings,S solo
(Seiffert, M.) "Nun Schweiget,
Winde, For Solo Voice And
Orchestra" BREITKOPF-W perf mat
rent   (H142)

Sinfonia, Act III *see Solomon:
Entrance Of The Queen Of Sheba

Solomon: Entrance Of The Queen Of
Sheba
LUCKS 09081 sc $4.50, set $6.75,
pts $.95, ea.   (H143)
"Sinfonia, Act III" string orch,2ob
soli/2vln soli BROUDE BR. study
sc $2.50, set $6.00, pts $.75,
ea.   (H144)

Suite In Vier Satzen, [arr.] (from
Alcides; Esther; Saul)
(Pearson) string orch,cont [13'] sc
PETERS H 276 f.s., perf mat rent
(H145)

Suite "Mit Dem Marsch, " [arr.]
"Suite With March, [arr.]" strings
without vla,cont KALMUS A1103 sc
$4.50, set $5.00, pts $1.00, ea.
(H146)

Suite With March, [arr.] *see Suite
"Mit Dem Marsch, " [arr.]

Terpsicore: Ballet Suite
(Mueller, H.) 2ob,strings,cont
KALMUS 5234 sc $3.00, perf mat
rent, set $8.00, pts $1.00, ea.
(H147)

Wassermusik - Feuerwerksmusik
(Redlich) sc DEUTSCHER 4018 f.s.
contains: Royal Fireworks Music
(Concerto Grosso No. 26); Water
Music (Concerto Grosso No. 25)
(H148)
Water Music (Concerto Grosso No. 25)
see Handel, George Frideric, Royal
Fireworks Music
see Wassermusik - Feuerwerksmusik
LUCKS 06119 sc $12.00, set $25.00,
min sc $3.00, pts $2.00, ea.
(H149)

Xerxes: Largo *see Serse: Ombra Mai
Fu, [arr.]

HANDELS ELITE QUADRILLE see Strauss,
Johann, [Jr.]

HANDOSHKIN, IVAN
see KHANDOSHKIN, IVAN

HANDS ACROSS THE SEA MARCH see Sousa,
John Philip

HANDWERKER-SUITE see Bortz, Alfred

HANNIKAINEN, ILMARI (1892-1955)
Erakkomaja, [arr.] *Op.8,No.3
(Koskimies E.) 1.2.2.2. 2.0.0.0.
timp,strings,solo voice [3']
FAZER perf mat rent   (H150)

Miksi Laulat Lintuseni, For Solo
Voice And Orchestra [6']
2.2.2.1. 3.1.0.0. strings,solo
voice
FAZER perf mat rent   (H151)

HANNIKAINEN, VAINO (1900-1960)
Onnen Ovi, For Solo Voice And
Orchestra *Op.3,No.2 [3']
1.1.2.1. 2.1.1.0. timp,strings,
solo voice

HANNIKAINEN, VAINO (cont'd.)

FAZER perf mat rent   (H152)

Tuutulaulu, For Solo Voice And
Orchestra *Op.80,No.1b [3']
0.0.2.0. 2.0.0.0. perc,harp,
strings,solo voice
FAZER perf mat rent   (H153)

HANS HEILING: OVERTURE see Marschner,
Heinrich (August)

HANS IM GLUCK, FOR CLARINET AND
ORCHESTRA see Schonherr, Max

HANSEATISCHE SUITE see Scheffler,
Siegfried

HANSEL AND GRETEL: SANDMAN'S SONG,
EVENING PRAYER, AND DREAM PANTOMIME
see Humperdinck, Engelbert, Hansel
Und Gretel: Lied Des Sandmannchens;
Abendsegen Und Traumpantomime

HANSEL UND GRETEL: LIED DES
SANDMANNCHENS; ABENDSEGEN UND
TRAUMPANTOMIME see Humperdinck,
Engelbert

HANSEL UND GRETEL: VORSPIEL see
Humperdinck, Engelbert

HANSON, GEOFFREY (1939-   )
Concertino for Oboe and String
Orchestra
string orch,ob solo
ROBERTON perf mat rent   (H154)

Concerto for Piano and Orchestra
ROBERTON perf mat rent   (H155)

HAPPY END see Faust, Willi

HARFENSPIELER I, FOR SOLO VOICE AND
ORCHESTRA see Wolf, Hugo

HARFENSPIELER II, FOR SOLO VOICE AND
ORCHESTRA see Wolf, Hugo

HARFENSPIELER III, FOR SOLO VOICE AND
ORCHESTRA see Wolf, Hugo

HARK THE HERALD ANGELS SING see
Mendelssohn-Bartholdy, Felix

HARK THE MERRY BELLS
(Luck, Andrew) LUCKS HYMNS 21 sc
$5.00, set $10.00, pts $.60, ea.
(H156)

HARLEKINADE see Woitschach, Paul

HARLEKINS OUVERTURE see Dressel, Erwin

HARMONIE MARCH see Luck, Arthur

HARPALYCE, FOR HARP AND STRING
ORCHESTRA see Constant, Marius

HARPER, EDWARD
Concerto for Piano and Orchestra
[10']
2.2.2.2. 2.2.1.0. strings,pno
solo
OXFORD perf mat rent   (H157)

Fantasia I [15']
fl,clar,2horn,trp,perc,strings
OXFORD perf mat rent   (H158)

Fantasia II [16']
6vln,2vla,2vcl,db
OXFORD perf mat rent   (H159)

Fern Hill [23']
2(alto fl).2.2.2. 2.2.0.0. harp,
strings
OXFORD perf mat rent   (H160)

Ricercari [16']
fl,clar,bass clar,horn,trp,perc,
harp,pno,vln,vla,db
study sc OXFORD 07.035 $12.00, sc,
pts OXFORD rent   (H161)

Seven Poems By e.e. cummings, For
Solo Voice And Orchestra [23']
2.2.2.2. 4.2.3.1. 3perc,harp,pno/
cel,strings,S solo
OXFORD perf mat rent   (H162)

Sonata for Chamber Orchestra [14']
fl,ob,clar,horn,strings
OXFORD perf mat rent   (H163)

Symphony [35']
2.3.3.2.alto sax. 4.3.3.1. timp,
2perc,harp,pno/cel,strings
OXFORD perf mat rent   (H164)

HARPZANGEN VAN KONING DAVID, FOR SOLO
VOICE AND ORCHESTRA see Bijvanck,
Henk

HARTMANN, BRUNO
Tanz Im Sonnenschein
LIENAU f.s.   (H165)

HARTMANN, PER J.
Permanent Wave *Op.30
0.1.2(bass clar).0. 0.0.0.0.
strings
NORGE   (H166)

HARU NO UMI see Ikebe, Shin-Ichiro

HASELBACH, JOSEF
Transtuli
HUG perf mat rent   (H167)

HASENPFLUG, CURT
Jolita
RIES f.s.   (H168)

Kleines Gondellied
RIES f.s.   (H169)

Konzert-Ouverture
RIES f.s.   (H170)

Spanische Skizze
RIES f.s.   (H171)

HASSAN: INTERMEZZO see Delius,
Frederick

HASSAN: SERENADE see Delius, Frederick

HASSLER, HANS LEO (1564-1612)
Intraden *CCU
2.1.2.0. 1.0.0.0. strings sc,pts
HARMONIA 1813 f.s.   (H172)

HATIKVAH
(Luck, Arthur) LUCKS HYMNS 20 set
$9.50, pts $.65, ea.   (H173)

HATRIK, JURAJ (1941-   )
Sans Souci *see Symphony No. 1

Symphony No. 1 [33']
2.2.2.2. 2.2.2.0. timp,strings
SLOV.HUD.FOND 0-496A perf mat rent
(H174)

HATTORI, KOH-ICHI (1933-   )
Two Movements For Strings
string orch
BOOSEY sc $5.50, set $22.00 (H175)

HATTORI, RYOICHI (1907-   )
American In Tokyo, An
2+pic.2.2.2. 4.3.3.1. timp,perc,
harp,cel,pno,strings
sc J.C.A. f.s.   (H176)

HATZIS, CHRISTOS
Kleidocymbalon I
string orch
SEESAW perf mat rent   (H177)

HAUBENSTOCK-RAMATI, ROMAN (1919-   )
Concerto Per Archi
string orch
sc HANSEN-DEN f.s.   (H178)

HAUER, JOSEF MATTHIAS (1883-1959)
Apokalyptische Phantasie *Op.5
[8'30"]
2.2.2.1+contrabsn. 2.2.1.0. timp,
pno,strings
study sc DOBLINGER STP. 490 f.s.,
sc,pts DOBLINGER 74 901 rent
(H179)

Suite No. 1, Op. 31 [18']
1+pic.2(English horn).1+bass
clar.1+contrabsn. 2.2.0.0. pno,
timp,strings
sc,pts LIENAU rent   (H180)

HAUG, HALVOR
Poema Sonora No. 4
3(pic).3(English horn).3(bass
clar).3(contrabsn). 4.3.3.1.
timp,perc,cel,harp,strings
NORGE   (H181)

HAUSEGGER, SIEGMUND VON (1872-1948)
Aufklänge [30']
3(pic).2+English horn.2+bass
clar.3(contrabsn). 6.3.0.0.
timp,2perc,2harp,cel,strings
RIES perf mat rent   (H182)

Wieland Der Schmied
2+pic.2+English horn.2+bass
clar.2+contrabsn. 4.3.3.1.
timp,2strings
RIES perf mat rent   (H183)

HAUTE VOLEE POLKA see Strauss, Johann,
[Jr.]

HAVANAISE, FOR VIOLIN AND ORCHESTRA see
Saint-Saens, Camille

HAVET see Wahlberg, Rune, Symphony No.
5

HAWAIIAN HOLIDAY see Kirchstein, Harold
M.

HAWK IS SET FREE, THE see Hoddinott,
Alun

HAWOK see Thomassen, Thomas

HAYDN, [FRANZ] JOSEPH (1732-1809)
Ah Crudel!, For Solo Voice And
Orchestra
2.0.0.0. 2.0.0.0. strings,S solo
(1780, additional aria to
Gazzaniga's "La Vendemmia") sc
UNIVER. HMP 112 $13.50, set
UNIVER. HMP 113 $11.00, pts
UNIVER. $3.00, ea.   (H184)

Ah, Tu Non Senti, For Solo Voice And
Orchestra
1.2.0.2. 2.0.0.0. strings,T solo
(1786, additional aria to Traetta's
"Ifigenia In Tauride") sc UNIVER.
HMP 100 $13.50, set UNIVER.
HMP 101 $20.00, pts UNIVER.
$3.00, ea.   (H185)

Ariadne Auf Naxos, For Solo Voice And
Orchestra, [arr.] *see Arianna A
Naxos, For Solo Voice And
Orchestra, [arr.]

Arianna A Naxos, For Solo Voice And
Orchestra *Hob.XXVIb:2
2.2.2.1. 2.0.0.0. strings,Mez
solo
[Ger] KALMUS A4582 sc $16.00, perf
mat rent, set $27.00, pts $1.50,
ea.   (H186)

Arianna A Naxos, For Solo Voice And
Orchestra, [arr.] *Hob.XXVIb:2
(Frank, E.) "Ariadne Auf Naxos, For
Solo Voice And Orchestra, [arr.]"
2.2.2.2. 2.2.0.0. timp,strings,S
solo [18'] BREITKOPF-W perf mat
rent   (H187)
(Link, Helmut) 1.2.2.2. 2.2.0.0.
timp,strings,solo voice [16']
RIES perf mat rent   (H188)

Armida: Overture
LUCKS 01370 set $15.00, pts $1.00,
ea.   (H189)

Bear Symphony *see Symphony No. 82
in C

Begli Occhi Vezzosi, For Solo Voice
And Orchestra
0.0.0.1. 2.0.0.0. strings,T solo
(1777?, additional aria to "Il
Mondo Della Luna") sc UNIVER.
HMP 122 $13.50, set UNIVER.
HMP 123 $5.50, pts UNIVER. $3.00,
ea.   (H190)

Cassation in D [13']
0.0.0.0. 4.0.0.0. strings
(Landon, H.C.R.) sc,pts DOBLINGER
DM 66 f.s., study sc DOBLINGER
STP. 285 f.s.   (H191)

Cassation in G [15']
0.2.0.0.opt bsn. 2.0.0.0. strings
(Landon, H.C.R.) (Hob. II:G1) sc,
pts DOBLINGER DM 47 f.s., study
sc DOBLINGER STP. 287 f.s.   (H192)

Chasse, La *see Symphony No. 73 in D

Chi Vive Amante, For Solo Voice And
Orchestra
1.2.0.2. 2.0.0.0. strings,S solo
(1787, additional aria to Bianchis'
"Alessandro Nell 'Indie") sc
UNIVER. HMP 132 $13.50, set
UNIVER. HMP 133 $13.50, pts
UNIVER. $3.00, ea.   (H193)

Christmas Symphony *see Symphony No.
26 in D minor

Clock Symphony *see Symphony No. 101
in D

Concerti For Violoncello And
Orchestra *CCU
(Gerlach, Sonja) sc,pap HENLE
HN 5201 $46.25, sc,cloth HENLE
HN 5202 $54.50 Joseph Haydn Werke
Series III, Volume 2   (H194)

Concerti Mit Orgelleiern *CCU
sc,pap HENLE 5231 $54.00, sc,cloth
HENLE 5232 $61.00 Joseph Haydn
Werke Series VI   (H195)

Concerto for Harpsichord and
Orchestra in D, Hob.XVIII: 2
2ob,2horn,strings,hpsd/pno solo
INTERNAT. perf mat rent   (H196)
LUCKS 00029 sc $5.00, set $11.00,
min sc $2.00, pts $.95, ea.
(H197)
(Soldan) 2ob,2horn,strings,hpsd/pno

HAYDN, [FRANZ] JOSEPH (cont'd.)

solo BROUDE BR. set $12.00, pts
$1.25, ea.   (H198)

Concerto for Harpsichord and
Orchestra in F, MIN 63 [12']
2fl,strings,hpsd/pno solo
(Hob. XVIII: F1) INTERNAT. perf mat
rent   (H199)
(Hob. XVIII:F1) KALMUS A3204 sc
$8.00, set $9.00, pts $1.00, ea.
(H200)

Concerto for Horn and Orchestra, No.
1, in D, Hob.VIId: 3
2ob,strings,horn solo
(Leloir, Edmond) (in this edition
oboes are optional) sc BILLAUDOT
$9.25, perf mat rent   (H201)

Concerto for Organ and Orchestra in
C, Hob.XVIII: 8
(Robbins Landon, H.C.) min sc
UNIVER. PH457 $6.00   (H202)

Concerto for Piano and Orchestra in
G, Hob.XVIII: 4
INTERNAT. perf mat rent   (H203)
KALMUS 5425 sc $9.00, set $9.00
(H204)
LUCKS 00138 sc $10.00, set $10.00,
pts $1.50, ea.   (H205)

Concerto for Piano and String
Orchestra in F, Hob.XVIII: 3
LUCKS 01136 sc $5.00, set $7.00,
pts $1.00, ea.   (H206)

Concerto for Trumpet and Orchestra in
E flat, Hob.VIIe: 1
LUCKS 00803 sc $9.75, set $14.00,
min sc $2.50, ea., pts $1.15, ea.
(H207)

Concerto for Viola and Orchestra in
D, [arr.] (from Concerto For
Violoncello And Orchestra)
2.2.2.2. 2.0.0.0. strings,vla solo
[28'] INTERNAT. perf mat rent
(H208)

Concerto for Violin and String
Orchestra, No. 1, in C, Hob.VIIa:
1
LUCKS 00407 sc $9.00, set $12.00,
pts $1.50, ea.   (H209)

Concerto for Violin and String
Orchestra, No. 2, in G, Hob.VIIa:
4 [20']
string orch,cont,vln solo
KALMUS 5235 sc $7.00, perf mat
rent, set $12.00, pts $1.50, ea.
(H210)
LUCKS 00417 sc $9.00, set $12.00,
min sc $2.00, pts $1.50, ea.
(H211)

Concerto for Violoncello and
Orchestra in C, Hob.VIIb: 1 [25']
2ob, 2horn,strings,vcl solo
(in this edition called Concerto In
E Minor) sc INTERNAT. 2326
$10.00, perf mat rent   (H212)

Concerto for Violoncello and
Orchestra in C, Hob.VIIb: 5
*reconstruction
(Popper, David) 2.2.2.2. 0.0.0.0.
strings,vcl solo [18'] KALMUS
5165 kbd pt $5.00, sc $20.00,
perf mat rent, set $26.00, pts
$1.75, ea.   (H213)

Concerto for Violoncello and
Orchestra, Op. 101, in D,
Hob.VIIb: 2
LUCKS 00631 sc $8.75, set $9.75,
pts $1.15, ea.   (H214)
(Gerlach, Sonja) (this edition is
scored for 2ob, bsn, 2horn, str)
BAREN. BA 4681 perf mat rent
(H215)
(Soldan) 2ob,2horn,strings,vcl solo
BROUDE BR. set $17.50, pts $1.50,
ea.   (H216)

Concerto for Violoncello and
Orchestra, Op. 101, in D,
Hob.VIIb: 2, [arr.]
(Gevaert, F.A.) 2.2.2.2. 2.0.0.0.
strings,vcl solo [28'] INTERNAT.
perf mat rent   (H217)
(Geveart) LUCKS 00605 sc $8.75, set
$9.75, pts $1.15, ea.   (H218)

Costretta A Piangere, For Solo Voice
And Orchestra
0.2(English horn).0.0. 2.0.0.0.
hpsd,strings,S solo
(1762, probably from a lost
Commedia) sc UNIVER. HMP 136
$13.50, set UNIVER. HMP 137
$13.50, pts UNIVER. $3.00, ea.
(H219)

Creation, The: In Native Worth *see
Schopfung, Die: Mit Wurd' Und
Hoheit Angetan, For Solo Voice
And Orchestra

HAYDN, [FRANZ] JOSEPH (cont'd.)

Creation, The: With Verdure Clad
  *see Schopfung, Die: Nun Beut Die
  Flur, For Solo Voice And
  Orchestra

Da Che Pensa A Maritarmi, For Solo
  Voice And Orchestra
  1.2.0.2. 2.0.0.0. strings,T solo
  (1790, additional aria to
  Gassmann's "L'amore Artigiano")
  sc UNIVER. HMP 126 $13.50, set
  UNIVER. HMP 127 $12.50, pts
  UNIVER. $3.00, ea.   (H220)

Deutsche Tanze, Sechs, MIN 36
  string orch
  sc,pts HEINRICH. 223 f.s.   (H221)

Deutschland Uber Alles
  (Luck, Arthur) LUCKS HYMNS 19 set
  $9.50, pts $.65, ea.   (H222)

Dice Benissimo, For Solo Voice And
  Orchestra
  0.0.0.0. 2.0.0.0. strings,Bar
  solo
  (1780, additional aria to Salieri's
  "La Scuola De 'Gelosi") sc
  UNIVER. HMP 104 $13.50, set
  UNIVER. HMP 105 $12.00, pts
  UNIVER. $3.00, ea.   (H223)

Distratto, Il *see Symphony No. 60
  in C

Divertimento for Harpsichord and
  String Orchestra in C
  string orch without vla,hpsd/pno
  solo
  (Landon, H.C.R.) (Hob.XIV: C2) sc,
  pts DOBLINGER DM 325 f.s. (H224)

Divertimento In G, Hob. II:G1 *see
  Cassation in G

Drum Roll Symphony *see Symphony No.
  103 in E flat

D'Una Sposa Meschinella, For Solo
  Voice And Orchestra
  0.2.0.0. 2.0.0.0. strings,S solo
  (1777, additional aria to
  Paisiello's "La Frascatana") sc
  UNIVER. HMP 128 $13.50, set
  UNIVER. HMP 129 $7.50, pts
  UNIVER. $3.00, ea.   (H225)

Farewell Symphony *see Symphony No.
  45 in F sharp minor

Fire Symphony *see Symphony No. 59
  in A

Hen Symphony *see Symphony No. 83 in
  G minor

Horn Signal Symphony *see Symphony
  No. 31 in D

Hunt, The, Symphony *see Symphony
  No. 73 in D

Imperial Symphony *see Symphony No.
  53 in D

Infelice Sventurata, For Solo Voice
  And Orchestra
  0.2.0.2. 2.0.0.0. strings,S solo
  (1789, additional aria to
  Cimarosa's "I Due Supposti
  Contri") sc UNIVER. HMP 102
  $13.50, set UNIVER. HMP 103
  $10.50, pts UNIVER. $3.00, ea.
                              (H226)

Jahreszeiten, Die: Schon Eilet Froh
  Der Ackersmann, For Solo Voice
  And Orchestra
  "Seasons, The: With Joy The
  Impatient Husbandman" LUCKS 03118
  sc $3.75, set $7.50, pts $.75,
  ea.   (H227)

Kindersinfonie
  "Toy Symphony" (attributed to
  Haydn) LUCKS 05758 sc $1.50, set
  $5.00, pts $.75, ea.   (H228)

Laudon Symphony *see Symphony No. 69
  in C

London Symphonies *see Symphony Nos.
  93-104

Magd, Ein Dienerin, Ein, For Solo
  Voice And Orchestra
  2horn,org,strings,S solo
  voc sc UNIVER. HMP 37 $9.00, sc
  UNIVER. HMP 38 $14.50, set
  UNIVER. HMP 39 $3.75, pts UNIVER.
  $2.00, ea.   (H229)

Maria Theresia Symphony *see
  Symphony No. 48 in C

HAYDN, [FRANZ] JOSEPH (cont'd.)

Meglio Mio Carattere, Il, For Solo
  Voice And Orchestra
  1.2.0.2. 2.0.0.0. strings,S solo
  (1790, additional aria to
  Cimarosa's "L'impressario In
  Angustie") sc UNIVER. HMP 118
  $13.50, set UNIVER. HMP 119
  $12.50, pts UNIVER. $4.00, ea.
                              (H230)

Menuette, Zwolf, Hob. IX:1
  0.2.0.0. 2.0.0.0. string orch
  without vla
  (Landon, R.H.C.) "Seitenstetten-
  Menuette" sc,pts DOBLINGER DM855
  f.s.   (H231)

Military Symphony *see Symphony No.
  100 in G

Miracle Symphony *see Symphony No.
  96 in D

Moglie Quandro E Buona, La, For Solo
  Voice And Orchestra
  1.2.0.2. 2.0.0.0. strings,S solo
  (1790, additional aria to
  Cimarosa's "Giannina E
  Bernadone") sc UNIVER. HMP 108
  $13.50, set UNIVER. HMP 109
  $19.00, pts UNIVER. $3.00, ea. (H232)

Orlando Paladino: Overture, [arr.]
  2.1.2.1. 0.0.0.0. strings sc,pts
  HARMONIA 1814 f.s.   (H233)

Ours, L', Symphony *see Symphony No.
  82 in C

Overture in D, MIN 74 [4']
  fl,2ob,2bsn,2horn,strings
  (Negrotti, N.) sc,pts ZANIBON D248
  rent   (H234)

Oxford Symphony *see Symphony No. 92
  in G

Passione, La, Symphony *see Symphony
  No. 49 in F minor

Poule, La, Symphony *see Symphony
  No. 83 in G minor

Quando La Rosa Non Ha Piu Spine, For
  Solo Voice And Orchestra
  1.0.0.1. 2.0.0.0. strings,S solo
  (1779, additional aria to Anfossis'
  "La Metilde Ritrovata") sc
  UNIVER. HMP 114 $10.00, set
  UNIVER. HMP 115 $6.00, pts
  UNIVER. $2.00, ea.   (H235)

Reine, La, Symphony *see Symphony
  No. 85 in B flat

Roxelane, La *see Symphony No. 63 in
  C

Schoolmaster Symphony *see Symphony
  No. 55 in E flat

Schopfung, Die: Mit Wurd' Und Hoheit
  Angetan, For Solo Voice And
  Orchestra
  "Creation, The: In Native Worth"
  LUCKS 03085 sc $3.75, set $7.50,
  pts $.75, ea.   (H236)

Schopfung, Die: Nun Beut Die Flur,
  For Solo Voice And Orchestra
  "Creation, The: With Verdure Clad"
  LUCKS 02285 sc $3.75, set $7.50,
  pts $.75, ea.   (H237)

Se Tu Mi Sprezzi, Ingrate, For Solo
  Voice And Orchestra
  0.2.0.2. 2.0.0.0. strings,T solo
  (1788, additional aria to Sarti's
  "Il Finti Erredi") sc UNIVER.
  HMP 124 $13.50, set UNIVER.
  HMP 125 $16.50, pts UNIVER.
  $3.00, ea.   (H238)

Seasons, The: With Joy The Impatient
  Husbandman *see Jahreszeiten,
  Die: Schon Eilet Froh Der
  Ackersmann, For Solo Voice And
  Orchestra

Seitenstetten—Menuette *see
  Menuette, Zwolf, Hob. IX:1

Serenade, [arr.]
  string orch LUCKS 05380 sc $2.00,
  set $3.00, pts $.75, ea.   (H239)

Signor, Voi Sapete, For Solo Voice
  And Orchestra
  2.2.0.2. 2.0.0.0. strings,S solo
  (1785, additional aria to Anfossis'
  "Il Matrimonio Per Inganno") sc
  UNIVER. HMP 116 $13.50, set
  UNIVER. HMP 117 $14.00, pts
  UNIVER. $3.00, ea.   (H240)

HAYDN, [FRANZ] JOSEPH (cont'd.)

Sinfonia Concertante for Violin,
  Violoncello, Oboe, Bassoon and
  Orchestra, Op. 84, in B flat,
  Hob.I: 105
  BAREN. BA 4683 perf mat rent (H241)
  min sc UNIVER. PH 805 $6.00 (H242)
  sc UNIVER. HMP 193 $43.00, set
  UNIVER. HMP 194 $46.00, pts
  UNIVER. $4.50, ea.   (H243)

Solo E Pensos, For Solo Voice And
  Orchestra
  0.0.2.2. 2.0.0.0. strings,S solo
  sc UNIVER. HMP 106 $13.50, set
  UNIVER. HMP 107 $12.00, pts
  UNIVER. $3.00, ea.   (H244)

Sono Alcina, E Sono Ancora Un Visino,
  For Solo Voice And Orchestra
  1.2.0.2. 2.0.0.0. strings,S solo
  (1786, additional aria to
  Gazzanigas' "L'Isola di Alcina")
  sc UNIVER. HMP 130 $13.50, set
  UNIVER. HMP 131 $12.50, pts
  UNIVER. $3.00, ea.   (H245)

Surprise Symphony *see Symphony No.
  94 in G

Symphonies, Vol.1 *CC14L
  (Robbins Landon, H.C.) min sc
  UNIVER. PH589 $36.00 contains
  Symphony No. 107 (Symphony A),
  Symphony No. 108 (Symphony B),
  Symphonies Nos.1-12   (H246)

Symphonies, Vol.2 *CC15L
  (Robbins Landon, H.C.) min sc
  UNIVER. PH590 $36.00 contains
  Symphonies Nos.13-27   (H247)

Symphonies, Vol.3 *CC13L
  (Robbins Landon, H.C.) min sc
  UNIVER. PH591 $36.00 contains
  Symphonies Nos.28-40   (H248)

Symphonies, Vol.4 *CC9L
  (Robbins Landon, H.C.) min sc
  UNIVER. PH592 $36.00 contains
  Symphonies Nos.41-49   (H249)

Symphonies, Vol.5 *CC8L
  (Robbins Landon, H.C.) min sc
  UNIVER. PH593 $36.00 contains
  Symphonies Nos.50-57   (H250)

Symphonies, Vol.6 *CC8L
  (Robbins Landon, H.C.) min sc
  UNIVER. PH594 $36.00 contains
  Symphonies Nos.58-65   (H251)

Symphonies, Vol.7 *CC8L
  (Robbins Landon, H.C.) min sc
  UNIVER. PH595 $36.00 contains
  Symphonies Nos.66-73   (H252)

Symphonies, Vol.8 *CC8L
  (Robbins Landon, H.C.) min sc
  UNIVER. PH596 $36.00 contains
  Symphonies Nos.74-81   (H253)

Symphonies, Vol.9 *CC6L
  (Robbins Landon, H.C.) min sc
  UNIVER. PH597 $36.00 contains
  Symphonies Nos.82-87   (H254)

Symphonies, Vol.10 *CC6L
  (Robbins Landon, H.C.) min sc
  UNIVER. PH598 $36.00 contains
  Symphonies Nos.88-92 and Sinfonia
  Concertante   (H255)

Symphonies, Vol.11 *CC6L
  (Robbins Landon, H.C.) min sc
  UNIVER. PH599 $36.00 contains
  Symphonies Nos.93-98   (H256)

Symphonies, Vol.12 *CC6L
  (Robbins Landon, H.C.) min sc
  UNIVER. PH600 $36.00 contains
  Symphonies Nos.99-104   (H257)

Symphony A *see Symphony No. 107 in
  B flat

Symphony B *see Symphony No. 108 in
  B flat

Symphony No. 1 in D
  min sc UNIVER. PH701 $4.00   (H258)
  LUCKS 01198 sc $4.75 set $9.75,
  min sc $2.00, pts $.95, ea.
                              (H259)

Symphony No. 2 in C
  min sc UNIVER. PH702 $4.00   (H260)

Symphony No. 3 in G
  min sc UNIVER. PH703 $4.00   (H261)

Symphony No. 4 in D
  min sc UNIVER. PH704 $4.00   (H262)
  LUCKS 08125 sc $5.00, set $10.00,
  min sc $2.00, pts $1.00, ea.
                              (H263)

HAYDN, [FRANZ] JOSEPH (cont'd.)

Symphony No. 5 in A
　min sc UNIVER. PH705 $4.00　　(H264)

Symphony No. 6 in D
　min sc UNIVER. PH706 $6.00　.(H265)

Symphony No. 7 in C
　(in this edition no cont part)
　BAREN. BA 4682 perf mat rent
　　　　　　　　　　　　　　　　(H266)
　min sc UNIVER. PH707 $6.00　　(H267)

Symphony No. 8 in G
　min sc UNIVER. PH708 $6.00　　(H268)

Symphony No. 9 in C
　min sc UNIVER. PH709 $4.00　　(H269)

Symphony No. 10 in D
　min sc UNIVER. PH710 $4.00　　(H270)

Symphony No. 11 in E flat
　min sc UNIVER. PH711 $4.00　　(H271)

Symphony No. 12 in E
　min sc UNIVER. PH712 $4.00　　(H272)

Symphony No. 13 in D
　min sc UNIVER. PH713 $4.00　　(H273)

Symphony No. 14 in A
　min sc UNIVER. PH714 $4.00　　(H274)

Symphony No. 15 in D
　min sc UNIVER. PH715 $4.00　　(H275)

Symphony No. 16 in B flat
　min sc UNIVER. PH716 $4.00　　(H276)

Symphony No. 17 in F
　min sc UNIVER. PH717 $4.00　　(H277)

Symphony No. 18 in G
　min sc UNIVER. PH718 $4.00　　(H278)

Symphony No. 19 in D
　min sc UNIVER. PH719 $4.00　　(H279)

Symphony No. 20 in C
　min sc UNIVER. PH720 $4.00　　(H280)

Symphony No. 21 in A
　min sc UNIVER. PH721 $4.00　　(H281)
　LUCKS 08507 sc $5.00, set $9.75,
　　min sc $2.00, pts $.95, ea.
　　　　　　　　　　　　　　　　(H282)

Symphony No. 22 in E flat
　min sc UNIVER. PH722 $4.00　　(H283)

Symphony No. 23 in G
　min sc UNIVER. PH723 $4.00　　(H284)

Symphony No. 24 in D
　min sc UNIVER. PH724 $4.00　　(H285)

Symphony No. 25 in C
　min sc UNIVER. PH725 $4.00　　(H286)

Symphony No. 26 in D minor
　min sc UNIVER. PH726 $4.00　　(H287)
　LUCKS 01344 sc $5.00, set $10.00,
　　min sc $2.00, pts $1.00, ea.
　　　　　　　　　　　　　　　　(H288)

Symphony No. 27 in G
　min sc UNIVER. PH727 $4.00　　(H289)

Symphony No. 28 in A
　min sc UNIVER. PH728 $4.00　　(H290)
　KALMUS A1560 sc $5.00, perf mat
　　rent, set $12.00, pts $1.50, ea.
　　　　　　　　　　　　　　　　(H291)
　LUCKS 05760 sc $4.75, set $9.75,
　　min sc $2.00, pts $1.00, ea.　(H292)

Symphony No. 29 in E
　min sc UNIVER. PH729 $4.00　　(H293)

Symphony No. 30 in C
　min sc UNIVER. PH730 $6.00　　(H294)

Symphony No. 31 in D
　min sc UNIVER. PH731 $6.00　　(H295)
　LUCKS 08899 sc $4.75, set $9.75,
　　min sc $2.00, pts $.90, ea.
　　　　　　　　　　　　　　　　(H296)

Symphony No. 32 in C
　min sc UNIVER. PH732 $4.00　　(H297)

Symphony No. 33 in C
　min sc UNIVER. PH733 $4.00　　(H298)

Symphony No. 34 in D minor
　min sc UNIVER. PH734 $4.00　　(H299)

Symphony No. 35 in B flat
　min sc UNIVER. PH735 $4.00　　(H300)

Symphony No. 36 in E flat
　min sc UNIVER. PH736 $4.00　　(H301)

Symphony No. 37 in C
　min sc UNIVER. PH737 $4.00　　(H302)

HAYDN, [FRANZ] JOSEPH (cont'd.)

Symphony No. 38 in C
　min sc UNIVER. PH738 $4.00　　(H303)

Symphony No. 39 in G minor
　min sc UNIVER. PH739 $4.00　　(H304)

Symphony No. 40 in F
　min sc UNIVER. PH740 $4.00　　(H305)

Symphony No. 41 in C
　min sc UNIVER. PH741 $4.00　　(H306)

Symphony No. 42 in D
　min sc UNIVER. PH742 $4.00　　(H307)

Symphony No. 43 in E flat
　min sc UNIVER. PH743 $4.00　　(H308)

Symphony No. 44 in E minor
　min sc UNIVER. PH744 $4.00　　(H309)

Symphony No. 45 in F sharp minor
　min sc UNIVER. PH745 $4.00　　(H310)
　min sc INTERNAT. 984 $3.50　　(H311)

Symphony No. 46 in B
　min sc UNIVER. PH746 $4.00　　(H312)

Symphony No. 47 in G
　min sc UNIVER. PH747 $4.00　　(H313)

Symphony No. 48 in C
　min sc UNIVER. PH748 $4.00　　(H314)
　min sc PETERS 539 $4.50　　　(H315)
　LUCKS 01581 sc $5.00, set $12.00,
　　min sc $2.00, pts $1.00, ea.
　　　　　　　　　　　　　　　　(H316)

Symphony No. 49 in F minor
　min sc UNIVER. PH749 $4.00　　(H317)
　LUCKS 08530 sc $6.50, set $17.00,
　　min sc $2.00, pts $1.40, ea.
　　　　　　　　　　　　　　　　(H318)

Symphony No. 50 in C [22']
　0.2.0.1. 2.2.0.0. timp,strings
　min sc UNIVER. PH750 $4.00　　(H319)
　sc UNIVER. HMP 57 $33.00, set
　　UNIVER. HMP 58 $32.00, pts
　　UNIVER. $2.75, ea.　　　　　(H320)

Symphony No. 51 in B flat [23']
　0.2.0.1. 2.0.0.0. strings
　min sc UNIVER. PH751 $4.00　　(H321)
　sc UNIVER. HMP 59 $23.00, set
　　UNIVER. HMP 60 $22.00, pts
　　UNIVER. $2.75, ea.　　　　　(H322)

Symphony No. 52 in C minor [23']
　0.2.0.1. 2.0.0.0. strings
　min sc UNIVER. PH752 $4.00　　(H323)
　sc UNIVER. HMP 40 $28.00, set
　　UNIVER. HMP 41 $9.50, pts UNIVER.
　　$2.75, ea.　　　　　　　　　(H324)

Symphony No. 53 in D [24']
　1.2.0.2. 2.0.0.0. timp,strings
　min sc UNIVER. PH753 $4.00　　(H325)
　(with 2 finales) sc UNIVER. HMP 61
　　$30.00, set UNIVER. HMP 62
　　$32.00, pts UNIVER. $3.75, ea.
　　　　　　　　　　　　　　　　(H326)
　sc CARISCH 20763 f.s., pts CARISCH
　　20870 rent　　　　　　　　　(H327)

Symphony No. 54 in G [34']
　2.2.0.2. 2.2.0.0. timp,strings
　min sc UNIVER. PH754 $4.00　　(H328)
　sc UNIVER. HMP 63 $23.00, set
　　UNIVER. HMP 64 $40.00, pts
　　UNIVER. $2.75, ea.　　　　　(H329)

Symphony No. 55 in E flat [21']
　0.2.0.1. 2.0.0.0. strings
　min sc UNIVER. PH755 $4.00　　(H330)
　(in this edition 2 bassoon parts)
　　sc UNIVER. HMP 65 $25.00, set
　　UNIVER. HMP 66 $25.00, pts
　　UNIVER. $2.75, ea.　　　　　(H331)
　KALMUS 5347 sc $12.00, perf mat
　　rent, set $15.00, pts $1.50, ea.
　　　　　　　　　　　　　　　　(H332)
　min sc PETERS 540 $4.50　　　(H333)

Symphony No. 56 in C [28']
　0.2.0.1. 2.2.0.0. timp,strings
　min sc UNIVER. PH756 $4.00　　(H334)
　sc UNIVER. HMP 55 $23.00, set
　　UNIVER. HMP 56 $36.00, pts
　　UNIVER. $3.75, ea.　　　　　(H335)

Symphony No. 57 in D [24']
　0.2.0.1. 2.0.0.0. opt timp,
　　strings
　min sc UNIVER. PH757 $4.00　　(H336)
　sc UNIVER. HMP 67 $23.00, set
　　UNIVER. HMP 68 $25.00, pts
　　UNIVER. $2.75, ea.　　　　　(H337)

Symphony No. 58 in F [22']
　0.2.0.1. 2.0.0.0. hpsd,strings
　min sc UNIVER. PH758 $4.00　　(H338)
　sc UNIVER. HMP 25 $14.50, set
　　UNIVER. HMP 26 $25.00, pts
　　UNIVER. $2.75, ea.　　　　　(H339)

HAYDN, [FRANZ] JOSEPH (cont'd.)

Symphony No. 59 in A [22']
　0.2.0.1. 2.0.0.0. hpsd,strings
　min sc UNIVER. PH759 $4.00　　(H340)
　sc UNIVER. HMP 27 $17.00, set
　　UNIVER. HMP 28 $13.25, pts
　　UNIVER. $2.75, ea.　　　　　(H341)

Symphony No. 60 in C [28']
　0.2.0.1. 2.2.0.0. timp,strings
　min sc UNIVER. PH760 $4.00　　(H342)
　sc UNIVER. HMP 29 $30.00, set
　　UNIVER. HMP 30 $32.00, pts
　　UNIVER. $3.25, ea.　　　　　(H343)

Symphony No. 61 in D [26']
　1.2.0.2. 2.0.0.0. timp,strings
　min sc UNIVER. PH761 $4.00　　(H344)
　sc UNIVER. HMP 31 $29.00, set
　　UNIVER. HMP 32 $36.00, pts
　　UNIVER. $3.75, ea.　　　　　(H345)

Symphony No. 62 in D [22']
　1.2.0.2. 2.0.0.0. strings
　min sc UNIVER. PH762 $4.00　　(H346)
　sc UNIVER. HMP 84 $23.00, set
　　UNIVER. HMP 85 $32.00, pts
　　UNIVER. $3.75, ea.　　　　　(H347)

Symphony No. 63 in C
　min sc UNIVER. PH763 $4.00　　(H348)
　(includes first version scored for
　　1202 2200, timp, str) sc UNIVER.
　　HMP 86 $33.00, set UNIVER. HMP 87
　　$43.00, pts UNIVER. $4.50, ea.
　　　　　　　　　　　　　　　　(H349)

Symphony No. 64 in A
　min sc UNIVER. PH764 $4.00　　(H350)
　sc UNIVER. HMP 88 $18.00, set
　　UNIVER. HMP 89 $25.00, pts
　　UNIVER. $3.75, ea.　　　　　(H351)

Symphony No. 65 in A [23']
　0.2.0.1. 2.0.0.0. strings
　min sc UNIVER. PH765 $4.00　　(H352)
　sc UNIVER. HMP 33 $17.00, set
　　UNIVER. HMP 34 $16.50, pts
　　UNIVER. $2.75, ea.　　　　　(H353)

Symphony No. 66 in B flat [21']
　0.2.0.2. 2.0.0.0. strings
　min sc UNIVER. PH766 $4.00　　(H354)
　sc UNIVER. HMP 90 $30.00, set
　　UNIVER. HMP 91 $32.00, pts
　　UNIVER. $3.75, ea.　　　　　(H355)

Symphony No. 67 in F [25']
　0.2.0.2. 2.0.0.0. strings
　min sc UNIVER. PH767 $4.00　　(H356)
　sc UNIVER. HMP 92 $30.00, set
　　UNIVER. HMP 93 $31.00, pts
　　UNIVER. $3.75, ea.　　　　　(H357)

Symphony No. 68 in B flat [23']
　0.2.0.2. 2.0.0.0. strings
　min sc UNIVER. PH768 $4.00　　(H358)
　sc UNIVER. HMP 94 $30.00, set
　　UNIVER. HMP 95 $32.00, pts
　　UNIVER. $3.75, ea.　　　　　(H359)

Symphony No. 69 in C [22']
　0.2.0.2. 2.2.0.0. timp,strings
　min sc UNIVER. PH769 $4.00　　(H360)
　sc UNIVER. HMP 150 $30.00, set
　　UNIVER. HMP 151 $46.00, pts
　　UNIVER. $4.50, ea.　　　　　(H361)

Symphony No. 70 in D
　min sc UNIVER. PH770 $4.00　　(H362)
　sc UNIVER. HMP 35 $23.00, set
　　UNIVER. HMP 36 $46.00, pts
　　UNIVER. $3.75, ea.　　　　　(H363)

Symphony No. 71 in B flat [21']
　1.2.0.2. 2.0.0.0. strings
　min sc UNIVER. PH771 $4.00　　(H364)
　sc UNIVER. HMP 152 $30.00, set
　　UNIVER. HMP 153 $32.00, pts
　　UNIVER. $3.75, ea.　　　　　(H365)

Symphony No. 72 in D [26']
　1.2.0.1. 4.0.0.0. hpsd,strings
　min sc UNIVER. PH772 $4.00　　(H366)
　sc UNIVER. HMP 142 $23.00, set
　　UNIVER. HMP 143 $40.00, pts
　　UNIVER. $3.75, ea.　　　　　(H367)

Symphony No. 73 in D
　min sc UNIVER. PH773 $4.00　　(H368)
　sc UNIVER. HMP 154 $30.00, set
　　UNIVER. HMP 155 $46.00, pts
　　UNIVER. $4.50, ea.　　　　　(H369)
　LUCKS 09036 sc $7.50, set $17.00,
　　pts $1.40, ea.　　　　　　　(H370)

Symphony No. 74 in E flat [21']
　1.2.0.2. 2.0.0.0. strings
　min sc UNIVER. PH774 $4.00　　(H371)
　sc UNIVER. HMP 156 $29.00, set
　　UNIVER. HMP 157 $32.00, pts
　　UNIVER. $3.75, ea.　　　　　(H372)

Symphony No. 75 in D
　min sc UNIVER. PH775 $4.00　　(H373)
　(in this edition 2 bassoon parts)

HAYDN, [FRANZ] JOSEPH (cont'd.)
    sc UNIVER. HMP 158 $29.00, set
    UNIVER. HMP 159 $36.00, pts
    UNIVER. $3.75, ea.   (H374)

Symphony No. 76 in E flat
    min sc UNIVER. PH776 $4.00   (H375)
    sc UNIVER. HMP 160 $27.00, set
    UNIVER. HMP 161 $28.00, pts
    UNIVER. $4.00, ea.   (H376)

Symphony No. 77 in B flat
    min sc UNIVER. PH777 $4.00   (H377)
    sc UNIVER. HMP 162 $30.00, set
    UNIVER. HMP 163 $36.00, pts
    UNIVER. $3.75, ea.   (H378)

Symphony No. 78 in C minor
    min sc UNIVER. PH778 $4.00   (H379)
    sc UNIVER. HMP 164 $29.00, set
    UNIVER. HMP 165 $36.00, pts
    UNIVER. $3.75, ea.   (H380)
    BROUDE BR. set $18.00, pts $1.50,
    ea.   (H381)

Symphony No. 79 in F
    min sc UNIVER. PH779 $4.00   (H382)
    sc UNIVER. HMP 166 $30.00, set
    UNIVER. HMP 167 $36.00, pts
    UNIVER. $3.75, ea.   (H383)

Symphony No. 80 in D minor [20']
    1.2.0.2. 2.0.0.0. strings
    min sc UNIVER. PH780 $4.00   (H384)
    sc UNIVER. HMP 195 $30.00, set
    UNIVER. HMP 196 $36.00, pts
    UNIVER. $3.75, ea.   (H385)

Symphony No. 81 in G
    min sc UNIVER. PH781 $4.00   (H386)
    sc UNIVER. HMP 96 $30.00, set
    UNIVER. HMP 97 $36.00, pts
    UNIVER. $3.75, ea.   (H387)

Symphony No. 82 in C
    min sc UNIVER. PH782 $4.00   (H388)
    sc UNIVER. HMP 144 $30.00, set
    UNIVER. HMP 145 $36.00, pts
    UNIVER. $3.75, ea.   (H389)
    LUCKS 05386 sc $10.00, set $18.00,
    pts $1.50, ea.   (H390)

Symphony No. 83 in G minor
    min sc UNIVER. PH783 $4.00   (H391)
    sc UNIVER. HMP 138 $29.00, set
    UNIVER. HMP 139 $32.00, pts
    UNIVER. $3.75, ea.   (H392)
    LUCKS 09061 sc $9.75, set $17.00,
    pts $1.40, ea.   (H393)

Symphony No. 84 in E flat
    min sc UNIVER. PH784 $4.00   (H394)
    sc UNIVER. HMP 140 $30.00, set
    UNIVER. HMP 141 $32.00, pts
    UNIVER. $3.75, ea.   (H395)

Symphony No. 85 in B flat
    min sc UNIVER. PH785 $4.00   (H396)
    sc UNIVER. HMP 146 $29.00, set
    UNIVER. HMP 147 $32.00, pts
    UNIVER. $3.75, ea.   (H397)
    min sc BOOSEY 274 $3.75   (H398)
    (Pommer) min sc PETERS 653 $4.50
                                (H399)

Symphony No. 86 in D
    min sc UNIVER. PH786 $4.00   (H400)
    sc UNIVER. HMP 148 $32.00, set
    UNIVER. HMP 149 $43.00, pts
    UNIVER. $4.50, ea.   (H401)
    LUCKS 05749 sc $7.50, set $17.00,
    pts $1.40, ea.   (H402)
    (Pommer) min sc PETERS 835 $4.50
                                (H403)

Symphony No. 87 in A
    min sc UNIVER. PH787 $4.00   (H404)
    sc UNIVER. HMP 168 $30.00, set
    UNIVER. HMP 169 $32.00, pts
    UNIVER. $3.75, ea.   (H405)

Symphony No. 88 in G
    min sc UNIVER. PH788 $4.00   (H406)
    sc UNIVER. HMP 170 $30.00, set
    UNIVER. HMP 171 $36.00, pts
    UNIVER. $3.75, ea.   (H407)
    LUCKS 05752 sc $6.75, set $17.00,
    pts $1.40, ea.   (H408)

Symphony No. 89 in F
    min sc UNIVER. PH789 $5.00   (H409)
    sc UNIVER. HMP 172 $30.00, set
    UNIVER. HMP 173 $36.00, pts
    UNIVER. $3.75, ea.   (H410)

Symphony No. 90 in C
    min sc UNIVER. PH790 $5.00   (H411)
    sc UNIVER. HMP 174 $30.00, set
    UNIVER. HMP 175 $46.00, pts
    UNIVER. $4.50, ea.   (H412)

Symphony No. 91 in E flat
    min sc UNIVER. PH791 $5.00   (H413)
    sc UNIVER. HMP 176 $30.00, set
    UNIVER. HMP 177 $36.00, pts
    UNIVER. $3.75, ea.   (H414)
    sc CARISCH 20989 perf mat rent

HAYDN, [FRANZ] JOSEPH (cont'd.)
                                (H415)
Symphony No. 92 in G
    min sc UNIVER. PH792 $5.00   (H416)
    sc UNIVER. HMP 98 $30.00, set
    UNIVER. HMP 99 $43.00, pts
    UNIVER. $4.50, ea.   (H417)
    LUCKS 05757 sc $8.00, set $19.00,
    pts $1.40, ea.   (H418)

Symphony No. 93 in D
    min sc UNIVER. PH793 $5.00   (H419)
    sc UNIVER. HMP 69 $29.00, set
    UNIVER. HMP 70 $46.00, pts
    UNIVER. $4.50, ea.   (H420)
    BROUDE BR. set $25.00, pts $1.50,
    ea.   (H421)
    (Pommer) min sc PETERS 654 $4.50
                                (H422)

Symphony No. 94 in G
    min sc UNIVER. PH794 $5.00   (H423)
    sc UNIVER. HMP 71 $30.00, set
    UNIVER. HMP 72 $46.00, pts
    UNIVER. $4.50, ea.   (H424)
    min sc PETERS 534 $4.50   (H425)
    min sc ZEN-ON 890301 f.s.   (H426)

Symphony No. 95 in C minor
    min sc UNIVER. PH795 $5.00   (H427)
    (in this edition 2 flute parts) sc
    UNIVER. HMP 73 $30.00, set
    UNIVER. HMP 74 $43.00, pts
    UNIVER. $4.50, ea.   (H428)

Symphony No. 96 in D
    min sc UNIVER. PH796 $5.00   (H429)
    sc UNIVER. HMP 75 $21.00, set
    UNIVER. HMP 76 $46.00, pts
    UNIVER. $4.50, ea.   (H430)

Symphony No. 97 in C
    min sc UNIVER. PH797 $5.00   (H431)
    sc UNIVER. HMP 77 $39.00, set
    UNIVER. HMP 78 $46.00, pts
    UNIVER. $4.50, ea.   (H432)
    BOOSEY 234 min sc $3.50, sc $28.00
                                (H433)
    (Pommer) min sc PETERS 831 $4.50
                                (H434)

Symphony No. 98 in B flat
    min sc UNIVER. PH798 $5.00   (H435)
    (in this edition 2 flute parts;
    solo cembalo in Finale) sc
    UNIVER. HMP 79 $33.00, set
    UNIVER. HMP 80 $43.00, pts
    UNIVER. $4.50, ea.   (H436)
    (Pommer) min sc PETERS 832 $6.00
                                (H437)

Symphony No. 99 in E flat
    min sc UNIVER. PH799 $5.00   (H438)
    sc UNIVER. HMP 178 $33.00, set
    UNIVER. HMP 179 $50.00, pts
    UNIVER. $4.50, ea.   (H439)
    BROUDE BR. set $22.50, pts $1.50,
    ea.   (H440)

Symphony No. 100 in G
    min sc UNIVER. PH800 $5.00   (H441)
    sc UNIVER. HMP 180 $34.00, set
    UNIVER. HMP 181 $50.00, pts
    UNIVER. $4.50, ea.   (H442)
    min sc ZEN-ON 890302 f.s.   (H443)

Symphony No. 101 in D
    min sc UNIVER. PH801 $5.00   (H444)
    sc UNIVER. HMP 182 $34.00, set
    UNIVER. HMP 183 $50.00, pts
    UNIVER. $4.50, ea.   (H445)

Symphony No. 102 in B flat
    min sc UNIVER. PH802 $5.00   (H446)
    sc UNIVER. HMP 184 $34.00, set
    UNIVER. HMP 185 $46.00, pts
    UNIVER. $4.50, ea.   (H447)
    BROUDE BR. set $22.50, pts $1.50,
    ea.   (H448)
    min sc PETERS 834 $6.00   (H449)
    LUCKS 05751 sc $6.00, set $20.00,
    pts $1.50, ea.   (H450)

Symphony No. 103 in E flat
    min sc UNIVER. PH803 $5.00   (H451)
    sc UNIVER. HMP 186 $34.00, set
    UNIVER. HMP 187 $50.00, pts
    UNIVER. $4.50, ea.   (H452)

Symphony No. 104 in D
    min sc UNIVER. PH804 $5.00   (H453)
    sc UNIVER. HMP 188 $34.00, set
    UNIVER. HMP 189 $50.00, pts
    UNIVER. $4.50, ea.   (H454)

Symphony No. 107 in B flat
    (Symphony A) min sc UNIVER. PH699
    $4.00   (H455)

Symphony No. 108 in B flat
    (Symphony B) min sc UNIVER. PH700
    $4.00   (H456)

Tergi I Vezzosi Rai, For Solo Voice
    And Orchestra
    0.2.0.2. 2.0.0.0. strings,Bar
    solo
    (1773, additional aria to "Acide E

HAYDN, [FRANZ] JOSEPH (cont'd.)
    Galatea" (2nd Version)) sc
    UNIVER. HMP 120 $14.00, set
    UNIVER. HMP 121 $18.00, pts
    UNIVER. $2.75, ea.   (H457)

Toy Symphony *see Kindersinfonie

Un Cor Si Tenero, For Solo Voice And
    Orchestra
    0.2.0.0. 2.0.0.0. strings,Bar
    solo
    (1787, additional aria to Bianchi's
    "Il Disertore") sc UNIVER. HMP 43
    $13.50, set UNIVER. HMP 44
    $13.50, pts UNIVER. $3.00, ea.
                                (H458)

Vada Adagio, Signorina, For Solo
    Voice And Orchestra
    0.2.0.2. 2.0.0.0. strings,S solo
    (1787, additional aria to
    Guglielmis' "La Quakera
    Spiritosa") sc UNIVER. HMP 46
    $14.00, set UNIVER. HMP 47
    $10.50, pts UNIVER. $1.75, ea.
                                (H459)

HAYDN, [JOHANN] MICHAEL (1737-1806)
    Concerto for Flute and Orchestra, MIN
    2
    (Vecsey) min sc EMB K47 $4.00
                                (H460)

    Concerto for 2 Horns and Orchestra,
    MIN 33
    2ob,2horn,strings,2horn soli
    (de Nys, Carl) COSTALL perf mat
    rent   (H461)

    O Worship The King
    (Luck, Arthur) LUCKS HYMNS 8 set
    $10.00, pts $.65, ea. contains
    also: Croft, William, Oh God, Our
    Help In Ages Past   (H462)

    Pastorello
    2fl,2clar,strings
    LUCKS 01139 sc $7.50, set $12.00,
    min sc $2.50, pts $1.00, ea.
                                (H463)
    sc,pts HARMONIA 1829 f.s.   (H464)

    Sechs Menuette, Perger 70
    1.2.0.1. 2.0.0.0. strings without
    vla
    (Sherman, Ch.) sc,pts DOBLINGER
    DM 806 f.s.   (H465)

    Symphonies, Five
    see SALZBURG, PART 2

    Zaire, Perger 13
    2.2(English horn).0.1. 2.1.0.0.
    timp,perc,strings
    (Rainer, W.) sc,pts DOBLINGER
    DM 577 f.s.   (H466)

HEART WOUNDS; LAST SPRING see Grieg,
    Edvard Hagerup, Elegiac Melodies

HEAVEN CAME DOWN
    (Mayfield, Larry; Skillings, Otis)
    SINGSPIR 7707 $19.95   (H467)

HEAVEN MEDLEY, [ARR.]
    (Kirkland, Camp) CRESPUB CP-IN 7+3
    $15.00 see also Seven+
    Orchestration Series, Group 1
                                (H468)

HEAVENTREE OF STARS, THE, FOR VIOLIN
    AND ORCHESTRA see Hoddinott, Alun

HEBRAIC SKETCHES: SUITE NO. 2 see
    Krein, Alexander

HEBREW SONGS see Bruch, Max

HEBRIDEN, DIE see Mendelssohn-
    Bartholdy, Felix

HEEGAARD, LARS
    Symphony No. 1
    3.3.3.2. 4.3.3.1. timp,perc,harp,
    pno,strings
    SAMFUNDET perf mat rent   (H469)

HEERENVEEN see Schouwman, Hans

HEI MET DE WOLKEN ZOO WIT see
    Andriessen, Willem

HEIDER, WERNER (1930-   )
    Nachdenken Uber, For Trumpet And
    Orchestra [22']
    3.3.3.3.sax. 4.3.3.1. 3perc,
    strings,trp solo
    study sc PETERS EP 8461 $60.00,
    perf mat rent   (H470)

HEILIGENSTADTER RENDEZVOUS POLKA, FOR
    SOLO VOICE AND ORCHESTRA see
    Strauss, Johann, [Jr.]

HEILMANN, HARALD (1924-)
Concertino for Recorder and String
Orchestra [15']
string orch,S rec solo
MULLER (H471)

Hymnus, For Violin And String
Orchestra [8']
string orch,vln solo
MULLER (H472)

Triptychon [15']
MULLER (H473)

HEIMISCHE KLANGE WALZER see Strauss,
Eduard

HEINZELMANNCHENS BRAUTFAHRT see
Hagelbauer, C.A.

HEITERE BEGEGNUNGEN see Dressel, Erwin

HEITERE SUITE see Lohse, Fred

HEJRE KATI see Hubay, Jeno, Scenes De
La Csarda No. 4, For Violin And
Orchestra

HEKSTER, WALTER (1937-)
Auroras Of Autumn, The, For Oboe And
Orchestra [12']
5perc,harp,pno,elec org,cel/pno,
6vln,3vla,2vcl,ob&ob
d'amore&English horn solo
sc DONEMUS f.s., perf mat rent
(H474)
Between Two Worlds, For Saxophone And
Orchestra [12']
1.1.2.1. 1.2.1.0. timp,3perc,pno,
acord,elec org,strings,sax
solo, elec bass gtr
sc DONEMUS f.s., perf mat rent
(H475)
Concerto for Guitar and Orchestra
[12']
2.1.2.1.sax. 1.1.1.0. 3perc,
strings,gtr solo
DONEMUS (H476)

Epitaphium
string orch
sc DONEMUS f.s., perf mat rent
(H477)
Nocturnal Conversation [11']
2.1.2.1. 2.2.1.1. timp,5perc,pno,
8vln,4vla,2vcl,db,opt
electronic tape
sc DONEMUS f.s., perf mat rent
(H478)
Parts Of A World, For Viola And
Orchestra [12']
1.1.2.1. 0.0.4.0. 3perc,harp,pno,
6vcl,6db,vla solo
sc DONEMUS f.s., perf mat rent
(H479)
Primavera, For Piano And Orchestra
[14']
2.1.2.2. 2.2.2.1. 3perc,strings,
pno solo
DONEMUS sc f.s., pts rent, solo pt
f.s. (H480)
Sea Surface Full Of Clouds [6']
12strings
DONEMUS perf mat rent (H481)
Sunday [11']
1.1.1.1. 1.0.0.0. 6vln,3vla,2vcl,
db
sc DONEMUS f.s., perf mat rent
(H482)
Transport To Summer, For Clarinet And
Orchestra [12']
perc,pno,6vln,3vla,2vcl,db,clar
solo
DONEMUS perf mat rent (H483)

HEKTOGRAF POLKA see Strauss, Eduard

HELDENLEBEN, EIN see Strauss, Richard

HELIOS see Mathias, William

HELIOS KINETIC see Gutche, Gene

HELLERMANN, WILLIAM (1939-)
Stop-Start
PRESSER 446-41038 sc $12.00, pts
rent (H484)

Time And Again
2.2.2.2. 4.2.2.0. perc,harp,pno,
strings
sc MERION $15.00 (H485)

HELM, JOSEF
Rennfieber
RIES f.s. (H486)

HELPS, ROBERT (1928-)
Gossamer Noons, For Solo Voice And
Orchestra [18']
2(pic).2.2.2. 4.3.3.0. timp,
3perc,pno,strings,S solo
PETERS P66649 perf mat rent (H487)

HEMEL, OSCAR VAN (1892-)
Concerto for Violin and Orchestra,
No. 3 [15']
2.2.2.2. 4.2.2.0. timp,3perc,
strings,vln solo
DONEMUS perf mat rent (H488)

Concerto for 2 Violins and String
Orchestra [11']
string orch,2vln soli
sc DONEMUS f.s., perf mat rent
(H489)
Tombeau De Kathleen Ferrier, Le, For
Solo Voice And Orchestra [20']
3.3.3.3. 4.3.3.1. timp,perc,cel,
strings,A solo
sc DONEMUS f.s., perf mat rent
(H490)
Trittico Liturgico, For Solo Voice
And String Orchestra
string orch,Mez solo
sc DONEMUS f.s., perf mat rent
(H491)

HEMINGWAY'S ADVENTURES OF A YOUNG MAN:
SUITE see Waxman, Franz

HEMY
Faith Of Our Fathers
see Dykes, Eternal Father Strong To
Save

HEN SYMPHONY see Haydn, [Franz] Joseph,
Symphony No. 83 in G minor

HENKEMANS, HANS (1913-)
Balade Pour Robert d'Estouteville
see Villonerie, For Solo Voice And
Orchestra

Ballade, For Solo Voice And Orchestra
[8']
2.1.2.0. 2.0.0.0. timp,harp,
12vln,4vla,3vcl,3db,A solo
sc DONEMUS f.s., perf mat rent
(H492)
Canzoni Amorose Del Duecento, For
Solo Voices And Orchestra
3.3.3.3. 4.0.0.0. timp,perc,harp,
pno,strings,SBar soli sc DONEMUS
f.s., perf mat rent
contains: Farso, Il; Partite,
Amore, Adeo; Sparvero, Lo
(H493)
Concerto for Horn and Orchestra [11']
3.3.3.3. 0.3.3.1. timp,2perc,pno,
2harp,strings,horn solo
sc DONEMUS f.s. (H494)

Debat Du Cuer Et Du Corps De Villon,
Le
see Villonerie, For Solo Voice And
Orchestra

Farso, Il
see Canzoni Amorose Del Duecento,
For Solo Voices And Orchestra

Partite, Amore, Adeo
see Canzoni Amorose Del Duecento,
For Solo Voices And Orchestra

Sparvero, Lo
see Canzoni Amorose Del Duecento,
For Solo Voices And Orchestra

Tetrastique
see Villonerie, For Solo Voice And
Orchestra

Villonerie, For Solo Voice And
Orchestra
3.3.3.3. 4.3.3.1. timp,perc,2harp,
pno,strings,Bar solo sc DONEMUS
f.s., perf mat rent
contains: Balade Pour Robert
d'Estouteville; Debat Du Cuer
Et Du Corps De Villon, Le;
Tetrastique (H495)

HENRICH, HERMANN (1891-)
Innsbruck *Op.43 [25']
2(pic).2.2.2. 4.2.3.1. 2timp,
perc,strings,opt men cor&boy
cor
RIES perf mat rent (H496)

HENRY VIII: THREE DANCES see German,
[Sir] Edward (Edward German Jones)

HENSELT, ADOLPH VON (1814-1889)
Ave Maria (from Op. 5)
see RICREAZIONI DI ANTICHE MUSICHE
CLASSICHE, SERIE IV: MUSICHE
ANTICHE ITALIANE

Concerto for Piano and Orchestra, Op.
16, in F minor [28']
2.2.2.2. 2.2.3.0. timp,strings,
pno solo
BREITKOPF-W perf mat rent (H497)

HENZE, HANS WERNER (1926-)
Aria De La Folia Espanola
2.2.1.2. 2.0.0.0. perc,cel,pno,
mand,strings
sc EUR.AM.MUS. 71 A6841 $43.00

HENZE, HANS WERNER (cont'd.)

(H498)
Barcarola
3(pic,alto fl).3(English horn,
Heckelphone).3(clar in E flat,
bass clar,contrabass
clar).3(contrabsn).soprano
sax.baritone sax. 6.4.3.1.
perc,2harp,cel,pno,strings
sc SCHOTTS ED 6899 $42.00 (H499)

HEPPENER, ROBERT (1925-)
Sweelinck Fanfare [5']
3.3.3.3. 4.3.3.1. timp,2perc,
harp,strings
DONEMUS perf mat rent (H500)
orch MOLENAAR 14.1559.08 f.s.
(H501)

HEPZIBAH see Buchtger, Fritz

HERBERT, VICTOR (1859-1924)
Babes In Toyland: March Of The Toys
LUCKS 05775 set $11.00, pts $.75,
ea. (H502)
set LUCKS $29.50 (H503)

Babes In Toyland: Selection
(Langey) LUCKS 05776 set $18.00,
pts $1.00, ea. (H504)

Babes In Toyland: Selections
set LUCKS $32.50 (H505)

Concerto for Violoncello and
Orchestra, No. 1, Op. 8
2.2.2.2. 4.2.3.0. timp,harp,
strings,vcl solo
(each movement available
separately) KALMUS A4350 sc
$30.00, perf mat rent, set
$45.00, pts $3.00, ea., solo pt
$3.00 (H506)

Concerto for Violoncello and
Orchestra, No. 2, Op. 30 [23']
2.2.2.2. 4.2.3.0. timp,strings,
vcl solo
INTERNAT. perf mat rent (H507)
(each movement available
separately) KALMUS A4351 sc
$15.00, perf mat rent, set
$35.00, pts $2.00, ea., solo pt
$3.00 (H508)
LUCKS 00654 sc $25.00, set $35.00,
pts $2.50, ea. (H509)

Fortune Teller, The: Gypsy Love Song,
For Solo Voice And Orchestra
(Langey) (C maj) LUCKS 02981 set
$15.00, pts $.75, ea. (H510)
(Luck) (A maj) LUCKS 02981 set
$15.00, pts $.75, ea. (H511)

Fortune Teller, The: Romany Life, For
Solo Voice And Orchestra
LUCKS 02444 set $28.00, pts $1.00,
ea. (H512)

Fortune Teller, The: Selection
(Langey; Luck) LUCKS 05790 set
$40.00, pts $1.50, ea. (H513)

Red Mill, The: Selections
LUCKS 05825 set $11.00, pts $.75,
ea. (H514)

Red Mill, The: Selections
set LUCKS $29.25 (H515)

Serenade for Violoncello and
Orchestra (from Suite, Op. 3)
LUCKS 00621 set $14.00, pts $1.15,
ea. (H516)

Serenade, Op. 12
string orch
LUCKS 07400 sc $9.00, set $12.00,
pts $2.50, ea. (H517)

HERBSTROSEN WALZER see Strauss, Josef

HERBSTSTURM see Gilse, Jan van

HERCHET, JÖRG (1943-)
Komposition, For Flute And Orchestra
[20']
0.0.0.0. 3.1.2.0. 4perc,harp,cel,
hpsd,strings,fl&alto fl solo
sc PETERS EP 9226 f.s., perf mat
rent (H518)

Kompositionen, For Trombone, Solo
Voice And Orchestra
3.3.4.3. 4.3.2.1. cel,harp,pno,
timp,perc,strings,trom solo,Bar
solo
DEUTSCHER perf mat rent (H519)

HERCULES: MY FATHER, FOR SOLO VOICE AND
STRING ORCHESTRA see Handel, George
Frideric

HERFST IN FRIESLAND see Schouwman, Hans

HERINNERING see Andriessen, Willem

HERINNERING AAN HOLLAND, FOR SOLO VOICE
AND ORCHESTRA see Voormolen,
Alexander Nicolas

HERMANN UND DOROTHEA: OVERTURE see
Schumann, Robert (Alexander)

HERMANS, NICO (1919-   )
Concerto for Clarinet and Orchestra
[20']
2.2.2.2. 2.2.0.0. perc,strings,
clar solo
DONEMUS   (H520)

Concerto for Harp and Orchestra [22']
2.2.2.2. 2.2.0.0. timp,strings,
harp solo
DONEMUS perf mat rent   (H521)

Deux Nocturnes, For Solo Voice And
Orchestra *Op.10
fl,strings,Mez solo sc DONEMUS
f.s., perf mat rent
contains: Nacht; Nacht-Stilte
(H522)

Festival Overture [8'30"]
3.2.2.2. 4.3.3.1. timp,3perc,
harp,strings
DONEMUS perf mat rent   (H523)

Nacht
see Deux Nocturnes, For Solo Voice
And Orchestra

Nacht-Stilte
see Deux Nocturnes, For Solo Voice
And Orchestra

HERMANSON, AKE (1923-   )
Utopia *Op.20 [16']
4.3.3.3. 6.4.3.1. cel,pno,strings
sc SUECIA ENO 314 perf mat rent
(H524)

HERODIADE: BALLET SUITE see Massenet,
Jules

HERODIADE: IL EST DOUX, IL EST BON, FOR
SOLO VOICE AND ORCHESTRA see
Massenet, Jules

HERODIADE: VISION FUGITIVE, FOR SOLO
VOICE AND ORCHESTRA see Massenet,
Jules

HEROLD, LOUIS-JOSEPH-FERDINAND
(1791-1833)
Symphonies In C And In D
(Schwarz, Boris; Schwarz, K.
Robert) ("The Symphony", Vol. D-
IX) sc GARLAND ISBN 0-8240-3808-8
$90.00 contains also: Onslow,
Georges, Symphonies, Op. 41 In A
And Op. 42 In D Minor   (H525)

Zampa: Overture
LUCKS 05854 sc $9.50, set $23.00,
pts $1.40, ea.   (H526)

HERO'S LIFE, A see Strauss, Richard,
Heldenleben, Ein

HERO'S SONG see Dvorak, Antonin

HERTEL, JOHANN WILHELM (1727-1789)
Concerti, For Trumpet And String
Orchestra, Three
string orch,trp solo
sc,pts COSTALL f.s.   (H527)

HERZEL POLKA see Strauss, Johann, [Jr.]

HERZLICH TUT MICH VERLAGEN, [ARR.] see
Bach, Johann Sebastian

HESELTINE, PHILIP ("PETER WARLOCK")
(1894-1930)
Capriol Suite, Version For String
Orchestra
min sc BOOSEY 57 $6.50   (H528)

HESPERUS POLKA see Strauss, Johann,
[Jr.]

HESPOS, HANS-JOACHIM (1938-   )
Stoub [11'32"]
1(pic).1(English horn).0.bass
clar.clar in E flat.1. 1.1.1.0.
timp,2vln,vla,vcl,db
MODERN 1919 rent   (H529)

HESS, WILLY (1906-   )
Concerto for Violin, Viola and
Orchestra, Op. 81, in F
2.2.2.2. 2.0.0.0. timp,perc,
strings,vln solo,vla solo
sc EULENBURG GM593 f.s., perf mat
rent   (H530)

Serenade, Op. 19
fl,ob,clar,2bsn,2horn,2vln,vla,
vcl
sc,pts AMADEUS GM 532 f.s.   (H531)

HESSENBERG, KURT (1908-   )
Concerto for Oboe and Orchestra, Op.
92
0.0.2.2. 0.0.0.0. timp,strings,ob
solo
[18'] LEUCKART perf mat rent (H532)

HEUBERGER, RICHARD (1850-1914)
Baby, Das: Overture
LUCKS 07407 sc $16.00, set $40.00,
pts $2.00, ea.   (H533)

Opernball, Der: Domino Waltz
LUCKS 05898 set $32.00, pts $1.50,
ea.   (H534)

Opernball, Der: Im Chambre Separee
LUCKS 07401 set $18.00, pts $.75,
ea.   (H535)

Opernball, Der: Overture
LUCKS 07405 sc $22.00, set $40.00,
pts $2.00, ea.   (H536)

Opernball, Der: Potpourri
LUCKS 07406 set $30.00, pts $1.50,
ea.   (H537)

Struwwelpeter: March
LUCKS 07403 set $18.00, pts $.75,
ea.   (H538)

Struwwelpeter: Overture
LUCKS 07404 set $30.00, pts $1.50,
ea.   (H539)

Struwwelpeter: Waltz
LUCKS 07857 set $30.00, pts $1.50,
ea.   (H540)

HEUSER, ERNST
Baskischer Tanz
RIES f.s.   (H541)

HIGHLAND OVERTURE, A see Wordsworth,
William

HILDACH, EUGEN (1849-1924)
Lenz, Der, For Solo Voice And
Orchestra
LUCKS 02913 set $7.50, pts $.60,
ea.   (H542)

HILDEBRAND, CAMILLO
Sanger-Fest-Ouverture
orch,opt cor
sc,pts RIES f.s.   (H543)

Vier Idyllen [22']
1(pic).1.2.1. 2.1.0.0. timp,perc,
strings
RIES perf mat rent   (H544)

HILDEBRAND, ERICH
Picador, El
RIES f.s.   (H545)

HILL, EDWARD BURLINGAME (1872-1960)
Sinfonietta, Op. 40a
string orch
sc BOOSEY $9.00   (H546)

HILLBORG, ANDERS (1954-   )
Lamento, For Clarinet And String
Orchestra
string orch,clar solo
STIM   (H547)

Untitled
ob,pno,7vln,3vla,2vcl,db
sc STIM PA-2804-18 rent, pts STIM
rent   (H548)

Worlds [11'30"]
3xylo&claves,3marimba,elec gtr,
2harp,2pno,strings
sc STIM perf mat rent   (H549)

HIMMEL VOLLER GEIGEN, DER see Ziehrer,
Carl Michael

HINA-UTA, NO. 2 see Koyama, Kiyoshige

HINTER DEN COULISSEN QUADRILLE see
Strauss, Johann, [Jr.]

HINUBER WALL'ICH, FOR SOLO VOICE AND
ORCHESTRA see Diepenbrock, Alphons

HIRNER, TEODOR (1910-1975)
Little Carapathian Overture *see
Malokarpatska Predohra

Malokarpatska Predohra
2.2.2.2. 4.2.3.0. timp,harp,
strings
"Little Carapathian Overture"
SLOV.HUD.FOND 0-176 perf mat rent
(H550)

Serenade
string orch
SLOV.HUD.FOND 0-138 perf mat rent
(H551)

Suite
1.1.1.1. 1.0.0.0. harp,cel,
strings

HIRNER, TEODOR (cont'd.)

SLOV.HUD.FOND 0-164 perf mat rent
(H552)

HIROSE, RYOHEI (1930-   )
Concerto For Shakuhachi And Orchestra
[23']
2.2.2.2. 4.2.3.1. 4perc,harp,pno,
cel,strings, Shakuhachi solo
ONGAKU perf mat rent   (H553)

Concerto for Violin and Orchestra
2.2.2.2. 4.2.3.0. perc,pno/cel,
harp,strings,vln solo
ONGAKU perf mat rent   (H554)

Festival Overture [8']
2+pic.2.2.2. 4.3.3.1. 4perc,harp,
cel,strings
ONGAKU perf mat rent   (H555)

HIRSCH, HANS LUDWIG (1937-   )
Concerto for Oboe, Bassoon and String
Orchestra
string orch,ob solo,bsn solo
sc PETERS 8153 $37.50   (H556)

HIRT, HERBERT
Schmetterling Im Pavillon
RIES f.s.   (H557)

HIVER, L', FOR SOLO VOICE AND ORCHESTRA
see Bon, Willem Frederik

HJARTER KUNG: GAGLIARDA DI GUSTAV VASA
see Eyser, Eberhard

HOCH, FRANCESCO (1943-   )
Figura Esposta [10']
1.1.2.1. 2.2.1.0. 2perc,pno&cel,
2vln,vla,vcl,db
sc ZERBONI 8412 f.s., pts ZERBONI
8413 rent   (H558)

HOCH LEBE DER WEIN see Blon, Franz von

HOCH OSTERREICH MARSCH see Strauss,
Johann, [Jr.]

HOCHETUS ET RONDELLUS see Chailly,
Luciano

HOCHQUELLE POLKA, DIE see Strauss,
Eduard

HOCHZEITSKLANGE. WALZER see Strauss,
Josef

HODDINOTT, ALUN (1929-   )
French Suite *Op.91 [18']
2.2.2.2. 2.2.0.0. timp,strings
OXFORD perf mat rent   (H559)

Hawk Is Set Free, The *Op.72,No.5
[14']
2.2.2.2. 4.2.3.0. timp,2perc,
harp,strings
OXFORD perf mat rent   (H560)

Heaventree Of Stars, The, For Violin
And Orchestra [15']
OXFORD perf mat rent   (H561)

Landscapes *Op.86 [20']
3.2.2.2. 4.2.3.1. timp,perc,
strings
sc OXFORD $35.00, perf mat rent
(H562)

Passaggio *Op.94 [15']
3.2+English horn.2+bass clar.2+
contrabsn. 4.3.3.1. timp,3perc,
harp,strings
OXFORD perf mat rent   (H563)

HOE SCHONE STAET DIE LINDE see Badings,
Henk

HOEMSNES, BJORN K.
Concerto for Bass Clarinet and String
Orchestra [10']
string orch,bass clar solo
NORGE   (H564)

HOFBALL QUADRILLE see Strauss, Johann,
[Jr.]

HOFBALLTANZE see Lanner, Josef

HOFBALLTANZE see Strauss, Johann, [Jr.]

HOFFMANN, ERNST THEODOR AMADEUS
(1776-1822)
Symphony in E flat
2.2.2.2. 2.2.0.0. timp,strings
DEUTSCHER perf mat rent   (H565)
(Hubsch, Lini) sc MULLER SM 1945
f.s., perf mat rent   (H566)

HOFFMEISTER, A.
Chasse, La *see Symphony in D

Symphony in D
sc,pts BOOSEY $52.50   (H567)

HOFFMEISTER, FRANZ ANTON (1754-1812)
Concerto for Double Bass and
Orchestra, No. 2, in D [16']
0.2.0.1. 2.0.0.0. timp,strings,db
solo
(Malaric, R.) sc,pts DOBLINGER rent
(H568)
Concerto for 2 Horns and String
Orchestra in E flat [6']
string orch,2horn soli
INTERNAT. perf mat rent (H569)

Concerto for Viola and Orchestra in
D, MIN 54 [17']
2ob,2horn,strings,vla solo
INTERNAT. perf mat rent (H570)

HOFFMEISTER, FRIEDRICH ANTON
(1782-1864)
Concerto for Clarinet and Orchestra
in B flat
0.2.0.0. 2.0.0.0. strings,clar
solo
(Balassa) sc,pts EULENBURG E10115
f.s. (H571)

HOFFSTETTER, ROMAN(US) (1742-1815)
Concerto for Viola and Orchestra in G
2fl,2horn,strings,vla solo, vcl
obligato
(Hoffman) sc,pts MOSELER 40.129
f.s. (H572)

HOFMANN, HEINRICH
Silhouetten Aus Ungarn [17']
2(pic).2.2.2. 4.2.3.1. timp,perc,
pno,harp,strings
(Dressel, Erwin) sc RIES f.s., perf
mat rent (H573)

HOFMANN, WOLFGANG (1922-   )
Ave Maria, For Solo Voice, Oboe And
String Orchestra [8']
string orch,S solo,ob solo
MANNHEIM E 4-74 f.s. (H574)

Concerto for Harp and Strings [17']
14strings,harp solo
PETERS perf mat rent (H575)

Concerto for Violoncello and Chamber
Orchestra [21']
0.2.0.1. 2.0.0.0. strings,vcl
solo
PETERS perf mat rent (H576)

Der Du Von Dem Himmel Bist, For Solo
Voice And Strings
see Drei Gesange, For Solo Voice
And Strings

Drei Gesange, For Solo Voice And
Strings
14strings,S solo MANNHEIM E 1-71
f.s.
contains: Der Du Von Dem Himmel
Bist, For Solo Voice And
Strings; Menschen Seele, Des,
For Solo Voice And Strings;
Uber Allen Gipfeln Ist Ruh',
For Solo Voice And Strings
(H577)
Droste Lieder, For Solo Voice And
Strings *CC4U
14strings,S solo MANNHEIM E 1-77
f.s. (H578)

Kammersinfonie [11']
1.2.0.2. 2.0.0.0. strings
PETERS perf mat rent (H579)

Menschen Seele, Des, For Solo Voice
And Strings
see Drei Gesange, For Solo Voice
And Strings

Uber Allen Gipfeln Ist Ruh', For Solo
Voice And Strings
see Drei Gesange, For Solo Voice
And Strings

HOJSGAARD, ERIK
Concerto for Violoncello and
Orchestra [23']
2.2.2.2. 2.2.2.0. mand,2harp,
timp,4perc,cel,strings,vcl solo
SAMFUNDET perf mat rent (H580)

Reflection [4']
2.1.2.2. 2.4.0.0. 2perc,harp,
strings
SAMFUNDET perf mat rent (H581)

HOLBERG SUITE see Grieg, Edvard Hagerup

HOLDERLIN-FRAGMENTE, FOR SOLO VOICE AND
ORCHESTRA see Rihm, Wolfgang

HOLEWA, HANS (1905-   )
Concertino No. 4 [15']
1.1.1.1. 1.1.1.0. perc,2vln,vla,
vcl,db
sc STIM perf mat rent (H582)

HOLEWA, HANS (cont'd.)

Concertino No. 5 [12']
1.1.1.1. 1.1.1.0. perc,pno,2vln,
vla,vcl,db
sc STIM perf mat rent (H583)

Concerto for Piano and Orchestra, No.
2
3.3.3.3. 4.3.3.0. timp,perc,
strings,pno solo
[25'] sc STIM (H584)

Symphony No. 4 [20']
3.2.2.2. 4.3.3.0. timp,perc,
strings
sc STIM (H585)

HOLIDAY FOR BOWS see Faust, Willi

HOLLAND, FOR SOLO VOICE AND ORCHESTRA
see Bordewijk-Roepman, Johanna

HOLLER, KARL (1907-   )
Divertimento for Flute and String
Orchestra, Op. 53a
string orch,fl solo
sc PETERS 8142 $17.50, pts PETERS
$3.00, ea., set PETERS $18.50
(H586)

HOLLER, YORK (1944-   )
Arcus [20']
1(pic).1(English horn).1+bass
clar.1+contrabsn. 1.1.1.0.
2perc,pno/elec org,2vln,vla,
vcl,db,electronic tape,
electronic equipment
BREITKOPF-W perf mat rent (H587)

Chroma [18']
4(pic).4(English horn).4(sax,bass
clar).2+2contrabsn. 6.4.4.0.
5perc,elec org,elec pno,elec
gtr,elec bass,strings,
sopranino
BREITKOPF-W perf mat rent (H588)

Concerto for Piano and Orchestra
[16']
2.2.2.2. 2.2.2.1. 2perc,harp,
strings,pno solo
BREITKOPF-W (H589)

Mythos [25']
1.0.2.0. 2.1.2.1. 2perc,pno/cel,
2vcl,db,electronic tape
BREITKOPF-W perf mat rent (H590)

Resonance [20']
2(pic,alto fl).2(English
horn).2(bass
clar).2(contrabsn). 2.2.2.1.
2perc,harp,pno/cel,3vln,2vla,
2vcl,db,electronic equipment
BREITKOPF-W perf mat rent (H591)

Umbra [21']
3(pic).2+English horn.3(2bass
clar).2+contrabsn. 4.3.3.1. 2-
3perc,harp,pno/cel,strings,
electronic tape
BREITKOPF-W perf mat rent (H592)

HOLLODEROH-MARSCH see Lorens, Carl

HOLLOWAY, ROBIN (1943-   )
Concertino No. 2, Op. 10 [25']
1.1(English horn).1.1. 2.0.0.0.
strings
BOOSEY perf mat rent (H593)

Concertino No. 3 [9']
1.0.1.1.alto sax. 1.1.1.0. 2perc,
2vln
min sc BOOSEY $10.00, perf mat rent
(H594)
Concerto for Orchestra [45']
2(pic).alto fl.1(English
horn).3(sax).1. 2.2.1.1. perc,
cel,strings
BOOSEY perf mat rent (H595)

Domination Of Black [50']
4.3.3.3. 4.4.3.2. timp,perc,
2harp,cel,org,strings
BOOSEY perf mat rent (H596)

Evening With Angels [33']
2(pic).1(English horn).2.1.
1.1.1.1. cel,2vln,vla,vcl,db
sc BOOSEY $28.00, perf mat rent
(H597)
Liederkreis - After Schumann's Opus
24 [28']
orch,pno
BOOSEY perf mat rent (H598)

Overture For K.W. [4']
1(pic).0.1.alto sax. 1.1.1.0.
2perc,2vln
BOOSEY perf mat rent (H599)

Romanza [13']
2.1.2.1. 2.0.0.0. harp,strings
min sc BOOSEY HPS 944 $17.00 (H600)

HOLLOWAY, ROBIN (cont'd.)

Souvenirs Of Schumann [22']
BOOSEY perf mat rent (H601)

Wind Shifts, The, For Solo Voice And
String Orchestra [20']
string orch,high solo
BOOSEY perf mat rent (H602)

HOLLYWOOD KINTOP see Kirchstein, Harold
M.

HOLM, MOGENS WINKEL (1936-   )
Concerto for Violoncello and
Orchestra
3.3.3.1. 3.2.3.0. perc,vibra,
harp,pno,strings
SAMFUNDET perf mat rent (H603)

Galgarien [20']
2.2+English horn.2.2+contrabsn.
2.2.2.0. perc,cel,harp,pno,
strings
sc HANSEN-DEN WH 29267 $67.75
(H604)
HOLST, GUSTAV (1874-1934)
Country Song
KALMUS 5558 sc $5.00, set $14.00
(H605)
Greeting
2.1.2.1. 0.0.0.0. strings
KALMUS 5230 set $8.00, pts $.75,
ea., cmplt ed rent (H606)

Marching Song
KALMUS 5559 sc $7.00, set $19.00
(H607)
Morning Of The Year, The: Dances
(Holst, Imogen; Matthews, Colin) 2+
pic.2+English horn.2+contrabsn.
4.2.3.1. timp,2-3perc,strings
[25'] OXFORD perf mat rent (H608)

Planets, The
min sc BOOSEY 22 $25.00 (H609)

Six Morris Dance Tunes, Set 1
fl,clar,strings
KALMUS 5231 set $14.00, pts $2.00,
ea., cmplt ed rent (H610)

Six Morris Dance Tunes, Set 2
fl,clar,strings
KALMUS 5232 set $14.00, pts $2.00,
ea., cmplt ed rent (H611)

Suite De Ballet *Op.10 [18'30"]
3(pic).2.2.2. 4.2.3.1. timp,perc,
harp,strings
KALMUS 5233 sc $25.00, perf mat
rent, set $75.00, pts $3.00, ea.
(H612)
HOLT, SIMEON TEN (1923-   )
..A-.TA-LON-, For Solo Voice And
Orchestra [20']
3.3.5.1. 2.3.1.0. harp,pno,gtr,
mand,marimba,vibra,3vln,3vla,
3vcl,3db,Mez solo
sc DONEMUS f.s., perf mat rent
(H613)
Centri-Fuga [25']
4.4.4.4. 4.4.4.0. 2pno,2elec org,
2marimba,strings
DONEMUS sc f.s., pts rent (H614)

Diagonaalmuziek [22']
string orch
sc DONEMUS f.s., perf mat rent
(H615)
Une Musique Blanche [20']
3.3.3.3.3sax. 3.3.3.0. elec org,
harp,cel,pno,glock,vibra,
2marimba,2claves,strings
DONEMUS (H616)

HOLTEN
Caccia
sc HANSEN-DEN WH 29631 $44.00
(H617)
HOLTEN, B0
Venetian Rhapsody [10']
fl,ob,clar,horn,bsn,3trp,2trom,
2vln,vla,vcl
sc,pts SAMFUNDET 302 f.s. (H618)

HOLVAST, JOHN (1942-   )
Concerto for Accordion and Orchestra
2.3.2.2. 2.2.2.0. timp,2perc,
strings,acord solo
sc DONEMUS f.s., perf mat rent
(H619)
HOLY, HOLY, HOLY see Dykes

HOLY WEEK, FOR SOLO VOICE AND ORCHESTRA
see Wolf, Hugo, Karwoche, For Solo
Voice And Orchestra

HOLZBAUER, IGNAZ (1711-1783)
Betulia Liberate, La: Sinfonia [5']
2.2.0.2. 2.0.0.0. strings
(Bodart, Eugen) MANNHEIM E 5-57
f.s. (H620)

HOLZBAUER, IGNAZ (cont'd.)

Concerto for Viola, Violoncello and
String Orchestra in E flat
string orch,vla solo,vcl solo
(Druener) sc,pts EULENBURG E10109
f.s.   (H621)

HOMAGE A CHARLES IVES see Grahn, Ulf

HOMAGE TO CASALS see Balada, Leonardo

HOMAGE TO SARASATE see Balada, Leonardo

HOME STRETCH see Anderson, Leroy

HOMMAGE A BIZET see Godron, Hugo

HOMMAGE A DIONYSOS see Terzakis,
Dimitri

HOMMAGE A MARCHAUT, FOR SOLO VOICE AND
ORCHESTRA see Thiele, Siegfried

HOMMAGE A WAGNER-REGENY see Schubert,
Manfred

HOMMAGE AAN DIMITRI SCHOSTAKOWITSCH see
Boer, Ed de

HOMOLA, BERNARD (1894-1975)
Variationen-Fantasie Uber Das
"Perpetuum Mobile" Von Johann
Strauss *Op.12 [6']
2(pic).2.2.2.2alto sax.opt
2soprano sax.tenor sax.
4.2.3.0. timp,perc,banjo,
strings
sc,pts LIENAU rent   (H622)

HOPKINS, JOHN HENRY, JR. (1820-1891)
We Three Kings Of Orient Are
see What Child Is This?

HOPSASSA see Rixner, Josef

HORA see Petersma, Wim

HORI, ETSUKO (1943-   )
Concerto for Timpani, Violoncello and
Orchestra
orch,timp solo,vcl solo
ZEN-ON 899155   (H623)

HORN BLOWS AT MIDNIGHT, THE, FOR
TRUMPET AND ORCHESTRA see Waxman,
Franz

HORN SIGNAL SYMPHONY see Haydn, [Franz]
Joseph, Symphony No. 31 in D

HOROLOGE, L' see Landowski, Marcel

HOROVITZ, JOSEPH (1926-   )
Fantasia On Theme Of Couperin
11strings
sc NOVELLO 2554 $12.50   (H624)

Jubilee Toy Symphony
perc,strings
sets NOVELLO $38.40, and up   (H625)

HORST, ANTON VAN DER (1899-1965)
Alre Lieffelicken Een, Een
see Drie Oud-Nederlandse Liederen,
For Solo Voice And Orchestra

Drie Oud-Nederlandse Liederen, For
Solo Voice And Orchestra *Op.17b
1.2.2.1. 0.0.0.0. perc,cel,8vln,
2vla,2vcl,2db,S solo sc DONEMUS
f.s., perf mat rent
contains: Alre Lieffelicken Een,
Een; Nu Laet Ons Allen Gode
Loven; Och Voor Den Doot (H626)

Nu Laet Ons Allen Gode Loven
see Drie Oud-Nederlandse Liederen,
For Solo Voice And Orchestra

Och Voor Den Doot
see Drie Oud-Nederlandse Liederen,
For Solo Voice And Orchestra

Oratio, For Solo Voice And Orchestra
*Op.19a [9']
2.3.3.3. 3.3.3.0. timp,2harp,
strings,S solo
sc DONEMUS f.s., perf mat rent
(H627)
Zeven Italiaansche Liederen, For Solo
Voice And Orchestra *Op.21a
[15']
3.3.4.2. 4.2.3.0. timp,perc,
2harp,strings,S solo
sc DONEMUS f.s., perf mat rent
(H628)

HORT IHR DEN TROMMELSCHLAG see Schwaen,
Kurt

HORVATH, JOSEF MARIA (1931-   )
Redundanz 3
0.2(English horn).2(bass
clar).2(contrabsn). 2.0.0.0.
2vln,vla,vcl
f.s. pts DOBLINGER 06 913, study sc

HORVATH, JOSEF MARIA (cont'd.)

DOBLINGER STP 257   (H629)

HOTTEPFERDCHEN see Robrecht, Carl

HOVHANESS, ALAN (1911-   )
Armenian Rhapsody No. 3
string orch
sc PETERS 6299 $8.00, pts PETERS
$.75, ea., set PETERS $4.50
(H630)

Khorhoort Nahadagats *Op.251
lute/gtr,strings,oud
sc PEER $8.00, perf mat rent (H631)

Odysseus Symphony *see Symphony No.
25, Op. 275

Psalm And Fugue
string orch
sc PETERS 6112A $7.00, pts PETERS
$1.50, ea., set PETERS $7.50
(H632)

Symphony No. 25, Op. 275 [36']
sc PEER $15.00   (H633)

Symphony No. 31, Op. 294
string orch
MT. TAHO sc $19.95, pts rent (H634)

Symphony No. 43, Op. 334
ob,trp,timp,strings
sc FUJIHARA $12.00   (H635)

Symphony No. 46, Op. 347
sc FUJIHARA $20.00   (H636)

HOVLAND, EGIL (1924-   )
Concerto for Trombone and Orchestra,
Op. 76 [19']
3.2.3.2. 2.0.0.0. 3perc,harp,
strings,trom solo
min sc NORSK NMO 8802 $31.50 (H637)

Tombeau De Bach *Op.95
NORSK   (H638)

HOW GREAT THOU ART
(Mayfield, Larry; Skillings, Otis)
SINGSPIR 7705 $19.95   (H639)

HRUSOVSKY, IVAN (1927-   )
Konfrontacie [14']
2.2.3.2. 4.3.4.0. timp,perc,pno,
xylo,strings
SLOV.HUD.FOND 0-491A perf mat rent
(H640)

HRY see Tandler, Juraj

HUB, FRANZ PETER
Impressionen In Moll
RIES f.s.   (H641)

Launige Groteske
RIES f.s.   (H642)

Nordland-Romanze
RIES f.s.   (H643)

Vergnugter Kobold
RIES f.s.   (H644)

HUBAY, JENO (1858-1937)
Czinka Panna Notaja, For Violin And
Orchestra [12']
2.2.2.2. 3.2.3.0. timp,harp,
strings,vln solo
manuscript CARISCH   (H645)

Hejre Kati *see Scenes De La Csarda
No. 4, For Violin And Orchestra

Nocturne for Violin and Orchestra,
[arr.]
(Dressel, Erwin) sc RIES f.s.
(H646)
Scenes De La Csarda No. 3, For Violin
And Orchestra *Op.18
LUCKS 00400 set $16.00, pts $1.15,
ea.   (H647)

Scenes De La Csarda No. 4, For Violin
And Orchestra *Op.32
"Hejre Kati" LUCKS 00512 set
$16.00, pts $1.15, ea.   (H648)

Symphony No. 2, Op. 93
3+pic.2+English horn.2+bass
clar.2+contrabsn. 6.3.3.1.
timp,glock,2perc,2harp,strings
BREITKOPF-W perf mat rent   (H649)

HUBER, NICOLAUS A. (1939-   )
Gespenster [17']
3(alto fl,pic).3(English horn,
Heckelphone).3(alto clar in E
flat,bass clar).3(contrabsn).
4.4(piccolo trp).4.0. timp,
perc,harp,cel,pno,glock,
strings,electronic tape,solo
voice
BREITKOPF-W perf mat rent   (H650)

HUBER, NICOLAUS A. (cont'd.)

Lernen Von [18']
3.3.3.3. 4.3.4.1. timp,perc,harp,
pno,strings
BREITKOPF-W perf mat rent   (H651)

Morgenlied [16'30"]
3(pic).3(English horn).3(clar in
E flat).3(contrabsn). 4.3.3.0.
timp,3perc,harp,pno/cel,strings
BREITKOPF-W perf mat rent   (H652)

Spharenmusik [16']
2(alto fl,pic).3(English
horn).3(soprano clar in E
flat).2(contrabsn). 2.3.2.0.
timp,3perc,cel,strings
BREITKOPF-W perf mat rent   (H653)

HUBERTUS-JAGD see Skibbe, Gustav

HUBICKA: OVERTURE see Smetana, Bedrich

HUBLER, KLAUS-K. (1955-   )
Wer Die Schonheit Angeschaut Mit
Augen
2basset horn,strings,vcl solo
MOECK 5228 study sc f.s., pts rent
(H654)

HUDEC, JIRI (1923-   )
E-A-D-G - Blues [2'30"]
pno,gtr,perc,strings
ORLANDO rent   (H655)

E-A-D-G - Boogie [2'30"]
pno,gtr,perc,strings
ORLANDO rent   (H656)

Kleine Skizzen [9'50"]
pno,harp,cel,elec gtr,gtr,perc,
strings
ORLANDO rent   (H657)

Rosalie [2'30"]
Hamm,hpsd,xylo,glock,gtr,perc,
strings
ORLANDO rent   (H658)

Sunny Boy [3']
Hamm,cel,gtr,perc,strings
ORLANDO rent   (H659)

Uschka, Wohin? [2'30"]
Hamm,hpsd,xylo,glock,gtr,perc,
strings
ORLANDO rent   (H660)

Zerrspiegel, Der [8']
pic,bass clar,xylo,glock,hpsd,
gtr,tuba,perc,strings
ORLANDO rent   (H661)

HUDECEK, RADOVAN (1945-   )
Fem Dagar I Paris [18']
ob,perc,strings
sc STIM perf mat rent   (H662)

HUGGLER, JOHN (1928-   )
Sinfonia, Op. 78 [12']
fl,ob,clar,bsn,trp,bass trom,
harp,pno,2perc,vln,vla,vcl
sc MARGUN BP 3009 $7.50, perf mat
rent   (H663)

Symphony [20']
2.2.2(bass clar).2. 4.3.3.1.
timp,2perc,harp,strings
PETERS 66859 perf mat rent   (H664)

HUHNER MASKEN QUADRILLE see Lumbye,
Hans Christian

HULDIGUNGEN WALZER see Strauss, Eduard

HULDIGUNGSMARSCH see Grieg, Edvard
Hagerup, Sigurd Jorsalfar:
Triumphal March

HUMAN see Marez Oyens, Tera de

HUMMEL, JOHANN NEPOMUK (1778-1837)
Concertino for Piano and Orchestra,
Op. 73, in G [17']
1.2.0.1. 2.0.0.0. strings,pno
solo
sc,pts LIENAU rent   (H665)

Concerto for Bassoon and Orchestra in
F
2ob,2horn,strings,bsn solo
sc,pts BUBONIC rent   (H666)

Concerto for Piano and Orchestra, Op.
85, in A minor [30']
1.2.2.2. 2.0.0.0. timp,strings,
pno solo
(each movement available
separately) KALMUS A4639 sc
$12.00, perf mat rent, set
$30.00, pts $2.00, ea.   (H667)
sc,pts LIENAU rent   (H668)

Concerto for Piano and Orchestra, Op.
89, in B minor
LUCKS 00088 sc $3.50, set $20.00,

HUMMEL, JOHANN NEPOMUK (cont'd.)

pts $1.50, ea. (H669)

Concerto for Piano and Orchestra, Op. 110, in E
1.2.2.2. 3.3.1.0. timp,strings, pno solo
KALMUS 5236 set $19.00, pts $1.50, ea., cmplt ed rent (H670)

Concerto for Piano and Orchestra, Op. 113, in A flat
2.0.2.2. 2.2.0.0. timp,strings, pno solo
KALMUS 5239 set $19.00, pts $1.50, ea., cmplt ed rent (H671)

Concerto for Trumpet and Orchestra [17']
1.2.2.2. 2.0.0.0. timp,strings, trp solo
(original version in E) sc UNIVER. UE 25A030 $33.00, set UNIVER. UE 25B030 $44.00, pts UNIVER. $2.50, ea., pno red UNIVER. UE 25C030 $22.00 (H672)
(original version in E) INTERNAT. perf mat rent (H673)
(original version in E) KALMUS 5238 sc $20.00, perf mat rent, set $50.00, pts $3.00, ea. (H674)
(Hann, Stefan de) (original version in E) min sc EULENBURG $13.50 (H675)

Rondo Brilliant For Piano And Orchestra *Op.56
1.2.2.2. 2.0.0.0. strings,pno solo
KALMUS A5503 solo pt $6.00, set $9.00, pts $1.00, ea., solo pt $6.00 (H676)

HUMMEL, JOSEPH FRIEDRICH (1841-1919)
Konzertstuck for Bassoon and Orchestra, Op. 201, in B flat
BREITKOPF-W perf mat rent (H677)

HUMORESKE see Bortz, Alfred

HUMORESKE see Humperdinck, Engelbert

HUMORESKE, FOR VIOLIN AND ORCHESTRA see Schonherr, Max

HUMORESQUE, FOR PIANO AND ORCHESTRA see Pick-Mangiagalli, Riccardo

HUMORESQUE, OP. 101, NO. 7, [ARR.] see Dvorak, Antonin

HUMPERDINCK, ENGELBERT (1854-1921)
Hansel And Gretel: Sandman's Song, Evening Prayer, And Dream Pantomime *see Hansel Und Gretel: Lied Des Sandmannchens; Abendsegen Und Traumptomime

Hansel Und Gretel: Lied Des Sandmannchens; Abendsegen Und Traumpantomime
"Hansel And Gretel: Sandman's Song, Evening Prayer, And Dream Pantomime" LUCKS 05897 sc $6.00, set $17.00, pts $.95, ea. (H678)

Hansel Und Gretel: Vorspiel
LUCKS 05901 sc $5.00, set $17.00, min sc $3.00, pts $.95, ea. (H679)

Humoreske
2.2.2.2. 2.2.0.0. timp,strings
sc,pts LIENAU rent (H680)

Straussle-Gavotte
RIES f.s. (H681)

HUNDSNES, SVEIN
Konsertfantasi No. 1: Rendevous
3.2.2.2. 4.4.3.1. perc,harp, strings
NORGE (H682)

HUNGARIAN DANCE NO. 4 see Brahms, Johannes, Ungarischer Tanz No. 4, [arr.]

HUNGARIAN DANCES NO. 1, 3, AND 10 see Brahms, Johannes, Ungarische Tanze Nos. 1, 3, And 10, [arr.]

HUNGARIAN DANCES NO. 5 AND 6 see Brahms, Johannes, Ungarische Tanze Nos. 5 And 6, [arr.]

HUNGARIAN DANCES NOS. 1, 3, AND 10 see Brahms, Johannes, Ungarische Tanze Nos. 1, 3, And 10, [arr.]

HUNGARIAN GYPSY AIRS, [ARR.] see Tchaikovsky, Piotr Ilyich

HUNGARIAN MARCH see Berlioz, Hector (Louis)

HUNGARIAN MARCH, [ARR.] see Liszt, Franz

HUNGARIAN MELODIES, FOR CORNET AND ORCHESTRA see Bach, Vincent

HUNGARIAN RHAPSODY see Popper, David, Ungarische Rhapsodie, For Violoncello And Orchestra

HUNGARIAN RHAPSODY NO. 2 see Liszt, Franz, Rhapsodie Hongroise No. 2, [arr.]

HUNGARIAN RHAPSODY NO. 3 see Liszt, Franz, Rhapsodie Hongroise No. 3, [arr.]

HUNT, THE, SYMPHONY see Haydn, [Franz] Joseph, Symphony No. 73 in D

HUNYADY LASZLO see Einem, Gottfried von

HURD, MICHAEL (1928-   )
Dance Diversions
sets NOVELLO 9103-04 $70.50, and up, sc NOVELLO 9102 $22.00, pts NOVELLO 9609 $1.50, ea. (H683)

HURSLEY
Sun Of My Soul
see Monk, Abide With Me

HUSITSKA OVERTURE see Dvorak, Antonin

HUTCHISON, (DAVID) WARNER (1930-   )
Prairie Sketch
2.1.2.1. 2.1.1.0. strings
SEESAW perf mat rent (H684)

HVIEZDNATA NOC see Cikker, Jan

HVOSLEF, KETIL
Antigone [21']
4(pic).4.4(bass clar).4(contrabsn). 4.4.3.1. timp,perc,harp,pno,strings
NORGE (H685)

Mi-Fi-Li
3(pic).2+English horn.3(bass clar).2. 4.2.0.0. timp,2perc, strings
sc NORSK NMO 9303 $35.00 (H686)

HYMN TO NIGHT, FOR SOLO VOICE AND CHAMBER ORCHESTRA see Schafer, R. Murray

HYMN TO NIGHT, FOR SOLO VOICE AND ORCHESTRA see Schafer, R. Murray

HYMN TO THAIS, FOR SOLO VOICE AND ORCHESTRA , [ARR.] see Sibelius, Jean

HYMN TO THE MEMORY OF DARIUS MILHAUD see Andriessen, Louis

HYMNAL see Gould, Morton

HYMNE A LA MORT see Markevitch, Igor

HYMNE AN DIE NACHT: GEHOBEN IST DER STERN, FOR SOLO VOICE AND ORCHESTRA see Diepenbrock, Alphons

HYMNE AN DIE NACHT: MUSS IMMER DER MORGEN WIEDERKOMMEN, FOR SOLO VOICE AND ORCHESTRA see Diepenbrock, Alphons

HYMNE AUS VATERLAND see Luck, Andrew H.

HYMNE "WENIGE WISSEN DAS GEHEIMNISS DER LIEBE, FOR SOLO VOICE AND ORCHESTRA see Diepenbrock, Alphons

HYMNES see Markevitch, Igor

HYMNISCHES KONZERT, FOR SOLO VOICES AND ORCHESTRA see Schubert, Heinz

HYMNUS see Klengel, Julius

HYMNUS, FOR SOLO VOICE AND ORCHESTRA see Flothuis, Marius

HYMNUS, FOR VIOLIN AND STRING ORCHESTRA see Heilmann, Harald

HYPERION see Wuorinen, Charles

HYPERION-FRAGMENTE, FOR SOLO VOICE AND ORCHESTRA see Matthus, Siegfried

HYPOTHESEN WALZER see Strauss, Eduard

I

I BREATHED THE BREATH OF BLOSSOMS RED see Mahler, Gustav, Sieben Lieder Aus Letzter Zeit: Ich Atmet' Einen Linden Duft, For Solo Voice And Orchestra

I FJOL GJAETT'E GJETTIN see Svendsen, Johan (Severin)

I GULT OCH ROTT see Strindberg, Henrik

I LOVE YOU, FOR SOLO VOICE AND ORCHESTRA, [ARR.] see Grieg, Edvard Hagerup

I SKOGSDUNKLET, FOR BASSOON AND ORCHESTRA see Lundkvist, Per

I' TIPFERL POLKA see Strauss, Johann, [Jr.]

I WANT TO DIE EASY, FOR VIOLIN AND STRING ORCHESTRA see May, Helmut W.

ICARUS see Gutche, Gene

ICARUS' FLIGHT, FOR PIANO AND CHAMBER ORCHESTRA see Laporte, Andre

ICH HAB IN PENNA EINEN LIEBSTEN WOHNEN, FOR SOLO VOICE AND ORCHESTRA see Wolf, Hugo

ICH RUF' ZU DIR, HERR JESUS, [ARR.] see Bach, Johann Sebastian

ICH SCHLAF, ICH WACH see Kubizek, Augustin

ICH WILL HIER BEI DIR STEHEN, [ARR.] see Bach, Johann Sebastian

ICHIYANAGI, TOSHI (1933-   )
Field, The, For Flute And Orchestra [13']
3.2.2.4. 4.3.3.1. perc,pno, strings,fl solo
PETERS P66146 perf mat rent (I1)

ICHOCHRONOS II see Terzakis, Dimitri

ICTHYON see Sherman, Norman

IDEALEN, DEM see Blon, Franz von

IDILLIO see Galliera, Alceo

IDOLS OF PERVERSITY, FOR VIOLA AND STRING ORCHESTRA see Mimaroglu, Ilhan Kamaleddin

IDOMENEO: ZEFFIRETTI LUSINGHIERI, FOR SOLO VOICE AND ORCHESTRA see Mozart, Wolfgang Amadeus

IDYLL, FOR HORN AND STRING ORCHESTRA see Nelson, Paul

IDYLLE, FOR VIOLIN AND ORCHESTRA see Matsushita, Shin-Ichi

IDYLLEN WALZER see Strauss, Johann, [Jr.]

IDYLLISCHE SUITE see Dressel, Erwin

IF I WERE KING: OVERTURE see Adam, Adolphe-Charles, Si J'Etais Roi: Overture

IFFEZHEIMER RENNEN see Kallies, Hanns

IFUKUBE, AKIRA (1914-   )
Lauda Concertata, For Marimba And Orchestra
2+pic.2+English horn.2+bass clar.2+contrabsn. 4.3.3.1. timp,perc,harp,strings,marimba solo
ONGAKU perf mat rent (I2)

Ritmica Ostinata, For Piano And Orchestra
orch,pno solo
ZEN-ON 899071 (I3)

IK BEN IN EENZAAMHEID NIET MEER ALLEEN see Diepenbrock, Alphons, Liederen Voor Sopraan En Orkest No. 2

IK DIE BIJ DE STERREN SLIEP, FOR SOLO VOICE AND ORCHESTRA see Dijk, Jan van

IK WENSCHE U, FOR SOLO VOICE AND STRING ORCHESTRA see Bordewijk-Roepman, Johanna

INTONING see Blomberg, Erik

INTRADA see Alkema, Henk

INTRADA see Koppel, Herman David

INTRADA FESTIVA see Strategier, Herman

INTRADA NO. 4 see Borris, Siegfried

INTRADE see Moser, Rudolf

INTRADEN see Hassler, Hans Leo

INTRO IN DUTCH STYLE see Wijdeveld, Wolfgang, Intro In Hollandse Trant

INTRO IN HOLLANDSE TRANT see Wijdeveld, Wolfgang

INTRODUCTIE, CHACONNE EN FINALE see Mulder, Herman

INTRODUCTIE EN RONDO see Felderhof, Jan

INTRODUCTION AND ALLEGRO, FOR STRING QUARTET AND STRING ORCHESTRA see Elgar, [Sir] Edward (William)

INTRODUCTION AUX CHOROS see Villa-Lobos, Heitor

INTRODUCTION ET RONDO CAPRICCIOSO, FOR VIOLIN AND ORCHESTRA see Saint-Saens, Camille

INTRODUKCIA A ALLEGRO see Martincek, Dusan

INTRODUKTION OCH FUGA see Robertsson, Stig

INTRODUKTION UND RONDO, FOR HORN AND ORCHESTRA see Kalliwoda, Johann Wenzel

INTRODUKTION UND RONDO UBER EIN FRANZOSISCHES KINDERLIED see Etti, Karl

INTRODUZIONE, ARIA E FINALE, FOR VIOLIN AND ORCHESTRA see Medin, N.

INTRODUZIONE E FUGA see Porpora, Nicola Antonio

INTRODUZIONE E SALTARELLO see Toni, Alceo

INTRODUZIONE PER UNA COMMEDIA GAIA see Soresina, Alberto

INTRODUZIONE, TEMA E SETTE VARIAZIONI see Massarani, Renzo

INTROITUS - EXODUS see Bialas, Gunter

INVASION see Rogers, Bernard

INVENZIONE, FOR FLUTE AND STRING ORCHESTRA see Dionisi, Renato

INVENZIONE, FOR FLUTE AND STRING ORCHESTRA see Giuffre, Gaetano

INVERNO IN-VER see Castiglioni, Niccolo

INVINCIBLE EAGLE MARCH, THE see Sousa, John Philip

INVITATION AU VOYAGE, L' see Scherchen, Tona

INVITATION AU VOYAGE, L', FOR SOLO VOICE AND ORCHESTRA see Andriessen, Hendrik

INVITATION AU VOYAGE, L', FOR SOLO VOICE AND ORCHESTRA see Duparc, Henri

INVITATION TO THE DANCE, [ARR.] see Weber, Carl Maria von, Aufforderung Zum Tanz, [arr.]

INVITO RESPINTO, FOR SOLO VOICES AND ORCHESTRA see Sinigaglia, Leone

INVOCAZIONE see Borstlap, John

IO LA VIDI, FOR SOLO VOICES AND ORCHESTRA see Verdi, Giuseppe

IO TI LASCIO, FOR SOLO VOICE AND ORCHESTRA see Mozart, Wolfgang Amadeus

IOANNIDES, YANNIS (1930-   )
Projections [8']
    2.2.2.2. 2.2.3.0. pno,strings
    NOMOS E.N. 109 perf mat rent   (I13)

IOLANTHE: ENTRANCE AND MARCH OF THE PEERS, "LOUDLY LET THE TRUMPETS BRAY" see Sullivan, [Sir] Arthur Seymour

IOLANTHE: LOVE, UNREQUITED ROBS ME OF MY REST, FOR SOLO VOICE AND ORCHESTRA see Sullivan, [Sir] Arthur Seymour

IOLANTHE: OH FOOLISH FAY, FOR SOLO VOICE AND ORCHESTRA see Sullivan, [Sir] Arthur Seymour

IOLANTHE: WER KANN MIT MATHILDEN SICH MESSEN AN MACHT, FOR SOLO VOICE AND ORCHESTRA see Tchaikovsky, Piotr Ilyich

IOWA SERENADE see Masseus, Jan

IPHIGENIE EN AULIDE: OVERTURE see Gluck, Christoph Willibald, Ritter von

IPPOLITOV-IVANOV, MIKHAIL MIKHAILOVICH (1859-1935)
Caucasian Sketches *Op.10
    min sc INTERNAT. 699 $6.00   (I14)

IRELAND, JOHN (1879-1962)
Concertino Pastorale
    string orch
    min sc BOOSEY 30 $2.00   (I15)

Overlanders, The
    min sc BOOSEY 869 $12.50   (I16)

Two Symphonic Studies *CC2U
    min sc BOOSEY 868 $6.50   (I17)

IRINO, YOSHIRO (1921-   )
Wandlungen
    JAPAN 8001   (I18)

IRIS POLKA see Strauss, Eduard

IRISCHE LUSTSPIEL-OUVERTURE see Brase, Fritz

IRISH FOLK SONG see Foote, Arthur

IRISH SYMPHONY see Cunningham, Michael Gerald

IRVING, ROBERT
Wits And Fancies
    2.2.2.2. 4.2.3.1. timp,perc,harp, strings
    BOOSEY perf mat rent   (I19)

ISAAC, HEINRICH (ca. 1450-1517)
Sechs Instrumentalsatze
    "Six Instrumental Pieces" KALMUS A1105 sc $3.00, set $6.00, pts $1.50, ea.   (I20)

Six Instrumental Pieces *see Sechs Instrumentalsatze

ISHII, MAKI (1936-   )
Concerto for Violin and Orchestra, Op. 34
    2.2.2.2. 4.2.2.1. 4perc,harp,pno, strings,vln solo
    [14'] sc,pts MOECK 5206   (I21)

Faint Dawn *see Sho-Ko

Jo
    MOECK 5186 study sc $23.00, pts rent   (I22)

Lost Sounds II, For Violin And Orchestra
    MOECK 5206 study sc f.s., pts rent   (I23)

Lost Sounds III, FOR VIOLIN AND ORCHESTRA *see Concerto for Violin and Orchestra, Op. 34

Mono-Prism [24']
    3.3.3.3. 6.4.3.1. 5perc,2harp, pno,cel,strings, Japanese drums (7 players)
    study sc MOECK 5192 f.s., perf mat rent   (I24)

Petite Symphonie [8']
    2(pic).2.2.2.alto sax. 4.2.2.0. timp,perc,strings
    ONGAKU perf mat rent   (I25)

Search In Grey I, For Violin, Piano, Percussion And Orchestra
    orch,vln solo,pno solo,perc solo
    pts MOECK 5215 rent   (I26)

Sho-Ko *Op.39
    3.3.3.3. 6.3.3.1. 5perc,2harp, pno,cel,strings
    "Faint Dawn" [15'30"] sc,pts MOECK 5235   (I27)

ISLAMEY, [ARR.] see Balakirev, Mily Alexeyevich

ISOLINE: PAVAUNE DES FEES, [ARR.] see Messager, Andre

ISOMERIE see Tessier, Roger

ISSE: SUITE see Destouches, Andre-Cardinal

ISTRIAN DANCES see Svara, Danilo, Istrski Plesi

ISTRIAN MOTIVES, FOR SOLO VOICES AND CHAMBER ORCHESTRA see Svara, Danilo, Istrski Motivi, For Solo Voices And Chamber Orchestra

ISTRIAN SUITE see Devcic, Natko

ISTRSKI MOTIVI, FOR SOLO VOICES AND CHAMBER ORCHESTRA see Svara, Danilo

ISTRSKI PLESI see Svara, Danilo

IT CAME UPON A MIDNIGHT CLEAR see Willis, Richard Storrs

ITALIAN SYMPHONY see Mendelssohn-Bartholdy, Felix, Symphony No. 4, Op. 90, in A

ITALIANA IN ALGERI, L': OVERTURE see Rossini, Gioacchino

ITALIANA IN LONDRA: OVERTURE see Cimarosa, Domenico

ITALIENISCHE SUITE, FUNF STUCKE VON PAGANINI, FOR VIOLIN AND ORCHESTRA see Wilhelmj, August

ITALIENISCHER KARNEVAL see Karrasch, Kurt

ITKISIT JOSKUS ILLOIN, FOR SOLO VOICE AND ORCHESTRA see Madetoja, Leevi

IVANOVICI, ION (1845-1902)
Waves Of The Danube
    LUCKS 08607 pno-cond sc $3.00, set $15.00, pts $1.00, ea.   (I28)

Waves Of The Danube, [arr.] [7']
    1.2.2.2.euphonium. 2.2.3.0. perc, strings
    (Balfour, S.V.) KALMUS A4643 sc $4.00, perf mat rent, set $15.00, pts $1.00, ea.   (I29)

IVES, CHARLES (1874-1954)
"Gyp The Blood" Or Hearst!? Which Is Worst?!
    (Singleton, Kenneth) set PEER $12.00   (I30)

March II: Son Of A Gambolier
    (Singleton, Kenneth) PEER sc $6.00, set $12.00   (I31)

Remembrance
    set PEER $4.00   (I32)

Set Of Pieces For Theatre Or Chamber Orchestra
    LUCKS 01593 sc $5.00, set $15.00, pts $2.00, ea.   (I33)

J

JA, SO SINGT UND TANZT MAN NUR IN WIEN,
FOR SOLO VOICE AND ORCHESTRA see
Strauss, Johann, [Jr.]

JA VISST GJOR DET ONT, FOR SOLO VOICE
AND CHAMBER ORCHESTRA see Kruse,
Bjorn

JACCHINI, GIUSEPPE MARIA
(ca. 1663-1727)
Sinfonia, Op. 5, No. 8
2trp,strings,cont
MUS. RARA 1960B f.s.   (J1)

Sonata in D, MIN 101
string orch,cont,trp solo
INTERNAT. perf mat rent   (J2)

Sonata in D, MIN 102
trp,strings,cont
(XII 5) MUS. RARA 1962B f.s.   (J3)

Sonata in D, MIN 103
trp,strings,cont
(XII 6) MUS. RARA 1961B f.s.   (J4)

Sonata, Op. 5, No. 1
2trp,strings,cont
MUS. RARA 1946B f.s.   (J5)

JACK TAR MARCH see Sousa, John Philip

JACOBSEN, JULIUS
Concerto in A for Trumpet, Trombone
and Orchestra [10'15"]
2.2.2.2. 4.3.2.0. timp,perc,pno,
strings,trp solo,trom solo
BUSCH HBM 019 perf mat rent   (J6)

JADIN, LOUIS EMANUEL (1768-1853)
Fantaisie Concertante, For Harp And
Orchestra
2clar,2bsn,2horn,strings,harp
solo
(Robert, F.) COSTALL perf mat rent
                                          (J7)

JAGD-OUVERTURE see Kunneke, Eduard

JAHN, THOMAS (1940-   )
Canto Por Victor Jara, For
Violoncello And Orchestra [20']
perc,strings,vcl solo
BREITKOPF-W perf mat rent   (J8)

JAHRESLAUF, DER see Stockhausen,
Karlheinz

JAHRESZEITEN, DIE see Kick-Schmidt,
Paul

JAHRESZEITEN, DIE: SCHON EILET FROH DER
ACKERSMANN, FOR SOLO VOICE AND
ORCHESTRA see Haydn, [Franz] Joseph

JAM LUCIS ORTO SIDERE, FOR SOLO VOICE
AND ORCHESTRA see Klerk, Albert de

JANACEK, LEOS (1854-1928)
Lachian Dances, Op. 2, Nos. 1 & 2
[8']
2+pic.2.2.2. 4.2.3.0. timp,perc,
harp,strings
"Valasske Tance" KALMUS A4657 sc
$15.00, perf mat rent, set
$40.00, pts $1.50, ea.   (J9)

Suite for String Orchestra
string orch
min sc INTERNAT. 3120 $5.25, pts
INTERNAT. 3119 $7.75   (J10)

Valasske Tance *see Lachian Dances,
Op. 2, Nos. 1 & 2

JANITSCH, JOHANN GOTTLIEB (1708-1763)
Concerto for Harpsichord and String
Orchestra
string orch,cont,hpsd solo
MCGIN-MARX perf mat rent   (J11)

JANSEN, PETER
Orchesterparade [4']
2(pic).2(English
horn).2.2(contrabsn). 4.3.3.0.
timp,perc,harp,pno/cel,strings
RIES perf mat rent   (J12)

Tandelei [7']
2.2.2.3. 3.2.3.0. timp,perc,harp,
strings
RIES perf mat rent   (J13)

JANSON, ALFRED (1937-   )
Concerto for Violin and Orchestra
HANSEN-DEN   (J14)

Forspill, For Violin And Orchestra
*see Concerto for Violin and
Orchestra

JANSSEN, GUUS (1951-   )
Gieter [17']
3.3.3.3.tenor sax. 4.3.3.1.
2perc,pno,elec gtr,strings
sc DONEMUS f.s., perf mat rent
                                          (J15)

Toonen [15']
2.2.2.2. 2.2.1.0. perc,pno,
strings
DONEMUS   (J16)

JANSSON, JOHANNES (1950-   )
Studie For Strakorkester (Study for
String Orchestra, Op. 13) [25']
string orch
sc STIM   (J17)

Study for String Orchestra, Op. 13
*see Studie For Strakorkester

JAPANISCHE LIEDER, FOR SOLO VOICE AND
CHAMBER ORCHESTRA see Zieritz,
Grete von

JAPANISCHER FRUHLING, FOR SOLO VOICE
AND ORCHESTRA see Jensen, Ludwig
Irgens

JARDANYI, PAL (1920-1966)
Sinfonietta
string orch
(special import only) sc,set EMB
5521 $33.00   (J18)

JARNEFELT, ARMAS (1869-1958)
Aallon Kehtolaulu, For Solo Voice And
Orchestra, [arr.]
(Pylkkanen, T.) 2.1.2.0. 2.0.0.0.
harp,strings,solo voice [14']
FAZER perf mat rent   (J19)

Berceuse [3']
0.0.2.1. 2.0.0.0. strings sc,pts
FAZER f.s.   (J20)
LUCKS 05922 sc $3.75, set $7.50,
pts $.75, ea.   (J21)

Prelude
BROUDE BR. set $10.00, pts $1.10,
ea.   (J22)
min sc INTERNAT. 1371 $1.50   (J23)
LUCKS 05923 sc $6.50, set $13.00,
pts $1.15, ea.   (J24)

JAROCH, JIRI (1920-   )
Symphony No. 3 for Violin and
Orchestra
sc PANTON 1664 f.s.   (J25)

JAUCHZET DEM HERRN, FOR SOLO VOICE AND
ORCHESTRA see Telemann, Georg
Philipp

JAUCHZET DEM HERRN ALLE WELT, FOR SOLO
VOICE AND STRING ORCHESTRA see
Bruhns, Nicholaus

JAZZ CONCERTO see Schaffer, Boguslaw

JAZZ SUITE see Martinu, Bohuslav

JE MARCHE SUR TOUS LES CHEMINS see
Massenet, Jules, Manon:
Introduction And Gavotte

JEAN DE PARIS: OVERTURE see Boieldieu,
Francois-Adrien

JEANNE D'ARC: ADIEU FORETS see
Tchaikovsky, Piotr Ilyich, Maid Of
Orleans, The: Farewell, Forests,
For Solo Voice And Orchestra

JEANNE D'ARC: SUITE NO. 1, VISION ET
DIEU LE VEUT see Gounod, Charles
Francois

JEANNE D'ARC: SUITE NO. 2, PRIERE DE
JEANNE D'ARC see Gounod, Charles
Francois

JEANNE D'ARC: SUITE NO. 3, MARCHE DU
SACRE see Gounod, Charles Francois

JEANNETTENS HOCHZEIT: WOLLT BLUHEN IHR
SEH'N, FOR SOLO VOICE AND ORCHESTRA
see Masse, Victor

JEANNIE WITH THE LIGHT BROWN HAIR, FOR
SOLO VOICE AND STRING ORCHESTRA,
[ARR.] see Foster, Stephen Collins

JELKY ANDRAS SUITE see Farkas, Ferenc

JENEY, ZOLTAN (1943-   )
Quemadmodum
string orch
(special import only) sc EMB 7954
f.s.   (J26)

JENSEN, GUSTAV (1843-1895)
Sinfonietta, Op. 22 [21']
string orch
LIENAU f.s.   (J27)

JENSEN, LUDWIG IRGENS (1894-1969)
Japanischer Fruhling, For Solo Voice
And Orchestra
2(pic).1(English horn).2.1.
2.2.0.0. perc,harp,cel,strings,
S solo
[Ger] [23'] sc NORSK NMO 9159
$31.50   (J28)

JENTSCH, WALTER (1900-   )
Baurische Festmusik [11']
1.1.2.1. 2.2.1.0. perc,strings
RIES perf mat rent   (J29)

Konzertante Serenade *Op.8 [10']
2.2.2.2. 2.2.0.0. timp,perc,
strings
RIES perf mat rent   (J30)

JERGER, WILHELM (1902-1978)
Partita, Op. 21 [12']
2(pic).2.2.2. 2.2.0.0. timp,perc,
harp,strings
RIES perf mat rent   (J31)

JERSILD, JORGEN (1913-   )
Pastorale [7']
string orch
min sc HANSEN-DEN WH 29400 B $7.75
                                          (J32)

JESU BLEIBET MEINE FREUDE, [ARR.] see
Bach, Johann Sebastian

JESU, JOY OF MAN'S DESIRING, [ARR.] see
Bach, Johann Sebastian, Jesu
Bleibet Meine Freude, [arr.]

JESU, WIJS EN WONDERMACHTIG see Dijk,
Jan van

JET D'EAU, LE, FOR SOLO VOICE AND
ORCHESTRA, [ARR.] see Debussy,
Claude

JEU D'AMOUR see Czernik, W.

JEUX CONCERTANTS, FOR FLUTE AND
ORCHESTRA see Petric, Ivo

JEUX D'ENFANTS, [ARR.] see Bizet,
Georges

JEWELS OF THE MADONNA: INTERMEZZO AND
SERENADE see Wolf-Ferrari, Ermanno,
Gioielli Della Madonna, I:
Intermezzo E Serenata

JEZ, JAKOB (1928-   )
Folk Tune And Intermezzo, For Violin
And Orchestra *see Narodna In
Intermezzo, For Violin And
Orchestra

Narodna In Intermezzo, For Violin And
Orchestra [10']
2(pic).2(English horn).2.2.
2.2.2.0. timp,2perc,strings,vln
solo
"Folk Tune And Intermezzo, For
Violin And Orchestra" DRUSTVO
DSS 774 perf mat rent   (J33)

Strune, Milo Se Glasite [13']
mand,18strings
"Sweet Strings" DRUSTVO DSS 855
perf mat rent   (J34)

Sweet Strings *see Strune, Milo Se
Glasite

JINGLE BELLS
see O Tannenbaum

JIRASEK, IVO (1920-   )
Mother Of Hope *see Symphony

Symphony
sc PANTON 1650 f.s.   (J35)

JO see Ishii, Maki

JOCELYN: BERCEUSE, FOR SOLO VOICE AND
ORCHESTRA see Godard, Benjamin
Louis Paul

JOCELYN: SUITE NO. 1 see Godard,
Benjamin Louis Paul

JOCELYN: SUITE NO. 2 see Godard,
Benjamin Louis Paul

JOHANNIS KAFERLN WALZER see Strauss,
Johann, [Jr.]

JOHANSEN, SVEND AAQUIST
Ketjak
2fl,2trp,horn,trom,tuba,2vcl,2db
sc,pts SAMFUNDET 273 perf mat rent
                                          (J36)

Sinfonia, Op. 33a [11']
2.2.2.2. 2.2.2.1. 2perc,harp,
10vln,3vla,2vcl,2db
SAMFUNDET perf mat rent   (J37)

JOHANSON, SVEN-ERIC (1919-   )
Nalle Puh, For Narrator And Orchestra
2.2.2.2. 2.2.2.1. timp,3perc,
harp,strings,narrator
sc STIM perf mat rent   (J38)

Sinfonia Concertante for Violin,
Balalaika and Chamber Orchestra
1.1.1.1. 0.0.0.0. strings,vln
solo,balalaika solo
STIM   (J39)

JOHNSEN, HALLVARD (1916-   )
Concerto for Trumpet and Orchestra,
Op. 50
NORSK   (J40)

JOHNSON, HUNTER (1906-   )
For An Unknown Soldier, For Flute And
String Orchestra
string orch,fl solo
NEW VALLEY 147 sc,pts $7.50, pts
$.75, ea.   (J41)

JOLAS, BETSY (1926-   )
Liring Ballade, For Solo Voice And
Orchestra [22']
3.3.3.3. 4.3.3.2. timp,4perc,pno,
cel,strings,Bar solo
RICORDI-FR R.2290 perf mat rent
                               (J42)

JOLITA see Hasenpflug, Curt

JOLLY OLD SAINT NICHOLAS
(Luck, Arthur) LUCKS HYMNS 24 set
$15.00, pts $.65, ea. contains
also: Fink, While Shepherds Watched
Their Flocks By Night   (J43)

JONGE DICHTER DENKT AAN DE GELIEFDE,
EEN see Pluister, Simon

JOPLIN, SCOTT (1868-1917)
Pleasant Moments, For Cornet And
Orchestra [4']
1.0.2.0. 2.0.1.0. perc,vln,vcl,
db,cornet solo, trap set
MARGUN BP 4007 sc $5.50, pts $9.50
                               (J44)

JORDAHL, ROBERT A. (1926-   )
Evocation
string orch
SEESAW perf mat rent   (J45)

JORGENSEN, ERIK
Notturno
sc,pts SAMFUNDET 220 perf mat rent
                               (J46)

JORNS, HELGE (1941-   )
Canti V, For Harpsichord And Chamber
Orchestra [17'30"]
orch,hpsd solo
MODERN 2163 rent   (J47)

Raumblocke
BUDDE perf mat rent   (J48)

Valse Paradox [10']
MODERN 2165 rent   (J49)

JOSEPHINE, FOR CORNET AND ORCHESTRA see
Kryl, Bohumir

JOSHUA: O HAD I JUBAL'S LYRE, FOR SOLO
VOICE AND ORCHESTRA see Handel,
George Frideric

JOTA ARAGONAISE, OP. 64 see Saint-
Saens, Camille

JOUR CONTRE JOUR see Grisey, Gerard

JOUR DE FETE see Glazunov, Alexander
Konstantinovich

JOURNEY OF OWAIN MADOC, THE see Polin,
Claire

JOURNEY TOWARDS THE LIGHT, FOR PIANO
AND ORCHESTRA see Selby, Philip

JOY TO THE WORLD see Handel, George
Frideric

JOYEUSE MARCHE see Chabrier, [Alexis-]
Emmanuel

JUBEL OUVERTURE see Weber, Carl Maria
von

JUBILATIO see Eder, Helmut

JUBILATION see Wordsworth, William

JUBILAUM see Stockhausen, Karlheinz

JUBILEE TOY SYMPHONY see Horovitz,
Joseph

JUBILEUMSSPEL see Wahlberg, Rune

JUBILO see Gould, Morton

JUBILUS SONUS see Rekola, Jukka

JUDAS MACCABAEUS: ARM, ARM YE BRAVE,
FOR SOLO VOICE AND ORCHESTRA see
Handel, George Frideric

JUDAS MACCABAEUS: OVERTURE see Handel,
George Frideric

JUDAS MACCABAEUS: SOUND AN ALARM, FOR
SOLO VOICE AND ORCHESTRA see
Handel, George Frideric

JUGENDUBERMUT see Bode, Hermann

JUHANNUSYO, FOR SOLO VOICE AND
ORCHESTRA see Sonninen, Ahti

JUIVE, LA: SI LA RIGEUR ET VENGEANCE,
FOR SOLO VOICE AND ORCHESTRA see
Halevy, Jacques

JUNG, HELGE (1943-   )
Trois Poesies Francaises, For Solo
Voice And Orchestra *Op.23 [20']
2.2.3.2. 4.3.3.1. timp,perc,
strings,Mez/Bar solo
PETERS perf mat rent   (J50)

JUNGFRU MARIA, FOR SOLO VOICE AND
ORCHESTRA see Frumerie, (Per)
Gunnar (Fredrik) de

JUON, PAUL (1872-1940)
Anmut Und Wurde *see Suite, Op. 94

Burletta *see Konzertstuck for
Violin and Orchestra, Op. 97

Concerto for Violin and Orchestra,
No. 1, Op. 42 [30']
3+pic.2.2.2+contrabsn. 4.2.0.0.
harp,timp,perc,strings,vln solo
sc,pts LIENAU f.s.   (J51)

Concerto for Violin and Orchestra,
No. 2, Op. 49 [32']
2.2.2.2. 4.2.3.0. timp,strings,
vln solo
sc,pts LIENAU rent   (J52)

Concerto for Violin, Violoncello,
Piano and Orchestra, Op. 45
2.2.2.2+contrabsn. 4.2.3.1. timp,
strings,vln solo,vcl solo,pno
solo
sc,pts LIENAU rent   (J53)

Fantasy, Op. 31 [30']
3+pic.2+English horn.2.2+
contrabsn. 6.2.3.1. harp,glock,
timp,perc,strings
sc,pts LIENAU rent   (J54)

Funf Kleine Stucke *Op.16 [15']
string orch,tamb,triangle
sc,pts LIENAU rent   (J55)

Kammersinfonie *Op.27
0.1.1.1. 1.0.0.0. pno,strings
sc,pts LIENAU rent   (J56)

Konzertstuck for Violin and
Orchestra, Op. 97 [12']
3(pic).2(English horn).2.2.
4.2.0.0. timp,perc,strings,vln
solo
sc,pts LIENAU f.s.   (J57)

Rhapsodische Sinfonie *Op.95 [30']
3(pic).2+English horn.2+bass
clar.2+contrabsn. 4.3.3.1.
harp,glock,timp,perc,strings
sc,pts LIENAU rent   (J58)

Serenadenmusik, Eine *Op.40 [30']
2.1.2.2. 2.0.0.0. timp,triangle,
strings
sc,pts LIENAU rent   (J59)

Sinfonietta Capricciosa *Op.98 [30']
3.2+English horn.2.2+contrabsn.
4.3.3.1. timp,perc,strings
sc,pts LIENAU rent   (J60)

Sinfonische Musik *Op.50a [30']
2.2.2.2. 3.0.0.0. glock,xylo,pno,
timp,triangle,strings
sc,pts LIENAU rent   (J61)

Suite, Op. 94 [18']
3.2.2.2+contrabsn. 4.2.3.1. timp,
perc,strings
sc,pts LIENAU f.s.   (J62)

Symphony, Op. 23 [35']
2+pic.2.2.2+contrabsn. 4.2.3.1.
harp,timp,strings
sc,pts LIENAU rent   (J63)

Tanz-Capricen *Op.96 [25']
4(2pic).3+English horn.2.2.
4.3.3.1. harp,glock,xylo,timp,
perc,strings
sc,pts LIENAU rent   (J64)

JUON, PAUL (cont'd.)

Vaegtervise *see Fantasy, Op. 31

JUPITER SYMPHONY see Mozart, Wolfgang
Amadeus, Symphony No. 41 in C, K.
551

JUSI see Kim, Yong Jin

JUST A MOMENT AGAIN... see Straesser,
Joep

JUXBRUDER WALZER see Strauss, Johann,
[Jr.]

K

K.U.K. MUSIK see Kupkovic, Ladislav

KA see Platz, Robert

KABALEVSKY, DMITRI BORISOVICH
   (1904-   )
   Colas Breugnon: Overture
      LUCKS 09059 sc $13.00, set $40.00,
      min sc $3.00, pts $1.75, ea. (K1)

   Comedians, The *Op.26
      LUCKS 08800 sc $14.00, set $35.00,
      min sc $4.00, pts $2.25, ea. (K2)

   Comedians, The: Galop
      LUCKS 05406 sc $10.00, set $12.00,
      pts $1.00, ea.   (K3)

   Symphony No. 1, Op. 18 [25']
      3.3.3.3. 4.3.3.1. timp,perc,
      strings
      KALMUS 5293 sc $30.00, perf mat
      rent, set $90.00, pts $3.00, ea.
                                         (K4)

KAFIG, DER see Globokar, Vinko

KAGEL, MAURICIO (1931-   )
   Vox Humana? [21']
      3.2.1.1. 0.1.1.1. 2perc,pno,3vcl,
      women's voices, loud-speaker
      PETERS perf mat rent   (K5)

KAI, N.
   Concerto for Violin and Orchestra
      sc ZEN-ON 899011 f.s.   (K6)

KAISER-ERIC, W.
   Donaustrand, Du Walzerland
      (Lohr, Hanns) WOITSCHACH f.s.   (K7)

   Fugger-Zeitbilder
      (Jugel-Janson, K.) WOITSCHACH f.s.
                                         (K8)

KAISER-WALZER see Strauss, Johann,
   [Jr.]

KAISER-WALZER, [ARR.] see Strauss,
   Johann, [Jr.]

KAISER WILHELM POLONAISE see Strauss,
   Johann, [Jr.]

KAISERLICHE BOTSCHAFT, EINE, FOR SOLO
   VOICE AND ORCHESTRA see Buchtger,
   Fritz

KAISERMARSCH see Wagner, Richard

KAIVOTIELLA, FOR SOLO VOICE AND
   ORCHESTRA see Pylkkanen, Tauno
   Kullervo

KAKUDU QUADRILLE see Strauss, Josef

KALINNIKOV, VASSILI SERGEIEVICH
   (1866-1901)
   Cedar And The Palm, The [7']
      2.2.0.2. 4.3.2.0. timp,harp,
      strings
      INTERNAT. perf mat rent   (K9)

   Chanson Triste, [arr.]
      string orch LUCKS 08421 sc,set
      $4.00, pts $.60, ea.   (K10)

   Symphony No. 2 in A [30']
      2.2.2.2. 4.2.3.1. timp,harp,
      strings
      BELAIEFF perf mat rent   (K11)

   Tsar Boris: Overture And Entr'actes
      [30']
      2+pic.2.2.2. 4.2.3.0.opt tuba.
      timp,perc,harp,strings
      KALMUS 4476 sc $45.00, set $100.00
                                        (K12)

KALIVODA, JAN KRTITEL
   see KALLIWODA, JOHANN WENZEL

KALLIES, HANNS
   Iffezheimer Rennen
      RIES f.s.   (K13)

   In Der Manege
      RIES f.s.   (K14)

KALLIWODA, JOHANN WENZEL (1801-1866)
   Introduktion Und Rondo, For Horn And
   Orchestra *Op.51
      2.0.2.2. 0.0.0.0. strings,horn
      solo
      MUS. RARA 41.918 perf mat rent
                                        (K15)

KALLSTENIUS, EDVIN (1881-1967)
   Drei Schwedische Volksweisen *CC3U
      string orch sc,pts RIES f.s.   (K16)

KALLSTENIUS, EDVIN (cont'd.)
   Via Ur Dalarapsodi
      sc SUECIA f.s.   (K17)

KALLUSCH, W.
   see KALUS, VACLAV

KALUS, VACLAV (W. KALLUSCH)
   Variacie, For Double Bass And
   Orchestra
      2ob,2horn,strings,db solo
      SLOV.HUD.FOND 0-449A perf mat rent
                                        (K18)

KAMMERKONZERT see Erbse, Heimo

KAMMERMUSIK I "HOMMAGE A MOZART" see
   Lehmann, Hans Ulrich

KAMMERMUSIK II see Lehmann, Hans Ulrich

KAMMERSINFONIE see Hofmann, Wolfgang

KAMMERSINFONIE see Juon, Paul

KAMMERSINFONIE see Pepusch, John
   Christopher

KAMMERSINFONIE NO. 2 see Domhardt, Gerd

KAMMERSUITE see Unger, Hermann

KAMP, HANS
   Tanz Auf Dem Regenbogen
      RIES f.s.   (K19)

   Waldgeister
      RIES f.s.   (K20)

KANAI, KIKUKO
   Capriccio Okinawa
      2(pic).2+English horn.1+bass
      clar.1+contrabsn. 4.3.3.1.
      timp,perc,harp,org,strings
      sc J.C.A. f.s.   (K21)

KANG, SUKHI (1949-   )
   Mega-Melos [32']
      4(pic).4(English horn).4(bass
      clar).4(contrabsn). 4.4.4.2.
      timp,4perc,pno,harp,strings
      BREITKOPF-W perf mat rent   (K22)

KANN ICH IM BUSEN HEISSE WUNSCHE
   TRAGEN?, FOR VOICE AND
   ORCHESTRA see Diepenbrock, Alphons

KANON see Penderecki, Krzysztof

KANON, [ARR.] see Pachelbel, Johann

KANONS, VIERZEHN, BWV 1087, [ARR.] see
   Bach, Johann Sebastian

KANONS, VIERZEHN, BWV 1087, [ARR.] see
   Bach, Johann Sebastian

KAPRIOLEN OUVERTURE see Dressel, Erwin

KAPRIZIOSE POLKA see Leschetizky,
   Walter

KARDOS, DEZIDER (1914-   )
   Groteskny Pochod [3']
      2.2.2.2. 2.2.1.0. timp,perc,pno,
      strings
      "Grotesque March" SLOV.HUD.FOND
      0-51 perf mat rent   (K23)

   Grotesque March *see Groteskny
      Pochod

   Sinfonietta Domestica *Op.50 [20']
      3.3.3.3. 4.3.3.1. timp,4perc,
      harp,cel,pno,strings
      SLOV.HUD.FOND 0-487A perf mat rent
                                        (K24)

   Slovakofonia *Op.46 [26']
      3.3.3.3. 4.3.3.1. timp,perc,harp,
      xylo,pno,strings
      SLOV.HUD.FOND 0-437A perf mat rent
                                        (K25)

KARELIA OVERTURE see Sibelius, Jean

KARELIA SUITE see Sibelius, Jean

KARJALAN NEIDON LAULUJA, FOR SOLO VOICE
   AND ORCHESTRA see Sonninen, Ahti

KARKOFF, INGVAR (1958-   )
   Tomorrow No One Knows
      fl/pic,alto fl,ob/soprano sax,
      bsn,4perc,gtr,elec gtr,pno,vln,
      db
      pts STIM perf mat rent   (K26)

KARKOFF, MAURICE (1927-   )
   Musica Seria *Op.146 [14']
      fl,clar,strings
      sc GEHRMANS   (K27)

   Symphony No. 8, Op. 145 [21']
      3.3.2.3. 4.3.3.1. timp,4perc,
      harp,strings
      sc STIM   (K28)

KARKOFF, MAURICE (cont'd.)
   Tre Capriskisser *Op.144 [10']
      1.0.2.0. 0.1.0.0. 3perc,strings
      sc STIM   (K29)

   Voices From The Past, For Solo Voices
   And String Orchestra *Op.148
   [18']
      string orch,ABar soli
      STIM   (K30)

KARKOSCHKA, ERHARD (1923-   )
   Teleologies [25']
      2(pic).2(English horn).2+bass
      clar.1. 4.2.2.0. 3perc,strings
      BREITKOPF-W perf mat rent   (K31)

KARLEKENS RINGDANS see Hallnas, Hilding

KARLINS, M. WILLIAM (1932-   )
   Concert Music V
      3.3.3.3.2sax. 4.4.2.2. timp,
      5perc,pno,strings
      SEESAW perf mat rent   (K32)

KARLOWICZ, MIECZYSLAW (1876-1909)
   Concerto for Violin and Orchestra,
   Op. 8 [23']
      2.2.2.2. 4.2.3.1. timp,strings,
      vln solo
      sc,pts LIENAU rent   (K33)

KARRASCH, KURT
   Italienischer Karneval
      RIES f.s.   (K34)

   Maurische Rhapsodie
      RIES f.s.   (K35)

KARWOCHE, FOR SOLO VOICE AND ORCHESTRA
   see Wolf, Hugo

KASCHUBEC, ERICH
   Kinderleben
      RIES f.s.   (K36)

   Liebes Wort, Ein
      RIES f.s.   (K37)

   Mexikanische Serenade
      RIES f.s.   (K38)

KASKI, HEINO (1885-1957)
   Niin Mustina Muratit Kiertaa, For
   Solo Voice And Orchestra, [arr.]
   *Op.54,No.4
      (Jalas, J.) 2.1.1.1. 2.0.0.0. timp,
      strings,solo voice [3'] FAZER
      perf mat rent   (K39)

KASSATIONEN, SERENADEN UND DIVERTIMENI,
   K. 136-138, 525, ANH. 69, ANH. 223
   see Mozart, Wolfgang Amadeus

KASSATIONEN, SERENADEN UND
   DIVERTIMENTI, K. 32, 63, 99, 63A,
   62, 100 see Mozart, Wolfgang
   Amadeus

KASSATIONEN, SERENADEN UND
   DIVERTIMENTI, K. 335, 320, 286 see
   Mozart, Wolfgang Amadeus

KATE DALRYMPLE see Whyte, Ian

KATHCHEN VON HEILBRONN: MELODRAM,
   ZWISCHENAKTMUSIK UND MARSCH see
   Pfitzner, Hans

KATHCHEN VON HEILBRONN: NACH DER
   HOLUNDERBUSCHSZENE see Pfitzner,
   Hans

KATHCHEN VON HEILBRONN: VORSPIEL ZUM
   III. AKT see Pfitzner, Hans

KATTNIGG, RUDOLF (1895-1955)
   Concerto for Flute, Piano and String
   Orchestra, Op. 28
      string orch,fl solo,pno solo
      sc MULLER 1678 f.s.   (K40)

KATZER, GEORG (1935-   )
   Concerto for Piano and Orchestra
   [25']
      3.3.3.2. 4.3.3.0. timp,3perc,
      harp,strings,pno solo
      sc PETERS EP 5568 f.s., perf mat
      rent   (K41)

   Concerto for Violoncello, Harp and
   Orchestra [30']
      2.2.2.1. 2.1.1.0. 3perc,cel,pno,
      strings,vcl solo,harp solo
      sc PETERS EP 5595 f.s., perf mat
      rent   (K42)

   Empfindsame Musik
      3perc,58strings
      sc PETERS EP 5527 f.s., perf mat
      rent   (K43)

   Sound-House [23']
      2+alto fl.2+English horn.2.2.
      4.3.3.1. timp,perc,harp,2mand,

KATZER, GEORG (cont'd.)

       hpsd,gtr,banjo,pno,strings,
       electronic tape, spinet
      sc PETERS EP 5548 f.s., perf mat
      rent   (K44)

KAUFMANN, DIETER (1941-   )
  Overture for Orchestra
    sc REIMERS f.s., perf mat rent
                      (K45)

KAUN, HUGO (1863-1932)
  Sir John Falstaff *Op.60 [16']
    3(pic).2.2+bass clar.2+contrabsn.
    4.3.3.1. timp,2perc,strings
    RIES perf mat rent   (K46)

KAVALKADE see Buder, Ernst Erich

KAY, HERSHY (1919-1981)
  Cakewalk: Suite
    sc BOOSEY $30.00   (K47)

  Western Symphony
    sc BOOSEY $30.00   (K48)

KAY, N.
  Concerto for Violin and Orchestra
    orch,vln solo   )
    ZEN-ON 899011   (K49)

KAY, ULYSSES SIMPSON (1917-   )
  Quiet One, The: Suite [16']
    2.1.1.1. 1.1.1.0. timp,perc,pno,
    strings
    PEMBROKE   (K50)

  Quintet Concerto, For Brass Quintet
    And Orchestra [17']
    3.2.3.2. 3.1.1.0. perc,strings,
    horn solo,2trp soli,bass trom/
    tuba solo, tenor trombone solo
    PEMBROKE   (K51)

  Southern Harmony [20']
    3.3.3.3. 4.3.3.1. timp,2perc,
    strings
    PEMBROKE sc $15.00, pts rent (K52)

  Western Paradise, The, For Narrator
    And Orchestra [16']
    3.3.3.3. 4.3.3.1. timp,perc,harp,
    strings,narrator
    PEMBROKE   (K53)

KAYN, ROLAND (1933-   )
  Aggregates Sonores [11']
    5.0.4.0. 6.5.5.2. 6perc,strings
    sc ZERBONI 7740 f.s., pts ZERBONI
    7741 rent   (K54)

KEEP GOING see Kornac, Hans

KEHTOLAULU KUOLLEELLE RATSUMIEHELLE see
  Sallinen, Aulis

KEIZER VAN ZWEDEN, DE see Beekhuis,
  Hanna

KELEMEN, MILKO (1924-   )
  Infinity [13']
    3.3.3.3. 4.3.3.1. perc,strings
    study sc PETERS EP 8477 f.s., perf
    mat rent   (K55)

  Mageia [11']
    3.2.3.2. 4.3.3.0. 3perc,strings
    study sc PETERS EP 8472 f.s., perf
    mat rent   (K56)

KELTERBORN, RUDOLF (1931-   )
  Chiaroscuro [16']
    3(pic).2(English horn).3(bass
    clar).2(contrabsn). 4.3.3.0.
    timp,1-2perc,harp,strings
    study sc BAREN. BA 6775 f.s., perf
    mat rent   (K57)

  Erinerungen An Orpheus
    sc BOTE $55.50   (K58)

  Phantasmen [10']
    2+pic.2+English horn.3(bass
    clar).2+contrabsn. 4.3.3.1.
    timp,3perc,harp,strings
    min sc BAREN. BA 3815 $26.50 (K59)

  Visions Sonores Fur Sechs
    Schlagzeuggruppen Und Sechs
    Obligate Instrumente [13']
    fl,clar,trp,trom,perc,vln,vcl
    BAREN. BA 6771 perf mat rent (K60)

KEMPFF, WILHELM (1895-   )
  Arkadische Suite *Op.42 [15']
    1.2.0.2. 0.0.0.0. triangle,
    strings
    sc RIES f.s., perf mat rent (K61)

  Epitaph *Op.72,No.1 [14']
    string orch
    sc RIES f.s., perf mat rent (K62)

KENNEDY, JOHN BRODBIN (1934-   )
  Symphonic Fantasy
    sc BOOSEY $7.50   (K63)

KENNST DU MICH? WALZER see Strauss,
  Johann, [Jr.]

KERMESSE see Bossi, [Marco] Enrico

KERSTLIED, FOR SOLO VOICE AND ORCHESTRA
  see Dresden, Sem

KERSTLIEDJE see Dijk, Jan van

KERSTLIEDJE, FOR SOLO VOICE AND
  ORCHESTRA see Voormolen, Alexander
  Nicolas

KESAILLALLA, FOR SOLO VOICE AND
  ORCHESTRA see Linnala, Eino

KESAYO KIRKKOMAALLA, FOR SOLO VOICE AND
  ORCHESTRA, [ARR.] see Kuula, Toivo

KESS, LUDWIG
  Capriccio Scivolando [6']
    2.2.2.2. 4.2.3.0. timp,perc,harp,
    strings
    sc RIES f.s., perf mat rent (K64)

  Reisestimmung [6']
    2.2.2.2. 4.2.3.0. timp,perc,harp,
    strings
    sc RIES f.s., perf mat rent (K65)

  Ritter Der Landstrasse
    RIES f.s.   (K66)

  Sonniger Morgen
    RIES f.s.   (K67)

KETJAK see Johansen, Svend Aaquist

KETTING, OTTO (1935-   )
  Adagio [18']
    0.0.3.0. 1.1.1.0. 2perc,pno,vln,
    vla,vcl
    sc DONEMUS f.s., perf mat rent
                      (K68)
  For Moonlight Nights, For Flute And
    Orchestra [20']
    0.0.0.0. 0.4.4.0. harp,marimba,
    8vln,5vcl,3db,fl&pic&alto fl
    solo
    sc DONEMUS f.s., perf mat rent
                      (K69)
  Light Of The Sun, The, For Solo Voice
    And Orchestra [35']
    3.3.2.2. 4.3.2.0. timp,2perc,
    harp,strings,solo voice
    DONEMUS perf mat rent   (K70)

  O, Gij, Rhinoceros, For Solo Voices
    And Chamber Orchestra [30']
    1.1.1.1. 0.1.0.0. perc,pno,2vln,
    vla,vcl,db,SMezTBar soli
    sc DONEMUS f.s., perf mat rent
                      (K71)
  Symphony for 4 Saxophones and
    Orchestra [28']
    0.0.0.0. 6.5.4.1. perc,pno,
    strings,4sax soli
    DONEMUS perf mat rent   (K72)

KETTING, PIET (1905-   )
  Clown
    see Vier Gedichten, For Solo Voice
    And Orchestra

  Concertone 1980, For Viola And
    Orchestra [22']
    2.2.3.2. 2.2.1.0. perc,vla solo
    DONEMUS f.s.   (K73)

  Schipper, De
    see Vier Gedichten, For Solo Voice
    And Orchestra

  Shakespeare's Winteravondsprookje
    see Vier Gedichten, For Solo Voice
    And Orchestra

  Tema Con 6 Variazioni, For Flute And
    Orchestra [17']
    0.3.3.2. 4.4.4.0. timp,perc,harp,
    cel,strings,fl solo
    sc DONEMUS f.s., perf mat rent
                      (K74)
  Twee Reddelozen
    see Vier Gedichten, For Solo Voice
    And Orchestra

  Vier Gedichten, For Solo Voice And
    Orchestra
    2.2.3.0. 0.0.0.0. perc,pno,acord,
    vln,2vla,vcl,Mez solo sc DONEMUS
    f.s., perf mat rent
    contains: Clown; Schipper, De;
    Shakespeare's
    Winteravondsprookje; Twee
    Reddelozen   (K75)

KEULEN, GEERT VAN (1943-   )
  Concerto for Violin and Orchestra
    [20']
    3.3.4.3.2sax. 2.2.2.0. 2perc,elec
    org,harp,strings,vln solo
    DONEMUS   (K76)

  Cors Et Cordes, For Bassethorn And
    Orchestra
    2English horn,opt ob,2horn,hpsd,
    strings,basset horn solo
    DONEMUS perf mat rent   (K77)

  Koraal [10']
    3.3.3.3. 4.3.3.0. perc,pno,
    strings
    DONEMUS perf mat rent   (K78)

  Sonatas [12']
    4.4.4.3. 6.4.3.1. 4perc,pno,
    strings
    DONEMUS perf mat rent   (K79)

  Souvenir Nostalgique
    string orch
    sc DONEMUS f.s., perf mat rent
                      (K80)

KEUNING, HANS P. (1926-   )
  Birth Of Music, The
    2.2.2.0. 0.2.0.0. perc,strings
    sc,pts HARMONIA 2256 f.s. (K81)

  Golden Age Dances
    2.1.2.0. 0.2.0.0. perc,strings
    sc,pts HARMONIA 2737 f.s. (K82)

  Sinfonietta Concertante
    2.2.2.2. 4.2.2.0. timp,perc,
    strings
    sc DONEMUS f.s., perf mat rent
                      (K83)

KEURIS, TRISTAN (1946-   )
  Capriccio [10']
    0.2.4.2. 4.0.0.0. db
    DONEMUS perf mat rent   (K84)

  Concerto for Piano and Orchestra
    [23']
    3.3.3.3. 4.2.3.1. 3perc,strings,
    pno solo
    DONEMUS   (K85)

  Concerto for Saxophone and Orchestra
    [11']
    3.2.3.2. 4.2.2.1. pno,cel,
    marimba,vibra,strings,alto sax
    solo
    sc DONEMUS f.s., perf mat rent
                      (K86)
  Movements [28']
    3.3.4.3. 4.3.3.1. timp,4perc,
    harp,strings
    DONEMUS   (K87)

  Serenade for Oboe and Orchestra [12']
    3.3.3.3. 4.2.2.1. harp,pno,
    marimba,vibra,strings,ob solo
    sc DONEMUS f.s., perf mat rent
                      (K88)
  Sinfonia [15']
    4.4.3.4.2sax. 8.4.3.2. perc,pno,
    strings
    DONEMUS perf mat rent   (K89)

KEVAT TULEE, FOR SOLO VOICE AND
  ORCHESTRA see Palmgren, Selim

KHACHATURIAN, ARAM ILYICH (1903-1978)
  Concerto for Piano and Orchestra
    sc RICORDI-IT PR922 f.s.   (K90)

  Concerto for Violin and Orchestra
    [34']
    3.3.2.2. 4.3.3.1. timp,perc,harp,
    strings,vln solo
    KALMUS 1055 sc $40.00, perf mat
    rent, set $80.00, pts $6.00, ea.
                      (K91)
    sc RICORDI-IT PR853 f.s.   (K92)

  Gayane: Sabre Dance
    "Gayaneh: La Danza Delle Sciabole"
    sc RICORDI-IT PR904 f.s. (K93)

  Gayane: Three Dances
    LUCKS 09112 sc $13.00, set $32.00,
    min sc $2.00, pts $1.60, ea.
                      (K94)
  Gayaneh: La Danza Delle Sciabole
    *see Gayane: Sabre Dance

  Masquerade Suite
    LUCKS 09116 sc $25.00, set $38.00,
    pts $2.25, ea.   (K95)

KHANDOSHKIN, IVAN (1747-1804)
  Concerto for Viola and String
    Orchestra [12']
    string orch,vla solo
    INTERNAT. perf mat rent   (K96)

KHORHOORT NAHADAGATS see Hovhaness,
  Alan

KHOVANTCHINA: OVERTURE see Mussorgsky, Modest Petrovich

KICK-KLETZKI
    Legende
        RIES f.s.   (K97)

KICK-SCHMIDT, PAUL
    Jahreszeiten, Die
        sc,pts RIES f.s.   (K98)

    Lied Im Volksmund
        RIES f.s.   (K99)

KIENZL, WILHELM (1857-1941)
    Tanzweisen Aus Osterreich [23']
        2.2.2.2. 2.2.0.0. timp,2perc,
        strings
        (Dressel, Erwin) sc RIES f.s., perf
        mat rent   (K100)

KIERMEIR, KURT
    Madchenbilder [8']
        1(pic).1(English horn).2.1.
        0.0.0.0. perc,harp/pno,strings
        (Mielenz, Hans) sc RIES f.s., perf
        mat rent   (K101)

KIESEWETTER, PETER (1945-   )
    Reveries Heroiques De Mme. de Meck,
        Les [19']
        clar,bsn,trp,trom,tuba,pno,org,
        vcl,db,2perc
        ORLANDO rent   (K102)

KIKIMORA see Liadov, Anatol Konstantinovich

KIKVORST, DE see Dijk, Jan van

KILPINEN, YRJO (1892-1959)
    Maassa Marjani Makaavi, For Solo
        Voice And Orchestra, [arr.]
        *Op.3,No.3
        (Funtek, L.) 1.1.2.1. 0.0.0.0.
        perc,harp,strings,solo voice [4']
        FAZER f.s.   (K103)

    Sa Dansa, For Solo Voice And
        Orchestra, [arr.] *Op.47,No.6,
        CC6U
        (Fougstedt, N-E.) 2.2.2.2. 2.2.0.0.
        perc,strings,solo voice FAZER
        perf mat rent   (K104)

KIM, YONG JIN
    Jusi
        18strings
        SEESAW perf mat rent   (K105)

KINDER-SYMPHONIE see Mozart, Leopold,
    Cassation in C

KINDERLEBEN see Kaschubec, Erich

KINDERLIEDJES II, FOR SOLO VOICE AND
    ORCHESTRA see Frid, Geza

KINDERSINFONIE see Haydn, [Franz]
    Joseph

KINDERSPIELE POLKA see Strauss, Johann,
    [Jr.]

KINDERTAG, EIN see Kludas, Erich

KINDERTAG, EIN, FOR SOLO VOICE AND
    ORCHESTRA see Kludas, Erich

KINDERTOTENLIEDER, FOR SOLO VOICE AND
    ORCHESTRA see Mahler, Gustav

KINDES SCHEIDEN, DES, FOR SOLO VOICE
    AND ORCHESTRA see Weingartner,
    (Paul) Felix von

KING, HAROLD C. (1895-   )
    Concerto for Organ and Orchestra
        [18']
        0.1.0.0. 0.3.3.0. timp,2vln,vla,
        vcl,db,org solo
        sc DONEMUS f.s., perf mat rent
                                          (K106)

KING ARTHUR: SUITE NO. 1, [ARR.] see
    Purcell, Henry

KING ARTHUR: SUITE NO. 2, [ARR.] see
    Purcell, Henry

KING ARTHUR: SUITE NO. 3, [ARR.] see
    Purcell, Henry

KING CHRISTIAN II, FOR SOLO VOICE AND
    ORCHESTRA see Sibelius, Jean

KING COTTON MARCH see Sousa, John
    Philip

KING LEAR OVERTURE see Berlioz, Hector
    (Louis)

KING STEPHEN: OVERTURE see Beethoven,
    Ludwig van, Konig Stephan: Overture

KINGMA, PIET (1926-   )
    Twee Dansen
        3.2.2.1. 2.2.0.0. timp,perc,
        strings
        sc DONEMUS f.s., perf mat rent
                                          (K107)

KING'S HUNT, THE see Bull, John

KIRCHSTEIN, HAROLD M. (1906-   )
    Hawaiian Holiday [14']
        ORLANDO rent   (K108)

    Hollywood Kintop [21']
        ORLANDO rent   (K109)

    Port d'Amour [4']
        harp,gtr,marimba,perc,strings
        ORLANDO rent   (K110)

    Temptation [3']
        fl,clar,cel,strings,vln solo
        ORLANDO rent   (K111)

KISS, THE see Arditi, Luigi, Bacio, Il,
    For Solo Voice And Orchestra

KISTENMACHER, ARTHUR
    Trinklied, For Solo Voice And
        Orchestra, [arr.]
        (Satow, Karl) 2.1.2.2. 4.2.3.0.
        timp,perc,harp,strings,solo voice
        [4'] RIES perf mat rent   (K112)
        (Schlemm, G.A.) 1.1.2.1. 3.2.1.0.
        timp,harp,strings,solo voice [4']
        RIES perf mat rent   (K113)

KJERULF, HALFDAN (1815-1868)
    Last Night The Nightingale Woke Me,
        For Solo Voice And Orchestra
        LUCKS 02860 sc $2.00, set $4.50,
        pts $.75, ea.   (K114)

KLAAS, JULIUS (1888-1965)
    Aus Galanter Zeit *Op.10 [22']
        fl,ob,strings
        sc RIES f.s., perf mat rent   (K115)

    Divertimento, Op. 66 [27']
        string orch
        sc RIES f.s., perf mat rent   (K116)

    Nachtmusik Im Garten *Op.62 [23']
        fl,ob,strings
        sc RIES f.s., perf mat rent   (K117)

KLAGE DER GARDE see Beekhuis, Hanna

KLANGBILD see Stranz, Ulrich

KLANGE DER PUSZTA see Muller, Pepi

KLANGFARBEN see Hamel, Peter Michael

KLARINETTEN-KAPRIOLEN see Loffler,
    Willy

KLEBE, GISELHER (1925-   )
    Begrussung [12']
        2+pic.2(English horn).1+bass
        clar.1+contrabsn. 4.5.5.0.
        timp,3perc,harp,strings
        "Salutations" BAREN. BA 6790 perf
        mat rent   (K118)

    Boogie Agitato [7']
        1+pic.1.1+bass clar.1+contrabsn.
        4.3.3.1. timp,2perc,harp,pno,
        strings
        BAREN. BA 6792 perf mat rent (K119)

    Concerto for Organ and Orchestra, Op.
        85 [30']
        3(pic).2+English horn.3(bass
        clar).2+contrabsn. 6.4.4.1.
        timp,2perc,2harp,strings
        BAREN. BA 6780 perf mat rent (K120)

    Orpheus *Op.73 [15']
        3(pic).3.3.3. 4.3.3.1. 3perc,
        harp,pno,strings
        BAREN. BA 6721 perf mat rent (K121)

    Salutations *see Begrussung

KLEIDOCYMBALON I see Hatzis, Christos

KLEINE, WERNER (1907-   )
    Bunte Lichter
        RIES f.s.   (K122)

    Goldsucher, Der [12']
        2.1+English horn.2.2. 2.2.1.0.
        timp,perc,harp,cel,strings
        (Dressel, Erwin) sc RIES f.s., perf
        mat rent   (K123)

    Taiga
        RIES f.s.   (K124)

    Westfalische Bauernhochzeit
        RIES f.s.   (K125)

    Wiener Pastell
        RIES f.s.   (K126)

KLEINE BALLETT-MUSIK, [ARR.] see
    Gretry, Andre Ernest Modeste

KLEINE BALLETTSTUDIE see Stolzenwald,
    Otto

KLEINE CARMEN see Bortz, Alfred

KLEINE CHRONIK POLKA see Strauss,
    Eduard

KLEINE DAGMUZIEK see Verhaar, Ary

KLEINE FESTMUSIK see Ebenhoh, Horst

KLEINE FESTMUSIK see Reuter, Fritz

KLEINE FESTMUSIK see Trenkner, Werner

KLEINE KOMODIE see Dressel, Erwin

KLEINE KONIGSTOCHTER, DIE see Schmidt-
    Wunstorf, Rudolf, Petite Reine, La

KLEINE KONZERTANTE SUITE see Burkhard,
    Willy

KLEINE MUHLE, DIE, FOR SOLO VOICE AND
    ORCHESTRA see Strauss, Josef

KLEINE NACHTMUSIK, EINE see Mozart,
    Wolfgang Amadeus

KLEINE OUVERTURE, FOR SOLO VOICE AND
    ORCHESTRA see Flothuis, Marius

KLEINE RHAPSODIE see Pero, Hans

KLEINE SINFONIE FUR MUSIKFREUNDE see
    Mozart, Leopold

KLEINE SKIZZEN see Hudec, Jiri

KLEINE SUITE see Biener, Gustav

KLEINE SUITE see Bund, Hans

KLEINE TANZE GROSSER MEISTER see
    Deutschmann, Gerhard

KLEINE TANZMUSIK see Niklas, Ferry

KLEINE THEATER-SUITE see Lothar, Mark

KLEINE ZUGABE see Kotscher, Edmund

KLEINES GONDELLIED see Hasenpflug, Curt

KLEINES SPIEL see Walden, Erich

KLENGEL, JULIUS (1859-1933)
    Hymnus *Op.57 [9']
        12vcl
        sc BREITKOPF-W EB 6846 f.s., pts
        BREITKOPF-W EB 6847 f.s.   (K127)

KLERK, ALBERT DE (1917-   )
    Jam Lucis Orto Sidere, For Solo Voice
        And Orchestra
        2.2.2.2. 2.2.3.0. timp,harp,
        strings,T solo
        sc DONEMUS f.s., perf mat rent
                                          (K128)

    Suite Concertante, For Organ And
        String Orchestra [18']
        string orch,org solo
        sc DONEMUS f.s., perf mat rent
                                          (K129)

KLETSCH, LUDWIG
    Arenas
        RIES f.s. contains also: Don Alonzo
                                          (K130)

    Don Alonzo
        see Kletsch, Ludwig, Arenas

    Eilpost
        RIES f.s.   (K131)

    Fischertanz
        RIES f.s.   (K132)

    Frohliches Spiel
        RIES f.s. contains also: Presto
                                          (K133)

    Konzertanter Tango
        RIES f.s. contains also: Langsamer
        Walzer   (K134)

    Langsamer Walzer
        see Kletsch, Ludwig, Konzertanter
        Tango

    Presto
        see Kletsch, Ludwig, Frohliches
        Spiel
        RIES f.s.   (K135)

    Schnellpolka
        RIES f.s.   (K136)

    Tanz-Suite
        string orch
        sc,pts RIES f.s.   (K137)

KLOPSTOCK-ODE, FOR SOLO VOICE AND
ORCHESTRA see Kunad, Rainer

KLUDAS, ERICH
Kindertag, Ein [8']
1.1.2.1. 2.1.0.0. timp,perc,harp,
strings
(Schreiter, Heinz) sc RIES f.s.,
perf mat rent   (K138)

Kindertag, Ein, For Solo Voice And
Orchestra [8']
1.1.2.1. 2.1.0.0. timp,perc,harp,
strings,solo voice
(Schreiter, Heinz) RIES perf mat
rent   (K139)

Slawische Melodie
RIES f.s.   (K140)

KLUGERE GIEBT NACH, DER. POLKA see
Strauss, Johann, [Jr.]

KNABEN WUNDERHORN, DES: DAS IRDISCHE
LEBEN, FOR SOLO VOICE AND ORCHESTRA
see Mahler, Gustav

KNABEN WUNDERHORN, DES: DER SCHILDWACHE
NACHTLIED, FOR SOLO VOICE AND
ORCHESTRA see Mahler, Gustav

KNABEN WUNDERHORN, DES: DES ANTONIUS
VON PADUA FISCHPREDIGT, FOR SOLO
VOICE AND ORCHESTRA see Mahler,
Gustav

KNABEN WUNDERHORN, DES: EARTHLY LIFE
see Mahler, Gustav, Knaben
Wunderhorn, Des: Das Irdische
Leben, For Solo Voice And Orchestra

KNABEN WUNDERHORN, DES: SENTINEL'S
NIGHT see Mahler, Gustav, Knaben
Wunderhorn, Des: Der Schildwache
Nachtlied, For Solo Voice And
Orchestra

KNABEN WUNDERHORN, DES: WO DIE SCHONEN
TROMPETEN BLASEN, FOR SOLO VOICE
AND ORCHESTRA see Mahler, Gustav

KNALL AUND FALL POLKA see Strauss,
Eduard

KNAP, ROLF (1937-   )
Materiam Superabat Opus Zelomaniana,
For Oboe And String Orchestra
*Op.2,No.38 [6']
string orch,ob solo
sc DONEMUS f.s., perf mat rent
(K141)

KNAPIK, EUGENIUSZ (1951-   )
Chant, Le, For Solo Voice And
Orchestra [11']
4.4.5.4. 6.4.4.1. perc,harp,
10vln,8db,S solo
[Fr] sc POLSKIE $34.40   (K142)

Flute De Jade, La, For Solo Voice And
Orchestra [21'-22']
4.0.0.0. 4.0.0.0. 2perc,pno,
strings,S solo
[Fr] sc,fac ed POLSKIE $24.96
(K143)

KNAPP, A.
In Memoriam, For Violin And String
Orchestra
string orch,vln solo
sc,pts HEINRICH. 794 f.s.   (K144)

KNAVERLEK, FOR TWO KEY FIDDLES AND
STRING ORCHESTRA see Alldahl, Per-
Gunnar

KNUMANN, JO
Balkan
RIES f.s. contains also: Slawisch
(K145)
Rumanisch
RIES f.s.   (K146)

Russisch
RIES f.s.   (K147)

Schottisch
RIES f.s.   (K148)

Slawisch
see Knumann, Jo, Balkan

Ungarisch
RIES f.s.   (K149)

Zwischen Zwei Flussen
RIES f.s.   (K150)

KNUSSEN, OLIVER (1952-   )
Chorale [9']
4(alto fl).4(English horn).4(clar
in E flat,bass clar).4.
8.3.4.1. 3perc,6db
MARGUN BP4005A perf mat rent (K151)

KOBLITZ, DAVID (1948-   )
Eight Three-Part Inventions [12']
string orch without db
MARGUN MM 43A set $23.00, perf mat
rent, sc $10.00   (K152)

Gris-Gris [8']
3(alto fl).0.3(clar in E flat).0.
2.3.0.0. 4perc,elec gtr,cel/
pno,strings
MARGUN BP 4001 perf mat rent (K153)

Trism [7']
2.2.3.2. 3.3.3.1. 4perc,harp,pno,
strings
MARGUN BP 4002 perf mat rent (K154)

KOCH, ERLAND VON (1910-   )
Concerto for Alto Saxophone and
String Orchestra [17']
string orch,alto sax solo
study sc PEER $6.00   (K155)

Concerto for Oboe and String
Orchestra
string orch,ob solo
sc GEHRMANS ENO 6061   (K156)

Concerto for Violin and Orchestra,
No. 2 [24']
2.2.2.2. 4.2.3.0. timp,2perc,
strings,vln solo
sc STIM perf mat rent   (K157)

KOCH, FREDERICK (1924-   )
Veltin Fantasy, For Oboe And String
Orchestra
string orch,ob solo
SEESAW perf mat rent   (K158)

KOCH-RAPHAEL, ERWIN (1949-   )
Land Der Nacht *Op.22
sc BOTE f.s.   (K159)

KOCHAN, GUNTER (1930-   )
Symphony No. 4
sc,quarto PETERS 9598 $27.50, perf
mat rent   (K160)

KOCHER
For The Beauty Of The Earth
(Luck, Arthur) LUCKS HYMNS 7 set
$10.00, pts $.65, ea. contains
also: Beautiful Saviour   (K161)

KOCHMANN, SPERO (1889-   )
Flirt
RIES f.s.   (K162)

KOCKELMANS, GERARD (1925-1965)
Diverterend
2.2.2.2. 2.2.2.0. timp,2perc,
harp,strings
DONEMUS   (K163)

KODAISHINSYO see Watanabe, Urato

KODALY, ZOLTAN (1882-1967)
Concerto for Orchestra
min sc BOOSEY 703 $16.00   (K164)

KOECHLIN, CHARLES (1867-1950)
Course De Printemps, La *Op.95
ESCHIG sc,pts rent, min sc f.s.
(K165)

KOESTER, WILLY
Darinka
RIES f.s.   (K166)

KOETSIER, JAN (1911-   )
Concertino Drammatico, For Violin,
Viola And String Orchestra
*Op.88 [16']
string orch,vln solo,vla solo
DONEMUS   (K167)

Concertino for Horn and String
Orchestra [15']
string orch,horn solo
DONEMUS perf mat rent   (K168)

Concertino for Trumpet and String
Orchestra, Op. 84 [16']
DONEMUS f.s.   (K169)

Concertino for Tuba and String
Orchestra, Op. 77 [15']
string orch,tuba solo
DONEMUS perf mat rent   (K170)

Concerto Capriccioso, For Piano And
Orchestra [18']
2.2.2.2. 2.2.3.0. timp,perc,
strings,pno solo
sc DONEMUS f.s., perf mat rent
(K171)

Skurrile Elegie Auf Richard W., For
Wagner Tuba And String Orchestra
*Op.86,No.2 [8']
string orch, Wagner tuba-bass
clar solo
DONEMUS   (K172)

Variationen Uber Ein
Altniederlandisches Minnelied
*Op.83 [7']

KOETSIER, JAN (cont'd.)

string orch
DONEMUS   (K173)

KOGLER, KARL (1918-   )
Concerto for Harpsichord and
Orchestra
1.0.1.1. 1.1.0.0. vibra,cel,xylo,
strings,hpsd solo
sc,pts DOBLINGER rent   (K174)

KOHLER, SIEGFRIED (1927-   )
Epitaph Fur Antigone (Sinfonia No. 4,
Op. 62) [17']
2.2.3.3. 4.3.3.1. timp,perc,harp,
pno,strings
sc PETERS EP 5550 f.s., perf mat
rent   (K175)

Gefesselte Orpheus, Der *Op.60 [11']
2.2.3.3. 4.3.3.1. timp,perc,
strings
sc PETERS EP 5493 f.s., perf mat
rent   (K176)

Kommentare Zu Drei Venezianischen
Madrigalen Des Heinrich Schutz
Aus Dem Jahre 1611 *Op.63
string orch
sc DEUTSCHER 1715 f.s., perf mat
rent   (K177)

Sinfonia No. 4, Op. 62 *see Epitaph
Fur Antigone

KOHN, KARL (1926-   )
Concerto for Horn and Orchestra [25']
fl,ob,clar,2bsn,vibra,pno,
strings,horn solo
FISCHER,C perf mat rent   (K178)

Sinfonia Concertante for Piano and
Orchestra [20']
2.2.2.2. 2.2.3.1. timp,strings,
pno solo
FISCHER,C perf mat rent   (K179)

KOHTALO, FOR SOLO VOICE AND ORCHESTRA,
[ARR.] see Kuula, Toivo

KOL NIDREI, FOR DOUBLE BASS AND
ORCHESTRA, [ARR.] see Bruch, Max

KOL NIDREI, FOR TROMBONE AND ORCHESTRA,
[ARR.] see Bruch, Max

KOL NIDREI, FOR VIOLA AND ORCHESTRA,
[ARR.] see Bruch, Max

KOL NIDREI, FOR VIOLIN AND ORCHESTRA,
[ARR.] see Bruch, Max

KOL NIDREI, FOR VIOLONCELLO AND
ORCHESTRA see Bruch, Max

KOLB, BARBARA (1939-   )
Soundings
min sc BOOSEY HPS 931 $35.00 (K180)

KOMISCHE VERFOLGUNG UND FLUCHT see
Becce, Giuseppe

KOMM, SUSSER TOD, [ARR.] see Bach,
Johann Sebastian

KOMM, SUSSER TOD. VARIATIONEN UBER EIN
THEMA VON J.S. BACH see Ahlgrimm,
Hans

KOMMENTARE ZU DREI VENEZIANISCHEN
MADRIGALEN DES HEINRICH SCHUTZ AUS
DEM JAHRE 1611 see Kohler,
Siegfried

KOMMST DU NUN, JESUS, VON HIMMEL
HERUNTER, [ARR.] see Bach, Johann
Sebastian

KOMODIANTEN see Mielenz, Hans

KOMODIE DER UNART see Kont, Paul

KOMOROUS, RUDOLF (1931-   )
Dustere Anmut [6']
1.1.1.0. 1.1.1.0. glock,vla,vcl,
db,electronic tape, prepared
piano
sc UNIVER. UE 15199 $6.25, perf mat
rent   (K181)

Rossi
pic,fl,ob,English horn,2clar,bass
clar,trp,vibra,snare drum,
harmonica,2vla,2vcl, Baroque
organ
study sc UNIVER. 51 15985 $25.00
(K182)

KOMPLIMENTE see Buder, Ernst Erich

KOMPOSITIE see Bondt, Cornelis de

KOMPOSITION, FOR FLUTE AND ORCHESTRA
see Herchet, Jorg

KOMPOSITIONEN, FOR TROMBONE, SOLO VOICE
AND ORCHESTRA see Herchet, Jorg

KONCERTANTNA GLASBA, FOR HORN AND
ORCHESTRA see Ajdic, Alojz

KONCERTANTNA GLASBA, FOR TIMPANI AND
ORCHESTRA see Ramovs, Primoz

KONCERTNA HUDBA, FOR CLARINET AND
ORCHESTRA see Tandler, Juraj

KONECNY, IVAN (1940-   )
Concerto for Piano and Orchestra, Op.
3
2trp,strings,pno solo
SLOV.HUD.FOND O-466 perf mat rent
(K183)

KONFRONTACIE see Hrusovsky, Ivan

KONIG IN THULE, DER, FOR SOLO VOICE AND
ORCHESTRA see Diepenbrock, Alphons

KONIG KRISTIAN II, FOR SOLO VOICE AND
ORCHESTRA see Sibelius, Jean, King
Christian II, For Solo Voice And
Orchestra

KONIG STEPHAN: OVERTURE see Beethoven,
Ludwig van

KONIGIN VON SABA, DIE: BALLET MUSIC see
Goldmark, Karl

KONIGSLIED, DAS see Gilse, Jan van

KONIGSLIEDER WALZER see Strauss,
Johann, [Jr.]

KONSERT-UVERTYR see Robertson, Karl-
Olof

KONSERTANTE MUZIEK, FOR VIOLA AND
ORCHESTRA see Beurden, Bernard van

KONSERTFANTASI NO. 1: RENDEVOUS see
Hundsnes, Svein

KONSTELLATIONEN II see Wengler, Marcel

KONT, PAUL (1920-   )
Concerto for Piano and Orchestra
[16']
2(pic).2+English horn.2+bass
clar.2+contrabsn. 4.2.3.1.
timp,perc,strings,pno solo
sc,pts DOBLINGER rent   (K184)

Drei Altosterreicher-Marsche [9'30"]
2(pic).2(English horn).2(clar in
E flat).2(contrabsn). 4.3.3.1.
perc,strings
sc,pts DOBLINGER rent   (K185)

Komodie Der Unart [16']
2(pic).2(English horn).2(bass
clar).2(contrabsn). 2.2.2.0.
strings
sc,pts DOBLINGER rent   (K186)

Vivaldi-Monument [18']
2(pic).2(English horn).2(bass
clar).2(contrabsn). 4.3.3.0.
strings
sc,pts DOBLINGER rent   (K187)

KONTEMPLATIVA VARIATIONER see
Fredriksson, Lennart

KONTRASTE see Stolzenwald, Otto

KONTRETANZE, ZWOLF see Beethoven,
Ludwig van

KONTRETANZE, ZWOLF, WOO. 14 see
Beethoven, Ludwig van

KONTSKI, ANTOINE DE (1817-1889)
Erwachen Des Lowen, Das *Op.115
1+pic.2.2.2. 4.2.3.0. timp,perc,
strings
sc,pts LIENAU rent   (K188)

KONZERT-ALLEGRO MIT INTRODUKTION, FOR
PIANO AND ORCHESTRA, OP. 134 see
Schumann, Robert (Alexander)

KONZERT-OUVERTURE see Hasenpflug, Curt

KONZERTANTE FANTASIE see Geissler,
Fritz

KONZERTANTE MUSIK, FOR VIOLIN,
VIOLONCELLO AND STRING ORCHESTRA
see Schlemm, Gustav Adolf

KONZERTANTE SERENADE see Jentsch,
Walter

KONZERTANTE SINFONIE see Berghorn,
Alfred

KONZERTANTER TANGO see Kletsch, Ludwig

KONZERTANTES QUARTETT, K. AHN. 9 see
Mozart, Wolfgang Amadeus, Sinfonia
Concertante in E flat, K. 297b

KONZERTARIE, FOR SOLO VOICE AND
ORCHESTRA see Rihm, Wolfgang

KONZERTOUVERTURE see Madsen, Trygve

KONZERTSATZ, FOR PIANO AND ORCHESTRA
(FRAGMENT), ANH. 64 see Mozart,
Wolfgang Amadeus

KONZERTSATZ FOR VIOLIN AND ORCHESTRA IN
C, [ARR.] see Beethoven, Ludwig van

KOPELENT, MAREK (1932-   )
Canto De Li Augei, Il, For Solo Voice
And Orchestra [14']
2(pic).2(English horn).2.2.
1.2.1.0. 4perc,harp,strings,S
solo
BREITKOPF-W perf mat rent   (K189)

Intimissimo [18']
clar,English horn,alto sax,trp,
trom,prepared pno,gtr,perc,
2vln,2vla,vcl,db,opt electronic
tape
BREITKOPF-W perf mat rent   (K190)

Liebliche Musik Mit Einem
Volkstumlichen Motiv, For Cymbal
And Orchestra [22']
2.2+English horn.2.2. 1.2.0.1.
2perc,prepared pno,strings,
cimbalom solo
BREITKOPF-W perf mat rent   (K191)

Plauderstundchen, For Saxophone And
Orchestra [22']
0.pic+alto fl.3+English horn.0.0.
0.5.3.1. 2perc,cimbalom,cel,
prepared pno,4db,alto sax solo
BREITKOPF-W perf mat rent   (K192)

Schweisstuch Der Veronika, Das
(Sonata for Strings) [14']
11strings
BREITKOPF-W perf mat rent   (K193)

Sonata for Strings *see Schweisstuch
Der Veronika, Das

Stilleben [10']
1.1.1.0. 1.1.1.0. perc,pno,
strings
BREITKOPF-W perf mat rent   (K194)

KOPER SYMPHONY, THE see Lovec,
Vladimir, Koprska Simfonija

KOPPEL, HERMAN DAVID (1908-   )
Concerto for Oboe and Orchestra
sc,pts SAMFUNDET 238 perf mat rent
(K195)

Concerto for Orchestra [23']
3.2.3.2. 4.3.3.1. timp,perc,cel,
harp,pno,strings
SAMFUNDET perf mat rent   (K196)

Intrada [8']
3.2.2.2. 4.3.3.1. timp,perc,
strings
SAMFUNDET perf mat rent   (K197)

Prelude To A Symphony
3.3.2.2. 4.3.3.1. timp,perc,
strings
SAMFUNDET perf mat rent   (K198)

KOPRSKA SIMFONIJA see Lovec, Vladimir

KORAAL see Keulen, Geert van

KORAALFANTASIE, OVER PSALM 91, FOR
TRUMPET AND STRING ORCHESTRA see
Braal, Andries de

KORAL IN TOKATA see Ramovs, Primoz

KORINEK, MILOSLAV (1925-   )
Allegro Brilante [5']
3.2.3.2. 4.2.4.1. timp,strings
SLOV.HUD.FOND O-435A perf mat rent
(K199)
Presli Roky, For Solo Voice And
Orchestra [7']
2.2.1.2. 2.2.0.0. timp,perc,cel,
strings,Bar solo
"Years Have Passed, The, For Solo
Voice And Orchestra"
SLOV.HUD.FOND O-488 perf mat rent
(K200)
Years Have Passed, The, For Solo
Voice And Orchestra *see Presli
Roky, For Solo Voice And
Orchestra

KORMANN, H.L.
Arena
RIES f.s.   (K201)

KORN, PETER JONA (1922-   )
Four Pieces *Op.46, CC4U
string orch sc PETERS 8155 $18.00,
pts PETERS $3.75, ea., set PETERS
$20.00   (K202)

Variations On A Tune From "The
Beggar's Opera"
sc BOOSEY $50.00   (K203)

KORNAC, HANS (1939-   )
Keep Going [2']
2.2.4.3.alto sax. 4.2.2.0. vln,
vcl,db
sc DONEMUS f.s., perf mat rent
(K204)

KORPUS ET ANTIKORPUS see Ribeiro,
Agnaldo

KOSKENLASKIAN MORSIAMET, FOR SOLO VOICE
AND ORCHESTRA see Sibelius, Jean

KOSMOCHROMIE I see Giltay, Berend

KOSMOCHROMIE II, FOR STRING QUARTET AND
CHAMBER ORCHESTRA see Giltay,
Berend

KOSUBEK, HERBERT
Blutenzauber
RIES f.s.   (K205)

KOTONSKI, WLODZIMIERZ (1925-   )
Bora
pts MOECK 5224 rent   (K206)

Sirocco
3.3.3.3. 4.3.3.1. 4perc,harp,cel,
strings
[15'] sc,pts MOECK 5242   (K207)

Windrose, Die [13']
2.2.3.2. 4.2.3.1. perc,harp,
strings
sc MOECK 5194 f.s., perf mat rent
(K208)

KOTSCHER, EDMUND
Auf Den Spuren Eines Rehes
RIES f.s.   (K209)

Drei Tempi
RIES f.s.   (K210)

Frisch, Frech, Federleicht
RIES f.s.   (K211)

Im Suden Von Spanien
RIES f.s.   (K212)

Kleine Zugabe
RIES f.s.   (K213)

Lustige Biene
(Plee, J.) RIES f.s.   (K214)

KOUMANS, RUDOLF (1929-   )
Symphony No. 2, Op. 53 [25']
2.2.2.2. 4.2.0.0. timp,strings
DONEMUS perf mat rent   (K215)

KOVACH, ANTON (1915-   )
Symphoniette
string orch
sc EULENBURG E10112 f.s., perf mat
rent   (K216)

KOVACI NA BASCARSIJI see Lavrin, Anton

KOVAROVIC, KAREL (1862-1920)
Slovacka Pisen, For Solo Voice And
Orchestra
LUCKS 02914 sc $3.50, set $7.50,
pts $.75, ea.   (K217)

KOVEN, REGINALD DE
see DE KOVEN, (HENRY LOUIS) REGINALD

KOWALSKI, JULIUS (1912-   )
Buffonesca Piccola
2.2.2.2. 4.3.2.0. timp,perc,
strings
SLOV.HUD.FOND O-436A perf mat rent
(K218)
Concerto for Violin and Chamber
Orchestra
1.1.1.1. 1.0.0.0. perc,strings,
vln solo
SLOV.HUD.FOND O-482A perf mat rent
(K219)
Divertimento in D
gtr,strings,2vln soli
SLOV.HUD.FOND O-476A perf mat rent
(K220)
Elegy
3.3.3.3. 4.2.3.1. timp,4perc,
harp,strings,vcl solo
SLOV.HUD.FOND O-70A perf mat rent
(K221)
Music for Violoncello and Chamber
Orchestra
fl,clar,bsn,4vln,2vla,2vcl,db,vcl
solo
SLOV.HUD.FOND KH-45 perf mat rent
(K222)

KOX, HANS (1930-   )
Allegria, L', For Solo Voice And
Orchestra
3.0.0.0. 0.1.0.0. strings,S solo sc
DONEMUS f.s., perf mat rent
contains: Peso; Sempre Notte;
Solitudine; Stasera; Universo
(K223)

Concertino Chitarristico [15']
2horn,8vln,2vla,2vcl,db,3gtr soli
DONEMUS   (K224)

Concerto for Violin and Orchestra,
No. 2 [18']
0.2.0.0. 2.0.0.0. strings,vln
solo
DONEMUS sc f.s., pts rent   (K225)

Cyclophony VIII
1.1.1.1. 1.0.0.0. strings
sc DONEMUS f.s., perf mat rent
(K226)

Dorian Gray Suite [15']
2.2.2.0. 2.2.0.0. timp,2perc,
harp,strings
DONEMUS sc f.s., pts rent   (K227)

Gedachtnislieder, For Solo Voice And
Orchestra
0.2.1.0. 4.0.0.0. 12vln,8vla,S/T
solo
sc DONEMUS f.s., perf mat rent
(K228)

Gothic Concerto, A, For Harp And
Orchestra [14']
1.0.1.0. 1.0.0.0. 2perc,3vln,
3vla,2vcl,db,harp solo
sc DONEMUS f.s., perf mat rent
(K229)

Peso
see Allegria, L', For Solo Voice
And Orchestra

Sempre Notte
see Allegria, L', For Solo Voice
And Orchestra

Sinfonia Concertante for Violin,
Violoncello and Orchestra
2.0.0.2. 0.2.2.0. strings,vln
solo,vcl solo
sc DONEMUS f.s., perf mat rent
(K230)

Solitudine
see Allegria, L', For Solo Voice
And Orchestra

Stasera
see Allegria, L', For Solo Voice
And Orchestra

Universo
see Allegria, L', For Solo Voice
And Orchestra

Vangoghiana [12']
9cornet,English horn,3perc,
strings, 2bombardon, 2helicon
DONEMUS perf mat rent   (K231)

KOYAMA, KIYOSHIGE (1914-   )
Hina-Uta, No. 2
3(pic).3(English horn).3(soprano
clar in E flat,bass
clar).3(contrabsn). 4.3.3.1.
timp,perc,strings
ONGAKU perf mat rent   (K232)

KOZELUCH, JOHANN ANTON (JAN
EVANGELISTA) (1738-1814)
Concerto for Bassoon and Orchestra in
C, MIN 14
MUS. RARA 41.932 perf mat rent
(K233)

KOZELUCH, LEOPOLD ANTON (1747-1818)
Concerto for Piano 4-Hands and
Orchestra, MIN 45
2ob,2horn,strings,pno 4-hands
soli
(Novak) sc ZANIBON 5699 rent, pts
ZANIBON 5700 rent   (K234)

KRAFT, WILLIAM (1923-   )
Avalanche: Suite [12']
NEW MUSIC WEST perf mat rent (K235)

Concertino for Percussion and Chamber
Orchestra [18']
fl/pic,ob,clar,bsn,horn,trp,trom,
vln,vla,vcl,perc solo
NEW MUSIC WEST perf mat rent (K236)

Concerto for Piano and Orchestra
[25']
NEW MUSIC WEST perf mat rent (K237)

Cornucopia, For Tuba And Orchestra
[18']
NEW MUSIC WEST perf mat rent (K238)

Dream Tunnel, For Narrator And
Orchestra [15']
NEW MUSIC WEST perf mat rent (K239)

KRAFT, WILLIAM (cont'd.)

Mobiles [8']
2pic,2fl,ob,English horn,3clar,
bass clar,Heckelphone,bsn,harp,
pno,vln,vcl,db
NEW MUSIC WEST perf mat rent (K240)

Silent Boughs, For Solo Voice And
String Orchestra [19'30"]
string orch,S solo
NEW MUSIC WEST perf mat rent (K241)

Tintinnabulations: Collage III [10']
NEW MUSIC WEST perf mat rent (K242)

KRATT: SUITE see Tubin, Eduard

KRATZSCHMAR, WILFRIED (1944-   )
Explosionen Und Cantus *see Symphony
No. 2

Symphony No. 1
3.3.3.3. 4.3.3.1. perc,strings
DEUTSCHER perf mat rent   (K243)

Symphony No. 2
4.4.4.4. 6.4.4.2. harp,cel,pno,
timp, perc,strings
sc DEUTSCHER 1714 f.s., perf mat
rent   (K244)

KRAUS, JOSEPH MARTIN (1756-1792)
Symphonies, Six
see SYMPHONY IN SWEDEN, THE, PART 1

Symphony in C minor, MIN 76
2.2.0.0. 4.0.0.0. strings
(Englander, Richard) sc,min sc,pts
REIMERS ER MMS 2 f.s.   (K245)

Symphony in C sharp, MIN 92
2fl,2horn,cont,strings without db
pts,fac ed AUTOGR AM 011 $13.00
(K246)

Symphony in E flat, MIN 91
fl,2ob,bsn,2horn,cont, strings
without vcl, db
fac ed AUTOGR AM 001 $19.00, sc
AUTOGR AM 002 $11.00   (K247)

Tragodie Olympia: Overture [8']
0.2.0.1. 2.0.0.0. strings
MANNHEIM E 3 f.s.   (K248)

KRAUZE, ZYGMUNT (1938-   )
Concerto for Piano and Orchestra
[20']
alto sax,tenor sax,baritone sax,
3horn,2trp,trom,2acord,2elec
gtr,strings,pno solo
sc UNIVER. UE 16805 f.s., solo pt
UNIVER. UE 16807 f.s., perf mat
rent   (K249)

Suite De Danses Et De Chansons, For
Harpsichord And Orchestra [18']
3.3.3.3. 0.0.0.0. 2acord,2mand,
strings,hpsd solo
UNIVER. perf mat rent   (K250)

KREIN, ALEXANDER (1883-1950)
Hebraic Sketches: Suite No. 2 *Op.13
KALMUS A3216 sc $5.00, perf mat
rent, set $12.00, pts $2.00, ea.
(K251)

KREISLER, FRITZ (1875-1962)
Caprice Viennois, [arr.]
(Leidzen) string orch sets FISCHER,
C F1461X $3.50, and up   (K252)

Liebesfreud, [arr.]
(Leidzen) string orch sets FISCHER,
C F1462X $3.50, and up   (K253)

Liebeslied, [arr.]
(Leidzen) string orch sets FISCHER,
C F1463X $3.50, and up   (K254)

Miniature Viennese March, [arr.]
(Leidzen) string orch sets FISCHER,
C F1465X $3.50, and up   (K255)

Schon Rosmarin, [arr.]
(Leidzen) string orch sets FISCHER,
C F1464X $3.50, and up   (K256)

Tambourin Chinois, [arr.]
(Leidzen) string orch sets FISCHER,
C F1466X $3.00, and up   (K257)

KRENEK, ERNST (1900-   )
Arc Of Life *Op.234 [17']
1(pic).1(English horn).1.1.
1.1.1.0. timp,5perc,pno,strings
"Lebensbogen" BAREN. BA 6791 perf
mat rent   (K258)

Concerto for Violin and Orchestra,
No. 1, Op. 29
min sc UNIVER. PH370 $11.00 (K259)

Im Tal Der Zeit *Op.232 [15']
1.1.1(clar in E flat,bass
clar).1. 1.1.1.0. 3perc,gtr,
pno,strings

KRENEK, ERNST (cont'd.)

BAREN. BA 6778 perf mat rent (K260)

Lebensbogen *see Arc Of Life

KREPELA, JOSEF
Paprika-Csardas
RIES f.s.   (K261)

Strasse In Toledo
RIES f.s.   (K262)

KRESANEK, JOZEF (1913-   )
Three Songs, For Solo Voice And
String Orchestra *see Tri
Piesne, For Solo Voice And String
Orchestra

Tri Piesne, For Solo Voice And String
Orchestra [12']
string orch,B solo
"Three Songs, For Solo Voice And
String Orchestra" SLOV.HUD.FOND
0-439A perf mat rent   (K263)

KRETZSCHMAR, CARL
Lustspiel-Ouverture
RIES f.s.   (K264)

KREUTZER, KONRADIN (1780-1849)
Nachtlager In Granada, Das: Evening
Prayer, For Solo Voice And
Orchestra
LUCKS 02983 set $7.50, pts $.75,
ea.   (K265)

Nachtlager In Granada, Das: Overture
BREITKOPF-W perf mat rent   (K266)

KREUZFIDEL POLKA see Strauss, Johann,
[Jr.]

KRIEGERS LIEBCHEN POLKA see Strauss,
Johann, [Jr.]

KRIMINALLEGRO see Bruchmann, Klaus
Peter

KROAIE ENDEN PUYT, DE, FOR SOLO VOICE
AND ORCHESTRA see Bordewijk-
Roepman, Johanna

KROLL, GEORG (1934-   )
Suite De Balades [12']
2.2.2.3.soprano sax. 3.3.3.0.
perc,harp,strings
MOECK 5204 sc f.s., pts rent (K267)

Tode Und Tore
3.3.3.3. 4.3.3.1. perc,harp,pno/
cel,strings,opt speaking voice
[12'-13'] sc,pts MOECK 5248 (K268)

KROMATA DA CAMERA DI PIUS MUSIAE see
Sagvik, Stellan

KRON'IKELZ 70 see Lanza, Alcides E.

KRONUNGSLIEDER. WALZER see Strauss,
Josef

KRONUNGSMARSCH see Meyerbeer, Giacomo

KRONUNGSMARSCH see Strauss, Johann,
[Jr.]

KRONUNGSMARSCH "WILHELM I" see
Meyerbeer, Giacomo

KROPFREITER, AUGUSTINIUS FRANZ
(1936-   )
Sinfonia Concertante for Wind Quintet
and String Orchestra
string orch,fl solo,ob solo,clar
solo,horn solo,bsn solo
sc,pts DOBLINGER rent   (K269)

KRUSE, BJORN
Ja Visst Gjor Det Ont, For Solo Voice
And Chamber Orchestra [8']
1.1.1.1. 3.0.0.0. perc,strings,A
solo
"Yes, It Sure Hurts, For Solo Voice
And Chamber Orchestra" NORGE
(K270)

Velvet And Hemp [7']
12vcl
NORGE   (K271)

Yes, It Sure Hurts, For Solo Voice
And Chamber Orchestra *see Ja
Visst Gjor Det Ont, For Solo
Voice And Chamber Orchestra

KRUYF, TON DE (1937-   )
Meditations On Poems By Dylan Thomas,
For Solo Voice And Orchestra
*Op.34 [25']
pno,strings,Bar solo
DONEMUS perf mat rent   (K272)

Oxnaltsinfonie [15']
4.0.4.0. 0.4.4.0. perc,2harp,pno,
strings
sc DONEMUS f.s., perf mat rent

KRUYF, TON DE (cont'd.)
                              (K273)
Pour Faire Le Portrait D'Un Oiseau,
   For Solo Voice And Orchestra
   1.1.1.1. 1.0.1.0. 2perc,harp,pno,
   vibra/xylo,vcl,db,Mez solo
   sc DONEMUS f.s., perf mat rent
                              (K274)
Quatre Pas De Deux, For Flute And
   Orchestra *Op.30 [15']
   0.0.0.0. 2.2.2.0. 4perc,2harp,
   pno,hpsd,cel,mand,gtr,strings,
   fl solo
   sc DONEMUS f.s., perf mat rent
                              (K275)
String-Time Fantasietta [3'30"]
   8vln,2vla,2vcl,db
   DONEMUS perf mat rent   (K276)

KRYL, BOHUMIR (1874-1961)
Josephine, For Cornet And Orchestra
   [6']
   1.0.2.0. 2.1.1.1. euphonium,perc,
   vln,vcl,db,cornet solo, trap
   set
   MARGUN BP 4010 sc $11.00, pts
   $12.50   (K277)

KUBELIK, RAFAEL (1914-   )
Orphikon [25']
   3.3.3.3. 4.3.3.1. perc,cel,harp,
   strings
   PETERS perf mat rent   (K278)

KUBIN, RUDOLF (1909-1973)
Concerto for Clarinet and Orchestra
   min sc PANTON 119 f.s.   (K279)

KUBIZEK, AUGUSTIN (1918-   )
Concertino De Motu Impari, For
   Clarinet And Orchestra *Op.44,
   No.1 [6']
   2.2.2.2. 2.2.1.0. timp,perc,
   strings,clar solo
   sc,pts DOBLINGER rent   (K280)

Hab Ich Lieb, For Solo Voice, Violin
   And String Orchestra *Op.14b
   string orch,S solo,vln solo sc,pts
   DOBLINGER rent
   contains: Hab Ich Lieb, So Hab
   Ich Not; Ich Schlaf, Ich Wach;
   Winter Ist Ein Scharfer Gast,
   Der; Wo Zwei Herzensliebe
                              (K281)
Hab Ich Lieb, So Hab Ich Not
   see Hab Ich Lieb, For Solo Voice,
   Violin And String Orchestra

Ich Schlaf, Ich Wach
   see Hab Ich Lieb, For Solo Voice,
   Violin And String Orchestra

Winter Ist Ein Scharfer Gast, Der
   see Hab Ich Lieb, For Solo Voice,
   Violin And String Orchestra

Wo Zwei Herzensliebe
   see Hab Ich Lieb, For Solo Voice,
   Violin And String Orchestra

KUGERL, H.
Brunnennymphe, For Violin And
   Orchestra
   KRENN perf mat rent   (K282)

Liebeslied, For Violin And Orchestra
   KRENN perf mat rent   (K283)

Rhapsody for Saxophone and Orchestra
   KRENN perf mat rent   (K284)

Serenade And Tarantella, For Clarinet
   And Orchestra
   KRENN perf mat rent   (K285)

KUHLAU, FRIEDRICH (1786-1832)
Elverhoj: Agnetes Drom
   3.2.2.2. 4.2.1.0. perc,strings
   sc,pts SAMFUNDET 241 perf mat rent
                              (K286)
Elverhoj: Overture
   min sc HANSEN-DEN f.s.   (K287)

KUHN, MAX (1908-1981)
Concierto De Tenerife, For Piano And
   Orchestra
   min sc HUG f.s., perf mat rent
                              (K288)

KUHN, SIEGFRIED
Suite in C [20']
   string orch
   RIES perf mat rent   (K289)

KUHNE, FERDINAND (1858-1939)
Geburtstagsmarsch *Op.41
   1+pic.2.2.2. 4.2.3.0. timp,perc,
   strings
   LIENAU f.s.   (K290)

KUHNL, CLAUS (1957-   )
Monodie *Op.12 [8']
   1.1.0.0. 0.1.1.0. perc,pno,
   strings without db
   sc BREITKOPF-W PB 5101 f.s., perf

KUHNL, CLAUS (cont'd.)

   mat rent   (K291)

Sinfonische Szenen
   1.1.1.1.(ad lib) 1.1.1.0., 3perc,
   pno, 12vln, 2vla, 4vcl, 2db
   BREITKOPF-W perf mat rent (K292)

KULLERVO UND SEINE SCHWESTER see
   Sibelius, Jean

KULLERVOS KLAGE, FOR SOLO VOICE AND
   ORCHESTRA see Sibelius, Jean

KUN PAIVA PAISTAA, FOR SOLO VOICE AND
   ORCHESTRA, [ARR.] see Merikanto,
   Oskar

KUNAD, RAINER (1936-   )
Klopstock-Ode, For Solo Voice And
   Orchestra
   2.2.2.2. 2.3.3.0. timp,perc,
   strings,Bar solo
   (conatum 69) DEUTSCHER perf mat
   rent   (K293)

KUNNEKE, EDUARD (1885-1953)
Jagd-Ouverture *Op.8 [10']
   3(pic).2.3.3. 4.2.3.1. timp,perc,
   strings
   sc RIES f.s., perf mat rent (K294)

KUNST, JOS (1936-   )
Marine, V [11']
   2.1.1.1. 0.2.2.0. 3perc,strings
   sc DONEMUS f.s., perf mat rent
                              (K295)
KUNST DER FUGE, DIE, [ARR.] see Bach,
   Johann Sebastian

KUNST DER FUGE, DIE: CONTRAPUNCTUS NO.
   1, (ARR.) see Bach, Johann
   Sebastian

KUNSTLER QUADRILLE see Strauss, Johann,
   [Jr.]

KUNSTLERLEBEN WALZER see Strauss,
   Johann, [Jr.]

KUNTERBUNT see Dressel, Erwin

KUOLEMAN JOUTSEN, FOR SOLO VOICE AND
   ORCHESTRA see Pylkkanen, Tauno
   Kullervo

KUPKOVIC, LADISLAV (1936-   )
K.u.K. Musik [25']
   4(2pic).4.4.3(contrabsn).
   4.4.5.0. timp,2perc,harp,pno&
   cel,strings
   UNIVER. perf mat rent   (K296)

Marsch, For Violin And Orchestra [6']
   2.2.2.2. 2.1.1.0. timp,perc,
   strings,vln solo
   UNIVER. perf mat rent   (K297)

Morceau De Genre [11']
   trp,timp,string orch,vln solo
   UNIVER. perf mat rent   (K298)

Souvenir, For Violin And String
   Orchestra [6']
   string orch,vln solo
   UNIVER. perf mat rent   (K299)

KUSS, DER: OVERTURE see Smetana,
   Bedrich, Hubicka: Overture

KUSS WALZER see Strauss, Johann, [Jr.]

KUULA, TOIVO (1883-1918)
Impi Ja Pajarin Poika, For Solo Voice
   And Orchestra *Op.18,No.1 [13']
   3.3.3.2. 4.2.3.0. timp,perc,harp,
   strings,S solo
   "Maiden And The Boyar's Son, The"
   FAZER perf mat rent   (K300)

Kesayo Kirkkomaalla, For Solo Voice
   And Orchestra, [arr.] *Op.6,No.1
   (Peter, H.A.) 0.2.2.2. 2.0.0.0.
   harp,strings,solo voice [3']
   FAZER perf mat rent   (K301)

Kohtalo, For Solo Voice And
   Orchestra, [arr.] *Op.23,No.4
   (Peter, H.A.) 1.2.2.2. 2.0.0.0.
   strings,solo voice [2'] FAZER
   perf mat rent   (K302)

Lauantai-Ilta, For Solo Voice And
   Orchestra, [arr.] *Op.24,No.1
   (Peter, H.A.) 2.2.2.2. 2.0.0.0.
   timp,harp,strings,solo voice [4']
   FAZER perf mat rent   (K303)

Lyo Sydan, For Solo Voice And
   Orchestra, [arr.]
   (Peter, H.A.) 0.2.2.2. 2.0.0.0.
   timp,strings,solo voice [1'30"]
   FAZER perf mat rent   (K304)

KUULA, TOIVO (cont'd.)

Maiden And The Boyar's Son, The *see
   Impi Ja Pajarin Poika, For Solo
   Voice And Orchestra

Merenkylpijaneidot, For Solo Voice
   And Orchestra *Op.12,No.1 [7']
   1.2.3.1. 2.2.1.0. timp,2perc,
   harp,strings,S solo
   "Sea-Bathing Maidens, The" FAZER
   perf mat rent   (K305)

Paimenet, For Solo Voice And
   Orchestra, [arr.] *Op.29a,No.3
   (Funtek, L.) 2.1.2.1. 3.2.0.0.
   timp,perc,harp,strings,solo voice
   [4'] FAZER f.s.   (K306)
   (Jalas, J.) 2.2.2.2. 4.3.3.1. timp,
   perc,strings,solo voice [4']
   FAZER f.s.   (K307)

Sea-Bathing Maidens, The *see
   Merenkylpijaneidot, For Solo
   Voice And Orchestra

Sinipiika, For Solo Voice And
   Orchestra, [arr.] *Op.23,No.1
   (Peter, H.A.) 2.2.2.2. 2.0.0.0.
   timp,harp,strings,solo voice [3']
   FAZER perf mat rent   (K308)

Suutelo, For Solo Voice And
   Orchestra, [arr.] *Op.8,No.1
   (Jalas, J.) 2.2.2.2. 2.3.2.0. perc,
   strings,solo voice [5'] FAZER
   perf mat rent   (K309)

Tuijotin Tulehen Kauan, For Solo
   Voice And Orchestra, [arr.]
   *Op.2,No.2
   (Merikanto, A.) 2.2.2.2. 2.2.2.0.
   strings,solo voice [5'] FAZER
   perf mat rent   (K310)

Tule Armaani, For Solo Voice And
   Orchestra, [arr.] *Op.29a,No.1
   (Funtek, L.) 2.2.3.3. 4.0.0.0.
   timp,strings,solo voice [4']
   FAZER perf mat rent   (K311)

Yli Kukkien, For Solo Voice And
   Orchestra, [arr.] *Op.23,No.3
   (Peter, H.A.) 2.2.2.2. 2.0.0.0.
   timp,harp,strings,solo voice [2']
   FAZER perf mat rent   (K312)

Yo-Natt, For Solo Voice And
   Orchestra, [arr.]
   (Peter, H.A.) 2.2.2.2. 2.0.0.0.
   strings,solo voice [2'] FAZER
   perf mat rent   (K313)

KVADE see Blomberg, Erik

KVAM, ODDVAR S.
Communication *see Symphony No. 2

Fra De Unges Verden *Op.46
   3.2.2.2. 4.2.2.1. timp,perc,gtr,
   elec bass,strings
   [14'] sc MUSIKK f.s.   (K314)

Gloselund, For Solo Voice And
   Orchestra *Op.56b [20']
   2.2.2.2(contrabsn). 2.2.2.1.
   perc,timp,strings,solo voice
   NORGE   (K315)

Symphony No. 2 [34']
   3(pic).3(English horn).3(bass
   clar).3(contrabsn). 4.3.3.1.
   timp,perc,harp,strings
   NORGE   (K316)

KVANDAL, JOHAN (1919-   )
Concerto for Oboe and String
   Orchestra, Op. 46
   string orch,ob solo
   sc NORSK NMO 9094A $15.75, perf mat
                              (K317)

Concerto for Violin and Orchestra,
   Op. 52
   2.2.2.2. 4.3.3.1. timp,perc,cel,
   strings,vln solo
   sc NORSK NMO 9293 $52.50   (K318)

Divertimento, Op. 3
   string orch
   NORSK   (K319)

Variations And Fugue *Op.14
   min sc NORSK NMO 8980 $31.50 (K320)

KVERNSLATT, OP. 22A, NO. 2 see
   Saeverud, Harald

KWATRIJNEN EN NACHTSTILTE, FOR SOLO
   VOICE AND STRING ORCHESTRA see
   Beekhuis, Hanna

KYROS see Levy, Marvin David

L

LA MONTAINE, JOHN (1920-)
Colloquy For Strings *Op.21 [13']
string orch
study sc FREDONIA $4.50, perf mat
rent (L1)

Early American Sampler, An *Op.43a
[9']
2+pic.2.2.2. 4.3.3.1. timp,2perc,
strings
FREDONIA sc,pts rent, study sc
$3.50 (L2)

Fragments From The Song Of Songs, For
Solo Voice And Orchestra *Op.29
[26']
2+pic.2+English horn.2.2.
4.3.3.1. timp,2perc,pno/harp,
strings,S solo
FREDONIA voc sc $25.00, sc,pts rent
(L3)

Recitative, Aria And Finale *Op.16a
string orch
study sc FREDONIA $4.50, perf mat
rent (L4)

Wilderness Journal: Symphony *Op.41
[45']
1+pic.1(English horn).2.1.
1.2.2.0. timp,3perc,harp,pno,
strings,B solo,org solo,tape
recorder
FREDONIA study sc $9.50, voc sc
$25.00, sc $135.00 (L5)

LA MOTTE, DIETER DE
see MOTTE, DIETER DE LA

LA ROTELLA, PASQUALE (1880-1963)
Corsaresca [29']
3.3.3.2. 4.3.3.1. timp,perc,
bells,cel,xylo,pno,harp,strings
manuscript CARISCH (L6)

LAAT DE LUIKEN GELOKEN ZIJN see Van
Lier, Bertus

**LAATOKKA, FOR SOLO VOICE AND ORCHESTRA,
[ARR.]** see Merikanto, Oskar

LABOR see Morthenson, Jan W.

LABURDA, JIRI (1931-)
Burlesca, For Horn And Orchestra [7']
2.2(English horn).0.2. 2.0.0.0.
strings,horn solo
RIES perf mat rent (L7)

Concertino for Trumpet and String
Orchestra
string orch,trp solo
sc PRESSER 114-40220 $9.00, perf
mat rent (L8)

**LACHENMANN, HELMUT FRIEDRICH
(1935-)**
Accanto, For Clarinet And Orchestra
[26']
2.0.3.0.contrabsn. 0.2.2.1. timp,
2perc,xylorimba,pno,elec gtr,
strings,electronic tape,clar
solo
BREITKOPF-W perf mat rent (L9)

Tanzsuite Mit Deutschlandlied [30']
4(pic).3.3+bass clar.3+contrabsn.
4.3.3.1. 4perc,harp,pno,
strings,string quar soli
BREITKOPF-W perf mat rent (L10)

LACHIAN DANCES, OP. 2, NOS. 1 & 2 see
Janacek, Leos

LACHMAN, HANS (1906-)
Ouverture "Con Brio" [15']
2.3.2.2. 4.3.3.1. timp,perc,
strings
sc DONEMUS f.s., perf mat rent
(L11)

**LACHRYMAE, FOR VIOLA AND STRING
ORCHESTRA** see Britten, [Sir]
Benjamin

LACOMBE, PAUL (1837-1927)
Aubade A Ninon
string orch,vln solo
KALMUS A4235 solo pt $1.00, sc
$3.00, set $4.00, pts $1.00, ea.
(L12)

Berceuse Gasconne *Op.102,No.1
string orch
KALMUS A5506 sc $2.00, set $5.00,
pts $1.00, ea. (L13)

LACRIMOSA see Castaldo, Joseph F.

LAGUNEN WALZER see Strauss, Johann,
[Jr.]

LAJOVIC, ALEKSANDER (1920-)
Preproste Popevke, For Solo Voice And
Chamber Orchestra [12']
1.1.1(bass clar).1. 1.0.0.0.
strings,solo voice
"Simple Songs, For Solo Voice And
Chamber Orchestra" DRUSTVO
DSS 795 perf mat rent (L14)

Simple Songs, For Solo Voice And
Chamber Orchestra *see Preproste
Popevke, For Solo Voice And
Chamber Orchestra

**LAKE IN ZELENGORA, THE, FOR SOLO VOICE
AND ORCHESTRA** see Markovic,
Adalbert

LAKE: TO ......, THE see Geist, John

**LAKME: AH! VIENS DANS LA FORET, FOR
SOLO VOICE AND ORCHESTRA** see
Delibes, Leo

**LAKME: AIR DES CLOCHETTES, FOR SOLO
VOICE AND ORCHESTRA** see Delibes,
Leo

LAKME: BALLET MUSIC see Delibes, Leo

LAKME: BELL SONG see Delibes, Leo,
Lakme: Air Des Clochettes, For Solo
Voice And Orchestra

**LAKME: FANTAISIE AUX DIVINS MENSONGES,
FOR SOLO VOICE AND ORCHESTRA** see
Delibes, Leo

**LAKME: POURQUOI DANS LES GRANDS BOIS,
FOR SOLO VOICE AND ORCHESTRA** see
Delibes, Leo

LALANDE, MICHEL RICHARD DE
see DELALANDE, MICHEL-RICHARD

LALO, EDOUARD (1823-1892)
Namouna: Suite No. 1
2.2.2.4. 4.0.3.1. timp,perc,
2harp,strings
sc,pts HAMELLE f.s. (L15)

Namouna: Suite No. 2
2.2.2.4. 4.4.3.1. timp,perc,
2harp,strings
pts HAMELLE f.s. (L16)

Namouna: Valse De La Cigarette
2.2.2.2. 4.0.0.0. timp,strings
sc,pts HAMELLE f.s. (L17)

Rhapsody
LUCKS 06025 sc $10.00, set $32.00,
pts $1.60, ea. (L18)

Roi D'Ys, Le: Vainement Ma Bien
Aimee, For Solo Voice And
Orchestra
LUCKS 02125 sc $3.75, set $7.50,
pts $.75, ea. (L19)

Symphonie Espagnole, For Violin And
Orchestra *Op.21
BROUDE BR. set $40.00, pts $1.75,
ea. (L20)
LUCKS 00515 sc $11.00, set $34.00,
min sc $3.75, pts $1.70, ea.
(L21)
Symphony in G minor
KALMUS 4475 sc $40.00, set $70.00
(L22)

LAMAN, WIM (1946-)
Canto Infernale, For Soprano And
Orchestra [20']
2.0.3.2.Heckelphone.baritone sax.
4.3.3.1. 2perc,strings without
db,S solo
DONEMUS perf mat rent (L23)

Contravolution [20'40"]
4.4.6.4.2A rec. 8.5.4.2. 3perc,
2harp,Hamm,strings,electronic
tape
DONEMUS perf mat rent (L24)

Fleurs Du Mal, For Solo Voice And
Orchestra [21']
2.2.3.2.2sax. 4.2.2.1. 3perc,
10vla,8vcl,vln solo,Mez/A solo
DONEMUS (L25)

Gevecht, Het, For Solo Voice And
Orchestra [27'30"]
1.0.2.0. 1.1.1.0. 2perc,hpsd/cel/
pno,harp,vln,vla,vcl,electronic
tape,Bar solo
"Struggle, The" DONEMUS perf mat
rent (L26)

Musica, Ars Subtilior, For Viola And
Orchestra [13']
0.2.3.2.basset horn.2alto sax.
2.2.2.0. perc, vla solo (ampl.)
sc DONEMUS f.s., perf mat rent
(L27)

LAMAN, WIM (cont'd.)
Rito [14']
2.2.3.2. 2.2.2.1. 3perc,harp,
strings
DONEMUS sc f.s., pts rent (L28)

Struggle, The *see Gevecht, Het, For
Solo Voice And Orchestra

Wahnfried [14']
3.3.3.3. 6.3.3.2. 5perc,strings
DONEMUS sc f.s., pts rent (L29)

LAMB, JOSEPH F. (1887-1960)
Ragtime Nightingale, [arr.]
(Schuller, Gunther) 1.1.1.1.
1.1.1.1. perc,pno,strings [4'30"]
sc,pts MARGUN MM-2 $12.00, sc
MARGUN $2.50, pts MARGUN $.75,
ea. (L30)

LAMBRO, PHILLIP (1935-)
Miraflores [5'30"]
string orch
WIMBLEDN W1180 sc $9.50, pts $1.00,
ea. (L31)

Structures [8'30"]
string orch
WIMBLEDN W1250 sc $20.00, pts
$2.50, ea. (L32)

Two Pictures For Percussionist And
Orchestra [13']
2.2.2.2. 2.2.2.0. cel,harp,pno,
strings,perc solo
sc WIMBLEDN $34.50, perf mat rent
(L33)

LAMENT, FOR SOLO VOICE AND ORCHESTRA
see Habbestad, Kjell

LAMENT FOR A MOON CHILD see Minor,
Eugene

LAMENTO see Tabakov, Emil

**LAMENTO, FOR CLARINET AND STRING
ORCHESTRA** see Hillborg, Anders

**LAMENTO "ACH, DASS ICH WASSERS GNUG
HATTE", FOR SOLO VOICE AND
ORCHESTRA** see Bach, Johann
Christoph

LAMENTO D'ARIANNA see Monteverdi,
Claudio

LAMENTO PER ARCHI see Visser, Peter

LAMIA, FOR SOLO VOICE AND ORCHESTRA see
Druckman, Jacob Raphael

LAMPARTER, OMAR
Budapest
RIES f.s. (L34)

Serrara Fontana
RIES f.s. (L35)

LAND DER BERGE, LAND AM STROME see
Mozart, Wolfgang Amadeus

LAND DER NACHT see Koch-Raphael, Erwin

**LAND OF THE LEAL, THE, FOR SOLO VOICE
AND ORCHESTRA**
LUCKS 03052 sc $4.00, set $12.00, pts
$.75, ea. (L36)

LANDES FARBEN see Strauss, Johann,
[Jr.]

LANDLERISCHE TANZE, SECHS, WOO. 15 see
Beethoven, Ludwig van

LANDLERMUSIK see Borschel, Erich

LANDLICHE HUMORESKE see Stanke, Willy

LANDLICHE SUITE see Buder, Ernst Erich

LANDLICHE TANZE see Paulsen, Helmut

LANDLICHER TANZ see Gutzeit, Erich

LANDOWSKI, MARCEL (1915-)
Horologe, L' [18']
SALABERT perf mat rent (L37)

LANDRE, GUILLAUME (1905-1968)
Groet Der Martelaren, For Solo Voice
And Orchestra [10']
3.2.2.2. 4.2.3.1. timp,perc,
strings,Bar solo
sc DONEMUS f.s., perf mat rent
(L38)

LANDSCAPE see Gaathaug, Morten

LANDSCAPES see Hoddinott, Alun

LANDSCAPES see Maros, Rudolf

LANG, ISTVAN (1933-　　)
　Concerto for Violin and Orchestra
　　orch,vln solo
　　(special import only) sc EMB 10225
　　f.s.　　　　　　　　　　　　(L39)

LANG, IVANA (1919-　　)
　Four Bagatelles
　　harp,strings
　　DRUS.HRVAT.SKLAD. f.s.　　　(L40)

LANG, JOHANN GEORG (1724-1794)
　Sinfonia in G
　　0.0.0.0. 2.0.0.0. strings
　　(Portius, F.) KALMUS A1106 set
　　$5.00, pts $.75, ea.　　　　(L41)

LANG, WALTER (1896-1966)
　Festliche Sonate *Op.25 [6']
　　string orch
　　RIES perf mat rent　　　　　(L42)

　Scherzo Fugato *Op.30
　　string orch sc HUG GH8550 f.s.,
　　perf mat rent　　　　　　　(L43)

LANGEY, OTTO
　Mandolina
　　(Puerner) LUCKS set $8.00, pts
　　$.75, ea.　　　　　　　　　(L44)

LANGGARD, RUED (1893-1953)
　Symphony No. 4
　　sc SAMFUNDET 187 perf mat rent
　　　　　　　　　　　　　　　(L45)

LANGSAMER WALZER see Kletsch, Ludwig

LANNER, JOSEF (1801-1843)
　Hofballtanze *Op.161
　　KALMUS 5201 pno-cond sc $2.00, set
　　$15.00, pts $1.00, ea., cmplt ed
　　rent　　　　　　　　　　　(L46)

　Schonbrunner Walzer, Die *Op.200
　　1+pic.1.2.1. 2.2+opt 4trp.1.1.
　　timp,perc,strings
　　sc,pts LIENAU rent　　　　　(L47)
　　LUCKS set $14.00, pts $.95, ea.
　　　　　　　　　　　　　　　(L48)
　　(Hruby, V.) CRANZ f.s.　　(L49)

LANZA, ALCIDES E. (1929-　　)
　Kron'ikelz 70 [15']
　　orch,2 narrators, electronic
　　sounds and electronic
　　extensions
　　BOOSEY perf mat rent　　　(L50)

LAPORTE, ANDRE (1931-　　)
　Icarus' Flight, For Piano And Chamber
　　Orchestra [10']
　　1(pic).1.1.1. 1.1.1.0. 2vln,vla,
　　vcl,db,pno solo
　　BREITKOPF-W perf mat rent　(L51)

　Morte Chitarre, Le, For Solo Voice
　　And Instrumental Ensemble
　　fl,14strings,T solo
　　TONOS 7242　　　　　　　　(L52)

　Transit [15']
　　24vln,10vla,8vcl,6db
　　BREITKOPF-W perf mat rent　(L53)

LARGE SINFONICO see Skalkottas, Nikos

LARGHETTO, [ARR.] see Handel, George
　Frideric

LARGHETTO (FRAGMENT), ANH. 69 see
　Mozart, Wolfgang Amadeus

LARGHETTO NACH MOZART, FOR VIOLIN AND
　ORCHESTRA see Wilhelmj, August

LARGO, [ARR.] see Handel, George
　Frideric, Serse: Ombra Mai Fu,
　[arr.]

L'ARGO (DECEMBER) IN B FLAT MINOR, FOR
　TENOR SAXOPHONE, PIANO AND STRING
　ORCHESTRA see Sivertsen, Kenneth

LARGO DOLOROSO, [ARR.] see Chopin,
　Frederic

LARGO TRAGICO, [ARR.] see Chopin,
　Frederic

LARSSON, S. ROGER (1955-　　)
　Aubade Marine, For Violoncello And
　　Orchestra
　　2.2.2.3. 2.1.2.1. perc,harp,
　　strings,vcl solo
　　STIM　　　　　　　　　　　(L54)

　Concerto for Piano and Orchestra
　　[35']
　　2.2.2.2. 1.2.2.1. timp,perc,
　　strings,pno solo
　　sc STIM perf mat rent　　　(L55)

LAST NIGHT THE NIGHTINGALE WOKE ME, FOR
　SOLO VOICE AND ORCHESTRA see
　Kjerulf, Halfdan

LAST SPRING see Grieg, Edvard Hagerup,
　Letzter Fruhling, For Solo Voice
　And String Orchestra

LATTUADA, FELICE (1882-1962)
　Cimitero Di Guerra [3']
　　2.3.3.3. 4.3.3.1. timp,perc,cel,
　　2harp,strings
　　manuscript CARISCH　　　　(L56)

LAUANTAI-ILTA, FOR SOLO VOICE AND
　ORCHESTRA, [ARR.] see Kuula, Toivo

LAUDA see Farina, Guido

LAUDA CONCERTATA, FOR MARIMBA AND
　ORCHESTRA see Ifukube, Akira

LAUDATE PUERI, FOR SOLO VOICES AND
　STRING ORCHESTRA see Lotti, Antonio

LAUDI see Mathias, William

LAUDON SYMPHONY see Haydn, [Franz]
　Joseph, Symphony No. 69 in C

LAUFER, KENNETH (1943-　　)
　Twelve Note Rag, The, [arr.]
　　(Schuller, Gunther) 1.1.1.1.
　　1.1.1.1. perc,pno,gtr,2vln,vla,
　　vcl,db, trap set [4'30"] sc
　　MARGUN BP 4011 $7.50, perf mat
　　rent　　　　　　　　　　　(L57)

LAULELMIA SAIMAALTA, FOR SOLO VOICE AND
　ORCHESTRA see Borg, Kim

LAULUA ALEKSIS KIVEN SANOIHIN, 7, FOR
　SOLO VOICE AND ORCHESTRA see Borg,
　Kim

LAUNIGE GROTESKE see Hub, Franz Peter

LAURO, ANTONIO (1917-　　)
　Concerto for Guitar and Orchestra
　　[20']
　　2.1+English horn.1.1. 2.1.0.0.
　　timp,cym,marimba,tamb,strings,
　　gtr solo
　　sc ZANIBON 5873 f.s., pts ZANIBON
　　5874 rent　　　　　　　　　(L58)

LAUSCHIGE NACHTE see Ailbout, Hans

LAUT UND TRAUT POLKA see Strauss,
　Eduard

LAUTENSCHLAGER, W.
　Sonntag Im Heidedorf
　　RIES f.s.　　　　　　　　　(L59)

LAVAGNINO, ANGELO FRANCESCO (1909-　　)
　Annunciazione, L' [3']
　　string orch
　　manuscript CARISCH　　　　(L60)

　Concerto for Oboe and Orchestra [14']
　　perc,cel,pno,strings,ob solo
　　manuscript CARISCH　　　　(L61)

　Concerto for Violin and Orchestra
　　[32']
　　2.2.2.2. 4.2.2.0. timp,perc,cel,
　　harp,strings,vln solo
　　manuscript CARISCH　　　　(L62)

　Ouverture Per La Locandiera Di
　　Goldoni [6']
　　2.2.2.2. 2.2.0.0. timp,perc,
　　strings
　　manuscript CARISCH　　　　(L63)

　Tempo Alto [18']
　　3.3.3.3. 4.3.3.1. timp,perc,cel,
　　2harp,strings
　　manuscript CARISCH　　　　(L64)

　Volo d'api [3']
　　3.2.2.2. 2.2.2.0. timp,perc,cel,
　　harp,strings
　　manuscript CARISCH　　　　(L65)

LAVRIN, ANTON (1908-1965)
　Bascarsija Blacksmiths, The *see
　　Kovaci Na Bascarsiji

　Kovaci Na Bascarsiji [12']
　　2(pic).2(English horn).2(bass
　　clar).2(contrabsn). 4.2.3.1.
　　timp,2perc,pno,harp,strings
　　"Bascarsija Blacksmiths, The"
　　DRUSTVO DSS 512 perf mat rent
　　　　　　　　　　　　　　　(L66)

LAWHEAD, D.V.
　Aleost
　　string orch
　　KERBY set $22.00, sc $4.00　(L67)

LAWSON'S MATES see Dreyfus, George

LAYERS OF TIME see Bloch, Augustyn,
　Warstwy Czasu

LAZAROF, HENRI (1932-　　)
　Concerto for Orchestra
　　study sc MERION $12.50　　(L68)

　Sinfonietta for Chamber Orchestra
　　study sc MERION $25.00　　(L69)

　Symphony
　　sc MERION 446-41036 $20.00　(L70)

LAZZARI, F.
　Sonata a 6
　　2trp,strings,cont
　　MUS. RARA 1922B f.s.　　　(L71)

LEBEN IST DOCH SCHON WALZER, DAS see
　Strauss, Eduard

LEBEN LANG, EIN see Crucius, Heinz

LEBENSBOGEN see Krenek, Ernst, Arc Of
　Life

LEBENSFREUDE see Schumann, Georg

LEBENSWECKER WALZER see Strauss,
　Johann, [Jr.]

LEBIC, LOJZE (1934-　　)
　Tangram [14']
　　1(pic,rec).1.1(bass clar).0.
　　1.1.1.0. perc,harp,pno,strings
　　DRUSTVO DSS 851 perf mat rent (L72)

LEBRUN, LUDWIG AUGUST (1746-1790)
　Concerto for Oboe and Orchestra, No.
　　1, in D minor
　　orch,ob solo sc EUR.AM.MUS. 71U0090
　　$24.00, set EUR.AM.MUS.
　　71U0090SET $22.00, pts
　　EUR.AM.MUS. $3.00, ea.　　(L73)

LECHNER, KONRAD (1911-　　)
　Facettes [13']
　　2.(ad lib:pic, alfl)
　　2.2(bsclr).2. 2.2.2.1. 2perc,
　　harp, cel, strings
　　BREITKOPF-W perf mat rent　(L74)

LECLAIR, JEAN MARIE (1697-1764)
　Concerto for Violin and String
　　Orchestra, Op. 7, No. 2, in D
　　string orch,cont,vln solo
　　(Paillard, J.F.) sc,pts COSTALL
　　f.s.　　　　　　　　　　　(L75)

　Concerto for Violin and String
　　Orchestra, Op. 7, No. 3, in C
　　string orch,cont,vln/fl/ob solo
　　pts RICORDI-IT 519 f.s., pno red
　　RICORDI-IT 518 f.s.　　　(L76)

　Concerto for Violin and String
　　Orchestra, Op. 10, No. 2, in A
　　string orch,cont,vln solo
　　(Paillard, J.F.) sc,pts COSTALL
　　f.s.　　　　　　　　　　　(L77)

　Concerto for Violin and String
　　Orchestra, Op. 10, No. 6, in G
　　minor
　　string orch,cont,vln solo
　　(Paillard, J.F.) sc,pts COSTALL
　　f.s.　　　　　　　　　　　(L78)

　Gavotte in C minor (from Le Tombeau,
　　[arr.])
　　(Simpson) string orch,cont [3']
　　PETERS H 75 f.s., perf mat rent
　　　　　　　　　　　　　　　(L79)

　Sonata, MIN 94, [arr.]
　　string orch KALMUS A1046 sc $7.50,
　　set $7.50, pts $1.50, ea.　(L80)

LEDENJOV, ROMAN (1930-　　)
　Notturni [7']
　　1.1.1.1. 1.0.0.0. strings
　　sc UNIVER. UE 15773 f.s., perf mat
　　rent　　　　　　　　　　　(L81)

LEES, BENJAMIN (1924-　　)
　Concerto for Orchestra
　　sc BOOSEY $40.00　　　　　(L82)

　Interlude
　　string orch
　　sc BOOSEY $10.00, ipr　　　(L83)

　Passacaglia [24']
　　3.2.2.3. 4.3.3.1. timp,perc,pno,
　　strings
　　min sc BOOSEY HPS 930 $17.00 (L84)

　Prologue, Capriccio And Epilogue
　　sc BOOSEY $20.00　　　　　(L85)

　Scarlatti Portfolio [25']
　　2.2.2.2. 2.2.1.0. timp,perc,
　　strings
　　BOOSEY perf mat rent　　　(L86)

　Spectrum
　　min sc BOOSEY 942 $12.00　(L87)

LEEUW, CHARLES VAN DER (1952-   )
Behind The Veils Of Words [25']
1.0.1.0.2sax. 0.1.1.1. timp,perc,
pno,strings,opt solo voice
sc DONEMUS f.s., perf mat rent
(L88)

LEEUW, REINBERT DE (1938-   )
Abschied [22']
4.4.5.5.2sax. 8.5.4.2. timp,perc,
2harp,pno,strings
DONEMUS perf mat rent   (L89)

LEEUW, TON DE (1926-   )
Brabant, For Solo Voice And Orchestra
[10']
3.3.3.3. 4.3.3.1. timp,2perc,
harp,cel,strings,med solo
sc DONEMUS f.s., perf mat rent
(L90)

Haiku II, For Solo Voice And
Orchestra [12']
4.4.4.4. 4.4.4.1. 4perc,strings,S
solo
sc DONEMUS f.s., perf mat rent
(L91)

LEFEBVRE, CLAUDE
Cheminements [6']
8vln,3vla,3vcl,2db
SALABERT   (L92)

LEGEND OF THE MEGALITHS see Dorward,
David

LEGENDE see Bleyle, Karl

LEGENDE see Kick-Kletzki

LEGENDE, FOR VIOLIN AND ORCHESTRA see
Wieniawski, Henryk

LEGENDE D'AMOUR see Becce, Giuseppe

LEGENDES see Rekola, Jukka

LEGGENDA E TRIPARTITA see Mortari,
Virgilio

LEGRENZI, GIOVANNI (1626-1690)
Totila: Tosto Dal Vicin Bosco, For
Solo Voice And Orchestra [5']
0.0.0.0. 0.1.0.0. timp,strings,
solo voice
manuscript CARISCH   (L93)

LEHAR, FRANZ (1870-1948)
Gold And Silver Waltz *see Gold Und
Silber Walzer

Gold Und Silber Walzer
KALMUS 5404 sc $1.50, perf mat
rent, set $23.00, pts $1.00, ea.
(L94)
"Gold And Silver Waltz" LUCKS 06073
set $24.00, pts $1.00, ea.   (L95)

Lustige Witwe, Die: Vilia, For Solo
Voice And Orchestra
"Merry Widow, The: Vilia" LUCKS
02838 sc $4.00, set $9.50, pts
$.75, ea.   (L96)

Merry Widow, The: Vilia *see Lustige
Witwe, Die: Vilia, For Solo Voice
And Orchestra

LEHMANN, HANS ULRICH (1937-   )
Kammermusik I "Hommage A Mozart"
[15']
2(pic,alto fl).2.1+bass clar.1.
3.2.1.0. timp,perc,cel,5vla,
4vcl,3db
BREITKOPF-W perf mat rent   (L97)

Kammermusik II [13']
2.2.2.1. 2.2.0.0. 2perc,2vcl,2db
BREITKOPF-W perf mat rent   (L98)

LEHNER, FRANZ XAVER (1904-   )
Veni Sancti Spiritu, For Organ And
Orchestra [20']
2.2.2.2. 4.2.3.1. timp,perc,harp,
16vln,4vla,4vcl,4db,org solo
ORLANDO f.s.   (L99)

LEIBOWITZ, RENE (1913-1972)
Concerto for Violoncello and
Orchestra, Op. 58 [16']
orch,vcl solo
MOBART sc $25.00, pts rent   (L100)

LEICHTE KAVALLERIE: OVERTURE see Suppe,
Franz von

LEICHTES BLUT see Strauss, Johann,
[Jr.]

LEITARTICKEL, DIE. WALZER see Strauss,
Johann, [Jr.]

LEKEU, GUILLAUME (1870-1894)
Adagio, Op. 3
string orch
LUCKS sc $3.00, set $4.75, pts
$.95, ea.   (L101)

LENAU-FANTASIEN, FOR VIOLONCELLO AND
CHAMBER ORCHESTRA see Winbeck,
Heinz

LENDVAY, KAMILLO (1928-   )
Pezzo Concertato, For Violoncello And
Orchestra
orch,vcl solo
(special import only) sc EMB 10203
f.s.   (L102)

LENOT, JACQUES (1945-   )
A.S.C. [20']
3.2.4.1. 0.0.0.0. 3vln,2vla,2vcl,
db
RICORDI-FR R.2222 perf mat rent
(L103)

Concerto for Piano and Orchestra
[22']
3.3.3.3. 4.4.3.1. harp,pno,cel/
org,6vln,3vla,3vcl,3db,pno solo
sc ZERBONI 8142 f.s., pts ZERBONI
8143 rent   (L104)

De Par Les Rues, La Memoire, For
Flute, Piano And String Orchestra
[17']
string orch,fl solo,pno solo
sc ZERBONI 8171 f.s., pts ZERBONI
8172 rent   (L105)

Esprit Des Lieux, L': Premiere Livre
[17']
alto fl,English horn,clar,bass
clar,bsn,2horn,trom,2vln,vla,
vcl,db,clar in A solo
SALABERT perf mat rent   (L106)

Im Frohlichen Ton [10']
12vcl
SALABERT   (L107)

Sonata da Camera [13']
fl,ob,clar,bsn,horn,pno,2vln,vla,
vcl,db
sc ZERBONI 8276 f.s., pts ZERBONI
8277 rent   (L108)

Symphony [46']
4.4.4.4. 6.4.4.1. timp,harp,pno&
cel,3perc,strings
sc ZERBONI 8224 f.s., pts ZERBONI
8225 rent   (L109)

LENTEDANS see Beekhuis, Hanna

LENTEREGEN, DE see Pluister, Simon

LENTZ, NICOLAAS
Concerto for Harpsichord and String
Orchestra, No. 2
string orch,hpsd solo
sc,pts HARMONIA 1884 f.s.   (L110)

LENZ, DER, FOR SOLO VOICE AND ORCHESTRA
see Hildach, Eugen

LENZWIND see Friis, Borge

LEO, LEONARDO (ORONZO SALVATORE DE)
(1694-1744)
Concerti, For Violoncello And String
Orchestra, Three *CC3U
(Geiringer, Karl) string orch,hpsd,
vcl solo sc,pts PRESSER $8.00
(L111)

Nozze Di Psiche Con Amore, Le:
Sinfonia [5']
2ob,2trp,cont,strings
(Pastore, G.A.) sc ZANIBON 4312
f.s., pts ZANIBON 4313 f.s.
(L112)

Olimpiade: Sinfonia [6']
2ob,2horn,cont,strings
(Pastore, G.A.) sc ZANIBON 4309
f.s., pts ZANIBON 4310 f.s.
(L113)

Santa Elena Al Calvario: Sinfonia,
[arr.]
(Kretzschmar) 2.2.2.2. 2.0.0.0.
strings [5'] KALMUS 5240 sc
$4.00, perf mat rent, set $10.00,
pts $.75, ea.   (L114)

LEONCAVALLO, RUGGIERO (1858-1919)
Mattinata, For Solo Voice And
Orchestra
"'Tis The Day" KALMUS 5320 pno-cond
sc $1.50, set $8.00, pts $.75,
ea., cmplt ed rent   (L115)
"Tis The Day" LUCKS 02093 sc $4.00,
set $8.00, pts $.75, ea.   (L116)

Pagliacci, I: Intermezzo
LUCKS 05440 sc $6.50, set $18.00,
pts $.95, ea.   (L117)

Pagliacci, I: Prologo, For Solo Voice
And Orchestra
(Jungnickel) LUCKS 02050 sc $7.50,
set $20.00, pts $1.15, ea. (L118)

Pagliacci, I: Qual Fiamma Avea Nel
Guardo, For Solo Voice And
Orchestra
LUCKS 02696 sc $3.75, set $7.50,

LEONCAVALLO, RUGGIERO (cont'd.)

pts $.75, ea.   (L119)

Pagliacci, I: Serenata, "O
Colombina", For Solo Voice And
Orchestra
LUCKS 03122 sc $3.75, set $5.00,
pts $.75, ea.   (L120)

Pagliacci, I: Vesti La Giubba - Ridi
Pagliaccio, For Solo Voice And
Orchestra
LUCKS 02023 sc $3.75, set $7.50,
pts $.75, ea.   (L121)

'Tis The Day *see Mattinata, For
Solo Voice And Orchestra

LEONORE OVERTURE NO. 1 see Beethoven,
Ludwig van

LEONORE OVERTURE NO.3 see Beethoven,
Ludwig van

LEONTOVICH, M.
Carol Of The Bells
2+pic.2.2.2. 4.3.3.1. timp,2perc,
harp,cel&pno,strings
(Wilhousky, Peter; Hayman, Richard)
FISCHER,C set $25.00, and up, pts
$1.00, ea., sc $5.00, pno-cond sc
$2.50   (L122)

LEOPOLDSTADTER POLKA see Strauss,
Johann, [Jr.]

LERNEN VON see Huber, Nicolaus A.

LERSEN, FRED
Frage Nicht
RIES f.s.   (L123)

Lied Des Fischers
RIES f.s.   (L124)

Schlafe Ein, Traume Suss
RIES f.s.   (L125)

LERSTAD, TERJE B.
Concerto for Clarinet and Orchestra,
No. 5, Op. 87 [17']
1.2(English horn).2.2(contrabsn).
2.2.0.2. perc,strings,clar solo
NORGE   (L126)

Concerto for Piccolo and Orchestra,
Op. 132 [31'30"]
0.2.0.4. 4.1.4.0. 2flugelhorn,
perc,strings,2rec,pic solo
NORGE   (L127)

Concerto for Trombone and Orchestra,
Op. 126 [23']
4.3.4.3.baritone sax. 4.2.0.2.
perc,strings,rec, saxhorn, trb
solo
NORGE   (L128)

Three Dances, For Clarinet And String
Orchestra *Op.12 [7']
string orch,clar solo
NORGE   (L129)

LESCHETIZKY, WALTER
Im Kurpark
RIES f.s.   (L130)

Kapriziose Polka
RIES f.s.   (L131)

LESUR, DANIEL (1908-   )
Symphonie "D'Ombre Et De Lumiere"
[20']
AMPHION A281 sc $95.00, pts rent
(L132)

Variations for Piano and String
Orchestra
string orch,pno solo
sc,pts COSTALL f.s.   (L133)

LETELIER LLONA, ALFONSO (1912-   )
Cuatro Canciones De Cuna, For Solo
Voice And Orchestra
fl,clar,harp/pno,strings,solo
voice
"Four Cradle Songs, For Solo Voice
And Orchestra" [Span] sc PEER
$8.00   (L134)

Four Cradle Songs, For Solo Voice And
Orchestra *see Cuatro Canciones
De Cuna, For Solo Voice And
Orchestra

LETTERS TO JANEK, FOR SOLO VOICE AND
ORCHESTRA see Mikula, Zdenko, Pisma
K Janeku, For Solo Voice And
Orchestra

LETTRE, FOR SOLO VOICE AND ORCHESTRA
see Mul, Jan

LETZTER FRUHLING, FOR SOLO VOICE AND
STRING ORCHESTRA see Grieg, Edvard
Hagerup

LEVINSON, GERALD (1951-   )
   Light Dances - Stones Sing [22']
      fl&pic,ob&English horn,2clar,bsn,
      2trp,horn,bass trom,3perc,pno&
      cel,2vln,vla,vcl,db
      sc MARGUN MM 49 $40.00, perf mat
         rent   (L135)

LEVY, MARVIN DAVID (1932-   )
   Canto De Los Marranos, For Solo Voice
      And Orchestra [28']
      2.2.2.2. 2.1.1.0. harp,pno,cel,
      timp,perc,strings,S solo, elec
      kbd
      BOOSEY perf mat rent   (L136)

   Kyros
      sc BOOSEY $7.50   (L137)

LEWALTER, JOHANN
   Schwalmer Tanze, [arr.]
      (Dressel, Erwin) sc RIES f.s.
                                     (L138)

LHASA see Rekola, Jukka

LHOTKA-KALINSKI, IVO (1913-   )
   Funeral Music, For Solo Voice And
      Orchestra
      2.1.1.2. 2.2.1.0. timp,perc,
      strings,solo voice
      DRUS.HRVAT.SKLAD. f.s.   (L139)

LIADOV, ANATOL KONSTANTINOVICH
      (1855-1914)
   Baba Yaga *Op.56
      LUCKS 09117 sc $8.50, set $28.00,
      pts $1.40, ea.   (L140)

   Eight Russian Folksongs *Op.58
      BROUDE BR. sc $15.00, set $22.50,
      pts $1.75, ea.   (L141)
      LUCKS 06087 sc $9.00, set $18.00,
      min sc $2.50, pts $1.40, ea.
                                     (L142)
      min sc INTERNAT. 685 $4.25   (L143)

   Enchanted Lake *Op.62
      LUCKS 06086 sc $8.50, set $18.00,
      min sc $2.00, pts $1.40, ea.
                                     (L144)
      min sc INTERNAT. 715 $4.25   (L145)

   Intermezzo, Op. 8
      INTERNAT. perf mat rent   (L146)

   Jour De Fete *see Glazunov,
      Alexander Konstantinovich

   Kikimora *Op.63
      LUCKS 08527 sc $8.50, set $23.00,
      min sc $2.50, pts $1.40, ea.
                                     (L147)
   Mazurka, Op. 19
      KALMUS A4624 sc $12.00, perf mat
      rent, set $23.00, pts $1.00, ea.
                                     (L148)
   Musical Snuff Box, The, [arr.]
      sc LUCKS 06088 $9.50   (L149)

   Vendredis Polka, Les *see Glazunov,
      Alexander Konstantinovich

LIBELLE, DIE see Strauss, Josef

LIBELLE, DIE, FOR SOLO VOICE AND
   ORCHESTRA, [ARR.] see Sibelius,
   Jean

LIBELLEN WALZER see Strauss, Johann,
   [Jr.]

LIBERATION see Zimmer, Jan, Oslobodenie

LIBERTY BELL MARCH, THE see Sousa, John
   Philip

LICHTZWANG, FOR VIOLIN AND ORCHESTRA
   see Rihm, Wolfgang

LIE UND WEIN see Strauss, Josef

LIEBES MANDEL, WO IS'S BANDEL, FOR SOLO
   VOICES AND ORCHESTRA see Mozart,
   Wolfgang Amadeus

LIEBES WORT, EIN see Kaschubec, Erich

LIEBESFREUD, [ARR.] see Kreisler, Fritz

LIEBESLIED see Erhardt, Siegfried

LIEBESLIED, FOR VIOLIN AND ORCHESTRA
   see Kugerl, H.

LIEBESLIED, [ARR.] see Kreisler, Fritz

LIEBESLIEDER OHNE WORTE see Geisler,
   Willy

LIEBESLIEDER WALZER see Strauss,
   Johann, [Jr.]

LIEBESLIEDERWALZER, [ARR.] see Brahms,
   Johannes

LIEBESPROBE ODER DIE REKRUTIERUNG, DIE
   see Mozart, Wolfgang Amadeus

LIEBESTRAUM see Blon, Franz von

LIEBESTRAUM, [ARR.] see Liszt, Franz

LIEBESVERBOT, DAS: OVERTURE see Wagner,
   Richard

LIEBESWERBEN see Derksen, Bernard

LIEBESZAUBER POLKA see Strauss, Eduard

LIEBLICHE MUSIK MIT EINEM
   VOLKSTUMLICHEN MOTIV, FOR CYMBAL
   AND ORCHESTRA see Kopelent, Marek

LIEBSTER JESU, DEINE LIEBE, FOR SOLO
   VOICE AND STRING ORCHESTRA see
   Stolzel, Gottfried Heinrich

LIEBSTER JESU, KEHRE WIEDER, FOR SOLO
   VOICE AND ORCHESTRA see Telemann,
   Georg Philipp

LIEBSTER JESUS, WIR SIND HIER, [ARR.]
   see Bach, Johann Sebastian

LIED, FOR SOLO VOICE AND INSTRUMENTAL
   ENSEMBLE see Bilucaglia, Claudio

LIED DER SPINNERIN, FOR SOLO VOICE AND
   ORCHESTRA see Diepenbrock, Alphons

LIED DER SPINNERIN, FOR SOLO VOICE AND
   STRINGS see Diepenbrock, Alphons

LIED DER WALKURE, FOR SOLO VOICE AND
   ORCHESTRA see Weingartner, (Paul)
   Felix von

LIED DES FISCHERS see Lersen, Fred

LIED IM VOLKSMUND see Kick-Schmidt,
   Paul

LIED UIT DE VERTE, FOR SOLO VOICE AND
   ORCHESTRA see Boehmer, Konrad

LIED VOM FISCHER FIDOLIN, DAS, FOR SOLO
   VOICE AND ORCHESTRA see Ebert,
   Wolfgang

LIEDER AUS ASIEN III, FOR SOLO VOICE
   AND ORCHESTRA see Verhaar, Ary

LIEDER DER KINDHEIT, FOR SOLO VOICE AND
   ORCHESTRA see Lothar, Mark

LIEDER DER LIEBE, FOR SOLO VOICE AND
   ORCHESTRA see Schwickert, Gustav

LIEDER EINES FAHRENDEN GESELLEN, FOR
   SOLO VOICE AND ORCHESTRA see
   Mahler, Gustav

LIEDER QUADRILLE see Strauss, Johann,
   [Jr.]

LIEDER UND TANZE DAS TODES, FOR SOLO
   VOICE AND ORCHESTRA, [ARR.] see
   Mussorgsky, Modest Petrovich, Songs
   And Dances Of Death, For Solo Voice
   And Orchestra, [arr.]

LIEDEREN, FOR SOLO VOICE AND ORCHESTRA
   see Mengelberg, Karel

LIEDEREN, FOR SOLO VOICE AND ORCHESTRA
   see Mesritz van Velthuysen, Anny

LIEDEREN VAN DOOD EN LEVEN, FOR SOLO
   VOICE AND ORCHESTRA see Badings,
   Henk

LIEDEREN VOOR SOPRAAN EN ORKEST NO. 2
   see Diepenbrock, Alphons

LIEDERKREIS - AFTER SCHUMANN'S OPUS 24
   see Holloway, Robin

LIEF GA NIET HEEN ZONDER AFSCHEID see
   Mengelberg, Karel

LIEF MIJN HART VERLANGT see Mengelberg,
   Karel

LIER, BERTUS VAN
   see VAN LIER, BERTUS

LIEUTENANT KIJE see Prokofiev, Serge

LIFE FOR THE TSAR, A: MAZURKA see
   Glinka, Mikhail Ivanovich

LIFE FOR THE TSAR, A: OVERTURE see
   Glinka, Mikhail Ivanovich

LIFE STUDY NO. 2 see Maw, Nicholas

LIGETI, GYORGY (1923-   )
   Fragment [8']
      contrabsn,bass trom,db tuba,perc,
      harp,hpsd,pno,3db
      study sc UNIVER. UE 13363 f.s.,

LIGETI, GYORGY (cont'd.)

      perf mat rent   (L150)

LIGHT see Machover, Tod

LIGHT CAVALRY: OVERTURE see Suppe,
   Franz von, Leichte Kavallerie:
   Overture

LIGHT DANCES - STONES SING see
   Levinson, Gerald

LIGHT OF LIFE, THE: MEDITATION see
   Elgar, [Sir] Edward (William)

LIGHT OF THE SUN, THE, FOR SOLO VOICE
   AND ORCHESTRA see Ketting, Otto

LIMA, JERONIMO FRANCISCO (1741-1822)
   Nozze d'Ercole Ed Ebe, Le *Overture
      2.2.0.2. 0.2.2.0. strings,hpsd
      (Leal, Luis Pereira) sc,pts
      PORT.MUS. PM 23 f.s.   (L151)

LINCKE, PAUL (1866-1946)
   Majolika
      LIENAU f.s.   (L152)

   Singvogelchen
      LIENAU f.s.   (L153)

LINDA DI CHAMOUNIX: O LUCE DI QUEST'
   ANIMA, FOR SOLO VOICE AND ORCHESTRA
   see Donizetti, Gaetano

LINDA DI CHAMOUNIX: OVERTURE see
   Donizetti, Gaetano

LINDBLAD, RUNE (1923-   )
   Concerto for String Orchestra, No. 1,
      Op. 170
      string orch
      sc STIM   (L154)

   Concerto for String Orchestra, No. 3,
      Op. 176 [12']
      STIM   (L155)

LINDE, BO (1933-1970)
   Gammalmodig Svit [11']
      string orch
      "Oldfashioned Suite" sc,pts BUSCH
      f.s.   (L156)

   Oldfashioned Suite *see Gammalmodig
      Svit

   Serenata Nostalgica *Op.30 [15'40"]
      11strings
      BUSCH perf mat rent   (L157)

LINDGREN, PAR (1952-   )
   Brutet Ackord [37']
      14strings
      STIM   (L158)

LINDROTH, PETER (1950-   )
   And So It Goes [10'30"]
      2perc,strings
      STIM   (L159)

LINKE, NORBERT (1933-   )
   Concerto for Violin and Orchestra
      [23']
      3(pic).3(English horn).3(bass
      clar).3(contrabsn). 4.3.3.1.
      2perc,harp,strings,vln solo
      BREITKOPF-W perf mat rent   (L160)

   Profit Tout Clair [12'30"]
      ob,clar,bsn,horn,strings
      BREITKOPF-W perf mat rent   (L161)

LINNALA, EINO (1896-1973)
   Fromm, For Solo Voice And Orchestra
      [3']
      2.0.2.0. 0.0.0.0. harp,strings,
      solo voice
      FAZER perf mat rent   (L162)

   Kesaillalla, For Solo Voice And
      Orchestra [2']
      1.1.1.0. 2.0.0.0. perc,strings,
      solo voice
      FAZER perf mat rent   (L163)

   Madrigal, For Solo Voice And
      Orchestra [3']
      1.1.1.0. 2.0.0.0. strings,solo
      voice
      FAZER perf mat rent   (L164)

   Med Sina Skonaste Sanger, For Solo
      Voice And Orchestra [3']
      2.1.1.0. 2.0.0.0. strings,solo
      voice
      FAZER perf mat rent   (L165)

LINTU, FOR SOLO VOICE AND ORCHESTRA see
   Pylkkanen, Tauno Kullervo

LINZ, MARTA
  Rumanische Rhapsodie, For Violin And
    Orchestra
    fl,clar,harp,strings,vln solo
    sc RIES f.s., perf mat rent   (L166)

LINZ SYMPHONY see Mozart, Wolfgang
  Amadeus, Symphony No. 36 in C, K.
  425

LION, THE see Luck, Arthur

LIONS see Rorem, Ned

LIRING BALLADE, FOR SOLO VOICE AND
  ORCHESTRA see Jolas, Betsy

LISZT, FRANZ (1811-1886)
  Angelus. Priere Aux Anges Gardiens
    string orch
    KALMUS 5344 sc $2.50, set $3.00,
      pts $.60, ea.   (L167)
    LUCKS 07455 sc $2.50, set $3.00,
      pts $.60, ea.   (L168)

  Christus: Hirtengesang
    2.2+English horn.2.2. 4.2.0.0.
      timp,harp,strings
    KALMUS A1649 sc $12.00, perf mat
      rent, set $22.00, pts $1.25, ea.
      (L169)
  Concerto for Piano and Orchestra, No.
    1, in E flat [18']
    2+pic.2.2.2. 2.2.3.0. timp,perc,
      strings,pno solo
    BROUDE BR. set $27.50, pts $1.25,
      ea.   (L170)
    sc,pts LIENAU f.s.   (L171)
    LUCKS 00034 sc $9.50, set $20.00,
      min sc $4.00, pts $.95, ea.   (L172)

  Festival Prelude
    2.2.2.2. 2.2.3.1. timp,perc,
      strings
    KALMUS 5291 sc $7.00, perf mat
      rent, set $25.00, pts $1.75, ea.
      (L173)
  Festklange [18']
    2.2.2.2. 4.3.3.1. timp,perc,
      strings
    KALMUS 5383 sc $30.00, perf mat
      rent, set $50.00, pts $2.50, ea.
      (L174)
  Hamlet [10']
    3.2.2.2. 4.2.3.1. timp,strings
    KALMUS 5335 sc $15.00, perf mat
      rent, set $22.00, pts $1.00, ea.
      (L175)
  Hungarian March, [arr.]
    (Atzler) KALMUS 5292 pno-cond sc
      $2.00, set $11.00, pts $.75, ea.,
      cmplt ed rent   (L176)

  Hungarian Rhapsody No. 2 *see
    Rhapsodie Hongroise No. 2, [arr.]

  Hungarian Rhapsody No. 3 *see
    Rhapsodie Hongroise No. 3, [arr.]

  Liebestraum, [arr.]
    (Schuller, Gunther) 3(alto
      fl).3.3.3. 4.3.3.1. perc,harp,
      gtr,pno,cel,strings, trap set
      [4'] MARGUN BP 4003 perf mat rent
      (L177)
  Mephisto Waltz
    LUCKS 07456 sc $14.00, set $28.00,
      pts $1.60, ea.   (L178)
  Orpheus
    LUCKS 08511 sc $10.50, set $28.00,
      min sc $3.00, pts $1.40, ea.
      (L179)
  Preludes, Les
    BROUDE BR. set $30.00, pts $1.50,
      ea.   (L180)
    min sc ZEN-ON 890951 f.s.   (L181)
    LUCKS 06108 sc $12.00, set $24.00,
      min sc $3.00, pts $1.15, ea.
      (L182)
  Rhapsodie Hongroise No. 2, [arr.]
    "Hungarian Rhapsody No. 2" LUCKS
      06104 sc $11.00, set $18.00, min
      sc $6.00, pts $1.15, ea.   (L183)
  Rhapsodie Hongroise No. 3, [arr.]
    "Hungarian Rhapsody No. 3" LUCKS
      05468 sc $10.00, set $30.00, min
      sc $6.00, pts $1.75, ea.   (L184)
    (Hutschenruyter, W.) "Ungarische
      Rhapsodie No. 3, [arr.]" 2+
      pic.2.2.2. 4.3.3.1. harp,timp,
      triangle,strings sc,pts LIENAU
      rent   (L185)

  Rhapsodie Hongroise No. 5, For Piano
    And Orchestra, [arr.]
    (Burmeister, Richard) 2.2.2.2.
      4.2.3.1. timp,strings,pno solo
    sc,pts LIENAU f.s.   (L186)
  Rhapsodie Hongroise No. 11, [arr.]
    (Hutschenruyter, W.) "Ungarische
      Rhapsodie No. 11, [arr.]"
      3.2.2.2. 4.3.3.1. timp,perc,
      strings [8'] sc,pts LIENAU f.s.

LISZT, FRANZ (cont'd.)
    (L187)
  Rhapsodie Hongroise No. 13, [arr.]
    (Hutschenruyter, W.) "Ungarische
      Rhapsodie No. 13, [arr.]"
      3(pic).2.2.2. 4.4.3.1. harp,
      glock,timp,perc,strings [8'] sc,
      pts LIENAU f.s.   (L188)
  Tarantelle, [arr.]
    (Muller-Berghaus) KALMUS 5334 sc
      $15.00, perf mat rent, set
      $30.00, pts $1.75, ea.   (L189)
  Totentanz, For Piano And Orchestra
    LUCKS 00091 sc $12.00, set $25.00,
      min sc $3.00, pts $1.40, ea.
      (L190)
  Ungarische Rhapsodie No. 3, [arr.]
    *see Rhapsodie Hongroise No. 3,
    [arr.]

  Ungarische Rhapsodie No. 11, [arr.]
    *see Rhapsodie Hongroise No. 11,
    [arr.]

  Ungarische Rhapsodie No. 13, [arr.]
    *see Rhapsodie Hongroise No. 13,
    [arr.]

  Ungarischer Sturmmarsch [4']
    2+pic.2.2.2. 4.2.3.1. timp,perc,
      strings
    sc,pts LIENAU f.s.   (L191)
  Vom Fels Zum Meer [6']
    2+pic.2.2.2. 4.2.3.1. timp,perc,
      strings
    sc,pts LIENAU f.s.   (L192)

LITHOSFEER see Schat, Peter

LITKIEWICZ, ALFRED
  Bella Rosita
    RIES f.s.   (L193)

LITTLE CARAPATHIAN OVERTURE see Hirner,
  Teodor, Malokarpatska Predohra

LITTLE CIRCUS, THE see Cohn, James
  Myron

LITTLE FANTASY see Schuller, Gunther

LITTLE LANE, FOR OBOE AND ORCHESTRA see
  Eisma, Will

LITTLE SUITE see Nielsen, Carl

LITTLE SUITE OF DANCES see Whyte, Ian

LITUANI, I: SINFONIA see Ponchielli,
  Amilcare

LITUANI OVERTURE see Ponchielli,
  Amilcare, Lituani, I: Sinfonia

LIVRE DES PRODIGES see Ohana, Maurice

LO, HERE THE GENTLE LARK, FOR SOLO
  VOICE AND ORCHESTRA see Bishop,
  [Sir] Henry (Rowley)

LO, HOW A ROSE E'ER BLOOMING see
  Brahms, Johannes, Chorale Prelude:
  Es Ist Ein Ros' Entsprungen, [arr.]

LO, IN THE GRAVE HE LAY
  (Kirkland, Camp) CRESPUB CP-IN 7+9
    $17.50   (L194)

LOB DER FRAUEN see Strauss, Johann,
  [Jr.]

LOCANDIERA, LA: OVERTURE see Martino,
  Aladino di

LOCATELLI, PIETRO (1695-1764)
  Concerto Grosso, Op. 1, No. 6, in C
    minor
    string orch,cont
    (Egidi) KALMUS 5241 sc $4.00, perf
      mat rent, set $9.00, pts $1.00,
      ea.   (L195)
  Trauer-Symphonie [15']
    string orch,cont
    (Schering) KALMUS 5242 sc $4.00,
      perf mat rent, set $9.00, pts
      $1.00, ea.   (L196)

LOCKE, MATTHEW (1630-1677)
  Psyche: Suite
    sets NOVELLO 9112-13 $25.00, and
      up, sc NOVELLO 9111 $4.25, pts
      NOVELLO 9612 $1.00, ea.   (L197)
  Tempest, The: Incidental Music [24']
    string orch,cont
    (Dennison, Peter) sc OXFORD 27.961
      $11.75, pts OXFORD f.s., rent
      (L198)
LOCKVOGEL see Strauss, Johann, [Jr.]

LODOISKA: OVERTURE see Cherubini, Luigi

LOEILLET, JACQUES (JACOB) (1685-1746)
  Concerto for Oboe and String
    Orchestra in E flat, MIN 77
    string orch,cont,ob solo
    MUS. RARA   (L199)

LOEVENDIE, THEO (1930-   )
  Flexio [17']
    3.3.4.3. 4.3.3.1. timp,4perc,
      2harp,pno,strings
    DONEMUS perf mat rent   (L200)

  Incantations, For Bass Clarinet And
    Orchestra [13']
    1.0.0.1. 4.3.2.0. perc,harp,pno,
      cel,strings,bass clar solo
    DONEMUS perf mat rent   (L201)

  Nachtegaal, De, For Solo Voice And
    Orchestra [35']
    1.1.2.1. 2.1.1.0. 2perc,harp,
      strings,narrator
    "Nightingale, The, For Solo Voice
      And Orchestra" DONEMUS   (L202)

  Nightingale, The, For Solo Voice And
    Orchestra *see Nachtegaal, De,
    For Solo Voice And Orchestra

  Orbits, For Horn Solo, 4 Horns
    Obligato And Orchestra [18']
    3.3.3.alto sax. 4.4.3.1. 4perc,
      harp,pno,strings,horn solo
    sc DONEMUS f.s., perf mat rent
      (L203)
LOEWE, CARL GOTTFRIED (1796-1869)
  Uhr, Die, For Solo Voice And
    Orchestra, [arr.] *Op.123,No.3
    (Braun, Ed.) 2.2(English
      horn).2.2(contrabsn). 2.2.1.0.
      timp,strings [6'] sc,pts LIENAU
      rent   (L204)

LOEWE, KARL
  see LOEWE, CARL GOTTFRIED

LOFFLER, WILLY
  Angelique
    RIES f.s.   (L205)

  Klarinetten-Kapriolen
    RIES f.s.   (L206)

  Romanze Rubato
    RIES f.s.   (L207)

  Sonnige Tage
    RIES f.s.   (L208)

  Tanz Der Geigen
    RIES f.s.   (L209)

LOFSANG, EX MINIMIS PATET IPSE DEUS,
  FOR SOLO VOICE AND ORCHESTRA see
  Voormolen, Alexander Nicolas

LOGIC OF DISTRACTION, THE, FOR PIANO
  AND ORCHESTRA see Hachimura, Yoshio

LOHENGRIN: EINSAM IN TRUBEN TAGEN, FOR
  SOLO VOICE AND ORCHESTRA see
  Wagner, Richard

LOHENGRIN: IN FERNEM LAND, FOR SOLO
  VOICE AND ORCHESTRA see Wagner,
  Richard

LOHENGRIN: LOHENGRINS ERMAHNUNG AN
  ELSA, FOR SOLO VOICE AND ORCHESTRA
  see Wagner, Richard

LOHENGRIN: MEIN LIEBER SCHWAN, FOR SOLO
  VOICE AND ORCHESTRA see Wagner,
  Richard

LOHENGRIN: PRELUDE, ACT I see Wagner,
  Richard

LOHENGRIN: PRELUDE, ACT III see Wagner,
  Richard

LOHENGRIN: PRELUDES, ACTS I AND III see
  Wagner, Richard

LOHSE, FRED (1908-   )
  Deutsche Reigen [18']
    2.2.2.2. 3.2.0.0. timp,triangle,
      strings
    RIES perf mat rent   (L210)

  Heitere Suite [18']
    2.2.2.2. 4.2.3.0. timp,triangle,
      strings
    RIES perf mat rent   (L211)

LOKKETRALL OG SOMAR-NATTA, FOR SOLO
  VOICE AND ORCHESTRA see Brevik, Tor

LOLA see Friedemann, Carl

LOMBARDI, LUCA (1945-   )
  Canzone [9']
      1.1.2.1. 1.1.0.0. perc,pno,2vln,
      vla,vcl,db
    sc MOECK 5177 f.s., perf mat rent
                                    (L212)
  Symphony No. 1
    pts MOECK 5176 rent   (L213)

LONDON SYMPHONIES see Haydn, [Franz]
  Joseph, Symphony Nos. 93-104

LONG DISTANCE, FOR PIANO AND
  INSTRUMENTAL ENSEMBLE see Finnissy,
  Michael

LONGO, ACHILLE (1900-1954)
  Bolero [5']
      2.2.2.2.2sax. 2.2.1.0. timp,perc,
      cel,harp,strings
    sc CARISCH 18917 perf mat rent
                                    (L214)

LONZA E LA LUPA, LA see Stallaert,
  Alphonse

LOOK, THE see Flothuis, Marius

LORELEI-RHEINKLANGE see Strauss,
  Johann, [Sr.]

LORENS, CARL (1851-1909)
  Holloderoh-Marsch
    LIENAU f.s.   (L215)

LORENTZEN, BENT (1935-   )
  Tide [12']
      2.2.2.2. 2.2.2.0. perc,strings
    sc HANSEN-DEN WH 29463 $26.25
                                    (L216)

LORENZ, CARL ADOLF (1837-1923)
  Symphonische Variationen Uber Ein
    Originalthema Und Fuge *Op.98
    sc LIENAU f.s.   (L217)

LORENZINI, DANILO (1952-   )
  Concerto for Piano and Orchestra
    [20']
      2.1.2.0. 0.1.0.0. perc,6vla,6vcl,
      pno solo,S solo
    sc ZERBONI 8255 f.s., pts ZERBONI
    8256 rent   (L218)

  Notturno
      3.3.3.3. 4.3.3.0. vibra,cel,
      2harp,strings
    sc ZERBONI 8184 f.s., pts ZERBONI
    8185 rent   (L219)

  Symphony No. 2 for Solo Voice and
    Orchestra [14']
      2.2.2.2. 2.2.0.0. perc,strings,
      solo voice
    sc ZERBONI 8342 f.s., pts ZERBONI
    8343 rent   (L220)

LORTZING, (GUSTAV) ALBERT (1801-1851)
  Czar And Carpenter: Overture *see
    Zar Und Zimmermann: Overture

  Waffenschmied, Der: Auch Ich War Ein
    Jungling, For Solo Voice And
    Orchestra
    BREITKOPF-W perf mat rent   (L221)

  Zar Und Zimmermann: Die Eifersucht
    Ist Eine Plage, For Solo Voice
    And Orchestra [8']
      2.2.0.2. 2.0.0.0. strings,S solo
    BREITKOPF-W perf mat rent   (L222)

  Zar Und Zimmermann: Leb Wohl, Mein
    Flandrisch Madchen, For Solo
    Voice And Orchestra [8']
      2.2.0.2. 2.0.0.0. strings,T solo
    BREITKOPF-W perf mat rent   (L223)

  Zar Und Zimmermann: Overture
    "Czar And Carpenter: Overture"
    LUCKS 06140 sc $5.00, set $11.50,
    pts $.95, ea.   (L224)

LOSLASSEN! see Ziehrer, Carl Michael

LOST CHORD, THE, FOR SOLO VOICE AND
  ORCHESTRA, [ARR.] see Sullivan,
  [Sir] Arthur Seymour

LOST FLUTE, THE, FOR NARRATOR AND
  ORCHESTRA see Tcherepnin, Alexander

LOST SOUNDS II, FOR VIOLIN AND
  ORCHESTRA see Ishii, Maki

LOST SOUNDS III, FOR VIOLIN AND
  ORCHESTRA see Ishii, Maki, Concerto
  for Violin and Orchestra, Op. 34

LOSTOMIGE WIND see Mulder, Herman

LOTHAR, MARK (1902-   )
  Altdeutsche Lieder, For Solo Voice
    And Orchestra *Op.41a [14']
      2(pic).1.2.2(contrabsn). 2.0.0.0.
      timp,perc,harp,cel,strings,S
      solo
    RIES perf mat rent   (L225)

LOTHAR, MARK (cont'd.)
  Eichendorff-Suite *Op.36 [16']
      2(pic).2(English horn).2(bass
      clar).2. 2.1.0.bass trom.0.
      timp,2perc,harp,strings
    RIES perf mat rent   (L226)

  Kleine Theater-Suite *Op.28 [15']
      2(pic).1.1.1. 2.2.0.0. timp,perc,
      cel,harp,opt 2mand,strings
    RIES perf mat rent   (L227)

  Lieder Der Kindheit, For Solo Voice
    And Orchestra *Op.38 [12']
      2(pic).2(English horn).3+bass
      clar.2(contrabsn). 4.3.3.1.
      timp,2perc,harp,pno,cel,
      strings,med solo
    RIES perf mat rent   (L228)

  Mittelalterliche Tanzsuite *Op.49
    [16']
      2(pic).2(English
      horn).2.2(contrabsn). 4.3.3.1.
      timp,2perc,harp,strings
    sc RIES f.s., perf mat rent (L229)

  Suite Aus Einem Kindermarchenspiel
    [12']
      1(pic).1.1.1. 2.1.1.0. timp,perc,
      pno,strings
    RIES perf mat rent   (L230)

  Tyll: Nele's Lied, For Solo Voice And
    Orchestra [3']
      2+pic.2+English horn.2+bass
      clar.2+contrabsn. 4.3.3.1.
      timp,harp,strings,high solo
    RIES perf mat rent   (L231)

LOTICHIUS, ERIK (1929-   )
  Variaties En Finale, On A Theme By
    Duke Ellington [10']
      2.2.2.2sax. 2.3.2.1. perc,
      strings
    DONEMUS   (L232)

LOTTI, ANTONIO (1667-1740)
  Laudate Pueri, For Solo Voices And
    String Orchestra [8']
      string orch,3 female soli
    sc CARISCH 21691 f.s., pts CARISCH
    21692 rent   (L233)

LOUISE: DEPUIS LE JOUR, FOR SOLO VOICE
  AND ORCHESTRA see Charpentier,
  Gustave

LOUISEN-QUADRILLE see Strauss, Johann,
  [Sr.]

LOUVIER, ALAIN (1945-   )
  Suite in C [20']
      2.1.2.1. 1.1.1.0. timp,perc,harp,
      pno,7vln,2vla,2vcl,db
    LEDUC perf mat rent   (L234)

  Trois Atmospheres, For Clarinet And
    Orchestra [25']
      4.2.5.4.2sax. 2.2.2.1. timp,
      4perc,harp,cel,2pno,6vln,3vla,
      2vcl,2db,clar solo
    LEDUC perf mat rent   (L235)

LOVE CHARM SONGS, FOR SOLO VOICE AND
  INSTRUMENTAL ENSEMBLE see Sermila,
  Jarmo

LOVE OF THREE ORANGES: MARCH AND
  SCHERZO see Prokofiev, Serge

LOVEC, VLADIMIR (1922-   )
  Concertino for Flute and Orchestra
    [16']
      1.0.2.2. 2.2.0.0. timp,harp,
      strings,fl solo
    DRUSTVO DSS 762 perf mat rent
                                    (L236)
  Koper Symphony, The *see Koprska
    Simfonija

  Koprska Simfonija [20']
      2(pic).2.2.2. 4.2.3.1. timp,perc,
      strings
    "Koper Symphony, The" DRUSTVO
    DSS 867 perf mat rent   (L237)

LUCIA DI LAMMERMOOR: MAD SCENE see
  Donizetti, Gaetano, Lucia Di
  Lammermoor: Scena Della Pazzia, For
  Solo Voice And Orchestra

LUCIA DI LAMMERMOOR: REGNAVA NEL
  SILENZIO, FOR SOLO VOICE AND
  ORCHESTRA see Donizetti, Gaetano

LUCIA DI LAMMERMOOR: SCENA DELLA
  PAZZIA, FOR SOLO VOICE AND
  ORCHESTRA see Donizetti, Gaetano

LUCIFER see El-Dabh, Halim

LUCIFER POLKA see Strauss, Johann,
  [Jr.]

LUCK, ANDREW H.
  Deep River, [arr.]
    string orch LUCKS 06127 sc $4.00,
    set $3.75, pts $.75. ea.   (L238)

  Grand March Funebre No. 2
    LUCKS 06145 sc $5.00, set $24.00,
    pts $1.00, ea.   (L239)

  Hymne Aus Vaterland
    LUCKS 02352 sc $8.00, set $16.00,
    pts $1.00, ea.   (L240)

  Sehnsucht, For Solo Voice And
    Orchestra
    LUCKS 02009 sc $4.50, set $8.50,
    pts $.75, ea.   (L241)

  Two Preludes On Bach Themes
    LUCKS 06547 sc $2.00, set $8.00,
    pts $.75, ea.   (L242)

  Wiegenlied, For Solo Voice And
    Orchestra
    LUCKS 02167 sc $1.50, set $3.75,
    pts $.75, ea.   (L243)

LUCK, ARTHUR
  Gavotte A La Henry
    LUCKS 08525 sc $1.00, set $4.00,
    pts $.60, ea.   (L244)

  Gavotte No. 2
    string orch
    LUCKS 06150 set $2.50, pts $.50,
    ea.   (L245)

  Harmonie March
    LUCKS 06151 set $9.00, pts $.60,
    ea.   (L246)

  Lion, The
    LUCKS 06152 sc $5.00, set $9.00,
    pts $.50, ea.   (L247)

  Thy Sweet Dreams, For Solo Voice And
    Orchestra
    LUCKS 02010 sc $2.00, set $10.00,
    pts $.50, ea.   (L248)

  Victory March
    LUCKS 06154 sc $5.00, set $9.00,
    pts $.50, ea.   (L249)

LUCKY, STEPAN (1919-   )
  Concerto for Violin, Piano and
    Orchestra
    sc PANTON 1550 f.s.   (L250)

LUCREZIA BORGIA see Grimm, Friedrich
  Karl

LUCTUS IN LUDIS, FOR SOLO VOICE AND
  ORCHESTRA see Dionisi, Renato

LUDEWIG, WOLFGANG (1926-   )
  Fantasie Uber Ein Thema Von Mozart
    [11']
      1.1.1.bass clar.0. 0.1.1.0. pno,
      marimba,2vln,vla,vcl,db
    BREITKOPF-W perf mat rent   (L251)

LUDI LEOPOLDINI see Einem, Gottfried
  von

LUFT, GERD
  Autobummel [3']
      2.2.2.2. 4.2.3.0. timp,perc,harp,
      cel,gtr,strings
    ORLANDO rent   (L252)

LUFTIG UND DUFTIG POLKA see Strauss,
  Eduard

LUIGINI, ALEXANDRE (1850-1906)
  Ballet Egyptien *Op.12
    LUCKS 06158 sc $18.00, set $35.00,
    pts $2.00, ea.   (L253)

LUISA MILLER: OVERTURE see Verdi,
  Giuseppe

LUISA MILLER: QUANDO LE SERE, FOR SOLO
  VOICE AND ORCHESTRA see Verdi,
  Giuseppe

LULLABY see Brahms, Johannes

LULLABY OF THE DRUMS see Anderson,
  Leroy

LULLY, JEAN-BAPTISTE (LULLI)
  (1632-1687)
  Ballet Music
    string orch without vla LUCKS 01172
    sc $3.00, set $4.00, pts $1.00,
    ea.   (L254)

  Gavotte
    LUCKS 05475 sc $2.00, set $6.00,
    pts $.75, ea.   (L255)

  Soupe Du Roy, Le, [arr.]
      2.2.2.0. 0.2.0.0. perc,strings
      without vla sc,pts HARMONIA 2406
      f.s.   (L256)

LUMBYE, HANS CHRISTIAN (1810-1874)
Donau-Blumen Quadrille
LUCKS 07895 set $15.00, pts $.75,
ea.   (L257)

Huhner Masken Quadrille
LUCKS 07899 set $15.00, pts $.75,
ea.   (L258)

Reunions Galop
LUCKS 07903 set $15.00, pts $.75,
ea.   (L259)

Skandinavische Quadrille
LUCKS 07466 set $25.00, pts $1.25,
ea.   (L260)

Sommernacht In Danemark, Eine
LUCKS 07896 set $13.00, pts $.75,
ea.   (L261)

LUMIERE ECLATEE, LA, FOR SOLO VOICE AND
ORCHESTRA see Bondon, Jacques

LUNDE, IVAR (1944-   )
Symphony No. 2, Op. 67
4(pic).4(English horn).4(2bass
clar).3(contrabsn). 4.4.3.1.
timp,perc,harp,strings,S solo
NORGE   (L262)

LUNDIN, DAG (1943-   )
Ebbe Skammelsson-Variationer
3.2.2.2. 3.3.3.1. timp,3perc,pno,
strings
[22'] pts STIM   (L263)

LUNDKVIST, PER (1916-   )
Blommande Ronn, For Solo Voice And
Orchestra [4']
1.1.2.1. 2.0.0.0. harp,strings,
solo voice
sc STIM perf mat rent   (L264)

Fagelsang, For Flute And Orchestra
[6'30"]
0.1.2.1. 2.0.0.0. harp,strings,fl
solo
sc STIM perf mat rent   (L265)

I Skogsdunklet, For Bassoon And
Orchestra
1.1.2.0. 2.0.0.0. strings,bsn
solo
sc STIM perf mat rent   (L266)

Smekande Vind, For Violin And
Orchestra [5']
1.1.2.1. 2.0.0.0. harp,strings,
vln solo
sc STIM perf mat rent   (L267)

Spelmansvisa, For Solo Voice And
Orchestra
2horn,strings,solo voice
sc STIM perf mat rent   (L268)

LUNDQUIST, TORBJORN (1920-   )
Anrop, For Solo Voice And Orchestra
study sc SUECIA f.s.   (L269)

Concertino for Accordion and
Orchestra [11']
2.1.2.1. 2.2.1.0. timp,perc,
strings,acord solo
STIM   (L270)

Intarzia, For Accordion And String
Orchestra [12']
string orch,acord solo
STIM   (L271)

Integration [17']
5perc,strings
STIM   (L272)

Serenade
string orch
sc STIM perf mat rent   (L273)

Symphony No. 5
2.2.2.2. 2.2.1.0. timp,perc,
strings
sc STIM perf mat rent   (L274)

Trumpet Music, For Trumpet And
Orchestra
perc,pno,strings,trp solo
sc,pts,solo pt STIM perf mat rent
                                 (L275)

LUPI, ROBERTO (1908-1971)
Tre Fughe E Due Interludi [15']
string orch
sc CARISCH 21632 f.s., perf mat
rent   (L276)

Viandante, Il, For Violoncello And
Orchestra [22']
3.2.2.2. 2.2.2.0. timp,perc,harp,
cel,pno,xylo,strings,vcl solo
manuscript CARISCH   (L277)

LURMANN, LUDWIG
Beschwingtes Zwischenspiel *Op.27
[5']
1.1.2.1. 2.2.1.0. timp,perc,harp/
pno,strings
RIES perf mat rent   (L278)

Festlicher Aufklang *Op.15 [4']
2.2.2.2+opt contrabsn. 4.3.3.1.
timp,perc,harp,strings
RIES perf mat rent   (L279)

Ruf Zur Freude *Op.20 [6']
2.2.2.2+opt contrabsn. 4.2.3.1.
timp,perc,harp,strings
RIES perf mat rent   (L280)

Serenadenmusik *Op.25 [14']
1.1.2.1. 2.2.1.0. timp,perc,
strings
RIES perf mat rent   (L281)

LUST'GER RATH. POLKA see Strauss,
Johann, [Jr.]

LUSTIG IM KREISE POLKA see Strauss,
Eduard

LUSTIGE BIENE see Kotscher, Edmund

LUSTIGE G'SCHICHTEN WALZER see Strauss,
Eduard

LUSTIGE KRIEG, DER. QUADRILLE see
Strauss, Johann, [Jr.]

LUSTIGE OUVERTURE see Strecke, Gerhard

LUSTIGE WITWE, DIE: VILIA, FOR SOLO
VOICE AND ORCHESTRA see Lehar,
Franz

LUSTIGEN WEIBER VON WINDSOR, DIE:
BALLETTMUSIK see Nicolai, Otto

LUSTIGEN WEIBER VON WINDSOR, DIE:
HORCH, DIE LERCHE SINGT IM HAIN,
FOR SOLO VOICE AND ORCHESTRA see
Nicolai, Otto

LUSTIGEN WEIBER VON WINDSOR, DIE:
OVERTURE see Nicolai, Otto

LUSTOBJEKT see Termos, Paul

LUSTSPIEL-OUVERTURE see Blumer, Theodor

LUSTSPIEL-OUVERTURE see Fiedler, Max

LUSTSPIEL-OUVERTURE see Kretzschmar,
Carl

LUSTSPIEL-OUVERTURE see Mielenz, Hans

LUSTSPIEL-OUVERTURE see Reznicek, Emil
Nikolaus von

LUTHER, MARTIN (1483-1546)
Away In A Manger
(Luck, Arthur) LUCKS HYMNS 22 set
$15.00, pts $.65, ea. contains
also: Willis, Richard Storrs, It
Came Upon A Midnight Clear (L282)

LUTOSLAWSKI, WITOLD (1913-   )
Concerto for Oboe, Harp and Chamber
Orchestra [20']
perc,strings,ob solo,harp solo
CHESTER J.W.C. 55410 perf mat rent
                                 (L283)
Espaces Du Sommeil, Les, For Solo
Voice And Orchestra
3.3.3.3. 4.3.2.1. timp,perc,harp,
pno,strings,Bar solo
min sc CHESTER $27.50   (L284)

Mi-Parti
min sc CHESTER $29.75   (L285)

Novelette [18']
3(2pic).3(English horn).3(bass
clar).3(contrabsn). 4.3.3.1.
timp,perc,2harp,cel,pno,strings
sc CHESTER JWC 55312 $22.75, rent,
pts CHESTER rent   (L286)

LYDISCHE NACHT, FOR SOLO VOICE AND
ORCHESTRA see Diepenbrock, Alphons

LYO SYDAN, FOR SOLO VOICE AND
ORCHESTRA, [ARR.] see Kuula, Toivo

LYRIC PIECE AND RONDO, FOR TUBA AND
STRING ORCHESTRA see Dennison, Sam

LYRIC PIECES, TWO, FROM OP. 68 see
Grieg, Edvard Hagerup

LYRISCHE TANZE see Dressel, Erwin

LYRISCHES KONZERT, FOR VIOLA AND
CHAMBER ORCHESTRA see Schubert,
Heinz

LYRISM see Blomberg, Erik

LYRO-SVIT see Hallnas, Eyvind

M

MA BOHEME see Escher, Rudolf George

MA VLAST: SARKA see Smetana, Bedrich

MA VLAST: TABOR see Smetana, Bedrich

MA VLAST: VITAVA see Smetana, Bedrich

MA VLAST: VYSEHRAD see Smetana, Bedrich

MA VLAST: Z CESKYCH LUHU A HAJU see
    Smetana, Bedrich

MAANLICHT see Badings, Henk

MAASSA MARJANI MAKAAVI, FOR SOLO VOICE
    AND ORCHESTRA, [ARR.] see Kilpinen,
    Yrjo

MAASZ, GERHARD (1906-   )
    Deutscher Choral
        string orch
        sc,pts RIES f.s.   (M1)

    Hamburgische Tafelmusik [12']
        1.2.0.1. 0.0.0.0. hpsd/pno,
            strings
        RIES perf mat rent   (M2)

    Marchenmusik, Eine [16']
        1+opt fl.1.2.1. 1.1+opt trp.1.0.
            perc,strings
        sc RIES f.s., perf mat rent   (M3)

    Musik No. I [12']
        fl,clar,strings
        RIES perf mat rent   (M4)

    Musik No. II [15']
        1.1.1.1. 0.1.0.0. strings
        RIES perf mat rent   (M5)

    Wir Sind Die Musikanten
        2.2.2.2. 2.2.1.1. timp,perc,harp,
            cel,strings,opt narrator,opt
            cor
        sc SCHOTTS 71 U0184 $13.00, set
        SCHOTTS 71 U0184SET $28.00, pts
        SCHOTTS $2.00, ea.   (M6)

MAAVAK see Feiler, Dror

MACBETH see Strauss, Richard

MACBRIDE, DAVID HUSTON (1951-   )
    Once Removed
        string orch
        SEESAW perf mat rent   (M7)

MCCABE, JOHN (1939-   )
    Concerto for Piano and Orchestra, No.
        3
        sc NOVELLO 2574 $15.25   (M8)

MACCHI, EGISTO (1928-   )
    Composizione 5, "No Han Muerto" [14']
        0.0.3.0. 3.3.3.0. 8perc,strings,
            narrator
        BRUZZI S-024 perf mat rent   (M9)

    Composizione No. 3 [7']
        1.1.1.1. 1.1.1.0. vln,2vla,vcl,db
        sc BRUZZI C-013 $12.00, perf mat
            rent   (M10)

MCCULLOH, BYRON B. (1927-   )
    Concerto for Trombone and Orchestra
        2.2.2.2. 2.2.0.1. timp,2perc,pno,
            strings,trom solo
        SEESAW perf mat rent   (M11)

    Dreamstreams, For Flute And String
        Orchestra
        string orch,fl solo
        SEESAW perf mat rent   (M12)

MACDOWELL, EDWARD ALEXANDER (1861-1908)
    To A Water Lily, [arr.]
        LUCKS 06172 sc $2.00, set $8.00,
            pts $.75, ea.   (M13)

    To A Wild Rose, [arr.]
        string orch LUCKS 06171 sc $1.50,
            set $3.75, pts $.75, ea.   (M14)

    Woodland Sketches, Nos. 1-5, [arr.]
        (Woodhouse) LUCKS 06174 set $14.00,
            pts $1.00, ea.   (M15)

    Woodland Sketches, Nos. 6-10, [arr.]
        (Woodhouse) LUCKS 06182 set $14.00,
            pts $1.00, ea.   (M16)

MCGUIRE, EDWARD
    Calgacus [20']
        3.3.3.3. 4.3.3.1. 2perc,harp,pno,
            bagpipe,strings
        SCOTUS 224-5   (M17)

MCGUIRE, EDWARD (cont'd.)
    Epitaph [15']
        3.3.3.3. 4.2.3.1. timp,3perc,
            harp,pno,strings
        SCOTUS 229-6   (M18)

    Symphony No. 1 [24']
        3(pic,alto fl).2.2+bass clar.2.
            4.2.2.1. timp,2perc,harp,pno,
            strings
        SCOTUS 239-3   (M19)

MACHA, OTMAR (1922-   )
    Sinfonietta No. 1
        sc PANTON 1726 f.s.   (M20)

MACHE, FRANCOIS BERNARD (1935-   )
    Naluan [22']
        1.0.1.0. 0.0.0.0. 4perc,pno,vln,
            vla,vcl,db
        AMPHION A 329 perf mat rent   (M21)

MACHOVER, TOD (1953-   )
    Concerto for Guitar and Chamber
        Orchestra [16']
        0.pic.0.English horn.0.bass
            clar.1. 1.0.1.0. perc,pno,
            string quin,gtr solo
        RICORDI-FR R.2298 perf mat rent
                                        (M22)

    Light [30']
        1.1.0.1. 1.1.1.0. 2perc,pno,harp,
            string quar,electronic
            equipment
        RICORDI-FR R.2268 perf mat rent
                                        (M23)

MACKENZIE, [SIR] ALEXANDER CAMPBELL
    (1847-1935)
    Benedictus
        KALMUS A1675 sc $4.00, set $10.00,
            pts $1.00, ea.   (M24)

MCKINLEY, WILLIAM THOMAS (1939-   )
    Concertino for Orchestra [7']
        4.6.5.4. 4.2.2.1. 4perc,strings
        sc MARGUN BP 5002 $12.00, perf mat
            rent   (M25)

    Concerto for Clarinet and Orchestra,
        No. 1 [23']
        2.2.3.3. 4.2.2.1. timp,2perc,
            strings,clar solo
        MARGUN BP 5003 perf mat rent   (M26)

    Symphony No. 1 [10']
        3.4.4.4. 4.2.2.1. perc,harp,pno,
            strings
        MARGUN BP 5004 perf mat rent   (M27)

MCLENNAN, JOHN STEWART (1915-   )
    Celebration [13']
        3.2.2.3. 4.3.3.1. perc,strings
        MARGUN BP 5005 perf mat rent   (M28)

MACRO FANTASY ON GRIEG'S A MINOR, FOR
    PIANO AND ORCHESTRA see Thommessen,
    Olav Anton

MADAME CHRYSANTHEME: BALLET SUITE,
    [ARR.] see Messager, Andre

MADCHENBILDER see Kiermeir, Kurt

MADCHENLAUNE POLKA see Strauss, Eduard

MADDERMARKET SUITE see Cockshott,
    Gerald Wilfred

MADERNA, BRUNO (1920-1973)
    Aura
        sc RICORDI-IT 131960 $20.00   (M29)

    Biogramma
        sc RICORDI-IT 131985 f.s.   (M30)

    Giardino Religioso
        sc RICORDI-IT 132049 $15.00   (M31)

    Venetian Journal, For Solo Voice And
        Orchestra
        sc RICORDI-IT 131987 f.s.   (M32)

MADETOJA, LEEVI (1887-1947)
    Elegy, Op. 4, No. 1 [5']
        string orch
        sc,pts FAZER f.s.   (M33)

    Ilta, For Solo Voice And String
        Orchestra *Op.60,No.3 [3']
        string orch,solo voice
        FAZER perf mat rent   (M34)

    Itkisit Joskus Illoin, For Solo Voice
        And Orchestra [3']
        2.0.2.1. 2.0.0.0. strings,solo
            voice
        FAZER perf mat rent   (M35)

    Merituuli, For Solo Voice And
        Orchestra, [arr.] *Op.26,No.4
        (Funtek, L.) 2.2.2.2. 2.2.0.0.
            timp,perc,strings,solo voice [2']
        FAZER perf mat rent   (M36)

MADETOJA, LEEVI (cont'd.)
    Suomen Puu, For Solo Voice And
        Orchestra *Op.49,No.2 [4']
        2.2.2.2. 4.3.3.1. timp,strings,
            solo voice
        FAZER perf mat rent   (M37)

    Terve Paiva Pohjolahan, For Solo
        Voice And Orchestra, [arr.]
        *Op.49,No.1
        (Funtek, L.) 2.2.2.2. 2.0.3.0.
            timp,perc,harp,strings,solo voice
        [3'] FAZER perf mat rent   (M38)

MADITACIA A TANEC, FOR PIANO AND
    ORCHESTRA see Suchon, Eugen

MADRIGAL see Chaminade, Cecile

MADRIGAL, FOR SOLO VOICE AND ORCHESTRA
    see Linnala, Eino

MADRIGALI, [ARR.] see Monteverdi,
    Claudio

MADRIGALILLOS, FOR SOLO VOICE AND
    CHAMBER ORCHESTRA see Eyser,
    Eberhard

MADSEN, TRYGVE (1940-   )
    Concerto for Oboe and Orchestra, Op.
        30
        sc,pts MUSIKK   (M39)

    Concerto for Piano and Orchestra, Op.
        27
        3(pic).2.2.2. 4.3.3.1. timp,perc,
            strings,pno solo
        sc MUSIKK   (M40)
        NORGE   (M41)

    Fancy For "Hardanger Fiddle" And
        String Orchestra *Op.31
        [12'] sc MUSIKK   (M42)

    Konzertouverture *Op.11
        2.2.2.2. 4.3.3.1. timp,perc,
            strings
        [12'] sc MUSIKK f.s.   (M43)

MAEGAARD, JAN (1926-   )
    Due Tempi
        1.1.3.1. 2.1.1.1. timp,8perc,cel,
            harp,pno,strings
        sc SAMFUNDET 289 f.s.   (M44)

MAESSEN, ANTOON (1919-   )
    Greensleeves-Phantasy [18']
        2.1.2.1. 3.2.2.1. timp,perc,
            strings,brass,rec,acord,opt
            solo voices
        DONEMUS   (M45)

MAESTOSA SONATA SENTIMENTALE, FOR
    VIOLIN AND ORCHESTRA see Paganini,
    Niccolo

MAGD, EIN DIENERIN, EIN, FOR SOLO VOICE
    AND ORCHESTRA see Haydn, [Franz]
    Joseph

MAGDALENIC, MIROSLAV (1906-1969)
    Symphony No. 1
        3.3.3.2. 4.3.3.1. timp,perc,harp,
            strings
        DRUS.HRVAT.SKLAD. f.s.   (M46)

MAGEIA see Kelemen, Milko

MAGIC ART, THE see Wuorinen, Charles

MAGIC ART, THE: SUITE see Wuorinen,
    Charles

MAGIC FLUTE, THE: LA DOVE PRENDE see
    Mozart, Wolfgang Amadeus,
    Zauberflote, Die: Bei Mannern, For
    Solo Voices And Orchestra

MAGIC FLUTE, THE: OVERTURE see Mozart,
    Wolfgang Amadeus, Zauberflote, Die:
    Overture

MAGYARENTANZ see Woitschach, Paul

MAHLER, GUSTAV (1860-1911)
    Anthony Of Padua's Fish Sermon *see
        Knaben Wunderhorn, Des: Des
        Antonius Von Padua Fischpredigt,
        For Solo Voice And Orchestra

    I Breathed The Breath Of Blossoms Red
        *see Sieben Lieder Aus Letzter
        Zeit: Ich Atmet' Einen Linden
        Duft, For Solo Voice And
        Orchestra

    Kindertotenlieder, For Solo Voice And
        Orchestra
        LUCKS 02295 sc $12.00, set $18.00,
            min sc $4.00, pts $1.40, ea.
                                        (M47)

    "Songs On The Death Of Children"
        min sc INTERNAT. 2029 $5.25   (M48)

MAHLER, GUSTAV (cont'd.)

Knaben Wunderhorn, Des: Das Irdische
   Leben, For Solo Voice And
   Orchestra [4']
   2.3.2.2. 3.1.0.0. cym,strings,
   solo voice
   LUCKS 11153 sc $6.00, set $12.00,
   pts $.60, ea.   (M49)
   "Knaben Wunderhorn, Des: Earthly
   Life" KALMUS 5254 sc $6.00, perf
   mat rent, set $12.00, pts $.60,
   ea.   (M50)

Knaben Wunderhorn, Des: Der
   Schildwache Nachtlied, For Solo
   Voice And Orchestra [6']
   3.3.2.2. 4.2.0.0. timp,3perc,
   harp,strings,solo voice
   LUCKS 11154 sc $6.00, set $12.00,
   pts $.75, ea.   (M51)
   "Knaben Wunderhorn, Des: Sentinel's
   Night" KALMUS 5253 sc $6.00, perf
   mat rent, set $18.00, pts $.75,
   ea.   (M52)

Knaben Wunderhorn, Des: Des Antonius
   Von Padua Fischpredigt, For Solo
   Voice And Orchestra
   "Anthony Of Padua's Fish Sermon"
   LUCKS 03287 sc $4.00, set $8.00,
   pts $.75, ea.   (M53)

Knaben Wunderhorn, Des: Earthly Life
   *see Knaben Wunderhorn, Des: Das
   Irdische Leben, For Solo Voice
   And Orchestra

Knaben Wunderhorn, Des: Sentinel's
   Night *see Knaben Wunderhorn,
   Des: Der Schildwache Nachtlied,
   For Solo Voice And Orchestra

Knaben Wunderhorn, Des: Wo Die
   Schonen Trompeten Blasen, For
   Solo Voice And Orchestra
   LUCKS 03302 sc $4.00, set $8.00,
   pts $.75, ea.   (M54)

Lieder Eines Fahrenden Gesellen, For
   Solo Voice And Orchestra [25']
   3.2.3.2. 4.2.3.0. timp,perc,harp,
   strings,solo voice
   "Songs Of A Wayfarer" BOOSEY perf
   mat rent   (M55)
   "Songs Of A Wayfarer" KALMUS 5175
   sc $18.00, perf mat rent, set
   $30.00, pts $1.50, ea.   (M56)
   "Songs Of A Wayfarer" LUCKS 03346
   sc $18.00, set $28.00, min sc
   $4.00, pts $1.40, ea.   (M57)
   "Songs Of A Wayfarer" min sc
   INTERNAT. 2047 $5.25   (M58)

Sieben Lieder Aus Letzter Zeit:
   Blicke Mir Nicht In Die Lieder,
   For Solo Voice And Orchestra
   LUCKS 02934 sc $4.00, set $8.00,
   pts $.75, ea.   (M59)

Sieben Lieder Aus Letzter Zeit: Der
   Tamboursg'sell, For Solo Voice
   And Orchestra
   LUCKS 03350 sc $5.00, set $8.00,
   pts $.75, ea.   (M60)

Sieben Lieder Aus Letzter Zeit: Ich
   Atmet Einen Linden Duft, For Solo
   Voice And Orchestra [2']
   1.1.2. 3.0.0.0. harp,cel,vln,
   vla,solo voice
   LUCKS 02208 sc $5.00, set $8.00,
   pts $.75, ea.   (M61)
   "I Breathed The Breath Of Blossoms
   Red" KALMUS 5252 sc $4.00, perf
   mat rent, set $10.00, pts $.60,
   ea.   (M62)

Sieben Lieder Aus Letzter Zeit: Ich
   Bin Der Welt Abhanden Gekommen,
   For Solo Voice And Orchestra
   LUCKS 03300 sc $4.00, set $8.00,
   pts $.75, ea.   (M63)

Sieben Lieder Aus Letzter Zeit:
   Liebst Du Um Schonheit, For Solo
   Voice And Orchestra
   LUCKS 03352 sc $4.00, set $12.00,
   pts $.75, ea.   (M64)

Sieben Lieder Aus Letzter Zeit:
   Revelge, For Solo Voice And
   Orchestra
   LUCKS 03349 sc $12.00, set $36.00,
   pts $1.50, ea.   (M65)

Sieben Lieder Aus Letzter Zeit: Um
   Mitternacht, For Solo Voice And
   Orchestra
   KALMUS A2890 sc $4.00, set $8.00,
   pts $.60, ea.   (M66)
   LUCKS 03301 sc $4.00, set $8.00,
   pts $.75, ea.   (M67)

MAHLER, GUSTAV (cont'd.)

Songs Of A Wayfarer *see Lieder
   Eines Fahrenden Gesellen, For
   Solo Voice And Orchestra

Songs On The Death Of Children *see
   Kindertotenlieder, For Solo Voice
   And Orchestra

Symphony No. 2 in C minor
   min sc ZEN-ON 891702 f.s.   (M68)

Symphony No. 3 in D minor
   min sc ZEN-ON 890703 f.s.   (M69)

Symphony No. 4 in G
   min sc INTERNAT. 1201 $8.25   (M70)

Symphony No. 5 in C sharp minor
   min sc UNIVER. PH458 $18.00   (M71)
   min sc ZEN-ON 890705 f.s.   (M72)

Symphony No. 5 in C sharp minor,
   Fourth Movement
   harp,strings
   (Adagietto) LUCKS 08450 sc $2.25,
   set $4.75, pts $.95, ea.   (M73)

Symphony No. 7 in E minor
   min sc UNIVER. PH473 $19.00   (M74)

Symphony No. 8 in E flat [90']
   min sc UNIVER. 53 490 $20.00   (M75)

What The Wild Flowers Tell Me, [arr.]
   (Britten) 2.2.2.2. 4.3.0.0. perc,
   harp,strings [8'] BOOSEY perf mat
   rent   (M76)

MAID OF ORLEANS, THE: FAREWELL,
   FORESTS, FOR SOLO VOICE AND
   ORCHESTRA see Tchaikovsky, Piotr
   Ilyich

MAIDEN AND THE BOYAR'S SON, THE see
   Kuula, Toivo, Impi Ja Pajarin
   Poika, For Solo Voice And Orchestra

MAILLART, LOUIS AIME (1817-1871)
   Dragons De Villars, Les: Overture
   [6']
   2.2.2.2. 4.2+2cornet.3.0. timp,
   perc,strings
   KALMUS 5250 pno-cond sc $4.00, set
   $25.00, pts $1.00, ea., cmplt ed
   rent   (M77)

MAJOLIKA see Lincke, Paul

MAJORETTEN see Schoonenbeek, Kees

MAL, LE see Escher, Rudolf George

MALDERE, PIERRE VAN (1729-1768)
   Overtures, Op. 4, Nos. 1-3
   2ob,2horn,hpsd,strings
   KALMUS 5436 set $16.00, pts $2.50,
   ea.   (M78)

   Overtures, Op. 4, Nos. 4-6
   2ob,2horn,hpsd,strings
   KALMUS 5437 set $16.00, pts $2.50,
   ea.   (M79)

MALEC, IVO (1925-   )
   Arco-11
   string orch
   study sc SALABERT $15.50   (M80)

MALINCONIA, FOR SOLO VOICES AND
   ORCHESTRA see Mihalovici, Marcel

MALIPIERO, GIAN FRANCESCO (1882-1973)
   Gabrieliana
   sc RICORDI-IT PR1228 $7.50   (M81)

   Impressioni Dal Vero, I
   min sc UNIVER. PH288 $7.00   (M82)

MALIPIERO, RICCARDO (1914-   )
   Antico Sole, For Solo Voice And
   Orchestra [30']
   2.2.2.2. 2.2.0.0. perc,pno,
   strings,solo voice
   manuscript CARISCH   (M83)

   Balletto [25']
   2.2.2.2. 4.4.4.0. timp,perc,pno,
   strings
   manuscript CARISCH   (M84)

   Concerto Breve, For Ballerina And
   Orchestra [16']
   1.1.1.1. 2.2.0.0. strings
   ZERBONI perf mat rent   (M85)

   Divertimento for Oboe, Bassoon and
   String Orchestra
   string orch,ob solo,bsn solo
   ZERBONI 8574   (M86)

   Due Pezzi Sacri [15']
   3.3.3.3. 6.4.4.1. perc,harp,pno,
   strings
   sc ZERBONI 8400 f.s., pts ZERBONI

MALIPIERO, RICCARDO (cont'd.)

   8401 rent   (M87)

   Piccolo Concerto, For Piano And
   Orchestra [15']
   1.1.1.1. 2.2.0.0. timp,perc,tam-
   tam,strings,pno solo
   manuscript CARISCH   (M88)

   Requiem For Orchestra [13']
   3.3.3.3. 4.4.4.0. harp,pno,perc,
   strings
   sc ZERBONI 8173 f.s., perf mat rent
                                    (M89)

   Sinfonia [25']
   2.2.2.2. 4.3.3.0. timp,perc,
   strings
   manuscript CARISCH   (M90)

MALOKARPATSKA PREDOHRA see Hirner,
   Teodor

MAMIYA, MICHIO (1929-   )
   Concerto for Orchestra
   JAPAN 7901   (M91)

   Concerto for Violin and Orchestra,
   No. 2
   orch,vln solo
   ZEN-ON 899126   (M92)

   Concerto for Violoncello and
   Orchestra
   orch,vcl solo
   ZEN-ON 899122   (M93)

MAMSELL UIBERMUTH see Ziehrer, Carl
   Michael

MAN BEHIND THE GUN MARCH, THE see
   Sousa, John Philip

MAN FROM MIDIAN, THE see Wolpe, Stefan

MAN LEBT NUR EINMAL. WALZER see
   Strauss, Johann, [Jr.]

MAN MADE FROM SLEEP see Sallinen,
   Aulis, Unesta Tehty Mies

MANASSEN, ALEX (1950-   )
   Concerto for Bass Clarinet and
   Orchestra [21']
   2.2.2.2.2sax. 2.2.2.1. timp,
   3perc,pno/cel,harp,strings,bass
   clar solo
   DONEMUS   (M94)

   Double Helix, For Clarinet, Piano And
   Symphony Orchestra [11']
   2.2.2.2.alto sax.tenor sax.
   2.2.2.2. timp,2perc,harp,pno/
   cel,strings,clar solo,pno solo
   DONEMUS perf mat rent   (M95)

MANDALA see Alkema, Henk

MANDELLI, EMANUELE (1891-   )
   Mila Di Codra
   3.3.3.3. 4.3.3.1. timp,perc,harp,
   strings
   manuscript CARISCH   (M96)

   Notturno
   3.2.2.1. 4.2.3.1. timp,perc,harp,
   bells,strings
   manuscript CARISCH   (M97)

MANDOLINA see Langey, Otto

MANFREDINI, FRANCESCO (1680-1748)
   Concerto Grosso, Op. 3, No. 12, in C
   [10']
   string orch,cont,2vln soli,vcl
   solo
   (Schering) KALMUS 5248 sc $5.00,
   set $6.00, pts $1.00, ea.   (M98)

   Sinfonia Pastorale Per Il Santissimo
   Natale *Op.2,No.12
   (Nielsen, Riccardo) sc DE SANTIS
   DS 781 f.s., pts DE SANTIS
   DS 782A-D f.s.   (M99)

MANHATTAN BEACH MARCH see Sousa, John
   Philip

MANNEKE, DAAN (1939-   )
   En Passant [5']
   2.2.2.2. 2.2.2.0. timp,perc,
   strings
   MOLENAAR 14.1566.08 f.s.   (M100)

   Motet
   2S rec,2A rec,2T rec,B rec, 4
   comorne, ranket or trb or
   cornett or dulcian, lute,
   bassgamba
   sc DONEMUS f.s., perf mat rent
                                    (M101)

   Ruimten [15']
   2.2.2.2. 4.3.3.0. strings
   "Spaces" DONEMUS perf mat rent
                                    (M102)

MANNEKE, DAAN (cont'd.)

Sinfonia, For 13 Solo Strings
8vln,2vla,2vcl,db
sc DONEMUS f.s., perf mat rent
(M103)

Sonatas, 4 [20']
4.2.0.1. 0.3.0.0. timp,perc,
12vln,3vla,2vcl
sc DONEMUS f.s., perf mat rent
(M104)

Spaces *see Ruimten

MANNINO, FRANCO (1924-   )
Concerto for Piano and Orchestra
sc DE SANTIS DS 934 f.s.   (M105)

Due Liriche Tedesche E Un Congedo Di
Giosue Carducci, For Solo Voice
And Orchestra *Op.66, CC2U
sc RICORDI-IT 131785 f.s.   (M106)

Music For Angels
sc RICORDI-IT 130849 f.s.   (M107)

Sinfonia No. 2 [26']
3.2.2.3. 4.3.3.1. timp,perc,
strings
sc CARISCH 21916 rent, pts CARISCH
21916A rent   (M108)

MANOIR DE ROSEMONDE, LE, FOR SOLO VOICE
AND ORCHESTRA see Duparc, Henri

MANON: AH! FUYEZ DOUCE IMAGE, FOR SOLO
VOICE AND ORCHESTRA see Massenet,
Jules

MANON: INTRODUCTION AND GAVOTTE see
Massenet, Jules

MANON: LE REVE, "EN FERMANT LES YEUX",
FOR SOLO VOICE AND ORCHESTRA see
Massenet, Jules

MANON LESCAUT: IN QUELLE TRINE MORBIDE,
FOR SOLO VOICE AND ORCHESTRA see
Puccini, Giacomo

MANON LESCAUT: INTERMEZZO see Puccini,
Giacomo

MANON LESCAUT: INTERMEZZO, ACT III see
Puccini, Giacomo

MANON LESCAUT: SOLA, PERDUTA,
ABBANDONATA, FOR SOLO VOICE AND
ORCHESTRA see Puccini, Giacomo

MANYANAS LIEBESLIEDER, FOR SOLO VOICE
AND ORCHESTRA see Beers, Jacques

MANZONI, GIACOMO (1932-   )
Multipli
sc RICORDI-IT 132059 f.s.   (M109)

Percorso C 2
bsn,11strings
sc RICORDI-IT 132530 f.s.   (M110)

Variabili
sc RICORDI-IT 132079 f.s.   (M111)

MAOMETTO, IL: SECONDO OVERTURE see
Rossini, Gioacchino

MARCELLO, ALESSANDRO
(ca. 1684-ca. 1750)
Concerto in D minor, MIN 13
string orch,cont,ob solo
sc,pts MUS. RARA 41.891-20 f.s.
(M112)

Concerto in D minor, MIN 25
string orch,cont,ob solo
(Fechner) sc PETERS P9483 $20.00,
ipa   (M113)

Concerto in G, MIN 26
S rec,A rec,T rec,B rec,strings
(Croci) HEINRICH. N3374 sc $15.00,
set $20.00, pts $2.25, ea. (M114)

MARCELLO, BENEDETTO (1686-1739)
Qual Turbine Improvviso, For Solo
Voice And String Orchestra [8']
string orch,S solo
sc ZANIBON 5576 rent, pts ZANIBON
5577 rent   (M115)

Sinfonia, No. 3, in G [4'30"]
strings,hpsd
(Guglielmo) sc,pts ZANIBON ZA5587
f.s.   (M116)

MARCH II: SON OF A GAMBOLIER see Ives,
Charles

MARCH OF THE FINNISH INFANTRY, OP. 91A
see Sibelius, Jean

MARCH OF THE JOLLY MARKSMEN see Faust,
Willi

MARCH OF THE LITTLE LEAD SOLDIERS see
Pierne, Gabriel, Marche Des Petits
Soldats De Plomb, [arr.]

MARCHE DE L'ARMEE FRANCAISE AU TONKIN
see Desormes, I.C.

MARCHE DE TRIOMPHE see Charpentier,
Marc-Antoine

MARCHE DES PETITS SOLDATS DE PLOMB,
[ARR.] see Pierne, Gabriel

MARCHE FUNEBRE D'UNE MARIONETTE see
Gounod, Charles Francois

MARCHE HEROIQUE see Saint-Saens,
Camille

MARCHE LORRAINE see Strauss, Josef

MARCHE NUPTIALE see Gounod, Charles
Francois

MARCHE SLAVE see Tchaikovsky, Piotr
Ilyich

MARCHE SOLENNELLE see Tchaikovsky,
Piotr Ilyich

MARCHEN AUS DEM ORIENT. WALZER see
Strauss, Johann, [Jr.]

MARCHEN AUS DER HEIMAT WALZER see
Strauss, Eduard

MARCHEN VON DER SCHONEN MELUSINE see
Mendelssohn-Bartholdy, Felix

MARCHENMUSIK, EINE see Maasz, Gerhard

MARCHING SONG see Holst, Gustav

MARCIA FUNEBRE PER UN PULCINO see
Guarino, Carmine

MARCIA NUZIALE see Bossi, [Marco]
Enrico

MAREN AARIA, FOR SOLO VOICE AND
ORCHESTRA see Pylkkanen, Tauno
Kullervo

MARESCOTTI, ANDRE FRANCOIS (1902-   )
Concerto for Violoncello and
Orchestra [23']
2.2.2.2. 4.2.2.1. timp,2perc,
vibra,xylo,cel,harp,strings,vcl
solo
JOBERT perf mat rent   (M117)

MAREZ OYENS, TERA DE (1932-   )
Concertino 'In Exile', For Piano And
Orchestra [9']
2fl,horn,strings,pno solo
DONEMUS perf mat rent   (M118)

Episodes [30']
2.2.2.2. 2.2.3.0. timp,perc,
strings
sc DONEMUS f.s., perf mat rent
(M119)

Human [27']
2.2.2.2. 2.1.1.1. timp,4perc,
strings,electronic tape
sc DONEMUS f.s., perf mat rent
(M120)

Shoshadre [8'-12']
string orch
sc DONEMUS f.s., perf mat rent
(M121)

Transformation [11']
1.1.1.1. 2.1.1.0. 6perc,harp,pno,
cel,xylo,strings
sc DONEMUS f.s., perf mat rent
(M122)

MARGINALS see Eberhard, Dennis

MARGOLA, FRANCO (1908-   )
Concerto for Guitar and String
Orchestra [10']
string orch,gtr solo
(Tagliavini, E.) sc ZANIBON 5567
f.s., pts ZANIBON 5568 f.s.
(M123)

Concerto for Trumpet and Orchestra
perc,strings,trp solo
sc,pts ZANIBON 5764-5 rent   (M124)

Concerto Per La Candida Pace [16']
3.3.3.3. 3.3.4.1. timp,perc,pno,
strings
manuscript CARISCH   (M125)

Partita for Flute and String
Orchestra [12']
string orch,fl solo
sc ZANIBON 4696 f.s., pts ZANIBON
4697 f.s.   (M126)

Passacaglia [12'30"]
pno,perc,strings
sc ZANIBON 4787 f.s., pts ZANIBON
4788 f.s.   (M127)

Piccolo Concerto, For Oboe And String
Orchestra
string orch,ob solo
f.s. sc CARISCH 21642, pts CARISCH
21643   (M128)

MARGOLA, FRANCO (cont'd.)

Sinfonia for String Orchestra [20']
sc CARISCH 20752 f.s., pts CARISCH
18884 f.s.   (M129)

Suite for Clarinet and String
Orchestra [15']
string orch,clar solo
sc ZANIBON 5334 f.s., pts ZANIBON
5335 f.s.   (M130)

Variazioni Su Un Tema Giocoso [18']
string orch
sc CARISCH 21761 perf mat rent
(M131)

MARGUERITE AT THE SPINNING WHEEL,
[ARR.] see Schubert, Franz (Peter),
Gretchen Am Spinnrade, [arr.]

MARGUERITE UND DER BAR, DIE see Grimm,
Hans Heinz

MARIA CATLINA, FOR SOLO VOICE AND
ORCHESTRA see Sinigaglia, Leone

MARIA THERESIA SYMPHONY see Haydn,
[Franz] Joseph, Symphony No. 48 in
C

MARIA ZART, VON EDLER ART, FOR SOLO
VOICE AND STRING ORCHESTRA see
Andriessen, Hendrik

MARIATTI, FRANCO
Giorni Delusi, I
sc CARISCH perf mat rent   (M132)

MARIENKLANGE. WALZER see Strauss, Josef

MARINE, V see Kunst, Jos

MARINI, BIAGIO (ca. 1595-1665)
Balletto, [arr.]
(Bonelli, E.) string orch [8'] sc
ZANIBON 4027 f.s., pts ZANIBON
4028 f.s.   (M133)

MARINUZZI, GINO, JR. (1920-   )
Concertino for Oboe, Saxophone, Piano
and String Orchestra [16'30"]
string orch,ob solo,sax solo,pno
solo
sc CARISCH 19459 f.s., perf mat
rent   (M134)

Concerto for Orchestra [28']
3.3.2.2. 4.3.2.1. timp,cel,pno,
strings
manuscript CARISCH   (M135)

Concerto for Piano and Orchestra
[25']
1.1.1.1. 2.1.1.0. timp,perc,
strings,pno solo
manuscript CARISCH   (M136)

Piccole Variazioni Su Fra Martino
Campanaro [12']
1.2.2.1. 2.1.1.0. timp,perc,xylo,
strings
manuscript CARISCH   (M137)

MARION DELORME: MARCIA FUNEBRE see
Ponchielli, Amilcare

MARIONETTES, LES see Filipucci, Edmond

MARIOTTI, MARIO (1889-   )
Odisseo [18']
3.3.2.2. 4.2.3.1. timp,perc,harp,
strings
manuscript CARISCH   (M138)

MARITINO, IL, FOR SOLO VOICES AND
ORCHESTRA see Sinigaglia, Leone

MARKET DAY, FOR SOLO VOICE AND
ORCHESTRA
LUCKS 03083 set $15.00, pts $.75, ea.
(M139)

MARKEVITCH, IGOR (1912-1983)
Hymne A La Mort [4']
2.2.2.1. 1.1.0.0. 2perc,pno,
strings,opt A solo
BOOSEY   (M140)

Hymnes [18']
2.2.3.2. 2.2.2.0. 2perc,pno,
strings
BOOSEY   (M141)

Petite Suite D'Apres Schumann [16']
1.2.2.2. 2.1.1.0. perc,pno,
strings
BOOSEY   (M142)

Taille De L'Homme, La, For Solo Voice
And Instrumental Ensemble [40']
1.1.1.1. 1.1.0.0. pno,2vln,vla,
vcl,db,S solo
BOOSEY   (M143)

MARKISCHE SEEN see Blume, Karl

MARKOVIC, ADALBERT (1929-   )
    Collage
        2.2.2.2. 2.3.3.1. timp,perc,pno,
        harp,strings
        DRUS.HRVAT.SKLAD. f.s.   (M144)

    Lake In Zelengora, The, For Solo
        Voice And Orchestra
        3.3.3.3. 4.3.3.1. timp,perc,pno,
        harp,strings,solo voice
        DRUS.HRVAT.SKLAD. f.s.   (M145)

MAROS, MIKLOS (1943-   )
    Coalottino II, For Bass Clarinet And
        String Orchestra [12']
        string orch,bass clar solo
        sc STIM   (M146)

    Concerto for Wind Quintet and
        Orchestra [12']
        2.2.2.2. 2.2.2.0. 2perc,strings,
        wind quin soli
        sc STIM   (M147)

MAROS, RUDOLF (1917-   )
    Landscapes
        string orch
        sc PEER $6.00, perf mat rent (M148)

    Musica Da Camera Per 11
        fl,alto fl,2clar,bass clar,perc,
        hpsd,harp,2vln,vla,vcl,db
        PEER sc $5.00, set $10.00   (M149)

    Notices
        string orch
        [8'] sc PEER $7.00   (M150)

    Sirato, For Solo Voice And Chamber
        Orchestra [6']
        alto fl,ob,clar,bsn,bells,
        marimba,harp,strings,S solo
        sc PEER $5.00   (M151)

MARRIAGE OF FIGARO, THE: OVERTURE see
    Mozart, Wolfgang Amadeus, Nozze Di
    Figaro, Le: Overture

MARSCH, FOR VIOLIN AND ORCHESTRA see
    Kupkovic, Ladislav

MARSCH DER LANDSKNECHTE see Siebert,
    Friedrich

MARSCH IN C, K. 214 see Mozart,
    Wolfgang Amadeus

MARSCH IN D, K. 189 see Mozart,
    Wolfgang Amadeus

MARSCH IN D, K. 215 see Mozart,
    Wolfgang Amadeus

MARSCH IN D, K. 237 see Mozart,
    Wolfgang Amadeus

MARSCH IN D, K. 249 see Mozart,
    Wolfgang Amadeus

MARSCH IN D, K. 290 see Mozart,
    Wolfgang Amadeus

MARSCH IN D, K. 445 see Mozart,
    Wolfgang Amadeus

MARSCH IN F, K. 248 see Mozart,
    Wolfgang Amadeus

MARSCHE, DREI, K. 408 see Mozart,
    Wolfgang Amadeus

MARSCHE, ZWEI, K. 335 see Mozart,
    Wolfgang Amadeus

MARSCHE, K. 62, 189, 214, 215, 237,
    248, 249, 290, 335, 408, 1-3, 445,
    544 see Mozart, Wolfgang Amadeus

MARSCHERA, F.
    Canzone
        string orch
        (Lenzewski, G.) sc,pts VIEWEG 1810
        f.s.   (M152)

MARSCHNER, HEINRICH (AUGUST)
    (1795-1861)
    Hans Heiling: Overture
        BREITKOPF-W perf mat rent   (M153)

MARSEILLAISE, LA see Rouget de l'Isle,
    Claude Joseph

MARTHA: ACH SO FROMM, FOR SOLO VOICE
    AND ORCHESTRA see Flotow, Friedrich
    von

MARTHA: DIE LETZTE ROSE, FOR SOLO VOICE
    AND ORCHESTRA see Flotow, Friedrich
    von

MARTHA: LASST MICH EUCH FRAGEN, FOR
    SOLO VOICE AND ORCHESTRA see
    Flotow, Friedrich von

MARTHA: M'APPARI TUTT' AMOR see Flotow,
    Friedrich von, Martha: Ach So
    Fromm, For Solo Voice And Orchestra

MARTHA: OVERTURE see Flotow, Friedrich
    von

MARTHA: PORTER SONG see Flotow,
    Friedrich von, Martha: Lasst Mich
    Euch Fragen, For Solo Voice And
    Orchestra

MARTHA-QUADRILLE see Strauss, Johann,
    [Sr.]

MARTHA: TIS THE LAST ROSE OF SUMMER see
    Flotow, Friedrich von, Martha: Die
    Letzte Rose, For Solo Voice And
    Orchestra

MARTI, HEINZ (1934-   )
    Aurora E Danza
        perc,strings sc HUG GH11239 f.s.,
        perf mat rent   (M154)

MARTINCEK, DUSAN (1936-   )
    Introdukcia A Allegro
        pno,strings
        SLOV.HUD.FOND 0-252A perf mat rent
                                      (M155)

MARTINI, G.M. (1925-   )
    Salmo Funebre [10']
        1.1.2.2. 0.0.0.0. strings
        CARISCH perf mat rent   (M156)

MARTINI, [PADRE] GIOVANNI BATTISTA
    (1706-1784)
    Aria Variata
        see RICREAZIONI DI ANTICHE MUSICHE
        CLASSICHE, SERIE II: MUSICHE
        ANTICHE ITALIANE

    Concerto for Trumpet and String
        Orchestra [8']
        string orch,trp solo
        (Sciannameo, Franco) sc,pts
        RARITIES $12.00   (M157)

    Fantasy, [arr.]
        (Maione, Rino) sc DE SANTIS DS 1057
        f.s.   (M158)

    Gavotte, [arr.]
        (Roques, L.) 1.2.1.1. 0.0.0.0.
        strings KALMUS 5317 set $5.00,
        pts $.50, ea.   (M159)

    Sinfonia Con Violoncello Obbligato
        [10']
        (Sciannameo, Franco) sc,pts
        RARITIES $8.00   (M160)

MARTINO, ALADINO DI (1908-   )
    Canto Di Terra d'Oro, Il [11']
        3.2.3.2. 4.3.4.0. timp,perc,cel,
        xylo,harp,pno,strings,Mez solo
        sc CARISCH 19874 perf mat rent
                                      (M161)

    Locandiera, La: Overture [7']
        3.2.2.2. 4.3.0.0. timp,perc,
        bells,strings
        sc CARISCH 18893 perf mat rent
                                      (M162)

    Prelude [6']
        2.2.2.2. 2.0.0.0. cel,harp,
        strings
        min sc CARISCH 20770 perf mat rent
                                      (M163)

    Suite for Violin and Orchestra [13']
        2.2.2.2. 2.2.0.0. timp,perc,pno,
        strings,vln solo
        manuscript CARISCH   (M164)

MARTINO, DONALD (1931-   )
    Concerto for 3 Clarinets and
        Orchestra [26']
        1.1.0.2. 1.1.2.0. 2perc,pno,cel,
        2vln,vla,vcl,db,clar solo,bass
        clar solo,contrabass clar solo
        sc DANTALIAN DSE105 $60.00, study
        sc DANTALIAN DSE105A $12.00, pts
        DANTALIAN rent   (M165)

    Ritorno [15']
        2.3.3.2. 4.3.3.1. 4perc,cel,pno,
        harp,strings
        sc DANTALIAN DSE104 $35.00, study
        sc DANTALIAN DSE104A $6.00, pts
        DANTALIAN rent   (M166)

MARTINOTTI, BRUNO (1936-   )
    Paradigmi [14']
        2.2.2.2. 2.2.2.0. 2perc,harp,cel,
        timp,strings,electronic tape
        sc ZERBONI 8151 f.s., pts ZERBONI
        8153 rent   (M167)

MARTINSON, ROLF (1956-   )
    Impression [18'30"]
        2.2.2.2. 2.0.0.0. timp,strings
        pts STIM   (M168)

MARTINSON-KANTAT, FOR SOLO VOICES AND
    CHAMBER ORCHESTRA see Glaser,
    Werner Wolf

MARTINU, BOHUSLAV (1890-1959)
    Divertimento for Piano Left-Hand and
        Orchestra
        sc PANTON 1667 f.s.   (M169)

    Jazz Suite
        sc PANTON 1070 f.s.   (M170)

    Sinfonia Concertante
        sc BOOSEY $20.00   (M171)

    Sonata da Camera for Violoncello and
        Orchestra
        1.1.2.2. 2.0.0.0. strings,vcl
        solo
        study sc BAREN. BA 4319 f.s., perf
        mat rent   (M172)

    Toccata E Due Canzoni
        sc BOOSEY $35.00   (M173)

MARTIRIO DEL S. TERENZIO, IL see
    Caldara, Antonio

MARTTINEN, TAUNO (1912-   )
    Concerto For Piano And Orchestra,
        1964
        2.2.2.2. 4.2.2.1. timp,perc,
        strings,pno solo
        SEESAW perf mat rent   (M174)

MARTUCCI, GIUSEPPE (1856-1909)
    Gavotta *Op.55,No.2
        sc RICORDI-IT PR225 f.s.   (M175)

MARTYRE, UNE, FOR SOLO VOICE AND
    ORCHESTRA see Orthel, Leon

MARVIA, EINARI (1915-   )
    Serenata, For Solo Voice And
        Orchestra *Op.9,No.4 [3']
        2.2.2.2. 2.2.1.0. timp,perc,
        strings,solo voice
        FAZER perf mat rent   (M176)

    Syyspaiva, For Solo Voice And
        Orchestra *Op.17,No.2 [3']
        2.0.2.0. 2.0.0.0. strings,solo
        voice
        FAZER perf mat rent   (M177)

    Tuulen Kehtolaulu, For Solo Voice And
        Orchestra [2']
        2.0.2.0. 0.0.0.0. strings,solo
        voice
        FAZER perf mat rent   (M178)

MARX, KARL (1897-   )
    Entschlafenen, Die, For Solo Voice
        And String Orchestra *Op.70,No.3
        string orch,med solo
        BAREN. BA 6705 perf mat rent (M179)

MARZVEILCHEN POLKA see Strauss, Eduard

MASANIELLO: OVERTURE see Auber, Daniel-
    Francois-Esprit, Muette De Portici,
    La: Overture

MASCAGNI, PIETRO (1863-1945)
    Amico Fritz, L': Intermezzo [4']
        2+pic.2.2.2. 4.2.3.1. timp,perc,
        harp,strings
        LUCKS 06199 sc $8.00, set $22.00,
        pts $.90, ea.   (M180)
        KALMUS A4875 sc $4.00, perf mat
        rent, set $13.00, pts $.75, ea.
                                      (M181)

    Amico Fritz, L': Preludio
        2+pic.2.2.2. 4.2.3.1. timp,perc,
        harp,strings
        KALMUS A4869 sc $8.00, perf mat
        rent, set $16.00, pts $.75, ea.
                                      (M182)

    Cavalleria Rusticana: Addio Alla
        Madre, For Solo Voice And
        Orchestra
        LUCKS 03548 sc $4.00, set $8.00,
        pts $.60, ea.   (M183)

    Cavalleria Rusticana: Bada Santuzza,
        For Solo Voices And Orchestra
        LUCKS 03544 sc $3.00, set $5.00,
        pts $.60, ea.   (M184)

    Cavalleria Rusticana: Brindisi, "Viva
        Il Vino Spumeggiante", For Solo
        Voice And Orchestra
        LUCKS 02250 sc $4.00, set $9.00,
        pts $.60, ea.   (M185)

    Cavalleria Rusticana: Il Cavallo
        Scalpita, For Solo Voice And
        Orchestra
        LUCKS 03542 sc $3.00, set $5.00,
        pts $.60, ea.   (M186)

    Cavalleria Rusticana: Intermezzo
        LUCKS 09029 sc $5.50, set $11.00,
        pts $.95, ea.   (M187)

    Cavalleria Rusticana: No, No Turiddu,
        Rimani, For Solo Voices And
        Orchestra
        LUCKS 03545 sc $4.00, set $9.00,
        pts $.60, ea.   (M188)

MASCAGNI, PIETRO (cont'd.)

Cavalleria Rusticana: Preludio E
Siciliana
LUCKS 09028 sc $5.50, set $16.00,
pts $.95, ea.   (M189)

Cavalleria Rusticana: Turiddu Mi
Tolse L'Onore, For Solo Voices
And Orchestra
LUCKS 03546 sc $4.00, set $9.00,
pts $.60, ea.   (M190)

Cavalleria Rusticana: Voi Lo Sapete,
For Solo Voice And Orchestra
LUCKS 02011 sc $3.75, set $7.50,
pts $.75, ea.   (M191)

Guglielmo Ratcliff: Intermezzo
(Prelude, Act IV)
2+pic.2+English horn.0.2.2basset
horn. 4.2.0.0. timp,perc,harp,
strings
"William Radcliffe: Intermezzo"
KALMUS A5507 sc $5.00, perf mat
rent, set $13.00, pts $.75, ea.
                                 (M192)

Guglielmo Ratcliff: Introduction
2+pic.2+English horn.2+bass
clar.2+contrabsn. 4.3.3.1.
timp,perc,2harp,strings
"William Radcliffe: Introduction"
KALMUS A5508 sc $5.00, perf mat
rent, set $16.00, pts $.75, ea.
                                 (M193)

Guglielmo Ratcliff: Sogno, Act III
"William Radcliffe: Radcliffe's
Dream" KALMUS A5509 sc $5.00,
perf mat rent, set $20.00, pts
$.75, ea.   (M194)
"William Ratcliff: Ratcliff's
Dream" LUCKS 07478 sc $5.00, set
$25.00, pts $.80, ea.   (M195)

William Radcliffe: Intermezzo *see
Guglielmo Ratcliff: Intermezzo
(Prelude, Act IV)

William Radcliffe: Introduction *see
Guglielmo Ratcliff: Introduction

William Radcliffe: Radcliffe's Dream
*see Guglielmo Ratcliff: Sogno,
Act III

William Ratcliff: Ratcliff's Dream
*see Guglielmo Ratcliff: Sogno,
Act III

MASETTI, ENZO (1893-1961)
Sagra [4']
3.3.3.3. 4.3.3.1. perc,cel,harp,
xylo,pno,strings
manuscript CARISCH   (M196)

MASKENZUG. POLKA see Strauss, Johann,
[Jr.]

MASONIC FUNERAL MUSIC see Mozart,
Wolfgang Amadeus, Maurerische
Trauermusik

MASQUERADE SUITE see Khachaturian, Aram
Ilyich

MASSARANI, RENZO (1898-1975)
Introduzione, Tema E Sette Variazioni
[18']
1.1.1.1. 1.1.1.0. pno,strings
sc CARISCH 17117 perf mat rent
                                 (M197)

MASSE, VICTOR (1822-1884)
Jeannettens Hochzeit: Wollt Bluhen
Ihr Seh'n, For Solo Voice And
Orchestra [8']
1+pic.2.2.2. 4.3.0.0. strings,S
solo
sc,pts LIENAU rent   (M198)

MASSENET, JULES (1842-1912)
Cendrillon Suite No. 1: Le Sommeil De
Cendrillon
KALMUS 5298 sc $3.00, perf mat
rent, set $8.00, pts $.50, ea.
                                 (M199)

Cendrillon Suite No. 2: Les Filles De
Noblesse
KALMUS 5321 sc $5.00, perf mat
rent, set $15.00, pts $.75, ea.
                                 (M200)

Cendrillon Suite No. 3: Menuet
KALMUS 5299 sc $8.00, perf mat
rent, set $12.00, pts $.60, ea.
                                 (M201)

Cendrillon Suite No.4: Les Tendres
Fiances
KALMUS 5300 sc $2.00, perf mat
rent, set $9.00, pts $.60, ea.
                                 (M202)

Cendrillon Suite No. 5: Les Mandores
KALMUS 5303 sc $5.00, perf mat
rent, set $10.00, pts $.60, ea.
                                 (M203)

Cendrillon Suite No. 6: La Florentine
KALMUS 5302 sc $5.00, perf mat
rent, set $12.00, pts $.75, ea.

MASSENET, JULES (cont'd.)
                                 (M204)
Cendrillon Suite No. 7: Marche Des
Princesses
KALMUS 5301 sc $8.00, perf mat
rent, set $15.00, pts $.75, ea.
                                 (M205)

Cid, Le: Ballet Suite [16']
2(pic).2(English horn).2.2. 4.2+
2cornet.3.1. timp,perc,2harp,
strings
KALMUS A1690 sc $22.00, perf mat
rent, set $65.00, pts $3.50, ea.
                                 (M206)

Cid, Le: Pleurez, Pleurez Mes Yeux,
For Solo Voice And Orchestra
LUCKS 02087 sc $6.00, set $12.00,
pts $.75, ea.   (M207)

Don Quichotte: Interlude No. 1,
"Serenade"
LUCKS 07145 sc $2.00, set $7.00,
pts $.60, ea.   (M208)

Don Quichotte: Interlude No. 2, "La
Tristesse De Dulcinee"
LUCKS 07137 sc $2.00, set $7.00,
pts $.60, ea.   (M209)

Herodiade: Ballet Suite
LUCKS 05481 sc $15.00, set $55.00,
pts $2.50, ea.   (M210)

Herodiade: Il Est Doux, Il Est Bon,
For Solo Voice And Orchestra
LUCKS 02012 sc $3.75, set $7.50,
pts $.75, ea.   (M211)

Herodiade: Vision Fugitive, For Solo
Voice And Orchestra
LUCKS 02031 sc $3.75, set $9.50,
pts $.75, ea.   (M212)

Je Marche Sur Tous Les Chemins *see
Manon: Introduction And Gavotte

Manon: Ah! Fuyez Douce Image, For
Solo Voice And Orchestra
LUCKS 02120 sc $3.75, set $9.50,
pts $.75, ea.   (M213)

Manon: Introduction And Gavotte
KALMUS 5180 sc $4.00, perf mat
rent, set $12.00, pts $.60, ea.
                                 (M214)
"Je Marche Sur Tous Les Chemins"
LUCKS 02353 sc $3.00, set $10.00,
pts $.75, ea.   (M215)

Manon: Le Reve, "En Fermant Les
Yeux", For Solo Voice And
Orchestra
LUCKS 02114 sc $3.75, set $7.50,
pts $.75, ea.   (M216)

Thais: Meditation
LUCKS 06217 sc $5.50, set $11.00,
pts $.95, ea.   (M217)

Werther: Pourquoi Me Reveiller, For
Solo Voice And Orchestra
LUCKS 02200 sc $3.75, set $9.50,
pts $.75, ea.   (M218)

MASSEUS, JAN (1913-   )
Akoetest *Op.45 [10']
3.3.3.3. 4.3.3.1. timp,perc,harp,
pno,strings
sc DONEMUS f.s., perf mat rent
                                 (M219)

Iowa Serenade *Op.56 [17']
2.2.2.1. 2.2.0.0. timp,2-3perc,
strings
DONEMUS   (M220)

MASSIMO, LEONE (1896-   )
Concerto for Violin and Orchestra
[15']
1.1.1.2. 1.1.0.0. timp,strings,
vln solo
manuscript CARISCH   (M221)

Concerto Grosso [12']
0.1.1.1. 0.1.1.0. timp,pno,
strings
manuscript CARISCH   (M222)

Divertimento No. 1 [17']
4.3.3.3. 4.3.3.0. timp,strings
manuscript CARISCH   (M223)

Divertimento No. 2 [18']
2.2.2.2. 2.1.1.0. timp,strings
manuscript CARISCH   (M224)

Quattro Pezzi Per Orchestra [20']
5.3.4.3. 4.3.2.1. timp,harp,
strings
manuscript CARISCH   (M225)

Serenade [16']
4.3.4.4. 4.3.3.0. timp,org,pno,
strings
manuscript CARISCH   (M226)

MASSON, GERARD (1936-   )
Concerto for Piano and Orchestra
3(2pic).2(English horn).2(bass
clar,contrabass
clar).2(contrabsn). 4.2.2.0.
perc,2harp,2cel,strings,pno
solo
SALABERT perf mat rent   (M227)

Pas Seulement Des Moments, Des Moyens
d'Amour [26']
4.4.4(bass clar,contrabass
clar).2(contrabsn). 4.3.2.1.
3perc,2pno,strings
SALABERT perf mat rent   (M228)

MATEJ, JOZKA (1922-   )
Symphony No. 3
sc PANTON 1330 f.s.   (M229)

MATEJ: INTERMEZZO see Rosinsky, Jozef

MATERI see Ukmar, Vilko

MATERIAM SUPERABAT OPUS ZELOMANIANA,
FOR OBOE AND STRING ORCHESTRA see
Knap, Rolf

MATHIAS, WILLIAM (1934-   )
Celtic Dances *Op.60 [14']
2.2.2.2. 4.2.3.0.opt tuba. timp,
3perc,cel,harp,strings
sc OXFORD 77.881 $17.50, perf mat
rent   (M230)

Dance Variations *Op.72 [20']
2.2.2.2. 2.2.0.0. timp,strings
sc OXFORD 77.155 $30.00, perf mat
rent   (M231)

Helios *Op.76 [16']
2.2.2.2. 4.3.3.1. timp,3perc,pno,
cel,harp,strings
OXFORD perf mat rent   (M232)

Laudi *Op.62 [13']
2.2.2.3. 4.2.3.0. timp,perc,pno,
cel,strings
study sc OXFORD 77.889 $18.00
                                 (M233)

Melos *Op.73 [14']
fl,harp,perc,strings
OXFORD perf mat rent   (M234)

Vistas *Op.69 [17']
2(pic).2.2.2. 4.3.3.1. timp,
3perc,harp,pno&cel,strings
study sc OXFORD 77.888 $12.00
                                 (M235)

MATI see Osterc, Slavko

MATICIC, JANEZ (1926-   )
Concerto for Piano and Orchestra
[25']
2(pic).2.2(bass clar).2. 4.3.3.1.
timp,2perc,strings,pno solo
DRUSTVO DSS 845 perf mat rent
                                 (M236)

Symphony [33']
2(pic).2.2(bass
clar).2(contrabsn). 4.2.3.1.
timp,perc,strings
DRUSTVO DSS 768 perf mat rent
                                 (M237)

MATROSENTANZ see Pranschke, Johannes

MATSUMURA, TEIZO (1929-   )
Concerto for Piano and Orchestra, No.
1
orch,pno solo
ZEN-ON 899162   (M238)

Concerto for Piano and Orchestra, No.
2
orch,pno solo
ZEN-ON 899163   (M239)

MATSUSHITA, SHIN-ICHI (1922-   )
Haleines Astrales [15']
1.1.1.1. 1.1.1.0. harp,pno,2vln,
vla,vcl
ONGAKU perf mat rent   (M240)

Idylle, For Violin And Orchestra
3(pic).2.2+bass clar.0. 4.3.3.1.
timp,pno/cel,vibra,harp,
strings,vln solo
ONGAKU perf mat rent   (M241)

Sinfonia Vita [18']
6perc,pno,strings
ONGAKU perf mat rent   (M242)

Three Tempi [18']
1.0.1+bass clar.0.alto sax.
0.1.1.0. vibra,pno,vla,vcl,db
ONGAKU perf mat rent   (M243)

MATTAUSCH, H.A.
Nymphenburger Schlossmusik [20']
2.1.2.1. 2.0.0.0. timp,triangle,
glock,strings
sc RIES f.s., perf mat rent   (M244)

MATTAUSCH, H.A. (cont'd.)

Spitzweg-Suite [20']
string orch
RIES perf mat rent   (M245)

MATTEI, STANISLAV (1750-1825)
Sinfonias, Five
(Longyear, Rey M.) ("The Symphony",
Vol. A-VIII) sc GARLAND
ISBN 0-8240-3802-9 $90.00
contains also: Zingarelli, Nicola
Antonio, Sinfonias, Seven   (M246)

MATTHEWS
Night Music
sc FABER $2.00   (M247)

MATTHUS, SIEGFRIED (1934-   )
Concerto for Flute and Orchestra
3.2.3.2. 0.0.3.0. timp,3perc,
harp,strings,fl solo
DEUTSCHER 1435 perf mat rent (M248)

Concerto for Violoncello and
Orchestra
3.3.3.3. 4.3.3.1. timp,perc,
strings,vcl solo
sc DEUTSCHER 1427 f.s.   (M249)

Hyperion-Fragmente, For Solo Voice
And Orchestra
3.3.3.3. 2.4.3.1. timp,perc,harp,
strings,B solo
DEUTSCHER perf mat rent   (M250)

Responso
sc DEUTSCHER DVFM 1706 f.s. (M251)

Visionen
string orch
sc DEUTSCHER DVFM 1708 f.s. (M252)

MATTINATA, FOR SOLO VOICE AND ORCHESTRA
see Leoncavallo, Ruggiero

MAURERISCHE TRAUERMUSIK see Mozart,
Wolfgang Amadeus

MAURISCHE RHAPSODIE see Karrasch, Kurt

MAUSOLEUM see Andriessen, Louis

MAW, NICHOLAS (1935-   )
Concert Music (from Rising Of The
Moon, The) [14']
3(pic).3(English horn).3(clar in
E flat).2. 4.3.2.1. timp,perc,
harp,cel,strings
BOOSEY perf mat rent   (M253)

Life Study No. 2 (from Life Studies)
[8']
string orch
BOOSEY perf mat rent   (M254)

Serenade [15']
1.2.0.2. 2.0.0.0. strings
BOOSEY perf mat rent   (M255)

MAXING TANZE. WALZER see Strauss,
Johann, [Jr.]

MAXWELL DAVIES, PETER
see DAVIES, PETER MAXWELL

MAY, HELMUT W.
I Want To Die Easy, For Violin And
String Orchestra [17']
string orch,vln solo
SCHOTTS CON 190 sc $13.00, pts
$2.50, ea.   (M256)

MAY NIGHT see Palmgren, Selim

MAYER, WILLIAM ROBERT (1925-   )
Andante For String Orchestra [6']
string orch
study sc MCA $1.00, perf mat rent
                             (M257)

M'AYMEREZ-VOUS BIEN? see Beekhuis,
Hanna

MAYO, FELIPE DE (1789- ?)
Sinfonia in F
see SYMPHONY IN MADRID, THE

MAYR, JOHANN SIMON (1763-1845)
Concerto Bergamasco [18']
1.2.1.1. 2.2.1.0. timp,strings,
pic&fl solo,clar&basset horn
solo
ORLANDO rent   (M258)

MAYUZUMI, TOSHIRO (1929-   )
Aria In G, For Violin And Orchestra
3.3.3.3. 4.3.3.1. timp,4perc,
harp,cel,strings,vln solo
PETERS P66771 perf mat rent (M259)

MAZEPPA: OVERTURE see Tchaikovsky,
Piotr Ilyich

MAZURKA see Bullerian, Hans

MAZURKA see Glazunov, Alexander
Konstantinovich

MAZURKA see Pogorelow, W.

MAZURKA, FOR VIOLIN AND ORCHESTRA,
[ARR.] see Mlynarski, Emil

MAZURKA, OP. 19 see Liadov, Anatol
Konstantinovich

MEALE, RICHARD (1932-   )
Viridian [16']
string orch
UNIVER. perf mat rent   (M260)

MECHEM, KIRKE LEWIS (1925-   )
Symphony No. 1, Op. 16
sc BOOSEY $15.00   (M261)

Symphony No. 2 [32']
2(pic).2(English horn).2(bass
clar).2(contrabsn). 4.3.3.1.
pno,timp,perc,strings
BOOSEY perf mat rent   (M262)

MED SINA SKONASTE SANGER, FOR SOLO
VOICE AND ORCHESTRA see Linnala,
Eino

MEDICUS, V. (1896-   )
Ultime Rose, For Solo Voice And
Orchestra [3']
1.1.1.1. 2.0.0.0. strings,solo
voice
manuscript CARISCH   (M263)

MEDIN, N. (1904-1969)
Danze Per I Cinque Cerchi [18']
3.2.2.2. 4.2.2.0. timp,perc,harp,
strings
manuscript CARISCH   (M264)

Introduzione, Aria E Finale, For
Violin And Orchestra [20']
1.1.1.1. 1.1.0.0. pno,strings,vln
solo
manuscript CARISCH   (M265)

Partita [11']
string orch
manuscript CARISCH   (M266)

Serenata Concertante, For Viola,
Double Bass And Orchestra [19']
1.1.2.2. 1.1.0.0. perc,cel,pno,
vibra,strings,vla solo,db solo
manuscript CARISCH   (M267)

Sinfonia No. 1 [28']
3.3.3.3. 4.3.3.1. timp,perc,
strings
manuscript CARISCH   (M268)

Sinfonia No. 2 [23']
3.2.2.2. 4.3.3.1. timp,perc,
strings
manuscript CARISCH   (M269)

MEDITATION see Gounod, Charles
Francois, Ave Maria, [arr.]

MEDITATION AND DANCE, FOR PIANO AND
ORCHESTRA see Suchon, Eugen,
Maditacia A Tanec, For Piano And
Orchestra

MEDITATION ON AN OLD BOHEMIAN CHORALE
see Suk, Josef, Meditation On The
Chorale "Saint Wenceslas"

MEDITATION ON THE CHORALE "SAINT
WENCESLAS" see Suk, Josef

MEDITATIONS see Berkeley, Michael

MEDITATIONS ON POEMS BY DYLAN THOMAS,
FOR SOLO VOICE AND ORCHESTRA see
Kruyf, Ton de

MEERESSTILLE UND GLUCKLICHE FAHRT see
Mendelssohn-Bartholdy, Felix

MEETING THE ORCHESTRA, FOR NARRATOR AND
ORCHESTRA see Brevik, Tor

MEFISTOFELE: ECCO IL MONDO, FOR SOLO
VOICE AND ORCHESTRA see Boito,
Arrigo

MEFISTOFELE: L'ALTRA NOTTE, FOR SOLO
VOICE AND ORCHESTRA see Boito,
Arrigo

MEFISTOFELE: SON LO SPIRITO, FOR SOLO
VOICE AND ORCHESTRA see Boito,
Arrigo

MEFISTOFELE: SONG OF THE WHISTLE see
Boito, Arrigo, Mefistofele: Son Lo
Spirito, For Solo Voice And
Orchestra

MEGA-MELOS see Kang, Sukhi

MEGLIO MIO CARATTERE, IL, FOR SOLO
VOICE AND ORCHESTRA see Haydn,
[Franz] Joseph

MEHUL, ETIENNE-NICOLAS (1763-1817)
Symphonies, Three
(Charlton, David; Caston, Anthony)
sc GARLAND ISBN 0-8240-3812-6
$90.00 "The Symphony", Vol. D-
VIII
contains: Symphony No. 3 in C;
Symphony No. 4 in E; Symphony
No. 5 in A   (M270)

Symphony No. 1 in G minor [25']
2.2.2.2. 2.0.0.0. timp,strings
BREITKOPF-W perf mat rent   (M271)

Symphony No. 3 in C
see Symphonies, Three

Symphony No. 4 in E
see Symphonies, Three

Symphony No. 5 in A
see Symphonies, Three

MEIJERING, CHIEL (1954-   )
Are All Americans Made Of Plastic?
[25']
3.3.3.4. 8.4.4.1. 5perc,2harp,
pno,strings
DONEMUS sc f.s., pts rent   (M272)

Bedouin Caravan In The Desert [11']
1.1.1.2. 2.2.2.1. timp,perc,
strings
DONEMUS perf mat rent   (M273)

End Of A Specimen, The [15']
3.3.3.3. 4.4.3.1. 6perc,pno,
2harp,strings
DONEMUS   (M274)

Suite 16 [15']
2.2.2.1.alto sax. 1.0.0.0.
strings, female voice
DONEMUS sc f.s., pts rent   (M275)

Zombies Awake, The [10']
2pic,2fl,2ob,2clar,perc,harp,pno,
strings
DONEMUS perf mat rent   (M276)

MEIN JESU, [ARR.] see Bach, Johann
Sebastian

MEIN JESU, WAS FUR SEELENWEH, [ARR.]
see Bach, Johann Sebastian

MEIN LEBENSLAUF IST LIEB' UND LUST see
Strauss, Josef

MEIN LIEBLINGSLIED see Geisler, Willy

MEIN SCHONES ERZGEBIRGE see Scheibe, W.

MEIN SCHONES UNGARLAND see Fridl, Hans

MEINE LIEBE IST GRUN, FOR SOLO VOICE
AND ORCHESTRA, [ARR.] see Brahms,
Johannes

MEINE SEELE ERHEBT DEN HERREN, FOR SOLO
VOICE AND ORCHESTRA see Telemann,
Georg Philipp

MEISTERSINGER VON NURNBERG, DIE:
MORGENLICH LEUCHTEND see Wagner,
Richard

MEISTERSINGER VON NURNBERG, DIE:
MORGENLICH LEUCHTEND, FOR SOLO
VOICE AND ORCHESTRA see Wagner,
Richard

MEISTERSINGER VON NURNBERG, DIE:
PRELUDE see Wagner, Richard

MEISTERSINGER VON NURNBERG, DIE: WAHN,
WAHN, UBERALL WAHN, FOR SOLO VOICE
AND ORCHESTRA see Wagner, Richard

MEISTERSINGER VON NURNBERG, DIE:
WALTER'S PRIZE SONG see Wagner,
Richard, Meistersinger Von
Nurnberg, Die: Morgenlich Leuchtend

MEISTERSINGER VON NURNBERG, DIE:
WALTHER'S PRIZE SONG see Wagner,
Richard, Meistersinger Von
Nurnberg, Die: Morgenlich
Leuchtend, For Solo Voice And
Orchestra

MELARTIN, ERKKI (1875-1937)
Sirkan Haamatka, For Solo Voice And
Orchestra [2']
2.1.2.1. 3.1.0.0. timp,strings,
solo voice
FAZER f.s.   (M277)

MELCHER, JOHN (1951-   )
  From Wood And Metal [9']
    1.1.1.1. 2.2.0.0. perc,pno,8vln,
    3vla,2vcl,2db
    sc ZERBONI 8125 f.s., pts ZERBONI
    8126 rent   (M278)

MELEK NATO, DAL CUORE LUMINOSO see De
  Grandis, Renato

MELENCOLIA I, FOR CLARINET, HARP AND
  STRING ORCHESTRA see Birtwistle,
  Harrison

MELITTA see Blon, Franz von

MELODIA see Geisler, Willy

MELODIA-RITMICA, OP. 59, NO. 2 see
  Eder, Helmut

MELODIE, FOR VIOLIN AND ORCHESTRA see
  Bird, Arthur

MELODIE ET SERENADE ESPAGNOLE, FOR
  VIOLONCELLO AND ORCHESTRA see
  Glazunov, Alexander Konstantinovich

MELODIE UND RHYTHMUS see Geisler, Willy

MELODIEN QUADRILLE, OP. 112 see
  Strauss, Johann, [Jr.]

MELODIEN QUADRILLE, OP. 254 see
  Strauss, Johann, [Jr.]

MELODY IN F, [ARR.] see Rubinstein,
  Anton

MELOS see Mathias, William

MEMOIRE see Benes, Juraj

MEMORIALS see Gould, Morton

MEMORIE see Bartolozzi, Bruno

MEMORIES OF YOU see Bruce

MENDELSSOHN-BARTHOLDY, FELIX
  (1809-1847)
  Athalie: Kriegsmarsch Der Priester
    "Athalie: War March Of Priests"
    LUCKS 06228 sc $10.00, set
    $14.00, pts $1.15, ea.   (M279)

  Athalie: War March Of Priests *see
    Athalie: Kriegsmarsch Der
    Priester

  Beautiful Melusine *see Marchen Von
    Der Schonen Melusine

  Calm Sea And Prosperous Voyage *see
    Meeresstille Und Gluckliche Fahrt

  Canzonetta *Op.14
    string orch
    LUCKS 06230 sc $2.50, set $5.00,
    pts $1.00, ea.   (M280)

  Capriccio Brillante, For Piano And
    Orchestra *Op.22
    LUCKS 00043 sc $8.50, set $14.00,
    pts $1.15, ea.   (M281)

  Concerto for Piano and Orchestra, No.
    1, Op. 25, in G minor
    BROUDE BR. set $22.50, pts $1.50,
    ea.   (M282)
    study sc INTERNAT. 464 $4.25 (M283)
    LUCKS 00041 sc $13.00, set $16.00,
    min sc $2.50, pts $1.40, ea.
                               (M284)
  Concerto for Piano and Orchestra, No.
    2, Op. 40, in D minor
    LUCKS 00042 sc $14.00, set $20.00,
    min sc $5.00, pts $1.60, ea.
                               (M285)
  Concerto for Violin and Orchestra,
    Op. 64, in E minor
    BROUDE BR. sc $15.00, set $25.00,
    pts $1.75, ea.   (M286)
    min sc ZEN-ON 891341 f.s. (M287)
    LUCKS 00520 sc $7.50, set $18.00,
    min sc $3.00, pts $1.60, ea.
                               (M288)
  Elias: Dann Werden Die Gerechten
    Leuchten, For Solo Voice And
    Orchestra
    "Elijah: Then Shall The Righteous
    Shine" LUCKS 03110 sc $3.75, set
    $7.75, pts $.75, ea.   (M289)

  Elias: Es Ist Genug, For Solo Voice
    And Orchestra
    "Elijah: It Is Enough" LUCKS 02208
    sc $3.75, set $7.50, pts $.75,
    ea.   (M290)

  Elias: Herr Gott Abrahams, Isaaks,
    Und Israels, For Solo Voice And
    Orchestra
    "Elijah: Lord God Of Abraham" LUCKS
    02969 sc $2.00, set $6.75, pts
    $.75, ea.   (M291)

MENDELSSOHN-BARTHOLDY, FELIX (cont'd.)

  Elias: Hore, Israel, For Solo Voice
    And Orchestra
    "Elijah: Hear Ye, Israel" LUCKS
    02325 sc $3.75, set $7.50, pts
    $.75, ea.   (M292)

  Elias: Ist Nicht Des Herren Wort Wie
    Ein Feuer?, For Solo Voice And
    Orchestra
    "Elijah: Is Not His Word Like A
    Fire?" LUCKS 03111 sc $3.75, set
    $7.50, pts $.75, ea.   (M293)

  Elias: Ja, Es Sollen Wohl Berge
    Weichen, For Solo Voice And
    Orchestra
    "Elijah: For The Mountains Shall
    Depart" LUCKS 03304 sc $3.75, set
    $7.50, pts $.75, ea.   (M294)

  Elias: Sei Stille Dem Herrn Und Warte
    Auf Ihn, For Solo Voice And
    Orchestra
    "Elijah: O Rest In The Lord" LUCKS
    02972 sc $2.00, set $6.00, pts
    $.75, ea.   (M295)

  Elias: So Ihr Mich Von Ganzem Herzen
    Suchet, For Solo Voice And
    Orchestra
    "Elijah: If With All Your Hearts"
    LUCKS 02397 sc $3.75, set $7.50,
    pts $.75, ea.   (M296)

  Elijah: For The Mountains Shall
    Depart *see Elias: Ja, Es Sollen
    Wohl Berge Weichen, For Solo
    Voice And Orchestra

  Elijah: Hear Ye, Israel *see Elias:
    Hore, Israel, For Solo Voice And
    Orchestra

  Elijah: If With All Your Hearts *see
    Elias: So Ihr Mich Von Ganzem
    Herzen Suchet, For Solo Voice And
    Orchestra

  Elijah: Is Not His Word Like A Fire?
    *see Elias: Ist Nicht Des Herren
    Wort Wie Ein Feuer?, For Solo
    Voice And Orchestra

  Elijah: It Is Enough *see Elias: Es
    Ist Genug, For Solo Voice And
    Orchestra

  Elijah: Lord God Of Abraham *see
    Elias: Herr Gott Abrahams,
    Isaaks, Und Israels, For Solo
    Voice And Orchestra

  Elijah: O Rest In The Lord *see
    Elias: Sei Stille Dem Herrn Und
    Warte Auf Ihn, For Solo Voice And
    Orchestra

  Elijah: Then Shall The Righteous
    Shine *see Elias: Dann Werden
    Die Gerechten Leuchten, For Solo
    Voice And Orchestra

  Fingal's Cave Overture *see
    Hebriden, Die

  Hark The Herald Angels Sing
    (Luck, Arthur) LUCKS HYMNS 3 set
    $10.00, pts $.65, ea. contains
    also: Wade, Adeste Fidelis (M297)

  Hebriden, Die *Op.26
    "Fingal's Cave Overture" BROUDE BR.
    set $22.50 pts $1.50, ea. (M298)
    "Fingal's Cave Overture" min sc
    PETERS 615 $5.00   (M299)
    "Fingal's Cave Overture" LUCKS
    06232 sc $7.50, set $18.00, min
    sc $3.00, pts $1.15, ea.   (M300)

  Italian Symphony *see Symphony No.
    4, Op. 90, in A

  Marchen Von Der Schonen Melusine
    *Op.32
    "Beautiful Melusine" LUCKS 07484 sc
    $10.00, set $17.00, min sc $2.50,
    pts $1.25, ea.   (M301)

  Meeresstille Und Gluckliche Fahrt
    *Op.27
    "Calm Sea And Prosperous Voyage"
    min sc PETERS 699 $5.00   (M302)
    "Calm Sea And Prosperous Voyage"
    LUCKS 06234 sc $10.00, set
    $17.00, pts $1.25, ea.   (M303)

  Midsummer Night's Dream: Dance Of The
    Clowns
    (Mayes) LUCKS 11206 sc $2.75, set
    $3.00, pts $.30, ea.   (M304)

  Midsummer Night's Dream: Five
    Excerpts
    min sc PETERS 698 $6.00   (M305)

MENDELSSOHN-BARTHOLDY, FELIX (cont'd.)

  Midsummer Night's Dream: Intermezzo
    LUCKS 06238 sc $4.00, set $10.00,
    pts $.95, ea.   (M306)

  Midsummer Night's Dream: Notturno
    LUCKS 06237 sc $4.00, set $9.50,
    pts $.95, ea.   (M307)

  Midsummer Night's Dream: Oh
    Glimmering Light, For Solo Voices
    And Orchestra
    LUCKS 03305 sc $3.75, set $7.50,
    pts $.75, ea.   (M308)

  Midsummer Night's Dream: Oh Spotted
    Snake, For Solo Voice And
    Orchestra
    LUCKS 03306 sc $4.75, set $9.50,
    pts $.75, ea.   (M309)

  Midsummer Night's Dream: Overture
    *Op.21 [12']
    2.2.2.2. 2.2.0.1. timp,strings
    BROUDE BR. set $22.50, pts $1.50,
    ea.   (M310)
    pts BREITKOPF-L OB 191 f.s. (M311)
    LUCKS 06236 sc $10.00, set $14.00,
    min sc $2.50, pts $1.15, ea.
                               (M312)
    "Sommernachtstraum: Overture" min
    sc UNIVER. PH16 $3.00   (M313)

  Midsummer Night's Dream: Scherzo
    LUCKS 06239 sc $4.00, set $11.00,
    pts $.95, ea.   (M314)

  Midsummer Night's Dream: Wedding
    March
    LUCKS 06240 sc $4.00, set $14.00,
    pts $.95, ea.   (M315)

  Octet, Op. 20, Scherzo, [arr.]
    (Mendelssohn-Bartholdy, Felix)
    2.2.2.2. 2.2.0.0. timp,strings
    [5'] KALMUS A4482 sc $7.00, perf
    mat rent, set $15.00, pts $1.00,
    ea.   (M316)

  Paulus: Gott Sei Mir Gnadig, For Solo
    Voice And Orchestra
    "St. Paul: O Lord Have Mercy" LUCKS
    02954 sc $4.00, set $8.00, pts
    $.60, ea.   (M317)

  Reformation Symphony *see Symphony
    No. 5, Op. 107, in D minor

  Romance in E, [arr.] (from Op. 19)
    (Salabert, F.) 1.1.1.1. 0.1.1.0.
    timp,harp,strings KALMUS A4558 sc
    $3.00, set $7.00, pts $.60, ea.
                               (M318)

  Ruy Blas Overture
    LUCKS 06243 sc $9.50, set $20.00,
    min sc $2.50, pts $1.15, ea.
                               (M319)

  St. Paul: O Lord Have Mercy *see
    Paulus: Gott Sei Mir Gnadig, For
    Solo Voice And Orchestra

  Sinfonia No. 9 in C
    string orch
    LUCKS 08995 sc $7.50, set $7.50,
    pts $1.40, ea.   (M320)

  Sommernachtstraum: Overture *see
    Midsummer Night's Dream: Overture

  Song Of The Venetian Gondelier, Op.
    19, No. 6, [arr.] *see
    Venezianisches Gondellied, Op.
    19, No. 6, [arr.]

  Spinnerlied, Op. 67, No. 4, [arr.]
    (Lux, F.) "Spinning Song, Op. 67,
    No. 4, [arr.]" 2.2.2.2. 2.2.3.1.
    timp,strings [5'] KALMUS A4623 sc
    $5.00, perf mat rent, set $20.00,
    pts $1.00, ea.   (M321)

  Spinning Song, Op. 67, No. 4, [arr.]
    *see Spinnerlied, Op. 67, No. 4,
    [arr.]

  Symphony No. 3, Op. 56, in A minor
    min sc PETERS 611 $7.00   (M322)
    min sc ZEN-ON 891303 f.s. (M323)

  Symphony No. 4, Op. 90, in A
    BROUDE BR. set $27.50, pts $1.75,
    ea.   (M324)
    min sc PETERS 612 $7.00   (M325)
    min sc ZEN-ON 891304 f.s. (M326)

  Symphony No. 5, Op. 107, in D minor
    BROUDE BR. study sc $10.00, set
    $32.50, pts $2.50, ea.   (M327)
    LUCKS 06226 sc $14.00, set $24.00,
    min sc $4.50, pts $2.00, ea.
                               (M328)

  Trompeten Ouverture *Op.101
    BREITKOPF-W perf mat rent (M329)

MENDELSSOHN-BARTHOLDY, FELIX (cont'd.)

Venezianisches Gondellied, Op. 19,
No. 6, [arr.]
(Salabert, F.) "Song Of The
Venetian Gondelier, Op. 19, No.
6, [arr.]" 1.1.1.0. 0.1.1.0.
timp,strings KALMUS A4584 sc
$3.00, set $6.00, pts $.50, ea.
(M330)

MENDOZA, EMILIO (1953-   )
Pasaje [8']
4vln,4vla,3vcl,2db
sc NOMOS E.N. 114 perf mat rent
(M331)

MENGELBERG, KAREL (1902-   )
Dag Aan Dag Komt Hij En Gaat
see Liederen, For Solo Voice And
Orchestra

Liederen, For Solo Voice And
Orchestra
2.2.2.2. 4.3.3.1. timp,perc,2harp,
cel,strings,S solo sc DONEMUS
f.s., perf mat rent
contains: Dag Aan Dag Komt Hij En
Gaat; Lief Ga Niet Heen Zonder
Afscheid; Lief Mijn Hart
Verlangt   (M332)

Lief Ga Niet Heen Zonder Afscheid
see Liederen, For Solo Voice And
Orchestra

Lief Mijn Hart Verlangt
see Liederen, For Solo Voice And
Orchestra

MENGELBERG, KURT RUDOLF (1892-1959)
Adoro Te, For Solo Voice And
Orchestra [10']
2.3.3.3. 3.2.0.0. strings,A solo
sc DONEMUS f.s., perf mat rent
(M333)

Magnificat for Solo Voice and
Orchestra [10']
2.2.3.2. 3.1.2.0. timp,strings,A
solo
sc DONEMUS f.s., perf mat rent
(M334)

MENGELBERG, MISJA (1935-   )
Onderweg [15']
2.2.2.3. 2.2.2.0. 4perc,strings,
"moulinette musicale"
sc DONEMUS f.s., perf mat rent
(M335)

MENNIN, PETER (MENNINI) (1923-   )
Symphony No. 8
study sc SCHIRM.G $22.50   (M336)

MENSCH, DER, FOR SOLO VOICE AND
INSTRUMENTAL ENSEMBLE see
Zimmermann, Udo

MENSCHEN SEELE, DES, FOR SOLO VOICE AND
STRINGS see Hofmann, Wolfgang

MENTRE TI LASCIO, O FIGLIA, FOR SOLO
VOICE AND ORCHESTRA see Mozart,
Wolfgang Amadeus

MENUET MET VARIATIES see Ruiter, Wim de

MENUETT IN C, K. 409 see Mozart,
Wolfgang Amadeus

MENUETT IN E FLAT, K. 122 see Mozart,
Wolfgang Amadeus

MENUETT IN G, K. 1, [ARR.] see Mozart,
Wolfgang Amadeus

MENUETTE, FUNF, UND SECHS TRIOS see
Schubert, Franz (Peter)

MENUETTE, NEUNZEHN, K. 103 see Mozart,
Wolfgang Amadeus

MENUETTE, SECHS, K. 61H see Mozart,
Wolfgang Amadeus

MENUETTE, SECHS, K. 104 see Mozart,
Wolfgang Amadeus

MENUETTE, SECHS, K. 105 see Mozart,
Wolfgang Amadeus

MENUETTE, SECHS, K. 164 see Mozart,
Wolfgang Amadeus

MENUETTE, SECHSZEHN, K. 176 see Mozart,
Wolfgang Amadeus

MENUETTE, ZWEI, MIT EINGEFUGTEN
CONTRETANZEN, K. 463 see Mozart,
Wolfgang Amadeus

MENUETTE, ZWOLF, WOO. 7 see Beethoven,
Ludwig van

MENUETTE, ZWOLF, HOB. IX:1 see Haydn,
[Franz] Joseph

MENUETTE MIT TRIO, SIEBEN, K. 65A see
Mozart, Wolfgang Amadeus

MEPHISTO MASQUE, [ARR.] see Dede,
Edmund

MEPHISTO WALTZ see Liszt, Franz

MER, LA see Debussy, Claude

MER, LA see Glazunov, Alexander
Konstantinovich, Sea, The

MERATH, SIEGFRIED (1923-   )
Inkognito
RIES f.s.   (M337)

Stechmucken
RIES f.s.   (M338)

MERCATOR SAPIENS see Strietman, Willem

MERCHANT OF VENICE: MASCARADE see
Sullivan, [Sir] Arthur Seymour

MERENKYLPIJANEIDOT, FOR SOLO VOICE AND
ORCHESTRA see Kuula, Toivo

MERIKANTO, OSKAR (1868-1924)
Kun Paiva Paistaa, For Solo Voice And
Orchestra, [arr.] *Op.24,No.1
(Fougstedt, N-E.) 2.2.2.2. 2.0.0.0.
harp,strings,solo voice [2']
FAZER perf mat rent   (M339)

Laatokka, For Solo Voice And
Orchestra, [arr.] *Op.83,No.1
(Sonninen, A.) 2.2.2.2. 4.2.3.1.
timp,strings,solo voice [3']
FAZER perf mat rent   (M340)

MERITUULI, FOR SOLO VOICE AND
ORCHESTRA, [ARR.] see Madetoja,
Leevi

MERKU, PAVLE (1927-   )
Sunny Sunshine [8']
string orch
(outside Yugoslavia this
publication can be obtained from
Gerig) study sc DRUSTVO f.s.,
perf mat rent   (M341)

MERLET, MICHEL (1939-   )
Moirures [13']
3(pic).3(English horn).3(bass
clar).3. 4.3.3.1. timp,2perc,
cel,strings
LEDUC perf mat rent   (M342)

Soiree A Nohant, Une, For Violoncello
And String Orchestra
string orch,vcl solo
LEDUC perf mat rent   (M343)

MERRY WIDOW, THE: VILIA see Lehar,
Franz, Lustige Witwe: Die: Vilia,
For Solo Voice And Orchestra

MERRY WIVES OF WINDSOR, THE: OVERTURE
see Nicolai, Otto, Lustigen Weiber
Von Windsor, Die: Overture

MERTENS, HARDY (1960-   )
Duodecimet No. 1 [4'30"]
3vln,2vla,2vla da gamba,3vcl,2db
DONEMUS   (M344)

MERULA, TARQUINO (fl. 1620-1650)
Sonata Cromatica
see RICREAZIONI DI ANTICHE MUSICHE
CLASSICHE, SERIE II: MUSICHE
ANTICHE ITALIANE

MESALLIANCE, FOR PIANO AND INSTRUMENTAL
ENSEMBLE see Rands, Bernard

MESCHWITZ, FRIEDER (1942-   )
Skizzen Zu Einem Frauenportrat, For
Piano And Orchestra [20']
3(pic).3(English
horn).3.3(contrabsn). 4.3.3.1.
timp,perc,strings,pno solo
sc,pts DOBLINGER rent   (M345)

MESRITZ VAN VELTHUYSEN, ANNY
(1897-1965)
Adieu
see Liederen, For Solo Voice And
Orchestra

Barque d'Or
see Liederen, For Solo Voice And
Orchestra

Bonheur, Le
see Liederen, For Solo Voice And
Orchestra

Liederen, For Solo Voice And
Orchestra
2.2.2.1. 2.2.0.0. harp,cel,strings,
S solo sc DONEMUS f.s., perf mat
rent
contains: Adieu; Barque d'Or;
Bonheur, Le   (M346)

MESSAGER, ANDRE (1853-1929)
Isoline: Pavaune Des Fees, [arr.]
(Delsaux) 2.1.2.2. 2.2.1.0. timp,
perc,strings KALMUS 5249 sc
$5.00, perf mat rent, set $14.00,
pts $.60, ea.   (M347)

Madame Chrysantheme: Ballet Suite,
[arr.]
(Gabriel-Marie) 2.1.2.1. 2.2.3.0.
timp,perc,harp,strings KALMUS
5251 sc $3.00, perf mat rent, set
$16.00, pts $.75, ea.   (M348)

MESSIAH: BUT WHO MAY ABIDE THE DAY OF
HIS COMING, FOR SOLO VOICE AND
ORCHESTRA see Handel, George
Frideric

MESSIAH: COMFORT YE - EVERY VALLEY
SHALL BE EXALTED, FOR SOLO VOICE
AND ORCHESTRA see Handel, George
Frideric

MESSIAH: HE SHALL FEED HIS FLOCK, FOR
SOLO VOICE AND ORCHESTRA see
Handel, George Frideric

MESSIAH: HE WAS DESPISED, FOR SOLO
VOICE AND ORCHESTRA see Handel,
George Frideric

MESSIAH: HOW BEAUTIFUL ARE THE FEET,
FOR SOLO VOICE AND ORCHESTRA see
Handel, George Frideric

MESSIAH: I KNOW THAT MY REDEEMER
LIVETH, FOR SOLO VOICE AND
ORCHESTRA see Handel, George
Frideric

MESSIAH: OVERTURE, [ARR.] see Handel,
George Frideric

MESSIAH: PASTORAL SYMPHONY see Handel,
George Frideric

MESSIAH: REJOICE GREATLY, FOR SOLO
VOICE AND ORCHESTRA see Handel,
George Frideric

MESSIAH: THE PEOPLE THAT WALKED IN
DARKNESS, FOR SOLO VOICE AND
ORCHESTRA see Handel, George
Frideric

MESSIAH: THE TRUMPET SHALL SOUND, FOR
SOLO VOICE AND ORCHESTRA see
Handel, George Frideric

MESSIAH: THOU SHALT BREAK THEM, FOR
SOLO VOICE AND ORCHESTRA see
Handel, George Frideric

MESSIAH: THUS SAITH THE LORD, FOR SOLO
VOICE AND ORCHESTRA see Handel,
George Frideric

MESSIAH: WHY DO THE NATIONS, FOR SOLO
VOICE AND ORCHESTRA see Handel,
George Frideric

MESTRAL, PATRICE (1945-   )
Courants, For Trombone And
Instrumental Ensemble [18'-20']
2.1.3.1.alto sax. 0.0.0.0. 3perc,
pno,harp,vln,vla,vcl,db,trom
solo
RICORDI-FR R.2233 perf mat rent
(M349)
Focales, For Double Bass And
Instrumental Ensemble [23']
2.2.3.0. 0.3.3.0. 4perc,pno,harp,
vln,vla,vcl,db solo
RICORDI-FR R.2228 perf mat rent
(M350)
Fusions-Diffusions [18']
2.2.3.2. 2.2.2.1. 3perc,pno,harp,
3vln,2vla,2vcl,db
RICORDI-FR R.2252 perf mat rent
(M351)
Rapports 3, For Piano, Percussion And
Orchestra [18']
0.alto fl.0.English horn.0.bass
clar.0.contrabsn. 2.2.2.1.
timp,2perc,6vln,3vla,3vcl,2db,
pno solo,perc solo
RICORDI-FR R.2242 perf mat rent
(M352)

MESTRES-QUADRENY, JOSEP MARIA
(1929-   )
Aronada
string orch
SEESAW perf mat rent   (M353)

Frigoli-Frigola
string orch
SEESAW perf mat rent   (M354)

METAMORPHOSE see Voss, Friedrich

METAMORPHOSE I see Raxach, Enrique

METAMORPHOSEN, FOR 2 TRUMPETS AND
ORCHESTRA see Bossler, Kurt

METAMORPHOSES DE DANSE see Bravnicar,
Matija

METAMORPHOSIS 4-6-2-1 see Ashkenazy,
Benjamin

METAMORPHOSIS - DANCE see Goehr,
Alexander

METASTASEIS see Xenakis, Yannis
(Iannis)

METRAL, PIERRE (1936-   )
Variations Sur Un Theme Elegiaque,
For Solo Voices And String
Orchestra
string orch,SMez soli
TONOS   (M355)

METSELWERK see Eisma, Will

METZL, WLADIMIR
Versunkene Glocke, Die *Op.12 [25']
3(pic).2+English horn.2+bass
clar.2+contrabsn. 4.3.3.1.
2harp,glock,timp,perc,strings
sc,pts LIENAU rent   (M356)

METZLER, FRIEDRICH (1910-   )
Dialog, For Trumpet And String
Orchestra
string orch,trp solo
BUDDE perf mat rent   (M357)

Geistliches Konzert, For Solo Voice
And Orchestra
BUDDE perf mat rent   (M358)

Symphony No. 2 [23']
3(pic).2.2.2. 4.2.3.1. timp,perc,
strings
RIES perf mat rent   (M359)

Symphony No. 3 [25']
2(pic).2(English horn).2(bass
clar).2(contrabsn). 4.2.3.0.
timp,perc,strings
RIES perf mat rent   (M360)

MEULEMANS, ARTHUR (1884-1966)
Concerto for Piano and Orchestra, No.
1 [23']
sc,solo pt MEULEMANS f.s., ipa
                                  (M361)

Dennen-Symfonie *see Symphony No. 3

Egmont: Overture [6']
sc,pts MEULEMANS f.s.   (M362)

Evasies [11']
sc MEULEMANS f.s.   (M363)

Plinius' Fontein [18']
sc,pts MEULEMANS f.s.   (M364)

Rembrandt Symfonie *see Symphony No.
13

Sinfonietta No. 3 [17']
sc,pts MEULEMANS f.s.   (M365)

Symphony No. 2 [19']
sc MEULEMANS f.s.   (M366)

Symphony No. 3 [20']
sc MEULEMANS f.s.   (M367)

Symphony No. 6 [40']
sc MEULEMANS f.s.   (M368)

Symphony No. 7 [30']
sc MEULEMANS f.s.   (M369)

Symphony No. 9 [30']
sc MEULEMANS f.s.   (M370)

Symphony No. 13 [30']
sc,pts MEULEMANS f.s.   (M371)

Zeesymfonie *see Symphony No. 6

Zwaneven *see Symphony No. 7

MEXICAN HAT DANCE
LUCKS 06123 sc $4.00, set $12.00, pts
$.75, ea.   (M372)

MEXIKANISCHE SERENADE see Kaschubec,
Erich

MEYER, ERNST HERMANN (1905-   )
Concerto for Viola and Orchestra
[17']
3.2.2.2. 4.3.3.0. timp,perc,harp,
strings,vla solo
sc PETERS EP 5565 f.s., perf mat
rent   (M373)

Sinfonietta for Orchestra [18']
3.3.3.2. 4.3.3.1. timp,2perc,
strings
sc PETERS EP 5593 f.s., perf mat
rent   (M374)

MEYER, KRZYSZTOF (1943-   )
Polish Chants, For Solo Voice And
Chamber Orchestra *see Spiewy
Polskie, For Solo Voice And
Chamber Orchestra

Spiewy Polskie, For Solo Voice And
Chamber Orchestra [25']
5perc,strings,S solo
"Polish Chants, For Solo Voice And
Chamber Orchestra" sc POLSKIE
$44.80   (M375)

Symphony No. 4, Op. 31
sc PETERS P8396 $60.00   (M376)

MEYER-HELMUND, ERIK (1861-1932)
Zauberlied, Das
RIES f.s.   (M377)

MEYERBEER, GIACOMO (1791-1864)
Africaine, L': O Paradis, For Solo
Voice And Orchestra
LUCKS 02067 sc $3.75, set $9.50,
pts $.75, ea.   (M378)

Coronation March *see Kronungsmarsch

Dinorah: Shadow Song *see Pardon De
Ploermel, Le: Ombre Legere, For
Solo Voice And Orchestra

Etoile Du Nord, L': Overture [8']
1+pic.2.2.2.2soprano sax.baritone
sax.2bass sax. 4.2.3.0. 2harp,
timp,perc,strings
"Nordstern, Der: Overture" sc,pts
LIENAU rent   (M379)

Festmarsch Zu Schillers 100jahriger
Geburtstagsfeier [7']
2+pic.2.2.4. 4.2+2cornet.3.1.
2harp,timp,perc,strings
sc,pts LIENAU rent   (M380)

Kronungsmarsch
"Coronation March" sets NOVELLO
9118-19 $41.00, and up, sc
NOVELLO 9117 $7.75, pts NOVELLO
9614 $1.00, ea.   (M381)

Kronungsmarsch "Wilhelm I"
sc,pts LIENAU rent   (M382)

Nordstern, Der: Overture *see Etoile
Du Nord, L': Overture

Pardon De Ploermel, Le: Ombre Legere,
For Solo Voice And Orchestra
"Dinorah: Shadow Song" LUCKS 02127
set $7.50, pts $.75, ea.   (M383)

Prophete, Le: Ah, Mon Fils, For Solo
Voice And Orchestra
LUCKS 02069 sc $3.75, set $7.50,
pts $.75, ea.   (M384)

Prophete, Le: Coronation March *see
Prophete, Le: Marche Du
Couronnement

Prophete, Le: Marche Du Couronnement
"Prophete, Le: Coronation March"
LUCKS 06262 sc $11.00, set
$30.00, pts $1.40, ea.   (M385)

Struensee: Overture, No.8 Polonaise
And No.9 Dorfschenke
2.2.2.2. 4.2.3.1. harp,timp,
strings
sc,pts LIENAU rent   (M386)

MI-FI-LI see Hvoslef, Ketil

MI-PARTI see Lutoslawski, Witold

MIA SPERANZA ADORATA, FOR SOLO VOICE
AND ORCHESTRA see Mozart, Wolfgang
Amadeus

MICHEL, WILFRIED (1940-   )
Ombre [20']
MODERN 2066 perf mat rent   (M387)

MICROSUITE see Baguena Soler, Jose

MIDDAY WITCH see Dvorak, Antonin

MIDDLETON, JEAN (1913-   )
Symphony in C
sc BOOSEY $9.00   (M388)

MIDGAARD GEDENKKLANK, DE, FOR VIOLIN
AND ORCHESTRA see Rottgering,
Martin Almar

MIDSOMMARVAKA - SWEDISH RHAPSODY NO. 1
see Alfven, Hugo

MIDST SILENT SHADES, FOR SOLO VOICE AND
ORCHESTRA see Bach, Johann
Christian

MIDSUMMER DAY see Cikker, Jan, Na Jana

MIDSUMMER NIGHT'S DREAM, A: INCIDENTAL
MUSIC, VOL. 1 see Purcell, Henry

MIDSUMMER NIGHT'S DREAM, A: INCIDENTAL
MUSIC, VOL. 2 see Purcell, Henry

MIDSUMMER NIGHT'S DREAM: DANCE OF THE
CLOWNS see Mendelssohn-Bartholdy,
Felix

MIDSUMMER NIGHT'S DREAM: FIVE EXCERPTS
see Mendelssohn-Bartholdy, Felix

MIDSUMMER NIGHT'S DREAM: INTERMEZZO see
Mendelssohn-Bartholdy, Felix

MIDSUMMER NIGHT'S DREAM: NOTTURNO see
Mendelssohn-Bartholdy, Felix

MIDSUMMER NIGHT'S DREAM: OH GLIMMERING
LIGHT, FOR SOLO VOICES AND
ORCHESTRA see Mendelssohn-
Bartholdy, Felix

MIDSUMMER NIGHT'S DREAM: OH SPOTTED
SNAKE, FOR SOLO VOICE AND ORCHESTRA
see Mendelssohn-Bartholdy, Felix

MIDSUMMER NIGHT'S DREAM: OVERTURE see
Mendelssohn-Bartholdy, Felix

MIDSUMMER NIGHT'S DREAM: SCHERZO see
Mendelssohn-Bartholdy, Felix

MIDSUMMER NIGHT'S DREAM: WEDDING MARCH
see Mendelssohn-Bartholdy, Felix

MIEG, PETER (1906-   )
Combray
string orch
AMADEUS GM 690 sc f.s., pts rent
                                  (M389)

Concerto Dans Le Gout Italien, For
Violin, Viola, Violoncello And
String Orchestra
string orch,vln solo,vla solo,vcl
solo
sc HUG f.s., perf mat rent   (M390)

Concerto for 2 Flutes and String
Orchestra
string orch,2fl soli
AMADEUS BP 2676 sc f.s., pts rent
                                  (M391)

Rondeau Symphonique
AMADEUS GM 592 sc f.s., pts rent
                                  (M392)

MIELENZ, H.
Bambolina
WOITSCHACH f.s.   (M393)

Blumen-Serenade
WOITSCHACH f.s.   (M394)

MIELENZ, HANS
Dascha
RIES f.s.   (M395)

Komodianten
RIES f.s.   (M396)

Lustspiel-Ouverture *Op.9 [7']
2+pic.2+English horn.2+bass
clar.2+contrabsn. 4.3.3.1.
timp,perc,harp,strings
RIES perf mat rent   (M397)

Spanische Serenade
RIES f.s.   (M398)

Wie Im Traum [6']
2.1+English horn.2+bass
clar.0.opt bsn. 3.3.3.0. timp,
perc,harp,strings,opt mix cor
sc RIES f.s., perf mat rent   (M399)
RIES f.s.   (M400)

MIETZNER, HEINZ
Bohmische Kirmes
RIES f.s.   (M401)

In Einer Rumanischen Tscharda
RIES f.s.   (M402)

MIGNON, FOR SOLO VOICE AND ORCHESTRA
see Diepenbrock, Alphons

MIGNON: CONNAIS-TU LE PAYS?, FOR SOLO
VOICE AND ORCHESTRA see Thomas,
Ambroise

MIGNON (FIRST VERSION), FOR SOLO VOICE
AND ORCHESTRA see Wolf, Hugo

MIGNON: JE SUIS TITANIA, FOR SOLO VOICE
AND ORCHESTRA see Thomas, Ambroise

MIGNON: LEGERES HIRONDELLES, FOR SOLO
VOICES AND ORCHESTRA see Thomas,
Ambroise

MIGNON: RONDO-GAVOTTE, "ME VOICI DANS
SON BOUDOIR", FOR SOLO VOICE AND
ORCHESTRA see Thomas, Ambroise

MIGNON (SECOND VERSION), FOR SOLO VOICE AND ORCHESTRA see Wolf, Hugo

MIGOT, GEORGES (1891-1976)
Symphonie D'Espace Et De Temps, De Musique Et De Danse *see Symphony No. 13

Symphony No. 13 [43'40"]
2.2.2.3. 2.2.2.0. timp,perc, 2harp,strings
LEDUC perf mat rent (M403)

MIGRACIONES, FOR SOLO VOICE AND ORCHESTRA see Pla, Francisco Llacer

MIHALOVICI, MARCEL (1898-)
Malinconia, For Solo Voices And Orchestra
sc HEUGEL f.s., perf mat rent (M404)

MIHELCIC, PAVLE (1937-)
Concerto for Horn and Orchestra [15']
0.2.1.2. 3.2.2.1. 3perc,cel, strings,horn solo
DRUSTVO DSS 800 perf mat rent (M405)

MIKADO, THE: THE MOON AND I, FOR SOLO VOICE AND ORCHESTRA see Sullivan, [Sir] Arthur Seymour

MIKADO, THE: WERE YOU NOT TO KOKO PLIGHTED?, FOR SOLO VOICES AND ORCHESTRA see Sullivan, [Sir] Arthur Seymour

MIKADO, THE: WILLOW, TIT-WILLOW, FOR SOLO VOICE AND ORCHESTRA see Sullivan, [Sir] Arthur Seymour

MIKI, MINORU (1930-)
Concerto for Marimba and Orchestra
3(pic).3(English horn).3(soprano clar in E flat).2(contrabsn). 4.3.3.1. timp,3perc,harp, strings,marimba solo
ONGAKU perf mat rent (M406)

MIKROKOSMOS: FIVE PIECES, [ARR.] see Bartok, Bela

MIKSI LAULAT LINTUSENI, FOR SOLO VOICE AND ORCHESTRA see Hannikainen, Ilmari

MIKULA, ZDENKO (1916-)
Ciganske Piesne, For Solo Voice And Orchestra
clar,cimbalom,strings,T solo
"Gypsy Songs, For Solo Voice And Orchestra" SLOV.HUD.FOND 0-173 perf mat rent (M407)

Gypsy Songs, For Solo Voice And Orchestra *see Ciganske Piesne, For Solo Voice And Orchestra

Letters To Janek, For Solo Voice And Orchestra *see Pisma K Janeku, For Solo Voice And Orchestra

Pisma K Janeku, For Solo Voice And Orchestra
1.1.1.1. 1.0.0.0. strings,Mez solo
"Letters To Janek, For Solo Voice And Orchestra" SLOV.HUD.FOND 0-105A perf mat rent (M408)

Rapsodicke Variacie [10']
fl,ob,clar,bsn,horn,strings
SLOV.HUD.FOND 0-432A, B perf mat rent (M409)

Tri Nokturna
string orch
SLOV.HUD.FOND 0-471 perf mat rent (M410)

MIKULICZ, LOTHAR
Zwei Stucke: Marchen Und Ein Volkslied [8']
harp,strings
RIES perf mat rent (M411)

MILA DI CODRA see Mandelli, Emanuele

MILANO, FRANCESCO DA see FRANCESCO DA MILANO

MILITARY SYMPHONY see Haydn, [Franz] Joseph, Symphony No. 100 in G

MILL-WHEEL TUNE see Saeverud, Harald, Kvernslatt, Op. 22a, No. 2

MILLER, CHARLES (1899-)
Carribean Islands
ESCHIG sc,pts rent, min sc f.s. (M412)

MILLIONS D'ARLEQUIN, LES: VALSE DES ALOUETTES see Drigo, Riccardo

MILLIONS D'ARLEQUIN, LES: VALSE DES ALOUETTES, [ARR.] see Drigo, Riccardo

MILNER, ANTHONY (1925-)
Sinfonia Pasquale [8']
string orch,opt woodwinds
sc UNIVER. UE 12990 f.s., perf mat rent (M413)

MIMAROGLU, ILHAN KAMALEDDIN (1926-)
Idols Of Perversity, For Viola And String Orchestra
string orch,vla solo
SEESAW perf mat rent (M414)

Romance for Trombone and String Orchestra
string orch,trom solo
SEESAW perf mat rent (M415)

MIMESIS, FOR INSTRUMENTAL QUINTET AND CHAMBER ORCHESTRA see Terpstra, Koos

MIMESIS 2 see Sermila, Jarmo

MINE EYES HAVE SEEN see Green, John

MINIATURE, FOR FLUTE AND STRING ORCHESTRA see Schonherr, Max

MINIATURE VIENNESE MARCH, [ARR.] see Kreisler, Fritz

MINNELIED, FOR SOLO VOICE AND ORCHESTRA (from Locheimer Liederbuch)
LUCKS 03255 sc $4.00, set $9.50, pts $.75, ea. (M416)

MINOR, EUGENE (1940-)
Lament For A Moon Child *Op.26a [11']
string orch
KALMUS A5512 sc $5.00, set $7.50, pts $1.50, ea. (M417)

MINUETTI, DUE, IN D AND E FLAT, [ARR.] see Boccherini, Luigi

MINUETTO
see Ricreazioni Di Antiche Musiche Classiche, Serie I: Musiche Antiche Italiane

MINUETTO see Bolzoni, Giovanni

MINUETTO IN G see Boccherini, Luigi

MINUETTO, MUSETTA E GAVOTTA, [ARR.] see Handel, George Frideric

MINUETTO NO. 1 see Puccini, Giacomo

MINUETTO NO. 2 see Puccini, Giacomo

MINUETTO, NOTTURNO E MARCIA see Mortari, Virgilio

MINUETTO, OP. 11 see Boccherini, Luigi

MIRACLE SYMPHONY see Haydn, [Franz] Joseph, Symphony No. 96 in D

MIRAFLORES see Lambro, Phillip

MIRAGE see Dolatshahi, Dariush

MIRAGE see Nystedt, Knut

MIRAGE, FOR TRUMPET AND STRING ORCHESTRA see Selig, Robert

MIRAGES see Risset, Jean Claude

MIRANDA, FOR SOLO VOICE AND ORCHESTRA, [ARR.] see Planck, Lillemor

MIREILLE: OVERTURE see Gounod, Charles Francois

MIROGLIO, FRANCIS (1924-)
Eclipses
string orch,opt hpsd
HINRICHSEN perf mat rent (M418)

MIRROR II see Gudmundsen-Holmgreen, Pelle

MIRROR OF WHITENING LIGHT, A see Davies, Peter Maxwell

MIRRORS FOR JAZZ TRIO AND ORCHESTRA see Giuffre, James Peter (Jimmy)

MISERA ME-HO SPAVENTO. SCENA ED ARIA D'ATALIA, FOR SOLO VOICE AND ORCHESTRA see Weber, Carl Maria von

MISERO! O SOGNO, FOR SOLO VOICE AND ORCHESTRA see Mozart, Wolfgang Amadeus

MR. SKEFFINGTON see Waxman, Franz

MISTLETOE BRIDE see Chihara, Paul Seiko

MIT DAMPF POLKA see Strauss, Eduard

MIT DER FEDER POLKA see Strauss, Eduard

MIT DER STRIEMUNG POLKA see Strauss, Eduard

MIT ZOPF UND REIFROCK see Ailbout, Hans

MITRIDATE: OVERTURE see Mozart, Wolfgang Amadeus

MITTELALTERLICHE TANZSUITE see Lothar, Mark

MIXTUM COMPOSITUM see Reinl, Franz

MIYOSHI, AKIRA (1933-)
Concerto for Piano and Orchestra
orch,pno solo
ZEN-ON 899115 (M419)

Concerto for Violoncello and Orchestra
orch,vcl solo
ZEN-ON 899111 (M420)

Noesis
ZEN-ON 899114 (M421)

Requiem
ZEN-ON 899001 (M422)

MIZAR see Halffter, Cristobal

MIZELLE, DARY JOHN
Primavera: Heterophony
24vcl
sc LINGUA (M423)

MLYNARSKI, EMIL (1870-1935)
Mazurka, For Violin And Orchestra, [arr.] (Dressel, Erwin) 2(pic).2.2.2. 4.2.3.0. timp,perc,harp,strings [5'] sc RIES f.s., perf mat rent (M424)

MOBILES see Kraft, William

MODE-QUADRILLE see Strauss, Johann, [Sr.]

MODULATIONS see Grisey, Gerard

MODULATIONS, FOR HARMONICA AND ORCHESTRA see Rypdal, Terje

MOGLIE QUANDRO E BUONA, LA, FOR SOLO VOICE AND ORCHESTRA see Haydn, [Franz] Joseph

MOIRA see Vogel, Ernst

MOIRURES see Merlet, Michel

MOLDAU, THE see Smetana, Bedrich, Ma Vlast: Vitava

MOLDAVA see Smetana, Bedrich, Ma Vlast: Vitava

MOLIQUE, (WILHELM) BERNHARD (1802-1869)
Concertino for Oboe and Orchestra in G minor [16']
2.0.2.2. 2.0.0.0. timp,strings,ob solo
BREITKOPF-W perf mat rent (M425)

Concertino for Violin and Orchestra in F minor
1.2.2.2. 2.2.0.0. timp,strings, vln solo
KALMUS A3071 solo pt $1.50, set $30.00, perf mat rent, pts $1.50, ea. (M426)

MOLTER, JOHANN MELCHIOR (1695-1765)
Concerto for Clarinet and String Orchestra in D, MIN 6
string orch,cont,clar solo
(Hofmann, K.) (MWV VI, 36) sc CARUS 40.502-01 f.s., pts CARUS (M427)
Concerto for Trumpet and Orchestra in D, MIN 114
2ob,strings,cont,trp solo
(in this edition, No. 1) sc,pts BRASS PRESS $10.00 (M428)

Concerto for Trumpet and Orchestra in D, MIN 115
2ob,strings,cont,trp solo
(in this edition, No. 2) BRASS PRESS sc,pts $10.00, fac ed $2.50 (M429)

Concerto in D, MIN 8
string orch,cont,2trp soli
(MWV IV, 9) sc,pts MUS. RARA 41.880-02 f.s. (M430)

Concerto in D, MIN 9
string orch,cont,2trp soli
(MWV IV, 7) sc,pts MUS. RARA 41.883-20 f.s. (M431)

Concerto in D, MIN 10
string orch,cont,2trp soli
(MWV IV, 11) sc,pts MUS. RARA

MOLTER, JOHANN MELCHIOR (cont'd.)

41.884-20 f.s.   (M432)

Concerto in D, MIN 11
string orch,cont,2trp soli
(MWV IV, 8) sc,pts MUS. RARA
41.885-20 f.s.   (M433)

Concerto in D, MIN 12
string orch,cont,2trp soli
(MWV IV, 10) sc,pts MUS. RARA
41.886-20 f.s.   (M434)

MOMENT MUSICAL, [ARR.] see Schubert,
Franz (Peter)

MOMENTO CAPRICCIOSO see Weber, Carl
Maria von

MONDONVILLE, JEAN-JOSEPH DE
(ca. 1711-1772)
Titon Et L'Aurore: Suite
2fl,2ob,2bsn,strings
COSTALL perf mat rent   (M435)

MONK
Abide With Me
(Luck, Arthur) LUCKS HYMNS 5 set
$9.50, pts $.65, ea. contains
also: Hursley, Sun Of My Soul
(M436)

MONNIKENDAM, MARIUS (1896-1977)
Concert For Organ And Orchestra,
MIN104 [17']
2.1.1.1. 2.1.1.0. timp,2perc,
strings,org solo
DONEMUS perf mat rent   (M437)

MONO-PRISM see Ishii, Maki

MONOCHROME OVERTURE, FOR PIANO AND
ORCHESTRA see Tautenhahn, Gunther

MONODIA see Morthenson, Jan W.

MONODIE see Kuhnl, Claus

MONT BLANC OVERTURE see Bavicchi, John
Alexander

MONTAGE, FOR PIANO AND INSTRUMENTAL
ENSEMBLE see Emmer, Huib

MONTESINOS, EDUARDO
Variaciones Caleidoscopicas
sc PILES 2090-P f.s.   (M438)

MONTEVERDI, CLAUDIO (ca. 1567-1643)
Combattimento Di Tancredi E Clorinda,
Il, For Solo Voices And String
Orchestra, [arr.]
string orch,2 solo voices&speaking
voice [25'] manuscript CARISCH
(M439)

Lamento d'Arianna
see RICREAZIONI DI ANTICHE MUSICHE
CLASSICHE, SERIE V: MUSICHE
ANTICHE ITALIANE

Madrigali, [arr.]
(Berio; Rands) fl,ob,horn,trp,perc,
strings [22'] sc UNIVER. UE 16186
f.s., perf mat rent   (M440)

Oh, Let Me Die, [arr.]
(Nelhybel, Vaclav) string orch sc,
pts BARTA B 115 $7.50, pts BARTA
$.60, ea.   (M441)

Orfeo: Overture
LUCKS 01625 sc $7.50, set $14.00,
pts $1.15, ea.   (M442)

MONTI, VITTORIO
Csardas, For Violin And Orchestra
1+pic.2.2.2. 4.2.3.0. timp,harp,
strings,vln solo
KALMUS 5435 pno-cond sc $3.00, perf
mat rent, set $12.00, pts $.60,
ea.   (M443)

MONTICO, MARIO (1885-1959)
Caccia, For Horn And Orchestra [3']
1.1.1.1. 0.0.0.0. timp,harp,pno,
strings,horn solo
sc CARISCH 21299 rent, pts CARISCH
21308 f.s.   (M444)

Elegy for Horn and Orchestra [3']
1.1.1.1. 0.0.0.0. timp,harp,pno,
strings,horn solo
sc CARISCH 21298 rent, pts CARISCH
21308 f.s.   (M445)

MONTSALVATGE, XAVIER (1912-   )
Cinco Invocaciones Al Crucificado,
For Solo Voice And Orchestra
[26']
PEER perf mat rent   (M446)

MOOR, EMANUEL (1863-1931)
Suite, Op. 103
2string quin,winds
study sc SALABERT $12.25   (M447)

MORAL, PABLO DEL (fl. 1765-1805)
Sinfonia in C
see SYMPHONY IN MADRID, THE

MORCEAU DE CONCERT, FOR HORN AND
ORCHESTRA see Saint-Saens, Camille

MORCEAU DE GENRE see Kupkovic, Ladislav

MORDET PA GUSTAV III ELLER
MASKERADBALEN I FICKFORMAT, FOR
VOICE AND STRING ORCHESTRA see
Eyser, Eberhard

MORENDO see Morthenson, Jan W.

MORENO, FRANCISCO JAVIER (1748-1836)
Sinfonias In C, D And E Flat
see SYMPHONY IN MADRID, THE

MORET, NORBERT
Suite A l'Image Du Temps
string orch
TONOS   (M448)

MORGEN see Badings, Henk

MORGEN, DER see Duvosel, Lieven

MORGEN, FOR SOLO VOICE AND ORCHESTRA
see Strauss, Richard

MORGEN, EIN MITTAG, EIN ABEND IN WIEN,
EIN: OVERTURE see Suppe, Franz von

MORGEN WAR VON DIR ERFULLT, DER see
Flothuis, Marius

MORGENBLATTER WALZER see Strauss,
Johann, [Jr.]

MORGENLIED see Huber, Nicolaus A.

MORILLO, ROBERTO GARCIA (1911-   )
Variaciones Olimpicas
sc BARRY-ARG $27.00   (M449)

MORNING JOURNALS see Strauss, Johann,
[Jr.], Morgenblatter Walzer

MORNING, NOON AND NIGHT IN VIENNA:
OVERTURE see Suppe, Franz von,
Morgen, Ein Mittag, Ein Abend In
Wien, Ein: Overture

MORNING OF THE YEAR, THE: DANCES see
Holst, Gustav

MORRICONE, ENNIO (1928-   )
Musique Pour 11 Violins
study sc SALABERT $14.50   (M450)

MORT DE CLEOPATRE, LA, FOR SOLO VOICE
AND ORCHESTRA see Berlioz, Hector
(Louis)

MORTARI, VIRGILIO (1902-   )
Allegra Piazzetta, L': Suite
2.2.2.2. 2.2.1.0. timp,perc,harp,
strings
sc CARISCH 20484 f.s., perf mat
rent   (M451)

Concertino for Harp and String
Orchestra (from Piccolo Concerto
For Guitar) [9']
string orch,harp solo
sc ZANIBON 5581 f.s., pts ZANIBON
5582 f.s.   (M452)

Concertino for Orchestra [14']
2.2.2.1. 2.0.0.0. timp,strings
manuscript CARISCH   (M453)

Concerto for Flute and Orchestra
[15']
2.2.2.2. 2.2.0.0. timp,perc,harp,
strings,fl solo
manuscript CARISCH   (M454)

Concerto for Harp and Orchestra [20']
2.2.2.2. 2.2.0.0. timp,3perc,
strings,harp solo
sc CARISCH 21921 rent, pts CARISCH
21921A rent   (M455)

Concerto for 2 Violins, Viola,
Violoncello and 2 Horns [24']
2horn,timp,harp,strings,2vln
soli,vla solo,vcl solo
sc CARISCH 18902 f.s., perf mat
rent   (M456)

Due Laude, For Solo Voice And
Orchestra
2.1.2.2. 2.1.0.0. pno,strings,
solo voice
sc CARISCH 21693 f.s., pts CARISCH
21694 rent   (M457)

Elegia E Capriccio, For Violin,
Doublebass And String Orchestra
string orch,vln solo,db solo
sc RICORDI-IT 132519 f.s.   (M458)

MORTARI, VIRGILIO (cont'd.)

Fantasy for Piano and Orchestra
FORLIVESI perf mat rent   (M459)

Intermezzo
FORLIVESI perf mat rent   (M460)

Leggenda E Tripartita [17']
3.3.3.3. 4.3.3.1. timp,4perc
sc CARISCH 21905 rent, pts CARISCH
21905A rent   (M461)

Minuetto, Notturno E Marcia [9']
3.2.2.2. 4.3.3.1. perc,harp,xylo,
strings
manuscript CARISCH   (M462)

Musica Per Archi [15']
string orch
sc CARISCH 20321 f.s., pts CARISCH
20094 f.s.   (M463)

Musica Per Un Balletto [10']
1.1.1.1. 0.1.0.0. strings
manuscript CARISCH   (M464)

Notturno Incantato [5']
1.1.2.2. 2.0.0.0. timp,harp,
strings
sc CARISCH 19887 f.s., perf mat
rent   (M465)

Padovana, For Harpsichord And String
Orchestra [18']
string orch,hpsd solo
sc ZANIBON 5418 f.s., pts ZANIBON
5419 rent   (M466)

Partita in G
FORLIVESI perf mat rent   (M467)

Piccola Serenata [8']
string orch
sc CARISCH 20967 f.s., pts CARISCH
20873 f.s.   (M468)

Piccolo Concerto, For Guitar And
String Orchestra [12']
string orch,gtr solo
(Diaz,A.) sc ZANIBON 5541 f.s.,
pts ZANIBON 5542 f.s.   (M469)

Sarabanda E Allegro, For Violoncello
And Orchestra [14']
2.2.2.2. 4.2.1.0. timp,xylo,harp,
strings,vcl solo
manuscript CARISCH   (M470)

Stabat Mater for Solo Voices and
Orchestra [20']
2horn,timp,perc,strings,2 female
soli
sc CARISCH 20972 f.s., perf mat
rent   (M471)

MORTE CHITARRE, LE, FOR SOLO VOICE AND
INSTRUMENTAL ENSEMBLE see Laporte,
Andre

MORTE D'ABEL, LA see Caldara, Antonio

MORTE E SEPULTURA DI CHRISTO see
Caldara, Antonio

MORTENSEN, FINN (1922-   )
Symphony No. 1, Op. 5
3.3.3.3. 4.3.3.1. timp,perc,
strings
min sc NORSK NMO 8804 $52.50 (M472)

MORTHENSON, JAN W. (1940-   )
Anticanti
string orch
REIMERS ER 5   (M473)

Concerto for Organ and Orchestra
sc REIMERS f.s., perf mat rent
(M474)

Five Pieces °CC5U
sc NORDISKA f.s.   (M475)

Labor [12']
fl,alto fl,ob,English horn,clar,
clar in E flat,bass clar,bsn,
horn,trom,pno,2vln,vla,vcl
sc UNIVER. UE 15623 $23.50, perf
mat rent   (M476)

Monodia
REIMERS ER 74   (M477)

Morendo [16']
REIMERS ER 42   (M478)

Video
string orch
sc,pts REIMERS ER 46   (M479)

MOSCHELES, IGNAZ (1794-1870)
Concertino for Flute, Oboe and
Orchestra [13']
2.2.2.2. 2.2.0.0. timp,strings,fl
solo,ob solo
(Wojciechowsky) PETERS perf mat
rent   (M480)

MOSCHELES, IGNAZ (cont'd.)

Concerto for Piano and Orchestra, No. 3, Op. 58, in G minor [31']
2.2.2.2. 4.2.1.0. timp,strings, pno solo
sc,pts LIENAU rent (M481)

MOSE: BALLET MUSIC see Rossini, Gioacchino

MOSER, RUDOLF (1892-1960)
Burleske *Op.42,No.1
2.2.2.2. 2.2.2.0. timp,perc,cel, strings
sc,pts MOSER f.s. (M482)

Concerto for Clarinet and String Orchestra, Op. 101
string orch,clar solo
sc,pts MOSER f.s. (M483)

Concerto for Oboe and String Orchestra, Op. 86
string orch,ob solo
sc,pts MOSER f.s. (M484)

Concerto for Organ and String Orchestra, Op. 37
string orch,org solo
sc,pts MOSER f.s. (M485)

Concerto for Piano and Orchestra, Op. 61
1.1.1.1. 2.1.0.0. timp,strings, pno solo
sc,pts MOSER f.s. (M486)

Concerto for Viola and Chamber Orchestra, Op. 62
fl,clar,bsn,strings,vla solo
sc,pts MOSER f.s. (M487)

Concerto for Viola d'Amore, Viola da Gamba and String Orchestra, Op. 74
string orch,vla d'amore solo,vla da gamba solo
sc,pts MOSER f.s. (M488)

Concerto for Violin, Viola, Violoncello and String Orchestra, Op. 46
string orch,vln solo,vla solo,vcl solo
sc,pts MOSER f.s. (M489)

Concerto for Violoncello and Orchestra, No. 2, Op. 71
1.1.1.1. 1.0.0.0. opt timp, strings,vcl solo
sc,pts MOSER f.s. (M490)

Concerto for Violoncello and Orchestra, Op. 44
timp,strings,vcl solo
sc,pts MOSER f.s. (M491)

Intrade *Op.38,No.2
string orch,hpsd
sc,pts MOSER f.s. (M492)

Passacaglia Uber "Es Ist Ein Schnitter, Der Heisst Tod" *Op.98
2.2.2.2. 2.2.0.0. timp,strings
sc,pts MOSER f.s. (M493)

Spielmusik *Op.57,No.4
string orch
sc,pts MOSER f.s. (M494)

Suite, Op. 38, No. 1
string orch,hpsd
sc,pts MOSER f.s. (M495)

Suite, Op. 40
string orch
sc,pts MOSER f.s. (M496)

Suite, Op. 47
string orch
sc,pts MOSER f.s. (M497)

Variations, Op. 42, No. 2
2.2.2.2. 2.2.0.0. timp,strings
sc,pts MOSER f.s. (M498)

MOSZKOWSKI, MORITZ (1854-1925)
Cortege In A Minor *Op.43,No.1
3.2.2.2. 4.2.3.0. timp,perc,harp, strings
KALMUS 5346 sc $8.00, perf mat rent, set $23.00, pts $1.00, ea. (M499)

Sarabande
string orch
LUCKS 07493 sc $3.00, set $4.75, pts $.95, ea. (M500)

Sarabande Und Minuette Scherzando, [arr.]
(Dressel, Erwin) sc RIES f.s. (M501)

MOSZKOWSKI, MORITZ (cont'd.)

Spanish Dances, Op. 12, Nos. 1, 3, And 4, [arr.]
LUCKS 06317 sc $10.00, set $25.00, pts $1.40, ea. (M502)

Spanish Dances, Op. 12, Nos. 2 And 5, [arr.]
LUCKS 06316 sc $10.00, set $27.00, pts $1.40, ea. (M503)

MOTHER see Osterc, Slavko, Mati

MOTHER OF HOPE see Jirasek, Ivo, Symphony

MOTO DI GIOIA, UN, FOR SOLO VOICE AND ORCHESTRA see Mozart, Wolfgang Amadeus

MOTO PERPETUO, [ARR.] see Paganini, Niccolo

MOTTE, DIETHER DE LA (1928-)
Concerto for Orchestra, No. 2 [25']
2+pic.2+English horn.2+bass clar.2+contrabsn. 4.3.3.1. 4timp,strings
BAREN. BA 6772 perf mat rent (M504)

Echokonzert, For Violoncello And Orchestra [18']
2(pic).2.2(clar in E flat).2(contrabsn). 2.2.2.0. perc,strings,vcl solo
BAREN. BA 6718 perf mat rent (M505)

MOUCHE, LA, [ARR.] see Bohm, Carl

MOUNTAIN TUNE, A see Sumsion, Herbert W.

MOURET, JEAN JOSEPH (1682-1738)
Suite De Symphonies No. 1
0.2.0.2. 0.2.0.0. timp,strings without vla,hpsd
(Viollier, R.) KALMUS A4676 sc $5.00, perf mat rent, set $14.00, pts $1.25, ea. (M506)

MOUSSORGSKY, MODEST PETROVITCH see MUSSORGSKY, MODEST PETROVICH

MOUTONS DE PANURGE, LES see Rzewski, Frederic Anthony

MOUVEMENTS CONCERTANTES, FOR TWO PIANOS AND STRING ORCHESTRA see Fontyn, Jacqueline

MOVEMENT FOR ORCHESTRA see Fountain, Primous

MOVEMENTS see Keuris, Tristan

MOVEMENTS see Vries, Klaas de, Bewegingen

MOVIMENTI see Tabachnik, Michel

MOVIMENTO SINFONICO see Bettinelli, Bruno

MOYZES, ALEXANDER (1906-)
Symphony No. 10, Op. 77
3.3.3.3. 4.3.3.1. timp,perc,harp, cel,xylo,carillon,strings
SLOV.HUD.FOND 0-477 perf mat rent (M507)

Symphony No. 11
3.3.3.3. 4.3.3.1. timp,perc,harp, cel,strings
SLOV.HUD.FOND 0-478 perf mat rent (M508)

MOZART, LEOPOLD (1719-1787)
Allegro, Menuett Und Rondino
string orch
(Schneider) sc,pts HEINRICH. 224 f.s. (M509)

Cassation in C
sc BREITKOPF-W PB 4905 f.s., pts BREITKOPF-W OB 4905 f.s. (M510)

Concerto for Trombone and Orchestra in D
0.2.2.2. 0.0.0.0. strings,trom/ vla solo
(Weinmann) (Movements 8, 6, 7 from Serenata) sc,pts EULENBURG E10139 f.s. (M511)

Concerto for Trumpet and Orchestra in D [14']
0.0.0.0. 2.0.0.0. strings,trp solo
(Weinmann) (Movements 4, 5 from Serenata) sc,pts EULENBURG E10138 f.s. (M512)

Kinder-Symphonie *see Cassation in C

Kleine Sinfonie Fur Musikfreunde
string orch
pts HEINRICH. 6032 f.s. (M513)

MOZART, LEOPOLD (cont'd.)

Wedding Minuet
0.0.0.0. 2.0.0.0. strings without vla,hpsd
KALMUS A1108 sc $4.00, set $8.75, pts $1.25, ea. (M514)

MOZART, WOLFGANG AMADEUS (1756-1791)
Abduction From The Seraglio, The: Overture *see Entfuhrung Aus Dem Serail, Die: Overture

Adagio for Violin and Orchestra in E, K. 261
LUCKS 01201 sc $5.00, set $9.00, pts $1.25, ea. (M515)

Adagio Und Fuge In C Minor, K. 546
see Einzelstucke, K. 409, 477, 527, 546
f.s. sc CARISCH 21016, pts CARISCH 21017 (M516)
BROUDE BR. study sc $5.00, set $5.00, pts $1.00, ea. (M517)

Ah Se In Ciel, Benigne Stelle, For Solo Voice And Orchestra *K.538
LUCKS 03194 sc $3.75, set $14.00, pts $1.15, ea. (M518)

Alcandro, Lo Confesso (I), For Solo Voice And Orchestra *K.294
LUCKS 03267 sc $3.75, set $9.75, pts $.95, ea. (M519)

Alma Grande E Nobil Core, For Solo Voice And Orchestra *K.578
LUCKS 03303 sc $4.00, set $10.00, pts $1.00, ea. (M520)

Andante For Flute And Orchestra In C *K.315
LUCKS 00820 sc $2.75, set $5.50, min sc $2.50, pts $.95, ea. (M521)

Apollo Und Hyacinthus: Prelude
LUCKS 05000 sc $3.75, set $11.00, min sc $2.50, pts $.75, ea. (M522)

Ascanio In Alba: Overture
BREITKOPF-W perf mat rent (M523)

Baccio Di Mano, Un, For Solo Voice And Orchestra *K.541
LUCKS 03237 sc $3.75, set $9.50, pts $.75, ea. (M524)
INTERNAT. perf mat rent (M525)

Bastien Und Bastienne: Overture
LUCKS 08307 sc $3.75, set $7.00, pts $.75, ea. (M526)

Bella Mia Fiamma, For Solo Voice And Orchestra *K.528
LUCKS 02847 sc $3.75, set $9.50, pts $.75, ea. (M527)

Cassation No. 1 in G, K. 63
see Kassationen, Serenaden Und Divertimenti, K. 32, 63, 99, 63a, 62, 100

Chi Sa, Chi Sa, Qual Sia, For Solo Voice And Orchestra *K.582
LUCKS 03307 sc $3.75, set $9.50, pts $.75, ea. (M528)

Ch'Io Mi Scordi Di Te, For Solo Voice And Orchestra *K.505
LUCKS 02910 sc $3.75, set $7.50, pts $.75, ea. (M529)

Clemenza Di Tito, La: Ecco Il Punto - Non Piu Di Fiori, For Solo Voice And Orchestra
LUCKS 02636 sc $4.75, set $9.50, pts $.75, ea. (M530)

Clemenza Di Tito, La: Overture
"Titus: Overture" LUCKS 07506 sc $3.75, set $9.50, pts $.75, ea. (M531)

Clemenza Di Tito, La: Parto, Ma Tu Ben Mio, For Solo Voice And Orchestra
LUCKS 02013 sc $3.75, set $9.50, pts $.95, ea. (M532)

Concerti For Piano And Orchestra, K. 175, 382, 238, 242
(Flothuis) sc DEUTSCHER 4563 f.s.
contains: Concerto for Piano and Orchestra, No. 5, in D, K. 175; Concerto for Piano and Orchestra, No. 6, in B flat, K. 238; Concerto for 3 Pianos and Orchestra, No. 7, in F, K. 242; Rondo for Piano and Orchestra in D, K. 382 (M533)

Concerti For Piano And Orchestra, K. 246, 271, 365
(Wolff) sc DEUTSCHER 4571 f.s.
contains: Concerto for Piano and Orchestra, No. 8, in C, K. 246;

MOZART, WOLFGANG AMADEUS (cont'd.)

Concerto for Piano and
Orchestra, No. 9, in E flat, K.
271; Concerto for 2 Pianos and
Orchestra, No. 10, in E flat,
K. 365   (M534)

Concerti For Piano And Orchestra, K.
414, 413, 415
(Wolff) sc DEUTSCHER 4575 f.s.
contains: Concerto for Piano and
Orchestra, No. 11, in F, K.
413; Concerto for Piano and
Orchestra, No. 12, in A, K.
414; Concerto for Piano and
Orchestra, No. 13, in C, K. 415
(M535)

Concerti For Piano And Orchestra, K.
449-451
(Flothius) sc DEUTSCHER 4572 f.s.
contains: Concerto for Piano and
Orchestra, No. 14, in E flat,
K. 449; Concerto for Piano and
Orchestra, No. 15, in B flat,
K. 450; Concerto for Piano and
Orchestra, No. 16, in D, K. 451
(M536)

Concerti For Piano And Orchestra, K.
453, 456, 459
(Badura-Skoda) sc DEUTSCHER 4552
f.s.
contains: Concerto for Piano and
Orchestra, No. 17, in G, K.
453; Concerto for Piano and
Orchestra, No. 18, in B flat,
K. 456; Concerto for Piano and
Orchestra, No. 19, in F, K. 459
(M537)

Concerti For Piano And Orchestra, K.
466, 467, 482
(Engel; Heussner) sc DEUTSCHER 4528
f.s.
contains: Concerto for Piano and
Orchestra, No. 20, in D minor,
K. 466; Concerto for Piano and
Orchestra, No. 21, in C, K.
467; Concerto for Piano and
Orchestra, No. 22, in E flat,
K. 482   (M538)

Concerti For Piano And Orchestra, K.
488, 491, 503
(Beck) sc DEUTSCHER 4519 f.s.
contains: Concerto for Piano and
Orchestra, No. 23, in A, K.
488; Concerto for Piano and
Orchestra, No. 24, in C minor,
K. 491; Concerto for Piano and
Orchestra, No. 25, in C, K. 503
(M539)

Concerti For Piano And Orchestra, K.
537, 595, 386, Anh. 64
(Rehm) sc DEUTSCHER 4524 f.s.
contains: Concerto for Piano and
Orchestra, No. 26, in D, K.
537; Concerto for Piano and
Orchestra, No. 27, in B flat,
K. 595; Konzertsatz, For Piano
And Orchestra (Fragment), Anh.
64; Rondo for Piano and
Orchestra in A, K. 386   (M540)

Concerti For Piano And Orchestra Nos.
17-22
study sc DOVER 23599-8 $10.95
reprint of Breitkopf and Hartel
edition, also contains cadenzas
for Concerti 17-19
contains: Concerto for Piano and
Orchestra, No. 17, in G, K.
453; Concerto for Piano and
Orchestra, No. 18, in B flat,
K. 456; Concerto for Piano and
Orchestra, No. 19, in F, K.
459; Concerto for Piano and
Orchestra, No. 20, in D minor,
K. 466; Concerto for Piano and
Orchestra, No. 21, in C, K.
467; Concerto for Piano and
Orchestra, No. 22, in E flat,
K. 482   (M541)

Concerti For Piano And Orchestra Nos.
23-27
study sc DOVER 23600-5 $8.95
reprint of Breitkopf and Hartel
edition, also contains cadenzas
for Concerti no. 23 and 27
contains: Concerto for Piano and
Orchestra, No. 23, in A, K.
488; Concerto for Piano and
Orchestra, No. 24, in C minor,
K. 491; Concerto for Piano and
Orchestra, No. 25, in C, K.
503; Concerto for Piano and
Orchestra, No. 26, in D, K.
537; Concerto for Piano and
Orchestra, No. 27, in B flat,
K. 595; Rondo For Piano And
Orchestra In D, K. 382   (M542)

Concerto for Bassoon and Orchestra in
B flat, K. 191
LUCKS 00775 sc $5.50, set $9.50,
min sc $2.50, pts $1.15, ea.

MOZART, WOLFGANG AMADEUS (cont'd.)

(M543)
Concerto for Clarinet and Orchestra
in A, K. 622 [31']
BROUDE BR. set $20.00, pts $1.75,
ea.   (M544)
min sc PETERS 819 $5.00   (M545)
min sc ZEN-ON 890447 f.s.   (M546)
(Giegling) sc DEUTSCHER 4576 f.s.
(M547)
(Giegling, Franz) sc,pts BAREN.
BA 4773 f.s.   (M548)

Concerto for Flute and Orchestra, No.
1, in G, K. 313
LUCKS 00778 sc $7.50, set $12.00,
min sc $2.50, pts $1.15, ea.,
solo pt $2.00   (M549)

Concerto for Flute and Orchestra, No.
2, in D, K. 314
min sc PETERS 818 $5.00   (M550)
LUCKS 00764 sc $5.50, set $9.50,
min sc $2.50, pts $.95, ea., solo
pt $2.00   (M551)

Concerto for Flute, Harp and
Orchestra in C, K. 299
LUCKS 00763 sc $5.00, set $9.50,
min sc $2.50, pts $1.15, ea.
(M552)

Concerto for Horn and Orchestra, No.
1, in D, K. 412
LUCKS 00779 sc $3.75, set $5.75,
min sc $2.50, pts $.95, ea., solo
pt $2.00   (M553)

Concerto for Horn and Orchestra, No.
1, in D, K. 412, Rondo
opt 2ob,opt 2bsn,strings,horn
solo
(Marguerre, Karl) sc BREITKOPF-W
PB 5069 f.s., pts BREITKOPF-W
OB 5069 f.s.   (M554)

Concerto for Horn and Orchestra, No.
2, in E flat, K. 417
LUCKS 00780 sc $3.75, set $8.00,
min sc $2.50, pts $.95, ea., solo
pt $2.00   (M555)

Concerto for Horn and Orchestra, No.
3, in E flat, K. 447
LUCKS 00773 sc $3.75, set $8.00,
min sc $2.50, pts $.95, ea., solo
pt $2.00   (M556)

Concerto for Horn and Orchestra, No.
4, in E flat, K. 495
LUCKS 00790 sc $3.75, set $8.00,
min sc $2.50, pts $.95, ea., solo
pt $2.00   (M557)

Concerto for Piano and Orchestra, No.
5, in D, K. 175
see Concerti For Piano And
Orchestra, K. 175, 382, 238, 242

Concerto for Piano and Orchestra, No.
6, in B flat, K. 238
see Concerti For Piano And
Orchestra, K. 175, 382, 238, 242

Concerto For Piano And Orchestra No.
7 *see Concerto for 3 Pianos and
Orchestra, No. 7, in F, K. 242

Concerto for Piano and Orchestra, No.
8, in C, K. 246
see Concerti For Piano And
Orchestra, K. 246, 271, 365

Concerto for Piano and Orchestra, No.
9, in E flat, K. 271
see Concerti For Piano And
Orchestra, K. 246, 271, 365
LUCKS 00049 sc $7.00, set $13.50,
min sc $2.50, pts $1.40, ea.
(M558)
Concerto For Piano And Orchestra No.
10 *see Concerto for 2 Pianos
and Orchestra, No. 10, in E flat,
K. 365

Concerto for Piano and Orchestra, No.
11, in F, K. 413
see Concerti For Piano And
Orchestra, K. 414, 413, 415

Concerto for Piano and Orchestra, No.
12, in A, K. 414
see Concerti For Piano And
Orchestra, K. 414, 413, 415
LUCKS 00010 sc $6.50, set $14.50,
min sc $2.50, pts $1.15, ea.
(M559)
Concerto for Piano and Orchestra, No.
13, in C, K. 415
see Concerti For Piano And
Orchestra, K. 414, 413, 415

Concerto for Piano and Orchestra, No.
14, in E flat, K. 449
see Concerti For Piano And
Orchestra, K. 449-451

MOZART, WOLFGANG AMADEUS (cont'd.)

study sc INTERNAT. 1097 $4.75
(M560)
LUCKS 00142 sc $8.00, set $15.50,
min sc $2.50, pts $1.60, ea.,
solo pt $5.00   (M561)

Concerto for Piano and Orchestra, No.
15, in B flat, K. 450
see Concerti For Piano And
Orchestra, K. 449-451
LUCKS 00052 sc $7.50, set $14.50,
min sc $2.50, pts $1.15, ea.
(M562)
Concerto for Piano and Orchestra, No.
16, in D, K. 451
see Concerti For Piano And
Orchestra, K. 449-451

Concerto for Piano and Orchestra, No.
17, in G, K. 453
see Concerti For Piano And
Orchestra, K. 453, 456, 459
see Concerti For Piano And
Orchestra Nos. 17-22
min sc PETERS 869 $6.00   (M563)
LUCKS 00053 sc $10.00, set $15.50,
min sc $2.50, pts $1.15, ea.
(M564)
Concerto for Piano and Orchestra, No.
18, in B flat, K. 456
see Concerti For Piano And
Orchestra, K. 453, 456, 459
see Concerti For Piano And
Orchestra Nos. 17-22
LUCKS 00054 sc $10.00, set $9.50,
min sc $2.50, pts $.95, ea.
(M565)
Concerto for Piano and Orchestra, No.
19, in F, K. 459
see Concerti For Piano And
Orchestra, K. 453, 456, 459
see Concerti For Piano And
Orchestra Nos. 17-22
min sc PETERS 892 $8.50   (M566)
LUCKS 00085 sc $8.00, set $13.50,
min sc $2.50, pts $1.40, ea.
(M567)
Concerto for Piano and Orchestra, No.
20, in D minor, K. 466
see Concerti For Piano And
Orchestra, K. 466, 467, 482
see Concerti For Piano And
Orchestra Nos. 17-22
min sc PETERS 663 $6.00   (M568)
min sc ZEN-ON 890442 f.s.   (M569)
LUCKS 00055 sc $8.00, set $14.50,
min sc $2.50, pts $1.40, ea.
(M570)
Concerto for Piano and Orchestra, No.
21, in C, K. 467
see Concerti For Piano And
Orchestra, K. 466, 467, 482
see Concerti For Piano And
Orchestra Nos. 17-22
min sc PETERS 812 $6.00   (M571)
LUCKS 00056 sc $9.50, set $15.50,
min sc $2.50, pts $1.25, ea.
(M572)
Concerto for Piano and Orchestra, No.
22, in E flat, K. 482
see Concerti For Piano And
Orchestra, K. 466, 467, 482
see Concerti For Piano And
Orchestra Nos. 17-22
LUCKS 00057 sc $10.00, set $16.00,
min sc $2.50, pts $1.15, ea.
(M573)
Concerto for Piano and Orchestra, No.
23, in A, K. 488
see Concerti For Piano And
Orchestra Nos. 23-27
see Concerti For Piano And
Orchestra, K. 488, 491, 503
min sc UNIVER. PH58 $4.00   (M574)
min sc BOOSEY 277 $6.00   (M575)
BROUDE BR. set $22.50, pts $1.75,
ea.   (M576)
min sc PETERS 548 $6.00   (M577)
min sc ZEN-ON 890443 f.s.   (M578)
LUCKS 00058 sc $10.50, set $16.00,
min sc $2.50, pts $1.40, ea.
(M579)
Concerto for Piano and Orchestra, No.
24, in C minor, K. 491
see Concerti For Piano And
Orchestra, K. 488, 491, 503
see Concerti For Piano And
Orchestra Nos. 23-27
min sc UNIVER. PH57 $4.00   (M580)
BROUDE BR. study sc $5.00, set
$11.50, pts $1.50, ea.   (M581)
LUCKS 00059 sc $11.00, set $14.50,
min sc $2.50, pts $1.15, ea.
(M582)
Concerto for Piano and Orchestra, No.
25, in C, K. 503
see Concerti For Piano And
Orchestra Nos. 23-27
see Concerti For Piano And
Orchestra, K. 488, 491, 503
min sc PETERS 810 $7.00   (M583)
LUCKS 00099 sc $8.00, set $14.50,
min sc $2.50, pts $.95, ea.
(M584)

MOZART, WOLFGANG AMADEUS (cont'd.)

Concerto for Piano and Orchestra, No.
26, in D, K. 537
see Concerti For Piano And
Orchestra, K. 537, 595, 386, Anh.
64
see Concerti For Piano And
Orchestra Nos. 23-27
min sc ZEN-ON 890441 f.s.   (M585)
LUCKS 00060 sc $10.00, set $11.50,
min sc $2.50, pts $1.15, ea.
(M586)

Concerto for Piano and Orchestra, No.
27, in B flat, K. 595
see Concerti For Piano And
Orchestra Nos. 23-27
see Concerti For Piano And
Orchestra, K. 537, 595, 386, Anh.
64
LUCKS 00061 sc $7.50, set $12.50,
min sc $2.50, pts $1.15, ea.
(M587)

Concerto For Piano And Orchestra No.
28 *see Rondo for Piano and
Orchestra in D, K. 382

Concerto for 2 Pianos and Orchestra,
No. 10, in E flat, K. 365
see Concerti For Piano And
Orchestra, K. 246, 271, 365
min sc INTERNAT. 985 $4.75   (M588)
min sc PETERS 891 $6.00   (M589)
LUCKS 00050 sc $7.50, set $11.50,
min sc $2.50, pts $.75, ea.
(M590)

Concerto for 3 Pianos and Orchestra,
No. 7, in F, K. 242
see Concerti For Piano And
Orchestra, K. 175, 382, 238, 242
LUCKS 00048 sc $10.00, set $13.50,
min sc $2.50, pts $1.40, ea.,
solo pt $5.00   (M591)

Concerto for Violin and Orchestra,
No. 1, in B flat, K. 207
BROUDE BR. set $15.00, pts $1.50,
ea.   (M592)

Concerto for Violin and Orchestra,
No. 2, in D, K. 211
BROUDE BR. set $15.00, pts $1.50,
ea.   (M593)
min sc PETERS 701 $4.00   (M594)

Concerto for Violin and Orchestra,
No. 3, in G, K. 216
min sc BOOSEY 280 $3.50   (M595)
BROUDE BR. set $17.50, pts $1.50,
ea.   (M596)
LUCKS 00521 sc $5.50, set $11.00,
min sc $2.50, pts $.95, ea.
(M597)

Concerto for Violin and Orchestra,
No. 4, in D, K. 218
BROUDE BR. set $15.00, pts $1.50,
ea.   (M598)
LUCKS 00522 sc $5.50, set $8.50,
min sc $2.50, pts $.95, ea.
(M599)

Concerto for Violin and Orchestra,
No. 5, in A, K. 219
BROUDE BR. set $17.50, pts $1.50,
ea.   (M600)
LUCKS 00523 sc $4.75, set $10.00,
min sc $2.50, pts $.95, ea.
(M601)

Concerto for Violin and Orchestra,
No. 6, in E flat, K. 268
LUCKS 00578 sc $4.75, set $10.00,
min sc $2.50, pts $.95, ea.
(M602)

Concertone For Two Violins And
Orchestra In C, K. 190
see Concertone, Sinfonia
Concertante, K. 190, 364
LUCKS 05508 sc $8.00, set $11.00,
min sc $5.00, pts $1.15, ea.
(M603)

Concertone, Sinfonia Concertante, K.
190, 364
(Mahling) sc DEUTSCHER 4569 f.s.
contains: Concertone For Two
Violins And Orchestra In C, K.
190; Sinfonia Concertante for
Violin, Viola and Orchestra in
E flat, K. 364   (M604)

Concervati Fedele, For Solo Voice And
String Orchestra *K.23 [7']
strings without vcl,S solo
BREITKOPF-W perf mat rent   (M605)

Contretanze, Funf, K. 609
LUCKS 05509 sc $3.75, set $3.50,
pts $.75, ea.   (M606)

Contretanze, Vier, K. 267
see Tanze, K. 65a, 103, 104, 105,
61h, 123, 164, 176, 101, 267,
122, 94

Contretanze, K. 123
see Tanze, K. 65a, 103, 104, 105,
61h, 123, 164, 176, 101, 267,
122, 94

Cosi Dunque Tradisci, For Solo Voice
And Orchestra *K.432
LUCKS 03234 sc $3.75, set $9.50,
pts $.75, ea.   (M607)

Cosi Fan Tutte: Ah Scotati - Smanie
Implacabile, For Solo Voice And
Orchestra
LUCKS 03158 sc $4.75, set $9.50,
pts $.75, ea.   (M608)

Cosi Fan Tutte: Come Scoglio Immoto,
For Solo Voice And Orchestra [4']
0.2.2.2. 0.2.0.0. strings,S solo
BREITKOPF-W perf mat rent   (M609)
LUCKS 02203 sc $3.75, set $7.50,
pts $.75, ea.   (M610)

Cosi Fan Tutte: Donne Mie, La Fate A
Tanti, For Solo Voice And
Orchestra
LUCKS 03152 sc $3.75, set $7.50,
pts $.75, ea.   (M611)

Cosi Fan Tutte: In Uomini, In
Soldati, For Solo Voice And
Orchestra
LUCKS 03199 sc $3.75, set $7.50,
pts $.75, ea.   (M612)

Cosi Fan Tutte: Overture
min sc UNIVER. PH15 $2.50   (M613)
BROUDE BR. set $17.50, pts $1.00,
ea.   (M614)
min sc BOOSEY 171 $2.00   (M615)
LUCKS 08535 sc $2.75, set $9.50,
min sc $1.50, pts $.95, ea.
(M616)

Cosi Fan Tutte: Per Pieta, Ben Mio,
For Solo Voice And Orchestra
LUCKS 03206 sc $3.75, set $11.50,
pts $.75, ea.   (M617)

Cosi Fan Tutte: Prendero Quel
Brunettino, For Solo Voices And
Orchestra
LUCKS 03169 sc $3.75, set $7.50,
pts $.75, ea.   (M618)

Cosi Fan Tutte: Rivolgete A Lui Lo
Sguardo, For Solo Voice And
Orchestra
LUCKS 03210 sc $6.50, set $11.50,
pts $.95, ea.   (M619)

Cosi Fan Tutte: Un' Aura Amorosa, For
Solo Voice And Orchestra
LUCKS 03023 sc $3.75, set $7.50,
pts $.75, ea.   (M620)

Dein Bin Ich *see Re Pastore, Il:
L'Amero Saro Costante, For Solo
Voice And Orchestra

Deutsche Tanze, Drei, K. 605
"German Dances, Three, K. 605"
LUCKS 08908 sc $4.00, set $17.00,
min sc $3.00, pts $.95, ea.
(M621)

Deutsche Tanze, Sechs, K. 571
"German Dances, Six, K. 571" LUCKS
01607 sc $7.00, set $18.00, min
sc $3.00, pts $1.50, ea.   (M622)

Divertimenti, Seventeen *CC17L
study sc DOVER 23862-8 $6.95
reprint of Breitkopf and Hartel
edition, 1878-1880   (M623)

Divertimento, K. 113, in E flat
see Serenades And Divertimenti, K.
113, 131, 189, 185
LUCKS 05516 sc $3.00, set $9.00,
pts $.95, ea.   (M624)

Divertimento, K. 131, in D
see Serenades And Divertimenti, K.
113, 131, 189, 185
LUCKS 07500 sc $6.00, set $10.00,
min sc $2.50, pts $.95, ea.
(M625)

Divertimento, K. 136, in D
see Kassationen, Serenaden Und
Divertimeni, K. 136-138, 525,
Anh. 69, Anh. 223

Divertimento, K. 137, in B flat
see Kassationen, Serenaden Und
Divertimeni, K. 136-138, 525,
Anh. 69, Anh. 223

Divertimento, K. 138, in F
see Kassationen, Serenaden Und
Divertimeni, K. 136-138, 525,
Anh. 69, Anh. 223

Divertimento, K. 205, in D
LUCKS 05529 sc $3.00, set $8.00,
min sc $2.50, pts $.75, ea.
(M626)

Divertimento, K. 287, in B flat
min sc PETERS 894 $5.00   (M627)

Divertimento, K. 334, in D
BROUDE BR. set $12.50, pts $1.50,
ea.   (M628)
LUCKS 08488 sc $8.00, set $10.00,
min sc $2.50, pts $1.25, ea.
(M629)

Don Giovanni: Batti, Batti, O Bel
Masetto, For Solo Voice And
Orchestra
LUCKS 02399 sc $3.75, set $7.50,
pts $.75, ea.   (M630)

Don Giovanni: Dalla Sua Pace, For
Solo Voice And Orchestra
LUCKS 03155 sc $3.75, set $7.50,
pts $.75, ea.   (M631)

Don Giovanni: Deh Vieni Alla
Finestra. Serenade, For Solo
Voice And Orchestra
LUCKS 02032 sc $3.75, set $7.50,
pts $.75, ea.   (M632)

Don Giovanni: Finch' Han Dal Vino,
For Solo Voice And Orchestra
LUCKS 02434 sc $3.75, set $7.50,
pts $.75, ea.   (M633)

Don Giovanni: Fuggi Crudele, For Solo
Voice And Orchestra
LUCKS 02990 sc $4.00, set $7.50,
pts $.75, ea.   (M634)

Don Giovanni: Il Mio Tesoro, For Solo
Voice And Orchestra
LUCKS 02279 sc $3.75, set $6.50,
pts $.75, ea.   (M635)

Don Giovanni: La Ci Darem La Mano,
For Solo Voices And Orchestra
[4']
1.2.0.2. 2.0.0.0. strings,SBar
soli
BREITKOPF-W perf mat rent   (M636)
LUCKS 02280 sc $3.75, set $7.50,
pts $.75, ea.   (M637)

Don Giovanni: Madamina! Il Catalogo,
For Solo Voice And Orchestra
LUCKS 02343 sc $3.75, set $7.50,
pts $.75, ea.   (M638)

Don Giovanni: Mi Tradi Quell'Alma
Ingrata, For Solo Voice And
Orchestra
LUCKS 02080 sc $3.75, set $8.00,
pts $.75, ea.   (M639)

Don Giovanni: Non Mi Dir Bell'Idol
Mio, For Solo Voice And Orchestra
LUCKS 02631 sc $3.75, set $7.50,
pts $.75, ea.   (M640)

Don Giovanni: Notte E Giorno, For
Solo Voice And Orchestra
LUCKS 03164 sc $4.00, set $7.50,
pts $.75, ea.   (M641)

Don Giovanni: Or Sai Chi L'Onore, For
Solo Voice And Orchestra
LUCKS 02938 sc $3.75, set $7.50,
pts $.75, ea.   (M642)

Don Giovanni: Overture
see Einzelstucke, K. 409, 477, 527,
546
LUCKS 06325 sc $3.00, set $10.00,
min sc $1.50, pts $.75, ea.
(M643)
BROUDE BR. set $15.50, pts $1.25,
ea.   (M644)
min sc BOOSEY 170 $2.50   (M645)
"Don Juan: Overture" min sc UNIVER.
PH14 $2.50   (M646)

Don Giovanni: Vedrai Carino, For Solo
Voice And Orchestra
LUCKS 02326 sc $3.75, set $7.50,
pts $.75, ea.   (M647)

Don Juan: Overture *see Don
Giovanni: Overture

Einzelstucke, K. 409, 477, 527, 546
(Plath) sc DEUTSCHER 4586 f.s.
contains: Adagio Und Fuge In C
Minor, K. 546; Don Giovanni:
Overture; Maurerische
Trauermusik, K.477; Menuett In
C, K. 409   (M648)

Entfuhrung Aus Dem Serail, Die: Ach
Ich Liebte, For Solo Voice And
Orchestra
LUCKS 03198 sc $3.75, set $10.50,
pts $.75, ea.   (M649)

Entfuhrung Aus Dem Serail, Die: Durch
Zartlichkeit, For Solo Voice And
Orchestra
LUCKS 02400 sc $2.00, set $3.00,
pts $.75, ea.   (M650)

MOZART, WOLFGANG AMADEUS (cont'd.)

Entfuhrung Aus Dem Serail, Die:
Frisch Zum Kampfe, For Solo Voice
And Orchestra
LUCKS 03217 sc $3.00, set $8.75,
pts $.75, ea.   (M651)

Entfuhrung Aus Dem Serail, Die: Ha!
Wie Will Ich Triumphieren, For
Solo Voice And Orchestra
LUCKS 03176 sc $3.75, set $7.50,
pts $.75, ea.   (M652)

Entfuhrung Aus Dem Serail, Die: Hier
Soll Ich Dich Denn Sehen, For
Solo Voice And Orchestra
LUCKS 02980 sc $2.00, set $6.50,
pts $.75, ea.   (M653)

Entfuhrung Aus Dem Serail, Die: Ich
Baue Ganz Auf Deine Starke, For
Solo Voice And Orchestra
LUCKS 02979 sc $3.75, set $7.50,
pts $.75, ea.   (M654)

Entfuhrung Aus Dem Serail, Die:
Martern Aller Arten, For Solo
Voice And Orchestra
LUCKS 02964 sc $8.00, set $12.00,
pts $.95, ea.   (M655)

Entfuhrung Aus Dem Serail, Die: O Wie
Angstlich, O Wie Feurig, For Solo
Voice And Orchestra
LUCKS 03091 sc $3.75, set $7.50,
pts $.75, ea.   (M656)

Entfuhrung Aus Dem Serail, Die:
Overture
"Abduction From The Seraglio, The:
Overture" min sc UNIVER. PH47
$2.50   (M657)
"Abduction From The Seraglio, The:
Overture" BROUDE BR. set $17.50,
pts $1.00, ea.   (M658)
"Seraglio, Il: Overture" LUCKS
06323 sc $3.75, set $9.50, min sc
$2.50, pts $.95, ea.   (M659)

Entfuhrung Aus Dem Serail, Die:
Solche Hergelauf'ne Laffen, For
Solo Voice And Orchestra
LUCKS 02635 sc $3.75, set $9.50,
pts $.75, ea.   (M660)

Entfuhrung Aus Dem Serail, Die: Welch
Ein Geschick; Meinetwegen Sollst
Du Sterben, For Solo Voices And
Orchestra
LUCKS 03137 sc $3.75, set $8.50,
pts $.75, ea.   (M661)

Entfuhrung Aus Dem Serail, Die:
Welcher Wechsel; Traurigkeit Ward
Mir Zum Loose, For Solo Voice And
Orchestra
LUCKS 03113 sc $3.75, set $7.50,
pts $.75, ea.   (M662)

Fantasy in F minor, [arr.]
(Schmitt, Alois) org,strings [10']
RIES perf mat rent   (M663)

Galimathias Musicum, K. 32
see Kassationen, Serenaden Und
Divertimenti, K. 32, 63, 99, 63a,
62, 100

German Dances, Six, K. 571 *see
Deutsche Tanze, Sechs, K. 571

German Dances, Three, K. 605 *see
Deutsche Tanze, Drei, K. 605

Haffner Symphony *see Symphony No.
35 in D, K. 385

Idomeneo: Zeffiretti Lusinghieri, For
Solo Voice And Orchestra
LUCKS 02848 sc $3.75, set $9.75,
pts $1.15, ea.   (M664)
BREITKOPF-W perf mat rent   (M665)

Impresario, The: Overture *see
Schauspieldirektor, Der: Overture

Io Ti Lascio, For Solo Voice And
Orchestra *K.621a
LUCKS 03308 sc $3.75, set $3.00,
pts $.75, ea.   (M666)

Jupiter Symphony *see Symphony No.
41 in C, K. 551

Kassationen, Serenaden Und
Divertimeni, K. 136-138, 525,
Anh. 69, Anh. 223
(Fussl; Schmid) sc DEUTSCHER 4544
f.s.
contains: Divertimento, K. 136,
in D; Divertimento, K. 137, in
B flat; Divertimento, K. 138,
in F; Kleine Nachtmusik, Eine,
K.525; Larghetto (Fragment),
Anh. 69; Sinfonia (Fragment),

MOZART, WOLFGANG AMADEUS (cont'd.)

Anh. 223   (M667)

Kassationen, Serenaden Und
Divertimenti, K. 32, 63, 99, 63a,
62, 100
(Hausswald; Plath) sc DEUTSCHER
4555 f.s.
contains: Cassation No. 1 in G,
K. 63; Galimathias Musicum, K.
32; Serenade No. 1 in D, K. 100
(M668)

Kassationen, Serenaden Und
Divertimenti, K. 335, 320, 286
(Senn) sc DEUTSCHER 4588 f.s.
contains: Marsche, Zwei, K. 335;
Serenade No. 8 in D, K. 286;
Serenade No. 9 in D, K. 320
(M669)

Kleine Nachtmusik, Eine *K.525
string orch
see Kassationen, Serenaden Und
Divertimeni, K. 136-138, 525,
Anh. 69, Anh. 223
min sc UNIVER. PH366 $2.50   (M670)
LUCKS 06327 sc $3.00, set $5.75,
pts $1.15, ea.   (M671)
BROUDE BR. sc $3.50, set $7.50, pts
$1.50, ea.   (M672)

Konzertantes Quartett, K. Ahn. 9
*see Sinfonia Concertante in E
flat, K. 297b

Konzertsatz, For Piano And Orchestra
(Fragment), Anh. 64
see Concerti For Piano And
Orchestra, K. 537, 595, 386, Anh.
64

Land Der Berge, Land Am Strome
(Luck, Arthur) LUCKS HYMNS 16 set
$9.50, pts $.65, ea.   (M673)

Larghetto (Fragment), Anh. 69
see Kassationen, Serenaden Und
Divertimeni, K. 136-138, 525,
Anh. 69, Anh. 223

Liebes Mandel, Wo Is's Bandel, For
Solo Voices And Orchestra
2.2.0.0. 2.0.0.0. strings,STB
soli
BREITKOPF-W perf mat rent   (M674)

Liebesprobe Oder Die Rekrutierung,
Die *K. Anh.28 [30']
2.2.0.2. 2.2.0.0. strings
BREITKOPF-W perf mat rent   (M675)

Linz Symphony *see Symphony No. 36
in C, K. 425

Magic Flute, The: La Dove Prende
*see Zauberflote, Die: Bei
Mannern, For Solo Voices And
Orchestra

Magic Flute, The: Overture *see
Zauberflote, Die: Overture

Marriage Of Figaro, The: Overture
*see Nozze Di Figaro, Le:
Overture

Marsch In C, K. 214
see Marsche, K. 62, 189, 214, 215,
237, 248, 249, 290, 335, 408, 1-
3, 445, 544

Marsch In D, K. 189
see Marsche, K. 62, 189, 214, 215,
237, 248, 249, 290, 335, 408, 1-
3, 445, 544
see Serenades And Divertimenti, K.
113, 131, 189, 185

Marsch In D, K. 215
see Marsche, K. 62, 189, 214, 215,
237, 248, 249, 290, 335, 408, 1-
3, 445, 544
see Serenades, K. 237, 203, 215,
204, 239

Marsch In D, K. 237
see Marsche, K. 62, 189, 214, 215,
237, 248, 249, 290, 335, 408, 1-
3, 445, 544
see Serenades, K. 237, 203, 215,
204, 239

Marsch In D, K. 249
see Marsche, K. 62, 189, 214, 215,
237, 248, 249, 290, 335, 408, 1-
3, 445, 544
see Serenades, K. 249, 250

Marsch In D, K. 290
see Marsche, K. 62, 189, 214, 215,
237, 248, 249, 290, 335, 408, 1-
3, 445, 544

Marsch In D, K. 445
see Marsche, K. 62, 189, 214, 215,
237, 248, 249, 290, 335, 408, 1-

MOZART, WOLFGANG AMADEUS (cont'd.)

3, 445, 544

Marsch In F, K. 248
see Marsche, K. 62, 189, 214, 215,
237, 248, 249, 290, 335, 408, 1-
3, 445, 544

Marsche, Drei, K. 408
see Marsche, K. 62, 189, 214, 215,
237, 248, 249, 290, 335, 408, 1-
3, 445, 544

Marsche, Zwei, K. 335
see Kassationen, Serenaden Und
Divertimenti, K. 335, 320, 286
see Marsche, K. 62, 189, 214, 215,
237, 248, 249, 290, 335, 408, 1-
3, 445, 544

Marsche, K. 62, 189, 214, 215, 237,
248, 249, 290, 335, 408, 1-3,
445, 544
(Plath) sc DEUTSCHER 4581 f.s.
contains: Marsch In C, K. 214;
Marsch In D, K. 189; Marsch In
D, K. 215; Marsch In D, K. 237;
Marsch In D, K. 249; Marsch In
D, K. 290; Marsch In D, K. 445;
Marsch In F, K. 248; Marsche,
Drei, K. 408; Marsche, Zwei, K.
335   (M676)

Masonic Funeral Music *see
Maurerische Trauermusik

Maurerische Trauermusik *K.477
see Einzelstucke, K. 409, 477, 527,
546
min sc UNIVER. PH60 $2.50   (M677)
"Masonic Funeral Music" LUCKS 08289
sc $4.00, set $5.50, min sc
$2.50, pts $.50, ea.   (M678)

Mentre Ti Lascio, O Figlia, For Solo
Voice And Orchestra *K.513
INTERNAT. perf mat rent   (M679)
LUCKS 03197 sc $3.75, set $9.50,
pts $.75, ea.   (M680)

Menuett In C, K. 409
see Einzelstucke, K. 409, 477, 527,
546
BREITKOPF-W perf mat rent   (M681)
LUCKS 05554 sc $2.00, set $6.00,
pts $.50, ea.   (M682)

Menuett In E Flat, K. 122
see Tanze, K. 65a, 103, 104, 105,
61h, 123, 164, 176, 101, 267,
122, 94

Menuett In G, K. 1, [arr.]
LUCKS 06334 sc $3.00, set $8.00,
pts $.75, ea.   (M683)

Menuette, Neunzehn, K. 103
see Tanze, K. 65a, 103, 104, 105,
61h, 123, 164, 176, 101, 267,
122, 94

Menuette, Sechs, K. 61h
see Tanze, K. 65a, 103, 104, 105,
61h, 123, 164, 176, 101, 267,
122, 94

Menuette, Sechs, K. 104
see Tanze, K. 65a, 103, 104, 105,
61h, 123, 164, 176, 101, 267,
122, 94

Menuette, Sechs, K. 105
see Tanze, K. 65a, 103, 104, 105,
61h, 123, 164, 176, 101, 267,
122, 94

Menuette, Sechs, K. 164
see Tanze, K. 65a, 103, 104, 105,
61h, 123, 164, 176, 101, 267,
122, 94

Menuette, Sechszehn, K. 176
see Tanze, K. 65a, 103, 104, 105,
61h, 123, 164, 176, 101, 267,
122, 94

Menuette, Zwei, Mit Eingefugten
Contretanzen, K. 463
"Two Minuets And Contra-Dances"
LUCKS 05623 sc $2.00, set $5.50,
pts $.75, ea.   (M684)

Menuette Mit Trio, Sieben, K. 65a
string orch
sc BREITKOPF-W PB 4747 f.s., pts
BREITKOPF-W OB 4747 f.s.   (M685)

Mia Speranza Adorata, For Solo Voice
And Orchestra *K.416
LUCKS 02900 sc $3.75, set $7.50,
pts $.75, ea.   (M686)

Misero! O Sogno, For Solo Voice And
Orchestra *K.431
LUCKS 03231 sc $3.75, set $9.50,

MOZART, WOLFGANG AMADEUS (cont'd.)

pts $.95, ea.   (M687)

Mitridate: Overture [5']
2.2.0.0. 2.0.0.0. strings
(Sontag, W.) f.s. sc CARISCH 21490,
pts CARISCH 21491   (M688)

Moto Di Gioia, Un, For Solo Voice And
Orchestra *K.579
LUCKS 03209 sc $3.75, set $7.50,
pts $.75, ea.   (M689)

Musical Joke, A *see Musikalischer
Spass, Ein

Musikalischer Spass, Ein *K.522
"Musical Joke, A" LUCKS 06326 sc
$3.75, set $8.50, min sc $2.50,
pts $1.40, ea.   (M690)

No, No, Che Non Sel Capace, For Solo
Voice And Orchestra *K.419
LUCKS 03232 sc $4.00, set $7.50,
pts $.75, ea.   (M691)

Nozze Di Figaro, Le: Aprite Un Po'
Quegl'Occhi, For Solo Voice And
Orchestra
LUCKS 03121 sc $3.75, set $7.50,
pts $.75, ea.   (M692)

Nozze Di Figaro, Le: Cinque, Dieci,
For Solo Voices And Orchestra
LUCKS 02961 sc $3.75, set $7.50,
pts $.75, ea.   (M693)

Nozze Di Figaro, Le: Crudel! Perche
Finora, For Solo Voices And
Orchestra
LUCKS 02633 sc $3.75, set $6.50,
pts $.75, ea.   (M694)

Nozze Di Figaro, Le: Deh, Vieni Non
Tardar, For Solo Voice And
Orchestra
LUCKS 02401 sc $3.75, set $7.50,
pts $.75, ea.   (M695)

Nozze Di Figaro, Le: Dove Sono, For
Solo Voice And Orchestra
LUCKS 02791 sc $3.75, set $7.50,
pts $.75, ea.   (M696)

Nozze Di Figaro, Le: La Vendetta, For
Solo Voice And Orchestra
LUCKS 03208 sc $4.00, set $10.00,
pts $.75, ea.   (M697)

Nozze Di Figaro, Le: Non Piu Andrai,
For Solo Voice And Orchestra
LUCKS 02239 sc $3.75, set $7.50,
pts $.75, ea.   (M698)

Nozze Di Figaro, Le: Non So Piu Cosa
Son, For Solo Voice And Orchestra
LUCKS 02323 sc $3.75, set $7.50,
pts $.75, ea.   (M699)

Nozze Di Figaro, Le: Overture
"Marriage Of Figaro, The: Overture"
LUCKS 06328 sc $2.75, set $9.50,
min sc $1.50, pts $.75, ea.
(M700)
"Marriage Of Figaro, The: Overture"
BROUDE BR. set $17.50, pts $1.25,
ea.   (M701)
"Marriage Of Figaro, The: Overture"
min sc UNIVER. PH13 $2.00   (M702)

Nozze Di Figaro, Le: Porgi Amor, For
Solo Voice And Orchestra
LUCKS 02205 sc $3.75, set $7.50,
pts $.75, ea.   (M703)

Nozze Di Figaro, Le: Se A Caso
Madama, For Solo Voices And
Orchestra
LUCKS 02965 sc $3.75, set $7.50,
pts $.75, ea.   (M704)

Nozze Di Figaro, Le: Se Vuol Ballare,
For Solo Voice And Orchestra
LUCKS 02278 sc $3.75, set $6.50,
pts $.75, ea.   (M705)

Nozze Di Figaro, Le: Sull' Aria! Che
Soave Zeffiretto, For Solo Voices
And Orchestra
LUCKS 02634 sc $3.75, set $7.50,
pts $.75, ea.   (M706)

Nozze Di Figaro, Le: Vedro Mentr'Io
Sospiro, For Solo Voice And
Orchestra
LUCKS 02795 sc $4.75, set $11.50,
pts $.75, ea.   (M707)

Nozze Di Figaro, Le: Venite,
Inginocchiatevi, For Solo Voice
And Orchestra
LUCKS 03145 sc $3.75, set $7.50,
pts $.75, ea.   (M708)

MOZART, WOLFGANG AMADEUS (cont'd.)

Nozze Di Figaro, Le: Voi Che Sapete,
For Solo Voice And Orchestra
LUCKS 02463 sc $3.75, set $7.50,
pts $.75, ea.   (M709)

Nun Liebes Weibchen, Ziehst Mit Mir,
For Solo Voices And Orchestra
*K.625
LUCKS 03309 sc $3.75, set $9.50,
pts $.75, ea.   (M710)

Ombra Felice, For Solo Voice And
Orchestra *K.255
LUCKS 03335 sc $7.50, set $12.50,
pts $1.50, ea.   (M711)

Overture in B flat, K. 311a
(Sandberger) sc,quarto PETERS L2843
$17.50   (M712)

Paris Symphony *see Symphony No. 31
in D, K. 297

Per Pieta, Non Ricercate, For Solo
Voice And Orchestra *K.420
LUCKS 03233 sc $3.75, set $9.50,
pts $.75, ea.   (M713)

Per Questa Bella Mano, For Solo Voice
And Orchestra *K.612
INTERNAT. perf mat rent   (M714)
KALMUS 5537 sc $4.00, set $8.00
(M715)
LUCKS 02240 sc $4.00, set $8.00,
pts $.75, ea.   (M716)

Petit Riens, Les *K. Anh.10
min sc PETERS 866 $5.00   (M717)

Petits Riens, Les, [arr.] *K. Anh.10
2.1.2.0. 0.2.0.0. strings sc,pts
HARMONIA 1575 f.s.   (M718)

Prague Symphony *see Symphony No. 38
in D, K. 504

Re Pastore, Il: L'Amero, Saro
Costante, For Solo Voice And
Orchestra
LUCKS 02235 sc $3.75, set $9.50,
pts $.75, ea.   (M719)
"Dein Bin Ich" ERES 2015 rent
(M720)

Re Pastore, Il: Overture
see Symphonies, K. 201, 202, 196,
297, 121, 208
BREITKOPF-W perf mat rent   (M721)
LUCKS 07304 sc $3.75, set $9.50,
pts $.95, ea.   (M722)

Rondo Concertante, For Piano And
Orchestra, [arr.] (from Concerto
For Piano And Orchestra No. 22 In
E Flat, K. 482)
(Busoni, F.) BREITKOPF-W perf mat
rent   (M723)

Rondo for Piano and Orchestra in A,
K. 386
see Concerti For Piano And
Orchestra, K. 537, 595, 386, Anh.
64

Rondo for Piano and Orchestra in D,
K. 382
see Concerti For Piano And
Orchestra, K. 175, 382, 238, 242
see Concerti For Piano And
Orchestra Nos. 23-27
min sc INTERNAT. 950 $3.50   (M724)
min sc PETERS 893 $5.00   (M725)
LUCKS 00095 sc $4.00, set $9.50,
min sc $2.50, pts $1.15, ea.
(M726)

Rondo for Violin and Orchestra in B
flat, K. 269
BREITKOPF-W perf mat rent   (M727)

Schauspieldirektor, Der: Overture
"Impresario, The: Overture" BROUDE
BR. study sc $3.50, set $17.50,
pts $1.00, ea.   (M728)
"Impresario, The: Overture" LUCKS
06336 sc $2.75, set $9.50, min sc
$2.00, pts $.95, ea.   (M729)

Seraglio, Il: Overture *see
Entfuhrung Aus Dem Serail, Die:
Overture

Serenade No. 1 in D, K. 100
see Kassationen, Serenaden Und
Divertimenti, K. 32, 63, 99, 63a,
62, 100

Serenade No. 2 In F, K. 101
see Tanze, K. 65a, 103, 104, 105,
61h, 123, 164, 176, 101, 267,
122, 94

Serenade No. 3 in D, K. 185
see Serenades And Divertimenti, K.
113, 131, 189, 185

MOZART, WOLFGANG AMADEUS (cont'd.)

Serenade No. 4 in D, K. 203
see Serenades, K. 237, 203, 215,
204, 239

Serenade No. 5 in D, K. 204
see Serenades, K. 237, 203, 215,
204, 239

Serenade No. 6 in D, K. 239
see Serenades, K. 237, 203, 215,
204, 239
min sc PETERS 867 $4.50   (M730)
LUCKS 06393 sc $5.00, set $9.50,
min sc $2.50, pts $.95, ea.
(M731)

Serenade No. 7 in D, K. 250
see Serenades, K. 249, 250
LUCKS 06331 sc $12.00, set $21.00,
min sc $2.50, pts $1.75, ea.
(M732)

Serenade No. 8 in D, K. 286
see Kassationen, Serenaden Und
Divertimenti, K. 335, 320, 286
min sc PETERS 896 $4.50   (M733)

Serenade No. 9 in D, K. 320 [35']
2.2.0.2. 2.2.0.0. timp,strings
see Kassationen, Serenaden Und
Divertimenti, K. 335, 320, 286
sc,pts BREITKOPF-W PB-OB 4900 f.s.
(M734)

Serenades And Divertimenti, K. 113,
131, 189, 185
(Hausswald) sc DEUTSCHER 4523 f.s.
contains: Divertimento, K. 113,
in E flat; Divertimento, K.
131, in D; Marsch In D, K. 189;
Serenade No. 3 in D, K. 185
(M735)

Serenades, K. 237, 203, 215, 204, 239
(Hausswald) sc DEUTSCHER 4531 f.s.
contains: Marsch In D, K. 237;
Marsch In D, K. 237; Serenade
No. 4 in D, K. 203; Serenade
No. 5 in D, K. 204; Serenade
No. 6 in D, K. 239   (M736)

Serenades, K. 249, 250
(Senn) sc DEUTSCHER 4580 f.s.
contains: Marsch In D, K. 249;
Serenade No. 7 in D, K. 250
(M737)

Sinfonia Concertante for Violin,
Viola and Orchestra in E flat, K.
364
see Concertone, Sinfonia
Concertante, K. 190, 364
BROUDE BR. set $17.50, pts $1.25,
ea.   (M738)
LUCKS 06343 sc $10.00, set $11.00,
pts $1.40, ea.   (M739)

Sinfonia Concertante in E flat, K.
297b *reconstruction
ob,clar,bsn,horn,orch LUCKS 08541
sc $8.50, set $15.00, pts $1.40,
ea.   (M740)

Sinfonia (Fragment), Anh. 223
see Kassationen, Serenaden Und
Divertimeni, K. 136-138, 525,
Anh. 69, Anh. 223

Sonata for Organ and Orchestra in G,
K. 241
see Sonatas For Organ And
Orchestra, K. 67-69, 144, 145,
212, 241, 224, 245, 263, 278,
329, 328, 338, 274

Sonata for Organ and Orchestra, No.
1, in E flat, K. 67
see Sonatas For Organ And
Orchestra, K. 67-69, 144, 145,
212, 241, 224, 245, 263, 278,
329, 328, 338, 274

Sonata for Organ and Orchestra, No.
2, in B flat, K. 68
see Sonatas For Organ And
Orchestra, K. 67-69, 144, 145,
212, 241, 224, 245, 263, 278,
329, 328, 338, 274

Sonata for Organ and Orchestra, No.
3, in D, K. 69
see Sonatas For Organ And
Orchestra, K. 67-69, 144, 145,
212, 241, 224, 245, 263, 278,
329, 328, 338, 274

Sonata for Organ and Orchestra, No.
4, in D, K. 144
see Sonatas For Organ And
Orchestra, K. 67-69, 144, 145,
212, 241, 224, 245, 263, 278,
329, 328, 338, 274

Sonata for Organ and Orchestra, No.
5, in F, K. 145
see Sonatas For Organ And
Orchestra, K. 67-69, 144, 145,
212, 241, 224, 245, 263, 278,
329, 328, 338, 274

MOZART, WOLFGANG AMADEUS (cont'd.)

Sonata for Organ and Orchestra, No.
6, in B flat, K. 212
see Sonatas For Organ And
Orchestra, K. 67-69, 144, 145,
212, 241, 224, 245, 263, 278,
329, 328, 338, 274

Sonata for Organ and Orchestra, No.
7, in F, K. 224
see Sonatas For Organ And
Orchestra, K. 67-69, 144, 145,
212, 241, 224, 245, 263, 278,
329, 328, 338, 274

Sonata for Organ and Orchestra, No.
9, in F, K. 244
see Sonatas For Organ And
Orchestra, K. 244, 245, 274, 328,
336

Sonata for Organ and Orchestra, No.
10, in D, K. 245
see Sonatas For Organ And
Orchestra, K. 244, 245, 274, 328,
336
see Sonatas For Organ And
Orchestra, K. 67-69, 144, 145,
212, 241, 224, 245, 263, 278,
329, 328, 338, 274

Sonata for Organ and Orchestra, No.
11, in G, K. 274
see Sonatas For Organ And
Orchestra, K. 67-69, 144, 145,
212, 241, 224, 245, 263, 278,
329, 328, 338, 274
see Sonatas For Organ And
Orchestra, K. 244, 245, 274, 328,
336

Sonata for Organ and Orchestra, No.
12, in C, K. 278
see Sonatas For Organ And
Orchestra, K. 67-69, 144, 145,
212, 241, 224, 245, 263, 278,
329, 328, 338, 274

Sonata for Organ and Orchestra, No.
13, in C, K. 328
see Sonatas For Organ And
Orchestra, K. 67-69, 144, 145,
212, 241, 224, 245, 263, 278,
329, 328, 338, 274
see Sonatas For Organ And
Orchestra, K. 244, 245, 274, 328,
336

Sonata for Organ and Orchestra, No.
14, in C, K. 329
see Sonatas For Organ And
Orchestra, K. 67-69, 144, 145,
212, 241, 224, 245, 263, 278,
329, 328, 338, 274

Sonata for Organ and Orchestra, No.
15, in C, K. 336
see Sonatas For Organ And
Orchestra, K. 67-69, 144, 145,
212, 241, 224, 245, 263, 278,
329, 328, 338, 274
see Sonatas For Organ And
Orchestra, K. 244, 245, 274, 328,
336

Sonata for Organ and Orchestra, No.
17, in C, K. 263
see Sonatas For Organ And
Orchestra, K. 67-69, 144, 145,
212, 241, 224, 245, 263, 278,
329, 328, 338, 274

Sonatas For Organ And Orchestra, K.
67-69, 144, 145, 212, 241, 224,
245, 263, 278, 329, 328, 338, 274
(Dounias) sc DEUTSCHER 4511 f.s.
contains: Sonata for Organ and
Orchestra in G, K. 241; Sonata
for Organ and Orchestra, No. 1,
in E flat, K. 67; Sonata for
Organ and Orchestra, No. 2, in
B flat, K. 68; Sonata for Organ
and Orchestra, No. 3, in D, K.
69; Sonata for Organ and
Orchestra, No. 4, in D, K. 144;
Sonata for Organ and Orchestra,
No. 5, in F, K. 145; Sonata for
Organ and Orchestra, No. 6, in
B flat, K. 212; Sonata for
Organ and Orchestra, No. 7, in
F, K. 224; Sonata for Organ and
Orchestra, No. 10, in D, K.
245; Sonata for Organ and
Orchestra, No. 11, in G, K.
274; Sonata for Organ and
Orchestra, No. 12, in C, K.
278; Sonata for Organ and
Orchestra, No. 13, in C, K.
328; Sonata for Organ and
Orchestra, No. 14, in C, K.
329; Sonata for Organ and
Orchestra, No. 15, in C, K.
336; Sonata for Organ and
Orchestra, No. 17, in C, K. 263
(M741)

MOZART, WOLFGANG AMADEUS (cont'd.)

Sonatas For Organ And Orchestra, K.
244, 245, 274, 328, 336
KALMUS A1110 sc $7.50, set $6.00,
pts $1.50, ea.
contains: Sonata for Organ and
Orchestra, No. 9, in F, K. 244;
Sonata for Organ and Orchestra,
No. 10, in D, K. 245; Sonata
for Organ and Orchestra, No.
11, in G, K. 274; Sonata for
Organ and Orchestra, No. 13, in
C, K. 328; Sonata for Organ and
Orchestra, No. 15, in C, K. 336
(M742)

Symphonies, K. 128-130, 132-134, 141a
(Fischer) sc DEUTSCHER 4502 f.s.
contains: Symphony in D, K. 161,
K. 163; Symphony No. 16 in C,
K. 128; Symphony No. 17 in G,
K. 129; Symphony No. 18 in F,
K. 130; Symphony No. 19 in E
flat, K. 132; Symphony No. 20
in D, K. 133; Symphony No. 21
in A, K. 134 (M743)

Symphonies, K. 162, 184, 181-183,
199, 200
(Beck) sc DEUTSCHER 4522 f.s.
contains: Symphony No. 22 in C,
K. 162; Symphony No. 23 in D,
K. 181; Symphony No. 24 in B
flat, K. 182; Symphony No. 25
in G minor, K. 183; Symphony
No. 26 in E flat, K. 184;
Symphony No. 27 in G, K. 199;
Symphony No. 28 in C, K. 200
(M744)

Symphonies, K. 201, 202, 196, 297,
121, 208
(Beck) sc DEUTSCHER 4508 f.s.
contains: Re Pastore, Il:
Overture; Symphony in D, K.
121; Symphony in D, K. 196;
Symphony No. 29 in A, K. 201;
Symphony No. 30 in D, K. 202;
Symphony No. 31 in D, K. 297
(M745)

Symphonies, K. 204, 250, 320
(Hausswald) sc DEUTSCHER 4518 f.s.
contains: Symphony in D, K. 204;
Symphony in D, K. 250; Symphony
in D, K. 320 (M746)

Symphonies, K. 318, 319, 338, 385
(Mahling; Schnapp) sc DEUTSCHER
4558 f.s.
contains: Symphony No. 32 in G,
K. 318; Symphony No. 33 in B
flat, K. 319; Symphony No. 34
in C, K. 338; Symphony No. 35
in D, K. 385 (M747)

Symphonies, K. 425, 504
(Schnapp; Somfai) sc DEUTSCHER 4561
f.s.
contains: Symphony No. 36 in C,
K. 425; Symphony No. 38 in D,
K. 504 (M748)

Symphonies, K. 543, 550, 551
(Landon) sc DEUTSCHER 4509 f.s.
contains: Symphony No. 39 in E
flat, K. 543; Symphony No. 40
in G minor, K. 550; Symphony
No. 41 in C, K. 551 (M749)

Symphony in C, K. 96
BREITKOPF-W perf mat rent (M750)

Symphony in D, K. 95
BREITKOPF-W perf mat rent (M751)

Symphony in D, K. 97
BREITKOPF-W perf mat rent (M752)

Symphony in D, K. 121
see Symphonies, K. 201, 202, 196,
297, 121, 208

Symphony in D, K. 161, K. 163
see Symphonies, K. 128-130, 132-
134, 141a

Symphony in D, K. 196
see Symphonies, K. 201, 202, 196,
297, 121, 208

Symphony in D, K. 204
see Symphonies, K. 204, 250, 320

Symphony in D, K. 250
see Symphonies, K. 204, 250, 320

Symphony in D, K. 320
see Symphonies, K. 204, 250, 320

Symphony in F, K. 76
BREITKOPF-W perf mat rent (M753)

Symphony in F, K. Anh. 223 [15']
2ob, 2horn, hpsd, strings
(Munster, Robert) sc BAREN. BA 4795
f.s., perf mat rent (M754)

MOZART, WOLFGANG AMADEUS (cont'd.)

Symphony No. 1 in E flat, K. 16
LUCKS 06337 sc $5.00, set $11.50,
min sc $2.50, pts $1.15, ea.
(M755)

Symphony No. 6 in F, K. 43
LUCKS 05571 sc $8.00, set $10.00,
min sc $2.50, pts $1.25, ea.
(M756)

Symphony No. 9 in C, K. 73
BREITKOPF-W perf mat rent (M757)

Symphony No. 10 in G, K. 74
BREITKOPF-W perf mat rent (M758)

Symphony No. 14 in A, K. 114
sc EUR.AM.MUS. 71U0101 $10.50, set
EUR.AM.MUS. 71U0101WS $10.50, pts
EUR.AM.MUS. $2.25, ea. (M759)
LUCKS 05573 sc $8.00, set $10.00,
min sc $2.50, pts $1.25, ea.
(M760)

Symphony No. 15 in G, K. 124
LUCKS 01830 sc $4.00, set $10.00,
min sc $2.50, pts $1.50, ea.
(M761)

Symphony No. 16 in C, K. 128
see Symphonies, K. 128-130, 132-
134, 141a

Symphony No. 17 in G, K. 129
see Symphonies, K. 128-130, 132-
134, 141a
BREITKOPF-W perf mat rent (M762)

Symphony No. 18 in F, K. 130
see Symphonies, K. 128-130, 132-
134, 141a

Symphony No. 19 in E flat, K. 132
see Symphonies, K. 128-130, 132-
134, 141a

Symphony No. 19 in E flat, K. 132,
[arr.]
2.1.2.0. 0.2.0.0. perc, strings sc,
pts HARMONIA 1805 f.s. (M763)

Symphony No. 20 in D, K. 133
see Symphonies, K. 128-130, 132-
134, 141a
LUCKS 05582 sc $5.00, set $15.00,
min sc $2.50, pts $1.25, ea.
(M764)

Symphony No. 21 in A, K. 134
see Symphonies, K. 128-130, 132-
134, 141a

Symphony No. 22 in C, K. 162
see Symphonies, K. 162, 184, 181-
183, 199, 200
LUCKS 05583 sc $4.00, set $10.00,
min sc $2.50, pts $1.15, ea.
(M765)

Symphony No. 23 in D, K. 181
see Symphonies, K. 162, 184, 181-
183, 199, 200

Symphony No. 24 in B flat, K. 182
see Symphonies, K. 162, 184, 181-
183, 199, 200
BROUDE BR. study sc $3.50, set
$12.50, pts $1.25, ea. (M766)
LUCKS 05593 sc $4.00, set $10.00,
min sc $2.50, pts $1.25, ea.
(M767)

Symphony No. 25 in G minor, K. 183
see Symphonies, K. 162, 184, 181-
183, 199, 200
BROUDE BR. set $15.00, pts $1.25,
ea. (M768)

Symphony No. 26 in E flat, K. 184
see Symphonies, K. 162, 184, 181-
183, 199, 200
LUCKS 08360 sc $7.50, set $9.50,
min sc $2.50, pts $.95, ea.
(M769)

Symphony No. 27 in G, K. 199
see Symphonies, K. 162, 184, 181-
183, 199, 200

Symphony No. 28 in C, K. 200 [15']
0.2.0.0. 2.2.0.0. strings
see Symphonies, K. 162, 184, 181-
183, 199, 200
min sc UNIVER. PH50 $3.50 (M770)
sc, pts BREITKOPF-W PB-OB 4401 f.s.
(M771)

Symphony No. 29 in A, K. 201
see Symphonies, K. 201, 202, 196,
297, 121, 208
BROUDE BR. set $15.00, pts $1.25,
ea. (M772)
LUCKS 08992 sc $5.00, set $10.50,
min sc $2.50, pts $1.15, ea.
(M773)

Symphony No. 30 in D, K. 202
see Symphonies, K. 201, 202, 196,
297, 121, 208

Symphony No. 31 in D, K. 297
see Symphonies, K. 201, 202, 196,
297, 121, 208
LUCKS 09062 sc $6.00, set $22.00,

MOZART, WOLFGANG AMADEUS (cont'd.)

min sc $2.50, pts $1.15, ea.
(M774)

Symphony No. 32 in G, K. 318
see Symphonies, K. 318, 319, 338,
385
LUCKS 09185 sc $4.50, set $16.00,
min sc $2.50, pts $1.25, ea.
(M775)
(Negrotti, N.) sc,pts ZANIBON D289
rent (M776)

Symphony No. 33 in B flat, K. 319
see Symphonies, K. 318, 319, 338,
385
BROUDE BR. study sc $4.50, set
$20.00, pts $1.25, ea. (M777)

Symphony No. 34 in C, K. 338
see Symphonies, K. 318, 319, 338,
385
BROUDE BR. study sc $5.50, set
$22.50, pts $1.50, ea. (M778)

Symphony No. 35 in D, K. 385 [17']
see Symphonies, K. 318, 319, 338,
385
min sc UNIVER. PH51 $3.00 (M779)
BROUDE BR. set $22.50, pts $1.50,
ea. (M780)
min sc PETERS 541 $5.00 (M781)
sc FABER $15.00 (M782)
min sc ZEN-ON 890401 f.s. (M783)
(Mahling, Christoph-Hellmut) pts
BAREN. BA 4781 f.s. (M784)

Symphony No. 36 in C, K. 425
see Symphonies, K. 425, 504
min sc UNIVER. PH49 $3.00 (M785)
min sc PETERS 543 $5.00 (M786)
min sc ZEN-ON 890402 f.s. (M787)
LUCKS 06339 sc $6.00, set $14.50,
min sc $2.50, pts $1.15, ea.
(M788)

Symphony No. 38 in D, K. 504
see Symphonies, K. 425, 504
min sc UNIVER. PH61 $3.50 (M789)
sc BOOSEY 164 $32.00 (M790)
min sc ZEN-ON 890403 f.s. (M791)
LUCKS 07502 sc $6.50, set $18.00,
min sc $2.50, pts $1.15, ea.
(M792)

Symphony No. 39 in E flat, K. 543
see Symphonies, K. 543, 550, 551
min sc UNIVER. PH56 $4.00 (M793)
min sc BOOSEY 165 $3.50 (M794)
BROUDE BR. study sc $4.50, set
$25.00, pts $2.00, ea. (M795)
min sc ZEN-ON 890404 f.s. (M796)
LUCKS 06340 sc $6.50, set $17.00,
min sc $2.50, pts $1.15, ea.
(M797)

Symphony No. 40 in G minor, K. 550
see Symphonies, K. 543, 550, 551
min sc UNIVER. PH27 $3.50 (M798)
BROUDE BR. set $22.50, pts $1.50,
ea. (M799)
(second version) min sc PETERS 544
$5.00 (M800)
min sc ZEN-ON 890405 f.s. (M801)
LUCKS 06341 sc $8.50, set $17.00,
min sc $2.50, pts $1.40, ea.
(M802)

Symphony No. 41 in C, K. 551
see Symphonies, K. 543, 550, 551
min sc UNIVER. PH6 $3.50 (M803)
min sc BOOSEY 167 $4.25 (M804)
BROUDE BR. sc $5.00, set $22.50,
pts $1.50, ea. (M805)
min sc ZEN-ON 890406 f.s. (M806)

Tanze Fur Orchester, [arr.] *CCU
(Smith, E.) 2.2.2.1. 2.2.0.0. timp,
perc,strings sc,pts DOBLINGER
74 003 (M807)

Tanze, K. 65a, 103, 104, 105, 61h,
123, 164, 176, 101, 267, 122, 94
(Elvers) sc DEUTSCHER 4517 f.s.
contains: Contretanze, Vier, K.
267; Contretanze, K. 123;
Menuett In E Flat, K. 122;
Menuette, Neunzehn, K. 103;
Menuette, Sechs, K. 61h;
Menuette, Sechs, K. 104;
Menuette, Sechs, K. 105;
Menuette, Sechs, K. 164;
Menuette, Sechszehn, K. 176;
Serenade No. 2 In F, K. 101
(M808)

Titus: Overture *see Clemenza Di
Tito, La: Overture

Turkischer Marsch, [arr.] (from
Sonata For Piano In A, K. 331)
(Pascal) LUCKS 06333 sc $3.00, set
$5.00, pts $.75, ea. (M809)

Turkish Concerto *see Concerto for
Violin and Orchestra, No. 5, in
A, K. 219

Two Minuets And Contra-Dances *see
Menuette, Zwei, Mit Eingefugten
Contretanzen, K. 463

MOZART, WOLFGANG AMADEUS (cont'd.)

Vado, Ma Dove, For Solo Voice And
Orchestra *K.583
LUCKS 03310 sc $4.00, set $10.00,
pts $1.00, ea. (M810)

Waltzes, Three, [arr.] *CC3U
(Tocchi, Gian Luca) harp,strings sc
DE SANTIS DS 571 f.s. (M811)

Zaide: Ruhe Sanft, For Solo Voice And
Orchestra
LUCKS 03193 sc $4.00, set $8.00,
min sc $2.50, pts $.75, ea. (M812)

Zauberflote, Die: Ach, Ich Fuhl's,
For Solo Voice And Orchestra
LUCKS 02331 sc $3.75, set $7.50,
pts $.75, ea. (M813)

Zauberflote, Die: Bei Mannern, For
Solo Voices And Orchestra
"Magic Flute, The: La Dove Prende"
LUCKS 02836 sc $3.75, set $7.50,
pts $.75, ea. (M814)

Zauberflote, Die: Der Holle Rache,
For Solo Voice And Orchestra
LUCKS 02014 sc $3.75, set $7.50,
pts $.75, ea. (M815)

Zauberflote, Die: Der Vogelfanger Bin
Ich Ja, For Solo Voice And
Orchestra
LUCKS 03218 sc $4.00, set $8.00,
pts $.75, ea. (M816)

Zauberflote, Die: Dies Bildnis Ist
Bezaubernd Schon, For Solo Voice
And Orchestra
LUCKS 02204 sc $3.75, set $7.50,
pts $.75, ea. (M817)

Zauberflote, Die: Ein Madchen Oder
Weibchen, For Solo Voice And
Orchestra
LUCKS 03203 sc $4.00, set $8.00,
pts $.75, ea. (M818)

Zauberflote, Die: In Diesen Heil'gen
Hallen, For Solo Voice And
Orchestra
LUCKS 02035 sc $3.75, set $6.50,
pts $.75, ea. (M819)

Zauberflote, Die: O Isis Und Osiris,
For Solo Voice And Orchestra
LUCKS 02115 sc $3.75, set $7.50,
pts $.75, ea. (M820)

Zauberflote, Die: O Zitt're Nicht,
For Solo Voice And Orchestra
LUCKS 02846 sc $3.75, set $7.50,
pts $.75, ea. (M821)

Zauberflote, Die: Overture
"Magic Flute, The: Overture" min sc
UNIVER. PH12 $3.00 (M822)
"Magic Flute, The: Overture" LUCKS
06332 sc $3.00, set $9.50, min sc
$2.00, pts $.75, ea. (M823)
"Magic Flute, The: Overture" BROUDE
BR. set $17.50, pts $1.00, ea.
(M824)

Zauberflote, Die: Pa-Pa-Pa-Papagena,
For Solo Voices And Orchestra
LUCKS 02960 sc $3.75, set $7.50,
pts $.75, ea. (M825)

Zauberflote, Die: Wie Stark Ist Nicht
Dein Zauberton, For Solo Voice
And Orchestra
LUCKS 03311 sc $3.75, set $7.50,
pts $.75, ea. (M826)

MRACZEK, KARL
Slavische Tanze [10']
3(pic).3.2+bass clar.2+contrabsn.
4.3.3.1. timp,perc,harp,strings
RIES perf mat rent (M827)

MUAK see Yun, Isang

MUDE SOLDAT, DER see Beekhuis, Hanna

MUETTE DE PORTICI, LA: OVERTURE see
Auber, Daniel-Francois-Esprit

MUFFAT, GEORG (ca. 1645-1704)
Important Wedding Suite *see
Splendidae Nuptiae

Splendidae Nuptiae
string orch
"Important Wedding Suite" LUCKS
01502 sc $3.00, set $6.25, pts
$1.25, ea. (M828)

MUHR, FERRY
An Den Ufern Der Wolga
RIES f.s. (M829)

Wogende Bluten
RIES f.s. (M830)

MUL, JAN (1911-1971)
Cuatro Coplas, For Solo Voice And
Orchestra [3']
2.2.2.2. 2.2.0.0. timp,strings,
high solo
sc DONEMUS f.s., perf mat rent
(M831)
Drie Latijnse Minneliederen, For Solo
Voice And Orchestra
1.0.1.0. 0.0.0.0. perc,strings,S
solo sc DONEMUS f.s., perf mat
rent
contains: Floret Silva; Stetit
Puella; Veni, Veni, Venias
(M832)
Floret Silva
see Drie Latijnse Minneliederen,
For Solo Voice And Orchestra

Galant Kwartet, For Solo Voice And
Orchestra [5']
1.1.1.1. 0.0.0.0. perc,strings,S
solo
sc DONEMUS f.s., perf mat rent
(M833)
Lettre, For Solo Voice And Orchestra
[9']
2.2.2.2. 2.2.2.0. timp,perc,harp,
strings,Bar solo
sc DONEMUS f.s., perf mat rent
(M834)
Old Familiar Faces, The, For Solo
Voice And Orchestra
1.0.1.0. 0.0.0.0. perc,strings,B
solo
sc DONEMUS f.s., perf mat rent
(M835)
Stetit Puella
see Drie Latijnse Minneliederen,
For Solo Voice And Orchestra

Veni, Veni, Venias
see Drie Latijnse Minneliederen,
For Solo Voice And Orchestra

MULDER, ERNEST W. (1898-1959)
Cleopatre I
see Trois Chansons, For Solo Voice
And Orchestra

Clepatre II
see Trois Chansons, For Solo Voice
And Orchestra

Sinfonietta for Solo Voice and
Orchestra
2.2.2.2. 2.2.0.0. timp,perc,harp,
strings,med solo
sc DONEMUS f.s., perf mat rent
(M836)
Soir
see Trois Chansons, For Solo Voice
And Orchestra

Trois Chansons, For Solo Voice And
Orchestra
1.1.1.1. 1.0.0.0. timp,pno,strings,
S solo sc DONEMUS f.s., perf mat
rent
contains: Cleopatre I; Clepatre
II; Soir (M837)

MULDER, HERMAN (1894-   )
Capriccio, Op. 159 [11']
3.3.3.3. 4.3.3.1. timp,2harp,
strings
sc DONEMUS f.s., perf mat rent
(M838)
Concertino, Op. 142 for Oboe and
Orchestra
2.1.2.0. 1.2.1.0. timp,perc,
strings,ob solo
sc DONEMUS f.s., perf mat rent
(M839)
Dreamland *see Droomland, For Solo
Voice And Orchestra

Droomland, For Solo Voice And
Orchestra *Op.74
3.3.3.2. 4.0.0.0. timp,perc,harp,
strings,Bar/A solo
"Dreamland" sc DONEMUS f.s., perf
mat rent (M840)
Duisternis
see Vier Liederen, For Solo Voice
And Orchestra

Introductie, Chaconne En Finale
*Op.174 [29']
3.3.3.3. 4.3.3.1. timp,perc,
strings
DONEMUS f.s. (M841)
Lostomige Wind
see Vier Liederen, For Solo Voice
And Orchestra

Sinfonia Concertante for Violin,
Viola, Violoncello and Orchestra,
Op. 172 [30']
3.3.2.2. 2.2.2.0. 2perc,harp,
strings,vln solo,vla solo,vcl
solo
DONEMUS perf mat rent (M842)

MULDER, HERMAN (cont'd.)
    Sinfonia No. 8, Op. 144 [45']
        3.3.3.3. 4.3.3.1. timp,perc,
        2harp,pno,strings
        sc DONEMUS f.s., perf mat rent
                                        (M843)
    Snaren Hebben Getrild, De, For Solo
        Voice And Orchestra *Op.173
        [20']
        3.3.3.3. 4.3.3.1. timp,2harp,
        strings,S solo
        "Strings Have Vibrated, The"
        DONEMUS perf mat rent   (M844)
    Sonnettenkring, For Solo Voice And
        Orchestra *Op.130,Op.130a
        2.2.3.2. 2.0.0.0. harp,strings,A/
        Bar solo
        sc DONEMUS f.s., perf mat rent
                                        (M845)
    Strijder, De
        see Vier Liederen, For Solo Voice
        And Orchestra
    Strings Have Vibrated, The *see
        Snaren Hebben Getrild, De, For
        Solo Voice And Orchestra
    Symphony No. 11, Op. 165 [40']
        3.3.3.3. 4.3.3.1. timp,perc,
        2harp,strings
        sc DONEMUS f.s., perf mat rent
                                        (M846)
    Symphony No. 12, Op. 169 [36']
        4.4.4.3. 6.4.3.1. timp,perc,
        2harp,strings
        sc DONEMUS f.s., perf mat rent
                                        (M847)
    Vier Liederen, For Solo Voice And
        Orchestra
        1.1.1.1. 1.1.1.0. timp,perc,harp,
        strings,Bar solo sc DONEMUS f.s.,
        perf mat rent
        contains: Duisternis; Lostomige
        Wind; Strijder, De; Winden
        Lachen Zacht, De   (M848)
    Winden Lachen Zacht, De
        see Vier Liederen, For Solo Voice
        And Orchestra

MULLER, PEPI
    Klange Der Puszta
        RIES f.s.   (M849)

MULLER-MARC, RAYM.
    Verliebtes Spiel
        RIES f.s.   (M850)

MULLER-ZURICH, PAUL (1898-   )
    Sinfonietta I *Op.66
        2.2.2.2. 2.2.1.0. timp,strings
        sc,pts EULENBURG E10086 f.s. (M851)

MULTIPLAY see Wimberger, Gerhard

MULTIPLI see Manzoni, Giacomo

MURMELN see Correggia, Enrico

MUSEN-QUADRILLE see Strauss, Johann,
    [Sr.]

MUSEN QUADRILLE see Strauss, Johann,
    [Jr.]

MUSETTA see Nordio, Cesare

MUSGRAVE, THEA (1928-   )
    Orfeo II, For Flute And String
        Orchestra
        string orch,fl solo
        sc NOVELLO 89.0081.07 f.s.   (M852)

MUSIC-BOX-GAVOTTE see Faust, Willi

MUSIC FOR A NON-EXISTING MUSICAL see
    Deursen, Anton van

MUSIC FOR A SOLEMN FESTIVAL, VOL. 1 see
    Musik Zu Ernsten Feiern, Heft 1

MUSIC FOR A SOLEMN FESTIVAL, VOL. 2 see
    Musik Zu Ernsten Feiern, Heft 2

MUSIC FOR ANGELS see Mannino, Franco

MUSIC FOR BRASS, STRINGS AND PERCUSSION
    see Cope, David

MUSIC FOR CLARINET AND STRING ORCHESTRA
    see Zador, Eugene (Jeno)

MUSIC FOR ORCHESTRA NO. 2 see Fritchie,
    Wayne

MUSIC FOR STRING INSTRUMENTS see
    Dessau, Paul

MUSIC FOR VIOLINS AND VIOLAS see Frid,
    Geza

MUSIC II see Wagemans, Peter-Jan

MUSIC OF THE SEA see Wagner, Joseph
    Frederick

MUSIC TO THE GUDBRANDSDALS PLAY, THE
    see Berge, Sigurd

MUSICA, ARS SUBTILIOR, FOR VIOLA AND
    ORCHESTRA see Laman, Wim

MUSICA DA CAMERA PER 11 see Maros,
    Rudolf

MUSICA DI CATASTO see Delden, Lex van

MUSICA IN MEMORIAM HONEGGER see Salva,
    Tadeas

MUSICA PER 12 see Bettinelli, Bruno

MUSICA PER ANTICHI POETI ITALIANI, FOR
    SOLO VOICE AND ORCHESTRA see
    Cattini, Umberto

MUSICA PER ARCHI see Mortari, Virgilio

MUSICA PER ARCHI see Rochat, Andree

MUSICA PER ORGANO TRENTUNISONO I NO. 4
    see Dijk, Jan van

MUSICA PER UN BALLETTO see Mortari,
    Virgilio

MUSICA PER VIOLINI, VIOLONCELLI E
    CONTRABASSI see Roos, Robert de

MUSICA SERIA see Karkoff, Maurice

MUSICAL JOKE, A see Mozart, Wolfgang
    Amadeus, Musikalischer Spass, Ein

MUSICAL OFFERING: RICERCARE, [ARR.] see
    Bach, Johann Sebastian,
    Musikalisches Opfer: Ricercare A 6,
    [arr.]

MUSICAL SNUFF BOX, THE, [ARR.] see
    Liadov, Anatol Konstantinovich

MUSIK FUR ORCHESTER see Dencker, Helmut

MUSIK NO. I see Maasz, Gerhard

MUSIK NO. II see Maasz, Gerhard

MUSIK ZU EINEM RITTERBALLETT, [ARR.]
    see Beethoven, Ludwig van

MUSIK ZU ERNSTEN FEIERN, HEFT 1
    (Altemark, J.) "Music For A Solemn
    Festival, Vol. 1" strings,kbd
    KALMUS A1112 sc $4.50, set $10.00,
    pts $1.00, ea.   (M853)

MUSIK ZU ERNSTEN FEIERN, HEFT 2
    (Altemark, J.) "Music For A Solemn
    Festival, Vol. 2" strings,kbd
    KALMUS A1113 sc $4.50, set $11.25,
    pts $1.00, ea.   (M854)

MUSIKALISCHER SPASS, EIN see Mozart,
    Wolfgang Amadeus

MUSIKALISCHES OPFER: RICERCARE A 6,
    [ARR.] see Bach, Johann Sebastian

MUSIKANTEN-SUITE see Geisler, Willy

MUSIQUE CONCERTANTE, FOR HORN AND
    ORCHESTRA see Ajdic, Alojz,
    Koncertantna Glasba, For Horn And
    Orchestra

MUSIQUE CONCERTANTE, FOR TIMPANI AND
    ORCHESTRA see Ramovs, Primoz,
    Koncertantna Glasba, For Timpani
    And Orchestra

MUSIQUE CREUSE LE CIEL, LA, FOR TWO
    PIANOS AND ORCHESTRA see Rihm,
    Wolfgang

MUSIQUE DE GESTE see Turchi, Guido

MUSIQUE POUR 11 VIOLINS see Morricone,
    Ennio

MUSIQUE POUR L'HOMME, FOR SOLO VOICES
    AND ORCHESTRA see Straesser, Joep

MUSIQUE POUR ORCHESTRE DE CHAMBRE see
    Baekers, Stephan

MUSIQUE POUR QUINZE see Sivic, Pavle

MUSSORGSKY, MODEST PETROVICH
    (1839-1881)
    Bilder Einer Ausstellung, [arr.]
        *see Pictures At An Exhibition,
        [arr.]
    Boris Godunov: Chanson De Varlaam
        LUCKS 02224 sc $5.00, set $14.00,
        pts $.75, ea.   (M855)

MUSSORGSKY, MODEST PETROVICH (cont'd.)
    Boris Godunov: Hallucination Scene.
        Scene Of The Clock, For Solo
        Voice And Orchestra
        LUCKS 03323 sc $6.00, set $13.00,
        pts $.75, ea.   (M856)
    Boris Godunov: Monologue Of Boris,
        For Solo Voice And Orchestra
        LUCKS 02333 sc $5.00, set $13.00,
        pts $.75, ea.   (M857)
    Cicaleccio Del Mercato
        see RICREAZIONI DI ANTICHE MUSICHE
        CLASSICHE, SERIE IV: MUSICHE
        ANTICHE ITALIANE
    Khovantchina: Overture
        min sc INTERNAT. 670 $3.00   (M858)
    Lieder Und Tanze Das Todes, For Solo
        Voice And Orchestra, [arr.] *see
        Songs And Dances Of Death, For
        Solo Voice And Orchestra, [arr.]
    Night On Bald Mountain
        3.2.2.2. 4.2.3.1. timp,perc,harp,
        strings
        INTERNAT. perf mat rent   (M859)
        min sc ZEN-ON 892251 f.s.   (M860)
        "Nuit Sur Le Mont Chauve, Une" sc,
        pts HAMELLE f.s.   (M861)
    Nuit Sur Le Mont Chauve, Une *see
        Night On Bald Mountain
    Pictures At An Exhibition, [arr.]
        (Becce, Giuseppe) "Bilder Einer
        Ausstellung, [arr.]" 2.1.2.2.
        2.2.3.0. timp,perc,strings [50']
        sc,pts LIENAU rent   (M862)
        (Dolan, James) [30'] NEW MUSIC WEST
        perf mat rent   (M863)
    Song Of The Flea, For Solo Voice And
        Orchestra
        LUCKS 02223 sc $4.00, set $7.50,
        pts $.75, ea.   (M864)
    Songs And Dances Of Death, For Solo
        Voice And Orchestra, [arr.]
        (Labinsky, S.; Ljapunow, A.;
        Rimsky-Korsakov, N.) "Lieder Und
        Tanze Das Todes, For Solo Voice
        And Orchestra, [arr.]"
        3(pic).2(English horn).2.2.
        4.2.3.1. timp,3perc,harp,strings,
        Bar/Mez solo BREITKOPF-W perf mat
        rent   (M865)
    Songs And Dances Of Death: Berceuse,
        For Solo Voice And Orchestra
        LUCKS 02935 set $7.50, pts $.75,
        ea.   (M866)

MUTACIONES see Rugeles, Alfredo

MUTATIONEN see Berg, Gunnar

MUTAZIONI see Nishimura, Akira

MUTTERTANDELEI, FOR SOLO VOICE AND
    ORCHESTRA see Strauss, Richard

MUZIEK TER BRUILOFT, FOR SOLO VOICE AND
    ORCHESTRA see Paap, Wouter

MUZYKA SYMFONICZNA I I II see Rychlik,
    Jozef

MY COUNTRY: FROM BOHEMIA'S MEADOWS AND
    FORESTS see Smetana, Bedrich, Ma
    Vlast: Z Ceskych Luhu A Haju

MY COUNTRY: MOLDAU see Smetana,
    Bedrich, Ma Vlast: Vitava

MY COUNTRY: SARKA see Smetana, Bedrich,
    Ma Vlast: Sarka

MY COUNTRY: TABOR see Smetana, Bedrich,
    Ma Vlast: Tabor

MY COUNTRY 'TIS OF THEE see America

MY COUNTRY: VYSEHRAD see Smetana,
    Bedrich, Ma Vlast: Vysehrad

MY JESUS, OH WHAT ANGUISH, [ARR.] see
    Bach, Johann Sebastian, Mein Jesu,
    Was Fur Seelenweh, [arr.]

MY LOVE, SHE'S BUT A LASSIE YET, FOR
    SOLO VOICE AND ORCHESTRA
    LUCKS 03240 sc $4.00, set $13.50, pts
    $.75, ea.   (M867)

MY ROMANCE see Schubert-Weber, S.

MY SPANISH GUITAR
    LUCKS 02862 set $24.00, pts $.75, ea.
                                     (M868)

MY TOY BALLOON see Slonimsky, Nicolas

MY TRIBUTE
   (Mayfield, Larry; Skillings, Otis)
   SINGSPIR 7709 $19.95   (M869)

MYRTHENBLUTHEN WALZER see Strauss,
   Johann, [Jr.]

MYRTHENSTRAUSSCHEN WALZER see Strauss,
   Eduard

MYSTERION, FOR ENGLISH HORN AND STRING
   ORCHESTRA see Rietz, Johannes

MYSTIC TRUMPETER, THE see Genzmer,
   Harald, Cantata for Solo Voice,
   Trumpet and String Orchestra

MYTHOS see Holler, York

N

NA JANA see Cikker, Jan

NABOKOV, NICOLAS (1903-1978)
   Don Quichotte: Suite
      3.3.3.3. 4.3.3.1. timp,2perc,
      harp,strings
      SEESAW perf mat rent   (N1)

NABOTH see Caldara, Antonio

NABUCCO: DIO DI GUIDA, FOR SOLO VOICE
   AND ORCHESTRA see Verdi, Giuseppe

NABUCCO: OVERTURE see Verdi, Giuseppe

NABUCCO: PREGHIERA DI FENENA, FOR SOLO
   VOICE AND ORCHESTRA see Verdi,
   Giuseppe

NACH KURZER POST POLKA see Strauss,
   Eduard

NACHDENKEN UBER, FOR TRUMPET AND
   ORCHESTRA see Heider, Werner

NACHT see Hermans, Nico

NACHT, DIE, FOR SOLO VOICE AND
   ORCHESTRA see Diepenbrock, Alphons

NACHT IN VENEDIG, EINE: LAGUNEN-WALZER
   see Strauss, Johann, [Jr.]

NACHT IN VENEDIG, EINE: OVERTURE see
   Strauss, Johann, [Jr.]

NACHT IN VENEDIG, EINE: SELECTION see
   Strauss, Johann, [Jr.]

NACHT-STILTE see Hermans, Nico

NACHTEGAAL, DE, FOR SOLO VOICE AND
   ORCHESTRA see Loevendie, Theo

NACHTEGAEL DIE SANCK EEN LIEDT, DE see
   Beekhuis, Hanna

NACHTFALTER WALZER see Strauss, Johann,
   [Jr.]

NACHTIGALL UND DIE ROSE, DIE see Voss,
   Friedrich

NACHTLAGER IN GRANADA, DAS: EVENING
   PRAYER, FOR SOLO VOICE AND
   ORCHESTRA see Kreutzer, Konradin

NACHTLAGER IN GRANADA, DAS: OVERTURE
   see Kreutzer, Konradin

NACHTLANDSCHAFT see Trede, Yngre Jan

NACHTLICHER BUMMEL see Taborski, H.

NACHTLIED, FOR SOLO VOICE AND ORCHESTRA
   see Frederich, Otto

NACHTMUSIK IM GARTEN see Klaas, Julius

NACHTORDNUNG see Rihm, Wolfgang

NACHTSCHATTEN see Strauss, Josef

NACHTSTILTE see Dijk, Jan van

NAGY-FARKAS, PETER (1933-   )
   Uprising, The
      3.3.3.3. 4.2.3.1. perc,pno,harp,
      strings
      SEESAW perf mat rent   (N2)

NAIADES, LES see Andersen, Alfred

NAJADEN-QUADRILLE see Strauss, Johann,
   [Sr.]

NAJADEN QUADRILLE see Strauss, Johann,
   [Jr.]

NALLE PUH, FOR NARRATOR AND ORCHESTRA
   see Johanson, Sven-Eric

NALUAN see Mache, Francois Bernard

NAMOUNA: SUITE NO. 1 see Lalo, Edouard

NAMOUNA: SUITE NO. 2 see Lalo, Edouard

NAMOUNA: VALSE DE LA CIGARETTE see
   Lalo, Edouard

NANA-SYMPHONIE see Constant, Marius

NAPRAVNIK, EDUARD (1839-1916)
   Fandango (from Deux Pieces
      Espagnoles)
      KALMUS A4642 sc $8.00, perf mat
      rent, set $24.00, pts $1.00, ea.
                                    (N3)

NAPRAVNIK, EDUARD (cont'd.)

   Romance (from Deux Pieces Espagnoles)
      KALMUS A4640 sc $4.00, perf mat
      rent, set $14.00, pts $.75, ea.
                                    (N4)

NARDINI, PIETRO (1722-1793)
   Concerto for Violin and Orchestra in
      E minor, [arr.]
      LUCKS 00570 sc $7.50, set $14.00,
      pts $1.15, ea.   (N5)

   Concerto for Violin and String
      Orchestra in A [24']
      string orch,cont,vln solo
      manuscript CARISCH   (N6)

   Concerto for Violin and String
      Orchestra in C, MIN 48 [10']
      string orch,vln solo
      sc,pts RARITIES $12.00   (N7)

NARODNA IN INTERMEZZO, FOR VIOLIN AND
   ORCHESTRA see Jez, Jakob

NARRATIVE, FOR VIOLONCELLO AND CHAMBER
   ORCHESTRA see Finney, Ross Lee

NASCIMBENE, M. (1913-   )
   Acqueforti Della Vecchia Milano [30']
      3.3.3.3. 4.3.3.1. timp,perc,
      bells,xylo,harp,cel,pno,strings
      manuscript CARISCH   (N8)

NASVELD, ROBERT (1955-   )
   Chamber Concerto [12']
      1.1.1.1. 1.1.1.0. perc,pno,2vln,
      vla,vcl,db
      DONEMUS sc f.s., pts rent   (N9)

   Concerto for 2 Pianos and Orchestra
      [17']
      3.3.3.3. 4.3.3.1. timp,2perc,
      strings,2pno soli
      DONEMUS   (N10)

NATALE, IL, FOR SOLO VOICES AND
   ORCHESTRA see Sinigaglia, Leone

NATIONAL EMBLEM MARCH see Bagley, E.E.

NATTSTYCKE see Osterling, Ulf

NATURE MEDITATION, A, FOR VIOLIN AND
   ORCHESTRA see Selby, Philip

NECKEREI see Wilcken, Eugen

NELHYBEL, VACLAV (1919-   )
   Agitato [9']
      string orch,pno,string quar soli
      KERBY 16835 sc,pts $25.00, sc $6.00
                                   (N11)
   Concertino Da Camera, For Violoncello
      And Orchestra [11']
      15winds,db,perc,vcl solo
      KERBY 5147 sc $10.00, pts rent
                                   (N12)
   Concerto for Viola and Orchestra
      2.2.2.2. 3.1.1.0. 2perc,strings,
      vla solo
      BARTA B 108 perf mat rent   (N13)

   Oratio III
      2.2.2.2. 0.0.0.0. strings
      sc,pts BARTA B 114 $30.00, pts
      BARTA $.50, ea.   (N14)

   Oratio IV
      0.0.0.0. 2.3.3.1. strings
      sc,pts BARTA B 131 $7.50, pts BARTA
      rent   (N15)

   Oratio V
      2.2.2.2. 1.0.0.0. strings
      sc BARTA B 132 $6.50, pts BARTA
      rent   (N16)

NELJA LAULUA UNESTA, FOR SOLO VOICE AND
   ORCHESTRA see Sallinen, Aulis

NELL GWYN: THREE DANCES see German,
   [Sir] Edward (Edward German Jones)

NELL'ANNO 1000: PRELUDIO see Bossi,
   Renzo

NELSON, BRADLEY
   Recantation, For Solo Voice And
      Orchestra
      1.1.2.1. 2.2.1.1. 4perc,strings,
      solo voice
      SEESAW perf mat rent   (N17)

NELSON, PAUL (1929-   )
   Idyll, For Horn And String Orchestra
      string orch,horn solo
      A MOLL DUR $5.00   (N18)

NENIA see Bossi, [Marco] Enrico

NENIA see Szabo, Csaba

NERI, MASSIMILIANO (ca. 1610-ca. 1666)
Sonata, MIN 75, [arr.]
(Bonelli, E.) string orch [9'] sc
ZANIBON 3693 f.s., pts ZANIBON
3694 f.s.   (N19)

NEUBERT, GUNTER (1936-   )
Notturno [13']
11vln,4vla,3vcl,db
sc PETERS EP 5665 f.s., perf mat
rent   (N20)

NEUE LIEBE, FOR SOLO VOICE AND
ORCHESTRA see Wolf, Hugo

NEUE WELT POLKA, EINE see Strauss,
Eduard

NEUES FEDERSPIEL NACH VERSEN AUS "DES
KNABEN WUNDERHORN", FOR SOLO VOICE
AND CHAMBER ORCHESTRA see
Braunfels, Walter

NEUES LEBEN. POLKA see Strauss, Johann,
[Jr.]

NEUN GEDICHTE AUS "SANGE EINES
FAHRENDEN SPIELMANNS" VON STEFAN
GEORGE, FOR SOLO VOICE AND CHAMBER
ORCHESTRA see Frommel, Gerhard

NEVER SEEK TO TELL THY LOVE see Brings,
Allen Stephen

NEW LOVE see Wolf, Hugo, Neue Liebe,
For Solo Voice And Orchestra

NEW TOWN SUITE see Thorpe Davie, Cedric

NEW YORK CONCERTO see Giuffre, Gaetano

NEWMAN, THEODORE SIMON (1933-1975)
"B" For Orchestra [6']
2+pic.2+English horn.2+bass
clar.2+contrabsn. 4.3.3.1.
timp,perc,harp,pno,strings
KALMUS A5486 sc $5.00, perf mat
rent, set $22.00, pts $.75, ea.
(N21)

Cain Ballet [19']
1+pic.1.2.1. 2.1.1.0. timp,perc,
pno,cel,strings
KALMUS A5487 sc $40.00, perf mat
rent, set $80.00, pts $5.00, ea.
(N22)

Discourse [14']
2+pic.2.2.2. 2.2.2.0. timp,perc,
strings
KALMUS A5488 sc $20.00, perf mat
rent, set $50.00, pts $2.50, ea.
(N23)

Double Piece [4']
2+pic.2+English horn.2+bass
clar.2+contrabsn. 4.3.3.1.
timp,perc,harp,pno,strings
KALMUS A5484 sc $5.00, perf mat
rent, set $30.00, pts $1.00, ea.
(N24)

Epilogue [2']
timp,perc,strings without vla
KALMUS A5483 sc $2.00, set $10.50,
pts $1.50, ea.   (N25)

Presto [4']
2+pic.2+English horn.2+bass
clar.2+contrabsn. 4.3.3.1.
timp,perc,harp,pno,strings
KALMUS A5485 sc $10.00, perf mat
rent, set $30.00, pts $1.00, ea.
(N26)

Psalm For String Orchestra [4']
string orch
KALMUS A5492 sc $5.00, set $7.00,
pts $1.00, ea.   (N27)

Symphonic Prelude [8']
2+pic.2+English horn.2+bass
clar.2+contrabsn. 4.3.3.1.
timp,perc,harp,pno,strings
KALMUS A5489 sc $25.00, perf mat
rent, set $75.00, pts $2.50, ea.
(N28)

Symphony No. 1 in F sharp [48']
2+pic.3.2+bass clar.2+contrabsn.
4.3.3.1. timp,perc,harp,pno,
strings
KALMUS A5490 sc $70.00, perf mat
rent, set $100.00, pts $3.50, ea.
(N29)

Toccata [10']
1+pic.1+English horn.1+bass
clar.1+contrabsn. 4.3.3.1.
timp,perc,pno,strings
KALMUS A5491 sc $25.00, perf mat
rent, set $80.00, pts $3.50, ea.
(N30)

NICOLAI, OTTO (1810-1849)
Lustigen Weiber Von Windsor, Die:
Ballettmusik [10']
2.2.2.2. 4.2.3.0. timp,perc,
strings
KALMUS 5438 sc $21.00, perf mat
rent, set $50.00, pts $2.50, ea.
(N31)

NICOLAI, OTTO (cont'd.)
Lustigen Weiber Von Windsor, Die:
Horch, Die Lerche Singt Im Hain,
For Solo Voice And Orchestra [4']
1+pic.1.1.2. 2.0.0.0. harp,
strings,T solo
BREITKOPF-W perf mat rent   (N32)

Lustigen Weiber Von Windsor, Die:
Overture
"Merry Wives Of Windsor, The:
Overture" min sc UNIVER. PH41
$2.00   (N33)
"Merry Wives Of Windsor, The:
Overture" PETERS 596 $5.00   (N34)
"Merry Wives Of Windsor, The:
Overture" min sc BOOSEY 291 $3.50
(N35)
"Merry Wives Of Windsor, The:
Overture" LUCKS 06369 sc $6.50,
set $23.00, min sc $1.50, pts
$1.40, ea.   (N36)

Merry Wives Of Windsor, The: Overture
*see Lustigen Weiber Von Windsor,
Die: Overture

NICOLINI, GIUSEPPE (1762-1842)
Sinfonias In F And E Minor
see NORTHERN ITALIAN SYMPHONY,
1800-1840, THE

NIEHAUS, MANFRED (1933-   )
Drei Tanze Aus Dem 14. Jahrhundert
[13']
2(pic).0.2(bass clar).2.alto sax.
2.1+bass trp.2.1. timp,2perc,
harp,cel,strings
BREITKOPF-W perf mat rent   (N37)

Pop And Art [12']
3.3.3.3. 6.3.4.0. timp,perc,2gtr,
2bass gtr,strings,opt cor
BREITKOPF-W perf mat rent   (N38)

NIELSEN, CARL (1865-1931)
Concerto for Clarinet and Orchestra,
Op. 57 [27']
0.0.0.2. 2.0.0.0. perc,strings,
clar solo
KALMUS 5354 solo pt $2.50, sc
$15.00, perf mat rent, set
$12.00, pts $1.00, ea.   (N39)

Little Suite *Op.1
string orch
LUCKS 05669 sc $6.00, set $7.00,
pts $1.40, ea.   (N40)

NIELSEN, JOHN
Variationer, 15 [13']
3.3.3.3. 4.3.2.1. perc,strings
sc,pts SAMFUNDET 250 perf mat rent
(N41)

NIELSEN, RICCARDO (1908-   )
Capriccio for Piano and Orchestra
[8']
1.1.1.1. 0.1.1.0. timp,perc,xylo,
strings,pno solo
manuscript CARISCH   (N42)

Sinfonia [21']
1.1.1.1. 2.1.1.0. timp,strings
manuscript CARISCH   (N43)

NIELSEN, TAGE
Giardino Magico, Il
sc,pts SAMFUNDET 225 perf mat rent
(N44)

NIEUWE LENTE OP HOLLANDS ERF, EEN, FOR
SOLO VOICE AND ORCHESTRA see
Voormolen, Alexander Nicolas

NIGHT IN THE TROPICS, A, [ARR.] see
Gottschalk, Louis Moreau

NIGHT IN VENICE: OVERTURE see Strauss,
Johann, [Jr.], Nacht In Venedig,
Eine: Overture

NIGHT IN VENICE: SELECTION see Strauss,
Johann, [Jr.], Nacht In Venedig,
Eine: Selection

NIGHT JOURNEY see Schuman, William
Howard

NIGHT MUSIC see Matthews

NIGHT MUSIC, FOR FLUTE AND ORCHESTRA
see Dorati, Antal

NIGHT ON BALD MOUNTAIN see Mussorgsky,
Modest Petrovich

NIGHT VOICES, FOR NARRATOR AND
ORCHESTRA see Epstein, David M.

NIGHTINGALE, THE, FOR SOLO VOICE AND
ORCHESTRA see Loevendie, Theo,
Nachtegaal, De, For Solo Voice And
Orchestra

NIGHTMUSIC see Schevikhoven, Henk van

NIIN MUSTINA MURATIT KIERTAA, FOR SOLO
VOICE AND ORCHESTRA, [ARR.] see
Kaski, Heino

NIKLAS, FERRY
Franzosische Suite [13']
1.1.1.1. 0.2.2.0. perc,harp,pno,
strings
(Mikulicz, Lothar) RIES perf mat
rent   (N45)

Kleine Tanzmusik
RIES f.s.   (N46)

Spanische Suite
sc RIES f.s.   (N47)

NILFLUTHEN WALZER see Strauss, Josef

NILSSON, ANDERS (1954-   )
Trois Pieces Pour Grand Orchestre:
Premier Mouvement [13'30"]
3.3.3.3. 4.3.3.1. timp,2perc,
harp,pno,cel,strings
pts STIM   (N48)

NILSSON, BO (1937-   )
Szene I-III
study sc SUECIA f.s.   (N49)

NILSSON, TORBJORN (1955-   )
Concerto for String Orchestra, No. 1
[22'30"]
string orch
sc STIM perf mat rent   (N50)

Concerto for String Orchestra, No. 2
[15']
string orch
sc STIM perf mat rent   (N51)

NINE AND A HALF FOR HENRY (AND WILBUR
AND ORVILLE) see Erickson, Robert

NINNA NANNA, FOR SOLO VOICE AND
ORCHESTRA see Soresina, Alberto

NINNA NANNA DI GESU BAMBINO, FOR SOLO
VOICES AND ORCHESTRA see
Sinigaglia, Leone

NISHIMURA, AKIRA (1953-   )
Mutazioni [17']
4.4.4.4. 6.4.4.1. 2perc,harp,
strings
sc ZERBONI 8436 f.s., pts ZERBONI
8437 rent   (N52)

NIXENTANZE see Bode, Hermann

NIXON, ROGER A. (1921-   )
Concerto for Viola and Orchestra
[30']
2(pic).2(English horn).2.2.
4.2.3.0. timp,perc,harp,cel,
strings,vla solo
study sc FISCHER,C $10.00   (N53)

NO, NO, CHE NON SEL CAPACE, FOR SOLO
VOICE AND ORCHESTRA see Mozart,
Wolfgang Amadeus

NOACK, WALTER
Schwabischer Landler
see Zwei Volkstanze

Schwarzwalder Polka
see Zwei Volkstanze

Zwei Volkstanze
RIES f.s.
contains: Schwabischer Landler;
Schwarzwalder Polka   (N54)

NOBRE, MARLOS (1939-   )
Concerto for String Orchestra, No. 1
string orch
TONOS   (N55)

Concerto for String Orchestra, No. 2
string orch
TONOS   (N56)

Desafio II, For Violoncello And
String Orchestra
string orch,vcl solo
TONOS 10242   (N57)

Desafio III, For Violin And String
Orchestra
string orch,vln solo
TONOS 10243   (N58)

Desafio IV, For Double Bass And
String Orchestra
string orch,db solo
TONOS 10244   (N59)

Desafio VII, For Piano And String
Orchestra
string orch,pno solo
TONOS 10250   (N60)

NOCTAMBULE see Bush, Geoffrey

NOCTURNAL CONVERSATION see Hekster, Walter

NOCTURNE FOR STRINGS see Proto, Frank

NOCTURNE FROM STRING QUARTET NO. 2, [ARR.] see Borodin, Alexander Porfirievich

NOCTURNE FROM STRING QUARTET NO. 2 FOR VIOLIN AND ORCHESTRA, [ARR.] see Borodin, Alexander Porfirievich

NOCTURNE- NEW YEAR MUSIC see Finzi, Gerald

NOCTURNEN, FOR SOLO VOICE AND ORCHESTRA see Andriessen, Louis

NOCTURNES see Debussy, Claude

NODA, TERUYUKI (1940-)
    Concerto for Piano and Orchestra [12']
        2(pic).2.2.2. 4.3.3.0. timp, 4perc,harp,strings,pno solo
        sc ONGAKU f.s., perf mat rent (N61)

NOELS POUR LES INSTRUMENTS see Charpentier, Marc-Antoine

NOESIS see Miyoshi, Akira

NOM D'OEDIPE, LE see Boucourechliev, Andre

NON NOVA see Devcic, Natko

NONE BUT THE LONELY HEART, FOR SOLO VOICE AND ORCHESTRA, [ARR.] see Tchaikovsky, Piotr Ilyich

NONNENKLAGE, FOR SOLO VOICE AND ORCHESTRA see Orthel, Leon

NONO, JOSE (1776-1845)
    Sinfonia in F
    see SYMPHONY IN MADRID, THE

NONO, LUIGI (1924-)
    Como Una Ola De Fuerza Y Luz, For Solo Voice, Piano And Orchestra
        sc RICORDI-IT 131983 $47.50 (N62)

NORBOTTEN-SYMPHONIE II see Degen, Johannes

NORBY, ERIK
    Capriccio [12']
        trp,pno,strings
        sc HANSEN-DEN WH 29533 $18.50 (N63)

    Corps Celeste [14']
        3.2.3.2. 4.4.3.1. timp,perc, vibra,harp,pno,strings
        sc SAMFUNDET 277 perf mat rent (N64)

    Illuminations-Capriccio For Flute And Orchestra
        2.2.2.2. 3.1.2.0. vibra,cel,harp, strings,fl solo
        sc HANSEN-DEN f.s. (N65)

NORD UND SUD. POLKA see Strauss, Johann, [Jr.]

NORDDEUTSCHE TANZE see Paulsen, Helmut

NORDENSTEN, FRANK T.
    Concerto for Violin and Orchestra, No. 1, Op. 31 [19']
        2(pic).2(English horn).0.2(contrabsn). 4.3.3.1. timp,perc,harp,hpsd,3db,vln solo
        NORGE (N66)

    Symphony No. 2 [46']
        3(pic).3(English horn).3(bass clar).3(contrabsn). 4.4.4.1. timp,perc,pno,strings
        NORGE (N67)

    Too This, Too That *Op.27 [17']
        3(pic).2(English horn).3(bass clar).2. 4.3.3.0. timp,perc, pno,strings
        NORGE (N68)

NORDENSTROM, GLADYS (1924-)
    Work For Orchestra III [15']
        2+pic.2.2+bass clar.2+contrabsn. 4.2.0.0. timp,perc,harp,pno, strings
        BAREN. BA 6709 perf mat rent (N69)

NORDGREN, PEHR HENRIK (1944-)
    Symphony, Op. 43
        string orch
        sc FAZER f.s. (N70)

NORDIC OVERTURE see Schultz, Svend S.

NORDIO, CESARE (1891-)
    Canzone [8']
        2.1.1.1. 2.2.0.0. timp,harp, strings
        manuscript CARISCH (N71)

    Elegia Romantica, For Solo Voice And Orchestra [11']
        2.2.2.2. 4.3.3.0. timp,harp,pno, strings,solo voice
        manuscript CARISCH (N72)

    Fantasia Notturna [12']
        2.3.2.2. 4.3.3.0. timp,2harp,cel, perc,strings
        manuscript CARISCH (N73)

    Festa Iontana [12']
        2.2.2.2. 2.2.2.0. timp,perc,harp, 3cel,strings
        manuscript CARISCH (N74)

    Musetta [3']
        1.1.1.1. 0.0.0.0. timp,harp, strings
        manuscript CARISCH (N75)

NORDISCHE LYRIK see Palmgren, Selim

NORDLAND-ROMANZE see Hub, Franz Peter

NORDRON see Simai, Pavol

NORDSEEBILDER WALZER see Strauss, Johann, [Jr.]

NORDSTERN, DER: OVERTURE see Meyerbeer, Giacomo, Etoile Du Nord, L': Overture

NORFOLK RHAPSODY NO. 1 IN E MINOR see Vaughan Williams, Ralph

NORGAARD, PER (1932-)
    Twilight
        3(pic).2+English horn.2+bass clar.2+contrabsn. 4.3.3.1. timp,4perc,harp,strings
        sc HANSEN-DEN $43.75 (N76)

NORGWEGIAN FOLK TUNES, 19, [ARR.] see Grieg, Edvard Hagerup

NORMA: CASTA DIVA, FOR SOLO VOICE AND ORCHESTRA see Bellini, Vincenzo

NORMA: DEH! CON TE, MIRA O NORMA, FOR SOLO VOICES AND ORCHESTRA see Bellini, Vincenzo

NORMA: SINFONIA see Bellini, Vincenzo

NORRSKEN, FOR ORGAN, ELECTRONIC EQUIPMENT AND STRING ORCHESTRA see Chini, Andre

NORSK STEMNING see Amdahl, Magne

NORTHERN ITALIAN SYMPHONY, 1800-1840, THE
    (Longyear, Rey M.) sc GARLAND ISBN 0-8240-3819-3 $90.00 "The Symphony", Vol. A-VI
    contains: Asioli, Bonifazio, Sinfonia Azione Teatrale Campestre; Basili, Francesco, Sinfonia in D minor; Nicolini, Giuseppe, Sinfonias In F And E Minor; Pavesi, Stefano, Sinfonias In C And B Flat; Polledro, Giovanni Battista, Sinfonias In D, Two; Pugni, Cesare, Sinfonia Per Una O Due Orchestre And Sinfonia In E; Rolla, Alessandro, Sinfonias In D And E Minor (N77)

NORWEGIAN ARTISTS' CARNIVAL IN ROME see Svendsen, Johan (Severin)

NORWEGIAN BRIDAL PROCESSION, [ARR.] see Grieg, Edvard Hagerup

NOSTALGIES, FOR SOLO VOICE AND ORCHESTRA see Escher, Rudolf George

NOTATIONS see Boulez, Pierre

NOTES 12-78 see Ridderstrom, Bo

NOTICES see Maros, Rudolf

NOTTE, LA see Vivaldi, Antonio, Concerto, RV 501, Op. 45, No. 8, in B flat, P. 401, F.VIII no. 1

NOTTE DI GETSEMANI, LA see De Zuccoli, G.

NOTTE, DIVINA NOTTE, FOR SOLO VOICE AND ORCHESTRA see Donati, Pino

NOTTETEMPO: DANZA DI BUFERA see Bussotti, Sylvano

NOTTURNI see Ledenjov, Roman

NOTTURNO see Fine, Irving

NOTTURNO see Lorenzini, Danilo

NOTTURNO CONCERTANTE, FOR VIOLIN, VIOLA, ENGLISH HORN AND ORCHESTRA see Pinelli, Carlo

NOTTURNO E TARANTELLA see Toni, Alceo

NOTTURNO INCANTATO see Mortari, Virgilio

NOVAK, JAN (1921-)
    Concentus Bijugis, For Piano 4-Hands And String Orchestra
        string orch,pno 4-hands soli
        sc ZANIBON 5674 rent, pts ZANIBON 5675 f.s. (N78)

    Concerto Per Euridice, For Guitar And String Orchestra [18']
        string orch,gtr solo
        (Diaz, A.) sc ZANIBON 5139 f.s., pts ZANIBON 5140 f.s. (N79)

    Odarum Concentus [12'30"]
        string orch
        sc ZANIBON 5329 f.s., pts ZANIBON 5330 f.s. (N80)

NOVAK, MILAN (1927-)
    Concerto for Violoncello and Orchestra [23']
        1.1.1.1. 1.0.0.0. perc,harp,pno, strings,vcl solo
        SLOV.HUD.FOND 0-454A perf mat rent (N81)

NOVARA LA BELLE, FOR SOLO VOICE AND ORCHESTRA see Sinigaglia, Leone

NOVELETTE see Lutoslawski, Witold

NOVELLETTA see Gandino

NOW THANK WE ALL OUR GOD see Cruger, Johann

NOW THE DAY IS OVER see Barnby, [Sir] Joseph

NOZZE DELL'ALPIGIANO, LE, FOR SOLO VOICE AND ORCHESTRA see Sinigaglia, Leone

NOZZE D'ERCOLE ED EBE, LE see Lima, Jeronimo Francisco

NOZZE DI FIGARO, LE: APRITE UN PO' QUEGL'OCCHI, FOR SOLO VOICE AND ORCHESTRA see Mozart, Wolfgang Amadeus

NOZZE DI FIGARO, LE: CINQUE, DIECI, FOR SOLO VOICES AND ORCHESTRA see Mozart, Wolfgang Amadeus

NOZZE DI FIGARO, LE: CRUDEL! PERCHE FINORA, FOR SOLO VOICE AND ORCHESTRA see Mozart, Wolfgang Amadeus

NOZZE DI FIGARO, LE: DEH, VIENI NON TARDAR, FOR SOLO VOICE AND ORCHESTRA see Mozart, Wolfgang Amadeus

NOZZE DI FIGARO, LE: DOVE SONO, FOR SOLO VOICE AND ORCHESTRA see Mozart, Wolfgang Amadeus

NOZZE DI FIGARO, LE: LA VENDETTA, FOR SOLO VOICE AND ORCHESTRA see Mozart, Wolfgang Amadeus

NOZZE DI FIGARO, LE: NON PIU ANDRAI, FOR SOLO VOICE AND ORCHESTRA see Mozart, Wolfgang Amadeus

NOZZE DI FIGARO, LE: NON SO PIU COSA SON, FOR SOLO VOICE AND ORCHESTRA see Mozart, Wolfgang Amadeus

NOZZE DI FIGARO, LE: OVERTURE see Mozart, Wolfgang Amadeus

NOZZE DI FIGARO, LE: PORGI AMOR, FOR SOLO VOICE AND ORCHESTRA see Mozart, Wolfgang Amadeus

NOZZE DI FIGARO, LE: SE A CASO MADAMA, FOR SOLO VOICES AND ORCHESTRA see Mozart, Wolfgang Amadeus

NOZZE DI FIGARO, LE: SE VUOL BALLARE, FOR SOLO VOICE AND ORCHESTRA see Mozart, Wolfgang Amadeus

NOZZE DI FIGARO, LE: SULL' ARIA! CHE SOAVE ZEFFIRETTO, FOR SOLO VOICES AND ORCHESTRA see Mozart, Wolfgang Amadeus

NOZZE DI FIGARO, LE: VEDRO MENTR'IO
    SOSPIRO, FOR SOLO VOICE AND
    ORCHESTRA see Mozart, Wolfgang
    Amadeus

NOZZE DI FIGARO, LE: VENITE,
    INGINOCCHIATEVI, FOR SOLO VOICE AND
    ORCHESTRA see Mozart, Wolfgang
    Amadeus

NOZZE DI FIGARO, LE: VOI CHE SAPETE,
    FOR SOLO VOICE AND ORCHESTRA see
    Mozart, Wolfgang Amadeus

NOZZE DI PSICHE CON AMORE, LE: SINFONIA
    see Leo, Leonardo (Oronzo Salvatore
    de)

NU LAET ONS ALLEN GODE LOVEN see Horst,
    Anton van der

NUIT DU NORD see Vecsey, Ferenc von

NUIT SUR LE MONT CHAUVE, UNE see
    Mussorgsky, Modest Petrovich, Night
    On Bald Mountain

NUITS D'ETE, LES, FOR SOLO VOICE AND
    ORCHESTRA see Berlioz, Hector
    (Louis)

NUMERIC SERENADE, FOR PIANO AND
    ORCHESTRA see Tautenhahn, Gunther

NUN LIEBES WEIBCHEN, ZIEHST MIT MIR,
    FOR SOLO VOICES AND ORCHESTRA see
    Mozart, Wolfgang Amadeus

NUN SCHWEIGET, WINDE, FOR SOLO VOICE
    AND ORCHESTRA see Handel, George
    Frideric, Silete Venti, For Solo
    Voice And Orchestra

NUR WER DIE SEHNSUCHT KENNT see
    Tchaikovsky, Piotr Ilyich, None But
    The Lonely Heart, For Solo Voice
    And Orchestra, [arr.]

NURMAHAL: OVERTURE see Spontini,
    Gaspare

NUTCRACKER: PAS DE DEUX see
    Tchaikovsky, Piotr Ilyich

NUTCRACKER: SUITE see Tchaikovsky,
    Piotr Ilyich

NUVOLE E COLORI, FOR SOLO VOICE AND
    ORCHESTRA see Renzi, Armando

NYMPHENBURGER SCHLOSSMUSIK see
    Mattausch, H.A.

NYSTEDT, KNUT (1915-   )
    Exultate *Op.74b [10']
        3(pic).2.2.2. 4.3.3.0. timp,perc,
        strings
        NORGE   (N82)

    Mirage *Op.71
        2.2.2.2. 4.3.3.4. perc,cel,pno,
        strings
        min sc NORSK NMO 9011 $29.50   (N83)

O

O AMANTISSIME SPONSE, JESU, FOR SOLO
    VOICE AND STRING ORCHESTRA see
    Ritter, Christian

O BONNE DOUCE FRANCE, FOR HARMONICA AND
    CHAMBER ORCHESTRA see Strietman,
    Willem

O' CANADA
    (Luck, Arthur) LUCKS HYMNS 17 set
    $9.50, pts $.65, ea.   (O1)

O, GIJ, RHINOCEROS, FOR SOLO VOICES AND
    CHAMBER ORCHESTRA see Ketting, Otto

O HOLY NIGHT see Adam, Adolphe-Charles,
    Cantique De Noel

O LITTLE TOWN OF BETHLEHEM see Redner,
    Lewis [Henry]

O LORD MOST HOLY see Franck, Cesar,
    Panis Angelicus, For Solo Voice And
    Orchestra

O LUNA CHE FAI LUME, FOR SOLO VOICE AND
    ORCHESTRA see Davico, Vincenzo

O MAN VAN SMARTE see Andriessen, Willem

O NACHT see Flothuis, Marius

O NOTTE, FOR SOLO VOICE AND ORCHESTRA
    see Rihm, Wolfgang

O, SCHONSTE DU see Rixner, Josef

O SOLE MIO, FOR SOLO VOICE AND
    ORCHESTRA, [ARR.] see Di Capua,
    Eduardo

O SOUL, CONSIDER!, FOR SOLO VOICE AND
    ORCHESTRA see Wolf, Hugo, Denk Es,
    O Seele, For Solo Voice And
    Orchestra

O TANNENBAUM
    (Luck, Arthur) LUCKS HYMNS 13 set
    $10.00, pts $.65, ea. contains
    also: Jingle Bells   (O2)

O WORSHIP THE KING see Haydn, [Johann]
    Michael

OBERON: OVERTURE see Weber, Carl Maria
    von

OBERON: OZEAN, DU UNGEHEUER, FOR SOLO
    VOICE AND ORCHESTRA see Weber, Carl
    Maria von

OBERSCHLESISCHE TANZSUITE see Strecke,
    Gerhard

OBERTO CONTE DI S. BONIFACIO: OVERTURE
    see Verdi, Giuseppe

OBOE AND ORCHESTRA see Feldman, Morton

OBSTINATO see Blomberg, Erik

OCENAS, ANDREJ (1911-   )
    Ceskoslovenska Predohra *Op.53 [10']
        3.2.2.3. 4.4.4.1. perc,harp,xylo,
        bells,pno,strings
        "Czechoslovak Overture"
        SLOV.HUD.FOND O-457 perf mat rent
                                          (O3)
    Concerto for Violoncello and
        Orchestra, No. 2, Op. 50 [30']
        3.2.2.2. 3.1.0.0. timp,2perc,
        harp,strings,vcl solo
        SLOV.HUD.FOND O-494A perf mat rent
                                          (O4)
    Czechoslovak Overture *see
        Ceskoslovenska Predohra

OCH VOOR DEN DOOT see Horst, Anton van
    der

OCHRE see Williamson, Malcolm

OCTET, OP. 20, SCHERZO, [ARR.] see
    Mendelssohn-Bartholdy, Felix

OCTOBER MUSIC see Bortz, Daniel

ODARUM CONCENTUS see Novak, Jan

ODE see Bon, Andre

ODE see Dorward, David

ODE, FOR SOLO VOICE AND ORCHESTRA see
    Zagwijn, Henri

ODE TO LORD BUCKLEY, FOR SAXOPHONE AND
    ORCHESTRA see Amram, David Werner

ODEFONIA see Consoli, Marc-Antonio

ODEON TANZE. WALZER see Strauss,
    Johann, [Jr.]

ODISSEO see Mariotti, Mario

ODYSSEUS SYMPHONY see Hovhaness, Alan,
    Symphony No. 25, Op. 275

OEDIPE A COLONNE: FURIE D'AVERNO, FOR
    SOLO VOICES AND ORCHESTRA see
    Sacchini, Antonio (Maria Gasparo
    Gioacchino)

OEDIPE A COLONNE: OVERTURE see
    Sacchini, Antonio (Maria Gasparo
    Gioacchino)

OEDIPUS TYRANNOS see Theodorakis, Mikis

OEIL DE CHAT see Scherchen, Tona

OF DREAMS AND NIGHTMARES see
    Tautenhahn, Gunther

OF NIGHT AND THE SEA, FOR SOLO VOICES
    AND INSTRUMENTAL ENSEMBLE see
    Palmer, Robert

OFFENBACH, JACQUES (1819-1880)
    Beautiful Helen, The: Overture *see
        Belle Helene, La: Overture

    Belle Helene, La: Overture
        "Beautiful Helen, The: Overture"
        LUCKS 06390 sc $8.50, set $20.00,
        pts $1.15, ea.   (O5)

    Contes d'Hoffmann, Les: Barcarolle,
        "O Belle Nuit, O Nuit d'Amour",
        For Solo Voice And Orchestra"
        "Tales Of Hoffmann: Barcarolle"
        LUCKS 03629 sc $6.00, set $15.00,
        pts $.95, ea.   (O6)

    Contes d'Hoffmann, Les: Il Etait Une
        Fois, For Solo Voice And
        Orchestra
        "Tales Of Hoffman: Legend Of
        Kleinzack" LUCKS 02402 sc $5.00,
        set $12.00, pts $.75, ea.   (O7)

    Contes d'Hoffmann, Les: Intermede Et
        Barcarolle
        "Tales Of Hoffmann: Intermezzo And
        Barcarolle" LUCKS 06387 sc $5.50,
        set $14.00, pts $.95, ea.   (O8)

    Contes d'Hoffmann, Les: Les Oiseaux
        Dans La Charmille, For Solo Voice
        And Orchestra
        "Tales Of Hoffmann: The Doll Song"
        LUCKS 02354 sc $4.75, set $11.50,
        pts $.75, ea.   (O9)

    Drei Stucke, For Violoncello And
        Orchestra, [arr.]
        (Waldenmaier, August P.) 2.2.2.2.
        2.0.0.0. timp,harp,strings,vcl
        solo ORLANDO rent
        contains: Serenade, For
        Violoncello And Orchestra,
        [arr.]; Soir, Le, For
        Violoncello And Orchestra,
        [arr.]; Souvenir Du Val, For
        Violoncello And Orchestra,
        [arr.]   (O10)

    Orphee Aux Enfers: Overture
        "Orpheus In The Underworld:
        Overture" LUCKS 06388 sc $7.00,
        set $20.00, pts $1.15, ea. (O11)

    Orpheus In The Underworld: Overture
        *see Orphee Aux Enfers: Overture

    Serenade, For Violoncello And
        Orchestra, [arr.]
        see Drei Stucke, For Violoncello
        And Orchestra, [arr.]

    Soir, Le, For Violoncello And
        Orchestra, [arr.]
        see Drei Stucke, For Violoncello
        And Orchestra, [arr.]

    Souvenir Du Val, For Violoncello And
        Orchestra, [arr.]
        see Drei Stucke, For Violoncello
        And Orchestra, [arr.]

    Tales Of Hoffman: Legend Of Kleinzack
        *see Contes d'Hoffmann, Les: Il
        Etait Une Fois, For Solo Voice
        And Orchestra

    Tales Of Hoffmann: Barcarolle *see
        Contes d'Hoffmann, Les:
        Barcarolle, "O Belle Nuit, O Nuit
        d'Amour", For Solo Voice And
        Orchestra

    Tales Of Hoffmann: Intermezzo And
        Barcarolle *see Contes
        d'Hoffmann, Les: Intermede Et

OFFENBACH, JACQUES (cont'd.)

Barcarolle

Tales Of Hoffmann: The Doll Song
*see Contes d'Hoffmann, Les: Les
Oiseaux Dans La Charmille, For
Solo Voice And Orchestra

OFFENE FENSTER, DAS see Gutzeit, Erich

OFFERTA DELLE ROSE, L', FOR SOLO VOICE
AND ORCHESTRA see Piccioli,
Giuseppe

OFFERTE POUR LES INSTRUMENTS see
Charpentier, Marc-Antoine

OFFRANDE A ERARD, FOR HARP AND
ORCHESTRA see Bernier, Rene

OFFRANDE A UNE OMBRE see Barraud, Henry

OGIVE, FOR HARPSICHORD AND STRINGS see
Gaussin, Allain

OGURA, ROH (1916-   )
Composition [8']
string orch
ONGAKU perf mat rent   (012)

Concerto for Violoncello and
Orchestra
sc ZEN-ON 899200 f.s.   (013)

OH GOD, OUR HELP IN AGES PAST see
Croft, William

OH, LET ME DIE, [ARR.] see Monteverdi,
Claudio

OHANA, MAURICE (1914-   )
Anneau Du Tamarit, L', For
Violoncello And Orchestra
2.2.2.2. 2.2.1.0. 3perc,pno,
strings,vcl solo
JOBERT perf mat rent   (014)

Concerto for Piano and Orchestra
[26']
sc JOBERT $31.50, perf mat rent
                                        (015)

Livre Des Prodiges [25']
JOBERT perf mat rent   (016)

OHLSSON, RICHARD (1874-1940)
Ett Narkes Bondbrollop
orch
STIM   (017)

OLD DUTCH SUITE see Riemsdijk, Johan
Cornelius Marius van

OLD ENGLISH LOVE SONGS, FOR SOLO VOICE
AND ORCHESTRA see Glaser, Werner
Wolf

OLD FAMILIAR FACES, THE, FOR SOLO VOICE
AND ORCHESTRA see Mul, Jan

OLD FOLKS AT HOME, [ARR.] see Foster,
Stephen Collins

OLD POLISH SUITE see Panufnik, Andrzej

OLDFASHIONED SUITE see Linde, Bo,
Gammalmodig Svit

OLIFANT-VARIATIES, OP EEN THEMA VAN
SAINT-SAENS, FOR DOUBLEBASS AND
ORCHESTRA see Frid, Geza

OLIMPIADE: OUVERTURE see Vivaldi,
Antonio

OLIMPIADE: SINFONIA see Leo, Leonardo
(Oronzo Salvatore de)

OLIVEROS, PAULINE (1932-   )
To Valerie Solanas And Marilyn Monroe
any instruments and-or voices SMITH
PUB $4.25   (018)

OLSEN, SPARRE (1903-   )
Canticum
sc NORSK f.s.   (019)

Six Old Village Songs From Lom In
Norway *CC6U
string orch,vln solo sc NORSK f.s.
                                        (020)

OLSSON, OTTO EMANUEL (1879-1964)
Symphony, Op. 11, in G minor [53']
3.2.2.3. 4.2.3.1. timp,perc,
strings
pts STIM perf mat rent   (021)

OLYMPIE: OUVERTURE see Spontini, Gaspare

OM MIJN OUD WOONHUIS PEPPELS STAAN see
Van Lier, Bertus

OMAGGIO A GESUALDO, FOR VIOLIN AND
ORCHESTRA see Vlijmen, Jan van

OMBRA FELICE, FOR SOLO VOICE AND
ORCHESTRA see Mozart, Wolfgang
Amadeus

OMBRE see Michel, Wilfried

OMBRE DI SOGNI: SARABANDA, GAVOTTA,
BARCAROLA see Pick-Mangiagalli,
Riccardo

OMBRE DI SOGNI: SERENATA see Pick-
Mangiagalli, Riccardo

OMIZZOLO, SILVIO (1905-   )
Concerto for Piano and Orchestra
[20']
2.2.2.2. 2.2.0.0. timp,bass drum,
strings,pno solo
sc ZANIBON 4851 rent, pts ZANIBON
4852 rent   (022)

ON KOLME UNTA SISAKKAIN see Sallinen,
Aulis

ON THE BEAUTIFUL BLUE DANUBE see
Strauss, Johann, [Jr.], An Der
Schonen Blauen Donau

ONCE A CANADIAN LAD see Coakley, Donald

ONCE REMOVED see MacBride, David Huston

ONDERWEG see Mengelberg, Misja

ONE HEART ONE MIND see Strauss, Johann,
[Jr.], Ein Herz Ein Sinn

ONNEN OVI, FOR SOLO VOICE AND ORCHESTRA
see Hannikainen, Vaino

ONSLOW, GEORGES (1784-1853)
Symphonies, Op. 41 In A And Op. 42 In
D Minor
see Herold, Louis-Joseph-Ferdinand,
Symphonies In C And In D

ONZE VISAGES OU L'ANTIFUGUE see
Chaynes, Charles

OOSTEN, ROEL VAN (1958-   )
She Weeps Over Rahoon, For Solo Voice
And Orchestra [10']
2.2.2.2. 4.2.3.1. timp,perc,harp,
pno,strings,S solo
DONEMUS   (023)

OOSTERVELD, ERNST (1951-   )
Applefonia [12']
2.2.2.2. 4.3.3.1. timp,2perc,
strings
DONEMUS   (024)

Exchanges [21'30"]
4.4.4.4.4sax. 6.4.4.1. 2pno,
2marimba/vibra,strings
DONEMUS   (025)

Transitions [13']
1.1.1.1. 1.1.1.0. perc,pno,2vln,
vla,vcl,db
DONEMUS   (026)

OPENINGSMUZIEK see Vis, Lucas

OPERNBALL, DER: DOMINO WALTZ see
Heuberger, Richard

OPERNBALL, DER: IM CHAMBRE SEPAREE see
Heuberger, Richard

OPERNBALL, DER: OVERTURE see Heuberger,
Richard

OPERNBALL, DER: POTPOURRI see
Heuberger, Richard

OPOJNO POLETJE see Skerl, Dane

OPRITCHNIK: OVERTURE see Tchaikovsky,
Piotr Ilyich

OPUS 21 see Testi, Flavio

OPUS 23 see Testi, Flavio

OPWAARTSCHE WEGEN see Bergeijk, Gilius
van

ORAGE, L': OVERTURE see Tchaikovsky,
Piotr Ilyich

ORAISON DU SOIR see Escher, Rudolf
George

ORANGE FLOWERS see Storrle, Heinz

ORANJE MAY-LIED, FOR SOLO VOICE AND
ORCHESTRA see Bordewijk-Roepman,
Johanna

ORATIO, FOR SOLO VOICE AND ORCHESTRA
see Horst, Anton van der

ORATIO III see Nelhybel, Vaclav

ORATIO IV see Nelhybel, Vaclav

ORATIO V see Nelhybel, Vaclav

ORATION see Bridge, Frank

ORBITS, FOR HORN SOLO, 4 HORNS OBLIGATO
AND ORCHESTRA see Loevendie, Theo

ORCHESTERPARADE see Jansen, Peter

ORCHESTERPROLOG see Chemin-Petit, Hans

ORCHESTERSTUCK see Goosen, Jacques

ORCHESTRA see Feldman, Morton

ORCHIDEA see Stein-Schneider, L.

ORDONEZ, CARLO D' (1737-1786)
Symphonies, Seven *CC7U
(Brown, A. Peter; Alexander, Peter
M.) sc GARLAND ISBN 0-8240-3800-2
$90.00 "The Symphony", Vol. B-IV
                                        (027)

ORE TRISTI E SERENE, FOR SOLO VOICE AND
STRING ORCHESTRA see Rossellini,
Renzo

ORFEO ED EURIDICE: AIR DE FURIES see
Gluck, Christoph Willibald, Ritter
von

ORFEO ED EURIDICE: BALLET DES OMBRES
HEUREUSES, [ARR.] see Gluck,
Christoph Willibald, Ritter von

ORFEO ED EURIDICE: CHE FARO SENZA
EURIDICE, FOR SOLO VOICE AND
ORCHESTRA see Gluck, Christoph
Willibald, Ritter von

ORFEO ED EURIDICE: OVERTURE see Gluck,
Christoph Willibald, Ritter von

ORFEO ED EURIDICE: SO KLAG ICH IHREN
TOD, FOR SOLO VOICE AND ORCHESTRA
see Gluck, Christoph Willibald,
Ritter von

ORFEO II, FOR FLUTE AND STRING
ORCHESTRA see Musgrave, Thea

ORFEO: LA DISPERAZIONE DI ORFEO, FOR
SOLO VOICE AND STRING ORCHESTRA see
Rossi, Luigi

ORFEO: OVERTURE see Monteverdi, Claudio

ORFEO: PEZZI CONCERTATI see Schenker,
Friedrich

ORGIA, L' see Rossini, Gioacchino

ORKESTSPEL see Bergeijk, Gilius van

ORLAND, HENRY (1918-   )
Epigram
3.3.3.2. 2.2.3.1. timp,perc,
strings
SEESAW perf mat rent   (028)

Symphony No. 4 for Solo Voices and
String Orchestra
string orch,narrator&S solo
SEESAW perf mat rent   (029)

ORLANDO PALADINO: OVERTURE, [ARR.] see
Haydn, [Franz] Joseph

ORLINSKI, HEINZ BERNHARD
Concerto for Organ and String
Orchestra
string orch,org solo
HEINRICH. sc f.s., pts rent   (030)

ORLOWSKI, MICHAL (fl. 1750-1800)
Symphony in F
see SYMPHONY IN POLAND, THE

ORPHEE AUX ENFERS: OVERTURE see
Offenbach, Jacques

ORPHEUS see Foss, Lukas

ORPHEUS see Klebe, Giselher

ORPHEUS see Liszt, Franz

ORPHEUS: DANCE OF THE BLESSED SPIRITS
see Gluck, Christoph Willibald,
Ritter von, Orfeo Ed Euridice:
Ballet Des Ombres Heureuses, [arr.]

ORPHEUS: DANCE OF THE FURIES see Gluck,
Christoph Willibald, Ritter von,
Orfeo Ed Euridice: Air De Furies

ORPHEUS IN THE UNDERWORLD: OVERTURE see
Offenbach, Jacques, Orphee Aux
Enfers: Overture

ORPHEUS QUADRILLE see Strauss, Johann,
[Jr.]

ORPHIKON see Kubelik, Rafael

ORTH
  In The Clock Store
    set LUCKS $28.00   (031)

ORTHEL, LEON (1905-   )
  Album Di Disegni *Op.81 [19']
    3.3.3.2. 4.3.3.0. timp,1-2perc,
    cel,harp,pno,strings
    DONEMUS   (032)

  Concertina Alla Burla, For Piano And
    Orchestra *Op.12 [11']
    3.2.2.2. 2.2.0.0. timp,perc,
    strings,pno solo
    sc,pts ALBERSEN rent   (033)

  Evocazione *Op.83 [5']
    3.3.3.2. 4.3.3.1. timp,3perc,
    strings
    MOLENAAR 14.1563.08 f.s.   (034)

  Martyre, Une, For Solo Voice And
    Orchestra *Op.71 [11']
    3.2.3.2. 4.2.3.0. timp,strings,S/
    T solo
    sc DONEMUS f.s., perf mat rent
                                      (035)
  Music for Double Bass and Orchestra,
    Op. 89 [16']
    3.2.3.2.sax. 4.3.3.1. timp,2perc,
    strings,db solo
    DONEMUS   (036)

  Nonnenklage, For Solo Voice And
    Orchestra *Op.25b [7']
    2.0.3.0. 2.0.0.0. harp,strings,S/
    Mez solo
    sc DONEMUS f.s., perf mat rent
                                      (037)
  Scherzo for Piano and Orchestra, Op.
    10 [7']
    2.2.2.2. 2.2.0.0. timp,strings
    sc,pts ALBERSEN rent   (038)

  Suite, No. 2, Op. 88 [15']
    2.2.2.2. 4.2.3.0. timp,2perc,
    strings
    DONEMUS   (039)

  Symphony No. 1, Op. 13 [28'30"]
    3.3.3.3. 4.3.3.1. timp,perc,
    strings
    sc,pts ALBERSEN rent   (040)

  Symphony No. 2, Op. 18 [16']
    3.3.3.3. 4.3.3.1. timp,perc,
    strings
    sc,pts ALBERSEN rent   (041)

  Symphony No. 3, Op. 24 [33']
    3.3.3.3. 4.3.3.1. timp,perc,
    strings
    sc,pts ALBERSEN rent   (042)

OSBORNE, NIGEL (1948-   )
  Concerto for Violoncello and
    Orchestra [17']
    3.2.3.2. 4.3.3.0. 4perc,harp,
    strings,vcl solo
    UNIVER. perf mat rent   (043)

  Sickle, The, For Solo Voice And
    Orchestra [11']
    2.2.2.2. 2.2.0.0. perc,harp,gtr,
    strings,S solo
    study sc UNIVER. UE 16215 f.s.,
    perf mat rent   (044)

OSIRIS see Fountain, Primous

OSLOBODENIE see Zimmer, Jan

OSTERC, SLAVKO (1895-1941)
  Concerto for Orchestra [20']
    2(pic).2(English horn).2(bass
    clar).2. 4.3.3.1. timp,2perc,
    pno,strings
    DRUSTVO DSS 841 perf mat rent (045)

  Dances
    (outside Yugoslavia this
    publication can be obtained from
    Gerig) study sc DRUSTVO 858 perf
    mat rent   (046)

  Four Pieces *see Stiri Skladbe

  Mati [7']
    2(pic).2.2.2.alto sax. 4.3.3.1.
    timp,perc,harp,strings
    "Mother" (outside Yugoslavia this
    publication can be obtained from
    Gerig (HG 1270)) min sc DRUSTVO
    DSS 778 f.s.   (047)

  Mother *see Mati

  Passacaglia And Chorale *see
    Passacaglia In Koral

  Passacaglia In Koral [10']
    2(pic).2(English horn).2(bass
    clar).2. 4.3.3.1. timp,2perc,
    strings

OSTERC, SLAVKO (cont'd.)

  "Passacaglia And Chorale" DRUSTVO
    DSS 842 perf mat rent   (048)

  Quatre Pieces Symphoniques [23']
    2(pic).2.2(bass clar).2. 4.3.3.1.
    timp,perc,harp,strings
    DRUSTVO DSS 767 perf mat rent (049)

  Stiri Skladbe [12']
    2.1(English horn).2.2. 4.2.3.1.
    timp,2perc,strings
    "Four Pieces" DRUSTVO DSS 843 perf
    mat rent   (050)

OSTERLING, ULF (1939-   )
  Fran Sally, For Solo Voice And
    Chamber Orchestra [7']
    1.1.1.1. 0.1.1.0. timp,perc,pno,
    2vln,vcl,A solo
    sc STIM   (051)

  Nattstycke [12']
    1.1.1.1. 1.1.1.1. timp,strings
    sc STIM perf mat rent   (052)

OTELLO: BALLABILI see Verdi, Giuseppe

OTELLO: CANZONE DEL SALCE see Verdi,
  Giuseppe

OTELLO: CREDO IN UN DIO CRUDEL, FOR
  SOLO VOICE AND ORCHESTRA see Verdi,
  Giuseppe

OTELLO: NIUN MI TEMA, FOR SOLO VOICE
  AND ORCHESTRA see Verdi, Giuseppe

OTELLO: ORA E PER SEMPRE ADDIO, FOR
  SOLO VOICE AND ORCHESTRA see Verdi,
  Giuseppe

OTELLO: SALCE! SALCE!, FOR SOLO VOICE
  AND ORCHESTRA see Verdi, Giuseppe,
  Otello: Canzone Del Salce

OTHELLO OVERTURE see Dvorak, Antonin

OURS, L', SYMPHONY see Haydn, [Franz]
  Joseph, Symphony No. 82 in C

OUTWARDS see Escher, Rudolf George

OUVERTURE 1975 see Weegenhuise, Johan

OUVERTURE ANACREONTIQUE see Francaix,
  Jean

OUVERTURE "CON BRIO" see Lachman, Hans

OUVERTURE D'ACHILLE EN SYMPHONIE see
  Paer, Ferdinando

OUVERTURE GIOCOSA see Ricci Signorini,
  Antonio

OUVERTURE IN D, MIN 72 see Telemann,
  Georg Philipp

OUVERTURE IN D, MIN 73 see Telemann,
  Georg Philipp

OUVERTURE MIGNONNE see Becce, Giuseppe

OUVERTURE PER LA LOCANDIERA DI GOLDONI
  see Lavagnino, Angelo Francesco

OUVERTURE PER UNA COMMEDIA DI GOLDONI
  "IL SERVO DI DUE PADRONI," OP.
  1.66 see Rosseau, Norbert

OUVERTURE ROMANTICA see Spagnoli, G.

OUVERTURE ROMANTIQUE see Groot, Hugo de

OUVERTURE SOLENNELLE see Tchaikovsky,
  Piotr Ilyich, Overture 1812

OUVERTURE ZU DER GEDULDIGE SOKRATES see
  Telemann, Georg Philipp

OUVERTURE ZU EINEM HEITEREN SPIEL see
  Andres, Walter

OUVERTURE ZU EINEM HEITEREN SPIEL see
  Schwickert, Gustav

OUVERTURE ZU EINEM MARCHENSPIEL see
  Dressel, Erwin

OUVERTURE ZU "TASSO" see Brambach,
  Caspar Joseph

OUVERTURE ZUR OPERETTE "FATINITZA" see
  Gaebel, Kurt

OUVRE TON COEUR, FOR SOLO VOICE AND
  ORCHESTRA see Bizet, Georges

OVERLANDERS, THE see Ireland, John

OVERTURE 1812 see Tchaikovsky, Piotr
  Ilyich

OVERTURE - CONFLICT see Wordsworth,
  William

OVERTURE FOR K.W. see Holloway, Robin

OVERTURE HALF HOLIDAY see Gardner, John
  Linton

OVERTURE IN C, "IN THE ITALIAN STYLE"
  see Schubert, Franz (Peter)

OVERTURE IN D, "IN THE ITALIAN STYLE"
  see Schubert, Franz (Peter)

OVERTURE IN D, OP. 43 see Boccherini,
  Luigi, Sinfonia, Ge. 521, Op. 43,
  in D

OVERTURE: LAURUS CRUENTAS see Croft,
  William

OVERTURE OF THE SEASON see Svoboda,
  Tomas

OVERTURE ON GREEK THEMES, NO. 1, OP. 3
  see Glazunov, Alexander
  Konstantinovich

OVERTURE ON THE THEMES OF THREE RUSSIAN
  FOLK SONGS see Balakirev, Mily
  Alexeyevich

OVERTURE TO A SUMMER NIGHT see Roskott,
  Carl

OVERTURE TO RIVER DOWNS see Proto,
  Frank

OVERTURES, OP. 3, NOS. 1-6 see Bach,
  Johann Christian, Sinfonia, Op. 3,
  Nos. 1-6

OVERTURES, OP. 3, NOS. 1-6 see Bach,
  Johann Christian, Sinfonias, Op. 3,
  Nos. 1-6

OXFORD SYMPHONY see Haydn, [Franz]
  Joseph, Symphony No. 92 in G

OXNALTSINFONIE see Kruyf, Ton de

OYENS, TERA DE MARZ
  see MAREZ OYENS, TERA DE

OZI, ETIENNE (1754-1813)
  Symphonies Concertantes In B Flat And
    In F
    see Deshayes, Prosper-Didier,
    Symphony in D

P

PA DIN TAERSKEL, FOR SOLO VOICE AND
ORCHESTRA see Colding-Jorgensen,
Henrik

PA GLYTT...:(AJAR), FOR DOUBLEBASS AND
ORCHESTRA see Am, Magnar, Concerto
for Double Bass and Orchestra

PAAP, WOUTER (1908-1981)
Muziek Ter Bruiloft, For Solo Voice
And Orchestra [14']
2.2.2.2. 2.0.0.0. timp,perc,harp,
strings,T solo
sc DONEMUS f.s., perf mat rent (P1)

PAASCH, LEOPOLD
Ballettprobe
RIES f.s. (P2)

PABLO, LUIS DE (1930-)
A Modo De Concierto [17']
pno,cel,glock,elec org,perc,8vln,
8vcl
sc ZERBONI 8292 f.s., perf mat rent
(P3)

PACHELBEL, JOHANN (1653-1706)
Kanon, [arr.]
(Paillard, Jean-Francois) hpsd,
strings COSTALL C.3625 f.s. (P4)

PACHERNEGG, ALOIS (1892-1964)
Deutsches Barock [10']
1.1.2.1. 2.1.1.0. timp,perc,
strings
RIES perf mat rent (P5)

Intermezzo Espagnole
RIES f.s. (P6)

Pusztastimmung [10']
2(pic).2.2.2. 4.2.3.0. timp,perc,
harp,strings
RIES perf mat rent (P7)
RIES f.s. (P8)

Unter Dampf [2']
2.2.2.2. 4.2.3.1. timp,perc,xylo,
strings
sc RIES f.s., perf mat rent (P9)
RIES f.s. (P10)

Wienerisch
RIES f.s. (P11)

PACIFIC SIRENS see Erickson, Robert

PACINI, GIOVANNI (1796-1867)
Falegname Di Livonia, Il: Sinfonia
[6'30"]
2.2.2.2. 2.2.0.0. timp,strings
(Negrotti, N.) sc,pts ZANIBON D288
rent (P12)

PADILLA
Cielito Lindo, For Solo Voice And
Orchestra
LUCKS 02866 sc $3.75, set $8.00,
pts $.75, ea. (P13)

PADOVANA, FOR HARPSICHORD AND STRING
ORCHESTRA see Mortari, Virgilio

PADOVANO, ANDREA (1920-)
Suite in E minor [16']
string orch
(in homage to Bach) sc ZANIBON 5453
f.s., pts ZANIBON 5454 rent (P14)

PAER, FERDINANDO (1771-1839)
Ouverture d'Achille En Symphonie
2.2.2.2. 2.2.0.0. timp,2perc,
strings
(Kuschy, H.) BREITKOPF-W perf mat
rent (P15)

Virtu Al Cimento, La: Sinfonia
[5'30"]
2fl,2ob,2bsn,2horn,strings
(Negrotti, N.) sc,pts ZANIBON D285
rent (P16)

PAGANINI, NICCOLO (1782-1840)
Concerto for Violin and Orchestra,
No. 1, Op. 6, in D
LUCKS 00415 sc $25.00, set $30.00,
pts $1.75, ea. (P17)

Concerto for Violin and Orchestra,
No. 1, Op. 6, in D
(Wilhelmj) LUCKS 00525 sc $7.50,
set $17.00, pts $1.15, ea. (P18)

Maestosa Sonata Sentimentale, For
Violin And Orchestra
(Vacchelli, Anna Maria Monterosso)
(Opere Di Niccolo Paganini,
Volume 2) fac ed,sc IISM f.s.
(P19)

PAGANINI, NICCOLO (cont'd.)
Moto Perpetuo, [arr.] *Op.11
LUCKS 06398 sc $10.00, set $20.00,
pts $1.25, ea. (P20)
(Dolan, James) "Perpetual Motion,
[arr.]" fl,ob,bsn,horn,perc,harp,
strings [5'] NEW MUSIC WEST perf
mat rent (P21)

Perpetual Motion, [arr.] *see Moto
Perpetuo, [arr.]

Rondo [5']
(Sciannameo, Franco) sc,pts
RARITIES $12.00 (P22)

PAGLIACCI, I: INTERMEZZO see
Leoncavallo, Ruggiero

PAGLIACCI, I: PROLOGO, FOR SOLO VOICE
AND ORCHESTRA see Leoncavallo,
Ruggiero

PAGLIACCI, I: QUAL FIAMMA AVEA NEL
GUARDO, FOR SOLO VOICE AND
ORCHESTRA see Leoncavallo, Ruggiero

PAGLIACCI, I: SERENATA, "O COLOMBINA",
FOR SOLO VOICE AND ORCHESTRA see
Leoncavallo, Ruggiero

PAGLIACCI, I: VESTI LA GIUBBA - RIDI
PAGLIACCIO, FOR SOLO VOICE AND
ORCHESTRA see Leoncavallo, Ruggiero

PAIMENET, FOR SOLO VOICE AND ORCHESTRA,
[ARR.] see Kuula, Toivo

PAISIELLO, GIOVANNI (1740-1816)
Barber Of Seville: Overture *see
Barbiere Di Siviglia, Il:
Overture

Barbiere Di Siviglia, Il: Overture
"Barber Of Seville: Overture"
2.2.0.1. 2.2.0.0.0. strings [5']
KALMUS A 4879 sc $6.00, perf mat
rent, set $18.00, pts $1.50, ea.
(P23)
(De Guarnieri, F.) 2.2.0.2.
2.0.0.0. timp,strings [6'] f.s.
sc CARISCH 18729, pts CARISCH
18802 (P24)

Belle Molinara, La: Duetto, For Solo
Voices And Orchestra
0.2.0.0. 2.0.0.0. strings, solo
voices
sc CARISCH 21770 rent, pts CARISCH
21771 rent (P25)

Quartet No. 1 in A, [arr.]
(Bonelli, E.) string orch [15'] sc
ZANIBON 3321 f.s., pts ZANIBON
3323 f.s. (P26)

Quartet No. 2 in E flat, [arr.]
(Bonelli, E.) string orch [16'] sc
ZANIBON 3324 f.s., pts ZANIBON
3326 f.s. (P27)

Quartet No. 3 in E flat, [arr.]
(Bonelli, E.) string orch [20'] sc
ZANIBON 3327 f.s., pts ZANIBON
3329 f.s. (P28)

Scuffiara, La: Overture [4']
2.2.0.2. 2.2.0.0. strings
KALMUS 5360 sc $5.00, perf mat
rent, set $12.00, pts $.75, ea.
(P29)

Zingare In Fiera, Le: Overture [4']
2fl,2ob,2bsn,2horn,strings
(Negrotti, N.) sc,pts ZANIBON D283
rent (P30)

PALAFUTI
Elevazione
see RICREAZIONI DI ANTICHE MUSICHE
CLASSICHE, SERIE V: MUSICHE
ANTICHE ITALIANE

PALAU, MANUEL (1893-1967)
Divertimento
sc PILES 2040-V f.s. (P31)

PALESTRINA: PRELUDES TO ACTS 1, 2, AND
3 see Pfitzner, Hans

PALINODIE III see Stuppner, Hubert

PALMER, ROBERT (1915-)
Of Night And The Sea, For Solo Voices
And Instrumental Ensemble
1.1.1+bass clar.1. 1.0.0.0.
strings,SATBar soli
PEER perf mat rent (P32)

PALMGREN, SELIM (1878-1951)
Aamun Auteréessa, For Solo Voice And
Orchestra *Op.106,No.2 [3']
2.0.2.0. 0.0.0.0. strings,solo
voice
FAZER perf mat rent (P33)

PALMGREN, SELIM (cont'd.)
Aus Finnland *see From Finland

From Finland *Op.24 [19']
2+pic.2.2.2. 4.3.3.1. harp,timp,
perc,strings
"Aus Finnland" sc,pts LIENAU rent
(P34)

Kevat Tulee, For Solo Voice And
Orchestra *Op.106,No.1 [8']
2.2.2.2. 4.2.0.0. timp,strings,
solo voice
FAZER perf mat rent (P35)

May Night
LUCKS 05705 pno-cond sc $2.00, set
$6.00, pts $.75, ea. (P36)

Nordische Lyrik
LIENAU f.s. (P37)

Sallsam Fagel, En, For Solo Voice And
Orchestra *Op.95 [7']
2.3.2.2. 4.2.3.1. timp,perc,harp,
cel,strings,solo voice
FAZER perf mat rent (P38)

PAN see Rosenberg, Hilding

PAN UND DIE NYMPHEN, FOR FLUTE, HARP
AND STRING ORCHESTRA see Daetwyler,
Jean

PAN UND ECHO see Sibelius, Jean

PANACEA KLANGE. WALZER see Strauss,
Johann, [Jr.]

PANIS ANGELICUS, FOR SOLO VOICE AND
ORCHESTRA see Franck, Cesar

PANNI, MARCELLO (1940-)
Allegro Brillante, For Piano And
Chamber Orchestra [5']
2.2.2.2. 2.2.0.0. timp,perc,6vln,
2vcl,2db,pno solo
sc ZERBONI 8169 f.s., pts ZERBONI
8170 rent (P39)

PANTA RHEI see Dallinger, Fridolin

PANTHER, DER see Stallaert, Alphonse

PANUFNIK, ANDRZEJ (1914-)
Old Polish Suite
string orch
BOOSEY 871 min sc $15.00, sc $6.00
(P40)
Polonia
sc BOOSEY $35.00 (P41)

Sinfonia Mistica [28']
2.2.2.2. 2.0.0.0. strings
sc BOOSEY $50.00 (P42)

PAPIOL see Ricci Signorini, Antonio

PAPPACODA. POLKA see Strauss, Johann,
[Jr.]

PAPRIKA-CSARDAS see Krepela, Josef

PAR FORCE POLKA see Strauss, Johann,
[Jr.]

PARADE see Hambraeus, Bengt

PARADE DE VOTRE FAUST see Pousseur,
Henri

PARADE QUADRILLE see Strauss, Josef

PARADEISER, MARIAN (CARL) (1747-1775)
Symphonies, Three
see AUSTRIAN CLOISTER SYMPHONISTS

PARADIGMI see Martinotti, Bruno

PARADINE CASE, THE, FOR PIANO AND
ORCHESTRA see Waxman, Franz

PARAFRASI SETTECENTESCA see Toni, Alceo

PARAPHRASE ON "A BIRD SANG IN THE
LINDEN TREE", OP. 48, [ARR.] see
Eberle, Frederick, Paraphrase On
"Ein Voglein Sang Im Lindenbaum",
Op. 48, [arr.]

PARAPHRASE ON "EIN VOGLEIN SANG IM
LINDENBAUM", OP. 48, [ARR.] see
Eberle, Frederick

PARCHMAN, GEN LOUIS (1929-)
Concerto For 6 Percussionists And
Orchestra
3.3.3.3. 4.3.3.1. strings,6perc
soli
SEESAW perf mat rent (P43)

Concerto for Marimba and Orchestra
2.3.3.3. 4.4.3.2. timp,3perc,
strings,marimba solo
SEESAW perf mat rent (P44)

PARCHMAN, GEN LOUIS (cont'd.)

Concerto for Timpani and Orchestra
3.3.3.3. 4.4.3.1. strings,timp
solo
SEESAW perf mat rent   (P45)

Symphony No. 5
2.2.2.2. 2.2.0.0. timp,perc,
strings
SEESAW perf mat rent   (P46)

PARDON DE PLOERMEL, LE: OMBRE LEGERE,
FOR SOLO VOICE AND ORCHESTRA see
Meyerbeer, Giacomo

PARIBENI, GIULIO CESARE (1881-1964)
Largo [3']
string orch
sc CARISCH 17716 rent, pts CARISCH
17116B f.s.   (P47)

PARIS SYMPHONY see Mozart, Wolfgang
Amadeus, Symphony No. 31 in D, K.
297

PARLA-WALZER see Arditi, Luigi

PARLA-WALZER, FOR SOLO VOICE AND
ORCHESTRA see Arditi, Luigi

PARNASSE OU L'APOTHEOSE DE CORELLI, LE,
[ARR.] see Couperin, Francois (le
Grand)

PAROLE DI SAN PAOLO, FOR SOLO VOICE AND
ORCHESTRA see Dallapiccola, Luigi

PARSIFAL: GLOCKEN- UND GRALSSZENE see
Wagner, Richard

PARSIFAL: KLINGSORS ZAUBERGARTEN UND
DIE BLUMENMADCHEN (CONCERT VERSION)
see Wagner, Richard

PARSIFAL: PRELUDE see Wagner, Richard

PARSIFAL: PRELUDE, ACT I see Wagner,
Richard

PARTITA ALLA POPOLARE see Bontempelli,
Massimo

PARTITE, AMORE, ADEO see Henkemans,
Hans

PARTS OF A WORLD, FOR VIOLA AND
ORCHESTRA see Hekster, Walter

PAS DE COLOMBINE see Stein-Schneider,
L.

PAS DE QUOI see Wilson, Thomas

PAS SEULEMENT DES MOMENTS, DES MOYENS
D'AMOUR see Masson, Gerard

PASAJE see Mendoza, Emilio

PASSACAGLIA AND CHORALE see Osterc,
Slavko, Passacaglia In Koral

PASSACAGLIA IN KORAL see Osterc, Slavko

PASSACAGLIA UBER "ES IST EIN SCHNITTER,
DER HEISST TOD" see Moser, Rudolf

PASSAGGIO see Hoddinott, Alun

PASSEPIEDS, TWO see Bach, Johann
Sebastian

PASSIONE, LA, SYMPHONY see Haydn,
[Franz] Joseph, Symphony No. 49 in
F minor

PASSIONE AMOROSA, FOR DOUBLE BASS AND
ORCHESTRA see Bottesini, Giovanni

PASSIONE DI GESU SIGNOR NOSTRO, LA see
Caldara, Antonio

PASTORA FEDELE, LA, FOR SOLO VOICES AND
ORCHESTRA see Sinigaglia, Leone

PASTORAL SYMPHONY see Vaughan Williams,
Ralph

PASTORALE SYMPHONY see Beethoven,
Ludwig van, Symphony No. 6, Op. 68,
in F

PASTORELLA see Sonnleithner, Christoph
von

PASTORELLO see Haydn, [Johann] Michael

PAT' MALYCH ELEGII PRE SLACIKY see
Bazlik, Miroslav

PATEJDL, VACLAV
Comedy Overture *see Veseloherna
Predohra

PATEJDL, VACLAV (cont'd.)

Veseloherna Predohra
3.2.2.2. 4.2.3.1. 2timp,perc,
strings
"Comedy Overture" SLOV.HUD.FOND
0-465 perf mat rent   (P48)

PATHETIQUE see Bank, Jacques

PATHETIQUE SYMPHONY see Tchaikovsky,
Piotr Ilyich, Symphony No. 6, Op.
74, in B minor

PATINEURS, LES see Waldteufel, Emil

PAULSEN, HELMUT (1909-1943)
Dorfmusik [12']
string orch
RIES perf mat rent   (P49)

Feiermusik [15']
fl,strings
RIES perf mat rent   (P50)

Landliche Tanze [12']
string orch
RIES perf mat rent   (P51)

Norddeutsche Tanze [10']
1.1.1.1. 1.1.0.0. timp,perc,
strings
RIES perf mat rent   (P52)

PAULUS: GOTT SEI MIR GNADIG, FOR SOLO
VOICE AND ORCHESTRA see
Mendelssohn-Bartholdy, Felix

PAUSENLOS IM RING see Cardello, Rolf

PAVANA see Barbetta Padovano, Julio
Cesare

PAVANE see Andriessen, Jurriaan

PAVANE see Ruders, Poul

PAVESI, STEFANO (1779-1850)
Sinfonias In C And B Flat
see NORTHERN ITALIAN SYMPHONY,
1800-1840, THE

PAVIA see Farina, Guido

PAWLOWSKI, JAKUB (fl. 1750-1800)
Symphony in B flat
see SYMPHONY IN POLAND, THE

PAZ-PAIZ-PEACE see Cordero, Roque

PECHEURS DE PERLES, LES: AU FOND DU
TEMPLE SAINT, FOR SOLO VOICES AND
ORCHESTRA see Bizet, Georges

PECHEURS DE PERLES, LES: COMME
AUTREFOIS DANS LA NUIT SOMBRE, FOR
SOLO VOICE AND ORCHESTRA see Bizet,
Georges

PECHEURS DE PERLES, LES: JE CROIS
ENTENDRE ENCORE, FOR SOLO VOICE AND
ORCHESTRA see Bizet, Georges

PECHEURS DE PERLES, LES: PRELUDE see
Bizet, Georges

PEDROLLO, ARRIGO (1878-1964)
Allegro Da Concerto, For Piano And
Orchestra [10']
2.1.1.1. 2.0.0.0. timp,xylo,harp,
strings,pno solo
manuscript CARISCH   (P53)

Castelli Di Giulietta E Romeo, I, For
Piano And Orchestra [30']
2+pic.2+English horn.2+bass
clar.2. 4.3.3.1. timp,perc,
harp,strings,pno solo
sc ZANIBON 4361 rent, pts ZANIBON
4362 rent   (P54)

Elegy [3']
string orch
sc CARISCH 18732 perf mat rent
(P55)

Intermezzi Per La Tragedia "Ifigenia
In Aulide" [14']
2.2.1.1. 2.2.0.0. timp,harp,
strings
sc CARISCH 18903 f.s., perf mat
rent   (P56)

PEER GYNT: OVERTURE see Grieg, Edvard
Hagerup

PEER GYNT: SUITE NO. 1 see Grieg,
Edvard Hagerup

PEER GYNT: SUITE NO. 2 see Grieg,
Edvard Hagerup

PEJHOVSKY, ANTON (1911-   )
Prelude and Fugue [10']
string orch
SLOV.HUD.FOND 0-21 perf mat rent
(P57)

PELICAN, LE see Stallaert, Alphonse

PELLEAS ET MELISANDE: SICILIENNE see
Faure, Gabriel-Urbain

PELLEAS ET MELISANDE: SUITE see Faure,
Gabriel-Urbain

PELLEAS ET MELISANDE: SUITE, [ARR.] see
Sibelius, Jean

PELLEGRINO DI S. GIACOMO, IL, FOR SOLO
VOICE AND ORCHESTRA see Sinigaglia,
Leone

PENA, ANGEL
Concerto for Double Bass and
Orchestra [20']
orch,db solo
PEER perf mat rent   (P58)

PENDERECKI, KRZYSZTOF (1933-   )
Kanon
string orch,electronic tape
study sc SCHOTTS 71 A6342 $14.00
(P59)
Sonata for Violoncello and Orchestra
[10']
sc KALMUS A7009 $15.00   (P60)

Symphony No. 1
3.3.4.3. 5.3.4.1. timp,perc,harp,
cel,pno,strings
study sc SCHOTTS 71 A6614 $25.00
(P61)
Threnody. To The Victims Of Hiroshima
sc KALMUS A7010 $12.00   (P62)

PENDULE HARMONIEUSE see Pick-
Mangiagalli, Riccardo

PENTAGON see Ramovs, Primoz

PENTAGRAM, FOR TRUMPET AND ORCHESTRA
see Sermila, Jarmo

PEPUSCH, JOHN CHRISTOPHER (1667-1752)
Kammersinfonie
string orch
sc,pts HEINRICH. 227 f.s.   (P63)

PER FUNZIONI RELIGIOSE E ACCADEMIE
*CC17U
(Bonelli, E.) string orch,org pts
ZANIBON 3792 f.s. contains works
by: Gounod; Wagner; Handel; Gluck;
Ignoto and others   (P64)

PER LA MESSA NUZIALE *CC10U
(Bonelli, E.) string orch,org pts
ZANIBON 3444 f.s. contains works
by: Mendelssohn; Mozzi; Wagner;
Gounod; Schumann and others (P65)

PER PIETA, NON RICERCATE, FOR SOLO
VOICE AND ORCHESTRA see Mozart,
Wolfgang Amadeus

PER QUESTA BELLA MANO, FOR SOLO VOICE
AND ORCHESTRA see Mozart, Wolfgang
Amadeus

PER SONARE ED ASCOLTARE, FOR FLUTE AND
ORCHESTRA see Flothuis, Marius

PERCORSO C 2 see Manzoni, Giacomo

PERGOLESI, GIOVANNI BATTISTA
(1710-1736)
Frate 'Nnamorato, Lo: Chi Disse Che
La Femmena, For Solo Voice And
String Orchestra [4']
string orch,solo voice
CARISCH perf mat rent   (P66)

Frate 'Nnamorato, Lo: Gnora
Creditemi, For Solo Voice And
String Orchestra [4']
string orch,solo voice
CARISCH perf mat rent   (P67)

Frate 'Nnamorato, Lo: Ogni Pena Cchiu
Spietata, For Solo Voice And
String Orchestra [5']
string orch,solo voice
CARISCH perf mat rent   (P68)

PERIODICAL OVERTURE see Dittersdorf,
Karl Ditters von

PERLE DU BRESIL, LA: CHARMANT OISEAU,
FOR SOLO VOICE AND ORCHESTRA see
David, Felicien-Cesar

PERMANENT WAVE see Hartmann, Per J.

PERNES, THOMAS (1956-   )
Concerto Per Orchestra Da Camera
2.0.2(bass clar).0. 2.3.4.1.
timp,perc,2pno,2vln,vla,3db
sc,pts DOBLINGER rent   (P69)

PERO, HANS
Andalusische Strassenmusik
RIES f.s. contains also: Stanke,
Willy, Sarello   (P70)

Fruhling Am Lago Maggiore
RIES f.s. contains also: Tessiner
Herbstlied   (P71)

Kleine Rhapsodie
RIES f.s.   (P72)

Tessiner Herbstlied
see Pero, Hans, Fruhling Am Lago
Maggiore

PERPETUAL MOTION, [ARR.] see Paganini,
Niccolo, Moto Perpetuo, [arr.]

PERPETUAL MOVEMENT see Andriessen,
Jurriaan

PERPETUUM MOBILE see Strauss, Johann,
[Jr.]

PERPETUUM MOBILE, FOR VIOLIN AND
ORCHESTRA see Ries, Franz

PERSEUS AND ANDROMEDA XX see Gutche,
Gene

PERSIAN MARCH see Strauss, Johann,
[Jr.], Persischer Marsch

PERSISCHER MARSCH see Strauss, Johann,
[Jr.]

PERT, MORRIS
Sun Dragon *Op.12 [17']
3.3.3.3. 4.3.3.1. timp,4perc,cel,
pno,strings,electronic tape
WEINBERGER perf mat rent   (P73)

Symphony, Op. 27
3.3.3.3. 5.3.3.1. hpsd,pno,cel,
timp,3perc,strings
WEINBERGER perf mat rent   (P74)

Xumbu-Ata *Op.5 [19']
2.2.3.2. 4.2.3.1. hpsd,pno,cel,
timp,5perc,strings
WEINBERGER perf mat rent   (P75)

PESCETTI, GIOVANNI BATTISTA (1704-1766)
Sonata
see RICREAZIONI DI ANTICHE MUSICHE
CLASSICHE, SERIE V: MUSICHE
ANTICHE ITALIANE

PESENTI, MARTINO (1600-1647)
Corrente E Gagliarda [6']
string orch
sc CARISCH 21409 rent, pts CARISCH
19373 rent   (P76)

PESO see Kox, Hans

PESTALOZZI, HEINRICH (1878-1940)
Ciribiribin, For Solo Voice And
Orchestra
LUCKS 02927 sc $3.75, set $8.00,
pts $.75, ea.   (P77)

PESTER CSARDAS, FOR SOLO VOICE AND
ORCHESTRA see Strauss, Johann,
[Jr.]

PETER AND THE WOLF, FOR NARRATOR AND
ORCHESTRA see Prokofiev, Serge

PETER SCHMOLL: OVERTURE see Weber, Carl
Maria von

PETERSMA, WIM (1942-   )
Hora
4.4.4.4. 4.4.3.1. strings
sc DONEMUS f.s., perf mat rent   (P78)

PETERSON, WAYNE TURNER (1927-   )
Exaltation, Dithyramb And Caprice
sc BOOSEY $12.50   (P79)

Free Variations
sc BOOSEY $8.50   (P80)

PETIT CONCERT, FOR PIANO AND CHAMBER
ORCHESTRA see Bjelinski, Bruno

PETIT CONCERT DE PRINTEMPS, FOR FLUTE
AND STRINGS see Voorn, Joop

PETIT RIENS, LES see Mozart, Wolfgang
Amadeus

PETITE GAVOTTE, [ARR.] see Pierne,
Gabriel

PETITE MUSIQUE see Stuhec, Igor, Drobna
Glasba

PETITE REINE, LA see Schmidt-Wunstorf,
Rudolf

PETITE SUITE, [ARR.] see Debussy,
Claude

PETITE SUITE D'APRES SCHUMANN see
Markevitch, Igor

PETITE SYMPHONIE see Ishii; Maki

PETITE SYMPHONIE see Pleyel, Ignace
Joseph

PETITS RIENS, LES, [ARR.] see Mozart,
Wolfgang Amadeus

PETRASSI, GOFFREDO (1904-   )
Sonata da Camera [14']
1.1.1.1. 0.0.0.0. hpsd,2vln,2vla,
vcl,db
ZERBONI perf mat rent   (P81)

PETRIC, IVO (1931-   )
Divertimento Za Slavka Osterca [15']
1.1.1.1. 1.0.0.0. perc,harp,pno,
string quin
DRUSTVO DSS 576 perf mat rent (P82)

Inlaid-Work *see Intarzije

Intarzije [13']
1.0.1.1. 1.1.1.0. perc,string
quin
"Inlaid-Work" DRUSTVO DSS 366 perf
mat rent   (P83)

Jeux Concertants, For Flute And
Orchestra [15']
0(pic).0(English horn).1(bass
clar).1(contrabsn). 3.0.0.0.
2perc,harp,pno/cel,strings,fl
solo
DRUSTVO DSS 892 perf mat rent (P84)

Tako Je Godel Kurent, For Viola And
Orchestra [22']
1+pic.1(English horn).2(bass
clar).1(contrabsn). 3.3.3.3.
3perc,harp,pno/cel,strings,vla
solo
"Thus Played Kurent, For Viola And
Orchestra" DRUSTVO DSS 769 perf
mat rent   (P85)

Thus Played Kurent, For Viola And
Orchestra *see Tako Je Godel
Kurent, For Viola And Orchestra

PETROUCHKA see Stravinsky, Igor

PETROUCHKA: AT THE MOOR see Stravinsky,
Igor

PETROUCHKA: CARNIVAL & DEATH OF
PETROUCHKA see Stravinsky, Igor

PETROUCHKA: DANSE RUSSE see Stravinsky,
Igor

PETROUCHKA: THE FAIR see Stravinsky,
Igor

PETTERSSON, ALLAN (1911-1980)
Symphony No. 14 [52']
3.2.3.3. 4.3.3.1. timp,4perc,
strings
pts STIM perf mat rent   (P86)

Symphony No. 15 [31']
3.2.3.3. 4.3.3.1. timp,4perc,
strings
STIM   (P87)

Symphony No. 16 [25']
3.2.2.3. 4.3.3.0. timp,perc,
strings,alto sax solo
solo pt STIM perf mat rent   (P88)

PETZOLD, RUDOLF (1908-   )
Prelude, Op. 51 [12']
2.2.2.2. 4.2.3.1. timp,perc,
strings
BREITKOPF-W perf mat rent   (P89)

PEYTON PLACE: SUITE see Waxman, Franz

PEZZO CAPRICCIOSO, FOR VIOLONCELLO AND
ORCHESTRA see Tchaikovsky, Piotr
Ilyich

PEZZO CONCERTATO, FOR VIOLONCELLO AND
ORCHESTRA see Lendvay, Kamillo

PEZZO CONCERTATO NO. 2, FOR CITARA AND
ORCHESTRA see Bozay, Attila

PEZZO D'ARCHI see Bozay, Attila

PFEIL, DER see Bode, Hermann

PFISTER, HUGO (1914-1969)
Five Sketches
2.2.2.2. 2.2.2.0. 2perc,strings
(Tschupp) sc EULENBURG GM110P f.s.,
perf mat rent   (P90)

PFITZNER, HANS (1869-1949)
Kathchen Von Heilbronn: Melodram,
Zwischenaktmusik Und Marsch [15']
3(pic).2.2.2. 4.3.3.1. timp,perc,
harp,strings

PFITZNER, HANS (cont'd.)

sc RIES f.s., perf mat rent   (P91)

Kathchen Von Heilbronn: Nach Der
Holunderbuschszene [5']
2.2.2.2. 4.2.3.1. timp,triangle,
harp,strings
RIES perf mat rent   (P92)

Kathchen Von Heilbronn: Vorspiel Zum
III. Akt [10']
3(pic).2.2.2. 4.0.3.1. timp,harp,
strings
RIES perf mat rent   (P93)

Palestrina: Preludes To Acts 1, 2,
And 3
study sc EUR.AM.MUS. 71 A4557
$13.50   (P94)

Uber Ein Stundlein, For Solo Voice
And Orchestra *Op.7,No.3 [3']
1.2.2.2. 1.0.0.0. timp,harp,
strings,low solo
RIES perf mat rent   (P95)

PFUNDT, REINHARD (1951-   )
Concerto for Orchestra
2.2.2.2. 4.3.3.1. perc,strings
DEUTSCHER perf mat rent   (P96)

De Profundis
0.0.0.0. 0.3.3.0. harp,strings
DEUTSCHER perf mat rent   (P97)

PHAEDRA, FOR SOLO VOICE AND ORCHESTRA
see Britten, [Sir] Benjamin

PHAETON see Saint-Saens, Camille

PHANOMENE WALZER see Strauss, Johann,
[Jr.]

PHANTASMEN see Kelterborn, Rudolf

PHIDYLE, FOR SOLO VOICE AND ORCHESTRA
see Duparc, Henri

PHILADELPHIA STORY, THE: SUITE see
Waxman, Franz

PHILHARMONIC WALTZES see Gould, Morton

PHILLIPS, ROBERT
Concerto for 2 Pianos and Orchestra
*see Poseidon

Poseidon (Concerto for 2 Pianos and
Orchestra)
SEESAW perf mat rent   (P98)

PHILOMELA: BERCEUSE, FOR SOLO VOICE AND
ORCHESTRA see Andriessen, Hendrik

PHRYNETTE see Filipucci, Edmond

PIANGO, FOR SOLO VOICE AND STRING
ORCHESTRA see Vivaldi, Antonio

PIANTO DELLE CREATURE, FOR SOLO VOICE
AND ORCHESTRA see Bucchi, Valentino

PIBERNIK, ZLATKO (1926-   )
Symphony
4.4.4.4. 4.6.4.1. timp,xylo,
vibra,marimba,pno,strings
DRUS.HRVAT.SKLAD. f.s.   (P99)

PICADOR, EL see Hildebrand, Erich

PICAYUNE SUITE see Dorward, David

PICCINNI, NICCOLO (1728-1800)
Concerto for Flute and Orchestra in D
1.2.0.0. 2.0.0.0. strings,fl solo
(Landon, H.C.R.) sc,pts DOBLINGER
DM 807 f.s.   (P100)

PICCIOLI, GIUSEPPE (1905-1961)
Burlesca, For Piano And Orchestra
[8']
2.2.2.2. 2.2.1.0. timp,strings,
pno solo
sc CARISCH 18897 f.s., perf mat
rent   (P101)

Intermezzi Secenteschi [12']
1.3.1.2. 0.0.0.0. harp,pno,
strings
min sc CARISCH 17146 perf mat rent
                                  (P102)

Offerta Delle Rose, L', For Solo
Voice And Orchestra [25']
3.3.2.2. 4.3.3.1. timp,perc,
bells,cel,harp,pno,strings,solo
voice
sc CARISCH 18736 f.s., perf mat
rent   (P103)

Siciliana [5']
2.3.3.2. 4.2.3.1. timp,harp,
strings
manuscript CARISCH   (P104)

PICCOLA SERENATA see Mortari, Virgilio

PICCOLA SUITE see Camussi, Ezio

PICCOLE SERENATE see Chailly, Luciano

PICCOLE VARIAZIONI SU FRA MARTINO
CAMPANARO see Marinuzzi, Gino, Jr.

PICCOLO-BAMBINO see Ritter, Helmut

PICCOLO CONCERTO, FOR GUITAR AND STRING
ORCHESTRA see Mortari, Virgilio

PICCOLO CONCERTO, FOR OBOE AND STRING
ORCHESTRA see Dionisi, Renato

PICCOLO CONCERTO, FOR OBOE AND STRING
ORCHESTRA see Margola, Franco

PICCOLO CONCERTO, FOR PIANO AND
ORCHESTRA see Malipiero, Riccardo

PICCOLO CONCERTO, FOR TUBA AND
ORCHESTRA see Steffaro, Julius

PICHL, WENZEL (VACLAV) (1741-1805)
  Concerto for Double Bass and
    Orchestra, No. 1, in D [17']
    0.2.0.0. 2.0.0.0. strings,db solo
    (Malaric, R.) sc,pts DOBLINGER rent
                                    (P105)

PICK-MANGIAGALLI, RICCARDO (1882-1949)
  Ecco Settembre, For Solo Voice And
    Orchestra [3']
    2.3.2.2. 4.0.0.0. harp,strings,
    solo voice
    manuscript CARISCH   (P106)

  Fiorile, For Solo Voice And Orchestra
    [3']
    2.2.2.2. 2.0.0.0. harp,strings,
    solo voice
    manuscript CARISCH   (P107)

  Humoresque, For Piano And Orchestra
    [14']
    3.2.2.2. 4.2.3.1. timp,perc,
    strings,pno solo
    sc CARISCH 17110 f.s., perf mat
    rent   (P108)

  Intermezzo [9']
    2.1.2.0. 1.0.0.0. harp,pno,
    strings
    sc CARISCH 19447 f.s., perf mat
    rent   (P109)

  Ombre Di Sogni: Sarabanda, Gavotta,
    Barcarola [8']
    2.2.2.2. 2.2.1.0. perc,harp,cel,
    pno,harmonium,strings
    manuscript CARISCH   (P110)

  Ombre Di Sogni: Serenata [5']
    2.1.2.1. 2.0.0.0. timp,perc,pno,
    strings
    manuscript CARISCH   (P111)

  Pendule Harmonieuse [3']
    string orch,cel
    manuscript CARISCH   (P112)

  Rapsodia Epica [18']
    3.2.3.3. 4.3.3.5. pno,bells,org,
    strings
    sc CARISCH 19891 f.s., perf mat
    rent   (P113)

PICTURES AT AN EXHIBITION, [ARR.] see
  Mussorgsky, Modest Petrovich

PIECE FOR ORCHESTRA see Wilder, Alec

PIECE FOR XYLOPHONE AND ORCHESTRA IN C
  see Skalkottas, Nikos

PIECE OF ORCHESTRA, A see Antonsen,
  Ivar

PIECE SYMPHONIQUE, FOR ORGAN AND
  ORCHESTRA see Purvis, Richard

PIECES ARRANGED IN THE FORM OF A SUITE
  see Bach, Johann Sebastian

PIERCE, (ANNE) ALEXANDRA (1934-   )
  Behemoth
    2.1.1.1. 2.1.1.0. timp,perc,harp,
    strings
    SEESAW perf mat rent   (P114)

PIERNE, GABRIEL (1863-1937)
  Ballet De Cour: La Canarie
    KALMUS 5542 sc $4.00, set $6.00
                                 (P115)

  Ballet De Cour: Menuet Du Roy
    KALMUS 5544 sc $3.00, set $3.75
                                 (P116)

  Ballet De Cour: Passa-Mezzo
    KALMUS 5545 sc $4.00, set $18.00
                                 (P117)

  Ballet De Cour: Passepied
    KALMUS 5541 sc $2.00, set $5.00
                                 (P118)

PIERNE, GABRIEL (cont'd.)
  Ballet De Cour: Pavane Et Saltarello
    KALMUS 5543 sc $5.00, set $11.00
                                 (P119)

  Ballet De Cour: Rigaudon
    KALMUS 5540 sc $5.00, set $12.00
                                 (P120)

  Canzonetta, For Clarinet And
    Orchestra *Op.19
    KALMUS 4549 sc $3.00, set $8.00
                                 (P121)

  Farandole, [arr.] *Op.14,No.2
    0.pic.1.1.1. 1.0.opt trp.0.0. perc,
    strings [3'] KALMUS 5540 sc
    $3.00, set $9.00   (P122)

  Konzertstuck for Harp and Orchestra,
    Op. 39
    orch,harp solo
    KALMUS 5440 solo pt $4.50, sc
    $24.00, perf mat rent, set
    $22.00, pts $1.00, ea.   (P123)

  March Of The Little Lead Soldiers
    *see Marche Des Petits Soldats De
    Plomb, [arr.]

  Marche Des Petits Soldats De Plomb,
    [arr.]
    "March Of The Little Lead Soldiers"
    LUCKS 06409 sc $4.00, set $11.50,
    pts $1.15, ea.   (P124)

  Petite Gavotte, [arr.] *Op.14,No.4
    1.1.1.0. 1.0.0.0. strings [3']
    KALMUS 4549 sc $3.00, set $6.00
                                 (P125)

  Veillee De L'Ange Gardien, La, [arr.]
    *Op.14,No.3
    string orch [3'] KALMUS 5547 sc
    $2.00, set $3.75   (P126)

PIETROWSKI, KAROL (fl. 1750-1800)
  Symphony in D
    see SYMPHONY IN POLAND, THE

PIJPER, WILLEM (1894-1947)
  Romance Sans Paroles, For Solo Voice
    And Orchestra
    3.2.3.1. 3.3.0.0. 2perc,2harp,
    pno,cel,gtr,2mand,strings,Mez
    solo
    sc DONEMUS f.s., perf mat rent
                                 (P127)

PILATI, MARIO (1903-1938)
  Bagatelle [20']
    1.1.1.1. 1.1.0.0. perc,pno,harp,
    strings
    sc CARISCH 19455 f.s., perf mat
    rent   (P128)

  Preludio, Aria E Tarantella, For
    Violin And Orchestra [9']
    3.3.3.2. 4.3.4.0. timp,perc,harp,
    cel,strings,vln solo
    sc CARISCH 18890 perf mat rent
                                 (P129)

  Quattro Canzoni Popolari [14']
    1.1.1.1. 1.1.0.0. perc,harp,
    strings
    sc CARISCH 18744 f.s., perf mat
    rent   (P130)

PILGER QUADRILLE, DIE see Strauss,
  Eduard

PILGRIMS see Rorem, Ned

PILGRIM'S SONG, FOR SOLO VOICE AND
  ORCHESTRA, [ARR.] see Tchaikovsky,
  Piotr Ilyich

PINELLI, CARLO (1911-   )
  Notturno Concertante, For Violin,
    Viola, English Horn And Orchestra
    study sc BSE $7.25   (P131)

PIONEERS, THE see Yashima, Hideaki

PIQUE DAME: OVERTURE see Suppe, Franz
  von

PIQUE DAME: PRINCE YELETSKY'S ARIA see
  Tchaikovsky, Piotr Ilyich, Queen Of
  Spades: I Love You, Dear, For Solo
  Voice And Orchestra

PIRATA, IL: SINFONIA see Bellini,
  Vincenzo

PIRATES OF PENZANCE, THE: I AM THE VERY
  PATTERN OF A MODERN MAJOR GENERAL,
  FOR SOLO VOICE AND ORCHESTRA see
  Sullivan, [Sir] Arthur Seymour

PIRATES OF PENZANCE: OVERTURE see
  Sullivan, [Sir] Arthur Seymour

PISANELLA, LA: SUITE see Pizzetti,
  Ildebrando

PISMA K JANEKU, FOR SOLO VOICE AND
  ORCHESTRA see Mikula, Zdenko

PISTORIUS, GUNTER (1940-   )
  Concerto for Percussion and Orchestra
    3.2.2.2. 4.3.3.1. harp,strings,
    4perc soli
    DEUTSCHER perf mat rent   (P132)

PIZZARCO see Schnelldorfer, Martin

PIZZETTI, ILDEBRANDO (1880-1968)
  Pisanella, La: Suite
    FORLIVESI perf mat rent   (P133)

  Santa Uliva: Ninna-Nanna, For Solo
    Voice And Orchestra [4']
    2.2.0.0. 1.0.0.0. pno,strings,S
    solo
    manuscript CARISCH   (P134)

PIZZICATI-ARABESKEN see Fanchetti, G.

PIZZICATO-POLKA see Strauss, Johann,
  [Jr.]

PIZZINI, CARLO ALBERTO (1905-   )
  Canti Sereni, I, For Solo Voice And
    Orchestra [11']
    2.2.2.2. 2.2.3.0. timp,harp,
    strings,S/T solo
    sc ZANIBON 4524 rent, pts ZANIBON
    4524A rent   (P135)

  Concierto Para Tres Hermanas, For
    Guitar And Orchestra [26']
    2.2.2.2. 2.2.3.0. timp,perc,
    strings,gtr solo
    sc ZANIBON 5219 f.s., pts ZANIBON
    5220 f.s.   (P136)

  Poema Delle Dolomiti, Il [15']
    2+pic.2+English horn.2+bass
    clar.2+contrabsn. 4.4.3.1.
    3timp,3perc,harp,cel,glock,org,
    strings
    sc ZANIBON 3173 f.s., pts ZANIBON
    3174 rent   (P137)

  Strapaese [6']
    3.3.4.2. 4.3.3.1. timp,perc,
    bells,xylo,acord,strings
    sc CARISCH 17118 f.s., perf mat
    rent   (P138)

PLA, FRANCISCO LLACER
  Migraciones, For Solo Voice And
    Orchestra
    sc PILES 2080-P f.s.   (P139)

PLACE IN THE SUN, A see Waxman, Franz

PLANCK, LILLEMOR (1926-   )
  Miranda, For Solo Voice And
    Orchestra, [arr.]
    (Samuelson, Lars) 2.2.2.2. 2.2.3.0.
    perc,strings,solo voice, jazz
    combo sc STIM   (P140)

PLANETS, THE see Holst, Gustav

PLANTES DE LA JEUNE FILLE, LES, [ARR.]
  see Schubert, Franz (Peter)

PLATZ, ROBERT
  Ka [22']
    MODERN 2070 perf mat rent   (P141)

PLAUDERSTUNDCHEN, FOR SAXOPHONE AND
  ORCHESTRA see Kopelent, Marek

PLAY GROUND see Crosse, Gordon

PLAYS, FOR TWELVE VIOLONCELLI, BRASS
  AND PERCUSSION see Wimberger,
  Gerhard

PLEASANT MOMENTS, FOR CORNET AND
  ORCHESTRA see Joplin, Scott

PLEASURE TRAIN see Strauss, Johann,
  [Jr.], Vergnugungszug

PLESNA BURLESKA see Bravnicar, Matija

PLEYEL, IGNACE JOSEPH (1757-1831)
  Petite Symphonie
    2.1.2.0. 0.2.0.0. strings
    sc,pts HARMONIA 1577 f.s.   (P142)

  Symphonie Concertante For Violin,
    Viola, And Orchestra In B Flat
    see Symphonies, Four And Symphonie
    Concertante

  Symphonie Periodique No. 10
    see Symphonies, Four And Symphonie
    Concertante

  Symphonie Periodique No. 20
    see Symphonies, Four And Symphonie
    Concertante

  Symphonie Periodique No. 25
    see Symphonies, Four And Symphonie
    Concertante

PLEYEL, IGNACE JOSEPH (cont'd.)

Symphonie Periodique No. 27
see Symphonies, Four And Symphonie
Concertante

Symphonies, Four And Symphonie
Concertante
(Smith, Raymond; Townsend, Douglas)
sc GARLAND ISBN 0-8240-3804-5
$90.00 "The Symphony", Vol. D-VI
contains: Symphonie Concertante
For Violin, Viola, And
Orchestra In B Flat; Symphonie
Periodique No. 10; Symphonie
Periodique No. 20; Symphonie
Periodique No. 25; Symphonie
Periodique No. 27   (P143)

PLINIUS' FONTEIN see Meulemans, Arthur

PLOTZLICH see Boer, Ed de

PLUCKING STRINGS see Steffaro, Julius

PLUIE, LA see David, Adolphe Isaac

PLUISTER, SIMON (1913-   )
Dans Der Goden, De
see Drie Chineesche Liederen, For
Solo Voice And Orchestra

Drie Chineesche Liederen, For Solo
Voice And Orchestra
2.2.2.2. 3.0.0.0. perc,cel,2harp,
strings,A solo sc DONEMUS f.s.,
perf mat rent
contains: Dans Der Goden, De;
Jonge Dichter Denkt Aan De
Geliefde, Een; Lenteregen, De
(P144)

Jonge Dichter Denkt Aan De Geliefde,
Een
see Drie Chineesche Liederen, For
Solo Voice And Orchestra

Lenteregen, De
see Drie Chineesche Liederen, For
Solo Voice And Orchestra

Ricercar E Giga, For Organ And String
Orchestra [14'30"]
string orch,org solo
DONEMUS   (P145)

Slaapliederen Voor Grote Mensen, For
Solo Voice And Orchestra [10']
2.2.2.2. 2.2.0.0. perc,harp,
strings,S solo
sc DONEMUS f.s., perf mat rent
(P146)

PODIUM SUITE, FOR VIOLIN AND ORCHESTRA
see Frid, Geza

PODPROCKY, JOZEF (1945-   )
Dramatic Study *see Dramaticka
Studia

Dramaticka Studia
3.3.2.3. 4.2.3.1. timp,4perc,cel,
xylo,strings
"Dramatic Study" SLOV.HUD.FOND
0-172 perf mat rent   (P147)

POEMA DELLE DOLOMITI, IL see Pizzini,
Carlo Alberto

POEMA LIGURE see Cantu, Mario

POEMA SONORA NO. 4 see Haug, Halvor

POEME, FOR VIOLIN AND ORCHESTRA see
Chausson, Ernest

POEME LYRIQUE, OP. 12 see Glazunov,
Alexander Konstantinovich

POEME POUR UN HOMME BIEN-AIME see
Dispa, Robert

POET AND PEASANT: OVERTURE see Suppe,
Franz von, Dichter Und Bauer:
Overture

POGORELOW, W.
Mazurka
RIES f.s.   (P148)

POHADKA SUITE see Suk, Josef

POHL'AD DO NEZNAMA, FOR SOLO VOICE AND
ORCHESTRA see Suchon, Eugen

POINTS AND DANCES FROM TAVERNER see
Davies, Peter Maxwell

POLE see Porcelijn, David

POLIN, CLAIRE
Journey Of Owain Madoc, The
3.3.3.2. 1.2.1.1. 5perc,pno,
strings
SEESAW perf mat rent   (P149)

POLIN, CLAIRE (cont'd.)

Scenes From Gilgamesh, For Flute And
String Orchestra
string orch,fl solo
SEESAW perf mat rent   (P150)

POLISH CHANTS, FOR SOLO VOICE AND
CHAMBER ORCHESTRA see Meyer,
Krzysztof, Spiewy Polskie, For Solo
Voice And Chamber Orchestra

POLLAROLO, CARLO FRANCESCO (1653-1722)
Fughetta
see RICREAZIONI DI ANTICHE MUSICHE
CLASSICHE, SERIE I: MUSICHE
ANTICHE ITALIANE

POLLEDRO, GIOVANNI BATTISTA (1781-1853)
Sinfonias In D, Two
see NORTHERN ITALIAN SYMPHONY,
1800-1840, THE

POLOLANIK, ZDENEK (1935-   )
Concerto Grosso [15']
string orch,clar in E flat/fl
solo,gtr solo,hpsd solo
sc ZANIBON 5081 f.s., pts ZANIBON
5082 f.s.   (P151)

POLONAISE, [ARR.] see Wagner, Richard

POLONAISE BRILLANTE, FOR PIANO AND
ORCHESTRA, [ARR.] see Weber, Carl
Maria von

POLONAISE BRILLANTE, FOR VIOLIN AND
ORCHESTRA see Wieniawski, Henryk

POLONAISE DE CONCERT, FOR VIOLIN AND
ORCHESTRA see Wieniawski, Henryk

POLONAISE IN D MAJOR, [ARR.] see
Dittersdorf, Karl Ditters von

POLONAISE, OP. 40, NO.1, [ARR.] see
Chopin, Frederic

POLONIA see Panufnik, Andrzej

POLYTOPE see Xenakis, Yannis (Iannis)

POMMERN-SUITE see Walter, Fried

POMP AND CIRCUMSTANCE MARCH NO. 1 IN D
see Elgar, [Sir] Edward (William)

POMP AND CIRCUMSTANCE MARCHES NOS. 1-5
see Elgar, [Sir] Edward (William)

PONANT 19, FOR PIANO AND INSTRUMENTAL
ENSEMBLE see Constant, Marius

PONCHIELLI, AMILCARE (1834-1886)
Elegy [12']
2.3.3.2. 4.2.4.0. timp,perc,harp,
strings
(Spada, P.) sc ZERBONI 8196 f.s.,
pts ZERBONI 8197 rent   (P152)

Gioconda, La: Cielo E Mar, For Solo
Voice And Orchestra
LUCKS 02772 sc $3.75, set $7.50,
pts $.75, ea.   (P153)

Gioconda, La: Ombre Di Mia Prosapia,
For Solo Voice And Orchestra
LUCKS 03190 sc $5.00, set $10.00,
pts $.75, ea.   (P154)

Gioconda, La: Selection
(Wiegand, G.) LUCKS 07518 sc $5.00,
set $10.00, pts $.75, ea.   (P155)

Gioconda, La: Suicidio - In Questi
Fieri Momenti, For Solo Voice And
Orchestra
LUCKS 02168 sc $3.75, set $7.50,
pts $.75, ea.   (P156)

Gioconda, La: Voce Di Donna, For Solo
Voice And Orchestra
LUCKS 02151 sc $3.75, set $7.50,
pts $.75, ea.   (P157)

Lituani, I: Sinfonia [6']
3.2.2.2. 4.2.3.1. timp,perc,harp,
strings
KALMUS 5257 sc $20.00, perf mat
rent, set $50.00, pts $2.50, ea.
(P158)
"Lituani Overture" LUCKS 11304 sc
$20.00, set $50.00, pts $2.00,
ea.   (P159)

Lituani Overture *see Lituani, I:
Sinfonia

Marion Delorme: Marcia Funebre [3']
3.2.2.2. 4.2.3.1. timp,perc,
strings
KALMUS 5256 sc $5.00, perf mat
rent, set $15.00, pts $.60, ea.
(P160)

PONSE, LUCTOR (1914-   )
Concerto for Piano and Orchestra, No.
1, Op. 39 [29']
2.2.3.3. 4.2.3.1. timp,4perc,
harp,strings,electronic tape,
pno solo
DONEMUS   (P161)

POP AND ART see Niehaus, Manfred

POP-SUITE see Quelle, Ernst August

POPPER, DAVID (1843-1913)
Hungarian Rhapsody *see Ungarische
Rhapsodie, For Violoncello And
Orchestra

Requiem *Op.66 [6'30"]
2.2.2.2. 2.0.0.0. perc,strings,
3vcl soli
INTERNAT. perf mat rent   (P162)

Tarentelle, For Violoncello And
Orchestra *Op.33
LUCKS 00607 sc $7.50, set $18.00,
pts $1.40, ea.   (P163)

Ungarische Rhapsodie, For Violoncello
And Orchestra *Op.68
"Hungarian Rhapsody" LUCKS 00609 sc
$8.00, set $18.00, pts $1.40, ea.
(P164)

PORCELIJN, DAVID (1947-   )
Concerto for Flute, Harp and
Orchestra [12']
0.0.0.0. 2.0.0.0. 4vln,4vla,4vcl,
2db,fl solo,harp solo
sc DONEMUS f.s., perf mat rent
(P165)

Confrontations And Indoctrinations,
For Jazz Quintet, Big Band And 19
Instruments
2.2.3.1. 3.0.0.1. perc,2pno,vln,
vla,vcl,db,electronic
equipment, jazz quintet and
jazz big band
sc DONEMUS f.s., perf mat rent
(P166)

Cybernetisch Objekt [24']
5.4.5.3.tenor sax. 2.2.2.1. cym,
vibra,xylo,pno,2vln,2vla,2vcl,
2db, harp (ampl.) and elec hpsd
sc DONEMUS f.s., perf mat rent
(P167)

For The Last Time...! I Repeat...,
For Flute And Orchestra
4.4.4.4.2alto sax.2tenor sax.
8.4.4.0. 4perc,strings,fl solo
sc DONEMUS f.s., perf mat rent
(P168)

Pole [20']
2alto fl,2bass fl,2bass clar,
2basset horn,2contrabass,2tenor
sax,2bass trom,2tuba,4vla,4db,
2 alto trb
sc DONEMUS f.s., perf mat rent
(P169)

Pulverization [12']
24vln,10vla,10vcl,8db
sc DONEMUS f.s., perf mat rent
(P170)

Pulverization II, For Saxophone And
Orchestra [15']
4.2.2.2.2tenor sax.2basset horn.
2.0.4.2. 5perc,strings,alto sax
solo
sc DONEMUS f.s., perf mat rent
(P171)

10-5-6-5-(a) [5'-9']
2string quar,wind quin,2vibra
sc DONEMUS f.s., perf mat rent
(P172)

Terrible Power [5']
4.4.4.4. 6.4.3.1. timp,perc,xylo,
marimba,pno,strings
MOLENAAR 14.1565.08 f.s.   (P173)

PORPORA, NICOLA ANTONIO (1686-1768)
Introduzione E Fuga
see RICREAZIONI DI ANTICHE MUSICHE
CLASSICHE, SERIE V: MUSICHE
ANTICHE ITALIANE

PORRINO, ENNIO (1910-1959)
Canti dell'Esilio, I, For Solo Voice
And Orchestra [40']
1.1.1.1. 0.0.0.0. perc,harp,
strings,solo voice
manuscript CARISCH   (P174)

Canti Di Stagione, For Solo Voice And
Orchestra [15']
2.1.1.2. 2.1.1.1. perc,harp,pno,
strings,S solo
manuscript CARISCH   (P175)

Due Pagine d'Album, For Solo Voice
And String Orchestra [6']
string orch,solo voice
manuscript CARISCH   (P176)

Tre Canti Regionali, For Solo Voice
And Orchestra [8']
1.1.1.1. 2.1.1.0. timp,perc,harp,
pno,strings,S solo
manuscript CARISCH   (P177)

PORT D'AMOUR see Kirchstein, Harold M.

PORTRAIT, FOR HARPSICHORD AND ORCHESTRA
see Donatoni, Franco

PORTRAIT OF STEPHEN FOSTER, A see
Proto, Frank

POSEIDON see Phillips, Robert

POSPISIL, JURAJ (1931-   )
Concerto Eroico, For Horn And
Orchestra *Op.31,No.2 [11']
2.2.2.2. 1.1.1.1. 3-4timp,perc,
strings,horn solo
SLOV.HUD.FOND 0-438A perf mat rent
(P178)
Symfonicka Freska *Op.32,No.2 [8']
1.2.2.2. 1.1.2.0. timp,perc,
strings
"Symphonic Fresco" SLOV.HUD.FOND
0-448A perf mat rent   (P179)

Symphonic Fresco *see Symfonicka
Freska

Symphony No. 4
2.3.3.3. 4.2.3.1. timp,4perc,
strings,mix cor
SLOV.HUD.FOND 0-497 perf mat rent
(P180)
Warzawa *see Symphony No. 4

POSSESSION FRANCAISE see Escher, Rudolf
George

POSTIL, FOR VIOLIN AND STRING ORCHESTRA
see Shackelford, Randolph Owens

POT POURRI see Benvenuti, Arrigo

POUL, FRANTISEK (1945-   )
Sinfonietta [15']
3.3.3.3. 4.3.3.1. timp,perc,harp,
cel,xylo,carillon,pno,strings
SLOV.HUD.FOND 0-470 perf mat rent
(P181)
POULE, LA, SYMPHONY see Haydn, [Franz]
Joseph, Symphony No. 83 in G minor

POUPEE DE NUREMBERG, LA: OVERTURE see
Adam, Adolphe-Charles

POUR FAIRE LE PORTRAIT D'UN OISEAU, FOR
SOLO VOICE AND ORCHESTRA see Kruyf,
Ton de

POUR LE TEMPS DE LA MOISSON see Royer,
Etienne

POUR LES BALEINES see Xenakis, Yannis
(Iannis)

POUR UN MONDE NOIR, FOR SOLO VOICE AND
ORCHESTRA see Chaynes, Charles

POUR UNE FETE DE JEUNESSE see Vuataz,
Roger

POUSSEUR, HENRI (1929-   )
Chronique Illustree: Grande Chronique
Illustree, For Solo Voice And
Orchestra [5']
4.4.4.0.sax. 4.4.3.1. harp,pno,
perc,strings,Bar solo
sc ZERBONI 8304 f.s., perf mat rent
(P182)
Chronique Illustree: Petite Chronique
Illustree [5']
4.4.4.0.sax. 4.4.3.1. harp,pno,
perc,strings
sc ZERBONI 8304 f.s., perf mat rent
(P183)
Parade De Votre Faust [12']
3.2+English horn.4.2.alto
sax.tenor sax. 4.3.4.1. timp,
3perc,harp,strings
UNIVER. perf mat rent   (P184)

PRADO, JOSE-ANTONIO (ALMEIDA)
(1943-   )
Concerto for Flute and String
Orchestra
string orch,fl solo
TONOS   (P185)

Cronica De Um Dia De Verao, For
Clarinet And String Orchestra
string orch,clar solo
TONOS 10351   (P186)

PRAELUDIUM see Stravinsky, Igor

PRAELUDIUM, FUGE UND GIGUE see Fischer,
Johann Caspar Ferdinand

PRAELUDIUM UND TOCCATA see Schubert,
Heinz

PRAGER ORGELKONZERT, FOR ORGAN AND
ORCHESTRA see Zechlin, Ruth

PRAGUE SYMPHONY see Mozart, Wolfgang
Amadeus, Symphony No. 38 in D, K.
504

PRAIRIE SKETCH see Hutchison, (David)
Warner

PRAISE MEDLEY, [ARR.]
(Kirkland, Camp) CRESPUB CP-IN 7+1
$15.00 see also Seven+
Orchestration Series, Group 1
(P187)

PRANSCHKE, JOHANNES (1913-1971)
Matrosentanz [5']
2.2.2.2. 4.2.3.0. timp,perc,
strings
sc RIES f.s., perf mat rent (P188)

PRAYER OF THANKSGIVING see Valerius,
Adrianus

PREAMBLE FOR A SOLEMN OCCASION see
Copland, Aaron

PRECIOSA: OVERTURE see Weber, Carl
Maria von

PREDIERI, LUCA ANTONIO (1688-1767)
Concerto in B minor
string orch,cont,vln solo
sc,pts HUG f.s.   (P189)

PRELUDE A L'APRES-MIDI D'UN FAUNE see
Debussy, Claude

PRELUDE AND FUGUE IN C MINOR, [ARR.]
see Bach, Johann Sebastian

PRELUDE AND IDYLL, FOR SOLO VOICES AND
ORCHESTRA see Delius, Frederick

PRELUDE AND MAZURKA see Delibes, Leo

PRELUDE. CHORAL AND FUGUE, [ARR.] see
Franck, Cesar

PRELUDE, CHORALE, AND FUGUE, [ARR.] see
Bach, Johann Sebastian

PRELUDE TO A SYMPHONY see Koppel,
Herman David

PRELUDE TO THE AFTERNOON OF A FAUN see
Debussy, Claude, Prelude A L'Apres-
Midi D'Un Faune

PRELUDES, LES see Liszt, Franz

PRELUDIO A UN DRAMMA see Becce,
Giuseppe

PRELUDIO, ARIA E TARANTELLA, FOR VIOLIN
AND ORCHESTRA see Pilati, Mario

PRELUDIO-CORALE-FUGA see Robbiani,
Igino

PRELUDIO E ALLEGRO see Vittorio, E.

PRELUDIO E ALLEGRO CONCERTANTE see
Gervasio, Raffaele

PRELUDIO EROICO see Zanon, Sante

PRELUDIO RELIGIOSO see Rossini,
Gioacchino

PRELUDIO SARABANDA E FINALE see
Dionisi, Renato

PRELUDIO SINFONICO see Grillo, Giovanni
Battista

PRELUDIUM OCH INTERMEZZO, FOR TRUMPET
AND STRING ORCHESTRA see Hallnas,
Eyvind

PREPROSTE POPEVKE, FOR SOLO VOICE AND
CHAMBER ORCHESTRA see Lajovic,
Aleksander

PRESENTIMENT see Carl, Gene, Voorgevoel

PRESLI ROKY, FOR SOLO VOICE AND
ORCHESTRA see Korinek, Miloslav

PRESTO see Kletsch, Ludwig

PRESTO see Newman, Theodore Simon

PRIELOM see Suchon, Eugen

PRIMAVERA see Berkeley, Michael

PRIMAVERA, FOR PIANO AND ORCHESTRA see
Hekster, Walter

PRIMAVERA D'OR, LA, FOR SOLO VOICE AND
ORCHESTRA see Glazunov, Alexander
Konstantinovich

PRIMAVERA: HETEROPHONY see Mizelle,
Dary John

PRINCE KHOLMSKY: OVERTURE AND INTERLUDE
see Glinka, Mikhail Ivanovich

PRINCE METHUSALEM: O LOVELY MAY see
Strauss, Johann, [Jr.], Prinz
Methusalem: O Schoner Mai

PRINCE METHUSALEM: OVERTURE see
Strauss, Johann, [Jr.], Prinz
Methusalem: Overture

PRINCE METHUSALEM: SELECTIONS see
Strauss, Johann, [Jr.], Prinz
Methusalem: Selections

PRINCE OF THE PAGODAS: PRELUDE AND
DANCES see Britten, [Sir] Benjamin

PRINCE VALIANT: SUITE see Waxman, Franz

PRINCESSE DE TREBIZONDE, LA. QUADRILLE
see Strauss, Johann, [Jr.]

PRINTEMPS, LE, FOR SOLO VOICE AND
ORCHESTRA see Bon, Willem Frederik

PRINZ METHUSALEM: O SCHONER MAI see
Strauss, Johann, [Jr.]

PRINZ METHUSALEM: OVERTURE see Strauss,
Johann, [Jr.]

PRINZ METHUSALEM: SELECTIONS see
Strauss, Johann, [Jr.]

PRISMES, FOR SOLO VOICE AND STRING
ORCHESTRA see Casagrande, E.

PROCACCINI, TERESA (1934-   )
Concerto for Organ and Orchestra
[27']
3.2.2.2. 4.3.0.0. timp,strings,
org solo
manuscript CARISCH   (P190)

Concerto for Violin, Violoncello,
Piano and Orchestra [27']
3.2.3.2. 4.3.0.0. timp,strings,
vln solo,vcl solo,pno solo
manuscript CARISCH   (P191)

Dannazione E Preghiera, For Solo
Voice And String Orchestra (from
Sentimento Nel Tempo) [13']
string orch,Mez solo
manuscript CARISCH   (P192)

Fantasy [13']
3.2.3.2. 4.0.3.1. timp,perc,xylo,
strings
manuscript CARISCH   (P193)

Sinfonietta [25']
2.2.2.2. 2.2.0.0. strings
manuscript CARISCH   (P194)

PROCESSIONAL AND CAPRICCIO FOR PICCOLO
AND ORCHESTRA see Sawyer, Wilson

PROCH, HEINRICH (1809-1878)
Deh, Torna, Mio Bene!, For Solo Voice
And Orchestra
LUCKS 02659 set $8.00, pts $.75,
ea.   (P195)

PROCHAZKA, RUDOLF (1864-1936)
Gluck, Das: Overture
sc LIENAU f.s.   (P196)

PRODANA NEVESTA: GERNE WILL ICH DIR
VERTRAUEN, FOR SOLO VOICE AND
ORCHESTRA see Smetana, Bedrich

PRODANA NEVESTA: O, WAS ICH MICH
BETRUBE, FOR SOLO VOICE AND
ORCHESTRA see Smetana, Bedrich

PRODANA NEVESTA: OVERTURE see Smetana,
Bedrich

PROFIEL, FOR HARPSICHORD AND ORCHESTRA
see Boogaard, Bernard van den

PROFIT TOUT CLAIR see Linke, Norbert

PROGRAMM see Wimberger, Gerhard

PROIMION IN ETHOS C see Terzakis,
Dimitri

PROJECTIONS see Ioannides, Yannis

PROKOFIEV, SERGE (1891-1953)
Classical Symphony (Symphony No. 1,
Op. 25)
BROUDE BR. set $35.00, pts $1.75,
ea.   (P197)
LUCKS 07217 sc $12.00, set $28.00,
pts $1.40, ea.   (P198)
study sc INTERNAT. 2275 $7.00
(P199)
Concerto for Piano and Orchestra, No.
1, Op. 10, in D flat
LUCKS 00146 sc $35.00, set $40.00,
min sc $6.00, pts $3.00, ea.
(P200)
Concerto for Violin and Orchestra,
No. 1, Op. 19, in D
min sc INTERNAT. 1442 $7.00 (P201)

Fiore Di Pietra, Il: Suite Nuziale
*see Tale Of The Stone Flower:
Wedding Suite

PROKOFIEV, SERGE (cont'd.)

Lieutenant Kije *Op.60
BROUDE BR. set $45.00, pts $2.50,
ea.   (P202)

Love Of Three Oranges: March And
Scherzo
LUCKS 08663 sc $13.00, set $27.00,
min sc $3.00, pts $1.40, ea.
                                 (P203)

Peter And The Wolf, For Narrator And
Orchestra *Op.67 [25']
1.1.1.1. 3.1.1.0. timp,perc,pno,
strings,narrator
min sc BOOSEY $17.50, perf mat rent
                                 (P204)
LUCKS 07249 sc $10.00, set $19.00,
min sc $5.00, pts $1.40, ea.
                                 (P205)
sc,quarto PETERS 5712 $35.00 (P206)
[Ger/Fr/Eng] min sc PETERS 5714
$17.00   (P207)

Romeo And Juliet: Suite No. 1
*Op.64a
sc PETERS 5741 $27.50   (P208)

Romeo And Juliet: Suite No. 2
*Op.64b
sc PETERS 5742 $27.50   (P209)

Romeo And Juliet: Suite No. 3
*Op.101
sc PETERS 5743 $24.50   (P210)

Symphony No. 1, Op. 25 *see
Classical Symphony

Symphony No. 5, Op. 100
sc RICORDI-IT PR908 f.s.   (P211)

Symphony No. 7, Op. 131
sc PETERS 5716 $26.50   (P212)

Tale Of The Stone Flower: Wedding
Suite
"Fiore Di Pietra, Il: Suite
Nuziale" sc RICORDI-IT PR925 f.s.
                                 (P213)

PROLOGUE AND FUGUE see Green, George C.

PROLOGUE, CAPRICCIO AND EPILOGUE see
Lees, Benjamin

PROLOOG see Bonsel, Adriaan

PROMENADE QUADRILLE see Strauss,
Johann, [Jr.]

PROMENADES: FANFARE see Godron, Hugo

PROMETEO see Caltabiano, Sebastiano

PROMETHEUS, FOR SOLO VOICE AND
ORCHESTRA see Wolf, Hugo

PROMETHEUS: OVERTURE see Beethoven,
Ludwig van, Geschopfe Des
Prometheus, Die: Overture

PROMISES OF DARKNESS, THE see Reynolds,
Roger

PROMOTIONEN WALZER see Strauss, Johann,
[Jr.]

PROMVARIATIES, VARIATIONS ON "THE
BRITISH GRENADIERS" see
Dirriwachter, Wim

PROPHETE, LE: AH, MON FILS, FOR SOLO
VOICE AND ORCHESTRA see Meyerbeer,
Giacomo

PROPHETE, LE: CORONATION MARCH see
Meyerbeer, Giacomo, Prophete, Le:
Marche Du Couronnement

PROPHETE, LE: MARCHE DU COURONNEMENT
see Meyerbeer, Giacomo

PROSPERI, CARLO (1921-   )
Concerto d'Infanzia, For Voice And
Orchestra [18']
4.3.4.2. 4.2.2.0. 2perc,xylo,cel,
pno,harp,strings,S solo
BRUZZI SV-003 perf mat rent (P214)

PROTO, FRANK (1941-   )
Bicentennial Fanfare
winds,perc,pno,harp,8db
LIBEN   (P215)

Concerto for Violoncello and
Orchestra
LIBEN   (P216)

Fanfare And Dance
LIBEN   (P217)

Four Seasons, The
tuba,perc,strings,electronic tape
LIBEN   (P218)

PROTO, FRANK (cont'd.)

Nocturne For Strings
string orch
LIBEN   (P219)

Overture To River Downs
LIBEN   (P220)

Portrait Of Stephen Foster, A
LIBEN   (P221)

Suite From The Opera "Carmen"
orch, jazz ensemble
LIBEN   (P222)

PROVENZALE, FRANCESCO (1627-1704)
Stellidaure Vendicata: Deh, Rendetemi
Ombre Care, For Solo Voice And
String Orchestra [5']
string orch,solo voice
manuscript CARISCH   (P223)

PROZESS-POLKA see Strauss, Johann,
[Jr.]

PRYOR, ARTHUR (1870-1942)
Whistler And His Dog, The
LUCKS 06421 set $9.00, pts $.75,
ea.   (P224)

PSALM AND FUGUE see Hovhaness, Alan

PSALM FOR STRING ORCHESTRA see Newman,
Theodore Simon

PSALM NO. 4 FOR SOLO VOICE AND
ORCHESTRA see Bettinelli, Bruno

PSALM NO. 5 see Beers, Jacques, Verba
Mea Auribus

PSALM NO. 23 see Beers, Jacques,
Dominus Regit Me

PSALM NO. 33 see Beers, Jacques,
Exultare Justi In Domino

PSALM NO. 100 see Bruhns, Nicholaus,
Jauchzet Dem Herrn Alle Welt, For
Solo Voice And String Orchestra

PSALM NO. 118 FOR SOLO VOICE AND
ORCHESTRA see Strategier, Herman

PSYCHE: 3. LES JARDINS D'EROS see
Franck, Cesar

PSYCHE: 4. PSYCHE ET EROS see Franck,
Cesar

PSYCHE: SUITE see Locke, Matthew

PUBLICISTEN, DIE. WALZER see Strauss,
Johann, [Jr.]

PUCCINI, GIACOMO (1858-1924)
Boheme, La: Addio Di Mimi, For Solo
Voice And Orchestra
LUCKS 03105 sc $3.75, set $7.50,
pts $.75, ea.   (P225)

Boheme, La: Che Gelida Manina, For
Solo Voice And Orchestra
LUCKS 02053 sc $3.00, set $7.00,
pts $.75, ea.   (P226)

Boheme, La: Mimi Tu Non Torni, For
Solo Voices And Orchestra
LUCKS 03635 sc $5.00, set $12.00,
pts $.75, ea.   (P227)

Boheme, La: Musetta's Waltz *see
Boheme, La: Quando Me'n Vo
Soletta, For Solo Voice And
Orchestra

Boheme, La: O Soave Fanciulla, For
Solo Voices And Orchestra
LUCKS 03068 sc $3.00, pts $8.50,
pts $.75, ea.   (P228)

Boheme, La: Quando Me'n Vo Soletta,
For Solo Voice And Orchestra
"Boheme, La: Musetta's Waltz" LUCKS
02054 sc $3.00, set $7.50, pts
$.75, ea.   (P229)

Boheme, La: Si, Mi Chiamano Mimi, For
Solo Voice And Orchestra
LUCKS 03067 sc $3.00, set $7.00,
pts $.75, ea.   (P230)

Boheme, La: Vecchia Zimarra, For Solo
Voice And Orchestra
LUCKS 03138 sc $3.00, set $7.50,
pts $.75, ea.   (P231)

Crisantemi
KALMUS A1117 sc $3.00, set $3.75,
pts $.75, ea.   (P232)

Manon Lescaut: In Quelle Trine
Morbide, For Solo Voice And
Orchestra
LUCKS 02075 sc $5.00, set $12.00,

PUCCINI, GIACOMO (cont'd.)

pts $.75, ea.   (P233)

Manon Lescaut: Intermezzo
KALMUS 5138 sc $5.00, perf mat
rent, set $15.00, pts $.75, ea.
                                (P234)

Manon Lescaut: Intermezzo, Act III
LUCKS 07520 sc $7.00, set $15.00,
pts $.75, ea.   (P235)

Manon Lescaut: Sola, Perduta,
Abbandonata, For Solo Voice And
Orchestra
LUCKS 03225 sc $7.00, set $12.00,
pts $.75, ea.   (P236)

Minuetto No. 1
string orch
KALMUS A1115 sc $3.00, set $3.75,
pts $.75, ea.
LUCKS 01498 sc $3.00, set $3.75,   (P237)
pts $.75, ea.   (P238)

Minuetto No. 2
string orch
KALMUS A1116 sc $3.00, set $3.75,
pts $.75, ea.   (P239)

Tosca: E Lucevan Le Stelle, For Solo
Voice And Orchestra
LUCKS 02776 sc $3.75, set $9.50,
pts $.75, ea.   (P240)

Tosca: Non La Sospiri La Nostra
Casetta, For Solo Voice And
Orchestra
LUCKS 02095 sc $4.00, set $10.00,
pts $.75, ea.   (P241)

Tosca: Recondita Armonia, For Solo
Voice And Orchestra
LUCKS 02076 sc $3.75, set $11.50,
pts $.75, ea.   (P242)

Tosca: Vissi D'Arte, For Solo Voice
And Orchestra
LUCKS 02775 sc $3.75, set $9.50,
pts $.75, ea.   (P243)

PUER NOBIS NASCITUR see Badings, Henk

PUGNI, CESARE (1802-1870)
Sinfonia Per Una O Due Orchestre And
Sinfonia In E
see NORTHERN ITALIAN SYMPHONY,
1800-1840, THE

PUISQUE L'AURE GRANDIT, FOR SOLO VOICE
AND ORCHESTRA see Diepenbrock,
Alphons

PULCINELLA: SUITE see Stravinsky, Igor

PULVERIZATION see Porcelijn, David

PULVERIZATION II, FOR SAXOPHONE AND
ORCHESTRA see Porcelijn, David

PUNCTUM CONTRA PUNCTUM see Sixta, Jozef

PUNCTUS CONTRA PUNCTUM, FOR SOLO VOICES
AND CHAMBER ORCHESTRA see
Tischhauser, Franz

PUPPEN-MENUETT see Blon, Franz von

PUPPENSPIELE, FOR PIANO AND ORCHESTRA
see Franko, Mladen

PURCELL, HENRY (1658 or 59-1695)
Dido And Aeneas: Farewell Of Dido,
[arr.]
(Rogers, Bernard) sets ACCURA
042, 043 $9.00, and up   (P244)

Dido And Aeneas: Overture, [arr.]
2.2.2.0. 0.2.0.0. perc,strings sc,
pts HARMONIA 2736 f.s.   (P245)

Dido And Aeneas: When I Am Laid In
Earth, For Solo Voice And String
Orchestra
LUCKS 02802 sc $2.00, set $3.00,
pts $.75, ea.   (P246)

Fairy Queen, The: Two Suites
string orch
KALMUS 5255 sc $4.00, set $5.00,
pts $1.00, ea.   (P247)

Fantasia On One Note
string orch
LUCKS 01504 sc $3.00, set $5.00,
pts $1.00, ea.   (P248)

Five Pieces, [arr.]
string orch KALMUS A4641 sc $3.00,
set $5.00, pts $1.00, ea.   (P249)

King Arthur: Suite No. 1, [arr.]
(Whittaker) string orch [15']
SCOTUS 485-X perf mat rent   (P250)

PURCELL, HENRY (cont'd.)

King Arthur: Suite No. 2, [arr.]
(Whittaker) string orch [15']
SCOTUS 495-7 perf mat rent (P251)

King Arthur: Suite No. 3, [arr.]
(Whittaker) string orch [15']
SCOTUS 401-9 perf mat rent (P252)

Midsummer Night's Dream, A:
Incidental Music, Vol. 1
string orch,cont
KALMUS A1118 sc $4.00, set $4.00,
pts $1.00, ea. (P253)

Midsummer Night's Dream, A:
Incidental Music, Vol. 2
string orch,cont
KALMUS A1119 sc $4.00, set $4.00,
pts $1.00, ea. (P254)

Three Pieces: Allemande, Sarabande,
Cebell
string orch
LUCKS 07801 sc $2.75, set $4.75,
pts $.95, ea. (P255)

Trumpet Prelude, [arr.]
(Luck) LUCKS 07236 sc $5.00, set
$10.50, pts $1.40, ea. (P256)

Trumpet Voluntary, [arr.]
(Westermann) 2+pic.2.2.2. 4.2.3.1.
timp,perc,strings KALMUS A1895 sc
$5.00, set $25.00, pts $1.50, ea.
(P257)

PURITANI, I: QUI LA VOCE; VIEN DILETTO,
FOR SOLO VOICE AND ORCHESTRA see
Bellini, Vincenzo

PURVIS, RICHARD
Piece Symphonique, For Organ And
Orchestra
timp,harp,strings,org solo
WORLD 2454 perf mat rent (P258)

PUSZTAI, TIBOR (1946-)
Folii III [11']
1(pic).1.1.1. 1.0.0.0. perc,pno,
strings
MARGUN BP 6002 perf mat rent (P259)

Requiem Profana, For Solo Voices And
Chamber Orchestra [13']
ob,clar,bsn,horn,trp,trom,perc,
harp,elec pno,pno,vln,vcl,db,
MezT soli
MARGUN BP 6010 perf mat rent (P260)

Three Pictures [7']
2.1.2.1. 2.2.2.1. perc,vibra,
strings
MARGUN BP 6001 perf mat rent (P261)

PUSZTASTIMMUNG see Pachernegg, Alois

PUTS see Blomberg, Erik

PYGMALION OVERTURE see Britain, Radie

PYLKKANEN, TAUNO KULLERVO (1918-)
Barcarolle *see Venhelaulu, For Solo
Voice And Orchestra

Kaivotiella, For Solo Voice And
Orchestra *Op.1,No.2 [5']
2.2.2.1. 2.2.1.0. timp,harp,
strings,solo voice
FAZER perf mat rent (P262)

Kuoleman Joutsen, For Solo Voice And
Orchestra *Op.21 [15']
2.2.3.2. 3.2.1.0. timp,perc,harp,
strings,solo voice
FAZER perf mat rent (P263)

Lintu, For Solo Voice And Orchestra
*Op.1,No.1 [3']
2.2.2.1. 2.0.0.0. harp,strings,
solo voice
FAZER perf mat rent (P264)

Maren Aaria, For Solo Voice And
Orchestra [3']
2.2.2.2. 4.3.3.1. timp,perc,
strings,S solo
FAZER perf mat rent (P265)

Tieda Muistatko Mua, En, For Solo
Voice And Orchestra [3']
2.1.2.1. 0.0.0.0. harp/pno,
strings,solo voice
FAZER perf mat rent (P266)

Venhelaulu, For Solo Voice And
Orchestra [3']
2.2.3.0. 2.0.0.0. harp,strings,
solo voice
"Barcarolle" FAZER perf mat rent
(P267)

Q

QUADRETTI INFANTILI see Toni, Alceo

QUADRIFOGLIO, FOR WOODWIND QUARTET AND
ORCHESTRA see Sutermeister,
Heinrich

QUADRILLE SUR DES AIRS FRANCAISE see
Strauss, Johann, [Jr.]

QUADRILLE UBER BELIEBTE MOTIVE AUS
AUBERS OPER "DES TEUFELS ANTEIL"
see Strauss, Johann, [Sr.]

QUADRO SONORO see Tocchi, Gian-Luca

QUAESTIO see Slangen, John

QUAL TURBINE IMPROVVISO, FOR SOLO VOICE
AND STRING ORCHESTRA see Marcello,
Benedetto

QUANDO LA ROSA NON HA PIU SPINE, FOR
SOLO VOICE AND ORCHESTRA see Haydn,
[Franz] Joseph

QUANTZ, JOHANN JOACHIM (1697-1773)
Concerto for Flute and String
Orchestra in G, MIN 27
string orch,cont,fl solo
(Augsbach) PETERS P9698 sc $23.50,
set $15.00, pts $3.00, ea. (Q1)

Concerto for Flute and String
Orchestra in G, MIN 829
LUCKS 00829 sc $6.00, set $7.50,
min sc $2.50, pts $1.60, ea. (Q2)

Concerto for Flute and String
Orchestra in G minor, MIN 28
string orch,cont,fl solo
(Burmeister) PETERS P9696 sc
$27.50, set $15.00, pts $3.00,
ea. (Q3)

QUARANTA, FELICE (1910-)
Concerto for Violin and Chamber
Orchestra [15']
1.1.1.1. 2.1.0.0. timp,strings,
vln solo
sc ZANIBON 5135 f.s., pts ZANIBON
5136 f.s. (Q4)

QUARTET: SLOW MOVEMENT, [ARR.] see
Borodin, Alexander Porfirievich,
Nocturne From String Quartet No. 2,
[arr.]

QUARTETS I-VIII, VERSION FOR 24 PLAYERS
see Cage, John

QUARTETS I-VIII, VERSION FOR 41 PLAYERS
see Cage, John

QUARTETS I-VIII, VERSION FOR 93 PLAYERS
see Cage, John

QUARTETTO PER UN VIOLINO SOLO, [ARR.]
see Bull, Ole Bornemann

QUASI IN MODO DI VALZER see Schuyt,
Nico

QUASI UNE SINFONIA see Stuppner, Hubert

QUATERNI see Vlijmen, Jan van

QUATRE BRAS, FOR CLARINET AND 4
QUARTETS see Smit, Sytze

QUATRE ETUDES see Stravinsky, Igor,
Four Etudes

QUATRE PAS DE DEUX, FOR FLUTE AND
ORCHESTRA see Kruyf, Ton de

QUATRE PIECES SYMPHONIQUES see Osterc,
Slavko

QUATTRO CANZONI POPOLARI see Pilati,
Mario

QUATTRO MOMENTI MUSICALI, FOR FLUTE AND
STRING ORCHESTRA see Dalla Vecchia,
Wolfango

QUATTRO PEZZI see Bossi, [Marco] Enrico

QUATTRO PEZZI PER ORCHESTRA see
Massimo, Leone

QUATTRO RUSTEGHI, I: PRELUDIO E
INTERMEZZO see Wolf-Ferrari,
Ermanno

QUATTRO STAGIONI, LE see Vivaldi,
Antonio

QUATTRO STAGIONI, LE see Vivaldi,
Antonio

QUEEN OF SHEBA, THE: BALLET MUSIC see
Goldmark, Karl, Konigin Von Saba,
Die: Ballet Music

QUEEN OF SPADES: I LOVE YOU, DEAR, FOR
SOLO VOICE AND ORCHESTRA see
Tchaikovsky, Piotr Ilyich

QUEEN'S LACE HANDKERCHIEF, THE:
OVERTURE see Strauss, Johann,
[Jr.], Spitzentuch Der Konigin,
Das: Overture

QUELLE, ERNST AUGUST (1931-)
Pop-Suite [9'30"]
1+alto fl.1.0.0. 3.2.2+bass
trom.0. timp,perc,harp,pno,gtr,
strings
ORLANDO rent (Q5)

QUELQUES ENFANTS QUELQUES SOLDATS...
see Ruyneman, Daniel

QUEMADMODUM see Jeney, Zoltan

QUIET ONE, THE: SUITE see Kay, Ulysses
Simpson

QUIETE MERIDIANA NELL'ALPE, LA, FOR
SOLO VOICE AND ORCHESTRA see
Sinigaglia, Leone

QUINTESSENCE, FOR WIND QUINTET AND
STRING ORCHESTRA see Hallberg,
Bengt

QUINTET CONCERTO, FOR BRASS QUINTET AND
ORCHESTRA see Kay, Ulysses Simpson

QUINTETS FOR ORCHESTRA see Foss, Lukas

QUINTUPLO FOR BRASS QUINTET AND
ORCHESTRA see Fennelley, Brian

QUODLIBET, OP. 9 see Weill, Kurt,
Zaubernacht, Op. 9: Orchestersuite

R

RACHMANINOFF, SERGEY VASSILIEVICH
(1873-1943)
Chanson Georgienne, For Solo Voice
And Orchestra, [arr.] *Op.4,No.4
(Leonardi) KALMUS 5444 sc $5.00,
perf mat rent, set $12.00, pts
$.60, ea.   (R1)

Concerto for Piano and Orchestra, No.
2, Op. 18, in C minor
BROUDE BR. set $47.50, pts $2.50,
ea.   (R2)

Prelude, Op. 3, No. 2, in C sharp
minor, [arr.]
KALMUS 5442 pno-cond sc $2.00, perf
mat rent, set $15.00, pts $.75,
ea.   (R3)

Rapsodie Sur Un Theme De Paganini For
Piano And Orchestra *Op.43
sc KALMUS A7007 $42.00   (R4)

Symphonic Dances, Op. 45
sc KALMUS A7006 $50.00   (R5)

Symphony No. 1, Op. 13 [40']
3.2.2.2. 4.3.3.1. timp,perc,
strings
KALMUS 5182 sc $25.00, perf mat
rent, set $125.00, pts $6.00, ea.
(R6)

Symphony No. 3, Op. 44, in A minor
sc KALMUS A7001 $70.00   (R7)

Vocalise, For Solo Voice And String
Orchestra, [arr.] *Op.34,No.14
(Braden) string orch,S solo KALMUS
5445 sc $3.00, set $7.00, pts
$1.00, ea.   (R8)

Vocalise, [arr.]
LUCKS 03229 set $10.50, pts $.75,
ea.   (R9)

RADAMISTO: ARIA DI POLISSENA, FOR SOLO
VOICE AND ORCHESTRA see Handel,
George Frideric

RADETZKY MARSCH see Strauss, Johann,
[Sr.]

RADICA, RUBEN (1931-   )
Concerto Abbreviato
3.3.3.3.2sax. 4.3.3.1. timp,perc,
xylo,cel,harp,pno,vcl solo
DRUS.HRVAT.SKLAD. f.s.   (R10)

RAGA DI NOTTE, FOR VIOLIN AND ORCHESTRA
see Ranki, Gyorgy

RAGNI, GUIDO (1899-1968)
Concerto for Violin and Orchestra
[25']
2.2.2.2. 4.2.3.0. timp,strings,
vln solo
manuscript CARISCH   (R11)

RAGNO SALTIMBANCO, IL, FOR SOLO VOICE
AND ORCHESTRA see Sabino, A.

RAGTIME, FOR ELEVEN INSTRUMENTS see
Stravinsky, Igor

RAGTIME NIGHTINGALE, [ARR.] see Lamb,
Joseph F.

RAIN, THE see David, Adolphe Isaac,
Pluie, La

RAMEAU, JEAN-PHILIPPE (1683-1764)
Ballet Suite, [arr.]
(Mottl) LUCKS 06436 sc $14.00, set
$24.00, pts $1.75, ea.   (R12)
(Mottl) 2(pic).2.2(English horn).2.
2.2.0.0. timp,perc,strings BROUDE
BR. study sc $6.00, set $27.50,
pts $2.00, ea.   (R13)

Guirlande, La
(Beck, G.; Lesure, F.) sc LEDUC
f.s., perf mat rent   (R14)

Indes Galantes, Les: Overture, [arr.]
1.1.1.0. 0.1.0.0. harp/pno,strings
without vla sc,pts HARMONIA 2657
f.s.   (R15)

RAMIREZ, LUIS ANTONIO (1923-   )
Fragmentos
3.3.3.2. 4.3.3.1. 4perc,pno,harp,
strings
SEESAW perf mat rent   (R16)

RAMOVS, PRIMOZ (1921-   )
Chorale And Toccata *see Koral In
Tokata

RAMOVS, PRIMOZ (cont'd.)
Concertino for Trumpet and Orchestra
[12']
2.0.2.2. 2.0.0.0. strings,trp
solo
DRUSTVO DSS 779 perf mat rent (R17)

Concerto for Piano and Orchestra
[23']
2(pic).2.2.2(contrabsn). 4.3.3.1.
timp,strings,pno solo
DRUSTVO DSS 880 perf mat rent (R18)

Concerto for 2 Pianos and Orchestra
[20']
DRUSTVO DSS 881 perf mat rent (R19)

Concerto for Tuba and Orchestra [10']
2.0.2.0. 0.2.2.0. timp,2perc,
strings,tuba solo
DRUSTVO DSS 882 perf mat rent (R20)

Koncertantna Glasba, For Timpani And
Orchestra [12']
2.2.2.2. 2.2.0.0. harp,timp
"Musique Concertante, For Timpani
And Orchestra" DRUSTVO DSS 884
perf mat rent   (R21)

Koral In Tokata [18']
2(pic).2(English horn).2(bass
clar).2(contrabsn).alto sax.
4.3.3.1. timp,4perc,strings
"Chorale And Toccata" DRUSTVO
DSS 879 perf mat rent   (R22)

Musique Concertante, For Timpani And
Orchestra *see Koncertantna
Glasba, For Timpani And Orchestra

Nocturne [9']
1.1.1.0. 0.0.0.0. strings
DRUSTVO DSS 885 perf mat rent (R23)

Pentagon [16']
pic,English horn,clar in E flat,
bass clar,3trp,3trom,tuba,timp,
5perc,strings
DRUSTVO DSS 883 perf mat rent (R24)

Sedem Skladb, For String Orchestra
[17']
string orch
"Seven Pieces, For String
Orchestra" DRUSTVO DSS 887 perf
mat rent   (R25)

Seven Pieces, For String Orchestra
*see Sedem Skladb, For String
Orchestra

Symphony No. 3 [42']
2(pic).2(English horn).2(bass
clar).2(contrabsn). 4.3.3.1.
timp,4perc,strings
DRUSTVO DSS 878 perf mat rent (R26)

Transformacije, For 2 Violas And
Strings [9']
10strings,2vla soli
"Transformations, For 2 Violas And
Strings" DRUSTVO DSS 886 perf mat
rent   (R27)

Transformations, For 2 Violas And
Strings *see Transformacije, For
2 Violas And Strings

RAMSIER, PAUL (1927-   )
Road To Hamelin, For Double Bass,
Narrator And Orchestra [16']
1.1.1.1. 1.1.0.0. perc,xylo,opt
harp,pno,strings,db solo,
narrator
BOOSEY perf mat rent   (R28)

RANA E IL ROSPO, LA, FOR SOLO VOICE AND
STRING ORCHESTRA see Sinigaglia,
Leone

RANDOM OR NOT RANDOM see Evangelisti,
Franco

RANDS, BERNARD (1935-   )
Mesalliance, For Piano And
Instrumental Ensemble [15']
1+alto fl.0.1+bass clar.0.
0.3.3.0. 2perc,vibra,marimba,
harp,cel,elec org,2vcl,db,pno
solo
sc UNIVER. 50 15482 $45.00   (R29)

Serenata 75b, For Flute And
Instrumental Ensemble [22']
clar,perc,cel,pno,elec pno,elec
org,strings,fl solo
sc UNIVER. UE 16103 f.s., perf mat
rent   (R30)

RANKI, GYORGY (1907-   )
Raga Di Notte, For Violin And
Orchestra
orch,vln solo
(special import only) sc EMB 8128
f.s.   (R31)

RANNOCH-CONCERTO, FOR HORN AND
ORCHESTRA see Furst, Paul Walter

RAPALO, UGO (1914-   )
Burlesca [7']
3.3.3.3. 4.3.3.1. perc,2harp,
strings
manuscript CARISCH   (R32)

RAPF, KURT (1922-   )
Concerto No. 2 *see Contrasts

Contrasts (Concerto No. 2) [8'30"]
2.1+English horn.2(bass
clar).2(contrabsn). 2.2.0.0.
perc,cel,glock,harp,strings
sc,pts DOBLINGER rent   (R33)

RAPHAEL, GUNTHER (1903-1960)
Symphonische Fantasie, For Violin And
Strings, Op. 59
3vln,3vla,3vcl,2db,vln solo
[20'] MULLER   (R34)

Symphony, Op. 60, in F
3.3.3.3. 4.4.4.1. timp,perc,harp,
strings
[45'] MULLER   (R35)

RAPPORTS 3, FOR PIANO, PERCUSSION AND
ORCHESTRA see Mestral, Patrice

RAPSODIA EPICA see Pick-Mangiagalli,
Riccardo

RAPSODICKE VARIACIE see Mikula, Zdenko

RAPSODIE CAMBODGIENNE see Bourgault-
Ducoudray, Louis-Albert

RAPSODIE CARTESIENNE see Barraud, Henry

RAPSODIE DIONYSIENNE see Barraud, Henry

RAPSODIE SUR UN THEME DE PAGANINI FOR
PIANO AND ORCHESTRA see
Rachmaninoff, Sergey Vassilievich

RASPONI, GIUSEPPE
Spagnoletta
see RICREAZIONI DI ANTICHE MUSICHE
CLASSICHE, SERIE II: MUSICHE
ANTICHE ITALIANE

RATHAUSBALL TANZE. WALZER see Strauss,
Johann, [Jr.]

RATIU, HORIA
Altitudes [15']
2(2pic).1.1(bass
clar).0(contrabsn). 1.1.1.0.
2perc,2vln,vla,vcl,db
SALABERT perf mat rent   (R36)

RATTENFANGER, DER, FOR SOLO VOICE AND
ORCHESTRA see Wolf, Hugo

RAUMBLOCKE see Jorns, Helge

RAUTAVAARA, EINOJUHANI (1928-   )
Concerto for Flute and Orchestra, Op.
69
0.0.0.2+contrabsn. 3.3.0.0. timp,
perc,harp,strings,fl solo
study sc BREITKOPF-W PB 5052 f.s.,
perf mat rent   (R37)

Concerto for Piano and Orchestra, Op.
45
2.0.2.0. 4.2.2.0. timp,perc,
strings,pno solo
study sc BREITKOPF-W PB 4860 f.s.,
perf mat rent   (R38)

RAVANELLO, ORESTE (1871-1938)
Andante *Op.118,No.2 [3']
string orch,opt org
sc ZANIBON 372 f.s., pts ZANIBON
372A f.s.   (R39)

Canto Mistico *Op.119,No.1 [4']
string orch,org
sc ZANIBON 371 f.s., pts ZANIBON
371A f.s.   (R40)

Due Pezzi *Op.11 [5']
string orch
sc ZANIBON 91 f.s., pts ZANIBON 92
f.s.   (R41)

Elegy [4']
string orch,opt org
sc ZANIBON 1416 f.s., pts ZANIBON
2060 f.s.   (R42)

RAVISHING SUMMER see Skerl, Dane,
Opojno Poletje

RAXACH, ENRIQUE (1932-   )
Ad Marginem, For Flute, Violin,
Viola, And Orchestra [14']
0.0.1.2. 4.3.3.0. timp,3perc,pno/
cel,harp,strings,fl solo,vln
solo,vla solo
sc DONEMUS f.s., perf mat rent
(R43)

RAXACH, ENRIQUE (cont'd.)

Am Ende Des Regenboges [25']
4.4.4.4. 4.4.4.1. timp,3perc,
strings
DONEMUS   (R44)

Erdenlicht [17']
2.2.2.2. 4.2.3.1. timp,2perc,
strings
DONEMUS perf mat rent   (R45)

Figuren In Einer Landschaft [23']
4.3.3.3. 4.4.4.1. timp,4perc,
harp,pno/cel,strings
DONEMUS perf mat rent   (R46)

Metamorphose I [27']
3.3.3.3. 4.3.3.1. timp,3perc,
harp,strings
DONEMUS perf mat rent   (R47)

Sine Nomine, For Solo Voice And
Orchestra [23']
2.2.2.2.alto sax. 2.2.2.0. 2perc,
harp,Hamm,hpsd,elec gtr,mand,
strings,S solo,opt pno/
synthesizer
sc DONEMUS f.s., perf mat rent
                                    (R48)

RE see Ruiter, Wim de

RE PASTORE, IL: L'AMERO, SARO COSTANTE,
FOR SOLO VOICE AND ORCHESTRA see
Mozart, Wolfgang Amadeus

RE PASTORE, IL: OVERTURE see Mozart,
Wolfgang Amadeus

REBECCA: SUITE see Waxman, Franz

REBELLE, LE, FOR SOLO VOICE AND
ORCHESTRA see Emmer, Huib

RECANTATION, FOR SOLO VOICE AND
ORCHESTRA see Nelson, Bradley

RECHBERGER, HERMANN (1947-   )
Consort Music 1 [20']
trom,perc,hpsd,strings,rec solo
sc JASE $18.00   (R49)

Consort Music 2 [20']
2trp,2trom,2perc,strings, 2
Renaissance instruments soli
sc JASE $35.00   (R50)

RECITAL see Ferrari, Giorgio

RECITATIVE AND RONDO, FOR ENGLISH HORN
AND ORCHESTRA see Reicha, Anton

RECITATIVE, ARIA AND FINALE see La
Montaine, John

RECITATIVES AND ARIAS, FOR PIANO AND
ORCHESTRA see Ruders, Poul

RECORD see Tocchi, Gian-Luca

RECORDERS, FOR RECORDER AND ORCHESTRA
see Bank, Jacques

RECUEILLEMENT, FOR SOLO VOICE AND
ORCHESTRA see Diepenbrock, Alphons

RED MILL, THE: SELECTIONS see Herbert,
Victor

RED MILL, THE: SELECTIONS see Herbert,
Victor

RED POPPY, THE: RUSSIAN SAILORS' DANCE
see Gliere, Reinhold Moritzovich

RED POPPY, THE: SUITE see Gliere,
Reinhold Moritzovich

REDEL, MARTIN CHRISTOPH (1947-   )
Concerto for Orchestra, Op. 27
sc BOTE $68.00   (R51)

REDEMPTION: MORCEAU SYMPHONIQUE NO. 5
see Franck, Cesar

REDNER, LEWIS [HENRY] (1831-1908)
O Little Town Of Bethlehem
see Gruber, Franz Xaver, Silent
Night

REDUNDANZ 3 see Horvath, Josef Maria

REED, ALFRED (1921-   )
Siciliana Notturno
string orch
sc MARKS MSO 16 $3.00, set MARKS
$15.00, pts MARKS $1.00, ea.
                                    (R52)
Suite Concertante
harp,strings
KALMUS 5028 sc $15.00, set $15.00
                                    (R53)

REFLECTED REALITIES see Farberman,
Harold

REFLECTION see Hojsgaard, Erik

REFLECTIONS see Svoboda, Tomas

REFLECTIONS see Vantus, I.

REFORMATION SYMPHONY see Mendelssohn-
Bartholdy, Felix, Symphony No. 5,
Op. 107, in D minor

REICHA, ANTON (1770-1836)
Recitative And Rondo, For English
Horn And Orchestra
MCGIN-MARX perf mat rent   (R54)

REICHA, JOSEPH (1746-1795)
Concerto for Violoncello and String
Orchestra in E
string orch,vcl solo
(Jerie, Marek) SCHOTTS CON 187 sc
$17.50, pts $3.50, ea.   (R55)

Symphony in D
see SEVEN SYMPHONIES FROM THE COURT
OF OETTINGEN-WALLERSTEIN (1773-
1795)

REICHEL, GERD
Goldrausch °see Elfers, Konrad

REIF, PAUL (1910-1978)
America 1776-1876-1976
2.2.2.2. 2.2.3.0. timp,perc,gtr,
strings
SEESAW perf mat rent   (R56)

REINBERGER, KARL (1933-   )
Im Gegenteil [9']
2(pic).2(English horn).2(bass
clar).1(contrabsn). 3.2.1.0+db
tuba. 4perc,vibra,xylorimba,
elec gtr,vln,vla,3db, electric
bass guitar
UNIVER. perf mat rent   (R57)

REINE, LA, SYMPHONY see Haydn, [Franz]
Joseph, Symphony No. 85 in B flat

REINL, FRANZ (1903-   )
Mixtum Compositum [14']
2.2(English horn).2.2. 2.2.0.0.
timp,perc,cel,harp,gtr,strings
sc RIES f.s., perf mat rent   (R58)

REISE NACH VENEDIG, DIE see Walter,
Fried

REISESTIMMUNG see Kess, Ludwig

REISSIGER, KARL GOTTLIEB (1798-1859)
Felsenmuhle, Die: Overture
BREITKOPF-W perf mat rent   (R59)

Solo for Horn and Orchestra in F
orch,horn solo
(Janetzky) PETERS perf mat rent
                                    (R60)

REIZENSTEIN, FRANZ (1911-1968)
Serenade in F
sc BOOSEY $25.00   (R61)

REKOLA, JUKKA (1948-   )
Jubilus Sonus [15']
string orch
STIM   (R62)

Legendes °Op.7 [20']
string orch
sc STIM perf mat rent   (R63)

Lhasa (Symphony No. 3, Op. 8) [24']
4.4.4.4. 6.4.3.1. timp,2perc,
harp,cel,strings
sc STIM   (R64)

Symphony No. 2 [42']
3.3.3.3. 4.3.3.2. timp,2perc,
harp,strings
sc STIM perf mat rent   (R65)

Symphony No. 3, Op. 8 °see Lhasa

RELIEF see Giefer, Willy

REMBRANDT SYMFONIE see Meulemans,
Arthur, Symphony No. 13

REMBRANDT'S "SAUL EN DAVID", FOR SOLO
VOICE AND ORCHESTRA see Dresden,
Sem

REMEMBRANCE see Ives, Charles

REMINISCENTIE III see Voortman, Roland

RENGA see Cage, John

RENNFIEBER see Helm, Josef

RENNQVIST, KARIN (1957-   )
Strak [10']
string orch
STIM   (R66)

RENOSTO, PAOLO (1935-   )
Gesta
6vln,2vla,2vcl,db
RICORDI-IT 132394 f.s.   (R67)

RENZI, ARMANDO
Adagio E Rondo Variato, For Piano And
Orchestra [19']
2+pic.2.2+bass clar.2+contrabsn.
4.2.3.1. timp,perc,glock,cel,
xylo,strings,pno solo
sc ZANIBON 4236 rent, pts ZANIBON
4237 rent   (R68)

Nuvole E Colori, For Solo Voice And
Orchestra [16']
2.2.2.2. 3.2.2.0. timp,2perc,cel,
pno,harp,harmonica,strings,S/T
solo
sc,pts ZANIBON 4216 rent   (R69)

REPUBLIQUE ARGENTINE-- LA PLATA see
Escher, Rudolf George

REQUIEM see Popper, David

REQUIEM FOR ORCHESTRA see Malipiero,
Riccardo

REQUIEM PROFANA, FOR SOLO VOICES AND
CHAMBER ORCHESTRA see Pusztai,
Tibor

RESONANCE see Holler, York

RESPONSO see Matthus, Siegfried

REST IS DROSS, THE see Sandstrom, Sven-
David

RETTUNG DER ANDROMEDA DURCH PERSEUS,
DIE see Dittersdorf, Karl Ditters
von, Sinfonia in F, Krebs 76

RETURN OF ULYSSES, THE see Skalkottas,
Nikos, Symphony in One Movement

REUNIONS GALOP see Lumbye, Hans
Christian

REUTER, FRITZ (1896-1963)
Concerto for Organ and String
Orchestra, Op. 32 [20']
string orch,org solo
RIES perf mat rent   (R70)

Kleine Festmusik [10']
2.2.2.2. 3.3.1.0. 2perc,strings
RIES perf mat rent   (R71)

REVELATION AND FALL, FOR SOLO VOICE AND
ORCHESTRA see Davies, Peter Maxwell

REVERIE see Boisdeffre, Charles-Henri-
Rene de

REVERIE see Scriabin, Alexander

REVERIE ET CAPRICE, FOR VIOLIN AND
ORCHESTRA see Berlioz, Hector
(Louis)

REVERIES HEROIQUES DE MME. DE MECK, LES
see Kiesewetter, Peter

REVOLUTIONARY SYMPHONY see Valek, Jiri,
Symphony No. 9

REYNOLDS, ROGER (1934-   )
Fiery Wind [15']
3(2pic).2(English
horn).2.2(contrabsn). 3.3.3.1.
4perc,pno,strings
sc PETERS P66765 $11.00, perf mat
rent   (R72)

Promises Of Darkness, The [22']
1.0.1.1. 1.1.1.0. perc,pno,vln,
vcl,db
sc PETERS P66655 $23.50, perf mat
rent   (R73)

REZNICEK, EMIL NIKOLAUS VON (1860-1945)
Donna Diana: Overture
min sc UNIVER. PH159 $7.75   (R74)

Lustspiel-Ouverture [10']
3(pic).2.2.2. 4.2.0.0. timp,
strings
RIES perf mat rent   (R75)
KALMUS A4652 sc $12.00, perf mat
rent, set $26.00, pts $1.50, ea.
                                    (R76)

Symphonische Suite In D [20']
3(pic).2.2.2+contrabsn. 4.2.3.0.
timp,strings
RIES perf mat rent   (R77)

Symphonische Suite In E Minor [25']
3(pic).2.2.2. 4.2.3.1. timp,perc,
strings
KALMUS 5259 sc $30.00, perf mat
rent, set $60.00, pts $2.50, ea.
                                    (R78)

REZNICEK, EMIL NIKOLAUS VON (cont'd.)

Tanz-Symphonie
3(pic).2+English horn.2+bass
clar.2+contrabsn. 4.3.3.1.
timp,perc,harp,cel,strings
KALMUS 5183 sc $30.00, perf mat
rent, set $100.00, pts $4.00, ea.
(R79)

RHAPSODIE CATALAN see Ailbout, Hans

RHAPSODIE HONGROISE NO. 2, [ARR.] see
Liszt, Franz

RHAPSODIE HONGROISE NO. 3, [ARR.] see
Liszt, Franz

RHAPSODIE HONGROISE NO. 5, FOR PIANO
AND ORCHESTRA, [ARR.] see Liszt,
Franz

RHAPSODIE HONGROISE NO. 11, [ARR.] see
Liszt, Franz

RHAPSODIE HONGROISE NO. 13, [ARR.] see
Liszt, Franz

RHAPSODIE NO. 2 see Rixner, Josef

RHAPSODISCHE SINFONIE see Juon, Paul

RHAPSODY BASED ON FOLK SONG FROM
OKINAWA see Toyama, Yuzo

RHEINBERGER, JOSEF (1839-1901)
Suite, Op. 149
string orch,vln solo,vcl solo,org
solo
KALMUS A4653 sc $12.00, perf mat
rent, set $19.00, pts $1.25, ea.
(R80)

RHINOW, H.J.
Cabo Raso-Gut So
RIES f.s. (R81)

RHODES, PHILLIP (1940-   )
Divertimento [12']
fl,trp,horn,bsn,strings
PETERS P66776 perf mat rent (R82)

RHYTHMIC IMPRESSIONS see Vrabec, Ubalo,
Ritmicne Impresije

RHYTHMISCHE OUVERTURE see Bruchmann,
Klaus Peter

RIBARI, ANTAL (1924-   )
Sinfonia No. 3
(special import only) sc EMB 10196
f.s. (R83)

RIBEIRO, AGNALDO (1943-   )
Korpus Et Antikorpus [14']
1(pic).0.1.1. 1.1.0.0. 2perc,pno,
2vln,vla,vcl,db
BREITKOPF-W perf mat rent (R84)

RICCI SIGNORINI, ANTONIO (1867-1965)
Canzone d'Estate, For Violin And
Orchestra [6']
2.2.2.2. 2.2.0.0. timp,harp,
bells,strings,vln solo
manuscript CARISCH (R85)

Due Canti, For Violin And Orchestra
[8']
2.2.2.2. 2.2.0.0. timp,harp,org,
strings,vln solo
manuscript CARISCH (R86)

Due Impressioni
string orch,2harp
manuscript CARISCH (R87)

Due Momenti Intimi, For Violoncello
And Orchestra
2.2.2.2. 2.0.0.0. timp,harp,
strings,vcl solo
manuscript CARISCH (R88)

Finale Farsesco [6']
3.2.2.2.sax. 4.2.3.1. timp,perc,
harp,xylo,strings
sc CARISCH f.s., perf mat rent
(R89)

Ouverture Giocosa [7']
3.2.2.3. 4.3.3.1. timp,perc,
strings
sc CARISCH 15765 perf mat rent
(R90)

Papiol [6']
4.2.2.3. 4.3.3.1. timp,perc,
strings
sc CARISCH 12549 perf mat rent
(R91)

Tre Pezzi Poetica [12']
string orch
sc CARISCH 14217 rent, pts CARISCH
14218 f.s. (R92)

RICE, THOMAS
Genesis
2.2.2.1. 2.2.0.0. perc,
synthesizer,strings
SEESAW perf mat rent (R93)

RICE, THOMAS (cont'd.)

Three Overtures (Toccata-Festival-
Pastoral)
2.2.2.2. 4.2.2.0. timp,2perc,
strings
SEESAW perf mat rent (R94)

RICERCAR E GIGA, FOR ORGAN AND STRING
ORCHESTRA see Pluister, Simon

RICERCARE see Chailly, Luciano

RICERCARI see Bettinelli, Bruno

RICERCARI see Harper, Edward

RICHARTZ, WILLY (1900-1972)
Zu Jeder Lederhos'n
RIES f.s. (R95)

RICHTER, FRANZ XAVER (1709-1789)
Concerto for Trumpet and String
Orchestra, MIN 105
string orch,hpsd,trp solo
(Munster, Robert) sc MULLER 2021
f.s. (R96)

Sinfonia, MIN 88
2.2.2.0. 0.2.0.0. strings
sc,pts HARMONIA 2431 f.s. (R97)

RICHTER-CAROLI, WOLFGANG (1948-   )
Suite for String Orchestra [13']
string orch
BREITKOPF-W perf mat rent (R98)

RICOMPOSIZIONE see Benvenuti, Arrigo

RICREAZIONI DI ANTICHE MUSICHE
CLASSICHE, SERIE I: MUSICHE ANTICHE
ITALIANE
(Bossi, Renzo) string orch sc CARISCH
16873 f.s., pts CARISCH 16873A f.s.
contains: Aria Fiamminga; Minuetto;
Francesco da Milano, Canzone
Degli Uccelli, La; Pollarolo,
Carlo Francesco, Fughetta;
Zipoli, Domenico, Elevazione
(R99)

RICREAZIONI DI ANTICHE MUSICHE
CLASSICHE, SERIE II: MUSICHE
ANTICHE ITALIANE
(Bossi, Renzo) string orch sc CARISCH
18896 f.s., pts CARISCH 19163 f.s.
contains: Barbetta Padovano, Julio
Cesare, Pavana; Frescobaldi,
Girolamo, Toccata Per La
Elevazione; Martini, [Padre]
Giovanni Battista, Aria Variata;
Merula, Tarquino, Sonata
Cromatica; Rasponi, Giuseppe,
Spagnoletta; Scarlatti, Domenico,
Sonata (R100)

RICREAZIONI DI ANTICHE MUSICHE
CLASSICHE, SERIE III: MUSICHE
ANTICHE ITALIANE
(Bossi, Renzo) string orch sc CARISCH
20157 f.s., pts CARISCH 20379 f.s.
contains: Arcadelt, Jacob, Ave
Maria; Bach, Johann Sebastian,
Fugue in C; Bach, Johann
Sebastian, Sinfonia No. 9;
Buxtehude, Dietrich, Fughetta;
Couperin, Francois (le Grand),
Soeur Monique Rondo; Handel,
George Frideric, Aria E Finale
(R101)

RICREAZIONI DI ANTICHE MUSICHE
CLASSICHE, SERIE IV: MUSICHE
ANTICHE ITALIANE
(Bossi, Renzo) string orch sc CARISCH
20320 f.s., pts CARISCH 20388 f.s.
contains: Bossi, [Marco] Enrico,
Angelus (from Op. 118, No. 4);
Bossi, [Marco] Enrico, Fatemi La
Grazia; Bossi, [Marco] Enrico,
Fughetta (from Op. 118, No. 2);
Henselt, Adolph von, Ave Maria
(from Op. 5); Mussorgsky, Modest
Petrovich, Cicaleccio Del
Mercato; Schumann, Robert
(Alexander), Canone I; Schumann,
Robert (Alexander), Canone II;
Wagner, Richard, Due Canti;
Weber, Carl Maria von, Momento
Capriccioso (from Op. 12) (R102)

RICREAZIONI DI ANTICHE MUSICHE
CLASSICHE, SERIE V: MUSICHE ANTICHE
ITALIANE
(Bossi, Renzo) string orch sc CARISCH
21339 rent, pts CARISCH 21340 rent
contains: Bach, Johann Sebastian,
Fughetta Sopra "Queste Sole Dieci
Sante Preci"; Caccini, Giulio,
Amarilli; Frescobaldi, Girolamo,
Canzona; Frescobaldi, Girolamo,
Fugue; Monteverdi, Claudio,
Lamento d'Arianna; Palafuti,
Elevazione; Pescetti, Giovanni
Battista, Sonata; Porpora, Nicola
Antonio, Introduzione E Fuga;
Scarlatti, Domenico, Fuga Del
Gatto (R103)

RICREAZIONI DI ANTICHE MUSICHE
CLASSICHE, SERIE VI: MUSICHE
ANTICHE ITALIANE see Bossi, [Marco]
Enrico

RID I NATT see Eyser, Eberhard

RIDDERSTROM, BO (1937-   )
Notes 12-78 [7']
1.1.1.1. 1.1.0.0. 2perc,2vln,vla,
vcl,db
sc,pts STIM perf mat rent (R104)

RIDOUT, ALAN (1934-   )
Concerto for Flute and Orchestra
[16']
0.2.2.2. 4.2.3.0. timp,2perc,pno,
strings,fl solo
SCOTUS 244-X f.s. (R105)

Elegiac Waltz [4']
fl,strings
SCOTUS 075-7 f.s. (R106)

Some Animals Noah Forgot, For
Narrator And Orchestra
fl,clar,horn,strings,narrator
sc,pts SCOTUS 249-0 f.s. (R107)

RIEDEL, GEORG (1934-   )
Concerto Burlesco, For Alto
Saxophone, Jazz Group And
Orchestra [18']
2.2.2.2. 4.2.2.1. timp,perc,
strings,alto sax solo, jazz
group
pts STIM (R108)

RIEDER, AMBROSIUS
Ave Maria, For Solo Voice And
Orchestra *Op.153
2horn,org,strings,S/T solo
pts LIENAU (R109)

Domine Meus Salutis Meae, For Solo
Voice And Orchestra *Op.122
2horn,org,strings,S/T solo,vln
solo
pts LIENAU (R110)

RIEGE, ERNST (1885-1976)
Burleske [10']
2(pic).2.3.2.opt contrabsn.
4.3.3.1. timp,perc,harp,opt
cel,strings
RIES perf mat rent (R111)

RIEMSDIJK, JOHAN CORNELIUS MARIUS VAN
(1841-1895)
Old Dutch Suite
2.1.2.0. 0.1.0.0. perc,strings
without vla
sc,pts HARMONIA 1838 f.s. (R112)

RIENZI: FINALE, ACT III see Wagner,
Richard

RIENZI: FRIEDENSMARSCH see Wagner,
Richard

RIENZI: OVERTURE see Wagner, Richard

RIES, FERDINAND (1784-1838)
Symphonies, Three
(Hill, Cecil) sc GARLAND
ISBN 0-8240-3817-7 $90.00 "The
Symphony", Vol. C-XII
contains: Symphony No. 1, Op. 23,
in D; Symphony No. 2, Op. 80,
in C minor; Symphony No. 7, Op.
181, in A minor (R113)

Symphony No. 1, Op. 23, in D
see Symphonies, Three

Symphony No. 2, Op. 80, in C minor
see Symphonies, Three

Symphony No. 7, Op. 181, in A minor
see Symphonies, Three

RIES, FRANZ (1846-1932)
Am Rhein, Am Deutschen Rhein, For
Solo Voice And Orchestra *Op.35
[7']
2.1.2.1. 2.2.3.0. timp,glock,
strings,solo voice
RIES perf mat rent (R114)

Bourree Und Gondoliera, For Violin
And Orchestra, [arr.]
(Dressel, Erwin) 2.2.2.2. 2.2.0.0.
timp,strings,vln solo [7'] sc
RIES f.s., perf mat rent (R115)

Capricciosa, La, For Violin And
Orchestra [5']
2.2.2.2. 2.2.0.0. timp,perc,
strings,vln solo
RIES perf mat rent (R116)

Gondoliera
see Crucius, Heinz, Elegie

RIES, FRANZ (cont'd.)

Perpetuum Mobile, For Violin And
Orchestra *Op.34,No.5 [5']
2(pic).2.2.2. 2.0.0.0. strings,
vln solo
RIES perf mat rent   (R117)

Wiegenlied, For Solo Voice And
Orchestra *Op.33,No.4 [5']
2.2.2.2. 2.0.0.0. timp,strings,
solo voice
RIES perf mat rent   (R118)

RIETZ, JOHANNES (1905-   )
Mysterion, For English Horn And
String Orchestra
string orch,English horn solo
TONOS   (R119)

RIETZ, JULIUS (1812-1877)
Konzertstuck for Oboe and Orchestra,
Op. 33
MUS. RARA 41.829 perf mat rent
                            (R120)

RIFUGIO, IL, FOR SOLO VOICE AND
ORCHESTRA see Sinigaglia, Leone

RIGACCI, BRUNO (1921-
Sciofar, For Solo Voice And Orchestra
[18']
3.2.2.2. 4.3.3.1. timp,perc,harp,
pno,strings,speaking voice
manuscript CARISCH   (R121)

RIGOLETTO: CARO NOME, FOR SOLO VOICE
AND ORCHESTRA see Verdi, Giuseppe

RIGOLETTO: CORTIGIANI, VIL RAZZA
DANNATA, FOR SOLO VOICE AND
ORCHESTRA see Verdi, Giuseppe

RIGOLETTO: LA DONNA E MOBILE, FOR SOLO
VOICE AND ORCHESTRA see Verdi,
Giuseppe

RIGOLETTO: PARLA SIAM - TUTTE LE FESTE
AL TEMPIO, FOR SOLO VOICES AND
ORCHESTRA see Verdi, Giuseppe

RIGOLETTO: PARMI VEDER LE LAGRIME, FOR
SOLO VOICE AND ORCHESTRA see Verdi,
Giuseppe

RIGOLETTO: PRELUDIO see Verdi, Giuseppe

RIGOLETTO: QUESTA O QUELLA, FOR SOLO
VOICE AND ORCHESTRA see Verdi,
Giuseppe

RIGOLETTO: SIGNOR NE PRINCIPE: E IL SOL
DELL' ANIMA, FOR SOLO VOICE AND
ORCHESTRA see Verdi, Giuseppe

RIHM, WOLFGANG (1952-   )
Cuts And Dissolves [20']
2.2.2(bass clar).2(contrabsn).
2.2.2.1. 3perc,harp,pno,3vln,
2vla,2vcl,2db
UNIVER. perf mat rent   (R122)

Holderlin-Fragmente, For Solo Voice
And Orchestra [10']
1(pic,alto fl).1+English horn.1+
bass clar.1+contrabsn.tenor
sax. 2.1.1.1. timp,perc,harp,
pno,8vln,4vla,4vcl,4db,solo
voice
sc UNIVER. UE 16771 f.s., perf mat
rent   (R123)

Konzertarie, For Solo Voice And
Orchestra [17']
4.3.3.3. 4.3.3.1. timp,4-5perc,
harp,strings,Mez solo
UNIVER. perf mat rent   (R124)

Lichtzwang, For Violin And Orchestra
[17']
4(pic).0.4.4. 4.2+bass trp.2.1.
timp,5perc,harp,10vla,8vcl,6db,
vln solo
sc UNIVER. UE 15058 $12.50, perf
mat rent   (R125)

Musique Creuse Le Ciel, La, For Two
Pianos And Orchestra [30']
4(pic).4.4.4. 6.4.4.1. 3perc,
2harp,strings,2pno soli
UNIVER. perf mat rent   (R126)

Nachtordnung [15']
9vln,3vla,2vcl,db
sc UNIVER. UE 16631 $7.00, perf mat
rent   (R127)

O Notte, For Solo Voice And Orchestra
[12']
fl,clar,bass clar,contrabsn,harp,
2vla,2vcl,db,Bar solo
UNIVER. perf mat rent   (R128)

Symphony No. 3 [60']
4(pic).4.4+2bass clar.4+
2contrabsn. 6.4.4.2. timp,6-
7perc,2harp,cel,pno,mand,

RIHM, WOLFGANG (cont'd.)
strings,SBar soli,mix cor
sc UNIVER. UE 16765 $48.00, perf
mat rent   (R129)

Trakt *Op.11 [10']
4.3.3+bass clar.2+contrabsn.
6.4.4.1. timp,perc,pno,strings
BREITKOPF-W perf mat rent   (R130)

RIISAGER, KNUDAGE (1897-1974)
To Apollo, The God Of Light [10']
3.2.2.2. 4.3.3.1. timp,perc,harp,
pno,strings
sc SAMFUNDET 293 f.s.   (R131)

RILEY, DENNIS (1943-   )
Concertante Music III [19']
3(pic,alto fl).3.3.2. 4.2.3.0.
timp,5perc,harp,pno,cel,
strings,vla solo
PETERS P66658 perf mat rent (R132)

Elegy for Violoncello and String
Orchestra [4']
string orch,vcl solo
PETERS P66696 perf mat rent (R133)

RIMPROVERO, IL see Rossini, Gioacchino

RIMSKY-KORSAKOV, NIKOLAI (1844-1908)
Aimant La Rose, For Solo Voice And
Orchestra
"Rose Enslaves The Nightingale,
The" LUCKS 02344 sc $3.00, set
$7.50, pts $.75, ea.   (R134)

Capriccio Espagnol *Op.34
min sc ZEN-ON 892452 f.s.   (R135)

Christmas Eve: Polonaise
LUCKS 08641 sc $9.50, pts $32.00,
pts $1.60, ea.   (R136)

Christmas Eve: Suite
LUCKS 05852 sc $17.00, set $50.00,
pts $2.25, ea.   (R137)

Conte Feerique *Op.29
"Fairy Tales" INTERNAT. perf mat
rent   (R138)

Coq D'Or, Le: Introduction And Bridal
Procession
"Coq D'Or, Le: Introduction And
Cortege" LUCKS 08619 sc $10.50,
set $32.00, pts $1.25, ea. (R139)

Coq D'Or, Le: Introduction And
Cortege *see Coq D'Or, Le:
Introduction And Bridal
Procession

Coq D'Or, Le: Suite
3.3.3.3. 4.3.3.1. timp,perc,
strings
min sc EULENBURG $15.00   (R140)

Dubinushka *Op.62
LUCKS 08697 sc $4.75, set $11.50,
pts $.75, ea.   (R141)

Fairy Tales *see Conte Feerique

Jour De Fete *see Glazunov,
Alexander Konstantinovich

Rose Enslaves The Nightingale, The
*see Aimant La Rose, For Solo
Voice And Orchestra

Sadko: Song Of India, For English
Horn And Orchestra, [arr.]
(Dolan, James) [5'] NEW MUSIC WEST
perf mat rent   (R142)

Sadko: Song Of India, For Solo Voice
And Orchestra
LUCKS 02090 set $7.50, pts $.75,
ea.   (R143)

Sadko: Song Of India, [arr.]
(Luck) LUCKS 06472 sc $5.00, set
$8.00, pts $.75, ea.   (R144)

Sadko: Song Of The Viking Quest, For
Solo Voice And Orchestra
LUCKS 03196 set $7.50, pts $.75,
ea.   (R145)

Scheherazade *Op.35
sc RICORDI-IT PR921 f.s.   (R146)
min sc ZEN-ON 892451 f.s.   (R147)

Symphony No. 3, Op. 32, in C
KALMUS 4992 sc $40.00, set $75.00
                            (R148)

Tsar Saltan: Flight Of The Bumblebee
LUCKS 06482 sc $3.75, set $9.50,
pts $.95, ea.   (R149)

RINALDO: LASCIA CH'IO PIANGA, FOR SOLO
VOICE AND ORCHESTRA see Handel,
George Frideric

RINALDO: LASS MICH MIT TRANEN MEIN LOS
BEKLAGEN, FOR SOLO VOICE AND
ORCHESTRA, [ARR.] see Handel,
George Frideric

RINDERSPACHER, JEAN
Wildschutzen-Marsch
1+pic.2.2.2. 4.2.3.0. perc,
strings
sc,pts LIENAU rent   (R150)

RING THE BELLS
(Mayfield, Larry; Skillings, Otis)
SINGSPIR 7702 $19.95   (R151)

RISSET, JEAN CLAUDE (1938-   )
Mirages [23']
2.1.1(bass clar).0. 1.0.2.0.
perc,harp,cel,pno,2vln,vla,vcl,
db,electronic tape
AMPHION A 378 perf mat rent (R152)

RITE OF SPRING, THE see Stravinsky,
Igor, Sacre Du Printemps, Le

RITMICA OSTINATA, FOR PIANO AND
ORCHESTRA see Ifukube, Akira

RITMICNE IMPRESIJE see Vrabec, Ubalo

RITO see Laman, Wim

RITORNELLI PER ARCHI see Wilson, Thomas

RITORNO see Martino, Donald

RITORNO DEGLI SNOVIDENIA, IL, FOR
VIOLONCELLO AND ORCHESTRA see
Berio, Luciano

RITORNO D'ORFEO, IL, FOR CELLO AND
ORCHESTRA see Slothouwer, Jochem

RITOURNELLE see Chaminade, Cecile

RITTER, CHRISTIAN (ca. 1640-ca. 1720)
O Amantissime Sponse, Jesu, For Solo
Voice And String Orchestra [15']
string orch,hpsd/org,S solo
BREITKOPF-W perf mat rent   (R153)

RITTER, HELMUT
Bewegtes Spiel
sc RIES f.s.   (R154)

Bunte Balle
RIES f.s.   (R155)

Gelbe Narzissen
RIES f.s.   (R156)

Piccolo-Bambino
RIES f.s.   (R157)

Sturmische Begegnung [5']
2(pic).1.2.1. 3.2.2.0. timp,perc,
harp,strings
sc RIES f.s., perf mat rent (R158)

RITTER DER LANDSTRASSE see Kess, Ludwig

RITTER PASMAN: POLKA see Strauss,
Johann, [Jr.]

RITTER PASMAN: WALZER see Strauss,
Johann, [Jr.]

RITUALS see Shapey, Ralph

RIXNER, JOSEF (1902-1973)
Bagatelle
RIES f.s.   (R159)

Bayrische Hochzeit
RIES f.s.   (R160)

Capriolen
RIES f.s.   (R161)

Goldner Becher
RIES f.s.   (R162)

Hopsassa
RIES f.s.   (R163)

O, Schonste Du
RIES f.s.   (R164)

Rhapsodie No. 2
RIES f.s.   (R165)

Tanz Der Maske
RIES f.s.   (R166)

Vision
RIES f.s.   (R167)

ROAD TO HAMELIN, FOR DOUBLE BASS,
NARRATOR AND ORCHESTRA see Ramsier,
Paul

ROBBIANI, IGINO (1884-1966)
Anna Karenina: Suite No. 1 [23']
3.3.3.3. 4.3.3.1. timp,perc,
bells,cel,xylo,harp,strings
sc CARISCH 18881 f.s., perf mat

ROBBIANI, IGINO (cont'd.)

   rent   (R168)

   Anna Karenina: Suite No. 2 [17']
     3.3.3.3. 4.3.3.1. timp,perc,xylo,
     cel,harp,strings
     sc CARISCH 18882 f.s., perf mat
     rent   (R169)

   Elegy [7']
     2.3.2.2. 4.0.0.0. timp,perc,harp,
     strings
     sc CARISCH 19465 f.s., perf mat
     rent   (R170)

   Guido Del Popolo: Frammenti Sinfonici
   [11']
     3.3.3.3. 4.3.3.1. timp,perc,cel,
     harp,strings
     min sc CARISCH 18879 perf mat rent
                                         (R171)

   Preludio-Corale-Fuga [15']
     3.3.3.3. 4.3.3.1. timp,perc,cel,
     harp,strings
     sc CARISCH 19872 f.s., perf mat
     rent   (R172)

   Roma Dei Cesari: Frammenti Sinfonici
   [15']
     3.3.3.3. 4.3.3.1. timp,perc,xylo,
     cel,pno,harp,strings
     sc CARISCH 18880 f.s., perf mat
     rent   (R173)

   Romanticismo: Frammenti [18']
     3.3.3.3. 4.3.3.1. timp,perc,cel,
     harp,strings
     sc CARISCH 18878 perf mat rent
                                         (R174)

   Scherzo [5']
     3.3.3.2. 4.3.3.1. timp,perc,
     strings
     sc CARISCH 19463 f.s., perf mat
     rent   (R175)

ROBERTSON, KARL-OLOF (1918-   )
   Konsert-Uvertyr [9']
     2.2.2.2. 3.2.2.0. timp,perc,harp,
     strings
     sc STIM   (R176)

ROBERTSSON, STIG (1940-   )
   Introduktion Och Fuga [7']
     string orch
     sc,pts STIM   (R177)

ROBIN HOOD: ARMORER'S SONG, FOR SOLO
   VOICE AND ORCHESTRA see De Koven,
   (Henry Louis) Reginald

ROBIN HOOD: O PROMISE ME, FOR SOLO
   VOICE AND ORCHESTRA see De Koven,
   (Henry Louis) Reginald

ROBRECHT, CARL (1888-1961)
   Festpolonaise
     RIES f.s.   (R178)

   Hottepferdchen
     RIES f.s.   (R179)

ROCCA, LODOVICO (1895-   )
   Cella Azzurra, La [12']
     3.3.3.3. 4.3.3.1. timp,perc,
     bells,cel,harp,pno,org,strings
     sc CARISCH 16155 perf mat rent
                                         (R180)

ROCHAT, ANDREE (1900-   )
   Musica Per Archi °Op.26 [16']
     string orch
     sc CARISCH 21282 rent, pts CARISCH
     21283 rent   (R181)

ROCOCO-CONCERTO, FOR CLARINET AND
   ORCHESTRA see Andriessen, Jurriaan

ROGERS, BERNARD (1893-1968)
   Amphitryon: Overture [9']
     3.3.3.3. 4.3.3.1. timp,perc,
     2harp,cel,strings
     MARGUN BP 6025 perf mat rent (R182)

   Colors Of Youth, The [11']
     3.2.3.3. 4.3.3.1. timp,perc,harp,
     pno,strings
     MARGUN BP 6026 perf mat rent (R183)

   Invasion [5']
     3.3.3.3. 4.3.3.1. timp,perc,harp,
     strings
     MARGUN BP 6027 perf mat rent (R184)

   Warrior, The: Prelude [5']
     2(pic).2(English horn).2(bass
     clar).2(contrabsn). 3.2.2.0.
     3perc,harp,pno,strings
     MARGUN BP 6024 perf mat rent (R185)

ROI D'YS, LE: VAINEMENT MA BIEN AIMEE,
   FOR SOLO VOICE AND ORCHESTRA see
   Lalo, Edouard

ROI LEAR OVERTURE see Berlioz, Hector
   (Louis), King Lear Overture

ROI MALGRE LUI, LE: FETE POLONAISE see
   Chabrier, [Alexis-] Emmanuel

ROI S'AMUSE, LE see Delibes, Leo

ROLLA, ALESSANDRO (1757-1841)
   Concertino for Viola and Orchestra,
   MIN 38
     orch,vla solo
     (Sciannameo, F.) KERBY perf mat
     rent   (R186)

   Concerto for Basset Horn and
   Orchestra in F minor
     2ob,2horn,strings,basset horn
     solo
     KNUS perf mat rent   (R187)

   Overture [6']
     (Sciannameo, Franco) sc,pts
     RARITIES $12.00   (R188)

   Rondo for Viola and Orchestra in G
   [8']
     2ob,2horn,strings,vla solo
     sc,pts RARITIES $6.50   (R189)

   Sinfonia No. 1 in D [4']
     2fl,2ob,2bsn,2horn,strings
     (Negrotti, N.) sc,pts ZANIBON D286
     rent   (R190)

   Sinfonia No. 2 in D [4']
     2fl,2ob,2bsn,2horn,strings
     (Negrotti, N.) sc,pts ZANIBON D287
     rent   (R191)

   Sinfonias In D And E Minor
     see NORTHERN ITALIAN SYMPHONY,
     1800-1840, THE

ROMA DEI CESARI: FRAMMENTI SINFONICI
   see Robbiani, Igino

ROMAN, JOHAN HELMICH (1694-1758)
   Concerto for Violin and Orchestra,
   MIN 37
     orch,vln solo
     KALMUS 5443 solo pt $2.00, kbd pt
     $2.00, sc $7.00, set $5.00, pts
     $1.00, ea.   (R192)

   Drottningholms-Musique
     fac ed AUTOGR AM 010 $30.00   (R193)

   Sinfonia in A, MIN 81 [8']
     string orch,cont
     sc,pts BUSCH f.s.   (R194)

   Sinfonias, Six
     see SYMPHONY IN SWEDEN, THE, PART 1

   Sinfonias Nos. 1-3 *CCU
     (Bengtsson, Ingmar) sc,min sc,pts
     REIMERS ER MMS 4 f.s.   (R195)

ROMAN CARNIVAL see Berlioz, Hector
   (Louis), Carnaval Romain, Le

ROMANCE SANS PAROLES, FOR SOLO VOICE
   AND ORCHESTRA see Pijper, Willem

ROMANS, FOR VIOLIN AND STRING ORCHESTRA
   see Fredriksson, Lennart

ROMANTIC ODE see Fine, Vivian

ROMANTICISMO: FRAMMENTI see Robbiani,
   Igino

ROMANTISKA MINIATYRER see Gullberg,
   Olof

ROMANZA see Holloway, Robin

ROMANZA SICILIANA, FOR FLUTE AND
   ORCHESTRA see Weber, Carl Maria von

ROMANZE RUBATO see Loffler, Willy

ROMANZETTA see Dressel, Erwin

ROMBERG, BERNHARD HEINRICH (1767-1841)
   Concerto for Flute and Orchestra, Op.
   30, in B minor [17']
     0.2.0.2. 2.0.0.0. strings,fl solo
     (Foerster) sc EULENBURG E10134
     f.s., perf mat rent   (R196)

ROMEO AND JULIET see Diamond, David

ROMEO AND JULIET see Svendsen, Johan
   (Severin)

ROMEO AND JULIET: LOVE SCENE see
   Berlioz, Hector (Louis), Romeo Et
   Juliette: Scene D'Amour

ROMEO AND JULIET: OVERTURE see Bellini,
   Vincenzo, Capuleti E I Montecchi,
   I: Sinfonia

ROMEO AND JULIET. OVERTURE-FANTASY see
   Tchaikovsky, Piotr Ilyich

ROMEO AND JULIET: QUEEN MAB, SCHERZO
   see Berlioz, Hector (Louis), Romeo
   Et Juliette: La Reine Mab, Scherzo

ROMEO AND JULIET: ROMEO ALONE -
   FESTIVITIES AT CAPULET'S see
   Berlioz, Hector (Louis), Romeo Et
   Juliette: Grand Fete Chez Capulet

ROMEO AND JULIET: SUITE NO. 1 see
   Prokofiev, Serge

ROMEO AND JULIET: SUITE NO. 2 see
   Prokofiev, Serge

ROMEO AND JULIET: SUITE NO. 3 see
   Prokofiev, Serge

ROMEO AND JULIET: WALTZ SONG see
   Gounod, Charles Francois, Romeo Et
   Juliette: Valse, "Je Veux Vivre
   Dans Ce Reve", For Solo Voice And
   Orchestra

ROMEO ET JULIETTE: BALLET MUSIC see
   Gounod, Charles Francois

ROMEO ET JULIETTE: GRAND FETE CHEZ
   CAPULET see Berlioz, Hector (Louis)

ROMEO ET JULIETTE: LA REINE MAB,
   SCHERZO see Berlioz, Hector (Louis)

ROMEO ET JULIETTE: NUIT D'HYMENEE, FOR
   SOLO VOICES AND ORCHESTRA see
   Gounod, Charles Francois

ROMEO ET JULIETTE: SCENE D'AMOUR see
   Berlioz, Hector (Louis)

ROMEO ET JULIETTE: VALSE, "JE VEUX
   VIVRE DANS CE REVE", FOR SOLO VOICE
   AND ORCHESTRA see Gounod, Charles
   Francois

ROMISCHER CARNEVAL see Berlioz, Hector
   (Louis), Carnaval Romain, Le

RONDA DEI LILLIPUZZI see Bossi, [Marco]
   Enrico

RONDEAU SYMPHONIQUE see Mieg, Peter

RONDEAUX AMOUREUX, FOR SOLO VOICE AND
   ORCHESTRA see Boer, Jan den

RONDINE IMPORTUNA, LA, FOR SOLO VOICE
   AND ORCHESTRA see Sinigaglia, Leone

RONDO BRILLIANT FOR PIANO AND ORCHESTRA
   see Hummel, Johann Nepomuk

RONDO CAPRICCIOSO, FOR VIOLIN AND
   ORCHESTRA see Hamann, Bernhard

RONDO CONCERTANTE, FOR PIANO AND
   ORCHESTRA, [ARR.] see Mozart,
   Wolfgang Amadeus

RONDO FINALE see Christensen, Bernhard

RONDO FOR PIANO AND ORCHESTRA IN D, K.
   382 see Mozart, Wolfgang Amadeus

RONDOBURLESKE see Dressel, Erwin

RONNES, ROBERT
   Concerto for Clarinet and Orchestra
     2(pic).2(2English horn).3(2bass
     clar).2(contrabsn). 2.0.0.1.
     flugelhorn,Ondes Martenot,perc,
     harp,strings,clar solo
     NORGE   (R197)

ROOD see Schat, Peter

ROOK see Schat, Peter

ROOS, ROBERT DE (1907-1976)
   Adagio, Allegretto En Allegro
     1.0.1.0. 0.0.0.0. perc,pno,12vln,
     4vcl,db
     sc DONEMUS f.s., perf mat rent
                                         (R198)

   Bekranzter Kahn
     see Zwei Lieder, For Solo Voice And
     Orchestra

   Drei Romantische Lieder, For Solo
   Voice And Orchestra
     2.3.3.2. 4.2.2.0. timp,perc,harp,
     strings,S solo
     sc DONEMUS f.s., perf mat rent
                                         (R199)

   Musica Per Violini, Violoncelli E
   Contrabassi [8']
     strings without vla
     sc DONEMUS f.s., perf mat rent
                                         (R200)

   Traurige Fruhlingsnacht
     see Zwei Lieder, For Solo Voice And
     Orchestra

   Zwei Lieder, For Solo Voice And
   Orchestra
     1.1.1.0. 0.0.0.0. perc,pno,cel,1-

ROOS, ROBERT DE (cont'd.)

   4vla,1-4vcl,Bar solo sc DONEMUS
   f.s., perf mat rent
   contains: Bekranzter Kahn;
      Traurige Fruhlingsnacht   (R201)

ROP see Blomberg, Erik

ROREM, NED (1923-   )
   Design
      sc BOOSEY $10.00   (R202)

   Eagles
      sc BOOSEY $5.00   (R203)

   Eleven Studies For Eleven Players
      1.1.1.0. 0.1.0.0. perc,harp,pno,
      vln,vla,db
      BOOSEY sc $17.00, pts rent   (R204)

   Lions
      sc BOOSEY $8.00   (R205)

   Pilgrims
      string orch
      sc BOOSEY $2.50   (R206)

   Sunday Morning [20']
      3(pic).3(English horn).3.3.
      6.3.3.1. timp,perc,harp,pno,opt
      cel,strings
      BOOSEY perf mat rent   (R207)

   Water Music
      sc BOOSEY $10.00   (R208)

ROSALIE see Hudec, Jiri

ROSAMUNDE: BALLET MUSIC see Schubert,
   Franz (Peter)

ROSAMUNDE: ENTR'ACTE AND BALLET MUSIC
   see Schubert, Franz (Peter),
   Rosamunde: Zwischenakt- Und
   Ballettmusik

ROSAMUNDE: OVERTURE see Schubert, Franz
   (Peter)

ROSAMUNDE: ZWISCHENAKT- UND
   BALLETTMUSIK see Schubert, Franz
   (Peter)

ROSAMUNDE: ZWISCHENAKTMUSIK see
   Schubert, Franz (Peter)

ROSE ENSLAVES THE NIGHTINGALE, THE see
   Rimsky-Korsakov, Nikolai, Aimant La
   Rose, For Solo Voice And Orchestra

ROSEN OHNE DORNE. WALZER see Strauss,
   Johann, [Jr.]

ROSENBERG, HILDING (1892-   )
   Dagdrivaren
      study sc SUECIA f.s.   (R209)

   Pan
      2.2.2.0. 1.0.0.0. timp,perc,
      strings
      sc STIM perf mat rent   (R210)

   Sinfonia Serena *see Symphony No. 8

   Symphony No. 8
      3.3.2.2. 4.3.3.1. timp,perc,harp,
      cel,strings
      STIM   (R211)

   Yttersta Domen
      sc SUECIA f.s.   (R212)

ROSENBOOM, DAVID (1947-   )
   Caliban Upon Setebos
      2.2.3.1. 2.2.2.0. timp,perc,pno,
      strings
      SEESAW perf mat rent   (R213)

ROSENFELD, GERHARD (1931-   )
   Concerto for Violin and Orchestra,
      No. 2
      sc PETERS 9551 $36.50, pts PETERS
      rent   (R214)

ROSETTI, FRANCESCO ANTONIO (1746-1792)
   Concerto for Horn and Orchestra in E
      flat, MIN 29 [15']
      0.2.0.0. 2.0.0.0. strings,horn
      solo
      (Paeuler) sc,pts EULENBURG E10128
      f.s.   (R215)

   Symphonies In F, B Flat And D
      see SEVEN SYMPHONIES FROM THE COURT
      OF OETTINGEN-WALLERSTEIN (1773-
      1795)

ROSIERE REPUBLICAINE, LA: BALLET MUSIC
   see Gretry, Andre Ernest Modeste

ROSINSKY, JOZEF (1897-1973)
   Matej: Intermezzo
      3.3.3.3. 4.2.3.1. timp,perc,harp,
      strings
      SLOV.HUD.FOND O-235 perf mat rent

ROSINSKY, JOZEF (cont'd.)

                                    (R216)

ROSKOTT, CARL (1952-   )
   Adagio [12']
      2.2.2.3. 4.2.3.1. timp,strings
      sc MARGUN BP 6003 $10.00, perf mat
      rent   (R217)

   Overture To A Summer Night [11']
      3.2.3.3. 4.3.3.1. timp,2perc,
      harp,cel,strings
      MARGUN BP 6004 perf mat rent (R218)

ROSLER, JOHANN JOSEPH (1771-1813)
   Concerto for Piano and Orchestra in D
      1.2.0.2. 2.2.0.0. timp,strings,
      pno solo
      (formerly attributed to Beethoven)
      BREITKOPF-W perf mat rent   (R219)

ROSSEAU, NORBERT (1907-1975)
   Ouverture Per Una Commedia Di Goldoni
      "Il Servo Di Due Padroni, " Op.
      1.66 [5'40"]
      CBDM   (R220)

ROSSELLINI, RENZO (1908-   )
   Ore Tristi E Serene, For Solo Voice
      And String Orchestra
      string orch,S solo
      sc RICORDI-IT 131890 f.s.   (R221)

ROSSI see Komorous, Rudolf

ROSSI, LUIGI (1597-1653)
   Orfeo: La Disperazione Di Orfeo, For
      Solo Voice And String Orchestra
      [7']
      string orch,cont,T/Mez solo
      (Spezzaferri, L.) sc,pts ZANIBON
      D309 rent   (R222)

ROSSINI, GIOACCHINO (1792-1868)
   Barber Of Seville, The: Overture
      *see Barbiere Di Siviglia, Il:
      Overture

   Barbiere Di Siviglia, Il: Dunque Io
      Son, For Solo Voices And
      Orchestra
      LUCKS 06342 sc $3.75, set $9.50,
      pts $.75, ea.   (R223)

   Barbiere Di Siviglia, Il: Ecco
      Ridente In Cielo, For Solo Voice
      And Orchestra
      LUCKS 03640 sc $3.75, set $9.75,
      pts $.75, ea.   (R224)

   Barbiere Di Siviglia, Il: La
      Calunnia, For Solo Voice And
      Orchestra
      LUCKS 02345 sc $3.75, set $7.50,
      pts $.75, ea.   (R225)

   Barbiere Di Siviglia, Il: Largo Al
      Factotum, For Solo Voice And
      Orchestra
      LUCKS 02253 sc $3.75, set $7.50,
      pts $.75, ea.   (R226)

   Barbiere Di Siviglia, Il: Overture
      min sc ZEN-ON 890752 f.s.   (R227)
      BROUDE BR. set $20.00, pts $1.25,
      ea.   (R228)
      "Barber Of Seville, The: Overture"
      min sc UNIVER. PH17 $2.50   (R229)
      "Barber Of Seville, The: Overture"
      LUCKS 06505 sc $7.50, set $7.00,
      min sc $2.50, pts $.75, ea.
                                    (R230)

   Barbiere Di Siviglia, Il: Una Voce
      Poco Fa, For Solo Voice And
      Orchestra
      LUCKS 02104 sc $3.75, set $7.50,
      pts $.75, ea.   (R231)

   Cambiale Di Matrimonio, La: Overture
      KALMUS A4903 sc $7.00, perf mat
      rent, set $13.00, pts $1.00, ea.
                                    (R232)

   Cenerentola, La: Nacqui All'Affanno -
      Non Piu Mesta, For Solo Voice And
      Orchestra
      LUCKS 02805 sc $3.75, set $7.50,
      pts $.75, ea.   (R233)

   Cenerentola, La: Overture
      LUCKS 06508 sc $9.50, set $18.00,
      min sc $5.00, pts $1.15, ea.
                                    (R234)

   Danza, La, For Solo Voice And
      Orchestra
      LUCKS 02092 sc $3.75, set $9.50,
      pts $.75, ea.   (R235)

   Diebische Elster, Die: Overture *see
      Gazza Ladra, La: Overture

   Eduardo E Cristina: Overture [7'30"]
      2.2.2.2. 2.2.1.0. timp,perc,
      strings
      (Gorgni, L.) sc,pts ZANIBON D343
      rent   (R236)

ROSSINI, GIOACCHINO (cont'd.)

   Gazza Ladra, La: Overture
      LUCKS 06509 sc $7.50, set $22.00,
      min sc $2.50, pts $1.40, ea.
                                    (R237)
      "Diebische Elster, Die: Overture"
      min sc UNIVER. PH112 $4.00   (R238)

   Grande Fanfare
      1+pic.1.2.2. 4.2.0.1. strings
      KALMUS A5499 sc $6.00, perf mat
      rent, set $15.00, pts $.75, ea.
                                    (R239)

   Guillaume Tell: Ballet, Pas De Six
      LUCKS 08429 sc $9.50, set $18.00,
      pts $1.15, ea.   (R240)

   Guillaume Tell: Overture
      min sc ZEN-ON 890751 f.s.   (R241)
      "William Tell: Overture" LUCKS
      06515 sc $8.50, set $23.00, min
      sc $3.00, pts $1.15, ea.   (R242)
      (Hoffmann) pts BROUDE BR. $1.50,
      ea.   (R243)

   Italiana In Algeri, L': Overture
      BROUDE BR. set $25.00, pts $1.00,
      ea.   (R244)

   Maometto, Il: Secondo Overture
      KALMUS 5258 sc $15.00, perf mat
      rent, set $30.00, pts $1.50, ea.
                                    (R245)

   Mose: Ballet Music
      KALMUS A4979   (R246)

   Orgia, L' (from Les Soirees
      Musicales, [arr.])
      (Waldenmaier, August P.) 2.2.2.2.
      4.3.3.0. timp,perc,harp,strings
      [3'] ORLANDO rent   (R247)

   Preludio Religioso [6']
      2.3.3.3. 4.3.3.1. strings
      (Toni, A.) sc CARISCH 18908, pts
      CARISCH 21397   (R248)

   Rimprovero, Il (from Les Soirees
      Musicales, [arr.])
      (Waldenmaier, August P.) 2.2.2.2.
      4.3.3.0. timp,perc,harp,strings
      [4'] ORLANDO rent   (R249)

   Scala Di Seta, La: Overture
      LUCKS 07587 sc $9.50, set $18.00,
      min sc $5.00, pts $1.15, ea.
                                    (R250)

   Semiramide: Ah, Quel Giorno, For Solo
      Voice And Orchestra
      LUCKS 02778 sc $7.00, set $8.00,
      pts $.75, ea.   (R251)

   Semiramide: Overture [12']
      2.2.2.2. 4.2.3.0. timp,perc,
      strings
      sc,pts BREITKOPF-W PB-OB 4396 f.s.
                                    (R252)
      LUCKS 06513 sc $8.50, set $22.00,
      pts $1.15, ea.   (R253)

   Signor Bruschino, Il: Overture
      LUCKS 08595 sc $9.50, set $20.00,
      min sc $3.00, pts $1.40, ea. (R254)

   Sonata No. 1 in G
      string orch
      KALMUS A1167 sc $6.00, set $10.00,
      pts $2.00, ea.   (R255)
      LUCKS 01509 sc $4.00, set $5.00,
      pts $1.25, ea.   (R256)
      (Malaric, R.) sc,pts,study sc
      DOBLINGER DM 251 f.s.   (R257)

   Sonata No. 2 in A
      string orch
      KALMUS A1168 sc $6.00, set $10.00,
      pts $2.00, ea.   (R258)
      (Malaric, R.) sc,pts,study sc
      DOBLINGER DM 252 f.s.   (R259)

   Sonata No. 3 in C
      string orch
      KALMUS A1169 sc $6.00, set $10.00,
      pts $2.00, ea.   (R260)
      (Malaric, R.) sc,pts,study sc
      DOBLINGER DM 253 f.s.   (R261)

   Sonata No. 4 in B flat
      string orch
      KALMUS A1170 sc $6.00, set $10.00,
      pts $2.00, ea.   (R262)
      (Malaric, R.) sc,pts,study sc
      DOBLINGER DM 254 f.s.   (R263)

   Sonata No. 5 in E flat
      string orch
      KALMUS A1171 sc $6.00, set $10.00,
      pts $2.00, ea.   (R264)
      (Malaric, R.) sc,pts,study sc
      DOBLINGER DM 255 f.s.   (R265)

   Sonata No. 6 in D
      string orch
      KALMUS A1172 sc $6.00, set $10.00,
      pts $2.00, ea.   (R266)

ROSSINI, GIOACCHINO (cont'd.)

(Malaric, R.) sc,pts,study sc
DOBLINGER DM 256 f.s.   (R267)

Tancredi: Overture
LUCKS 06514 sc $10.00, set $20.00,
min sc $5.00, pts $.95, ea.
(R268)
Turco In Italia, Il: Overture
KALMUS A4153 sc $14.00, perf mat
rent, set $17.00, pts $1.00, ea.
(R269)
Variations for Clarinet and Orchestra
LUCKS 01657 sc $5.50, set $11.50,
pts $.95, ea.   (R270)

William Tell: Overture *see
Guillaume Tell: Overture

ROSSLER, FRANZ ANTON
see ROSETTI, FRANCESCO ANTONIO

ROSSMANN, RICHARD
Tarantella
RIES f.s.   (R271)

ROTA, NINO (1911-1979)
Divertimento for Double Bass and
String Orchestra [23'21"]
string orch,db solo
sc,pts CARISCH 21922 perf mat rent
(R272)
Fantasia Sopra 12 Note Del "Don
Giovanni", For Piano And
Orchestra [12']
2.2.2.2. 2.2.0.0. timp,harp,cel,
strings,pno solo
sc CARISCH 21891 rent, pts CARISCH
21891A rent   (R273)

ROTE KAPPCHEN, DAS: OVERTURE see
Dittersdorf, Karl Ditters von

ROTE TULPEN see Fridl, Hans

ROTTGERING, MARTIN ALMAR (1926-   )
Concerto for Piano and Orchestra
2.2.2.2. 4.2.0.0. timp,perc,
strings,pno solo
sc DONEMUS f.s., perf mat rent
(R274)
Midgaard Gedenkklank, De, For Violin
And Orchestra
2.2.2.2. 2.2.0.0. timp,strings,
vln solo
sc DONEMUS f.s., perf mat rent
(R275)

ROUGET DE L'ISLE, CLAUDE JOSEPH
(1760-1836)
Marseillaise, La
(Luck, Arthur) LUCKS HYMNS 18 set
$9.50, pts $.65, ea.   (R276)

ROUNDEL see Chaminade, Cecile

ROWLAND, DAVID (1939-   )
Consorts [15']
12vcl
sc DONEMUS f.s., perf mat rent
(R277)
Easter Stanzas, For Solo Voice And
Orchestra [22']
2.2.2.2. 2.2.2.1. 3perc,pno,6vla,
6vcl,4db,S solo
DONEMUS perf mat rent   (R278)

Serenade [20']
string orch
DONEMUS perf mat rent   (R279)

Tableaux [17']
3.3.3.3. 4.3.3.1. 3perc,cel,harp,
strings
DONEMUS   (R280)

ROXELANE, LA see Haydn, [Franz] Joseph,
Symphony No. 63 in C

ROYAL FIREWORKS MUSIC see Handel,
George Frideric

ROYAL INVITATION see Argento, Dominick

ROYAL MILE see Thorpe Davie, Cedric

ROYER, ETIENNE (1882-1928)
Pour Le Temps De La Moisson
string orch
study sc SALABERT $11.25   (R281)

ROZSA, MIKLOS (1907-   )
Concerto for Viola and Orchestra, Op.
37
2.2.2.2. 4.3.3.0.db tuba. timp,
perc,harp,cel,strings,vla solo
BREITKOPF-W perf mat rent   (R282)

RUBEZAHL see Czernik, Willy

RUBIN, MARCEL (1905-   )
Concertino for 12 Violoncelli
12vcl f.s. sc DOBLINGER 06 264, pts
DOBLINGER 06 265, study sc
DOBLINGER STP 506   (R283)

RUBIN, MARCEL (cont'd.)

Concerto for Bassoon and Orchestra
[21']
1+pic.1.1.1. 2.1.1.1. timp,perc,
strings,bsn solo
sc,pts DOBLINGER rent   (R284)
Variationen Uber Ein Franzosisches
Revolutionslied [11']
2+pic.2.2.2. 4.2.2.1. xylo,perc,
strings
sc,pts DOBLINGER rent   (R285)
Variationen Uber Einen Bach-Choral
[20']
2+pic.2.2.2. 4.2.2.1. timp,perc,
strings
sc,pts DOBLINGER rent   (R286)

RUBINSTEIN, ANTON (1829-1894)
Concerto for Piano and Orchestra, No.
3, Op. 45 [35']
2.2.2.2. 2.2.0.0. perc,strings,
pno solo
KALMUS 5355 solo pt $15.00, sc
$40.00, perf mat rent, set
$27.00, pts $1.50, ea.   (R287)
LUCKS 00136 sc $40.00, set $27.00,
pts $1.50, ea., solo pt $15.00
(R288)
Concerto for Piano and Orchestra, No.
4, Op. 70
LUCKS 00068 sc $20.00, set $35.00,
pts $2.75, ea.   (R289)

Concerto for Violin and Orchestra,
Op. 46, in G [25']
2.2.2.2. 4.0.0.0. timp,strings,
vln solo
PETERS perf mat rent   (R290)

Melody In F, [arr.] *Op.3,No.1
(D'Indy) LUCKS 06528 sc $5.75, set
$9.50, pts $.95, ea.   (R291)

Trot De Cavalerie [3']
3(pic).2.2.2. 4.2.3.1. timp,perc,
strings
RIES perf mat rent   (R292)

RUDERS, POUL
Capriccio Pian' E Forte [20']
3.3.3.3. 4.3.3.1. timp,perc,harp,
pno,strings
SAMFUNDET perf mat rent   (R293)

Pavane [11']
2.0.2.0. 2.2.2.0. perc,elec gtr,
harp,pno,elec org,cel,strings
sc SAMFUNDET 281 perf mat rent
(R294)
Recitatives And Arias, For Piano And
Orchestra [15']
1.1.1.1. 1.1.1.0. perc,harp,
strings,pno solo
SAMFUNDET perf mat rent   (R295)

RUDORFF, ERNST (1840-1916)
Symphony No. 2, Op. 40 [28']
2.2.2.2. 4.2.3.0. timp,strings
sc,pts LIENAU rent   (R296)

RUE DE PLAISIR see Bund, Hans

RUF ZUR FREUDE see Lurmann, Ludwig

RUGELES, ALFREDO (1949-   )
Mutaciones [12']
string orch
sc NOMOS E.N. 112 perf mat rent
(R297)
RUGGLES, CARL SPRAGUE (1876-1971)
Sun-Treader
sc PRESSER 416-41104 $6.50, perf
mat rent   (R298)

RUHE MEINE SEELE, FOR SOLO VOICE AND
ORCHESTRA, [ARR.] see Strauss,
Richard

RUIMTEN see Manneke, Daan

RUINEN VON ATHEN, DIE: OVERTURE see
Beethoven, Ludwig van

RUINEN VON ATHEN, DIE: TURKISCHER
MARSCH see Beethoven, Ludwig van

RUINS OF ATHENS, THE: OVERTURE see
Beethoven, Ludwig van, Ruinen Von
Athen, Die: Overture

RUINS OF ATHENS, THE: TURKISH MARCH see
Beethoven, Ludwig van, Ruinen Von
Athen, Die: Turkischer Marsch

RUITER, WIM DE (1943-   )
Allegro, Adagio En Variaties [20'25"]
1.1.1.1. 1.1.1.0. perc,pno,2vln,
vla,vcl,db
DONEMUS   (R299)

Menuet Met Variaties [12'30"]
2.2.2.2. 2.1.0.0. perc,strings
DONEMUS f.s.   (R300)

RUITER, WIM DE (cont'd.)

Re [10']
4.4.4.4. 4.4.4.1. perc,strings
sc DONEMUS f.s., perf mat rent
(R301)

Spectrum [10'30"]
2.2.2.2. 2.2.2.0. 3perc,strings
DONEMUS perf mat rent   (R302)

RULE BRITTANIA see Wagner, Richard

RUMANISCH see Knumann, Jo

RUMANISCHE RHAPSODIE, FOR VIOLIN AND
ORCHESTRA see Linz, Marta

RUNNSTROM, WILLIAM (1951-   )
Bisatta *Op.10 [10']
2.2.2.2. 4.3.3.0. strings
STIM   (R303)

RURALIA see Schiavo, Gregorio de

RUSALKA: SONG TO THE MOON, FOR SOLO
VOICE AND ORCHESTRA see Dvorak,
Antonin

RUSCELLO, IL see Bolzoni, Giovanni

RUSES D'AMOUR: GRAND PAS DES FIANCES
see Glazunov, Alexander
Konstantinovich

RUSSELL, ARMAND KING (1932-   )
Ecophony
string orch
SEESAW perf mat rent   (R304)

RUSSIAN GYPSY SONG, FOR SOLO VOICE AND
ORCHESTRA
LUCKS 02932 set $11.50, pts $.75, ea.
(R305)

RUSSIAN PIECES see Dodgson

RUSSISCH see Knumann, Jo

RUSSISCHER MARSCH FANTASIE see Strauss,
Johann, [Jr.]

RUSSLAN AND LUDMILLA: OVERTURE see
Glinka, Mikhail Ivanovich

RUST, FRIEDRICH WILHELM (1739-1796)
Auf Sonnigen Strassen
RIES f.s.   (R306)

RUY BLAS OVERTURE see Mendelssohn-
Bartholdy, Felix

RUYNEMAN, DANIEL (1886-1963)
Adieu
see Trois Chansons Des Maquisards
Condamnes, For Solo Voice And
Orchestra

In Claghen
see Vier Liederen, For Solo Voice
And Orchestra

Quelques Enfants Quelques Soldats...
see Trois Chansons Des Maquisards
Condamnes, For Solo Voice And
Orchestra

Soefisch
see Vier Liederen, For Solo Voice
And Orchestra

Sous Le Ciel Immobile J'ai Compte
Jusqu'a Mille
see Trois Chansons Des Maquisards
Condamnes, For Solo Voice And
Orchestra

Sous Le Pont Mirabeau, For Solo
Voices And Chamber Orchestra [6']
fl,harp,strings,SA soli
sc DONEMUS f.s., perf mat rent
(R307)
Symphonia
see Vier Liederen, For Solo Voice
And Orchestra

Trois Chansons Des Maquisards
Condamnes, For Solo Voice And
Orchestra
2.3.3.2. 2.2.2.0. timp,perc,harp,
strings,A/Bar solo sc DONEMUS
f.s., perf mat rent
contains: Adieu; Quelques Enfants
Quelques Soldats...; Sous Le
Ciel Immobile J'ai Compte
Jusqu'a Mille   (R308)

Vier Liederen, For Solo Voice And
Orchestra
2.2.2.1. 2.0.0.0. timp,perc,harp,
cel,strings,T solo sc DONEMUS
f.s., perf mat rent
contains: In Claghen; Soefisch;
Symphonia   (R309)

RYCHLIK, JOZEF (1946-   )
    Muzyka Symfoniczna I i II [7'30"-
    8'30"]
        alto sax,tenor sax,baritone sax,
        3trp,perc,harp,2pno,hpsd,9vcl,
        2string quar
        "Symphonic Music I And II" fac ed
        POLSKIE f.s.   (R310)

    Symphonic Music I And II *see Muzyka
        Symfoniczna I i II

RYPDAL, TERJE
    A.B.C. Or Adventure - Bedtime Story -
    Celebration [6'45"]
        0.0.1(bass clar).0.
        4.4(flugelhorn).4.0. perc,
        acord,2kbd,elec bass,strings
        NORGE   (R311)

    Concerto No. 3 for Solo Voice and
    Orchestra
        2.2.1.1. 2.1.1.0. timp,perc,2kbd,
        strings,Mez solo
        NORGE   (R312)

    Modulations, For Harmonica And
    Orchestra [14']
        2.0.0.1. 2.0.1.0. strings,
        harmonica solo
        NORGE   (R313)

    Symphony No. 3
        4(2alto fl).4(2English
        horn).4(2bass
        clar).3(contrabsn). 6.4.4.2.
        euphonium,2kbd,timp,perc,harp,
        strings,2elec bass, alto horn
        NORGE   (R314)

    Thoughts, For Solo Voice And
    Orchestra
        0.0.0.1. 2.0.1.0. perc,harp,elec
        gtr,elec bass,strings,solo
        voice
        NORGE   (R315)

RYTTERKVIST, HANS (1926-   )
    Saggio II [12']
        2.1.2.1. 2.2.1.0. 2perc,gtr,pno,
        strings
        sc STIM perf mat rent   (R316)

RZEWSKI, FREDERIC ANTHONY (1938-   )
    Moutons De Panurge, Les
        any number of melody instruments
        sc ZEN-ON 899153 $3.50   (R317)

S

SA DANSA, FOR SOLO VOICE AND ORCHESTRA,
    [ARR.] see Kilpinen, Yrjo

SAAT UND ERNTE POLKA see Strauss,
    Eduard

SABINO, A. (1898-1946)
    Falso Pellegrino, Il, For Solo Voice
    And Orchestra [4']
        2.2.2.2. 2.2.0.0. timp,perc,
        strings,solo voice
        manuscript CARISCH   (S1)

    Ragno Saltimbanco, Il, For Solo Voice
    And Orchestra [4']
        2.2.2.2. 2.2.0.0. timp,perc,pno,
        strings,solo voice
        manuscript CARISCH   (S2)

SACCHINI, ANTONIO (MARIA GASPARO
    GIOACCHINO) (1730-1786)
    Oedipe A Colonne: Furie d'Averno, For
    Solo Voices And Orchestra [6']
        0.2.0.2. 2.2.0.0. timp,strings,
        solo voices
        manuscript CARISCH   (S3)

    Oedipe A Colonne: Overture [6']
        2ob,2horn,timp,strings
        KALMUS 5305 sc $4.00, perf mat
        rent, set $15.00, pts $1.50, ea.
                                       (S4)

SACRE DU PRINTEMPS, LE see Stravinsky,
    Igor

SADKO: SONG OF INDIA, FOR ENGLISH HORN
    AND ORCHESTRA, [ARR.] see Rimsky-
    Korsakov, Nikolai

SADKO: SONG OF INDIA, FOR SOLO VOICE
    AND ORCHESTRA see Rimsky-Korsakov,
    Nikolai

SADKO: SONG OF INDIA, [ARR.] see
    Rimsky-Korsakov, Nikolai

SADKO: SONG OF THE VIKING QUEST, FOR
    SOLO VOICE AND ORCHESTRA see
    Rimsky-Korsakov, Nikolai

SAEVERUD, HARALD (1897-   )
    Kvernslatt, Op. 22a, No. 2
        "Mill-Wheel Tune" MUSIKK perf mat
        rent   (S5)

    Mill-Wheel Tune *see Kvernslatt, Op.
        22a, No. 2

    Siljustoel March *see
        Siljustolmarsj, Op. 21a, No. 5

    Siljustolmarsj, Op. 21a, No. 5
        "Siljustoel March" [6'] MUSIKK perf
        mat rent   (S6)

SAGA, EN see Sibelius, Jean

S'AGARO see Erhardt, Siegfried

SAGGIO II see Rytterkvist, Hans

SAGRA see Masetti, Enzo

SAGVIK, STELLAN (1952-   )
    Anagramma *Op.104 [4'30"]
        string orch
        sc STIM   (S7)

    Analgetika *Op.109 [18']
        2.2.2.1. 2.2.3.0. 2perc,strings
        sc STIM   (S8)

    Annaca, For Solo Voices And Chamber
    Orchestra *Op.108 [29']
        1.1.1.1. 1.0.0.0. perc,2vln,vla,
        vcl,db,AT soli
        STIM   (S9)

    Kromata Da Camera Di Pius Musiae
    *Op.87 [7']
        pic,ob,alto clar in E flat,bass
        clar,alto sax,trp,trom,perc,
        2vln,vcl,db
        sc STIM perf mat rent   (S10)

SAILOR'S LIFE, FOR SOLO VOICE AND
    ORCHESTRA see Bjorlin, Ulf

SAINT-GEORGES, CHEVALIER DE
    see SAINT-GEORGES, JOSEPH BOULOGNE DE

SAINT-GEORGES, JOSEPH BOULOGNE DE
    (1739-1799)
    Concerti for Violin and Orchestra,
    Op. 2, Nos. 1-2
        see Violin Concertos And Two
        Simphonies Concertantes

SAINT-GEORGES, JOSEPH BOULOGNE DE
    (cont'd.)
    Concerti for Violin and Orchestra,
    Op. 5, Nos. 1-2
        see Violin Concertos And Two
        Simphonies Concertantes

    Concerti for Violin and Orchestra,
    Op. 7, Nos. 1-2
        see Violin Concertos And Two
        Simphonies Concertantes

    Concerto for Violin and Orchestra,
    Op. 2, No. 1, in G
        (Lerma, Dominique-Rene de) 2ob,
        2horn,strings,vln solo sc PEER
        $12.00, perf mat rent   (S11)

    Ernestine: Scena, For Solo Voice And
    Orchestra
        2ob,2bsn,2horn,strings,S solo
        (Lerma, Dominique-Rene de) PEER
        perf mat rent   (S12)

    Symphonie Concertante for 2 Violins
    and String Orchestra, Op. 13, in
    G
        string orch,2vln soli
        (Paillard, J.F.) sc,pts COSTALL
        f.s.   (S13)

    Symphonies Concertantes, For 2
    Violins And String Orchestra, Two
        see Violin Concertos And Two
        Simphonies Concertantes

    Violin Concertos And Two Simphonies
    Concertantes
        (Banat, Gabriel) pts JOHNSON $75.00
        "Masters of the Violin", Vol. 3
        contains: Concerti for Violin and
        Orchestra, Op. 2, Nos. 1-2;
        Concerti for Violin and
        Orchestra, Op. 5, Nos. 1-2;
        Concerti for Violin and
        Orchestra, Op. 7, Nos. 1-2;
        Symphonies Concertantes, For 2
        Violins And String Orchestra,
        Two   (S14)

ST. PAUL: O LORD HAVE MERCY see
    Mendelssohn-Bartholdy, Felix,
    Paulus: Gott Sei Mir Gnadig, For
    Solo Voice And Orchestra

SAINT-SAENS, CAMILLE (1835-1921)
    Allegro Appassionato For Piano And
    Orchestra *Op.70
        LUCKS 00071 sc $12.00, set $24.00,
        pts $1.25, ea.   (S15)

    Allegro Appassionato For Violoncello
    And Orchestra *Op.43
        LUCKS 00622 sc $10.50, set $14.00,
        pts $.95, ea., solo pt $2.00
                                       (S16)

    Caprice En Forme De Valse, [arr.]
    *Op.52
        (Ysaye) 2(pic).2.2.2. 2.2.0.0.
        timp,perc,strings [5'] KALMUS
        5210 sc $20.00, set $18.00   (S17)

    Carnaval Des Animaux, Le
        min sc ZEN-ON 891951 f.s.   (S18)
        "Carnival Of The Animals" sc,quarto
        PETERS 9293 $6.00, perf mat rent
                                       (S19)
        (Pommer) "Carnival Of The Animals"
        min sc PETERS 9293A $12.00   (S20)

    Carnival Of The Animals *see
        Carnaval Des Animaux, Le

    Concerto for Piano and Orchestra, No.
    2, Op. 22, in G minor
        LUCKS 00069 sc $22.00, set $33.00,
        pts $2.25, ea.   (S21)

    Concerto for Violin and Orchestra,
    No. 1, Op. 20, in A
        2.2.2.2. 2.2.0.0. timp,strings,
        vln solo
        [13'] LEUCKART perf mat rent   (S22)
        sc,pts HAMELLE f.s.   (S23)

    Concerto for Violoncello and
    Orchestra, No. 1, Op. 33, in A
    minor
        study sc INTERNAT. 2276 $8.75 (S24)
        LUCKS 00610 sc $15.00, set $25.00,
        min sc $6.00, pts $1.60, ea.,
        solo pt $2.00   (S25)

    Danse Macabre *Op.40
        LUCKS 06540 sc $12.00, set $26.00,
        min sc $3.50, pts $1.60, ea.
                                       (S26)

    Deluge, Le: Prelude
        BROUDE BR. study sc $3.00, set
        $5.00, pts $1.00, ea.   (S27)
        LUCKS 06543 sc $4.00, set $3.75,
        pts $.75, ea.   (S28)
        "Flood, The: Prelude" INTERNAT.
        perf mat rent   (S29)

SAINT-SAENS, CAMILLE (cont'd.)

Flood, The: Prelude *see Deluge, Le:
Prelude

Havanaise, For Violin And Orchestra
*Op.83
LUCKS 00593 sc $5.00, set $12.00,
pts $.95, ea.   (S30)

Introduction Et Rondo Capriccioso,
For Violin And Orchestra *Op.28
LUCKS 00528 sc $9.00, set $20.00,
min sc $4.00, pts $1.40, ea.
(S31)
INTERNAT. perf mat rent   (S32)

Jota Aragonaise, Op. 64 [4']
2+pic.2.2.2. 4.2+2cornet.3.0.
timp,perc,harp,strings
KALMUS A1959 sc $8.00, perf mat
rent, set $20.00, pts $1.00, ea.
(S33)

Marche Heroique *Op.34
LUCKS 06545 sc $6.00, set $18.00,
pts $1.15, ea.   (S34)

Morceau De Concert, For Horn And
Orchestra *Op.94
LUCKS 00839 sc $6.00, set $11.00,
pts $.95, ea.   (S35)

Phaeton *Op.39
LUCKS 06547 sc $10.00, set $30.00,
pts $1.60, ea.   (S36)

Romance for Horn and Orchestra, Op.
36
INTERNAT. perf mat rent   (S37)
LUCKS 00799 sc $2.75, set $10.50,
pts $.95, ea.   (S38)

Romance for Violoncello and
Orchestra, Op. 36, [arr.]
2.1.2.1. 0.0.0.0. strings,vcl solo
[4'] INTERNAT. perf mat rent
(S39)

Samson Et Dalila: Amour, Viens Aider
Ma Faiblesse, For Solo Voice And
Orchestra
LUCKS 02085 sc $3.00, set $5.00,
pts $.75, ea.   (S40)

Samson Et Dalila: Bacchanale
LUCKS 06550 sc $12.00, set $20.00,
pts $1.60, ea.   (S41)

Samson Et Dalila: Dalila And High
Priest, For Solo Voices And
Orchestra
LUCKS 03655 sc $9.00, set $18.00,
pts $1.00, ea.   (S42)

Samson Et Dalila: Mon Coeur S'Ouvre A
Ta Voix, For Solo Voice And
Orchestra
"Samson Et Dalila: My Heart At Thy
Sweet Voice" LUCKS 02020 sc
$3.75, set $7.50, pts $.75, ea.
(S43)

Samson Et Dalila: My Heart At Thy
Sweet Voice *see Samson Et
Dalila: Mon Coeur S'Ouvre A Ta
Voix, For Solo Voice And
Orchestra

Samson Et Dalila: Printemps Qui
Commence, For Solo Voice And
Orchestra
LUCKS 02147 sc $3.00, set $6.00,
pts $.75, ea.   (S44)

Suite Algerienne *Op.60
LUCKS 06539 sc $18.00, set $50.00,
pts $2.50, ea.   (S45)

Symphony No. 1, Op. 2, in E flat
[32']
3.2.2.2. 4.4.3.0. timp,perc,
4harp,strings, 2saxhorns
KALMUS 5148 sc $40.00, perf mat
rent, set $75.00, pts $2.50, ea.
(S46)
Symphony No. 3, Op. 78, in C minor
study sc INTERNAT. 2122 $9.50 (S47)

Tarentelle, For Flute, Clarinet And
Orchestra *Op.6
LUCKS 07544 sc $6.00, set $11.50,
pts $1.25, ea.   (S48)

SAISON QUADRILLE see Strauss, Johann,
[Jr.]

SAKAC, BRANIMIR (1918-1979)
Barasou, For Solo Voice And Chamber
Orchestra
DRUS.HRVAT.SKLAD. f.s.   (S49)

Serenade for Strings
string orch
DRUS.HRVAT.SKLAD. f.s.   (S50)

Solo No. 1, For Piano And Orchestra
BREITKOPF-W perf mat rent   (S51)

SALIERI, ANTONIO (1750-1825)
Concertino Da Camera, For Flute And
String Orchestra In G, MIN30
[12']
string orch,fl solo
(Koch, R.J.) sc,pts ZANIBON ZA5521
f.s.   (S52)

Concerto for Organ and Orchestra in C
0.2.0.0. 0.2.0.0. timp,strings,
org solo
sc,pts DOBLINGER DM 829 f.s. (S53)

Variazioni Sulla "Follia Di Spagna"
2.2.2.2. 2.2.3.0. timp,drums,
harp,strings
(Spada, Pietro) sc BSE $10.75 (S54)

SALLINEN, AULIS (1935-   )
Cradle Song For A Dead Horseman *see
Kehtolaulu Kuolleelle
Ratsumiehelle

Ei Mikaan Virta
"There Is No Stream" see Nelja
Laulua Unesta, For Solo Voice And
Orchestra

Kehtolaulu Kuolleelle Ratsumiehelle
"Cradle Song For A Dead Horseman"
see Nelja Laulua Unesta, For Solo
Voice And Orchestra

Man Made From Sleep *see Unesta
Tehty Mies

Nelja Laulua Unesta, For Solo Voice
And Orchestra
3.3.3.3. 4.3.3.0. timp,2perc,harp,
cel,strings,S solo FAZER perf mat
rent
contains: Ei Mikaan Virta, "There
Is No Stream"; Kehtolaulu
Kuolleelle Ratsumiehelle,
"Cradle Song For A Dead
Horseman"; On Kolme Unta
Sisakkain, "Three Dreams Each
Within Each"; Unesta Tehty
Mies, "Man Made From Sleep"
(S55)
On Kolme Unta Sisakkain
"Three Dreams Each Within Each" see
Nelja Laulua Unesta, For Solo
Voice And Orchestra

Symphony No. 3
4.3.4.3. 4.3.3.1. timp,perc,harp,
pno,cel,strings
sc NOVELLO 2718-90 $22.00, perf mat
rent   (S56)

Symphony No. 4, Op. 49
sc NOVELLO 2588 $16.50   (S57)

There Is No Stream *see Ei Mikaan
Virta

Three Dreams Each Within Each *see
On Kolme Unta Sisakkain

Unesta Tehty Mies
"Man Made From Sleep" see Nelja
Laulua Unesta, For Solo Voice And
Orchestra

SALLSAM FAGEL, EN, FOR SOLO VOICE AND
ORCHESTRA see Palmgren, Selim

SALM see Cresswell, Lyell

SALMO DI DAVID, FOR SOLO VOICE AND
ORCHESTRA see Salviucci, Giovanni

SALMO FUNEBRE see Martini, G.M.

SALOME, OP.54: SALOMES TANZ see
Strauss, Richard

SALOMON ROSSI SUITE see Foss, Lukas

SALUT D'AMOUR see Elgar, [Sir] Edward
(William)

SALUTATIONS see Klebe, Giselher,
Begrussung

SALVA, TADEAS (1937-   )
Canticum Zachariae, For Solo Voice
And Orchestra [5']
1.1.1.1. 1.1.1.0. perc,cel,xylo,
strings,S solo
SLOV.HUD.FOND 0-339 perf mat rent
(S58)

Musica In Memoriam Honegger [20']
trp,org,strings
SLOV.HUD.FOND 0-479A perf mat rent
(S59)

Sinfonia Concertante [20']
2.2.2.2. 2.1.1.0. strings
SLOV.HUD.FOND 0-486 perf mat rent
(S60)

SALVIUCCI, GIOVANNI (1907-1937)
Overture in C sharp minor [10']
3.3.3.0. 4.3.3.0. timp,strings
sc CARISCH 17107 perf mat rent
(S61)

SALVIUCCI, GIOVANNI (cont'd.)

Salmo Di David, For Solo Voice And
Orchestra [4']
1.1.1.1. 1.1.1.0. pno,strings,S
solo
min sc CARISCH 17145 perf mat rent
(S62)

SALZBURG, PART 2
sc GARLAND ISBN 0-8240-3818-5 $90.00
"The Symphony", Vol. B-VIII
contains: Adlgasser, Anton Cajetan,
Symphonies, Four (Rainer,
Werner); Eberlin, Johann Ernst,
Symphonies, Three (Cuvay-
Schneider, Michaela); Haydn,
[Johann] Michael, Symphonies,
Five (Sherman, Charles H.) (S63)

SAMAMA, LEO (1951-   )
Spleen Et Ideal *Op.10 [20']
3-4perc,strings,vla solo,fl solo
DONEMUS   (S64)

Tombeau Concertant, For 2 Violins And
String Orchestra [13']
string orch,2vln soli
DONEMUS perf mat rent   (S65)

SAMARITANA, LA: PRELUDIO see Furlotti,
Arnaldo

SAMIOTISSA see Bresgen, Cesar

SAMMARTINI, GIOVANNI BATTISTA
(1701-1775)
Concerto, Op. 6, No. 1, in G [10']
string orch,cont
(Cooper, Barry) sc OXFORD 27.959
$11.50   (S66)

SAMSON ET DALILA: AMOUR, VIENS AIDER MA
FAIBLESSE, FOR SOLO VOICE AND
ORCHESTRA see Saint-Saens, Camille

SAMSON ET DALILA: BACCHANALE see Saint-
Saens, Camille

SAMSON ET DALILA: DALILA AND HIGH
PRIEST, FOR SOLO VOICES AND
ORCHESTRA see Saint-Saens, Camille

SAMSON ET DALILA: MON COEUR S'OUVRE A
TA VOIX, FOR SOLO VOICE AND
ORCHESTRA see Saint-Saens, Camille

SAMSON ET DALILA: MY HEART AT THY SWEET
VOICE see Saint-Saens, Camille;
Samson Et Dalila: Mon Coeur S'Ouvre
A Ta Voix, For Solo Voice And
Orchestra

SAMSON ET DALILA: PRINTEMPS QUI
COMMENCE, FOR SOLO VOICE AND
ORCHESTRA see Saint-Saens, Camille

SAMSON: HONOUR AND ARMS, FOR SOLO VOICE
AND ORCHESTRA see Handel, George
Frideric

SAMSON: HOW WILLING MY PATERNAL LOVE,
FOR SOLO VOICE AND ORCHESTRA see
Handel, George Frideric

SAMSON: LET THE BRIGHT SERAPHIM, FOR
SOLO VOICE AND ORCHESTRA see
Handel, George Frideric

SAMSON: THY GLORIOUS DEEDS INSPIR'D MY
TONGUE, FOR SOLO VOICE AND
ORCHESTRA see Handel, George
Frideric

SAMSON: TOTAL ECLIPSE, FOR SOLO VOICE
AND ORCHESTRA see Handel, George
Frideric

SAMSON: WHY DOES THE GOD OF ISRAEL
SLEEP, FOR SOLO VOICE AND ORCHESTRA
see Handel, George Frideric

SAMSON: WITH PLAINTIVE NOTES, FOR SOLO
VOICE AND ORCHESTRA see Handel,
George Frideric

SAMUEL, GERHARD (1924-   )
Three Hymns To Apollo [15']
fl,ob,clar,vln,vla,vcl,perc,
glock,vibra,harp,vcl solo
BELWIN rent   (S67)

SAN ZENO-VERONA see Boone, Charles N.

SANDSTROM, JAN (1954-   )
Era [10']
3.2.3.3. 4.3.3.1. timp,2perc,
harp,pno,strings
sc STIM perf mat rent   (S68)

SANDSTROM, SVEN-DAVID (1942-   )
Rest Is Dross, The [8']
string orch
pts STIM perf mat rent   (S69)

SANDYS
First Noel, The
(Luck, Arthur) LUCKS HYMNS 25 set
$15.00, pts $.65, ea. contains
also: Good King Wenceslas   (S70)

SANGER-FEST-OUVERTURE see Hildebrand,
Camillo

SANGERSLUST POLKA see Strauss, Johann,
[Jr.]

SANS SOUCI see Hatrik, Juraj, Symphony
No. 1

SANS SOUCI MENUET see Claassen, Arthur

SANTA CATERINA DA SIENA see Bossi,
[Marco] Enrico

S. ELENA AL CALVARIO see Caldara,
Antonio

SANTA ELENA AL CALVARIO: SINFONIA,
[ARR.] see Leo, Leonardo (Oronzo
Salvatore de)

SANTA LUCIA, FOR SOLO VOICE AND
ORCHESTRA see Braga, Gaetano

SANTA ULIVA: NINNA-NANNA, FOR SOLO
VOICE AND ORCHESTRA see Pizzetti,
Ildebrando

SANTINI, DALMAZIO
Concerto for Trombone and Orchestra
[20']
orch,trom solo
RYDET EMS 1942 $5.50   (S71)

S. PIETRO IN CESAREA see Caldara,
Antonio

SANTOLIQUIDO, FRANCESCO (1883-1971)
Ferhuda: 2 Intermezzi
FORLIVESI perf mat rent   (S72)

Sinfonia No. 1
FORLIVESI perf mat rent   (S73)

Tre Miniature Per I Piccoli
FORLIVESI perf mat rent   (S74)

SAPIEYEVSKI, JERZY (1945-   )
Concerto for Trumpet and Orchestra
[14']
3.3.3.3. 4.3.3.1. timp,3perc,
strings,trp solo
sc PETERS P66662 $15.00, perf mat
rent   (S75)

SARABANDA E ALLEGRO, FOR VIOLONCELLO
AND ORCHESTRA see Mortari, Virgilio

SARABANDA, GIGA E BADINERIE see
Corelli, Arcangelo

SARABANDE see Moszkowski, Moritz

SARABANDE UND MINUETTE SCHERZANDO,
[ARR.] see Moszkowski, Moritz

SARAGOSSA see Crucius, Heinz

SARAI, TIBOR (1919-   )
Symphony No. 2
(special import only) sc EMB 10173
f.s.   (S76)

SARASATE, PABLO DE (1844-1908)
Danse Espagnole, For Violin And
Orchestra *Op.37
2.2.2.2. 2.0.0.0. timp,harp,
strings,vln solo
(based on L. Zortzico's "Adios
Montanas") INTERNAT. perf mat
rent   (S77)

Gypsy Airs *see Zigeunerweisen, For
Violin And Orchestra

Zigeunerweisen, For Violin And
Orchestra *Op.20
BROUDE BR. study sc $6.00, set
$17.50, pts $1.25, ea.   (S78)
INTERNAT. perf mat rent   (S79)
"Gypsy Airs" LUCKS 00529 sc $5.00,
set $14.00, pts $1.15, ea.   (S80)

SARATOGA QUICKSTEP see Gould, Morton

SARELLO see Stanke, Willy

SARI, JOZSEF (1935-   )
Fossilien
string orch
(special import only) sc EMB 10206
f.s.   (S81)

SARKOZY, ISTVAN (1920-   )
Concerto Semplice, For Violin And
Orchestra
orch,vln solo
(special import only) sc EMB 10187
f.s.   (S82)

SATANELLA POLKA see Strauss, Johann,
[Jr.]

SATIE, ERIK (1866-1925)
Gnossiennes, Trois, [arr.]
(Bon, Willem Frederik) 2.2.2.2.alto
sax. 3.2.0.0. perc,harp,strings
[9'] sc DONEMUS f.s., perf mat
rent   (S83)

Gymnopedies Nos. 1 And 3, [arr.]
(Debussy) LUCKS 07547 sc $4.50, set
$10.50, pts $1.15, ea.   (S84)
(Debussy) 2.1.0.0. 4.0.0.0. cym,
2harp,strings BROUDE BR. set
$12.50, pts $1.25, ea.   (S85)

SATO, KIMI (1949-   )
Ailleurs [10']
1.1.1.1. 1.1.1.0. 2perc,string
quin
RICORDI-FR R.2264 perf mat rent
(S86)

SATOW, KARL (1884-1966)
Serenade [14']
string orch
RIES perf mat rent   (S87)

SAWYER, WILSON (1917-1979)
Alaskan Symphony *see Symphony No. 1

Processional And Capriccio For
Piccolo And Orchestra [12']
3.3.3.3. 4.3.3.1. timp,perc,
strings
MARGUN BP 7129 perf mat rent   (S88)

Symphony No. 1, Op. 19 [29']
3.3.2.3. 4.3.3.1. timp,perc,
strings,Bar solo
MARGUN BP 7128 perf mat rent   (S89)

SAY CHEESE see Andriessen, Jurriaan

SCALA DI SETA, LA: OVERTURE see
Rossini, Gioacchino

SCALERO, ROSARIO (1870-1954)
Divina Foresta, La [7']
2.3.3.3. 4.3.3.1. timp,strings
sc CARISCH 16178 perf mat rent
(S90)

SCARLATTI, ALESSANDRO (1660-1725)
Concerto Grosso No. 1 in F minor
string orch,cont
LUCKS 01516 sc $4.00, set $5.75,
pts $1.15, ea.   (S91)
(Upmeyer) KALMUS A1173 sc $4.00,
set $7.50, pts $1.50, ea.   (S92)

Concerto Grosso No. 2 in C minor
string orch,cont
LUCKS 07498 sc $4.00, set $5.75,
pts $1.15, ea.   (S93)
(Upmeyer) KALMUS A1174 sc $4.00,
set $7.50, pts $1.50, ea.   (S94)

Concerto Grosso No. 3 in F
string orch,cont
LUCKS 01518 sc $4.00, set $5.75,
pts $1.15, ea.   (S95)
(Lenzewski) KALMUS A1175 sc $4.00,
set $7.50, pts $1.50, ea.   (S96)

Sedecia, Re Di Gerusalemme, Il: Caldo
Sangue, For Solo Voice And String
Orchestra [5']
string orch,T solo
manuscript CARISCH   (S97)

Sinfonia No. 1 in F [6']
2A rec/2fl,strings,cont
KALMUS 5275 sc $6.00, set $6.00,
pts $.75, ea.   (S98)

Sinfonia No. 2 in D [7']
2fl,strings,cont
KALMUS 5276 sc $6.00, perf mat
rent, set $8.00, pts $1.00, ea.
(S99)

Sinfonia No. 4 in E minor [9']
fl,ob,strings,cont
KALMUS 5277 sc $6.00, perf mat
rent, set $8.00, pts $1.00, ea.
(S100)

Sinfonia No. 5 in D minor [9']
2fl,strings,cont
KALMUS 5278 sc $6.00, perf mat
rent, set $8.00, pts $1.00, ea.
(S101)

Sinfonia No. 12 in C minor [6']
fl,strings,cont
KALMUS 5279 sc $5.00, set $7.00,
pts $1.00, ea.   (S102)

Sinfonie d'oratorio
(from "La Colpa", "La Giuditta",
"Caino", "Il David", "L'Abramo",
"Il Sedecia") sc DE SANTIS
DS 1110 f.s.   (S103)

Su Le Sponde Del Tebro, For Solo
Voice And Orchestra
trp/ob,hpsd,strings without vla,S
solo
[It] MULLER sc $13.00, set $10.00,

SCARLATTI, ALESSANDRO (cont'd.)

pts $2.00, ea.   (S104)

SCARLATTI, DOMENICO (1685-1757)
Allegro Marciale, Pastorale Und Fuge
string orch
sc,pts MOSELER M 10.011 f.s. (S105)

Capriccio Fugato [8']
string orch,cont
(Winter, P.) sc,pts GERIG BG 678
f.s.   (S106)

Fuga Del Gatto
see RICREAZIONI DI ANTICHE MUSICHE
CLASSICHE, SERIE V: MUSICHE
ANTICHE ITALIANE

Sinfonia No. 1
strings,cont
(Geoffroy-Dechaume, Antoine) sc,pts
FRANCAIS $22.50   (S107)

Sinfonia No. 2
2fl,ob,strings,cont
(Geoffroy-Dechaume, Antoine) sc,pts
FRANCAIS $22.50   (S108)

Sinfonia No. 3
strings,cont
(Geoffroy-Dechaume, Antoine) sc,pts
FRANCAIS $22.50   (S109)

Sinfonia No. 4
ob,strings,cont
(Geoffroy-Dechaume, Antoine) sc,pts
FRANCAIS $22.50   (S110)

Sinfonia No. 5
strings,cont
(Geoffroy-Dechaume, Antoine) sc,pts
FRANCAIS $22.50   (S111)

Sinfonia No. 6
ob,strings,cont
(Geoffroy-Dechaume, Antoine) sc,pts
FRANCAIS $22.50   (S112)

Sinfonia No. 7
strings,cont
(Geoffroy-Dechaume, Antoine) sc,pts
FRANCAIS $22.50   (S113)

Sinfonia No. 8
ob,strings,cont
(Geoffroy-Dechaume, Antoine) sc,pts
FRANCAIS $22.50   (S114)

Sinfonia No. 9
ob,strings,cont
(Geoffroy-Dechaume, Antoine) sc,pts
FRANCAIS $22.50   (S115)

Sinfonia No. 10
ob,strings,cont
(Geoffroy-Dechaume, Antoine) sc,pts
FRANCAIS $22.50   (S116)

Sinfonia No. 11
ob,strings,cont
(Geoffroy-Dechaume, Antoine) sc,pts
FRANCAIS $22.50   (S117)

Sinfonia No. 12
ob,strings,cont
(Geoffroy-Dechaume, Antoine) sc,pts
FRANCAIS $22.50   (S118)

Sinfonia No. 13
ob,strings,cont
(Geoffroy-Dechaume, Antoine) sc,pts
FRANCAIS $22.50   (S119)

Sinfonia No. 14
fl,ob,strings,cont
(Geoffroy-Dechaume, Antoine) sc,pts
FRANCAIS $22.50   (S120)

Sinfonia No. 15
ob,strings,cont
(Geoffroy-Dechaume, Antoine) sc,pts
FRANCAIS $22.50   (S121)

Sinfonia No. 16
ob,strings,cont
(Geoffroy-Dechaume, Antoine) sc,pts
FRANCAIS $22.50   (S122)

Sinfonia No. 17
2ob,strings,cont
(Geoffroy-Dechaume, Antoine) sc,pts
FRANCAIS $22.50   (S123)

Sonata
see RICREAZIONI DI ANTICHE MUSICHE
CLASSICHE, SERIE II: MUSICHE
ANTICHE ITALIANE

SCARLATTI PORTFOLIO see Lees, Benjamin

SCENE see Berio, Luciano

SCENE DE BALLET, FOR VIOLIN AND
ORCHESTRA see Beriot, Charles-
August de

SCENE IN MONOCHROME see Siekmann, Frank

SCENE PASSIONNEE see Becce, Giuseppe

SCENES DE BALLET see Stravinsky, Igor

SCENES DE LA CSARDA NO. 3, FOR VIOLIN
AND ORCHESTRA see Hubay, Jeno

SCENES DE LA CSARDA NO. 4, FOR VIOLIN
AND ORCHESTRA see Hubay, Jeno

SCENES FROM BACHO see Yuasa, Joji

SCENES FROM GILGAMESH, FOR FLUTE AND
STRING ORCHESTRA see Polin, Claire

SCHAATSENRIJDERS see Schouwman, Hans

SCHAFE KONNEN SICHER WEIDEN, [ARR.] see
Bach, Johann Sebastian

SCHAFER, R. MURRAY (1933-   )
Adieu, Robert Schumann, For Solo
Voice And Orchestra [18'-20']
2.2.2.2. 2.2.2.0. 2perc,pno,
strings,electronic tape,solo
voice
sc UNIVER. UE 16520 $25.00, perf
mat rent   (S124)

Arcana, For Solo Voice And Chamber
Orchestra
2.2.2.2. 2.2.2.0. 2perc,harp,pno&
elec org,solo voice
study sc UNIVER. UE 16019 f.s.,
perf mat rent   (S125)

Cortege [15']
2.2.2.2. 2.2.0.0. perc,strings
sc UNIVER. UE 16531 f.s., perf mat
rent, study sc UNIVER. UE 16533
$29.00   (S126)

Hymn To Night, For Solo Voice And
Chamber Orchestra
fl,ob,trp,trom,2perc,harp,pno&
elec org,vln,vcl,db,S solo
sc UNIVER. UE 16524 $36.00, perf
mat rent   (S127)

Hymn To Night, For Solo Voice And
Orchestra [16']
1.1.1.1. 1.1.1.0. 2perc,harp,pno&
elec org,strings,S solo
sc UNIVER. UE 16522 f.s., perf mat
rent   (S128)

SCHAFER-QUADRILLE see Strauss, Johann,
[Sr.]

SCHAFFER, BOGUSLAW (1929-   )
Jazz Concerto [17']
4.0.0.4. 0.4.4.0. 4vcl,4db, and
jazz ensemble: clar, soprano
sax, alto sax, tenor sax,
baritone sax, trp, horn, trom,
vibra, pno, perc, db
sc POLSKIE $16.50, perf mat rent
                                 (S129)

SCHAT, PETER (1935-   )
Brons
see Cryptogamen, For Solo Voice And
Orchestra

Cryptogamen, For Solo Voice And
Orchestra
3.2.4.3. 4.3.2.1. timp,4perc,harp,
pno/cel,strings,Bar solo sc
DONEMUS f.s., perf mat rent
contains: Brons; Lithosfeer;
Rood; Rook; Steen   (S130)

Lithosfeer
see Cryptogamen, For Solo Voice And
Orchestra

Rood
see Cryptogamen, For Solo Voice And
Orchestra

Rook
see Cryptogamen, For Solo Voice And
Orchestra

Steen
see Cryptogamen, For Solo Voice And
Orchestra

Stemmen Uit Het Labyrint, For Solo
Voices And Orchestra [30']
3.3.3.3.sarrusophone. 4.3.3.2.
timp,4perc,harp,pno,13vla,
10vcl,8db,ATB soli
sc DONEMUS f.s., perf mat rent
                                 (S131)

Symphony No. 1, Op. 27 [40']
3.3.4.4. 4.3.3.2. timp,4perc,
2harp,strings,harmonica
DONEMUS perf mat rent   (S132)

SCHAUSPIELDIREKTOR, DER: OVERTURE see
Mozart, Wolfgang Amadeus

SCHEFFLER, SIEGFRIED (1892-1969)
Hanseatische Suite [15']
2(pic).1.2.2. 2.2.1.1. perc,harp,
strings
sc RIES f.s., perf mat rent   (S133)

SCHEHERAZADE see Rimsky-Korsakov,
Nikolai

SCHEIBE, W.
Czardas No. 3
(Jugel-Janson, K.) WOITSCHACH f.s.
                                 (S134)

Mein Schones Erzgebirge
(Jubel-Janson, K.) WOITSCHACH f.s.
                                 (S135)

Wunder Der Berge
WOITSCHACH f.s.   (S136)

SCHELB, JOSEF (1894-   )
Concerto for Flute and Orchestra
timp,strings,fl solo
sc MULLER 2007 f.s.   (S137)

SCHEMI E CADENZE see Benvenuti, Arrigo

SCHENKER, FRIEDRICH (1942-   )
Concerto for Double Bass and
Orchestra
sc DEUTSCHER DVFM 1428 f.s., perf
mat rent   (S138)

Orfeo: Pezzi Concertati [30']
3.3.3.3. 4.3.3.1. harp,cel,timp,
perc,strings
DEUTSCHER perf mat rent   (S139)

Sonate Fur JSB [42']
4.4.4.4. 5.4.4.1. timp,perc,pno/
org,hpsd,harp,strings
DEUTSCHER perf mat rent   (S140)

SCHERCHEN, TONA (1938-   )
Invitation Au Voyage, L' [22']
1(pic).1.2(bass clar).1. 1.2.2.0.
pno,harp,perc,vln,vla,vcl,db
BOOSEY perf mat rent   (S141)

Oeil De Chat [13']
4.4.4.4. 6.4.4.1. timp,perc,
strings
BOOSEY perf mat rent   (S142)

SCHERZO A LA RUSSE see Stravinsky, Igor

SCHERZO FUGATO see Lang, Walter

SCHERZO-TARENTELLE, FOR VIOLIN AND
ORCHESTRA see Wieniawski, Henryk

SCHERZO UND FINALE see Wolf, Hugo

SCHEVIKHOVEN, HENK VAN (1947-   )
Nightmusic [7']
3.3.3.3. 4.3.3.1. timp,perc,harp,
cel,vibra,xylo,strings
sc DONEMUS f.s., perf mat rent
                                 (S143)

SCHIASSI, GAETANO MARIA (ca. 1690-1754)
Christmas Symphony *see Sinfonia
Pastorale

Sinfonia Pastorale
"Christmas Symphony" LUCKS 08379 sc
$4.00, set $6.25, pts $1.25, ea.
                                 (S144)

SCHIAVO, GREGORIO DE (1900-   )
Ruralia [9']
2.2.2.2. 2.2.0.0. timp,cel,harp,
strings
sc CARISCH 15984 perf mat rent
                                 (S145)

Theme and Variations [11']
2.2.2.2. 2.2.0.0. perc,strings
sc CARISCH 15985 perf mat rent
                                 (S146)

SCHICHTEN-BOGEN see Buchtger, Fritz

SCHILLING, HANS LUDWIG (1927-   )
Exzentrischer Marsch
pts MOECK 3015 rent   (S147)

SCHILLINGS, MAX VON (1868-1933)
Zwiegesprach, Ein, For Violin,
Violoncello And Orchestra [20']
2.2.2.2. 4.2.0.0. triangle,opt
harp,strings,vln solo,vcl solo
RIES perf mat rent   (S148)

SCHIPPER, DE see Ketting, Piet

SCHLACHT-SINFONIE see Winter, Peter von

SCHLAFE EIN, TRAUME SUSS see Lersen,
Fred

SCHLAFENDES JESUSKIND, FOR SOLO VOICE
AND ORCHESTRA see Wolf, Hugo

SCHLEMM, GUSTAV ADOLF (1902-   )
Capriccio for Violin and Orchestra
sc,pts RIES f.s.   (S149)

Konzertante Musik, For Violin,
Violoncello And String Orchestra
string orch,vln solo,vcl solo

SCHLEMM, GUSTAV ADOLF (cont'd.)

sc,pts RIES f.s.   (S150)

Veranderungen Uber Ein Thema Von
Couperin, For Violin And String
Orchestra
string orch,vln solo
TONOS   (S151)

SCHLENKERMANN, FRITZ (1907-   )
Schneewalzer
LEUCKART f.s.   (S152)

SCHLENSOG, MARTIN
Gartenfest, Ein [17']
2.1.1.1. 0.0.0.0. timp,triangle,
strings
RIES perf mat rent   (S153)

SCHLITTENPFERDE, DIE see Bruyns, Henk

SCHMELZER, JOHANN HEINRICH (1623-1680)
Balletto
2trp,3trom,bsn,strings,cont
MUS. RARA 1712 f.s.   (S154)

SCHMERZEN, FOR SOLO VOICE AND
ORCHESTRA, [ARR.] see Wagner,
Richard

SCHMETTERLING IM PAVILLON see Hirt,
Herbert

SCHMIDT, CHRISTFRIED (1932-   )
Concerto for Violoncello and
Orchestra
3.2.2.2.sax. 2.2.2.0. timp,perc,
hpsd,strings,vcl solo
sc DEUTSCHER 1429 f.s.   (S155)

SCHMIDT-WUNSTORF, RUDOLF (1916-   )
Escaliers De Piranese, Les [8']
3.2+English horn.2+bass clar.3.
3.3.0.0. harp,strings
"Treppen Des Piranesi, Die" sc RIES
f.s., perf mat rent   (S156)

Kleine Konigstochter, Die *see
Petite Reine, La

Petite Reine, La [15']
2(pic).2(English horn).2.2.
4.2.3.0. timp,2perc,harp,
strings
"Kleine Konigstochter, Die" RIES
perf mat rent   (S157)

Treppen Des Piranesi, Die *see
Escaliers De Piranese, Les

SCHMITT, GEORG ALOIS (1827-1902)
Konzertstuck for Oboe and Orchestra,
Op. 29 [11']
2.0.2.2. 2.2.0.0. timp,strings,ob
solo
sc,pts LIENAU f.s.   (S158)

Konzertstuck for 2 Pianos and String
Orchestra, Op. 23 [11']
string orch,2pno soli
sc,pts LIENAU rent   (S159)

SCHMUCKE DICH, O LIEBE SEELE, FOR
VIOLONCELLO AND STRING ORCHESTRA,
[ARR.] see Bach, Johann Sebastian

SCHNABEL, ARTUR (1882-1951)
Duodecimet, [arr.]
(Lebowitz) min sc BOOSEY 587 $3.00
                                 (S160)

SCHNEESTERNCHEN POLKA see Strauss,
Eduard

SCHNEEWALZER see Schlenkermann, Fritz

SCHNEIDER, FRANZ (1737-1812)
Symphony
see AUSTRIAN CLOISTER SYMPHONISTS

SCHNELLDORFER, MARTIN
Pizzarco [3'30"]
2.2.2.1. 2.2.2.0. glock,xylo,
harp,cel,pno,gtr,strings
ORLANDO rent   (S161)

SCHNELLPOLKA see Kletsch, Ludwig

SCHOECK, OTHMAR (1886-1957)
Concerto for Violin and Orchestra,
Op. 21
min sc HUG GH 5026 f.s., perf mat
rent   (S162)

Concerto for Violoncello and
Orchestra, Op. 61
sc,pts HUG GH 9373 f.s., perf mat
rent   (S163)

Festlicher Hymnus *Op.64
sc HUG GH 9765 f.s., perf mat rent
                                 (S164)

Sommernacht *Op.58
string orch
sc HUG A168 f.s., perf mat rent
                                 (S165)

SCHOENBERG, ARNOLD (1874-1951)
Chamber Symphony No.2 *Op.38
min sc UNIVER. PH461 $20.00 (S166)

Concerto for Violin and Orchestra,
Op. 36
min sc UNIVER. PH460 $26.00 (S167)

SCHOLLUM, ROBERT (1913-   )
Seestuck *Op.108
2+pic.2+English horn.2.2+
contrabsn.alto sax. 4.2.2.0.
timp,perc,glock,xylo,vibra,pno,
strings
sc,pts DOBLINGER rent (S168)

SCHON ROHTRAUT POLKA see Strauss,
Eduard

SCHON ROSMARIN, [ARR.] see Kreisler,
Fritz

SCHONBERG, STIG GUSTAV (1933-   )
Concerto for Organ and Orchestra, Op.
100 [20']
2.2.2.2. 4.3.3.0. timp,perc,
strings,org solo
STIM (S169)

SCHONBRUNNER WALZER, DIE see Lanner,
Josef

SCHONHERR, MAX (1903-   )
A Capriccio, For Violin And Orchestra
KRENN perf mat rent (S170)

Hans Im Gluck, For Clarinet And
Orchestra
KRENN perf mat rent (S171)

Humoreske, For Violin And Orchestra
KRENN perf mat rent (S172)

Im Duett, For Clarinet And Orchestra
KRENN perf mat rent (S173)

Miniature, For Flute And String
Orchestra
string orch,fl solo
KRENN sc f.s., pts f.s., rent
(S174)

Walzer Poesie, For Piano And
Orchestra
KRENN perf mat rent (S175)

SCHONTHAL, RUTH
Concerto for Piano and Orchestra, No.
2 [26']
2+pic.2.2.3. 4.2.2.1. timp,
strings,pno solo
OXFORD perf mat rent (S176)

SCHOOL FOR FATHERS: PRELUDE AND
INTERMEZZO see Wolf-Ferrari,
Ermanno, Quattro Rusteghi, I:
Preludio E Intermezzo

SCHOOLMASTER SYMPHONY see Haydn,
[Franz] Joseph, Symphony No. 55 in
E flat

SCHOONENBEEK, KEES (1947-   )
Brabantse Rapsodie [6']
3.2.2.2. 3.3.3.1. 3perc,strings
DONEMUS perf mat rent (S177)

Concerto for Piano and Orchestra
[15']
3.2.3.3. 3.3.3.1. timp,3perc,
xylo,strings,pno solo
sc DONEMUS f.s., perf mat rent
(S178)

Majoretten [11']
3.2.2.2. 3.3.3.1. timp,4perc,
strings
DONEMUS sc f.s., pts rent (S179)

Serenade for Oboe and Orchestra [20']
1.1.2.1. 2.1.1.0. perc,harp,
strings,ob solo
DONEMUS (S180)

SCHOPENHAUER-CANTATE, FOR SOLO VOICE
AND ORCHESTRA see Frid, Geza

SCHOPFUNG, DIE: MIT WURD' UND HOHEIT
ANGETAN, FOR SOLO VOICE AND
ORCHESTRA see Haydn, [Franz] Joseph

SCHOPFUNG, DIE: NUN BEUT DIE FLUR, FOR
SOLO VOICE AND ORCHESTRA see Haydn,
[Franz] Joseph

SCHOSTAKOWITSCH, DMITRI
see SHOSTAKOVICH, DMITRI

SCHOTTISCH see Knumann, Jo

SCHOTTISCHE FANTASIE, FOR VIOLIN AND
ORCHESTRA see Bruch, Max

SCHOUWMAN, HANS (1902-1967)
Friesland *Op.44,No.1
see Friesland, For Solo Voice And
Orchestra

SCHOUWMAN, HANS (cont'd.)

Friesland, For Solo Voice And
Orchestra
2.2.2.2. 1.0.0.0. perc,harp,
strings,low solo sc DONEMUS f.s.,
perf mat rent
contains: Friesland, Op.44,No.1;
Heerenveen, Op.44,No.3; Herfst
In Friesland, Op.44,No.4;
Schaatsenrijders, Op.44,No.2
(S181)

Heerenveen *Op.44,No.3
see Friesland, For Solo Voice And
Orchestra

Herfst In Friesland *Op.44,No.4
see Friesland, For Solo Voice And
Orchestra

Schaatsenrijders *Op.44,No.2
see Friesland, For Solo Voice And
Orchestra

SCHREINER, ALEXANDER (1901-   )
Verwandte Seelen, For Two Clarinets
And Orchestra
LUCKS 00769 set $16.00, pts $.75,
ea. (S182)

Worried Drummer, The
LUCKS 08592 sc $6.00, set $12.00,
pts $1.00, ea. (S183)

SCHRODER, HANNING (1896-   )
Sinfonia
string orch,tam-tam
BUDDE perf mat rent (S184)

Varianten, For Flute And Orchestra
BUDDE perf mat rent (S185)

SCHUBACK, PETER (1947-   )
Chanson Du Desespoir, For Violoncello
And Orchestra [20']
1.1.1.1. 1.1.1.0. timp,2perc,
strings,vcl solo
sc STIM perf mat rent (S186)

SCHUBERT, FERDINAND (1794-1859)
Sechs Walzer [11']
1+pic.2.2.2. 2.2.1.0. timp,perc,
strings
(Fuhrer, R.) sc,pts DOBLINGER rent
(S187)

SCHUBERT, FRANZ (PETER) (1797-1828)
Allmacht, Die, "Gross Ist Jehova",
For Solo Voice And Orchestra,
[arr.] *Op.79,No.2
(Mottl) KALMUS A5146 sc $5.00, perf
mat rent, set $21.00, pts $1.00,
ea. (S188)

An Die Musik, For Solo Voice And
Orchestra, [arr.]
LUCKS 02002 sc $3.75, set $7.50,
pts $.75, ea. (S189)

Ave Maria, For Solo Voice And
Orchestra, [arr.]
LUCKS 02255 sc $4.00, set $8.00,
pts $.75, ea. (S190)

Ave Maria, [arr.]
(Barison, C.) 2.2.2.2. 0.0.0.0.
2harp,bells,strings [3'] sc
CARISCH 20542 f.s., pts CARISCH
20622 f.s. (S191)

Claudine Von Villa Bella: Overture
BREITKOPF-W perf mat rent (S192)

Des Teufels Lustschloss: Overture
KALMUS A5494 sc $6.00, perf mat
rent, set $20.00, pts $1.50, ea.
(S193)

Deutsche Tanze, Funf, Mit Coda Und
Sieben Trios *D.90
string orch
"Five German Dances, Coda And Trio"
BROUDE BR. sc $4.25, set $7.50,
pts $1.50, ea. (S194)
"Five German Dances With Coda And
Seven Trios" LUCKS 01521 sc
$2.75, set $7.00, pts $1.40, ea.
(S195)

Deutscher Mit Zwei Trios, [arr.]
(Clementi, A.) 1.1.1.1. 1.1.1.0.
gtr,cel,vln,vla,vcl [8'] sc
ZERBONI 7167 f.s., pts ZERBONI
7168 rent (S196)

Du Bist Die Ruh, For Solo Voice And
Orchestra, [arr.]
LUCKS 02317 set $7.50, pts $.75,
ea. (S197)

Duo, Op. 140, [arr.]
(Leibowitz, R.) 2.2.2.2. 4.2.3.0.
timp,strings [50'] manuscript
CARISCH (S198)

Fantasia For Piano And Orchestra In
C, "Der Wanderer", [arr.]
*Op.15,D.760
(Liszt) "Wanderer Fantasy" LUCKS sc

SCHUBERT, FRANZ (PETER) (cont'd.)

$22.00, set $35.00, pts $2.50,
ea. (S199)

Five German Dances, Coda And Trio
*see Deutsche Tanze, Funf, Mit
Coda Und Sieben Trios

Five German Dances With Coda And
Seven Trios *see Deutsche Tanze,
Funf, Mit Coda Und Sieben Trios

Five Minuets And Six Trios *see
Menuette, Funf, Und Sechs Trios

Gretchen Am Spinnrade, [arr.] *Op.2
(Liszt) 2.2.2.2. 2.0.0.0. timp,
harp,strings [3'30"] KALMUS 5293
sc $9.00, set $17.00 (S200)
(Offenbach, J.) "Marguerite At The
Spinning Wheel, [arr.]" 1.1.2.1.
2.1.0.0. timp,strings KALMUS
A5336 set $10.00, pts $1.00, ea.
(S201)

Impatience *see Ungeduld, For Solo
Voice And Orchestra, [arr.]

Marguerite At The Spinning Wheel,
[arr.] *see Gretchen Am
Spinnrade, [arr.]

Menuette, Funf, Und Sechs Trios
*D.89
string orch
"Five Minuets And Six Trios" LUCKS
01520 sc $3.75, set $5.75, pts
$1.15, ea. (S202)

Moment Musical, [arr.]
LUCKS 06591 sc $4.00, set $13.00,
pts $1.15, ea. (S203)

Overture In C, "In The Italian Style"
*D.591
LUCKS 09180 sc $6.50, set $14.00,
pts $.95, ea. (S204)

Overture in C minor, D. 8, [arr.]
(Hofmann) 1.0.2.1. 2.0.0.0. strings
PETERS P8053 sc $17.50, set
$22.00, pts $2.50, ea. (S205)

Overture in D, D. 26
BREITKOPF-W perf mat rent (S206)

Overture In D, "In The Italian Style"
*D.590 [8']
2.2.2.2. 2.2.0.0. timp,strings
KALMUS 5379 sc $6.00, perf mat
rent, set $17.00, pts $1.25, ea.
(S207)
LUCKS 06039 sc $8.00, set $25.00,
pts $2.00, ea. (S208)

Plantes De La Jeune Fille, Les,
[arr.]
(Offenbach, J.) 1.2.2.1. 2.0+
2cornet.0.0. timp,strings KALMUS
A5316 sc $1.50, set $10.00, pts
$1.00, ea. (S209)

Rondo for Violin and String Orchestra
in A, D. 438
LUCKS 01522 sc $3.75, set $5.50,
pts $.95, ea. (S210)

Rosamunde: Ballet Music
BROUDE BR. sc $4.50, set $22.50,
pts $1.25, ea. (S211)
LUCKS 06593 sc $4.50, set $17.00,
pts $1.75, ea. (S212)

Rosamunde: Entr'acte And Ballet Music
*see Rosamunde: Zwischenakt- Und
Balletmusik

Rosamunde: Overture *D.644
min sc UNIVER. PH24 $2.50 (S213)
LUCKS 06592 sc $9.50, set $24.00,
min sc $2.50, pts $1.15, ea.
(S214)
BROUDE BR. set $30.00, pts $1.25,
ea. (S215)

Rosamunde: Zwischenakt- Und
Balletmusik
"Rosamunde: Entr'acte And Ballet
Music" min sc PETERS 520 $5.00
(S216)

Rosamunde: Zwischenaktmusik
LUCKS 06594 sc $6.50, set $17.00,
pts $1.75, ea. (S217)

Salve Regina, Op. 153 for Solo Voice
and String Orchestra
string orch,S solo
sc HANSSLER 47.010-01 f.s., pts
HANSSLER 47.010-11:14 f.s. (S218)
[Lat] KNUS K14 sc $9.00, set $8.75,
pts $1.75, ea. (S219)

Serenade *see Standchen, For Solo
Voice And Orchestra, [arr.]

SCHUBERT, FRANZ (PETER) (cont'd.)

Sinfonia No. 9, [arr.] *see Duo, Op. 140, [arr.]

Standchen, For Solo Voice And Orchestra, [arr.] (Serenade) LUCKS 02228 sc $3.00, set $7.50, pts $.75, ea. (S220)

Symphony No. 2 in B flat, D. 125 BROUDE BR. sc $10.00, set $30.00, pts $2.00, ea. (S221)

Symphony No. 4 in C minor, D. 417 LUCKS 08433 sc $12.50, set $28.00, min sc $4.00, pts $1.60, ea. (S222)

(Brahms, Johannes) (reprint of Breitkopf and Hartel edition) study sc DOVER 23681-1 $6.50 contains also: Symphony No. 5 in B flat, D. 485; Symphony No. 7 in C, D. 944; Symphony No. 8 in B minor, D. 759 (S223)

Symphony No. 5 in B flat, D. 485 see Schubert, Franz (Peter), Symphony No. 4 in C minor, D. 417 min sc UNIVER. PH91 $4.00 (S224)

Symphony No. 6 in C, D. 589 min sc PETERS 511 $6.00 (S225) LUCKS 09004 sc $16.00, set $28.00, min sc $4.00, pts $1.75, ea. (S226)

Symphony No. 7 in C, D. 944 see Schubert, Franz (Peter), Symphony No. 4 in C minor, D. 417 min sc UNIVER. PH92 $6.00 (S227) min sc PETERS 513 $12.00 (S228)

Symphony No. 8 in B minor, D. 759 see Schubert, Franz (Peter), Symphony No. 4 in C minor, D. 417 BROUDE BR. set $27.50, pts $1.50, ea. (S229) min sc ZEN-ON 890601 f.s. (S230) LUCKS 06600 sc $6.00, set $16.00, min sc $2.50, pts $1.15, ea. (S231) min sc UNIVER. PH2 $3.00 (S232)

Symphony No. 9 In C *see Symphony No. 7 in C, D. 944

Tragic Symphony *see Symphony No. 4 in C minor, D. 417

Trauermarsch *Op.55 LUCKS 08332 sc $8.00, set $18.00, pts $.75, ea. (S233)

Unfinished Symphony *see Symphony No. 8 in B minor, D. 759

Üngeduld, For Solo Voice And Orchestra, [arr.] "Impatience" LUCKS 02404 sc $3.00, set $8.00, pts $.75, ea. (S234)

Wanderer, Der, For Solo Voice And Orchestra, [arr.] (Luck) LUCKS 02195 sc $4.00, set $15.50, pts $.75, ea. (S235)

Wanderer Fantasy *see Fantasia For Piano And Orchestra In C, "Der Wanderer", [arr.]

Whither *see Wohin?, For Solo Voice And Orchestra, [arr.]

Who Is Sylvia, For Solo Voice And Orchestra, [arr.] LUCKS 02016 sc $4.00, set $9.00, pts $.75, ea. (S236)

Wohin?, For Solo Voice And Orchestra, [arr.] "Whither" LUCKS 02895 sc $3.00, set $8.00, pts $.75, ea. (S237)

SCHUBERT, HEINO (1928-) Concerto for Woodwinds and Strings study sc BREITKOPF-W HG3 1276 f.s., perf mat rent (S238)

SCHUBERT, HEINZ (1908-1945) Concertante Suite, For Violin And Chamber Orchestra [18'] 2.1.0.0. 0.0.0.0. strings,vln solo RIES perf mat rent (S239)

Hymnisches Konzert, For Solo Voices And Orchestra [33'] 1.1.0.1. 0.3.0.0. org,strings,ST soli RIES perf mat rent (S240)

Lyrisches Konzert, For Viola And Chamber Orchestra [27'] 0.0.1.0. 1.0.0.0. strings without db,vla solo RIES perf mat rent (S241)

SCHUBERT, HEINZ (cont'd.)

Praeludium Und Toccata [13'] string orch,vln solo,vla solo,vcl solo RIES perf mat rent (S242)

Sinfonietta [20'] 2.2.2.2. 4.2.0.0. timp,2perc, strings RIES perf mat rent (S243)

Vom Unendlichen, For Solo Voice And String Orchestra [15'] string orch,S solo RIES perf mat rent (S244)

SCHUBERT, MANFRED (1937-) Evocazioni clar,bsn,horn,2perc,harp,vln,vla, vcl,db DEUTSCHER perf mat rent (S245)

Hommage a Wagner-Regeny perc,harp,cel,13strings sc DEUTSCHER 1437 f.s., perf mat rent (S246)

SCHUBERT-WEBER, S. Berceuse ob,harp,strings sc,pts RIES f.s. (S247)

My Romance RIES f.s. (S248)

Valse Caprice, For Piano And Orchestra [3'] 2(pic).2.2.2. 2.2.1.0. timp,perc, strings,pno solo (Dressel, Erwin) RIES perf mat rent (S249)

SCHULLER, GUNTHER (1925-) Concerto for Horn and Orchestra, No. 1 [14'] 3.3.3.3. 4.3.3.1. timp,perc,harp, cel,strings,horn solo MARGUN BP 7001 perf mat rent (S250)

Little Fantasy [4'] 1.1.1.1. 2.1.1.0. timp,perc MARGUN BP 7002 perf mat rent (S251)

Six Early Songs, For Solo Voice And Orchestra [18'] 3.3.4.3. 4.2.2.1. perc,harp,pno, cel,strings,S solo MARGUN BP 7003 $6.00, perf mat rent (S252)

Suite for Chamber Orchestra [8'] 2.2.2.2. 2.1.1.0. strings MARGUN BP 7004 perf mat rent (S253)

Variants On A Theme Of Thelonious Monk [15'] fl,tenor sax&fl&bass clar,vibra, gtr,pno,drums,2vln,vla,vcl,2db MARGUN BP 7050 perf mat rent (S254)

Vertige d'Eros [14'] 3(alto fl).2.3.2. 4.3.3.1. timp, perc,2harp,pno,cel,strings MARGUN BP 7005 perf mat rent (S255)

SCHULTZ, SVEND S. (1913-) Nordic Overture 2.2.2.2. 4.3.3.0. timp,perc, strings sc HANSEN-DEN $18.00 (S256)

SCHUMAN, WILLIAM HOWARD (1910-) Night Journey fl,ob,clar,bsn,horn,pno,4vln, 2vla,2vcl,db sc PRESSER 444-41011 $20.00, perf mat rent (S257)

Three Colloquies, For Horn And Orchestra 3.2.3.2. 0.3.0.0. timp,perc,harp, pno&cel,strings,horn solo sc PRESSER 144-40085 $26.00, perf mat rent (S258)

SCHUMANIANA see Toni, Alceo

SCHUMANN, GEORG (1886-1952) Drei Deutsche Tanze *Op.79 [16'] 2+pic.2.2.2. 4.2.1.0. timp,drums, strings sc,pts LIENAU f.s. (S259)

Elegy for Solo Voice and Orchestra, Op. 78b [13'] 2.2.2.2+contrabsn. 4.1.3.1. harp, timp,strings,S solo sc LIENAU (S260)

Lebensfreude *Op.54 [18'] 4(pic).3.3.2+contrabsn. 4.3.3.1. timp,perc,harp,strings RIES perf mat rent (S261)

Variationen Und Gigue Uber Ein Thema Von Handel *Op.72 [36'] 2+pic.2.2+bass clar.2+contrabsn.

SCHUMANN, GEORG (cont'd.)

4+opt 2horn.3.3.1. 2harp,timp, perc,strings sc,pts LIENAU f.s. (S262)

Vita Somnium *Op.78a [20'] 2.2.2.2+contrabsn. 4.2.3.1. harp, timp,perc,strings sc,pts LIENAU rent (S263)

SCHUMANN, ROBERT (ALEXANDER) (1810-1856) Abendlied, [arr.] *Op.85,No.12 (Luck) "Evening Song" string orch LUCKS 06606 sc $1.25, set $3.75, pts $.75, ea. (S264) (Saint-Saens) "Evening Song" LUCKS 10209 sc $2.00, set $5.00, pts $.75, ea. (S265)

Beiden Grenadiere, Die, For Solo Voice And Orchestra, [arr.] *Op.49,No.1 LUCKS 02171 sc $6.00, set $10.00, pts $.75, ea. (S266)

Canone I see RICREAZIONI DI ANTICHE MUSICHE CLASSICHE, SERIE IV: MUSICHE ANTICHE ITALIANE

Canone II see RICREAZIONI DI ANTICHE MUSICHE CLASSICHE, SERIE IV: MUSICHE ANTICHE ITALIANE

Concerto for Piano and Orchestra, Op. 54, in A minor see Works For Piano And Orchestra min sc UNIVER. PH424 $8.00 (S267) BROUDE BR. sc $17.50, set $30.00, pts $1.50, ea. (S268)

Concerto for Violoncello and Orchestra, Op. 129, in A minor LUCKS 00612 sc $8.50, set $18.00, min sc $3.00, pts $1.40, ea. (S269)

Dedication *see Widmung, For Solo Voice And Orchestra, [arr.]

Evening Song *see Abendlied, [arr.]

Hermann Und Dorothea: Overture KALMUS 5534 sc $6.00, set $15.00 (S270)

Konzert-Allegro Mit Introduktion, For Piano And Orchestra, Op. 134 see Works For Piano And Orchestra

Konzertstuck for Piano and Orchestra, Op. 92, in G see Works For Piano And Orchestra

Spanisches Liederspiel, [arr.] *Op.74 (Hermann) string orch,string quar soli [13'] KALMUS 5270 sc $10.00, set $10.00 (S271)

Spring Symphony *see Symphony No. 1, Op. 38, in B flat

Symphonies Nos. 1-4 (republication of original Breitkopf and Hartel editions) pap DOVER 24013-4 $11.95 (S272)

Symphony No. 1, Op. 38, in B flat min sc PETERS 551 $8.50 (S273) LUCKS 06612 sc $18.00, set $30.00, min sc $5.00, pts $1.50, ea. (S274)

Symphony No. 2, Op. 61, in C min sc PETERS 552 $8.50 (S275)

Symphony No. 3, Op. 97, in E flat min sc PETERS 553 $8.50 (S276)

Symphony No. 4, Op. 120, in D minor PETERS perf mat rent (S277) min sc PETERS 554 $7.00 (S278)

Traumerei, [arr.] string orch LUCKS 06610 sc $2.00, set $3.00, pts $.75, ea. (S279)

Widmung, For Solo Voice And Orchestra, [arr.] "Dedication" LUCKS 02892 sc $4.00, set $7.50, pts $.75, ea. (S280)

Works For Piano And Orchestra pap DOVER ISBN 0-486-24340-0 $7.50 contains: Concerto for Piano and Orchestra, Op. 54, in A minor; Konzert-Allegro Mit Introduktion, For Piano And Orchestra, Op. 134; Konzertstuck for Piano and Orchestra, Op. 92, in G (S281)

SCHURMANN, GERARD (1928-   )
    Concerto for Piano and Orchestra
        sc NOVELLO 2589 $29.00   (S282)

    Concerto for Violin and Orchestra
        NOVELLO study sc $27.50, sc,pts
        rent   (S283)

SCHUYT, NICO (1922-   )
    Concerto [20']
        2.0.0.opt clar.0. 0.0.opt
        trp.0.0. 2perc,pno 4-hands,
        strings
        sc DONEMUS f.s., perf mat rent
                                      (S284)

    Festa Seria [16']
        3.3.3.3. 3.4.3.1. timp,4perc,
        harp,pno,strings
        DONEMUS   (S285)

    Greetings From Holland [15']
        2.2.2.2. 2.1.0.0. timp,perc,harp/
        cel/pno,strings
        sc DONEMUS f.s., perf mat rent
                                      (S286)

    Quasi In Modo Di Valzer [9']
        3.3.3.3. 4.3.3.1. timp,3perc,
        harp,cel,strings
        sc DONEMUS f.s., perf mat rent
                                      (S287)

SCHWABISCHER LANDLER see Noack, Walter

SCHWAEN, KURT (1909-   )
    Hort Ihr Den Trommelschlag
        string orch
        sc,pts DEUTSCHER 32 073A, B f.s.
                                      (S288)

SCHWALMER TANZE, [ARR.] see Lewalter,
    Johann

SCHWAN, EIN see Grieg, Edvard Hagerup,
    Swan, A, For Solo Voice And
    Orchestra, [arr.]

SCHWANTNER, JOSEPH (1943-   )
    Aftertones Of Infinity [14']
        2(pic).2(English horn).2.2.
        4.2.3.1. timp,2perc,pno,cel,
        strings
        sc PETERS P66790 $15.00, perf mat
        rent   (S289)

    Canticle Of The Evening Bells, For
        Flute And Orchestra [20']
        0.1(English horn).1.1. 1.1.1.0.
        perc,pno,vln,vla,vcl,db,fl solo
        PETERS P66678 perf mat rent   (S290)

SCHWARTZ, OTTO (1871-1940)
    Fraulein Teufel: Satanella Walzer
        2.2.2.2. 4.2.3.0. harp,timp,
        strings
        sc,pts LIENAU rent   (S291)

SCHWARZE LAUTE, DIE see Bordewijk-
    Roepman, Johanna

SCHWARZWALDER POLKA see Noack, Walter

SCHWARZWALDER UHREN see Dressel, Erwin

SCHWATZERIN, DIE see Strauss, Josef

SCHWEDISCHE HOCHZEITSREISE see Dixie
    Joe

SCHWEDISCHER REITERSIGNAL-MARSCH see
    Grawert, Theodor

SCHWEISSTUCH DER VERONIKA, DAS see
    Kopelent, Marek

SCHWERTSIK, KURT (1935-   )
    Concerto for Violin and Orchestra,
        Op. 31 [20']
        1(pic).1.1(bass clar,clar in E
        flat).2. 2.1.0.1. harp,timp,
        perc,strings,vln solo
        min sc BOOSEY HPS 943 $23.00 (S292)

    Epilog Zu Rosamunde [12']
        2.2.2.2. 2.2.3.0. timp,strings
        BOOSEY perf mat rent   (S293)

SCHWICKERT, GUSTAV
    Concertino for Flute and String
        Orchestra, Op. 9 [9']
        string orch,fl solo
        RIES perf mat rent   (S294)

    Funf Lieder, For Solo Voice And
        Orchestra *Op.14a [12']
        1.1.2.1. 1.0.0.0. strings,med
        solo
        RIES perf mat rent   (S295)

    Lieder Der Liebe, For Solo Voice And
        Orchestra *Op.6a [10']
        2.1.2.2. 2.0.0.0. strings,high
        solo
        RIES perf mat rent   (S296)

    Ouverture Zu Einem Heiteren Spiel
        *Op.11 [7']
        2(pic).2.2.2. 4.2.3.0. timp,perc,
        strings

SCHWICKERT, GUSTAV (cont'd.)

    RIES perf mat rent   (S297)

    Sinfonietta, Op. 10, in C minor [25']
        2(pic).2.2.2. 4.2.3.1. timp,perc,
        strings
        RIES perf mat rent   (S298)

    Sturmnacht, For Solo Voice And
        Orchestra *Op.12 [16']
        2(pic).1.2.1. 2.1.1.0. timp,
        strings,med solo
        RIES perf mat rent   (S299)

SCIARRINO, SALVATORE (1947-   )
    Clair De Lune, For Piano And
        Orchestra *Op.25
        sc RICORDI-IT 132426 f.s.   (S300)

    Variazioni, For Violoncello And
        Orchestra
        sc RICORDI-IT 132227 f.s.   (S301)

SCIOFAR, FOR SOLO VOICE AND ORCHESTRA
    see Rigacci, Bruno

SCIOSTAKOVIC, DMITRI
    see SHOSTAKOVICH, DMITRI

SCIPIONE: HEAR ME! YE WINDS AND WAVES!,
    FOR SOLO VOICE AND ORCHESTRA see
    Handel, George Frideric

SCORE AND 23 PARTS see Cage, John

SCOTCH FANTASY see Bruch, Max,
    Schottische Fantasie, For Violin
    And Orchestra

SCOTT, CYRIL MEIR (1879-1970)
    Early One Morning, For Piano And
        Orchestra
        sc BOOSEY $15.00   (S302)

SCOTTISH WALTZ see Dorward, David

SCRIABIN, ALEXANDER (1872-1915)
    Reverie *Op.24
        LUCKS 06619 sc $7.50, set $25.00,
        min sc $3.50, pts $1.60, ea.
                                      (S303)

    Scriabin Settings, [arr.]
        (Knussen, Oliver) 1.1.2.1. 2.0.0.0.
        cel,strings [11'] MARGUN BP 7130
        perf mat rent   (S304)

SCRIABIN SETTINGS, [ARR.] see Scriabin,
    Alexander

SCUFFIARA, LA: OVERTURE see Paisiello,
    Giovanni

SE TU MI SPREZZI, INGRATE, FOR SOLO
    VOICE AND ORCHESTRA see Haydn,
    [Franz] Joseph

SEA, THE see Glazunov, Alexander
    Konstantinovich

SEA, THE see Skalkottas, Nikos

SEA-BATHING MAIDENS, THE see Kuula,
    Toivo, Merenkylpijaneidot, For Solo
    Voice And Orchestra

SEA IN SPRINGTIME, THE see Ikebe, Shin-
    Ichiro, Haru No Umi

SEA PICTURES, FOR SOLO VOICE AND
    ORCHESTRA see Elgar, [Sir] Edward
    (William)

SEA SURFACE FULL OF CLOUDS see Hekster,
    Walter

SEAL WOMAN, THE see Flothuis, Marius

SEARCH IN GREY I, FOR VIOLIN, PIANO,
    PERCUSSION AND ORCHESTRA see Ishii,
    Maki

SEASON OF DARKNESS see Frank, Andrew

SEASONS, THE, [ARR.] see Tchaikovsky,
    Piotr Ilyich

SEASONS, THE, OP. 67: SPRING see
    Glazunov, Alexander Konstantinovich

SEASONS, THE, OP. 67: SUMMER see
    Glazunov, Alexander Konstantinovich

SEASONS, THE: WITH JOY THE IMPATIENT
    HUSBANDMAN see Haydn, [Franz]
    Joseph, Jahreszeiten, Die: Schon
    Eilet Froh Der Ackersmann, For Solo
    Voice And Orchestra

SECHS INSTRUMENTALSATZE see Isaac,
    Heinrich

SECHS MENUETTE, PERGER 70 see Haydn,
    [Johann] Michael

SECHS SINFONIEN UND SECHS CONCERTI, OP.
    5 see Torelli, Giuseppe

SECHS WALZER see Schubert, Ferdinand

SECRET OF SUZANNE: OVERTURE see Wolf-
    Ferrari, Ermanno, Segreto Di
    Susanna, Il: Overture

SECUNDEN POLKA see Strauss, Johann,
    [Jr.]

SEDECIA see Caldara, Antonio

SEDECIA, RE DI GERUSALEMME, IL: CALDO
    SANGUE, FOR SOLO VOICE AND STRING
    ORCHESTRA see Scarlatti, Alessandro

SEDEM SKLADB, FOR STRING ORCHESTRA see
    Ramovs, Primoz

SEECADET QUADRILLE see Strauss, Eduard

SEESTUCK see Schollum, Robert

SEGERSTAM, LEIF (1944-   )
    Concerto Serioso, For Violin And
        Orchestra [20'45"]
        2.2(English horn).2(bass clar).2.
        2.3.3.0. timp,perc,cel,harp,
        strings,vln solo
        BUSCH DM 054 perf mat rent   (S305)

    Divertimento [12']
        string orch
        sc,pts BUSCH f.s.   (S306)

    Seven Red Moments, For Trumpet And
        Orchestra [20']
        2.2.2.2. 2.3.3.0. timp,4perc,
        harp,cel,strings,trp solo
        FAZER f.s.   (S307)

SEGRETO DI SUSANNA, IL: OVERTURE see
    Wolf-Ferrari, Ermanno

SEHNSUCHT, FOR SOLO VOICE AND ORCHESTRA
    see Luck, Andrew H.

SEI GETROST see Bordewijk-Roepman,
    Johanna

SEI VARIAZIONI SU UN TEMA DI A. CORELLI
    see Bonelli, Ettore

SEID UMSCHLUNGEN MILLIONEN WALZER see
    Strauss, Johann, [Jr.]

SEIDL, KURT
    Feierliches Adagio *Op.4 [9']
        2.2.2.2. 4.3.3.1. timp,perc,harp,
        strings
        RIES perf mat rent   (S308)

SEITENSTETTEN-MENUETTE see Haydn,
    [Franz] Joseph, Menuette, Zwolf,
    Hob. IX:1

SELBY, PHILIP
    Concerto for Guitar and Orchestra
        ROBERTON perf mat rent   (S309)

    From The Fountain Of Youth, For
        Guitar And Orchestra
        ROBERTON perf mat rent   (S310)

    Journey Towards The Light, For Piano
        And Orchestra
        ROBERTON perf mat rent   (S311)

    Nature Meditation, A, For Violin And
        Orchestra
        ROBERTON perf mat rent   (S312)

    Symphonic Dance
        ROBERTON perf mat rent   (S313)

SELECTION OF SONGS, [ARR.] see
    Chaminade, Cecile

SELIG, ROBERT (1938-   )
    Concerto For Rock Group And Orchestra
        [28']
        3.3.3.3. 4.3.3.1. perc,strings,
        rock group (elec gtr, org, elec
        bass, drums)
        MARGUN BP 7006 perf mat rent (S314)

    Earth Colors *see Symphony No. 2

    Mirage, For Trumpet And String
        Orchestra [14']
        string orch,trp solo
        MARGUN BP 7008 perf mat rent (S315)

    Symphony No. 2 [35']
        3.3.3.3. 4.3.3.1. timp,perc,harp,
        strings
        MARGUN BP 7131 perf mat rent (S316)

SEMELE: O SLEEP WHY DOST THOU LEAVE
    ME?, FOR SOLO VOICE AND ORCHESTRA
    see Handel, George Frideric

SEMELE: WHERE'ER YOU WALK, FOR SOLO
VOICE AND ORCHESTRA see Handel,
George Frideric

SEMI DI GRAMSCI, I see Bussotti,
Sylvano

SEMIRAMIDE: AH, QUEL GIORNO, FOR SOLO
VOICE AND ORCHESTRA see Rossini,
Gioacchino

SEMIRAMIDE: OVERTURE see Rossini,
Gioacchino

SEMPER FIDELIS MARCH see Sousa, John
Philip

SEMPRE NOTTE see Kox, Hans

SENALES see Alsina, Carlos Roque

SENTENS PRO UTOPIA see Ahlund, Ulrik

SENTIMENT see Blomberg, Erik

SENTIMENTO DEL SOGNO, FOR SOLO VOICE
AND ORCHESTRA see Bartolozzi, Bruno

SENTIMENTO DEL TEMPO, FOR 3 WOODWINDS
AND ORCHESTRA see Baur, Jurg

SERAGLIO, IL: OVERTURE see Mozart,
Wolfgang Amadeus, Entfuhrung Aus
Dem Serail, Die: Overture

SEREBRIER, JOSE (1938-   )
Fantasy for String Orchestra [12']
string orch
sc PEER $6.00   (S317)

SERENADE see Becce, Giuseppe

SERENADE, FOR VIOLONCELLO AND
ORCHESTRA, [ARR.] see Offenbach,
Jacques

SERENADE AND TARANTELLA, FOR CLARINET
AND ORCHESTRA see Kugerl, H.

SERENADE D'AMALFI see Becce, Giuseppe

SERENADE DE MANDOLINES see Desormes,
I.C.

SERENADE LOINTAINE see Filipucci,
Agostino

SERENADE MELANCOLIQUE, OP. 26, FOR HORN
AND ORCHESTRA, [ARR.] see
Tchaikovsky, Piotr Ilyich

SERENADE NO. 2 IN F, K. 101 see Mozart,
Wolfgang Amadeus

SERENADE OF CAROLS see Gould, Morton

SERENADENMUSIK see Lurmann, Ludwig

SERENADENMUSIK, EINE see Juon, Paul

SERENADES AND DIVERTIMENTI, K. 113,
131, 189, 185 see Mozart, Wolfgang
Amadeus

SERENADES, K. 237, 203, 215, 204, 239
see Mozart, Wolfgang Amadeus

SERENADES, K. 249, 250 see Mozart,
Wolfgang Amadeus

SERENATA, FOR SOLO VOICE AND ORCHESTRA
see Marvia, Einari

SERENATA, LA, FOR SOLO VOICE AND
ORCHESTRA see Tosti, Francesco
Paolo

SERENATA 75B, FOR FLUTE AND
INSTRUMENTAL ENSEMBLE see Rands,
Bernard

SERENATA CONCERTANTE, FOR VIOLA, DOUBLE
BASS AND ORCHESTRA see Medin, N.

SERENATA CONCERTANTE, FOR VIOLA, PIANO
AND STRING ORCHESTRA see Werdin,
Eberhard

SERENATA DELLA LAGUNA see Becce,
Giuseppe

SERENATA MIGNONNE see Becce, Giuseppe

SERENATA NAPOLITANA see Becce, Giuseppe

SERENATA NOSTALGICA see Linde, Bo

SERMILA, JARMO (1939-   )
Counterbass, For Double Bass And
String Orchestra [11']
string orch,db solo
sc JASE $14.00   (S318)

Love Charm Songs, For Solo Voice And
Instrumental Ensemble [13']
woodwind quin,string quin,2perc,S

SERMILA, JARMO (cont'd.)

solo
[Eng] sc JASE $5.50   (S319)

Mimesis 2 [14']
sc JASE $16.00   (S320)

Pentagram, For Trumpet And Orchestra
[11'-12']
2bsn,2horn,3perc,6vcl,2db,trp
solo
JASE sc f.s., solo pt f.s.   (S321)

SEROCKI, KAZIMIERZ (1922-1981)
Ad Libitum [18']
3.3.3.3. 4.3.3.0. 3perc,2harp,
pno,cel,strings
study sc MOECK 5196 f.s., perf mat
rent   (S322)

SERRARA FONTANA see Lamparter, Omar

SERSE: OMBRA MAI FU, FOR SOLO VOICE AND
ORCHESTRA see Handel, George
Frideric

SERSE: OMBRA MAI FU, [ARR.] see Handel,
George Frideric

SERSE: OVERTURE AND SINFONIA see
Handel, George Frideric

SESSIONS, ROGER (1896-   )
Concerto for Violin, Violoncello and
Orchestra [20']
3.2.3.2. 3.1.2.0. timp,perc,pno,
strings,vln solo,vcl solo
sc MERION 446-41032 $30.00   (S323)

Symphony No. 1
sc KALMUS A7017 $30.00   (S324)

SESTAK, ZDENEK (1925-   )
Symphony No. 2
sc PANTON 1589 f.s.   (S325)

SET OF PIECES FOR THEATRE OR CHAMBER
ORCHESTRA see Ives, Charles

SETTE VARIAZIONI SU UN'ALLEMANDA DI
JOHN BULL see Guerrini, Guido

SEUFZER, FOR SOLO VOICE AND ORCHESTRA
see Wolf, Hugo

SEVEN+ ORCHESTRATION SERIES, GROUP 1
(Kirkland, Camp) cmplt ed CRESPUB
CP-IN 7+P $50.00
contains & see also: Heaven Medley,
[arr.]; I'll Fly Away, [arr.];
Praise Medley, [arr.]; Worship
Medley, [arr.]   (S326)

SEVEN+ ORCHESTRATION SERIES, GROUP 2
(Kirkland, Camp) cmplt ed CRESPUB
CP-IN 7+P2 $62.50
contains & see also: Children's
Songs, [arr.]; Christ Arose,
[arr.]; Cross Songs, [arr.]; When
The Morning Comes, [arr.]; When
The Roll Is Called Up Yonder,
[arr.]   (S327)

SEVEN PIECES, FOR STRING ORCHESTRA see
Ramovs, Primoz, Sedem Skladb, For
String Orchestra

SEVEN POEMS BY E.E. CUMMINGS, FOR SOLO
VOICE AND ORCHESTRA see Harper,
Edward

SEVEN RED MOMENTS, FOR TRUMPET AND
ORCHESTRA see Segerstam, Leif

SEVEN SYMPHONIES FROM THE COURT OF
OETTINGEN-WALLERSTEIN (1773-1795)
(Murray Sterling) sc GARLAND
ISBN 0-8240-3806-1 $90.00 "The
Symphony", Vol. C-VI
contains: Beecke, (Franz) Ignaz
von, Symphony in C minor; Fiala,
Joseph, Symphony in C; Reicha,
Joseph, Symphony in D; Rosetti,
Francesco Antonio, Symphonies In
F, B Flat And D; Wineberger,
Paul, Symphony in F   (S328)

SHACKELFORD, RANDOLPH OWENS (1941-   )
Excerpt, For Piano And Chamber
Orchestra
ZANIBON 5729 f.s.   (S329)

Postil, For Violin And String
Orchestra
string orch,vln solo
ZANIBON 5727 f.s.   (S330)

SHADOWS see Arrigo, Girolamo

SHAKESPEARE MUSIC see Davies, Peter
Maxwell

SHAKESPEARE'S WINTERAVONDSPROOKJE see
Ketting, Piet

SHAPEY, RALPH (1921-   )
Rituals
study sc PRESSER $15.00   (S331)

SHE WEEPS OVER RAHOON, FOR SOLO VOICE
AND ORCHESTRA see Oosten, Roel van

SHEEP MAY SAFELY GRAZE, [ARR.] see
Bach, Johann Sebastian, Schafe
Konnen Sicher Weiden, [arr.]

SHERMAN, NORMAN (1926-   )
Icthyon [10']
13strings
KERBY NS 2 sc $37.50, set $60.00
                               (S332)

SHIMIZU, YASUO (1910-   )
Symphoniquepoeme Asuka
2+pic.2+English horn.2+bass
clar.2+contrabsn. 4.3.3.1.
timp,perc,harp,strings
sc J.C.A. f.s.   (S333)

SHISHIDO, MUTSUO
Concerto for Piano and Orchestra, No.
3(pic).3.3.3. 4.3.3.1. 4perc,cel,
harp,strings,pno solo
ONGAKU perf mat rent   (S334)

SHO-KO see Ishii, Maki

SHORT SYMPHONY, [ARR.] see Beethoven,
Ludwig van

SHORT SYMPHONY (TESTAMENT TO A BIG
CITY) see Bazelon, Irwin Allen

SHOSHADRE see Marez Oyens, Tera de

SHOSTAKOVICH, DMITRI (1906-1975)
Concerto for Piano and Orchestra, No.
1, Op. 35, in C minor
BROUDE BR. set $15.00, pts $2.25,
ea.   (S335)

Concerto for Piano and Orchestra, No.
2, Op. 102, in F
sc RICORDI-IT PR1040 f.s.   (S336)

Concerto for Violin and Orchestra,
No. 1, Op. 99, in A minor
(Collected Works, Vol. 14;
designated by the composer as Op.
77) sc MEZ KNIGA $60.00 contains
also: Concerto for Violin and
Orchestra, No. 2, Op. 129 (1+
pic.2.2.2+contrabsn. 4.0.0.0.
timp,perc,strings,vln solo)   (S337)

Concerto for Violin and Orchestra,
No. 2, Op. 129
see Shostakovich, Dmitri, Concerto
for Violin and Orchestra, No. 1,
Op. 99, in A minor

Festive Overture *Op.96
sc RICORDI-IT PR901 f.s.   (S338)

Golden Age, The: Polka
KALMUS A5145 sc $5.00, perf mat
rent, set $15.00, pts $1.00, ea.
                               (S339)

Hamlet: Incidental Music [16']
1.1.1.1. 2.2.1.1. timp,perc,
strings
KALMUS A2040 sc $22.00, perf mat
rent, set $50.00, pts $3.00, ea.
                               (S340)

Prelude in E flat minor, [arr.]
(Stokowski, Leopold) 4.2+English
horn.3+bass clar.3+contrabsn.
4.4.4.1. timp,2perc,harp,strings
[3'] KALMUS A5523 sc $3.00, perf
mat rent, set $15.00, pts $.60,
ea.   (S341)

Symphony No. 1, Op. 10, in F minor
sc PETERS 5740 $24.50   (S342)
LUCKS 07250 sc $30.00, set $40.00,
min sc $4.00, pts $3.25, ea.
                               (S343)
Symphony No. 5, Op. 47, in D minor
(Collected Works, Vol. 3) MEZ
KNIGA $60.00 contains also:
Symphony No. 6, Op. 53-54, in B
minor   (S344)
LUCKS 08889 sc $35.00, set $60.00,
min sc $7.50, pts $3.25, ea.
                               (S345)
Symphony No. 6, Op. 53-54, in B minor
see Shostakovich, Dmitri, Symphony
No. 5, Op. 47, in D minor
sc KALMUS A5482 $40.00   (S346)

Symphony No. 7, Op. 60, in C [70']
3(alto fl,pic).2+English
horn.3(clar in E flat).bass
clar.2+contrabsn. 8.6.6.1.
timp,perc,2harp,pno,strings
sc KALMUS A3403 $40.00   (S347)
sc PETERS 5727 $32.50   (S348)
(Collected Works, Vol. 4) sc MEZ
KNIGA $60.00 contains also:
Symphony No. 8, Op. 65, in C
minor   (S349)

SHOSTAKOVICH, DMITRI (cont'd.)
Symphony No. 8, Op. 65, in C minor
[60']
4.3.4.3. 4.3.3.1. timp,perc,
strings
see Shostakovich, Dmitri, Symphony
No. 7, Op. 60, in C
KALMUS 5185 sc $35.00, perf mat
rent, set $100.00, pts $4.00, ea.
(S350)
Symphony No. 9, Op. 70, in E flat
(Collected Works, Vol. 5) sc MEZ
KNIGA $60.00 contains also:
Symphony No. 10, Op. 93, in E
minor (S351)
Symphony No. 10, Op. 93, in E minor
see Shostakovich, Dmitri, Symphony
No. 9, Op. 70, in E flat

Symphony No. 11, Op. 103, in G minor
sc RICORDI-IT PR907 f.s. (S352)
(Collected Works, Vol. 6) sc MEZ
KNIGA $60.00 contains also:
Symphony No. 12, Op. 112, in D
minor (S353)

Symphony No. 12, Op. 112, in D minor
see Shostakovich, Dmitri, Symphony
No. 11, Op. 103, in G minor

Symphony No. 14, Op. 135
(Collected Works, Vol. 8) sc MEZ
KNIGA $60.00 contains also:
Symphony No. 15, Op. 141 (S354)

Symphony No. 15, Op. 141
see Shostakovich, Dmitri, Symphony
No. 14, Op. 135

SHYLOCK SUITE: NOCTURNE see Faure,
Gabriel-Urbain

SI J'ETAIS ROI: OVERTURE see Adam,
Adolphe-Charles

SIBELIUS, JEAN (1865-1957)
Arioso, For Solo Voice And String
Orchestra [5']
string orch,solo voice
FAZER perf mat rent (S355)

Belshazzar's Feast: Suite, [arr.]
*Op.51
(Pagel, Alfr.) LIENAU f.s. (S356)

Concerto for Violin and Orchestra,
Op. 47, in D minor
study sc INTERNAT. 2277 $7.75
(S357)
LUCKS 00597 sc $10.50, set $32.00,
min sc $5.00, pts $2.00, ea.
(S358)
Ferryman's Bride, The, For Solo Voice
And Orchestra *see Koskenlaskian
Morsiamet, For Solo Voice And
Orchestra

Finlandia *Op.26
LUCKS 06636 sc $8.00, set $23.00,
min sc $1.00, pts $1.15, ea.
(S359)
BROUDE BR. set $30.00, pts $1.25,
ea. (S360)

Fruhlingslied *see Spring Song

Hymn To Thais, For Solo Voice And
Orchestra , [arr.]
(Jalas, J.) 2.2.2.2. 0.0.0.0. timp,
strings,solo voice [4'] FAZER
perf mat rent (S361)

Karelia Overture *Op.10 [9']
3.2.2.2. 4.3.3.1. timp,perc,
strings
KALMUS 5395 sc $10.00, perf mat
rent, set $22.00, pts $1.00, ea.
(S362)
Karelia Suite *Op.11
LUCKS 06637 sc $10.00, set $32.00,
pts $1.15, ea. (S363)

King Christian II, For Solo Voice And
Orchestra *Op.27 [27']
2.2.2.2. 4.2.3.0. timp,2perc,
harp,strings,A solo
"Konig Kristian II, For Solo Voice
And Orchestra" BREITKOPF-W perf
mat rent (S364)

Konig Kristian II, For Solo Voice And
Orchestra *see King Christian
II, For Solo Voice And Orchestra

Koskenlaskian Morsiamet, For Solo
Voice And Orchestra *Op.33
"Ferryman's Bride, The, For Solo
Voice And Orchestra" KALMUS A5504
sc $18.00, perf mat rent, set
$25.00, pts $1.50, ea. (S365)

Kullervo Und Seine Schwester *Op.7,
No.3
study sc BREITKOPF-W PB 5015 f.s.

SIBELIUS, JEAN (cont'd.)
(S366)
Kullervos Klage, For Solo Voice And
Orchestra [3']
1+pic.2.2.2. 4.3.3.1. timp,perc,
strings,Bar solo
BREITKOPF-W perf mat rent (S367)

Libelle, Die, For Solo Voice And
Orchestra, [arr.] *Op.17,No.5
[3']
(Borg, K.) "Slanda, En, For Solo
Voice And Orchestra, [arr.]"
2.0.2.2. 0.0.0.0. timp,harp,
strings,B solo BREITKOPF-W perf
mat rent (S368)

March Of The Finnish Infantry, Op.
91a
2.2.2+bass clar.2. 4.3.3.0. timp,
perc,strings
KALMUS A5455 sc $3.00, perf mat
rent, set $12.00, pts $.60, ea.
(S369)
Pan Und Echo *Op.53a
2.2.2.2. 4.2.3.0. timp,perc,
strings
sc LIENAU f.s. (S370)

Pelleas Et Melisande: Suite, [arr.]
*Op.46
(Pagel, Alfr.) LIENAU f.s. (S371)

Romance, Op. 42, in C [5']
string orch
KALMUS 5369 sc $5.00, set $3.75,
pts $.75, ea. (S372)
LUCKS 06640 sc $2.00, set $3.75,
pts $.75, ea. (S373)

Saga, En *Op.9
LUCKS 07683 sc $15.00, set $45.00,
min sc $3.00, pts $2.50, ea.
(S374)
Serenade for Violin and Orchestra,
No. 2, Op. 69b, in G minor
BREITKOPF-W perf mat rent (S375)

Slanda, En, For Solo Voice And
Orchestra, [arr.] *see Libelle,
Die, For Solo Voice And
Orchestra, [arr.]

Souda, Souda Sinisorsa, For Solo
Voice And Orchestra, [arr.]
(Jalas, J.) 2.1.2.2. 4.0.0.0. timp,
strings,solo voice [2'] FAZER
perf mat rent (S376)

Spring Song *Op.16 [10']
2.2.2.2. 4.3.3.1. timp,perc,
strings
"Fruhlingslied" KALMUS 5280 sc
$8.00, perf mat rent, set $20.00,
pts $.60, ea. (S377)
Swan Of Tuonela, The *Op.22,No.2
BROUDE BR. set $15.00, pts $1.00,
ea. (S378)
LUCKS 06641 sc $3.75, set $10.50,
min sc $2.50, pts $.75, ea.
(S379)
Symphony No. 1, Op. 39, in E minor
LUCKS 06642 sc $30.00, set $45.00,
min sc $5.00, pts $2.75, ea.
(S380)
Symphony No. 3, Op. 52, in C
LUCKS 05247 sc $19.00, set $45.00,
min sc $6.00, pts $2.75, ea.
(S381)
Tanz-Intermezzo *Op.45,No.2 [3']
2.1.2.1. 4.2.0.0. timp,perc,harp,
strings
BREITKOPF-W perf mat rent (S382)

Valse Triste (from Kuolema, Op. 44)
BROUDE BR. set $9.00, pts $1.00,
ea. (S383)
LUCKS 06643 sc $3.75, set $7.50,
pts $.75, ea. (S384)

SICILIANA see Piccioli, Giuseppe

SICILIANA NOTTURNO see Reed, Alfred

SICILIANA see Boccherini, Luigi

SICILIANO FROM SONATA IN C MINOR, BWV
1017, [ARR.] see Bach, Johann
Sebastian

SICILIANO NACH BACH, FOR VIOLIN AND
ORCHESTRA see Wilhelmj, August

SICKLE, THE, FOR SOLO VOICE AND
ORCHESTRA see Osborne, Nigel

SIEBEN, JEDENFALLS SIEBEN see Bon,
Maarten

SIEBEN LIEDER AUS LETZTER ZEIT: BLICKE
MIR NICHT IN DIE LIEDER, FOR SOLO
VOICE AND ORCHESTRA see Mahler,
Gustav

SIEBEN LIEDER AUS LETZTER ZEIT: DER
TAMBOURSG'SELL, FOR SOLO VOICE AND
ORCHESTRA see Mahler, Gustav

SIEBEN LIEDER AUS LETZTER ZEIT: ICH
ATMET EINEN LINDEN DUFT, FOR SOLO
VOICE AND ORCHESTRA see Mahler,
Gustav

SIEBEN LIEDER AUS LETZTER ZEIT: ICH BIN
DER WELT ABHANDEN GEKOMMEN, FOR
SOLO VOICE AND ORCHESTRA see
Mahler, Gustav

SIEBEN LIEDER AUS LETZTER ZEIT: LIEBST
DU UM SCHONHEIT, FOR SOLO VOICE AND
ORCHESTRA see Mahler, Gustav

SIEBEN LIEDER AUS LETZTER ZEIT:
REVELGE, FOR SOLO VOICE AND
ORCHESTRA see Mahler, Gustav

SIEBEN LIEDER AUS LETZTER ZEIT: UM
MITTERNACHT, FOR SOLO VOICE AND
ORCHESTRA see Mahler, Gustav

SIEBERT, FRIEDRICH (1906-)
Marsch Der Landsknechte
RIES f.s. (S385)

SIEBERT, WILHELM DIETER (1931-)
Trunk Des Poseidon, Der, For Solo
Voices And Orchestra
fl,2ob,bsn,2horn,2trp,timp,perc,
strings,T&speaking voice
BUDDE perf mat rent (S386)

SIEGFRIED: FOREST MURMURS see Wagner,
Richard, Siegfried: Waldweben

SIEGFRIED: HOHO! HOHO! SCHMIEDE MEIN
HAMMER, FOR SOLO VOICE AND
ORCHESTRA see Wagner, Richard

SIEGFRIED IDYLL see Wagner, Richard

SIEGFRIED: SCHMIEDELIEDER, FOR SOLO
VOICE AND ORCHESTRA see Wagner,
Richard, Siegfried: Hoho! Hoho!
Schmiede Mein Hammer, For Solo
Voice And Orchestra

SIEGFRIED: WALDWEBEN see Wagner,
Richard

SIEGMEISTER, ELIE (1909-)
Symphony No. 5 [17'30"]
2(2pic).2(English horn).2+bass
clar.2(contrabsn). 4.3.3.1.
timp,4perc,harp,pno,strings
sc FISCHER,C $15.00 (S387)

Visions Of Time *see Symphony No. 5

SIEKMANN, FRANK
Concerto for Trombone and Orchestra
2.1.2.1. 1.2.1.0. timp,4perc,
harp,strings,trom solo
SEESAW perf mat rent (S388)

Scene In Monochrome
string orch
SEESAW perf mat rent (S389)

SIETE CANCIONES POPULARES ESPANOLAS,
FOR SOLO VOICE AND ORCHESTRA,
[ARR.] see Falla, Manuel de

SIGH, A, FOR SOLO VOICE AND ORCHESTRA
see Wolf, Hugo, Seufzer, For Solo
Voice And Orchestra

SIGLIED see Ferrero

SIGNOR BRUSCHINO, IL: OVERTURE see
Rossini, Gioacchino

SIGNOR, VOI SAPETE, FOR SOLO VOICE AND
ORCHESTRA see Haydn, [Franz] Joseph

SIGNORE DAL VOLTO LUMINOSO ALLA TERRA,
IL see De Grandis, Renato

SIGURD JORSALFAR: TRIUMPHAL MARCH see
Grieg, Edvard Hagerup

SIKORSKI, KAZIMIERZ (1895-)
Cztery Polonezy Wersalskie [28']
string orch
"Four Polonaises Of Versailles" sc,
pts POLSKIE $9.28 (S390)

Four Polonaises Of Versailles *see
Cztery Polonezy Wersalskie

SILBURY AIR see Birtwistle, Harrison

SILENT BOUGHS, FOR SOLO VOICE AND
STRING ORCHESTRA see Kraft, William

SILENT NIGHT see Gruber, Franz Xaver

SILETE VENTI, FOR SOLO VOICE AND
ORCHESTRA see Handel, George
Frideric

SILHOUETTEN AUS UNGARN see Hofmann,
  Heinrich

SILJUSTOEL MARCH see Saeverud, Harald,
  Siljustolmarsj, Op. 21a, No. 5

SILJUSTOLMARSJ, OP. 21A, NO. 5 see
  Saeverud, Harald

SILLAGES see Tabachnik, Michel

SILVANA: OVERTURE see Weber, Carl Maria
  von

SILVER RING, THE see Chaminade, Cecile,
  Anneau d'Argent, L'

SIMAI, PAVOL (1930-   )
  Nordron [13']
    3.3.3.3. 4.4.3.1. timp,4perc,
      harp,strings
    sc STIM perf mat rent   (S391)

SIMFONICNA ANTITEZA see Bravnicar,
  Matija

SIMON, HERMANN (1896-1948)
  Sinfonische Gesange, For Solo Voice
    And Orchestra
    orch,Bar solo
    sc LIENAU f.s.   (S392)

SIMPLE SONGS, FOR SOLO VOICE AND
  CHAMBER ORCHESTRA see Lajovic,
  Aleksander, Preproste Popevke, For
  Solo Voice And Chamber Orchestra

SINE NOMINE see Weis, Flemming

SINE NOMINE, FOR SOLO VOICE AND
  ORCHESTRA see Raxach, Enrique

SINFONIA, FOR 13 SOLO STRINGS see
  Manneke, Daan

SINFONIA 1-6 see Glaser, Jan Pieter

SINFONIA, ACT III see Handel, George
  Frideric, Solomon: Entrance Of The
  Queen Of Sheba

SINFONIA ALL'ITALIANA see Gnecco,
  Francesco

SINFONIA AZIONE TEATRALE CAMPESTRE see
  Asioli, Bonifazio

SINFONIA COME UN GRANDE LAMENTO see
  Zimmermann, Udo

SINFONIA CON VIOLONCELLO OBBLIGATO see
  Martini, [Padre] Giovanni Battista

SINFONIA DA CAMERA see Steffen,
  Wolfgang

SINFONIA DELL'AUTUNNO PAVESE see
  Farina, Guido

SINFONIA ECOLOGICA see Brandstrom,
  Christer, Symphony No. 1, Op. 25

SINFONIA (FRAGMENT), ANH. 223 see
  Mozart, Wolfgang Amadeus

SINFONIA IN MEMORIAM MAURICE RAVEL see
  Escher, Rudolf George

SINFONIA JUBILATA, NO. 1 see Booren, Jo
  van den

SINFONIA MISTICA see Panufnik, Andrzej

SINFONIA NO. 9, [ARR.] see Schubert,
  Franz (Peter), Duo, Op. 140, [arr.]

SINFONIA PASQUALE see Milner, Anthony

SINFONIA PASTORALE see Schiassi,
  Gaetano Maria

SINFONIA PASTORALE IN D, OP. 4, NO. 2
  see Stamitz, Johann Wenzel Anton

SINFONIA PASTORALE IN F see Cannabich,
  Christian

SINFONIA PASTORALE PER IL SANTISSIMO
  NATALE see Manfredini, Francesco

SINFONIA PATETICA see Graner, Georg,
  Symphony No. 2

SINFONIA PER UNA O DUE ORCHESTRE AND
  SINFONIA IN E see Pugni, Cesare

SINFONIA PERIODIQUE NO. 2 see Fils,
  [Johann] Anton

SINFONIA PICCOLA see Giltay, Berend

SINFONIA SACRA, FOR SOLO VOICE AND
  ORCHESTRA see Thyrestam, Gunnar

SINFONIA SEMPLICE see Wordsworth,
  William

SINFONIA SERENA see Rosenberg, Hilding,
  Symphony No. 8

SINFONIA VITA see Matsushita, Shin-Ichi

SINFONIAS, FIVE see Mattei, Stanislav

SINFONIAS, SEVEN see Zingarelli, Nicola
  Antonio

SINFONIAS, SIX see Roman, Johan Helmich

SINFONIAS IN C AND B FLAT see Pavesi,
  Stefano

SINFONIAS IN C, D AND E FLAT see
  Moreno, Francisco Javier

SINFONIAS IN D, TWO see Polledro,
  Giovanni Battista

SINFONIAS IN D AND E MINOR see Rolla,
  Alessandro

SINFONIAS IN F AND E MINOR see
  Nicolini, Giuseppe

SINFONIAS NOS. 1-3 see Roman, Johan
  Helmich

SINFONIAS, OP. 3, NOS. 1-3 see Bach,
  Johann Christian

SINFONIAS, OP. 3, NOS. 1-6 see Bach,
  Johann Christian

SINFONIAS, OP. 3, NOS. 4-6 see Bach,
  Johann Christian

SINFONIE D'ORATORIO see Scarlatti,
  Alessandro

SINFONIE POLIZIANE see Blackford,
  Richard

SINFONIE SINGULIERE see Berwald, Franz

SINFONIETTA CAPRICCIOSA see Juon, Paul

SINFONIETTA CONCERTANTE see Keuning,
  Hans P.

SINFONIETTA DOMESTICA see Kardos,
  Dezider

SINFONIETTA GIOCOSA see Ebel, Arnold

SINFONIETTA I see Muller-Zurich, Paul

SINFONIETTA SERENA see Dressel, Erwin

SINFONISCHE GESANGE, FOR SOLO VOICE AND
  ORCHESTRA see Simon, Hermann

SINFONISCHE METAMORPHOSEN UBER GESUALDO
  see Baur, Jurg

SINFONISCHE MUSIK see Juon, Paul

SINFONISCHE SUITE see Ehrenberg, Carl
  Emil Theodor

SINFONISCHE SZENEN see Kuhnl, Claus

SINGER, M.
  Concerto for Violin and String
    Orchestra [20']
    hpsd,strings,vln solo
    sc SCOTUS 259-8 f.s.   (S393)

  Time Must Have A Stop, For Piano And
    Orchestra [11']
    2.3.2.2. 2.3.2.1. xylo,marimba,
      strings,pno solo
    sc SCOTUS 254-7 f.s.   (S394)

SINGVOGELCHEN see Lincke, Paul

SINIGAGLIA, LEONE (1868-1944)
  Aria Del Molino, L', For Solo Voices
    And Orchestra *Op.40,No.10 [3']
    2.1.2.2. 2.0.0.0. timp,string
      quar,2 female soli
    manuscript CARISCH   (S395)

  Baruffe Chiozzotte, Le: Overture
    BREITKOPF-W perf mat rent   (S396)

  Canto Dell'Ospite, For Solo Voice And
    Orchestra *Op.37,No.1
    2.3.2.2. 4.2.0.0. timp,harp,
      strings,solo voice
    manuscript CARISCH   (S397)

  Cecilia, For Solo Voice And Orchestra
    *Op.40,No.6 [3']
    2.2.2.2. 2.2.0.0. timp,triangle,
      strings,solo voice
    manuscript CARISCH   (S398)

  Donna Bianca, For Solo Voice And
    Orchestra *Op.40,No.31 [3']
    2.2.2.2. 3.2.0.0. timp,strings,

SINIGAGLIA, LEONE (cont'd.)
  solo voice
    manuscript CARISCH   (S399)

  Due Pezzi: Humoreske, For Horn And
    Orchestra
    see Sinigaglia, Leone, Due Pezzi:
      Lied, For Horn And Orchestra

  Due Pezzi: Lied, For Horn And
    Orchestra
    2.1.2.2. 4.0.0.0. timp,harp,
      strings,horn solo
    manuscript CARISCH contains also:
      Due Pezzi: Humoreske, For Horn
      And Orchestra (2.2.2.2. 4.0.0.0.
      timp,harp,strings,horn solo)
                                   (S400)

  Falciatori, I, For Solo Voice And
    Orchestra *Op.40,No.13 [3']
    2.1.2.2. 2.0.0.0. strings,solo
      voice
    manuscript CARISCH   (S401)

  Figlio Del Re, Il, For Solo Voice And
    Orchestra *Op.40,No.35 [3']
    2.2.2.2. 2.2.0.0. timp,harp,
      strings,solo voice
    manuscript CARISCH   (S402)

  Grillo E La Formica, Il, For Solo
    Voice And Orchestra *Op.40,No.5
    [3']
    2.1.2.2. 1.0.0.0. timp,perc,
      strings,solo voice
    manuscript CARISCH   (S403)

  Invito Respinto, For Solo Voices And
    Orchestra *Op.40,No.27 [3']
    0.1.1.1. 1.0.0.0. strings,SA soli
    manuscript CARISCH   (S404)

  Maria Catlina, For Solo Voice And
    Orchestra *Op.40,No.11 [3']
    2.2.2.2. 2.2.0.0. timp,harp,
      strings,solo voice
    manuscript CARISCH   (S405)

  Maritino, Il, For Solo Voices And
    Orchestra *Op.40,No.3 [3']
    2.1.2.2. 2.1.0.0. timp,triangle,
      string quar,2 female soli
    manuscript CARISCH   (S406)

  Natale, Il, For Solo Voices And
    Orchestra *Op.6 [3']
    2.2.2.2. 2.2.0.0. timp,perc,
      strings,4 solo voices
    manuscript CARISCH   (S407)

  Ninna Nanna Di Gesu Bambino, For Solo
    Voices And Orchestra *Op.40,
    No.32 [3']
    2.0.2.0. 1.0.0.0. harp,triangle,
      strings,SSS soli
    manuscript CARISCH   (S408)

  Novara La Belle, For Solo Voice And
    Orchestra *Op.40,No.36 [3']
    2.2.2.2. 2.2.0.0. timp,perc,
      strings,solo voice
    manuscript CARISCH   (S409)

  Nozze Dell'Alpigiano, Le, For Solo
    Voice And Orchestra *Op.40,No.28
    [3']
    2.2.2.2. 2.0.0.0. timp,triangle,
      strings,solo voice
    manuscript CARISCH   (S410)

  Pastora Fedele, La, For Solo Voices
    And Orchestra *Op.40,No.1 [3']
    2.1.2.0. 2.0.0.0. timp,triangle,
      string quar,2 female soli
    manuscript CARISCH   (S411)

  Pellegrino Di S. Giacomo, Il, For
    Solo Voice And Orchestra *Op.40,
    No.30 [3']
    1.1.1.1. 1.0.0.0. triangle,
      strings,solo voice
    CARISCH   (S412)

  Quiete Meridiana Nell'Alpe, La, For
    Solo Voice And Orchestra *Op.37,
    No.2 [3']
    2.3.2.2. 2.0.0.0. harp,triangle,
      strings,solo voice
    manuscript CARISCH   (S413)

  Rana E Il Rospo, La, For Solo Voice
    And String Orchestra *Op.40,
    No.16 [3']
    string orch,solo voice
    manuscript CARISCH   (S414)

  Rifugio, Il, For Solo Voice And
    Orchestra *Op.37,No.3 [3']
    2.2.2.2. 2.0.0.0. harp,strings,
      solo voice
    manuscript CARISCH   (S415)

  Rondine Importuna, La, For Solo Voice
    And Orchestra *Op.40,No.15 [3']
    1.1.2.1. 0.0.0.0. harp,triangle,

SINIGAGLIA, LEONE (cont'd.)

strings,solo voice
manuscript CARISCH (S416)

Serenade, Op. 23, No. 2 for Solo
Voice and Orchestra [3']
2.1.2.2. 0.0.0.0. timp,triangle,
strings,solo voice
manuscript CARISCH (S417)

Sposa Di Beltramo, La, For Solo Voice
And Orchestra *Op.40,No.33 [3']
2.2.2.2. 4.2.0.0. timp,perc,
strings,solo voice
manuscript CARISCH (S418)

Tregua, La, For Solo Voice And
Orchestra *Op.23,No.3 [3']
2.3.2.2. 4.2.0.0. timp,harp,pno,
strings,solo voice
manuscript CARISCH (S419)

Triste Sera, For Solo Voice And
Orchestra *Op.23,No.1 [3']
1.2.2.2. 4.0.0.0. timp,strings,
solo voice
manuscript CARISCH (S420)

Uccellino Del Bosco, L', For Solo
Voice And String Orchestra
*Op.40,No.19 [3']
string orch,solo voice
manuscript CARISCH (S421)

SINIPIIKA, FOR SOLO VOICE AND
ORCHESTRA, [ARR.] see Kuula, Toivo

SINOPOLI, GIUSEPPE (1946-   )
Souvenirs A La Memoire, For Solo
Voices And Orchestra
sc RICORDI-IT 132267 f.s. (S422)

Tombeau D'Armor
sc RICORDI-IT 132351 f.s. (S423)

SIR JOHN FALSTAFF see Kaun, Hugo

SIRATO, FOR SOLO VOICE AND CHAMBER
ORCHESTRA see Maros, Rudolf

SIRENETTA E IL PESCE TURCHINO see
Castelnuovo-Tedesco, Mario

SIRENS, THE see Gliere, Reinhold
Moritzovich

SIRKAN HAAMATKA, FOR SOLO VOICE AND
ORCHESTRA see Melartin, Erkki

SIROCCO see Kotonski, Wlodzimierz

SITUATIONEN see Zechlin, Ruth

SIVERTSEN, KENNETH
Largo (December) In B Flat Minor, For
Tenor Saxophone, Piano And String
Orchestra
string orch,tenor sax solo,pno
solo
NORGE (S424)

SIVIC, PAVLE (1908-   )
Musique Pour Quinze [12']
1.1.1.1. 1.1.1.0. harp,pno,timp,
perc,string quin
DRUSTVO DSS 895 perf mat rent
(S425)

SIX EARLY SONGS, FOR SOLO VOICE AND
ORCHESTRA see Schuller, Gunther

SIX EPIGRAPHES ANTIQUES, [ARR.] see
Debussy, Claude

SIX GREEK DANCES see Skalkottas, Nikos

SIX INSTRUMENTAL PIECES see Isaac,
Heinrich, Sechs Instrumentalsatze

SIX MORRIS DANCE TUNES, SET 1 see
Holst, Gustav

SIX MORRIS DANCE TUNES, SET 2 see
Holst, Gustav

SIX OLD VILLAGE SONGS FROM LOM IN
NORWAY see Olsen, Sparre

SIX SEQUENCES FOR DANCE see Cervetti,
Sergio

SIX VIOLIN CONCERTOS AND SIXTY-FOUR
CADENZAS see Borghi, Luigi

SIXTA, JOZEF (1940-   )
Four Orchestral Compositions
2.2.2.2. 2.2.0.0. strings
SLOV.HUD.FOND 0-403 perf mat rent
(S426)

Punctum Contra Punctum
3.3.3.3. 4.3.3.0. strings
SLOV.HUD.FOND 0-441 perf mat rent
(S427)

SIZILIETTA see Blon, Franz von

SJOBLOM, HEIMER (1910-   )
Concertino for Organ and String
Orchestra [18'30"]
string orch,org solo
sc,pts STIM perf mat rent (S428)

SKALKOTTAS, NIKOS (1904-1949)
Ancient Greek March
MARGUN BP 7009 perf mat rent (S429)

Classical Symphony In A
MARGUN BP 7010 perf mat rent (S430)

Concertino for 2 Pianos and Orchestra
MARGUN BP 7012 perf mat rent (S431)

Concerto for Double Bass and
Orchestra [20']
MARGUN BP 7013 perf mat rent (S432)

Concerto for Piano and Orchestra in C
MARGUN BP 7011 perf mat rent (S433)

Concerto for Piano and Orchestra, No.
1 [25']
MARGUN BP 7014 perf mat rent (S434)

Concerto for Piano and Orchestra, No.
2 [35']
MARGUN BP 7015 perf mat rent (S435)

Dance Suite
MARGUN BP 7016 perf mat rent (S436)

Large Sinfonico [25']
MARGUN BP 7017 perf mat rent (S437)

Piece For Xylophone And Orchestra In
C
MARGUN BP 7018 perf mat rent (S438)

Return Of Ulysses, The *see Symphony
in One Movement

Sea, The
MARGUN BP 7019 perf mat rent (S439)

Sinfonietta in B flat
MARGUN BP 7020 perf mat rent (S440)

Six Greek Dances
MARGUN BP 7021 perf mat rent (S441)

Symphonic Suite No. 1 [40']
MARGUN BP 7022 perf mat rent (S442)

Symphony in One Movement [25']
MARGUN BP 7023 perf mat rent (S443)

SKANDINAVISCHE QUADRILLE see Lumbye,
Hans Christian

SKARABEE see Bois, Rob du

SKATERS' WALTZ, THE see Waldteufel,
Emil, Patineurs, Les

SKERJANC, LUCIJAN MARIJA (1900-1973)
Symphony No. 5 [38']
2(pic).2.2(bass clar).2. 4.3.3.1.
timp,2perc,harp,strings
DRUSTVO DSS 816 perf mat rent
(S444)

SKERL, DANE (1931-   )
Opojno Poletje
2(pic).2(English horn).2(bass
clar).2(contrabsn). 4.3.3.1.
timp,3perc,vibra,xylo,harp,cel,
strings
"Ravishing Summer" DRUSTVO DSS 519
perf mat rent (S445)

Ravishing Summer *see Opojno Poletje

SKETCH, FOR SOLO VOICE, VIOLIN AND
ORCHESTRA see Freso, Tibor, Skica,
For Solo Voice, Violin And
Orchestra

SKIBBE, GUSTAV
Hubertus-Jagd
RIES f.s. (S446)

SKICA, FOR SOLO VOICE, VIOLIN AND
ORCHESTRA see Freso, Tibor

SKIZZEN ZU EINEM FRAUENPORTRAT, FOR
PIANO AND ORCHESTRA see Meschwitz,
Frieder

SKOLD, YNGVE (1899-   )
Elegy [8']
1.0.2.0. 1.2.1.0. opt pno,strings
sc STIM perf mat rent (S447)

SKURRILE ELEGIE AUF RICHARD W., FOR
WAGNER TUBA AND STRING ORCHESTRA
see Koetsier, Jan

SKY see Conyngham, Barry

SLAAPLIEDEREN VOOR GROTE MENSEN, FOR
SOLO VOICE AND ORCHESTRA see
Pluister, Simon

SLANDA, EN, FOR SOLO VOICE AND
ORCHESTRA, [ARR.] see Sibelius,
Jean, Libelle, Die, For Solo Voice
And Orchestra, [arr.]

SLANGEN, JOHN (1951-   )
Quaestio [16']
string orch
DONEMUS (S448)

SLAVA! see Bernstein, Leonard

SLAVISCHE RHAPSODIE NO. 1 see
Friedemann, Carl

SLAVISCHE RHAPSODIE NO. 3 see
Friedemann, Carl

SLAVISCHE TANZE see Mraczek, Karl

SLAVONIAN MARCH see Tchaikovsky, Piotr
Ilyich, Marche Slave

SLAVONIC DANCE, OP. 72, NO. 2, [ARR.]
see Dvorak, Antonin

SLAVONIC DANCES, NOS. 4 AND 6 see
Dvorak, Antonin

SLAVONIC DANCES, OP. 46 see Dvorak,
Antonin

SLAWIA see Franko, Mladen

SLAWISCH see Knumann, Jo

SLAWISCHE MELODIE see Kludas, Erich

SLEEPING BEAUTY, THE: PAS DE DEUX, ACT
III see Tchaikovsky, Piotr Ilyich

SLEEPING BEAUTY, THE: PAS DE QUATRE,
"BLUEBIRD" see Tchaikovsky, Piotr
Ilyich

SLITS see Gefors, Hans

SLONIMSKY, NICOLAS (1894-   )
My Toy Balloon [6']
3.2.2.2. 2.2.3.1. timp,perc,xylo,
cel/pno,harp/pno,strings
SHAWNEE J 66 $20.00 (S449)

SLOTHOUWER, JOCHEM (1938-   )
Ritorno D'Orfeo, Il, For Cello And
Orchestra [15']
harp,strings,vcl solo
DONEMUS perf mat rent (S450)

SLOVACKA PISEN, FOR SOLO VOICE AND
ORCHESTRA see Kovarovic, Karel

SLOVAKOFONIA see Kardos, Dezider

SLOVANKA QUADRILLE see Strauss, Johann,
[Jr.]

SLOW MOVEMENT FOR STRING ORCHESTRA see
Imbrie, Andrew Welsh

SLOW PIECE, FOR STRING ORCHESTRA see
Finney, Ross Lee

SLUNOVRAT see Brozak, Daniel

SMART, GARY (1943-   )
Del Diario De Un Papagayo [9']
0(pic).2.1.2. 2.0.0.0. pno,strings,
electronic tape sc MARGUN BP 7025
$15.00, perf mat rent (S451)

SMEKANDE VIND, FOR VIOLIN AND ORCHESTRA
see Lundkvist, Per

SMETANA, BEDRICH (1824-1884)
Bartered Bride, The: Overture *see
Prodana Nevesta: Overture

Doktor Faust: Overture
KALMUS 1183 sc $6.00, set $10.00
(S452)

Dve Vdovy: Samostatne Vladnu Ja
Vsemi, For Solo Voice And
Orchestra
LUCKS 02897 sc $4.00, set $8.00,
pts $.75, ea. (S453)

From Bohemia's Meadows And Forests
*see Ma Vlast: Z Ceskych Luhu A
Haju

Hubicka: Overture
"Kuss, Der: Overture" min sc
UNIVER. PH73 $3.00 (S454)

Kuss, Der: Overture *see Hubicka:
Overture

Ma Vlast: Sarka
"My Country: Sarka" LUCKS 08691 sc
$17.00, set $36.00, min sc $4.50,
pts $2.00, ea. (S455)

Ma Vlast: Tabor
"My Country: Tabor" LUCKS 05933 sc
$20.00, set $40.00, min sc $5.50,

SMETANA, BEDRICH (cont'd.)

    pts $2.25, ea. (S456)

Ma Vlast: Vitava
  "Moldau, The" min sc ZEN-ON 892151
    f.s. (S457)
  "Moldava" sc RICORDI-IT PR518 f.s. (S458)
  "My Country: Moldau" pts BROUDE BR.
    $1.50, ea. (S459)

Ma Vlast: Vysehrad
  "My Country: Vysehrad" LUCKS 05932
    sc $17.00, set $34.00, min sc
    $4.50, pts $2.00, ea. (S460)

Ma Vlast: Z Ceskych Luhu A Haju
  "From Bohemia's Meadows And
    Forests" min sc PETERS 822 $7.00 (S461)
  "My Country: From Bohemia's Meadows
    And Forests" LUCKS 06655 sc
    $13.00, set $20.00, min sc $6.50,
    pts $.95, ea. (S462)

Moldau, The *see Ma Vlast: Vitava

Moldava *see Ma Vlast: Vitava

My Country: From Bohemia's Meadows
  And Forests *see Ma Vlast: Z
  Ceskych Luhu A Haju

My Country: Moldau *see Ma Vlast:
  Vitava

My Country: Sarka *see Ma Vlast:
  Sarka

My Country: Tabor *see Ma Vlast:
  Tabor

My Country: Vysehrad *see Ma Vlast:
  Vysehrad

Prodana Nevesta: Gerne Will Ich Dir
  Vertrauen, For Solo Voice And
  Orchestra
  LUCKS 02337 sc $4.00, set $8.00,
    pts $.75, ea. (S463)

Prodana Nevesta: O, Was Ich Mich
  Betrube, For Solo Voice And
  Orchestra
  LUCKS 02373 sc $4.00, set $8.00,
    pts $.75, ea. (S464)

Prodana Nevesta: Overture
  "Bartered Bride, The: Overture"
    LUCKS 06656 sc $8.00, set $20.00,
    min sc $2.50, pts $1.15, ea. (S465)
  "Bartered Bride, The: Overture" min
    sc BOOSEY 287 $3.50 (S466)
  "Verkaufte Braut, Die: Overture"
    min sc UNIVER. PH72 $2.00 (S467)

Verkaufte Braut, Die: Overture *see
  Prodana Nevesta: Overture

SMIT, SYTZE (1944-)
  Charsigaud [20']
    string orch,alto fl solo,bass
    clar solo,contrabsn solo,string
    quar soli
  DONEMUS (S468)

  Concerto for Violin, Saxophone and
    Orchestra [35']
    2.2.2.2. 3.1.3.0. drums,strings,
    vln solo,sax solo
  DONEMUS perf mat rent (S469)

  Quatre Bras, For Clarinet And 4
    Quartets
    0.2.0.2. 2.2.3.0. 2vln,vla,vcl,
    db,clar solo
    sc DONEMUS f.s., perf mat rent (S470)

SMITH, JOHN STAFFORD (1750-1836)
  Star-Spangled Banner, The
    see Ward, America The Beautiful

SNAREN HEBBEN GETRILD, DE, FOR SOLO
  VOICE AND ORCHESTRA see Mulder,
  Herman

SNEEUW LIGT IN DEN MORGEN VROEG, EEN
  see Van Lier, Bertus

SO GEHST DU NUN, MEIN JESU, HIN, [ARR.]
  see Bach, Johann Sebastian

SO WIE MEIN WIEN see Fridl, Hans

SODERBERG, HANS (1937-)
  Concerto for Marimba and Orchestra
    [20']
    2.1.2.2. 2.0.0.0. strings,marimba
    solo
  STIM (S471)

  Concerto for Orchestra, Op. 61
    2.2.2.2. 4.3.3.1. timp,perc,
    strings

SODERBERG, HANS (cont'd.)

  sc STIM (S472)

  Concerto for Violin and Orchestra,
    No. 1, Op. 59
    2.2.2.2. 2.0.0.0. timp,perc,
    strings,vln solo
    sc STIM perf mat rent (S473)

SODERLIND, RAGNAR
  Symphony No. 2, Op. 30
    3(pic).3(English horn).3(bass
    clar).3(contrabsn). 4.4.3.1.
    timp,perc,pno/cel,harp,strings
  NORGE (S474)

  Trauermusik *Op.12
    3(pic).2.3(soprano clar in E
    flat).2. 4.3.3.0. 3-4perc,harp,
    org,strings
    [8'30"] sc NORSK NMO 8861 $21.00 (S475)

SODERLUNDH, LILLE BROR (1912-1957)
  Concerto for Violin and Orchestra
    [21']
    2.1.2.2. 2.2.2.0. timp,perc,
    strings,vln solo
    BUSCH HBM 053 perf mat rent (S476)

SODERSTEN, GUNNO (1920-)
  Concerto for Organ and String
    Orchestra, No. 2 [18']
    string orch,org solo
  STIM (S477)

SOEFISCH see Ruyneman, Daniel

SOEUR MONIQUE RONDO see Couperin,
  Francois (le Grand)

SOFIEN QUADRILLE see Strauss, Josef

SOIR see Mulder, Ernest W.

SOIR, LE, FOR VIOLONCELLO AND
  ORCHESTRA, [ARR.] see Offenbach,
  Jacques

SOIREE A NOHANT, UNE, FOR VIOLONCELLO
  AND STRING ORCHESTRA see Merlet,
  Michel

SOKOLOV, NIKOLAI ALEXANDROVICH
  (1859-1922)
  Vendredis Polka, Les *see Glazunov,
  Alexander Konstantinovich

SOLDATENGRUSS POLKA see Strauss, Eduard

SOLEN BOR I LONNEN, FOR SOLO VOICE AND
  STRING ORCHESTRA see Sorenson,
  Torsten

SOLER, [PADRE] ANTONIO (1729-1783)
  Sonatas, Two, [arr.]
    (Palau, Manual) sc PILES 2060-V
    f.s. (S478)

SOLER, JOSE BAGUENA
  see BAGUENA SOLER, JOSE

SOLITUDE, [ARR.] see Ellington, Edward
  Kennedy (Duke)

SOLITUDINE see Kox, Hans

SOLITUDINE, FOR SOLO VOICE AND
  ORCHESTRA see Wolf, Hugo

SOLMISATION see Chailley, Jacques

SOLO E PENSOS, FOR SOLO VOICE AND
  ORCHESTRA see Haydn, [Franz] Joseph

SOLO NO. 1, FOR PIANO AND ORCHESTRA see
  Sakac, Branimir

SOLOMON: ENTRANCE OF THE QUEEN OF SHEBA
  see Handel, George Frideric

SOLSTICE, THE see Brozak, Daniel,
  Slunovrat

SOLVEJG'S SONG, FOR SOLO VOICE AND
  ORCHESTRA see Grieg, Edvard Hagerup

SOMBRERO see Dixie Joe

SOME ANIMALS NOAH FORGOT, FOR NARRATOR
  AND ORCHESTRA see Ridout, Alan

SOME OTHER WHERE see Togni, Camillo

SOMMER IN AMALFI see Crucius, Heinz

SOMMERFELDT, OISTEIN (1919-)
  Waltz For Hege
    2.2.2.2. 3.0.0.0. vibra,strings
  NORGE (S479)

SOMMERLATTE, ULRICH
  Festlicher Aufruf [11']
    2.2.2.2. 4.3.3.1. timp,perc,
    strings
    RIES perf mat rent (S480)

SOMMERNACHT see Schoeck, Othmar

SOMMERNACHT IN DANEMARK, EINE see
  Lumbye, Hans Christian

SOMMERNACHTSTRAUM: OVERTURE see
  Mendelssohn-Bartholdy, Felix,
  Midsummer Night's Dream: Overture

SONATA A 6 see Lazzari, F.

SONATA A 7 see Forster, K.

SONATA AL DIVINO CLAUDIO see Farina,
  Edoardo

SONATA CONCERTANTE see Dorward, David

SONATA CROMATICA see Merula, Tarquino

SONATA DI VIOLE see Stradella,
  Alessandro

SONATA IN BIANCO MINORE, FOR SOLO
  VOICES AND ORCHESTRA see Gubitosi,
  Emilia

SONATA NOTTURNA, FOR FLUTE, VIOLIN AND
  STRINGS see Carpi, Fiorenzo

SONATA SANCTI IOANNIS NEPOMUNCENI see
  Biber, Carl

SONATA TRITEMATICA NO. 7 see Chailly,
  Luciano

SONATAS see Keulen, Geert van

SONATAS, TWO, [ARR.] see Soler, [Padre]
  Antonio

SONATAS, 4 see Manneke, Daan

SONATAS FOR CLARINO, THREE see Biber,
  Carl

SONATAS FOR CLARINO, TWO see Biber,
  Carl

SONATAS FOR ORGAN AND ORCHESTRA, K. 67-
  69, 144, 145, 212, 241, 224, 245,
  263, 278, 329, 328, 338, 274 see
  Mozart, Wolfgang Amadeus

SONATAS FOR ORGAN AND ORCHESTRA, K.
  244, 245, 274, 328, 336 see Mozart,
  Wolfgang Amadeus

SONATAS FOR TRUMPETS, TWO see Biber,
  Carl

SONATE FUR JSB see Schenker, Friedrich

SONG see Brings, Allen Stephen

SONG AND DANCE see Washburn, Robert
  Brooks

SONG OF THE FLEA, FOR SOLO VOICE AND
  ORCHESTRA see Mussorgsky, Modest
  Petrovich

SONG OF THE VALKYR see Weingartner,
  (Paul) Felix von, Lied Der Walkure,
  For Solo Voice And Orchestra

SONG OF THE VENETIAN GONDELIER, OP. 19,
  NO. 6, [ARR.] see Mendelssohn-
  Bartholdy, Felix, Venezianisches
  Gondellied, Op. 19, No. 6, [arr.]

SONG TO SPRING, FOR SOLO VOICE AND
  ORCHESTRA see Wolf, Hugo, Er Ist's,
  "Fruhling Lasst Sein Blaues Band",
  For Solo Voice And Orchestra

SONGFEST, FOR SOLO VOICES AND ORCHESTRA
  see Bernstein, Leonard

SONGS AND DANCES OF DEATH, FOR SOLO
  VOICE AND ORCHESTRA, [ARR.] see
  Mussorgsky, Modest Petrovich

SONGS AND DANCES OF DEATH: BERCEUSE,
  FOR SOLO VOICE AND ORCHESTRA see
  Mussorgsky, Modest Petrovich

SONGS FOR DOV, FOR SOLO VOICE AND
  ORCHESTRA see Tippett, [Sir]
  Michael

SONGS FOR PATRICIA, FOR SOLO VOICE AND
  ORCHESTRA see Wilder, Alec

SONGS OF A WAYFARER see Mahler, Gustav,
  Lieder Eines Fahrenden Gesellen,
  For Solo Voice And Orchestra

SONGS OF THE CROSS
  (Kirkland, Camp) CRESPUB CP-IN 7+7
    $17.50
    contains: At The Cross; When I
    Survey The Wondrous Cross (S481)

SONGS ON THE DEATH OF CHILDREN see Mahler, Gustav, Kindertotenlieder, For Solo Voice And Orchestra

SONNAMBULA, LA: CARA COMPAGNE; COME PER ME SERENO; SOVRA IL SEN, FOR SOLO VOICE AND ORCHESTRA see Bellini, Vincenzo

SONNE IM LAUB see Blume, Karl

SONNETTENKRING, FOR SOLO VOICE AND ORCHESTRA see Mulder, Herman

SONNIGE TAGE see Loffler, Willy

SONNIGER MORGEN see Kess, Ludwig

SONNINEN, AHTI (1914-   )
Juhannusyo, For Solo Voice And Orchestra *Op.21 [11']
2.0.2.0. 4.0.0.0. timp,perc,harp, cel,strings,solo voice
FAZER perf mat rent   (S482)

Karjalan Neidon Lauluja, For Solo Voice And Orchestra *Op.24 [6']
3.1.2.2. 4.0.0.0. timp,harp, strings,solo voice
FAZER perf mat rent   (S483)

SONNLEITHNER, CHRISTOPH VON
Pastorella
string orch
sc,pts HARMONIA 3190 f.s.   (S484)

SONNTAG IM HEIDEDORF see Lautenschlager, W.

SONO ALCINA, E SONO ANCORA UN VISINO, FOR SOLO VOICE AND ORCHESTRA see Haydn, [Franz] Joseph

SONORES NASCENTES ET MORIENTES see Szekely, Endre

SONORITA see Szollosy, Andras

SOPRONI, JOZSEF (1930-   )
Symphony No. 1
(special import only) sc EMB 10213 f.s.   (S485)

SORCERER'S APPRENTICE, THE see Dukas, Paul, Apprenti Sorcier, L'

SORENSON, TORSTEN (1908-   )
Brokiga Blad [20']
string orch
STIM   (S486)

Solen Bor I Lonnen, For Solo Voice And String Orchestra [10']
string orch,S solo
STIM   (S487)

SORESINA, ALBERTO (1911-   )
Aria E Burlesca [5']
harp,cel,pno,strings
sc,pts ZANIBON D163 rent   (S488)

Concerto for Piano and Orchestra [20']
2.2.2.2. 2.2.0.0. timp,pno, strings,pno solo
manuscript CARISCH   (S489)

Concerto for String Orchestra [17']
string orch
sc,pts ZANIBON D282 rent   (S490)

Due Notturni [8']
harp,strings
sc,pts ZANIBON D264 rent   (S491)

Favole, For Solo Voices And Orchestra [15']
1.1.1.1. 1.1.1.0. pno,strings,SB& child solo
sc CARISCH 21964 perf mat rent   (S492)

Introduzione Per Una Commedia Gaia [4']
1+pic.1.1.1. 2.2.2.0. timp,perc, harp,cel,strings
sc,pts ZANIBON D168 rent   (S493)

Ninna Nanna, For Solo Voice And Orchestra [2'30"]
pno,cel,strings,solo voice
sc,pts ZANIBON D164 rent   (S494)

Tempo E Fantasia, For Piano And String Orchestra [10']
string orch,pno solo
sc,pts ZANIBON D248 rent   (S495)

SORGENBRECHER WALZER see Strauss, Johann, [Jr.]

SORTIE VERS LA LUMIERE DU JOUR see Grisey, Gerard

SOSPIRI see Elgar, [Sir] Edward (William)

SOUDA, SOUDA SINISORSA, FOR SOLO VOICE AND ORCHESTRA, [ARR.] see Sibelius, Jean

SOUND-HOUSE see Katzer, Georg

SOUNDINGS see Kolb, Barbara

SOUNDS OF PRAISE INSTRUMENTAL PARTS *CCU
(Red, Buryl) sc BROADMAN 4573-11 $6.95, pts BROADMAN 4573-12 $2.75, ea.   (S496)

SOUPE DU ROY, LE, [ARR.] see Lully, Jean-Baptiste (Lulli)

SOUPIRS DE GENEVIEVE, LES see Vacchi, F.

SOUS LE CIEL IMMOBILE J'AI COMPTE JUSQU'A MILLE see Ruyneman, Daniel

SOUS LE PONT MIRABEAU, FOR SOLO VOICES AND CHAMBER ORCHESTRA see Ruyneman, Daniel

SOUSA, JOHN PHILIP (1854-1932)
Bride Elect March, The
LUCKS 06668 set $12.00, pts $.50, ea.   (S497)

Capitan March, El
LUCKS 06672 set $12.00, pts $.75, ea.   (S498)

Capitan Spectacular, El, [arr.]
string orch
(Gordon) sc MARKS MSO 15 $2.00, set MARKS $10.00, pts MARKS $1.00, ea.   (S499)

Charlatan March, The
LUCKS 06669 set $12.00, pts $.75, ea.   (S500)

Diplomat March, The
LUCKS 08196 set $12.00, pts $.75, ea.   (S501)

Directorate March, The
LUCKS 08195 set $12.00, pts $.75, ea.   (S502)

Free Lance March
LUCKS 11485 set $12.00, pts $.50, ea.   (S503)

Gladiator March, The
LUCKS 08198 set $12.00, pts $.75, ea.   (S504)

Hail To The Spirit Of Liberty March
LUCKS 11486 set $12.00, pts $.75, ea.   (S505)

Hands Across The Sea March
LUCKS 06677 set $12.00, pts $.75, ea.   (S506)

Imperial Edward March
LUCKS 11487 set $12.00, pts $.50, ea.   (S507)

Invincible Eagle March, The
LUCKS 08199 set $10.00, pts $.75, ea.   (S508)

Jack Tar March
LUCKS 08200 set $12.00, pts $.75, ea.   (S509)

King Cotton March
LUCKS 08690 set $12.00, pts $.75, ea.   (S510)

Liberty Bell March, The
LUCKS 06681 set $12.00, pts $.75, ea.   (S511)

Man Behind The Gun March, The
LUCKS 08202 set $12.00, pts $.75, ea.   (S512)

Manhattan Beach March
LUCKS 08203 set $12.00, pts $.75, ea.   (S513)

Semper Fidelis March
LUCKS 06683 set $12.00, pts $.75, ea.   (S514)

Stars And Stripes Forever March, The
LUCKS 06684 set $12.00, pts $.75, ea.   (S515)

Three Quotations: A: The King Of France
LUCKS 06685 set $10.00, pts $.75, ea.   (S516)

Three Quotations: B: I, Too, Was Born In Arcadia
LUCKS 06686 set $10.00, pts $.75, ea.   (S517)

SOUSA, JOHN PHILIP (cont'd.)

Three Quotations: C: In Darkest Africa
LUCKS 10084 set $10.00, pts $.75, ea.   (S518)

Thunderer March, The
LUCKS 08206 set $12.00, pts $.75, ea.   (S519)

Washington Post March, The
LUCKS 06682 set $12.00, pts $.75, ea.   (S520)

SOUSA OVERTURE, A see Turok, Paul Harris

SOUTHERN HARMONY see Kay, Ulysses Simpson

SOUVENIR see Booren, Jo van den

SOUVENIR, FOR VIOLIN AND STRING ORCHESTRA see Kupkovic, Ladislav

SOUVENIR DE BADE POLKA see Strauss, Eduard

SOUVENIR DE PHILADELPHIA see Gungl, Joseph

SOUVENIR DE VILLINGEN, [ARR.] see Grappelli, Stephane

SOUVENIR DU SILENCE see Dusapin, Pascal

SOUVENIR DU VAL, FOR VIOLONCELLO AND ORCHESTRA, [ARR.] see Offenbach, Jacques

SOUVENIR D'UN LIEU CHER: MEDIATATION, FOR VIOLIN AND ORCHESTRA, [ARR.] see Tchaikovsky, Piotr Ilyich

SOUVENIR D'UN LIEU CHER: SCHERZO, FOR VIOLIN AND ORCHESTRA, [ARR.] see Tchaikovsky, Piotr Ilyich

SOUVENIR NOSTALGIQUE see Keulen, Geert van

SOUVENIRS A LA MEMOIRE, FOR SOLO VOICES AND ORCHESTRA see Sinopoli, Giuseppe

SOUVENIRS OF SCHUMANN see Holloway, Robin

SPACES see Manneke, Daan, Ruimten

SPAGNOLETTA see Rasponi, Giuseppe

SPAGNOLI, G. (1896-   )
Due Intermezzi [6']
3.3.2.2. 4.2.3.0. timp,pno,harp, strings
manuscript CARISCH   (S521)

Ouverture Romantica
2.2.2.2. 2.2.3.0. timp,strings
manuscript CARISCH   (S522)

Suite In Tre Tempi [12']
3.3.4.3. 4.3.3.1. perc,cel,harp, pno,xylo,bells,strings
manuscript CARISCH   (S523)

SPANISCHE SERENADE see Mielenz, Hans

SPANISCHE SKIZZE see Hasenpflug, Curt

SPANISCHE SUITE see Niklas, Ferry

SPANISCHER TANZ see Bund, Hans

SPANISCHES LIEDERSPIEL, [ARR.] see Schumann, Robert (Alexander)

SPANISH DANCE see Bird, Arthur

SPANISH DANCES, OP. 12, NOS. 1, 3, AND 4, [ARR.] see Moszkowski, Moritz

SPANISH DANCES, OP. 12, NOS. 2 AND 5, [ARR.] see Moszkowski, Moritz

SPANNENDER DIALOG MIT PAUSEN see Becce, Giuseppe

SPARVERO, LO see Henkemans, Hans

SPAZIERGANG see Eisbrenner, Werner

SPECTRUM see Lees, Benjamin

SPECTRUM see Ruiter, Wim de

SPEKTRUM see Erdmann, Dietrich

SPELMANSSTAMMA see Blomberg, Erik

SPELMANSVISA, FOR SOLO VOICE AND ORCHESTRA see Lundkvist, Per

SPHARENKLANGE see Strauss, Josef

SPHARENKLANGE, FOR SOLO VOICE AND ORCHESTRA see Strauss, Josef

SPHARENMUSIK see Huber, Nicolaus A.

SPIEGELZEIT see Egk, Werner

SPIEL ZU 45 see Bredemeyer, Reiner

SPIELMUSIK see Moser, Rudolf

SPIEWY POLSKIE, FOR SOLO VOICE AND CHAMBER ORCHESTRA see Meyer, Krzysztof

SPIJTIG KLAARTJE see Voormolen, Alexander Nicolas

SPINNER, LEOPOLD (1906-   )
  Concerto for Piano and Orchestra, Op. 4
    sc BOOSEY $15.00   (S524)

SPINNERLIED, OP. 67, NO. 4, [ARR.] see Mendelssohn-Bartholdy, Felix

SPINNING SONG, OP. 67, NO. 4, [ARR.] see Mendelssohn-Bartholdy, Felix, Spinnerlied, Op. 67, No. 4, [arr.]

SPIRALEN WALZER see Strauss, Johann, [Jr.]

SPIRITUALS see Gould, Morton

SPITZENTUCH DER KONIGIN, DAS: OVERTURE see Strauss, Johann, [Jr.]

SPITZWEG-SUITE see Mattausch, H.A.

SPLEEN see Vuursteen, Frans

SPLEEN ET IDEAL see Samama, Leo

SPLENDIDAE NUPTIAE see Muffat, Georg

SPOHR, LUDWIG (LOUIS) (1784-1859)
  Alchymist, Der: Overture [9']
    2+pic.2.2.2. 4.2.3.0. timp,perc, strings
    sc,pts LIENAU rent   (S525)
    KALMUS 5447 set $18.00, pts $1.00, ea., cmplt ed rent   (S526)

  Concerto for Violin and Orchestra, No. 2, Op. 2, in D minor
    LUCKS 00404 set $18.00, pts $1.40, ea.   (S527)

  Concerto for Violin and Orchestra, No. 6, Op. 28, in G minor [20']
    2.2.2.2. 3.0.0.0. strings,vln solo
    sc,pts LIENAU f.s.   (S528)

  Concerto for Violin and Orchestra, No. 12, Op. 79, in A [19']
    2.2.2.2. 2.2.0.0. timp,strings, vln solo
    sc,pts LIENAU rent   (S529)

  Faust: Overture
    BREITKOPF-W perf mat rent   (S530)

  Symphonies, Three
    (Berrett, Joshua) sc GARLAND ISBN 0-8240-3803-7 $90.00 "The Symphony", Vol. C-IX
    contains: Symphony No. 4, Op. 86, in F; Symphony No. 6, Op. 116, in G; Symphony No. 7, Op. 121, in C   (S531)

  Symphony No. 3, Op. 78, in C minor [31']
    2.2.2.2. 4.2.3.0. timp,strings
    sc,pts LIENAU rent   (S532)

  Symphony No. 4, Op. 86, in F [40']
    2.2.2.2. 4.2.3.0. timp,perc, strings
    see Symphonies, Three
    sc,pts LIENAU rent   (S533)

  Symphony No. 5, Op. 102, in C minor [30']
    2.2.2.2. 4.2.3.0. timp,strings
    sc,pts LIENAU rent   (S534)

  Symphony No. 6, Op. 116, in G
    see Symphonies, Three

  Symphony No. 7, Op. 121, in C
    see Symphonies, Three

  Weihe Der Tone, Die *see Symphony No. 4, Op. 86

SPONTINI, GASPARE (1774-1851)
  Borussia Marsch
    2+pic.2.2+2basset horn.2+ contrabsn. 4.2.3.1. timp,perc, strings
    sc,pts LIENAU rent   (S535)

SPONTINI, GASPARE (cont'd.)
  Eroismo Ridicolo, L': Overture [4'30"]
    1.2.1.1. 2.0.0.0. timp,strings
    (Negrotti, N.) sc,pts ZANIBON D290 rent   (S536)

  Nurmahal: Overture [8']
    2+pic.2.2.2. 4.2.3.0. harp,timp, perc,strings
    sc,pts LIENAU rent   (S537)

  Olympie: Overture [7']
    2+pic.2.2.4. 4.2.3.0. timp, strings
    sc,pts LIENAU rent   (S538)

  Vestale, La: Overture [7']
    2+pic.2.2.2. 4.2.3.0. timp, strings
    "Vestalin, Die: Overture" sc,pts LIENAU rent   (S539)

  Vestalin, Die: Overture *see Vestale, La: Overture

SPOSA DI BELTRAMO, LA, FOR SOLO VOICE AND ORCHESTRA see Sinigaglia, Leone

SPOSALIZIO, FOR VIOLIN, VIOLONCELLO AND ORCHESTRA see Bossi, [Marco] Enrico

SPRING FESTIVAL OVERTURE, A see Wordsworth, William

SPRING IN MY HEART, FOR SOLO VOICE AND ORCHESTRA see Strauss, Johann, [Jr.]

SPRING SONG see Sibelius, Jean

SPRING SYMPHONY see Schumann, Robert (Alexander), Symphony No. 1, Op. 38, in B flat

SPRINGTIME IN THE AIR, FOR SOLO VOICE AND ORCHESTRA see Strauss, Johann, [Jr.]

SPRUHTEUFELCHEN see Bode, Hermann

ST-48-1, 240162 see Xenakis, Yannis (Iannis)

STAAT, DE, FOR SOLO VOICES AND ORCHESTRA see Andriessen, Louis

STADT UND LAND. POLKA see Strauss, Johann, [Jr.]

STALLAERT, ALPHONSE (1920-   )
  Aep, De Hond En De Vis, Den
    see Internationale Dierentuin, For Solo Voice And Orchestra

  Internationale Dierentuin, For Solo Voice And Orchestra
    bass trom,pno,strings,S solo
    DONEMUS sc f.s., pts rent
    contains: Aep, De Hond En De Vis, Den; Lonza E La Lupa, La; Panther, Der; Pelican, Le; Toro, El; Tyger, The   (S540)

  Lonza E La Lupa, La
    see Internationale Dierentuin, For Solo Voice And Orchestra

  Panther, Der
    see Internationale Dierentuin, For Solo Voice And Orchestra

  Pelican, Le
    see Internationale Dierentuin, For Solo Voice And Orchestra

  Toro, El
    see Internationale Dierentuin, For Solo Voice And Orchestra

  Tyger, The
    see Internationale Dierentuin, For Solo Voice And Orchestra

STAM, HENK (1922-   )
  Funf Bagatellen [6']
    1.1.1.1. 0.0.0.0. perc,strings without db
    sc DONEMUS f.s., perf mat rent   (S541)

STAMITZ, ANTON (1754-ca. 1809)
  Concerto for Flute and String Orchestra in D, MIN 50
    string orch,fl solo
    sc AMADEUS BP 2452 f.s., pts AMADEUS f.s.   (S542)

  Concerto for Viola and Orchestra, No. 4, in D [25']
    (Lebermann, W.) sc BREITKOPF-W PB 4865 f.s., pts BREITKOPF-W OB 4865 f.s.   (S543)

STAMITZ, ANTON (cont'd.)
  Concerto for Viola and String Orchestra, No. 4, in D
    string orch,vla solo
    (Lebermann, Walter) (with cadenzas)
    sc,pts NAGELS NMA 238 f.s.   (S544)

  Sinfonia Concertante for 2 Flutes and Orchestra in D
    0.1.0.0. 1.0.0.0. strings,2fl soli
    (Gronefeld) sc,pts EULENBURG E10141 f.s.   (S545)

STAMITZ, CARL (1745-1801)
  Concerto for Clarinet and Orchestra in B flat, MIN 35
    2horn,strings,clar solo
    sc EUR.AM.MUS. 71U0141 $16.00, pts EUR.AM.MUS. $3.00, ea.   (S546)

  Concerto for Clarinet and Orchestra in B flat, MIN 68
    2horn,strings,clar solo
    (Balassa, Gyorgy) (2nd Darmstadter Konzert) SCHOTTS CON 192 sc $13.50, pts $2.50   (S547)

  Concerto for Viola and Orchestra, Op. 1, in D
    LUCKS 00844 sc $9.00, set $10.50, pts $1.15, ea.   (S548)
    (David, Hans T.) 0.0.2.0. 2.0.0.0. strings,vla solo KALMUS A2072 sc $9.00, perf mat rent, set $12.00, pts $1.50, ea., solo pt $1.50   (S549)

  Concerto for Viola d'Amore and Orchestra, No. 1, in D
    sc,pts KRENN f.s.   (S550)

  Concerto for Viola d'Amore and Orchestra, No. 2
    sc,pts KRENN f.s.   (S551)

  Sinfonia, Op. 35, No. 2, in D
    2fl,opt ob,2clar,perc,strings
    sc,pts HARMONIA 2257 f.s.   (S552)

STAMITZ, JOHANN WENZEL ANTON (1717-1757)
  Concerto for Flute and String Orchestra in D, MIN 3
    (Lebermann, W.) KALMUS A2071 sc $8.00, set $8.00, pts $1.50, ea., solo pt $1.50   (S553)

  Concerto for Harpsichord and Orchestra, Op. 10, No. 1, in D
    2fl/2ob, 2horn,strings,hpsd/pno solo
    (Schultz-Hauser, Karlheinz) SCHOTTS CON 189 sc $8.75, pts $3.00, ea.   (S554)

  Concerto for Violin and String Orchestra in G, MIN 64
    string orch,cont,vln solo
    (in this edition called Concerto No. 8) sc,pts HUG f.s.   (S555)

  Sinfonia Pastorale In D, Op. 4, No. 2
    (Upmeyer, W.) KALMUS A2070 sc $7.00, set $10.00, pts $1.00, ea.   (S556)

STANDCHEN, FOR SOLO VOICE AND ORCHESTRA, [ARR.] see Schubert, Franz (Peter)

STANDCHEN AN COLOMBINE see Winkler, Gerhard

STANKE, WILLY
  Fahrt Nach Trento
    RIES f.s.   (S557)

  Furiade
    RIES f.s.   (S558)

  Landliche Humoreske
    RIES f.s.   (S559)

  Sarello
    see Pero, Hans, Andalusische Strassenmusik

STANZAS OF CHARLES II, FOR SOLO VOICE AND ORCHESTRA see Voormolen, Alexander Nicolas

STAR-SPANGLED BANNER, THE see Smith, John Stafford

STAR-SPANGLED OVERTURE see Gould, Morton

STARK, WILHELM (1913-   )
  Concertino Mediterraneo, For Flute And Orchestra
    bass clar,perc,hpsd,strings,fl solo
    BUDDE perf mat rent   (S560)

STARRY NIGHT see Cikker, Jan, Hviezdnata Noc

STARS AND STRIPES FOREVER MARCH, THE
   see Sousa, John Philip

START AND FINISH see Stolzenwald, Otto

STASERA see Kox, Hans

STATUE OF III, THE see Tsubonoh,
   Katsuhiro

STAVENHAGEN, BERNHARD
   Concerto for Piano and Orchestra, Op.
      4
      2(pic).2.2.2+contrabsn. 4.2.3.1.
         timp,perc,strings,pno solo
      RIES perf mat rent   (S561)

STECHMUCKEN see Merath, Siegfried

STEEN see Schat, Peter

STEEN, GERT VAN DER (1907-   )
   Divertimento [12']
      2.0.0.0. 0.0.0.0. perc, strings
         without vla, db
      sc DONEMUS f.s., perf mat rent
                                   (S562)

STEENHUIS, FRANCOIS (1918-1956)
   Serenade, Op. 8 [15']
      1.0.1.0. 0.1.0.0. perc,pno 4-
         hands, strings without vla, db
      sc DONEMUS f.s., perf mat rent
                                   (S563)

STEFFAN, JOSEPH ANTON (1726-1797)
   Concerto in D [30']
      2horn,pno,strings
      (Picton, Howard) sc OXFORD 77.886
         $23.00, pts OXFORD $3.00   (S564)

STEFFARO, JULIUS (1927-   )
   Danse De Fete [5'10"]
      2.2.2.2. 4.3.3.1. perc,harp,pno,
         strings
      ORLANDO rent   (S565)

   Galopping Strings [3']
      1.1.2.1. 0.0.0.0. perc,gtr,
         strings
      ORLANDO rent   (S566)

   Piccolo Concerto, For Tuba And
      Orchestra [6']
      2.2.2.2. 4.3.3.0. timp,2perc,
         harp,strings,tuba solo
      sc DONEMUS f.s., perf mat rent
                                   (S567)

   Plucking Strings [2'30"]
      perc,gtr,strings
      ORLANDO rent   (S568)

   Suite Pastorale, For English Horn And
      Chamber Orchestra [9']
      harp,strings,English horn solo
      ORLANDO rent   (S569)

STEFFE, WILLIAM
   Battle Hymn Of The Republic
      (Luck, Arthur) LUCKS HYMNS 14 set
         $8.50, pts $.65   (S570)

STEFFEN, WOLFGANG (1923-   )
   Sinfonia Da Camera
      1.1.1.1. 2.1.1.1. timp,perc,
         strings
      BUDDE perf mat rent   (S571)

STEGER, WERNER (1932-   )
   Prelude and Fugue [8']
      string orch
      MANNHEIM E 31-60 f.s.   (S572)

STEHE STILL, FOR SOLO VOICE AND
   ORCHESTRA, [ARR.] see Wagner,
   Richard

STEIN, LEON (1910-   )
   Dance Of The Enraptured
      sc TRANSCON. 990084 $2.99, perf mat
         rent   (S573)

   Dance Of The Exultant
      sc TRANSCON. 990085 $2.50, perf mat
         rent   (S574)

   Dance Of The Joyous
      sc TRANSCON. 990083 $2.00, perf mat
         rent   (S575)

STEIN-SCHNEIDER, L.
   Orchidea
      RIES f.s. contains also: Pas De
         Colombine   (S576)

   Pas De Colombine
      see Stein-Schneider, L., Orchidea

STELLIDAURE VENDICATA: DEH, RENDETEMI
   OMBRE CARE, FOR SOLO VOICE AND
   STRING ORCHESTRA see Provenzale,
   Francesco

STEMMEN UIT HET LABYRINT, FOR SOLO
   VOICES AND ORCHESTRA see Schat,
   Peter

STENHAMMAR, WILHELM (1871-1927)
   Serenade, Op. 31, in F
      min sc NORDISKA f.s.   (S577)

STERNDALE BENNETT, WILLIAM
   see BENNETT, [SIR] WILLIAM STERNDALE

STERNENGESANG see Barolsky, Michael

STETIT PUELLA see Mul, Jan

STEWART, DON
   Two Hundred Bar Passacaglia
      2.2.2.2. 4.3.3.1. 5perc,harp,
         strings
      SEESAW perf mat rent   (S578)

STHAMER, HEINRICH (1885-1955)
   Concerto for Piano and Orchestra, Op.
      9 [30']
      2.2+English horn.2.2. 4.2.3.1.
         harp,timp,perc,strings,pno solo
      sc,pts LIENAU rent   (S579)

STIL ENDE VREDSAEM see Badings, Henk

STILL WIE DIE NACHT, FOR SOLO VOICE AND
   ORCHESTRA see Bohm, Karl

STILLEBEN see Kopelent, Marek

STIMMEN AUS DEM PUBLICUM. WALZER see
   Strauss, Johann, [Jr.]

STIMMEN AUS DEM PUBLIKUM see Strauss,
   Eduard

STIMMEN AUS DER FERNE, FOR SOLO VOICE
   AND ORCHESTRA see Baird, Tadeusz

STIMULI POUR SOURCES SONORES ALEATOIRES
   ET INSTRUMENTS see Capdenat,
   Philippe

STIRB UND WERDE see Tiessen, Heinz,
   Symphony, Op. 17

STIRI SKLADBE see Osterc, Slavko

STOCK, DAVID (1939-   )
   Inner Space [13']
      3.2.2.2. 4.3.3.1. timp,3perc,
         strings
      MARGUN BP 7026 perf mat rent (S580)

   Triflumena [9']
      3.2.3.2. 4.3.3.1. perc,strings
      MARGUN BP 7027 perf mat rent (S581)

   Zohar [18']
      3.3.3.3. 4.3.3.1. perc,strings
      MARGUN BP 7028 perf mat rent (S582)

STOCKHAUSEN, KARLHEINZ (1928-   )
   Inori, For One Or Two Soloists And
      Orchestra *No.38
      STOCKHAUS   (S583)

   Jahreslauf, Der *No.47 (from Licht)
      STOCKHAUS rent   (S584)

   Jubilaum *No.45
      STOCKHAUS   (S585)

   Tierkreis [23']
      clar,horn,bsn,strings
      sc STOCKHAUS $18.00   (S586)

   Trans *No.35 [26']
      sc STOCKHAUS $52.00   (S587)

STOLTE, SIEGFRIED (1925-   )
   Concertino for Recorder and String
      Orchestra
      string orch,S rec solo
      sc DEUTSCHER DVFM 32 069A f.s., pts
         DEUTSCHER DVFM 32 069B f.s.
                                   (S588)

STOLZEL, GOTTFRIED HEINRICH (1690-1749)
   Concerto Grosso A Quattro Cori
      1.3.0.1. 0.6.0.0. timp,hpsd,
         strings
      (Darvas) PETERS P8141 sc $22.50,
         set $35.00, pts $2.50, ea. (S589)

   Liebster Jesu, Deine Liebe, For Solo
      Voice And Orchestra [9']
      string orch,org,A solo
      (Bachmair, J.) BREITKOPF-W perf mat
         rent   (S590)

STOLZENWALD, OTTO
   Frischer Wind
      RIES f.s.   (S591)

   Frohliche Geigen
      RIES f.s.   (S592)

   Kleine Ballettstudie [4']
      2.2.2.2. 4.2.3.0. timp,perc,harp,
         strings
      RIES f.s.   (S593)
      RIES perf mat rent   (S594)

STOLZENWALD, OTTO (cont'd.)
   Kontraste
      RIES f.s.   (S595)

   Start And Finish
      RIES f.s.   (S596)

   Streiflichter [5']
      2.2.2.2. 4.2.3.0. timp,2perc,
         harp,strings
      sc RIES f.s., perf mat rent (S597)

STONY BROOK see Bales, Richard Horner

STOP-START see Hellermann, William

STORBEKKEN, EGIL
   Festintrade *see Brevik, Tor

   Lokketrall Og Somar-Natta, For Solo
      Voice And Orchestra *see Brevik,
      Tor

STORIES see Back, Sven-Erik

STORM, THE see Tchaikovsky, Piotr
   Ilyich, Orage, L': Overture

STORRLE, HEINZ (1932-   )
   Orange Flowers [7']
      2.1.1+bass clar.1. 4.2.3.0.
         glock/vibra,harp,elec pno,elec
         gtr,elec bass,strings
      ORLANDO rent   (S598)

   Your Melody [6']
      2.1.1+bass clar.2. 2.2.2.0. perc,
         harp,elec gtr,elec bass,strings
      ORLANDO rent   (S599)

STOUB see Hespos, Hans-Joachim

STRADELLA, ALESSANDRO (1645-1682)
   Barcheggio, Il: Serenata A Tre, For
      Solo Voices And Orchestra
      [96'40"]
      0.0.0.0. 0.1.1.0. hpsd,strings,
         SAB soli
      manuscript CARISCH   (S600)

   Barcheggio, Il: Sinfonia
      string orch,cont,trp solo
      (Tarr, E.H.) sc,pts COSTALL f.s.
                                   (S601)

   Damone, Il: Sinfonia
      string orch,lute,cont,2vln soli,
         2vcl soli
      (Tarr, E.H.) sc,pts COSTALL f.s.
                                   (S602)

   Floridoro, Il: Per Pieta, For Solo
      Voice And Orchestra
      LUCKS 02830 set $8.00, pts $.75,
         ea.   (S603)
      KALMUS A3021 set $8.00, pts $.60,
         ea.   (S604)

   Sonata Di Viole [7'30"]
      strings,2vln soli,lute solo
      (Tarr, E.H.) COSTALL C.3466 f.s.
                                   (S605)

STRAESSER, JOEP (1934-   )
   Canterbury Concerto, For Piano And
      Orchestra [12']
      2.2.3.2. 2.2.2.0. 3perc,pno,
         strings,pno solo
      DONEMUS perf mat rent   (S606)

   Chorai Revisited [12']
      4.2.4.2.2sax. 2.2.2.0. 3perc,
         harp,pno,cel,strings
      sc DONEMUS f.s., perf mat rent
                                   (S607)

   Just A Moment Again...
      2perc,pno,strings
      DONEMUS perf mat rent   (S608)

   Musique Pour L'Homme, For Solo Voices
      And Orchestra [26']
      4.4.4.4. 4.4.4.1. 5perc,strings,
         SATB soli
      sc DONEMUS f.s., perf mat rent
                                   (S609)

   Summerconcerto, For Oboe And
      Orchestra [11']
      2.2.2.2. 2.2.2.0. 3perc,harp,
         strings,ob solo
      sc DONEMUS f.s., perf mat rent
                                   (S610)

   Twenty-Two Pages, For Solo Voices And
      Orchestra [11']
      4.4.4.4. 4.4.4.1. 3perc,harp,pno&
         cel,vibra&xylo,8db,TBarB soli
      sc DONEMUS f.s., perf mat rent
                                   (S611)

STRAK see Rennqvist, Karin

STRANGE TENDERNESS OF NAKED LEAPING see
   Dlugoszewski, Lucia

STRANZ, ULRICH (1946-   )
   Contrasubjekte. Passacaglia Uber BACH
      [9']
      8vln,3vla,2vcl,db
      BAREN. BA 6787 perf mat rent (S612)

STRANZ, ULRICH (cont'd.)

Klangbild [15']
3+pic.3+English horn.3+bass
clar.3+contrabsn. 6.4.4.1.
timp,3perc,harp,cel,strings
BAREN. BA 6715 perf mat rent (S613)

STRAPAESE see Pizzini, Carlo Alberto

STRASSE IN TOLEDO see Krepela, Josef

STRATEGIER, HERMAN (1912-   )
Concerto for Basset Horn and
Orchestra [14']
1.1.1.1. 1.1.0.0. perc,cel,harp,
strings,basset horn solo
DONEMUS   (S614)

Intrada Festiva
3.3.3.2. 4.3.3.1. timp,perc,harp,
cel,strings
sc DONEMUS f.s., perf mat rent
(S615)

Psalm No. 118 for Solo Voice and
Orchestra [28']
2.2.2.2. 3.3.3.0. timp,perc,harp,
cel,strings,Bar/A solo
sc DONEMUS f.s., perf mat rent
(S616)

Sonatina [12']
2.2.2.2. 2.2.0.0. timp,strings
DONEMUS perf mat rent (S617)

STRAUSS, EDUARD (1835-1916)
Abonnenten Walzer *Op.116
LUCKS 07924 set $23.50, pts $1.25,
ea.   (S618)

Angot Quadrille *Op.110
LUCKS 07970 set $13.50, pts $.75,
ea.   (S619)

Augensprache *Op.119
LUCKS 07954 set $11.00, pts $.75,
ea.   (S620)

Aula-Lieder Walzer *Op.113
LUCKS 07925 set $23.50, pts $1.25,
ea.   (S621)

Aus Dem Rechtsleben Walzer *Op.126
LUCKS 07923 set $25.00, pts $1.25,
ea.   (S622)

Aus Der Studienzeit Walzer *Op.141
LUCKS 07926 set $22.50, pts $1.25,
ea.   (S623)

Aus Lieb' Zu Ihr Polka *Op.135
LUCKS 07953 set $13.50, pts $.75,
ea.   (S624)

Bahn Frei Polka *Op.45
LUCKS 07570 set $14.00, pts $.75,
ea.   (S625)
"Fast Track Polka" 1+pic.2.2.2.
4.4.3.1. perc,strings [3'] KALMUS
A2077 sc $3.00, perf mat rent,
set $15.00, pts $.75, ea. (S626)
(Hruby, V.) 2.2.2.2. 4.2.3.0. perc,
harp,strings CRANZ f.s.   (S627)

Ball Promessen Walzer *Op.82
LUCKS 07927 set $25.00, pts $1.25
ea.   (S628)

Ballchronik Walzer *Op.167
LUCKS 06717 set $26.00, pts $1.25,
ea.   (S629)

Bessere Zeiten Walzer *Op.130
LUCKS 07928 set $23.50, pts $1.25,
ea.   (S630)

Boccaccio Quadrille *Op.180
LUCKS 06718 set $20.00, pts $1.00,
ea.   (S631)

Bruder Studio Polka *Op.78
LUCKS 07574 set $15.00, pts $.75,
ea.   (S632)

Colombine Polka *Op.89
LUCKS 07963 set $15.00, pts $.75,
ea.   (S633)

Consequenzen Walzer *Op.143
LUCKS 06720 set $15.00, pts $.75,
ea.   (S634)

Deutsche Herzen Walzer *Op.65
LUCKS 06721 set $31.00, pts $1.25,
ea.   (S635)

Doctrinen Walzer *Op.79
2.2.2.0. 4.2.3.0. perc,harp,strings
CRANZ f.s.   (S636)
LUCKS 06722 set $26.00, pts $1.25,
ea.   (S637)

Ehret Die Frauen Walzer *Op.80
LUCKS 06723 set $21.00, pts $1.25,
ea.   (S638)

STRAUSS, EDUARD (cont'd.)

En Miniatur Polka *Op.181
LUCKS 06724 set $14.00, pts $.75,
ea.   (S639)

Fast Track Polka *see Bahn Frei
Polka

Fatinitza Quadrille *Op.136
LUCKS 06751 set $16.50, pts $.75,
ea.   (S640)

Fesche Geister *Op.75
2.2.2.2. 4.2.3.0. perc,harp,strings
CRANZ f.s.   (S641)

Fidele Bursche Walzer *Op.124
LUCKS 07931 set $25.00, pts $1.25,
ea.   (S642)

Flottes Leben Polka *Op.115
LUCKS 07956 set $15.00, pts $.75,
ea.   (S643)

Fur Lustige Leut' *Op.255
LUCKS 07932 set $15.50, pts $.75,
ea.   (S644)

Fusionen Walzer *Op.74
LUCKS 07933 set $23.50, pts $1.25,
ea.   (S645)

Goldfischlein Polka *Op.77
LUCKS 07965 set $14.00, pts $.75,
ea.   (S646)

Heimische Klange Walzer *Op.252
LUCKS 07934 set $22.50, pts $1.25,
ea.   (S647)

Hektograf Polka *Op.186
LUCKS 07571 set $13.50, pts $.75,
ea.   (S648)

Hochquelle Polka, Die *Op.114
LUCKS 07964 set $15.75, pts $.75,
ea.   (S649)

Huldigungen Walzer *Op.88
LUCKS 07935 set $31.00, pts $1.25,
ea.   (S650)

Hypothesen Walzer *Op.72
LUCKS 07936 set $25.00, pts $1.25,
ea.   (S651)

In Lieb Entbrannt Polka *Op.117
LUCKS 07957 set $14.00, pts $.75,
ea.   (S652)

Iris Polka *Op.9
LUCKS 07958 set $13.50, pts $.75,
ea.   (S653)

Kleine Chronik Polka *Op.128
LUCKS 07947 set $15.00, pts $.75,
ea.   (S654)

Knall Aund Fall Polka *Op.132
LUCKS 07948 set $15.00, pts $.75,
ea.   (S655)

Laut Und Traut Polka *Op.106
LUCKS 07576 set $15.00, pts $.75,
ea.   (S656)

Leben Ist Doch Schon Walzer, Das
*Op.150
LUCKS 07929 set $23.50, pts $1.25,
ea.   (S657)

Liebeszauber Polka *Op.84
LUCKS 07967 set $15.00, pts $.75,
ea.   (S658)

Luftig Und Duftig Polka *Op.206
LUCKS 07572 set $15.00, pts $.75,
ea.   (S659)

Lustig Im Kreise Polka *Op.93
LUCKS 07949 set $15.50, pts $.75,
ea.   (S660)

Lustige G'schichten Walzer *Op.227
LUCKS 07938 set $23.50, pts $1.25,
ea.   (S661)

Madchenlaune Polka *Op.99
LUCKS 07968 set $14.00, pts $.75,
ea.   (S662)

Marchen Aus Der Heimat Walzer
*Op.155
LUCKS 07939 set $26.00, pts $1.25,
ea.   (S663)

Marzveilchen Polka *Op.129
LUCKS 07959 set $15.00, pts $.75,
ea.   (S664)

Mit Dampf Polka *Op.70
LUCKS 07950 set $15.00, pts $.75,
ea.   (S665)

STRAUSS, EDUARD (cont'd.)

Mit Der Feder Polka *Op.69
LUCKS 07579 set $15.00, pts $.75,
ea.   (S666)

Mit Der Striemung Polka *Op.174
LUCKS 06728 set $15.50, pts $.75,
ea.   (S667)

Myrthenstrausschen Walzer *Op.87
LUCKS 07940 set $25.00, pts $1.25,
ea.   (S668)

Nach Kurzer Post Polka *Op.100
LUCKS 07960 set $12.00, pts $.75,
ea.   (S669)

Neue Welt Polka, Eine *Op.86
LUCKS 07946 set $15.00, pts $.75,
ea.   (S670)

Pilger Quadrille, Die *Op.91
LUCKS 08103 set $15.50, pts $.75,
ea.   (S671)

Saat Und Ernte Polka *Op.159
LUCKS 06729 set $14.00, pts $.75,
ea.   (S672)

Schneesternchen Polka *Op.157
LUCKS 06730 set $11.00, pts $.75,
ea.   (S673)

Schon Rohtraut Polka *Op.145
LUCKS 07578 set $15.50, pts $.75,
ea.   (S674)

Seecadet Quadrille *Op.151
LUCKS 06731 set $14.00, pts $.75,
ea.   (S675)

Soldatengruss Polka *Op.85
LUCKS 07961 set $14.00, pts $.75,
ea.   (S676)

Souvenir De Bade Polka *Op.146
LUCKS 07951 set $15.00, pts $.75,
ea.   (S677)

Stimmen Aus Dem Publikum *Op.104
LUCKS 06732 set $17.00, pts $.75,
ea.   (S678)

Studentenball-Tanze Walzer *Op.101
LUCKS 07941 set $14.00, pts $.75,
ea.   (S679)

Thauperle Polka *Op.42
LUCKS 07577 set $14.00, pts $.75,
ea.   (S680)

Theorien Walzer *Op.111
LUCKS 07942 set $15.00, pts $.75,
ea.   (S681)

Tour Un Retour Polka *Op.125
LUCKS 07962 set $13.50, pts $.75,
ea.   (S682)

Traumerin Polka, Die *Op.208
LUCKS 07575 set $13.50, pts $.75,
ea.   (S683)

Traumgebilde Walzer *Op.170
LUCKS 07943 set $23.50, pts $1.25,
ea.   (S684)

Treuliebchen Polka *Op.152
LUCKS 06734 set $13.50, pts $.75,
ea.   (S685)

Unter Der Enns Polka *Op.121
LUCKS 07952 set $13.50, pts $.75,
ea.   (S686)

Verdicte Walzer *Op.137
LUCKS 07944 set $14.00, pts $.75,
ea.   (S687)

STRAUSS, JOHANN, [SR.] (1804-1849)
Lorelei-Rheinklange *Op.154
LUCKS 08002 set $10.00, pts $.75,
ea.   (S688)

Louisen-Quadrille *Op.234
1+pic.1.2.1. 2.2.1.0. timp,perc,
strings
sc,pts LIENAU rent   (S689)

Martha-Quadrille *Op.215
1+pic.1.2.1. 2.2.1.0. timp,perc,
strings
sc,pts LIENAU rent   (S690)

Mode-Quadrille *Op.138
1+pic.1.2.1. 2.2.0.0. timp,perc,
strings
sc,pts LIENAU rent   (S691)

Musen-Quadrille *Op.174
1+pic.1.2.1. 2.2.1.0. timp,perc,
strings
sc,pts LIENAU rent   (S692)

STRAUSS, JOHANN, [SR.] (cont'd.)

Najaden-Quadrille *Op.206
   1+pic.1.2.1. 2.2.1.0. timp,
   strings
   sc,pts LIENAU rent   (S693)

Quadrille Uber Beliebte Motive Aus
   Aubers Oper "Des Teufels Anteil"
   *Op.211
   1+pic.1.2.1. 2.2.1.0. timp,perc,
   strings
   sc,pts LIENAU rent   (S694)

Radetzky Marsch *Op.228
   (Luck) LUCKS 06801 sc $8.00, set
   $16.00, pts $1.00, ea.   (S695)
   (Winter) set BOOSEY $51.00   (S696)

Schafer-Quadrille *Op.217
   1+pic.1.2.1. 2.2.1.0. timp,perc,
   strings
   sc,pts LIENAU rent   (S697)

STRAUSS, JOHANN, [JR.] (1825-1899)
Adepten Walzer, Die *Op.216
   LUCKS 07983 set $12.50, pts $1.25,
   ea.   (S698)

Afrikanerin Quadrille, Die *Op.299
   LUCKS 08065 set $15.00, pts $.75,
   ea.   (S699)
   (Racek, F.) 1+pic.2.2.2. 4.2.3.1.
   timp,perc,strings sc,pts
   DOBLINGER DM 689 f.s.   (S700)

Alexandrine Polka *Op.198
   LUCKS 08021 set $20.00, pts $1.00,
   ea.   (S701)

Almacks Quadrille *Op.243
   LUCKS 08057 set $11.00, pts $.75,
   ea.   (S702)

An Der Moldau Polka *Op.366
   LUCKS 07593 set $13.50, pts $.75,
   ea.   (S703)

An Der Schonen Blauen Donau *Op.314
   "On The Beautiful Blue Danube"
   2.2.2.2. 4.2.1.1. timp,perc,harp,
   strings pts BROUDE BR. $1.25, ea.
                                   (S704)
   (Racek, F.) 2(pic).2.2.2. 4.2.1.1.
   timp,perc,harp,strings sc,pts
   DOBLINGER DM 845 f.s.   (S705)

An Der Schonen Blauen Donau, [arr.]
   *Op.314
   (Zinn, William) "Blue Danube Waltz,
   [arr.]" string orch EXCELSIOR
   $8.00   (S706)

An Der Wolga Polka *Op.425
   LUCKS 06736 set $12.50, pts $.75,
   ea.   (S707)

Annen-Polka *Op.117
   2.2.2.2. 4.2.3.0. perc,strings
      KRENN f.s.   (S708)
   set LUCKS 08391 $30.00   (S709)
   LIENAU f.s.   (S710)

Armen Ball Polka *Op.167
   LUCKS 08023 set $11.00, pts $.75,
   ea.   (S711)

Artist's Life *see Kunstlerleben
   Walzer

Auf Der Jagd *Op.373
   LUCKS 06739 set $12.00, pts $.70,
   ea.   (S712)

Auf Zum Tanze *Op.436
   LUCKS 07591 set $14.25, pts $.75,
   ea.   (S713)

Aus Den Bergen Walzer *Op.292
   LUCKS 07971 set $13.50, pts $.75,
   ea.   (S714)
   (Racek, F.) 1+pic.2.2.2. 4.2.1.1.
   timp,perc,strings sc,pts
   DOBLINGER DM 800 f.s.   (S715)

Austria Marsch *Op.20
   2.2.2.2. 4.2.1.1. perc,strings
      KRENN f.s.   (S716)

Autograph Walzer
   LUCKS 06738 set $13.50, pts $.75,
   ea.   (S717)

Bal Champetre Quadrille *Op.303
   LUCKS 08059 set $13.50, pts $.75,
   ea.   (S718)

Ball Geschichten Walzer *Op.150
   LUCKS 07972 set $21.00, pts $1.25,
   ea.   (S719)

Ballstrausschen Polka *Op.380
   LUCKS 07592 set $14.00, pts $.75,
   ea.   (S720)

STRAUSS, JOHANN, [JR.] (cont'd.)

Banditen Galopp Polka *Op.378
   2.2.2.2. 4.2.3.0. perc,timp,strings
      KRENN f.s.   (S721)
   LUCKS 08049 set $16.00, pts $.75,
   ea.   (S722)

Bat, The: Laughing Song *see
   Fledermaus, Die: Mein Herr
   Marquis, For Solo Voice And
   Orchestra

Bat, The: Overture *see Fledermaus,
   Die: Overture

Bauern Polka *Op.276
   LUCKS 08024 set $16.00, set $.75,
   ea.   (S723)
   LIENAU f.s.   (S724)

Beau Monde Quadrille, Le *Op.199
   LUCKS 08080 set $14.00, pts $.75,
   ea.   (S725)

Bei Uns Z'Haus *Op.391
   LUCKS 07973 set $25.00, pts $1.25,
   ea.   (S726)

Berceuse, La *Op.194
   LUCKS 08078 set $13.50, pts $.75,
   ea.   (S727)

Bijouterie Quadrille *Op.169
   LUCKS 08061 set $11.00, pts $.70,
   ea.   (S728)

Bijoux Polka *Op.242
   LUCKS 08025 set $16.00, pts $.75,
   ea.   (S729)

Bitte Schon Polka *Op.372
   LUCKS 06726 set $14.00, pts $.75,
   ea.   (S730)

Blue Danube Waltz, [arr.] *see An
   Der Schonen Blauen Donau, [arr.]

Bluette Polka *Op.271
   LUCKS 08027 set $12.50, pts $.75,
   ea.   (S731)

Bouquet Quadrille *Op.135
   LUCKS 08060 set $11.50, pts $.75,
   ea.   (S732)

Brautshau Polka *Op.417
   LUCKS 06741 set $14.00, pts $.75,
   ea.   (S733)

Burgersinn Walzer *Op.295
   LUCKS 07974 set $21.00, pts $1.25,
   ea.   (S734)

Burschenwanderung Polka *Op.389
   LUCKS 07595 set $13.50, pts $.75,
   ea.   (S735)

Cagliostro In Wien: Overture
   LUCKS 11911 sc $15.00, set $12.00,
   pts $1.50, ea.   (S736)

Cagliostro Quadrille *Op.369
   LUCKS 06742 set $13.50, pts $.75,
   ea.   (S737)

Camelien Polka *Op.248
   LUCKS 08028 set $12.50, pts $.75,
   ea.   (S738)

Carnivalsbilder *Op.357
   LUCKS 07975 set $10.00, pts $1.00,
   ea.   (S739)

Centennial Waltz
   LUCKS 07977 set $14.00, pts $.75,
   ea.   (S740)

Champagner-Polka *Op.211
   LUCKS 08030 sc $8.00, set $11.50,
   pts $.75, ea.   (S741)

Charivari Quadrille *Op.196
   LUCKS 08064 set $12.50, pts $.75,
   ea.   (S742)

Colonnen Walzer *Op.262
   LUCKS 07978 set $20.00, pts $1.25,
   ea.   (S743)

Concurrenzen Walzer *Op.267
   LUCKS 07979 set $21.00, pts $1.25,
   ea.   (S744)

Cycloiden Walzer *Op.207
   LUCKS 07981 set $22.50, pts $1.25,
   ea.   (S745)

Cytheren Quadrille *Op.6
   LUCKS 08056 set $11.00, pts $.75,
   ea.   (S746)

Damen Souvenir Polka *Op.236
   LUCKS 08031 set $16.00, pts $.75,
   ea.   (S747)

STRAUSS, JOHANN, [JR.] (cont'd.)

Damenspende *Op.305
   (Racek, F.) 1+pic.2.2.2. 4.2.1.0.
   timp,perc,strings sc,pts
   DOBLINGER DM 801 f.s.   (S748)

Demi Fortune Polka *Op.186
   LUCKS 08029 set $12.50, pts $.75,
   ea.   (S749)

Demolirer Polka *Op.269
   LUCKS 08032 set $15.00, pts $.75,
   ea.   (S750)

Diabolin Polka *Op.244
   LUCKS 08033 set $15.50, pts $.75,
   ea.   (S751)

Dinorah Quadrille *Op.224
   LUCKS 08067 set $12.00, pts $.75,
   ea.   (S752)

Donauweibchen Waltzer *Op.427
   KALMUS 4514 set $16.00, pts $1.00,
   ea., cmplt ed rent   (S753)

Egyptian March *see Egyptischer
   Marsch

Egyptischer Marsch *Op.335
   "Egyptian March" LUCKS 06744 sc
   $7.50, set $11.50 pts $.75, ea. (S754)
   (Racek, F.) 1+pic.2.2.2. 4.2.3.0.
   perc,strings sc,pts DOBLINGER
   DM 1004 f.s.   (S755)

Ein Herz Ein Sinn *Op.323
   "One Heart One Mind" LUCKS 07580
   set $20.00, pts $.75, ea.   (S756)

Elektrophor-Polka *Op.297
   (Racek, F.) 1+pic.2.2.2. 4.2.1.1.
   timp,perc,strings sc,pts
   DOBLINGER DM 790 f.s.   (S757)

Elfen Polka *Op.74
   LUCKS 06122 sc $4.00, set $11.00,
   pts $.75, ea.   (S758)

Elisen Polka *Op.151
   LUCKS 08034 set $13.50, pts $.75,
   ea.   (S759)

Eljen A Magyar Polka *Op.332
   KALMUS 5203 sc $2.00, perf mat
   rent, set $12.00, pts $.60, ea. (S760)
   2.2.2.2. 4.2.3.1. perc,strings
      KRENN f.s.   (S761)

Emperor Waltz *see Kaiser-Walzer

Emperor Waltz, The, [arr.] *see
   Kaiser-Walzer, [arr.]

Entweder Oder Polka *Op.403
   LUCKS 06746 set $14.00, pts $.75,
   ea.   (S762)

Episode Polka *Op.296
   (Racek, F.) 1+pic.2.2.2. 4.2.1.1.
   timp,perc,strings sc,pts
   DOBLINGER DM 893 f.s.   (S763)

Erinnerung An Covent Garden Walzer
   *Op.329
   LUCKS 07989 set $23.50, pts $1.25,
   ea.   (S764)
   (Racek, F.) 1+pic.2.2.2. 4.2.3.1.
   timp,perc,strings sc,pts
   DOBLINGER DM 686 f.s.   (S765)

Ersten Curen Walzer, Die *Op.261
   LUCKS 07984 set $22.50, pts $1.25,
   ea.   (S766)

Express Polka *Op.311
   (Racek, F.) 1+pic.2.2.2. 4.2.1.1.
   timp,perc,strings sc,pts
   DOBLINGER DM 690 f.s.   (S767)

Extravaganten Walzer, Die *Op.205
   LUCKS 06747 set $27.00, pts $1.25
                                   (S768)

Fata Morgana *Op.330
   LUCKS 08054 set $17.00, pts $.75,
   ea.   (S769)
   (Racek, F.) 1+pic.2.2.2. 4.3.3.0.
   timp,perc,harp,strings [3'] sc
   DOBLINGER JSGA 21-1 f.s., pts
   DOBLINGER DM 1002 f.s.   (S770)

Feenmarchen Walzer *Op.312
   LUCKS 07988 set $22.50, pts $1.25,
   ea.   (S771)
   (Racek, F.) 2(pic).2.2.2. 4.2.1.0.
   timp,perc,harp,strings sc,pts
   DOBLINGER DM 895 f.s.   (S772)

Ferdinand Quadrille *Op.151
   LUCKS 08068 set $12.50, pts $.75,
   ea.   (S773)

STRAUSS, JOHANN, [JR.] (cont'd.)

Fest Quadrille *Op.165
    LUCKS 08069 set $12.50, pts $.75,
    ea.   (S774)

Fledermaus, Die: Czardas, For Solo
    Voice And Orchestra
    LUCKS 02319 sc $3.75, set $7.50,
    pts $.75, ea.   (S775)

Fledermaus, Die: Du Und Du
    LUCKS 06748 sc $5.50, set $11.50,
    pts $.75, ea.   (S776)

Fledermaus, Die: Ich Lade Gern Mir
    Gaste Ein, For Solo Voice And
    Orchestra
    LUCKS 03661 sc $3.00, set $7.00,
    pts $.75, ea.   (S777)

Fledermaus, Die: Mein Herr Marquis,
    For Solo Voice And Orchestra
    "Bat, The: Laughing Song" LUCKS
    02405 sc $3.75, set $7.50, pts
    $.75, ea.   (S778)

Fledermaus, Die: Overture
    "Bat, The: Overture" 2(pic).2.2.2.
    4.2.3.0. timp,perc,strings BROUDE
    BR. set $17.50, pts $1.00, ea.
                                     (S779)
    "Bat, The: Overture" min sc
    INTERNAT. 1036 $3.50   (S780)

Fledermaus, Die: Polka Francaise
    LUCKS 08035 sc $4.75, set $16.00,
    pts $.75, ea.   (S781)

Fledermaus, Die: Selection
    LUCKS 06750 set $21.00, pts $1.25,
    ea.   (S782)

Fledermaus, Die: Tick-Tack Polka
    *see Tik-Tak Polka

Fledermaus, Die: Watch Duet, Act 2,
    For Solo Voices And Orchestra
    LUCKS 03665 set $7.00, set $14.50,
    pts $.75, ea.   (S783)

Flugschriften Walzer *Op.300
    LUCKS 07992 set $12.00, pts $.75,
    ea.   (S784)
    (Racek, F.) 1+pic.2.2.2. 4.2.1.0.
    timp,perc,harp,strings sc,pts
    DOBLINGER DM 896 f.s.   (S785)

Frauen Kaferin *Op.99
    LUCKS 07993 set $20.00, pts $1.25,
    ea.   (S786)

Frederika Polka *Op.239
    LUCKS 08036 set $12.00, pts $.75,
    ea.   (S787)

Freikugeln Polka *Op.326
    (Racek, F.) 1+pic.2.2.2. 4.3.3.1.
    timp,perc,strings sc,pts
    DOBLINGER DM 685 f.s.   (S788)

Freiwillige Vor! Marsch
    LUCKS 07589 set $14.00, pts $.75,
    ea.   (S789)

Freuet Euch Des Lebens Walzer
    *Op.340
    LUCKS 06752 set $29.50, pts $1.25,
    ea.   (S790)

Frisch Heran Polka *Op.386
    LUCKS 06753 set $13.50, pts $.75,
    ea.   (S791)

Fruhlingsstimmen Walzer *Op.410
    2.2.2.2. 4.2.3.0. perc,harp,strings
    KRENN f.s.   (S792)
    "Voices Of Spring" LUCKS 06788 sc
    $6.50, set $15.00, pts $.95, ea.
                                     (S793)

Furioso Polka *Op.260
    LUCKS 08050 sc $5.50, set $11.50,
    pts $.75   (S794)

Furst Bariatinsky Marsch *Op.212
    LUCKS 08098 set $12.50, pts $.75,
    ea.   (S795)

Furstin Ninetta; Neue Pizzicato Polka
    *Op.449
    LUCKS 09051 sc $1.50, set $4.75,
    pts $.75, ea.   (S796)

Geschichten Aus Dem Wienerwald Walzer
    *Op.325
    "Tales From The Vienna Woods" LUCKS
    06782 sc $8.00, set $18.00, min
    sc $3.00, pts $.95, ea.   (S797)

Geschichten Aus Dem Wienerwald
    Walzer, For Solo Voice And
    Orchestra
    "Tales From The Vienna Woods, For
    Solo Voice And Orchestra" LUCKS
    02919 sc $12.00, set $25.00, pts
    $1.25, ea.   (S798)

STRAUSS, JOHANN, [JR.] (cont'd.)

Glucklich Ist, Wer Vergisst *Op.368
    LUCKS 06785 set $14.00, pts $.75,
    ea.   (S799)

Gross Wien Walzer *Op.440
    LUCKS 08370 set $25.00, pts $1.25,
    ea.   (S800)

Gypsy Baron, The: Overture *see
    Zigeunerbaron, Der: Overture

Gypsy Baron, The: Selection *see
    Zigeunerbaron, Der: Selection

Gypsy Baron, The: Treasure Waltz
    *see Zigeunerbaron, Der: Schatz
    Walzer

Haimanskinder Quadrille *Op.169
    LUCKS 08071 set $12.50, pts $.75,
    ea.   (S801)

Handels Elite Quadrille *Op.166
    LUCKS 08072 set $12.00, pts $.75,
    ea.   (S802)

Haute Volee Polka *Op.155
    LUCKS 08038 set $12.50, pts $.75,
    ea.   (S803)

Heiligenstadter Rendezvous Polka, For
    Solo Voice And Orchestra
    KRENN perf mat rent   (S804)

Herzel Polka *Op.188
    LUCKS 08039 set $14.00, pts $.75,
    ea.   (S805)

Hesperus Polka *Op.249
    LUCKS 08040 set $12.00, pts $.75,
    ea.   (S806)

Hinter Den Coulissen Quadrille
    LUCKS 08073 set $14.00, pts $.75,
    ea.   (S807)

Hoch Osterreich Marsch *Op.371
    LUCKS 06759 set $14.00, pts $.75,
    ea.   (S808)

Hofball Quadrille *Op.116
    LUCKS 08074 set $12.00, pts $.75,
    ea.   (S809)

Hofballtanze *Op.298
    LUCKS 07994 set $23.50, pts $1.25,
    ea.   (S810)
    (Racek, F.) 1+pic.2.2.2. 4.2.1.1.
    timp,perc,harp,strings sc,pts
    DOBLINGER DM 897 f.s.   (S811)

I' Tipferl Polka *Op.377
    LUCKS 06755 set $15.00, pts $.75,
    ea.   (S812)

Idyllen Walzer *Op.95
    LUCKS 06758 sc $21.00, pts $1.25,
    ea.   (S813)

Illustrationen Walzer *Op.331
    LUCKS 06757 set $29.50, pts $1.25,
    ea.   (S814)
    (Racek, F.) 1+pic.2.2.2. 4.2.3.0.
    timp,perc,strings sc DOBLINGER
    JSGA 21-2 f.s., pts DOBLINGER
    DM 1001 f.s.   (S815)

Im Russischen Dorfe *Op.355
    "In A Russian Village" LUCKS 11918
    sc $15.00, set $12.00, pts $1.50,
    ea.   (S816)

Immer Heiterer Walzer *Op.235
    LUCKS 07995 set $12.00, pts $.75,
    ea.   (S817)

In A Russian Village *see Im
    Russischen Dorfe

Inconnue, L'. Polka *Op.182
    LUCKS 08037 set $15.00, pts $.75,
    ea.   (S818)

Indigo Marsch *Op.349
    LUCKS 06756 set $13.50, pts $.75,
    ea.   (S819)

Indigo Quadrille *Op.344
    LUCKS 08075 set $15.00, pts $.75,
    ea.   (S820)

Ja, So Singt Und Tanzt Man Nur In
    Wien, For Solo Voice And
    Orchestra
    KRENN perf mat rent   (S821)

Johannis Kaferln Walzer *Op.82
    LUCKS 07581 set $28.00, pts $.75,
    ea.   (S822)

Juxbruder Walzer *Op.208
    LUCKS 07997 set $21.00, pts $1.25,
    ea.   (S823)

STRAUSS, JOHANN, [JR.] (cont'd.)

Kaiser-Walzer *Op.437
    "Emperor Waltz" LUCKS 06745 sc
    $4.00, set $12.00, min sc $3.00,
    pts $.75, ea.   (S824)

Kaiser-Walzer, [arr.] *Op.437
    (Zinn, William) "Emperor Waltz,
    The, [arr.]" string orch
    EXCELSIOR $8.00   (S825)

Kaiser Wilhelm Polonaise *Op.352
    LUCKS 07586 set $22.50, pts $1.25,
    ea.   (S826)

Kennst Du Mich? Walzer *Op.381
    LUCKS 07582 set $26.00, pts $1.25,
    ea.   (S827)

Kinderspiele Polka *Op.304
    LUCKS 08041 set $28.00, pts $.75,
    ea.   (S828)

Klugere Giebt Nach, Der. Polka
    *Op.401
    LUCKS 06761 set $18.00, pts $.75,
    ea.   (S829)

Konigslieder Walzer *Op.334
    LUCKS 06797 set $23.50, pts $1.25
                                     (S830)

Kreuzfidel Polka *Op.301
    (Racek, F.) 1+pic.2.2.2. 4.2.1.0.
    timp,perc,strings sc,pts
    DOBLINGER DM 894 f.s.   (S831)

Kriegers Liebchen Polka *Op.379
    LUCKS 08055 set $12.50, pts $.75,
    ea.   (S832)

Kronungsmarsch *Op.183
    LUCKS 08099 set $15.50, pts $.75,
    ea.   (S833)

Kunstler Quadrille *Op.201
    LUCKS 08077 set $18.00, pts $1.00,
    ea.   (S834)

Kunstlerleben Walzer *Op.316
    "Artist's Life" LUCKS 06737 sc
    $7.00, set $18.00, min sc $2.00,
    pts $1.15, ea.   (S835)
    (Racek, F.) 1+pic.2.2.2. 4.2.1.0.
    timp,perc,strings sc,pts
    DOBLINGER DM 687 f.s.   (S836)

Kuss Walzer *Op.400
    LUCKS 09032 set $14.00, pts $.95,
    ea.   (S837)

Lagunen Walzer *Op.411
    3(pic).2.2.2. 4.2.3.1. timp,perc,
    harp,strings [7'] KALMUS A3247
    set $20.00, perf mat rent, pts
    $1.00, ea.   (S838)

Landes Farben *Op.232
    LUCKS 07998 set $12.50, pts $.75,
    ea.   (S839)

Lebenswecker Walzer *Op.232
    LUCKS 07999 set $15.00, pts $1.25,
    ea.   (S840)

Leichtes Blut *Op.319
    (Racek, F.) 1+pic.2.2.2. 4.2.1.0.
    timp,perc,strings sc,pts
    DOBLINGER DM 683 f.s.   (S841)

Leitartickel, Die. Walzer *Op.273
    LUCKS 07584 set $22.50, pts $1.25,
    ea.   (S842)

Leopoldstadter Polka *Op.168
    LUCKS 07261 set $14.00, pts $.75,
    ea.   (S843)

Libellen Walzer *Op.180
    LUCKS 08000 set $13.50, pts $1.25,
    ea.   (S844)

Liebeslieder Walzer *Op.114
    LUCKS 08001 sc $2.00, set $10.00,
    pts $.75, ea.   (S845)

Lieder Quadrille *Op.275
    LUCKS 08081 set $16.50, pts $.75,
    ea.   (S846)

Lob Der Frauen *Op.315
    (Racek) 1+pic.2.2.2. 4.2.1.1. timp,
    perc,strings sc DOBLINGER $13.50
                                     (S847)

Lockvogel *Op.118
    LUCKS 06763 set $18.50, pts $1.25,
    ea.   (S848)

Lucifer Polka *Op.265
    LUCKS 08042 set $14.00, pts $.75,
    ea.   (S849)

Lust'ger Rath. Polka *Op.350
    LUCKS 06765 set $18.00, pts $.75,
    ea.   (S850)

STRAUSS, JOHANN, [JR.] (cont'd.)

Lustige Krieg, Der. Quadrille
   *Op.402
   LUCKS 06766 set $18.00, pts $.75,
   ea.   (S851)

Man Lebt Nur Einmal. Walzer *Op.167
   LUCKS 08003 set $20.00, pts $1.25,
   ea.   (S852)

Marchen Aus Dem Orient. Walzer
   *Op.444
   LUCKS 08303 set $22.50, pts $1.25,
   ea.   (S853)

Maskenzug. Polka *Op.240
   LUCKS 08044 set $14.00, pts $.75,
   ea.   (S854)

Maxing Tanze. Walzer *Op.79
   LUCKS 08004 set $16.50, pts $.75,
   ea.   (S855)

Melodien Quadrille, Op. 112 (from
   Motives Of Verdi)
   LUCKS 08082 set $15.50, pts $.75,
   ea.   (S856)

Melodien Quadrille, Op. 254
   LUCKS 08083 set $15.50, pts $.75,
   ea.   (S857)

Morgenblatter Walzer *Op.279
   2.2.2.2. 4.2.3.1. perc,harp,strings
   [10'] KALMUS 5392 sc $15.00, perf
   mat rent, set $17.00, pts $1.00,
   ea., pno-cond sc $3.00   (S858)
   "Morning Journals" LUCKS 06767 set
   $25.00, pts $1.25, ea.   (S859)

Morning Journals *see Morgenblatter
   Walzer

Musen Quadrille *Op.174
   LUCKS 08085 set $16.00, pts $1.25,
   ea.   (S860)

Myrthenbluthen Walzer *Op.395
   LUCKS 06769 sc $4.50, set $20.50,
   pts $.75, ea.   (S861)

Nacht In Venedig, Eine: Lagunen-
   Walzer
   LUCKS 07204 set $21.00, pts $1.25,
   ea.   (S862)

Nacht In Venedig, Eine: Overture
   2.2.2.2. 4.2.3.0. perc,harp,strings
   KRENN f.s.   (S863)
   "Night In Venice: Overture" LUCKS
   08900 pno-cond sc $1.25, set
   $20.00, pts $1.25, ea.   (S864)

Nacht In Venedig, Eine: Selection
   "Night In Venice: Selection " LUCKS
   06793 set $21.00, pts $1.25, ea.
                                (S865)

Nachtfalter Walzer *Op.157
   LUCKS 08007 set $17.50, pts $1.25,
   ea.   (S866)

Najaden Quadrille *Op.206
   LUCKS 08086 set $12.50, pts $.75,
   ea.   (S867)

Neues Leben. Polka *Op.278
   LUCKS 08045 set $16.50, pts $.75,
   ea.   (S868)

Night In Venice: Overture *see Nacht
   In Venedig, Eine: Overture

Night In Venice: Selection *see
   Nacht In Venedig, Eine: Selection

Nord Und Sud. Polka *Op.405
   LUCKS 06770 set $13.50, pts $.75,
   ea.   (S869)

Nordseebilder Walzer *Op.390
   LUCKS 08008 set $20.00, pts $1.25,
   ea.   (S870)

Odeon Tanze. Walzer *Op.172
   LUCKS 08009 set $13.50, pts $.75,
   ea.   (S871)

On The Beautiful Blue Danube *see An
   Der Schonen Blauen Donau

One Heart One Mind *see Ein Herz Ein
   Sinn

Orpheus Quadrille *Op.162
   LUCKS 08088 set $17.00, pts $1.00,
   ea.   (S872)

Panacea Klange. Walzer *Op.61
   LUCKS 08010 set $21.00, pts $1.25,
   ea.   (S873)

Pappacoda. Polka *Op.412
   LUCKS 07594 set $14.00, pts $.75,
   ea.   (S874)

STRAUSS, JOHANN, [JR.] (cont'd.)

Par Force Polka *Op.308
   (Racek, F.) 1+pic.2.2.2. 4.2.1.1.
   timp,perc,strings sc,pts
   DOBLINGER DM 682 f.s.   (S875)

Perpetuum Mobile *Op.257
   2(pic).2.2.2. 4.2.3.0. timp,perc,
   strings sc,pts LIENAU rent (S876)
   LUCKS 06771 sc $7.50, set $14.00,
   pts $.95, ea.   (S877)

Persian March *see Persischer Marsch

Persischer Marsch *Op.289
   "Persian March" LUCKS 05372 set
   $16.00, pts $.95, ea.   (S878)

Pester Csardas, For Solo Voice And
   Orchestra
   KRENN perf mat rent   (S879)

Phanomene Walzer *Op.193
   LUCKS 08011 set $21.00, pts $1.25,
   ea.   (S880)

Pizzicato-Polka (composed with
   Strauss, Josef)
   LUCKS 06780 sc $4.50, set $9.00,
   pts $.95, ea.   (S881)

Pleasure Train *see Vergnugungszug

Prince Methusalem: O Lovely May *see
   Prinz Methusalem: O Schoner Mai

Prince Methusalem: Overture *see
   Prinz Methusalem: Overture

Prince Methusalem: Selections *see
   Prinz Methusalem: Selections

Princesse De Trebizonde, La.
   Quadrille
   LUCKS 08079 set $28.00, pts $.75,
   ea.   (S882)

Prinz Methusalem: O Schoner Mai
   *Op.375
   "Prince Methusalem: O Lovely May"
   LUCKS 06764 set $13.50, pts $.75,
   ea.   (S883)

Prinz Methusalem: Overture
   "Prince Methusalem: Overture" LUCKS
   06772 sc $2.50, set $22.50, pts
   $1.00, ea.   (S884)

Prinz Methusalem: Selections
   "Prince Methusalem: Selections "
   LUCKS 07459 set $15.00, pts
   $1.25, ea.   (S885)

Promenade Quadrille *Op.98
   LUCKS 08039 set $11.00, pts $.75,
   ea.   (S886)

Promotionen Walzer *Op.221
   LUCKS 06777 set $22.00, pts $1.25,
   ea.   (S887)

Prozess-Polka *Op.294
   (Racek, F.) 1+pic.2.2.2. 4.2.1.1.
   timp,glock,perc,strings sc,pts
   DOBLINGER DM 694 f.s.   (S888)

Publicisten, Die. Walzer *Op.321
   LUCKS 07985 set $25.00, pts $.75,
   ea.   (S889)

Quadrille Sur Des Airs Francaise
   *Op.290
   LUCKS 08093 set $14.00, pts $.75,
   ea.   (S890)

Queen's Lace Handkerchief, The:
   Overture *see Spitzentuch Der
   Konigin, Das: Overture

Rathausball Tanze. Walzer *Op.438
   LUCKS 08371 set $23.50, pts $1.25,
   ea.   (S891)

Ritter Pasman: Polka
   LUCKS 05093 sc $5.00, set $15.00,
   pts $1.00, ea.   (S892)

Ritter Pasman: Walzer
   LUCKS 08302 set $25.00, pts $1.25,
   ea.   (S893)

Romance for Violoncello and
   Orchestra, Op. 255, in G minor,
   [arr.]
   1.1.2.0. 2.0.0.0. timp,harp,
   strings,vcl solo KRENN f.s. (S894)

Rosen Ohne Dorne. Walzer *Op.166
   LUCKS 06774 set $18.50, pts $1.25,
   ea.   (S895)

Russischer Marsch Fantasie *Op.353
   LUCKS 08096 set $15.50, pts $.75,
   ea.   (S896)

STRAUSS, JOHANN, [JR.] (cont'd.)

Saison Quadrille *Op.148
   LUCKS 08090 set $12.50, pts $.75,
   ea.   (S897)

Sangerslust Polka *Op.328
   (Racek, F.) 1+pic.2.2.2. 4.3.3.1.
   timp,perc,strings sc,pts
   DOBLINGER DM 789 f.s.   (S898)

Satanella Polka *Op.124
   LUCKS 08046 set $10.50, pts $.75,
   ea.   (S899)

Secunden Polka *Op.258
   LUCKS 08047 set $16.50, pts $.75,
   ea.   (S900)

Seid Umschlungen Millionen Walzer
   *Op.443
   LUCKS 06798 sc $7.50, set $14.00,
   pts $1.00, ea.   (S901)

Slovanka Quadrille *Op.338
   LUCKS 08091 set $15.50, pts $.75,
   ea.   (S902)

Sorgenbrecher Walzer *Op.230
   LUCKS 06776 set $25.00, pts $1.25,
   ea.   (S903)

Spiralen Walzer *Op.209
   LUCKS 08013 set $21.50, pts $1.25,
   ea.   (S904)

Spitzentuch Der Konigin, Das:
   Overture
   "Queen's Lace Handkerchief, The:
   Overture" LUCKS 06778 set $15.00,
   pts $1.40, ea.   (S905)

Spring In My Heart, For Solo Voice
   And Orchestra
   LUCKS 02893 set $24.00, pts $.75,
   ea.   (S906)

Springtime In The Air, For Solo Voice
   And Orchestra
   LUCKS 02890 set $16.00, pts $.75,
   ea.   (S907)

Stadt Und Land. Polka *Op.322
   LUCKS 07590 set $15.00, pts $.75,
   ea.   (S908)

Stimmen Aus Dem Publicum. Walzer
   *Op.104
   LUCKS 06732 set $17.50, pts $.75,
   ea.   (S909)

Sturmisch In Lieb Und Tanz *Op.393
   LUCKS 06799 set $14.00, pts $.75,
   ea.   (S910)

Sylphen-Polka *Op.309
   (Racek, F.) 1+pic.2.2.2. 4.2.1.1.
   timp,perc,strings sc,pts
   DOBLINGER DM 695 f.s.   (S911)

Sympathie Polka *Op.246
   LUCKS 08048 set $12.00, pts $.75,
   ea.   (S912)

Tales From The Vienna Woods *see
   Geschichten Aus Dem Wienerwald
   Walzer

Tales From The Vienna Woods, For Solo
   Voice And Orchestra *see
   Geschichten Aus Dem Wienerwald
   Walzer, For Solo Voice And
   Orchestra

Tausend Und Eine Nacht Walzer
   *Op.346
   "Thousand And One Nights Waltz"
   LUCKS 06784 set $15.00, pts
   $1.15, ea.   (S913)

Telegrafische Depeschen. Walzer
   *Op.195
   LUCKS 08014 set $23.50, pts $1.25,
   ea.   (S914)

Telegramme Walzer *Op.318
   LUCKS 08015 set $23.50, pts $1.25,
   ea.   (S915)
   (Racek, F.) 2(pic).2.2.2. 4.2.1.1.
   timp,perc,strings sc,pts
   DOBLINGER DM 688 f.s.   (S916)

Thousand And One Nights Waltz *see
   Tausend Und Eine Nacht Walzer

Thunder And Lightning *see Unter
   Donner Und Blitz

Tik-Tak Polka *Op.365
   "Fledermaus, Die: Tick-Tack Polka"
   LUCKS 07945 sc $5.50, set $13.00,
   pts $.95, ea.   (S917)

Trau-Schau-Wem
   KALMUS 5448 cmplt ed rent, set
   $18.00, pts $1.00, ea.   (S918)

STRAUSS, JOHANN, [JR.] (cont'd.)

Tritsch-Tratsch Polka *Op.214
2.2.2.2. 4.2.3.0. perc,strings
KRENN f.s.   (S919)
LIENAU f.s.   (S920)
LUCKS 07770 set $10.00, pts $.75,
ea.   (S921)

Unter Donner Und Blitz *Op.324
"Thunder And Lightning" LUCKS 06787
sc $6.00, set $14.00, pts $.75,
ea.   (S922)
(Racek, F.) 1+pic.2.2.2. 4.3.3.1.
perc,strings sc,pts DOBLINGER
DM 684 f.s.   (S923)

Vaterlandischer Marsch (composed with
Strauss, Josef)
LUCKS 08102 set $12.50, pts $.75,
ea.   (S924)

Vergessenes Lied, For Solo Voice And
Orchestra
KRENN perf mat rent   (S925)

Vergnugungszug *Op.281
"Pleasure Train" LUCKS 07588 set
$9.50, pts $.75, ea.   (S926)

Vibrationen Walzer *Op.204
LUCKS 06786 set $23.50, pts $1.25,
ea.   (S927)

Vienna Life *see Wiener Blut Walzer

Voices Of Spring *see
Fruhlingsstimmen Walzer

Von Der Borse *Op.337
(Racek, F.) 1+pic.2.2.2. 4.2.3.0.
timp,perc,harp,strings [3'] sc
DOBLINGER JSGA 21-8 f.s., pts
DOBLINGER DM 1003 f.s.   (S928)

Wahlstimmen Walzer *Op.250
LUCKS 08016 set $15.50, pts $.75,
ea.   (S929)

Was Sich Liebt Neckt Sich *Op.399
LUCKS 06791 set $14.00, pts $.75,
ea.   (S930)

Wein, Weib, Und Gesang *Op.333,
Waltz
"Wine, Women, And Song" LUCKS 06800
sc $7.00, set $22.00, min sc
$3.00, pts $1.15, ea.   (S931)

Where The Citrons Bloom *see Wo Die
Zitronen Bluhn

Wien, Mein Sinn. Walzer *Op.192
LUCKS 08018 set $21.00, pts $1.25,
ea.   (S932)

Wiener Blut Walzer *Op.354
"Vienna Life" LUCKS 06794 sc $7.00,
set $17.00, min sc $3.00, pts
$.95, ea.   (S933)

Wiener Bonbons Walzer *Op.307
LUCKS 06799 set $23.50, pts $1.25,
ea.   (S934)
(Racek, F.) 1+pic.2.2.2. 4.2.1.1.
timp,perc,strings sc,pts
DOBLINGER DM 692 f.s.   (S935)

Wiener Carnevals Quadrille *Op.124
LUCKS 08100 set $12.50, pts $.75,
ea.   (S936)

Wiener Chronik Walzer *Op.268
LUCKS 08017 set $17.50, pts $1.25,
ea.   (S937)

Wienerblut Muss Was Eigenes Sein, For
Solo Voice And Orchestra
KRENN perf mat rent   (S938)

Wienerwald Lerchen, For Solo Voice
And Orchestra
KRENN perf mat rent   (S939)

Wildfeuer *Op.313
(Racek, F.) 1+pic.2.2.2. 4.2.1.0.
timp,perc,strings sc,pts
DOBLINGER DM 693 f.s.   (S940)

Windsor Klange. Walzer *Op.104
LUCKS 08020 set $17.50, pts $1.25,
ea.   (S941)

Wine, Women, And Song *see Wein,
Weib, Und Gesang

Wo Die Zitronen Bluhn *Op.364
"Where The Citrons Bloom" LUCKS
06792 set $14.00, pts $.75, ea.
                                 (S942)

Wo Die Zitronen Bluhn, For Solo Voice
And Orchestra
2.2.2.2. 4.2.2.0. perc,harp,
strings,S solo KRENN perf mat
rent   (S943)

STRAUSS, JOHANN, [JR.] (cont'd.)

Zigeunerbaron, Der: Overture
"Gypsy Baron, The: Overture" LUCKS
06795 sc $10.00, set $14.00, min
sc $2.00, pts $1.15, ea.   (S944)

Zigeunerbaron, Der: Schatz Walzer
"Gypsy Baron, The: Treasure Waltz"
LUCKS 06796 sc $8.50, set $14.00,
pts $1.50, ea.   (S945)

Zigeunerbaron, Der: Selection
"Gypsy Baron, The: Selection" LUCKS
06760 set $21.00, pts $1.25, ea.
                                 (S946)

STRAUSS, JOSEF (1827-1870)
Abendstern *Op.160
LUCKS 07596 set $10.00, pts $.75,
ea.   (S947)

Actionen Walzer *Op.174
LUCKS 08104 set $13.50, pts $.75,
ea.   (S948)

Auf Ferienreisen *Op.133
LUCKS 08029 set $7.50, pts $.75,
ea.   (S949)

Blaubart Quadrille *Op.206
LUCKS 08134 set $13.50, pts $.75,
ea.   (S950)

Brennende Liebe *Op.129
2.2.2.2. 4.2.3.0. perc,harp,strings
KRENN f.s.   (S951)
LUCKS 08052 set $13.50, pts $.75,
ea.   (S952)
1+pic.2.2.2. 4.2.1.0. harp,timp,
perc,strings LIENAU f.s.   (S953)

Consortien Walzer *Op.260
LUCKS 08105 set $22.50, pts $1.25,
ea.   (S954)

Crispino Quadrille *Op.224
LUCKS 08135 set $16.50, pts $.75,
ea.   (S955)

Debaradeurs Quadrille *Op.97
LUCKS 08106 set $12.50, pts $.75,
ea.   (S956)

Disputationen Walzer *Op.243
LUCKS 08112 set $26.00, pts $1.25,
ea.   (S957)

Dithyrambe *Op.236
LUCKS 06727 set $11.00, pts $.75,
ea.   (S958)

Dorfschwalben Aus Osterreich *Op.164
"Village Swallows Waltz" LUCKS
06808 sc $9.50, pts $14.00, pts
$1.15, ea.   (S959)

Dorfschwalben Aus Osterreich, For
Solo Voice And Orchestra
"Village Swallows" LUCKS 03243 set
$22.00, pts $.75, ea.   (S960)

Ernst Und Humor. Walzer *Op.254
LUCKS 08109 set $27.50, pts $1.25,
ea.   (S961)

Feuerfest *Op.269
LUCKS 08128 sc $7.00, set $9.50,
pts $.75, ea.   (S962)

Frauenherz *Op.166
LUCKS 06762 set $12.50, pts $.75,
ea.   (S963)

Frauenwurde Walzer *Op.277
LUCKS 08113 set $25.00, pts $1.25,
ea.   (S964)

Friedenspalmen Walzer *Op.207
LUCKS 08114 set $21.25, pts $1.25,
ea.   (S965)

Frohes Leben Walzer *Op.272
LUCKS 08115 set $27.50, pts $1.25,
ea.   (S966)

Gablenz Marsch *Op.159
LUCKS 07598 set $12.50, pts $.75,
ea.   (S967)

Gazelle, Die *Op.155
LUCKS 07596 set $12.50, pts $.75,
ea.   (S968)

Gedenkblatter Walzer *Op.178
LUCKS 08116 set $22.50, pts $1.25,
ea.   (S969)

Herbstrosen Walzer *Op.232
LUCKS 08117 set $23.50, pts $1.25,
ea.   (S970)

Hochzeitsklange. Walzer *Op.242
LUCKS 06805 set $26.00, pts $1.25,
ea.   (S971)

STRAUSS, JOSEF (cont'd.)

Kakudu Quadrille *Op.276
LUCKS 08137 set $15.00, pts $.75,
ea.   (S972)

Kleine Muhle, Die, For Solo Voice And
Orchestra
KRENN perf mat rent   (S973)

Kronungslieder. Walzer *Op.226
LUCKS 06806 set $27.50, pts $1.25,
ea.   (S974)

Libelle, Die *Op.204
LUCKS 06803 set $14.00, pts $.75,
ea.   (S975)

Lie Und Wein *Op.122
LUCKS 08133 set $13.50, pts $.75,
ea.   (S976)

Marche Lorraine
LUCKS 05568 set $13.50, pts $.75,
ea.   (S977)

Marienklange. Walzer *Op.214
LUCKS 08118 set $22.50, pts $1.25,
ea.   (S978)

Mein Lebenslauf Ist Lieb' Und Lust
*Op.263
LUCKS 06807 set $20.00, pts $1.00,
ea.   (S979)

Nachtschatten *Op.229
LUCKS 07625 set $15.50, pts $.75,
ea.   (S980)

Nilfluthen Walzer *Op.275
LUCKS 08119 set $16.50, pts $.75,
ea.   (S981)

Parade Quadrille *Op.45
LUCKS 08120 set $14.00, pts $.75,
ea.   (S982)

Pizzicato-Polka *see Strauss,
Johann, [Jr.]

Schwatzerin, Die *Op.144
LUCKS 08132 set $12.50, pts $.75,
ea.   (S983)

Sofien Quadrille *Op.137
LUCKS 08121 set $12.50, pts $.75,
ea.   (S984)

Spharenklange *Op.235
LUCKS 08122 sc $9.00, pts $14.00,
pts $1.15, ea.   (S985)

Spharenklange, For Solo Voice And
Orchestra
2.2.2.2. 4.4.3.1. perc,harp,
strings,S solo KRENN perf mat
rent   (S986)

Studentenraume Walzer *Op.222
LUCKS 08123 set $22.50, pts $1.25,
ea.   (S987)

Tanz Adressen Walzer *Op.234
LUCKS 08124 set $27.50, pts $1.25,
ea.   (S988)

Tanz Prioritaten Walzer *Op.280
LUCKS 06783 set $38.50, pts $1.25,
ea.   (S989)

Theater Quadrille *Op.213
LUCKS 08141 set $12.50, pts $.75,
ea.   (S990)

Transactionen *Op.184
LUCKS 07600 set $21.00, pts $1.25,
ea.   (S991)

Vaterlandischer Marsch *see Strauss,
Johann, [Jr.]

Verliebte Augen
LUCKS 08130 set $13.50, pts $.75,
ea.   (S992)

Victoria Polka *Op.228
LUCKS 08131 set $13.50, pts $.75,
ea.   (S993)

Village Swallows *see Dorfschwalben
Aus Osterreich, For Solo Voice
And Orchestra

Village Swallows Waltz *see
Dorfschwalben Aus Osterreich

Vorwarts *Op.127
LUCKS 08051 set $21.00, pts $1.25,
ea.   (S994)

Wiener Fresken Walzer *Op.249
LUCKS 07597 set $24.50, pts $1.25,
ea.   (S995)

STRAUSS, JOSEF (cont'd.)

Wiener Kinder Singen Gern, For Solo
　Voice And Orchestra
　KRENN perf mat rent　　　(S996)

Wiener Stimmen. Walzer　*Op.239
　LUCKS 08127 set $15.50, pts $.75,
　ea.　　　　　　　　(S997)

STRAUSS, RICHARD (1864-1949)
Also Sprach Zarathustra
　see Tone Poems, Series 2

Aus Italien　*Op.16
　see Symphonic Poems, Vol. 1
　(each movement available
　separately) KALMUS A4638 sc
　$50.00, perf mat rent, set
　$75.00, pts $3.00, ea.　　(S998)

Burleske, For Piano And Orchestra
　LUCKS 00077 sc $18.00, set $32.00,
　pts $2.25, ea.　　　　(S999)

Concerto for Horn and Orchestra, No.
　1, Op. 11, in E flat
　min sc UNIVER. PH367 $7.50　(S1000)
　LUCKS 00806 sc $12.00, set $18.00,
　pts $1.40, ea., solo pt $2.00
　　　　　　　　　　　(S1001)
Death And Transfiguration　*see Tod
　Und Verklarung

Divertimento, Op. 86
　KALMUS 5237 sc $30.00, set $75.00
　　　　　　　　　　　(S1002)
Don Juan　*Op.20
　see Symphonic Poems, Vol. 1
　see Tone Poems, Series 1
　pts BROUDE BR. $3.00, ea.　(S1003)

Don Quixote　*Op.35
　see Symphonic Poems, Vol. 2
　see Tone Poems, Series 1

Feierlicher Einzug [7']
　2+pic.2.2.2+contrabsn. 4.3.3.1.
　opt org, timp, perc, strings
　sc, pts LIENAU f.s.　　　(S1004)

Festmarsch In E Flat　*Op.1 [9']
　3.2.2.2. 4.2.3.1. timp, strings
　KALMUS 5271 sc $5.00, perf mat
　rent, set $24.00, pts $1.00, ea.
　　　　　　　　　　　(S1005)
Four Last Songs, For Solo Voice And
　Orchestra　*see Vier Letzte
　Lieder, For Solo Voice And
　Orchestra

Heldenleben, Ein　*Op.40
　see Tone Poems, Series 2
　"Hero's Life, A" study sc INTERNAT.
　1325 $8.75　　　　　(S1006)

Hero's Life, A　*see Heldenleben, Ein

Macbeth　*Op.23
　see Symphonic Poems, Vol. 1

Morgen, For Solo Voice And Orchestra
　*Op.27,No.4
　LUCKS 02209 sc $3.00, set $5.00,
　pts $.75, ea.　　　　(S1007)

Muttertandelei, For Solo Voice And
　Orchestra　*Op.43,No.2
　LUCKS 03290 sc $3.00, set $12.00,
　pts $.75, ea.　　　　(S1008)

Ruhe Meine Seele, For Solo Voice And
　Orchestra, [arr.]　*Op.27,No.1
　LUCKS 03291 set $22.00, pts $.75,
　ea.　　　　　　　(S1009)

Salome, Op.54: Salomes Tanz
　sc INTERNAT. 2097 $6.00　(S1010)

Symphonic Poems, Vol. 1
　min sc, bds PETERS 8362A $100.00
　contains: Aus Italien, Op.16; Don
　　Juan, Op.20; Macbeth, Op.23
　　　　　　　　　　　(S1011)
Symphonic Poems, Vol. 2
　min sc, bds PETERS 8362B $100.00
　contains: Don Quixote, Op.35;
　　Till Eulenspiegels Lustige
　　Streiche, Op.28; Tod Und
　　Verklarung, Op.24　　(S1012)

Till Eulenspiegels Lustige Streiche
　*Op.28
　see Symphonic Poems, Vol. 2
　see Tone Poems, Series 2
　"Till Eulenspiegel's Merry Pranks"
　pts BROUDE BR. $3.00, ea. (S1013)

Till Eulenspiegel's Merry Pranks
　*see Till Eulenspiegels Lustige
　Streiche

Tod Und Verklarung　*Op.24
　see Symphonic Poems, Vol. 2
　see Tone Poems, Series 1
　"Death And Transfiguration" LUCKS

STRAUSS, RICHARD (cont'd.)

　06816 sc $20.00, set $40.00, pts
　$2.25, ea.　　　　　(S1014)
　"Death And Transfiguration" pts
　BROUDE BR. $3.00, ea.　(S1015)

Tone Poems, Series 1
　study sc DOVER 23754-0 $8.95
　contains: Don Juan; Don Quixote;
　　Tod Und Verklarung　(S1016)

Tone Poems, Series 2
　study sc DOVER 23755-9 $8.95
　contains: Also Sprach
　　Zarathustra; Heldenleben, Ein;
　　Till Eulenspiegels Lustige
　　Streiche　　　　　(S1017)

Vier Letzte Lieder, For Solo Voice
　And Orchestra
　4.3.3.3. 4.3.3.1. timp, perc, harp,
　cel, strings, high solo
　"Four Last Songs, For Solo Voice
　And Orchestra" min sc BOOSEY 667
　$15.00　　　　　　(S1018)

Zueignung, For Solo Voice And
　Orchestra, [arr.]　*Op.10,No.1
　LUCKS 02256 sc $3.00, set $8.00,
　pts $.75, ea.　　　　(S1019)

Zwei Militarmarsche　*Op.57
　KALMUS 5242 sc $8.00, set $25.00
　　　　　　　　　　　(S1020)
STRAUSSLE-GAVOTTE see Humperdinck,
　Engelbert

STRAVAGANZA, LA, VOL. 1 see Vivaldi,
　Antonio

STRAVAGANZA, LA, VOL. 2 see Vivaldi,
　Antonio

STRAVINSKY, IGOR (1882-1971)
Baiser De La Fee, Le: Divertimento
　BOOSEY 665 min sc $15.00, sc $35.00
　　　　　　　　　　　(S1021)
Chant De Rossignol, Le
　KALMUS A4349 sc $16.00, perf mat
　rent, set $50.00, pts $2.00, ea.
　　　　　　　　　　　(S1022)
Faune Et La Bergere, Le, For Solo
　Voice And Orchestra　*Op.2 [9']
　3.2.2.2. 4.2.3.1. timp, perc,
　strings, high solo
　KALMUS 5261 sc $8.00, perf mat
　rent, set $16.00, pts $1.00, ea.
　　　　　　　　　　　(S1023)
Firebird: Suite, 1919 Version
　LUCKS 06817 sc $20.00, set $42.00,
　pts $2.25, ea.　　　　(S1024)

Fireworks　*Op.4
　LUCKS 05949 sc $11.00, set $28.00,
　min sc $2.00, pts $1.40, ea.
　　　　　　　　　　　(S1025)
　study sc INTERNAT. 903 $3.50
　　　　　　　　　　　(S1026)
Four Etudes [12']
　3.3.3.2. 4.3.3.1. timp, harp, pno,
　strings
　BOOSEY 631 min sc $7.25, sc $15.00
　　　　　　　　　　　(S1027)
　"Quatre Etudes" KALMUS 5273 sc
　$15.00, perf mat rent, set
　$30.00, pts $1.00, ea.　(S1028)

Greeting Prelude
　sc BOOSEY $7.00　　　(S1029)

Petrouchka
　BOOSEY 639 min sc $13.00, sc $95.00
　　　　　　　　　　　(S1030)
Petrouchka: At The Moor
　4(2pic).4(English horn).4(bass
　clar).4(contrabsn). 4.2+
　2cornet.3.1. timp, perc, 2harp,
　cel, pno, strings
　KALMUS A4119 sc $18.00, perf mat
　rent, set $35.00, pts $2.00, ea.
　　　　　　　　　　　(S1031)
Petrouchka: Carnival & Death Of
　Petrouchka
　4(2pic).4(English horn).4(bass
　clar).4(contrabsn). 4.2+
　2cornet.3.1. timp, perc, 2harp,
　cel, pno, strings
　KALMUS A4120 sc $18.00, perf mat
　rent, set $35.00, pts $2.00, ea.
　　　　　　　　　　　(S1032)
Petrouchka: Danse Russe
　4(2pic).4(English horn).4(bass
　clar).4(contrabsn). 4.2+
　2cornet.3.1. timp, perc, 2harp,
　cel, pno, strings
　KALMUS A4118 sc $18.00, perf mat
　rent, set $35.00, pts $2.00, ea.
　　　　　　　　　　　(S1033)
Petrouchka: The Fair
　4(2pic).4(English horn).4(bass
　clar).4(contrabsn). 4.2+
　2cornet.3.1. timp, perc, 2harp,
　cel, pno, strings
　KALMUS A4117 sc $18.00, perf mat
　rent, set $35.00, pts $2.00, ea.

STRAVINSKY, IGOR (cont'd.)

　　　　　　　　　　　(S1034)
Praeludium
　sc BOOSEY $6.00　　　(S1035)

Pulcinella: Suite
　(Spalding, A.) KALMUS A 4543 sc
　$15.00, perf mat rent, set
　$50.00, pts $4.00, ea.　(S1036)

Quatre Etudes　*see Four Etudes

Ragtime, For Eleven Instruments
　KALMUS A4541 sc $5.00, perf mat
　rent, set $15.00, pts $1.25, ea.
　　　　　　　　　　　(S1037)
Rite Of Spring, The　*see Sacre Du
　Printemps, Le

Sacre Du Printemps, Le
　"Rite Of Spring, The" sc INTERNAT.
　3082 $11.75　　　　(S1038)

Scenes De Ballet
　min sc BOOSEY HPS 938 $9.50 (S1039)

Scherzo A La Russe
　min sc BOOSEY HPS 937 $4.50 (S1040)

Suite No. 1
　LUCKS 05970 sc $11.00, set $25.00,
　min sc $4.00, pts $2.00, ea.
　　　　　　　　　　　(S1041)
Suite No. 2
　LUCKS 05971 sc $11.00, set $25.00,
　pts $2.00, ea.　　　　(S1042)

STRECKE, GERHARD (1890-1968)
Konzertstuck for Violin and
　Orchestra, Op. 87 [7']
　1(pic).1.2.1. 2.1.1.0. timp,
　triangle, strings, vln solo
　RIES perf mat rent　　(S1043)

Lustige Ouverture　*Op.44 [10']
　2(pic).2.2.2. 4.2.2.1. timp, perc,
　strings
　RIES perf mat rent　　(S1044)

Oberschlesische Tanzsuite　*Op.43
　[16']
　2.2.2.2. 2.2.2.1. timp, perc,
　strings
　RIES perf mat rent　　(S1045)

Suite No. 2 for Orchestra [11']
　2(pic).1.2.1. 2.2.1.1. timp,
　glock, triangle, strings
　RIES perf mat rent　　(S1046)

Suite No. 7, Op. 86 for Orchestra
　[15']
　1(pic).1.2.1. 2.1.1.0. timp, perc,
　harp/pno, strings
　sc RIES f.s., perf mat rent (S1047)

STREIFLICHTER see Stolzenwald, Otto

STRIETMAN, WILLEM (1918-　　)
Mercator Sapiens [8']
　3.3.3.3. 4.3.3.1. timp, 4perc, cel,
　2harp, strings
　DONEMUS perf mat rent　(S1048)

O Bonne Douce France, For Harmonica
　And Chamber Orchestra [31']
　1.1.1.1.alto sax(opt soprano
　sax). 1.1.1.0. perc, harp, pno/
　cel, gtr/elec gtr, 14vln, 4vla,
　4vcl, 2db, harmonica solo
　sc DONEMUS f.s., perf mat rent
　　　　　　　　　　　(S1049)
STRIJDER, DE see Mulder, Herman

STRINDBERG, HENRIK (1954-　　)
I Gult Och Rott [10']
　2.2.2.2. 2.2.1.0. timp, 2perc,
　strings
　sc, pts STIM perf mat rent　(S1050)

STRING-TIME FANTASIETTA see Kruyf, Ton
　de

STRINGS HAVE VIBRATED, THE see Mulder,
　Herman, Snaren Hebben Getrild, De,
　For Solo Voice And Orchestra

STRUCTURES see Lambro, Phillip

STRUENSEE: OVERTURE, NO.8 POLONAISE AND
　NO.9 DORFSCHENKE see Meyerbeer,
　Giacomo

STRUGGLE, THE see Laman, Wim, Gevecht,
　Het, For Solo Voice And Orchestra

STRUNE, MILO SE GLASITE see Jez, Jakob

STRUNGK, NICOLAUS ADAM (1640-1700)
Sonata, MIN 95
　string orch, cont
　KALMUS A1124 sc $2.00, set $5.25,
　pts $.75, ea.　　　　(S1051)

STRUWWELPETER: MARCH see Heuberger,
    Richard

STRUWWELPETER: OVERTURE see Heuberger,
    Richard

STRUWWELPETER: WALTZ see Heuberger,
    Richard

STUCKE see Alsina, Carlos Roque

STUDENTENBALL-TANZE WALZER see Strauss,
    Eduard

STUDENTENRAUME WALZER see Strauss,
    Josef

STUDI IN FORMA DI VARIAZIONI see
    Fellegara, Vittorio

STUDIE FOR STRAKORKESTER see Jansson,
    Johannes

STUDIEN, FOR PIANO AND ORCHESTRA see
    Wallmann, Johannes

STUDIO see Bettinelli, Bruno

STUDY IN A see Twardowski, Romuald

STUHEC, IGOR (1932-   )
    Chanson Sans Paroles [11']
        1.1.1.0. 1.1.1.0. 3perc,2pno,
        string quin
        DRUSTVO DSS 797 perf mat rent
                                    (S1052)
    Drobna Glasba [15']
        2(pic).2.2.2. 4.3.3.1. timp,
        4perc,harp,pno,strings
        "Petite Musique" DRUSTVO DSS 763
        perf mat rent   (S1053)

    Petite Musique *see Drobna Glasba

STUPPNER, HUBERT (1944-   )
    Bal Lunaire
        1(pic).0.2.0. 1.0.1.0. perc,pno,
        2vln,vla,vcl,db
        [20'] MODERN 2201 f.s.   (S1054)

    Espressivo, For Solo Voice And
        Strings [12']
        5vln,2vla,3vcl,db,S solo
        MODERN 1892 rent   (S1055)

    Espressivo II [15']
        timp,strings
        MODERN 2052 rent   (S1056)

    Gesang Zur Nacht, For Solo Voice And
        Orchestra [18']
        1(pic).0.2.0. 1.1.1.0. perc,cel,
        strings,S solo
        MODERN 2024 rent   (S1057)

    Palinodie III [20']
        MODERN 2176 rent   (S1058)

    Quasi Une Sinfonia
        3.2.3.2. 4.4.2.0. 4perc,harp,cel,
        strings
        [20'] MODERN 2207 f.s.   (S1059)

STURMISCH IN LIEB UND TANZ see Strauss,
    Johann, [Jr.]

STURMISCHE BEGEGNUNG see Ritter, Helmut

STURMNACHT, FOR SOLO VOICE AND
    ORCHESTRA see Schwickert, Gustav

STURZ PHAETONS, DER see Dittersdorf,
    Karl Ditters von, Sinfonia in B
    flat, Krebs 74

STYX see Douw, Andre

STYX, FOR VIOLIN AND STRING ORCHESTRA
    see Douw, Andre

SU LE SPONDE DEL TEBRO, FOR SOLO VOICE
    AND ORCHESTRA see Scarlatti,
    Alessandro

SUCHON, EUGEN (1908-   )
    Breakthrough *see Prielom

    Concertino for Clarinet and Orchestra
        [30']
        3.2.2.3. 4.3.3.1. 2timp,5perc,
        pno,strings,clar solo
        SLOV.HUD.FOND O-463A perf mat rent
                                    (S1060)
    Glimpse Into The Unknown, For Solo
        Voice And Orchestra *see Pohl'ad
        Do Neznama, For Solo Voice And
        Orchestra

    Maditacia A Tanec, For Piano And
        Orchestra
        timp,perc,cel,strings,pno solo
        "Meditation And Dance, For Piano
        And Orchestra" SLOV.HUD.FOND
        O-415A, B perf mat rent   (S1061)

SUCHON, EUGEN (cont'd.)

    Meditation And Dance, For Piano And
        Orchestra *see Maditacia A
        Tanec, For Piano And Orchestra

    Pohl'ad Do Neznama, For Solo Voice
        And Orchestra [9']
        timp,perc,cel,pno,strings,T solo
        "Glimpse Into The Unknown, For Solo
        Voice And Orchestra" sc
        SLOV.HUD.FOND f.s., perf mat rent
                                    (S1062)
    Prielom [24']
        3.3.3.2. 4.3.3.1. timp,perc,harp,
        strings
        "Breakthrough" SLOV.HUD.FOND O-447A
        perf mat rent   (S1063)
    Sonatina [14']
        2horn,2trp,timp,perc,strings
        SLOV.HUD.FOND O-112A perf mat rent
                                    (S1064)
    Three Movements From Contemplations,
        For Piano And Orchestra *see Tri
        Casti Z Kontemplacii, For Piano
        And Orchestra

    Three Romantic Pieces, For Piano And
        Orchestra *see Tri Romanticke
        Kusy, For Piano And Orchestra

    Tri Casti Z Kontemplacii, For Piano
        And Orchestra
        fl,timp,perc,strings,pno solo
        "Three Movements From
        Contemplations, For Piano And
        Orchestra" SLOV.HUD.FOND
        O-416A, B perf mat rent   (S1065)

    Tri Romanticke Kusy, For Piano And
        Orchestra
        timp,perc,cel,strings,pno solo
        "Three Romantic Pieces, For Piano
        And Orchestra" SLOV.HUD.FOND
        O-414A, B perf mat rent   (S1066)

SUGAR, REZSO (1919-   )
    Concertino for Chamber Orchestra
        (special import only) sc EMB 8131
        f.s.   (S1067)

    Epilogue For Orchestra
        (special import only) sc EMB 7734
        f.s.   (S1068)

    Suite For String Orchestra
        EMB K59 min sc $7.00, sc $15.00
                                    (S1069)

SUITE 16 see Meijering, Chiel

SUITE A L'IMAGE DU TEMPS see Moret,
    Norbert

SUITE ACCADEMICA see Dalla Vecchia,
    Wolfango

SUITE ALGERIENNE see Saint-Saens,
    Camille

SUITE AUS EINEM KINDERMARCHENSPIEL see
    Lothar, Mark

SUITE CONCERTANTE, FOR ORGAN AND STRING
    ORCHESTRA see Klerk, Albert de

SUITE DANS LE STYLE ANCIEN, OP. 24 see
    Indy, Vincent d'

SUITE DE BALADES see Kroll, Georg

SUITE DE BALLET see Holst, Gustav

SUITE DE DANSES ET DE CHANSONS, FOR
    HARPSICHORD AND ORCHESTRA see
    Krauze, Zygmunt

SUITE DE SYMPHONIES NO. 1 see Mouret,
    Jean Joseph

SUITE DER MASKEN see Dressel, Erwin

SUITE FOR STRING ORCHESTRA see Sugar,
    Rezso

SUITE FROM THE OPERA "CARMEN" see
    Proto, Frank

SUITE IN FORMA DI VARIAZIONI see Toni,
    Alceo

SUITE IN TRE TEMPI see Spagnoli, G.

SUITE IN VIER SATZEN, [ARR.] see
    Handel, George Frideric

SUITE LORRAINE see Boisdeffre, Charles-
    Henri-Rene de

SUITE MINIATURE see Dubois, Theodore

SUITE "MIT DEM MARSCH, " [ARR.] see
    Handel, George Frideric

SUITE MODERNE see Baumann, Max

SUITE NO. 3 IN D, BWV 1068, SECOND
    MOVEMENT, [ARR.] see Bach, Johann
    Sebastian

SUITE OF DUTCH DANCES NO. 2 see
    Badings, Henk

SUITE ON ENGLISH FOLK TUNES "A TIME
    THERE WAS..." see Britten, [Sir]
    Benjamin

SUITE PASTORALE, FOR ENGLISH HORN AND
    CHAMBER ORCHESTRA see Steffaro,
    Julius

SUITE SPORTIVE see Breit, Bert

SUITE TSUGARU see Watanabe, Urato

SUITE WITH MARCH, [ARR.] see Handel,
    George Frideric, Suite "Mit Dem
    Marsch, " [arr.]

SUITES NOS.1-4, BWV 1066-1069 see Bach,
    Johann Sebastian

SUITES NOS. 5, OP. 34 AND NO. 6, OP. 40
    see Eisler, Hanns

SUK, JOSEF (1874-1935)
    Fairy-Tale Suite *see Pohadka Suite

    Meditation On An Old Bohemian Chorale
        *see Meditation On The Chorale
        "Saint Wenceslas"

    Meditation On The Chorale "Saint
        Wenceslas" *Op.35a
        string orch
        "Meditation On An Old Bohemian
        Chorale" LUCKS 08666 sc $3.75,
        set $3.75, pts $.75, ea.   (S1070)

    Pohadka Suite *Op.16 [31']
        "Fairy-Tale Suite" KALMUS A2141 sc
        $17.00, perf mat rent, set
        $50.00, pts $2.50, ea.   (S1071)

SULLIVAN, [SIR] ARTHUR SEYMOUR
    (1842-1900)
    H.M.S. Pinafore: I'm Called Little
        Buttercup, For Solo Voice And
        Orchestra
        LUCKS 11912 set $9.00, pts $.75,
        ea.   (S1072)

    H.M.S. Pinafore: Refrain, Audacious
        Tar, For Solo Voice And Orchestra
        LUCKS 11916 set $9.00, pts $.75,
        ea.   (S1073)

    H.M.S. Pinafore: When I Was A Lad,
        For Solo Voice And Orchestra
        LUCKS 11915 set $14.00, pts $.75,
        ea.   (S1074)

    Iolanthe: Entrance And March Of The
        Peers, "Loudly Let The Trumpets
        Bray"
        LUCKS 02807 set $19.00, pts $1.00,
        ea.   (S1075)

    Iolanthe: Love, Unrequited Robs Me Of
        My Rest, For Solo Voice And
        Orchestra
        LUCKS 11921 set $17.00, pts $1.00,
        ea.   (S1076)

    Iolanthe: Oh Foolish Fay, For Solo
        Voice And Orchestra
        LUCKS 11919 set $14.00, pts $.75,
        ea.   (S1077)

    Lost Chord, The, For Solo Voice And
        Orchestra, [arr.]
        LUCKS 02289 set $10.00, pts $.75,
        ea.   (S1078)

    Merchant Of Venice: Mascarade
        KALMUS 5274 sc $20.00, perf mat
        rent, set $35.00, pts $1.50, ea.
                                    (S1079)
    Mikado, The: The Moon And I, For Solo
        Voice And Orchestra
        LUCKS 03688 sc $4.00, set $8.00,
        pts $.60, ea.   (S1080)

    Mikado, The: Were You Not To Koko
        Plighted?, For Solo Voices And
        Orchestra
        LUCKS 02888 sc $4.00, set $8.00,
        pts $.75, ea.   (S1081)

    Mikado, The: Willow, Tit-Willow, For
        Solo Voice And Orchestra
        LUCKS 03332 sc $4.00, set $8.00,
        pts $.60, ea.   (S1082)

    Pirates Of Penzance, The: I Am The
        Very Pattern Of A Modern Major
        General, For Solo Voice And
        Orchestra
        LUCKS 03785 set $14.00, pts $.75,
        ea.   (S1083)

SULLIVAN, [SIR] ARTHUR SEYMOUR
(cont'd.)

Pirates Of Penzance: Overture
sets NOVELLO 9127-28 $59.50, and
up, sc NOVELLO 9126 $12.50, pts
NOVELLO 9617 $1.50, ea.   (S1084)

Symphony in E
2.2.2.2. 4.2.3.0. timp,strings
KALMUS 5342 sc $60.00, perf mat
rent, set $100.00, pts $4.00, ea.
(S1085)

Tempest, The [45']
2+pic.2.2.2. 2.2.3.0. timp,perc,
strings
KALMUS 5526 sc $60.00, set $90.00
(S1086)

Yeomen Of The Guard, The: Overture
2.1.2.2. 2.2.3.0. timp,strings
(Lloyd-Jones; Mackerras) min sc
EULENBURG $9.00   (S1087)

SUMMER INTERLUDES see Dorward, David

SUMMERCONCERTO, FOR OBOE AND ORCHESTRA
see Straesser, Joep

SUMSION, HERBERT W. (1899-   )
Mountain Tune, A [6']
string orch
SCOTUS 156-7 f.s.   (S1088)

SUN DRAGON see Pert, Morris

SUN OF MY SOUL see Hursley

SUN RISING, THE see Brown, Christopher

SUN-TREADER see Ruggles, Carl Sprague

SUNDAY see Hekster, Walter

SUNDAY MORNING see Rorem, Ned

SUNNY BOY see Hudec, Jiri

SUNNY SUNSHINE see Merku, Pavle

SUNRISE AT CAMPOBELLO: SUITE see
Waxman, Franz

SUNSET BOULEVARD: SUITE see Waxman,
Franz

SUOMALAISTA KANSANLAULUA, 20, FOR SOLO
VOICE AND ORCHESTRA see Borg, Kim

SUOMEN PUU, FOR SOLO VOICE AND
ORCHESTRA see Madetoja, Leevi

SUONI PER ARCHI see Ferrari, Giorgio

SUPERNOVAE see Tabachnik, Michel

SUPPE, FRANZ VON (1819-1895)
Banditenstreiche: Overture [7']
2.2.2.2. 4.3.3.0. timp,perc,harp,
strings
KALMUS 5449 sc $15.00, perf mat
rent, set $30.00, pts $1.50, ea.
(S1089)

Boccaccio: Hab Ich Nur Deine Liebe,
For Solo Voices And Orchestra
LUCKS 02408 set $13.50, pts $.75,
ea.   (S1090)

Dichter Und Bauer: Overture
"Poet And Peasant: Overture" min sc
PETERS 823 $5.00
"Poet And Peasant: Overture" LUCKS
06840 sc $9.50, set $22.00, min
sc $4.50, pts $1.15, ea.   (S1092)

Fatinitza: Overture [7']
2(pic).2.2.2. 4.2.3.0. timp,perc,
strings
KALMUS 5290 sc $20.00, perf mat
rent, set $12.00, pts $.75, ea.
(S1093)

Leichte Kavallerie: Overture
"Light Cavalry: Overture" LUCKS
06836 sc $6.00, set $18.00, pts
$1.15, ea.   (S1094)

Light Cavalry: Overture *see Leichte
Kavallerie: Overture

Morgen, Ein Mittag, Ein Abend In
Wien, Ein: Overture
"Morning, Noon And Night In Vienna:
Overture" LUCKS 06837 sc $7.50,
set $18.00, pts $.95, ea. (S1095)

Morning, Noon And Night In Vienna:
Overture *see Morgen, Ein
Mittag, Ein Abend In Wien, Ein:
Overture

Pique Dame: Overture
LUCKS 06839 sc $9.50, set $22.00,
pts $1.15, ea.   (S1096)

Poet And Peasant: Overture *see
Dichter Und Bauer: Overture

SUPPLIANTS D'ESCHYLE see Zemlinsky,
Alexander von

SURINACH, CARLOS (1915-   )
Concerto for String Orchestra
string orch
sc AMP $15.00   (S1097)

SURPRISE SYMPHONY see Haydn, [Franz]
Joseph, Symphony No. 94 in G

SUSANNA'S SECRET: OVERTURE see Wolf-
Ferrari, Ermanno, Segreto Di
Susanna, Il: Overture

SUTER, ROBERT (1919-   )
Airs Et Ritournelles [17'45"]
clar,clar in E flat,bass clar,
alto sax,baritone sax,3trp,
3trom,6perc,2pno,cel,6db
BREITKOPF-W perf mat rent (S1098)

SUTERMEISTER, HEINRICH (1910-   )
Quadrifoglio, For Woodwind Quartet
And Orchestra [26']
2.2.2.2. 4.3.3.1. timp,perc,harp,
strings,fl solo,ob solo,clar
solo,bsn solo
sc SCHOTTS 71 A6787 $37.00 (S1099)

SUUTELO, FOR SOLO VOICE AND ORCHESTRA,
[ARR.] see Kuula, Toivo

SVARA, DANILO (1902-   )
Ballabili In Modo Istriano [16']
2(pic).2(English horn).2(bass
clar).2. 4.3.3.1. timp,2perc,
harp,strings
DRUSTVO DSS 839 perf mat rent
(S1100)

Borec – Uvertura Na Partizanske Teme
[9']
2(pic).2.2.2. 4.3.3.1. timp,
2perc,strings
"Fighter – Overture On Partizan
Themes" DRUSTVO DSS 766 perf mat
rent   (S1101)

Concertato, For Piano And Orchestra
[15']
3(pic).2(English horn).2(bass
clar).2. 4.2.3.1. timp,2perc,
cel,strings,pno solo
DRUSTVO DSS 793 perf mat rent
(S1102)

Concerto for Clarinet and Orchestra
[15']
1.1(English horn).0(bass clar).1.
1.1.1.0. harp,strings,clar solo
DRUSTVO DSS 872 perf mat rent
(S1103)

Concerto for Oboe and Orchestra [19']
2(pic).0(English horn).2(bass
clar).2. 4.2.3.0. timp,3perc,
harp,strings,ob solo
DRUSTVO DSS 871 perf mat rent
(S1104)

Eseji [16']
2(pic).2(English horn).2(bass
clar).2. 4.3.3.1. timp,3perc,
harp,strings
"Essays" DRUSTVO DSS 873 perf mat
rent   (S1105)

Essays *see Eseji

Fantasia Doppia, For Violin,
Violoncello And Orchestra [9']
2(pic).2.2(bass clar).2. 2.2.0.0.
timp,2perc,strings,vln solo,vcl
solo
DRUSTVO DSS 772 perf mat rent
(S1106)

Fighter – Overture On Partizan Themes
*see Borec – Uvertura Na
Partizanske Teme

Istrian Dances *see Istrski Plesi

Istrian Motives, For Solo Voices And
Chamber Orchestra *see Istrski
Motivi, For Solo Voices And
Chamber Orchestra

Istrski Motivi, For Solo Voices And
Chamber Orchestra [20']
2.2.2.1. 0.0.0.0. 2perc,strings,
AA soli, tamburica
"Istrian Motives, For Solo Voices
And Chamber Orchestra" DRUSTVO
DSS 840 perf mat rent   (S1107)

Istrski Plesi [15']
2(pic).2(English horn).2(bass
clar).2. 4.3.3.1. timp,3perc,
harp,strings
"Istrian Dances" DRUSTVO DSS 874
perf mat rent   (S1108)

Suite Concertante No. 1 [25']
fl,ob,horn,strings
DRUSTVO DSS 764 perf mat rent
(S1109)

Suite Concertante No. 2 [20']
clar,bsn,trom,strings
DRUSTVO DSS 765 perf mat rent

SVARA, DANILO (cont'd.)

(S1110)

Symphony No. 2 [27']
2(pic).2(English horn).2(bass
clar).2. 4.2.3.1. timp,2perc,
strings
DRUSTVO DSS 876 perf mat rent
(S1111)

SVENDSEN, JOHAN (SEVERIN) (1840-1911)
Andante Funebre [9']
2.2.2.2. 4.2.3.1. timp,strings
KALMUS 5345 sc $4.00, perf mat
rent, set $12.00, pts $.50, ea.
(S1112)

Carnival In Paris *Op.9 [10']
2+pic.2.2.2. 4.2.3.1. timp,perc,
strings
KALMUS 5264 sc $12.00, perf mat
rent, set $32.00, pts $1.50, ea.
(S1113)

Festival Polonaise *Op.12 [8']
2+pic.2.2.2. 4.3.3.1. timp,perc,
strings
KALMUS 5265 sc $14.00, perf mat
rent, set $28.00, pts $1.00, ea.
(S1114)

I Fjol Gjaett'e Gjettin
string orch
LUCKS 06849 sc $1.75, set $3.75,
pts $.75, ea.   (S1115)

Norwegian Artists' Carnival In Rome
*Op.14
LUCKS 07213 sc $7.50, set $22.00,
pts $1.15, ea.   (S1116)

Romeo And Juliet *Op.18 [28']
2.2.2.2. 4.2.3.1. timp,strings
BREITKOPF-W perf mat rent (S1117)
KALMUS 5263 sc $14.00, perf mat
rent, set $30.00, pts $1.50, ea.
(S1118)

Two Icelandic Melodies
string orch
LUCKS 06853 sc $1.75, set $3.75,
pts $.75, ea.   (S1119)

Zorahayda *Op.11
min sc NORSK f.s.   (S1120)

SVENSK BOLERO see Blomberg, Erik

SVENSK BOUREE see Blomberg, Erik

SVOBODA, TOMAS (1939-   )
Concertino for Violin and Orchestra,
Op. 77 [19']
2.2.2.2. 2.2.3.0. timp,strings,
vln solo
sc,pts STANGLAND rent   (S1121)

Concerto for Piano and Orchestra, Op.
71 [18']
1.1.1.1. 1.1.0.0. timp,strings,
pno solo
sc,pts STANGLAND rent   (S1122)

Eugene Overture *Op.103 [9']
3.2.2.2. 4.4.4.1. timp,5perc,
strings
STANGLAND perf mat rent (S1123)

Nocturne, Op. 100 [19'30"]
2.2.2.2. 4.2.3.0. timp,2perc,gtr,
harp,pno,strings
STANGLAND perf mat rent (S1124)

Overture Of The Season *Op.89 [8']
3.2.2.2. 4.3.3.1. timp,2perc,
chimes,strings
sc,pts STANGLAND rent   (S1125)

Prelude and Fugue, Op. 67 [9']
string orch
sc,pts STANGLAND rent   (S1126)

Reflections *Op.53 [25']
4.3.4.3. 4.3.4.0. timp,5perc,
xylo,pno,strings
sc,pts STANGLAND rent   (S1127)

Sinfonietta, Op. 60 [20']
3.2.2.2. 4.3.3.1. timp,4perc,
strings
sc,pts STANGLAND rent   (S1128)

Symphony No. 3 for Organ and
Orchestra, Op. 43 [30']
3.2.5.2.sax. 4.3.4.1. timp,5perc,
xylo,pno,strings,org solo
sc,pts STANGLAND rent   (S1129)

Symphony No. 4, Op. 69 [27']
3.2.4.2.sax. 4.3.4.1. timp,5perc,
marimba,vibra,cel,glock,harp,
strings
sc,pts STANGLAND rent   (S1130)

Symphony No. 5, Op. 92 [28']
2+pic+alto fl.2+English horn.2+
clar in E flat+bass clar.2.
4.3.3.1. timp,4perc,harp,pno,
strings
sc,pts STANGLAND rent   (S1131)

SVOBODA, TOMAS (cont'd.)

Three Pieces *Op.45 [9']
3.2.2.2. 4.2.3.1. timp,2perc,
strings
sc,pts STANGLAND rent (S1132)

SWAN, A, FOR SOLO VOICE AND ORCHESTRA,
[ARR.] see Grieg, Edvard Hagerup

SWAN LAKE: OVERTURE, ACT II see
Tchaikovsky, Piotr Ilyich

SWAN LAKE: PAS DE DEUX, "BLACK SWAN"
see Tchaikovsky, Piotr Ilyich

SWAN LAKE: PAS DE DEUX, "WHITE SWAN"
see Tchaikovsky, Piotr Ilyich

SWAN LAKE: PAS DE TROIS see
Tchaikovsky, Piotr Ilyich

SWAN LAKE: SUITE see Tchaikovsky, Piotr
Ilyich

SWAN OF TUONELA, THE see Sibelius, Jean

SWEELINCK FANFARE see Heppener, Robert

SWEET STRINGS see Jez, Jakob, Strune,
Milo Se Glasite

SYDEMAN, WILLIAM J. (1928-   )
Divertimento
fl,clar,bsn,strings
SEESAW perf mat rent (S1133)

Fugue
string orch
SEESAW perf mat rent (S1134)

SYLPHEN-POLKA see Strauss, Johann,
[Jr.]

SYLPHIDES, LES, [ARR.] see Chopin,
Frederic

SYMFONICKA FRESKA see Pospisil, Juraj

SYMFONIE VOOR LOSSE SNAREN see
Andriessen, Louis

SYMPATHIE POLKA see Strauss, Johann,
[Jr.]

SYMPHONIA see Ruyneman, Daniel

SYMPHONIC ANTITHESIS see Bravnicar,
Matija, Simfonicna Antiteza

SYMPHONIC DANCE see Selby, Philip

SYMPHONIC DANCES ON NORWEGIAN THEMES
see Grieg, Edvard Hagerup

SYMPHONIC DANCES, OP. 45 see
Rachmaninoff, Sergey Vassilievich

SYMPHONIC FANTASY see Kennedy, John
Brodbin

SYMPHONIC FRESCO see Pospisil, Juraj,
Symfonicka Freska

SYMPHONIC METAMORPHOSIS ON A BACH
CHORALE see Ben-Haim, Paul

SYMPHONIC MOVEMENT see Giuffre, James
Peter (Jimmy)

SYMPHONIC MUSIC I AND II see Rychlik,
Jozef, Muzyka Symfoniczna I i II

SYMPHONIC POEMS, VOL. 1 see Strauss,
Richard

SYMPHONIC POEMS, VOL. 2 see Strauss,
Richard

SYMPHONIC PRELUDE see Newman, Theodore
Simon

SYMPHONIC SKETCHES see Chadwick, George
Whitefield

SYMPHONIC SKETCHES: A VAGROM BALLAD see
Chadwick, George Whitefield

SYMPHONIC SKETCHES: HOBGOBLIN see
Chadwick, George Whitefield

SYMPHONIC SKETCHES: JUBILEE AND NOEL
see Chadwick, George Whitefield

SYMPHONIC SUITE NO. 1 see Skalkottas,
Nikos

SYMPHONIE "CAPELLA" see Wayenberg,
Daniel

SYMPHONIE CEVENOLE, FOR PIANO AND
ORCHESTRA see Indy, Vincent d'

SYMPHONIE CONCERTANTE, FOR HARP AND
INSTRUMENTAL ENSEMBLE see
Bancquart, Alain

SYMPHONIE CONCERTANTE FOR VIOLIN,
VIOLA, AND ORCHESTRA IN B FLAT see
Pleyel, Ignace Joseph

SYMPHONIE DE CHAMBRE see Bancquart,
Alain

SYMPHONIE D'ESPACE ET DE TEMPS, DE
MUSIQUE ET DE DANSE see Migot,
Georges, Symphony No. 13

SYMPHONIE "D'OMBRE ET DE LUMIERE" see
Lesur, Daniel

SYMPHONIE ESPAGNOLE, FOR VIOLIN AND
ORCHESTRA see Lalo, Edouard

SYMPHONIE FANTASTIQUE see Berlioz,
Hector (Louis)

SYMPHONIE FANTASTIQUE: MARCH TO THE
SCAFFOLD, [ARR.] see Berlioz,
Hector (Louis)

SYMPHONIE FUNEBRE ET TRIOMPHALE see
Berlioz, Hector (Louis)

SYMPHONIE PERIODIQUE NO. 10 see Pleyel,
Ignace Joseph

SYMPHONIE PERIODIQUE NO. 20 see Pleyel,
Ignace Joseph

SYMPHONIE PERIODIQUE NO. 25 see Pleyel,
Ignace Joseph

SYMPHONIE PERIODIQUE NO. 27 see Pleyel,
Ignace Joseph

SYMPHONIE SPIRITUELLE NO. 6 see
Hamerik, Asger

SYMPHONIES, FIFTEEN see Wagenseil,
Georg Christoph

SYMPHONIES, FIVE see Albrechtsberger,
Johann Georg

SYMPHONIES, FIVE see Haydn, [Johann]
Michael

SYMPHONIES, FIVE see Wanhal, Johann
Baptist (Jan Krtitel)

SYMPHONIES, FOUR see Adlgasser, Anton
Cajetan

SYMPHONIES, FOUR AND SYMPHONIE
CONCERTANTE see Pleyel, Ignace
Joseph

SYMPHONIES, NINE see Brunetti, Gaetano

SYMPHONIES, SEVEN see Gassmann, Florian
Leopold

SYMPHONIES, SEVEN see Ordonez, Carlo d'

SYMPHONIES, SIX see Kraus, Joseph
Martin

SYMPHONIES, SIX see Bach, Carl Philipp
Emanuel

SYMPHONIES, THREE see Eberlin, Johann
Ernst

SYMPHONIES, THREE see Paradeiser,
Marian (Carl)

SYMPHONIES, THREE see Spohr, Ludwig
(Louis)

SYMPHONIES, THREE see Ries, Ferdinand

SYMPHONIES, THREE see Mehul, Etienne-
Nicolas

SYMPHONIES, THREE see Bennett, [Sir]
William Sterndale

SYMPHONIES, TWO see Zechner, Johann
Georg

SYMPHONIES CONCERTANTES, FOR 2 VIOLINS
AND STRING ORCHESTRA, TWO see
Saint-Georges, Joseph Boulogne de

SYMPHONIES CONCERTANTES IN B FLAT AND
IN F see Ozi, Etienne

SYMPHONIES CONCERTANTES IN F AND B FLAT
see Devienne, Francois

SYMPHONIES IN C AND IN D see Herold,
Louis-Joseph-Ferdinand

SYMPHONIES IN C, IN F AND IN C see
Franzl, Ignaz

SYMPHONIES IN F, B FLAT AND D see
Rosetti, Francesco Antonio

SYMPHONIES, K. 128-130, 132-134, 141A
see Mozart, Wolfgang Amadeus

SYMPHONIES, K. 162, 184, 181-183, 199,
200 see Mozart, Wolfgang Amadeus

SYMPHONIES, K. 201, 202, 196, 297, 121,
208 see Mozart, Wolfgang Amadeus

SYMPHONIES, K. 204, 250, 320 see
Mozart, Wolfgang Amadeus

SYMPHONIES, K. 318, 319, 338, 385 see
Mozart, Wolfgang Amadeus

SYMPHONIES, K. 425, 504 see Mozart,
Wolfgang Amadeus

SYMPHONIES, K. 543, 550, 551 see
Mozart, Wolfgang Amadeus

SYMPHONIES, NOS. 1-4 see Brahms,
Johannes

SYMPHONIES NOS. 1-4 see Schumann,
Robert (Alexander)

SYMPHONIES, NOS. 1-5 see Beethoven,
Ludwig van

SYMPHONIES NOS.1-8 see Boyce, William

SYMPHONIES, NOS. 6-9 see Beethoven,
Ludwig van

SYMPHONIES, OP. 41 IN A AND OP. 42 IN D
MINOR see Onslow, Georges

SYMPHONIES POUR LES SOUPERS DU ROI:
DEUXIEME CAPRICE OU CAPRICE QUE LE
ROY DEMANDOIT SOUVENT, [ARR.] see
Delalande, Michel-Richard

SYMPHONIES POUR LES SOUPERS DU ROI:
PREMIER CAPRICE OU CAPRICE DE
VILLERS-COTTERETS, [ARR.] see
Delalande, Michel-Richard

SYMPHONIES POUR LES SOUPERS DU ROI:
TROISIEME CAPRICE, [ARR.] see
Delalande, Michel-Richard

SYMPHONIES, VOL.1 see Haydn, [Franz]
Joseph

SYMPHONIES, VOL.2 see Haydn, [Franz]
Joseph

SYMPHONIES, VOL.3 see Haydn, [Franz]
Joseph

SYMPHONIES, VOL.4 see Haydn, [Franz]
Joseph

SYMPHONIES, VOL.5 see Haydn, [Franz]
Joseph

SYMPHONIES, VOL.6 see Haydn, [Franz]
Joseph

SYMPHONIES, VOL.7 see Haydn, [Franz]
Joseph

SYMPHONIES, VOL.8 see Haydn, [Franz]
Joseph

SYMPHONIES, VOL.9 see Haydn, [Franz]
Joseph

SYMPHONIES, VOL.10 see Haydn, [Franz]
Joseph

SYMPHONIES, VOL.11 see Haydn, [Franz]
Joseph

SYMPHONIES, VOL.12 see Haydn, [Franz]
Joseph

SYMPHONIETTE see Kovach, Anton

SYMPHONIQUEPOEME ASUKA see Shimizu,
Yasuo

SYMPHONISCHE FANTASIE, FOR VIOLIN AND
STRINGS, OP. 59 see Raphael,
Gunther

SYMPHONISCHE IMPRESSION see Hamann,
Bernhard

SYMPHONISCHE SUITE IN D see Reznicek,
Emil Nikolaus von

SYMPHONISCHE SUITE IN E MINOR see
Reznicek, Emil Nikolaus von

SYMPHONISCHE VARIATIONEN UBER EIN
ORIGINALTHEMA UND FUGE see Lorenz,
Carl Adolf

SYMPHONY see Aumann, Franz Josef

SYMPHONY see Schneider, Franz

SYMPHONY A see Haydn, [Franz] Joseph,
Symphony No. 107 in B flat

SYMPHONY B see Haydn, [Franz] Joseph, Symphony No. 108 in B flat

SYMPHONY FOR OPEN STRINGS see Andriessen, Louis, Symfonie Voor Losse Snaren

SYMPHONY FROM SILENCE see Thorne, Nicholas C.K.

SYMPHONY IN MADRID, THE
(Shadko, Jacqueline A.) sc GARLAND ISBN 0-8240-3809-6 $90.00 "The Symphony", Vol. F-IV
contains: Balado, Juan, Sinfonia in D minor; Mayo, Felipe de, Sinfonia in F; Moral, Pablo del, Sinfonia in C; Moreno, Francisco Javier, Sinfonias In C, D And E Flat; Nono, Jose, Sinfonia in F (S1135)

SYMPHONY IN NORWAY, THE
(Kortsen, Bjarne) sc GARLAND ISBN 0-8240-3810-X $90.00 "The Symphony", Vol. F-I
contains: Berlin, Johan Daniel, Symphony in D; Berlin, Johan Henrich, Symphony in C; Falbe, Hans Hagerup, Symphony in D (S1136)

SYMPHONY IN POLAND, THE
sc GARLAND ISBN 0-8240-3820-7 $90.00 "The Symphony", Vol. F-VII
contains: Bohdanowicz, Bazyli, Symphony in D (Swierczek, Wendelin); Dobrzynski, Ignacy Feliks, Symphony, Op. 15, in C minor (Smialek, William); Golabek, Jakub, Symphony in D (Muchenberg, Bohdan); Orlowski, Michal, Symphony in F (Muchenberg, Bohdan); Pawlowski, Jakub, Symphony in B flat (Prosnak, Jan); Pietrowski, Karol, Symphony in D (Berwaldt, Jacek); Wanski, Jan, Symphony in D (Dabrowski, Florian) (S1137)

SYMPHONY IN SWEDEN, THE, PART 1
sc GARLAND ISBN 0-8240-3811-8 $90.00 "The Symphony", Vol. F-II
contains: Kraus, Joseph Martin, Symphonies, Six (Boer, Bertil H. van, Jr.); Roman, Johan Helmich, Sinfonias, Six (Bengtsson, Ingmar) (S1138)

SYMPHONY NO. 9 IN C see Schubert, Franz (Peter), Symphony No. 7 in C, D. 944

SYMPHONY OF SPIRITUALS see Gould, Morton

SYMPHONY OF THREE ORCHESTRAS, A see Carter, Elliott Cook, Jr.

SYMPHONY ON A FRENCH MOUNTAIN AIR see Indy, Vincent d', Symphonie Cevenole, For Piano And Orchestra

SYMPOSIUM see Wordsworth, William

SYYSPAIVA, FOR SOLO VOICE AND ORCHESTRA see Marvia, Einari

SYZYGY see Del Tredici, David

SZABO, CSABA
Nenia
(special import only) sc EMB 10176 f.s. (S1139)

SZEKELY, ENDRE (1912-   )
Concerto for Trumpet and Orchestra orch,trp solo
(special import only) sc EMB 10170 f.s. (S1140)

Sonores Nascentes Et Morientes
(special import only) sc EMB 10224 f.s. (S1141)

SZENE I-III see Nilsson, Bo

SZENEN, FOR VIOLONCELLO, HARP AND ORCHESTRA see Baird, Tadeusz

SZENEN EINER MONDNACHT see Bortz, Alfred

SZOLLOSY, ANDRAS (1921-   )
Concerto for Harpsichord and String Orchestra
string orch,hpsd solo
(special import only) sc EMB 10227 f.s. (S1142)

Sonorita
(special import only) sc EMB 7408 f.s. (S1143)

T

T.H.T. see Decoust, Michel

TABACHNIK, MICHEL
Cosmogonie Pour Une Rose [20']
SALABERT perf mat rent (T1)

Fresque
sc RICORDI-IT 131825 f.s. (T2)

Movimenti
sc RICORDI-IT 132113 f.s. (T3)

Sillages
32strings
sc RICORDI-IT 131973 f.s. (T4)

Supernovae
fl,clar,trp,trom,perc,cel,2harp, 2pno,vla,vcl
sc NOVELLO 2599 $55.00 (T5)

TABAKOV, EMIL
Lamento [8']
12db
YORKE 0080 perf mat rent (T6)

TABLEAUX see Rowland, David

TABORSKI, H.
Nachtlicher Bummel
(Plee, J.) RIES f.s. (T7)

TAFELMUSIK see Fischer, Johann Augsburgiensis

TAFELMUSIK III, NO. 3 see Telemann, Georg Philipp

TAGLIONI, LA see Vittadini, Franco

TAIGA see Kleine, Werner

TAILLE DE L'HOMME, LA, FOR SOLO VOICE AND INSTRUMENTAL ENSEMBLE see Markevitch, Igor

TAKEMITSU, TORU (1930-   )
Coral Island, For Solo Voice And Orchestra
study sc SALABERT $24.75 (T8)

Eucalypts, For Flute, Harp, Oboe And Orchestra
study sc SALABERT $23.75 (T9)

TAKO JE GODEL KURENT, FOR VIOLA AND ORCHESTRA see Petric, Ivo

TAL, JOSEPH (1910-   )
Concerto for Violoncello and String Orchestra [17']
string orch,vcl solo
study sc ISR.MUS.INST. IMI 007 $5.50 (T10)

TALARCZYK, JOZEF (1919-   )
aBaCaDa [15']
3.2.2.2. 0.3.4.0. perc,harp, 12vcl,8db
sc,fac ed POLSKIE $15.36 (T11)

TALE OF THE STONE FLOWER: WEDDING SUITE see Prokofiev, Serge

TALES FROM THE VIENNA WOODS see Strauss, Johann, [Jr.], Geschichten Aus Dem Wienerwald Walzer

TALES FROM THE VIENNA WOODS, FOR SOLO VOICE AND ORCHESTRA see Strauss, Johann, [Jr.], Geschichten Aus Dem Wienerwald Walzer, For Solo Voice And Orchestra

TALES OF HOFFMAN: LEGEND OF KLEINZACK see Offenbach, Jacques, Contes d'Hoffmann, Les: Il Etait Une Fois, For Solo Voice And Orchestra

TALES OF HOFFMANN: BARCAROLLE see Offenbach, Jacques, Contes d'Hoffmann, Les: Barcarolle, "O Belle Nuit, O Nuit d'Amour", For Solo Voice And Orchestra

TALES OF HOFFMANN: INTERMEZZO AND BARCAROLLE see Offenbach, Jacques, Contes d'Hoffmann, Les: Intermede Et Barcarolle

TALES OF HOFFMANN: THE DOLL SONG see Offenbach, Jacques, Contes d'Hoffmann, Les: Les Oiseaux Dans La Charmille, For Solo Voice And Orchestra

TAMBOURIN CHINOIS, [ARR.] see Kreisler, Fritz

TANCREDI: OVERTURE see Rossini, Gioacchino

TANDELEI see Jansen, Peter

TANDLER, JURAJ (1934-   )
Concert Music, For Clarinet And Orchestra *see Koncertna Hudba, For Clarinet And Orchestra

Games *see Hry

Hry
3.3.3.3. 4.1.1.1. perc,strings
"Games" SLOV.HUD.FOND 0-473 perf mat rent (T12)

Koncertna Hudba, For Clarinet And Orchestra
1.1.1.1. 0.1.1.1. timp,perc, strings,clar solo
"Concert Music, For Clarinet And Orchestra" SLOV.HUD.FOND 0-467 perf mat rent (T13)

TANGRAM see Lebic, Lojze

TANNHAUSER: DICH TEURE HALLE, FOR SOLO VOICE AND ORCHESTRA see Wagner, Richard

TANNHAUSER: EINZUG DER GASTE AUF DER WARTBURG see Wagner, Richard

TANNHAUSER: O DU MEIN HOLDER ABENDSTERN, FOR SOLO VOICE AND ORCHESTRA see Wagner, Richard

TANNHAUSER: OVERTURE see Wagner, Richard

TANNHAUSER: PRELUDE, ACT III see Wagner, Richard

TANTUM ERGO, FOR SOLO VOICE AND ORCHESTRA see Verdi, Giuseppe

TANZ ADRESSEN WALZER see Strauss, Josef

TANZ AUF DEM REGENBOGEN see Kamp, Hans

TANZ-CAPRICEN see Juon, Paul

TANZ DER GEIGEN see Loffler, Willy

TANZ DER MASKE see Rixner, Josef

TANZ IM SONNENSCHEIN see Hartmann, Bruno

TANZ-INTERMEZZO see Sibelius, Jean

TANZ PRIORITATEN WALZER see Strauss, Josef

TANZ-SUITE see Kletsch, Ludwig

TANZ-SYMPHONIE see Reznicek, Emil Nikolaus von

TANZE FUR ORCHESTER, [ARR.] see Mozart, Wolfgang Amadeus

TANZE, K. 65A, 103, 104, 105, 61H, 123, 164, 176, 101, 267, 122, 94 see Mozart, Wolfgang Amadeus

TANZMINIATUREN see Dressel, Erwin

TANZSUITE MIT DEUTSCHLANDLIED see Lachenmann, Helmut Friedrich

TANZWEISEN AUS OSTERREICH see Kienzl, Wilhelm

TAORMINA see Erhardt, Siegfried

TARANTELLA see Rossmann, Richard

TARANTELLE, [ARR.] see Liszt, Franz

TARAS BULBA: SUITE see Waxman, Franz

TARENTELLE, FOR FLUTE, CLARINET AND ORCHESTRA see Saint-Saens, Camille

TARENTELLE, FOR VIOLONCELLO AND ORCHESTRA see Popper, David

TARENTINA, LA see Winkler, Gerhard

TARP, SVEND ERIK (1908-   )
Symphony No. 5
2.2.2.2. 4.3.3.0. perc,cel, strings
SAMFUNDET perf mat rent (T14)

Symphony No. 6 [27']
2.2.2.2. 4.3.3.0. timp,perc,pno, strings
SAMFUNDET perf mat rent (T15)

Symphony No. 7
2.2.2.2. 4.3.3.0. timp,2perc,pno, strings
SAMFUNDET perf mat rent (T16)

TARPEJA: TRIUMPH-MARSCH see Beethoven,
Ludwig van

TARTINI, GIUSEPPE (1692-1770)
Concerto for Violin and String
Orchestra in A, Dounias 96 [18']
string orch,cont,vln solo
(Farina, Edoardo) sc,pts CARISCH
CM 21877 f.s.   (T17)

Concerto for Violin and String
Orchestra in B flat, Dounias 117
[16']
string orch,cont,vln solo
(Scimone, Claudio) sc,pts CARISCH
CM 21962 f.s.   (T18)

Concerto for Violin and String
Orchestra in C, Dounias 12 [15']
string orch,cont,vln solo
(Scimone, Claudio) sc,pts CARISCH
CM 21948 f.s.   (T19)

Concerto for Violin and String
Orchestra in D, Dounias 21 [12']
string orch,cont,vln solo
(Scimone, C.) sc CARISCH 21971
f.s., pts CARISCH 21971A f.s.
                                   (T20)

Concerto for Violin and String
Orchestra in D, Dounias 24 [15']
string orch,cont,vln solo
(Farina, Edoardo) sc,pts CARISCH
CM 21866 f.s.   (T21)

Concerto for Violin and String
Orchestra in D minor, MIN 96
string orch,vln solo
(Scherchen, H.) KALMUS A3250 solo
pt $1.50, sc $2.50, set $5.00,
pts $1.00, ea.   (T22)

Concerto for Violin and String
Orchestra in E minor, Dounias 56
[18']
string orch,cont,vln solo
(Scimone, C.) sc CARISCH 21885
f.s., pts CARISCH 21885A f.s.
                                   (T23)

Concerto for Violin and String
Orchestra in F, Dounias 67 [11']
string orch,cont,vln solo
(Farina, Edoardo) sc,pts CARISCH
CM 21878 f.s.   (T24)

Concerto for Violin and String
Orchestra in G, Dounias 78 [15']
string orch,cont,vln solo
(Scimone, Claudio) sc,pts CARISCH
CM 21884 f.s.   (T25)

Concerto for Violin and String
Orchestra in G, Dounias 83 [15']
string orch,cont,vln solo
(Farina, Edoardo) sc,pts CARISCH
CM 21953 f.s.   (T26)

Sinfonia in A, MIN 527
string orch
LUCKS 01527 sc $3.00, set $5.00,
pts $1.00, ea.   (T27)

TASHI see Wuorinen, Charles

TAUBE, EVERT (1890-1976)
Taube-Suite, For Solo Voice And
Orchestra, [arr.]
(Bjorlin, Ulf) 2.2.2.2. 4.3.3.1.
timp,perc,harp,strings,solo voice
STIM perf mat rent   (T28)

TAUBE-SUITE, FOR SOLO VOICE AND
ORCHESTRA, [ARR.] see Taube, Evert

TAUBERT, [KARL GOTTFRIED] WILHELM
(1811-1891)
Concerto for Piano and Orchestra, No.
2, Op. 189 [23']
2.0.2.2. 2.0.0.0. strings,pno
solo
sc,pts LIENAU rent   (T29)

TAURIELLO, ANTONIO (1931-   )
Serenade, No. 2
fl,ob,clar,perc,strings
sc BARRY-ARG $9.00   (T30)

TAUSEND UND EINE NACHT WALZER see
Strauss, Johann, [Jr.]

TAUTENHAHN, GUNTHER (1938-   )
Chromatic Square [3']
2(pic).2(English horn).2(bass
clar).2(contrabsn). 5.4.2.1.
timp,3perc,harp,pno,strings
SEESAW   (T31)

Concerto for Saxophone and Orchestra
[25']
2(pic).2(English
horn).2.2(contrabsn). 6.3.2.1.
2perc,harp,pno,strings,alto sax
solo
SEESAW   (T32)

TAUTENHAHN, GUNTHER (cont'd.)

Concerto for Trumpet and Instrumental
Ensemble [12']
0(pic).0(English horn).0(alto
sax).1. 1.0.0.0. perc,harp,vln,
vla,vcl,trp solo
SEESAW   (T33)

Concerto for Viola and Orchestra
[15']
1(pic).1(English horn).1(bass
clar).1(contrabsn). 2.0.0.0.
perc,harp,vln,vcl,vla solo
SEESAW   (T34)

Monochrome Overture, For Piano And
Orchestra [9']
1.1(English horn).1(bass
clar).1.tenor sax.
1.1(cornet).2.1. 2perc,gtr,pno,
5vln,4vla,3vcl,pno solo
SEESAW   (T35)

Numeric Serenade, For Piano And
Orchestra [9']
2(pic).2(English
horn).2.2(contrabsn). 4.2.1.0.
perc,timp,harp,strings,pno solo
SEESAW   (T36)

Of Dreams And Nightmares [12']
1.1.1.1. 0.2.0.0. pno,2vln,vla,
vcl
SEESAW   (T37)

Prelude [5']
2.2.2.1. 2.2.1.1. 2perc,harp,
strings
SEESAW   (T38)

TCHAIKOVSKY, PIOTR ILYICH (1840-1893)
Andante Cantabile, [arr.] (from
String Quartet No. 1, Op. 11)
LUCKS 06884 sc $2.00, set $4.75,
pts $.95, ea.   (T39)

Capriccio Italien *Op.45
pts BROUDE BR. $1.50, ea.   (T40)
min sc PETERS 566 $6.00   (T41)

Concerto for Piano and Orchestra, No.
1, Op. 23, in B flat minor
BROUDE BR. pts $1.75, ea., set
$35.00   (T42)
min sc PETERS 564 $9.00   (T43)
min sc ZEN-ON 891641 f.s.   (T44)

Concerto for Piano and Orchestra, No.
2, Op. 44, in G
LUCKS 00079 sc $28.00, set $55.00,
min sc $5.50, pts $2.00, ea.   (T45)

Concerto for Violin and Orchestra,
Op. 35, in D
BROUDE BR. set $32.50, pts $1.75,
ea.   (T46)
min sc ZEN-ON 891645 f.s.   (T47)

Eugene Onegin: Aria Of Lenski, For
Solo Voice And Orchestra
"Eugene Onegin: Wohin, Wohin Seid
Ihr Entschwunden" LUCKS 02410 sc
$4.00, set $8.00, pts $.60, ea.
                                   (T48)

Eugene Onegin: Letter Scene, For Solo
Voice And Orchestra
LUCKS 02146 sc $6.00, set $14.00,
pts $.95, ea.   (T49)

Eugene Onegin: Polonaise
LUCKS 06890 sc $8.50, set $18.00,
pts $1.15, ea.   (T50)

Eugene Onegin: Waltz
LUCKS 08596 sc $8.50, set $20.00,
pts $1.15, ea.   (T51)

Eugene Onegin: Wohin, Wohin Seid Ihr
Entschwunden *see Eugene Onegin:
Aria Of Lenski, For Solo Voice
And Orchestra

Francesca Da Rimini. Fantasy *Op.32
min sc INTERNAT. 618 $7.00   (T52)

Hamlet, [arr.] *Op.67
(Andreae, M.) 2.2.2.2. 2.0.3.0.
timp,perc,strings [5'] BELAIEFF
perf mat rent   (T53)

Hungarian Gypsy Airs, [arr.]
(Menter, Sophie) KALMUS 5450 sc
$25.00, perf mat rent, set
$60.00, pts $3.00, ea.   (T54)

Iolanthe: Wer Kann Mit Mathilden Sich
Messen An Macht, For Solo Voice
And Orchestra
LUCKS 02682 set $15.50, pts $.75,
ea.   (T55)

Jeanne D'Arc: Adieu Forets *see Maid
Of Orleans, The: Farewell,
Forests, For Solo Voice And
Orchestra

TCHAIKOVSKY, PIOTR ILYICH (cont'd.)

Maid Of Orleans, The: Farewell,
Forests, For Solo Voice And
Orchestra
"Jeanne D'Arc: Adieu Forets" LUCKS
02017 sc $5.00, set $7.50, pts
$.75, ea.   (T56)

Marche Slave *Op.31
LUCKS 06894 sc $12.00, set $23.00,
min sc $3.00, pts $1.15, ea.
                                   (T57)
"Slavonian March" min sc ZEN-ON
891652 f.s.   (T58)

Marche Solennelle *Op. Posth.
2+pic.2+English horn.2.2.
4.2.3.1. timp,perc,2harp,
strings
KALMUS A5502 sc $9.00, perf mat
rent, set $30.00, pts $1.50, ea.
                                   (T59)

Mazeppa: Overture [8']
3(pic).2+English horn.2.2. 4.2+
2cornet.3.1. timp,perc,strings
KALMUS A2433 sc $15.00, perf mat
rent, set $32.00, pts $1.50, ea.
                                   (T60)

None But The Lonely Heart, For Solo
Voice And Orchestra, [arr.]
"Nur Wer Die Sehnsucht Kennt" LUCKS
02234 sc $2.75, set $7.50, pts
$.75, ea.   (T61)

Nur Wer Die Sehnsucht Kennt *see
None But The Lonely Heart, For
Solo Voice And Orchestra, [arr.]

Nutcracker: Pas De Deux
LUCKS 07156 set $35.00, pts $2.00,
ea.   (T62)

Nutcracker: Suite *Op.71a
pts BROUDE BR. $2.50, ea.   (T63)
LUCKS 06897 sc $15.00, set $28.00,
min sc $4.50, pts $1.50, ea.
                                   (T64)

Opritchnik: Overture
KALMUS 5161 sc $5.00, perf mat
rent, set $35.00, pts $1.50, ea.
                                   (T65)

Orage, L': Overture *Op.76
"Storm, The" KALMUS A5140 sc
$16.00, perf mat rent, set
$35.00, pts $1.50, ea.   (T66)

Ouverture Solennelle *see Overture
1812

Overture 1812 *Op.49 [16']
3.3.2.2. 4.2+2cornet.3.1. timp,
perc,strings
pts BROUDE BR. $1.75   (T67)
"Ouverture Solennelle" sc,pts
BREITKOPF-W PB-OB 4895 f.s. (T68)
"Ouverture Solennelle" min sc ZEN-
ON 891651 f.s.   (T69)

Pathetique Symphony *see Symphony
No. 6, Op. 74, in B minor

Pezzo Capriccioso, For Violoncello
And Orchestra *Op.62
LUCKS 00614 sc $6.00, set $15.00,
pts $1.00, ea.   (T70)

Pilgrim's Song, For Solo Voice And
Orchestra, [arr.]
LUCKS 02684 set $8.50, pts $.75,
ea.   (T71)

Pique Dame: Prince Yeletsky's Aria
*see Queen Of Spades: I Love You,
Dear, For Solo Voice And
Orchestra

Queen Of Spades: I Love You, Dear,
For Solo Voice And Orchestra
"Pique Dame: Prince Yeletsky's
Aria" LUCKS 02683 sc $5.00, set
$12.00, pts $.75, ea.   (T72)

Romeo And Juliet. Overture-Fantasy
BROUDE BR. set $35.00, pts $2.25,
ea.   (T73)
LUCKS 06904 sc $15.00, set $28.00,
min sc $4.00, pts $1.75, ea.
                                   (T74)

Seasons, The, [arr.] *Op.37a
(Hofmann) sc,quarto PETERS 8370
$23.50, perf mat rent   (T75)

Serenade Melancolique, Op. 26, For
Horn And Orchestra, [arr.]
(Heermann, Walter) 2.1.2.2.
3.0.0.0. strings,horn solo [8']
MARGUN BP 7029 perf mat rent
                                   (T76)

Serenade, Op. 48, in C
BROUDE BR. sc $5.00, set $11.25,
pts $2.25, ea.   (T77)
min sc ZEN-ON 891672 f.s.   (T78)

TCHAIKOVSKY, PIOTR ILYICH (cont'd.)

Slavonian March *see Marche Slave

Sleeping Beauty, The: Pas De Deux,
   Act III
   2+pic.2+English horn.2.2. 4.2+
   2cornet.3.1. timp,perc,strings
   KALMUS A4190 sc $16.00, perf mat
   rent, set $35.00, pts $2.00, ea.
                                        (T79)

Sleeping Beauty, The: Pas De Quatre,
   "Bluebird"
   3+pic.2.2.2. 2.2.2.0. timp,
   strings
   KALMUS A4352 sc $12.00, perf mat
   rent, set $35.00, pts $2.00, ea.
                                        (T80)

Souvenir D'Un Lieu Cher: Mediatation,
   For Violin And Orchestra, [arr.]
   *Op.42,No.1
   (Glazunow) LUCKS 00545 sc $5.00,
   set $10.00, pts $1.00, ea.   (T81)

Souvenir D'Un Lieu Cher: Scherzo, For
   Violin And Orchestra, [arr.]
   *Op.42,No.2
   (Glazunow) LUCKS 00546 sc $5.50,
   set $11.00, pts $.95, ea.   (T82)

Storm, The *see Orage, L': Overture

Suite No. 1, Op. 43, [excerpt]
   2+pic.2.2.2. 4.2.0.0. timp,
   strings
   (Intermezzo) KALMUS A5158 sc
   $25.00, perf mat rent, set
   $60.00, pts $1.00, ea.   (T83)
   (Marche Miniature) LUCKS 06906 sc
   $4.50, set $7.50, pts $.95, ea.
                                        (T84)

Swan Lake: Overture, Act II
   2.2.2.2. 4.2.3.1. timp,harp,
   strings
   KALMUS A4544 sc $6.00, perf mat
   rent, set $20.00, pts $1.00, ea.
                                        (T85)

Swan Lake: Pas De Deux, "Black Swan"
   [5']
   2+pic.2.2.2. 4.2+2cornet.3.1.
   timp,perc,strings
   KALMUS A4637 sc $12.00, perf mat
   rent, set $30.00, pts $1.50, ea.
                                        (T86)

Swan Lake: Pas De Deux, "White Swan"
   2+pic.2.2.2. 4.2+2cornet.3.1.
   timp,perc,harp,strings
   KALMUS A5461 sc $15.00, perf mat
   rent, set $30.00, pts $1.50, ea.
                                        (T87)

Swan Lake: Pas De Trois
   2+pic.2.2.2. 4.2+2cornet.3.1.
   timp,perc,harp,strings
   KALMUS A4033 sc $10.00, perf mat
   rent, set $40.00, pts $2.00, ea.
                                        (T88)

Swan Lake: Suite
   min sc BOOSEY 301 $6.00   (T89)

Symphony No. 1, Op. 13, in G minor
   LUCKS 09138 sc $30.00, set $60.00,
   min sc $6.00, pts $3.50, ea.
                                        (T90)

Symphony No. 2, Op. 17, in C minor
   min sc BOOSEY 627 $7.50   (T91)

Symphony No. 4, Op. 36, in F minor
   pts BROUDE BR. $2.75, ea.   (T92)
   min sc PETERS 561 $8.50   (T93)
   (reprint of Breitkopf and Hartel
   edition) study sc DOVER 23861-X
   $12.95 contains also: Symphony
   No. 5, Op. 64, in E minor;
   Symphony No. 6, Op. 74, in B
   minor   (T94)
   min sc ZEN-ON 891601 f.s.   (T95)

Symphony No. 5, Op. 64, in E minor
   see Tchaikovsky, Piotr Ilyich,
   Symphony No. 4, Op. 36, in F
   minor
   min sc ZEN-ON 891602 f.s.   (T96)
   min sc UNIVER. PH63 $8.00   (T97)
   min sc BOOSEY 194 $6.00   (T98)
   pts BROUDE BR. $2.25, ea.   (T99)
   min sc PETERS 562 $8.50   (T100)

Symphony No. 6, Op. 74, in B minor
   see Tchaikovsky, Piotr Ilyich,
   Symphony No. 4, Op. 36, in F
   minor
   min sc ZEN-ON 891603 f.s.   (T101)
   pts BROUDE BR. $2.75, ea.   (T102)
   min sc PETERS 563 $8.50   (T103)

Symphony No. 7 in E flat
   *reconstruction
   [38'] INTERNAT. perf mat rent
                                       (T104)

Triumphal Overture On A Danish
   National Hymn *Op.15 [15']
   2+pic.2.2.2. 4.2.3.1. timp,perc,
   strings
   KALMUS 5187 sc $15.00, perf mat
   rent, set $40.00, pts $2.00, ea.
                                       (T105)

TCHAIKOVSKY, PIOTR ILYICH (cont'd.)

Valse Scherzo, For Violin And
   Orchestra *Op.34
   LUCKS 01678 sc $7.50, set $18.00,
   pts $.75, ea.   (T106)

Variations On A Rococo Theme, For
   Violoncello And Orchestra *Op.33
   "Variations Sur Un Theme Rococo"
   LUCKS 00618 sc $16.00, set
   $23.00, min sc $5.50, pts $1.75,
   ea.   (T107)

Variations Sur Un Theme Rococo *see
   Variations On A Rococo Theme, For
   Violoncello And Orchestra

Voyevode, Op. 3: Overture
   KALMUS A2434 sc $15.00, perf mat
   rent, set $30.00, pts $1.50, ea.
                                       (T108)

Was I Not A Blade, For Solo Voice And
   Orchestra, [arr.] *Op.47,No.7
   LUCKS 02191 sc $4.00, set $12.50,
   pts $.75, ea.   (T109)

TCHEREPNIN, ALEXANDER (1899-1977)
Lost Flute, The, For Narrator And
   Orchestra
   2.4.2.2. 0.2.1.0. timp,perc,harp,
   strings,speaking voice
   BELAIEFF perf mat rent   (T110)

**TCHEREPNIN, IVAN ALEXANDROVITCH
   (1943-)**
Va Et Le Vient, Le
   3.3.3.3.sax. 4.3.3.1. 4perc,harp,
   strings
   BELAIEFF perf mat rent   (T111)

TECUM PRINCIPIUM, FOR SOLO VOICE AND
   ORCHESTRA see Bellini, Vincenzo

TELEGRAFISCHE DEPESCHEN. WALZER see
   Strauss, Johann, [Jr.]

TELEGRAMME WALZER see Strauss, Johann,
   [Jr.]

TELEMANN, GEORG PHILIPP (1681-1767)
Concerto in A, MIN 69
   2fl,bsn,strings,cont
   (Fleischhauer, G.) sc BREITKOPF-W
   PB 4058 f.s., pts BREITKOPF-W
   OB 4058 f.s.   (T112)

Concerto in B flat, MIN 31
   2fl,ob,strings,cont
   (Fleischhauer) PETERS P9411 sc
   $23.50, set $25.00, pts $2.25,
   ea.   (T113)

Concerto in B flat, MIN 70
   2fl,2ob,strings,cont
   (Komma, K.M.) sc BREITKOPF-W
   PB 3886 f.s., pts BREITKOPF-W
   OB 3886 f.s.   (T114)

Concerto in C minor, MIN 71
   string orch,cont,ob solo,vln solo
   (Beckmann, K.) sc BREITKOPF-W
   PB 4062 f.s., pts BREITKOPF-W
   OB 4062 f.s.   (T115)

Concerto in D, MIN 32
   string orch,cont,trp solo
   (Thilde, Jean) (in this edition
   called Concerto No. 2) sc
   BILLAUDOT $7.25, perf mat rent
                                       (T116)

Concerto in D, MIN 66
   string orch,cont,vln solo
   (Kross, Siegfried) sc,pts NAGELS
   NMA 244 f.s.   (T117)

Concerto in D, MIN 110
   2fl,strings,cont,vln solo,vcl
   solo
   (Fleischhauer) sc,pts PETERS
   EP 9823 f.s.   (T118)

Concerto in E flat, MIN 3 *see
   Tafelmusik III, No. 3

Concerto in E minor, MIN 11
   (Schroeder) KALMUS A2159 sc $10.00,
   set $10.00, pts $1.50, ea. (T119)

Concerto in F, MIN 65
   string orch,cont,ob solo,vln solo
   sc,pts MUS. RARA 41.940-20 f.s.
                                       (T120)

Concerto in F, MIN 815
   (Angerhofer, G.) sc BREITKOPF-W
   PB 3948 f.s., pts BREITKOPF-W
   OB 3948 f.s.   (T121)

Concerto in G, [arr.], MIN 97
   string orch,cont,vla solo [11']
   KALMUS A3267 solo pt $1.00, sc
   $5.00, set $5.00, pts $1.00, ea.
                                       (T122)

Concerto in G, MIN 40
   string orch,cont,vla solo
   LUCKS 00855 sc $3.00, set $4.75,

TELEMANN, GEORG PHILIPP (cont'd.)

   pts $.95, ea.   (T123)

Concerto in G, MIN 51
   string orch,cont,fl solo
   sc AMADEUS BP 2662 f.s., pts
   AMADEUS f.s.   (T124)

Concerto in G, MIN 55 [10']
   string orch,vla solo
   INTERNAT. perf mat rent   (T125)

Concerto in G, MIN 671
   orch,vln solo LUCKS 01671 sc $7.50,
   set $11.50, min sc $2.00, pts
   $1.40, ea.   (T126)

Don Quichotte Suite (Suite in G, No.
   10)
   string orch,cont
   BROUDE BR. sc $6.00, set $15.00,
   pts $1.25, ea.   (T127)
   "Don Quixote Suite" LUCKS 08903 sc
   $5.50, set $10.00, pts $.95, ea.
                                       (T128)

Don Quixote Suite *see Don Quichotte
   Suite

Franzosische Ouverture, In A Minor
   string orch
   [7'] PETERS H 72 perf mat rent
                                       (T129)

Jauchzet Dem Herrn, For Solo Voice
   And Orchestra
   ob/trp,strings,cont,B solo
   (Schroeder, F.) sc,pts LEUCKART 43
   f.s.   (T130)

Liebster Jesu, Kehre Wieder, For Solo
   Voice And Orchestra
   2fl,org,strings,S solo
   [Ger] VIEWEG V133 sc $6.50, set
   $12.00, pts $1.75, ea.   (T131)

Meine Seele Erhebt Den Herren, For
   Solo Voice And Orchestra
   fl,strings,cont,S solo
   (known as "Kleines Madnificat" by
   J.S. Bach) sc HANSSLER 10.139-01
   f.s., pts HANSSLER
   10.139-11:14, 21 f.s.   (T132)

Ouverture In D, Min 72 (Suite in D,
   No. 22)
   opt 2ob,3trp,timp,strings,cont
   (Hobohm, W.) (WV 55, D22) sc
   BREITKOPF-W PB-4060 f.s., pts
   BREITKOPF-W OB-4060 f.s.   (T133)

Ouverture In D, Min 73 (Suite in D,
   No. 18)
   opt 2ob,2trp,timp,strings,cont
   (Thom, E.; Maertens, W.) (TWV 55,
   D18) sc BREITKOPF-W PB-4061 f.s.,
   pts BREITKOPF-W OB-4061 f.s.
                                       (T134)

Ouverture Zu Der Geduldige Sokrates
   2ob,strings,cont
   (Baselt, Bernd) BAREN. BA 6553 perf
   mat rent   (T135)

Overture in A minor, MIN 89
   2rec,2ob,strings
   sc,pts HARMONIA 2084 f.s.   (T136)

Sonata in G, MIN 56 [11']
   string orch,cont,vla solo
   INTERNAT. perf mat rent   (T137)

Suite in A minor, MIN 62
   string orch,cont,A rec/fl solo
   sc,pts LEDUC f.s.   (T138)

Suite in A minor, No. 1
   string orch,cont
   LUCKS 01529 sc $3.00, set $3.75,
   pts $.75, ea.   (T139)
   (Schering, A.) KALMUS A1125 kbd pt
   $2.00, sc $3.00, set $3.75, pts
   $.75, ea.   (T140)

Suite in A minor, No. 2
   string orch,cont,fl solo
   LUCKS 07118 sc $5.50, set $8.70,
   pts $.95, ea.   (T141)

Suite in D, MIN 15
   string orch,cont,trp solo
   sc,pts MUS. RARA 41.935-20 f.s.
                                       (T142)

Suite in D, No. 6
   (Schulz) LUCKS 01311 sc $13.50, set
   $22.50, min sc $13.50, pts $3.00,
   ea.   (T143)

Suite in D, No. 18 *see Ouverture In
   D, Min 73

Suite in D, No. 22 *see Ouverture In
   D, Min 72

Suite in F, MIN 4
   (Buettner) KALMUS A5282 sc $5.00,
   set $6.00, pts $1.00, ea.   (T144)

TELEMANN, GEORG PHILIPP (cont'd.)

Suite in G, No. 10 *see Don Quichotte Suite

Tafelmusik III, No. 3 (Concerto in E flat, MIN 3)
KALMUS A2158 sc $15.00, set $8.00, pts $1.50, ea.   (T145)

TELEOLOGIES see Karkoschka, Erhard

TEMA CON 6 VARIAZIONI, FOR FLUTE AND ORCHESTRA see Ketting, Piet

TEMA CON VARIAZIONI see Ettorre, Igino

TEMA CON VARIAZIONI see Zagwijn, Henri

TEMA VARIATO see Alessandro, Rafaele d'

TEMA, VARIAZIONI E FUGA see Toni, Alceo

TEMPELWEIHE see Becce, Giuseppe

TEMPEST, THE see Sullivan, [Sir] Arthur Seymour

TEMPEST, THE: INCIDENTAL MUSIC see Locke, Matthew

TEMPETE, LA see Chausson, Ernest

TEMPO ALTO see Lavagnino, Angelo Francesco

TEMPO DI CARNEVALE: OVERTURE see Farina, Guido

TEMPO DI CONCERTO, FOR TRUMPET AND ORCHESTRA see Bossi, Renzo

TEMPO DI SCHERZO see Bossi, [Marco] Enrico

TEMPO DI SONATA, [ARR.] see Bach, Johann Sebastian

TEMPO E FANTASIA, FOR PIANO AND STRING ORCHESTRA see Soresina, Alberto

TEMPO SINFONICO, FOR PIANO AND ORCHESTRA see Casagrande, Alessandro

TEMPTATION see Kirchstein, Harold M.

TEMPUS IMPLETUM see Denhoff, Michael

10-5-6-5-(A) see Porcelijn, David

TERGI I VEZZOSI RAI, FOR SOLO VOICE AND ORCHESTRA see Haydn, [Franz] Joseph

TERMOS, PAUL (1942-   )
Lustobjekt
3.1.3.2.soprano sax. 1.2.2.0. pno,strings
DONEMUS perf mat rent   (T146)

TERPSICORE: BALLET SUITE see Handel, George Frideric

TERPSTRA, KOOS (1948-   )
Arpino-Ouverture [4']
2.0.1.0. 0.1.1.0. 2perc,pno, strings without vla
sc DONEMUS f.s., perf mat rent   (T147)
Impossible Future, For Soli And Small Orchestra
2.2.2.0. 1.1.1.0. pno/elec org, strings, soli: mobile ensemble
sc DONEMUS f.s., perf mat rent   (T148)
Mimesis, For Instrumental Quintet And Chamber Orchestra [10']
0.0.0.0.soprano sax. 2.2.3.0. 3perc,bass gtr,6vln,3vla,2vcl, db,pic solo,fl solo,alto fl solo,ob solo,clar solo, 7 saw-blades
sc DONEMUS f.s., perf mat rent   (T149)

TERRE EST UN HOMME, LA see Ferneyhough, Brian

TERRIBLE POWER see Porcelijn, David

TERVE PAIVA POHJOLAHAN, FOR SOLO VOICE AND ORCHESTRA, [ARR.] see Madetoja, Leevi

TERZAKIS, DIMITRI (1938-   )
Hommage A Dionysos [13']
2.2.2.2. 2.2.2.1. 2perc,harp, strings
BREITKOPF-W perf mat rent   (T150)

Ichochronos II [9']
fl,clar,horn,tuba,timp,perc,2vln, vla,vcl,db, lotosflote
BREITKOPF-W perf mat rent   (T151)

TERZAKIS, DIMITRI (cont'd.)

Proimion In Ethos C [10']
1.1.1.1. 1.1.1.0. perc,strings
BREITKOPF-W perf mat rent   (T152)

Tropi [15']
2.2.2.2. 2.2.2.0. 2perc,harp, strings
BREITKOPF-W perf mat rent   (T153)

TESSIER, ROGER (1939-   )
Isomerie [16'30"]
9vln,3vla,2vcl,db
SALABERT   (T154)

TESSINER HERBSTLIED see Pero, Hans

TESTAMENT, FOR SOLO VOICE AND ORCHESTRA see Duparc, Henri

TESTI, FLAVIO (1923-   )
Opus 21
sc RICORDI-IT 131905 f.s.   (T155)

Opus 23
sc RICORDI-IT 132044 f.s.   (T156)

TETRASTIQUE see Henkemans, Hans

THAIS: MEDITATION see Massenet, Jules

THANKSGIVING OVERTURE, A see George, Earl Robert

THAUPERLE POLKA see Strauss, Eduard

THEATER QUADRILLE see Strauss, Josef

THEME AND VARIATIONS, FOR VIOLA AND ORCHESTRA see Weber, Carl Maria von

THEODORAKIS, MIKIS (1925-   )
Oedipus Tyrannos
string orch
sc BOOSEY $10.00   (T157)

THEORIEN WALZER see Strauss, Eduard

THERE IS NO STREAM see Sallinen, Aulis, Ei Mikaan Virta

THEY ARE TELLING US see Brons, Carel

THIELE, SIEGFRIED (1934-   )
Concerto for Organ and Orchestra
3trp,4trom,timp,perc,org solo
sc DEUTSCHER 1430 f.s.   (T158)

Hommage A Marchaut, For Solo Voice And Orchestra [25']
2.2.1.1. 0.2.1.0. perc,harp, strings,A/Bar solo
sc PETERS EP 9215 f.s., perf mat rent   (T159)

Ubungen Im Verwandeln [20']
string orch
DEUTSCHER perf mat rent   (T160)

Wolkenbilder [14']
1.2.0.0. 2.0.0.0. strings
sc DEUTSCHER DVFM 1703 f.s., perf mat rent   (T161)

THIRTY PIECES FOR FIVE ORCHESTRAS see Cage, John

THOMAS, AMBROISE (1811-1896)
Caid, Le: Le Tambour-Major, For Solo Voice And Orchestra
LUCKS 02042 set $7.50, pts $.75, ea.   (T162)

Hamlet: Chanson Bachique, For Solo Voice And Orchestra
LUCKS 02320 sc $10.00, set $11.00, pts $.75, ea.   (T163)

Mignon: Connais-Tu Le Pays?, For Solo Voice And Orchestra
LUCKS 02153 sc $4.00, set $8.00, pts $.75, ea.   (T164)

Mignon: Je Suis Titania, For Solo Voice And Orchestra
LUCKS 02068 sc $4.75, set $8.50, pts $.75, ea.   (T165)

Mignon: Legeres Hirondelles, For Solo Voices And Orchestra
LUCKS 02973 sc $4.00, set $7.50, pts $.75, ea.   (T166)

Mignon: Rondo-Gavotte, "Me Voici Dans Son Boudoir", For Solo Voice And Orchestra
LUCKS 02467 sc $4.00, set $7.50, pts $.75, ea.   (T167)

THOMASSEN, THOMAS
Hawok
RIES f.s.   (T168)

THOMMESSEN, OLAV ANTON (1946-   )
Barbaresk *Op.15b
2.2.2.2.alto sax. 4.3.3.1. timp, perc,strings
[10'] sc MUSIKK f.s.   (T169)

Macro Fantasy On Grieg's A Minor, For Piano And Orchestra
3(pic).3(English horn).3(bass clar).3(contrabsn). 4.2.3.1. timp,perc,org,strings,pno solo
NORGE   (T170)

Two Sizes For Strings
string orch
NORGE   (T171)

THOMSON, VIRGIL GARNETT (1896-   )
Collected Poems, For Solo Voices And Orchestra
1.1.1.1. 0.1.0.0. perc,strings, SBar soli
PEER perf mat rent   (T172)

From Byron's Don Juan: Shipwreck And Love Scene, For Solo Voice And Orchestra
4.3+English horn.4.4. 4.4.4.1. timp,perc,harp,pno,strings,T solo
sc PEER $16.00, perf mat rent   (T173)

THORNE, NICHOLAS C.K. (1953-   )
Symphony From Silence
MARGUN   (T174)

THORPE DAVIE, CEDRIC (1913-   )
Fantasia No. 1 [13']
3.3.3.3. 4.3.3.1. timp,perc,harp, strings
sc SCOTUS 264-4 f.s.   (T175)

Fantasia No. 2 [19']
3.3.3.3. 4.3.3.1. timp,perc,harp, strings
sc SCOTUS 269-5 f.s.   (T176)

New Town Suite [22']
2+pic.2.2.2. 4.2.3.0. timp,perc, strings
sc SCOTUS 274-1 f.s.   (T177)

Royal Mile [9']
3.2.2.2. 4.3.3.1. timp,perc, strings
sc SCOTUS 297-0 f.s.   (T178)

Symphony in C [18']
3.2.3.2. 4.3.3.1. timp,perc, strings
sc SCOTUS 279-2 f.s.   (T179)

THOUGHTS, FOR SOLO VOICE AND ORCHESTRA see Rypdal, Terje

THOUSAND AND ONE NIGHTS WALTZ see Strauss, Johann, [Jr.], Tausend Und Eine Nacht Walzer

THREE COLLOQUIES, FOR HORN AND ORCHESTRA see Schuman, William Howard

THREE DANCE SEQUENCES 'THE CONTINUING STORY' see Carpenter, Gary

THREE DANCES see Bokes, Vladimir, Tri Tance

THREE DANCES see Wagemans, Peter-Jan

THREE DANCES, FOR CLARINET AND STRING ORCHESTRA see Lerstad, Terje B.

THREE DREAMS EACH WITHIN EACH see Sallinen, Aulis, On Kolme Unta Sisakkain

THREE ENTRADAS FOR ADVENT AND CHRISTMAS see Altenburg, Michael, Drei Intraden Zu Advent Und Weihnacht

THREE HYMNS TO APOLLO see Samuel, Gerhard

THREE IRISH PICTURES see Victory, Gerard

THREE LUTE FANTASIES, [ARR.] see Bakfark, Balint (Valentin)

THREE MOVEMENTS FROM CONTEMPLATIONS, FOR PIANO AND ORCHESTRA see Suchon, Eugen, Tri Casti Z Kontemplacii, For Piano And Orchestra

THREE NIGERIAN DANCES see Akpabot, Samuel

THREE NORWEGIAN PIECES see Grieg, Edvard Hagerup

THREE ORCHESTRAL PIECES see Delius, Frederick

THREE OVERTURES (TOCCATA-FESTIVAL-
PASTORAL) see Rice, Thomas

THREE PICTURES see Pusztai, Tibor

THREE PIECES see Fongaard, Bjorn

THREE PIECES see Grieg, Edvard Hagerup

THREE PIECES see Svoboda, Tomas

THREE PIECES: ALLEMANDE, SARABANDE,
CEBELL see Purcell, Henry

THREE QUESTIONS WITH TWO ANSWERS see
Dallapiccola, Luigi

THREE QUOTATIONS: A: THE KING OF FRANCE
see Sousa, John Philip

THREE QUOTATIONS: B: I, TOO, WAS BORN
IN ARCADIA see Sousa, John Philip

THREE QUOTATIONS: C: IN DARKEST AFRICA
see Sousa, John Philip

THREE ROMANTIC PIECES, FOR PIANO AND
ORCHESTRA see Suchon, Eugen, Tri
Romanticke Kusy, For Piano And
Orchestra

THREE SONGS, FOR SOLO VOICE AND
ORCHESTRA see Bagin, Pavel, Tri
Spevy, For Solo Voice And Orchestra

THREE SONGS, FOR SOLO VOICE AND STRING
ORCHESTRA see Kresanek, Jozef, Tri
Piesne, For Solo Voice And String
Orchestra

THREE SONGS OF BLAKE AND DONNE, FOR
SOLO VOICE AND ORCHESTRA see
Brings, Allen Stephen

THREE TALES FOR A YOUNG PIANIST, FOR
PIANO AND STRING ORCHESTRA see
Arnic, Blaz, Tri Pravljice, For
Piano And String Orchestra

THREE TEMPI see Matsushita, Shin-Ichi

THRENODY see Wilson, Thomas

THRENODY. TO THE VICTIMS OF HIROSHIMA
see Penderecki, Krzysztof

THUNDER AND LIGHTNING see Strauss,
Johann, [Jr.], Unter Donner Und
Blitz

THUNDERER MARCH, THE see Sousa, John
Philip

THUS DO YOU FARE, MY JESUS, [ARR.] see
Bach, Johann Sebastian, So Gehst Du
Nun, Mein Jesu, Hin, [arr.]

THUS PLAYED KURENT, FOR VIOLA AND
ORCHESTRA see Petric, Ivo, Tako Je
Godel Kurent, For Viola And
Orchestra

THY BLACK IS FAIREST, FOR SOLO VOICE
AND ORCHESTRA see Andriessen,
Jurriaan

THY SWEET DREAMS, FOR SOLO VOICE AND
ORCHESTRA see Luck, Arthur

THYRESTAM, GUNNAR (1900-   )
Sinfonia Sacra, For Solo Voice And
Orchestra
2.2.2.2. 2.2.2.0. timp,strings,S
solo
pts STIM perf mat rent   (T180)

TIDE see Lorentzen, Bent

TIEDA MUISTATKO MUA, EN, FOR SOLO VOICE
AND ORCHESTRA see Pylkkanen, Tauno
Kullervo

TIERKREIS see Stockhausen, Karlheinz

TIESSEN, HEINZ (1887-1971)
Amsel, Die, For Solo Voice And
Orchestra *Op.62 [15']
1.1.2.2. 2.2.0.0. pno,strings,S
solo
RIES perf mat rent   (T181)

Stirb Und Werde *see Symphony, Op.
17

Symphony, Op. 17 [25']
3(pic).2+English horn.3.2+
contrabsn. 6.3.3.1. timp,cym,
harp,strings
RIES perf mat rent   (T182)

Visionen, For Violin And Orchestra
[16']
2(pic).1.2.2. 2.1.0.0. timp,
2perc,strings,vln solo
RIES perf mat rent   (T183)

TIESSEN, HEINZ (cont'd.)

Vorspiel Zu Einem Revolutionsdrama
*Op.33 [8']
2(pic).2.2.2+contrabsn. 4.2.2+
bass trom.1. timp,perc,strings
sc RIES f.s., perf mat rent   (T184)

TIJ EN ONTIJ see Delden, Lex van

TIJD, DE see Andriessen, Louis

TIK-TAK POLKA see Strauss, Johann,
[Jr.]

TILL EULENSPIEGELS LUSTIGE STREICHE see
Strauss, Richard

TILL EULENSPIEGEL'S MERRY PRANKS see
Strauss, Richard, Till
Eulenspiegels Lustige Streiche

TIMBRES, ESPACE, MOUVEMENT see
Dutilleux, Henri

TIME see Andriessen, Louis, Tijd, De

TIME AND AGAIN see Hellermann, William

TIME MUST HAVE A STOP, FOR PIANO AND
ORCHESTRA see Singer, M.

TIME OF ORCHESTRAL TIME see Yuasa, Joji

TIMEE see Dusapin, Pascal

TINTINNABULATIONS: COLLAGE III see
Kraft, William

TIPPETT, [SIR] MICHAEL (1905-   )
Concerto for Piano and Orchestra
2.2.2.2. 4.2.3.0. timp,cel,
strings,pno solo
study sc SCHOTT 75 A10925 $24.00
                                (T185)
Songs For Dov, For Solo Voice And
Orchestra
2.2.2.2. 3.1.1.0. timp,perc,harp,
pno,gtr,4vln,2vla,3vcl,2db,T
solo
study sc SCHOTT 75 A11135 $18.50
                                (T186)
Symphony No. 3
3.3.3.3. 4.2.3.1. perc,harp,cel,
pno,strings
study sc SCHOTT 75 A11148 $47.00
                                (T187)
Symphony No. 4
study sc SCHOTT 75 A11395 $15.00
                                (T188)
'TIS THE DAY see Leoncavallo, Ruggiero,
Mattinata, For Solo Voice And
Orchestra

TISCHHAUSER, FRANZ (1921-   )
Dr. Bircher Und Rossi
string orch,hpsd
sc HUG f.s., perf mat rent   (T189)

Eve's Meditation On Love, For Solo
Voice, Tuba And String Orchestra
[27']
string orch,tuba solo,S solo
MARGUN BP 7125 perf mat rent   (T190)

Punctus Contra Punctum, For Solo
Voices And Chamber Orchestra
[16']
chamber orch,TB soli
MARGUN BP 7124 perf mat rent   (T191)

TITL, ANTON EMIL (1809-1882)
Serenade
LUCKS 06866 set $10.00, pts $.75,
ea.   (T192)

TITON ET L'AURORE: SUITE see
Mondonville, Jean-Joseph de

TITUS: OVERTURE see Mozart, Wolfgang
Amadeus, Clemenza Di Tito, La:
Overture

TIVOLI-OUVERTURE see Wellejus, Henning

TO A WATER LILY, [ARR.] see MacDowell,
Edward Alexander

TO A WILD ROSE, [ARR.] see MacDowell,
Edward Alexander

TO AN OLD LOVE, FOR SOLO VOICE AND
ORCHESTRA see Flothuis, Marius

TO APOLLO, THE GOD OF LIGHT see
Riisager, Knudage

TO VALERIE SOLANAS AND MARILYN MONROE
see Oliveros, Pauline

TOCCATA AND FUGUE IN C FOR ORGAN:
ADAGIO, [ARR.] see Bach, Johann
Sebastian

TOCCATA AND FUGUE IN C: LARGO, [ARR.]
see Bach, Johann Sebastian

TOCCATA E DUE CANZONI see Martinu,
Bohuslav

TOCCATA E FUGA see Ziino, Ottavio

TOCCATA IN C: ADAGIO E FUGA, [ARR.] see
Bach, Johann Sebastian

TOCCATA PER LA ELEVAZIONE see
Frescobaldi, Girolamo

TOCCHI, GIAN-LUCA (1901-   )
Divertimento
string orch
sc DE SANTIS DS 567 f.s.   (T193)

Quadro Sonoro
sc DE SANTIS DS 580 f.s.   (T194)

Record [6']
4.3.3.3. 4.4.4.0. timp,perc,
strings
sc CARISCH 17130 f.s., perf mat
rent   (T195)

TOD UND VERKLARUNG see Strauss, Richard

TODE UND TORE see Kroll, Georg

TOEBOSCH, LOUIS (1916-   )
Cantatorium Carnevale, For Solo
Voices And Orchestra *Op.62
[17']
2.2.2.2. 4.2.3.1. timp,perc,cel,
strings,TBar soli
sc DONEMUS f.s., perf mat rent
                                (T196)

TOESCHI, CARLO GIUSEPPE (1731-1788)
Sinfonia in D, MIN 107 [12']
0.2.0.0.opt 2bsn. 2.2.0.0. timp,
hpsd,strings
(Munster, Robert) ORLANDO rent
                                (T197)

TOFFOLETTI, MASSIMO (1913-   )
Invention [11']
string orch
manuscript CARISCH   (T198)

Sonata for String Orchestra [8']
string orch
sc,pts ZANIBON D219 rent   (T199)

TOGNI, CAMILLO (1922-   )
Some Other Where [6']
2.2.3.2. 2.2.0.0. vibra,harp,pno,
perc,strings
sc ZERBONI 8357 f.s., perf mat rent
                                (T200)

TOLEDANISCHE NACHT see Fischer-Larsen,
Eric

TOMBEAU see Vries, Klaas de

TOMBEAU CONCERTANT, FOR 2 VIOLINS AND
STRING ORCHESTRA see Samama, Leo

TOMBEAU D'ARMOR see Sinopoli, Giuseppe

TOMBEAU DE BACH see Hovland, Egil

TOMBEAU DE KATHLEEN FERRIER, LE, FOR
SOLO VOICE AND ORCHESTRA see Hemel,
Oscar van

TOMMASINI, VINCENZO (1878-1950)
Scherzo for Violoncello and Orchestra
[8']
2.0.2.1. 2.1.0.0. harp,strings,
vcl solo
(Silva, L.) sc ZANIBON 3203A f.s.,
pts ZANIBON 3203B rent   (T201)

TOMORROW NO ONE KNOWS see Karkoff,
Ingvar

TON THAT, TIET (1933-   )
Images Lointaines II, For Solo Voice
And Orchestra [20']
sc JOBERT $31.25, perf mat rent
                                (T202)

TONADAS see Eyser, Eberhard

TONE POEMS, SERIES 1 see Strauss,
Richard

TONE POEMS, SERIES 2 see Strauss,
Richard

TONI, ALCEO (1884-1969)
Cavaliere Romantico, Il [11']
3.2.2.2. 4.2.3.1. timp,perc,
strings
manuscript CARISCH   (T203)

Fantocci Ribelli, I [25']
3.2.2.2. 4.2.3.1. perc,cel,harp,
xylo,strings
manuscript CARISCH   (T204)

Inno Trionfale [8']
2.2.2.2. 4.3.4.0. timp,perc,harp,
strings
manuscript CARISCH   (T205)

TONI, ALCEO (cont'd.)

   Introduzione E Saltarello [5']
     3.2.2.3. 4.4.4.0. perc,harp,cel,
     pno,strings
     sc CARISCH 18749 f.s., perf mat
     rent   (T206)

   Notturno E Tarantella [9']
     4.3.3.3. 4.2.3.1. timp,perc,
     2harp,strings
     manuscript CARISCH   (T207)

   Overture No. 2 [8']
     3.2.2.2. 4.4.3.1. timp,perc,
     strings
     sc CARISCH 17144 perf mat rent
                                       (T208)

   Overture No. 3 [6']
     3.2.2.2. 4.3.4.0. strings
     sc CARISCH 19438 f.s., perf mat
     rent   (T209)

   Parafrasi Settecentesca [27']
     string orch,org
     sc CARISCH 19875 perf mat rent
                                       (T210)

   Quadretti Infantili [14']
     3.2.3.3. 4.3.3.1. perc,xylo,cel,
     strings
     manuscript CARISCH   (T211)

   Schumaniana [8']
     2.1.2.1. 2.0.0.0. harp,strings
     manuscript CARISCH   (T212)

   Serenade [4']
     1.1.2.1. 2.0.0.0. strings
     manuscript CARISCH   (T213)

   Sinfonia [35']
     3.2.2.2. 4.3.3.1. timp,cel,perc,
     harp,pno,strings
     sc CARISCH 17104 perf mat rent
                                       (T214)

   Suite In Forma Di Variazioni [22']
     3.3.3.3. 4.2.4.1. timp,perc,cel,
     2harp,strings,sistrum
     sc CARISCH 17102 perf mat rent
                                       (T215)

   Tema, Variazioni E Fuga [15']
     3.2.2.2. 4.3.3.1. timp,perc,cel,
     harp,strings
     sc CARISCH 17121 perf mat rent
                                       (T216)

TOO THIS, TOO THAT see Nordensten,
   Frank T.

TOONEN see Janssen, Guus

TORELLI, GIUSEPPE (1658-1709)
   Concertino in C, MIN 59 [6'30"]
     string orch,trp solo
     INTERNAT. perf mat rent   (T217)

   Concerto in C, MIN 61 [12']
     string orch,2trp soli
     INTERNAT. perf mat rent   (T218)

   Concerto in D, Giegling 2, No. 3
     string orch,cont,trp solo
     (Paillard, J.F.) sc,pts COSTALL
     f.s.   (T219)

   Concerto in D, MIN 60 [6']
     string orch,trp solo
     INTERNAT. perf mat rent   (T220)

   Concerto No. 1 in D minor
     string orch,cont
     (Kolneder, W.) (TV. 118) sc,pts
     DOBLINGER DM 641 f.s. see from
     Sechs Sinfonien Und Sechs
     Concerti, Op. 5   (T221)

   Concerto No. 2 in A
     string orch,cont
     (Kolneder, W.) (TV. 120) sc,pts
     DOBLINGER DM 643 f.s. see from
     Sechs Sinfonien Und Sechs
     Concerti, Op. 5   (T222)

   Concerto No. 3 in D
     string orch,cont
     (Kolneder, W.) (TV. 122) sc,pts
     DOBLINGER DM 645 f.s. see from
     Sechs Sinfonien Und Sechs
     Concerti, Op. 5   (T223)

   Concerto No. 4 in G minor
     string orch,cont
     (Kolneder, W.) (TV. 124) sc,pts
     DOBLINGER DM 647 f.s. see from
     Sechs Sinfonien Und Sechs
     Concerti, Op. 5   (T224)

   Concerto No. 5 in F
     string orch,cont
     (Kolneder, W.) (TV. 126) sc,pts
     DOBLINGER DM 649 f.s. see from
     Sechs Sinfonien Und Sechs
     Concerti, Op. 5   (T225)

   Concerto No. 6 in G
     string orch,cont
     (Kolneder, W.) (TV. 128) sc,pts

TORELLI, GIUSEPPE (cont'd.)

     DOBLINGER DM 651 f.s. see from
     Sechs Sinfonien Und Sechs
     Concerti, Op. 5   (T226)

   Concerto, Op. 6, No. 1
     string orch,cont
     (Piccioli, Giuseppe) sc DE SANTIS
     DS 854 f.s., pts DE SANTIS DS 855
     f.s.   (T227)

   Concerto, Op. 6, No. 10, in D minor
     KALMUS A3251 sc $2.00, set $5.00,
     pts $1.00, ea.   (T228)

   Concerto, Op. 8, No. 1, in C
     string orch,cont,2vln soli
     (Kolneder, W.) (TV. 153) sc,pts
     DOBLINGER DM 595 f.s.   (T229)

   Concerto, Op. 8, No. 2, in A minor
     string orch,cont,2vln soli
     (Kolneder, W.) (TV. 154) sc,pts
     DOBLINGER DM 596 f.s.   (T230)

   Concerto, Op. 8, No. 3, in E
     string orch,cont,2vln soli
     (Kolneder, W.) (TV. 155) sc,pts
     DOBLINGER DM 597 f.s.   (T231)

   Concerto, Op. 8, No. 4, in B
     string orch,cont,2vln soli
     (Kolneder, W.) (TV. 156) sc,pts
     DOBLINGER DM 598 f.s.   (T232)

   Concerto, Op. 8, No. 5, in G
     string orch,cont,2vln soli
     sc RICORDI-IT 129930 f.s.   (T233)
     (Kolneder, W.) (TV. 157) sc,pts
     DOBLINGER DM 599 f.s.   (T234)

   Concerto, Op. 8, No. 6, in G minor
     string orch,cont,2vln soli
     (Kolneder, W.) (TV. 158) sc,pts
     DOBLINGER DM 600 f.s.   (T235)

   Concerto, Op. 8, No. 7, in D minor
     string orch,cont,vln solo
     (Kolneder, W.) (TV. 159) sc,pts
     DOBLINGER DM 633 f.s.   (T236)

   Concerto, Op. 8, No. 8, in C minor
     string orch,cont,vln solo
     (Kolneder, W.) (TV. 160) sc,pts
     DOBLINGER DM 634 f.s.   (T237)

   Concerto, Op. 8, No. 9, in E minor
     string orch,cont,vln solo
     (Kolneder, W.) (TV. 161) sc,pts
     DOBLINGER DM 635 f.s.   (T238)

   Concerto, Op. 8, No. 10, in A
     string orch,cont,vln solo
     (Kolneder, W.) (TV. 162) sc,pts
     DOBLINGER DM 636 f.s.   (T239)

   Concerto, Op. 8, No. 11, in F
     string orch,cont,vln solo
     (Kolneder, W.) (TV. 163) sc,pts
     DOBLINGER DM 637 f.s.   (T240)

   Concerto, Op. 8, No. 12, in D
     string orch,cont,vln solo
     (Kolneder, W.) (TV. 164) sc,pts
     DOBLINGER DM 638 f.s.   (T241)

   Sechs Sinfonien Und Sechs Concerti,
     Op. 5 *see Concerto No. 1 in D
     minor; Concerto No. 2 in A;
     Concerto No. 3 in D; Concerto No.
     4 in G minor; Concerto No. 5 in
     F; Concerto No. 6 in G; Sinfonia
     No. 1 in A minor; Sinfonia No. 2
     in C; Sinfonia No. 3 in G minor;
     Sinfonia No. 4 in A; Sinfonia No.
     5 in D; Sinfonia No. 6 in E minor
                                       (T242)

   Sinfonia No. 1 in A minor
     string orch,cont
     (Kolneder, W.) (TV. 117) sc,pts
     DOBLINGER DM 640 f.s. see from
     Sechs Sinfonien Und Sechs
     Concerti, Op. 5   (T243)

   Sinfonia No. 2 in C
     string orch,cont
     (Kolneder, W.) (TV. 119) sc,pts
     DOBLINGER DM 642 f.s. see from
     Sechs Sinfonien Und Sechs
     Concerti, Op. 5   (T244)

   Sinfonia No. 3 in G minor
     string orch,cont
     (Kolneder, W.) (TV. 121) sc,pts
     DOBLINGER DM 644 f.s. see from
     Sechs Sinfonien Und Sechs
     Concerti, Op. 5   (T245)

   Sinfonia No. 4 in A
     string orch,cont
     (Kolneder, W.) (TV. 123) sc,pts
     DOBLINGER DM 646 f.s. see from
     Sechs Sinfonien Und Sechs
     Concerti, Op. 5   (T246)

TORELLI, GIUSEPPE (cont'd.)

   Sinfonia No. 5 in D
     string orch,cont
     (Kolneder, W.) (TV. 125) sc,pts
     DOBLINGER DM 648 f.s. see from
     Sechs Sinfonien Und Sechs
     Concerti, Op. 5   (T247)

   Sinfonia No. 6 in E minor
     string orch,cont
     (Kolneder, W.) (TV. 127) sc,pts
     DOBLINGER DM 650 f.s. see from
     Sechs Sinfonien Und Sechs
     Concerti, Op. 5   (T248)

TORO, EL see Stallaert, Alphonse

TORRENGA, BENNO (1953-   )
   Concerto for Oboe and Orchestra [21']
     2.2.2.2. 2.2.2.0. timp,2perc,
     strings,ob solo
     DONEMUS   (T249)

   Serenade for Viola and Instrumental
     Ensemble [7']
     2.2.3.2. 2.0.0.0. 2vcl,db,vla
     solo
     DONEMUS perf mat rent   (T250)

TORRI, M.
   Due Liriche, For Solo Voice And
     Orchestra [8']
     1.2+English horn.1.2. 3.2.0.0.
     harp,timp,perc,strings,A solo
     sc,pts ZANIBON D276 f.s.   (T251)

TORTELIER, PAUL (1914-   )
   Concerto for Violin, Violoncello and
     Orchestra
     2.2.2.2. 4.2.0.0. timp,harp,
     strings,vln solo,vcl solo/2vcl
     soli/2vln soli
     sc CHESTER $22.50, perf mat rent
                                       (T252)

TOSCA: E LUCEVAN LE STELLE, FOR SOLO
   VOICE AND ORCHESTRA see Puccini,
   Giacomo

TOSCA: NON LA SOSPIRI LA NOSTRA
   CASETTA, FOR SOLO VOICE AND
   ORCHESTRA see Puccini, Giacomo

TOSCA: RECONDITA ARMONIA, FOR SOLO
   VOICE AND ORCHESTRA see Puccini,
   Giacomo

TOSCA: VISSI D'ARTE, FOR SOLO VOICE AND
   ORCHESTRA see Puccini, Giacomo

TOSTI, FRANCESCO PAOLO (1846-1916)
   Serenata, La, For Solo Voice And
     Orchestra
     LUCKS 02728 sc $3.00, set $7.00,
     pts $.75, ea.   (T253)

TOTENTANZ, FOR PIANO AND ORCHESTRA see
   Liszt, Franz

TOTILA: TOSTO DAL VICIN BOSCO, FOR·SOLO
   VOICE AND ORCHESTRA see Legrenzi,
   Giovanni

TOUCH AFTER FINISH see Dijk, Jan van

TOUCHSTONE see Wilson, Thomas

TOUR UN RETOUR POLKA see Strauss,
   Eduard

TOUT A PARIS see Waldteufel, Emil

TOY SYMPHONY see Haydn, [Franz] Joseph,
   Kindersinfonie

TOYAMA, YUZO (1931-   )
   Rhapsody Based On Folk Song From
     Okinawa
     3(pic).2.2.3. 4.3.3.1. timp,perc,
     harp,cel,strings
     ONGAKU perf mat rent   (T254)

TRAGEN VINNER see Eyser, Eberhard

TRAGIC OVERTURE see Brahms, Johannes,
   Tragische Ouverture

TRAGIC SYMPHONY see Schubert, Franz
   (Peter), Symphony No. 4 in C minor,
   D. 417

TRAGISCHE INTERMEZZO see Becce,
   Giuseppe

TRAGISCHE OUVERTURE see Brahms,
   Johannes

TRAGISCHE OUVERTURE see Vierling, Georg

TRAGODIE OLYMPIA: OVERTURE see Kraus,
   Joseph Martin

TRAIL OF BEAUTY, THE, FOR SOLO VOICE
   AND ORCHESTRA see Amram, David
   Werner

TRAJKOVIC, VLASTIMIR
  Duo for Piano and Orchestra
  ESCHIG sc,pts rent, min sc f.s.
                                    (T255)

TRAKT see Rihm, Wolfgang

TRANS see Stockhausen, Karlheinz

TRANSACTIONEN see Strauss, Josef

TRANSFORMACIJE, FOR 2 VIOLAS AND
  STRINGS see Ramovs, Primoz

TRANSFORMATION see Marez Oyens, Tera de

TRANSFORMATIONS, FOR 2 VIOLAS AND
  STRINGS see Ramovs, Primoz,
  Transformacije, For 2 Violas And
  Strings

TRANSIT see Laporte, Andre

TRANSIT, FOR SOLO VOICES AND CHAMBER
  ORCHESTRA see Ferneyhough, Brian

TRANSITIONS see Oosterveld, Ernst

TRANSITOIRES see Grisey, Gerard

TRANSLUCENT II see Bruynel, Ton

TRANSPORT TO SUMMER, FOR CLARINET AND
  ORCHESTRA see Hekster, Walter

TRANSTULI see Haselbach, Josef

TRAU-SCHAU-WEM see Strauss, Johann,
  [Jr.]

TRAUER-SYMPHONIE see Locatelli, Pietro

TRAUERMARSCH see Schubert, Franz
  (Peter)

TRAUERMARSCH, [ARR.] see Beethoven,
  Ludwig van

TRAUERMUSIK see Soderlind, Ragnar

TRAUM, EIN, FOR SOLO VOICE AND
  ORCHESTRA, [ARR.] see Grieg, Edvard
  Hagerup

TRAUME, FOR SOLO VOICE AND ORCHESTRA
  see Wagner, Richard

TRAUMEREI, [ARR.] see Schumann, Robert
  (Alexander)

TRAUMERIN POLKA, DIE see Strauss,
  Eduard

TRAUMGEBILDE WALZER see Strauss, Eduard

TRAURIGE FRUHLINGSNACHT see Roos,
  Robert de

TRAVIATA, LA: ADDIO DEL PASSATO, FOR
  SOLO VOICE AND ORCHESTRA see Verdi,
  Giuseppe

TRAVIATA, LA: AH! DITE ALLA GIOVINE,
  MORRO! LA MIA MEMORIA, FOR SOLO
  VOICES AND ORCHESTRA see Verdi,
  Giuseppe

TRAVIATA, LA: AH FORS' E LUI; SEMPRE
  LIBERA, FOR SOLO VOICE AND
  ORCHESTRA see Verdi, Giuseppe

TRAVIATA, LA: DE' MIEI BOLLENTI
  SPIRITI, FOR SOLO VOICE AND
  ORCHESTRA see Verdi, Giuseppe

TRAVIATA, LA: DI PROVENZA IL MAR, FOR
  SOLO VOICE AND ORCHESTRA see Verdi,
  Giuseppe

TRAVIATA, LA: LIBIAMO, NE' LIETI
  CALICI, FOR SOLO VOICES AND
  ORCHESTRA see Verdi, Giuseppe

TRAVIATA, LA: PARIGI, O CARA, FOR SOLO
  VOICES AND ORCHESTRA see Verdi,
  Giuseppe

TRAVIATA, LA: PRELUDIO, ACT I see
  Verdi, Giuseppe

TRAVIATA, LA: PRELUDIO, ACT III see
  Verdi, Giuseppe

TRAVIATA, LA: UN DI FELICE, ETEREA, FOR
  SOLO VOICES AND ORCHESTRA see
  Verdi, Giuseppe

TRE CANTI REGIONALI, FOR SOLO VOICE AND
  ORCHESTRA see Porrino, Ennio

TRE CAPRISKISSER see Karkoff, Maurice

TRE DIVERTIMENTI see Casagrande,
  Alessandro

TRE EPISODI PER FANFARA E ORCHESTRA see
  Chailly, Luciano

TRE FUGHE E DUE INTERLUDI see Lupi,
  Roberto

TRE GAVOTTE ANTICHE DI LULLY, RAMEAU E
  HANDEL [6']
  string orch
  (Nordio, Cesare) manuscript CARISCH
                                    (T256)

TRE LIRICHE, FOR SOLO VOICE AND
  ORCHESTRA see Alfano, Franco

TRE LIRICHE, FOR SOLO VOICE AND STRING
  ORCHESTRA see Farina, Guido

TRE MINIATURE PER I PICCOLI see
  Santoliquido, Francesco

TRE MOMENTI FRANCESCANI see Bossi,
  [Marco] Enrico

TRE MOVIMENTI see Broggi, A.M.

TRE PEZZI see Bois, Rob du

TRE PEZZI POETICA see Ricci Signorini,
  Antonio

TRE PEZZI SINFONICI see Bossi, [Marco]
  Enrico

TRE POESIE DI SALVATORE QUASIMODO, FOR
  SOLO VOICE AND ORCHESTRA see
  Cattini, Umberto

TRE PRELUDI see Gianferrari, Vincenzo

TRE PSALMI, FOR SOLO VOICE AND
  ORCHESTRA see Beers, Jacques

TRE RIFRAZIONI SONORE see Bossi, Renzo

TRE SALMI, FOR SOLO VOICE AND ORCHESTRA
  see Cortese, Luigi

TRE SYMFONISKA POEM see Wahlberg, Rune

TREDE, YNGRE JAN
  Nachtlandschaft [20']
    2.2.3.2. 2.2.2.0. timp,perc,cel,
    harp,pno,strings
  SAMFUNDET perf mat rent   (T257)

TREGUA, LA, FOR SOLO VOICE AND
  ORCHESTRA see Sinigaglia, Leone

TREIBMANN, KARL OTTOMAR (1936-   )
  Symphony for Strings
    9vln,3vla,2vcl,db
  sc DEUTSCHER 1713 f.s., perf mat
  rent   (T258)

TRENKNER, WERNER
  Kleine Festmusik *Op.29 [10']
    2(pic).2.2.2. 2.2.3.0. timp,perc,
    harp,strings
  RIES perf mat rent   (T259)

  Variationen-Suite Uber Eine
    Lumpensammlerweise *Op.27 [15']
    2(pic).2.2.2. 4.2.1.0. timp,perc,
    strings
  RIES perf mat rent   (T260)

  Variationen Uber Ein Thema Aus Der
    "Zauberflote" [12']
    2.2.2.2. 2.2.0.0. timp,cel/pno,
    strings
  RIES perf mat rent   (T261)

  Variationen Und Fuge Uber Ein Eigenes
    Thema *Op.2 [26']
    3.2.2.2+contrabsn. 4.2.3.0. timp,
    harp,strings
  RIES perf mat rent   (T262)

  Variationen Und Fuge Uber Ein
    Romantisches Thema *Op.30 [16']
    2.2.2.2. 4.2.3.0. timp,perc,
    strings
  RIES perf mat rent   (T263)

TREPPEN DES PIRANESI, DIE see Schmidt-
  Wunstorf, Rudolf, Escaliers De
  Piranese, Les

TRES DANZAS ESPANOLAS, [ARR.] see
  Granados, Enrique

TREULIEBCHEN POLKA see Strauss, Eduard

TRI CASTI Z KONTEMPLACII, FOR PIANO AND
  ORCHESTRA see Suchon, Eugen

TRI NOKTURNA see Mikula, Zdenko

TRI PIESNE, FOR SOLO VOICE AND STRING
  ORCHESTRA see Kresanek, Jozef

TRI PRAVLJICE, FOR PIANO AND STRING
  ORCHESTRA see Arnic, Blaz

TRI ROMANTICKE KUSY, FOR PIANO AND
  ORCHESTRA see Suchon, Eugen

TRI SPEVY, FOR SOLO VOICE AND ORCHESTRA
  see Bagin, Pavel

TRI TANCE see Bokes, Vladimir

TRIAS-SYMPHONY II see Ikebe, Shin-
  Ichiro

TRIFLUMENA see Stock, David

TRILOGIA CRISTIANA, FOR VIOLONCELLO AND
  ORCHESTRA see Bossi, Renzo

TRINKLIED, FOR SOLO VOICE AND
  ORCHESTRA, [ARR.] see Kistenmacher,
  Arthur

TRIOLOGIA 2 see Glaser, Werner Wolf

TRIPARTITA see Diethelm, Caspar

TRIPLUM NO. 1 FOR VIOLIN, HARPSICHORD
  AND STRING ORCHESTRA see Chailly,
  Luciano

TRIPLUM NO. 2 FOR VIOLIN, PIANO AND
  ORCHESTRA see Chailly, Luciano

TRIPP-TRAPP, GALOPP see Dixie Joe

TRIPTYCHON see Fortner, Wolfgang

TRIPTYCHON see Heilmann, Harald

TRIPTYCHON, FOR FLUTE AND ORCHESTRA see
  Bossler, Kurt

TRISM see Koblitz, David

TRISTAN UND ISOLDE: PRELUDE AND
  LIEBESTOD see Wagner, Richard

TRISTE SERA, FOR SOLO VOICE AND
  ORCHESTRA see Sinigaglia, Leone

TRITSCH-TRATSCH POLKA see Strauss,
  Johann, [Jr.]

TRITTICO see Delden, Lex van

TRITTICO GALANTE, FOR OBOE AND STRING
  ORCHESTRA see Carlstedt, Jan

TRITTICO LITURGICO, FOR SOLO VOICE AND
  STRING ORCHESTRA see Hemel, Oscar
  van

TRIUMPHAL MARCH see Glazunov, Alexander
  Konstantinovich

TRIUMPHAL OVERTURE ON A DANISH NATIONAL
  HYMN see Tchaikovsky, Piotr Ilyich

TROIS ATMOSPHERES, FOR CLARINET AND
  ORCHESTRA see Louvier, Alain

TROIS CHANSONS, FOR SOLO VOICE AND
  ORCHESTRA see Mulder, Ernest W.

TROIS CHANSONS DES MAQUISARDS
  CONDAMNES, FOR SOLO VOICE AND
  ORCHESTRA see Ruyneman, Daniel

TROIS CHANTS DU CREPUSCULE, FOR SOLO
  VOICES AND STRING ORCHESTRA see
  Douw, Andre

TROIS MELODIES, FOR SOLO VOICE AND
  ORCHESTRA see Diepenbrock, Alphons

TROIS PASTORALES, FOR SOLO VOICE AND
  ORCHESTRA see Andriessen, Hendrik

TROIS PIECES POUR GRAND ORCHESTRE:
  PREMIER MOUVEMENT see Nilsson,
  Anders

TROIS POESIES FRANCAISES, FOR SOLO
  VOICE AND ORCHESTRA see Jung, Helge

TROIS SERENADES, FOR SOLO VOICE AND
  ORCHESTRA see Beekhuis, Hanna

TROJAHN, MANFRED (1949-   )
  Berceuse [12']
    2(pic,alto fl).2(English horn).3+
    bass clar.2. 4.2.2.0. timp,
    perc,cel/pno,harp,strings
  BAREN. BA 6786 perf mat rent (T264)

  Drittes Seebild "Gegen Norden", For
    Solo Voice And Orchestra
    3(pic,alto fl).2+English horn.3+
    bass clar.2+contrabsn. 4.4.3.1.
    timp,2perc,harp,strings,Mez
    solo
  BAREN. BA 6789 perf mat rent (T265)

  Erstes See-Bild Fur Grosses Orchester
    [17']
    3(pic,alto fl).2+English horn.3+
    bass clar.3(contrabsn).
    4.4.3.1. timp,4perc,harp,

TROJAHN, MANFRED (cont'd.)
    strings
      BAREN. BA 6779 perf mat rent (T266)

    Zweites Seebild "Schatten Von
      Kahnen", For Solo Voice And
      Orchestra
      0.bass fl+alto fl.0.English
        horn.2+bass clar.2+contrabsn.
        2.0.1.1. perc,harp,strings
        without vln,Mez solo
      BAREN. BA 6788 perf mat rent (T267)

TROMPETEN OUVERTURE see Mendelssohn-
    Bartholdy, Felix

TROPI see Terzakis, Dimitri

TROT DE CAVALERIE see Rubinstein, Anton

TROVATORE, IL: AH SI, BEN MIO, FOR SOLO
    VOICE AND ORCHESTRA see Verdi,
    Giuseppe

TROVATORE, IL: D'AMOR SULL' ALI ROSEE,
    FOR SOLO VOICE AND ORCHESTRA see
    Verdi, Giuseppe

TROVATORE, IL: DI QUELLA PIRA, FOR SOLO
    VOICE AND ORCHESTRA see Verdi,
    Giuseppe

TROVATORE, IL: IL BALEN DEL SUO
    SORRISO, FOR SOLO VOICE AND
    ORCHESTRA see Verdi, Giuseppe

TROVATORE, IL: MIRA, DI ACERBE LAGRIME;
    VIVRA! CONTENDE IL GIUBILO, FOR
    SOLO VOICES AND ORCHESTRA see
    Verdi, Giuseppe

TROVATORE, IL: SI, LA STANCHEZZA; AI
    NOSTRI MONTI, FOR SOLO VOICES AND
    ORCHESTRA see Verdi, Giuseppe

TROVATORE, IL: STRIDE LA VAMPA, FOR
    SOLO VOICE AND ORCHESTRA see Verdi,
    Giuseppe

TROVATORE, IL: TACEA LA NOTTE PLACIDA;
    DI TALE AMOR, FOR SOLO VOICE AND
    ORCHESTRA see Verdi, Giuseppe

TRUE LOVE see Brahms, Johannes

TRUMPET MUSIC, FOR TRUMPET AND
    ORCHESTRA see Lundquist, Torbjorn

TRUMPET PRELUDE, [ARR.] see Purcell,
    Henry

TRUMPET VOLUNTARY, [ARR.] see Purcell,
    Henry

TRUMPY, BALZ (1946-   )
    Wellenspiele [20']
      1.1(English horn).1(bass clar).1.
      2.2.1.0. pno,vla,vcl,db,
      electronic equipment
      RICORDI-FR R.2254 perf mat rent
                        (T268)

TRUNK DES POSEIDON, DER, FOR SOLO
    VOICES AND ORCHESTRA see Siebert,
    Wilhelm Dieter

TSAR BORIS: OVERTURE AND ENTR'ACTES see
    Kalinnikov, Vassili Sergeievich

TSAR SALTAN: FLIGHT OF THE BUMBLEBEE
    see Rimsky-Korsakov, Nikolai

TSCHAIKOWSKY, PJOTR ILJITSCH
    see TCHAIKOVSKY, PIOTR ILYICH

TSUBONOH, KATSUHIRO (1947-   )
    Statue Of III, The
      JAPAN 8002   (T269)

TSUKAHARA, SETSUO (1921-1978)
    Symphony No. 1
      ZEN-ON 899041   (T270)

TU MANCAVI A TORMENTARMI CRUDELISSIMA
    SPERANZA, [ARR.] see Cesti, Marc'
    Antonio

TUBIN, EDUARD (1905-   )
    Kratt: Suite [25']
      2.2.2.1. 2.2.2.0. timp,perc,harp,
      pno,strings
      sc,pts SUECIA ENO 307   (T271)

    Sinfonietta
      2.2.2.2. 2.2.1.0. timp,harp,
      strings
      sc STIM   (T272)

    Symphony No. 6 [36']
      3.3.3.3.tenor sax. 4.3.3.1. timp,
      4perc,pno,strings
      sc STIM perf mat rent   (T273)

TUIJOTIN TULEHEN KAUAN, FOR SOLO VOICE
    AND ORCHESTRA, [ARR.] see Kuula,
    Toivo

TULE ARMAANI, FOR SOLO VOICE AND
    ORCHESTRA, [ARR.] see Kuula, Toivo

TULL, FISHER AUBREY (1934-   )
    Capriccio [8'30"]
      2.1.1.1. 2.1.1.0. timp,perc,pno,
      strings
      BOOSEY perf mat rent   (T274)

    Concertino for Oboe and String
      Orchestra
      string orch,ob solo
      BOOSEY HSS 306 set $33.00,
      augmented set $55.00   (T275)

    Concerto for Trumpet and Orchestra,
      No. 2 [17']
      3.2.3.2. 4.3.3.1. timp,perc,harp,
      strings,trp solo
      BOOSEY perf mat rent   (T276)

TUNDER, FRANZ (1614-1667)
    Ach Herr, Lass Deine Lieben Engelein,
      For Solo Voice And String
      Orchestra [11']
      string orch,org/hpsd,S solo
      (Gohler, G.) BREITKOPF-W perf mat
      rent   (T277)

TURANDOT: INCIDENTAL MUSIC see Weber,
    Carl Maria von

TURANDOT: OVERTURE see Weber, Carl
    Maria von

TURCHI, GUIDO (1916-   )
    Concerto for String Orchestra
      string orch
      sc DE SANTIS DS 806 f.s.   (T278)

    Dedalo
      sc RICORDI-IT 131975 f.s.   (T279)

    Musique De Geste
      sc RICORDI-IT 131644 f.s.   (T280)

TURCO IN ITALIA, IL: OVERTURE see
    Rossini, Gioacchino

TURINI, FERDINANDO GASPARO (1749-1812)
    Concerto for Harpsichord and String
      Orchestra in C minor [10']
      string orch,hpsd solo
      (Sartori) sc,pts ZANIBON ZA5416
      f.s.   (T281)

TURKISCHER MARSCH, [ARR.] see Mozart,
    Wolfgang Amadeus

TURKISH CONCERTO see Mozart, Wolfgang
    Amadeus, Concerto for Violin and
    Orchestra, No. 5, in A, K. 219

TURNER ILLUSTRATIONS, FOR VIOLIN AND
    INSTRUMENTAL ENSEMBLE see Durko,
    Zsolt

TUROK, PAUL HARRIS (1929-   )
    Sousa Overture, A
      study sc SCHIRM.G $14.00   (T282)

    Symphony
      3.3.3.2. 4.2.3.1. timp,2perc,pno,
      strings
      SEESAW perf mat rent   (T283)

TUTINO, MARCO
    Andrea O I Ricongiunti
      ZERBONI 8784   (T284)

TUULEN KEHTOLAULU, FOR SOLO VOICE AND
    ORCHESTRA see Marvia, Einari

TUUTULAULU, FOR SOLO VOICE AND
    ORCHESTRA see Hannikainen, Vaino

TUZUN, FERIT (1929-1977)
    Anatolia-Orchestersuite
      3(pic).2+English horn.2+bass
      clar.2+contrabsn. 4.3.3.1.
      3perc,harp,pno,strings, S solo
      or klavioline solo or soprano
      sax solo
      [19'] LEUCKART perf mat rent (T285)

TWARDOWSKI, ROMUALD (1930-   )
    Study In A [13'40"]
      3.2.2.2. 4.3.3.0. 4perc,harp,pno,
      strings
      fac ed POLSKIE $17.10   (T286)

TWEE BALLADEN, FOR SOLO VOICE AND
    ORCHESTRA see Diepenbrock, Alphons

TWEE DANSEN see Kingma, Piet

TWEE REDDELOZEN see Ketting, Piet

TWELVE BEST LOVED SONGS, [ARR.] see
    Foster, Stephen Collins

TWELVE CHRISTMAS CAROLS
    string orch
    (Zinn, William) EXCELSIOR $18.00
                        (T287)

TWELVE ENGLISH SONGS, [ARR.] *CC12U
    (de Witt) KALMUS 5281 pno-cond sc
    $3.00, set $15.00, pts $1.00, ea.,
    cmplt ed rent   (T288)

TWELVE NOTE RAG, THE, [ARR.] see
    Laufer, Kenneth

TWENTY-TWO PAGES, FOR SOLO VOICES AND
    ORCHESTRA see Straesser, Joep

TWILIGHT see Norgaard, Per

TWO HUNDRED BAR PASSACAGLIA see
    Stewart, Don

TWO ICELANDIC MELODIES see Svendsen,
    Johan (Severin)

TWO MELODIES see Grieg, Edvard Hagerup

TWO MINUETS AND CONTRA-DANCES see
    Mozart, Wolfgang Amadeus, Menuette,
    Zwei, Mit Eingefugten Contretanzen,
    K. 463

TWO MOMENTS MUSICAL see Wagner, Joseph
    Frederick

TWO MOVEMENTS FOR STRINGS see Bergel,
    Bernd

TWO MOVEMENTS FOR STRINGS see Hattori,
    Koh-Ichi

TWO NORDIC MELODIES see Grieg, Edvard
    Hagerup

TWO NORWEGIAN AIRS see Grieg, Edvard
    Hagerup, Two Nordic Melodies

TWO-PART SYMPHONY see Wuorinen, Charles

TWO PICTURES FOR PERCUSSIONIST AND
    ORCHESTRA see Lambro, Phillip

TWO PIECES see Copland, Aaron

TWO PIECES, FOR FLUTE AND ORCHESTRA see
    Bird, Arthur

TWO PIECES FOR CELLO AND ORCHESTRA see
    Glazunov, Alexander
    Konstantinovich, Melodie Et
    Serenade Espagnole, For Violoncello
    And Orchestra

TWO PIECES FOR ORCHESTRA see Brings,
    Allen Stephen

TWO POEMS FOR ORCHESTRA see Bird,
    Arthur

TWO PRELUDES ON BACH THEMES see Luck,
    Andrew H.

TWO SACRED SONGS FROM THE "SPANISCHES
    LIEDERBUCH", [ARR.] see Wolf, Hugo,
    Zwei Lieder Aus Dem Spanischen
    Liederbuch, For Solo Voice And
    Orchestra, [arr.]

TWO SIZES FOR STRINGS see Thommessen,
    Olav Anton

TWO SYMPHONIC STUDIES see Ireland, John

TWO WALTZES, [ARR.] see Dvorak, Antonin

TYGER, THE see Stallaert, Alphonse

TYLL: NELE'S LIED, FOR SOLO VOICE AND
    ORCHESTRA see Lothar, Mark

U

UBER ALLEN GIPFELN IST RUH', FOR SOLO
    VOICE AND STRINGS see Hofmann,
    Wolfgang

UBER EIN STUNDLEIN, FOR SOLO VOICE AND
    ORCHESTRA see Pfitzner, Hans

UBER LANDER UND MEERE see Geisler,
    Willy

UBUNGEN IM VERWANDELN see Thiele,
    Siegfried

UCCELLINI, MARCO (ca. 1603-1680)
    Aria, For Two Violin And String
        Orchestra [6']
        string orch,2vln soli
        (Bossi, E.) sc ZANIBON 4415 f.s.,
        pts ZANIBON 4416 f.s.   (U1)

UCCELLINO DEL BOSCO, L', FOR SOLO VOICE
    AND STRING ORCHESTRA see
    Sinigaglia, Leone

UHL, ALFRED (1909-   )
    Drei Stucke [15']
        2(pic).2.2+bass clar.2. 3.3.3.1.
        timp,perc,strings
        sc,pts DOBLINGER rent   (U2)

UHR, DIE, FOR SOLO VOICE AND ORCHESTRA,
    [ARR.] see Loewe, Carl Gottfried

UKMAR, VILKO (1905-   )
    Concerto for Violoncello and
        Orchestra [25']
        2.2.2.2. 4.3.3.1. timp,2perc,
        strings,vcl solo
        DRUSTVO DSS 798 perf mat rent (U3)

    Fiddler *see Godec

    For Mother *see Materi

    Godec
        2(pic).2.2(bass clar).2. 4.3.3.0.
        timp,perc,harp,strings
        "Fiddler" DRUSTVO DSS 406 perf mat
        rent   (U4)

    Materi [12']
        2.2.2.2. 4.3.3.0. timp,2perc,
        strings
        "For Mother" DRUSTVO DSS 782 perf
        mat rent   (U5)

ULLMAN, BO (1929-   )
    Giorno Della Vita, Un [15']
        3.3.4.3. 2.3.3.1. timp,2perc,
        harp,cel,pno,mand,gtr,strings,
        campanella
        sc STIM perf mat rent   (U6)

ULTIME ROSE, FOR SOLO VOICE AND
    ORCHESTRA see Medicus, V.

ULTIMO CANTO see Bossi, [Marco] Enrico

UMBRA see Holler, York

UMBRAE IN MEMORIAM B.A. ZIMMERMANN, FOR
    VIOLIN, VIOLONCELLO AND ORCHESTRA
    see Denhoff, Michael

UN COR SI TENERO, FOR SOLO VOICE AND
    ORCHESTRA see Haydn, [Franz] Joseph

UNDER THE DOUBLE EAGLE MARCH see
    Wagner, Joseph Frederick

UNE MUSIQUE BLANCHE see Holt, Simeon
    ten

UNESTA TEHTY MIES see Sallinen, Aulis

UNFINISHED SYMPHONY see Schubert, Franz
    (Peter), Symphony No. 8 in B minor,
    D. 759

UNG, CHINARY (1942-   )
    Anicca [10']
        5.3.4.2. 4.2.3.1. 7perc,harp,cel,
        pno,strings
        PETERS perf mat rent   (U7)

UNGARISCH see Knumann, Jo

UNGARISCHE RHAPSODIE, FOR VIOLONCELLO
    AND ORCHESTRA see Popper, David

UNGARISCHE RHAPSODIE NO. 3, [ARR.] see
    Liszt, Franz, Rhapsodie Hongroise
    No. 3, [arr.]

UNGARISCHE RHAPSODIE NO. 11, [ARR.] see
    Liszt, Franz, Rhapsodie Hongroise
    No. 11, [arr.]

UNGARISCHE RHAPSODIE NO. 13, [ARR.] see
    Liszt, Franz, Rhapsodie Hongroise
    No. 13, [arr.]

UNGARISCHE SERENADE see Fuchs, Carl
    Emil

UNGARISCHE TANZE NOS. 1, 3, AND 10,
    [ARR.] see Brahms, Johannes

UNGARISCHE TANZE NOS. 5 AND 6, [ARR.]
    see Brahms, Johannes

UNGARISCHE VISION see Crucius, Heinz

UNGARISCHER STURMMARSCH see Liszt,
    Franz

UNGARISCHER TANZ NO. 4, [ARR.] see
    Brahms, Johannes

UNGEDULD, FOR SOLO VOICE AND ORCHESTRA,
    [ARR.] see Schubert, Franz (Peter)

UNGER, HERMANN (1886-1958)
    Alt-Niederland °Op.77 [16']
        2(pic).2(English horn).2.2.
        4.2.0.0. timp,perc,strings
        RIES perf mat rent   (U8)

    Kammersuite
        string orch
        sc,pts RIES f.s.   (U9)

UNITY AT THE CROSSROAD see El-Dabh,
    Halim

UNIVERS DE RIMBAUD, FOR SOLO VOICE AND
    ORCHESTRA see Escher, Rudolf George

UNIVERSO see Kox, Hans

UNTER DAMPF see Pachernegg, Alois

UNTER DER ENNS POLKA see Strauss,
    Eduard

UNTER DONNER UND BLITZ see Strauss,
    Johann, [Jr.]

UNTER STERNEN, FOR SOLO VOICE AND
    ORCHESTRA see Weingartner, (Paul)
    Felix von

UNTITLED see Hillborg, Anders

UP ON THE HOUSETOP
    see God Rest Ye, Merry Gentlemen

UPHEAVAL see Firat, Ertugrul

UPPSTROM, TORE (1937-   )
    Suite for Orchestra [15']
        3.2.2.2. 4.3.3.1. timp,4perc,
        harp,strings
        sc STIM perf mat rent   (U10)

UPRISING see Berkeley, Michael

UPRISING, THE see Nagy-Farkas, Peter

URACK, OTTO
    Alter Bauerntanz [3']
        1.1.2.1. 2.2.0.0. timp,strings
        RIES perf mat rent   (U11)

    Burlesca [5']
        1.1.2.1. 0.0.0.0. strings
        RIES perf mat rent   (U12)

URBANNER, ERICH (1936-   )
    Concerto for Saxophone and
        Instrumental Ensemble [13'30"]
        3.0.0.0. 1.0.0.0. 3perc,2pno,
        3vcl,db,alto sax solo
        sc,pts DOBLINGER rent   (U13)

USCHKA, WOHIN? see Hudec, Jiri

UTOPIA see Hermanson, Ake

UTSPEL see Blomberg, Erik

UTTONING see Blomberg, Erik

V

VA ET LE VIENT, LE see Tcherepnin, Ivan
    Alexandrovitch

VACCHI, F.
    Soupirs De Genevieve, Les
        11strings soli
        sc RICORDI-IT 132606 f.s.   (V1)

VADA ADAGIO, SIGNORINA, FOR SOLO VOICE
    AND ORCHESTRA see Haydn, [Franz]
    Joseph

VADO, MA DOVE, FOR SOLO VOICE AND
    ORCHESTRA see Mozart, Wolfgang
    Amadeus

VAEGTERVISE see Juon, Paul, Fantasy,
    Op. 31

VAGSPEL see Blomberg, Erik

VAGUE ET LA CLOCHE, LA, FOR SOLO VOICE
    AND ORCHESTRA see Duparc, Henri

VALASSKE TANCE see Janacek, Leos,
    Lachian Dances, Op. 2, Nos. 1 & 2

VALEDICTION see Wordsworth, William

VALEK, JIRI (1923-   )
    Revolutionary Symphony *see Symphony
        No. 9

    Symphony No. 9
        sc PANTON 1591 f.s.   (V2)

VALERIUS, ADRIANUS (1575-1625)
    Prayer Of Thanksgiving
        LUCKS 02294 sc $6.00, set $10.50,
        pts $.75, ea.   (V3)

VALOUCH, JOZEF (1930-   )
    Divertimento
        3.2.2.2. 4.2.3.0. timp,perc,harp,
        strings
        SLOV.HUD.FOND 0-78 perf mat rent
                                       (V4)

VALSE CAPRICE, FOR PIANO AND ORCHESTRA
    see Schubert-Weber, S.

VALSE-FANTAISIE see Glinka, Mikhail
    Ivanovich

VALSE PARADOX see Jorns, Helge

VALSE SCHERZO, FOR VIOLIN AND ORCHESTRA
    see Tchaikovsky, Piotr Ilyich

VALSE TRISTE see Sibelius, Jean

VALZER POETICI, OP. 5, [ARR.] see
    Converse, Frederick Shepherd

VAN DELDEN, LEX
    see DELDEN, LEX VAN

VAN DIJK, JAN
    see DIJK, JAN VAN

VAN LIER, BERTUS (1906-1972)
    In Claghen
        see Vier Verzen, For Solo Voice And
        Orchestra

    Laat De Luiken Geloken Zijn
        see Vier Verzen, For Solo Voice And
        Orchestra

    Om Mijn Oud Woonhuis Peppels Staan
        see Vier Verzen, For Solo Voice And
        Orchestra

    Sneeuw Ligt In Den Morgen Vroeg, Een
        see Vier Verzen, For Solo Voice And
        Orchestra

    Vier Verzen, For Solo Voice And
        Orchestra
        2.1.1.0. 1.0.0.0. harp,strings,S
        solo sc DONEMUS f.s., perf mat
        rent
        contains: In Claghen; Laat De
            Luiken Geloken Zijn; Om Mijn
            Oud Woonhuis Peppels Staan;
            Sneeuw Ligt In Den Morgen
            Vroeg, Een   (V5)

VAN VACTOR, DAVID (1906-   )
    Symphony No. 6 [13']
        2+pic.2+English horn.2+bass
        clar.2. 4.3.3.1. timp,perc,
        harp,strings
        RHODES,R   (V6)

VANDA see Dvorak, Antonin

VANGOGHIANA see Kox, Hans

VANHAL, JOHANN BAPTIST
see WANHAL, JOHANN BAPTIST

VANHALL, JAN KRTITEL
see WANHAL, JOHANN BAPTIST

VANTUS, I.
Reflections
(special import only) sc EMB 8274
f.s. (V7)

VARIABILI see Manzoni, Giacomo

VARIACIE, FOR DOUBLE BASS AND ORCHESTRA
see Kalus, Vaclav (W. Kallusch)

VARIACIONES CALEIDOSCOPICAS see
Montesinos, Eduardo

VARIACIONES ENIGMATICAS see Zorzi, Juan
Carlos

VARIACIONES OLIMPICAS see Morillo,
Roberto Garcia

VARIACIONES SOBRE LA RESONANCIA DE UN
GRITO see Halffter, Cristobal

VARIANTEN, FOR FLUTE AND ORCHESTRA see
Schroder, Hanning

VARIANTI see Bettinelli, Bruno

VARIANTI see Carpi, Fiorenzo

VARIANTS ON A THEME OF THELONIOUS MONK
see Schuller, Gunther

VARIANTS ON AN IRISH HYMN
(Tatgenhorst, John) BECKEN set
$15.00, pts $1.00, ea., min sc
$2.00 (V8)

VARIATI AMOROSI MOMENTI see Dalla
Vecchia, Wolfango

VARIATIES EN FINALE, ON A THEME BY DUKE
ELLINGTON see Lotichius, Erik

VARIATIES, OP EEN TERSCHELLINGER
MINNELIED see Vredenburg, Max

VARIATIONEN-FANTASIE UBER DAS
"PERPETUUM MOBILE" VON JOHANN
STRAUSS see Homola, Bernard

VARIATIONEN-SERENADE, FOR PIANO AND
ORCHESTRA see Dressel, Erwin

VARIATIONEN-SUITE UBER EINE
LUMPENSAMMLERWEISE see Trenkner,
Werner

VARIATIONEN UBER "ALL MEIN GEDANKEN"
see Werner, Hans

VARIATIONEN UBER EIN
ALTNIEDERLANDISCHES MINNELIED see
Koetsier, Jan

VARIATIONEN UBER EIN EIGENES THEMA see
Frommel, Gerhard

VARIATIONEN UBER EIN FRANZOSISCHES
REVOLUTIONSLIED see Rubin, Marcel

VARIATIONEN UBER EIN THEMA AUS DER
"ZAUBERFLOTE" see Trenkner, Werner

VARIATIONEN UBER EIN THEMA VON JOSEPH
HAYDN see Brahms, Johannes

VARIATIONEN UBER EIN THEMA VON MOZART
see Gress, Richard

VARIATIONEN UBER EINEN BACH-CHORAL see
Rubin, Marcel

VARIATIONEN UND FUGE UBER EIN EIGENES
THEMA see Trenkner, Werner

VARIATIONEN UND FUGE UBER EIN
ROMANTISCHES THEMA see Trenkner,
Werner

VARIATIONEN UND GIGUE UBER EIN THEMA
VON HANDEL see Schumann, Georg

VARIATIONER, 15 see Nielsen, John

VARIATIONER, FOR PIANO AND INSTRUMENTAL
ENSEMBLE see Gullberg, Olof

VARIATIONS AND FUGUE see Kvandal, Johan

VARIATIONS CHROMATIQUES, [ARR.] see
Bizet, Georges

VARIATIONS FOR 2 INSTRUMENTAL CHOIRS
see Deursen, Anton van

VARIATIONS FOR 4 INSTRUMENTAL CHOIRS
see Deursen, Anton van

VARIATIONS ON A HUNGARIAN FOLKSONG [9']
3.3.3.3. 4.3.3.1. timp,perc,2harp,
pno,strings
sc RIES RE65 f.s., perf mat rent (V9)

VARIATIONS ON A ROCOCO THEME, FOR
VIOLONCELLO AND ORCHESTRA see
Tchaikovsky, Piotr Ilyich

VARIATIONS ON A RUSSIAN FOLK TUNE
string orch
(variations by Arcibuscheff;
Blumenfeld; Ewald; Glazunoff;
Liadoff; Rimsky-Korsakoff;
Scriabine; Sokoloff; Wihtol and
Winkler) BELAIEFF BEL413 study sc
$10.00, sc f.s., perf mat rent
(V10)

VARIATIONS ON A RUSSIAN THEME
(variations by Artzibushev; Wihtol;
Liadov; Rimsky-Korsakov; Sokolov
and Glazunov) BELAIEFF perf mat
rent (V11)

VARIATIONS ON A RUSSIAN THEME
3.2.2.2. 4.2.3.1. timp,perc,harp,
strings
(variations by Artzibushev; Wihtol;
Liadov; Rimsky-Korsakov; Sokolov
and Glazunov) KALMUS 5451 sc
$18.00, set $40.00, pts $1.75, ea.
(V12)

VARIATIONS ON A THEME BY HAYDN see
Brahms, Johannes, Variationen Uber
Ein Thema Von Joseph Haydn

VARIATIONS ON A THEME BY VALERIUS see
Broekman, David

VARIATIONS ON A THEME OF TCHAIKOVSKY
see Arensky, Anton Stepanovich

VARIATIONS ON A TUNE FROM "THE BEGGAR'S
OPERA" see Korn, Peter Jona

VARIATIONS ON AN OLD SCOTS AIR see
Dorward, David

VARIATIONS ON "LA CI DAREM LA MANO",
FOR PIANO AND ORCHESTRA see Chopin,
Frederic

VARIATIONS SUR UN THEME ELEGIAQUE, FOR
SOLO VOICES AND STRING ORCHESTRA
see Metral, Pierre

VARIATIONS SUR UN THEME ROCOCO see
Tchaikovsky, Piotr Ilyich,
Variations On A Rococo Theme, For
Violoncello And Orchestra

VARIAZIONI, FOR VIOLONCELLO AND
ORCHESTRA see Sciarrino, Salvatore

VARIAZIONI E NOTTURNI, FOR SOLO VOICE
AND ORCHESTRA see Contilli, Gino

VARIAZIONI SINFONICHE see Giltay,
Berend

VARIAZIONI SU UN TEMA GIOCOSO see
Margola, Franco

VARIAZIONI SULLA "FOLLIA DI SPAGNA" see
Salieri, Antonio

VARII CAPRICCI see Walton, [Sir]
William (Turner)

VATERLANDISCHER MARSCH see Strauss,
Johann, [Jr.]

VAUGHAN WILLIAMS, RALPH (1872-1958)
Fantasia On A Theme By Tallis
min sc BOOSEY 59 $12.00 (V13)

Norfolk Rhapsody No. 1 In E Minor
KALMUS A4542 sc $10.00, perf mat
rent, set $25.00, pts $1.00, ea.
(V14)
Pastoral Symphony (Symphony No. 3)
min sc BOOSEY 73 $14.00 (V15)

Symphony No. 3 *see Pastoral
Symphony

Wasps, The
min sc BOOSEY 60 $11.00 (V16)
LUCKS 09094 sc $13.00, set $20.00,
pts $1.40, ea. (V17)

VEA, KETIL
Concerto for Piano and Orchestra, No.
2
4(pic).2(English horn).2.2.
4.3.3.1. timp,perc,strings,pno
solo
NORGE (V18)

Romance for Violin and Orchestra
2.2.2.2. 2.2.2.0. timp,perc,
strings,vln solo
NORGE (V19)

VECSEY, FERENC VON (1893-1935)
Nuit Du Nord
LIENAU f.s. (V20)

VEILLEE DE L'ANGE GARDIEN, LA, [ARR.]
see Pierne, Gabriel

VEJVANOVSKY, PAVEL JOSEF (1640-1693)
Sonata in G minor, MIN 78
trp,strings,cont
MUS. RARA f.s. (V21)

VELTIN FANTASY, FOR OBOE AND STRING
ORCHESTRA see Koch, Frederick

VELVET AND HEMP see Kruse, Bjorn

VENDREDIS POLKA, LES see Glazunov,
Alexander Konstantinovich

VENETIAN JOURNAL, FOR SOLO VOICE AND
ORCHESTRA see Maderna, Bruno

VENETIAN RHAPSODY see Holten, Bo

VENEZIANISCHES GONDELLIED, OP. 19, NO.
6, [ARR.] see Mendelssohn-
Bartholdy, Felix

VENHELAULU, FOR SOLO VOICE AND
ORCHESTRA see Pylkkanen, Tauno
Kullervo

VENI SANCTI SPIRITU, FOR ORGAN AND
ORCHESTRA see Lehner, Franz Xaver

VENI, VENI, VENIAS see Mul, Jan

VERACINI, FRANCESCO MARIA (1690-1768)
Largo, [arr.]
(Corti-Molinari) string orch,org
[5'] sc CARISCH 14248 f.s., pts
CARISCH 14249 f.s. (V22)

VERANDERUNGEN UBER EIN THEMA VON
COUPERIN, FOR VIOLIN AND STRING
ORCHESTRA see Schlemm, Gustav Adolf

VERBA MEA AURIBUS see Beers, Jacques

VERBORGENHEIT, FOR SOLO VOICE AND
ORCHESTRA see Wolf, Hugo

VERDI, GIUSEPPE (1813-1901)
Aida: Celeste Aida, For Solo Voice
And Orchestra
LUCKS 02024 sc $3.75, set $7.50,
pts $.75, ea. (V23)

Aida: Finale, Act 4, Scene 2, For
Solo Voices And Orchestra
LUCKS 02739 sc $6.00, set $9.00,
pts $.75, ea. (V24)

Aida: Marcia
"Aida: Triumphal March And Ballet"
LUCKS 02109 sc $35.00, set
$20.00, pts $1.75, ea. (V25)

Aida: O Patria Mia, For Solo Voice
And Orchestra
LUCKS 02037 sc $3.75, set $7.50,
pts $.75, ea. (V26)

Aida: Preludio, Act I
KALMUS A4554 sc $3.00, perf mat
rent, set $12.00, pts $.60, ea.
(V27)

Aida: Ritorna Vincitor, For Solo
Voice And Orchestra
LUCKS 02161 sc $3.75, set $7.50,
pts $.75, ea. (V28)

Aida: Triumphal March And Ballet
*see Aida: Marcia

Aroldo: Overture
KALMUS A5007 sc $20.00, perf mat
rent, set $30.00, pts $1.50, ea.
(V29)

Attila: Oh Dolore!, For Solo Voice
And Orchestra [6']
1.2.2.2. 4.0.0.0. harp,strings,T
solo
(Spada, P.) sc ZERBONI 8209 f.s.,
pts ZERBONI 8210 rent (V30)

Ballo In Maschera, Un: Di Tu Se
Fedele, For Solo Voice And
Orchestra
LUCKS 03187 sc $5.00, set $12.00,
pts $.75, ea. (V31)

Ballo In Maschera, Un: Eri Tu Che
Macchiavi, For Solo Voice And
Orchestra
LUCKS 02217 sc $3.75, set $7.50,
pts $.75, ea. (V32)

Ballo In Maschera, Un: Ma Dall' Arido
Stelo Divulsa, For Solo Voice And
Orchestra
LUCKS 02991 sc $3.75, set $9.50,
pts $.75, ea. (V33)

VERDI, GIUSEPPE (cont'd.)

Ballo In Maschera, Un: Ma Se M'e
Forza Perderti, For Solo Voice
And Orchestra
LUCKS 03144   (V34)

Ballo In Maschera, Un: Saper
Vorreste, For Solo Voice And
Orchestra
LUCKS 02088 sc $3.75, set $7.50,
pts $.75, ea.   (V35)

Battaglia Di Legnano, La: Overture
KALMUS A5085 sc $15.00, perf mat
rent, set $30.00, pts $1.50, ea.
(V36)

Don Carlos: Ella Giammai M'Amo, For
Solo Voice And Orchestra
LUCKS 02051 sc $4.00, set $8.00,
pts $.75, ea.   (V37)

Don Carlos: O Don Fatale, For Solo
Voice And Orchestra
LUCKS 02089 sc $3.75, set $7.50,
pts $.75, ea.   (V38)

Don Carlos: Per Me Giunto, O Carlo,
Ascolta, For Solo Voice And
Orchestra
LUCKS 02411 sc $6.00, set $11.00,
pts $.75, ea.   (V39)

Due Foscari, I: Cabaletta Di Jacopo,
For Solo Voice And Orchestra [6']
2.2.2.2. 4.2.3.1. strings,T solo
(Spada, P.) sc ZERBONI 8266 f.s.,
pts ZERBONI 8267 rent   (V40)

Ernani: Ernani Involami, For Solo
Voice And Orchestra
LUCKS 02291 sc $3.75, set $7.50,
pts $.75, ea.   (V41)

Ernani: Infelice, E Tu Credevi, For
Solo Voice And Orchestra
LUCKS 02113 sc $7.00, set $12.00,
pts $.75, ea.   (V42)

Ernani: Preludio
KALMUS A4555 sc $3.00, perf mat
rent, set $12.00, pts $.75, ea. (V43)

Falstaff: E Sogno? O Realta?, For
Solo Voice And Orchestra
LUCKS 02742 sc $6.00, set $12.00,
pts $.75, ea.   (V44)

Finto Stanislao, Il: Overture [6']
2.2.2.2. 4.2.3.1. timp,perc,
strings
KALMUS 5283 sc $15.00, perf mat
rent, set $35.00, pts $1.50, ea.
(V45)

Forza Del Destino, La: O Tu Che In
Seno Agli Angeli, For Solo Voice
And Orchestra
LUCKS 03221 sc $3.75, set $9.50,
pts $.75, ea.   (V46)

Forza Del Destino, La: Overture
LUCKS 06934 sc $9.50, set $18.00,
min sc $3.00, pts $1.15, ea.   (V47)
(Spada, P.) 3.2.2.2. 4.2.3.1. timp,
bass drum,strings [5'] sc ZERBONI
8316 f.s., pts ZERBONI 8317 rent
(V48)

Forza Del Destino, La: Pace, Pace,
Mio Dio, For Solo Voice And
Orchestra
LUCKS 02121 sc $3.00, set $7.50,
pts $.75, ea.   (V49)

Forza Del Destino, La: Solenne In
Quest'Ora, For Solo Voices And
Orchestra
LUCKS 02827 sc $3.00, set $7.50,
pts $.75, ea.   (V50)

Giovanna d'Arco: Overture
KALMUS A5053 sc $10.00, perf mat
rent, set $30.00, pts $1.50, ea.
(V51)

Io La Vidi, For Solo Voices And
Orchestra [12']
2.2.2.2. 2.2.3.0. strings,TT soli
(Spada, P.) sc ZERBONI 8198 f.s.,
pts ZERBONI 8199 rent   (V52)

Luisa Miller: Overture
KALMUS A5101 sc $12.00, perf mat
rent, set $35.00, pts $1.75, ea.
(V53)

Luisa Miller: Quando Le Sere, For
Solo Voice And Orchestra
LUCKS 03192 sc $3.00, set $12.00,
pts $.60, ea.   (V54)

Nabucco: Dio Di Guida, For Solo Voice
And Orchestra
LUCKS 03312 sc $4.75, set $8.75,
pts $.75, ea.   (V55)

VERDI, GIUSEPPE (cont'd.)

Nabucco: Overture
LUCKS 06939 sc $9.50, set $20.00,
min sc $2.00, pts $1.15, ea.   (V56)

Nabucco: Preghiera Di Fenena, For
Solo Voice And Orchestra [5']
2.2.2.2. 4.2.0.0. harp,strings,S
solo
(Spada, P.) sc ZERBONI 8307 f.s.,
pts ZERBONI 8416 rent   (V57)

Oberto Conte Di S. Bonifacio:
Overture [8']
2.2.2.2. 4.2.3.1. timp,perc,
strings
KALMUS 5284 sc $12.00, perf mat
rent, set $35.00, pts $1.50, ea.
(V58)

Otello: Ballabili [6']
3.2.2.4. 4.2+2cornet.4.0. timp,
perc,2harp,strings
KALMUS 5285 sc $10.00, perf mat
rent, set $40.00, pts $1.50, ea.
(V59)

Otello: Canzone Del Salce
"Otello: Salce! Salce!, For Solo
Voice And Orchestra" LUCKS 02794
sc $6.00, set $14.00, pts $1.00,
ea.   (V60)

Otello: Credo In Un Dio Crudel, For
Solo Voice And Orchestra
LUCKS 02221 sc $3.75, set $8.50,
pts $.75, ea.   (V61)

Otello: Niun Mi Tema, For Solo Voice
And Orchestra
LUCKS 03850 sc $3.00, set $8.00,
pts $.75, ea.   (V62)

Otello: Ora E Per Sempre Addio, For
Solo Voice And Orchestra
LUCKS 02025 sc $5.00, set $13.00,
pts $.75, ea.   (V63)

Otello: Salce! Salce!, For Solo Voice
And Orchestra *see Otello:
Canzone Del Salce

Quartet, [arr.]
(Dolan, James) string orch [30']
NEW MUSIC WEST perf mat rent
(V64)

Rigoletto: Caro Nome, For Solo Voice
And Orchestra
LUCKS 02036 sc $3.75, set $7.50,
pts $.75, ea.   (V65)

Rigoletto: Cortigiani, Vil Razza
Dannata, For Solo Voice And
Orchestra
LUCKS 02413 sc $4.00, set $10.00,
pts $.75, ea.   (V66)

Rigoletto: La Donna E Mobile, For
Solo Voice And Orchestra
LUCKS 02081 sc $3.75, set $7.50,
pts $.75, ea.   (V67)

Rigoletto: Parla Siam – Tutte Le
Feste Al Tempio, For Solo Voices
And Orchestra
LUCKS 02903 sc $3.75, set $7.50,
pts $.75, ea.   (V68)

Rigoletto: Parmi Veder Le Lagrime,
For Solo Voice And Orchestra
LUCKS 03168 sc $3.75, set $8.50,
pts $.75, ea.   (V69)

Rigoletto: Preludio
1+pic.2.2.2. 4.2.3.1. timp,perc,
strings
KALMUS A4550 sc $3.00, perf mat
rent, set $12.00, pts $.60, ea.
(V70)

Rigoletto: Questa O Quella, For Solo
Voice And Orchestra
LUCKS 02260 sc $3.75, set $7.50,
pts $.75, ea.   (V71)

Rigoletto: Signor Ne Principe: E Il
Sol Dell' Anima, For Solo Voice
And Orchestra
LUCKS 03852 sc $4.00, set $8.00,
pts $1.25, ea.   (V72)

Tantum Ergo, For Solo Voice And
Orchestra [10']
1.0.2.1. 2.2.1.0. strings,T solo
(Spada, P.) sc ZERBONI 8234 f.s.,
pts ZERBONI 8235 rent   (V73)

Traviata, La: Addio Del Passato, For
Solo Voice And Orchestra
LUCKS 02261 sc $3.75, set $7.50,
pts $.75, ea.   (V74)

Traviata, La: Ah! Dite Alla Giovine,
Morro! La Mia Memoria, For Solo
Voices And Orchestra
LUCKS 02939 sc $4.75, set $9.50,
pts $.75, ea.   (V75)

VERDI, GIUSEPPE (cont'd.)

Traviata, La: Ah Fors' E Lui; Sempre
Libera, For Solo Voice And
Orchestra
LUCKS 02052 sc $3.75, set $7.50,
pts $.75, ea.   (V76)

Traviata, La: De' Miei Bollenti
Spiriti, For Solo Voice And
Orchestra
LUCKS 02894 sc $3.75, set $7.50,
pts $.75, ea.   (V77)

Traviata, La: Di Provenza Il Mar, For
Solo Voice And Orchestra
LUCKS 02141 sc $3.75, set $7.50,
pts $.75, ea.   (V78)

Traviata, La: Libiamo, Ne' Lieti
Calici, For Solo Voices And
Orchestra
LUCKS 02443 sc $3.75, set $7.50,
pts $.75, ea.   (V79)

Traviata, La: Parigi, O Cara, For
Solo Voices And Orchestra
LUCKS 02692 sc $5.00, set $8.00,
pts $.75, ea.   (V80)

Traviata, La: Preludio, Act I
LUCKS 06936 sc $4.75, set $9.50,
pts $.95, ea.   (V81)

Traviata, La: Preludio, Act III
LUCKS 06937 sc $4.75, set $9.50,
pts $.95, ea.   (V82)

Traviata, La: Un Di Felice, Eterea,
For Solo Voices And Orchestra
LUCKS 02822 sc $5.75, set $14.50,
pts $1.00, ea.   (V83)

Trovatore, Il: Ah Si, Ben Mio, For
Solo Voice And Orchestra
LUCKS 03204 sc $4.00, set $9.00,
pts $.75, ea.   (V84)

Trovatore, Il: D'Amor Sull' Ali
Rosee, For Solo Voice And
Orchestra
LUCKS 03184 sc $3.75, set $7.50,
pts $.75, ea.   (V85)

Trovatore, Il: Di Quella Pira, For
Solo Voice And Orchestra
LUCKS 03205 sc $4.00, set $9.00,
pts $.75, ea.   (V86)

Trovatore, Il: Il Balen Del Suo
Sorriso, For Solo Voice And
Orchestra
LUCKS 02172 sc $3.75, set $8.50,
pts $.75, ea.   (V87)

Trovatore, Il: Mira, Di Acerbe
Lagrime; Vivra! Contende Il
Giubilo, For Solo Voices And
Orchestra
LUCKS 02828 sc $3.75, set $7.50,
pts $.75, ea.   (V88)

Trovatore, Il: Si, La Stanchezza; Ai
Nostri Monti, For Solo Voices And
Orchestra
LUCKS 02829 sc $3.75, set $7.50,
pts $.75, ea.   (V89)

Trovatore, Il: Stride La Vampa, For
Solo Voice And Orchestra
LUCKS 02412 sc $3.75, set $7.50,
pts $.75, ea.   (V90)

Trovatore, Il: Tacea La Notte
Placida; Di Tale Amor, For Solo
Voice And Orchestra
LUCKS 03071 sc $4.75, set $11.50,
pts $.75, ea.   (V91)

Vespri Siciliani, I: Ballabili "Le
Quattro Stagioni", Act III [29']
2.2.2.2. 4.2+2cornet.3.1. timp,
perc,harp,strings
"Vespri Siciliani, I: The Four
Seasons" KALMUS A4540 sc $40.00,
perf mat rent, set $70.00, pts
$3.50, ea.   (V92)

Vespri Siciliani, I: Nouvelle
Romance, For Solo Voice And
Orchestra [6']
1.2.2.2. 4.0.0.0. strings,T solo
(Spada, P.) (composed for M.
Villaret) sc ZERBONI 8221 f.s.,
pts ZERBONI 8222 rent   (V93)

Vespri Siciliani, I: O Tu, Palermo,
Terra Adorata, For Solo Voice And
Orchestra
LUCKS 03174 sc $4.00, set $12.00,
pts $.75, ea.   (V94)

Vespri Siciliani, I: Overture
LUCKS 06942 sc $12.00, set $20.00,
min sc $2.00, pts $1.15, ea.   (V95)

VERDI, GIUSEPPE (cont'd.)

Vespri Siciliani, I: The Four Seasons
*see Vespri Siciliani, I:
Ballabili "Le Quattro Stagioni",
Act III

VERDICTE WALZER see Strauss, Eduard

VERGESSENES LIED, FOR SOLO VOICE AND
ORCHESTRA see Strauss, Johann,
[Jr.]

VERGNUGTER KOBOLD see Hub, Franz Peter

VERGNUGUNGSZUG see Strauss, Johann,
[Jr.]

VERHAAR, ARY (1900-   )
Auflosung
see Lieder Aus Asien III, For Solo
Voice And Orchestra

Drei Geisha Lieder, For Solo Voice
And Orchestra
1.0.1.0. 0.0.0.0. pno,strings,A
solo
sc DONEMUS f.s., perf mat rent
(V96)
Du Bist
see Lieder Aus Asien III, For Solo
Voice And Orchestra

Kleine Dagmuziek [13']
2.2.2.2. 2.2.2.0.opt tuba. timp,
perc,opt cel,2db
sc DONEMUS f.s., perf mat rent
(V97)
Lieder Aus Asien III, For Solo Voice
And Orchestra *Op.11
1.0.1.0. 0.0.0.0. pno,strings,S
solo sc DONEMUS f.s., perf mat
rent
contains: Auflosung; Du Bist;
Verlassene, Die   (V98)

Verlassene, Die
see Lieder Aus Asien III, For Solo
Voice And Orchestra

VERKAUFTE BRAUT, DIE: OVERTURE see
Smetana, Bedrich, Prodana Nevesta:
Overture

VERLASSENE, DIE see Verhaar, Ary

VERLIEBTE AUGEN see Strauss, Josef

VERLIEBTES SPIEL see Muller-Marc, Raym.

VERSCHOLLENE SOLOKONZERTE IN
REKONSTRUKTIONEN see Bach, Johann
Sebastian

VERSTEINERUNG DER PHINEUS, DIE see
Dittersdorf, Karl Ditters von,
Sinfonia in D, Krebs 77

VERSUNKENE GLOCKE, DIE see Metzl,
Wladimir

VERTIGE D'EROS see Schuller, Gunther

VERWANDLUNG DER LYCISCHEN BAUERN see
Dittersdorf, Karl Ditters von,
Sinfonia in A, Krebs 78

VERWANDTE SEELEN, FOR TWO CLARINETS AND
ORCHESTRA see Schreiner, Alexander

VESELOHERNA PREDOHRA see Patejdl,
Vaclav

VESPRI SICILIANI, I: BALLABILI "LE
QUATTRO STAGIONI", ACT III see
Verdi, Giuseppe

VESPRI SICILIANI, I: NOUVELLE ROMANCE,
FOR SOLO VOICE AND ORCHESTRA see
Verdi, Giuseppe

VESPRI SICILIANI, I: O TU, PALERMO,
TERRA ADORATA, FOR SOLO VOICE AND
ORCHESTRA see Verdi, Giuseppe

VESPRI SICILIANI, I: OVERTURE see
Verdi, Giuseppe

VESPRI SICILIANI, I: THE FOUR SEASONS
see Verdi, Giuseppe, Vespri
Siciliani, I: Ballabili "Le Quattro
Stagioni", Act III

VESTALE, LA: OVERTURE see Spontini,
Gaspare

VESTALIN, DIE: OVERTURE see Spontini,
Gaspare, Vestale, La: Overture

VIA CRUCIS DI UN'ANIMA, SETTE STAZIONI
PER ORGANO E ORCHESTRA D'ARCHI see
Viezzer, M.

VIA UR DALARAPSODI see Kallstenius,
Edvin

VIANDANTE, IL see Bossi, [Marco] Enrico

VIANDANTE, IL, FOR VIOLONCELLO AND
ORCHESTRA see Lupi, Roberto

VIBRATIONEN WALZER see Strauss, Johann,
[Jr.]

VICTOR-VON-SCHEFFEL-MARSCH see
Friedemann, Carl

VICTORIA POLKA see Strauss, Josef

VICTORIS LAUS see Dalla Vecchia,
Wolfango

VICTORY, GERARD (1921-   )
Three Irish Pictures
sc BOTE f.s.   (V99)

VICTORY MARCH see Luck, Arthur

VIDEO see Morthenson, Jan W.

VIE ANTERIEURE, LA, FOR SOLO VOICE AND
ORCHESTRA see Duparc, Henri

VIENNA LIFE see Strauss, Johann, [Jr.],
Wiener Blut Walzer

VIER ERNSTE GESANGE, FOR SOLO VOICE AND
ORCHESTRA, [ARR.] see Brahms,
Johannes

VIER GEDICHTEN, FOR SOLO VOICE AND
ORCHESTRA see Ketting, Piet

VIER IDYLLEN see Hildebrand, Camillo

VIER LETZTE LIEDER, FOR SOLO VOICE AND
ORCHESTRA see Strauss, Richard

VIER LIEDEREN, FOR SOLO VOICE AND
ORCHESTRA see Flothuis, Marius

VIER LIEDEREN, FOR SOLO VOICE AND
ORCHESTRA see Mulder, Herman

VIER LIEDEREN, FOR SOLO VOICE AND
ORCHESTRA see Ruyneman, Daniel

VIER LIEDEREN, NAAR AANLEIDING VAN OUD-
HOLLANDSCHE MELODIEEN, FOR SOLO
VOICE AND ORCHESTRA see Beekhuis,
Hanna

VIER OUVERTUREN, BWV 1066-1069 see
Bach, Johann Sebastian, Suites Nos.
1-4, BWV 1066-1069

VIER REVIUS LIEDEREN, FOR SOLO VOICE
AND STRING ORCHESTRA see
Andriessen, Jurriaan

VIER TANZE see Franckenstein, Clemens
von

VIER TEMPERAMENTE, DIE see Degen,
Johannes

VIER VERZEN, FOR SOLO VOICE AND
ORCHESTRA see Van Lier, Bertus

VIER WIEGELIEDJES, FOR SOLO VOICE AND
STRING ORCHESTRA, [ARR.] see
Badings, Henk

VIERLING, GEORG (1820-1901)
Tragische Ouverture *Op.61 (from
Hexe, Die) [10']
2.2.2.2. 2.2.3.0. timp,strings
sc,pts LIENAU rent   (V100)

VIERUNDFUNFZIG ENDUNGEN see Detoni,
Dubravko

VIEUXTEMPS, HENRI (1820-1881)
Concerto for Violin and Orchestra,
No. 5, Op. 37, in A minor
LUCKS 00534 sc $14.50, set $28.00,
pts $1.40, ea.   (V101)

Elegy for Viola and Orchestra, Op.
30, [arr.]
(Blendinger, Herbert) 2.2.2.2.
3.0.0.0. timp,harp,strings,vla
solo [7'] ORLANDO rent   (V102)

VIEZZER, M. (1925-   )
Giorno In Conservatorio, Un [9']
2.2.2.2. 2.1.0.0. timp,perc,
strings
sc,pts ZANIBON 5091 rent   (V103)

Via Crucis Di Un'Anima, Sette
Stazioni Per Organo E Orchestra
D'archi [17']
strings,org solo
sc,pts ZANIBON 5090 rent   (V104)

VIJF LIEDEREN, FOR SOLO VOICE AND
ORCHESTRA see Dijk, Jan van

VILLA-LOBOS, HEITOR (1887-1959)
Bachianas Brasileiras No. 7
ESCHIG sc,pts rent, min sc f.s.
(V105)
Introduction Aux Choros
sc,pts ESCHIG rent   (V106)

Suite for String Orchestra
string orch
sc,pts ESCHIG rent   (V107)

VILLAGE, THE see Flosman, Oldrich,
Partita No. 2

VILLAGE ROMEO AND JULIET, A: THE WALK
TO PARADISE GARDEN see Delius,
Frederick

VILLAGE SWALLOWS see Strauss, Josef,
Dorfschwalben Aus Osterreich, For
Solo Voice And Orchestra

VILLAGE SWALLOWS WALTZ see Strauss,
Josef, Dorfschwalben Aus Osterreich

VILLONERIE, FOR SOLO VOICE AND
ORCHESTRA see Henkemans, Hans

VILLOTTA see Bossi, Renzo

VINTAGE ALICE, FOR SOLO VOICE AND
ORCHESTRA see Del Tredici, David

VIOLIN CONCERTOS AND TWO SIMPHONIES
CONCERTANTES see Saint-Georges,
Joseph Boulogne de

VIOLINS OF AUTUMN, THE see Dorward,
David

VIOLON DE LA MORT, LE, FOR VIOLIN,
PIANO AND ORCHESTRA see Zieritz,
Grete von

VIOTTI, GIOVANNI BATTISTA (1755-1824)
Concerto for Violin and Orchestra,
No. 22, in A minor
min sc PETERS 825 $7.00   (V108)
LUCKS 00536 sc $17.00, set $20.00,
min sc $4.50, pts $1.40, ea.
(V109)
Concerto for Violin and Orchestra,
No. 23, in G
LUCKS 00581 set $14.00, pts $1.40,
ea.   (V110)

Concerto for Violoncello and
Orchestra [15']
0.2.0.0. 2.0.0.0. strings,vcl
solo
sc BRUZZI S-062 $8.00, perf mat
rent   (V111)

Symphonie Concertante in B flat
see Deshayes, Prosper-Didier,
Symphony in D

Symphonie Concertante No. 2 for 2
Violins and Orchestra [20']
2.2.2.2. 2.0.0.0. strings,2vln
soli
sc CARISCH 19897 f.s., pts CARISCH
20199 f.s.   (V112)

VIRIDIAN see Meale, Richard

VIRTU AL CIMENTO, LA: SINFONIA see
Paer, Ferdinando

VIRTUOSA IN MERGELLINA, LA: TERZETTO,
FOR SOLO VOICES AND ORCHESTRA see
Guglielmi, Pietro Alessandro

VIS, LUCAS (1947-   )
Openingsmuziek [2']
1.0.1.1. 2.0.0.0. perc,strings
sc DONEMUS f.s., perf mat rent
(V113)

VISION see Rixner, Josef

VISIONE DI S. MARTINO see Caltabiano,
Sebastiano

VISIONE EROICA see Bonelli, Ettore

VISIONE ORIENTALE see Becce, Giuseppe

VISIONEN see Matthus, Siegfried

VISIONEN, FOR VIOLIN AND ORCHESTRA see
Tiessen, Heinz

VISIONS OF FRANCESCO PETRARCA, THE, FOR
SOLO VOICE, INSTRUMENTAL ENSEMBLE
AND SCHOOL ORCHESTRA see
Birtwistle, Harrison

VISIONS OF TERROR AND WONDER, FOR SOLO
VOICE AND ORCHESTRA see Wernick,
Richard

VISIONS OF TIME see Siegmeister, Elie,
Symphony No. 5

VISIONS SONORES FUR SECHS
    SCHLAGZEUGGRUPPEN UND SECHS
    OBLIGATE INSTRUMENTE see
    Kelterborn, Rudolf

VISSER, PETER (1939-   )
    Concertino Da Primavera, For Piano
      And Orchestra [23']
      1.1.1.1. 1.0.0.0. timp,strings,
      pno solo
      DONEMUS sc f.s., pno red f.s., pts
      rent   (V114)

    Lamento Per Archi [11']
      string orch
      DONEMUS   (V115)

VISTAS see Mathias, William

VITA SOMNIUM see Schumann, Georg

VITRAUX POUR NOTRE DAME, FOR SOLO VOICE
    AND STRING ORCHESTRA see
    Charpentier, Jacques

VITTADINI, FRANCO (1884-1948)
    Taglioni, La
      3.3.3.3. 4.3.3.1. timp,perc,
      2harp,cel,xylo,pno,strings
      manuscript CARISCH   (V116)

VITTORIO, E. (1908-1969)
    Preludio E Allegro [10']
      string orch
      sc CARISCH 20912 f.s., perf mat
      rent   (V117)

VIVALDI, ANTONIO (1678-1741)
    Canta In Prato, For Solo Voice And
      String Orchestra [6']
      string orch,cont,solo voice
      (Mortari, V.) sc,pts CARISCH rent
                                        (V118)
    Canta In Prato, For Solo Voice And
      String Orchestra, RV 636
      string orch,cont,S solo
      (Graulich) sc CARUS 40.006-01 f.s.,
      pts CARUS f.s.   (V119)

    Cardellino, Il *see Concerto, RV
      428, Op. 10, No. 3, in D, P. 155,
      F.VI no. 14

    Cessate Omai Cessate, For Solo Voice
      And String Orchestra [4']
      string orch,A solo
      manuscript CARISCH   (V120)

    Cimento Dell'Armonia E
      Dell'Invenzione, Il, Vol. 1
      sc RICORDI-IT PR1235 f.s.
        contains: Concerto, RV 180, Op.
        8, No. 6, in C, P. 7, F.I no.
        27; Concerto, RV 253, Op. 8,
        No. 5, in E flat, P. 415, F.I
        no. 26; Concerto, RV 269, Op.
        8, No. 1, in E, P. 241, F.I no.
        22; Concerto, RV 293, Op. 8,
        No. 3, in F, P. 257, F.I no.
        24; Concerto, RV 297, Op. 8,
        No. 4, in F minor, P. 442, F.I
        no. 25; Concerto, RV 315, Op.
        8, No. 2, in G minor, P. 336,
        F.I no. 23   (V121)

    Cimento Dell'Armonia E
      Dell'Invenzione, Il, Vol. 2
      sc RICORDI-IT PR1236 f.s.
        contains: Concerto, RV 178, Op.
        8, No. 12, in C, P. 8, F.I no.
        31; Concerto, RV 210, Op. 8,
        No. 11, in D, P. 153, F.I no.
        30; Concerto, RV 242, Op. 8,
        No. 7, in D minor, P. 258, F.I
        no. 28; Concerto, RV 332, Op.
        8, No. 8, in G minor, P. 337,
        F.I no. 16; Concerto, RV 362,
        Op. 8, No. 10, in B flat, P.
        338, F.I no. 29; Concerto, RV
        454, Op. 8, No. 9, in D minor,
        P. 259, F.VII no. 1   (V122)

    Concerto Alla Rustica [5']
      string orch,cont
      sc CARISCH 19453 f.s., pts CARISCH
      19804 f.s.   (V123)

    Concerto in B, MIN 111 [15']
      string orch,cont,vln solo
      sc CARISCH 20530 f.s., pts CARISCH
      18634 f.s.   (V124)

    Concerto in C minor, [arr.] (from RV
      17)
      string orch,ob solo,vln solo MUS.
      RARA 1642B f.s.   (V125)

    Concerto in D, MIN 3 [10']
      string orch,cont,gtr solo
      (Scheit, K.) sc,pts DOBLINGER
      GKM 41 f.s.   (V126)

    Concerto in D, MIN 67
      string orch,cont,vcl solo
      (Rapp) SCHOTTS ANT 121 sc $10.50,
      pts $2.50, ea., kbd pt $3.50

VIVALDI, ANTONIO (cont'd.)

                                        (V127)
    Concerto in D, MIN 113
      orch,gtr solo
      SPAN.MUS.CTR. perf mat rent   (V128)

    Concerto in D minor, MIN 20, [arr.]
      (Siloti) 2.2.2.2+contrabsn.
      0.0.0.0. org,strings BROUDE BR.
      set $20.00, pts $1.25, ea., sc
      $10.00   (V129)

    Concerto in E flat, [arr.] (from F. X
      Nos. 1 And 2)
      string orch,2trp soli [9']
      INTERNAT. perf mat rent   (V130)

    Concerto, MIN 39 [15']
      string orch,hpsd,3vln soli
      (Schumann, Georg) sc,pts LIENAU
      f.s.   (V131)

    Concerto, RV 112, in C, F.XI no. 47
      string orch,cont
      sc RICORDI-IT PR1182 $4.00   (V132)

    Concerto, RV 113, in C, P. 94, F.XI
      no. 48
      string orch,cont
      sc RICORDI-IT PR1184 $4.00   (V133)

    Concerto, RV 116, in C, F.XI no. 46
      string orch,cont
      sc RICORDI-IT PR1181 $4.00   (V134)

    Concerto, RV 132, in E, F.XI no. 50
      string orch,cont
      sc RICORDI-IT PR1190 $4.00   (V135)

    Concerto, RV 137, in F, F.XI no. 51
      string orch,cont
      sc RICORDI-IT PR1191 $4.00   (V136)

    Concerto, RV 144, in G, P. 145, F.XI
      no. 49
      string orch,cont
      sc RICORDI-IT PR1187 $4.00   (V137)

    Concerto, RV 148, in G, F.XII no. 49
      string orch,cont,fl solo
      sc RICORDI-IT PR1010 $4.00   (V138)

    Concerto, RV 151, Op. 51, No. 4, in
      G, P. 143, F.XI no. 11 [4']
      string orch,cont
      LUCKS 01747 sc $5.75, set $9.00,
      min sc $2.00, pts $1.40, ea.
                                        (V139)
    Concerto, RV 168, in B minor, F.XI
      no. 52
      string orch,cont
      sc RICORDI-IT PR1193 $4.00   (V140)

    Concerto, RV 175, in C, P. 93, F.I
      no. 232
      string orch,cont,vln solo
      sc RICORDI-IT PR1183 $4.00   (V141)

    Concerto, RV 178, Op. 8, No. 12, in
      C, P. 8, F.I no. 31
      see Cimento Dell'Armonia E
      Dell'Invenzione, Il, Vol. 2

    Concerto, RV 180, Op. 8, No. 6, in C,
      P. 7, F.I no. 27
      see Cimento Dell'Armonia E
      Dell'Invenzione, Il, Vol. 1

    Concerto, RV 185, Op. 4, No. 7, in C,
      P. 4, F.I no. 186
      see Stravaganza, La, Vol. 2

    Concerto, RV 196, Op. 4, No. 10, in C
      minor, P. 413, F.I no. 189
      see Stravaganza, La, Vol. 2

    Concerto, RV 204, Op. 4, No. 11, in
      D, P. 149, F.I no. 190
      see Stravaganza, La, Vol. 2

    Concerto, RV 210, Op. 8, No. 11, in
      D, P. 153, F.I no. 30
      see Cimento Dell'Armonia E
      Dell'Invenzione, Il, Vol. 2

    Concerto, RV 212a, Op. 35, No. 19, in
      D, P. 165, F.I no. 136 [11']
      string orch,cont,vln solo
      LUCKS 01749 sc $5.00, set $12.00,
      pts $1.25, ea.   (V142)
      (Jenkins) KALMUS A2217 kbd pt
      $3.00, sc $5.00, set $7.50, pts
      $1.25, ea.   (V143)

    Concerto, RV 227, in D, P. 211, F.I
      no. 234
      string orch,cont,vln solo
      sc RICORDI-IT PR1188 $4.50   (V144)

    Concerto, RV 230, Op. 3, No. 9, in D,
      P. 147, F.I no. 178
      see Estro Armonico, L', Vol. 2
      (Heller) sc,quarto PETERS 9459
      $24.50, ipa   (V145)

VIVALDI, ANTONIO (cont'd.)

    Concerto, RV 237, Op. 61, No. 2, in D
      minor, P. 277, F.I no. 143
      (Heller) sc,quarto PETERS 9463
      $21.50   (V146)
      (Heller; Held) sc,pts PETERS
      EP 9063 f.s.   (V147)

    Concerto, RV 242, Op. 8, No. 7, in D
      minor, P. 258, F.I no. 28
      see Cimento Dell'Armonia E
      Dell'Invenzione, Il, Vol. 2

    Concerto, RV 249, Op. 4, No. 8, in D
      minor, P. 253, F.I no. 187
      see Stravaganza, La, Vol. 2

    Concerto, RV 253, Op. 8, No. 5, in E
      flat, P. 415, F.I no. 26
      see Cimento Dell'Armonia E
      Dell'Invenzione, Il, Vol. 1

    Concerto, RV 256, in E flat, F.I no.
      231
      string orch,cont,vln solo
      sc RICORDI-IT PR1177 $4.50   (V148)

    Concerto, RV 265, Op. 3, No. 12, in E
      minor, P. 240, F.I no. 179
      see Estro Armonico, L', Vol. 2

    Concerto, RV 269, Op. 8, No. 1, in E,
      P. 241, F.I no. 22 [12']
      string orch,cont,vln solo
      see Cimento Dell'Armonia E
      Dell'Invenzione, Il, Vol. 1
      see Quattro Stagioni, Le
      see Quattro Stagioni, Le
      LUCKS 07113 sc $4.00, set $7.00,
      min sc $2.50, pts $1.15, ea.
                                        (V149)
      (Kolneder) PETERS P9056A sc $16.50,
      set $12.50, pts $2.50, ea. (V150)

    Concerto, RV 275, Op. 16, No. 2, in E
      minor, P. 109, F.I no. 220
      string orch,cont,vln solo
      MOSELER 40.132 sc,pts f.s., solo pt
      f.s.   (V151)

    Concerto, RV 279, Op. 4, No. 2, in E
      minor, P. 98, F.I no. 181
      see Stravaganza, La, Vol. 1

    Concerto, RV 284, Op. 4, No. 9, in F,
      P. 251, F.I no. 188
      see Stravaganza, La, Vol. 2

    Concerto, RV 293, Op. 8, No. 3, in F,
      P. 257, F.I no. 24 [11']
      string orch,cont,vln solo
      see Cimento Dell'Armonia E
      Dell'Invenzione, Il, Vol. 1
      see Quattro Stagioni, Le
      see Quattro Stagioni, Le
      LUCKS 07115 sc $4.00, set $7.00,
      min sc $2.50, pts $1.15, ea.
                                        (V152)
      (Kolneder) PETERS P9056C sc $16.50,
      set $12.50, pts $2.50, ea. (V153)

    Concerto, RV 297, Op. 8, No. 4, in F
      minor, P. 442, F.I no. 25 [12']
      string orch,cont,vln solo
      see Cimento Dell'Armonia E
      Dell'Invenzione, Il, Vol. 1
      see Quattro Stagioni, Le
      see Quattro Stagioni, Le
      LUCKS 07116 sc $4.00, set $7.00,
      min sc $2.50, pts $1.15, ea.
                                        (V154)
      (Kolneder) PETERS P9056D sc $16.50,
      set $12.50, pts $2.50, ea. (V155)

    Concerto, RV 298, Op. 4, No. 12, in
      G, P. 100, F.I no. 191
      see Stravaganza, La, Vol. 2

    Concerto, RV 301, Op. 4, No. 3, in G,
      P. 99, F.I no. 182
      see Stravaganza, La, Vol. 1

    Concerto, RV 310, Op. 3, No. 3, in G,
      P. 96, F.I no. 173
      string orch,cont,vln solo
      see Estro Armonico, L', Vol. 1
      sc AMADEUS BP 2450 f.s., pts
      AMADEUS f.s.   (V156)
      (Heller) sc,quarto PETERS 9453
      $24.50, ipa   (V157)

    Concerto, RV 315, Op. 8, No. 2, in G
      minor, P. 336, F.I no. 23 [11']
      string orch,cont,vln solo
      see Cimento Dell'Armonia E
      Dell'Invenzione, Il, Vol. 1
      see Quattro Stagioni, Le
      see Quattro Stagioni, Le
      LUCKS 07114 sc $4.00, set $7.00,
      min sc $2.50, pts $1.15, ea.
                                        (V158)
      (Kolneder) PETERS P9056B sc $16.50,
      set $12.50, pts $2.50, ea. (V159)

VIVALDI, ANTONIO (cont'd.)

Concerto, RV 316a, Op. 4, No. 6, in G
    minor, P. 328, F.I no. 185
    see Stravaganza, La, Vol. 1

Concerto, RV 332, Op. 8, No. 8, in G
    minor, P. 337, F.I no. 16
    see Cimento Dell'Armonia E
    Dell'Invenzione, Il, Vol. 2

Concerto, RV 347, Op. 4, No. 5, in A,
    P. 213, F.I no. 184
    see Stravaganza, La, Vol. 1

Concerto, RV 354, Op. 7, No. 4, in A
    minor, P. 6, F.I no. 200
    (Fechner) sc,quarto PETERS 9834
    $19.50, ipa   (V160)

Concerto, RV 355, in A minor, P. 92,
    F.I no. 236
    string orch,cont,vln solo
    sc RICORDI-IT PR1194 $4.00   (V161)

Concerto, RV 356, Op. 3, No. 6, in A
    minor, P. 1, F.I no. 176 [11']
    string orch,cont,vln solo
    see Estro Armonico, L', Vol. 1
    sc AMADEUS BP 2468 f.s., pts
    AMADEUS f.s.   (V162)
    (Einstein) LUCKS 01329 set $12.00,
    min sc $3.50, pts $1.50, ea.
                                    (V163)

Concerto, RV 357, Op. 4, No. 4, in A
    minor, P. 3, F.I no. 183
    see Stravaganza, La, Vol. 1

Concerto, RV 362, Op. 8, No. 10, in B
    flat, P. 338, F.I no. 29
    see Cimento Dell'Armonia E
    Dell'Invenzione, Il, Vol. 2

Concerto, RV 369, Op. 33, No. 4, in B
    flat, P. 356, F.I no. 65
    (Heller) sc,quarto PETERS 9464
    $19.50, ipa   (V164)

Concerto, RV 381, in B flat, P. 327,
    F.I no. 235
    string orch,cont,vln solo
    sc RICORDI-IT PR1189 $4.00   (V165)

Concerto, RV 382, in B flat, P. 412,
    F.I no. 233
    string orch,cont,vln solo
    sc RICORDI-IT PR1186 $4.00   (V166)

Concerto, RV 383a, Op. 4, No. 1, in B
    flat, P. 327, F.I no. 180
    see Stravaganza, La, Vol. 1

Concerto, RV 402, in C minor, F.III
    no. 27
    string orch,cont,vcl solo
    sc RICORDI-IT PR1202 $4.00   (V167)

Concerto, RV 405, in D minor, F.III
    no. 24
    string orch,cont,vcl solo
    sc RICORDI-IT PR1199 $4.00   (V168)

Concerto, RV 407, in D minor, F.III
    no. 23
    string orch,cont,vcl solo
    sc RICORDI-IT PR1198 $4.00   (V169)

Concerto, RV 415, in G, F.III no. 22
    string orch,cont,vcl solo
    sc RICORDI-IT PR1197 $4.00   (V170)

Concerto, RV 416, in G minor, F.III
    no. 26
    string orch,cont,vcl solo
    sc RICORDI-IT PR1201 $4.00   (V171)

Concerto, RV 420, in A minor, F.III
    no. 21
    string orch,cont,vcl solo
    sc RICORDI-IT PR1196 $4.00   (V172)

Concerto, RV 422, Op. 26, No. 2, in A
    minor, P. 24, F.III no. 4 [10']
    string orch,cont,vcl solo
    LUCKS 01848 sc $3.00, set $4.75,
    set $.95, ea.   (V173)
    (Mezo) SCHOTTS CON 173 sc $3.50,
    pts $2.50, ea., solo pt $3.50
                                    (V174)
    (Upmeyer) KALMUS A3252 sc $4.00,
    set $6.00, pts $1.00, ea.   (V175)

Concerto, RV 423, in B flat, F.III
    no. 25
    string orch,cont,vcl solo
    sc RICORDI-IT PR1200 $4.00   (V176)

Concerto, RV 428, Op. 10, No. 3, in
    D, P. 155, F.VI no. 14
    BROUDE BR. sc $5.00, set $8.75, pts
    $1.10, ea.   (V177)

Concerto, RV 433, Op. 10, No. 1, in
    F, P. 261, F.VI no. 12
    min sc ZEN-ON 890142 f.s.   (V178)

VIVALDI, ANTONIO (cont'd.)

Concerto, RV 434, Op. 10, No. 5, in
    F, P. 262, F.VI no. 1 [10']
    string orch,cont,fl solo
    (Redel) KALMUS A2209 sc $6.00, set
    $7.50, pts $1.25, ea.   (V179)
    (Redel) sc,pts ZIMMER. ZM1093 f.s.
                                    (V180)
    (Redel) LUCKS 01374 sc $6.00, set
    $12.00, pts $1.00, ea.   (V181)

Concerto, RV 444, Op. 44, No. 9, in
    C, P. 78, F.VI no. 5
    MUS. RARA 1529 f.s.   (V182)

Concerto, RV 445, Op. 44, No. 26, in
    A minor, P. 83, F.VI no. 9
    MUS. RARA 1184 f.s.   (V183)

Concerto, RV 452, in C, P. 91, F.VII
    no. 17
    string orch,cont,ob solo
    sc RICORDI-IT 1195 $4.00   (V184)

Concerto, RV 454, Op. 8, No. 9, in D
    minor, P. 259, F.VII no. 1
    string orch,cont,ob solo
    see Cimento Dell'Armonia E
    Dell'Invenzione, Il, Vol. 2
    sc,pts MUS. RARA 41.945-20 f.s.
                                    (V185)

Concerto, RV 455, Op. 39, No. 6, in
    F, P. 306, F.VII no. 2
    MUS. RARA 1956B f.s.   (V186)

Concerto, RV 461, Op. 39, No. 2, in A
    minor, P. 42, F.VII no. 5
    MUS. RARA 1955B f.s.   (V187)

Concerto, RV 463, Op. 57, No. 1, in A
    minor, P. 89, F.VII no. 13
    MUS. RARA 1963B f.s.   (V188)

Concerto, RV 501, Op. 45, No. 8, in B
    flat, P. 401, F.VIII no. 1
    INTERNAT. perf mat rent   (V189)

Concerto, RV 509, Op. 21, No. 4, in C
    minor, P. 436, F.I no. 12
    KALMUS A2210 sc $4.00 set $10.00,
    pts $1.50, ea., kbd pt $3.00
                                    (V190)

Concerto, RV 510, Op. 21, No. 2, in C
    minor, P. 435, F.I no. 14 [7']
    string orch,cont,2vln soli
    LUCKS 06029 sc $4.00, set $9.00,
    pts $1.15, ea.   (V191)

Concerto, RV 519, Op. 3, No. 5, in A,
    P. 212, F.I no. 175
    see Estro Armonico, L', Vol. 1
    (Heller) sc,quarto PETERS 9455
    $21.00, ipa   (V192)

Concerto, RV 522, Op. 3, No. 8, in A
    minor, P. 2, F.I no. 177 [11']
    string orch,cont,2vln soli
    see Estro Armonico, L', Vol. 2
    INTERNAT. perf mat rent   (V193)
    LUCKS 06031 sc $5.75, set $14.00,
    min sc $3.50, pts $1.40, ea.
                                    (V194)
    (Eller) sc,quarto PETERS 9458
    $24.50, ipa   (V195)

Concerto, RV 531, Op. 58, No. 3, in G
    minor, P. 411, F.III no. 2
    INTERNAT. perf mat rent   (V196)

Concerto, RV 533, Op. 47, No. 2, in
    C, P. 76, F.VI no. 2 [8']
    string orch,cont,2fl soli
    INTERNAT. perf mat rent   (V197)
    LUCKS 06032 sc $4.75, set $11.00,
    pts $1.15, ea.   (V198)

Concerto, RV 537, Op. 46, No. 1, in
    C, P. 75, F.IX no. 1
    INTERNAT. perf mat rent   (V199)

Concerto, RV 540, Op. 63, No. 2, in D
    minor, P. 266, F.XII no. 38
    (Benko, Daniel) string orch,vla
    solo,gtr solo SCHOTTS CON 191 sc
    $10.50, pts $2.50, ea.   (V200)

Concerto, RV 549, Op. 3, No. 1, in D,
    P. 146, F.IV no. 7
    see Estro Armonico, L', Vol. 1
    (Heller) sc,quarto PETERS 9451
    $25.00, ipa   (V201)

Concerto, RV 550, Op. 3, No. 4, in E
    minor, P. 97, F.I no. 174
    see Estro Armonico, L', Vol. 1
    (Heller) sc,quarto PETERS 9454
    $24.50, ipa   (V202)

Concerto, RV 563, in D, P. 210, F.XII
    no. 50
    string orch,cont,2ob soli,vln
    solo
    sc RICORDI-IT PR1185 $4.00   (V203)

VIVALDI, ANTONIO (cont'd.)

Concerto, RV 565, Op. 3, No. 11, in D
    minor, P. 250, F.IV no. 11
    see Estro Armonico, L', Vol. 2
    (Einstein) KALMUS A4535 sc $5.00,
    set $9.00, pts $1.25, ea.   (V204)

Concerto, RV 567, Op. 3, No. 7, in F,
    P. 249, F.IV no. 9
    see Estro Armonico, L', Vol. 2
    (Heller) sc,quarto PETERS 9457
    $24.50, ipa   (V205)

Concerto, RV 578, Op. 3, No. 2, in G
    minor, P. 326, F.IV no. 8 [12']
    string orch,cont,2vln soli,vcl
    solo
    see Estro Armonico, L', Vol. 1
    KALMUS 5286 sc $5.00, perf mat
    rent, set $12.00, pts $1.50, ea.
                                    (V206)
    LUCKS 01325 sc $5.00, set $12.00,
    pts $1.50, ea.   (V207)

Concerto, RV 580, Op. 3, No. 10, in B
    minor, P. 148, F.IV no. 10 [11']
    string orch,cont,4vln soli
    see Estro Armonico, L', Vol. 2
    (Eller) sc,quarto PETERS 9460
    $24.50, ipa   (V208)
    (Woehl) LUCKS 00538 sc $12.00, set
    $15.00, min sc $3.50, pts $1.50,
    ea.   (V209)

Concerto, RV 582, Op. 54, No. 2, in
    D, P. 164, F.I no. 62
    (Schroeder) KALMUS A2211 kbd pt
    $4.00, ea., sc $8.00, set $12.00,
    pts $1.50, ea.   (V210)

Concerto, RV 761, in C minor
    string orch,cont,vln solo
    (Talbot, Michael) (Amato Bene) sc
    OXFORD 27.013 $15.00, perf mat
    rent   (V211)

Concerto, RV Anh. 9, in D, F.I no.
    237 [8']
    string orch,cont,vln solo
    (Zanotelli, A.; Raffaelli, P.)
    (authenticity doubtful) sc
    ZANIBON 5783 f.s., pts ZANIBON
    5784 f.s.   (V212)

Dorilla: Balletti [8']
    0.2.0.0. 2.0.0.0. strings
    (Mortari, V.) CARISCH perf mat rent
                                    (V213)

Estro Armonico, L', Vol. 1
    sc RICORDI-IT PR1231 f.s.
    contains: Concerto, RV 310, Op.
    3, No. 3, in G, P. 96, F.I no.
    173; Concerto, RV 356, Op. 3,
    No. 6, in A minor, P. 1, F.I
    no. 176; Concerto, RV 519, Op.
    3, No. 5, in A, P. 212, F.I no.
    175; Concerto, RV 549, Op. 3,
    No. 1, in D, P. 146, F.IV no.
    7; Concerto, RV 550, Op. 3, No.
    4, in E minor, P. 97, F.I no.
    174; Concerto, RV 578, Op. 3,
    No. 2, in G minor, P. 326, F.IV
    no. 8   (V214)

Estro Armonico, L', Vol. 2
    sc RICORDI-IT PR1232 f.s.
    contains: Concerto, RV 230, Op.
    3, No. 9, in D, P. 147, F.I no.
    178; Concerto, RV 265, Op. 3,
    No. 12, in E minor, P. 240, F.I
    no. 179; Concerto, RV 522, Op.
    3, No. 8, in A minor, P. 2, F.I
    no. 177; Concerto, RV 565, Op.
    3, No. 11, in D minor, P. 250,
    F.IV no. 11; Concerto, RV 567,
    Op. 3, No. 7, in F, P. 249,
    F.IV no. 9; Concerto, RV 580,
    Op. 3, No. 10, in B minor, P.
    148, F.IV no. 10   (V215)

Four Seasons, The *see Concerti, RV
    269, RV 315, RV 293, RV 297

Giustino, Il: Sinfonia [6']
    string orch,cont
    (Bruni, M.) sc CARISCH 21415 f.s.,
    pts CARISCH 21416 f.s.   (V216)

In Turbato Mare Irato, For Solo Voice
    And String Orchestra *RV 627
    string orch,cont,S solo
    sc DEUTSCHER 9520 f.s., pts
    DEUTSCHER 9520A f.s.   (V217)

Notte, La *see Concerto, RV 501, Op.
    45, No. 8, in B flat, P. 401,
    F.VIII no. 1

Olimpiade: Ouverture [6']
    string orch
    (Mortari, V.) f.s. sc CARISCH
    19449, pts CARISCH 19605   (V218)

VIVALDI, ANTONIO (cont'd.)

Piango, For Solo Voice And String
Orchestra [8']
string orch,cont,solo voice
sc CARISCH 21955 rent, pts CARISCH
21955A rent   (V219)

Quattro Stagioni, Le
sc RICORDI-IT PR1230 f.s.
contains: Concerto, RV 269, Op.
8, No. 1, in E, P. 241, F.I no.
22; Concerto, RV 293, Op. 8,
No. 3, in F, P. 257, F.I no.
24; Concerto, RV 297, Op. 8,
No. 4, in F minor, P. 442, F.I
no. 25; Concerto, RV 315, Op.
8, No. 2, in G minor, P. 336,
F.I no. 23   (V220)

Quattro Stagioni, Le
min sc ZEN-ON 890141 f.s.
contains: Concerto, RV 269, Op.
8, No. 1, in E, P. 241, F.I no.
22; Concerto, RV 293, Op. 8,
No. 3, in F, P. 257, F.I no.
24; Concerto, RV 297, Op. 8,
No. 4, in F minor, P. 442, F.I
no. 25; Concerto, RV 315, Op.
8, No. 2, in G minor, P. 336,
F.I no. 23   (V221)

Sonata for Violoncello and String
Orchestra in A minor, [arr.]
(from Sonata, Op. 14, No. 3)
(Kelemen) string orch,vcl solo sc
PETERS 8107 $15.00, pts PETERS
$2.50, ea., set PETERS $15.00
(V222)

Sonata, RV 40, Op. 17, No. 5, in E
minor, F.XIV no. 5, [arr.]
1.2.1.2. 1.1.0.0. strings,db solo
[16'] INTERNAT. perf mat rent
(V223)

1.2.1.2. 1.1.0.0. harp,strings,vla
solo [12'] (in this edition
called Concerto In E Minor)
INTERNAT. perf mat rent   (V224)
2.3.2.2. 2.2.0.0. strings,vcl solo
[12'] INTERNAT. perf mat rent
(V225)
1.2.1.2. 1.1.0.0. strings,trom solo
[12'] INTERNAT. perf mat rent
(V226)
1.2.1.2. 1.1.0.0. strings,bsn solo
[12'] INTERNAT. perf mat rent
(V227)

Sonata, RV 43, Op. 17, No. 3, in A
minor, F.XIV no. 3, [arr.]
1.2.1.2. 2.2.0.0. strings without
vcl,bsn solo [17'] INTERNAT. perf
mat rent   (V228)
2.3.2.2. 2.2.0.0. harp,strings,vcl
solo [17'] INTERNAT. perf mat
rent   (V229)
1.2.1.2. 1.1.0.0. harp,strings,vla
solo [17'] INTERNAT. perf mat
rent   (V230)
1.2.1.2. 1.1.0.0. strings,db solo
[12'] INTERNAT. perf mat rent
(V231)
1.2.1.2. 1.1.0.0. harp,strings,trom
solo [17'] INTERNAT. perf mat
rent   (V232)

Sonata, RV 46, Op. 17, No. 6, in B
flat, F.XIV no. 6, [arr.]
0.2.1.1. 0.0.0.0. harp,strings,trom
solo [16'] INTERNAT. perf mat
rent   (V233)
0.2.1.1. 0.0.0.0. harp,strings,db
solo [17'] INTERNAT. perf mat
rent   (V234)
0.2.1.1. 0.0.0.0. harp,strings,vla
solo [16'] INTERNAT. perf mat
rent   (V235)
2.3.2.2. 2.2.0.0. harp,strings,vcl
solo [16'] INTERNAT. perf mat
rent   (V236)
0.2.1.1. 1.0.0.0. strings without
vla, vcl, bsn solo [16']
INTERNAT. perf mat rent   (V237)

Stravaganza, La, Vol. 1
sc RICORDI-IT PR1233 f.s.
contains: Concerto, RV 279, Op.
4, No. 2, in E minor, P. 98,
F.I no. 181; Concerto, RV 301,
Op. 4, No. 3, in G, P. 99, F.I
no. 182; Concerto, RV 316a, Op.
4, No. 6, in G minor, P. 328,
F.I no. 185; Concerto, RV 347,
Op. 4, No. 5, in A, P. 213, F.I
no. 184; Concerto, RV 357, Op.
4, No. 4, in A minor, P. 3, F.I
no. 183; Concerto, RV 383a, Op.
4, No. 1, in B flat, P. 327,
F.I no. 180   (V238)

Stravaganza, La, Vol. 2
sc RICORDI-IT PR1234 f.s.
contains: Concerto, RV 185, Op.
4, No. 7, in C, P. 4, F.I no.
186; Concerto, RV 196, Op. 4,
No. 10, in C minor, P. 413, F.I
no. 189; Concerto, RV 204, Op.

VIVALDI, ANTONIO (cont'd.)

4, No. 11, in D, P. 149, F.I
no. 190; Concerto, RV 249, Op.
4, No. 8, in D minor, P. 253,
F.I no. 187; Concerto, RV 284,
Op. 4, No. 9, in F, P. 251, F.I
no. 188; Concerto, RV 298, Op.
4, No. 12, in G, P. 100, F.I
no. 191   (V239)

Vos Aurae, For Solo Voice And String
Orchestra
string orch,cont,S solo
(Grossato, Elisa) [15'] f.s. sc
ZANIBON 5901, pts ZANIBON 5902
(V240)

VIVALDI-MONUMENT see Kont, Paul

VIVIANE see Chausson, Ernest

VLIET, HENK VAN DER (1928-   )
Cinq Etudes [15']
3.3.3.2. 3.3.3.0. timp,4perc,pno,
strings
sc DONEMUS f.s., perf mat rent
(V241)
Sinfonietta [18']
1.1.1.1. 2.1.0.0. strings
DONEMUS perf mat rent   (V242)

VLIJMEN, JAN VAN (1935-   )
Omaggio A Gesualdo, For Violin And
Orchestra [17']
4.4.3.4. 4.2.3.0. harp,gtr,2vln,
4vcl,db,vln solo
sc DONEMUS f.s., perf mat rent
(V243)
Quaterni [30']
3.3.5.5. 4.3.4.1. 2harp,cym,mand,
marimba,strings
DONEMUS sc f.s., pts rent   (V244)

VOCALISE, FOR SOLO VOICE AND STRING
ORCHESTRA, [ARR.] see Rachmaninoff,
Sergey Vassilievich

VOCALISE, [ARR.] see Rachmaninoff,
Sergey Vassilievich

VOGEL, ERNST (1926-   )
Concerto for Saxophone and Orchestra
[23']
2+pic.2.English
horn.2.2.contrabsn. 4.2.3.1.
timp,perc,strings,sax solo
sc,pts DOBLINGER rent   (V245)

Moira [18']
2+pic.2.2.2+contrabsn. 2.2.2.1.
timp,perc,strings
DOBLINGER perf mat rent   (V246)

Symphony No. 1 [28']
2+pic.2+English horn.2+clar in E
flat+bass clar.2+contrabsn.
4.2.3.1. timp,perc,cel,strings
DOBLINGER perf mat rent   (V247)

VOGEL, HELMUT (1925-   )
Sinfonietta
string orch
ASSMANN sc f.s., pts rent   (V248)

VOGEL, WILLEM (1920-   )
Concertino for Organ and String
Orchestra
string orch,org solo
sc DONEMUS f.s., perf mat rent
(V249)

VOGEL, WLADIMIR (1896-   )
Abschied
string orch
sc HUG f.s., perf mat rent   (V250)

VOGELS, DE: LIED VAN DEN HOP, FOR SOLO
VOICE AND ORCHESTRA see
Diepenbrock, Alphons

VOGLER, [ABBE] GEORG JOSEPH (1749-1814)
Exultet Orbis Gaudiis [8']
1.1.0.1. 2.0.0.0. strings
(Bodart, Eugen) MANNHEIM E 27-56
f.s.   (V251)

VOICES see Wilson, Olly

VOICES FROM THE PAST, FOR SOLO VOICES
AND STRING ORCHESTRA see Karkoff,
Maurice

VOICES OF SPRING see Strauss, Johann,
[Jr.], Fruhlingsstimmen Walzer

VOICI LA DOUCE NUIT DE MAI see
Beekhuis, Hanna

VOILES, LES see Brozak, Daniel, Zavoje

VOLKMANN, ROBERT (1815-1883)
Serenade No. 1, Op. 62, in C
string orch
LUCKS 08337 sc $3.50, set $5.75,
pts $1.15, ea.   (V252)

VOLKMANN, ROBERT (cont'd.)

Serenade No. 2, Op. 63, in F
string orch
LUCKS 06951 sc $5.00, set $4.75,
pts $.95, ea.   (V253)

Serenade No. 3, Op. 69, in D minor
string orch,vcl solo
LUCKS 00623 sc $2.75, set $4.75,
pts $.95, ea.   (V254)

VOLKSSINFONIE see Avidom, Menachem

VOLO D'API see Lavagnino, Angelo
Francesco

VOM FELS ZUM MEER see Liszt, Franz

VOM MENUETT ZUM WALZER see Geisler,
Willy

VOM UNENDLICHEN, FOR SOLO VOICE AND
STRING ORCHESTRA see Schubert,
Heinz

VON DER BORSE see Strauss, Johann,
[Jr.]

VON DER EITELKEIT DER WELT, FOR SOLO
VOICE AND ORCHESTRA see Chemin-
Petit, Hans

VONDEL'S VAART NAAR AGRIPPINE, FOR SOLO
VOICE AND ORCHESTRA see
Diepenbrock, Alphons

VOORGEVOEL see Carl, Gene

VOORMOLEN, ALEXANDER NICOLAS
(1895-1980)
Amsterdam, For Solo Voice And
Orchestra
2.3.3.2. 4.0.0.0. perc,harp,cel,
strings,Mez/Bar solo
sc DONEMUS f.s., perf mat rent
(V255)
Appelona
see Drie Gedichten, For Solo Voice
And Orchestra

Ave Maria, For Solo Voice And String
Orchestra
string orch,S/T solo [5'] sc
DONEMUS f.s., perf mat rent
(V256)
string orch,A/B/Bar solo [5'] sc
DONEMUS f.s., perf mat rent
(V257)

Drie Gedichten, For Solo Voice And
Orchestra
2.1.2.2. 2.0.0.0. perc,pno,cel,
strings,S solo sc DONEMUS f.s.,
perf mat rent
contains: Appelona; Spijtig
Klaartje; Zomerzang   (V258)

From: The Recollection, For Solo
Voice And String Orchestra [4']
cel,strings,Mez/Bar solo
sc DONEMUS f.s., perf mat rent
(V259)
Herinnering Aan Holland, For Solo
Voice And Orchestra
bass clar,strings,Mez/Bar solo
sc DONEMUS f.s., perf mat rent
(V260)
Kerstliedje, For Solo Voice And
Orchestra
2.0.0.2. 2.0.0.0. harp,cel,
strings,Mez/Bar solo
sc DONEMUS f.s., perf mat rent
(V261)
Lofsang, Ex Minimis Patet Ipse Deus,
For Solo Voice And Orchestra
cel,strings,med solo
sc DONEMUS f.s., perf mat rent
(V262)
Nieuwe Lente Op Hollands Erf, Een,
For Solo Voice And Orchestra
3.2.2.2. 4.3.3.0. timp,perc,harp,
org,strings,S solo
sc DONEMUS f.s., perf mat rent
(V263)
Spijtig Klaartje
see Drie Gedichten, For Solo Voice
And Orchestra

Stanzas Of Charles II, For Solo Voice
And Orchestra
1.2.0.0. 0.0.0.0. perc,cel,
strings,Bar solo
sc DONEMUS f.s., perf mat rent
(V264)
Zomerzang
see Drie Gedichten, For Solo Voice
And Orchestra

VOORN, JOOP (1932-   )
Immobile, Music For Tutankhamun [12']
4.3.3.3. 4.4.4.0.0. 4perc,2harp,
strings
sc DONEMUS f.s., perf mat rent
(V265)

W

VOORN, JOOP (cont'd.)

Petit Concert De Printemps, For Flute
And Strings
7vln,2vla,2vcl,db,fl&alto fl solo
sc DONEMUS f.s., perf mat rent
(V266)

VOORTMAN, ROLAND (1953-   )
Reminiscentie III [15']
string orch
DONEMUS perf mat rent   (V267)

VOR DER TUR, FOR SOLO VOICE AND
ORCHESTRA see Buchtger, Fritz

VOR EINER TAVERNE see Ailbout, Hans

VORSPIEL ZU EINEM REVOLUTIONSDRAMA see
Tiessen, Heinz

VORSPIEL ZU EINER KOMODIE see
Eisbrenner, Werner

VORWARTS see Strauss, Josef

VOS AURAE, FOR SOLO VOICE AND STRING
ORCHESTRA see Vivaldi, Antonio

VOSS, FRIEDRICH (1930-   )
Metamorphose [20']
3(pic).3.3.3(contrabsn).
4.4.3.1(db tuba). timp,perc,
strings
BREITKOPF-W perf mat rent   (V268)

Nachtigall Und Die Rose, Die [24']
1.1+English horn.2.1. 2.2.2.0.
timp,perc,harp,strings
BREITKOPF-W perf mat rent   (V269)

VOUS QUI FAITES L'ENORMIE see Gounod,
Charles Francois, Faust: Serenade
De Mephisto, For Solo Voice And
Orchestra

VOX HUMANA? see Kagel, Mauricio

VOYAGE see Corigliano, John

VOYEVODE, OP. 3: OVERTURE see
Tchaikovsky, Piotr Ilyich

VRABEC, UBALO (1905-   )
Rhythmic Impressions *see Ritmicne
Impresije

Ritmicne Impresije [19']
2.2.2.2. 4.3.3.0. timp,3perc,
harp,strings
"Rhythmic Impressions" DRUSTVO
DSS 771 perf mat rent   (V270)

VREDE-OORLAG-VREDE?, MOTO-PERPETUO? see
Bonsel, Adriaan

VREDENBURG, MAX (1904-1976)
Akiba, For Solo Voice And Orchestra
1.0.1.2. 2.0.1.0. harp,cel,
strings,Mez/Bar solo
sc DONEMUS f.s., perf mat rent
(V271)
Variaties, Op Een Terschellinger
Minnelied
2.1.1.0. 0.1.0.0. strings
sc DONEMUS f.s., perf mat rent
(V272)

VRIEND, JAN (1938-   )
Worlds [35']
2.2.2.2. 2.2.2.0. 4perc,harp,
2vln,2vla,2vcl,2db
DONEMUS perf mat rent   (V273)

VRIES, KLAAS DE (1944-   )
Bewegingen [8']
1.1.1.1. 1.0.0.0. 2perc,harp,cel,
pno,2vln,vla,vcl,db
"Movements" DONEMUS perf mat rent
(V274)
Movements *see Bewegingen

Tombeau [8']
string orch
DONEMUS   (V275)

VRIES ROBBE, WILLEM DE (1902-   )
Concertino for Flute, Harp and
Orchestra
0.2.2.2. 2.2.0.0. timp,strings,fl
solo,harp solo
sc DONEMUS f.s., perf mat rent
(V276)

VUATAZ, ROGER (1898-   )
Pour Une Fete De Jeunesse [9']
4.3.4.4. 4.3.3.1. timp,carillon,
strings
sc CARISCH 20761 perf mat rent
(V277)

VUURSTEEN, FRANS (1945-   )
Spleen [10'30"]
0.2.0.0. 2.0.0.0. 9vln,3vla,2vcl,
db
DONEMUS f.s.   (V278)

VYCHODOSLOVENSKY VERBUNK see Cikker,
Jan

WACHTERLIED see Beekhuis, Hanna

WADE
Adeste Fidelis
see Mendelssohn-Bartholdy, Felix,
Hark The Herald Angels Sing

WAFFENSCHMIED, DER: AUCH ICH WAR EIN
JUNGLING, FOR SOLO VOICE AND
ORCHESTRA see Lortzing, (Gustav)
Albert

WAGEMANS, PETER-JAN (1952-   )
Music II *Op.10 [30']
0.0.0.0. 0.3.4.0. perc,strings
DONEMUS perf mat rent   (W1)

Romance for Violin and Orchestra, Op.
17 [25']
3.3.3.3. 4.2.3.1. 3perc,2harp,
strings,vln solo
DONEMUS   (W2)

Symphony No. 3 [15']
4.4.4.4.3sax. 5.4.4.1. 5-6perc,
harp,strings
sc DONEMUS f.s., perf mat rent (W3)

Three Dances [15']
2.1.2.2. 2.1.1.0. perc,harp,pno,
strings
DONEMUS perf mat rent   (W4)

Zangen Van Maldoror, De [25']
3.3.3.3. 4.4.4.0. timp,perc,harp,
pno,strings
sc DONEMUS f.s., perf mat rent (W5)

WAGENAAR, BERNARD (1894-1971)
Sinfonietta
sc BOOSEY rent   (W6)

WAGENSEIL, GEORG CHRISTOPH (1715-1777)
Sinfonia, MIN 52 [15']
0.2.0.0. 0.0.0.0. hpsd,strings
sc UNIVER. UE 25A019 $12.50, set
UNIVER. UE 25B019 $17.50, pts
UNIVER. $2.00, ea.   (W7)

Symphonies, Fifteen *CC15U
(Kucaba, John) sc GARLAND
ISBN 0-8240-3805-3 $90.00 "The
Symphony", Vol. B-III   (W8)

WAGNER, JOSEF (1856-1908)
Aquamarin
RIES f.s.   (W9)

WAGNER, JOSEPH FREDERICK (1900-1974)
Music Of The Sea
string orch
SEESAW perf mat rent   (W10)

Two Moments Musical
string orch
SEESAW perf mat rent   (W11)

Under The Double Eagle March *Op.159
LUCKS 06962 set $13.00, pts $.75,
ea.   (W12)

WAGNER, RICHARD (1813-1883)
Adagio for Clarinet and String
Orchestra
string orch,clar solo
(formerly attributed to Wagner;
actually composed by H.J.
Barmann) LUCKS 06964 sc $3.75,
set $4.75, pts $.95, ea.   (W13)

Christoph Columbus [13']
3.2.2.2. 4.6.3.1. timp,strings
KALMUS 5452 sc $12.00, perf mat
rent, set $25.00, pts $1.00, ea.
(W14)
Due Canti
see RICREAZIONI DI ANTICHE MUSICHE
CLASSICHE, SERIE IV: MUSICHE
ANTICHE ITALIANE

Engel, Der, For Solo Voice And
Orchestra, [arr.] (from Wesendonk
Lieder, No. 1)
LUCKS 03136 sc $3.75, set $8.50,
pts $.75, ea.   (W15)

Fliegende Hollander, Der: Die Frist
Ist Um; Wie Oft In Meeres Tiefen
Schlund, For Solo Voice And
Orchestra
LUCKS 02293 sc $4.00, set $12.00,
pts $.75, ea.   (W16)

Fliegende Hollander, Der: Overture
min sc ZEN-ON 892356 f.s.   (W17)
"Flying Dutchman, The: Overture"
LUCKS 06967 sc $9.50, set $20.00,
min sc $2.00, pts $.95, ea. (W18)

WAGNER, RICHARD (cont'd.)

Flying Dutchman, The: Overture *see
Fliegende Hollander, Der:
Overture

Gotterdammerung: Brunnhilda's Self-
Immolation *see Gotterdammerung:
Brunnhilde Schlussgesang, For
Solo Voice And Orchestra

Gotterdammerung: Brunnhilde
Schlussgesang, For Solo Voice And
Orchestra
"Gotterdammerung: Brunnhilda's
Self-Immolation" LUCKS 09139 sc
$10.00, set $20.00, pts $1.75,
ea.   (W19)

Gotterdammerung: Siegfrieds
Rheinfahrt
"Gotterdammerung: Siegfried's Rhine
Journey" (Humperdinck ending)
LUCKS 06971 sc $11.00, set
$32.00, pts $1.60, ea.   (W20)
"Gotterdammerung: Siegfried's Rhine
Journey" KALMUS A4556 sc $15.00,
perf mat rent, set $50.00, pts
$2.00, ea.   (W21)

Gotterdammerung: Siegfried's Rhine
Journey *see Gotterdammerung:
Siegfrieds Rheinfahrt

Gotterdammerung: Trauermusik Beim
Tode Siegfrieds
min sc UNIVER. PH125 $1.50   (W22)

Gotterdammerung: Waltraute's Scene
LUCKS 02947 sc $10.00, set $20.00,
pts $1.50, ea.   (W23)

Grosser Festmarsch [12']
4.3.3.4. 4.4.3.1. timp,perc,
strings
KALMUS 5356 sc $12.00, perf mat
rent, set $36.00, pts $1.50, ea.
(W24)

LUCKS 06973 sc $12.00, set $36.00,
pts $1.50, ea.   (W25)

Im Treibhaus, For Solo Voice And
Orchestra, [arr.] (from Wesendonk
Lieder, No. 3)
LUCKS 02219 sc $3.75, set $8.50,
pts $.75, ea.   (W26)

Kaisermarsch [10']
2+pic.3.3.3. 4.3.3.1. timp,perc,
strings
KALMUS 5162 sc $8.00, perf mat
rent, set $18.00, pts $.60, ea. (W27)

Liebesverbot, Das: Overture
KALMUS 5560 sc $18.00, set $40.00
(W28)

Lohengrin: Einsam In Truben Tagen,
For Solo Voice And Orchestra
LUCKS 02220 sc $4.75, set $7.50,
pts $.75   (W29)

Lohengrin: In Fernem Land, For Solo
Voice And Orchestra
LUCKS 02206 sc $3.75, set $9.50,
pts $.75, ea.   (W30)

Lohengrin: Lohengrins Ermahnung An
Elsa, For Solo Voice And
Orchestra
LUCKS 02231 sc $4.00, set $8.00,
pts $.75, ea.   (W31)

Lohengrin: Mein Lieber Schwan, For
Solo Voice And Orchestra
LUCKS 02216 sc $4.00, set $9.00,
pts $.75, ea.   (W32)

Lohengrin: Prelude, Act I
LUCKS 08053 sc $3.00, set $22.00,
min sc $2.00, pts $1.15, ea. (W33)

Lohengrin: Prelude, Act III
LUCKS 06975 sc $9.00, set $28.00,
pts $1.40, ea.   (W34)

Lohengrin: Preludes, Acts I And III
min sc ZEN-ON 892354 f.s.   (W35)
min sc UNIVER. PH39 $2.00   (W36)

Meistersinger Von Nurnberg, Die:
Morgenlich Leuchtend
2.2.2.2. 4.2.3.1. timp,harp,
strings
"Meistersinger Von Nurnberg, Die:
Walter's Prize Song" KALMUS A2238
sc $6.00, perf mat rent, set
$20.00, pts $1.00, ea.   (W37)

Meistersinger Von Nurnberg, Die:
Morgenlich Leuchtend, For Solo
Voice And Orchestra
"Meistersinger Von Nurnberg, Die:
Walther's Prize Song" LUCKS 02027
sc $5.00, set $14.00, pts $.75,
ea.   (W38)

WAGNER, RICHARD (cont'd.)

Meistersinger Von Nurnberg, Die:
  Prelude
  min sc UNIVER. PH19 $3.00   (W39)
  min sc ZEN-ON 892351 f.s.   (W40)
  pts BROUDE BR. $1.50, ea.   (W41)
  LUCKS 06981 sc $5.50, set $22.00,
  pts $1.15, ea.   (W42)

Meistersinger Von Nurnberg, Die:
  Wahn, Wahn, Uberall Wahn, For
  Solo Voice And Orchestra
  LUCKS 02376 sc $4.00, set $9.00,
  pts $.75, ea.   (W43)

Meistersinger Von Nurnberg, Die:
  Walter's Prize Song *see
  Meistersinger Von Nurnberg, Die:
  Morgenlich Leuchtend

Meistersinger Von Nurnberg, Die:
  Walther's Prize Song *see
  Meistersinger Von Nurnberg, Die:
  Morgenlich Leuchtend, For Solo
  Voice And Orchestra

Parsifal: Glocken- Und Gralsszene
  KALMUS A3255 sc $5.00, perf mat
  rent, set $22.00, pts $1.00, ea.
                                 (W44)

Parsifal: Klingsors Zaubergarten Und
  Die Blumenmadchen (Concert
  Version) [13']
  3.2+English horn.3.2. 4.2.3.1.
  timp,strings
  (Steinbach) KALMUS A2242 sc $10.00,
  perf mat rent, set $41.00, pts
  $2.00, ea.   (W45)

Parsifal: Prelude
  min sc ZEN-ON 892358 f.s.   (W46)
  LUCKS 06986 sc $9.50, set $17.00,
  min sc $2.50, pts $1.15, ea.
                                 (W47)

Parsifal: Prelude, Act I
  min sc UNIVER. PH70 $3.00   (W48)

Polonaise, [arr.]
  (Hoffmann) 2(pic).2(English
  horn).2.2. 4.2.3.1. timp,perc,
  harp,strings KALMUS 5289 pno-cond
  sc $4.00, set $12.00, pts $.60,
  ea., cmplt ed rent   (W49)

Rienzi: Finale, Act III
  KALMUS 5288 sc $6.00, perf mat
  rent, set $25.00, pts $.75, ea.
                                 (W50)

Rienzi: Friedensmarsch [5']
  2.2.2.2. 4.2.3.1. timp,strings
  KALMUS 5287 sc $5.00, perf mat
  rent, set $15.00, pts $.60, ea.
                                 (W51)

Rienzi: Overture
  LUCKS 06990 sc $10.00, set $28.00,
  min sc $2.50, pts $1.40, ea.   (W52)

Rule Brittania
  (Mottl) KALMUS A4557 sc $12.00,
  perf mat rent, set $37.00, pts
  $1.50, ea.   (W53)

Schmerzen, For Solo Voice And
  Orchestra, [arr.] (from Wesendonk
  Lieder, No. 4)
  LUCKS 02160 sc $3.75, set $8.50,
  pts $.75, ea.   (W54)

Siegfried: Forest Murmurs *see
  Siegfried: Waldweben

Siegfried: Hoho! Hoho! Schmiede Mein
  Hammer, For Solo Voice And
  Orchestra
  (Kistler) "Siegfried:
  Schmiedelieder, For Solo Voice
  And Orchestra" LUCKS 07646 sc
  $12.00, set $30.00, pts $1.50,
  ea.   (W55)

Siegfried Idyll
  min sc UNIVER. PH68 $2.00   (W56)
  min sc ZEN-ON 892357 f.s.   (W57)
  LUCKS 06992 sc $5.00, set $14.00,
  min sc $2.50, pts $1.15, ea.
                                 (W58)

Siegfried: Schmiedelieder, For Solo
  Voice And Orchestra *see
  Siegfried: Hoho! Hoho! Schmiede
  Mein Hammer, For Solo Voice And
  Orchestra

Siegfried: Waldweben
  "Siegfried: Forest Murmurs" LUCKS
  06993 sc $7.00, set $20.00, pts
  $1.15, ea.   (W59)

Stehe Still, For Solo Voice And
  Orchestra, [arr.] (from Wesendonk
  Lieder, No. 2)
  LUCKS 02374 sc $3.75, set $8.50,
  pts $.75, ea.   (W60)

WAGNER, RICHARD (cont'd.)

Symphony in C
  LUCKS 08483 sc $20.00, set $50.00,
  pts $3.00, ea.   (W61)

Tannhauser: Dich Teure Halle, For
  Solo Voice And Orchestra
  LUCKS 02041 sc $4.00, set $10.00,
  pts $.75, ea.   (W62)

Tannhauser: Einzug Der Gaste Auf Der
  Wartburg
  BREITKOPF-W perf mat rent   (W63)

Tannhauser: O Du Mein Holder
  Abendstern, For Solo Voice And
  Orchestra
  LUCKS 02047 sc $3.75, set $8.50,
  pts $.75, ea.   (W64)

Tannhauser: Overture
  min sc ZEN-ON 892355 f.s.   (W65)

Tannhauser: Prelude, Act III
  INTERNAT. perf mat rent   (W66)

Traume, For Solo Voice And Orchestra
  (from Wesendonk Lieder, No. 5)
  LUCKS 02159 sc $3.75, set $8.50,
  pts $.75, ea.   (W67)

Tristan Und Isolde: Prelude And
  Liebestod
  min sc UNIVER. PH40 $2.00   (W68)
  min sc ZEN-ON 892352 f.s.   (W69)
  BREITKOPF-W perf mat rent   (W70)
  LUCKS 07000 sc $7.50, set $23.00,
  min sc $2.00, pts $1.15, ea.
                                 (W71)

Walkure, Die: Du Bist Der Lenz, For
  Solo Voice And Orchestra
  LUCKS 02346 sc $4.00, set $10.00,
  pts $.75, ea.   (W72)

Walkure, Die: Ein Schwert Verhiess
  Mir Der Vater, For Solo Voice And
  Orchestra
  LUCKS 02959 sc $4.75, set $15.00,
  pts $.75, ea.   (W73)

Walkure, Die: Hojo-To-Ho, For Solo
  Voice And Orchestra
  LUCKS 02229 sc $4.00, set $10.00,
  pts $.75, ea.   (W74)

Walkure, Die: Ritt Der Walkuren
  min sc ZEN-ON 892353 f.s.   (W75)

Walkure, Die: Siegmund! Sieh' Auf
  Mich, For Solo Voices And
  Orchestra
  LUCKS 02921 sc $6.00, set $15.00,
  pts $1.00, ea.   (W76)

Walkure, Die: Wintersturme Wichen Dem
  Wonnemond, For Solo Voice And
  Orchestra
  LUCKS 02241 sc $4.00, set $10.00,
  pts $.75, ea.   (W77)

Walkure, Die: Wotans Abschied Und
  Feuerzauber
  "Walkure, Die: Wotan's Farewell And
  Magic Fire Music" min sc PETERS
  649 $6.00   (W78)
  "Walkure, Die: Wotan's Farewell And
  The Magic Fire Scene" LUCKS 02375
  sc $17.00, set $28.00, min sc
  $2.50, pts $1.60, ea.   (W79)

Walkure, Die: Wotan's Farewell And
  Magic Fire Music *see Walkure,
  Die: Wotans Abschied Und
  Feuerzauber

Walkure, Die: Wotan's Farewell And
  The Magic Fire Scene *see
  Walkure, Die: Wotans Abschied Und
  Feuerzauber

Works Of Richard Wagner, Vol. 7:
  Orchesterwerke
  (Balling, Michael) study sc DA CAPO
  $75.00 reprint of Breitkopf and
  Hartel edition   (W80)

WAHLBERG, RUNE (1910-   )
Canzone, For Violin And Orchestra
  [7']
  1.1.2.1. 1.0.0.0. strings,vln
  solo
  sc,solo pt STIM   (W81)

Episoder *see Symphony No. 6

Havet *see Symphony No. 5

Jubileumsspel
  2.2.2.2. 2.2.1.0. timp,perc,
  strings
  sc STIM perf mat rent   (W82)

Symphony No. 5 [25'30"]
  3.2.2.2. 4.2.3.1. timp,perc,harp,
  strings,men cor

WAHLBERG, RUNE (cont'd.)

  sc STIM perf mat rent   (W83)

Symphony No. 6 [17'30"]
  3.2.2.2. 4.2.3.1. timp,2perc,
  strings
  sc STIM perf mat rent   (W84)

Tre Symfoniska Poem [16']
  2.2.2.2. 4.2.3.1. timp,perc,
  strings
  STIM   (W85)

WAHLSTIMMEN WALZER see Strauss, Johann,
  [Jr.]

WAHNFRIED see Laman, Wim

WAHREN, KARL HEINZ (1933-   )
Circulus Virtuosus, For Flute, Oboe,
  Clarinet, Bassoon And Orchestra
  BUDDE perf mat rent   (W86)

WALDEN, ERICH
Kleines Spiel
  RIES f.s.   (W87)

WALDESRUHE see Dvorak, Antonin, From
  The Bohemian Forest: Silent Woods,
  For Violoncello And Orchestra,
  [arr.]

WALDGEISTER see Kamp, Hans

WALDTEUFEL, EMIL (1837-1915)
Espana Waltz *Op.236
  LUCKS 07012 set $16.00, pts $1.00,
  ea.   (W88)

Estudiantina Waltz *Op.191
  LUCKS 07155 set $15.00, pts $.95,
  ea.   (W89)

Patineurs, Les
  "Skaters' Waltz, The" LUCKS 07026
  sc $12.00, set $15.00, pts $.95,
  ea.   (W90)

Skaters' Waltz, The *see Patineurs,
  Les

Tout A Paris *Op.240
  LUCKS 07045 set $15.00, pts $.95,
  ea.   (W91)

WALKURE, DIE: DU BIST DER LENZ, FOR
  SOLO VOICE AND ORCHESTRA see
  Wagner, Richard

WALKURE, DIE: EIN SCHWERT VERHIESS MIR
  DER VATER, FOR SOLO VOICE AND
  ORCHESTRA see Wagner, Richard

WALKURE, DIE: HOJO-TO-HO, FOR SOLO
  VOICE AND ORCHESTRA see Wagner,
  Richard

WALKURE, DIE: RITT DER WALKUREN see
  Wagner, Richard

WALKURE, DIE: SIEGMUND! SIEH' AUF MICH,
  FOR SOLO VOICES AND ORCHESTRA see
  Wagner, Richard

WALKURE, DIE: WINTERSTURME WICHEN DEM
  WONNEMOND, FOR SOLO VOICE AND
  ORCHESTRA see Wagner, Richard

WALKURE, DIE: WOTANS ABSCHIED UND
  FEUERZAUBER see Wagner, Richard

WALKURE, DIE: WOTAN'S FAREWELL AND
  MAGIC FIRE MUSIC see Wagner,
  Richard, Walkure, Die: Wotans
  Abschied Und Feuerzauber

WALKURE, DIE: WOTAN'S FAREWELL AND THE
  MAGIC FIRE SCENE see Wagner,
  Richard, Walkure, Die: Wotans
  Abschied Und Feuerzauber

WALLMANN, JOHANNES (1952-   )
Studien, For Piano And Orchestra
  2.2.2.2. 4.3.3.0. perc,strings,
  pno solo
  DEUTSCHER perf mat rent   (W92)

WALTER, FRIED (1907-   )
Pommern-Suite
  string orch
  sc,pts RIES f.s.   (W93)

Reise Nach Venedig, Die [9']
  2.2+English horn.2.2. 4.3.3.0.
  timp,2perc,pno,harp,strings
  (reduced scoring available) sc RIES
  f.s., perf mat rent   (W94)

WALTON, [SIR] WILLIAM (TURNER)
  (1902-1983)
Prelude for Orchestra [5']
  3.3.3.3. 4.3.3.1. 3perc,harp,
  strings
  OXFORD perf mat rent   (W95)

WALTON, [SIR] WILLIAM (TURNER)
(cont'd.)

Varii Capricci [14']
3(pic).3(English horn).3(bass
clar).2. 4.3.3.1. timp,3perc,
harp,strings
sc OXFORD 77.219 $25.00   (W96)

WALTZ AROUND THE SCALE see Anderson,
Leroy

WALTZ FOR HEGE see Sommerfeldt, Oistein

WALTZES, THREE, [ARR.] see Mozart,
Wolfgang Amadeus

WALTZING MATILDA
(Luck, Arthur) LUCKS HYMNS 15 sc
$8.00, set $16.00, pts $.75, ea.
(W97)

WALZER POESIE, FOR PIANO AND ORCHESTRA
see Schonherr, Max

WALZERREIGEN see Dressel, Erwin

WANDERER, DER, FOR SOLO VOICE AND
ORCHESTRA, [ARR.] see Schubert,
Franz (Peter)

WANDERER FANTASY see Schubert, Franz
(Peter), Fantasia For Piano And
Orchestra In C, "Der Wanderer",
[arr.]

WANDLUNGEN see Irino, Yoshiro

WANHAL, JOHANN BAPTIST (JAN KRTITEL)
(1739-1813)
Symphonies, Five
see Gassmann, Florian Leopold,
Symphonies, Seven

WANSKI, JAN (1762-ca. 1800)
Symphony in D
see SYMPHONY IN POLAND, THE

WARD
America The Beautiful
(Luck, Arthur) LUCKS HYMNS 12 set
$8.00, pts $.65, ea. contains
also: Smith, John Stafford, Star-
Spangled Banner, The   (W98)

WARD, ROBERT (1917-   )
Symphony No. 4
sc HIGHGATE 7.0261.6 $15.00   (W99)

WARLOCK, PETER
see HESELTINE, PHILIP

WARREN, GEORGE WILLIAM (1828-1902)
God Of Our Fathers
(Luck, Arthur) LUCKS HYMNS 10 set
$10.00, pts $.65, ea. contains
also: Dykes, Holy, Holy, Holy
(W100)

WARRIOR, THE: PRELUDE see Rogers,
Bernard

WARSTWY CZASU see Bloch, Augustyn

WARZAWA see Pospisil, Juraj, Symphony
No. 4

WAS GOTT TUT, DAS IST WOHLGETAN, [ARR.]
see Bach, Johann Sebastian

WAS I NOT A BLADE, FOR SOLO VOICE AND
ORCHESTRA, [ARR.] see Tchaikovsky,
Piotr Ilyich

WAS SAG ICH ZU "LODOISKA" VON
CHERUBINI, FOR SOLO VOICE AND
ORCHESTRA see Weber, Carl Maria von

WAS SICH LIEBT NECKT SICH see Strauss,
Johann, [Jr.]

WASHBURN, ROBERT BROOKS (1928-   )
Elegy
2.2.2.2. 4.3.3.1. timp,harp,
strings
BOOSEY set $24.00, augmented set
$40.00   (W101)

Song And Dance
string orch
BOOSEY set $10.00, sc $2.50   (W102)

WASHINGTON POST MARCH, THE see Sousa,
John Philip

WASPS, THE see Vaughan Williams, Ralph

WASSERFALL BEI NACHT see Flothuis,
Marius

WASSERMUSIK - FEUERWERKSMUSIK see
Handel, George Frideric

WAT BEN IK, DAN EEN VOGEL IN DE
SCHEMERING?, FOR SOLO VOICE AND
ORCHESTRA see Dijk, Jan van

WATANABE, URATO (1909-   )
Kodaishinsyo
1.1.1.1.alto sax.tenor sax.
2.2.3.0. timp,perc,harp,pno,
strings
sc J.C.A. f.s.   (W103)

Suite Tsugaru
JAPAN 8010   (W104)

WATER BIRD TALK, A see Argento,
Dominick

WATER CARRIER, THE: OVERTURE see
Cherubini, Luigi, Deux Journees,
Les: Overture

WATER MUSIC see Handel, George Frideric

WATER MUSIC see Rorem, Ned

WATKINS, MICHAEL BLAKE (1948-   )
Concerto for Violin and Orchestra
sc NOVELLO 2600 $15.25   (W105)

WAVERLEY OVERTURE see Berlioz, Hector
(Louis)

WAVES OF THE DANUBE see Ivanovici, Ion

WAVES OF THE DANUBE, [ARR.] see
Ivanovici, Ion

WAXMAN, FRANZ (1906-1967)
Carmen Fantasie, For Violin And
Orchestra [9'25"]
FIDELIO   (W106)

Creation Of The Female Monster, The:
Suite [7'17"]
FIDELIO   (W107)

Dr. Jekyll And Mr. Hyde: Suite
[10'5"]
FIDELIO   (W108)

Elegy for String Orchestra [3'30"]
string orch
FIDELIO   (W109)

Goyana: Four Sketches, For Piano And
String Orchestra [13'24"]
string orch,pno solo
FIDELIO   (W110)

Hemingway's Adventures Of A Young
Man: Suite [10'16"]
FIDELIO   (W111)

Horn Blows At Midnight, The, For
Trumpet And Orchestra [4'37"]
FIDELIO   (W112)

Mr. Skeffington [3'48"]
FIDELIO   (W113)

Paradine Case, The, For Piano And
Orchestra [11'25"]
FIDELIO   (W114)

Peyton Place: Suite [13'17"]
FIDELIO   (W115)

Philadelphia Story, The: Suite
[3'30"]
FIDELIO   (W116)

Place In The Sun, A [8'30"]
FIDELIO   (W117)

Prince Valiant: Suite [9'46"]
FIDELIO   (W118)

Rebecca: Suite [7'45"]
FIDELIO   (W119)

Sunrise At Campobello: Suite [6'30"]
FIDELIO   (W120)

Sunset Boulevard: Suite [7'44"]
FIDELIO   (W121)

Taras Bulba: Suite [10']
FIDELIO   (W122)

WAYENBERG, DANIEL (1929-   )
Symphonie "Capella" [32']
4.4.4.4. 6.4.4.1. timp,5perc,2harp,
pno/cel,strings sc DONEMUS f.s.,
perf mat rent   (W123)

WE BELONG see Dreyfus, George

WE THREE KINGS OF ORIENT ARE see
Hopkins, John Henry, Jr.

WE WISH YOU A MERRY CHRISTMAS
see Deck The Halls

WEBER, CARL MARIA VON (1786-1826)
Abu Hassan: Overture [3']
1+pic.2.2.2. 2.2.1.0. timp,perc,
strings
sc,pts LIENAU f.s.   (W124)
min sc PETERS 841 $4.00   (W125)
LUCKS 07056 sc $7.50, set $18.00,

WEBER, CARL MARIA VON (cont'd.)

min sc $2.00, pts $.95, ea.

Ah, Se Edmondo Zu "Helene" Von Mehul,
For Solo Voice And Orchestra
*Op.52
2.2.2.2. 2.2.0.0. timp,strings,S
solo
sc,pts LIENAU rent   (W127)

Andante Und Rondo Ungarese, For
Bassoon And Orchestra *Op.35
[5']
2.2.0.2. 2.2.0.0. timp,strings,
bsn solo
LIENAU perf mat rent   (W128)
KALMUS 5453 sc $4.00, perf mat
rent, set $11.00, pts $1.00, ea.
(W129)
LUCKS 00814 sc $15.00, set $27.00,
pts $2.00, ea.   (W130)

Aufforderung Zum Tanz, [arr.] *Op.65
(Berlioz) "Invitation To The Dance,
[arr.]" 1+pic.2.2.4. 4.2+
2cornet.3.0. timp,2harp,strings
pts BROUDE BR. $1.50, ea.   (W131)
(Berlioz) "Invitation To The Dance,
[arr.]" LUCKS 07060 sc $6.50, set
$22.00, min sc $3.00, pts $1.15,
ea.   (W132)

Beherrscher Der Geister, Der:
Overture [5']
1+pic.2.2.2. 4.2.3.0. timp,
strings
sc,pts LIENAU rent   (W133)

Concertino for Clarinet and
Orchestra, Op. 26, in E flat
[10']
1.2.0.2. 2.2.0.0. timp,strings,
clar solo
sc,pts LIENAU rent   (W134)
LUCKS 00771 sc $5.50, set $6.50,
pts $.95, ea.   (W135)

Concertino for Horn and Orchestra,
Op. 45, in E minor [15']
1.0.2.2. 2.2.0.0. timp,strings,
horn solo
sc,pts LIENAU rent   (W136)

Concerto for Bassoon and Orchestra,
Op. 75, in F [16']
2.2.0.2. 2.2.0.0. timp,strings,
bsn solo
sc,pts LIENAU rent   (W137)
LUCKS 00802 sc $10.00, set $17.00,
pts $1.15, ea.   (W138)

Concerto for Clarinet and Orchestra,
[arr.] (from Quintet, Op. 34)
(Kutsch, Bernhard) 2.2.1.2.
2.2.1.0. timp,strings,clar solo
[25'] sc,pts LIENAU rent   (W139)

Concerto for Clarinet and Orchestra,
No. 1, Op. 73, in F minor [19']
2.2.0.2. 3.2.0.0. timp,strings,
clar solo
sc,pts LIENAU rent   (W140)
LUCKS 00791 sc $8.50, set $15.50,
min sc $3.00, pts $1.00, ea.
(W141)

Concerto for Clarinet and Orchestra,
No. 2, Op. 74, in E flat [24']
2.2.0.2. 2.2.0.0. timp,strings,
clar solo
sc,pts LIENAU rent   (W142)
LUCKS 00807 sc $8.50, set $15.50,
min sc $3.00, pts $1.00, ea.
(W143)

Concerto for Piano and Orchestra, No.
1, Op. 11, in C [20']
2.2.0.2. 2.2.0.0. timp,strings,
pno solo
sc,pts LIENAU rent   (W144)

Concerto for Piano and Orchestra, No.
2, Op. 32, in E flat [21']
2.0.2.2. 2.2.0.0. timp,strings,
pno solo
sc,pts LIENAU rent   (W145)

Euryanthe: Overture [9']
2.2.2.2. 4.2.3.0. timp,strings
min sc UNIVER. PH77 $3.00   (W146)
LUCKS 07057 sc $6.50, set $18.00,
min sc $2.50, pts $.95, ea.
(W147)
sc,pts LIENAU f.s.   (W148)
BROUDE BR. set $27.50, pts $1.25,
ea.   (W149)

Freischutz, Der: Durch Die Walder,
Durch Die Auen, For Solo Voice
And Orchestra
LUCKS 02414 sc $3.75, set $9.50,
pts $.75, ea.   (W150)

Freischutz, Der: Overture [10']
2.2.2.2. 4.2.3.0. timp,strings
LUCKS 07058 sc $6.50, set $18.00,
min sc $2.50, pts $.95, ea.

WEBER, CARL MARIA VON (cont'd.)

    min sc ZEN-ON 892751 f.s. (W151)
    sc,pts LIENAU f.s. (W152)
    min sc UNIVER. PH22 $2.50 (W153)
    (W154)

Freischutz, Der: Schweig', Schweig'
    Damit, For Solo Voice And
    Orchestra
    LUCKS 02355 sc $4.00, set $8.00,
    pts $.75, ea. (W155)

Freischutz, Der: Und Ob Die Wolke Sie
    Verhulle, For Solo Voice And
    Orchestra
    LUCKS 02760 sc $3.75, set $7.50,
    pts $.75, ea. (W156)

Freischutz, Der: Wie Nahte Mir Der
    Schlummer, For Solo Voice And
    Orchestra
    LUCKS 02119 sc $3.75, set $8.50,
    pts $.75, ea. (W157)

Ines De Castro: Non Paventar Mia
    Vita-Sei Tu Sempre Il Mio Tesoro,
    For Solo Voice And Orchestra
    *Op.51
    2.0.2.2. 2.0.0.0. strings,S solo
    sc,pts LIENAU rent (W158)

Invitation To The Dance, [arr.] *see
    Aufforderung Zum Tanz, [arr.]

Jubel Ouverture *Op.59 [10']
    4.2.2.2. 4.2.3.0. timp,perc,
    strings
    (in this edition, 2 flute parts)
    sc,pts LIENAU rent (W159)
    LUCKS 07061 sc $11.00, set $23.00,
    min sc $2.00, pts $1.25, ea.
    (W160)

Konzertstuck for Piano and Orchestra,
    Op. 79, in F minor [15']
    2.2.2.2. 2.2.1.0. timp,strings,
    pno solo
    BROUDE BR. set $20.00, pts $1.25,
    ea. (W161)
    sc,pts LIENAU rent (W162)
    LUCKS 00080 sc $8.00, set $15.00,
    min sc $3.00, pts $.95, ea. (W163)

Misera Me-Ho Spavento. Scena Ed Aria
    d'Atalia, For Solo Voice And
    Orchestra *Op.50 [7']
    2.0.2.0. 2.2.0.0. timp,strings,S
    solo
    sc,pts LIENAU rent (W164)

Momento Capriccioso (from Op. 12)
    see RICREAZIONI DI ANTICHE MUSICHE
    CLASSICHE, SERIE IV: MUSICHE
    ANTICHE ITALIANE

Oberon: Overture [8']
    2.2.2.2. 4.2.3.0. timp,strings
    sc,pts LIENAU f.s. (W165)

Oberon: Ozean, Du Ungeheuer, For Solo
    Voice And Orchestra
    sc LIENAU f.s., rent (W166)

Peter Schmoll: Overture [10']
    2.2.2.2. 2.2.1.0. timp,strings
    KALMUS 1054 sc $15.00, perf mat
    rent, set $20.00, pts $1.00, ea.
    (W167)
    min sc PETERS 842 $4.00 (W168)
    sc,pts LIENAU f.s. (W169)
    (Margis-Berger) LUCKS 07064 set
    $20.00, pts $1.00, ea. (W170)

Polonaise Brillante, For Piano And
    Orchestra, [arr.] *Op.72
    (Liszt) LUCKS 00081 sc $8.00, set
    $10.00, pts $.95, ea. (W171)
    (Liszt, Franz) 2.2.2.2. 2.2.3.0.
    timp,perc,strings,pno solo [10']
    sc,pts LIENAU rent (W172)

Preciosa: Overture [8']
    2.2.2.2. 2.2.0.0. timp,perc,
    strings
    sc,pts LIENAU f.s. (W173)
    LUCKS 07065 sc $10.00, set $18.00,
    min sc $2.00, pts $1.15, ea.
    (W174)
    min sc PETERS 843 $4.00 (W175)

Romanza Siciliana, For Flute And
    Orchestra *Op.Posth.2 [4']
    0.2.2.0. 2.0.1.0. timp,strings,fl
    solo
    sc,pts LIENAU f.s. (W176)

Silvana: Overture [7']
    2.2.2.2. 2.2.1.0. timp,strings
    sc,pts LIENAU rent (W177)

Symphony No. 1 in C [22']
    1.2.0.2. 2.2.0.0. timp,strings
    sc,pts LIENAU rent (W178)
    LUCKS 06056 sc $30.00, set $40.00,
    min sc $10.50, pts $3.00, ea.
    (W179)

WEBER, CARL MARIA VON (cont'd.)

Symphony No. 2 in C [20']
    1.2.0.2. 2.2.0.0. timp,strings
    sc,pts LIENAU rent (W180)

Theme And Variations, For Viola And
    Orchestra
    1.2.0.2. 2.0.0.0. strings,vla
    solo
    (Druener) sc EULENBURG E10123 f.s.,
    perf mat rent (W181)

Turandot: Incidental Music *Op.37
    3.2.2.2. 2.2.1.0. timp,perc,
    strings
    (Schoenzeler) sc EULENBURG E10120
    f.s., perf mat rent (W182)

Turandot: Overture [5']
    1+pic.2.2.2. 2.2.1.0. timp,perc,
    strings
    sc,pts LIENAU rent (W183)

Waltz, [arr.]
    (Dubensky, A.) string orch KALMUS
    A1090 sc $3.00, set $3.75, pts
    $.75, ea. (W184)

Was Sag Ich Zu "Lodoiska" Von
    Cherubini, For Solo Voice And
    Orchestra *Op.56
    2.0.2.2. 2.2.0.0. timp,strings,S
    solo
    sc,pts LIENAU rent (W185)

WEDDING DAY AT TROLDHAUGEN, [ARR.] see
    Grieg, Edvard Hagerup

WEDDING MINUET see Mozart, Leopold

WEEGENHUISE, JOHAN (1910-   )
    Ouverture 1975
    2.2.2.2. 2.2.0.0. timp,strings
    sc DONEMUS f.s., perf mat rent
    (W186)

WEG NACH EISENSTADT, DER see Bialas,
    Gunter

WEIGEL, EUGENE (1910-   )
    Sonata for Strings
    string orch
    sc NEW VALLEY 149 $4.00 (W187)

WEIHE DER TONE, DIE see Spohr, Ludwig
    (Louis), Symphony No. 4, Op. 86

WEIHE DES HAUSES, DIE see Beethoven,
    Ludwig van

WEILL, KURT (1900-1950)
    Quodlibet, Op. 9 *see Zaubernacht,
    Op. 9: Orchestersuite

    Zaubernacht, Op. 9: Orchestersuite
    [23']
    2.2.2.2. 2.2.2.0. perc,strings
    "Quodlibet, Op. 9" sc UNIVER.
    47 08348 $22.00 (W188)

WEIN, WEIB, UND GESANG see Strauss,
    Johann, [Jr.]

WEINER, STANLEY (1925-   )
    Concerto for Violin and Orchestra,
    No. 1 [26']
    2.2.2.2. 4.3.2.0. timp,3perc,
    strings,vln solo
    MCA rent (W189)

WEINGARTNER, (PAUL) FELIX VON
    (1863-1942)
    Among The Stars *see Unter Sternen,
    For Solo Voice And Orchestra

    Kindes Scheiden, Des, For Solo Voice
    And Orchestra *Op.36,No.3
    LUCKS 02905 sc $12.00, set $60.00,
    pts $2.25, ea. (W190)

    Lied Der Walkure, For Solo Voice And
    Orchestra *Op.36,No.4 [4']
    2.2.2.2. 4.2.3.1. timp,harp,
    strings,S solo
    BREITKOPF-W perf mat rent (W191)
    "Song Of The Valkyr" LUCKS 02904 sc
    $9.00, set $25.00, pts $1.25, ea.
    (W192)

    Serenade [10']
    string orch
    RIES perf mat rent (W193)

    Song Of The Valkyr *see Lied Der
    Walkure, For Solo Voice And
    Orchestra

    Symphony No. 2, Op. 29, in E flat
    [50']
    3(pic).3.3.3(contrabsn). 4.3.3.1.
    timp,harp,strings
    BREITKOPF-W perf mat rent (W194)

    Unter Sternen, For Solo Voice And
    Orchestra *Op.22,No.12 [3']
    2.2.2.2. 4.2.3.0. timp,harp,
    strings,S solo

WEINGARTNER, (PAUL) FELIX VON (cont'd.)

    BREITKOPF-W perf mat rent (W195)
    "Among The Stars" LUCKS 02899 sc
    $7.00, set $20.00, pts $1.25, ea.
    (W196)

WEINZWEIG, JOHN (1913-   )
    Divertimento No. 1 for Flute and
    String Orchestra
    min sc BOOSEY 913 $4.00 (W197)

    Divertimento No. 2 for Oboe and
    String Orchestra
    min sc BOOSEY 914 $4.00 (W198)

WEIS, FLEMMING (1898-   )
    Sine Nomine [14']
    2.2.2.2. 2.0.0.0. strings
    sc,pts SAMFUNDET 292 perf mat rent
    (W199)

WEISS, MANFRED (1935-   )
    Concerto for Organ and Orchestra
    perc,strings,org solo
    sc DEUTSCHER 1432 f.s., perf mat
    rent (W200)

    Concerto for Violin and Orchestra
    2.2.2.2. 4.2.3.0. timp,perc,harp,
    strings,vln solo
    DEUTSCHER perf mat rent (W201)

    Symphony No. 3 [20']
    3.2.3.3. 4.3.3.1. timp,4perc,cel,
    pno,harp,strings
    DEUTSCHER perf mat rent (W202)

WELLEJUS, HENNING (1919-   )
    Concerto for Oboe and Orchestra
    2.0.2.2. 2.0.0.0. timp,perc,
    strings,ob solo
    SAMFUNDET perf mat rent (W203)

    Tivoli-Ouverture *Op.40
    4.4.4.3. 7.6.6.2. timp,perc,
    strings
    SAMFUNDET perf mat rent (W204)

WELLENSPIELE see Trumpy, Balz

WENGLER, MARCEL
    Konstellationen II [22']
    3.3.3.3. 4.4.3.1. pno,cel,harp,
    perc,strings
    study sc VOGT VF 2007 f.s., perf
    mat rent (W205)

WENN AUS 1000 BLUTENKELCHEN see Blon,
    Franz von

WENN ICH IHN NUR HABE, FOR SOLO VOICE
    AND ORCHESTRA see Diepenbrock,
    Alphons

WER DIE SCHONHEIT ANGESCHAUT MIT AUGEN
    see Hubler, Klaus-K.

WERDIN, EBERHARD (1911-   )
    Balletto For Orchester
    sc SCHWANN S 2362 f.s. (W206)

    Serenata Concertante, For Viola,
    Piano And String Orchestra
    string orch,vla solo,pno solo
    MOSELER 11.452 perf mat rent (W207)

WERLE, LARS-JOHAN (1926-   )
    Animalen, For Solo Voice And
    Orchestra
    1.1.2. 2.2.2.1. perc,harp,
    strings,solo voice
    STIM (W208)

WERNER, HANS
    Variationen Uber "All Mein Gedanken"
    fl,strings
    sc PETERS S 2249 f.s., pts PETERS
    f.s. (W209)

WERNER, SVEN ERIK
    Concerto for Violoncello and
    Orchestra
    3.3.3.3. 4.3.3.1. 5perc,cel,harp,
    pno,strings,vcl solo
    SAMFUNDET perf mat rent (W210)

    Ground, For Flute And Orchestra
    3.3.3.3. 4.3.3.1. perc,cel,harp,
    pno,strings,fl solo
    SAMFUNDET perf mat rent (W211)

WERNICK, RICHARD (1934-   )
    Visions Of Terror And Wonder, For
    Solo Voice And Orchestra [30']
    4.4.4.4. 4.3.3.1. timp,5perc,
    harp,cel,strings,Mez solo
    sc PRESSER 416-41097 $25.00 (W212)

WERTHER: POURQUOI ME REVEILLER, FOR
    SOLO VOICE AND ORCHESTRA see
    Massenet, Jules

WESTERGAARD, SVEND (1922-   )
    Concerto for Violoncello and
    Orchestra, Op. 26 [31']
    2.2.2.2. 4.3.0.0. timp,4perc,
    strings,vcl solo

WESTERGAARD, SVEND (cont'd.)

min sc HANSEN-DEN WH 29453 B $57.00
(W213)

WESTERN PARADISE, THE, FOR NARRATOR AND
ORCHESTRA see Kay, Ulysses Simpson

WESTERN SYMPHONY see Kay, Hershy

WESTFALISCHE BAUERNHOCHZEIT see Kleine,
Werner

WEYSE, CHRISTOPH ERNST FRIEDRICH
(1774-1842)
Symphony No. 6
sc,pts SAMFUNDET 217 perf mat rent
(W214)

WHAT CHILD IS THIS?
(Luck, Arthur) LUCKS HYMNS 26 set
$15.00. pts $.65. ea. contains
also: Hopkins, John Henry, Jr., We
Three Kings Of Orient Are   (W215)

WHAT THE CHILDREN TOLD ME see Cikker,
Jan, Co Mi Deti Rozpravali

WHAT THE WILD FLOWERS TELL ME, [ARR.]
see Mahler, Gustav

WHEN I SURVEY THE WONDROUS CROSS
see Songs Of The Cross

WHEN THE MORNING COMES, [ARR.]
(Kirkland, Camp) CRESPUB CP-IN 7+6
$15.00 see also Seven+
Orchestration Series, Group 2
(W216)

WHEN THE ROLL IS CALLED UP YONDER,
[ARR.]
(Kirkland, Camp) CRESPUB CP-IN 7+5
$15.00 see also Seven+
Orchestration Series, Group 2
(W217)

WHERE THE CITRONS BLOOM see Strauss,
Johann, [Jr.], Wo Die Zitronen
Bluhn

WHILE SHEPHERDS WATCHED THEIR FLOCKS BY
NIGHT see Fink

WHISTLER AND HIS DOG, THE see Pryor,
Arthur

WHITE CHRYSANTHEMUM, FOR SOLO VOICES
AND ORCHESTRA see Bozic, Darijan,
Bela Krizantema, For Solo Voices
And Orchestra

WHITGIFT SUITE see Cleeve, Stewart
Montagu

WHITHER see Schubert, Franz (Peter),
Wohin?, For Solo Voice And
Orchestra, [arr.]

WHO IS SYLVIA, FOR SOLO VOICE AND
ORCHESTRA, [ARR.] see Schubert,
Franz (Peter)

WHYTE, IAN (1901-   )
Kate Dalrymple [6']
string orch
SCOTUS 376-4 perf mat rent   (W218)

Little Suite Of Dances [10']
string orch
SCOTUS 381-0 perf mat rent   (W219)

WI' A HUNDRED PIPERS, FOR SOLO VOICE
AND ORCHESTRA
LUCKS 02748 set $5.50, pts $.75, ea.
(W220)

WIDMUNG, FOR SOLO VOICE AND ORCHESTRA,
[ARR.] see Schumann, Robert
(Alexander)

WIE IM TRAUM see Mielenz, Hans

WIEDERHERGESTELLTE RUHE, DIE see Boer,
Ed de

WIEGENLIED, FOR SOLO VOICE AND
ORCHESTRA see Luck, Andrew H.

WIEGENLIED, FOR SOLO VOICE AND
ORCHESTRA see Ries, Franz

WIEGENLIED, FOR SOLO VOICE AND
ORCHESTRA, [ARR.] see Brahms,
Johannes

WIEGENLIED, OP. 32, NO. 1 see Fiby, H.

WIELAND DER SCHMIED see Hausegger,
Siegmund von

WIEN, MEIN SINN. WALZER see Strauss,
Johann, [Jr.]

WIENER BLUT WALZER see Strauss, Johann,
[Jr.]

WIENER BONBONS WALZER see Strauss,
Johann, [Jr.]

WIENER CARNEVALS QUADRILLE see Strauss,
Johann, [Jr.]

WIENER CHRONIK WALZER see Strauss,
Johann, [Jr.]

WIENER FRESKEN WALZER see Strauss,
Josef

WIENER KINDER SINGEN GERN, FOR SOLO
VOICE AND ORCHESTRA see Strauss,
Josef

WIENER PASTELL see Kleine, Werner

WIENER STIMMEN. WALZER see Strauss,
Josef

WIENER TANZE, ELF see Beethoven, Ludwig
van

WIENERBLUT MUSS WAS EIGENES SEIN, FOR
SOLO VOICE AND ORCHESTRA see
Strauss, Johann, [Jr.]

WIENERISCH see Pachernegg, Alois

WIENERWALD LERCHEN, FOR SOLO VOICE AND
ORCHESTRA see Strauss, Johann,
[Jr.]

WIENIAWSKI, HENRYK (1835-1880)
Concerto for Violin and Orchestra,
No. 1, Op. 14, in F sharp minor
[25']
2.2.2.2. 2.2.3.0. timp,strings,
vln solo
KALMUS 5163 sc $22.00, perf mat
rent, set $30.00, pts $1.50, ea.,
solo pt $3.00   (W221)

Concerto for Violin and Orchestra,
No. 2, Op. 22, in D minor
LUCKS 00541 sc $13.00, set $22.00,
pts $1.40, ea.   (W222)

Legende, For Violin And Orchestra
*Op.17
LUCKS 00599 sc $8.00, set $16.00,
pts $1.00, ea.   (W223)

Polonaise Brillante, For Violin And
Orchestra *Op.21
LUCKS 00543 sc $12.00, set $10.50,
pts $.75, ea.   (W224)

Polonaise De Concert, For Violin And
Orchestra *Op.4
LUCKS 00588 set $15.00, pts $1.00,
ea.   (W225)

Scherzo-Tarentelle, For Violin And
Orchestra *Op.16
LUCKS 00542 sc $7.50, set $11.00,
pts $.95, ea.   (W226)

WIJDEVELD, WOLFGANG (1910-   )
Concertstuk [15']
1.1.1.1. 1.0.0.0. 3vln,2vla,2vcl,
db
sc DONEMUS f.s., perf mat rent
(W227)
Intro In Dutch Style *see Intro In
Hollandse Trant

Intro In Hollandse Trant *Op.82
[13']
2.2.2.2. 4.2.3.1. timp,2perc,
strings
"Intro In Dutch Style" DONEMUS
(W228)
WIJDING AAN MIJN VADER, FOR SOLO VOICE
AND ORCHESTRA see Dijk, Jan van

WILCKEN, EUGEN
Neckerei
RIES f.s.   (W229)

WILD DOVE, THE see Dvorak, Antonin,
Wood Dove

WILD WINDS, THE see Berkeley, Michael

WILDBERGER, JACQUES (1922-   )
...Die Stimme, Die Alte, Schwacher
Werdende Stimme..., For Solo
Voice, Violoncello And Orchestra
[22']
3(pic).1(English horn)+English
horn.2.2+contrabsn. 4.3.4.0.
perc,harp,cel,elec org,strings,
electronic tape,vcl solo,S solo
BREITKOPF-W perf mat rent   (W230)

WILDER, ALEC (1907-1980)
Air for Bassoon and String Orchestra
string orch,bsn solo
WILDER W 504 perf mat rent   (W231)

Concert Piece for Piano and Chamber
Orchestra
1.1.2.1. 2.2.1.0. perc,strings,
pno solo
WILDER W 547 perf mat rent   (W232)

WILDER, ALEC (cont'd.)

Concerto for Clarinet and Chamber
Orchestra
2.2.1.2. 3.0.3.0. perc,strings,
clar solo
WILDER W 538 perf mat rent   (W233)

Concerto for Flute and Chamber
Orchestra
0.2.2.2. 3.1.1.0. perc,strings,fl
solo
WILDER W 535 perf mat rent   (W234)

Concerto for Horn and Chamber
Orchestra, No. 1
2.2.2.2. 2.0.0.0. strings,horn
solo
WILDER W 502 perf mat rent   (W235)

Concerto for Saxophone and Chamber
Orchestra
1.1.2.1. 2.2.1.0. perc,strings,
tenor sax solo
WILDER W 519 perf mat rent   (W236)

Concerto for Violoncello and
Orchestra
2.2.2.3. 4.3.3.1. timp,perc,
strings,vcl solo
WILDER W 554 perf mat rent   (W237)

Effie Suite *see Suite for Tuba and
Orchestra, No. 1

Elegy For The Whale
2.2.2.2. 4.3.3.1. harp,perc,
strings,tuba solo
sc WILDER W 545 $8.00, perf mat
rent   (W238)

Entertainment No. 2
2.2.2.2. 2.2.0.0. strings
sc WILDER W 546 $7.50, perf mat
rent   (W239)

Entertainment No. 4 For Horn And
Chamber Orchestra
1.2.1.1. 1.0.3.0. timp,perc,
strings
WILDER W 531 perf mat rent   (W240)

Entertainment No. 6
2.2.2.2. 4.3.3.1. timp,perc,
strings
study sc MARGUN MM 18 $20.00, perf
mat rent   (W241)

Four Sentiments
3.3.3.2. 4.3.3.1. timp,perc,harp
WILDER W 540 perf mat rent   (W242)

Piece For Orchestra
2.2.2.3. 4.3.3.1. timp,perc,harp,
strings
WILDER W 521 perf mat rent   (W243)

Songs For Patricia, For Solo Voice
And Orchestra
1.2.2.1. 2.1.1.0. perc,harp,
strings
WILDER W 530 perf mat rent   (W244)

Suite for Brass Quintet and Strings
string orch,brass quin sc WILDER
W 537 $6.50, perf mat rent (W245)

Suite for Clarinet and Strings
string orch,clar solo
WILDER W 513 perf mat rent   (W246)

Suite for Flute and Strings
string orch,fl solo
WILDER W 528 perf mat rent   (W247)

Suite for Horn and Strings
string orch,horn solo
WILDER W 512 perf mat rent   (W248)

Suite for Saxophone and Strings, No.
1
string orch,tenor sax solo
sc WILDER W 511 $7.50, perf mat
rent   (W249)

Suite for Saxophone and Strings, No.
2
string orch,tenor sax solo
WILDER W 526 perf mat rent   (W250)

Suite for String Orchestra
string orch
WILDER W 525 perf mat rent   (W251)

Suite for Tuba and Orchestra, No. 1
2.2.2.2. 4.3.3.1. perc,strings,
tuba solo
sc WILDER W 510 $7.50, perf mat
rent   (W252)

WILDERNESS JOURNAL: SYMPHONY see La
Montaine, John

WILDFEUER see Strauss, Johann, [Jr.]

WILDSCHUTZEN-MARSCH see Rinderspacher, Jean

WILHELMINA V. BAYREUTH
Concerto for Harpsichord and Orchestra
fl,strings,hpsd solo
sc,pts LEUCKART f.s.   (W253)

WILHELMJ, AUGUST (1845-1908)
All' Ungherese, For Violin And Orchestra [5']
2.2.2.2. 4.2.1.0. timp,triangle, strings,vln solo
sc,pts LIENAU f.s.   (W254)

Alla Polacca, For Violin And Orchestra [6']
2.2.2.2. 4.2.3.0. timp,strings, vln solo
sc,pts LIENAU rent   (W255)

In Memoriam, For Violin And Orchestra
orch,vln solo
sc LIENAU f.s.   (W256)

Italienische Suite, Funf Stucke Von Paganini, For Violin And Orchestra
2.2.2.2. 2.0.0.0. timp,strings, vln solo
sc,pts LIENAU rent   (W257)

Larghetto Nach Mozart, For Violin And Orchestra [3']
1.1.2.2. 2.0.0.0. strings,vln solo
sc,pts LIENAU rent   (W258)

Romance for Violin and Orchestra, Op. 10, in E
orch,vln solo
sc LIENAU f.s.   (W259)

Siciliano Nach Bach, For Violin And Orchestra [3']
2ob/2clar,strings,vln solo
sc,pts LIENAU f.s.   (W260)

WILLIAM RADCLIFFE: INTERMEZZO see Mascagni, Pietro, Guglielmo Ratcliff: Intermezzo (Prelude, Act IV)

WILLIAM RADCLIFFE: INTRODUCTION see Mascagni, Pietro, Guglielmo Ratcliff: Introduction

WILLIAM RADCLIFFE: RADCLIFFE'S DREAM see Mascagni, Pietro, Guglielmo Ratcliff: Sogno, Act III

WILLIAM RATCLIFF: RATCLIFF'S DREAM see Mascagni, Pietro, Guglielmo Ratcliff: Sogno, Act III

WILLIAM TELL: OVERTURE see Rossini, Gioacchino, Guillaume Tell: Overture

WILLIAMS, ADRIAN
Explorations And Metamorphoses [26']
2.0.English horn.2.3.tenor sax. 2.1.1.0. timp,perc,harp,strings
OXFORD perf mat rent   (W261)

WILLIAMS, RALPH VAUGHAN
see VAUGHAN WILLIAMS, [SIR] RALPH

WILLIAMSON, MALCOLM (1931-   )
Concerto for Harp and String Orchestra [24']
string orch,harp solo
('Au Tombeau Du Mortgre Juif Inconnu') BOOSEY perf mat rent
                                        (W262)
Display, The: Dance Symphony [45']
2.2.2.2. 4.3.3.1. timp,perc,harp, pno,strings
WEINBERGER perf mat rent   (W263)

Hammarskjold Portrait, For Solo Voice And Orchestra [30']
string orch,S solo
BOOSEY perf mat rent   (W264)

Ochre [9']
3.3.3.3. 4.3.3.1. timp,perc,harp, strings,opt org
OXFORD perf mat rent   (W265)

WILLIS, RICHARD STORRS (1819-1900)
It Came Upon A Midnight Clear
see Luther, Martin, Away In A Manger

WILSON, OLLY (1937-   )
Akwan [16']
2.2.3.3. 4.3.3.1. 4perc,strings, pno/elec pno solo, ampl strings (4 vln, 2 vla, 2 vcl)
MARGUN BP 8001 perf mat rent (W266)

Voices [15']
2.2.3.3. 4.3.3.1. timp,4perc, strings

WILSON, OLLY (cont'd.)
sc MARGUN BP 8002 $15.00, perf mat rent   (W267)

WILSON, THOMAS
Concerto for Orchestra [17']
3.3.3.3. 4.3.3.1. timp,perc,cel, pno,strings
sc SCOTUS 289-X f.s.   (W268)

Pas De Quoi [11']
string orch
sc SCOTUS 294-6 f.s.   (W269)

Ritornelli Per Archi [19']
string orch
SCOTUS 299-7 f.s.   (W270)

Symphony No. 2 [25']
3.2.2.2. 4.2.3.1. perc,harp,cel, pno,strings
sc SCOTUS 300-4 f.s.   (W271)

Symphony No. 3 [25']
3.3.3.3. 4.3.3.1. timp,3perc, harp,cel,pno,strings
sc SCOTUS 305-5 f.s.   (W272)

Threnody [17']
3.3.3.3. 4.3.3.1. timp,perc,harp, cel,pno,strings
sc SCOTUS 310-1 f.s.   (W273)

Toccata [8']
3.2.2.2. 4.2.3.1. timp,harp, strings
sc SCOTUS 315-2 f.s.   (W274)

Touchstone [10']
3.3.3.3. 4.3.3.1. timp,perc,harp, cel,pno,strings
SCOTUS 445-0   (W275)

Variations [18']
2.2.2.2. 4.2.3.1. perc,harp,cel, strings
sc SCOTUS 320-9 f.s.   (W276)

WIMBERGER, GERHARD (1923-   )
Concertino for Orchestra [11']
2.2.2.1+contrabsn. 3.2.1.0. timp, perc,cel,strings
BAREN. BA 6795   (W277)

Multiplay [13']
1.1.1.1. 1.1.1.0. cel,strings, marimba,vibra
study sc BAREN. BA 6275 f.s., perf mat rent   (W278)

Plays, For Twelve Violoncelli, Brass And Percussion [20']
2.2.2.1+contrabsn. 2.2.2.1. 4timp,2perc,12vcl
study sc BAREN. BA 6711 f.s., perf mat rent   (W279)

Programm
3(alto fl,pic).2+English horn.2+ bass clar.2+contrabsn. 4.3.3.1. timp,3perc,harp,gtr,org,strings
study sc BAREN. BA 6744 f.s., perf mat rent   (W280)

WINBECK, HEINZ (1946-   )
Entgegengesang [16']
6.1.0.0. 0.0.0.0. 3perc,hpsd, harmonium,cel,harp,strings, 3zither
BAREN. BA 6797   (W281)

Lenau-Fantasien, For Violoncello And Chamber Orchestra [15']
clar,tenor sax,perc,harmonium, cel,strings
BAREN. BA 6798   (W282)

WIND SHIFTS, THE, FOR SOLO VOICE AND STRING ORCHESTRA see Holloway, Robin

WINDEN LACHEN ZACHT, DE see Mulder, Herman

WINDROSE, DIE see Kotonski, Wlodzimierz

WINDSONGS, FOR PIANO AND ORCHESTRA see Wuorinen, Charles

WINDSONGS, FOR PIANO AND ORCHESTRA see Zupko, Ramon

WINDSOR KLANGE. WALZER see Strauss, Johann, [Jr.]

WINDSTRING SOLILOQUIES, FOR SPEAKER AND CHAMBER ORCHESTRA see Cytron, Warren A.

WINE, WOMEN, AND SONG see Strauss, Johann, [Jr.], Wein, Weib, Und Gesang

WINEBERGER, PAUL (1758-1821)
Symphony in F
see SEVEN SYMPHONIES FROM THE COURT OF OETTINGEN-WALLERSTEIN (1773-1795)

WINKLER, GERHARD
Al Fine
RIES f.s.   (W283)

Im Kerzenschimmer
RIES f.s. contains also: Standchen An Colombine   (W284)

Standchen An Colombine
see Winkler, Gerhard, Im Kerzenschimmer

Tarentina, La
see Crucius, Heinz, Saragossa

WINTER, PETER VON (1754-1825)
Colmal Overture
see Franzl, Ignaz, Symphonies In C, In F And In C

Schlacht-Sinfonie
see Franzl, Ignaz, Symphonies In C, In F And In C

Symphonie Concertante, Op. 20
see Franzl, Ignaz, Symphonies In C, In F And In C

WINTER IST EIN SCHARFER GAST, DER see Kubizek, Augustin

WIR GLAUBEN ALL' AN EINEM GOTT, [ARR.] see Bach, Johann Sebastian

WIR SIND DIE MUSIKANTEN see Maasz, Gerhard

WIRBELWIND see Golde, Adolf

WISMAR, R.
Blumen Und Sterne
RIES f.s.   (W285)

Es Fiel Ein Stern
RIES f.s.   (W286)

Geige Weint, Die
RIES f.s.   (W287)

WISSMER, PIERRE (1915-   )
Symphony No. 6 [30']
2.2.2.2. 4.4.3.1. timp,perc,xylo, vibra,harp,cel,strings
AMPHION A 376 perf mat rent   (W288)

WITS AND FANCIES see Irving, Robert

WITT, FRIEDRICH (1770-1837)
Concertino for 2 Horns and Orchestra in E flat [8']
2.2.2.2. 2.2.0.0. timp,strings, 2horn soli
PETERS perf mat rent   (W289)

WITTINGER, ROBERT (1945-   )
Concerto Entusiastico *Op.33
MOECK 5201 study sc f.s., pts rent
                                        (W290)
Concerto for 2 Pianos and Orchestra, Op. 36
4.3.4.3. 4.3.3.0. timp,3perc, strings,2pno soli
[20'] sc,pts MOECK 5251   (W291)

Concerto Lirico *Op.32 [12']
3.3.3.3. 4.3.3.1. 4perc,harp,pno, strings
study sc MOECK 5200 f.s., perf mat rent   (W292)

Symphony No. 2, Op. 35
MOECK 5202 study sc f.s., pts rent
                                        (W293)

WO DIE TROMPETE DAS THEMA BEGINNT', FOR VIOLONCELLO AND ORCHESTRA see Eder, Helmut

WO DIE ZITRONEN BLUHN see Strauss, Johann, [Jr.]

WO DIE ZITRONEN BLUHN, FOR SOLO VOICE AND ORCHESTRA see Strauss, Johann, [Jr.]

WO FIND ICH TROST, FOR SOLO VOICE AND ORCHESTRA see Wolf, Hugo

WO ZWEI HERZENSLIEBE see Kubizek, Augustin

WOCKE, ERICH (1906-   )
Choralfantasie In A Minor [13']
fl,ob,clar,bsn,trp,strings
MANNHEIM E 43-60 f.s.   (W294)

WOGENDE BLUTEN see Muhr, Ferry

WOHIN?, FOR SOLO VOICE AND ORCHESTRA, [ARR.] see Schubert, Franz (Peter)

WOITSCHACH, PAUL
Harlekinade
WOITSCHACH f.s. (W295)

Magyarentanz
WOITSCHACH f.s. (W296)

WOLF, HUGO (1860-1903)
Anakreons Grab, For Solo Voice And
Orchestra
KALMUS A4659 sc $3.00, set $7.00,
pts $.60, ea. (W297)

Auf Ein Altes Bild "In Gruner
Landschaft", For Solo Voice And
Orchestra
0.2.2.2. 0.0.0.0. S solo
BREITKOPF-W perf mat rent (W298)

Denk Es, O Seele, For Solo Voice And
Orchestra
"O Soul, Consider!, For Solo Voice
And Orchestra" KALMUS A4625 sc
$3.00, perf mat rent, set $11.00,
pts $.60, ea. (W299)

Elfenlied, For Solo Voice And
Orchestra
KALMUS A4662 sc $6.00, set $10.00,
pts $.60, ea. (W300)

Er Ist's, "Fruhling Lasst Sein Blaues
Band", For Solo Voice And
Orchestra
"Song To Spring, For Solo Voice And
Orchestra" KALMUS A4658 sc $4.00,
perf mat rent, set $12.00, pts
$.60, ea. (W301)

Gebet, For Solo Voice And Orchestra
KALMUS A4664 sc $3.00, set $8.00,
pts $.60, ea. (W302)

Gesang Weylas "Du Bist Orplid, Mein
Land", For Solo Voice And
Orchestra [2']
0.0.1.0. 1.0.0.0. harp/pno,S solo
BREITKOPF-W perf mat rent (W303)

Harfenspieler I, For Solo Voice And
Orchestra
KALMUS A 4632 sc $3.00, set $9.00,
pts $.60, ea. (W304)

Harfenspieler II, For Solo Voice And
Orchestra
KALMUS A4633 sc $3.00, set $6.00,
pts $.60, ea. (W305)

Harfenspieler III, For Solo Voice And
Orchestra
KALMUS A4634 sc $3.00, set $10.00,
pts $.60, ea. (W306)

Holy Week, For Solo Voice And
Orchestra *see Karwoche, For
Solo Voice And Orchestra

Ich Hab In Penna Einen Liebsten
Wohnen, For Solo Voice And
Orchestra
KALMUS A4627 sc $3.00, set $10.00,
pts $.60, ea. (W307)

In Der Fruhe, For Solo Voice And
Orchestra
"In The Early Morning, For Solo
Voice And Orchestra" KALMUS
A 4626 sc $3.00, perf mat rent,
set $11.00, pts $.60, ea. (W308)

In The Early Morning, For Solo Voice
And Orchestra *see In Der Fruhe,
For Solo Voice And Orchestra

Karwoche, For Solo Voice And
Orchestra
"Holy Week, For Solo Voice And
Orchestra" KALMUS A4629 sc $5.00,
perf mat rent, set $12.00, pts
$.60, ea. (W309)

Mignon (First Version), For Solo
Voice And Orchestra
LUCKS 02422 sc $8.00, set $21.00,
pts $1.00, ea. (W310)
KALMUS A4636 sc $8.00, perf mat
rent, set $21.00, pts $1.00, ea.
(W311)

Mignon (Second Version), For Solo
Voice And Orchestra
LUCKS 03739 sc $8.00, set $20.00,
pts $1.00, ea. (W312)

Neue Liebe, For Solo Voice And
Orchestra
"New Love" LUCKS 02423 set $17.50,
pts $.75, ea. (W313)

New Love *see Neue Liebe, For Solo
Voice And Orchestra

O Soul, Consider!, For Solo Voice And
Orchestra *see Denk Es, O Seele,
For Solo Voice And Orchestra

WOLF, HUGO (cont'd.)

Prometheus, For Solo Voice And
Orchestra
LUCKS 00277 sc $8.00, set $34.50,
pts $1.25, ea. (W314)

Rattenfanger, Der, For Solo Voice And
Orchestra
LUCKS 02417 set $21.00, pts $1.00,
ea. (W315)

Scherzo Und Finale [15']
3.2.2.2. 4.3.3.1. timp,perc,
strings
sc MUSIKWISS. f.s. (W316)

Schlafendes Jesuskind, For Solo Voice
And Orchestra
KALMUS A4663 sc $3.00, set $7.00,
pts $.60, ea. (W317)

Seufzer, For Solo Voice And Orchestra
"Sigh, A, For Solo Voice And
Orchestra" KALMUS A4630 sc $3.00,
set $6.00, pts $.60, ea. (W318)

Sigh, A, For Solo Voice And Orchestra
*see Seufzer, For Solo Voice And
Orchestra

Solitudine, For Solo Voice And
Orchestra
2.2.2.2. 2.0.0.0. strings,solo
voice
manuscript CARISCH (W319)

Song To Spring, For Solo Voice And
Orchestra *see Er Ist's,
"Fruhling Lasst Sein Blaues
Band", For Solo Voice And
Orchestra

Two Sacred Songs From The "Spanisches
Liederbuch", [arr.] *see Zwei
Lieder Aus Dem Spanischen
Liederbuch, For Solo Voice And
Orchestra, [arr.]

Verborgenheit, For Solo Voice And
Orchestra
KALMUS A4628 sc $3.00, set $9.50,
pts $.60, ea. (W320)

Wo Find Ich Trost, For Solo Voice And
Orchestra
KALMUS A4661 sc $3.00, perf mat
rent, set $15.00, pts $.60, ea.
(W321)

Zwei Lieder Aus Dem Spanischen
Liederbuch, For Solo Voice And
Orchestra, [arr.]
(Stravinsky, Igor) "Two Sacred
Songs From The "Spanisches
Liederbuch", [arr.]" sc BOOSEY
$7.50 (W322)

WOLF-FERRARI, ERMANNO (1876-1948)
Campiello, Il: Intermezzo, Act II;
Ritornello, Act III
sc RICORDI-IT 129805 f.s. (W323)

Donne Curiose, Le: Overture
"Inquisitive Women: Overture" min
sc WEINBERGER W151 $7.00 (W324)

Gioielli Della Madonna, I: Intermezzo
E Serenata
"Jewels Of The Madonna: Intermezzo
And Serenade" min sc WEINBERGER
W150 $7.00 (W325)

Inquisitive Women: Overture *see
Donne Curiose, Le: Overture

Jewels Of The Madonna: Intermezzo And
Serenade *see Gioielli Della
Madonna, I: Intermezzo E Serenata

Quattro Rusteghi, I: Preludio E
Intermezzo
"School For Fathers: Prelude And
Intermezzo" min sc WEINBERGER
W149 $5.25 (W326)

School For Fathers: Prelude And
Intermezzo *see Quattro
Rusteghi, I: Preludio E
Intermezzo

Secret Of Suzanne: Overture *see
Segreto Di Susanna, Il: Overture

Segreto Di Susanna, Il: Overture
"Secret Of Suzanne: Overture" LUCKS
07095 sc $10.50, set $20.00, min
sc $5.00, pts $1.15, ea. (W327)
"Susanna's Secret: Overture" min sc
WEINBERGER W147 $5.25 (W328)

Susanna's Secret: Overture *see
Segreto Di Susanna, Il: Overture

WOLFE, STANLEY ANDREW (1924-   )
Symphony No. 3, Op. 14
sc BOOSEY $8.00 (W329)

WOLKENBILDER see Thiele, Siegfried

WOLPE, STEFAN (1902-1972)
Man From Midian, The
MCGIN-MARX perf mat rent (W330)

WOLSCHINA, REINHARD (1952-   )
Drei Dialoge, For Horn And Strings
15strings, horn solo
sc DEUTSCHER DVFM 1436 f.s. (W331)

WOOD DOVE see Dvorak, Antonin

WOODLAND SKETCHES, NOS. 1-5, [ARR.] see
MacDowell, Edward Alexander

WOODLAND SKETCHES, NOS. 6-10, [ARR.]
see MacDowell, Edward Alexander

WORDSWORTH, WILLIAM (1908-   )
Concerto for Violoncello and
Orchestra [30']
2.2.2.2. 4.2.3.0. timp,perc,harp,
cel,strings,vcl solo
sc SCOTUS 171-0 f.s. (W332)

Confluence [13']
3.3.3.3. 4.3.3.1. timp,harp,pno,
strings
SCOTUS 345-4 perf mat rent (W333)

Highland Overture, A [8']
2.2.2.2. 2.2.0.0. timp,perc,harp,
cel,strings
sc SCOTUS 330-6 f.s. (W334)

Jubilation [8']
2.2.2.2. 4.3.3.0. timp,perc,harp,
strings
sc SCOTUS 355-1 f.s. (W335)

Overture - Conflict [9']
2.2.2.2. 4.3.3.0. timp,perc,harp,
pno,strings
sc SCOTUS 360-8 f.s. (W336)

Sinfonia Semplice [12']
string orch
SCOTUS 306-3 f.s. (W337)

Sinfonietta [25']
1.1.1.1. 2.1.0.0. pno,strings
sc SCOTUS 370-5 f.s. (W338)

Spring Festival Overture, A [19']
2.2.2.2. 4.2.3.0. timp,perc,harp,
strings
sc SCOTUS 335-7 f.s. (W339)

Symphony No. 5 in A minor [34']
3.3.3.3. 4.3.3.1. timp,perc,harp,
cel,strings
SCOTUS 395-0 f.s. (W340)

Symposium [13']
pno,electronic tape,strings,vln
solo
SCOTUS 386-1 f.s. (W341)

Valediction [9']
2.3.2.3. 4.3.3.0. timp,perc,harp,
pno,cel,strings
SCOTUS 331-4 f.s. (W342)

WORK FOR ORCHESTRA III see Nordenstrom,
Gladys

WORKS FOR PIANO AND ORCHESTRA see
Schumann, Robert (Alexander)

WORKS OF RICHARD WAGNER, VOL. 7:
ORCHESTERWERKE see Wagner, Richard

WORLDS see Hillborg, Anders

WORLDS see Vriend, Jan

WORRIED DRUMMER, THE see Schreiner,
Alexander

WORSHIP MEDLEY, [ARR.]
(Kirkland, Camp) CRESPUB CP-IN 7+2
$15.00 see also Seven+
Orchestration Series, Group 1
(W343)

WORTHY IS THE LAMB
(Mayfield, Larry; Skillings, Otis)
SINGSPIR 7708 $19.95 (W344)

WREN, THE see Benedict, [Sir] Julius,
Capinera, La, For Solo Voice And
Orchestra

WUNDER DER BERGE see Scheibe, W.

WUORINEN, CHARLES (1938-   )
Ecclesiastical Symphonies [12'30"]
3(pic).3.3.3. 4.3.3.1. timp,
4perc,harp,pno,strings
PETERS P66851A perf mat rent (W345)

WUORINEN, CHARLES (cont'd.)

    Hyperion [16']
        1.1.1.1. 1.1.1.0. pno,vln,vla,
          vcl,db
        PETERS P66657 perf mat rent (W346)

    Magic Art, The [140']
        1(pic).2(English horn).1(bass
          clar).2. 2.2.1.0. timp,harp,
          pno,strings
        PETERS P66809 perf mat rent (W347)

    Magic Art, The: Suite [25']
        1(pic).2(English horn).1(bass
          clar).2. 2.0.0.0. pno,strings
        PETERS P66809A perf mat rent (W348)

    Tashi [30'30"]
        3.2.3.3. 4.3.3.1. timp,5perc,
          harp,strings,clar solo,vln
          solo,vcl solo,pno solo
        PETERS P66697 perf mat rent (W349)

    Two-Part Symphony [21']
        3.2.2.2. 4.2.2.1. timp,4perc,
          harp,pno,strings
        PETERS P66779 perf mat rent (W350)

    Windsongs, For Piano And Orchestra
        [23']
        4.3.3.3. 4.3.3.1. timp,2perc,
          harp,pno,strings,pno solo
        PETERS perf mat rent   (W351)

WYMAN, DAN C.
    Serenade
        string orch
        SEESAW perf mat rent   (W352)

X

XENAKIS, YANNIS (IANNIS) (1922-   )
    Metastaseis
        sc BOOSEY $25.00   (X1)

    Polytope
        sc BOOSEY $30.00   (X2)

    Pour Les Baleines [2'30"]
        string orch
        SALABERT   (X3)

    ST-48-1, 240162
        sc BOOSEY $22.00   (X4)

XERXES: LARGO see Handel, George
    Frideric, Serse: Ombra Mai Fu,
    [arr.]

XUMBU-ATA see Pert, Morris

Y

YASHIMA, HIDEAKI (1915-   )
    Pioneers, The
        2+pic.2+English horn.2+bass
          clar.2+contrabsn. 4.3.3.1.
          timp,perc,harp,strings
        sc J.C.A. f.s.   (Y1)

YEARS HAVE PASSED, THE, FOR SOLO VOICE
    AND ORCHESTRA see Korinek,
    Miloslav, Presli Roky, For Solo
    Voice And Orchestra

YEOMEN OF THE GUARD, THE: OVERTURE see
    Sullivan, [Sir] Arthur Seymour

YES, IT SURE HURTS, FOR SOLO VOICE AND
    CHAMBER ORCHESTRA see Kruse, Bjorn,
    Ja Visst Gjor Det Ont, For Solo
    Voice And Chamber Orchestra

YESTERDAY, TODAY AND TOMORROW
    (Mayfield, Larry; Skillings, Otis)
    SINGSPIR 7700 $19.95   (Y2)

YLI KUKKIEN, FOR SOLO VOICE AND
    ORCHESTRA, [ARR.] see Kuula, Toivo

YO-NATT, FOR SOLO VOICE AND ORCHESTRA,
    [ARR.] see Kuula, Toivo

YOUR ADVICE IS GOOD, FOR SOLO VOICE AND
    ORCHESTRA, [ARR.] see Grieg, Edvard
    Hagerup

YOUR MELODY see Storrle, Heinz

YTTERSTA DOMEN see Rosenberg, Hilding

YUASA, JOJI (1929-   )
    Scenes From Bacho
        ZEN-ON 899068   (Y3)

    Time Of Orchestral Time
        ZEN-ON 899067   (Y4)

YUN, ISANG (1917-   )
    Concerto for Clarinet and Orchestra
        sc BOTE f.s.   (Y5)

    Concerto for Violin and Orchestra
        sc BOTE f.s.   (Y6)

    Exemplum
        study sc BOTE f.s.   (Y7)

    Fanfare And Memorial
        sc BOTE f.s.   (Y8)

    Muak
        sc BOTE $42.25   (Y9)

Z

ZADOR, EUGENE (JENO) (1894-1977)
Music For Clarinet And String
Orchestra [16']
string orch,clar solo
sc EULENBURG E10027 f.s., perf mat
rent (Z1)

Suite for Horn, Strings and
Percussion
perc,pno,strings,horn solo
sc EULENBURG E10026 f.s., perf mat
rent (Z2)

ZAGWIJN, HENRI (1878-1954)
Fuszwaschung, Die, For Solo Voice And
Orchestra [10']
1.1.1.1. 1.0.0.0. timp,perc,pno,
Hamm,cel,strings,S solo
sc DONEMUS f.s., perf mat rent (Z3)

Ode, For Solo Voice And Orchestra
[7']
2.3.2.2. 4.2.1.0. timp,perc,
strings,A solo
sc DONEMUS f.s., perf mat rent (Z4)

Tema Con Variazioni [10']
strings without vla, db
sc DONEMUS f.s., perf mat rent (Z5)

ZAHIDE see Geisler, Willy

**ZAIDE: RUHE SANFT, FOR SOLO VOICE AND
ORCHESTRA see Mozart, Wolfgang
Amadeus**

**ZAIRE, PERGER 13 see Haydn, [Johann]
Michael**

**ZAMPA: OVERTURE see Herold, Louis-
Joseph-Ferdinand**

ZANABONI, GIUSEPPE (1927-)
Meditation
org,strings
sc CARISCH 22064 f.s. (Z6)

**ZANAIDA: OVERTURE, [ARR.] see Bach,
Johann Christian**

ZANDER, H.
Im Cafe Hungaria
WOITSCHACH f.s. (Z7)

ZANETTOVICH, DANIELE (1950-)
Estadio Nacional: Lager 1973, For
Flute And Orchestra
snare drum,strings,fl solo
LEDUC perf mat rent (Z8)

**ZANGEN VAN MALDOROR, DE see Wagemans,
Peter-Jan**

ZANON, SANTE (1899-1965)
Preludio Eroico [10']
3.3.2.2. 4.2.2.1. timp,harp,
strings
manuscript CARISCH (Z9)

Sinfonia [15']
2.2.1.1. 4.2.1.1. timp,perc,pno,
harp,strings
sc CARISCH 19441 perf mat rent
(Z10)

**ZAR UND ZIMMERMANN: DIE EIFERSUCHT IST
EINE PLAGE, FOR SOLO VOICE AND
ORCHESTRA see Lortzing, (Gustav)
Albert**

**ZAR UND ZIMMERMANN: LEB WOHL, MEIN
FLANDRISCH MADCHEN, FOR SOLO VOICE
AND ORCHESTRA see Lortzing,
(Gustav) Albert**

**ZAR UND ZIMMERMANN: OVERTURE see
Lortzing, (Gustav) Albert**

**ZAUBERFLOTE, DIE: ACH, ICH FUHL'S, FOR
SOLO VOICE AND ORCHESTRA see
Mozart, Wolfgang Amadeus**

**ZAUBERFLOTE, DIE: BEI MANNERN, FOR SOLO
VOICES AND ORCHESTRA see Mozart,
Wolfgang Amadeus**

**ZAUBERFLOTE, DIE: DER HOLLE RACHE, FOR
SOLO VOICE AND ORCHESTRA see
Mozart, Wolfgang Amadeus**

**ZAUBERFLOTE, DIE: DER VOGELFANGER BIN
ICH JA, FOR SOLO VOICE AND
ORCHESTRA see Mozart, Wolfgang
Amadeus**

**ZAUBERFLOTE, DIE: DIES BILDNIS IST
BEZAUBERND SCHON, FOR SOLO VOICE
AND ORCHESTRA see Mozart, Wolfgang
Amadeus**

**ZAUBERFLOTE, DIE: EIN MADCHEN ODER
WEIBCHEN, FOR SOLO VOICE AND
ORCHESTRA see Mozart, Wolfgang
Amadeus**

**ZAUBERFLOTE, DIE: IN DIESEN HEIL'GEN
HALLEN, FOR SOLO VOICE AND
ORCHESTRA see Mozart, Wolfgang
Amadeus**

**ZAUBERFLOTE, DIE: O ISIS UND OSIRIS,
FOR SOLO VOICE AND ORCHESTRA see
Mozart, Wolfgang Amadeus**

**ZAUBERFLOTE, DIE: O ZITT'RE NICHT, FOR
SOLO VOICE AND ORCHESTRA see
Mozart, Wolfgang Amadeus**

**ZAUBERFLOTE, DIE: OVERTURE see Mozart,
Wolfgang Amadeus**

**ZAUBERFLOTE, DIE: PA-PA-PA-PAPAGENA,
FOR SOLO VOICES AND ORCHESTRA see
Mozart, Wolfgang Amadeus**

**ZAUBERFLOTE, DIE: WIE STARK IST NICHT
DEIN ZAUBERTON, FOR SOLO VOICE AND
ORCHESTRA see Mozart, Wolfgang
Amadeus**

ZAUBERLIED, DAS see Meyer-Helmund, Erik

**ZAUBERNACHT, OP. 9: ORCHESTERSUITE see
Weill, Kurt**

ZAVOJE see Brozak, Daniel

ZECHLIN, RUTH (1926-)
Concerto for Piano and Orchestra
sc,quarto,fac ed PETERS 9684 $25.00
(Z11)

Music for Orchestra [12']
3.3.3.3. 4.4.3.1. perc,strings
PETERS perf mat rent (Z12)

Prager Orgelkonzert, For Organ And
Orchestra [21']
0.0.0.0. 0.4.3.1. perc,strings,
org solo
PETERS perf mat rent (Z13)

Situationen [13']
3.3.3.3. 4.4.3.1. timp,perc,
strings
PETERS $15.00 (Z14)
sc PETERS perf mat rent (Z15)

ZECHNER, JOHANN GEORG (1716-1778)
Symphonies, Two
see AUSTRIAN CLOISTER SYMPHONISTS

**ZEESYMFONIE see Meulemans, Arthur,
Symphony No. 6**

ZELENKA, JAN DISMAS (1679-1745)
Concerto A 5ol [17']
0.1.0.1. 0.0.0.0. hpsd,strings
sc UNIVER. UE 12853 $37.00, set
UNIVER. UE 12854 $17.50, pts
UNIVER. $2.00, ea. (Z16)

Suite, MIN 53 [25']
0.2.0.1. 0.0.0.0. hpsd,strings
sc UNIVER. UE 12843 $33.00, set
UNIVER. UE 12844 $19.00, pts
UNIVER. $5.25, ea. (Z17)

ZELJENKA, ILJA (1932-)
Epilog [14']
2.2.2.1. 2.2.1.0. timp,strings
SLOV.HUD.FOND 0-495A perf mat rent
(Z18)
Music for Piano and String Orchestra
[20']
string orch,pno solo
SLOV.HUD.FOND KH-135 perf mat rent
(Z19)

ZEMLINSKY, ALEXANDER VON (1871-1942)
Suppliants D'Eschyle
2trp,2trom,strings without vla
study sc SALABERT $19.00 (Z20)

ZERRSPIEGEL, DER see Hudec, Jiri

ZETTLER, RICHARD
Concertino in F for Horn and
Orchestra
fl,ob,2clar,bsn,timp,harp,
strings,horn solo
BUDDE perf mat rent (Z21)

**ZEVEN ITALIAANSCHE LIEDEREN, FOR SOLO
VOICE AND ORCHESTRA see Horst,
Anton van der**

ZIEHRER, CARL MICHAEL (1843-1922)
Himmel Voller Geigen, Der *Op.34
LIENAU f.s. (Z22)

Loslassen! *Op.386
1+pic.2.2.2. 4.2.3.0. timp,perc,
strings
sc,pts DOBLINGER DM 901 f.s. (Z23)

ZIEHRER, CARL MICHAEL (cont'd.)

Mamsell Uibermuth *Op.69
1+pic.2.2.1. 4.2.1.0. timp,perc,
strings
sc,pts LIENAU rent (Z24)

**ZIEKE BUUR, UIT: "FANTOMEN" VAN F.
PAUWELS, DE, FOR SOLO VOICE AND
ORCHESTRA see Beyerman-Walraven,
Jeanne**

ZIERITZ, GRETE VON
Bilder Vom Jahrmarkt, For Flute And
Orchestra [14']
2.2.2.2. 2.0.0.0. timp,2perc,
harp,strings,fl solo
RIES perf mat rent (Z25)

Japanische Lieder, For Solo Voice And
Chamber Orchestra [28']
1.1.1.1. 0.0.0.0. harp,cel,2perc,
strings,S solo
RIES perf mat rent (Z26)

Violon De La Mort, Le, For Violin,
Piano And Orchestra [26']
2(pic).2(English horn).2(bass
clar).2. 4.3.2.0. timp,3perc,
harp,strings,vln solo,pno solo
RIES perf mat rent (Z27)

**ZIGEUNERBARON, DER: OVERTURE see
Strauss, Johann, [Jr.]**

**ZIGEUNERBARON, DER: SCHATZ WALZER see
Strauss, Johann, [Jr.]**

**ZIGEUNERBARON, DER: SELECTION see
Strauss, Johann, [Jr.]**

**ZIGEUNERWEISEN, FOR VIOLIN AND
ORCHESTRA see Sarasate, Pablo de**

ZIINO, OTTAVIO (1909-)
Toccata E Fuga [12']
3.3.3.2. 4.3.3.1. strings
manuscript CARISCH (Z28)

**ZIJ SLUIMERT, FOR SOLO VOICE AND
ORCHESTRA see Diepenbrock, Alphons**

ZILCHER, HERMANN (1881-1948)
Suite, Op. 4, in G [25']
2(pic).2.2.2. 4.2.3.0. timp,perc,
strings
RIES perf mat rent (Z29)

ZIMMER, JAN (1926-)
Liberation *see Oslobodenie

Oslobodenie *Op.78 [23']
3.3.3.3. 4.3.3.1. timp,perc,harp,
cel,pno,strings,speaking voice
"Liberation" SLOV.HUD.FOND 0-64
perf mat rent (Z30)

ZIMMERMAN, ANTON (1741-1781)
Concerto for Double Bass and
Orchestra in D, MIN 5 [16']
0.2.0.0. 2.0.0.0. strings,db solo
(Malaric, R.) sc,pts DOBLINGER rent
(Z31)

ZIMMERMANN, BERND ALOIS (1918-1970)
Concerto for Violoncello and
Orchestra
orch,vcl solo
study sc SCHOTTS 71 A6329 $21.00
(Z32)

ZIMMERMANN, UDO (1943-)
Mensch, Der, For Solo Voice And
Instrumental Ensemble
alto fl,English horn,clar,horn,
trp,trom,perc,harp,5vcl,S solo
DEUTSCHER perf mat rent (Z33)

Sinfonia Come Un Grande Lamento
3.3.3.3. 4.4.4.1. 7timp,4perc,
strings
sc DEUTSCHER 1707 f.s., perf mat
rent (Z34)

**ZINGARE IN FIERA, LE: OVERTURE see
Paisiello, Giovanni**

ZINGARELLI, NICOLA ANTONIO (1752-1837)
Sinfonias, Seven
see Mattei, Stanislav, Sinfonias,
Five

ZINSSTAG, GERARD (1941-)
Alteration
fl,ob,clar,horn,trom,tuba,pno,
perc,vla,vcl,db
[21'] MODERN 2191 f.s. (Z35)

Innanzi, For Double Bass And
Orchestra [23'-25']
orch,db solo
MODERN 2073 perf mat rent (Z36)

ZIPOLI, DOMENICO (1688-1726)
Adagio
string orch,org,ob solo,vcl solo
(Paillard, J.F.) sc,pts COSTALL
f.s. (Z37)

ZIPOLI, DOMENICO (cont'd.)

  Elevazione
    see RICREAZIONI DI ANTICHE MUSICHE
      CLASSICHE, SERIE I: MUSICHE
      ANTICHE ITALIANE

  Suite in F, MIN 116
    (Lauth, A.) org/hpsd,strings,trp/
      vln solo [12'35"] COSTALL perf
      mat rent   (Z38)

ZODIAC see Bennett, Richard Rodney

ZOHAR see Stock, David

ZOLLNER, HEINRICH (1854-1941)
  Serenade for Flute and String
    Orchestra, Op. 95 [15']
      string orch,fl solo
      RIES perf mat rent   (Z39)

ZOMBIES AWAKE, THE see Meijering, Chiel

ZOMERZANG see Voormolen, Alexander
  Nicolas

ZORAHAYDA see Svendsen, Johan (Severin)

ZORZI, JUAN CARLOS (1935-   )
  Variaciones Enigmaticas
    sc BARRY-ARG $15.00   (Z40)

ZOSI, GIULIANO (1940-   )
  B 9 634 Oradour Sur Glane [12'-16']
    1.0.2.0.sax. 1.1.1.0. pno&cel,
      5perc,vln,vcl,db
    sc ZERBONI 8246 f.s., pts ZERBONI
      8247 rent   (Z41)

ZU JEDER LEDERHOS'N see Richartz, Willy

ZU WEM SPRECHE ICH HEUTE?, FOR SOLO
  VOICE AND ORCHESTRA see Bijl, Theo
  van der

ZUEIGNUNG, FOR SOLO VOICE AND
  ORCHESTRA, [ARR.] see Strauss,
  Richard

ZUM RENDEZ-VOUS see Blon, Franz von

ZUPKO, RAMON (1932-   )
  Windsongs, For Piano And Orchestra
    [23']
      4.3.3.3. 4.3.3.1. timp,2perc,
      harp,strings,pno solo
      PETERS 66863 perf mat rent (Z42)

ZWANEVEN see Meulemans, Arthur,
  Symphony No. 7

ZWEI GRIECHISCHE TANZE see Eichinger,
  Hans

ZWEI LIEDER, FOR SOLO VOICE AND
  ORCHESTRA see Roos, Robert de

ZWEI LIEDER AUS DEM SPANISCHEN
  LIEDERBUCH, FOR SOLO VOICE AND
  ORCHESTRA, [ARR.] see Wolf, Hugo

ZWEI MILITARMARSCHE see Strauss,
  Richard

ZWEI STUCKE, FOR VIOLIN AND ORCHESTRA
  see Hamann, Bernhard

ZWEI STUCKE: ALLEGRO UND ADAGIO see
  Eisbrenner, Werner

ZWEI STUCKE: MARCHEN UND EIN VOLKSLIED
  see Mikulicz, Lothar

ZWEI VOLKSTANZE see Noack, Walter

ZWEITES SEEBILD "SCHATTEN VON KAHNEN",
  FOR SOLO VOICE AND ORCHESTRA see
  Trojahn, Manfred

ZWIEGESPRACH, EIN, FOR VIOLIN,
  VIOLONCELLO AND ORCHESTRA see
  Schillings, Max von

ZWILICH, ELLEN TAAFFE (1939-   )
  Symphony No. 1
    MARGUN   (Z43)

ZWISCHEN ZWEI FLUSSEN see Knumann, Jo

EDUCATIONAL
ORCHESTRAL MUSIC

A BICYCLETTE see Amiot, Jean-Claude

ACCENTS see Frost, Robert S.

ACHTTOURIGER see Lehmann, S.

ADAGIO FROM SEXTET, OP 81B, [ARR.] see
Beethoven, Ludwig van

ADAM, ADOLPHE-CHARLES (1803-1856)
Oh Holy Night, [arr.]
(Whitney, John C.) set COLUMBIA
PIC. 24090B7X $20.00   (1)

AFRICAN TRILOGY see Diamond, Neil

AFTERNOON IN MONTREAL see Creston, Paul

AHLBERG, GUNNAR (1942-   )
Entrata
1.0.0.0. 0.1.0.0. perc,pno,strings
[5'30"] STIM perf mat rent   (2)

Macchie
2.2.2.2. 0.2.0.0. timp,pno,strings
[7'] STIM perf mat rent   (3)

Parentes
2.2.2.2. 2.2.0.0. perc,strings [9']
STIM perf mat rent   (4)

AIR DE BALLET, [ARR.] see Gluck,
Christoph Willibald, Ritter von

AIR, MINUET AND RONDO, [ARR.] see
Purcell, Henry

AIRS AND DANCES see Lully, Jean-
Baptiste (Lulli)

ALBINONI, TOMASO (1671-1750)
Three Balletti For Strings, [arr.]
(Polnauer, Frederick) string orch,
pno ELKAN-V $37.50   (5)

ALBUM FOR THE YOUNG: SUITE 1, [ARR.]
see Tchaikovsky, Piotr Ilyich

ALBUM FOR THE YOUNG: SUITE 2, [ARR.]
see Tchaikovsky, Piotr Ilyich

ALBUMS DU PETIT ORCHESTRE, LES, 2 VOLS.
*CCU
(Dourson, P.) LEDUC   (6)

ALFVEN, HUGO (1872-1960)
Swedish Rhapsody, [arr.]
(Isaac, Merle J.) string orch (med
easy) sets WYNN $16.00, and up
(7)

ALLA DANZA, [ARR.] see Zehm, Friedrich

ALLEGRO, [ARR.] see Leclair, Jean Marie

ALLEGRO IN C MAJOR, [ARR.] see Mozart,
Wolfgang Amadeus

ALPHA-BETA SET see Teuber, Fred

ALSHIN, HARRY
Hoedown In 5
(gr. III) BOWM   (8)

Miracle At The Stream, A
orch,narrator
(gr. III) BOWM   (9)

Quiet Tribute
string orch
(gr. III/gr. IV) BOWM   (10)

Renaissance Suite, A
string orch
(gr. III/gr. IV) BOWM   (11)

South American Holiday
2.1.2.1.opt alto sax.opt tenor sax.
2.2.1.0.opt tuba. perc,opt pno,
strings (gr. II) KENDOR sets
$16.00, and up, sc $3.00   (12)

Suite Chinoise
(gr. III) BOWM   (13)

ALSO SPRACH ZARATHUSTRA: THEMES, [ARR.]
see Strauss, Richard

AMELLER, ANDRE (CHARLES-GABRIEL)
(1912-   )
Petite Suite
(med easy) BILLAUDOT sc $6.50, pts
$25.50   (14)

AMERICAN FOLK SONG SUITE
(Errante, Belisario) string orch (gr.
III) sets ETLING,F $18.00, and up
(15)

AMERICAN FOLK SONG SUITE NO. 1 see
Isaac, Merle John, Editor

AMERICAN FOLK SONG SUITE NO. 2 see
Isaac, Merle John, Editor

AMERICAN FOLK SONG SUITE NO. 3 see
Isaac, Merle John, Editor

AMERICAN HYMN see Keller

AMERICAN PATROL, [ARR.] see Meacham

AMIOT, JEAN-CLAUDE
A Bicyclette (composed with John,
Chris)
see Mon Deuxieme Concert

Ballade Du Petit Tato (composed with
John, Chris)
see Mon Premier Concert

Black Cat Rag (composed with John,
Chris)
see Mon Deuxieme Concert

Chaconne Pour Un Film Imaginaire
(composed with John, Chris)
see Mon Deuxieme Concert

Cirque Zouzou, Le (composed with
John, Chris)
see Mon Deuxieme Concert

Five O'Clock (composed with John,
Chris)
see Mon Deuxieme Concert

Mon Deuxieme Concert (composed with
John, Chris)
2.1.2.1.soprano sax.alto sax.tenor
sax.baritone sax.
2.2.2.1.baritone horn. perc,gtr,
strings MARTIN pno-cond sc f.s.,
pts f.s.
contains: A Bicyclette; Black Cat
Rag; Chaconne Pour Un Film
Imaginaire; Cirque Zouzou, Le;
Five O'Clock   (16)

Mon Premier Concert (composed with
John, Chris)
2.1.2.1.soprano sax.2alto sax.tenor
sax.baritone sax.
2.2.2.1.baritone horn. perc,gtr,S
rec,strings MARTIN pno-cond sc
f.s., pts f.s.
contains: Ballade Du Petit Tato;
On The Mississippi River; Petit
Tato Va Chez Le Roy; Petite
Marche; Western Music   (17)

On The Mississippi River (composed
with John, Chris)
see Mon Premier Concert

Petit Tato Va Chez Le Roy (composed
with John, Chris)
see Mon Premier Concert

Petite Marche (composed with John,
Chris)
see Mon Premier Concert

Western Music (composed with John,
Chris)
see Mon Premier Concert

ANAGRAM FOR STRINGS see Forsblad,
Leland

ANDANTE FOR STRINGS, [ARR.] see
Schubert, Franz (Peter)

ANTAR, THIRD MOVEMENT, [ARR.] see
Rimsky-Korsakov, Nikolai, Symphony
No. 2, Op. 9, Third Movement,
[arr.]

ANTIPHONAL VOLUNTARY, [ARR.] see
Purcell, Henry

APARTMENT, THE, THEME FROM, [ARR.] see
Williams

APPALACHIAN FESTIVAL
(Gordon, Philip) set ALFRED 1932
$20.00   (18)

APPLEBAUM, SAMUEL
Away We Go (composed with Gordon,
Louis)
string orch,pno BELWIN sc $6.00,
kbd pt $4.00, pts $2.00, ea. (19)

Flying High (composed with Gordon,
Louis)
string orch,pno BELWIN sc $6.00,
kbd pt $4.00, pts $2.00, ea. (20)

ARCADELT, JACOB (ca. 1505-1568)
Hymn Of Faith, [arr.]
sets STAFF 0-6 $10.00, and up (21)

AROUND A LINE see Sandstrom, Sven-David

ASPEN FANTASY see Feese, Francis L.

AVISON, CHARLES (1709-1770)
Concerto in E minor, [arr.]
(Isaac) string orch,pno [2'30"]
(gr. II) sets ETLING,F $13.00,
and up   (22)

AWAY IN A MANGER
see Christmas Carol Kit, Set 2
(Frost, Robert) string orch,opt pno
KENDOR sc $2.50, sets $11.00, and
up   (23)

AWAY WE GO see Applebaum, Samuel

BACH, CARL PHILIPP EMANUEL (1714-1788)
Three Sonatas And Six Marches *CC9U
strings without vla,kbd,opt 2horn
LIENAU   (24)

BACH, JOHANN SEBASTIAN (1685-1750)
Beginning Bach
(Wieloszynski, Stephen) string
orch,opt pno (gr. I) sets KENDOR
$14.00, and up
contains: March, [arr.]; Minuet,
[arr.]; Musette, [arr.]   (25)

Bourree, [arr.]
(Muller, Frederick; Fink, Lorraine)
string orch,opt pno [2'10"] (gr.
III) set KJOS SO-31B $11.00   (26)

Brandenburg Concerto No. 5, [arr.]
(Isaac, Merle J.) string orch (gr.
III) sets ETLING,F $18.00, and up
(27)

Brandenburg Sinfonia, [arr.]
(Isaac) 2.1.2+bass clar.0.alto
sax.tenor sax. 2.2.2.1. timp,
perc,pno,strings [3'] (gr. III)
sets ETLING,F $24.00, and up (28)

Come, Blessed Peace, [arr.]
sets STAFF 0-10 $10.00, and up (29)

Fugue in G minor, [arr.], MIN 200
(Temianka, H.) string orch set
BELWIN BSO 32 $15.00   (30)

Fugue in G minor, [arr.], MIN 201
(Isaac, Merle J.) string orch (gr.
III) sets ETLING,F $26.00, and up
(31)

Goin' Baroque
(Bauernschmidt, Robert) (med) sets
WYNN $22.00, and up   (32)

King Of Glory *chorale
sets STAFF 0-17 $10.00, and up (33)

Kleine Spielmusik I (from Gradus Ad
Symphoniam)
LIENAU   (34)

Kleine Spielmusik II (from Gradus Ad
Symphoniam)
LIENAU   (35)

Little Bach Suite, [arr.]
sets STAFF 0-14 $10.00, and up (36)

March, [arr.]
see Beginning Bach

Menuet And March, [arr.] (from Little
Note Book For Anna Magdalena
Bach)
(Nelhybel, Vaclav) strings,kbd CHRI
ABC 8 f.s.   (37)

Minuet, [arr.]
see Beginning Bach

Musette, [arr.]
see Beginning Bach

Now Let Every Tongue, [arr.]
sets STAFF 0-8 $10.00, and up (38)

Prelude in C, [arr.] (from Well-
Tempered Clavier)
(Nelhybel, Vaclav) strings,kbd CHRI
ABC 7 f.s.   (39)

Three Bach Minuets, [arr.]
(Fink, Lorraine; Muller, Fred)
[5'45"] (gr. III) KJOS SO36B
$16.00   (40)

Toccata In G Major, [arr.]
(Hause) 2.2.2.2. 4.2.3.1. timp,
strings set SHAWNEE $20.00   (41)

Vierzehn Kanons, BWV 1087 Uber Die
Ersten Acht Fundamentalnoten Der
Aria Aus Den "Goldberg-
Variationen", [arr.]
(Meylan, Raymond) sc,pts NAGELS
NMA 242 f.s.   (42)

Werke Von Bach (from Gradus Ad
Symphoniam) CCU
LIENAU   (43)

BALLADE DU PETIT TATO see Amiot, Jean-
Claude

BAMBA, LA
(Isaac, Merle) 1.1.2.1.opt alto
sax.opt tenor sax. 2.2.1.0.opt
tuba. opt timp,2perc,opt pno,
strings [4'15"] (gr. II) sets
KENDOR $26.00, and up   (44)

BAROQUE FUGUE see Siennicki, Edmund
John

BAROUH
Man And A Woman, A, [arr.]
MCA UB129 set $17.50, sc $4.00,
pno-cond sc $2.00, pts $.75, ea.
(45)

BARRY MANILOW SELECTIONS see Manilow,
Barry

BART, LIONEL
Oliver: Medley, [arr.]
(Frackenpohl, Arthur; Frackenpohl,
Steven) 1.1.2.1.opt alto sax.opt
tenor sax. 2.2.1.1. perc,strings
[6'] (gr. II) sets KENDOR $28.00,
and up   (46)

Oliver: Where Is Love?, [arr.]
(Caponegro, John) string orch,opt
perc,opt pno [2'40"] (gr. II)
sets KENDOR $11.00, and up   (47)

BARTOK, BELA (1881-1945)
Dance Of The Slovaks, [arr.]
(Dishinger, R. Christian) set
STUDIO X7710 $10.00   (48)

Peasant Suite, [arr.]
(Bauernschmidt, Robert) (med easy)
sets WYNN $24.00, and up   (49)

BAUERNSCHMIDT, ROBERT
Bear Dance
2.1.2.0. 2.2.1.1. perc,strings set
LYDIAN ORCH $14.00   (50)

Christmas Eve Is Here
(med) sets WYNN $18.00, and up (51)

Country Festival
(med easy) sets WYNN $24.00, and up
(52)

BEAR DANCE see Bauernschmidt, Robert

BEATLES MEDLEY see Lennon, John

BEATLES MEET THE STRING ORCHESTRA, THE
see Lennon, John

BEAUTIFUL NOISE (CONCERT HIGHLIGHTS)
see Diamond, Neil

BEETHOVEN, LUDWIG VAN (1770-1827)
Adagio From Sextet, Op 81b, [arr.]
see HAUSKAPELLE, DIE, BOOK 1

Choral Symphony Theme, [arr.] *see
Symphony No. 9, Op. 125,
[excerpt], [arr.]

Fidelio: March, [arr.]
sets STAFF 0-16 $10.00, and up (53)

Fidelio: Overture, [arr.]
(Isaac) (med diff) sets WYNN
$30.00, and up   (54)

Heavens Resound, The, [arr.]
(Smith, Claude T.) string orch set
WINGERT $10.00   (55)

Symphony No. 1, Op. 21, First
Movement, [arr.]
(Isaac, Merle J.) (med) sets WYNN
$30.00, and up   (56)

Symphony No. 5, Op. 67, Finale,
[arr.]
(Matesky) (med diff) sets WYNN
$30.00, and up   (57)

Symphony No. 9, Op. 125, [excerpt],
[arr.]
MIDDLE CMK 205 f.s.   (58)

Turkischer Marsch From Die Ruinen Von
Athen, [arr.]
see HAUSKAPELLE, DIE, BOOK 1

BEETHOVEN'S FIFTH see Holcombe, Bill

BEGINNING BACH see Bach, Johann
Sebastian

BELL AND CEREMONIAL MUSIC, [ARR.] see
Purcell, Henry

BELVEDERE SUITE see Isaac, Merle John

BEMBO, D. BALDAN
Melody (Aria), [arr.]
(Stephan, Richard) set COLUMBIA
PIC. 1454MB7X $20.00   (59)

BERCEUSE, FOR VIOLIN AND ORCHESTRA see
Skold, Yngve

BERLIN, IRVING (1888-   )
God Bless America, [arr.]
(Kerr) (gr. IV) set LEONARD-US
04500425 $18.00   (60)

White Christmas, [arr.]
(Chase, Bruce) string orch (gr. II)
LEONARD-US 04849900 $15.00   (61)
(Chase, Bruce) (gr. II) LEONARD-US
04798814 $20.00   (62)

BICYCLE BUILT FOR TWO, [ARR.] see
Dacre, Harry

BILLINGS, WILLIAM (1746-1800)
Chester, [arr.]
(Gardner) sets STAFF 0-21 $15.00,
and up   (63)

BIZET, GEORGES (1838-1875)
Carmen: Prelude, [arr.]
(Kriechbaum, Casey B.) string orch
(gr. III) sets ETLING,F $26.00,
and up   (64)

Farandole, [arr.]
(Isaac) string orch,pno [3'10"]
(gr. III) sets ETLING,F $13.00,
and up   (65)

March And Impromptu, [arr.] (from
Jeux d'Enfants)
(Stone, David) 2.2.2.1. 2.2.2.0.
timp,perc,strings BOOSEY set
$33.00, augmented set $55.00 (66)

Symphony No. 1, First Movement,
[arr.]
(Isaac, Merle J.) string orch (gr.
IV) sets ETLING,F $32.00, and up (67)

BLACK CAT RAG see Amiot, Jean-Claude

BLOMBERG, ERIK (1922-   )
Uppspel
2.2.2.0. 0.2.0.0. timp,strings
[2'30"] STIM perf mat rent   (68)

BLUEBERRY HILL see Lewis, Al

BOCA GRANDE, LA see Kriechbaum, Casimer
B.

BOLZONI, GIOVANNI (1841-1919)
Minuetto, [arr.]
(Isaac) string orch,pno [2'30"]
(gr. II) sets ETLING,F $13.00,
and up   (69)

BON, MAARTEN (1933-   )
Ephemere Espagnol, Un
5.0.2.2.alto sax. 0.1.0.0. 11perc,
pno 4-hands,strings [5'] DONEMUS
(70)

BOOREN, JO VAN DEN (1935-   )
Brabant
MOLENAAR 14.1605.08   (71)

BORTZ, DANIEL (1943-   )
Concerto Grosso No. 1
2.2.2.2. 2.2.2.0. 2perc,pno 4-
hands,strings, Concertino: 2clar,
2trom, pno 4-hands, vln, vcl, str
octet [35'] STIM perf mat rent
(72)

BOURREE, [ARR.] see Bach, Johann
Sebastian

BOW-REGARD'S PARADE see Caponegro, John

BOYLE, RORY
Suite Of English Folk Songs, A
string orch sc CHESTER 55344 $6.75,
pts CHESTER 55345 $23.75   (73)

BRABANT see Booren, Jo van den

BRAHMS, JOHANNES (1833-1897)
Hungarian Dance No. 4, [arr.]
(Isaac, Merle J.) string orch (gr.
III) sets ETLING,F $18.00, and up
(74)
Hungarian Dance No. 5, [arr.]
(Isaac, Merle J.) string orch (gr.
III) sets ETLING,F $18.00, and up
(75)
Hymn Of Freedom, [arr.]
sets STAFF 0-3 $10.00, and up (76)

St. Anthony Chorale, [arr.] (from
Variations On A Theme Of Haydn)
MIDDLE CMK 202 f.s.   (77)

Waltz And Dance, [arr.]
(Lehmeier) (easy) set LEONARD-US
$20.00   (78)

BRANDENBURG CONCERTO NO. 5, [ARR.] see
Bach, Johann Sebastian

BRANDENBURG SINFONIA, [ARR.] see Bach,
Johann Sebastian

BRIGADOON: EXCERPTS see Loewe,
Frederick

BRIGHTON FESTIVAL OVERTURE see Platts,
Kenneth

BROADWAY TONIGHT!, [ARR.]
(Chase, Bruce) (gr. III) LEONARD-US
04499785 $40.00
contains: Everything's Coming Up
Roses; My Favorite Things;
People; Soon It's Gonna Rain;
That's Entertainment; Try To
Remember   (79)

BROWNE, PHILIP (1933-   )
Serenade
2.2.2+bass clar.2. 4.3.2.1. timp,
perc,strings [6'40"] (gr. IV)
sets ETLING,F $24.00, and up (80)

BRUNETTE, LA, [ARR.] see Severn, Edmund

BURLESCA see Sevius, Sven

CAHN, SAMMY (1913-   )
Let It Snow! Let It Snow! Let It
Snow!, [arr.] *see Styne, Jule
(Jules Stein)

CAJKOVSKIJ, PETR ILJIC
see TCHAIKOVSKY, PIOTR ILYICH

CANDLE ON THE WATER
see Disney Magic, [arr.]

CANTATE CANTICA SOCII (from Piae
Cantiones)
(Sonninen, Ahti) string orch FAZER
f.s.   (81)

CANTO ALLA LEGGENDA see Forsberg,
Roland

CANZONA see Lundquist, Torbjorn

CAPONEGRO, JOHN
Bow-Regard's Parade
string orch,opt perc,opt pno sc
KENDOR $2.50   (82)

Disco Strings
string orch,pno,opt perc (gr. II)
sets KENDOR $11.00, and up (83)
1.1.2.1. 2.2.1.0.opt tuba. perc,
pno,strings [3'] (gr. II) sets
KENDOR $16.00, and up   (84)

Swingin' Strings
string orch,opt perc,opt pno (gr.
I) sets KENDOR f.s.   (85)

Tropical Serenade
string orch,pno (gr. II) KENDOR
sets $11.00, and up, sc $2.50 (86)

CAPRICE NO. 9, [ARR.] see Paganini,
Niccolo

CAREFREE CAPER see Frost, Robert S.

CARIBBEAN CARNIVAL see Feese, Francis
L.

CARMEN: PRELUDE, [ARR.] see Bizet,
Georges

CARNIVAL SCENE see Forsblad, Leland

CAROUSEL: SELECTIONS, [ARR.] see
Rodgers, Richard

CAUCASIAN SKETCHES: PROCESSION, [ARR.]
see Ippolitov-Ivanov, Mikhail
Mikhailovich

CAVATINA, [ARR.] see Myers, Stanley A.

CELEBRATION OVERTURE see Lane, Philip

CHACONNE, [ARR.] see Purcell, Henry

CHACONNE POUR UN FILM IMAGINAIRE see
Amiot, Jean-Claude

CHAIKOVSKII, PETR IL'ICH
see TCHAIKOVSKY, PIOTR ILYICH

CHANUKAH CELEBRATION
(Feldstein, Sandy) set ALFRED 1927
$18.00   (87)

CHANUKAH MUSIC FOR STRINGS
(Shapiro) string orch (gr. II) sets
ETLING,F $18.00, and up   (88)

CHATSCHATURJAN, ARAM
see KHACHATURIAN, ARAM

CHESTER, [ARR.] see Billings, William

CHESTER VARIATIONS see Nelhybel, Vaclav

CHILD IS BORN, A see Jones

CHIM CHIM CHER-EE
see Disney Magic, [arr.]

CHOPIN, FREDERIC (1810-1849)
Two Preludes, [arr.]
(Etling, Forest R.) string orch
(gr. II) sets ETLING,F $18.00,
and up   (89)

CHORAL SYMPHONY THEME, [ARR.] see
Beethoven, Ludwig van, Symphony No.
9, Op. 125, [excerpt], [arr.]

CHORALE VARIATIONS see Smith, Claude
Thomas

CHORUS LINE, A: SELECTIONS, [ARR.] see
Hamlisch, Marvin F.

CHRISTENSEN, JAMES HARLAN (1935-   )
Season's Greetings
(gr. III) set LEONARD-US 04501450
$18.00   (90)

CHRISTIANSEN, JAMES
Hey Ride!
1(pic).1.2.1.opt alto sax.opt tenor
sax.opt baritone sax. 2.3.3.1.
2perc,opt pno,strings [2'10"]
(gr. V) set KENDOR $25.00   (91)

Three To Get Ready
1.1.2.1. 1.3.3.1. perc,opt gtr,pno,
strings [3'15"] (gr. V) set
KENDOR $22.00   (92)

CHRISTMAS CAROL KIT, SET 1
MIDDLE f.s.
contains: First Nowell, The; O Come
All Ye Faithful; Once In Royal
David's City; While Shepherds
Watched   (93)

CHRISTMAS CAROL KIT, SET 2
MIDDLE f.s.
contains: Away In A Manger; Ding
Dong Merrily On High; Hark The
Herald Angels Sing; O Little Town
Of Bethlehem   (94)

CHRISTMAS CAROLS, SET 1 see Isaac,
Merle John, Editor

CHRISTMAS CAROLS, SET 2 see Isaac,
Merle John, Editor

CHRISTMAS EVE IS HERE see
Bauernschmidt, Robert

CHRISTMAS FAVORITES
(Chase, Bruce) (med) set LEONARD-US
$35.00   (95)

CHRISTMAS FESTIVAL see Dickson, Richard

CHRISTMAS MEDLEY, A
(Frost, Robert S.) [3'15"] (gr. II)
KJOS S042B $14.50   (96)

CHRISTMAS MEMORIES, [ARR.] *Xmas
(Chase, Bruce) (gr. III) LEONARD-US
04500010 $35.00
contains: Frosty The Snow Man; Have
Yourself A Merry Little
Christmas; I Saw Mommy Kissing
Santa Claus; Santa Claus Is
Comin' To Town   (97)

CHRISTMAS SHOWCASE, A, [ARR.]
string orch set COLUMBIA PIC.
2481CB4X $10.00   (98)
(Fink, Philip) set COLUMBIA PIC.
2481CB7X $20.00   (99)

CHRISTMAS SONG, THE, [ARR.] see Torme,
Melvin Howard (Mel)

CHRISTMAS SUITE see Etling, Forest R.

CHRISTMAS SUITE FOR STRINGS see
Giammario, Matteo

CHRISTMAS TRADITIONALS
(Frost, Robert S.) string orch,opt
pno (gr. II) sets KENDOR f.s. (100)

CHRISTMAS WALTZ, [ARR.] see
Tchaikovsky, Piotr Ilyich

CHRISTMAS WISHES see Holcombe, Bill

CIAIKOVSKI, PIETRO
see TCHAIKOVSKY, PIOTR ILYICH

CIRCUS COMES TO TOWN, THE see Townsend,
Jill

CIRQUE ZOUZOU, LE see Amiot, Jean-
Claude

CLASS IN CONCERT see Salaman, William

CLASS IN CONCERT CHRISTMAS EXTRA
(Salaman, William) MIDDLE f.s.
contains: Coventry Carol; Good King
Wenceslas; Holly And The Ivy,
The; Jingle Bells; Lullaby,
Jesus, My Dear One, Be Sleeping;
Silent Night   (101)

CLASS IN CONCERT ENCORE see Salaman,
William

CLINE, THORNTON
Northeast Return
string orch (gr. III) sets ETLING,F
$18.00, and up   (102)

COHAN, GEORGE MICHAEL (1878-1942)
Give My Regards To Broadway, [arr.]
(Leideg, Vernon; Niehaus, Lennie)
set HIGHLAND $15.00   (103)

I'm A Yankee Doodle Dandy, [arr.]
(Leideg, Vernon; Niehaus, Lennie)
set HIGHLAND $15.00   (104)

Star Spangled Spectacular, [arr.]
(Gordon) MARKS M0145 set $16.00, sc
$4.00, pno-cond sc $1.50, pts
$.75, ea.   (105)

COME, BLESSED PEACE, [ARR.] see Bach,
Johann Sebastian

COMPOSER'S BAG OF TRICKS, THE see
Ervin, Max T.

CONCERTO BAROCCO, FOR VIOLIN AND STRING
ORCHESTRA see Wahlberg, Rune

CONCERTO FOR PIANO AND ORCHESTRA NO. 1,
OP. 23: THEMES, [ARR.] see
Tchaikovsky, Piotr Ilyich

CONCERTO FOR PIANO AND ORCHESTRA NO.
15: THEMES, [ARR.] see Mozart,
Wolfgang Amadeus

CONCERTO FOR PIANO AND ORCHESTRA, OP.
16: THEMES, [ARR.] see Grieg,
Edvard Hagerup

CONCERTO FOR VIOLIN AND ORCHESTRA NO.
22: THEMES, [ARR.] see Viotti,
Giovanni Battista

CONCERTO FOR VIOLINS AND ORCHESTRA,
[ARR.] see Mendelssohn-Bartholdy,
Felix

CONDOR PASA, EL
MIDDLE MK 02 f.s.   (106)

CONTI, BILL
Rocky: Musical Highlights
(Lowden, R.W.) set BIG3 $40.00
                               (107)

CONTRASTS IN E MINOR see Feese, Francis
L.

COOPER, MARTY
Little Bit Country, A Little Bit Rock
'n Roll, A
(Higgins, John) 1.1.2.1. 2.2.2.1.
perc,strings set JENSON 501-12020
$16.50   (108)

COPACABANA see Manilow, Barry

CORELLI, ARCANGELO (1653-1713)
Suite, [arr.]
(Bauernschmidt, Robert) (med easy)
sets WYNN $24.00, and up   (109)

CORIGLIANO, JAMES
Reverie
string orch set SHAWNEE $6.00 (110)

CORONATION CHORUS, [ARR.] see
Mussorgsky, Modest Petrovich

CORY, GEORGE C. (1920-   )
I Left My Heart In San Francisco,
[arr.] (composed with Cross,
Douglass)
(Bennett, Robert Russell) (gr. IV)
set LEONARD-US 04854050 $25.00
                               (111)

COULD IT BE MAGIC see Manilow, Barry

COUNTRY FESTIVAL see Bauernschmidt,
Robert

COUPERIN, FRANCOIS (LE GRAND)
(1668-1733)
Suite, MIN 7 (from Gradus Ad
Symphoniam)
LIENAU   (112)

COVENTRY CAROL
see Class In Concert Christmas Extra

CRESTON, PAUL (1906-   )
Afternoon In Montreal
3(pic).3.3(bass clar).2+contrabsn.
4.1.0.0. timp,perc,strings set
TEMPLETN $12.00   (113)

CRESTON, PAUL (cont'd.)

Night In Mexico
3(pic).3.3(bass clar).2+contrabsn.
4.3.3.1. timp,perc,strings, bass
clarinet may be substituted for
bassoon set TEMPLETN $20.00   (114)

CROSS, DOUGLASS (1920-   )
I Left My Heart In San Francisco,
[arr.] *see Cory, George C.

CRYSTAL FALLS see Frost, Robert S.

CZECH FOLK SONG SUITE
(Isaac, Merle J.) string orch (gr.
III) sets ETLING,F $26.00, and up
                               (115)

CZECH SONG AND DANCE see Townsend, Jill

DACRE, HARRY
Bicycle Built For Two, [arr.]
(Leideg, Vernon; Niehaus, Lennie)
set HIGHLAND $15.00   (116)

DANCE AND MUSETTE, [ARR.] see Gluck,
Christoph Willibald, Ritter von

DANCE MOVEMENTS see Mele, Frank

DANCE OF THE SLOVAKS, [ARR.] see
Bartok, Bela

DANCE SUITE see Townsend, Jill

DANCING BASSES see Isaac, Merle John

DANIELS, MELVIN L. (1931-   )
Elegy
string orch [3'] (gr. III) sets
ETLING,F $15.00, and up   (117)

Pendleton Suite
string orch [7'] (gr. III) sets
ETLING,F $15.00, and up   (118)

Prelude And Dance
string orch (gr. II) sets ETLING,F
$18.00, and up   (119)

DANS VOOR SCHOOLORKEST see Strategier,
Herman

DAVIES, PETER MAXWELL (1934-   )
Five Voluntaries
sc SCHOTT 75 A10994 $5.75, pts
SCHOTT 75 A10994A $2.00, ea.
                               (120)

DAY, NIGHT, AND DAY see Frost, Robert
S.

DAYBREAK see Manilow, Barry

DE PROFUNDIS see Heilmann, Harald

DECK THE HALLS
(Holcombe; Rothrock) string orch set
MUSICIANS PUB $12.00   (121)

DECSENYI, JANOS (1927-   )
Concertino for Violoncello and
Orchestra
orch,vcl solo EMB 8597 set $16.00,
augmented set $28.00   (122)

DEDEN, OTTO (1925-   )
Suite Minuscule
BANK DED 6 f.s.   (123)

DEGEN, JOHANNES (1910-   )
Episoder Kring Ett Tema
2.2.2.1.2sax. 1.1.1.0. strings STIM
perf mat rent   (124)

DENVER, JOHN
see DEUTSCHENDORF, HENRY JOHN

DESTINO see Errante, Belisario Anthony

DEURSEN, ANTON VAN (1922-   )
Little Triptych
string orch sc,pts HARMONIA 2334
f.s.   (125)

Three Dances
2S rec,A rec,2vln,vcl,pno,gtr sc,
pts HARMONIA 2613 f.s.   (126)

DEUTSCHENDORF, HENRY JOHN (1943-   )
I Want To Live
(Solomon, Murray) string orch,opt
pno,opt elec bass,opt drums,opt
gtr set CHERRY $14.00   (127)

John Denver Meets The String Section
*CC7L
(Solomon, Murray) string orch,opt
pno,opt elec bass,opt drums,opt
gtr CHERRY sc $5.50, pts $2.95,
ea.   (128)

DEUTSCHER TANZ, [ARR.] see Dittersdorf,
Karl Ditters von

DEUX PIECES FACILES see Gartenlaub,
Odette

DIABELLI, ANTON (1781-1858)
Three Pieces For Strings, [arr.]
(from Melodious Exercises, Op.
149)
(Hewitt-Jones, A.) string orch sc
CHESTER 55338 $6.75, pts CHESTER
55339 $23.75   (129)

DIALOGUE see Frost, Robert S.

DIAMOND, NEIL (1941-   )
African Trilogy
(Gold) set ALFRED 1926 $45.00 (130)

Beautiful Noise (Concert Highlights)
(O'Reilly, John) set ALFRED 1674
$28.00   (131)

September Morn
(O'Reilly, John) set ALFRED 1930
$18.00   (132)

You Don't Bring Me Flowers
(Forbes) set ALFRED 1163 $18.00
                                  (133)
(O'Reilly, John) set ALFRED 1175
$20.00   (134)

DICKERSON, ROGER DONALD (1934-   )
Ten Concert Pieces
string orch PEER sc $10.00, set
$20.00   (135)

DICKSON, RICHARD
Christmas Festival
perc,pno,strings set SHAWNEE $18.00
                                  (136)

DING DONG MERRILY ON HIGH
see Christmas Carol Kit, Set 2

DISCO STRINGS see Caponegro, John

DISNEY MAGIC, [ARR.]
(Lowden, Bob) (gr. III) LEONARD-US
04500048 $40.00
contains: Candle On The Water; Chim
Chim Cher-Ee; Dream Is A Wish
Your Heart Makes, A; It's A Small
World; Zip-A-Dee-Doo-Dah   (137)

DITTERSDORF, KARL DITTERS VON
(1739-1799)
Deutscher Tanz, [arr.]
see HAUSKAPELLE, DIE, BOOK 1

DIVERTISSEMENT BAROQUE see Joubert,
Claude-Henry

DIXIE SHOWBOAT
(Jurey, Edward) 1.1.2.1.alto
sax.tenor sax. 1.3.1.1. timp,perc,
strings GORDON sc $3.50, sets
$10.00, and up, pts $1.00, ea.
                                  (138)

DOBSZAY, L.
English Songs From The 17th Century
(special import only) sc,pts EMB
4483 f.s.   (139)

DOUBLE EAGLE POLKA, [ARR.] see Wagner,
Josef

DREAM IS A WISH YOUR HEART MAKES, A
see Disney Magic, [arr.]

DREAM OF A LOST CENTURY, A see Grahn,
Ulf

DREAM OF SCIPONE, [ARR.] see Mozart,
Wolfgang Amadeus, Sogno Di Scipone,
Il, [arr.]

DREI SATZE see Fheodoroff, Nikolaus

DREI STUCKE see Handel, George Frideric

DVORAK, ANTONIN (1841-1904)
Humoresque, [arr.]
(Isaac) string orch,pno [4'] (gr.
III) sets ETLING,F $13.00, and up
                                  (140)
Psalm Of Praise, [arr.]
sets STAFF 0-18 $10.00, and up
                                  (141)
Slavonic Dance No. 10, [arr.]
*Op.72,No.2
(Carlin, Sidney) string orch,pno,
includes parts for advanced vln,
vln III CARLIN sc $3.00, sets
$15.00, and up, pts $1.00, ea.
                                  (142)
Three Slavonic Dances, [arr.] *CC3U
(Isaac) string orch,pno (gr. III)
sets ETLING,F $15.00, and up (143)

EBONY AND IVORY, [ARR.] see McCartney,
[John] Paul

ECKERBERG, SIXTEN (1909-   )
Fran Sommen
2.2.2.2. 2.2.1.0. timp,perc,harp,
strings [19'] STIM perf mat rent
                                  (144)

EDELWEISS, [ARR.] see Rodgers, Richard

EKLUND, HANS (1927-   )
Facce
2.2.2.2. 2.2.1.0. timp,perc,strings
[15'] STIM perf mat rent   (145)

Interludio
2.2.2.2. 2.2.1.0. timp,perc,strings
[9'] GEHRMANS ENO 5740 perf mat
rent   (146)

Lamento
2.0.2.0. 0.0.0.0. strings [6']
GEHRMANS perf mat rent   (147)

ELEANOR RIGBY, [ARR.] see Lennon, John

ELGAR, [SIR] EDWARD (WILLIAM)
(1857-1934)
Pomp And Circumstance March, [arr.]
sets STAFF 0-7 $10.00, and up (148)

ELIZABETHAN DANCES see Platts, Kenneth

EMPEROR WALTZ, [ARR.] see Strauss,
Johann, [Jr.]

EN FA POUR ENFANTS see Joubert, Claude-
Henry

EN VACANCES see Vredenburg, Max

ENGLISH SONGS FROM THE 17TH CENTURY see
Dobszay, L.

ENGVICK, WILLIAM
While We're Young, [arr.] *see
Wilder, Alec

ENSEMBLE TIME FOR STRINGS, BOOK 1 *CCU
(Isaac, Merle J.) string orch ETLING,
F sc $6.00, sets $38.50, and up
                                  (149)
ENSEMBLE TIME FOR STRINGS, BOOK 2 *CCU
(Siennicki, Edmund J.) string orch
ETLING,F sc $6.00, sets $38.50, and
up   (150)

ENTERTAINER, THE
MIDDLE MK 05 f.s.   (151)

ENTERTAINER, THE, [ARR.] see Joplin,
Scott

ENTRATA see Ahlberg, Gunnar

EPHEMERE ESPAGNOL, UN see Bon, Maarten

EPISODER KRING ETT TEMA see Degen,
Johannes

EQUINOX see Rohn

ERICA see Kelch, Carleton

ERRANTE, BELISARIO ANTHONY (1920-   )
Destino
2.1.2+bass clar.0.alto sax.tenor
sax. 4.3.3.1. timp,perc,strings
[4'] (gr. III) sets ETLING,F
$18.00, and up   (152)

ERVIN, MAX T.
Composer's Bag Of Tricks, The
string orch,opt gtr,pno min sc
KENDOR $1.50   (153)

Jumpin' In July
string orch,pno (gr. I) KENDOR sets
$10.00, and up, sc $2.50   (154)

Mello-Cello
string orch,opt gtr,pno min sc
KENDOR $1.50   (155)

Readers Cha Cha
string orch,pno (gr. I) KENDOR sets
$10.00, and up, sc $2.50   (156)

Summer Waltz
string orch,pno (gr. I) KENDOR sets
$10.00, and up, sc $2.50   (157)

ESPRESSIVO see Nelhybel, Vaclav

ETLING, FOREST R. (? -1982)
Christmas Suite
1.1.2+bass clar.1.alto sax.tenor
sax. 2.2.1.0. timp,pno,strings
[3'] (gr. III) sets ETLING,F
$24.00, and up   (158)

Snow Flakes
string orch (gr. II) sets ETLING,F
$26.00, and up   (159)

EVANS, COLIN
Sounds For Swinging Strings
string orch,opt gtr,opt perc
NOVELLO sc $4.00, sc,pts $8.05
                                  (160)

EVEN NOW see Manilow, Barry

EVENING AT POPS, AN
(Holcombe, Bill) (med) set LEONARD-US
$35.00   (161)

EVERYTHING'S COMING UP ROSES
see Broadway Tonight!, [arr.]

EXPANDO see Rosell, Lars-Erik

EYE LEVEL
MIDDLE MK 03 f.s.   (162)

EYSER, EBERHARD (1932-   )
Hjarter Kung Gustav Wasas Hovmusik
string orch [14'] STIM perf mat
rent   (163)

Petit Nocturne
hpsd,strings,opt winds,db solo [7']
STIM perf mat rent   (164)

Sinfonietta No. 1
string orch [20'] STIM perf mat
rent   (165)

FACCE see Eklund, Hans

FAIR AT SOROTCHINSK, THE: GOPAK, [ARR.]
see Mussorgsky, Modest Petrovich

FAIREST ISLE, [ARR.] see Purcell, Henry

FANFARE AND CELEBRATION see Smith,
Claude Thomas

FANFARE AND RONDO, [ARR.] see Purcell,
Henry

FANTASIA PASTORALE see Hansgardh, Allan

FANTASIA SOPRA VENI REDEMPTOR SPIRITUS
see Hedwall, Lennart

FARANDOLE, [ARR.] see Bizet, Georges

FARIS, ALEXANDER
Upstairs Downstairs, [arr.]
(Frazer, Alan) string orch,opt pno,
opt perc sc,pts MIDDLE f.s. (166)

FARKAS, FERENC (1905-   )
Partita All'Ungaresca
string orch SCHOTTS 71 U0182 sc
$10.50, pts $3.00   (167)

FECKER, A.
Kleine Orchester, Das *CC7U
S rec,A rec,vln,vcl,opt triangle,
opt cym perf sc HEINRICH. 772
f.s.   (168)

Musik Zu Einem Krippenspiel
strings,opt triangle,opt cym sc,pts
HEINRICH. 3067 f.s.   (169)

FEESE, FRANCIS L. (1926-   )
Aspen Fantasy
(gr. III) YOUNG WORLD CO 83 sets
$28.00, and up, pts $1.00, ea.
                                  (170)
Caribbean Carnival
(gr. III) YOUNG WORLD CO 108 sets
$30.00, and up, pts $1.25, ea.
                                  (171)
Contrasts In E Minor
string orch (gr. III) YOUNG WORLD
SO 92 sets $15.00, and up, pts
$1.25, ea.   (172)
Performing Strings *CCU
string orch,pno (gr. I) YOUNG WORLD
SF 1503 sc $6.00, pts $2.25, ea.
                                  (173)
Saison De Cordes
string orch (gr. III) YOUNG WORLD
SO 210 sets $18.00, and up, pts
$1.25, ea.   (174)
Strings On Stage *CCU
string orch YOUNG WORLD SF 1102 sc
$6.00, pts $2.25, ea.   (175)

FELDSTEIN, SAUL (SANDY) (1940-   )
Pizzicato Rock
set ALFRED 1928 $18.00   (176)

FESTPOLONAS see Skold, Yngve

FEUERWERKSMUSIK II, [ARR.] see Handel,
George Frideric, Royal Fireworks
Music, [arr.]

FHEODOROFF, NIKOLAUS (1931-   )
  Drei Satze
    string orch,vln solo,vla solo,vcl
    solo [8'] sc,pts DOBLINGER rent
                                      (177)

FIDELIO: MARCH, [ARR.] see Beethoven,
  Ludwig van

FIDELIO: OVERTURE, [ARR.] see
  Beethoven, Ludwig van

FIRST NOWELL, THE
  see Christmas Carol Kit, Set 1

FIRST PERFORMANCE see Jurey, Edward B.,
  Editor

FISH FRY see Kelch, Carleton

FIVE NORDIC MELODIES
  (Sonninen, Ahti) "Viisi Pohjoismaista
  Savelmaa" string orch FAZER   (178)

FIVE O'CLOCK see Amiot, Jean-Claude

FIVE VOLUNTARIES see Davies, Peter
  Maxwell

FLUTE WALTZ see Frackenpohl, Arthur
  Roland

FLYING HIGH see Applebaum, Samuel

FOGELBERG, DANIEL GRAYLING (1951-   )
  Longer, [arr.]
    (Lehmeier) (easy) set LEONARD-US
    $20.00   (179)

FOGGY DAY, A see Gershwin, George

FOLK SONG FANTASY see Rusch, Harold W.

FOLKSONG OVERTURE see Tassone, Pasquale

FORSBERG, ROLAND (1939-   )
  Canto Alla Leggenda
    string orch [15'] STIM perf mat
    rent   (180)

FORSBLAD, LELAND
  Anagram For Strings
    string orch (gr. II) LEONARD-US
    04840300 $12.00   (181)

  Carnival Scene
    string orch (gr. II) LEONARD-US
    04841700 $15.00   (182)

FOUR CHARACTERISTIC DANCES, [ARR.]
  (Alshin, Harry) 2+opt pic.1.2.1.opt
  alto sax.opt tenor sax. 2.2.1.0.opt
  tuba. 2perc,opt pno,strings [4'30"]
  (gr. II) sets KENDOR $16.00, and up
                                    (183)
FOUR EASY PIECES see Groot, Hugo de

FRACKENPOHL, ARTHUR ROLAND (1924-   )
  Flute Waltz
    3fl,perc,gtr,elec bass,pno,strings
    [3'] (gr. IV) set ALMITRA $18.00
                                    (184)

  Prelude And Polka
    2.1.2.1. 2.2.2.1. timp,perc,strings
    set SHAWNEE $18.00   (185)

FRAN SOMMEN see Eckerberg, Sixten

FRANKE-BLOM, LARS-AKE (1941-   )
  Rorelser
    2.2.2.2. 4.2.3.0. timp,perc,harp,
    strings [15'] STIM perf mat rent
                                    (186)

  Sinfonia For Stor Ungdoms
    4.3.4.2. 4.3.3.1. timp,3perc,pno,
    strings [16'] STIM   (187)

FREE AMERICAY, A
  (Halen, Walter J.) string orch (gr.
  II) sets KENDOR $11.00, and up
                                    (188)

FRENCH MILITARY MARCH, [ARR.] see
  Saint-Saens, Camille

FROST, ROBERT S. (1942-   )
  Accents
    string orch (gr. II) KJOS S039B
    $15.00   (189)

  Carefree Caper
    [3'50"] (gr. III) KJOS S033B $14.50
                                    (190)
  Crystal Falls
    string orch,pno (gr. I) KENDOR sets
    $10.00, and up, sc $2.50   (191)

  Day, Night, And Day
    string orch,pno (gr. I) KENDOR sets
    $10.00, and up, sc $2.50   (192)

  Dialogue
    [2'] (gr. III) KJOS S034B $14.50
                                    (193)
  Heber Creeper, The
    string orch,pno (gr. II) KENDOR
    sets $11.00, and up, sc $2.50
                                    (194)

FROST, ROBERT S. (cont'd.)

  Hour Glass
    string orch,opt pno (gr. I) sets
    KENDOR f.s.   (195)

  Just For Strings
    string orch,pno (gr. II) KENDOR
    sets $11.00, and up, sc $2.50
                                    (196)
  Majestic March
    string orch,opt pno [2'15"] (gr. I)
    sets KENDOR $10.00, and up (197)

  Mini-Overture
    string orch [2'20"] (gr. II) set
    KENDOR $11.00, and up   (198)

  Peaceful Night
    string orch (gr. II) sets KENDOR
    $11.00, and up   (199)

  Petite Rondo
    string orch (gr. II) sets KENDOR
    $11.00, and up   (200)

  Pulsations
    string orch (gr. III) YOUNG WORLD
    SO 82 sets $12.00, and up, pts
    $1.00, ea.   (201)

  Raindrops
    string orch (gr. II) sets KENDOR
    $11.00, and up   (202)

  Rhythmical Transformations
    string orch (gr. III) YOUNG WORLD
    SO 91 sets $12.00, and up, pts
    $1.00, ea.   (203)

  Shadow Of The Wind, The
    string orch (gr. II) sets KENDOR
    $11.00, and up   (204)

  Simplicity
    string orch (gr. I) sets KENDOR
    $10.00, and up   (205)

  Snowflakes
    string orch,opt pno (gr. I) sets
    KENDOR $10.00, and up   (206)

  Song Of The Stranger
    string orch (gr. II) sets KENDOR
    $11.00, and up   (207)

  Step Ladder
    string orch,pno (gr. I) KENDOR sc
    $2.50, sets $10.00, and up (208)

  Stepping-Stones
    string orch [1'55"] (gr. I) set
    KENDOR $10.00, and up   (209)

FROSTY THE SNOW MAN
  see Christmas Memories, [arr.]

FRYSKE VARIATIES see Haan, J. de

FUNF MINIATUREN see Mullich

FUNNY FIDDLIN' see Nunez, Carold

GANNON, JAMES KIMBALL (KIM) (1900-1974)
  I'll Be Home For Christmas, [arr.]
    (composed with Kent)
    (Marsh, Gerry Jon) string orch (gr.
    II) LEONARD-US 04849350 $15.00
                                    (210)
GARTENLAUB, ODETTE
  Deux Pieces Faciles
    CHAPPELL-FR f.s.
      contains: Lento (clar,strings
      without db); Scherzetto (ob,
      tamb,strings without db) (211)

  Lento
    see Deux Pieces Faciles

  Scherzetto
    see Deux Pieces Faciles

GAST, LOTHAR (1928-   )
  Intervall, Das
    string orch set ERES f.s.   (212)

GAVOTTE, [ARR.] see Gossec, Francois
  Joseph

GEDULDIGE SOKRATES, DER: OVERTURE see
  Telemann, Georg Philipp

GEFORS, HANS (1952-   )
  Portrattsamling *Op.18, Suite
    2.2.2.2. 2.2.3.0. timp,perc,strings
    [10'] STIM perf mat rent   (213)

GENZMER, HARALD (1909-   )
  Sinfonia Per Giovani
    3.2.2.2.4sax. 4.2.3.1. timp,perc,
    3gtr,6rec,strings sc PETERS
    EP 8448 $50.00, ipa   (214)

GERSHWIN, GEORGE (1898-1937)
  Foggy Day, A
    (Reisman, Joe) (gr. IV) KENDOR set
    $24.00, sc $3.00   (215)

  I Loves You, [arr.] (from Porgy And
    Bess)
    (Wright, Rayburn)
    2(pic).1.0.1.soprano sax.alto
    sax.tenor sax.baritone sax.
    4.4.4.1. timp,perc,harp,elec gtr,
    pno,strings, clarinets may be
    substituted for saxophones [6']
    (gr. IV) set KENDOR $34.00 (216)

GIAMMARIO, MATTEO
  Christmas Suite For Strings
    string orch sets MUSICIANS PUB
    $12.00, and up   (217)

  Happy Robin, The
    string orch,pno sets MUSICIANS PUB
    $8.00, and up   (218)

  Jamaican Holiday
    string orch sets MUSICIANS PUB
    $8.00, and up   (219)

GIMBEL
  So Nice, [arr.]
    (Ployhar) MCA U083 set $16.00, sc
    $4.00, pno-cond sc $1.50, pts
    $.75, ea.   (220)

GIOVANNINI, CAESAR (1925-   )
  Northridge Drive
    string orch sets MUSICIANS PUB
    $8.00, and up   (221)

GIRL FROM IPANEMA, THE, [ARR.] see
  Jobim

GIVE MY REGARDS TO BROADWAY, [ARR.] see
  Cohan, George Michael

GLASER, WERNER WOLF (1910-   )
  Divertimento No. 1
    1.1.1.1. 1.1.0.0. strings [15']
    STIM perf mat rent   (222)

  Suite
    1.1.1.1. 1.1.1.0. timp,strings
    perf mat rent   (223)

  Tva Korta Orkesterstycken
    1.1.1.1. 1.1.0.0. timp,strings STIM
    perf mat rent   (224)

GLUCK, CHRISTOPH WILLIBALD, RITTER VON
  (1714-1787)
  Air De Ballet, [arr.]
    (Etling, Forest R.) string orch
    (gr. III) sets ETLING,F $18.00,
    and up   (225)

  Dance And Musette, [arr.]
    (Etling, Forest R.) string orch
    (gr. II) sets ETLING,F $18.00,
    and up   (226)

  Hymn To Diana, [arr.]
    (Etling, Forest R.) string orch
    (gr. II) sets ETLING,F $18.00,
    and up   (227)

  Sicilienne And Overture, [arr.]
    (Isaac, Merle J.) string orch (gr.
    III) sets ETLING,F $26.00, and up
                                    (228)
GOD BLESS AMERICA, [ARR.] see Berlin,
  Irving

GOD OF OUR FATHERS see Smith, Claude
  Thomas

GOIN' BAROQUE see Bach, Johann
  Sebastian

GOLD COUNTRY see Keuning, Ken

GOLDSMITH, JERRY (1929-   )
  Star Trek: Main Theme, [arr.]
    (Simeone, Harry) 2.1.2.1. 2.2.2.0.
    timp,perc,strings set SHAWNEE
    $25.00   (229)

GOOD KING WENCESLAS *Xmas
  see Class In Concert Christmas Extra
  (Gould, Morton) sets SCHIRM.G $15.00,
  and up   (230)
  (Wieloszynski) string orch,opt pno
  (gr. I) sets KENDOR f.s.   (231)

GORDON, LOUIS
  Away We Go *see Applebaum, Samuel

  Flying High *see Applebaum, Samuel

GOSSEC, FRANCOIS JOSEPH (1734-1829)
  Gavotte, [arr.]
    see HAUSKAPELLE, DIE, BOOK 1

GRAHN, ULF (1942-   )
Concertino for Piano and String
    Orchestra
    string orch,pno solo STIM perf mat
    rent   (232)

Concerto for Double Bass and Chamber
    Orchestra
    1.0.1.0. 0.0.1.0. 6vln,3vla,db solo
    [11'] STIM perf mat rent   (233)

Dream Of A Lost Century, A
    1.1.1.0. 0.0.0.0. pno,strings [15']
    STIM perf mat rent   (234)

Wind Of Dawn, The
    1.1.1.1. 0.1.1.0. perc,strings,
    electronic tape [11'] STIM perf
    mat rent   (235)

GRAINER, RON
Theme From Steptoe And Son
    (Frazer, Alan) MIDDLE MK 11 f.s.
                                        (236)

GREAT GATE OF KIEV AND HOPAK, [ARR.]
    see Mussorgsky, Modest Petrovich

GREAT MUPPET CAPER, THE, [ARR.]
    (Holcombe, Bill) (gr. III) LEONARD-US
    04500440 $35.00   (237)

GRIEG, EDVARD HAGERUP (1843-1907)
Concerto For Piano And Orchestra, Op.
    16: Themes, [arr.]
    (Palange, Louis S.) 1.1.2.1.2alto
    sax.tenor sax. 3.2.2.0. timp,pno,
    strings GORDON sc $5.00, sets
    $12.00, and up, pts $1.00, ea.,
    min sc $2.50   (238)

Grieg Suite, [arr.]
    (Etling, Forest R.) string orch
    (gr. III) sets ETLING,F $18.00,
    and up   (239)

Holberg Suite: Prelude, [arr.]
    (Isaac) string orch (med) sets WYNN
    $12.00, and up   (240)

Homage March, [arr.] (from Sigurd
    Jorsalfar, Op. 56)
    (Carter, Anthony) 2+pic.2.3.2.
    2.3.3.1. timp,perc,opt pno,
    strings [10'] sc OXFORD 77.890
    $11.00, set OXFORD 77.890-70
    $27.00, pts OXFORD $1.50, ea.   (241)

Patriotic Song, [arr.] *Op.12,No.8
    see Two Melodies Of Grieg, [arr.]

Two Melodies Of Grieg, [arr.]
    (Frost, Robert S.) string orch,opt
    pno (gr. II) sets KENDOR $11.00,
    and up
    contains: Patriotic Song, [arr.],
    Op.12,No.8; Waltz in E minor,
    Op. 38, No. 7, [arr.]   (242)

Waltz in E minor, Op. 38, No. 7,
    [arr.]
    see Two Melodies Of Grieg, [arr.]

GRIEG SUITE, [ARR.] see Grieg, Edvard
    Hagerup

GRISEY, GERARD (1946-   )
Manifestations Pour Echapper A La
    Television
    2fl,2clar,2perc,2gtr,pno,8vln,4vcl,
    opt db,4 solo voices [1'15"] sc,
    pts RICORDI-FR R.2237-38 f.s.   (243)

Manifestations Pour Obtenir Une Aire
    De Jeux
    2fl,2clar,2perc,4gtr,pno,8vln,4vcl,
    8 solo voices [11'] sc,pts
    RICORDI-FR R.2258-59 f.s.   (244)

Manifestations Pour Trouver Le
    Silence
    2fl,2clar,2perc,8vln,4vcl,opt db
    [6'] sc,pts RICORDI-FR R.2235-36
    f.s.   (245)

GROOT, HUGO DE (1914-   )
Four Easy Pieces
    string orch sc,pts HARMONIA 2683
    f.s.   (246)

Kaleidoscope Suite
    string orch sc,pts HARMONIA 2625
    f.s.   (247)

GRUBER, FRANZ XAVER (1787-1863)
Silent Night, [arr.]
    (Wieloszynski, Stephen) string
    orch,opt pno (gr. I) sets KENDOR
    $10.00, and up   (248)

GRUBER, HEINZ KARL (1943-   )
Phantom Bilder
    "Photo-Fit Pictures" [12'30"]
    BOOSEY HSS-303 set $36.00,
    augmented set $58.00   (249)

GRUBER, HEINZ KARL (cont'd.)

Photo-Fit Pictures *see Phantom
    Bilder

GULLBERG, OLOF (1931-   )
Prelude Et Berceuse, For Oboe And
    String Orchestra
    string orch,ob/fl/clar solo
    NORDISKA NMS 5482 perf mat rent
                                        (250)

GUNSENHEIMER, GUSTAV (1934-   )
Concertino for Recorder and String
    Orchestra
    string orch,A rec/fl solo [8'] sc,
    pts VOGT VF 1001 f.s.   (251)

Concerto for Harpsichord and
    Orchestra
    orch,hpsd solo [14'] sc,pts VOGT
    VF 1004 f.s.   (252)

HAAG, HANNO
Concertino, Op. 15
    ob,bsn,string orch sc,pts MOSELER
    M11.451 f.s.   (253)

HAAN, J. DE
Fryske Variaties
    MOLENAAR 14.1607.05   (254)

HAHNENTANZ see Lehmann, S.

HALEN, WALTER J. (1930-   )
Promenade And Hoe-Down
    string orch set SHAWNEE $9.00   (255)

HALLNAS, HILDING (1903-   )
Pastoral Och Scherzo *Op.9
    1.1.1. 1.0.0.0. strings [10']
    STIM perf mat rent   (256)

HAMBURGER SUITE, [ARR.]
    (Marsh, Gerry Jon) (gr. III) LEONARD-
    US 04854000 $20.00   (257)

HAMLISCH, MARVIN F. (1944-   )
Chorus Line, A: Selections, [arr.]
    (Lowden) (med) set LEONARD-US
    $40.00   (258)

Ice Castles: Theme, [arr.]
    string orch,pno set COLUMBIA PIC.
    2617TA4X $7.50   (259)
    (Fink) string orch set COLUMBIA
    PIC. 2617TB4X $10.00   (260)
    (Fink, Philip) string orch set COLUMBIA PIC.
    2617TB7X $20.00   (261)

Marvin Hamlisch In Concert, [arr.]
    (Lowden, Bob) (gr. V) LEONARD-US
    04500480 $40.00   (262)

They're Playing Our Song, [arr.]
    (Chase) (easy) set LEONARD-US
    $20.00   (263)

They're Playing Our Song: Selections,
    [arr.]
    (Lowden) (med easy) set LEONARD-US
    $35.00   (264)

What I Did For Love, [arr.]
    (Lehmeier) (easy) set LEONARD-US
    $20.00   (265)

HANDEL, GEORGE FRIDERIC (1685-1759)
Drei Stucke (from Gradus Ad
    Symphoniam)
    LIENAU   (266)

Feuerwerksmusik II, [arr.] *see
    Royal Fireworks Music, [arr.]

Fugue in F, [arr.]
    (Frost, Robert S.*) string orch
    (gr. III/gr. IV) KJOS S040B
    $15.00   (267)

Harmonius Blacksmith, [arr.]
    (Isaac) string orch,pno [4'25"]
    (gr. II) sets ETLING,F $13.00,
    and up   (268)

Judas Maccabaeus: March, [arr.]
    see Two Handel Melodies

Judas Maccabaeus: Suite, [arr.]
    (Isaac) 2.2.2+bass clar.1.tenor
    sax. 4.2.3.1. timp,pno,strings
    [7'50"] (gr. III) sets ETLING,F
    $24.00, and up   (269)

Larghetto, [arr.]
    see Two Handel Melodies

Largo, [arr.]
    see HAUSKAPELLE, DIE, BOOK 1

March And Minuet, [arr.]
    BOOSEY HSS-204 set $33.00,
    augmented set $54.00   (270)

HANDEL, GEORGE FRIDERIC (cont'd.)

Messiah: Selections, [arr.]
    (Isaac, Merle J.) string orch (gr.
    III) sets ETLING,F $26.00, and up
                                        (271)

Royal Fireworks Music, [arr.]
    (Twarz) "Feuerwerksmusik II,
    [arr.]" 2fl,strings sc,pts
    HEINRICH. 147 f.s.   (272)

Sarabande And Crusaders' March,
    [arr.]
    (Isaac) 2.1.2+bass clar.1.alto
    sax.tenor sax. 2.2.2.1. timp,
    perc,pno,strings [3'] (gr. III)
    sets ETLING,F $24.00, and up   (273)

Suite, MIN 2 (from Gradus Ad
    Symphoniam)
    LIENAU   (274)

Two Handel Melodies
    (Frost, Robert S.) string orch,opt
    pno (gr. II) sets KENDOR $11.00,
    and up
    contains: Judas Maccabaeus:
    March, [arr.]; Larghetto,
    [arr.]   (275)

Water Music: Suite, [arr.]
    (Etling, Forest R.) string orch
    (gr. III) sets ETLING,F $18.00,
    and up   (276)

HANSGARDH, ALLAN (1926-   )
Fantasia Pastorale
    2.2.2.2. 2.2.0.0. timp,strings
    [10'] STIM perf mat rent   (277)

Scherzo
    2.2.2.2. 2.0.0.0. timp,strings STIM
    perf mat rent   (278)

HAPPY FARMER, THE, [ARR.] see Schumann,
    Robert (Alexander)

HAPPY HANUKKAH!
    (Ward, Norman) string orch,pno (gr.
    II) KENDOR sets $11.00, and up, sc
    $2.50   (279)

HAPPY ROBIN, THE see Giammario, Matteo

HARBURG, E.Y. (YIP) (1896-   )
Old Devil Moon *see Lane, Burton

HARE, NICHOLAS
Three Tunes From Shakespeare's
    England
    string orch sc CHESTER 55340 $6.75,
    pts CHESTER 55341 $23.75   (280)

HARK THE HERALD ANGELS SING
    see Christmas Carol Kit, Set 2

HARMONIUS BLACKSMITH, [ARR.] see
    Handel, George Frideric

HARTEWENS-HYMNE see Keuning, Hans P.

HAUG, LUKAS (1920-   )
Wettlauf Zwischen Dem Hasen Und Dem
    Igel, Der
    strings,pno,speaking voice
    HEINRICH. 1835 f.s.   (281)

HAUSKAPELLE, DIE, BOOK 1
    (Zanger, Gustav) fl,pno,strings pts
    BRATFISCH f.s.
    contains: Beethoven, Ludwig van,
    Adagio From Sextet, Op 81b,
    [arr.]; Beethoven, Ludwig van,
    Turkischer Marsch From Die Ruinen
    Von Athen, [arr.]; Dittersdorf,
    Karl Ditters von, Deutscher Tanz,
    [arr.]; Gossec, Francois Joseph,
    Gavotte, [arr.]; Handel, George
    Frideric, Largo, [arr.]   (282)

HAVE YOURSELF A MERRY LITTLE CHRISTMAS
    see Christmas Memories, [arr.]

HAYDN, [FRANZ] JOSEPH (1732-1809)
Kindersinfonie
    string orch,opt pno, children's
    instruments (attributed to Haydn;
    probable composer Leopold Mozart)
    sc HEINRICH. 974 $6.50, set
    HEINRICH. 975 $9.00, pts
    HEINRICH. 506 $1.50, ea.   (283)

Menuet, [arr.]
    (Siennicki, Edmund J.) string orch
    (gr. III) sets ETLING,F $18.00,
    and up   (284)

Midnight Minuet, [arr.]
    (Klotman) string orch set ALFRED
    2297 $18.00   (285)

Speziale, Lo: Overture, [arr.]
    (Bauernschmidt, Robert) (med) sets
    WYNN $24.00, and up   (286)

HAYDN, [FRANZ] JOSEPH (cont'd.)

Symphony No. 14, First Movement,
   [arr.]
   (Gordon, Philip) string orch,pno
   (gr. II) KENDOR sets $16.00, and
   up, sc $2.50   (287)
   (Gordon, Philip) 2.1.2.1.opt alto
   sax.opt tenor sax. 2.2.1.0.opt
   tuba. timp,opt pno,strings (gr.
   II) KENDOR sets $24.00, and up,
   sc $3.00   (288)

Symphony No. 14, Minuet, [arr.]
   (Gordon, Philip) 2.1.2.1.opt alto
   sax.opt tenor sax. 2.2.1.1. opt
   timp,perc,opt pno,strings [4'25"]
   sets KENDOR $24.00, and up   (289)
   (Gordon, Philip) string orch
   [4'25"] (gr. II) sets KENDOR
   $16.00, and up   (290)

Symphony No. 96, Minuet, [arr.]
   (Carlin, Sidney) string orch,pno,
   includes parts for advanced vln,
   vln III CARLIN sc $3.00, sets
   $15.00, and up, pts $1.00, ea.
                                   (291)

Symphony No. 102, Minuet, [arr.]
   (Rogers, David) string orch,pno,
   includes parts for advanced vln,
   vln III CARLIN sc $3.00, sets
   $15.00, and up, pts $1.00, ea.
                                   (292)

HEAVENS RESOUND, THE, [ARR.] see
   Beethoven, Ludwig van

HEBER CREEPER, THE see Frost, Robert S.

HEDWALL, LENNART (1932-   )
   Fantasia Sopra Veni Redemptor
      Spiritus
      string orch STIM perf mat rent
                                   (293)

   Music For String Orchestra No. 2
      string orch [13'] STIM perf mat
      rent   (294)

HEIDI see Kelch, Carleton

HEILMANN, HARALD (1924-   )
   De Profundis
      [11'] MULLER   (295)

HELLDEN, DANIEL (1917-   )
   Divertimento
      pno,strings GEHRMANS perf mat rent
                                   (296)

HERBERT, VICTOR (1859-1924)
   Toyland, [arr.]
      (Caponegro, John) string orch (gr.
      I) sets KENDOR $10.00, and up (297)

HEY RIDE! see Christiansen, James

HJARTER KUNG GUSTAV WASAS HOVMUSIK see
   Eyser, Eberhard

HOEDOWN IN 5 see Alshin, Harry

HOHENHEIMER TANZE see Schneider, Willy

HOLBERG SUITE: PRELUDE, [ARR.] see
   Grieg, Edvard Hagerup

HOLCOMBE, BILL
   Beethoven's Fifth (composed with
      Rothrock, Carson)
      set MUSICIANS PUB $15.00   (298)
      string orch,pno sets MUSICIANS PUB
      $8.00, and up   (299)

   Christmas Wishes
      set MUSICIANS PUB $20.00   (300)
      string orch,pno sets MUSICIANS PUB
      $12.00, and up   (301)

HOLIDAY FOR STRINGS, [ARR.] see Rose,
   David

HOLLY AND THE IVY, THE
   see Class In Concert Christmas Extra

HOMAGE MARCH, [ARR.] see Grieg, Edvard
   Hagerup

HOMMAGE A BIHARI see Vary, Ferenc

HOOK, JAMES (1746-1827)
   Simple Symphony, [arr.] *Op.99
      2S rec,A rec,2vln,vcl,pno sc,pts
      HARMONIA 2771 f.s.   (302)

HOROVITZ, JOSEPH (1926-   )
   Jubilee Toy Symphony
      perc,strings NOVELLO sc $11.40, set
      $46.65   (303)

   Suite for Strings
      string orch (easy) sc,pts BELWIN
      $6.00   (304)

HORT IHR DEN TROMMELSCHLAG see Schwaen,
   Kurt

HOSTSANG see Wahlberg, Rune

HOUR GLASS see Frost, Robert S.

HUBBELL, FRED M.
   Two By Two
      string orch,pno [2'] (gr. I) sets
      ETLING,F $10.00, and up   (305)

HUMORESQUE, [ARR.] see Dvorak, Antonin

HUNGARIAN DANCE NO. 4, [ARR.] see
   Brahms, Johannes

HUNGARIAN DANCE NO. 5, [ARR.] see
   Brahms, Johannes

HYMN OF FAITH, [ARR.] see Arcadelt,
   Jacob

HYMN OF FREEDOM, [ARR.] see Brahms,
   Johannes

HYMN TO DIANA, [ARR.] see Gluck,
   Christoph Willibald, Ritter von

HYMNS OF THE CHURCH, SET 1 see Isaac,
   Merle John, Editor

I LEFT MY HEART IN SAN FRANCISCO,
   [ARR.] see Cory, George C.

I LOVES YOU, [ARR.] see Gershwin,
   George

I SAW MOMMY KISSING SANTA CLAUS
   see Christmas Memories, [arr.]

I WANT TO HOLD YOUR HAND, [ARR.] see
   Lennon, John

I WANT TO LIVE see Deutschendorf, Henry
   John

ICE CASTLES: THEME, [ARR.] see
   Hamlisch, Marvin F.

IF EVER I WOULD LEAVE YOU, [ARR.] see
   Loewe, Frederick

I'LL BE AROUND, [ARR.] see Wilder, Alec

I'LL BE HOME FOR CHRISTMAS, [ARR.] see
   Gannon, James Kimball (Kim)

I'M A YANKEE DOODLE DANDY, [ARR.] see
   Cohan, George Michael

IMPROVISATION I see Smedeby, Sune

IMPROVISATION II see Smedeby, Sune

INTERLUDE see Sevius, Sven

INTERLUDIO see Eklund, Hans

INTERNATIONAL JINGLE BELLS
   (Caponegro, John) string orch,opt
   perc,opt pno KENDOR sc $2.50, sets
   $14.00, and up   (306)

INTERVALL, DAS see Gast, Lothar

INTRODUCTION AND ALLEGRO, [ARR.] see
   Vitali, Giovanni Battista

IPPOLITOV-IVANOV, MIKHAIL MIKHAILOVICH
   (1859-1935)
   Caucasian Sketches: Procession,
      [arr.]
      (Wolfe) (very easy) sets WYNN
      $18.00, and up   (307)

ISAAC, BURTON
   Student String Festival Series
      string orch MEL BAY 93490 sc $3.95,
      pts $2.00, ea.   (308)

ISAAC, MERLE JOHN (1898-   )
   Belvedere Suite
      string orch,pno [6'20"] (gr. II)
      sets ETLING,F $13.00, and up (309)

   Dancing Basses
      string orch (gr. II) sets ETLING,F
      $18.00, and up   (310)

   Lazy Blues Suite
      string orch (med) sets WYNN $22.00,
      and up   (311)

   Tango Avila
      string orch (gr. II) sets ETLING,F
      $18.00, and up   (312)

   Tarantella
      (med easy) sets WYNN $18.00, and up
                                   (313)

ISAAC, MERLE JOHN, EDITOR
   American Folk Song Suite No. 1
      string orch (gr. I) sets KENDOR
      $14.00, and up   (314)

   American Folk Song Suite No. 2
      string orch (gr. I) sets KENDOR
      $14.00, and up   (315)

   American Folk Song Suite No. 3
      string orch,pno (gr. I) KENDOR sets
      $14.00, and up, sc $2.50   (316)

   Christmas Carols, Set 1
      string orch,pno [4'] (gr. III) sets
      ETLING,F $15.00, and up   (317)

   Christmas Carols, Set 2
      string orch (gr. III) sets ETLING,F
      $18.00, and up   (318)

   Hymns Of The Church, Set 1 *CCU
      string orch,pno (gr. III) sets
      ETLING,F $15.00, and up   (319)

   Lively And Rhythmic Suite No. 1
      string orch,opt pno sc KENDOR $2.50
                                   (320)

   Lively And Rhythmic Suite No. 2
      string orch,opt pno sc KENDOR $2.50
                                   (321)

   Lively And Rhythmic Suite No. 3
      string orch,opt pno (gr. I) sets
      KENDOR f.s.   (322)

   Sailing Songs
      2.1.2+bass clar.1.alto sax.tenor
      sax. 2.2.1.1. timp,perc,pno,
      strings (gr. II) sets KENDOR f.s.
                                   (323)

IT CAME UPON THE MIDNIGHT CLEAR
   (Gould, Morton) string orch set
   SCHIRM.G $10.00   (324)

IT'S A SMALL WORLD
   see Disney Magic, [arr.]

IT'S NOT UNUSUAL, [ARR.] see Mills

IT'S SO PEACEFUL IN THE COUNTRY see
   Wilder, Alec

JACKSON, JILL (1913-   )
   Let There Be Peace On Earth *see
      Miller, Seymour (Sy)

JACOB'S LADDER, [ARR.]
   (Norman) sets STAFF 0-11 $10.00, and
   up   (325)

JAMAICAN HOLIDAY see Giammario, Matteo

JAN STEEN: SUITE OF OLD DUTCH DANCES,
   [ARR.] see Keuning, Hans P.

JAZZ SUITE see Tiffault, Leighton

JEPPSSON, KERSTIN (1948-   )
   Tre Sentenzi
      2.1.1.1. 2.0.0.0. 2perc,strings
      STIM perf mat rent   (326)

JESSE POLKA, [ARR.] *folk song,Mex
   (Isaac, Merle J.) string orch (med
   easy) sets WYNN $16.00, and up
                                   (327)

JICARILLA TERRITORY see Keuning, Ken

JINGLE BELLS
   see Class In Concert Christmas Extra
   (Gould, Morton) set SCHIRM.G $10.00
                                   (328)

JINGLE BELLS, [ARR.] see Pierpont,
   James

JOBIM
   Girl From Ipanema, The, [arr.]
      (Ployhar) MCA U085 set $16.00, sc
      $4.00, pno-cond sc $2.00, pts
      $.75, ea.   (329)

JOEL, WILLIAM MARTIN (BILLY)
   (1949-   )
   Just The Way You Are
      (Chase, Bruce) (easy) set LEONARD-
      US $20.00   (330)

JOHN, CHRIS
   A Bicyclette *see Amiot, Jean-Claude

   Ballade Du Petit Tato *see Amiot,
      Jean-Claude

   Black Cat Rag *see Amiot, Jean-
      Claude

   Chaconne Pour Un Film Imaginaire
      *see Amiot, Jean-Claude

   Cirque Zouzou, Le *see Amiot, Jean-
      Claude

JOHN, CHRIS (cont'd.)

Five O'Clock *see Amiot, Jean-Claude

Mon Deuxieme Concert *see Amiot, Jean-Claude

Mon Premier Concert *see Amiot, Jean-Claude

On The Mississippi River *see Amiot, Jean-Claude

Petit Tato Va Chez Le Roy *see Amiot, Jean-Claude

Petite Marche *see Amiot, Jean-Claude

Western Music *see Amiot, Jean-Claude

JOHN DENVER MEETS THE STRING SECTION see Deutschendorf, Henry John

JONES
Child Is Born, A
(Wright, Rayburn) (gr. V) KENDOR set $22.00, sc $3.00   (331)

JOPLIN, SCOTT (1868-1917)
Entertainer, The, [arr.]
(Buchtel, Forrest L.) [2'30"] (gr. III/gr. IV) KJOS S037B $12.50   (332)
(Frazer, Alan) 1+opt fl.0+opt ob.2.0+opt bsn. 1+opt horn.2.1.0. opt 3perc,pno,strings sc,pts MIDDLE f.s.   (333)

Strenuous Life, The, [arr.]
(Buchtel, Forrest L.) [2'30"] (gr. III/gr. IV) KJOS S038B $12.50   (334)

JOUBERT, CLAUDE-HENRY
Divertissement Baroque
string orch sc,pts MARTIN f.s.   (335)

En Fa Pour Enfants
wind and string parts suitable for various combinations sc,pts MARTIN f.s.   (336)

Romance
string orch sc,pts MARTIN f.s.   (337)

JUBILEE TOY SYMPHONY see Horovitz, Joseph

JUDAS MACCABAEUS: MARCH, [ARR.] see Handel, George Frideric

JUDAS MACCABAEUS: SUITE, [ARR.] see Handel, George Frideric

JUMPIN' IN JULY see Ervin, Max T.

JUON, PAUL (1872-1940)
Kleine Sinfonie *Op.87 (from Gradus Ad Symphoniam)
string orch,opt pno LIENAU   (338)

Serenade, Op. 85 (from Gradus Ad Symphoniam)
string orch,opt pno LIENAU   (339)

JUREY, EDWARD B.
Program Builder
string orch,pno,perc BOURNE B232348 sc $12.00, pts $3.00, ea., kbd pt $6.00   (340)

JUREY, EDWARD B., EDITOR
First Performance *CC7L
string orch,opt perc HIGHLAND sc $6.00, pts $2.50, ea.   (341)

Performance Now *CCU
1.1.2.1.alto sax.tenor sax. 1.3.2.0. perc,pno,strings BELWIN sc $6.00, kbd pt $4.00, pts $2.00, ea.   (342)

JUST FOR STRINGS see Frost, Robert S.

JUST THE WAY YOU ARE see Joel, William Martin (Billy)

KALEIDOSCOPE SUITE see Groot, Hugo de

KARKOFF, MAURICE (1927-   )
Musical Contrasts *see Musikantiska Kontraster

Musikantiska Kontraster
"Musical Contrasts" 1.0.1.0. 0.1.0.0. perc,gtr,pno,strings [5'] NORDISKA ENO 6497 perf mat rent   (343)

KARKOFF, MAURICE (cont'd.)

Tre Capriskisser *Op.144
1.0.2.0. 0.1.0.0. 3perc,strings [9'30"] STIM perf mat rent   (344)

Tre Colori *Op.142
string orch GEHRMANS ENO 6040 perf mat rent   (345)

KEGEL see Lehmann, S.

KELCH, CARLETON
Erica
string orch [1'] set TEN TIMES $5.00   (346)

Fish Fry
string orch [1'15"] set TEN TIMES $5.00   (347)

Heidi
string orch [1'30"] set TEN TIMES $10.00   (348)

Orchestra Warm-Up Patterns
orch/string orch sets TEN TIMES $10.00, and up   (349)

Two Hands
string orch [1'] set TEN TIMES $3.00   (350)

KELLER
American Hymn
(Bruce) 1.1.2+bass clar.1.alto sax.tenor sax. 2.3.1.0. timp, perc,strings [2'30"] (gr. II) sets ETLING,F $18.00, and up   (351)

KENDELL, IAIN (1931-   )
Sonata for Strings
string orch CHESTER sc $7.00, pts f.s.   (352)

KENT
I'11 Be Home For Christmas, [arr.]
*see Gannon, James Kimball (Kim)

KEUNING, HANS P. (1926-   )
Hartewens-Hymne
4.2.4.0. 0.2.0.0. timp,perc,pno, strings sc DONEMUS f.s., perf mat rent   (353)

Jan Steen: Suite Of Old Dutch Dances, [arr.]
2S rec,A rec,2vln,vcl,pno sc,pts HARMONIA 2347 f.s.   (354)

Sinfonia Classica
string orch sc,pts HARMONIA 2287 f.s.   (355)

Stringtime
string orch sc,pts HARMONIA 2910 f.s.   (356)

Suite Ridicule
2S rec,A rec,2vln,vcl,pno sc,pts HARMONIA 2822 f.s.   (357)

To Begin
string orch sc,pts HARMONIA 2275 f.s.   (358)

KEUNING, KEN
Gold Country
string orch,pno (gr. II) YOUNG WORLD SO 221 sets $18.00, and up, pts $1.25, ea.   (359)

Jicarilla Territory
string orch (gr. II) YOUNG WORLD SO 107 sets $18.00, and up, pts $1.25, ea.   (360)

San Joaquin Delta Suite
string orch (gr. III) YOUNG WORLD SO 119 sets $15.00, and up, pts $1.25, ea.   (361)

KHACHATURIAN, ARAM ILYICH (1903-1978)
Sabre Dance
(Frost, Robert S.) [2'15"] (gr. III) KJOS S035B $14.50   (362)

Spartacus: Adagio, [arr.]
(Stone) BOOSEY HSS-205 set $30.00, augmented set $50.00   (363)

KINDERSINFONIE see Haydn, [Franz] Joseph

KINDERSINFONIE see Romberg, Bernhard

KINDERSINFONIE IN C see Thiele, Richard

KING OF GLORY see Bach, Johann Sebastian

KLEINE NACHTMUSIK, EINE, [ARR.] see Mozart, Wolfgang Amadeus

KLEINE ORCHESTER, DAS see Fecker, A.

KLEINE SINFONIE see Juon, Paul

KLEINE SPIELMUSIK I see Bach, Johann Sebastian

KLEINE SPIELMUSIK II see Bach, Johann Sebastian

KOCH, ERLAND VON (1910-   )
Rytmiska Strakbagateller, [arr.]
(Kallberg, E.) string orch GEHRMANS perf mat rent   (364)

KOCH, JOHN
Elegy for String Orchestra
string orch NEW VALLEY 148 sc,pts $7.50, pts $.75, ea.   (365)

KOWALSKI, JULIUS (1912-   )
Little Children's Suite, For Piano And String Orchestra *see Mala Detska Suita, For Piano And String Orchestra

Little Episodes, For Piano And String Orchestra *see Male Epizody, For Piano And String Orchestra

Mala Detska Suita, For Piano And String Orchestra
"Little Children's Suite, For Piano And String Orchestra" string orch,pno solo SLOV.HUD.FOND f.s.   (366)

Male Epizody, For Piano And String Orchestra
"Little Episodes, For Piano And String Orchestra" string orch,pno solo SLOV.HUD.FOND perf mat rent   (367)

KOX, HANS (1930-   )
Maskerades
MOLENAAR 14.1604.08   (368)

KRIECHBAUM, CASIMER B. (1923-   )
Boca Grande, La
string orch [2'30"] (gr. III) set KJOS WSO-1B $12.00   (369)

LAMENTO see Eklund, Hans

LANE, BURTON (1912-   )
Old Devil Moon (composed with Harburg, E.Y. (Yip))
(Reisman, Joe) (gr. IV) KENDOR set $22.00, sc $3.00   (370)

LANE, PHILIP
Celebration Overture
[8'30"] sc,pts ASHDOWN f.s.   (371)

Suite Of Cotswold Folkdances
[13'] sc,pts ASHDOWN f.s.   (372)

LANTLIG SVIT see Wahlberg, Rune

LARGHETTO, [ARR.] see Handel, George Frideric

LARGO, [ARR.] see Handel, George Frideric

LARSSON, FOLKE
Uvertyr Till "Hemsoborna" *Op.26
2.2.2.2. 2.2.2.0. timp,strings [10'] STIM perf mat rent   (373)

LAWLOR, CHARLES B. (1852-1925)
Sidewalks Of New York, [arr.]
(Leideg, Vernon; Niehaus, Lennie) set HIGHLAND $15.00   (374)

LAZY BLUES SUITE see Isaac, Merle John

LECLAIR, JEAN MARIE (1697-1764)
Allegro, [arr.]
(Errante, Belisario) string orch (gr. III) sets ETLING,F $18.00, and up   (375)

LECUONA, ERNESTO (1896-1963)
Malaguena, [arr.]
(Marsh) string orch (easy) set LEONARD-US $15.00   (376)

LEHAR, FRANZ (1870-1948)
Merry Widow Waltz
see TWO WALTZES, [ARR.]

LEHMANN, S.
Achttouriger
see Vier Volkstanze

Hahnentanz
see Vier Volkstanze

Kegel
see Vier Volkstanze

LEHMANN, S. (cont'd.)

Schumpel-Kontra
see Vier Volkstanze

Sieben Volkstanze *CC7L
fl,clar,bsn,strings without vla sc
HEINRICH. 8867 f.s., pts
HEINRICH. 8868 f.s.   (377)

Vier Volkstanze
fl,clar,strings without vla sc
HEINRICH. 8865 f.s., pts
HEINRICH. 8866 f.s.
contains: Achttouriger;
Hahnentanz; Kegel; Schumpel-
Kontra   (378)

LENNON, JOHN (1940-1980)
Beatles Medley (composed with
McCartney, [John] Paul)
(Mendelson) 2(pic).1.2+bass
clar.1.opt alto sax.opt tenor
sax.opt baritone sax. 2.3.3.1.
timp,perc,pno,opt harp,strings
(gr. V) set KENDOR f.s.   (379)

Beatles Meet The String Orchestra,
The (composed with McCartney,
[John] Paul) *CC7L
(Brockner, Charles) string orch,opt
pno,opt elec bass,opt drums,opt
gtr ATV sc $5.50, pno-cond sc
$4.50, pts $2.50, ea.   (380)

Eleanor Rigby, [arr.] (composed with
McCartney, [John] Paul)
(Chase, Bruce) string orch (gr. II)
LEONARD-US 00348704 $10.00 (381)

I Want To Hold Your Hand, [arr.]
MCA UB128 set $17.50, sc $4.00,
pno-cond sc $2.00, pts $.75, ea.
(382)
Let It Be, [arr.] (composed with
McCartney, [John] Paul)
(Chase, Bruce) string orch (gr.
III) LEONARD-US 00348760 $10.00 (383)
Long And Winding Road, The, [arr.]
(composed with McCartney, [John]
Paul)
(Chase, Bruce) string orch (gr.
III) LEONARD-US 00348773 $10.00 (384)
Norwegian Wood, [arr.] (composed with
McCartney, [John] Paul)
(Chase, Bruce) string orch (gr.
III) LEONARD-US 00348819 $10.00 (385)

LENTO see Gartenlaub, Odette

LET IT BE, [ARR.] see Lennon, John

LET IT SNOW! LET IT SNOW! LET IT SNOW!,
[ARR.] see Styne, Jule (Jules
Stein)

LET THERE BE PEACE ON EARTH see Miller,
Seymour (Sy)

LEWIS, AL (1924-   )
Blueberry Hill (composed with Stock,
Larry; Rose, Vincent)
(Reisman, Joe) (gr. IV) KENDOR set
$22.00, sc $3.00   (386)

LIMBURGSE VLA see Penders, J.

LINCOLN SCENE see Nelhybel, Vaclav

LINDEN, R. VAN DEN
Structures Combo I
ALBERSEN f.s.   (387)

Structures Combo II
ALBERSEN f.s.   (388)

Structures Combo III
ALBERSEN f.s.   (389)

LITEN VAGGVISA see Skold, Yngve

LITET POEM see Wahlberg, Rune

LITET STYCKE, ETT, FOR VIOLONCELLO AND
STRING ORCHESTRA see Rosenberg,
Hilding

LITTLE BACH SUITE, [ARR.] see Bach,
Johann Sebastian

LITTLE BIT COUNTRY, A LITTLE BIT ROCK
'N ROLL, A see Cooper, Marty

LITTLE CHILDREN'S SUITE, FOR PIANO AND
STRING ORCHESTRA see Kowalski,
Julius, Mala Detska Suita, For
Piano And String Orchestra

LITTLE EPISODES, FOR PIANO AND STRING
ORCHESTRA see Kowalski, Julius,
Male Epizody, For Piano And String
Orchestra

LITTLE TRIPTYCH see Deursen, Anton van

LIVELY AND RHYTHMIC SUITE NO. 1 see
Isaac, Merle John, Editor

LIVELY AND RHYTHMIC SUITE NO. 2 see
Isaac, Merle John, Editor

LIVELY AND RHYTHMIC SUITE NO. 3 see
Isaac, Merle John, Editor

LJUSA SKYAR see Lundkvist, Per

LOEWE, FREDERICK (1904-   )
Brigadoon: Excerpts
(Gordon) set BIG3 $20.00   (390)

If Ever I Would Leave You, [arr.]
(from Camelot)
(Forsblad, Leland) string orch (gr.
II) LEONARD-US 04843500 $15.00
(391)

LONG AND WINDING ROAD, THE, [ARR.] see
Lennon, John

LONGER, [ARR.] see Fogelberg, Daniel
Grayling

LORD OF THE RINGS, THE: THEME, [ARR.]
see Rosenman, Leonard

LULLABY, JESUS, MY DEAR ONE, BE
SLEEPING
see Class In Concert Christmas Extra

LULLY, JEAN-BAPTISTE (LULLI)
(1632-1687)
Airs And Dances (from Phaeton And
Alceste) CCU
(Steinitz, Paul) string orch, 3rd
violin required sc OXFORD 27.146
$8.75, pts OXFORD $2.00, ea.
(392)
March For King's Regiment, [arr.]
sets STAFF 0-12 $10.00, and up
(393)
Suite, MIN 4 (from Gradus Ad
Symphoniam)
LIENAU   (394)

LUNDKVIST, PER (1916-   )
Ljusa Skyar
2.2.2.2. 2.0.0.0. strings [12']
STIM perf mat rent   (395)

LUNDQUIST, TORBJORN (1920-   )
Canzona
1.1.0.0. 0.1.0.0. strings [8'] STIM
perf mat rent   (396)

Divertimento *Op.1
1.1.1.1. 0.0.0.0. strings [10']
STIM perf mat rent   (397)

Schatten
2.2.2.2. 2.2.2.0. timp,perc,harp,
pno,strings [8'] STIM perf mat
rent   (398)

Variationssvit
string orch STIM perf mat rent
(399)
LUNDSTEN, RALPH (1936-   )
Pompata, [arr.]
(Lundquist, G.) GEHRMANS perf mat
rent   (400)

LYRISKT MELLANSPEL see Wahlberg, Rune

LYRISKT POEM, FOR VIOLIN AND ORCHESTRA
see Skold, Yngve

MAASZ, GERHARD (1906-   )
Sinfonietta Facile
S rec,A rec,ob/clar,trp,perc,glock,
pno,strings sc,pts MOSELER
M 10.464 f.s.   (401)

MCCARTNEY, [JOHN] PAUL (1942-   )
Beatles Medley *see Lennon, John

Beatles Meet The String Orchestra,
The *see Lennon, John

Ebony And Ivory, [arr.]
(Holcombe, Bill) string orch (gr.
II) LEONARD-US 04849083 $15.00
(402)
(Marsh, Gerry Jon) (gr. II)
LEONARD-US 04792287 $20.00 (403)

Eleanor Rigby, [arr.] *see Lennon,
John

Let It Be, [arr.] *see Lennon, John

Long And Winding Road, The, [arr.]
*see Lennon, John

Norwegian Wood, [arr.] *see Lennon,
John

MACCHIE see Ahlberg, Gunnar

MACDOWELL, EDWARD ALEXANDER (1861-1908)
To A Wild Rose, [arr.]
(Rizzo, Jacques) string orch,pno
(gr. II) KENDOR sets $11.00, and
up, sc $2.50   (404)

MACLELLAN, GENE
Put Your Hand In The Hand, [arr.]
(Ward, Norman) orch/string orch set
STUDIO X721 $10.00   (405)

MADAME BUTTERFLY, [ARR.] see Puccini,
Giacomo

MAJESTIC MARCH see Frost, Robert S.

MALA DETSKA SUITA, FOR PIANO AND STRING
ORCHESTRA see Kowalski, Julius

MALAGUENA, [ARR.] see Lecuona, Ernesto

MALE EPIZODY, FOR PIANO AND STRING
ORCHESTRA see Kowalski, Julius

MAN AND A WOMAN, A, [ARR.] see Barouh

MANCINI, HENRY (1924-   )
Pink Panther, The, [arr.]
(Caponegro, John) string orch,opt
perc,opt pno (gr. II) sets KENDOR
f.s.   (406)

White Dawn, [arr.]
(Williams, Linda) (gr. IV) LEONARD-
US 04502050 $35.00   (407)

MANIFESTATIONS POUR ECHAPPER A LA
TELEVISION see Grisey, Gerard

MANIFESTATIONS POUR OBTENIR UNE AIRE DE
JEUX see Grisey, Gerard

MANIFESTATIONS POUR TROUVER LE SILENCE
see Grisey, Gerard

MANILOW, BARRY
Barry Manilow Selections
(Lowden, R.W.) set BIG3 $45.00
contains: Copacabana; Could It Be
Magic; Daybreak; Even Now;
Weekend In New England   (408)

Copacabana
see Barry Manilow Selections

Could It Be Magic
see Barry Manilow Selections

Daybreak
see Barry Manilow Selections

Even Now
see Barry Manilow Selections

Weekend In New England
see Barry Manilow Selections

MARCATO see Nelhybel, Vaclav

MARCH AND IMPROMPTU, [ARR.] see Bizet,
Georges

MARCH AND MINUET, [ARR.] see Handel,
George Frideric

MARCH AND SONATINA, [ARR.] see Mozart,
Wolfgang Amadeus

MARCH, [ARR.] see Bach, Johann
Sebastian

MARCH FOR KING'S REGIMENT, [ARR.] see
Lully, Jean-Baptiste (Lulli)

MARCH FOR YOUNG PEOPLE, [ARR.] see
Shostakovich, Dmitri

MARCH OF THE PEERS, [ARR.] see
Sullivan, [Sir] Arthur Seymour

MARCH OF THE PRIESTS, [ARR.] see
Mendelssohn-Bartholdy, Felix

MARCHE SLAVE, [ARR.] see Tchaikovsky,
Piotr Ilyich

MARCIA ANTIQUA see Nelhybel, Vaclav

MARSH, GERRY
Modal Festival, A
string orch (easy) set LEONARD-US
$15.00   (409)

Spiritual
string orch (easy) set LEONARD-US
$15.00   (410)

MARTIN, HUGH (1914-   )
Scenes From The New England Suite
(Wilder, Alec) 1(pic).1.opt English
horn.2(bass clar).1. 2.0.0.0.
perc,2hpsd/2pno,opt harp,strings
(gr. IV) KENDOR set $35.00, sc
$3.00   (411)

MARVIN HAMLISCH IN CONCERT, [ARR.] see
   Hamlisch, Marvin F.

MASKERADES see Kox, Hans

MASSENET, JULES (1842-1912)
   Meditation From Thais, [arr.]
      (Siennicki, Edmund J.) string orch
      sets ETLING,F $26.00, and up
                                       (412)

MAXWELL DAVIES, PETER
   see DAVIES, PETER MAXWELL

MAY TOMORROW BE A PERFECT DAY see
   Osmond, A.

MEACHAM
   American Patrol, [arr.]
      (Isaac, Merle J.) string orch (med
      easy) sets WYNN $16.00, and up
                                       (413)

MEDITATION FROM THAIS, [ARR.] see
   Massenet, Jules

MEISTERSINGER, DIE: PROCESSION OF THE
   MEISTERSINGERS, [ARR.] see Wagner,
   Richard

MELE, FRANK
   Dance Movements *CC10U
      string orch PRESSER 414-41119 sc
      $4.50, set $29.50, pts $2.50, ea.
                                       (414)
   Two Country Moods
      string orch [5'30"] (easy) PRESSER
      116-40018 sc,pts $17.50, sc
      $7.50, pts $1.00, ea., augmented
      set $5.00   (415)

MELLNAS, ARNE (1933-   )
   Capriccio
      2.1.2.1. 2.2.2.0. 2perc,strings
      [11'] GEHRMANS perf mat rent
                                       (416)
   Moments Musicaux
      2.2.2.2. 2.2.2.0. timp,perc,strings
      [15'] STIM perf mat rent   (417)

MELLO-CELLO see Ervin, Max T.

MELODIC SOUNDS *CC12U
   (Leideg, Vernon; Niehaus, Lennie)
   orch/string orch HIGHLAND $2.95
                                       (418)

MELODY (ARIA), [ARR.] see Bembo, D.
   Baldan

MENDELSSOHN-BARTHOLDY, FELIX
   (1809-1847)
   Concerto For Violins And Orchestra,
      [arr.]
      (Herfurth) 2.1.2.2. 2.2.2.0. timp,
      perc,pno,strings set SHAWNEE
      $25.00   (419)
   March Of The Priests, [arr.]
      (Etling, Forest R.) string orch
      (gr. III) sets ETLING,F $18.00,
      and up   (420)
   Midsummer Night's Dream: Nocturne,
      [arr.]
      (Frost, Robert S.) string orch,opt
      pno (gr. II) sets KENDOR f.s.
                                       (421)

MENUET AND MARCH, [ARR.] see Bach,
   Johann Sebastian

MENUET, [ARR.] see Haydn, [Franz]
   Joseph

MERLE, JOHN
   see ISAAC, MERLE JOHN

MERRY WIDOW WALTZ see Lehar, Franz

MESSIAH: SELECTIONS, [ARR.] see Handel,
   George Frideric

MIDNIGHT MINUET, [ARR.] see Haydn,
   [Franz] Joseph

MIDSUMMER NIGHT'S DREAM: NOCTURNE,
   [ARR.] see Mendelssohn-Bartholdy,
   Felix

MIGHTY FORTRESS IS OUR GOD, A, [ARR.]
   sets STAFF 0-2 $10.00, and up (422)

MIKADO, THE: SELECTIONS, [ARR.] see
   Sullivan, [Sir] Arthur Seymour

MILLER, SEYMOUR (SY) (1908-1971)
   Let There Be Peace On Earth (composed
      with Jackson, Jill)
      (Higgins, John) 1.1.2.1. 2.2.2.1.
      perc,strings set JENSON 501-12010
      $16.50   (423)

MILLS
   It's Not Unusual, [arr.]
      MCA UB132 set $17.50, sc $4.00,
      pno-cond sc $2.00, pts $.75, ea.
                                       (424)

MILLS, FRANK
   Music Box Dancer
      (Lowden, Bob) set MUSIC BOX
      E001727-503 $18.50   (425)

MIN FEMTE see Welin, Karl-Erik

MINI-OVERTURE see Frost, Robert S.

MINUET, [ARR.] see Bach, Johann
   Sebastian

MINUETTO, [ARR.] see Bolzoni, Giovanni

MIRACLE AT THE STREAM, A see Alshin,
   Harry

MITHRANDIR, [ARR.] see Rosenman,
   Leonard

MODAL FESTIVAL, A see Marsh, Gerry

MOLDAU, THE, [ARR.] see Smetana,
   Bedrich

MOLDAU, THE: THEMES, [ARR.] see
   Smetana, Bedrich

MOMENTS MUSICAUX see Mellnas, Arne

MON DEUXIEME CONCERT see Amiot, Jean-
   Claude

MON PREMIER CONCERT see Amiot, Jean-
   Claude

MORTENSEN, FINN (1922-   )
   Music For Amateur String Players
      *Op.22,No.5
      string orch sc,pts NORSK f.s. (426)

MOUSSORGSKY, MODEST PETROVITCH
   see MUSSORGSKY, MODEST PETROVICH

MOZART, LEOPOLD (1719-1787)
   Musikalische Schlittenfahrt, Die
      strings, children's instruments
      HEINRICH. sc $8.00, set $17.50,
      pts $1.75, ea.   (427)

MOZART, WOLFGANG AMADEUS (1756-1791)
   Allegro In C Major, [arr.]
      (Isaac, Merle J.) string orch (gr.
      III) sets ETLING,F $18.00, and up
                                       (428)
   Concerto For Piano And Orchestra No.
      15: Themes, [arr.]
      (Rogers, David) string orch,pno,
      includes parts for advanced vln,
      vln III CARLIN sc $3.00, sets
      $15.00, and up, pts $1.00, ea.
                                       (429)
   Divertimento No. 12, K. 252, [arr.]
      (Keuning) 2fl,2ob,2clar,2rec,2trp,
      timp,strings sc,pts HARMONIA
      HU 3383 f.s.   (430)
   Dream Of Scipone, [arr.] *see Sogno
      Di Scipone, Il, [arr.]
   Kleine Nachtmusik, Eine, [arr.]
      *K.525
      (Isaac) string orch,pno [4'] (gr.
      III) sets ETLING,F $15.00, and up
                                       (431)
      (Isaac) 2.1.2+bass clar.1.alto
      sax.tenor sax. 2.2.1.0. timp,
      perc,pno,strings [4'] (gr. III)
      sets ETLING,F $24.00, and up
                                       (432)
   March And Sonatina, [arr.]
      (Isaac, Merle J.) string orch (gr.
      III) sets ETLING,F $26.00, and up
                                       (433)
   Musical Joke, A, [arr.] *see
      Musikalischer Spass, Ein, [arr.]
   Musikalischer Spass, Ein, [arr.]
      "Musical Joke, A, [arr.]" MIDDLE
      CMK 206 f.s.   (434)
   Sinfonietta, MIN 3 (from Gradus Ad
      Symphoniam)
      LIENAU   (435)
   Sogno Di Scipone, Il, [arr.]
      (Isaac) "Dream Of Scipone, [arr.]"
      (med) sets WYNN $30.00, and up
                                       (436)
   Symphony No. 12 in G, K. 110, [arr.]
      (Rikhof) 2fl,2ob,2clar,2rec,2trp,
      timp,strings sc,pts HARMONIA
      HU 3348 f.s.   (437)
   Tanz Und Kontretanz, [arr.]
      (Walter) 2.2.2.0. 2.2.1.1. timp,
      perc,strings set SHAWNEE $16.00
                                       (438)
   Titus Overture, [arr.]
      (Isaac, Merle J.) string orch (gr.
      IV) sets ETLING,F $26.00, and up
                                       (439)

MULL OF KINTYRE
   MIDDLE MK 07 f.s.   (440)

MULLICH
   Funf Miniaturen (from Gradus Ad
      Symphoniam)
      string orch LIENAU   (441)

MUPPET MEDLEY, THE
   (Chase, Bruce) (med easy) set
   LEONARD-US $35.00   (442)

MURTAUGH, JOHN EDWARD (1927-   )
   Wildflower
      fl,strings (gr. IV) KENDOR set
      $18.00, sc $3.00   (443)

MUSETTE, [ARR.] see Bach, Johann
   Sebastian

MUSIC BOX DANCER see Mills, Frank

MUSIC FOR AMATEUR STRING PLAYERS see
   Mortensen, Finn

MUSIC FOR AQUARIUS see Visser, Peter

MUSIC FOR STRING ORCHESTRA NO. 2 see
   Hedwall, Lennart

MUSICAL CONTRASTS see Karkoff, Maurice,
   Musikantiska Kontraster

MUSICAL JOKE, A, [ARR.] see Mozart,
   Wolfgang Amadeus, Musikalischer
   Spass, Ein, [arr.]

MUSIK ZU EINEM KRIPPENSPIEL see Fecker,
   A.

MUSIK ZU EINEM MARCHENSPIEL see
   Schafer, K.

MUSIKALISCHE SCHLITTENFAHRT, DIE see
   Mozart, Leopold

MUSIKALISCHER SPASS, EIN, [ARR.] see
   Mozart, Wolfgang Amadeus

MUSIKANTISKA KONTRASTER see Karkoff,
   Maurice

MUSSORGSKY, MODEST PETROVICH
   (1839-1881)
   Coronation Chorus, [arr.]
      (Kohut) 2+pic.1.2.1.alto sax.tenor
      sax. 2.4.1.1. perc,strings
      [2'30"] (gr. II) sets ETLING,F
      $18.00, and up   (444)
   Fair At Sorotchinsk, The: Gopak,
      [arr.]
      (Stone, David) 2.2.2.1. 2.2.3.0.
      timp,perc,strings BOOSEY HSS-203
      set $30.00, augmented set $50.00
                                       (445)
   Great Gate Of Kiev And Hopak, [arr.]
      (Siennicki, Edmund J.) string orch
      (gr. II) sets ETLING,F $26.00,
      and up   (446)

MY FAVORITE THINGS
   see Broadway Tonight!, [arr.]

MYERS, STANLEY A. (1908-   )
   Cavatina, [arr.]
      (Frazer, Alan) 2.1.2.1. 2.0.0.0.
      perc,harp/pno,strings sc,pts
      MIDDLE f.s.   (447)

NACHTMUSIK, FOR GUITAR AND ORCHESTRA
   see Weiss, Harald

NELHYBEL, VACLAV (1919-   )
   Chester Variations
      string orch CHRI ABC 31 set $14.00,
      sc $2.00, pts $1.00, ea.   (448)
   Espressivo
      string orch CHRI ABC 17 f.s.   (449)
   Lincoln Scene
      CHRI JCMC 21 f.s.   (450)
   Marcato
      string orch CHRI ABC 16 f.s.   (451)
   Marcia Antiqua
      fl,perc,strings CHRI ABC 22 f.s.
                                       (452)
   Overture
      3(pic).2.2.2. 2.2.2.1. timp,2perc,
      strings CHRI JCMC 22 set $35.00,
      sc $3.00, pts $1.00, ea.   (453)
   Polyphonic Variations
      trp,strings CHRI JCMC 7 f.s.   (454)
   Suite No. 1
      CHRI ABC 18 f.s.   (455)
   Suite No. 2
      CHRI ABC 19 f.s.   (456)

NELHYBEL, VACLAV (cont'd.)

Suite No. 3
fl,2clar,bells,strings CHRI ABC 20
f.s.   (457)

Suite No. 4
2fl/2ob/2vln,gtr/pno,strings CHRI
ABC 21 f.s.   (458)

Triptych
string orch,opt trp CHRI ABC 23
f.s.   (459)

NEW PHASES FOR STRINGS *CCU
(Klevenow, Spencer; Pierce, Ransford)
string orch,opt wood blocks BIG3
pno-cond sc $5.95, pts $3.95, ea.
                                        (460)

NEW PIECES FOR STRING ORCHESTRA, [ARR.]
see Purcell, Henry

NIGHT IN MEXICO see Creston, Paul

NORTHEAST RETURN see Cline, Thornton

NORTHRIDGE DRIVE see Giovannini, Caesar

NORWEGIAN WOOD, [ARR.] see Lennon, John

NOW LET EVERY TONGUE, [ARR.] see Bach,
Johann Sebastian

NUNEZ, CAROLD
Funny Fiddlin'
string orch set SHAWNEE $7.50 (461)

String Swing
string orch set SHAWNEE $6.00 (462)

NUTCRACKER SUITE: DANCE OF THE SUGAR
PLUM FAIRY AND WALTZ OF THE
FLOWERS, [ARR.] see Tchaikovsky,
Piotr Ilyich

NUTCRACKER SUITE: MARCH OF THE
NUTCRACKER AND TREPAK, [ARR.] see
Tchaikovsky, Piotr Ilyich

NUTCRACKER SUITE: WALTZ, [ARR.] see
Tchaikovsky, Piotr Ilyich

O COME ALL YE FAITHFUL
see Christmas Carol Kit, Set 1

O LITTLE TOWN OF BETHLEHEM
see Christmas Carol Kit, Set 2

OBERON: WALTZ, [ARR.] see Weber, Carl
Maria von

OFFENBACH, JACQUES (1819-1880)
Orpheus In The Underworld: Can Can,
[arr.]
(Isaac, Merle J.) string orch (med
easy) sets WYNN $16.00, and up
                                        (463)
Orpheus In The Underworld: Galop,
[arr.]
MIDDLE CMK 201 f.s.   (464)

OH HOLY NIGHT, [ARR.] see Adam,
Adolphe-Charles

OLD DEVIL MOON see Lane, Burton

OLIVER: MEDLEY, [ARR.] see Bart, Lionel

OLIVER: WHERE IS LOVE?, [ARR.] see
Bart, Lionel

ON THE MISSISSIPPI RIVER see Amiot,
Jean-Claude

ONCE IN ROYAL DAVID'S CITY
see Christmas Carol Kit, Set 1

ORCHESTRA WARM-UP PATTERNS see Kelch,
Carleton

ORCHESTRAL SUITE FOR OLD ST. NICK
(Feldstein, Sandy) set ALFRED 1931
$18.00   (465)

ORPHEUS IN THE UNDERWORLD: CAN CAN,
[ARR.] see Offenbach, Jacques

ORPHEUS IN THE UNDERWORLD: GALOP,
[ARR.] see Offenbach, Jacques

OSMOND, A.
May Tomorrow Be A Perfect Day
(composed with Osmond, M.;
Osmond, W.)
(Higgins, John) 1.1.2.1. 2.2.2.1.
perc,strings set JENSON 501-13010
$16.50   (466)

OSMOND, M.
May Tomorrow Be A Perfect Day *see
Osmond, A.

OSMOND, W.
May Tomorrow Be A Perfect Day *see
Osmond, A.

OSTINATO see Smedeby, Sune

OWENS, DON (1942-   )
Stringfest (composed with Williams,
Linda) *CC22L
string orch sc LEONARD-US 04850050
$8.00, pts LEONARD-US $3.00.
                                        (467)

PACHELBEL, JOHANN (1653-1706)
Pachelbel Canon, The, [arr.]
(Alshin, Harry) 2.1.2.1.opt alto
sax.opt tenor sax. 2.2.1.0.opt
tuba. timp,opt pno,strings (gr.
II/gr. IV) KENDOR sets $20.00,
and up, sc $3.00   (468)

PACHELBEL CANON, THE, [ARR.] see
Pachelbel, Johann

PAGANINI, NICCOLO (1782-1840)
Caprice No. 9, [arr.]
(Sopkin) HIGHLAND sc $6.00, sets
$23.00, and up, pts $1.25, ea.
                                        (469)

PALESTRINA, GIOVANNI PIERLUIGI DA
(1525-1594)
Three Chorales, [arr.] *CC3U
sets STAFF 0-15 $10.00, and up (470)

PALITZ, MORTY
While We're Young, [arr.] *see
Wilder, Alec

PARENTES see Ahlberg, Gunnar

PARTITA ALL'UNGARESCA see Farkas,
Ferenc

PASSACAGLIA, FOR TWO SOLO INSTRUMENTS,
GUITAR AND ORCHESTRA see Schaper,
Heinz-Christian

PASTORAL OCH SCHERZO see Hallnas,
Hilding

PATRIOTIC SONG, [ARR.] see Grieg,
Edvard Hagerup

PEACEFUL NIGHT see Frost, Robert S.

PEASANT SUITE, [ARR.] see Bartok, Bela

PENDERS, J.
Limburgse Vla
MOLENAAR 14.1606.05   (471)

PENDLETON SUITE see Daniels, Melvin L.

PEOPLE
see Broadway Tonight!, [arr.]

PERFORMANCE NOW see Jurey, Edward B.,
Editor

PERFORMING STRINGS see Feese, Francis
L.

PETIT NOCTURNE see Eyser, Eberhard

PETIT TATO VA CHEZ LE ROY see Amiot,
Jean-Claude

PETITE MARCHE see Amiot, Jean-Claude

PETITE RONDO see Frost, Robert S.

PETITE SUITE see Ameller, Andre
(Charles-Gabriel)

PETZ, JOHANN CHRISTOPH (PEZ)
(1664-1716)
Sonata in B flat (from Gradus Ad
Symphoniam)
LIENAU   (472)

PEZ, JOHANN CHRISTOPH
see PETZ, JOHANN CHRISTOPH

PHANTOM BILDER see Gruber, Heinz Karl

PHASE ONE FOR STRINGS, VOL. 2, [ARR.]
*CC12L
string orch, vln III may be
substituted for vla pno-cond sc,pts
BIG3 f.s.   (473)

PHOTO-FIT PICTURES see Gruber, Heinz
Karl, Phantom Bilder

PIERPONT, JAMES (1822-1893)
Jingle Bells, [arr.]
(Wieloszynski, Stephen) string
orch,opt pno (gr. I) sets KENDOR
$10.00, and up   (474)

PINK PANTHER, THE, [ARR.] see Mancini,
Henry

PIZZICATO ROCK see Feldstein, Saul
(Sandy)

PLATTS, KENNETH (1946-   )
Brighton Festival Overture *Op.32
3(pic).2.2.2. 4.3.2+bass trom.1.
timp,3perc,opt harp,opt cel,
strings [9'] ASHDOWN perf mat
rent   (475)

Elizabethan Dances *Op.33
3(pic).2.2.2. 4.3.2+bass trom.1.
timp,3perc,opt harp,strings [12']
sc,pts ASHDOWN f.s.   (476)

Saturday Overture
2fl,opt ob,2clar,opt bsn,2trp,
2trom,perc,strings [4'] sc,pts
ASHDOWN f.s.   (477)

Sussex Overture *Op.34
2fl,opt ob,2clar,opt bsn,2trp/
2cornet,2trom,2perc,strings
[3'30"] sc,pts ASHDOWN f.s.   (478)

PLEYEL, IGNACE JOSEPH (1757-1831)
Sinfonietta, MIN 5 (from Gradus Ad
Symphoniam)
LIENAU   (479)

POLYPHONIC VARIATIONS see Nelhybel,
Vaclav

POMP AND CIRCUMSTANCE MARCH, [ARR.] see
Elgar, [Sir] Edward (William)

POMPATA, [ARR.] see Lundsten, Ralph

POP! GOES THE WEASEL
(Levenson, David M.) string orch set
SHAWNEE $10.00   (480)

PORTRATTSAMLING see Gefors, Hans

PORTSMOUTH
MIDDLE MK 09 f.s.   (481)

PRELUDE AND DANCE see Daniels, Melvin
L.

PRELUDE AND POLKA see Frackenpohl,
Arthur Roland

PRELUDE ET BERCEUSE, FOR OBOE AND
STRING ORCHESTRA see Gullberg, Olof

PROGRAM BUILDER see Jurey, Edward B.

PROMENADE AND HOE-DOWN see Halen,
Walter J.

PSALM OF PRAISE
(Jurey, Edward) 1.1.2.1.alto
sax.tenor sax. 1.3.1.1. timp,perc,
strings GORDON sc $3.50, sets
$10.00, and up, pts $1.00, ea.
                                        (482)

PSALM OF PRAISE, [ARR.] see Dvorak,
Antonin

PUCCINI, GIACOMO (1858-1924)
Madame Butterfly, [arr.]
(Errante, Belisario) string orch
(gr. III) sets ETLING,F $26.00,
and up   (483)

PULSATIONS see Frost, Robert S.

PURCELL, HENRY (1658 or 59-1695)
Air, Minuet And Rondo, [arr.]
(Isaac) string orch,pno [4'] (gr.
III) sets ETLING,F $15.00, and up
                                        (484)
Antiphonal Voluntary, [arr.]
sets STAFF 0-20 $12.00, and up (485)
Bell And Ceremonial Music, [arr.]
(Alshin, Harry A.) 2.1.2.0.opt
bsn.opt alto sax.opt tenor sax.
2.2.1.0.opt tuba. opt timp,2perc,
opt pno,strings sc KENDOR $3.00
                                        (486)
Chaconne, [arr.]
(Nelhybel, Vaclav) string orch CHRI
ABC 14 f.s.   (487)
Fairest Isle, [arr.]
see Two Songs From King Arthur,
[arr.]
Fanfare And Rondo, [arr.]
sets STAFF 0-5 $10.00, and up (488)
New Pieces For String Orchestra,
[arr.] (from Distressed Innocence
And Amphitryon)
(Hockner) string orch HANSEN-DEN sc
$9.00, pts f.s.   (489)
Purcell Suite, [arr.]
(Siennicki, Edmund J.) string orch
(gr. III) sets ETLING,F $26.00,
and up   (490)

PURCELL, HENRY (cont'd.)

Shepherd, Shepherd, [arr.]
see Two Songs From King Arthur,
[arr.]

Trumpet Tune And Air, [arr.]
sets STAFF 0-4 $10.00, and up (491)

Trumpet Voluntary, [arr.]
sets STAFF 0-100 $10.00, and up
(492)

Two Songs From King Arthur, [arr.]
(Frost, Robert S.) string orch,opt
pno (gr. I) sets KENDOR $10.00,
and up
contains: Fairest Isle, [arr.];
Shepherd, Shepherd, [arr.]
(493)

Voluntary And March, [arr.]
(Caponegro, John) string orch,opt
pno,opt perc (gr. I) sets KENDOR
f.s.   (494)

Voluntary, [arr.]
(Nelhybel, Vaclav) string orch CHRI
ABC 15 f.s.   (495)

PURCELL SUITE, [ARR.] see Purcell,
Henry

PUT YOUR HAND IN THE HAND, [ARR.] see
MacLellan, Gene

QUATUORS POUR TOUS *CC14L
(Rougeron, Philippe) wind and string
parts suitable for various
combinations sc,pts MARTIN f.s.
(496)

QUIET TRIBUTE see Alshin, Harry

RADETZKY MARCH, [ARR.] see Strauss,
Johann, [Sr.]

RAINBOW CONNECTION, THE, [ARR.]
(Forsblad, Leland) string orch (easy)
set LEONARD-US $15.00   (497)

RAINDROPS see Frost, Robert S.

READERS CHA CHA see Ervin, Max T.

REBIKOV, VLADIMIR IVANOVICH (1866-1920)
Silhouettes, [arr.]
(Ahronheim) [3'30"] (easy) PRESSER
116-40019 set $20.00, pts $.75,
ea., augmented set $5.00, sc
$5.00   (498)

RECUERDOS DE LA ALHAMBRA, [ARR.] see
Tarrega, Francisco

RENAISSANCE SUITE, A see Alshin, Harry

REVERIE see Corigliano, James

RHYTHMICAL TRANSFORMATIONS see Frost,
Robert S.

RICHIE, LIONEL
Three Times A Lady, [arr.]
string orch,pno set COLUMBIA PIC.
2596TA4X $7.50   (499)
(Fink, Philip) set COLUMBIA PIC.
2596TB7X $20.00   (500)

RIMSKY-KORSAKOV, NIKOLAI (1844-1908)
Antar, Third Movement, [arr.] *see
Symphony No. 2, Op. 9, Third
Movement, [arr.]

Symphony No. 2, Op. 9, Third
Movement, [arr.]
(Leidig, Vernon F.) (gr. IV) KJOS
WO3B $32.00   (501)

ROCKIN' CHRISTMAS
(Feldstein, Sandy) set ALFRED 1929
$18.00   (502)

ROCKY: MUSICAL HIGHLIGHTS see Conti,
Bill

RODGERS, RICHARD (1902-1979)
Carousel: Selections, [arr.]
(Applebaum) set HARMS,TB HMO 36
$15.00   (503)

Edelweiss, [arr.] (from Sound Of
Music)
(Lehmeier) (easy) set LEONARD-US
$20.00   (504)

ROGERS, KENNETH RAY (KENNY)
Through The Years, [arr.]
(Marsh, Gerry Jon) (gr. II)
LEONARD-US 04797800 $20.00   (505)
(Rosenhaus, Steve) string orch (gr.

ROGERS, KENNETH RAY (KENNY) (cont'd.)

II) LEONARD-US 04849800 $15.00
(506)

ROHN
Equinox
PRO ART PRO ORCH 56 set $14.50, sc
$3.00, kbd pt $2.50, pts $.75,
ea.   (507)

ROMBERG, BERNHARD (1865-1913)
Kindersinfonie *Op.62
strings without vla,pno, 7
children's instruments LIENAU
(508)

RONELL, ANN
Willow Weep For Me
(Lieb, Dick) 2(pic).0.opt ob.2+bass
clar.1.opt 2alto sax.opt 2tenor
sax.opt baritone sax. 4.3.opt
trp.3.opt trom.1. perc,elec bass,
opt harp,opt gtr,pno,strings (gr.
IV) KENDOR set $35.00, sc $3.00
(509)

RORELSER see Franke-Blom, Lars-Ake

ROSAMUNDE: BALLET, [ARR.] see Schubert,
Franz (Peter)

ROSE, DAVID (1919-   )
Holiday For Strings, [arr.]
set COLUMBIA PIC. 4743HB7X $25.00
(510)

ROSE, VINCENT (1880-1944)
Blueberry Hill *see Lewis, Al

ROSELL, LARS-ERIK (1944-   )
Expando
2.2.2.2. 2.2.2.0. 2perc,pno,strings
[7'] STIM perf mat rent   (511)

ROSENBERG, HILDING (1892-   )
Litet Stycke, Ett, For Violoncello
And String Orchestra
string orch,vcl/vla solo [4']
SUECIA perf mat rent   (512)

ROSENMAN, LEONARD (1924-   )
Lord Of The Rings, The: Theme, [arr.]
(Fink, Philip) 2.1.2+bass clar.1.
2.2.2.0. timp,2perc,pno,strings
set COLUMBIA PIC. 2614TB7X $20.00
(513)

Mithrandir, [arr.]
(Fink, Philip H.) set COLUMBIA PIC.
2794MB7X $20.00   (514)

ROSSINI, GIOACCHINO (1792-1868)
William Tell: Overture, [arr.]
(Isaac, Merle J.) string orch (med
easy) sets WYNN $16.00, and up
(515)

(Lehmeier) 2.2.2.2. 4.3.2.1. timp,
perc,strings [6'] (gr. III) sets
ETLING,F $24.00, and up   (516)

ROTHROCK, CARSON
Beethoven's Fifth *see Holcombe,
Bill

ROYAL FIREWORKS MUSIC, [ARR.] see
Handel, George Frideric

RUSCH, HAROLD W. (1908-   )
Folk Song Fantasy
2.1.2+bass clar.1.alto sax.tenor
sax. 3.3.3.1. timp,perc,pno,
strings [2'30"] (gr. II) sets
ETLING,F $18.00, and up   (517)

RUSSIAN FOLK DANCES, [ARR.]
(Alshin, Harry) 2.1.2.1.alto
sax.tenor sax. 2.2.1.0.opt tuba.
2perc,opt pno,strings [3'] (gr. II)
sets KENDOR $16.00, and up   (518)

RYTMISKA STRAKBAGATELLER, [ARR.] see
Koch, Erland von

SABRE DANCE see Khachaturian, Aram
Ilyich

SAILING SONGS see Isaac, Merle John,
Editor

ST. ANTHONY CHORALE, [ARR.] see Brahms,
Johannes

SAINT-SAENS, CAMILLE (1835-1921)
French Military March, [arr.] (from
Suite Algerienne)
(Isaac, Merle J.) string orch (med
easy) sets WYNN $12.00, and up
(519)

SAISON DE CORDES see Feese, Francis L.

SALAMAN, WILLIAM
Class In Concert *CCU
MIDDLE f.s.   (520)

SALAMAN, WILLIAM (cont'd.)

Class In Concert Encore *CCU
MIDDLE f.s.   (521)

SAN JOAQUIN DELTA SUITE see Keuning,
Ken

SANDSTROM, SVEN-DAVID (1942-   )
Around A Line
2.2.2.2. 2.2.2.0. 2perc,pno,strings
[12'] NORDISKA perf mat rent
(522)

SANFILIPPO, MARGHERITA MARIE
(1927-   )
Young Orchestra-String Orchestra
Concert Book, The *CC12L
1.1.2.1.alto sax.tenor sax.
2.2.1.1. perc,strings,opt solo
voices sc STUDIO X7711 $4.95, pts
STUDIO $2.50, ea.   (523)

SANTA CLAUS IS COMIN' TO TOWN
see Christmas Memories, [arr.]

SARABAND AND VARIATIONS, [ARR.] see
Steenwick, Gisbert

SARABANDE AND CRUSADERS' MARCH, [ARR.]
see Handel, George Frideric

SATURDAY OVERTURE see Platts, Kenneth

SCARBOROUGH FAIR
MIDDLE MK 01 f.s.   (524)

SCARLATTI
Sinfonia, [arr.]
(Errante, Belisario) string orch
(gr. III) sets ETLING,F $26.00,
and up   (525)

SCENES FROM THE NEW ENGLAND SUITE see
Martin, Hugh

SCHAFER, K.
Musik Zu Einem Marchenspiel
fl,4vln,vcl,db,opt perc sc,pts
HEINRICH. 3002 f.s.   (526)

SCHAPER, HEINZ-CHRISTIAN (1927-   )
Passacaglia, For Two Solo
Instruments, Guitar And Orchestra
4rec,2fl,ob,2clar,bsn,2trp,trom,
timp,perc,gtr,strings sc,pts
MOSELER M 43.502 f.s.   (527)

Schneller Marsch, Tanzstuck Und
Strassenmusik
4rec,2fl,ob,2clar,bsn,2trp,trom,
timp,perc,gtr,strings sc,pts
MOSELER M 43.504 f.s.   (528)

Sonata, For Two Solo Instruments,
Guitar And Orchestra
sc MOSELER M 43.501 f.s.   (529)

SCHATTEN see Lundquist, Torbjorn

SCHEIDT, SAMUEL (1587-1654)
Suite For Strings, [arr.]
(Klotman) string orch set ALFRED
2296 $25.00   (530)

SCHERZETTO see Gartenlaub, Odette

SCHERZO PIZZICATO, [ARR.] see
Tchaikovsky, Piotr Ilyich

SCHNEIDER, WILLY (1907-   )
Hohenheimer Tanze *Op.48
strings,pno sc,pts HEINRICH. 231
f.s.   (531)

SCHNELLER MARSCH, TANZSTUCK UND
STRASSENMUSIK see Schaper, Heinz-
Christian

SCHONBERG, STIG GUSTAV (1933-   )
Un Po' Ostinato
NORDISKA perf mat rent   (532)

SCHOSTAKOWITSCH, DMITRI
see SHOSTAKOVICH, DMITRI

SCHOUWMAN, HANS (1902-1967)
Sonatina
2.2.2.0. 0.0.0.0. Orff inst,perc,
pno,strings without db [17'] sc
DONEMUS f.s., perf mat rent   (533)

SCHUBERT, FRANZ (PETER) (1797-1828)
Andante For Strings, [arr.] (from
Sonata, Op. 137)
(Alshin, Harry) string orch,pno
(gr. II) KENDOR sets $11.00, and
up, sc $2.50   (534)

March, Op. 40, No. 2, in G minor,
[arr.]
(Wilkinson, Philip) 1+opt fl.0+opt
ob.2+opt clar.0+opt bsn. 1+opt
horn.2.1+opt trom.0. opt timp,opt
perc,strings [5'] sc OXFORD
77.894 $10.00, set OXFORD $28.00,
pts OXFORD $1.75, ea.   (535)

SCHUBERT, FRANZ (PETER) (cont'd.)

Rosamunde: Ballet, [arr.]
MIDDLE CMK 203 f.s.   (536)

Schubert Dance Suite, [arr.]
(Frost, Robert S.) string orch,opt
pno (gr. II) sets KENDOR $16.00,
and up   (537)

Valse Nobles, [arr.]
(Fortner, Wolfgang) string orch sc
SCHOTT 71 U0183 $10.50, pts
SCHOTT $2.50, ea.   (538)

SCHUBERT DANCE SUITE, [ARR.] see
Schubert, Franz (Peter)

SCHUMANN, ROBERT (ALEXANDER)
(1810-1856)
Concerto for Piano and Orchestra,
[excerpt], [arr.]
(Carlin, Sidney) string orch,pno,
includes parts for advanced vln,
vln III (Intermezzo) CARLIN sc
$3.00, sets $15.00, and up, pts
$1.00, ea.   (539)

Happy Farmer, The, [arr.]
see Three Vocations

Soldier's March, [arr.]
see Three Vocations

Song Of The Reaper, [arr.]
see Three Vocations

Three Vocations
(Wieloszynski, Stephen) string
orch,opt pno (gr. I) sets KENDOR
$14.00, and up
contains: Happy Farmer, The,
[arr.]; Soldier's March,
[arr.]; Song Of The Reaper,
[arr.]   (540)

Two Moods, [arr.] *Op.68,No.7
(Frost, Robert) string orch [2'40"]
(gr. II) sets KENDOR $11.00, and
up   (541)

SCHUMPEL-KONTRA see Lehmann, S.

SCHWAEN, KURT (1909-   )
Hort Ihr Den Trommelschlag
string orch sc DEUTSCHER 32 073A
f.s.   (542)

SCIOSTAKOVIC, DMITRI
see SHOSTAKOVICH, DMITRI

SEASON'S GREETINGS see Christensen,
James Harlan

SEBESKY, GERALD JOHN (1941-   )
Very First Recital Book *CC38U
string orch,pno sc STUDIO X7801
$8.00, pts STUDIO $2.50, ea.
                             (543)

SEITZ, FRIEDRICH (1848-1918)
Concerto for Violin and Orchestra,
No. 5, Op. 22, Third Movement,
[arr.]
string orch,pno [2'] (gr. III) sets
ETLING,F $13.00, and up   (544)

SEND IN THE CLOWNS, [ARR.] see
Sondheim, Stephen

SEPTEMBER MORN see Diamond, Neil

SEVEN PIECES FOR ELEMENTARY STRING
ENSEMBLE see Strachan, Brian

SEVERN, EDMUND (1862-1942)
Brunette, La, [arr.]
(Isaac, Merle J.) string orch (gr.
III) sets ETLING,F $18.00, and up
                             (545)

SEVIUS, SVEN (1928-   )
Burlesca
2.2.2.2. 2.2.1.0. timp,perc,strings
STIM perf mat rent   (546)

Interlude
2.2.2.2. 2.2.1.0. timp,perc,strings
[6'] STIM perf mat rent   (547)

SHADES OF YELLOW see Walker, William

SHADOW OF THE WIND, THE see Frost,
Robert S.

SHEPHERD, SHEPHERD, [ARR.] see Purcell,
Henry

SHOSTAKOVICH, DMITRI (1906-1975)
March For Young People, [arr.]
(Matesky) set ALFRED 1675 $18.50
                             (548)

SICILIENNE AND OVERTURE, [ARR.] see
Gluck, Christoph Willibald, Ritter
von

SIDEWALKS OF NEW YORK, [ARR.] see
Lawlor, Charles B.

SIEBEN VOLKSTANZE see Lehmann, S.

SIENNICKI, EDMUND JOHN (1920-   )
Baroque Fugue
string orch (gr. II) sets ETLING,F
$18.00, and up   (549)

Spirituals
string orch,pno [3'30"] (gr. III)
sets ETLING,F $15.00, and up (550)

Suite for Strings
string orch (gr. II) sets ETLING,F
$18.00, and up   (551)

Suite No. 1
string orch (gr. I) sets ETLING,F
$18.00, and up   (552)

SIGMAN, CARL (1909-   )
Summertime In Venice, [arr.]
(Ployhar) MCA U087 set $16.00, sc
$4.00, pno-cond sc $1.50, pts
$.75, ea.   (553)

SILENT NIGHT
see Class In Concert Christmas Extra

SILENT NIGHT, [ARR.] see Gruber, Franz
Xaver

SILHOUETTES, [ARR.] see Rebikov,
Vladimir Ivanovich

SILVER STRINGS, BOOK 1 *CCU
(Isaac, Merle J.) string orch ETLING,
F sc $8.00, pts $3.00, ea., sets
$77.00, and up   (554)

SILVER STRINGS, BOOK 2 *CCU
(McLeod, James) string orch ETLING,F
sc $8.00, pts $3.00, ea., sets
$77.00, and up   (555)

SILVER STRINGS, BOOK 3 *CCU
(Isaac, Merle J.) string orch ETLING,
F sc $8.00, pts $3.00, ea., sets
$77.00, and up   (556)

SILVER STRINGS, BOOK 4 *CCU
(McLeod, James) string orch ETLING,F
sc $8.00, pts $3.00, ea., sets
$77.00, and up   (557)

SIMPLE SYMPHONY, [ARR.] see Hook, James

SIMPLICITY see Frost, Robert S.

SINFONIA CLASSICA see Keuning, Hans P.

SINFONIA DA CHIESA NO. 1 see Sorenson,
Torsten

SINFONIA DA CHIESA NO. 2 see Sorenson,
Torsten

SINFONIA FOR STOR UNGDOMS see Franke-
Blom, Lars-Ake

SINFONIA PER GIOVANI see Genzmer,
Harald

SINFONIETTA FACILE see Maasz, Gerhard

SIXTEEN MARCHES *CC16U
KALMUS A1122 sc $5.00, set $8.75, pts
$1.75, ea. contains works by:
Telemann; Bach; Handel; Gluck;
Mozart; Beethoven and others (558)

SKATER'S WALTZ, THE see Waldteufel,
Emil

SKOLD, YNGVE (1899-   )
Berceuse, For Violin And Orchestra
1.0.1.0. 0.1.1.0. strings,vln solo
[4'] ELKAN&SCH perf mat rent (559)

Festpolonas
2.2.2.2. 4.2.3.1. timp,perc,strings
[7'] STIM perf mat rent   (560)

Intermezzo
2.2.2.2. 4.2.3.0. timp,strings [8']
STIM perf mat rent   (561)

Liten Vaggvisa
1.0.1.0. 0.0.0.0. strings [3']
GEHRMANS perf mat rent   (562)

Lyriskt Poem, For Violin And
Orchestra *Op.34
2.2.2.2. 2.2.1.0. timp,strings [7']
STIM perf mat rent   (563)

Suite No. 1 for Orchestra, Op. 30
2.2.2.2. 2.2.1.0. timp,perc,harp,
strings [16'] STIM perf mat rent
                             (564)

Suite No. 1 for String Orchestra, Op.
39
string orch [19'] BUSCH ENO 59 perf
mat rent   (565)

SKOLD, YNGVE (cont'd.)

Suite No. 2 for String Orchestra, Op.
48
string orch [23'] STIM perf mat
rent   (566)

SLAVONIC DANCE NO. 10, [ARR.] see
Dvorak, Antonin

SLOOP JOHN B
MIDDLE MK 10 f.s.   (567)

SMALLS, CHARLES
Wiz, The: Selections, [arr.]
(Fink, Philip) set COLUMBIA PIC.
1453SB7X $20.00   (568)

SMEDEBY, SUNE (1934-   )
Improvisation I
NORDISKA perf mat rent   (569)

Improvisation II
NORDISKA perf mat rent   (570)

Ostinato
STIM perf mat rent   (571)

SMETANA, BEDRICH (1824-1884)
Moldau, The, [arr.]
(Brown) PRO ART PRO ORCH 55 set
$11.00, sc $3.00, kbd pt $1.50,
pts $.50, ea.   (572)

Moldau, The: Themes, [arr.]
(Frost, Robert S.) string orch,opt
pno (gr. II) sets KENDOR $16.00,
and up   (573)

SMITH, CLAUDE THOMAS (1932-   )
Chorale Variations
string orch set WINGERT   (574)

Fanfare And Celebration
set WINGERT $20.00   (575)

God Of Our Fathers
set WINGERT $20.00   (576)

SNOW FLAKES see Etling, Forest R.

SNOWFLAKES see Frost, Robert S.

SO NICE, [ARR.] see Gimbel

SOGNO DI SCIPONE, IL, [ARR.] see
Mozart, Wolfgang Amadeus

SOLDIER'S MARCH, [ARR.] see Schumann,
Robert (Alexander)

SOMETIMES I FEEL LIKE A MOTHERLESS
CHILD
(Murtaugh, John) alto fl/sax,strings
(gr. V) KENDOR set $18.00, sc $3.00
                             (577)

SONATA, FOR TWO SOLO INSTRUMENTS,
GUITAR AND ORCHESTRA see Schaper,
Heinz-Christian

SONDHEIM, STEPHEN (1930-   )
Send In The Clowns, [arr.]
(Chase) (easy) set LEONARD-US
$20.00   (578)
(Forsblad) string orch (easy) set
LEONARD-US $18.00   (579)
(Lowden) (med) set LEONARD-US
$25.00   (580)

SONG OF THE REAPER, [ARR.] see
Schumann, Robert (Alexander)

SONG OF THE STRANGER see Frost, Robert
S.

SOON IT'S GONNA RAIN
see Broadway Tonight!, [arr.]

SORENSON, TORSTEN (1908-   )
Sinfonia Da Chiesa No. 1 *Op.32
string orch [14'] STIM perf mat
rent   (581)

Sinfonia Da Chiesa No. 2
string orch [13'] STIM perf mat
rent   (582)

SOUNDS FOR SWINGING STRINGS see Evans,
Colin

SOUNDS OF HANUKKAH, THE
(Ward) string orch,pno (gr. I) KENDOR
sets $10.00, and up, sc $2.50 (583)

SOUTH AMERICAN HOLIDAY see Alshin,
Harry

SPARTACUS: ADAGIO, [ARR.] see
Khachaturian, Aram Ilyich

SPEZIALE, LO: OVERTURE, [ARR.] see
Haydn, [Franz] Joseph

SPIRITUAL see Marsh, Gerry

SPIRITUALS see Siennicki, Edmund John

STAR SPANGLED SPECTACULAR, [ARR.] see
    Cohan, George Michael

STAR TREK: MAIN THEME, [ARR.] see
    Goldsmith, Jerry

STAR WARS (MAIN THEME), [ARR.] see
    Williams, John

STAR WARS MEDLEY see Williams, John

STEENWICK, GISBERT
    Saraband And Variations, [arr.]
        (LaPlante) string orch (med easy)
        sets WYNN $12.00, and up   (584)

STEIN, JULES
    see STYNE, JULE (JULES STEIN)

STEP LADDER see Frost, Robert S.

STEPPING-STONES see Frost, Robert S.

STEWART, JOSEPH ANTHONY (1924-   )
    Tone Poems
        string orch (gr. IV) KENDOR sets
        $14.00, and up, sc $2.50   (585)

STOCK, LARRY (1896-   )
    Blueberry Hill *see Lewis, Al

STRACHAN, BRIAN
    Seven Pieces For Elementary String
        Ensemble *CC7U
        string orch THOMP.G sc $3.50, pts
        $1.00, ea.   (586)

    Strings On Stage, Set 1
        string orch THOMP.G sc $4.25, pts
        $1.00, ea.   (587)

    Strings On Stage, Set 2
        string orch THOMP.G sc $4.25, pts
        $1.00, ea.   (588)

STRATEGIER, HERMAN (1912-   )
    Dans Voor Schoolorkest
        sc,pts ALBERSEN f.s.   (589)

STRAUSS, JOHANN, [SR.] (1804-1849)
    Radetzky March, [arr.]
        MIDDLE CMK 204 f.s.   (590)

STRAUSS, JOHANN, [JR.] (1825-1899)
    Emperor Waltz, [arr.]
        (Isaac, Merle J.) string orch (gr.
        III) sets ETLING,F $18.00, and up
                                    (591)
    Tritsch-Tratsch Polka, [arr.]
        (Isaac) (med) sets WYNN $24.00, and
        up   (592)

STRAUSS, RICHARD (1864-1949)
    Also Sprach Zarathustra: Themes,
        [arr.]
        (Lehmeier, Jerry) (med) set
        LEONARD-US $25.00   (593)

STRENUOUS LIFE, THE, [ARR.] see Joplin,
    Scott

STRING SWING see Nunez, Carold

STRING THINGS see Ward, Norman, Editor

STRINGFEST see Owens, Don

STRINGLETS *CC12U
    (Carey) string orch HIGHLAND $12.50
                                    (594)
STRINGS IN THE ROUND, [ARR.] *CC10U
    (Frost, Robert S.) string orch (gr.
    I) sets KENDOR $14.00, and up (595)

STRINGS ON STAGE see Feese, Francis L.

STRINGS ON STAGE, SET 1 see Strachan,
    Brian

STRINGS ON STAGE, SET 2 see Strachan,
    Brian

STRINGTIME see Keuning, Hans P.

STRUCTURES COMBO I see Linden, R. van
    den

STRUCTURES COMBO II see Linden, R. van
    den

STRUCTURES COMBO III see Linden, R. van
    den

STUDENT STRING FESTIVAL SERIES see
    Isaac, Burton

STYNE, JULE (JULES STEIN) (1905-   )
    Let It Snow! Let It Snow! Let It
        Snow!, [arr.] (composed with
        Cahn, Sammy)
        (Rosenhaus, Steve) (gr. II)
        LEONARD-US 04794575 $20.00   (596)
        (Rosenhaus, Steve) string orch (gr.
        II) LEONARD-US 04849425 $15.00

STYNE, JULE (JULES STEIN) (cont'd.)
                                    (597)
SUITE CHINOISE see Alshin, Harry

SUITE FOR STRINGS, [ARR.] see Scheidt,
    Samuel

SUITE FUR JUGEND-STREICHORCHESTER see
    Walter, Fried

SUITE MINUSCULE see Deden, Otto

SUITE OF COTSWOLD FOLKDANCES see Lane,
    Philip

SUITE OF ENGLISH FOLK SONGS, A see
    Boyle, Rory

SUITE RIDICULE see Keuning, Hans P.

SULLIVAN, [SIR] ARTHUR SEYMOUR
    (1842-1900)
    March Of The Peers, [arr.]
        (Isaac, Merle J.) string orch (gr.
        III) sets ETLING,F $32.00, and up
                                    (598)
    Mikado, The: Selections, [arr.]
        (Isaac, Merle J.) string orch (gr.
        II) sets ETLING,F $18.00, and up
                                    (599)
SUMMER WALTZ see Ervin, Max T.

SUMMERTIME IN VENICE, [ARR.] see
    Sigman, Carl

SUNDAY SYMPHONY ARRANGEMENTS *CCU
    (Mayfield, Larry) sc,pts SINGSPIR
    f.s.   (600)

SUSSEX OVERTURE see Platts, Kenneth

SWEDISH RHAPSODY, [ARR.] see Alfven,
    Hugo

SWEENEY, THE
    MIDDLE MK 06 f.s.   (601)

SWINGIN' STRINGS see Caponegro, John

TANGO AVILA see Isaac, Merle John

TANNHAUSER: SUITE, [ARR.] see Wagner,
    Richard

TANZ UND KONTRETANZ, [ARR.] see Mozart,
    Wolfgang Amadeus

TARANTELLA see Isaac, Merle John

TARREGA, FRANCISCO (1852-1909)
    Recuerdos De La Alhambra, [arr.]
        (Bauernschmidt, Robert) (med) sets
        WYNN $24.00, and up   (602)

TASSONE, PASQUALE
    Folksong Overture
        2(pic).1.2+bass clar.1. 2.2.2.1.
        2perc,opt pno,strings (gr. II)
        KENDOR sets $22.00, and up, sc
        $3.00   (603)

TCHAIKOVSKY, PIOTR ILYICH (1840-1893)
    Album For The Young: Suite 1, [arr.]
        fl,clar,opt perc,strings sc,pts
        MOSELER M10.009 f.s.   (604)

    Album For The Young: Suite 2, [arr.]
        fl,2clar,trp,opt perc,strings sc,
        pts MOSELER M10.010 f.s.   (605)

    Christmas Waltz, [arr.] (from The
        Seasons)
        (Stone, David) 2.2.2.1. 2.3.0.0.
        timp,perc,strings BOOSEY HSS-207
        set $27.00, augmented set $45.00
                                    (606)
    Concerto For Piano And Orchestra No.
        1, Op. 23: Themes, [arr.]
        (Palange, Louis S.) 1.1.2.1.2alto
        sax.tenor sax. 3.2.2.0. timp,pno,
        strings GORDON sc $5.00, sets
        $12.00, and up, pts $1.00, ea.,
        min sc $2.50   (607)

    Marche Slave, [arr.]
        (Tomlinson, Geoffrey) 2.opt
        pic.2.2.2. 2.2.2.0.opt tuba.
        timp,perc,strings sc OXFORD
        77.893 $12.95, set OXFORD
        77.893-70 $24.00, pts OXFORD
        $1.50, ea.   (608)

    Nutcracker Suite: Dance Of The Sugar
        Plum Fairy and Waltz Of The
        Flowers, [arr.]
        (Isaac) set BELWIN CO 154 $20.00
                                    (609)
    Nutcracker Suite: March Of The
        Nutcracker and Trepak, [arr.]
        (Isaac) set BELWIN CO 155 $20.00
                                    (610)

TCHAIKOVSKY, PIOTR ILYICH (cont'd.)
    Nutcracker Suite: Waltz, [arr.]
        (Alshin, Harry) (gr. III) BOWM
                                    (611)
    Scherzo Pizzicato, [arr.]
        (Frost, Robert S.) string orch (gr.
        IV) KJOS S041B $15.00   (612)

    Symphony No. 2, [excerpt], [arr.]
        (Andante Marziale) sets STAFF 0-9
        $10.00, and up   (613)

    Symphony No. 6, [excerpt]
        (Carlin, Sidney) 1.1.2.1.alto
        sax.tenor sax. 2.2.2.0. timp,
        perc,pno,strings (Themes from
        Pathetique Symphony, arr.) CARLIN
        sets $25.00, and up, pts $1.00,
        ea.   (614)

    Symphony No. 6, [excerpt], [arr.]
        (Errante) 2+pic.2.2.2. 4.2.3.1.
        timp,perc,strings [4'] (gr. III,
        March) sets ETLING,F $24.00, and
        up   (615)

TELEMANN, GEORG PHILIPP (1681-1767)
    Geduldige Sokrates, Der: Overture
        (Baselt, Bernd) 2ob,strings,cont
        BAREN. BA 6553 perf mat rent
                                    (616)
    Suite for Strings, [arr.]
        (Taylor, Barnett) string orch
        HARRIS $3.95   (617)

TEN CONCERT PIECES see Dickerson, Roger
    Donald

TEUBER, FRED
    Alpha-Beta Set
        string orch sc,pts GALAXY 1.2873
        $20.00, pts GALAXY 1.2911 $2.00,
        ea.   (618)

THAT'S ENTERTAINMENT
    see Broadway Tonight!, [arr.]

THEME AND VARIATIONS ON A MEXICAN
    FOLKSONG see Track, Gerhard

THEME FROM STEPTOE AND SON see Grainer,
    Ron

THEME FROM Z CARS
    MIDDLE MK 08 f.s.   (619)

THEY'RE PLAYING OUR SONG, [ARR.] see
    Hamlisch, Marvin F.

THEY'RE PLAYING OUR SONG: SELECTIONS,
    [ARR.] see Hamlisch, Marvin F.

THIELE, RICHARD
    Kindersinfonie In C
        fl,strings, 9 children's
        instruments LIENAU   (620)

THREE BACH MINUETS, [ARR.] see Bach,
    Johann Sebastian

THREE BALLETTI FOR STRINGS, [ARR.] see
    Albinoni, Tomaso

THREE CHORALES, [ARR.] see Palestrina,
    Giovanni Pierluigi da

THREE DANCES see Deursen, Anton van

THREE MODERN DANCES see Wierda, Sietze

THREE PIECES FOR STRINGS, [ARR.] see
    Diabelli, Anton

THREE SIXTEENTH CENTURY CHORALES,
    [ARR.] *CC3U
    sets STAFF 0-19 $10.00, and up (621)

THREE SLAVONIC DANCES, [ARR.] see
    Dvorak, Antonin

THREE SONATAS AND SIX MARCHES see Bach,
    Carl Philipp Emanuel

THREE TIMES A LADY, [ARR.] see Richie,
    Lionel

THREE TO GET READY see Christiansen,
    James

THREE TUNES FROM SHAKESPEARE'S ENGLAND
    see Hare, Nicholas

THREE VOCATIONS see Schumann, Robert
    (Alexander)

THROUGH THE YEARS, [ARR.] see Rogers,
    Kenneth Ray (Kenny)

TIE A YELLOW RIBBON
    MIDDLE MK 04 f.s.   (622)

TIFFAULT, LEIGHTON
  Jazz Suite
    set ALFRED 1933 $24.00   (623)

TILL THERE WAS YOU, [ARR.] see Willson,
  Meredith

TITUS OVERTURE, [ARR.] see Mozart,
  Wolfgang Amadeus

TO A WILD ROSE, [ARR.] see MacDowell,
  Edward Alexander

TO BEGIN see Keuning, Hans P.

TOCCATA IN G MAJOR, [ARR.] see Bach,
  Johann Sebastian

TONE POEMS see Stewart, Joseph Anthony

TORME, MELVIN HOWARD (MEL) (1925-   )
  Christmas Song, The, [arr.]
    (Forsblad, Leland) string orch (gr.
    II) LEONARD-US 04841900 $15.00
                                    (624)
    (Muller) (gr. III) set LEONARD-US
    $20.00   (625)

TOWNSEND, JILL
  Circus Comes To Town, The
    string orch sc CHESTER 55342 $6.75,
    pts CHESTER 55343 $23.75   (626)

  Czech Song And Dance
    string orch sc CHESTER 55348 $5.50,
    pts CHESTER 55349 $11.50   (627)

  Dance Suite
    string orch sc CHESTER 55346 $6.75,
    pts CHESTER 55347 $20.25   (628)

TOYLAND, [ARR.] see Herbert, Victor

TRACK, GERHARD (1934-   )
  Theme And Variations On A Mexican
    Folksong
    [11'] (gr. V) set KJOS WO-1B $50.00
                                    (629)

TRE CAPRISKISSER see Karkoff, Maurice

TRE COLORI see Karkoff, Maurice

TRE SENTENZI see Jeppsson, Kerstin

TRIPTYCH see Nelhybel, Vaclav

TRITSCH-TRATSCH POLKA, [ARR.] see
  Strauss, Johann, [Jr.]

TROPICAL SERENADE see Caponegro, John

TRUMPET TUNE AND AIR, [ARR.] see
  Purcell, Henry

TRUMPET VOLUNTARY, [ARR.] see Purcell,
  Henry

TRY TO REMEMBER
  see Broadway Tonight!, [arr.]

TSCHAIKOWSKY, PJOTR ILJITSCH
  see TCHAIKOVSKY, PIOTR ILYICH

TURKISCHER MARSCH FROM DIE RUINEN VON
  ATHEN, [ARR.] see Beethoven, Ludwig
  van

TVA KORTA ORKESTERSTYCKEN see Glaser,
  Werner Wolf

TVA ORKESTERSTYCKEN see Wiren, Dag Ivar

TWELVE BEST LOVED CHRISTMAS CAROLS
  *CC12L
  (Zinn, William) string orch EXCELSIOR
  $18.00   (630)

TWO BY TWO see Hubbell, Fred M.

TWO COUNTRY MOODS see Mele, Frank

TWO HANDEL MELODIES see Handel, George
  Frideric

TWO HANDS see Kelch, Carleton

TWO MELODIES OF GRIEG, [ARR.] see
  Grieg, Edvard Hagerup

TWO MOODS, [ARR.] see Schumann, Robert
  (Alexander)

TWO PRELUDES, [ARR.] see Chopin,
  Frederic

TWO SONGS FROM KING ARTHUR, [ARR.] see
  Purcell, Henry

TWO WALTZES, [ARR.]
  (Caponegro, John) string orch (gr. I)
  sets KENDOR $10.00, and up
    contains: Lehar, Franz, Merry Widow
    Waltz; Waldteufel, Emil, Skater's
    Waltz, The   (631)

UN PO' OSTINATO see Schonberg, Stig
  Gustav

UPPSPEL see Blomberg, Erik

UPSTAIRS DOWNSTAIRS, [ARR.] see Faris,
  Alexander

UVERTYR TILL "HEMSOBORNA" see Larsson,
  Folke

VALSE NOBLES, [ARR.] see Schubert,
  Franz (Peter)

VARIATIONEN UBER DAS WEIHNACHTSLIED
  "KNECHT RUPRECHT AUS DEM WALDE" see
  Zipp, Friedrich

VARIATIONS ON AN AMERICAN HYMN TUNE
  (Wilson, Kathryn) SHAWNEE set $12.00,
  pts $.75, ea.   (632)

VARIATIONS ON JOY TO THE WORLD
  (Christensen, James) 2.2.2+bass
  clar.2. 4.3.3.1. timp,2perc,harp/
  pno,strings KENDOR sc $3.00, set
  $30.00   (633)

VARIATIONSSVIT see Lundquist, Torbjorn

VARY, FERENC (1928-   )
  Hommage A Bihari
    (special import only) sc,pts EMB
    8329 f.s.   (634)

VERSUCHE UBER EINEN MARSCH see Wengler,
  Marcel

VERY FIRST RECITAL BOOK see Sebesky,
  Gerald John

VIER VOLKSTANZE see Lehmann, S.

VIERZEHN KANONS, BWV 1087 UBER DIE
  ERSTEN ACHT FUNDAMENTALNOTEN DER
  ARIA AUS DEN "GOLDBERG-
  VARIATIONEN", [ARR.] see Bach,
  Johann Sebastian

VIISI POHJOISMAISTA SAVELMAA see Five
  Nordic Melodies

VILLAGE DANCES FROM LOWER SAXONY *CCU
  (Hoffmann, A.) strings without vla,
  opt kbd KALMUS A1129 sc $5.00, set
  $7.50, pts $1.50, ea.   (635)

VIOTTI, GIOVANNI BATTISTA (1755-1824)
  Concerto For Violin And Orchestra No.
    22: Themes, [arr.]
    (Carlin, Sidney) string orch,pno,
    includes parts for advanced vln,
    vln III CARLIN sc $3.00, sets
    $15.00, and up, pts $1.00, ea.
                                    (636)

VISSER, PETER (1939-   )
  Music For Aquarius
    [17'] DONEMUS   (637)

VITALI, GIOVANNI BATTISTA (1632-1692)
  Introduction And Allegro, [arr.]
    (Alshin, Harry) string orch,opt pno
    (gr. IV) KENDOR sets $12.00, and
    up, sc $2.50   (638)

VIVALDI, ANTONIO (1678-1741)
  Concerto Grosso in D minor, MIN 1,
    [arr.]
    (Isaac) 2.2.2+bass clar.1. 4.2.3.1.
    timp,pno,strings [5'] (gr. IV)
    sets ETLING,F $24.00, and up   (639)

  Sonata da Camera in E minor, MIN 6
    (from Gradus Ad Symphoniam)
    LIENAU   (640)

VOLUNTARY AND MARCH, [ARR.] see
  Purcell, Henry

VOLUNTARY, [ARR.] see Purcell, Henry

VREDENBURG, MAX (1904-1976)
  En Vacances
    s recs, a recs or fl or ob or
    clar, strings without vla, db,
    opt school chorus
    sc DONEMUS f.s., perf mat rent
                                    (641)

WAGNER, ALFRED (1918-   )
  Concertino for Clarinet and Orchestra
    sc DEUTSCHER DVFM 32062 f.s., pts
    DEUTSCHER DVFM 32062A f.s.   (642)

WAGNER, JOSEF (1856-1908)
  Double Eagle Polka, [arr.]
    (Isaac, Merle J.) string orch (med)
    sets WYNN $16.00, and up   (643)

WAGNER, RICHARD (1813-1883)
  Meistersinger, Die: Procession Of The
    Meistersingers, [arr.]
    (Carlin, Sidney) 1.1.2.1.alto
    sax.tenor sax. 2.2.2.0. timp,
    perc,pno,strings CARLIN sets
    $25.00, and up, pts $1.00, ea.
                                    (644)

  Tannhauser: Suite, [arr.]
    (Isaac, Merle J.) string orch (gr.
    III) sets ETLING,F $26.00, and up
                                    (645)

WAHLBERG, RUNE (1910-   )
  Concerto Barocco, For Violin And
    String Orchestra
    string orch,vln solo [12'] STIM
    perf mat rent   (646)

  Hostsang
    2.2.2.2. 2.2.1.0. timp,strings [3']
    STIM perf mat rent   (647)

  Lantlig Svit
    string orch [11'] STIM perf mat
    rent   (648)

  Litet Poem
    string orch,solo voice [3']
    GEHRMANS perf mat rent   (649)

  Lyriskt Mellanspel
    2.2.2.2. 2.2.1.0. timp,strings [3']
    STIM perf mat rent   (650)

  Symphony No. 4
    2.2.2.2. 2.2.1.0. timp,strings
    [20'] STIM perf mat rent   (651)

WALDTEUFEL, EMIL (1837-1915)
  Skater's Waltz, The
    see TWO WALTZES, [ARR.]

WALKER, WILLIAM
  Shades Of Yellow
    2.1.2.1. 2.3.1.0. timp,perc,gtr,
    bass gtr,pno,strings set SHAWNEE
    $20.00   (652)

WALTER, FRIED (1907-   )
  Suite Fur Jugend-Streichorchester
    string orch,opt gtr,perc [12'] sc,
    pts RIES f.s.   (653)

WALTZ AND DANCE, [ARR.] see Brahms,
  Johannes

WARD, NORMAN, EDITOR
  String Things *CC18L
    string orch,opt perc sc STUDIO
    X7701 $4.95, pts STUDIO $2.50,
    ea.   (654)

WATER MUSIC: SUITE, [ARR.] see Handel,
  George Frideric

WEBER, CARL MARIA VON (1786-1826)
  Oberon: Waltz, [arr.]
    (Jurey, Edward) 1.1.2.1.alto
    sax.tenor sax. 1.3.1.1. timp,
    perc,strings GORDON sc $3.50,
    sets $10.00, and up, pts $1.00,
    ea.   (655)

WEEKEND IN NEW ENGLAND see Manilow,
  Barry

WEISS, HARALD (1949-   )
  Nachtmusik, For Guitar And Orchestra
    2perc,6-18gtr,strings,gtr solo
    SCHOTTS 71 U0180 sc $10.50, set
    $35.00   (656)

WELIN, KARL-ERIK (1934-   )
  Min Femte
    string orch GEHRMANS perf mat rent
                                    (657)

WENGLER, MARCEL
  Concerto for Harpsichord and
    Orchestra
    1.1.1.1. 1.0.0.0. strings,hpsd/pno
    solo [18'] study sc,sc,pts VOGT
    VF 2006 f.s.   (658)

  Versuche Uber Einen Marsch
    2.2.2.2. 2.2.2.1. perc,strings
    [16'30"] study sc,sc,pts VOGT
    VF 2008 f.s.   (659)

WERKE VON BACH see Bach, Johann
  Sebastian

WERKE VON BACH, BOCCHERINI, HANDEL
  (from Gradus Ad Symphoniam) CCU
  LIENAU   (660)

WERKE VON BACH, GLUCK, HANDEL (from
   Gradus Ad Symphoniam) CCU
   LIENAU   (661)

WERKE VON BACH, GLUCK, HANDEL, PURCELL
   (from Gradus Ad Symphoniam) CCU
   LIENAU   (662)

WERKE VON BACH UND HANDEL I (from
   Gradus Ad Symphoniam) CCU
   LIENAU   (663)

WERKE VON BACH UND HANDEL II (from
   Gradus Ad Symphoniam) CCU
   LIENAU   (664)

WERKE VON BEETHOVEN, HANDEL, LULLY,
   PERGOLESI (from Gradus Ad
   Symphoniam) CCU
   LIENAU   (665)

WERKE VON COUPERIN, GOSSEC, HAYDN (from
   Gradus Ad Symphoniam) CCU
   LIENAU   (666)

WERKE VON COUPERIN UND FIORE (from
   Gradus Ad Symphoniam) CCU
   LIENAU   (667)

WERKE VON DITTERSDORF, HANDEL, MOZART,
   VALENSIN (from Gradus Ad
   Symphoniam) CCU
   LIENAU   (668)

WERKE VON HAYDN, MENDELSSOHN, SCHUBERT,
   SPOHR (from Gradus Ad Symphoniam)
   CCU
   LIENAU   (669)

WESTERN MUSIC see Amiot, Jean-Claude

WETTLAUF ZWISCHEN DEM HASEN UND DEM
   IGEL, DER see Haug, Lukas

WHAT I DID FOR LOVE, [ARR.] see
   Hamlisch, Marvin F.

WHEN THE BOAT COMES IN
   (Mason, Tony) MIDDLE MK 12 f.s. (670)

WHEN THE SAINTS GO MARCHING IN
   (Isaac, Merle J.) string orch (gr.
   III) sets ETLING,F $18.00, and up
                                             (671)

WHILE SHEPHERDS WATCHED
   see Christmas Carol Kit, Set 1

WHILE WE'RE YOUNG, [ARR.] see Wilder,
   Alec

WHITE CHRISTMAS, [ARR.] see Berlin,
   Irving

WHITE DAWN, [ARR.] see Mancini, Henry

WIERDA, SIETZE
   Three Modern Dances
   2S rec,A rec,2vln,vcl,pno sc,pts
   HARMONIA 2503 f.s.   (672)

WILDER, ALEC (1907-1980)
   I'll Be Around, [arr.]
   (Wright, Rayburn) 2(pic).0.opt
      ob.opt English horn.2+opt
      clar.opt bass clar.1+opt bsn.
      4.3+opt trp.3.1. timp,perc,opt
      harp,pno,strings [6'] (gr. IV)
      set KENDOR $35.00   (673)

   It's So Peaceful In The Country
   (Mendelson, Manny) 2(pic).0.opt
      ob.2+bass clar.0.opt bsn.opt alto
      sax.opt tenor sax.opt baritone
      sax. 2.3.opt trp.3.opt trom.1.
      2perc,elec bass,opt harp,opt gtr,
      pno,strings (gr. IV) KENDOR set
      $35.00, sc $3.00   (674)

   While We're Young, [arr.] (composed
      with Palitz, Morty; Engvick,
      William)
   (Mendelson, Manny) 2(pic).0+opt
      ob.0.2+opt bsn. 4.4.4.1. timp,
      perc,opt harp,pno,strings [3'30"]
      (gr. IV) KENDOR set $32.00, sc
      $3.00   (675)

WILDFLOWER see Murtaugh, John Edward

WILLIAM TELL: OVERTURE, [ARR.] see
   Rossini, Gioacchino

WILLIAMS
   Apartment, The, Theme From, [arr.]
   (Cacavas) BELWIN 89317 set $16.00,
      sc $4.00, pno-cond sc $1.50, pts
      $.75, ea.   (676)

WILLIAMS, JOHN
   Star Wars (Main Theme), [arr.]
   (Fink, Philip H.) string orch,pno
      set COLUMBIA PIC. 0122MA4X $7.50
                                   (677)
   Star Wars Medley
   (Lowden, Bob) (gr. III) set
      COLUMBIA PIC. 6498SJOX $20.00

WILLIAMS, JOHN (cont'd.)
                                   (678)

WILLIAMS, LINDA
   Stringfest *see Owens, Don

WILLOW WEEP FOR ME see Ronell, Ann

WILLSON, MEREDITH (1902-   )
   Till There Was You, [arr.] (from The
      Music Man)
   (Forsblad, Leland) string orch (gr.
      II) LEONARD-US 04847600 $15.00
                                   (679)

WIND OF DAWN, THE see Grahn, Ulf

WIREN, DAG IVAR (1905-   )
   Tva Orkesterstycken *Op.7b
   2.2.2.2. 2.2.1.0. timp,strings [9']
      GEHRMANS perf mat rent   (680)

WIZ, THE: SELECTIONS, [ARR.] see
   Smalls, Charles

YANKEE DOODLE
   (Halen, Walter) string orch,pno (gr.
      I) KENDOR sets $10.00, and up, sc
      $2.50   (681)

YOU DON'T BRING ME FLOWERS see Diamond,
   Neil

YOU NEEDED ME, [ARR.]
   (Forsblad, Leland) string orch (easy)
      set LEONARD-US $15.00   (682)

YOUNG ORCHESTRA-STRING ORCHESTRA
   CONCERT BOOK, THE see Sanfilippo,
   Margherita Marie

YULETIDE FOR STRINGS *CCU
   string orch PRO ART pno-cond sc
      $6.00, pts $2.00, ea.   (683)

ZEHM, FRIEDRICH (1923-   )
   Alla Danza, [arr.]
   orch/string orch sc SCHOTTS
      71 A6755 $17.50, pts SCHOTTS
      71 A6755-11-19 $2.50, ea.   (684)

ZIP-A-DEE-DOO-DAH
   see Disney Magic, [arr.]

ZIPP, FRIEDRICH (1914-   )
   Variationen Uber Das Weihnachtslied
      "Knecht Ruprecht Aus Dem Walde"
   string orch,opt woodwinds sc
      HEINRICH. 3307 f.s., pts
      HEINRICH. 3308 f.s.   (685)

Publisher Directory

The list of publishers which follows contains the code assigned for each publisher, the name and address of the publisher, and U.S. agents who distribute the publications. This is the master list for the Music-In-Print series and represents all publishers who have submitted information for inclusion in the series. Therefore, all of the publishers do not necessarily occur in the present volume.

Code	Publisher	U.S. Agent
A COEUR JOIE	Éditions A Coeur Joie 21, rue Ste-Geneviève F-69006 Lyon France	
A MOLL DUR	A Moll Dur Publishing House P.O. Box 2258 Virginia Beach, VA 23452	
A-R ED	A-R Editions, Inc. 315 West Gorham Street Madison, WI 53703	
ABC	ABC Music Co.	BOURNE
ABER.GRP.	The Aberbach Group	BIG3
ABERDEEN	Aberdeen Music, Inc. 170 N.E. 33rd Street Fort Lauderdale, FL 33334	
ABINGDON	Abingdon Press 201 Eighth Avenue South Nashville, TN 37202	
ABRSM	Associated Board of the Royal Schools of Music 14 Bedford Square London WC1B 3JG England	
ACADEM	Academia Music Ltd. 16-5, Hongo 3-Chome Bunkyo-ku Tokyo, 113 Japan	KALMUS,A
ACCURA	Accura Music P.O. Box 887 Athens, OH 45701	
ACORD	Edizioni Accordo	CURCI
ACSB	Antigua Casa Sherry-Brener, Ltd. of Madrid 3145 West 63rd Street Chicago, IL 60629	
ADD.PRESS	Addington Press	ROYAL
ADD.-WESLEY	Addison-Wesley Publishing Co., Inc. 2725 Sand Hill Road Menlo Park, CA 94025	
AEOLUS	Aeolus Publishing Co. 60 Park Terrace West New York, NY 10034	
AGAPE	Agape	HOPE
AHLINS	Ahlins Musikförlag Box 26072 S-100 41 Stockholm Sweden	
AHN	Ahn & Simrock Wiedenmayerstraße 6 D-6 München 22 Germany	SCHIRM.G

Code	Publisher	U.S. Agent
AKADEM	Akademiska Musikförlaget Sirkkalagatan 7 B 48 SF-20500 Åbo 50 Finland	
ALBERSEN	Muziekhandel Albersen & Co. Groot Hertoginnelaan 182 NL-2517 EV Den Haag Netherlands	DONEMUS
ALBERT	J. Albert & Son Pty. Ltd. 139 King Street Sydney, N.S.W. Australia 2000	BELWIN
ALCOVE	Alcove Music	WESTERN
ALEX.HSE.	Alexandria House P.O. Box 300 Alexandria, IN 46001	
ALFRED	Alfred Publishing Co. 15335 Morrison Street Sherman Oaks, CA 91403	
ALKOR	Alkor Edition	BAREN.
ALLANS	Allans Music Australia Ltd. Box 513J, G.P.O. Melbourne 3001 Australia	
ALLOWAY	Alloway Publications P.O. Box 25 Santa Monica, CA 90406	
ALMITRA	Almitra	KENDOR
ALMO	Almo Publications	COLUMBIA PIC.
ALPEG	Alpeg	PETERS
ALPHENAAR	W. Alphenaar	DONEMUS
ALPUERTO	Editorial Alpuerto Caños del Peral 7 Madrid 13 Spain	
ALSBACH	G. Alsbach & Co. P.O. Box 338 Bussum Netherlands	PETERS
ALSBACH&D	Alsbach & Doyer	PETERS
AM.COMP.ALL.	American Composers Alliance 170 West 74th Street New York, NY 10023	
AM.INST.MUS.	American Institute of Musicology	HANSSLER
AM.MUS.ED.	American Music Edition 263 East Seventh Street New York, NY 10009	FISCHER,C

Code	Publisher	U.S. Agent	Code	Publisher	U.S. Agent
AMADEUS	Amadeus Verlag Bernhard Päuler Möttelistraße 62 CH-8400 Winterthur Switzerland	PETERS	APOLLO	Apollo-Verlag Paul Lincke Ostpreussendamm 26 D-1000 Berlin 45 Germany	
	American Musicological Society 201 South 34th Street Philadelphia, PA 19174	SCHIRM.EC	ARCADIA	Arcadia Music Publishing Co., Ltd. P.O. Box 1 Rickmansworth Herts WD3 3AZ England	
	American String Teachers Association see ASTA		ARCO	Arco Music Publishers	WESTERN
AMICI	Gli Amici della Musica da Camera Via Bocca di Leone 25 Roma Italy		ARGM	Editorial Argentina de Musica & Editorial Saraceno	PEER
AMP	Associated Music Publishers 866 Third Avenue New York, NY 10022		ARIEL	Ariel Verlag Am Industriehof 7-9 D-6000 Frankfurt Germany	
AMPHION	Éditons Amphion 12, rue Rougement F-75009 Paris France	KERBY	ARION	Coleccion Arion	MEXICANAS
AMS PRESS	AMS Press, Inc. 56 East 13th Street New York, NY 10003		ARION PUB	Arion Publications, Inc. 4964 Kathleen Avenue Castro Valley, CA 94546	
AMSCO	AMSCO Music Publishing Co. 33 West 60th Street New York, NY 10023		ARNOLD	Edward Arnold Series	NOVELLO
AMSI	Art Masters Studios, Inc. 2614 Nicollet Avenue Minneapolis, MN 55408		ARS NOVA	Ars Nova Publications 121 Washington San Diego, CA 92103	PRESSER
ANDEL	Edition Andel Madeliefjeslaan, 26 B-8400 Oostende Belgium		ARS POLONA	Ars Polona Krakowskie Przedmieście 7 Skrytka pocztowa 1001 00-950 Warszawa Poland	
ANDERSONS	Anderssons Musikförlag Sodra Forstadsgatan 6 Box 17018 S-200 10 Malmö Sweden		ARS VIVA	Ars Viva Verlag GmbH.	EUR.AM.MUS.
ANDRE	Johann André Musikverlag Frankfurterstraße 28, Postfach 141 D-6050 Offenbach-am-Main Germany		ARSIS	Arsis Press 1719 Bay Street SE Washington, DC 20003	PLYMOUTH
ANERCA	Anerca Music 35 St. Andrew's Garden Toronto, Ontario M4W 2C9 Canada		ARTHUR	J. Arthur Music The University Music House 4290 North High Street Columbus, OH 43214	
ANFOR	Anfor Music Publishers (Div. of Terminal Music Supply) 1619 East Third Street Brooklyn, NY 11230		ARTIA	Artia Prag Ve Smečkách 30 Praha 2 Czechoslovakia	BOOSEY (rental)
				Artist Production & Management see APM	
ANGELO	Peter Angelo 140 East 40th Street New York, NY 10016		ARTRANSA	Artransa Music	WESTERN
ANTICO	Antico Edition North Harton, Lustleigh Newton Abbot Devon TQ13 9SG England		ASCHERBERG	Ascherberg, Hopwood & Crew Ltd. 50 New Bond Street London W1A 2BR England	BELWIN
			ASHDOWN	Edwin Ashdown Ltd. 275-281 Cricklewood Broadway London NW2 6QR England	BOOSEY
APM	Artist Production & Management	VIERT	ASHLEY	Ashley Publications, Inc.	CENTURY
APNM	Association for Promotion of New Music 2002 Central Avenue Ship Bottom, NJ 08008		ASSMANN	Hermann Assmann, Musikverlag Franz-Werfel-Straße 36 D-6000 Frankfurt 50 Germany	
				Associated Board of the Royal Schools of Music see ABRSM	
				Associated Music Publishers see AMP	
APOGEE	Apogee Press	WORLD		Association for Promotion of New Music see APNM	

Code	Publisher	U.S. Agent	Code	Publisher	U.S. Agent
ASTA	American String Teachers Association	PRESSER	BEIAARD	Beiaardschool Belgium	PETERS
ATV	ATV Music Publications	CHERRY	BELAIEFF	M.P. Belaieff Kennedyallee 101 D-6000 Frankfurt-am-Main 70 Germany	PETERS
AUGSBURG	Augsburg Publishing House 426 South Fifth Street P.O. Box 1209 Minneapolis, MN 55440			Centre Belge de Documentation Musicale see CBDM	
AULOS	Aulos Music Publishers P.O. Box 54 Montgomery, NY 12549		BELLA	Bella Roma Music 1442A Walnut Street Suite 197 Berkeley, CA 94709	
AUTOGR	Autographus Musicus Ardalavägen 158 S-124 32 Bandhagen Sweden		BELMONT	Belmont Music Publishers P.O. Box 49961 Los Angeles, CA 90049	
AUTRY	Gene Autry's Publishing Companies	BIG3	BELWIN	Belwin-Mills Publishing Corp. 25 Deshon Drive Melville, NY 11747	
AVANT	Avant Music	WESTERN			
BAGGE	Jacob Bagge	STIM			
BANK	Annie Bank Musiek Anna Vondelstraat 13 NL-1054 GX Amsterdam Netherlands		BENJ	Anton J. Benjamin Werderstraße 44 Postfach 2561 D-2000 Hamburg 13 Germany	AMP
BANKS	Banks Music Publications 139 Holgate Road York YO2 4DF England		BENNY	Claude Benny Press 1401½ State Street Emporia, KS 66801	
BAREN.	Bärenreiter Verlag Heinrich Schütz Allee 31-37 Postfach 100329 D-3500 Kassel-Wilhelmshöhe Germany	MAGNAMUSIC	BENSON	John T. Benson 1625 Broadway Nashville, TN 37202	
BARNHS	C.L. Barnhouse 110 B Avenue East Oskaloosa, IA 52577		BERANDOL	Berandol Music Ltd. 11 St. Joseph Street Toronto, Ontario M4Y 1J8 Canada	
BARON,M	M. Baron Co. P.O. Box 149 Oyster Bay, NY 11771		BERBEN	Edizioni Musicali Berben Via Redipuglia 65 I-60100 Ancona Italy	PRESSER
BARRY-ARG	Barry & Cia Talcahuano 860, Bajo B Buenos Aires 1013-Cap. Federal Argentina	BOOSEY	BERGMANS	W. Bergmans	BANK
BARTA	Barta Music Company	JERONA	BERKLEE	Berklee Press Publications 1265 Boylston Street Boston, MA 02215	FRANK
BASART	Les Éditions Internationales Basart	GENERAL			
BASEL	Musik-Akademie der Stadt Basel Leonhardsstraße 6 CH-4051 Basel Switzerland		BERLIN	Irving Berlin Music Corp. 1290 Avenue of the Americas New York, NY 10019	
BAUER	Georg Bauer Musikverlag Luisenstraße 47-49 Postfach 1467 D-7500 Karlsruhe Germany		BERNOUILLI	Ed. Bernouilli	DONEMUS
			BESSEL	Éditions Bessel & Cie 78, rue Monceau Paris 8 France	BELWIN
BAVTON	Bavariaton-Verlag München Germany	ORLANDO	BEUSCH	Éditions Paul Beuscher Arpège 27, Boulevard Beaumarchais F-75004 Paris France	
			BEZIGE BIJ	De Bezige Bij	DONEMUS
BEACON HILL	Beacon Hill Music	LILLENAS	BIELER	Edmund Bieler Musikverlag Thürmchenswall 72 D-5 Köln 1 Germany	
BECKEN	Beckenhorst Press P.O. Box 14273 Columbus, OH 43214	ARTHUR	BIG BELL	Big Bells, Inc. 33 Hovey Avenue Trenton, NJ 08610	
BEECHWD	Beechwood Music Corporation 1750 Vine Street Hollywood, CA 90028	BIG3	BIG3	Big Three Music Corp. 729 Seventh Avenue New York, NY 10019	
BEEK	Beekman Music, Inc.	PRESSER			

Code	Publisher	U.S. Agent	Code	Publisher	U.S. Agent
BILLAUDOT	Éditions Billaudot 14, rue de l'Echiquier F-75010 Paris France	PRESSER	BORNEMANN	Éditions Bornemann 15 rue de Tournon F-75006 Paris France	BELWIN
BIRCH	Robert Fairfax Birch	PRESSER	BOSSE	Gustav Bosse Verlag Von der Tann Straße 38 Postfach 417 D-8400 Regensburg 1 Germany	MAGNAMUSIC EUR.AM.MUS.
BIRNBACH	Richard Birnbach Musikverlag Aubingerstraße 9 D-8032 Lochheim bei München Germany				
BIZET	Bizet Productions and Publications	PRESSER	BOSTON	Boston Music Co. 116 Boylston Street Boston, MA 02116	
BMI	Broadcast Music, Inc. 320 West 57th Street New York, NY 10019	SCHIRM.G	BOSWORTH	Bosworth & Company, Ltd. 14-18 Heddon Street London W1R 8DP England	
	Boccaccini and Spada Editori see BSE		BOTE	Bote & Bock Hardenbergstraße 9A D-1000 Berlin 12 Germany	AMP
BOCK	Fred Bock Music Co. P.O. Box 333 Tarzana, CA 91356	ALEX.HSE.	BOURNE	Bourne Co. 1212 Avenue of the Americas New York, NY 10036	SCHIRM.G
BODENS	Edition Ernst Fr. W. Bodensohn Dr. Rumpfweg 1 D-7570 Baden-Baden 21 Germany see also ERST		BOWDOIN	Bowdoin College Music Press Department of Music Bowdoin College Brunswick, ME 04011	
BOEIJENGA	Boeijenga Muziekhandel Kleinzand 89 NL-8601 BG Sneek Netherlands		BOWM	Bowmaster Productions 5300 Ocean Boulevard Sarasota, FL 33581	
BOELKE-BOM	Boelke-Bomart Music Publications Hillsdale, NY 12529	JERONA	BR.CONT.MUS.	British And Continental Music Agencies Ltd.	EMI
BOETHIUS	Boethius Press Little Oxton, Clarabricken 2 Clifton Co. Kilkenny Ireland		BRADLEY	Bradley Publications 43 West 61st Street New York, NY 10023	
BOHM	Anton Böhm & Sohn Postfach 110369 Lange Gasse 26 D-8900 Augsburg 11 Germany		BRANCH	Harold Branch Publishing, Inc. 95 Eads Street West Babylon, NY 11704	
BOIS	Bureau de Musique Mario Bois 5, rue Jarry F-75010 Paris France		BRANDEN	Branden Press, Inc. P.O. Box 843, Brookline Village Boston, MA 02147	
BOMART	Bomart Music Publications	BOELKE-BOM	BRASS PRESS	The Brass Press 136 8th Avenue North Nashville, TN 37203	
BONART	Bonart Publications	CAN.MUS. CENT.	BRATFISCH	Musikverlag Georg Bratfisch Kressenstein Straße 12 Postfach 1105 D-8650 Kulmbach Germany	
BONGIOVANI	Casa Musicale Francesco Bongiovanni Via Rizzoli 28E I-40125 Bologna Italy	BELWIN	BRAUER	Les Éditions Musicales Herman Brauer 30, rue St. Christophe Bruxelles Belgium	
BOONIN	Joseph Boonin, Inc.	EUR.AM.MUS.			
BOOSEY	Boosey & Hawkes Inc. 200 Smith Street Farmingdale, NY 11735		BRAUN-PER	St. A. Braun-Peretti Hahnchenpassage D-53 Bonn Germany	
BOOSEY-CAN	Boosey & Hawkes Ltd. 279 Yorkland Boulevard Willowdale, Ontario Canada	BOOSEY	BREITKOPF-L	Breitkopf & Härtel Karlstraße 10 DDR-701 Leipzig Germany	BROUDE,A
BOOSEY-ENG	Boosey & Hawkes The Hyde, Edgware Road London NW9 6JN England	BOOSEY	BREITKOPF-LN	Breitkopf & Härtel 20 Earlham Street London WC2H 9LN England	BROUDE,A

Code	Publisher	U.S. Agent	Code	Publisher	U.S. Agent
BREITKOPF-W	Breitkopf & Härtel Walkmühlstraße 52 Postfach 1707 D-6200 Wiesbaden 1 Germany	AMP	BUDAPEST	Editio Musica Budapest (Kultura) P.O.B. 322 H-1370 Budapest Hungary see also EMB	BOOSEY PRESSER
BRENT	Michael Brent Publications, Inc. P.O. Box 1186 Port Chester, NY 10573		BUDDE	Rolf Budde Musikverlag Hohenzollerndamm 54A D-1000 Berlin 33 Germany	
BRENTWOOD	Brentwood Publishing Group P.O. Box 220033 Dallas, TX 75222		BUSCH	Hans Busch Musikförlag Stubbstigen 3 S-18146 Lidingö Sweden	STIM
BRIDGE	Bridge Music Publishing Co. 1350 Villa Street Mountain View, CA 94042				
BRIGHT STAR	Bright Star Music Publications	WESTERN	BUSCH,E	Ernst Busch Verlag Schlüterstraße 14 Postfach 13225 D-2000 Hamburg 13 Germany	
	British and Continental Music Agencies Ltd. see BR.CONT.MUS.		CAILLET	Lucien Cailliet	SOUTHERN
	Broadcast Music, Inc. see BMI		CAMBIATA	Cambiata Press P.O. Box 1151 Conway, AR 72032	
BROADMAN	Broadman Press 127 Ninth Avenue, North Nashville, TN 37234		CAMPUS	Campus Publishers 713 Ellsworth Road West Ann Arbor, MI 48104	
BRODT	Brodt Music Co. 1409 East Independence Boulevard Charlotte, NC 28201		CAN.MUS.CENT.	Canadian Music Centre 1263 Bay Street Toronto, Ontario M5R 2C1 Canada	
BROEKMANS	Broekmans & Van Poppel Badhoevelaan 78 NL-1171 DE Badhoevedorp Netherlands		CANAAN	Canaanland Publications	WORD
BROGNEAUX	Éditions Musicales Brogneaux 73, Avenue Paul Janson B-1070 Bruxelles Belgium		CANYON	Canyon Press, Inc. P.O. Box 447 Islamorada, FL 33036	KERBY
			CAPELLA	Capella Music, Inc.	BOURNE
BROOK	Brook Publishing Co. 3602 Cedarbrook Road Cleveland Heights, OH 44118		CAPPR	Capital Press	PODIUM
BROUDE,A	Alexander Broude, Inc. 225 West 57th Street New York, NY 10019		CARABO	Carabo-Cone Method Foundation 1 Sherbrooke Road Scarsdale, NY 10583	
BROUDE BR.	Broude Brothers Ltd. 141 Light Oaks Road Williamstown, MA 01267		CARISCH	Carisch S.p.A. Via General Fara, 39 Casella Postale 10170 I-20124 Milano Italy	BOOSEY
BROWN	Brown University Choral Series	BOOSEY			
BROWN,R	Rayner Brown 2423 Panorama Terrace Los Angeles, CA 90039		CARLIN	Carlin Publications P.O. Box 2289 Oakhurst, CA 93644	
BROWN,WC	William C. Brown Co. 2460 Kerper Boulevard Dubuque, IA 52001		CARLTON	Carlton Musikverlag	BREITKOPF-W
			CARUS	Carus-Verlag	HANSSLER
BRUCK	Musikverlag M. Bruckbauer "Biblioteca de la Guitarra" Postfach 18 D-7953 Bad Schussenried Germany			Catholic Conference see U.S.CATH	
			CAVATA	Cavata Music Publishers, Inc.	PRESSER
BRUCKNER	Bruckner Verlag Austria	PETERS	CAVELIGHT	Cavelight Music P.O. Box 85 Oxford, NJ 07863	
BRUZZI	Aldo Bruzzichelli, Editore Lungarno Guicciardini 27r I-50124 Firenze Italy	MARGUN	CBC	Cundey Bettoney Co.	FISCHER,C
			CBDM	CeBeDeM rue de l'Hopital, 31 B-1000 Bruxelles Belgium	ELKAN,H
BSE	Boccaccini and Spada Editori	PRESSER			
BUBONIC	Bubonic Publishing Co. 706 Lincoln Avenue St. Paul, MN 55105		CCMP	Colorado College Music Press Publications Colorado Springs, CO 80903	

Code	Publisher	U.S. Agent
CEL	Celesta Publishing Co. P.O. Box 560603, Kendall Branch Miami, FL 33156	
CENTURY	Century Music Publishing Co. 263 Veterans Boulevard Carlstadt, NJ 07072	
	Centre Belge de Documentation Musicale see CBDM	
	Éditions du Centre Nationale de la Recherche Scientifique see CNRS	
CENTURY PR	Century Press Publishers 412 North Hudson Oklahoma City, OK 73102	
CESKY HUD.	Cesky Hudebni Fond Parizska 13 110 00 Praha 1 Czechoslovakia	BOOSEY (rental)
CHANT	Éditions Le Chant du Monde 164 rue Constant-Coquelin F-94600 Choisy-Le-Roi France	MCA
CHANTRY	Chantry Music Press, Inc. Wittenberg University P.O. Box 1101 Springfield, OH 45501	
CHAPLET	Chaplet Music Corp.	PARAGON
CHAPPELL	Chappell & Co., Inc. 810 Seventh Avenue New York, NY 10019	LEONARD-US
CHAPPELL-CAN	Chappell & Co., Ltd. Canada	LEONARD-US
CHAPPELL-ENG	Chappell & Co., Ltd. Printed Music Division 60-70 Roden Street Ilford, Essex IG1 2AQ England	LEONARD-US
CHAPPELL-FR	Chappell S.A. 25, rue d'Hauteville F-75010 Paris France	LEONARD-US
CHAR CROS	Charing Cross Music, Inc.	BIG BELL
CHARTER	Charter Publications, Inc. P.O. Box 850 Valley Forge, PA 19482	
CHENANGO	Chenango Valley Music Press P.O. Box 251 Hamilton, NY 13346	
CHERRY	Cherry Lane Music Co. P.O. Box 430 Port Chester, NY 10573	
CHESTER	J. & W. Chester, Ltd. Chester Music-Edition Wilhelm Hansen Eagle Court London EC1M 5QD England	BROUDE,A (sales only) MAGNAMUSIC (sales-rental)
CHOIR	Choir Publishing Co. 564 Columbus Street Salt Lake City, UT 84103	
CHORISTERS	Choristers Guild 2834 West Kingsley Road Garland, TX 75041	

Code	Publisher	U.S. Agent
CHOUDENS	Édition Choudens 38, rue Jean Mermoz F-75008 Paris France	BARON,M PETERS PRESSER
CHRI	Christopher Music Co. 380 South Main Place Carol Stream, IL 60187	
CHRIS	Christophorus-Verlag Herder Hermann-Herder-Straße 4 D-7800 Freiburg Breisgau Germany	
CHURCH	John Church Co.	PRESSER
CJC	Creative Jazz Composers, Inc. P.O. Box K Odenten, MD 21113	
CLARK	Clark and Cruickshank Music Publishers	BERANDOL
CMP	CMP Library Service MENC Historical Center/SCIM Music Library/Hornbake University of Maryland College Park, MD 20742	
CNRS	Éditions du Centre National de la Recherche Scientifique 15, quai Anatole-France F-75700 Paris France	SMPF
COBURN	Coburn Press	PRESSER
CODERG	Coderg-U.C.P. sàrl 42 bis, rue Boursault F-75017 Paris France	
COLE	M.M. Cole Publishing Co. 919 North Michigan Avenue Chicago, IL 60611	
COLEMAN	Dave Coleman Music, Inc. P.O. Box 230 Montesano, WA 98563	
COLFRANC	Colfranc Music Publishing Corp.	SCHIRM.G
COLIN	Charles Colin 315 West 53rd Street New York, NY 10019	
COLOMBO	Franco Colombo Publications	BELWIN
	Colorado College Music Press see CCMP	
COLUM UNIV	Columbia University Press 562 West 113th Street New York, NY 10025	SCHIRM.EC
COLUMBIA	Columbia Music Co.	PRESSER
COLUMBIA PIC.	Columbia Pictures Publiations P.O. Box 4340 16333 N.W. 54th Avenue Hialeah, FL 33014	
COMBRE	Consortium Musical, Marcel Combre Editeur 24, Boulevard Poissonnière F-75009 Paris France	PRESSER
COMP.FAC.	Composers Facsimile Edition	AM.COMP.AL.
COMP.LIB.	Composer's Library Editions	BROUDE,A
COMP-PERF	Composer/Performer Edition 2101 22nd Street Sacramento, CA 95818	

Code	Publisher	U.S. Agent	Code	Publisher	U.S. Agent
COMP.PR.	The Composers Press, Inc.	SEESAW	CRESPUB	Crescendo Publications, Inc. 2580 Gus Thomasson Road P.O. Box 28218 Dallas, TX 75228	
CONCERT	Concert Music Publishing Co. c/o Studio P-R, Inc. 16333 N.W. 54th Avenue Hialeah, FL 33014	STUDIO			
			CRITERION	Criterion Music Corp. P.O. Box 660 Lynbrook, NY 11563	
CONCORD	Concord Music Publishing Co.	ELKAN,H			
CONCORDIA	Concordia Publishing House 3558 South Jefferson Avenue St. Louis, MO 63118		CROATICA	Croatian Music Institute	DRUS.HRVAT. SKLAD.
CONSOL	Consolidated Music Publishers, Inc. 33 West 60th Street New York, NY 10023		CRON	Edition Cron Luzern Zinggentorstraße 5 CH-6006 Luzern Switzerland	
CONSORT	Consort Music, Inc. (Division of Magnamusic, Inc.) Sharon, CT 06069		CROWN	Crown Music Press 4119 North Pittsburgh Chicago, IL 60634	
CONSORT	Consort Press	FOSTER		Cundey Bettoney Co. see CBC	
CONSORT TR	Consort Trios P.O. Box 124 New York, NY 10025		CURCI	Edizioni Curci Galleria del Corso 4 I-20122 Milano Italy	BIG3(partial)
CONSORTIUM	Consortium Musical	ELKAN-V			
	Consortium Musical, Marcel Combre Editeur see COMBRE		CURTIS	Curtis Music Press P.O. Box 19320 Minneapolis, MN 55419	
CONTINUO	Continuo Music Press, Inc.	BROUDE,A	CURWEN	J. Curwen & Sons	SCHIRM.G
	Editorial Cooperativa Inter-Americana de Compositores see ECOAM		CZECH	Czechoslovak Music Information Centre Besední 3 118 00 Praha 1 Czechoslovakia	BOOSEY (rental)
COR PUB	Cor Publishing Co. 67 Bell Place Massapequa, NY 11758				
			DA CAPO	Da Capo Press, Inc. 227 West 17th Street New York, NY 10011	
CORONA	Edition Corona-Rolf Budde Hohenzollerndamm 54A D-1 Berlin 33 Germany			Samfundet til udgivelse af Dansk Musik see SAMFUNDET	
COROZINE	Vince Corozine Music Publishing Co. 6 Gabriel Drive Peekskill, NY 10566		DANTALIAN	Dantalian, Inc. Eleven Pembroke Street Newton, MA 02159	
COSTALL	Éditions Costallat 60 rue de la Chaussée d'Antin F-75441 Paris Cedex 09 France	BELWIN PRESSER	DAVIMAR	Davimar Music M. Productions 159 West 53rd Street New York, NY 10019	
COVENANT	Covenant Press 3200 West Foster Avenue Chicago, IL 60625		DCM	Le Droict Chemin de Musique 5 rue Fondary F-75015 Paris France	
COVENANT,MUS	Covenant Music P.O. Box 220033 Dallas, TX 75222		DE SANTIS	Edizioni de Santis Viale Mazzini, 6 I-00195 Roma Italy	
CRAMER	J.B. Cramer & Co., Ltd. 99 St. Martin's Lane London WC2N 4AZ England	BRODT	DEAN	Roger Dean Publishing Co. 324 West Jackson Macomb, IL 61455	
CRANZ	Éditions Cranz 30, rue St-Christophe B-1000 Bruxelles Belgium	PEER (study scores only)	DEIRO	Pietro Deiro Publications 133 Seventh Avenue South New York, NY 10014	
	Creative Jazz Composers see CJC		DELRIEU	Georges Delrieu & Cie Palais Bellecour B 14, rue Trachel F-06000 Nice France	SCHIRM.EC
CRES.-NETH	Uitgeverij Crescendo	DONEMUS			
CRESCENDO	Crescendo Music Sales Co. P.O. Box 395 Naperville, IL 60540		DEMONTE	Uitgeverij De Monte Naamse Straat 178 B-3000 Leuven 8 Belgium	

Code	Publisher	U.S. Agent
DENNER	Erster Bayerischer Musikverlag Joh. Dennerlein KG Beethovenstraße 7 D-8032 Lochham Germany	
DESHON	Deshon Music, Inc.	BELWIN
DESSAIN	Éditions Dessain Belgium	PETERS
DEUTSCHER	Deutscher Verlag für Musik Postschließfach 147 Karlstraße 10 DDR-701 Leipzig Germany	BROUDE,A
DEWOLF	DeWolfe Ltd. 80/88 Wardour Street London W1V 3LF England	DONEMUS
DIESTERWEG	Verlag Moritz Diesterweg Hochstraße 31 D-6000 Frankfurt-am-Main Germany	
	Dilia Prag see DP	
DIP PROV	Diputacion Provincal de Barcelona Servicio de Bibliotecas Carmen 47 Barcelona 1 Spain	
DITSON	Oliver Ditson Co.	PRESSER
DOBER	Les Éditions Doberman, Inc. 100 Ninth Avenue Richelieu, Quebec J3L 3N7 Canada	
DOBLINGER	Ludwig Doblinger Verlag Dorotheergasse 10 A-1011 Wien Austria	AMP
DONEMUS	Donemus Foundation Paulus Potterstraat 14 NL-1071 CZ Amsterdam Netherlands	PRESSER
DOORWAY	Doorway Music 2509 Buchanan Street Nashville, TN 37028	
DORABET	Dorabet Music Co.	HIGHLAND
DORING	Musikverlag Döring GmbH Hasenplatz 5-6 D-7033 Herrenburg 1 Germany	
DOUBLDAY	Doubleday & Co., Inc. 501 Franklin Avenue Garden City, NY 11530	
DOUGLAS,B	Byron Douglas	BELWIN
DOVEHOUSE	Dovehouse Editions 32 Glen Avenue Ottawa K1S 2Z7 Canada	
DOVER	Dover Publications, Inc. 180 Varick Street New York, NY 10014	
DOXO	Doxology Music P.O. Box M Aiken, SC 29801	
DP	Dilia Prag	BAREN.

Code	Publisher	U.S. Agent
DREIK	Dreiklang-Dreimasken Bühnen- und Musikverlag D-8000 München Germany	ORLANDO
	Le Droict Chemin de Musique see DCM	
DRUS.HRVAT. SKLAD.	Drustvo Hrvatskih Skladatelja Berislavićeva 9 Zagreb Yugoslavia	
DRUSTVO	Edicije Društva Slovenskih Skladateljev Trg Francoske Revolucije 6 61000 Ljubljana Yugoslavia	
DRZAVNA	Drzavna Zalozba Slovenije	DRUSTVO
DUCKWORTH	Gerald Duckworth & Co., Ltd. 43 Gloucester Crescent London, NW1 England	
DURAND	Durand & Cie 4 Place de la Madeleine F-75008 Paris France	ELKAN-V
DUTTON	E.P. Dutton & Co., Inc. 201 Park Avenue South New York, NY 10003	
DUX	Edition Dux Lockham D-8000 München Germany	DENNER
EAR.MUS.FAC.	Early Music Facsimiles P.O. Box 1813 Ann Arbor, MI 48106	
	East West Publications see EWP	
EASTMAN	Eastman School of Music	FISCHER,C
EBLE	Eble Music Co. P.O. Box 246 Iowa City, IA 52240	
ECK	Van Eck & Zn.	DONEMUS
ECOAM	Editorial Cooperativa Inter-Americana de Compositores Casilla de Correa No. 540 Montevideo Uruguay	PEER
EDI-PAN	Edi-Pan	DE SANTIS
EDUTAIN	Edu-tainment Publications (Div. of the Evolve Music Group) P.O. Box 767, Radio City Station New York, NY 10019	
EERSTE	Eerste Muziekcentrale	DONEMUS
EGTVED	Edition EGTVED P.O. Box 20 DK-6040 Egtved Denmark	EUR.AM.MUS.
EHRLING	Thore Ehrling Musik AB Linnegatan 9-11 Box 5268 S-102 45 Stockholm Sweden	
EIGEN UITGAVE	Eigen Uitgave van de Componist (Composer's Own Publication)	DONEMUS
ELITE	Elite Edition	SCHAUR

Code	Publisher	U.S. Agent	Code	Publisher	U.S. Agent
ELKAN,H	Henri Elkan Music Publisher 1316 Walnut Street Philadelphia, PA 19107		ESCHIG	Éditions Max Eschig 48 rue de Rome F-75008 Paris France	AMP
ELKAN&SCH	Elkan & Schildknecht Vastmannagatan 95 S-113 43 Stockholm Sweden			Editorial de Musica Española Contemporanea see EMEC	
ELKAN-V	Elkan-Vogel, Inc. Presser Place Bryn Mawr, PA 19010			Union Musical Española see UNION ESP	
ELKIN	Elkin & Co., Ltd	NOVELLO	ESSEX	Clifford Essex Music Musicsales, Ltd. Blenheim Park Estate Newmarket Road Bury-St.-Edmunds Suffolk 1P 333YB England	
EMB	Editio Musica Budapest P.O.B. 322 H-1370 Budapest Hungary see also BUDAPEST	BOOSEY PRESSER			
			ESSO	Van Esso & Co.	DONEMUS
EMEC	Editorial de Musica Española Contemporanea Ediciones Quiroga Alcalá, 70 Madrid 9 Spain		ETLING,F	Forest R. Etling, Publisher 14751 Carmenita Road Norwalk, CA 90650	
			ETOILE	Etoile Music, Inc. Publications Division Shell Lake, WI 54871	
EMERSON	Emerson Edition Windmill Farm Ampleforth York YO6 4DD England	EBLE GROVE KING,R WOODWIND	EULENBURG	Editon Eulenburg Gruetstraße 28 CH-8134 Adliswil-Zürich Switzerland	EUR.AM.MUS. (pocket scores)
EMI	EMI Music Publishing Ltd. 138-140 Charing Cross Road London WC2H OLD England		EUR.AM.MUS.	European American Music Corp. 11 West End Road Totowa, NJ 07512	
ENGELS	Musikverlag Carl Engels	TONGER	EWP	East West Publications	BROUDE,A
ENGSTROEM	Engstroem & Soedering Palaegade 6 DK-1261 København K Denmark	PETERS	EXCELSIOR	Excelsior Music Publishing Co.	PRESSER
			EXPO PR	Exposition Press 325 Kings Highway Smithtown, NY 11787	
ENOCH	Enoch & Cie 27 Boulevard des Italiens F-75002 Paris France	AMP BARON,M BRODT. PEER	FABER	Faber Music Ltd. 3 Queen Street London WC1N 3AU England	SCHIRM.G
ENSEMB	Ensemble Publications P.O. Box 98, Bidwell Station Buffalo, NY 14222		FAIR	Fairfield Publishing, Ltd.	NOVELLO
			FAITH	Faith Music	LILLENAS
ENSEMB PR	Ensemble Music Press	FISCHER,C	FAR WEST	Far West Music	WESTERN
EPHROS	Gershon Ephros Cantorial Anthology Foundation, Inc	TRANSCONTI- NENTAL	FARRELL	The Wes Farrell Organization	BIG3
ERDMANN	Rudolf Erdmann, Musikverlag Adolfsallee 34 D-62 Wiesbaden Germany		FAZER	Musik Fazer Post Box 260 SF-00101 Helsinki 10 Finland	MAGNAMUSIC
ERES	Edition Eres Feldhäuser Straße 94 Postfach 12 20 D-2804 Lilienthal/Bremen Germany		FEEDBACK	Feedback Studio Verlag	BAREN.
			FELDMAN,B	B. Feldman & Co., Ltd	EMI
			FEMA	Fema Music Publications P.O. Box 395 Naperville, IL 69540	CRESCENDO
ERICKSON	E.J. Erickson Music Co. 606 North Fourth Street P.O.Box 97 St. Peter, MN 56082		FENETTE	Fenette Music Ltd.	BROUDE,A
ERIKS	Eriks Musikhandel & Förlag AB Karlavägen 40 S-114 49 Stockholm Sweden		FENTONE	Fentone Music Ltd. Fleming Road, Earlstrees Corby, Northants England	BROUDE,A
ERST	Erstausgaben Bodensohn see also BODENS		FEREOL	Fereol Publications Route 8, Box 510C Gainesville, GA 30501	

Code	Publisher	U.S. Agent
FEUCHT	Feuchtinger & Gleichauf Schwarze Bärenstraße 5 D-8400 Regensburg 11 Germany	
FIDELIO	Fidelio Music Publishing Co. 39 Danbury Avenue Westport, CT 06880	
FIDULA	Fidula-Verlag Ahornweg, Postfach 250 D-5407 Boppard/Rhein Germany	HARGAIL
FILLMH	Fillmore Music House	FISCHER,C
FINE ARTS	Fine Arts Music Press P.O. Box 220128 Dallas, TX 75222	
FINN MUS	Finnish Music Information Center Runeberginkatu 15 A SF-00100 Helsinki 10 Finland	
FISCHER,C	Carl Fischer, Inc. 56-62 Cooper Square New York, NY 10003	
FISCHER, J	J. Fischer & Bro.	BELWIN
FISHER	Fisher Music Co.	PLYMOUTH
FITZSIMONS	H.T. FitzSimons Co., Inc. 357 West Erie Street Chicago, IL 60610	
FLAMMER	Harold Flammer, Inc.	SHAWNEE
FMA	Florilegium Musicae Antiquae	HANSSLER
FOETISCH	Foetisch Frères Grand Pont 2 bis CH-1003 Lausanne Switzerland	SCHIRM.EC
FOG	Dan Fog Musikforlag	PETERS
FOLEY,CH	Charles Foley, Inc.	BELWIN
FORBERG	Rob. Forberg-P. Jurgenson, Musikverlag Mirbachstraße 9 D-5300 Bonn-Bad Godesberg Germany	PETERS
FORLIVESI	A. Forlivesi & C. Via Roma 4 Firenze Italy	
FORNI	Arnaldo Forni Editore Via Gramsci 164 I-40010 Sala Bolognese Italy	
FORSTER	Forster Music Publisher, Inc. 216 South Wabash Avenue Chicago, IL 60604	
FORTEA	Biblioteca Fortea Fucar 10 Madrid 14 Spain	
FORTISSIMO	Fortissimo Musikverlag Margaretenplatz 4 A-1050 Wien Austria	
FORTRESS PR	Fortress Press 2900 Queen Lane Philadelphia, PA 19129	

Code	Publisher	U.S. Agent
FOSTER	Mark Foster Music Co. 28 East Springfield Avenue P.O. Box 4012 Champaign, IL 61820	
FOUR ST	Four Star Publishing Co.	BIG3
FOX,S	Sam Fox Publishing Co. P.O. Box 850 Valley Forge, PA 19482	CHERRY
FRANCAIS	Éditions Françaises de Musique	PRESSER
FRANCE	France Music	AMP
FRANCIS	Francis, Day & Hunter Ltd.	BIG3
FRANG	Frangipani Press P.O. Box 669 Bloomington, IN 47402	
FRANTON	Franton Music 4620 Sea Isle Memphis, TN 38117	
FREDONIA	Fredonia Press	SIFLER
FREEMAN	H. Freeman & Co., Ltd.	EMI
FROHLICH	Friedrich Wilhelm Fröhlich Musikverlag Ansbacher Straße 52 D-1000 Berlin 30 Germany	
FUJIHARA	Fujihara	BROUDE,A
FURST	Fürstner Ltd.	BOOSEY
GAITHER	Gaither Music Company	ALEX.HSE.
GALAXY	Galaxy Music Corp. 131 West 86th Street New York, NY 10024	SCHIRM.EC
GALLEON	Galleon Press 17 West 60th Street, 8th Fl. New York, NY 10023	
GALLERIA	Galleria Press 170 N.E. 33rd Street Fort Lauderdale, FL 33334	
GALLIARD	Galliard Ltd. Queen Anne's Road Southtown, Gt. Yarmouth Norfolk England	SCHIRM.EC
GARLAND	Garland Publishing, Inc. 136 Madison Avenue New York, NY 10016	
GARZON	Éditions J. Garzon 13 rue de l'Échiquier F-75010 Paris France	
GEHRMANS	Carl Gehrmans Musikförlag Apelbergsgatan 58 Postfack 505 S-10126 Stockholm 1 Sweden	BOOSEY PEER
GEMINI	Gemini Press Music Div. of the Pilgrim Press 132 West 31st Street New York, NY 10001	
GENERAL	General Music Publishing Co., Inc. 145 Palisade Street Dobbs Ferry, NY 10522	
GENERAL WDS	General Words and Music Co.	KJOS

Code	Publisher	U.S. Agent	Code	Publisher	U.S. Agent
GENESIS	Genesis	PLYMOUTH	GROSCH	Edition Grosch Phillip Grosch Lisztstraße 18 D-8000 München 80 Germany	THOMI
GENTRY	Gentry Publications	HINSHAW			
GERIG	Musikverlage Hans Gerig Drususgasse 7-11 (Am Museum) D-5000 Köln 1 Germany	BIG3 BREITKOPF-W MCA	GROVEN	Eivind Grovens Institutt for Reinstemming Ekebergveien 59 Oslo 11 Norway	
GIA	GIA Publications 7404 South Mason Avenue Chicago, IL 60638		GUARANI	Ediciones Musicals Mundo Guarani Sarmiento 444 Buenos Aires Argentina	
GILBERT	Gilbert Publications 4209 Manitou Way Madison, WI 53711		HA MA R	Ha Ma R Percussion Publications, Inc. 333 Spring Road Huntington, NY 11743	BOOSEY
GILLMAN	Gillman Publications P.O. Box 155 San Clemente, CA 92672		HAMBLEN	Stuart Hamblen Music Co. 26101 Ravenhill Road Canyon Country, CA 91351	
GLOCKEN	Glocken Verlag Theobaldgasse 16 A-1060 Wien Austria	BROUDE,A	HAMELLE	Hamelle & Cie	LEDUC
GLOUCHESTER	Glouchester Press P.O. Box 1044 Fairmont, WV 26554		HAMPTON	Hampton Edition	MARKS
GOLDEN	Golden Music Publishing Co. P.O. Box 383 Golden, CO 80401		HANSEN-DEN	Wilhelm Hansen Musikforlag Gothersgade 9-11 DK-1123 København Denmark	BROUDE,A (sales only) MAGNAMUSIC (sales-rental)
GOODMAN	Goodman Group (formerly Regent, Arc & Goodman)	CHERRY	HANSEN-ENG	Hansen, London see CHESTER	
GOODWIN	Goodwin & Tabb Publishing, Ltd.	NOVELLO	HANSEN-GER	Edition Wilhelm Hansen Eschersheimer Landstraße 12 D-6000 Frankfurt 1 Germany	BROUDE,A (sales only) MAGNAMUSIC (sales-rental)
GORDON	Gordon Music Co. 12111 Strathern Street, No. 113 North Hollywood, CA 91605				
GORNSTON	David Gornston	FOX,S	HANSEN-NY	Edition Wilhelm Hansen New York, NY	BROUDE,A (sales only) MAGNAMUSIC (sales-rental)
GOSPEL	Gospel Publishing House 1445 Boonville Avenue Springfield, MO 65802				
GRAHL	Grahl & Nicklas Braubachstraße 24 D-6 Frankfurt-am-Main Germany		HANSEN-SWED	Edition Wilhelm Hansen Warfvinges Vag 32 Box 32 S-101 30 Stockholm Sweden	WALTON
GRAS	Éditions Gras 36 rue Pape-Carpentier F-72200 La Flèche (Sarthe) France	BARON,M	HANSEN-US	Hansen House Publications, Inc. 1860 West Avenue Miami Beach, FL 33139	
GRAY	H.W. Gray Co., Inc.	BELWIN	HANSSLER	Hänssler-Verlag Bismarckstraße 4 Postfach 1220 D-7303 Neuhausen-Stuttgart Germany	FOSTER
GREENE ST.	Greene Street Music 354 Van Duzer Street Stapleton, NY 10304				
GREENWOOD	Greenwood Press, Inc. 88 Post Road West P.O. Box 5007 Westport, CT 06881	WORLD	HARGAIL	Hargail Music Press 51 East 12th Street New York, NY 10003	
GREGG	Gregg International Publishers, Ltd. 1 Westmead, Farnborough Hants GU14 7RU England		HARMONIA	Harmonia-Uitgave P.O. Box 126 NL-1200 AC Hilversum Netherlands	
GREGM	Gregg Music Sources P.O. Box 868 Novato, CA 94947		HARMS,TB	T.B. Harms	CHERRY
	Gregorian Institute of America see GIA		HARMUSE	Harmuse Publications 529 Speers Road Oakville, Ontario L6K 2G4 Canada	
GROEN	Muziekuitgeverij Saul B. Groen Ferdinand Bolstraat 6 NL-1072 LJ Amsterdam Netherlands		HARP PUB	Harp Publications 3437-2 Tice Creek Drive Walnut Creek, CA 94595	

Code	Publisher	U.S. Agent	Code	Publisher	U.S. Agent
HARRIS	Frederick Harris Music Co., Ltd. 529 Speers Road Oakville, Ontario L6K 2G4 Canada	BRODT	HENN	Editions Henn 8 rue de Hesse Genève Switzerland	
HARRIS,R	Ron Harris Publications P.O. Box 220033 Dallas, TX 75222		HENREES	Henrees Music Ltd.	EMI
			HERITAGE	Heritage Music Press	LORENZ
HARRISON	The Rev. Benjamin Harrison 2211 South Bluff Street Wichita, KS 67218		HERITAGE PUB	Heritage Music Pulishing Co.	CENTURY
HART	F. Pitman Hart & Co., Ltd.	BRODT	HEUGEL	Heugel & Cie 34, rue Montpensier F-75001 Paris France	LEDUC
HARTH	Harth Musikverlag Karl-Liebknecht-Straße 12 DDR-701 Leipzig Germany	PRO MUSICA	HEUWEKE.	Edition Heuwekemeijer & Zoon Dorpsstraat 16 NL-1746 AC Dirkshorn Netherlands	PRESSER
HASLINGER	Verlag Carl Haslinger Tuchlauben 11 A-1010 Wien Austria		HHP	Hollow Hills Press 7 Landview Drive Dix Hills, NY 11746	
HASTINGS	Hastings Music Corp.	BIG3	HIEBER	Musikverlag Max Hieber KG Kaufingerstraße 23 D-8000 München 33 Germany	
HATIKVAH	Hatikvah Publications	TRANSCON.			
HAWK	Hawk Music Press 668 Fairmont Avenue Oakland, CA 94611		HIGHGATE	Highgate Press 2121 Broadway New York, NY 10023	SCHIRM.EC
HAYMOZ	Haydn-Mozart Presse	EUR.AM.MUS.	HIGHLAND	Highland Music Co. 14751 Carmenita Road Norwalk, CA 90650	
	Hebrew Union College Sacred Music Press see SAC.MUS.PR.		HINRICHSEN	Hinrichsen Edition, Ltd.	PETERS
HEER	Joh. de Heer & Zn. B.V. Muziek-Uitgeverij en Groothandel Rozenlaan 113 NL-3051 LP Rotterdam Netherlands	PETERS	HINSHAW	Hinshaw Music, Inc. P.O. Box 470 Chapel Hill, NC 27514	
			HINZ	Hinz Fabrik Verlag Lankwitzerstraße 17-18 D-1000 Berlin 42 Germany	
HEIDELBERGER	Heidelberger	BAREN.			
HEINRICH.	Heinrichshofen's Verlag Liebigstraße 16 Postfach 620 D-2940 Wilhelmshaven Germany	PETERS	HIRSCHS	Abr. Hirschs Forlag Box 505 S-101 26 Stockholm Sweden	GEHRMANS
HELBING	Edition Helbling Kaplanstraße 9 A-6021 Neu-Rum b. Innsbruck Austria		HISPAVOX	Ediciones Musicales Hispavox Cuesta Je Santo Domingo 11 Madrid Spain	
HELBS	Helbling Edition Pffäfikerstraße 6 CH-8604 Volketswil-Zürich Switzerland		HOFFMAN,R	Raymond A. Hoffman Co. c/o Fred Bock Music Co. P.O. Box 333 Tarzana, CA 91356	HINSHAW
HELICON	Helicon Music Corp.	EUR.AM.MUS.	HOFMEISTER	VEB Friedrich Hofmeister, Musikverlag, Leipzig Karlstraße 10 DDR-701 Leipzig East Germany	DE,A
HELIOS	Editio Helios	FOSTER			
HENKLE	Ted Henkle 5415 Reynolds Street Savannah, GA 31405		HOFMEISTER-W	Friedrich Hofmeister Musikverlag, Taunus Ubierstraße 20 D-6238 Hofheim am Taunus West Germany	
HENLE	G. Henle Verlag Forstenrieder Allee 122 Postfach 710 466 D-8000 München 71 Germany		HOHLER	Heinrich Hohler Verlag	SCHNEIDER,H
	G. Henle USA, Inc. 10370 Page Industrial Boulevard St. Louis, MO 63132			Hollow Hills Press see HHP	
			HOLLY-PIX	Holly-Pix Music Publishing Co.	WESTERN
HENMAR	Henmar Press	PETERS	HONOUR	Honour Publications	WESTERN

Code	Publisher	U.S. Agent
HOPE	Hope Publishing Co. 380 South Main Place Carol Stream, IL 60187	
HORNPIPE	Hornpipe Music Publishing Co. 400 Commonwealth Avenue P.O. Box CY577 Boston, MA 02215	
HUEBER	Hueber-Holzmann Pädagogischer Verlag Krausstraße 30 D-8045 Ismaning, München Germany	
HUG	Hug & Co. Limmatquai 26 CH-8022 Zürich Switzerland	
HUHN	W. Huhn Musikalien-Verlag Jahnstraße 9 D-5880 Lüdenshied Germany	
HUNTZINGER	R.L. Huntzinger Publications	WILLIS
HURON	Huron Press P.O. Box 2095 London, Ontario N6A 4E1 Canada	
ICELAND	Iceland Music Information Centre Laufasveg 40 Reykjavik Iceland	ELKAN,H
IISM	Istituto Italiano per la Storia della Musica Academia Nazionale di Santa Cecilia Via Vittoria, 6 I-00187 Roma Italy	
IMB	Internationale Musikbibliothek	BAREN.
IMC	Indiana Music Center P.O. Box 582 322 South Swain Bloomington, IN 47401	
IMPERO	Impero-Verlag	PRESSER
INDEPENDENT	Independent Publications P.O. Box 162 Park Station Paterson, NJ 07513	
INDIANA	Indiana University Press Tenth & Morton Streets Bloomington, IN 47405	
INST ANT	Instrumenta Antiqua, Inc. 2530 California Street San Francisco, CA 94115	
INST.CO.	Instrumentalist Company 1418 Lake Street Evanston, IL 60204	
	Institute Of Stringed Instruments Guitar & Lute see ISI	
	Editorial Cooperativa Inter-Americana de Compositores see ECOAM	
INTERLOCH	Interlochen Press	CRESCENDO
INTERNAT.	International Music Co. 545 Fifth Avenue New York, NY 10017	
	Internationale Musikbibliothek see IMB	

Code	Publisher	U.S. Agent
INTERNAT.S.	International Music Service P.O. Box 66, Ansonia Station New York, NY 10023	
IONA	Iona Music Publishing Service P.O. Box 8131 San Marino, CA 91108	
IONE	Ione Press	SCHIRM.EC
IRIS	Iris Verlag Hernerstraße 64A Postfach 740 D-4350 Recklinghausen Germany	
IROQUOIS PR	Iroquois Press P.O. Box 2121 London, Ontario N6A 4E3 Canada	
ISI	Institute of Stringed Instruments, Guitar & Lute Poststraße 30 4 Düsseldorf Germany	SANDVOSS
	Aux Presses d'Isle-de-France see PRESSES	
ISR.MUS.INST.	Israel Music Institute P.O. Box 11253 Tel-Aviv Israel	
ISR.PUB.AG.	Israel Publishers Agency 7, Arlosoroff Street Tel-Aviv Israel	BOOSEY
ISRAELI	Israeli Music Publications, Ltd. P.O. Box 6011 Tel Aviv Israel	PRESSER
	Istituto Italiano per la Storia della Musica see IISM	
J.B.PUB	J.B. Publications 404 Holmes Circle Memphis TN 38111	
J.C.A.	Japan Composers Association 3-7-15, Akasaka Minato-Ku Tokyo Japan	
JACKMAN	Jackman Music Corp.	MUSICART
JAPAN	Japan Federation of Composers Shinanomachi Building 602 33 Shinanomachi Shinjuku-Ku Tokyo Japan	
JAREN	Jaren Music Co. 9691 Brynmar Drive Villa Park, CA 92667	
JASE	Jasemusiikki Ky Box 136 SF-13101 Hämeenlinna 10 Finland	
JAZZ ED	Jazz Education Publications P.O. Box 802 Manhattan, KS 66502	
JEANNETTE	Ed. Jeannette	DONEMUS
JEHLE	Jehle	HANSSLER

Code	Publisher	U.S. Agent
JENSON	Jenson Publications, Inc. P.O. Box 248 2880 171st Street New Berlin, WI 53151	
JERONA	Jerona Music Corp. 81 Trinity Place Hackensack, NJ 07601	
JOBERT	Editions Jean Jobert 76, rue Quincampoix F-75003 Paris France	PRESSER
JOHNSON	Johnson Reprint Corp. 757 3rd Avenue New York, NY 10017	
JOHNSON,P	Paul Johnson Productions P.O. Box 220033 Dallas, TX 75222	
JOSHUA	Joshua Corp.	GENERAL
JRB	JRB Music Education Materials Distributor	PRESSER
JUNNE	Otto Junne GmbH Sendlinger-Tor-Platz 10 D-8000 München Germany	
JUS-AUTOR	Jus-Autor Bulgaria	BREITKOPF-W
JUSKO	Jusko Publications	WILLIS
KAHNT	C.F. Kahnt, Musikverlag Hohenstraße 52 D-8992 Wasserburg A.B. Germany	PETERS
KALMUS	Edwin F. Kalmus Miami-Dade Industrial Park P.O. Box 1007 Opa Locka, FL 33054	BELWIN (miniature scores only)
KALMUS,A	Alfred A. Kalmus Ltd. c/o Universal Edition (London) Ltd 38 Eldon Way, Paddock Wood Tonbridge, Kent TN12 6BE England	
KAMMEN	J. & J. Kammen Music Co.	CENTURY
KANE	Walter Kane & Son, Inc. 351 West 52nd Street New York, NY 10019	
KAPLAN	Ida R. Kaplan 1308 Olivia Avenue Ann Arbor, MI 48104	
KARTHAUSE	Karthause Verlag Adamstraße 7 D-8000 München 19 Germany	
KAWE	Edition KaWe Brederodestraat 90 NL-1054 VC Amsterdam 13 Netherlands	KING,R
KAY PR	Kay Press 612 Vicennes Court Cincinnati, OH 45231	
KELTON	Kelton Publications 1343 Amalfi Drive Pacific Palisades, CA 90272	
KENDOR	Kendor Music Inc. Main & Grove Streets P.O. Box 278 Delevan, NY 14042	

Code	Publisher	U.S. Agent
KENSING.	Kensington Music Service P.O. Box 471 Tenafly, NJ 07670	
KENYON	Kenyon Publications	PLYMOUTH
KERBY	E.C. Kerby Ltd. 198 Davenport Road Toronto, Ontario M5R 1J2 Canada	
KING	King Music Publishing Co.	KANE
KING,R	Robert King Music Co. 7 Canton Street North Easton, MA 02356	
KISTNER	Fr. Kistner & C.F.W. Siegel & Co. Am Kielshof 2 D-5000 Köln 90 Germany	CONCORDIA
KJOS	Neil A. Kjos Music Co. 4382 Jutland Drive San Diego, CA 92117	
KLIMENT	Musikverlag Johann Kliment Kolingasse 15 A-1090 Wien 9 Austria	
KNOPF	Alfred A. Knopf 201 East 50th Street New York, NY 10022	
KNUF	Frits Knuf Uitgeverij Rodeheldenstraat 13 P.O. Box 720 NL-4116 ZJ Buren Netherlands	PENDRGN
KNUS	Edition Kneusslin Amselstraße 43 CH-4059 Basel Switzerland Edition Kneusslin, U.S.A. 84-A Centre Street Nutley, NJ 07110	
KODALY	Kodaly Center of America, Inc. 1326 Washington Street West Newton, MA 02165	JERONA
KON BOND	Kon. Bond van Chr. Zang- en Oratoriumverenigingen	DONEMUS
KONINKLIJK	Koninklijk Nederlands Zangersverbond	DONEMUS
KOPER	Musikverlag Karl-Heinz Köper Schneekoppenweg 12 D-3001 Isernhagen NB/Hannover Germany	
KRENN	Ludwig Krenn Verlag Reindorfergasse 42 A-1150 Wien 45 Austria	
KROMPHOLZ	Krompholz & Co Spitalgasse 28 CH-3001 Bern Switzerland	
KRUSEMAN	Ed. Philip Kruseman	DONEMUS
KYSAR	Michael Kysar 1250 South 211th Place Seattle, WA 98148	
LAMP	Latin-American Music Pub. Co. Ltd. 8 Denmark Street London England	

Code	Publisher	U.S. Agent	Code	Publisher	U.S. Agent
LAND	A. Land & Zn. Muziekuitgevers	DONEMUS	LIENAU	Robert Lienau, Musikverlag Lankwitzerstraße 9 D-1000 Berlin 45 Germany	
LANDES	Landesverband Evangelischer Kirchenchöre in Bayern	HANSSLER			
LANG	Lang Music Publications P.O. Box 11021 Indianapolis, IN 46201		LILLENAS	Lillenas Publishing Co. P.O. Box 527 Kansas City, MO 64141	
LANSMAN	Länsmansgarden PL-7012 S-762 00 Rimbo Sweden		LINDSAY	Lindsay Music Brookhouse 24 Royston Street Potton, Sandy Beds 5G19 2LP England	PRESSER
	Latin-American Music Pub. Co. Ltd. see LAMP		LINGUA	Lingua Press P.O. Box 481 Ramona, CA 92065	
LAUDINELLA	Laudinella Reihe	HANSSLER			
LAUMANN	Laumann Verlag Alter Gartenweg 14 Postfach 1360 D-4408 Dülmen Germany		LISTER	Mosie Lister	LILLENAS
			LITOLFF,H	Henry Litolff's Verlag Kennedy Allee 101 Postfach 700906 D-6000 Frankfurt 70 Germany	PETERS
LAVENDER	Lavender Publications, Ltd. Borough Green Sevenoaks, Kent TN15 8DT England		LITURGICAL	Liturgical Press St. Johns Abbey Collegeville, MN 56321	
LAWSON	Lawson-Gould Music Publishers, Inc.	SCHIRM.G			
LEA	Lea Pocket Scores P.O. Box 138, Audubon Station New York, NY 10032		LLUQUET	Guillermo Lluquet Almacen General de Musica Avendida del Oeste 43 Valencia Spain	
LEDUC	Alphonse Leduc 175 rue Saint-Honoré F-75040 Paris Cedex 01 France	BARON,M BRODT PRESSER (rental)	LONG ISLE	Long Island Music Publishers	BRANCH
			LOOP	Loop Music Co.	KJOS
LEEDS	Leeds Music Ltd. Canada	BELWIN	LORENZ	Lorenz Industries 501 East Third Street Dayton, OH 45401	
LEMOINE	Henry Lemoine & Cie 17, rue Pigalle F-75009 Paris France	PRESSER	LPME	The London Pro Musica Edition	SCHIRM.EC
LENGNICK	Alfred Lengnick & Co., Ltd. Purley Oaks Studios 421a Brighton Road South Croydon CR2 6YR, Surrey England	HARRIS	LUCKS	Luck's Music Library P.O. Box 407 Madison Heights, MI 48071	
			LUDWIG	Ludwig Music Publishing Co. 557-67 East 140th Street Cleveland, OH 44110	
LEONARD-ENG	Leonard, Gould & Bolttler	LESLIE	LUNDEN	Edition Lundén Bromsvagen 25 S-125 30 Alvsjö Sweden	
LEONARD-US	Hal Leonard Music 8112 West Bluemound Road Milwaukee, WI 53213				
LESLIE	Leslie Music Supply	BRODT	LUNDQUIST	Abr. Lundquist Musikförlag AB Katarina Bangata 17 S-116 25 Stockholm Sweden	
LEUCKART	F.E.C. Leuckart Nibelungenstraße 48 D-8000 München Germany	AMP			
			LYCHE	Harald Lyche Postboks 2171 Strømsø N-3001 Drammen Norway	
LEXICON	Lexicon Music P.O. Box 2222 Newbury Park, CA 91320		LYDIAN ORCH	Lydian Orchestrations 31000 Ruth Hill Road Orange Cove, CA 93646	
LIBEN	Liben Music Publications 6265 Dawes Lane Cincinnati, OH 45230		LYRA	Lyra Music Co. 133 West 69th Street New York, NY 10023	
LIBER	Svenska Utbildningsförlaget Liber AB Utbildningsförlaget, Centrallagret 13601 Handen Stockholm Sweden			Mac Murray Publications see MMP	
			MAGNAMUSIC	Magnamusic-Baton, Inc. 10370 Page Industrial Boulevard St. Louis, MO 63132	
LICHTENAUER	W.F. Lichtenauer	DONEMUS			

Code	Publisher	U.S. Agent
MALCOLM	Malcolm Music Ltd.	SHAWNEE
MANNA	Manna Music, Inc. 2111 Kenmere Avenue Burbank, CA 91504	
MANNHEIM	Mannheimer Musikverlag Richard Wagner Straße 6 Postfach 1504 D-6800 Mannheim 1 Germany	
MANU. PUB	Manuscript Publications 120 Maple Street Wrightsville, PA 17368	
MAPA MUNDI	Mapa Mundi	WORLDWIDE
MARBOT	Edition Marbot GmbH Bornstraße 12 D-2000 Hamburg 13 Germany	
MARCHAND	Marchand, Paap en Strooker	DONEMUS
MARGUN	Margun Music, Inc. 167 Dudley Road Newton Centre, MA 02159	
MARI	E. & O. Mari, Inc. 38-01 23rd Avenue Long Island City, NY 11105	
MARK	Mark Publications	CRESPUB
MARKS	Edward B. Marks Music Corp. 1790 Broadway New York, NY 10019	BELWIN
MARSEG	Marseg, Ltd. 18 Farmstead Road Willowdale, Ontario M2L 2G2 Canada	
MARTIN	Editions Robert Martin 106, Grande rue de la Coupée F-71009 Charnay-les-Macon France	
MASTER	Master Music	CRESPUB
MAURER	J. Maurer Watermanlaan 7 B-1150 Brussel Belgium	
MAURRI	Edizioni Musicali Ditta R. Maurri Via del Corso 1 (17R.) Firenze Italy	
MCA	MCA and Mills/MCA Joint Venture Editions 445 Park Avenue New York, NY 10022	BELWIN
MCAFEE	McAfee Music Corp.	BELWIN
MCGIN-MARX	McGinnis & Marx P.O. Box 229, Planetarium Station New York, NY 10024	DEIRO
MDV	Mitteldeutscher Verlag	PETERS
MEDIT	Mediterranean	GALAXY
MEL BAY	Mel Bay Publications, Inc. #4 Industrial Drive Dailey Industrial Park Pacific, MO 63069	
MELE LOKE	Mele Loke Publishing Co. Box 7142 Honolulu, Hawaii 96821	HIGHLAND (continental U.S.A.)

Code	Publisher	U.S. Agent
MELODI	Casa Editrice Melodi S.A. Galleria Del Corso 4 Milano Italy	
MENC	Music Educators National Conference Publications Division 1902 Association Drive Reston, VA 22091	
MERCATOR	Mercator Verlag & Wohlfahrt (Gert) Verlag Köhnenstraße 5-11, Postfach 100609 D-4100 Duisberg 1 Germany	
MERCURY	Mercury Music Corp.	PRESSER
MERIDIAN	Les Nouvelles Éditions Meridian 5, rue Lincoln F-75008 Paris 8 France	
MERION	Merion Music, Inc.	PRESSER
MERRYMOUNT	Merrymount Music, Inc.	PRESSER
MERSEBURG	Merseburger Verlag Motzstraße 13 D-3500 Kassel Germany	BAREN. PETERS
METRO	Metro Muziek Bernard Zweerskade 18 Amsterdam Netherlands	
METROPOLIS	Editions Metropolis Van Ertbornstraat, 5 B-2000 Antwerpen Belgium	ELKAN,H
MEULEMANS	Arthur Meulemans Fonds Charles de Costerlaan, 6 2050 Antwerpen Belgium	
MEXICANAS	Ediciones Mexicanas de Musica Avenida Juarez 18 Mexico City Mexico	PEER
MEZ KNIGA	Mezhdunarodnaja Kniga Moscow 121200 U.S.S.R.	SCHIRM,G
MIDDLE	Middle Eight Music 7 Garrick Street London, WC2E 9AR England	EMI
MILLER	Miller Music Corp.	BIG3
MILL MUSIC	Mills Music Jewish Catalogue	TRANSCON- TINENTAL
MINKOFF	Minkoff Reprints Chemin de la Mousse 46 CH-1225 Chêne-Bourg-Genève Switzerland	
MIRA	Mira Music Associates 199 Mountain Road Wilton, CT 06897	
	Mitteldeutscher Verlag see MDV	
MJQ	M.J.Q. Music, Inc. 1697 Broadway #1100 New York, NY 10019	FOX,S
MMP	Mac Murray Publications	MUS.SAC.PRO.
MMS	Monumenta Musica Svecicae	STIM

Code	Publisher	U.S. Agent	Code	Publisher	U.S. Agent
MOBART	Mobart Music Publications	BOELKE-BOM	MUS.SUR	Musica del Sur Apartado 5219 Barcelona Spain	
MODERN	Edition Modern Musikverlag Hans Wewerka Elisabethstraße 38 D-8000 München 40 Germany		MUS.VIVA	Musica Viva 262 King's Drive Eastbourne Sussex, BN21 2XD England	
MOECK	Hermann Moeck Velag Postfach 143 D-3100 Celle 1 Germany	EUR.AM.MUS.	MUS.VIVA HIST.	Musica Viva Historica	BOOSEY
MOLENAAR	Molenaar's Muziekcentrale Industrieweg 23 Postbus 19 NL-1520 AA Wormerveer Netherlands		MUSANT	Musantiqua Distribution, Inc. 100, Ninth Avenue Richelieu Quebec Canada	
MONDIAL	Mondial-Verlag KG 8 rue de Hesse Genève Switzerland		MUSIA	Musia	PETERS
MORAVIAN	Moravian Music Foundation	ABINGDON BELWIN BOOSEY BRODT PETERS	MUSIC	Music Sales Corp. 33 West 60th Street New York, NY 10023	
			MUSIC BOX	Music Box Dancer Publications Ltd.	PRESSER
				Music Educators National Conference see MENC	
MOSELER	Karl Heinrich Möseler Verlag Hoffman-von-Fallersleben-Straße 8-10 Postfach 460 D-3340 Wolfenbüttel Germany	MAGNAMUSIC	MUSIC-ENG	Music Sales Ltd. 78 Newman Street London W1P 3LA England	
MOSER	Verlag G. Moser Kirschweg 8 CH-4144 Arlesheim Switzerland		MUSIC INFO	Muzički Informativni Centar	BREITKOPF-W
			MUSIC SEV.	Music 70, Music Publishers 170 N.E. 33rd Street Fort Lauderdale, FL 33334	
MOWBRAY	Mowbray Music Publications The Alden Press Osney Mead Oxford OX2 OEG England			Société d'Éditions Musicales Internationales see SEMI	
MSM	MSM Music Publishers	BROUDE,A	MUSICAM	Music and Methods 15 North Mojave Road Las Vegas, NV 89101	
MT.SALUS	Mt. Salus Music 709 East Leake Street Clinton, MS 39056		MUSICART	Musicart West 733 East 840 North Circle Orem, UT 84057	
MT.TAHO	Mt. Tahoma	BROUDE,A			
MULLER	Willy Müller, Süddeutscher Musikverlag Marzgasse 5 D-6900 Heidelberg Germany	PETERS	MUSICIANS PUB	Musicians Publications P.O. Box 7160 West Trenton, NJ 08628	
			MUSICO	Musico Muziekuitgeverij	DONEMUS
MUNSTER	Van Munster Editie	DONEMUS	MUSICPRINT	Musicprint Corporation P.O. Box 767 Radio City Station New York, NY 10019	BROUDE,A
MURPHY	Spud Murphy Publications	WESTERN			
MUS.ANT.BOH.	Musica Antiqua Bohemica	BOOSEY			
MUS.ART	Music Art Publications P.O. Box 1744 Chula Vista, CA 92010		MUSICUS	Edition Musicus P.O. Box 1341 Stamford, CT 06904	
MUS.PERC.	Music For Percussion, Inc. 17 West 60th Street New York, NY 10023		MUSIKAL.	Musikaliska Konstföreningen	STIM
			MUSIKHOJ	Musikhojskolens Forlag ApS	EUR.AM.MUS.
MUS.RARA	Musica Rara Le Traversier Chemin de la Buire F-84170 Monteux France	Musica Rara, U.S.A. 305 Bloomfield Ave. Nutley, NJ 07110	MUSIKINST	Verlag das Musikinstrument Klüberstraße 9 D-6000 Frankfurt-am-Main Germany	
MUS.SAC.PRO	Musica Sacra et Profana P.O. Box 7248 Berkeley, CA 94707		MUSIKK	Musik-Huset A/S Karl Johansgaten 45 Oslo Norway	PETERS

Code	Publisher	U.S. Agent
MUSIKWISS.	Musikwissenschaftlicher Verlag Wien Dorotheergasse 10 A-1010 Wien 1 Austria	MAGNAMUSIC
	Eerste Muziekcentrale see EERSTE	
MYRRH	Myrrh Music	WORD
MYRTLE	Myrtle Monroe Music 2600 Tenth Street Berkeley, CA 94710	COLUMBIA PIC.
NAGELS	Nagels Verlag	AMP MAGNAMUSIC
NATIONAL	National Music Publishers P.O. Box 868 Tustin, CA 92680	
NEUE	Verlag Neue Musik Leipziger Straße 26 Postfach 1306 DDR-1080 Berlin Germany	
NEW HORIZON	New Horizon Publications	TRANSCONTINENTAL
NEW MUSIC	The New Music Co., Inc. P.O. Box 31757 Aurora, CO 80041	
NEW MUSIC WEST	New Music West P.O. Box 7434 Van Nuys, CA 91409	
NEW VALLEY	New Valley Music Press of Smith College Sage Hall 49 Northampton, MA 01063	
NIEUWE	De Nieuwe Muziekhandel	DONEMUS
NIPPON	Nippon Hosu	PRESSER
NME	New Music Edition	PRESSER
NO.AM.LIT.	North American Liturgy Resources Choral Music Department 10802 North 23rd Avenue Phoenix, AZ 85029	
NOETZEL	Noetzel Musikverlag	PETERS
NOMOS	Edition Nomos	BREITKOPF-W
NOORDHOFF	P. Noordhoff	DONEMUS
NORDISKA	AB Nordiska Musikförlaget Édition Wilhelm Hansen, Stockholm Box 745, Warfvinges Vag 32 S-101 30 Stockholm Sweden See also HANSEN-SWEDEN	BROUDE,A MAGNAMUSIC (sales-rental) WALTON (choral)
NORGE	Norsk Musikkinformasjon Tordenskioldsgatan 6B Oslo 1 Norway	
NORSK	Norsk Musikforlag AS Karl Johansgaten 39 P.O. Box 1499 Vika Oslo Norway	MAGNAMUSIC
NORTHRIDGE	Northridge Music, Inc.	CHERRY
NORTON	W.W. Norton & Co., Inc. 500 Fifth Avenue New York, NY 10003	
	Norwegian Music Information Center see NORGE	

Code	Publisher	U.S. Agent
NOSKE	A.A. Noske	DONEMUS
NOTERIA	Noteria S-890 30 Borensberg Sweden	STIM
NOVELLO	Novello & Co., Ltd. Borough Green Sevenoaks, Kent TN15 8DT England	BELWIN (rentals) PRESSER (sales)
NOW VIEW	Now View	PLYMOUTH
NYMPHEN	Edition Nymphenberg	PETERS
OAK	Oak Publications	MUSIC
OCTAVA	Octava Music Co., Ltd.	WEINBERGER
OISEAU	Éditions de L'Oiseau-Lyre Les Remparts Monaco	
OKRA	Okra Music Corp.	SEESAW
OLIVIAN	Olivian Press	ARCADIA
OLMS	G. Olms Verlag Hagentorwall 7 D-3200 Hildesheim Germany	
ONGAKU	Ongaku-No-Tomo Sha Co., Ltd. Kagurazaka 6-30, Shinjuku-ku Tokyo Japan	PRESSER
OPUS	Opus Music Publishers, Inc. 1880 Holste Northbrook, IL 60062	
OPUS-CZ	Opus Ceskoslavenske Hudobne Vydaratelstro Dunajska 18 Bratislava Czechoslovakia	BOOSEY (rental)
OR-TAV	Or-Tav Music Publications Israel Composers League P.O. Box 3200 Tel-Aviv Israel	
ORGAN	Organ Music Co.	WESTERN
ORGMS	Organmaster Music Series 282 Stepstone Hill Guilford, CT 06437	
ORION MUS	Orion Music Press P.O. Box 75 Berrien Springs, MI 49103	
ORLANDO	Orlando Musikverlag Kaprunerstraße 1 D-8000 München 21 Germany	
ORPHEUM	Orpheum Music 10th & Parker Berkeley, CA 94710	
OSTARA	Ostara Press, Inc.	WESTERN
OSTER	Österreichischer Bundesverlag Industriezentrum Nö-Sud Strassi, Object 34 Postanschrift: A-2351 Wiener Neudorf, Postfach Austria	AMP
OTOS	Otos Edizioni Musicali Via Marsillo Ficino, 10 I-50132 Firenze Italy	BELWIN

Code	Publisher	U.S. Agent	Code	Publisher	U.S. Agent
OUVRIERES	Les Éditions Ouvrières 12, Avenue Soeur-Rosalie F-75621 Paris Cedex 13, France	LEDUC	PENGUIN	Penguin Books 72 Fifth Avenue New York, NY 10011	
OXFORD	Oxford University Press 44 Conduit Street London W1R ODE England 1600 Pollitt Drive Fair Lawn, NJ 07410		PENN STATE	Pennsylvania State University Press 215 Wagner Building University Park, PA 16802	
PAGANI	O. Pagani & Bro., Inc. 289 Bleecker Street New York, NY 10014		PENOLL	Penoll Goteberg, Sweden	STIM
			PEPPER	J.W. Pepper And Son, Inc. P.O. Box 850 Valley Forge, PA 19482	
PAGANINI PUB	Paganiniana Publications, Inc. P.O. Box 27 Neptune City, NJ 07753		PERMUS	Permus Publications P.O. Box 02033 Columbus, OH 43202	
PALLMA	Pallma Music Co.	KJOS	PETERS	Edition Peters C.F. Peters Corp. 373 Park Avenue South New York, NY 10016	
PAN	Editions Pan Postfach 260 Zürich Switzerland		PETERS,K	Kermit Peters 1515 90th Street Omaha, NE 68124	
PAN AM	Pan American Union	PEER	PETERS,M	Mitchell Peters 3231 Benda Place Los Angeles, CA 90068	
PANTON	Panton Ricni 12 115 39 Praha 1 Czechoslovakia		PFAUEN	Pfauen Verlag Adolfsallee 34 Postfach 471 D-6200 Wiesbaden Germany	PETERS
PARAGON	Paragon Music Publishers	CENTURY			
PARAGON ASS.	Paragon Associates	ALEX.HSE.	PHILH	Philharmonia	EUR.AM.MUS.
PARIS	Uitgeverij H.J. Paris	DONEMUS	PHILIPPO	Editions Philippo	ELKAN-V
PARKS	Parks Music Corp.	KJOS	PIEDMONT	Piedmont Music Co.	MARKS
PASTORALE	Pastorale Music Company 235 Sharon Drive San Antonio, TX 78216		PILES	Piles Editorial de Musica Archena 33 Valencia 14 Spain	
PASTORINI	Musikhaus Pastorini AG Kasinostraße 25 CH-5000 Aarau Switzerland		PILLIN	Pillin Music	WESTERN
PATERSON	Paterson's Publications, Ltd. 36-40 Wigmore Street London, W1H OEX England	FISCHER,C	PIPER	Piper Music Co. P.O. Box 1713 Cincinnati, OH 45201	
			PIZKA	Pizka Edition	
PAXTON	Paxton Publications	NOVELLO	PLAINSONG	Plainsong & Medieval Music Society David Hiley, Hon. Sec. 46 Bond Street Englefield Green Surrey TW20 0PY England	
PEER	Peer International Corp. 1740 Broadway New York, NY 10019				
PEER MUSIK	Peer Musikverlag GmbH Muhlenkamp 43 Postfach 602129 D-2000 Hamburg Germany		PLAYER	Player Press 139-22 Caney Lane Rosedale, NY 11422	
PEG	Pegasus Musikverlag Liebig Straße 16 Postfach 620 D-2940 Wilhelmshaven Germany	PETERS	PLENUM	Plenum Publishing Corp. 227 West 17th Street New York, NY 10011	DA CAPO
			PLESNICAR	Don Plesnicar P.O. Box 4880 Albuquerque, NM 87106	
PELIKAN	Musikverlag Pelikan	BAREN.	PLOUGH	Plough Publishing House Rifton, NY 12471	
PEMBROKE	Pembroke Music Co., Inc.	FISCHER,C	PLYMOUTH	Plymouth Music Co., Inc. 170 N.E. 33rd Street Fort Lauderdale, FL 33334	
PENADES	José Penadés En Sanz 12 Valencia Spain				
PENDRGN	Pendragon Press 162 West 13th Street New York, NY 10011		PODIUM	Podium Music, Inc. 360 Port Washington Boulevard Port Washington, NY 11050	

Code	Publisher	U.S. Agent	Code	Publisher	U.S. Agent
POLSKIE	Polskie Wydawnictwo Muzyczne Al. Krasinskiego 11a 31-111 Cracow Poland		PSI	PSI Press P.O. Box 2320 Boulder, CO 80306	
POLYPH MUS	Polyphone Music Co.	ARCADIA	PUSTET	Verlag Friedrich Pustet Gutenbergstraße 8 Postfach 339 D-8400 Regensburg 11 Germany	
POLYPHON	Polyphon Musikverlag	BREITKOPF-W			
PORT.MUS.	Portugaliae Musicae	BAREN.	PYRAMINX	Pyraminx Publications	ACCURA
POWER	Power and Glory Music Co.	NEW MUSIC	QUIROGA	Ediciones Quiroga Alcalá, 70 Madrid 9 Spain	PRESSER
PRAEGER	Praeger Publications 383 Madison Avenue New York, NY 10017				
PREISSLER	Musikverlag Josef Preissler Postfach 521 Bräuhausstraße 8 D-8000 München 2 Germany		RAHTER	D. Rahter	AMP
			RAMSEY	Basil Ramsey Publisher of Music	BROUDE,A
			RARITIES	Rarities For Strings Publications 11300 Juniper Drive University Circle Cleveland, OH 44106	
PRELUDE	Prelude Publications 150 Wheeler Street Glouchester, MA 01930				
PRENTICE	Prentice-Hall, Inc. Englewood Cliffs, NJ 07632		RECITAL	Recital Publications, Ltd. P.O. Box 1697 Huntsville, TX 77340	
PRESSER	Theodore Presser Co. Presser Place Bryn Mawr, PA 19010		REGENT	Regent Music Corp.	BIG BELL
			REGINA	Regina Verlag Schumannstraße 35 Postfach 6148 D-6200 Wiesbaden 1 Germany	
PRESSES	Aux Presses d'Isle-de-France 12, rue de la Chaise F-75007 Paris France				
PRICE,P	Paul Price Publications 470 Kipp Street Teaneck, NJ 07666		REGUS	Regus Publisher 10 Birchwood Lane White Bear Lake, MN 55110	
PRIMAVERA	Editions Primavera	GENERAL	REIMERS	Edition Reimers AB Box 15030 S-16115 Bromma Sweden	
PRINCE	Prince Publications 1125 Francisco Street San Francisco, CA 94109				
PRO ART	Pro Art Publications, Inc.	BELWIN	REINHARDT	Reinhardt Verlag Sommergasse 46 CH-4000 Basel 12 Switzerland	
PRO MUSICA	Pro Musica Verlag Karl-Liebknecht-Straße 12 Postfach 467 DDR-7010 Leipzig Germany				
			REN	Les Editions Renaissantes	EUR.AM.MUS.
			RENK	Musikverlag Renk "Varia Edition" Herzog-Heinrich-Straße 21 D-8000 München 2 Germany	
PROCLAM	Proclamation Productions, Inc. Orange Square Port Jervis, NY 12771				
PROGRESS	Progress Press P.O. Box 12 Winnetka, IL 60093		RESEARCH	Research Publications, Inc. Lunar Drive Woodbridge, CT 06525	
PROSVETNI	Prosvetni Servis	DRUSTVO	REUTER	Reuter & Reuter Förlags AB Box 26072 S-100 41 Stockholm Sweden	
PROVIDENCE	Providence Music Press P.O. Box 2362 East Side Station Providence, RI 02906				
PROVINCTWN	Provincetown Bookshop Editions 246 Commercial Street Provincetown, MA 02657		RHODES,R	Roger Rhodes Music, Ltd. P.O. Box 855, Radio City Station New York, NY 10019	
PROWSE	Keith Prowse Music Publishing Co. 138-140 Charing Cross Road London, WC2H 0LD England	FOX,S	RICHMOND	Richmond Music Press, Inc. P.O. Box 465 P. P. Station Richmond, IN 47374	
			RICHMOND ORG.	The Richmond Organization	PLYMOUTH
PRUETT	Pruett Publishing Co. 3235 Prairie Avenue Boulder, CO 80302		RICORDI-ARG	Ricordi Americana S.A. Cangallo, 1558 Buenos Aires Argentina	SCHIRM.G
PSALTERY	Psaltery P.O. Box 220033 Dallas, TX 75222		RICORDI-BR	Ricordi Brasileira S.A. R. Conselheiro Nebias 773 1° S-10-12 Sao Paolo, Brazil	SCHIRM.G

Code	Publisher	U.S. Agent	Code	Publisher	U.S. Agent
RICORDI-CAN	G. Ricordi & Co. Toronto, Canada	SCHIRM.G	ROZSAVO.	Rozsavölgi & Co.	BUDAPEST
RICORDI-ENG	G. Ricordi & Co., Ltd. The Bury, Church Street Chesham, Bucks HP5 1JG England	SCHIRM.G	RUBANK	Rubank, Inc. 16215 N.W. 15th Avenue Miami, FL 33169	
RICORDI-FR	Société Anonyme des Éditions Ricordi 12, rue Rougemont F-75009 Paris France	SCHIRM.G	RUBATO	Rubato Musikverlag Hollandstraße 18 A-1020 Wien Austria	DONEMUS
RICORDI-GER	G. Ricordi & Co. Gewürzmühlstraße 5 D-8000 München 22 Germany	SCHIRM.G	RUH,E	Emil Ruh Musikverlag Zürichstraße 33 CH-8134 Adliswil - Zürich Switzerland	
RICORDI-IT	G. Ricordi & Co. Via Berchet 2 Milano Italy	SCHIRM.G	RUMAN.COMP.	Uniunea Compozitorilor din R.S. România (Union of Rumanian Composers) Str. C. Esarcu No. 2 București, Sector 1 Rumania	BAREN.
RIDEAU	Les Éditions Rideau Rouge 24, rue de Longchamp F-75016 Paris France	ELKAN-V	RUTGERS	Rutgers University Editions	BROUDE,A
RIES	Ries & Erler Charlottenbrunner Straße 42 D-1000 Berlin 33 (Grunewald) Germany		RYDET	Rydet Music Publishers P.O. Box 477 Purchase, NY 10577	
RILEY	Dr. Maurice W. Riley Eastern Michigan University 512 Roosevelt Boulevard Ypsilanti, MI 48197		SAC.MUS.PR.	Sacred Music Press of Hebrew Union College One West Fourth Street New York, NY 10012	TRANSCON.
ROBBINS	Robbins Music Corp.	BIG3	SACRED	Sacred Music Press	LORENZ
ROBERTON	Roberton Publications The Windmill, Wendover Aylesbury, Bucks, HP22 6JJ England	PRESSER	SACRED SNGS	Sacred Songs, Inc.	WORD
ROBERTS,L	Lee Roberts Music Publications, Inc. P.O. Box 225 Katonah, NY 10536	SCHIRM.G	SALABERT	Francis Salabert Éditions 22 rue Chauchat F-75009 Paris France	SCHIRM.G
ROBITSCHEK	Adolf Robitschek Musikverlag Graben 14 (Bräunerstraße 2) Postfach 42 A-1014 Wien Austria		SAMFUNDET	Samfundet til udgivelse af Dansk Musik Graabrodretorv 7 DK-1154 København Denmark	PETERS
ROCHESTER	Rochester Music Publishers, Inc.	ACCURA	SAN ANDREAS	San Andreas Press 3732 Laguna Avenue Palo Alto, CA 94306	
RODEHEAVER	Rodeheaver Publications	WORD	SANDSTONE	Sandstone Music Associates 7110 36th Avenue North, #109 Minneapolis, MN 55427	
ROLLAND	Rolland String Research Associates P.O. Box 35 Silver Cliff, CO 81249	BOOSEY	SANDVOSS	F.K. Sandvoss Musikverlag Poststraße 30 D-4000 Düsseldorf Germany	
RONCORP	Roncorp, Inc. P.O. Box 724 Cherry Hill, NJ 08003		SANJO	Sanjo Music Co. P.O. Box 700-104 Palos Verdes Peninsula, CA 90274	
RONGWEN	Rongwen Music, Inc.	BROUDE BR.	SAUL AVE	Saul Avenue Publishing Co. P.O. Box 37156 Cincinnati, OH 45222	
ROSSUM	Wed. J.R. van Rossum	PETERS			
ROUART	Rouart-Lerolle & Cie	SCHIRM.G	SCARECROW	The Scarecrow Press, Inc. 52 Liberty Street P.O. Box 656 Metuchen, NJ 08840	
ROW	R.D. Row Music Co.	FISCHER,C			
ROYAL	Royal School of Church Music Addington Palace Croydon, Surrey CR9 5AD England	BRODT	SCHAUR	Richard Schauer, Music Publishers 67 Belsize Lane, Hampstead London NW3 5AX England	AMP
	Royal School of Church Music in America Mr. Robert Kennedy P.O. Cornwall Bridge Warren, CT 06754		SCHEIDT	Altonaer Scheidt-Ausgabe	HANSS
			SCHERZANDO	Muziekuitgeverij Scherzando Antwerpen Belgium	ELKAN,H
	Associated Board of the Royal Schools of Music see ABRSM		SCHIRM.EC	E.C. Schirmer Music Co. 112 South Street Boston, MA 02111	

Code	Publisher	U.S. Agent	Code	Publisher	U.S. Agent
SCHIRM.G.	G. Schirmer, Inc. 866 Third Avenue New York, NY 10022		SERENUS	Serenus Corp. 145 Palisade Street Dobbs Ferry, NY 10522	
SCHMIDT,H	Musikverlag Hermann Schmidt Berliner Straße 26 D-6000 Frankfurt-am-Main 1 Germany		SERVANT	Servant Publications P.O. Box 8617 840 Airport Boulevard Ann Arbor, MI 48107	
SCHMITT	Schmitt Music Editions	BELWIN	SESAC	Sesac, Inc. 10 Columbus Circle New York, NY 10019	
SCHNEIDER,H	Musikverlag Hans Schneider Mozartstraße 6 D-8132 Tutzing Germany		SHALL-U-MO	Shall-U-Mo Publications P.O. Box 2824 Rochester, NY 14626	
SCHOLA	Éditions Musicales de la Schola Cantorum 76 bis, rue des Saints-Pères F-75007 Paris 7 France	PRESSER	SHAPIRO	Shapiro, Bernstein & Co., Inc. 10 East 53 Street New York, NY 10022	PLYMOUTH
SCHOTT	Schott & Co. Ltd. 48 Great Marlborough Street London W1V 2BN England	EUR.AM.MUS.	SHATTINGER	Shattinger Music Co. 252 Paul Brown Building St. Louis, MO 63101	
SCHOTT-FRER	Schott Frères 30 rue Saint-Jean B-1000 Bruxelles Belgium	EUR.AM.MUS.	SHAWNEE	Shawnee Press, Inc. Delaware Water Gap, PA 18327	
			SHEPPARD	John Sheppard Music Press	EUR.AM.MUS.
SCHOTT,J	Schott & Co. Japan	EUR.AM.MUS.		Antigua Casa Sherry-Brener, Ltd. see ACSB	
SCHOTTS	B. Schotts Söhne Weihergarten 5 Postfach 3640 D-6500 Mainz Germany	EUR.AM.MUS.	SIDEMTON	Sidemton Verlag	BREITKOPF-W
			SIFLER	Paul J. Sifler 3947 Fredonia Drive Hollywood, CA 90068	
SCHUBERTH	Edward Schuberth & Co., Inc.	ASHLEY	SIJN	D. van Sijn & Zonen Banorstraat 1 Rotterdam Netherlands	
SCHUL	Carl L. Schultheiß Denzenbergstraße 35 D-7400 Tübingen Germany	PETERS	SIKORSKI	Hans Sikorski Verlag Johnsallee 23 Postfach 132001 D-2000 Hamburg 13 Germany	SCHIRM.G
SCHULZ,FR	Blasmusikverlag Fritz Schulz Am Märzengraben 6 D-7800 Freiburg-Tiengen Germany		SIMROCK	N. Simrock	AMP
SCHWANN	Musikverlag Schwann	PETERS	SINGSPIR	Singspiration Music The Zondervan Corp. 1415 Lake Drive S.E. Grand Rapids, MI 49506	
SCHWEIZER.	Schweizerische Kirchengesangbund	HANSSLER	SIRIUS	Sirius-Verlag	PETERS
SCOTT	G. Scott Music Publishing Co.	WESTERN	SKAND.	Skandinavisk Musikforlag Gothersgade 9-11 DK-1123 København K. Denmark	MAGNAMUSIC
SCOTT MUSIC	Scott Music Publications	ALFRED			
SCOTUS	Scotus Music Publications, Ltd. 28 Dalrymple Crescent Edinburgh, EH9 2NX Scotland		SLOV.AKA.	Slovenska Akademija Znanosti in Umetnosti Trg Francoske Revolucije 6 Ljubljana Yugoslavia	DRUSTVO
SCREEN	Screen Gems-Columbia Publications	COLUMBIA PIC.	SLOV.HUD. FOND.	Slovenský Hudobný Fond Fucikova 29 801 00 Bratislava Czechoslovakia	BOOSEY (rental)
SEESAW	Seesaw Music Corp. 2067 Broadway New York, NY 10023		SLOV.MAT.	Slovenska Matica	DRUSTVO
SELMER	Selmer Éditions 18, rue de la Fontaine-au-Roi F-75011 Paris France		SMITH PUB	Smith Publications-Sonic Art Editions 2617 Gwynndale Avenue Baltimore, MD 21207	
SEMI	Société d'Editions Musicales Internationales	MERIDIAN			
SENART	Ed. Maurice Senart 22 rue Chauchat F-75009 Paris France	SCHIRM.G	SMITH,WJ	William J. Smith Co., Inc. 2611 Skidmore Road P.O. Box 217 Deer Park, NY 11729	

Code	Publisher	U.S. Agent	Code	Publisher	U.S. Agent
SMPF	SMPF, Inc. 14 East 60th Street New York, NY 10022		STEIN	Edition Steingräber Auf der Reiswiese 9 D-6050 Offenbach/M. Germany	
SOC.PUB.AM.	Society for the Publication of American Music	PRESSER	STIM	STIMs Informationcentral för Svensk Musik (Swedish Music Information Center) Birger Jarlsgatan 6 B Box 5091 S-102 42 Stockholm Sweden	
	Société d'Éditions Musicales Internationales see SEMI				
	Society of Finnish Composers see SUOMEN		STOCKHAUS	Stockhausen-Verlag Kettenberg 15 D-5067 Kürten Germany	
SOLAR	The Solar Studio 178 Cowles Road Woodbury, CT 06798			Stockhausen-Verlag, U.S. 2832 Maple Lane Fairfax, VA 22030	
SOMERSET	Somerset Press	HOPE	STOCKTON	Fred Stockton P.O. Box 814 Grass Valley, CA 95945	
SONANTE	Sonante Publications P.O. Box 74, Station F Toronto, Ontario M4Y 2L4 Canada				
SONOS	Sonos Music Resources, Inc. P.O. Box 9490 Salt Lake City, UT 84109		STUD	Studio 224	STUDIO
SONSHINE	Sonshine Productions	LORENZ	STUDIO	Studio P/R, Inc. 16333 N.W. 54th Avenue Hialeah, FL 33014	
SONZOGNO	Casa Musicale Sonzogno Via Bigli 11 I-20121 Milano Italy	BELWIN	STYRIA	Verlag Styria Schönaugasse 64 Postfach 435 A-8011 Graz Austria	
SOUTHERN	Southern Music Co. 1100 Broadway P.O. Box 329 San Antonio, TX 78292		SUECIA	Edition Suecia	STIM
			SUISEISHA	Suiseisha Editions	ONGAKU
SOUTHRN PUB	Southern Music Publishing Co., Inc.	PEER	SUMMIT	Summit Music Ltd. 497 Eglington Avenue West Toronto, Ontario M5N 1A8 Canada	
SOUTHWEST	Southwest Music Publications Box 4552 Santa Fe, NM 87501				
SPAN.MUS.CTR.	Spanish Music Center, Inc. Belvedere Hotel 319 West 48th Street New York, NY 10036		SUMMY	Summy-Birchard Co. P.O. Box 2027 Princeton, NJ 08540	
			SUOMEN	Suomen Säveltäjät ry (Society of Finnish Composers) Runeberginkatu 15 A 00100 Helsinki 10 Finland	
SPIRE	Spire Editions	FISCHER,C WORLD			
SPRATT	Spratt Music Publishers 17 West 60th Street 8th Fl. New York, NY 10023		SUPRAPHON	Supraphon Pulackeho 1 112 99 Praha Czechoslovakia	BOOSEY (rental)
ST.GREG.	St. Gregory Publishing Co. 64 Pineheath Road High Kelling, Holt Norfolk, NR25 6RH England	ROYAL		Svenska Utbildningsförlaget Liber AB see LIBER	
ST. MARTIN	St. Martin Music Co., Inc.	ROYAL	SWAN	Swan & Co. P.O. Box 1 Rickmansworth, Herts WD3 3AZ England	ARCADIA
STAFF	Staff Music Publishing Co., Inc. 5640 Collins Avenue, Apt. 7-D Miami Beach, FL 33140	PLYMOUTH			
STAINER	Stainer & Bell Ltd. 82 High Road East Finchley London N2 9PW England	SCHIRM.EC	SWAND	Swand Publications 120 North Longcross Road Linthicum Heights, MD 21090	
				Swedish Music Information Center see STIM	
STAMPS	Stamps-Baxter Music Publications Box 4007 Dallas, TX 75208	SINGSPIR	SYMPHON	Symphonia Verlag	BELWIN
STANDARD	Standard Music Publishing, Inc.	SCHIRM.G	TARPINIAN	Tarpinian Music Associates, Inc. 618 Sixth Street Brooklyn, NY 11215	
STANGLAND	Thomas C. Stangland Co. P.O. Box 19263 Portland, OR 97219		TAUNUS	Taunus	HOFMEIS- TER-W

Code	Publisher	U.S. Agent
TAYLOR	Robert Sample Taylor 600 Price Street Forest City, NC 28043	
TECLA	Tecla Editions Preacher's Court, Charterhouse London EC1M 6AS England	
TEESELING	Muziekuitgeverij van Teeseling Buurmansweg 29B NL-6524 RV Nijmegen Netherlands	
TEMPLETN	Templeton Publishing Co., Inc.	SHAWNEE
TEMPO	Tempo Music Publications P.O. Box 220113 Dallas, TX 75222	
TEN TIMES	Ten Times A Day P.O. Box 230 Deer Park, L.I., NY 11729	
TENUTO	Tenuto Publications see also TRI-TEN	PRESSER
TETRA	Tetra Music Corp.	BROUDE,A
TFS	Things For Strings Publishing Co. P.O. Box 9263 Alexandria, VA 22304	
THOMAS	Thomas Music House 1381 Franquette Avenue P.O. Box 6023 Concord, CA 94520	DEAN
THOMI	E. Thomi-Berg Musikverlag Postfach 322 D-8000 München 60 Germany	
THOMP.	Thompson Music House P.O. Box 12463 Nashville, TN 37212	
THOMP.G	Gordon V. Thompson, Ltd. 29 Birch Avenue Toronto, Ontario M4V 1E2 Canada	WALTON (choral)
TIEROLFF	Tierolff Muziek Centrale Markt 90-92 NL-4701 PJ Roosendaal Netherlands	
TISCHER	Tischer und Jagenberg Musikverlag Nibelungenstraße 48 D-8000 München 19 Germany	AMP
TOA	Toa Editions	ONGAKU
TONGER	P.J. Tonger, Musikverlag Auf dem Brand 3 Postfach 501865 D-5000 Köln 50 Germany	
TONOS	Editions Tonos Ahastraße 7 D-6100 Darmstadt Germany	SEESAW
TOORTS	Uitgeverij De Toorts	DONEMUS
TRANSAT.	Éditions Musicales Transatlantiques 50, rue Joseph-de-Maistre F-75018 Paris France	PRESSER
TRANSCON.	Transcontinental Music Publications 838 Fifth Avenue New York, NY 10021	

Code	Publisher	U.S. Agent
TREKEL	Joachim-Trekel-Verlag Postfach 620428 D-2000 Hamburg 62 Germany	
TRI-TEN	Tritone Press and Tenuto Publications P.O. Box 5081, Southern Station Hattiesburg, MS 39401	PRESSER
TRIGON	Trigon Music Inc.	TRIUNE
TRINITY	Trinity House Publishing	CRESPUB
TRIUNE	Triune Music, Inc. 824 19th Avenue-South Nashville, TN 37203	
TRO	Tro Songways Service, Inc. 10 Columbus Circle New York, NY 10019	PLYMOUTH
TROY	Troy State University Library Troy, AL 36081	
TUSKEGEE	Tuskegee Institute Music Press	KJOS
U.S.CATH	United States Catholic Conference Publications Office 1312 Massachusetts Avenue N.W. Washington, D.C. 20005	
UBER,D	David Uber Music Department Trenton State College Trenton, NJ 08625	
UFATON	Ufaton-Verlag	ORLANDO
UNICORN	Unicorn Music Company, Inc. 170 N.E. 33rd Street Fort Lauderdale, FL 33334	
UNION ESP.	Union Musical Española Carrera de San Jeronimo 26 Madrid Spain	AMP
UNITED ART	United Artists Group	BIG3
UNITED MUS.	United Music Publishers Ltd. 1 Montague Street Russell Square London WC1B 5BS England	PRESSER
UNIV. ALA	University of Alabama Press Drawer 2877 University, AL 35486	
UNIV.CAL	University of California Press 2223 Fulton Street Berkeley, CA 94720	
UNIV.CH	University of Chicago Press 5801 South Ellis Avenue Chicago, IL 60637	
UNIV.EVAN	University of Evansville Press P.O. Box 329 Evansville, IN 47702	
UNIV.IOWA	University of Iowa Press Iowa City, IA 52242	
UNIV.MIAMI	University of Miami Music Publications P.O. Box 8163 Coral Gables, FL 33124	FOX,S
UNIV.MICRO	University Microfilms 300 North Zeeb Road Ann Arbor, MI 48106	
UNIV.MINN	University of Minnesota Press 2037 University Avenue S.E. Minneapolis, MN 55455	

Code	Publisher	U.S. Agent	Code	Publisher	U.S. Agent
UNIV.MUS.ED.	University Music Editions P.O. Box 192-Ft. George Station New York, NY 10040		VOLKWEIN	Volkwein Brothers, Inc. 117 Sandusky Street Pittsburgh, PA 15212	
UNIV.NC	University of North Carolina Press P.O. Box 2288 Chapel Hill, NC 27514		WADSWORTH	Wadsworth Publishing Co. 10 Davis Street Belmont, CA 94002	
UNIV.OTAGO	University of Otago Press P.O. Box 56 Dunedin New Zealand		WAGENAAR	J.A.H. Wagenaar Oude Gracht 109 NL-3511 AG Utrecht Netherlands	ELKAN,H
UNIV.TEXAS	University of Texas Press P.O. Box 7819 Austin TX 78712		WAI-TE-ATA	Wai-te-ata Press	CAN.MUS. CENT.
UNIV.UTAH	University of Utah Press Salt Lake City, UT 84112		WALKER	Walker Publications P.O. Box 61 Arnold, MD 21012	
UNIV.WASH	University of Washington Press Seattle, WA 98105		WALTON	Walton Music Corp.	LORENZ
UNIVER.	Universal Edition Bösendorfer Straße 12 Postfach 130 A-1015 Wien Austria	EUR.AM.MUS.	WARNER	Warner Brothers Publications, Inc. 75 Rockefeller Plaza - 14th Fl. New York, NY 10019	
UP WITH	Up With People 3103 North Campbell Avenue Tucson, AZ 85719	LORENZ	WATERLOO	Waterloo Music Co. Ltd. 3 Regina Street North Waterloo, Ontario N2J 2Z7 Canada	
VALANDO	Valando Music, Inc.	PLYMOUTH	WEHMAN BR.	Wehman Brothers, Inc. Ridgedale Avenue Morris County Mall Cedar Knolls, NJ 07927	
VAMO	Musikverlag Vamö Leebgasse 52-25 Wien 10 Austria		WEINBERGER	Josef Weinberger Ltd. 12-14 Mortimer Street London W1N 8EL England	AMP BOOSEY FOX MARKS SCHIRM.G SHAPIRO
VANDEN-RUP	Vandenhoeck & Ruprecht Robert-Bosch-Breite 6 Postfach 77 D-3400 Göttingen Germany		WEINTRAUB	Weintraub Music Co.	MUSIC
VANDERSALL	Vandersall Editions	EUR.AM.MUS.	WELT	Welt Musik Josef Hochmuth Verlage Hegergasse 21 A-1030 Wien Austria	
VANGUARD	Vanguard Music Corp. 1595 Broadway, Room 313 New York, NY 10019				
VER.HUIS.	Vereniging voor Huismuziek Catharijnesingel 85 Utrecht Netherlands		WESSMAN	Wessmans Musikforlag S-620 Slite Sweden	STIM
VIERT	Viertmann Verlag Lübecker Straße 2 D-5000 Köln 1 Germany		WESTEND	Westend	PETERS
			WESTERN	Western International Music, Inc. 2859 Holt Avenue Los Angeles, CA 90034	
VIEWEG	Chr. Friedrich Vieweg, Musikverlag Nibelungenstraße 48 D-8000 München 19 Germany		WESTMINSTER	The Westminster Press 925 Chestnut Street Philadelphia, PA 19107	
VIKING	Viking Press, Inc. 625 Madison Avenue New York, NY 10022		WESTWOOD	Westwood Press, Inc. 2145 Central Parkway Cincinnati, OH 45214	WORLD
VIOLA	Viola World Publications 14 Fenwood Road Huntington Station, NY 11746		WHITE HARV.	White Harvest Music Publications P.O. Box 1144 Independence, MO 64051	
VOGGEN	Voggenreiter Verlag Viktoriastraße 25 D-5300 Bonn Germany		WIDE WORLD	Wide World Music, Inc. Box B Delaware Water Gap, PA 18327	
VOGT	Musikverlag Vogt & Fritz Friedrich-Stein-Straße 10 D-8720 Schweinfurt Germany		WIEN BOH.	Wiener Boheme Verlag GmbH Sonnenstraße 19 D-8000 München 2 Germany	
VOLK	Arno Volk Verlag	BREITKOPF-W	WIENER	Wiener Urtext Edition	EUR.AM.MUS.

Code	Publisher	U.S. Agent
WILDER	Wilder	MARGUN
WILHELM.	Wilhelmiana Musikverlag Edition Wilhelm Hansen, Frankfurt Eschersheimer Landstraße 12 D-6000 Frankfurt-am-Main Germany	MAGNAMUSIC
	Williams School of Church Music see WSCM	
WILLIAMSN	Williamson Music, Inc.	BOSTON
WILLIS	Willis Music Co. 7380 Industrial Highway Florence, KY 41042	
WILLSHIRE	Willshire Press Music Foundation, Inc.	WESTERN
WILSHORN	Wilshorn	HOPE
WILSON	Wilson Editions 36 John Dalton Street Manchester M2 6LE England	
WIMBLEDN	Wimbledon Music Inc. 1888 Century Park East Suite 10 Century City, CA 90067	
WIND MUS	Wind Music, Inc. 153 Highland Parkway Rochester, NY 14620	KALMUS,A
WINGERT	Wingert-Jones Music, Inc. 2026 Broadway P.O. Box 1878 Kansas City, MO 64141	
WINKEL	Alfred Winkelbauer Milchstraße 8 D-807 Ingolstadt Germany	
WOITSCHACH	Paul Woitschach Radio-Musikverlag Bregenzer Straße 13a D-1000 Berlin 15 Germany	
WOLF	Wolf-Mills Music	WESTERN
WOLLEN-WEBER	Verlag Walter Wollenweber Postfach 1165 D-8032 Gräfelfing vor München Germany	EUR.AM.MUS
WOODBURY	Woodbury Music Co. 33 Grassy Hill Road P.O. Box 447 Woodbury, CT 06798	
WOODWIND	Woodwind Editions P.O. Box 148 Bloomfield, CT 06002	
WORD	Word, Incorporated 4800 West Waco Drive Waco, TX 76703	
WORD GOD	The Word of God Music	SERVANT
WORLD	World Library of Sacred Music, Inc. 5040 North Ravenswood Avenue Chicago, IL 60640	
WORLDWIDE	Worldwide Music Services P.O. Box 995, Ansonia Station New York, NY 10023	

Code	Publisher	U.S. Agent
WSCM	Williams School of Church Music The Bourne Harpenden England	
WYE	WYE Music Publications	EMERSON
WYNN	Wynn/Music Publications P.O. Box 739 Orinda, CA 94563	
XYZ	Muziekuitgeverij XYZ 1e Wormenseweg 65 NL-7331 DB Apeldoorn Netherlands	
YAHRES	Yahres Publications 1315 Vance Avenue Coraopolis, PA 15108	
YBARRA	Ybarra Music P.O. Box 665 Lemon Grove, CA 92045	
YORKE	Yorke Editions 31 Thornhill Square London N1 1BQ England	SCHIRM.EC
YOUNG WORLD	Young World Publications 10485 Glennon Drive Lakewood, CO 80226	
	Yugoslavian Music Information Center see MUSIC INFO	
ZALO	Zalo Publications & Services P.O. Box 913 Bloomington, IN 47402	
ZANIBON	G. Zanibon Edition Piazza dei Signori, 44 I-35100 Padova Italy	
ZEN-ON	Zen-On Music Co., Ltd. 3-14 Higashi Gokencho Shinjuku-ku Tokyo 162 Japan	
ZENEM.	Zenemukiado Vallalat	BOOSEY GENERAL
ZENGERINK	Herman Zengerink, Amsterdam, Netherlands	PETERS
ZERBONI	Edizioni Suvini Zerboni Via Quintiliano 40 I-20138 Milano Italy	BOOSEY
ZIMMER.	Wilhelm Zimmermann, Musikverlag Gaugrafenstraße 19-23 D-6000 Frankfurt 90 Germany	SCHIRM.G
ZIMMER.PUBS.	Oscar Zimmerman Publications 90 Westminster Road Rochester, NY 14607	
	The Zondervan Corp. see SINGSPIR	
ZURFLUH	Éditions Zurfluh 73, Boulevard Raspail F-75006 Paris France	

Advertisements

Index to Advertisers

The OPERA Quarterly

a new journal devoted to all aspects of opera

Edited by Sherwin and Irene Sloan

Designed for both opera lovers and professionals, *The Opera Quarterly* combines the efforts of performing artists, producers, and scholars to provide an in-depth look at one of our richest art forms.

Four times a year, *The Opera Quarterly* presents original articles on history, composing, conducting, singing, staging, lighting, producing, and directing. Each issue is approximately 150–200 pages in length and includes columns by John Ardoin, M. Owen Lee, and Maria F. Rich; "The Opera Workshop," edited by Natalie Limonick; recording reviews edited by David Hamilton and Dale Harris; and book reviews edited by George Martin. One issue each year will focus on a special topic. The 1983 topic, for the third issue, is Richard Wagner, on the centennial of his death.

Opera is both a living, performing art and an academic pursuit of scholars, yet, until now, there was no journal for creative exchange between performing and producing experts and academicians. *The Opera Quarterly* will increase our knowledge of opera and further our understanding and appreciation of this exceptional art. It is a virtuoso performance.

SUBSCRIPTIONS

U.S. and Canada: $24/4 issues

Foreign: $29/4 issues

We require prepayment from individuals. Library orders may be billed.

Yes, please enter _____ subscription(s) to *The Opera Quarterly*.

☐ Library order. Please bill.

☐ My check for $_____ is enclosed.

☐ Charge my _____Visa _____MasterCard.

   # _____

   Expiration Date _____

   Name _____

   Address _____

   City, State, Zip _____

   _____

☐ Gift Subscription

   Name _____

   Address _____

   City, State, Zip _____

   _____

Return to:

The Opera Quarterly
Subscription Department
University of North Carolina Press
Post Office Box 2288
Chapel Hill, NC 27514

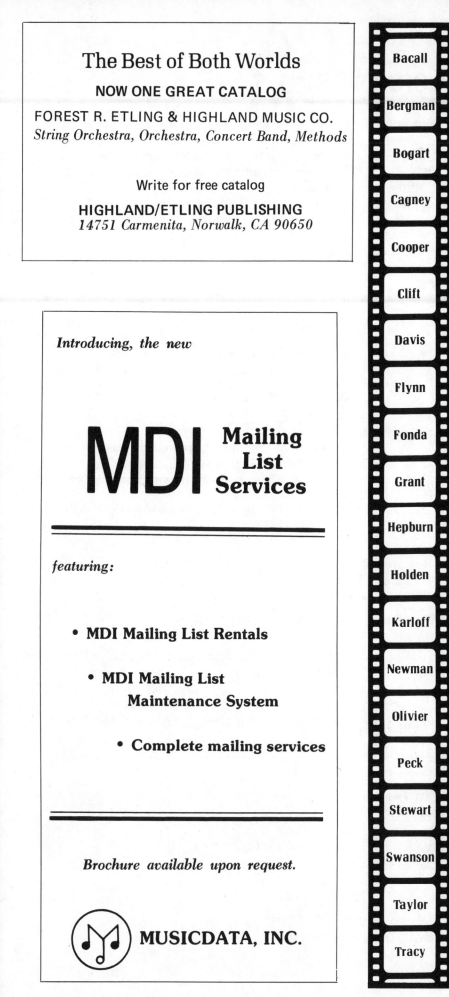

The MUSIC-IN-PRINT Series

The goal of the Music-In-Print series is to provide a complete and up-to-date 'in print' service for all areas of printed music, worldwide. Currently, the Music-In-Print series totals some 4,700 pages which list 240,000 editions from the catalogs of over 900 international music publishers. The entries include composer, arranger, title, instrumentation, publisher, publisher's number, and more. Titles of works are given in their original language; translated titles, if given, appear below the original title and are cross-referenced to it. Standard musical abbreviations have been used to facilitate use of the catalogs worldwide. All abbreviations are explained in a special list, and a publisher directory is included as well.

The Music-In-Print series publications are essential reference tools for libraries, music dealers, performing ensembles and schools, as well as for individual musicians.

Music-In-Print Series publications to date:

Vol. 1. Choral Music In Print - Sacred Choral Music (1974)
ISBN 0-88478-000-7 **$85.00**

Vol. 2. Choral Music In Print - Secular Choral Music (1974)
ISBN 0-88478-002-3 **$85.00**

Sacred Choral Music In Print: 1981 Supplement
ISBN 0-88478-012-0 **$54.00**

Secular Choral Music In Print: 1982 Supplement
ISBN: 0-88478-013-9 **$54.00**

Vol. 3. Organ Music In Print (1975)
ISBN 0-88478-006-6 **$54.00**

Vol. 4. Classical Vocal Music In Print (1976)
ISBN 0-88478-008-2 **$80.00**

Vol. 5. Orchestral Music In Print (1979)
ISBN 0-88478-010-4 **$115.00**

Orchestral Music In Print: 1983 Supplement
ISBN 0-88478-014-7 **$54.00**

Educational Section of Orchestral Music In Print (1978) (also included in Vol. 5)
ISBN 0-88478-009-0 (paperbound) **$10.00**

Vol. 6. String Music In Print, Second Edition (1973)
ISBN 0-88478-011-2 **$69.00**

Standing orders for the Music-In-Print series are invited. When placing a standing order, please state which volumes you already have.

The Music-In-Print Annual Supplement

Musicdata, Inc. offers a service designed to update the Music-In-Print series on an annual basis.

Musicdata has published, since 1979, a combined Annual Supplement to the Music-In-Print series. The Supplement contains separate sections to update each volume published in the Music-In-Print series. The large, paperbound supplements are cumulative, so that the user need only refer to the current year's issue, in conjunction with the base volumes of the series, to get complete, up-to-date information.

Three ways to order:

- **1983 Supplement** (alone) **$80.00**

- **Standing order: 1983 Supplement $80.00 and future supplements at special discount prices.**

- **Subscriptions:** (Subscriptions *must* be prepaid)
  2-year Subscription 1983-1984 $144.00
  3-year Subscription 1983-1985 $192.00

Musicdata, Inc.
3 Maplewood Mall
Philadelphia, PA 19144, U.S.A.

SYMPHONY MAGAZINE

Symphony Magazine, the official publication of the American Symphony Orchestra League, keeps you in touch with more than 1,500 symphony orchestras in the United States and Canada.

Enjoy articles on musicians, orchestra managers, and conductors, concert programming, fund-raising, management trends, technological developments, the state of classical music and the orchestral art.

Become a member of the American Symphony Orchestra League and receive *Symphony Magazine* plus informational newsletters and discounts on League publications, workshops, and seminars.

Yes! Please make me a member of the American Symphony Orchestra League today so that I will receive a full year subscription to *Symphony Magazine*. I enclose a check for $25.00 payable to the American Symphony Orchestra League. (U.S. Funds only).

NAME _____

ADDRESS _____

CITY_____ STATE _____ ZIP_____

SIGNATURE_____

SEND TO: American Symphony Orchestra League
           Symphony Magazine Offer
           633 E Street N.W.
           Washington, D.C. 20004

MUSIC, MUSIC, & MORE MUSIC

Our full line of music services has proven time and again to be of unqualified value to musicians and musicologists the world over. Our staff is unsurpassed in its knowledge, and our performance in providing immediate access to all domestic and foreign publishers, scholarly editions, rare and avant-garde works, and books on music, has earned us encore after encore.

Write for our monthly new publications listing or place your next order with: European American Retail Music, Dept. MD, P.O. Box 850, Valley Forge, PA 19482; 215/666-5771.

EUROPEAN AMERICAN RETAIL MUSIC, INC.